South African

Multi-Language Dictionary

AND PHRASE BOOK

South African

Multi-Language Dictionary
AND PHRASE BOOK

ENGLISH
AFRIKAANS
NORTHERN SOTHO
SESOTHO
TSWANA
XHOSA
ZULU

Published by
The Reader's Digest Association South Africa (Pty) Limited, Cape Town 8001

CONTRIBUTORS

The African translations and introductions were prepared in consultation with the Department of African Languages at the University of South Africa, Pretoria.

Northern Sotho   A E Kotzé and G M M Grobler
Sesotho   R H Moeketsi
Tswana   J C le Roux
Xhosa   N Saule
Zulu   P C Taljaard

The Afrikaans translation was prepared by Prof Johan Combrink of the University of Stellenbosch; and the Xhosa introduction was prepared in consultation with Dr D S Gxilishe, of the Department of African Languages and Literature at the University of Cape Town.

First edition © 1991. Third printing © 1994
The Reader's Digest Association South Africa (Pty) Limited,
130 Strand Street, Cape Town 8001

ISBN 0-947008-67-5

For The Reader's Digest Association South Africa (Pty) Limited:
Editor   Cecile Reynierse
Art Editor   Christabel Hardacre
Project co-ordinator   Carol Adams
Proofreader   Neilah Miller
Illustrators   David Thorpe, David Snook
Production designer   Mandy Moss

CONTENTS

USING THE COLOUR CODE
Each language in the book has a different colour key, as indicated below,
making it easy for you to find the particular section you need.

Note: 'Eyeliner' colour strips have been used in order to make the translations easier to follow.
However, where a word requires a longer translation, it continues onto the line below.

HOW TO USE THIS BOOK

HOW THE BOOK IS ORGANISED

This book is designed to help you achieve a basic level of understanding in the seven major languages of South Africa. It does this in four ways:

1 A visual dictionary, to help you identify a variety of everyday objects and situations in the different languages.

2 A 5 000-word dictionary that translates English and Afrikaans into Northern Sotho, Sesotho, Tswana, Xhosa and Zulu, and translates them back into Afrikaans and English (you can translate a word from one African language to another by first looking up the English meaning, and then turning to the English section to check its other African language equivalent).

3 Five hundred common phrases translated from English into the different languages.

4 Basic grammar and pronunciation rules of each African language, explained in English (the working language of the book) and a pronunciation guide to Afrikaans.

Each explanation precedes its own language in the dictionary section:
Afrikaans: page 137
Northern Sotho: page 225
Sesotho: page 273
Tswana: page 321
Xhosa: page 369
Zulu: page 417

In order to make these sections easier to follow, there is a glossary of grammatical terms starting on the page opposite.

SOTHO AND NGUNI GROUPINGS

The African languages of South Africa are split into two main groups:
1 Sotho, consisting of Northern Sotho, Sesotho and Tswana (spoken predominantly in the Transvaal and Orange Free State); and
2 Nguni, consisting of Xhosa and Zulu (spoken predominantly in Natal and the eastern and western Cape).

In order to make it easy to see the similarities between the two groupings, the Sotho languages are grouped together first (in alphabetical order), followed by the Nguni languages (also in alphabetical order).

USING THE DICTIONARY

When using the word lists, it is important to remember that no language translates literally into another — and where no simple translation exists in a particular African language, our contributors have chosen not to translate the word in that language.

If the word you want is not shown in a particular language, try using its nearest equivalent within the Sotho or Nguni groups — using the groupings indicated above.

Bear in mind, too, that this book is aimed at helping you achieve some understanding and use of the home language of another South African.

Shades of meaning and interpretations specific to the culture of one language are often lost in another. This problem is obviously compounded when a word is translated through six other languages. Anyone wanting to speak an African language fluently should register for a suitable course at a school, university or technikon.

PARTS OF SPEECH

In order to aid understanding, the part of speech of each word in the dictionary is listed in English.

(a) adjective

(adv) adverb

(conj) conjunction

(n) noun

(prep) preposition

(pron) pronoun

(v) verb

THE IMPORTANCE OF GRAMMAR

If you think of language as a building, it's easy to see why grammar is important: if words are the bricks, then grammar cements them together. Neither can function without the other.

This is why grammar is so important in the understanding of languages. While it may be true that we use our own language instinctively, it is equally true that a knowledge of grammar is vital to an understanding of a second or third language.

Each African language section in this book is preceded by a brief overview of how the grammar and syntax (sentence construction) works in that language. In order to help you to understand these sections, you need to be familiar with the more common grammatical terms.

ADJECTIVE Words that describe a noun or a noun substitute are adjectives. Adjectives can be simple (a **sweet** orange) or compound (a **bitter-sweet** grapefruit). Other parts of speech – for example, verbs and various combinations of verbs, nouns, prepositions and so on – may be used as adjectives: a **running** man; a **first-rate** meal; a **sit-in** strike.

ADVERB An adverb is a word that qualifies a verb, an adjective or another adverb: he **rarely** works; he is **particularly** clever; she sang **extremely** well this afternoon.

There are two types of adverbs: original adverbs (soon, rather, always) and adverbs formed from adjectives by adding **-ly** (sad, **sadly**; fierce, **fiercely**).

AGREEMENT A term used to describe the correspondence of words in number, gender and person.
Number: the little boy [s] sleeps [s]; kangaroos [pl] are [pl] marsupials [pl].
Gender: the little boy [m] sleeps in his [m] bed; she [f] has left her [f] home.
Person: I am, you are, he is, etc.

ARTICLE There are three kinds of articles: definite, indefinite and demonstrative.

The definite article (the) makes specific reference to a noun:
There is **the** boy we were seeking.

The indefinite article (a/an) points to a person or thing without fixing its identity:
There is **a** boy with **an** orange.

The demonstrative article (this/that, these/those) points out or specifies a person, thing or idea:
Which do you prefer: **this** chair by the window or **that** one near the fireplace?

AUXILIARY VERB As their name suggests, auxiliary verbs help the main verb to express various aspects of tense, voice and mood, and other precise meanings. The most common are: be, do, have, can, dare, let, may, must, need, ought, shall, used and will:
He **is** going.
I **had been** told about it.
May I borrow your pencil?
You **ought** to have come.

CASE A term used to describe the relationship of nouns and pronouns with other words in sentences. English has three distinct cases: the nominative or subjective, the genitive or possessive, and the accusative or objective.

The nominative case refers to the basic form of a noun or pronoun, singular or plural: boy, children, she, who, they. It indicates the subject in a sentence:
She and **her sisters** have gone on holiday.

The genitive case indicates possession. Nouns form their genitives by adding an **apostrophe** and s in the singular and an **apostrophe** in the plural or by a special order of words linked by the preposition **of**:
The **boy's** father.
The **boys'** fathers.
The father **of the boy**.

Some pronouns form their genitives by adding an **apostrophe** and s; others take **of**:
One always has **one's** doubts.
It is **anybody's** guess.
She bought two handbags, the colours **of which** matched her dresses.

Personal pronouns and the pronoun **who** have special genitive forms: my (mine), your(s), his, her(s), it(s), our(s), their(s), whose.

The accusative case marks a noun or pronoun as the object of a verb, preposition or adjective.
I like **him**.
He said he would come with **me**.
He built a large **boat**.

Only personal pronouns (except you and it) and the pronoun **who** have separate accusative forms: me, him, her, us, them, whom. All other pronouns and all nouns keep their basic singular or plural form when used as objects.

COMPARISON There are three degrees of comparison: the positive, the comparative and the superlative.

The positive denotes equality:
I am **as good as** you are.

The comparative degree indicates greater or smaller degrees of quality, quantity or manner. It is formed by the ending **-er** or by the use of the modifiers **more** and **less**:
Our garden is **smaller** than yours.
I'm **more** tired than ever.
She works **less** efficiently than anyone I know.

The superlative degree expresses the highest degree of quality, quantity or manner. It is formed by the ending **-est** or by the use of the modifiers **most** and **least**:
Our garden is the **smallest** in the neighbourhood.
He is the **most** in debt of us all.
She works the **least** efficiently.

CONCORD Agreement between words in person, number, gender or case.

CONJUGATION When the form of a verb is changed to show tense, voice, mood, person or number, it is being conjugated: he talks, we talked, you have been talking; it will be done.

CONJUNCTION A word that links words, groups of words or sentences:
Roses **and** camellias are my favourites.
Wait **until** you meet him.
He went to bed **but** she stayed up late.

Conjunctions fall into two main categories:
Co-ordinating conjunctions, such as **and, but, for, or, either, neither, yet**, which link sentence parts of equal rank; and
Subordinating conjunctions, such as **if, since, because, as, although, while, until** which join dependent clauses to main clauses.

COPULATIVE Serving to connect coordinate words or clauses.

DIRECT SPEECH The reporting of what someone has said or written by quoting his exact words:
'I must finish my work,' he said.

ENUMERATIVE Mentioned separately or in order; named one by one; listed.

GENDER English has three genders: masculine, feminine and neuter.

Masculine gender in a noun or pronoun denotes the male sex: man, boy, he, his, himself.
Feminine gender in a noun or pronoun denotes the female sex: woman, lioness, lass, she.

Neuter gender in a noun or pronoun denotes no sex: house, rain, courage, child, it, they.

Note that the common gender is sometimes applied to nouns and pronouns that do not define sex but could be understood as either masculine or feminine: friend, person, child, it, they.

GERUND This is formed from a verb by adding -ing, the same as the present participle. It is used as a noun:
Swimming is fun.
I didn't like the loud **shouting** next door.

IDEOPHONE Sound group which conveys a specific idea.

IMPERATIVE Denoting a mood of verbs used in giving orders, making requests etc.

INDIRECT SPEECH A restatement by one person of a direct statement made by someone else:
'How do you know?' (direct).
Michelle asked how I knew (indirect).

INFINITIVE The basic form of a verb, usually introduced by to (though sometimes the **to** is omitted): to walk, to hear, to be.

An infinitive may function as a verb (I must **work**), as a noun (**to work** in hot weather is tedious), as an adjective (the man **to see** is my boss) and as an adverb (she is going **to swim**).

INTERJECTION A word or remark expressing emotion; exclamation: **Oh!** I spilt the soup.

IRREGULAR VERB Verbs that do not follow a consistent pattern in forming their principal parts are called irregular. The most familiar irregular verb in English is the verb **to be**, which changes its form in person as well as in tense: am, are, is, was, were, been.

Most other verbs are irregular only in forming their past tenses and past participles: write, wrote, written, sing, sang, sung.

NOUN The name of any living being, lifeless thing, concept or idea: boy, dog, yacht, sugar, beauty, loneliness. Nouns may be singular or plural in number (boy, boys; child, children) and simple or compound in form (life, lifetime, lifejacket).

The names of particular beings or things are called proper nouns and begin with a capital letter: John, Shakespeare, Queenstown, Friday, New Year. The rest of the nouns are called common nouns: editor, president, bird, tree.

NUMBER Nouns, pronouns and verbs change form to show whether one person or thing, or more than one, is indicated: child, children; she, they; was, were; walks, walk.

OBJECT A noun, pronoun, noun clause, or noun phrase following a transitive verb or preposition:
John loves his **work**. (noun)
The dog ran after **me**. (pronoun)
I know **what he has done**. (noun clause)
I know **what to do**. (noun phrase)
    If a verb has only one object, as in the examples above, it is called a **direct object**. A noun or pronoun that either precedes or follows the direct object is called an **indirect object**:
I gave **him** a present.
He wrote a letter to the **city council**.
She cooked a roast for **him**.
    Note that when the indirect object follows the direct object, as in the last two examples, the prepositions **to** or **for** must be used. Thus, you can say either I wrote **him a letter** or I wrote **a letter to him**.

PARTICIPLE A form of the verb used in combination with auxiliary verbs to indicate tense, mood and voice.
    The present participle is the **-ing** form of a verb and indicates continuous action:
He is **singing**.
    The past participle, either regular (wounded, painted) or irregular (sung, broken), indicates past or perfect tense:
He had **sung**.
    The perfect participle combines the **-ing** form of the verb **to have** and the **past participle** of the main verb (having sung; having been sung) and indicates a completed past action:
Having sung, he went out.
    Participles can function as nouns and adjectives:
The **wounded** and the **dying** were carried from the battlefield. (nouns)
We watched the **singing** children around the **lighted** fire. (adjectives)

PART OF SPEECH A term used to describe any one of the classes of words that are combined to make up a sentence. English has nine parts of speech: adjectives, adverbs, articles, conjunctions, interjections, nouns, prepositions, pronouns and verbs.

PREDICATE The term predicate is used in two senses. Basically, it is the verb form in a sentence that expresses the state or action of the subject:
He **is** tired.
We **haven't done** it yet.

In a larger sense, the predicate includes both the verb and all the words and modifiers that follow, such as objects, adjectives, adverbs, phrases and so on:
I **have just written a letter**.
He **sang beautifully**.
They **vanished into thin air**.

PREPOSITION English uses a large number of prepositions (for example at, about, by, for, from, to, with) to specify the relationships of words in a sentence.
    Prepositions are used to show the relationship between various parts of speech (nouns, pronouns, verbs, adjectives) and nouns and pronouns:
The man **behind** the chair.
I know **about** the man.
She is fond **of** music.

PRONOUN Pronouns are used to replace nouns or noun phrases in a sentence. They are divided into personal, demonstrative, indefinite, interrogative, relative, reflexive and reciprocal pronouns. Many have forms for different functions.
    Personal pronouns can be singular (I, you, he, she, it) or plural (we, you, they) in number. The third person singular pronoun has three genders: the masculine **he**, the feminine **she** and the neuter **it**.
    Demonstrative pronouns are the singular **this**, **that** and the plural **these**, **those**. They are different from the demonstrative articles in that they can stand alone:
This is a camellia, **that** is an azalea and **those** are roses.
    Indefinite pronouns include **any**, **some**, **every**, **no** and their combinations with **-one**, **-body**, and **-thing**; and such pronouns as **many**, **few**, **none**, **several**, **another**, etc.
    Interrogative pronouns are **who**, **what** and **which** and are used in questions:
Who are you? **Which** do you want?
    Relative pronouns fall into two categories according to use. **Who**, **that** and **which** are used with an antecedent noun, pronoun or phrase:
This is the little girl **who** will recite the poem **that** I wrote for the children's party.
    Who, whoever, what, whatever, which and **whichever** are used in a more indefinite and general sense without an antecedent:
I don't know **who** did it.
You can choose **whichever** you like.
    Reflexive pronouns are **myself, yourself, himself, herself, oneself, itself, ourselves, yourselves** and **themselves**. They refer to or stand for a noun or pronoun, or pass the action of a verb back to the subject:
The child cried **himself** to sleep.
    Reciprocal pronouns are **each other** and **one another**. They express mutual action:
Those two always quarrel with **each other**.

QUANTITATIVE Involving or relating to considerations of amount or size.

REFLEXIVE VERB When a transitive verb has a reflexive pronoun as its object so that the action passes back to the subject or the doer of the action, the verb is called reflexive:
I **dressed myself** with care.
He is always **praising himself**.
We **talked ourselves** into the deal.

REGULAR VERB Verbs that form their past tenses and past participles according to certain language rules are called regular, for example, walk, walked; promise, promised; laugh, laughed.

RELATIVE CLAUSE A relative clause usually begins with a relative pronoun (who, that, which), which refers to the antecedent noun, pronoun, phrase or clause:
Tom is the boy **who** won the prize.
You can have this book or any other **that** you like.
I got up early, **which** was a good thing.

There are two main types of relative clauses: restrictive (defining) and non-restrictive (non-defining). Restrictive clauses define or identify their antecedents and are usually essential to the meaning of a sentence. They are not separated from their antecedents by commas.
A man **who owns a farm** gets up early.
I prefer a theatre **that has a late show**.

Non-restrictive clauses give additional information about the antecedent and may be separated by commas.
My father, **who owns a farm**, gets up early.
We went to the theatre, **which was crowded**.

SEQUENCE OF TENSES The tense of the verb in a subordinate clause usually follows that of the verb in the main clause. For example, if the verb in the main clause is in the past tense, the verb in the subordinate clause should also be in the past tense.
He **convinced** me that he **loved** his work.
I **told** him that I **knew** it.
She **asked** me whether I **walked** home.

SUBJECT The subject of a sentence is the doer of an action or the being or thing about which a statement is made:
Birds eat worms.
The boys seemed happy.

Many different parts of speech can act as subjects, for example,
The **sun** is setting (noun).
She loves flowers (pronoun).
To sleep well is a blessing (infinitive).
Reading improves the mind (gerund).
Whatever I say makes him angry (clause).

SYNTAX The meaningful arrangement of words into larger units, such as clauses and phrases, within a sentence.

TENSE The tense of a verb indicates the time when the action of the verb takes place. English verbs have six tenses in both the active and passive voice:
Present: I live; it is done.
Past: I lived; it was done.
Present perfect: I have lived; it has been done.
Past perfect: I had lived; it had been done.
Future: I will/shall live; it will be done.
Future perfect: I will/shall have lived; it will have been done.

Each tense can also have a progressive form: I am living, it is being done, and so on.

VERB A verb expresses a state of an action and is used to make a statement or demand, or to ask a question:
The dog **barks**.
Come as soon as you can!
Do you **visit** them often?

Verbs are either singular (he is/has/sings) or plural (they are/have/sing) in number, and simple (lift, nourish, take) or compound (uplift, undernourish, take part) in form.

According to the way they are used in a sentence, verbs can be either transitive or intransitive. Transitive verbs can take an object: I **saw** him today.
Some − such as **detest, dislike, prefer, outwit** − are always transitive (they must be used with an object):
Do you **dislike** him?
This year we **outwitted** our competitors.

Intransitive verbs can never be used with an object:
He **arrived** late.
The boys **remained** behind.

It is important to remember that many transitive verbs can be used with or without an object:
He **sells** books (transitive), BUT The books **sell** well (intransitive).
We **sang** a song (transitive), BUT Birds **sing** (intransitive).

VOICE English verbs have two voices, the active and the passive.

The active voice indicates that the subject of the sentence does, is or becomes something:
The gardener cut the lawn.

The passive voice indicates that the subject of the sentence is being acted upon. Note that when an active sentence is made passive, the active subject becomes the passive agent and the active object becomes the passive subject:
The lawn was cut by the gardener.

Many passive constructions do not require an agent or any doer of an action:
The lawn was cut yesterday.

VISUAL DICTIONARY

The human body

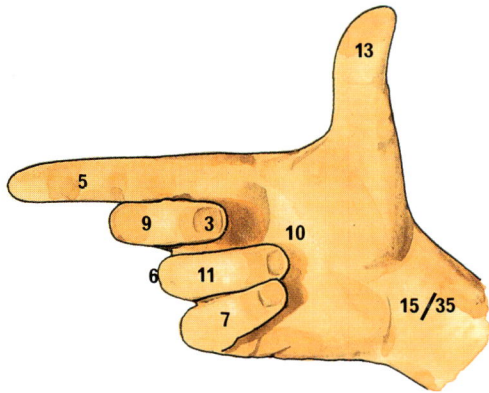

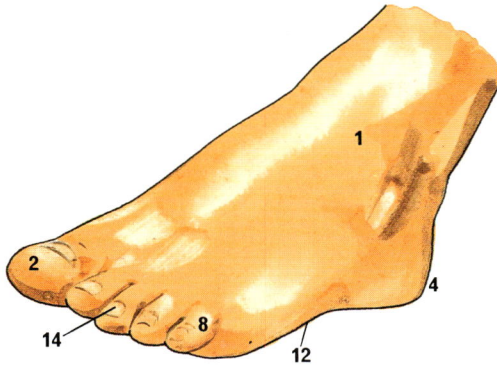

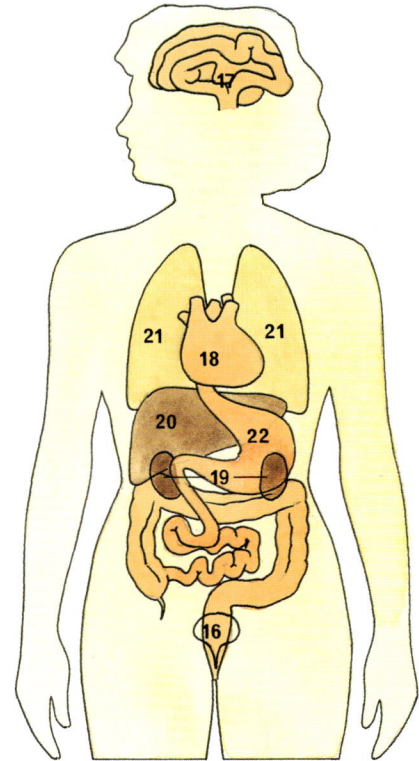

English	Afrikaans	N Sotho	Sesotho	Tswana	Xhosa	Zulu
The foot and hand	**Die voet en hand**	**Leoto le seatla**	**Leoto le seatla**	**Leoto le seatla**	**Unyawo nesandla**	**Unyawo nesandla**
1 ankle	enkel	kokoilane	leqaqailane	lenginana	iqatha	iqakala
2 big toe	groottoon	monwana wo mogolo	monwana a moholo wa leoto	monwana o mogolo	ubhontsi	uqukula
3 fingernail	vingernael	lenala	lenala	lonala	uzipho	uzipho
4 heel	hak	serethe	serethe	serethe	isithende	isithende
5 index finger (forefinger)	wysvinger	tšhupabaloi	monwana o supang	supabaloi	umnwe wokwalatha	unkomba
6 knuckle	kneukel	senoko	senoko	noko	iquphele	iqupha
7 little finger	pinkie	manapanyane	monwana o monyenyane	monnyennye	ucikicane	ucikicane
8 little toe	kleintoontjie	monwana wo monyane wa leoto	monwana wa leoto o monyenyane	monnyennye	ucikicane wozwane	uzwane oluncane
9 middle finger	middelvinger	monwanagare	monwana o mahareng	monogare	umnwe ophakathi	umunwe omude
10 palm	palm	legoswi	seatla	legofi	intende yesandla	impama
11 ring finger	ringvinger	monwana wa palamonwana	monwana wa reng	podile	umnwe womsesane	ifica
12 sole	sool	bogato	bohato	pato	isoli	intende
13 thumb	duim	mogogorupa	monwana o motona	kgonojwe	ubhontsi	isithupha
14 toenail	toonnael	lenala la monwana wa leoto	lenala la leoto	lonala lwa leoto	uzipho lozwane	uzipho lozwane
15 wrist	polsgewrig	manakaila	leqaqailane la letsoho	letlhalela	isihlahla	isihlakala

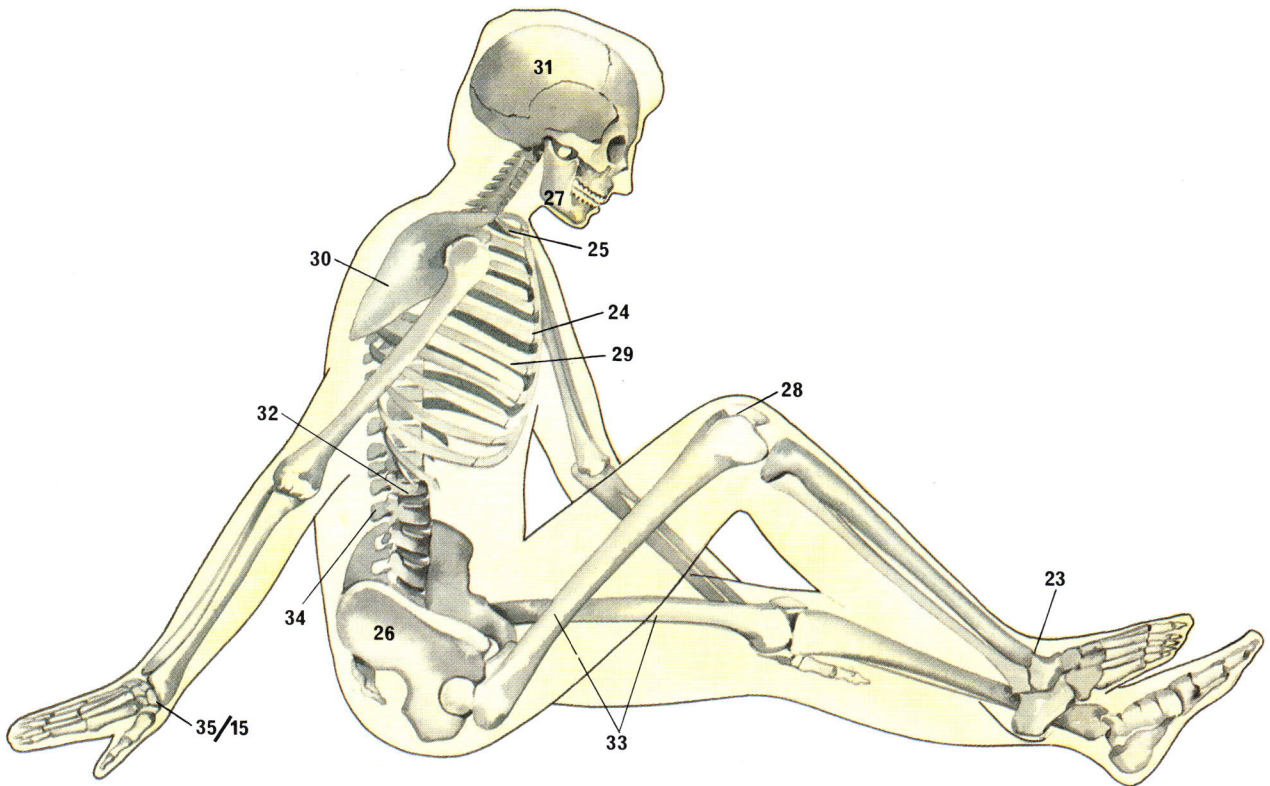

English	Afrikaans	N Sotho	Sesotho	Tswana	Xhosa	Zulu
The major organs	**Die groter organe**	**Ditho tše bohlokwa**	**Ditho tsa bohlokwa**	**Diretlo**	**Amalungu angundoqo**	**Izitho ezimqoka**
16 bladder	blaas	sebudula	senya	setlha	isinyi	isinye
17 brain	brein	bjoko	boko	boko	ubuchopho	ubuchopho
18 heart	hart	pelo	pelo	pelo	intliziyo	inhliziyo
19 kidney	nier	pshio	phio	philo	intso	inso
20 liver	lewer	sebete	sebete	sebete	isibindi	isibindi
21 lung	long	leswafo	letshwafo	lekgwafo	umphunga	iphaphu
22 stomach	maag	dimpa	mohodu	mogodu	isisu	isisu
The human skeleton	**Die menslike geraamte**	**Marapo a mmele wa motho**	**Mosohlo wa motho**	**Letlhotlholo la motho**	**Uphahla lwamathambo**	**Uhlaka lomzimba**
23 ankle joint	enkelgewrig	tokollo ya kokoilane	lenonyeletso la leqaqailane	lelokololo la lenginana	ekudibaneni kweqatha	ilunga leqakala
24 breastbone	borsbeen	kgara	lesapo la sefuba	kgara	ingqoba	ungiklane
25 collarbone	sleutelbeen	kgetlane	lepetu la molala	kgetlana	ingqosha	inqwababa
26 hipbone (pelvis)	heupbeen	letheka	lesapo la noka	lerapo la noka	ihleza	ithebe
27 jawbone	kakebeen	lerapo la mohlagare	lesapo la mohlahare	motlhagare	umhlathi	ithambo
28 kneecap	knieskyf	khurumelatolo	theledi	theledi	ilivi	ivi
29 ribs	ribbe	dikgopo	dikgopo	dikgopo	iimbambo	izimbambo
30 shoulderblade	skouerblad	segetla	sephaka	legetla	igxalaba	isiphanga
31 skull	skedel	legata	lehata	legata	ukhakhayi	ugebhezi lwekhanda
32 spine	ruggraat	mokokotlo	mokokotlo	mokokotlo	umnqonqo	umhlandla
33 thighbone	dybeen	lešukhukoto	lesufu	lerapo la serope	uthambo-fuphi	ugalo
34 vertebra	werwel	mokolo	masapo a mokokotlo	kidikidi	ithambo lomqolo	ithambo lomfunkulo
35 wrist	polsgewrig	manakaila	leqaqailane la letsoho	letlhalela	isihlahla	isihlakala

13

The human body

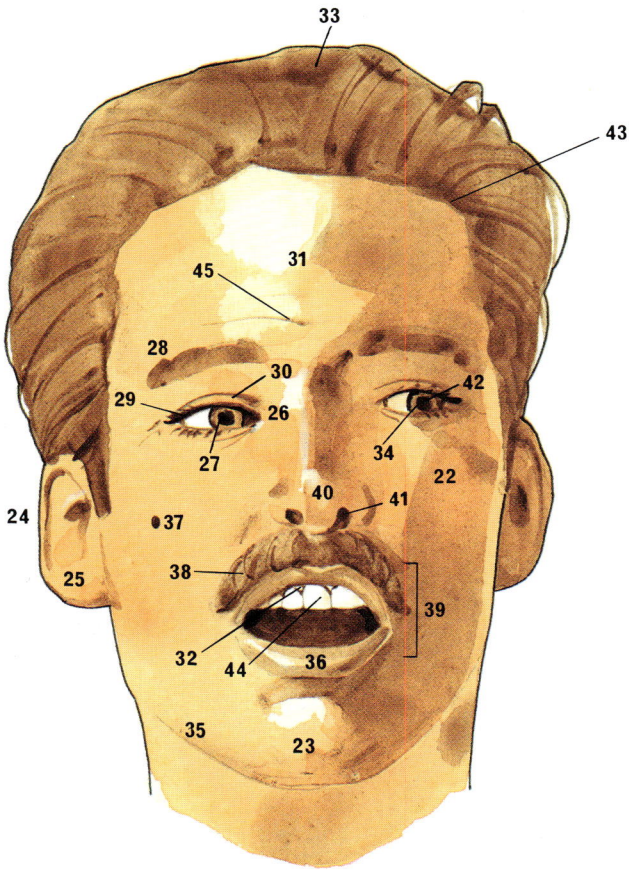

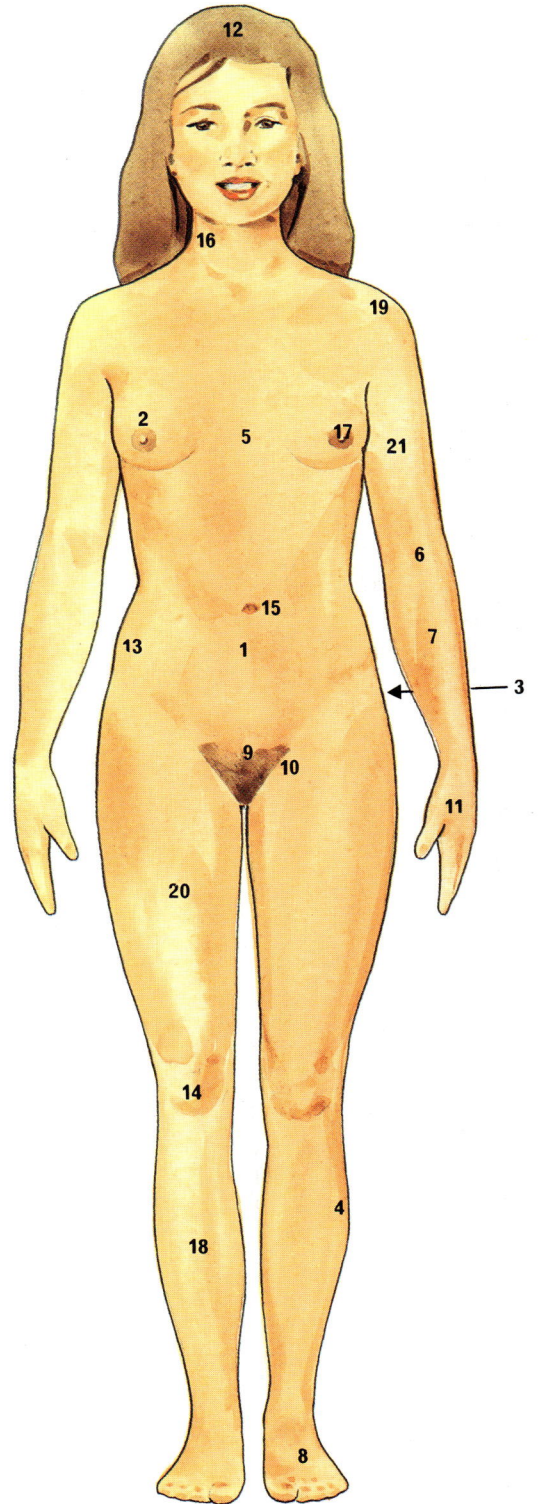

33
43
45
31
28
30
29
26
42
27
34
22
24
40
41
37
38
39
25
32
44
36
35
23

12
16
19
2
5
17
21
6
7
15
13
1
3
9
10
11
20
14
4
18
8

14

English	Afrikaans	N Sotho	Sesotho	Tswana	Xhosa	Zulu
	The human body	**Die menslike liggaam**	**Mmele wa motho**	**Mmele wa motho**	**Mmele wa motho**	**Umzimba womntu**	**Umzimba womuntu**
1	abdomen	buik	mpa	mpa	mpa	isisu	isisu
2	breast	bors	letswele	lebele	lebele	ibele	ibele
3	buttock	boud	lerago	sebono	lerago	intsula	isinqe
4	calf	kuit	potana	tlhafu	letlhau	ithole	isihluzu
5	chest	borskas	sehuba	sefuba	sefuba	isifuba	isifuba
6	elbow	elmboog	setšu	setswe	sejabana	ingqiniba	indololwane
7	forearm	voorarm	letsogo	letsoho	mokgono	ingalo	umkhono
8	foot	voet	leoto	leoto	leoto	unyawo	unyawo
9	genitals	geslagsorgane	dithobong	mapele	mapele	impahla enqabileyo	izitho zokuzala
10	groin	lies	lengamu	tshwelesa	lengamu	umphakatho	imbilapho
11	hand	hand	seatla	seatla	seatla	isandla	isandla
12	head	kop	hlogo	hlooho	tlhogo	intloko	ikhanda
13	hip	heup	letheka	noka	noka	inyonga	inqulu
14	knee	knie	letolo	lengole	lengole	idolo	idolo
15	navel	naeltjie	mokhubu	mokgubu	khubu	inkaba	inkaba
16	neck	nek	molala	molala	molala	intamo	intamo
17	nipple	tepel	tlhoko	tlhoko	tlhoko	ingono	isibele
18	shin	maermerrie	lenotlo	moomo	motwane	uxhongo	umbala
19	shoulder	skouer	legetla	lehetla	legetla	igxalaba	ihlombe
20	thigh	dy	serope	serope	serope	ithanga	ithanga
21	upper arm	boarm	sefaka	sephaka	lesufutsogo	ingalo engentla	umkhono ongenhla
	The head and face	**Die kop en gesig**	**Hlogo le sefahlego**	**Hlooho le sefahleho**	**Tlhogo le sefatlhago**	**Intloko nobuso**	**Ikhanda nobuso**
22	cheek	wang	lerama	lerama	lerama	isidlele	isihlathi
23	chin	ken	seledu	seledu	seledu	isilevu	isilevu
24	ear	oor	tsebe	tsebe	tsebe	indlebe	indlebe
25	earlobe	oorlel	lerethe	rete la tsebe	lereto	idlebe	isicube sendlebe
26	eye	oog	leihlo	leihlo	leitlho	iliso	iso
27	eyeball	oogappel	thaka ya leihlo	thaka e tshweu	kgolokweitlho	ukhozo lweliso	inhlamvu yeso
28	eyebrow	wenkbrou	ntšikgolo	dintshi	losi	ishiyi	ishiya
29	eyelash	ooghaar	ntši	dintshi	ntshi	umsebe	ukhophe
30	eyelid	ooglid	phuphu	dintshi	lesi	inkophe	ijwabu leso
31	forehead	voorkop	phatla	phatla	phatla	ibunzi	ibunzi
32	gums	tandvleis	marinini	marinini	marinini	iintsini	izinsini
33	hair	hare	moriri	moriri	moriri	unwele	unwele
34	iris	iris	leratladi la leihlo	irise	molathaka	isangqa seliso	isiyinge seso
35	jaw	kaak	mohlagare	mohlahare	motlhagare	umhlathi	umhlathi
36	lip	lip	molomo	mkolomo	pounama	umlebe	udebe
37	mole	moesie	tlhokobelé	sehloba	setlhoba	umkhango	umkhangu
38	moustache	snor	ditedu	tedu	tedu	udevu	amadevu
39	mouth	mond	molomo	molomo	molomo	umlomo	umlomo
40	nose	neus	nko	nko	nko	impumlo	ikhala
41	nostril	neusgat	lešobana la nko	dinko	lerobananko	iphumlo	ikhala
42	pupil	pupil	thaka ya leihlo	thaka ya leihlo	thaka	ukhozo lweliso	inhlamvu yeso
43	scalp	kopvel	letlalo la hlogo	letlalo la hlooho	letlalo la tlhogo	ufele lwentloko	isikhumba sekhanda
44	tooth	tand	leino	leino	leino	izinyo	izinyo
45	wrinkle	plooi	lešošo	maswebe	letsutsuba	umbimbi	umxhiliba

The house: plan

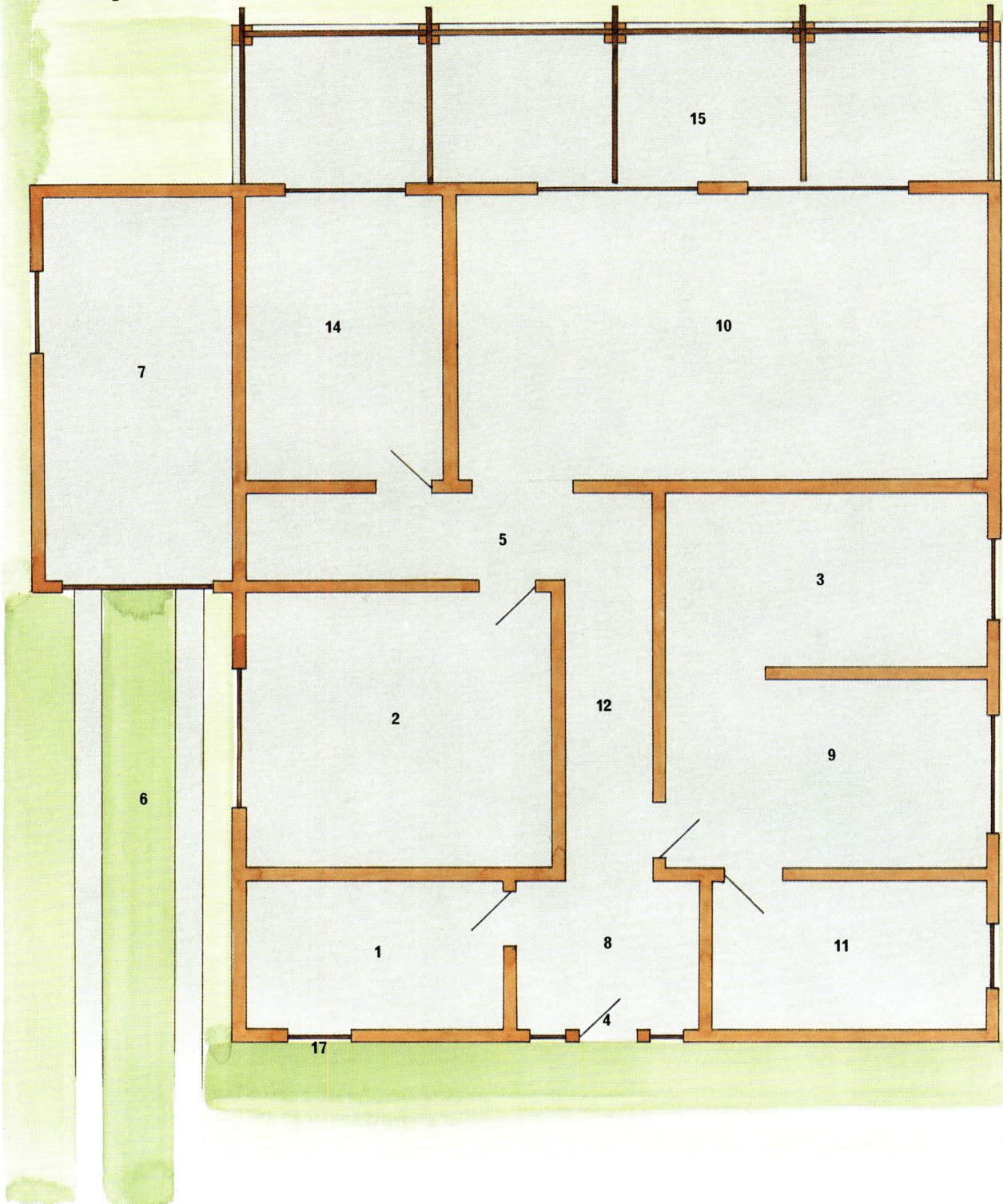

English	Afrikaans	N Sotho	Sesotho	Tswana	Xhosa	Zulu
House plan	**Huisplan**	**Polane ya ngwako**	**Polane ya ntlo**	**Thalo ya ntlo**	**Iplani yendlu**	**Okwasendlini**
1 bathroom	badkamer	bohlapelo	batekamore	botlhapelo	igumbi lokuhlambela	ibhavulumu
2 bedroom	slaapkamer	borobalelo	kamore	borobalo	igumbi lokulala	ibhedilumu
3 dining room	eetkamer	bojelo	phaposi ya ho jela	bojelo	igumbi lokutyela	ikamelo lokudlela
4 door	deur	lemati	lemati	lebati	ucango	umnyango
5 floor	vloer	lebato	foluru	bodilo	umgangatho	ifulo
6 driveway	inrit	mokgotha	tselana ya koloi	mmila	indledlana	idrayiviweyi
7 garage	motorhuis	karatše	karatjhe	karatše	igaraji	igalaji
8 hallway	voorportaal	matseno	sebae	ntlolehalala	iholwana yokungena	ihholo
9 kitchen	kombuis	khitši	kitjhene	boapeelo	ikhitshi	ikhishi
10 lounge	sitkamer	boitišetšo	phaposi ya boikgathollo	kamore ya boitapoloso	igumbi lokuhlala	ilawunji
11 pantry	spens	bobolokeladijo	sepense	polokelo ya dijo	ipentri	iphentri
12 passage	gang	phasetše	gang	peseje	ipaseji	iphasiji
13 roof	dak	tlhaka	marulelo	marulelo	uphahla	uphahla
14 study	studeerkamer	phapošiboithutelo	phaposi ya dibuka	boithuto	istudy	isitadi
15 veranda	veranda	mathudi	foranteng	mathudi	iveranda	uvulanda
16 wall	muur	leboto	lebota	lobota	udonga	udonga
17 window	venster	lefastere	fensetere	fensetere	ifestile	ifasitela

English	Afrikaans	N Sotho	Sesotho	Tswana	Xhosa	Zulu
Lounge	Sitkamer	Boitišetšo	Phaposi ya boikgathollo	Boitapoloso le bojelo	Igumbi loluhlala nelokutyela	Ilawunji
1 aerial	lugdraad	eriele	ereyale	eriele	ieriyali	uthi lomsakazo
2 armchair	leunstoel	setulo sa boiketlo	setulo sa maikeho	setulo	isitulo sokuhlala	isihlalo
3 ashtray	asbakkie	sethinthelamolora	setshelamolora	selatlhelamolora	isityana sothuthu	i-eshithreyi
4 burglar bars	diefysters	ditshipi tša go thibela mahodu	dithibelamashodu	dithibelabagodu	iintsimbi zokuthintela amasela	ibheglagadi
5 ceiling	plafon	siling	siling	sileng	isilingi	isilingi
6 coffee table	koffietafel	tafolana ya kofi	tafole ya kofi	tafole	itafilana	itafulo lekhofi
7 curtain rod	gordynstok	mphegelo wa garetene	sefala sa kgaretene	kota ya gatene	intsimbi ejinga umkhusane	induku yamakhethini
8 curtains	gordyne	digaretene	dikgaretene	gatene	imikhusane	amakhethini
9 cushion	kussing	mosamelo	mosamonyana	mosamo	umqamelo	ikhushini
10 firegrate	kaggelrooster	segoletšamollo	sehadiki sa leifo	gerate ya iso	iintsinjana zokubasela	uhlaka lokubasela
11 fireplace	kaggel	sebešo	leifo	leiso	iziko	iziko
12 firescreen	vuurskerm	seširetšamollo	sesireletsamollo	sesireletso sa molelo	isikhuse li-mlilo	umpheme womlilo
13 grandfather clock	staanhorlosie	sešupanako se segolo sa go emelela	watjhe e tjepameng	sesupanako	iwotshi engasahambiyo	ikilogo elikhulu
14 mantelpiece	kaggelrak	raka ya sebešo	mohaolwana wa leifo	raka ya leiso	ithalana eliphezu kweziko	ishelufu eliphezu kweziko
15 picture	prent	seswantšho	setshwantsho	setshwantsho	umfanekiso	isithombe
16 reclining chair	lêstoel	setulo sa go kanama	setulo se kakallang	setulo sa go robala	isitulo esiqethukayo	isihlalo sokuqhiyama
17 record player	platespeler	seralokadirekoto	sebapala direkoto	setshameka diraikoto	isidlala-zipleyiti	isidlali-marekhodi
18 rocking chair	rystoel		setulo se pholletsang	setulo sa go itisa	isitulo esishukumayo	untenga
19 rug	mat	mmete	mmata	mata	imethi	umata
20 settee	rusbank	panka ya boikhutšo	sofa	banka	isitulo sokuphumla	usofa
21 speaker	luidspreker	spikara	sepikara	sebusakgolo	ispikha	isandisilizwi
22 tape deck	bandspeler	seralokadikhasete	theiperekotara	setshameka dikasete	isidlali-teyiphu	ithephurikhoda
23 television set	televisiestel	thelebišene	thelebishine	thelebišhene	ithelevizhini	ithelevishini
24 tuner/amplifier	instemmer/versterker	segodiši/seoketši	empolifaya	segodisimodumo	ityhuna	i-amplifaya
25 vase	blompot	sebjana sa matšoba	sejana sa dipalesa	morufašeše	ivazi	ivazi
26 video recorder	video-opnemer	motšhene wa video	rekotara ya video	setshameka diwidio	ivideo	ividiyorekhoda
27 wall-to-wall carpet	volvloertapyt	khapete ye e tlalago lebato	khapete ya motlalantlo	dimata tse di tletseng	ikhapethi egqibe indlu yonke	ikhaphethi engugu-dludonga
28 window	venster	lefastere	fensetere	fensetere	ifestile	ifasitela
29 windowsill	vensterbank	lerakwana la lefastere	mohaolwana wa fensetere	sebopelo sa fensetere	indawo emthebelele ngasefestileni	iwindosili

The house: dining room

20

English	Afrikaans	N Sotho	Sesotho	Tswana	Xhosa	Zulu
Dining room	**Eetkamer**	**Bojelo**	**Phaposi ya boikgathollo**	**Boitapoloso le bojelo**	**Igumbi loluhlala nelokutyela**	**Ilawunji**
1 carving set	voorsnystel	sete ya dithipapetlo	diseti	dithipa	iseti yeemela	imimese yokusika inyama
2 chair back	stoelrug	marago a setulo	mokokotlo wa setulo	setulo sa go itshegetsa	indawo yolung-qiyamisa umhlana	umuvu wesihlalo
3 chair leg	stoelpoot	leoto la setulo	leoto la setulo	leoto la setulo	umlenze wesitulo	umlenze wesihlalo
4 cup	koppie	kopi	kopi	kopi	ikopi	inkomishi
5 dessert bowl	dessertbakkie	sebjana sa phuting	sekotlolo sa dijeli	sejana	isityana sesimun-cumunca	isitsha sephudingi
6 dessert spoon	dessertlepel	lepola la phuting	kgaba ya dijeli	leswana	icephe lesimuncumuncu	isipunu sephudingi
7 dining table	eettafel	tafola ya go jela	tafole ya ho jela	tafole	itafile yokutyela	itafula lokudlela
8 display cabinet	vertoonkas	lekasepontšho	khabinete ya mekgabiso	lekase	idisipleyi	ikhabethe lokukhangisa
9 dresser	buffet	lekase la khitši	teresara	kase	ikhabhathana yasegumbini lokulala	idresa
10 fish fork	visvurk	foroko ya hlapi	fereko ya tlhapi	foroko ya go ja tlhapi	ifolokhwe yentlanzi	imfologo yokudla inhlanzi
11 fish knife	vismes	thipa ya hlapi	thipa ya tlhapi	thipa ya go ja tlhapi	imela yentlanzi	ummese wokudla inhlanzi
12 floorboard	vloerplank	lepolanka la lebato	fuluru ya meapolanka	polanka ya bodilo	umgangatho weplanga	amapulangwe efulo
13 fork	vurk	foroko	fereko	foroko	ifolokhwe	imfologo
14 knife	mes	thipa	thipa	thipa	imela	ummese
15 placemat	tafelmatjie	mmetana wa tafola	mmatanyana wa tafole	sealo sa tafole	imethi yetafile	
16 plate	bord	poroto	poleite	poliete	ipleyiti	ipuleti
17 saucer	piering	piring	pirinki	pirinki	isosara	isosa
18 serviette	servet	sebiete	seviete	sephimola	iphetshana lokusula izandla	isafethe
19 sideboard	buffet	saepoto	saeboroto	kase	isayibhothi	isayidibhodi
20 soup bowl	sopbord	poroto ya sopo	sejana sa sopo	boroto ya sopo	isityana sesuphu	isitsha sesobho
21 soup spoon	soplepel	lepola la sopo	kgaba ya sopo	leswana la sopo	icephe lesuphu	ukhezo lwesobho
22 tablecloth	tafeldoek	tafoletuku	tafole tuku	tafoletuku	ilaphu letafile	indwangu yetafula
23 tea trolley	teewaentjie	troli ya teye	kolotsana ya tee	koloi ya tee	itroli yeti	inqolana yetiye

English	Afrikaans	N Sotho	Sesotho	Tswana	Xhosa	Zulu
Kitchen	**Kombuis**	**Khitšhi**	**Kitjhine**	**Boapeelo**	**Igumbi lokutyela**	**Ikhishi**
1 breadbin	broodblik	bobolokelo bja borotho	sejaka sa borotho	sa borotho	isigcini-sonka	isiphathisinkwa
2 breadboard	broodbord	lepolanka la go segela borotho	boroto ya borotho	sesegelaborotho	iplanga lesonka	uqwembe lokusikela isinkwa
3 breadslicer	broodsnyer	sesegaborotho	sekgabelaborotho	sesegaborotho	umashini wokusika isonka	ummese wesinkwa
4 coffee percolator	sypelkan	motšhene wa go dira kofi	kane ya kofi	seapayakofi	umashini wokubisisa ikofu	isibilisikhofi
5 deepfreeze	vrieskas	tipifrisi	forisara	setsidifatshe	idipfrizi	idiphufrizi
6 dishcloth	vadoek	fatuku	fatuku	fatuku	ilaphu lezitya	imfaduko
7 dishwasher	skottelgoedwasser	motšhene wa go hlatswa dibjana	sehlatswadijana	setlhatswadijelo	umashini wokuhlamba izitya	isihlanzizitsha
8 draining board	droogplank	lepolanka la go omišetša	lepolanka la ho omisa	polanka ya go omisa	idraining board	ipulangwe lokomisela
9 extractor fan	suigwaaier	segogamoya	sebutswelasemonyi	sefoki se se gogang	ifeni yomoya	ifeni esashimula
10 fire extinguisher	brandblusser	setimamollo	setimamollo	setimamolelo	isicimi-mlilo	isicimimlilo
11 grill	rooster	segadikelo	sehadiki	kwamisa	irostile	igrili
12 jug	beker	lebekere	lebekere	bekere	ijoko	ijeke
13 kettle	ketel	ketlele	ketlele	ketlele	iketile	igedlela
14 microwave oven	mikrogolfoond	onto ya maekroweife	onto ya maekoroweife	onto ya dimaekerowaefe	ioveni eyimak-hroweyivi	uhhavini oyima-khrowevi
15 peppermill	pepermeul	tšhilo ya pherefere	lewala la pepere	tshilo ya pepere	ilitye lokusila ipepile	isigayo sikapelepele
16 power plug	kragprop	polaka ya mohlagase	polaka	polaka	iplagi yombane	iplagi yamandla
17 power socket	kragpunt	polaka ya mohlagase	setsi sa motlakase	tokelo ya poropo	isokethi yombane	isokhethi yamandla
18 refrigerator	yskas	fritši	forije	setsidifatshe	ifriji	ifiliji
19 rubbish bin	vullisblik	seolelelamatlakala	motou wa dithole	motomo wa matlakala	umgqomo wenkunkuma	isiphathizibi
20 saltcellar	soutpotjie	sebjana sa letswai	pitsana ya letswai	poto ya letswai	imbizana yetyuwa	isiphathatswayi
21 sink	wasbak	sehlatswetšo	sinke	setlhatswetso	isinki	izinki
22 spice	spesery	senoko	dinoki	seloki	isinongo	isipayisi
23 stove	stoof	setofo	setofo	setofo	isitovu	isitofu
24 switch	skakelaar	switši	sewitjhe	switshi	iqhosha	iswishi
25 tap	kraan	pompi	pompo	thepe	itepu	umpompi
26 tea caddy	teeblik	boleke bja teye	kane ya tee	thini ya tee	itoti yeti	ithini letiye
27 tea cosy	teemus		lepae la ketlele		isigcini-bushushu	ithikhosi
28 teapot	teepot	ketlele ya teye	ketlele ya tee	ketlele ya tee	itipoti	ithibhothi
29 teastrainer	teesiffie	sefo ya teye	sefe ya tee	sefo ya tee	istreyina seti	isisefo setiye
30 tin opener	bliksnyer	sebulathini	sebuladithine	sebulathini	isixhobo sokuvula inkonkxa	isivulithini
31 toast	roosterbrood	senkgwabešwa	borotho bo besitsweng	borotho bo bo besitsweng	ithowusti	ithosi
32 toaster	broodrooster	sebešasenkgwa	sebesaborotho	sebesaborotho	ithowusta	ithositha
33 toast rack	broodstander	seswarasenkgwabešwa	raka ya ho besa borotho		ithala lesonka esirhawuliweyo	isiphathithosi
34 tumbledrier	tuimeldroër	motšhene wa go omiša mašela	seomisakamoya	seomisamatsela	umatshini wokomisa impahla	umshini wokukhama
35 washing machine	wasmasjien	motšhene wa go hlatswa mašela	motjhine wa ho hlatswa	setlhatswadiaparo	umashini wokuhlamba impahla	umshini wokuwasha

The house: pantry

English	Afrikaans	N Sotho	Sesotho	Tswana	Xhosa	Zulu
Pantry	**Spens**	**Bobolokelo bja dijo**	**Sepense**	**Polokelo ya dijo**	**Ipentri**	**Iphandolo**
1 broom	besem	leswielo	lefielo	lefeelo	umtshayelo	umshanelo
2 casserole dish	bakskottel	sekotlelo sa go pakela	sekotlolo sa hlama	sekotlele sa go besa	isitya sokubhaka	indishi yokupheka
3 corkscrew	kurktrekker	sentšhaporopo	sehulaporopo	segogakoroko	isikrufu sokuvula ipropu	isivulikhokho
4 dustpan	skoppie	seolelatlakala	pane ya dithole	seolatlakala	idastpani	ipani lezibi
5 eggbeater	eierklitser	sefehlamae	sefehlamahe	sefatlhamae	isiqhuqhi-qanda	isiphehli maqanda
6 egg cup	eierkelkie	sebjana sa lee	kopi ya lehe	sejelalee	ikopi yeqanda	inkomishi yeqanda
7 eggtimer	sandlopertjie		sekopalehe	sesupanako sa go apaya lee	ieggtimer	isibilisiqanda
8 electric mixer	elektriese menger	setswakanyi sa mohlagase	sedubi sa motlakase	setlhakanya	isixubi sikagesi	umshini wokuxuba
9 frying pan	braaipan	pane ya go gadikela	pane ya ho hadika	pane ya go gadika	ipani yokuqhotsa	ipani lokosa
10 grater	rasper	segohlo	rasepere	segotlhane	igreyitha	igretha
11 iron	strykyster	aene	aene	aene	iayini	i-ayini
12 ironing board	strykplank	lepolanka la go aenela	boto ya ho aena	sesedilelo	iplanga lokuayinela	ipulangwe loku-ayina
13 ladle	potlepel	leho	lesokwana	leswana	umcephe	ukhezo lokuphakela
14 liquidiser	versapper	motšhene wa go dira seela	sephofodifatsi	seedisa	ilikhwidayiza	isenzaluketshezi
15 measuring jug	maatbeker	lebekere la kelo	jeke ya ho metha	bekere ya go lekeletsa	ijoko yokumeta	ijeke lokulinganisa
16 mincer	vleismeul	tšhilo ya nama	sesilanama	tshilo	umatshini wokucumza inyama	isigayo senyama
17 mop	stokdweil	mopo	mopo	mopo	imophu	isesuli
18 polisher	poleerder	motšhene wa go pholeša mabato	sepolishe	sephatshimisi	isigudisi	umshini wokupholisha
19 pressure cooker	drukkastrol	pitšakgatelelo	kasetorole ya kgatello	kaseterole ya phufudi	imbiza epheka ngomphunga	iphreshakhukha
20 salad bowl	slaaibak	sebjana sa selae	sejana sa disalate	baka ya selete	ingqoko yesaladi	isitsha sesaladi
21 saucepan	kastrol	kastrolo	kesetorole	kaseterole	ipani	isosipani
22 sieve	sif	sefo	sefe	sefo	intluzo	isisefo
23 tinned food	blikkieskos	sejobolekana	dijo tsa dithine		ukutya okunkonk-xiweyo	ukudla kwasethinini
24 tray	skinkbord	threi	sekenkeboroto	terei	itreyi	ithileyi
25 vacuum cleaner	stofsuier	motšhene wa go hlwekiša mebete	semonyadithole	segogalorole	umatshini wokucoca womoya	umshini wekhaphethi

The house: bedroom

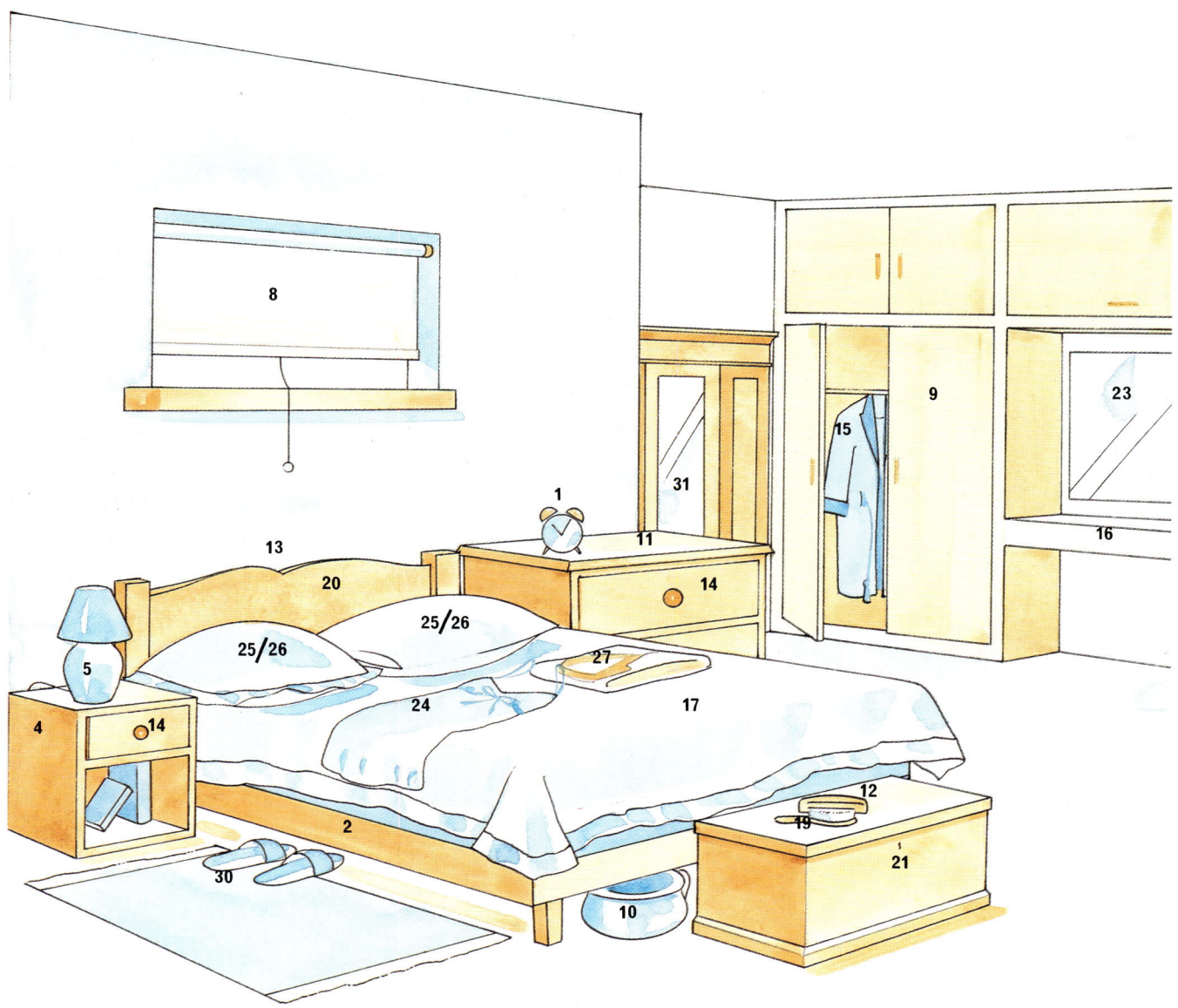

English	Afrikaans	N Sotho	Sesotho	Tswana	Xhosa	Zulu
Bedroom	**Slaapkamer**	**Borobalelo**	**Phaposi ya boroko**	**Borobalo**	**Igumbi lokulala**	**Ibhedilumu**
1 alarm clock	wekker	tšhupanakophafoša	watjhe ya ho tsosa borokong	sesupanako	iwotshi ekhalayo	ikilogo
2 bed	bed	bolao	bethe	bolao	ibhedi	umbhede
3 bedlinen	beddegoed	mašela a malao	mealo	dialo	amashiti	izingubo zombhede
4 bedside cabinet	bedkassie	lekasana la bolaong	lebokosana la pela bethe	kase ya bolao	ikhabhathi yangaseb-hedini	ikhabethe elisecakombhede
5 bedside lamp	bedlamp	lebone la bolaong	lebone la pela bethe	lobone fa bolaong	isibane sangasebhedini	isibane sasembhedeni
6 bedspread	deken	tekene	betheseporete	dekene	ibhedspredi	isipredi
7 blanket	kombers	kobo	kobo	kobo	ingubo	ingubo
8 rollerblind	rolblinding	seširo sa rolare	kgaratene ya rolara		ikhethini esongwayo	isisithalanga
9 built-in cupboard	muurkas	khapoto ye e agetšwego lebotong	wateropo ya leboteng	lekase	ikhabhathi eyakhelwe eludongeni	ikhabethe
10 chamber pot	kamerpot	sebjana sa mohlapologo	thuana		isitya sasebusuku	ishembe
11 chest of drawers	laaikas	lekase la dilaiki	lebokose la dilae	lekase la dilai	ikasi yeedrowa	ikhabethe elinamadilowa
12 comb	kam	kamo	kama	kamo	ikama	ikamu
13 double bed	dubbelbed	bolao bja ba babedi	bethe ya ba babedi	bolao bo bo tona	idabul-bhedi	umbhede oyidabuli
14 drawer	laai	laiki	lae	lai	idrowa	idilowa
15 dressing gown	kamerjas	kamorejase	jase ya kamoreng	japono	igawuni yokuvuka	igawuni yasekuseni
16 dressing table	spieëltafel	spilekase	tafolana ya ho itshasa	tafole ya seipone	itafile yokunxibela	idresingithebuli
17 duvet	duvet	tekene	duvete	duwei	iduveyi	iduveyi
18 eiderdown	donskombers	sekika	eidadawone	kobo ya mafofa	iayidadawuni	i-adadawuni
19 hairbrush	haarborsel	poraše ya meriri	borosolo ya moriri	boratshe ya moriri	ibrashi yeenwele	ibhulashi lezinwele
20 headboard	kopstuk	dihlogo tša bolao	heteboto		ihedibhodi	ihedibhodi
21 kist	kis	lekese	kisete	kese	ityesi	umphongolo
22 mattress	matras	matrase	materase	materase	umatrasi	umatrasi
23 mirror	spieël	seipone	seipone	seipone	isipili	isibuko
24 nightgown	nagrok	seaparo sa go robala	mose wa boroko	mosese wa go robala	igawuni yasebusuku	ilokwe lokulala
25 pillow	kussing	mosamelo	mosamo	mosamo	umqamelo	umcamelo
26 pillowslip	kussingsloop	mokotlana wa mosamelo	mokotlana mosamo	sekhupetsa mosamo	isilophu somqamelo	isikhwama somcamelo
27 pyjamas	pajamas	ditšwarwamalaong	dipijama	diaparo tsa go robala	impahla yokulala	amapijama
28 sheet	laken	lakane	lakene	llakane	ishiti	ishidi
29 single bed	enkelbed	bolao bja motho o tee	bethe ya motho ya mong	bolao bo bonnye	isingili bhedi	umbhede wesingili
30 slippers	pantoffels	disilipere	meqathatso		izihlangu zokulala	amahliphisi
31 wardrobe	hangkas	watropo	wateropo	lekase la diaparo	iwodrophu	ikhabethe lezingubo

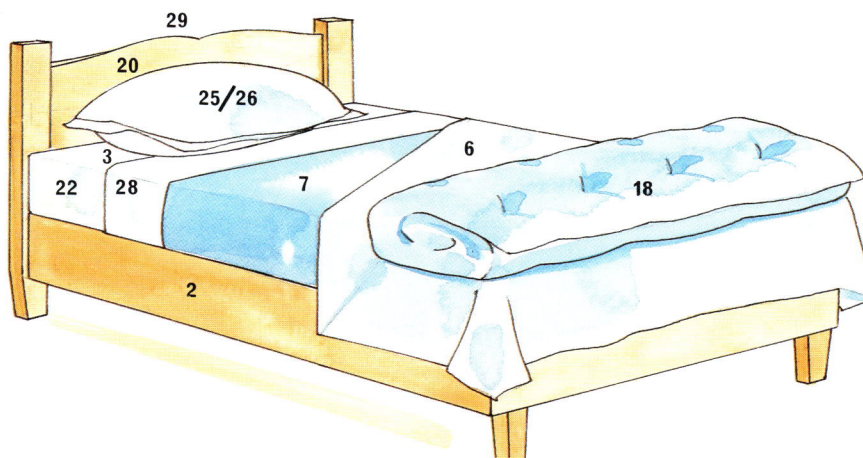

	English	Afrikaans	N Sotho	Sesotho	Tswana	Xhosa	Zulu
	Bathroom	**Badkamer**	**Bohlapelo**	**Batekamore**	**Botlhapelo**	**Igumbi lokuhlambela**	**Ibhavulumu**
1	bath	bad	pafo	bate	bata	ibhafu	ubhavu
2	bathmat	badmat	mmetana wa pafo	mmata wa bate	mata ya bata	imethi yebhafu	umata webhavu
3	bathplug	badprop	poropo ya pafo	polaka ya bate	poropo ya bata	isivingco sebhafu	isivalo sobhavu
4	cistern	waterbak	sehlapelo	nkgwana ntlwana	baka ya metsi	ithobhi	itangi
5	cold-water tap	kouewaterkraan	pompi ya meetse a go tonya	pompo ya metsi a batang	thepe ya metsi a mat-sididi	itepu yamanzi abandayo	umpompi wamanzi abandayo
6	facecloth	waslap	lešela la go hlapa	baselapa	waselapa	ivasi-laphu	indwangu yokugeza
7	handcream	room	setlolo sa diatla	setlolo sa matsoho	mafura	amafutha ezandla	ukhilimu
8	hot-water tap	warmwaterkraan	pompi ya meetse a go fiša	pompo ya metsi a tjhesang	thepe ya metsi a a bolelo	itepu yamanzi ashushu	umpompi wamanzi ashisayo
9	make-up	grimering	ditlolo	ho itshasa sefahleho	ditshasetsasefatlhego	ukuzenza	imekhaphu
10	medicine cabinet	medisynekassie	lepokisana la dihlare	lebokose la meriana	kase ya setlhare	indawo yamayeza	ikasi lomuthi
11	nailbrush	naelborsel	poraše ya dinala	borosolo ya dinala	boratshe ya dinala	ibrashi yeenzipho	ibhulashi lezinzipho
12	overflow	oorloop	sefaladišo	ho kgaphatseha	tshologo	ukuphuphuma	ukuchichima
13	pedestal	voetstuk	lepolanka la maotong	lepolanka la maot ong	leoto	isizinzi	isigqiki
14	plughole	propgat	lešoba la polaka	lesoba la polaka	mosima wa poropo	isivingco	umgodi
15	razor	skeermes	motšhene wa go beola	lehare	reisara	ireyiza	ireyiza
16	sewage pipe	rioolpyp	phaepe ya kelatšhila	phaepe ya mantle	peipe ya maswe	umbhobho wesureji	ipayipi lendle
17	shampoo	sjampoe	sešepe sa moriri	shampo	sesepa sa moriri	isihlambi-nwele	ishampu
18	shaving brush	skeerkwas	poraše ya go beola	borosolo ya ho beola	boratshe ya go poma	ibrashi yokutsheva	ibhulashi lokusheva
19	shaving cream	skeerroom	sešepe sa go beola	sesepa sa ho beola	sesepa sa go poma	ikhrim yokutsheva	insipho yokusheva
20	shower	stortbad	šawara	shawara	seawere	ishawari	ishawa
21	shower cubicle	storthokkie	lefelo la šawara	sekgutlwana sa shawara	seawere	igunjana leshawa	indawo yokushawa
22	shower curtain	stortgordyn	seširo sa šawara	kgarete ne ya shawara	gartene ya seawere	umkhusane weshawari	ikhetheni leshawa
23	soapdish	seepbakkie	seswarasešepe	sejana sa sesepa	baki ya sesepa	isityana sesepha	isiphathinsipho
24	sponge	spons	sepontšhe	sepontjhe	sepontshe	isiponji	
25	toilet bowl	toiletbak	tshipi ya boithomelo	sekotlolo sa ntlwana	baka ya boithusetso	ithobhi	ilavathi
26	toilet roll	toiletpapier	pampiri ya go itlhakola	pampiri ya ntlwana	pampiri ya boithusetso	iphepha lasese	iphepha laselavathi
27	toilet seat	bril	bodulelo bja boithomelo	setulo sa ntlwana	manno a boithusetso	isihlalo sasese	isihlalo selavathi
28	toothbrush	tandeborsel	poraše ya meno	borosolo ya meno	segatlhameno	ibhrashi yamazinyo	ibhulashi lamazinyo
29	toothpaste	tandepasta	sešepe sa meno	sesepa sa meno	sesepa sa meno	intlama yamazinyo	umuthi wamazinyo
30	towel	handdoek	toulo	thaole	toulo	itawuli	ithawula
31	towel rail	handdoekreëling	bofegelo bja toulo	sefala sa dithaole	maanego a ditoulo	intsimbi yokuxhoma itawuli	isilengisithawula
32	wall tile	muurteël	thaele ya leboto	thaele ya leboteng	ditaile tsa lebota	ithayile yodonga	itayili
33	washbasin	wasbak	lehlapelo	sekotlolo sa ho hlapa	botlhapelo	isitya sokuhlambela	iwashibheseni
34	waterpipe	waterpyp	phaepe ya meetse	phaepe ya metsi	leela la metsi	umbhobho wamanzi	ipayipi lamanzi

The house: garden

English	Afrikaans	N Sotho	Sesotho	Tswana	Xhosa	Zulu
Garden	**Tuin**	**Serapa**	**Serapa**	**Tshingwana**	**Igadi**	**Ingadi**
1 braai	vleisbraaiplek	bobešetšo	sebesetsong	bobesanama	indawo yokoja	indawo yokosa
2 compost	kompos	podišwa	kompose	motsetelo	ikhomposi	ikhomposi
3 deckchair	dekstoel	setulo sa ka ntle	setulo sa deke	setulo	isitulo esisongwayo	isihlalo saphandle
4 diving board	duikplank	lepolankatlompela	lepolanka la ho qwela	polanka ya go tlolela	iplanga lokuntywilela	ibhodi lokutshuza
5 edge trimmer	randafwerker	sesegamathoko	sekgabisadintlha	sesega dieje	umatshini wokuphetha	isiphundli
6 fence	heining	legora	fense	legora	ubiyelo	ifensi
7 filter	filter	mohlotlo	sesireletsi	motlhotlho	intluzo	ifiltha
8 flowerbed	blombedding	seloto sa matšoba	sebakana sa dipalesa	lekidi la disese	ibhedi yeentyatyambo	umbhede wezimbali
9 flowers	blomme	matšoba	dipalesa	disese	iintyatyambo	izimbali
10 garden fork	tuinvurk	foroko ya serapa	fereko ya serapa	foroko	ifolokhwe yegadi	imfologo yengadi
11 garden hose	tuinslang	lethopo la serapa	lethopo	leela	ithumbu legadi	ithumbu lokunisela
12 garden umbrella	sonsambreel	samporele ya serapa	samporele sa serapa	sekhukhu	isambreni sasegadini	isambulela
13 greenhouse	kweekhuis	ntlo ya go medišetša	ntlo ya dimela	ntlo ya go tlhogisa dijwalo	indlwana yokuntshulisa izityalo	indlu eluhlaza
14 grid	rooster	sebešetšo	rostere	kerete	irostile	insimbi yokosa enezikhala
15 hand fork	tuinvurkie	forokwana ya serapa	fereko ya letsoho	forokwana	ifolokhwana yesandla	imfologo yesandla
16 hedge	heining	legora	seotlwana	legora	intendelezo	uthango
17 lawn	grasperk	bjang bjo bo bjetšwego	lono	bojang	ibala lengca	ingilazi

English	Afrikaans	N Sotho	Sesotho	Tswana	Xhosa	Zulu
18 lawnmower	grassnyer	motšhene wa go sega bjang	sekutajwang	sesegabojang	umashini wokusika ingca	umshini wokusika utshani
19 potplant	potplant	semela sa ka pitšeng	palesa ya pitsaneng	setlhogapotong	isityalo esikhula enkonkxeni	
20 rake	hark	hareka	haraka	haraka	iharika	ihhala
21 secateurs	snoeiskêr	sekero sa go kgothakgotha	sefaodi	sekero	isikere sokuthena imithi	isikelo semithi
22 shears	tuinskêr	sekero sa serapa	sekere sa serapa	sekero	isikere	isikelo sengadi
23 shrub	struik	mohlašana	sehlahla	setlhatsana	isigcume	isihlahlana
24 spade	graaf	garafo	kgarafu	garawe	umhlakulo	isipete
25 sprinkler	sproeier	sefotšhedi	senyanyatsi	segasametsi	isiprinkila	isifafazi
26 stepladder	trapleer	llere	lere	llere	ileri emfutshane	isitebhisi
27 swimming pool	swembad	boruthelo	letangwana la ho sesa	bothumelo	iqula lasemakhaya lokuqubha	idamu lokubhukuda
28 tree	boom	sehlare	sefate	setlhare	umthi	umuthi
29 trowel	tuingrafie	garafšana ya serapa	kgarafunyana	garawe	umhlakulwana	itrofela
30 watering can	gieter	tšhitere	kgitere	gitere	inkonkxa yokunkcenk-ceshela	iketela
31 weedkiller	onkruiddoder	sebolayasekoro	sebolayalehola	sebolayamofero	isibulali-khula	isibulalikhula
32 weeds	onkruid	sekoro	lehola	mofero	ukhula	ukhula
33 wheelbarrow	kruiwa	kiribane	keribaye	kiriba	ikiriva	ibhala

31

The office

English	Afrikaans	N Sotho	Sesotho	Tswana	Xhosa	Zulu
Office	Kantoor	Ofisi	Kantoro	Ofisi	Iofisi	Ihhovisi
1 adhesive tape	kleefband	segomaretši	theipe e kgomarelang	theipi ya kgomaretso	iseloteyipi	ithephu enamathelayo
2 bookcase	boekkas	lekase la dipuku	raka ya dibuka	lekase la dibuka	ikasi yeencwadi	ikhabethe lamabhuku
3 calculator	sakrekenaar	sebaledi	sekopanyi	sebalela	ikhaltyuleyitha	isibali
4 calendar	almanak	almanaka	alemenaka	alemanaka	ikhalenda	ikalenda
5 carbon paper	koolpapier	pampiri ya khapone	pampiri ya khabone	pampiri ya karobono	ikhabhoni	ikhabhoniphepha
6 desk	lessenaar	teske	deseke	banka	idesika	ideski
7 diary	dagboek	pukutšatši	daeri	buka ya malatsi	idayari	idayari
8 dictaphone	diktafoon	diktafone	diketafouno	sebiletso	itheyiphurekhoda	isiqophalizwi
9 eraser	uitveër	sephumodi	raba	sephimodi	into yokucima	iraba
10 fan	waaier	fene	sefehlamoya	sefoki	ifeni	ifeni
11 file	lêer	faele	faele	faile	ifayile	ifayili
12 filing cabinet	lêerkabinet	lekase la difaele	kabinete ya difaele	lekase la difaile	ikhabhathi egcina iifayile	ikhabethe lamafayili
13 keyboard	toetsbord	khiipoto	boroto ya dinotlolo	boroto ya tekeletso	ikhibhodi	ikhibhodi
14 notebook	notaboek	puku ya go ngwalela	noutebuka	buka ya dinoutu	incwadana yamanqaku	inothibhuku
15 paperclip	skuifspeld	sepatiši sa dipampiri	sepelete sa pampiri	kgokelo ya dipampiri	into yokunqakula amaphepha	isiqhano samaphepha
16 paperweight	papierdrukker	segateletši sa dipampiri	sehatisapampiri	segatisa dipampiri	isicinzeli-phepha	isicindezeli maphepha
17 pencil sharpener	potloodskerper	selootšaphensele	seleotsapensele	selootsadiphesele	umashini wokulola epensile	isilolipensele
18 personal computer (PC)	persoonlike rekenaar (PR)	khomputa ye e lego ya gago	khomputa ya haoe	kompiutara	ikhompiyutha yakho	ikomphiyuta
19 printer	drukker	motšhene wa go gatiša	mohatisi	segatisi	isishicileli	iphrinta
20 ruler	liniaal	rula	rula	rula	irula	irula
21 screen	skerm	seswantšhetšo	seotlwana	sesireletso	umkhusane	umpheme
22 software	programmatuur	mananeo a khomputa	sepampiri	tsa porougeramo	impahla yekhompiyutha	isoftiweya
23 staple	kram	kgokaganyi ya dipampiri	seteipola	kgokelo	isteyipile	isitephuli
24 stapler	krammer	segokaganyi sa dipampiri	seteipolara	sa go kgokela	isteyipula	isitephula
25 stationery	skryfbehoeftes	dingwalelo	tsa ho ngola	tsa go kwala	izinto zokubhala	okokubhala
26 telephone	telefoon	thelefomo	telefouno	mogala	ifoni	ucingo
27 telephone directory	telefoongids	pukunomoro ya thelefomo	buka ya ditelefouno	buka ya dinomoro tsa mogala	incwadi yefoni	incwadi yezinamba zocingo
28 typewriter	tikmasjien	setlanyi	setlapisi	setlanyi	umashini wokuchwetheza	umshini wokuthayipha
29 typist's chair	tiksterstoel	setulo sa motlanyi	setulo sa motlapisi	setulo sa motlanyi	isitulo somchwethezi	isihlalo sikathayiphisi
30 wastepaper basket	snippermandjie	mmanki wa dipampiri	seroto sa dipampiri	bolatlhelo jwa dipampiri	ibhaskiti yenkunkuma	ibhasikede lezibi

The car

SERVICE STATION

English	Afrikaans	N Sotho	Sesotho	Tswana	Xhosa	Zulu
The car	**Die motor**	**Koloi**	**Mmotorakara**	**Mmotorokara**	**Imoto**	**Imoto**
1 jack	domkrag	tomkraga	jeke	jeke	ujek	ujeke
2 petrol pump	petrolpomp	pompi ya peterolo	pompo ya peterole	pompo ya peterolo	impompo yepetroli	iphampu likapetroli
3 service station	vulstasie	karatšhe	peterolong	karatšhe	isikhululo sokutha ipetroli	igalaji
4 spare wheel	noodwiel	leotwanadutwa	sepewili	lekgwatlho	ivili	isipele
5 workshop	werkswinkel	bošomelo	ntlo ya ho tehela	bodirelo	igumbi lokulungisela iimoto	ishabhu
Bodywork	**Bakwerk**	**Mmele**	**Bodi**	**Baka**	**Ibhodi**	**Umzimba wemoto**
6 bonnet/hood	enjinkap	ponete	bonete	bonete	ibhonethi	ibhonethe
7 boot	bagasiebak	putu	butu	butu	ibhuti	ibhuthi lemoto
8 bumper	stamper	pampara	bampara	sethulo	ibhampari	ibhampa
9 clearance certificate	klaringsbewys	setifikeiti ya tokelo	lengolo la laesense	seretifikaiti ya tshiamo	iphepha-mvume	isitifiketu sobuninimoto
10 door handle	deurknop	seswaro sa lemati	hentlele ya lemati	setshwaro	isiphatho socango	isibambo somnyango
11 headlight	koplig	lebone le legolo	lebone la ka pele	lebone	isibane	isibane sangaphambili
12 hubcap	naafdop	sekhurumelo sa hapo	wilekhepe	topo ya leotwana	isiciko sevili	iwilikhephu
13 indicator light	rigtingwyser	lebonepanyapanyi	lebone la paipai	pontshi	i-indikheyitha	inkomba
14 mudguard	modderskerm	sethibaleraga	sethibelaseretse	sesiraretse	imargathi	umadigadi
15 numberplate	nommerplaat	polatanomoro	polata ya dinomoro	nomoropolata	icwecwe lenambari	inambapuleti
16 parking light	parkeerlig	lebonephaka	lebone la ho paka	lebone la go phaka	ipaki layithi	izibani zokupaka
17 rearview mirror	truspieël	seiponeponatšamorago	seipone sa tse morao	seipone sa go bona kwa morago	isipili sokujonga ngemva	isibuko semoto
18 rear window	agterruit	lefastere la morago	fensetere ya ka morao	sesiraphefo sa kwa morago	ifestile yangasemva	ifasitela langemuva
19 roof	dak	bogodimo bja koloi	marulelo	bogodimo	uphahla	uphahla
20 safety belt	veiligheidsgordel	lepanta la tšhireletšo	lebanta la boipoloko	mabanta a polokego	ibhanti yesinqe	ibhande lokuphepha
21 sunroof	sondak	sanrufu	marulelo a nang le lemati	bodilo jwa go tsensa letsatsi	isanrufu	uphahla olukhanyayo
22 tread (of tyre)	loopvlak	makgwakgwa a thaere	sole	botsamayo	amaqoqo ethayara	ugqinsi lwethaya
23 wheel	wiel	leotwana	lebidi	leotwana	ivili	isondo
24 windscreen	voorruit	seširaphefo	fensetere ya ka pele	sesiraphefo	ifestile yangaphambili	ifasitela langaphambili

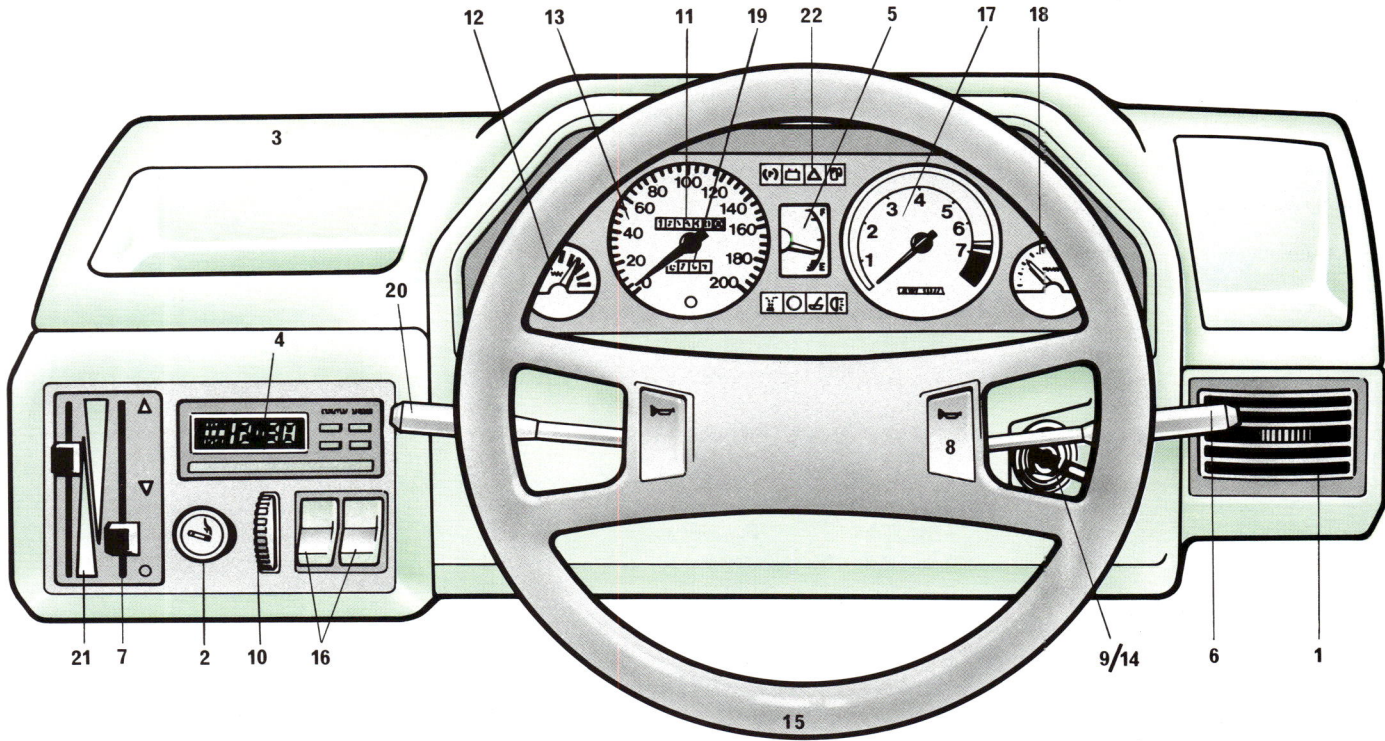

English	Afrikaans	N Sotho	Sesotho	Tswana	Xhosa	Zulu
Instruments	**Instrumente**	**Didirišwa**	**Disebediswa**	**Disupa**	**Izixhobo**	**Amathuluzi**
1 air vent	lugopening	lešoba la moya	lesobana la moya	setsentsaphefo	intunja yomoya	isingenisamoya
2 cigarette lighter	sigaretaansteker	sethumašasekerete	sehotetsi sa sakarete	setshuba	icwilika	ilayithela
3 dashboard	intrumentpaneel	tešepoto	mohaolwana wa ka pele	boroto ya disupetso	ideshibhodi	udeshibhodi
4 digital clock	digitale horlosie	sešupanako sa go panyapanya	watjhe ya dinomoro	sesupanako	ixesha	iwashi
5 fuel gauge	brandstofmeter	selekanyapeterolo	semethamafura	sesupamafura	isilinganisi mafutha	igeji likapetroli
6 headlight switch	kopligskakelaar	switšhi ya mabone a magolo	sehotetsamabone	setshubamabone	iswitshi yezibane	iswishi lezibani
7 heater control	verwarmerbeheer	selaolaseruthufatši	selaolamofuthu	sa go setela bothito	indawo yokulawula isifudumezi	izilawuli zesifudumezi
8 hooter	toeter	hutara	phala	lenaka	uphondo	ihuta
9 ignition switch	onstekingskakelaar	switšhikgotetši sa entšene	sekgwathaenjene	sefamollo	iswitshi yokuchukumisa imoto	iswishi sesitatha
10 instrument dimmer	instrumentverdowwer	sefokotšalesedi la tešepoto	selaolakganya	setimalobone	isiqhwanyazisi	isifiphazi
11 odometer	odometer	odometara	odomethara	odometara	isixhobo sokubala umgama	isibali-makhilomitha
12 oil-pressure gauge	oliedrukmeter	selekanyakgatelelo sa oli	semethamatla-a-oli	metara ya ole	usiba lweoyile	igeji lika-oyela
13 speedometer	spoedmeter	tšhupetšobelo	semethalebelo	sesupalobelo	usiba lwamendu	ispidomitha
14 steering lock	stuurslot	sekgonyasetering	senotlelasetering	senotlelalebili	isitshixo sesiqhubo	isikhiye sesitelingi
15 steering wheel	stuurwiel	setering	setering	lebili	isiqhubo	isitelingi
16 switches	skakelaars	diswitšhi	dihotetsi	diswitšhi	iswitshi	amaswishi
17 tachometer/rev counter	tagometer/ revolusieteller	sebaladitikologo	semethamodumo	sesupatikologo	irevkhawunta	iwashi lokureva kwemoto
18 temperature gauge	temperatuurmeter	seelathemperetšha	semethathemperetjha	sesupathemperetšha	usiba lobushuhhu	igeji lokushisa
19 trip odometer	toer-odometer	metara ya leeto	semethamaeto	odometara ya mo-tsamayo	isibali sobude bohambo	isibali-makhilomitha ohambo
20 turning indicator	rigtingwyser	lebonepanyapanyi	paipai ya ho thinya	pontshi	isalathisi sokujika	inkombajika
21 ventilator control	ventilasiebeheer	selaolatsenyomoya	selaolamoya	go laola phefo	isilawuli singenisi moya	isilawuli sesi-ngenisamoya
22 warning lights	klikligte	mabonetemošo	mabone a tshohanyetso	mabone a go supa kotsi	izibane zengozi	amahazadi

The car: mechanics

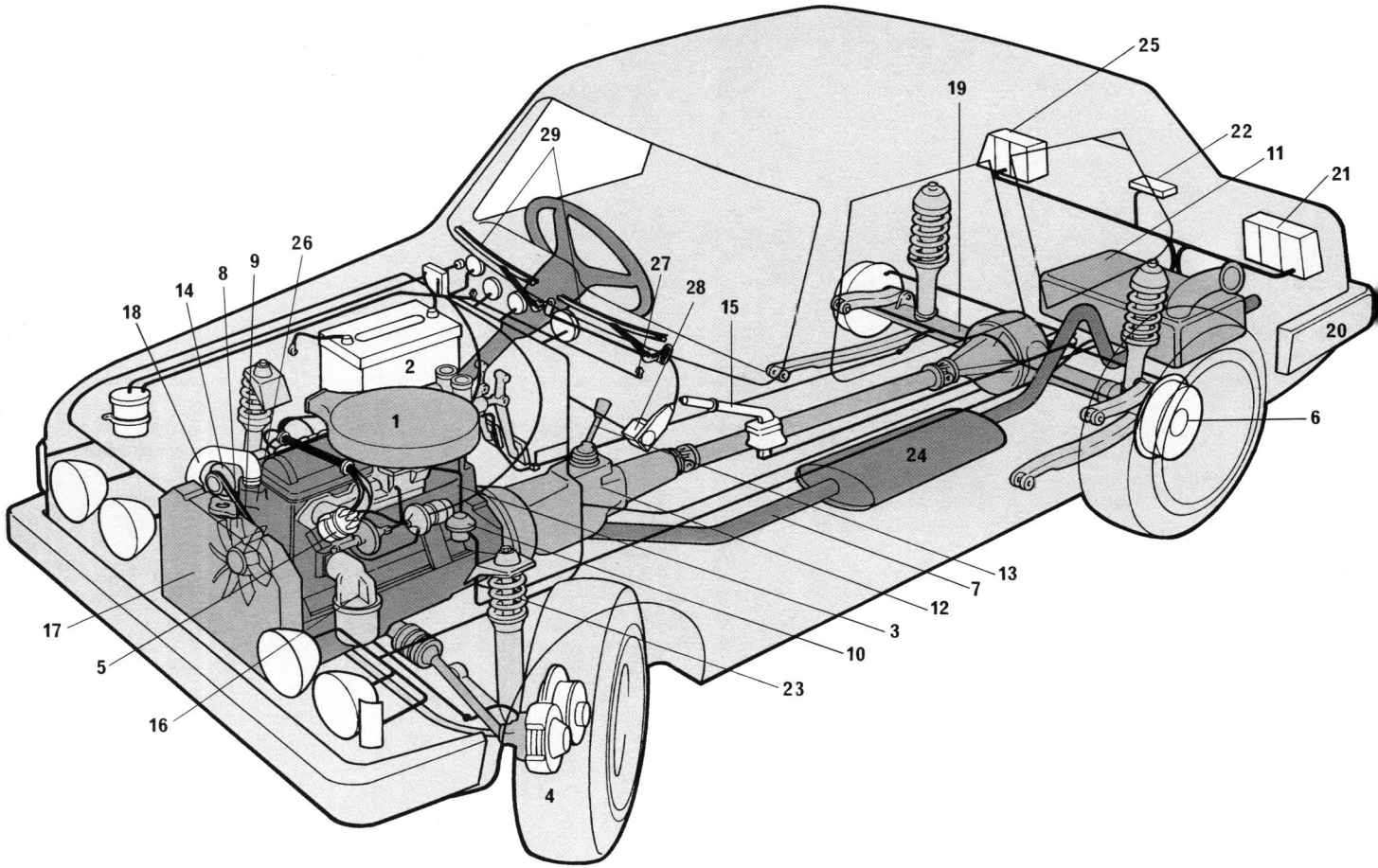

English	Afrikaans	N Sotho	Sesotho	Tswana	Xhosa	Zulu
Mechanics	**Meganieka**	**Bomotšhene**	**Botehi**	**Ssemotshini**	**uKhando**	**uBukhenikha**
1 air cleaner	lugfilter	sehlwekišamoya	sehlwekisamoya	setshekisamowa	isihluzi-moya	i-eliklina
2 battery	battery	peteri	bateri	lelatlha	ibhetri	ibhetri
3 carburettor	vergasser	khabareita	khabareitara	semowafatsi	ikhabhareyitha	ikhaburetha
4 disc brakes	skyfremme	diporiki tša phaphathi	mariki a diseke	diborikiphaphatshana	idisk breki	amabhuliki
5 distributor	verdeler	seabaganyi	seqhalamollo	seabi	isixhobo esihambisa umbane	idistribhutha
6 drum brake	tromrem	poriki ya teramo	mariki a diseke	boriki	idram breki	ibhuliki elisedilamini
7 exhaust pipe	uitlaatpyp	sentšhamuši	ekesose	sentshamosi	umbhobho woku-khupha umsi ngemva	ipayipi lesayilensa
8 fan	waaier	fene	sefehlamoya	sefoki	ifeni	ifeni
9 fanbelt	waaierband	lepanta la sefokišamoya	lebanta la sefehlamoya	lebanta la sefoki	ifanbelt	ibhande lefeni
10 fuel pump	brandstofpomp	pompi ya peterolo	pompo ya mafura	pompo ya mafura	impompo yepetroli	iphamphu likapetroli
11 fuel tank	brandstoftenk	tanka ya peterolo	tanka ya mafura	tanka ya mafura	itenki yepetroli	ithangi likapetroli
12 gearbox	ratkas	kerepokisi	kerebokose	kerebokoso	igiyebhoksi	igelibhoksi
13 gear lever	rathefboom	libara ya dikere	selaolakere	sefetoladikere	igqudu lokutshintsha	iliva legeli
14 generator/alternator	ontwikkelaar	tšenereithara	jenereitara	sefetlhi	ijenereyitha	ijeneretha
15 handbrake	handrem	porikitsogo	boriki ba letsoho	boriki jwa seatla	ibhreki yesandla	ibhuliki lesandla
16 oil filter	oliefilter	sehlwekišaoli	sesefaoli	motlhotlho wa ole	isihluzi-oyile	ifilita lika-oyela
17 radiator	verkoeler	radietara	sephodisi	setsidifatsi	iradiyeyitha	irediyetha
18 radiator hose	verkoelerslang	lethopo la radietara	lethopo la sephodisi	peipi ya setsidifatsi	umbhobho weradiyeyitha	ipayipi lerediyetha
19 rear axle	agteras	ase ya morago	ase ya ka morao	ase ya kwa morago	iasi yangasemva	i-ekseli yangemuva
20 rear bumper	agterstamper	pampara ya morago	bampara ya ka morao	sethulo sa morago	ibhampari yangasemva	ibhampa yangemuva
21 rear light	agterlig	lebone la morago	lebone la ka morao	lebone la morago	isibane sangemva	isibane sangemuva
22 reversing light	trulig	lebone la ribese	lebone la ho tjhetjha	lebone la morago	isibane sokubuya umva	isibane sokulivesa
23 shock absorber	skokbreker	semetšašoko	sefokotsa ho tlolatlola	soko	ishok-abzobha	ishoka
24 silencer	knaldemper	saelensara	setheolamodumo	sethulamisa modumo	isayilensa	isayilensa
25 stoplight	stoplig	setopolaete	lebone le lefubedu	mabone a a supang go ema	istoplayiti	isibane samabhuliki
26 thermostat	termostaat	selaolathempheretša	selaolamotjheso	selaolabolelo	ithemostati	ithemostati
27 windscreen washer	ruitwasser	sehlwekišamafastere	sehlatswafensetere	setlhatswasesiraphefo	isihlambi sefestile yan-gaphambili	isigezafasitela
28 windscreen wiper motor	ruitveërmotor	sesepediši sa sephumulaseširaphefo	motjhine wa seh-lakolafensetere	motshini wa setlha-tswasesiraphefo	umatshinana wezisuli-festile	umshini wamawayipha
29 windscreen wiper blade	ruitveërblad	phaphati ya sephumulaseširaphefo	leleme la seh-lakolafensetere	bolate ya setlha-tswasesiraphefo	ukutya kwezisuli-festile	iwayipha

Sport: soccer

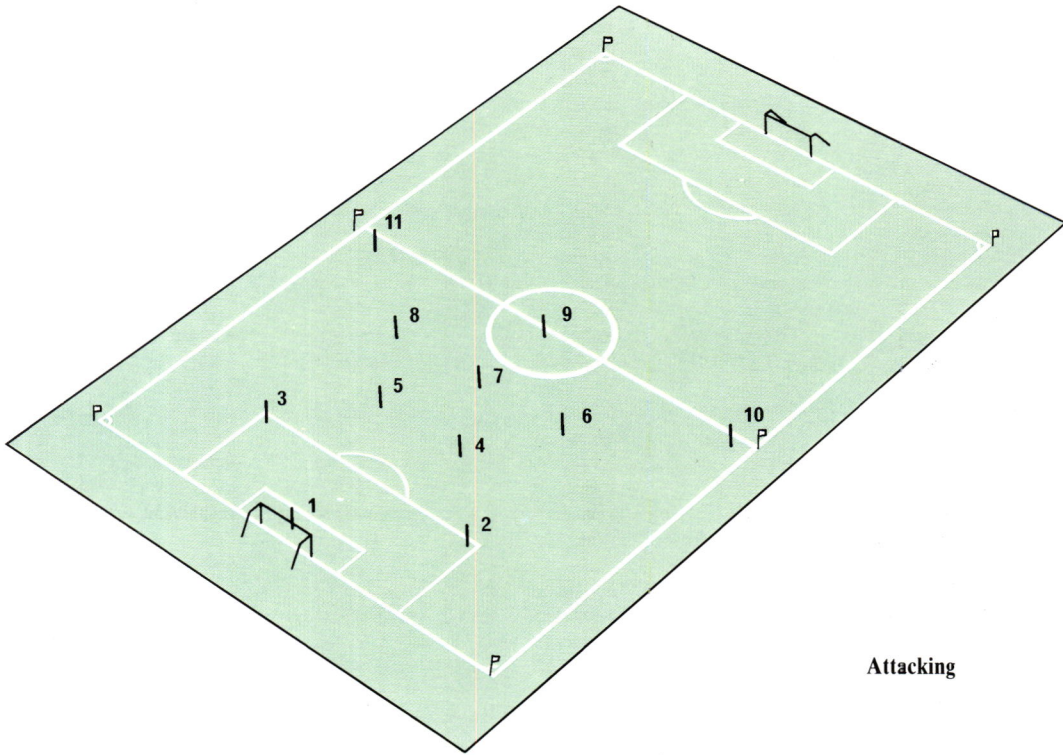

Attacking

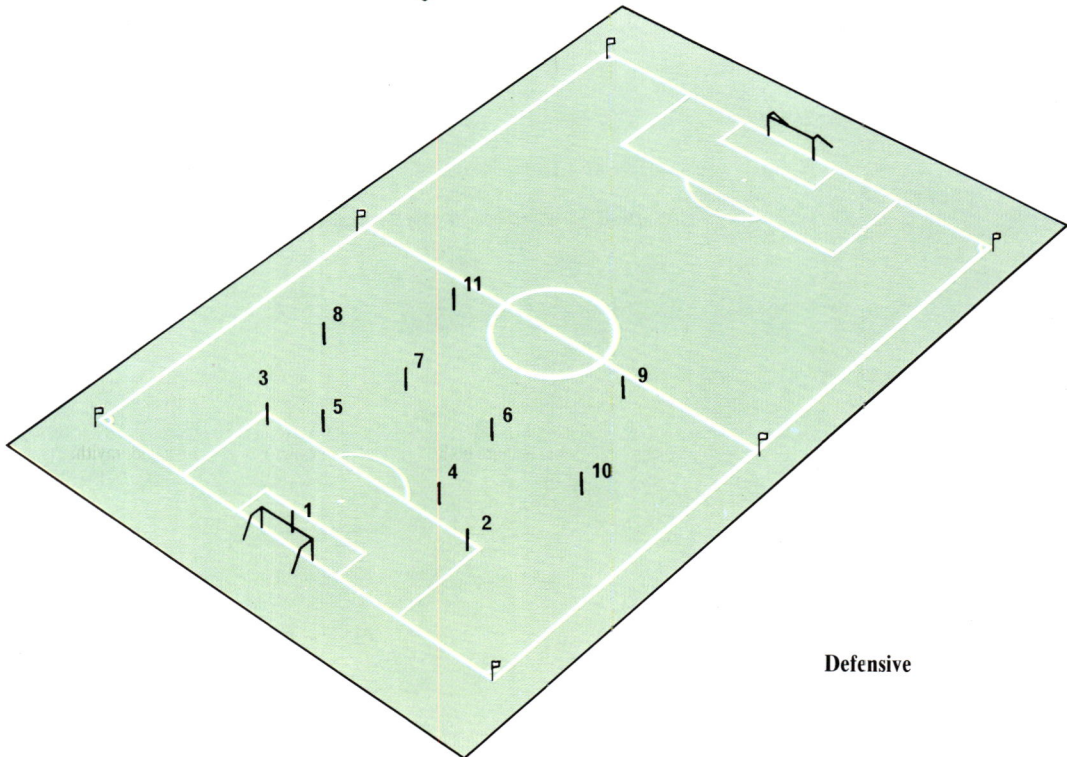

Defensive

40

	English	Afrikaans	N Sotho	Sesotho	Tswana	Xhosa	Zulu
	Soccer	**Sokker**	**Kgwele ya maoto**	**Bolo**	**Kgwele ya dinao**	**Ibhola ekhatywayo**	**Unobhutshuzwayo**
	The players	**Die spelers**	**Baraloki**	**Dibapadi**	**Batshameki**	**Abadlali**	**Abadlali**
	formation 4:3:3	formasie 4:3:3	tlhamo 4:3:3	tlhophiso 4:3:3	tshameko ya 4:3:3	ihlelo 4:3:3	iphethini elingu 4:3:3
	(attacking)	(aanvallend)	(ya tlhaselo)	(tlhaselo)	(e e tlhaselang)	(bayahlasela)	(ukuhlasela)
1	goalkeeper (goalie)	doelwagter	radino	sethibathibane	motshwaradino	umgcini-pali	unozinti
	defenders:	verdedigers:	bahlabanedi:	basireletsi:	basireletsi:	abakhuseli:	amadifenda:
4	centreback	middelagter	mothušabahlabanedi	mosireletsi ya mahareng	motshamekagaremorago	isentabhekhi	isentabhekhi
5	centrehalf	middelskakel	motlemaganyi	motlatsamosiretletsi ya mahareng	mothusa-motshamekagare	isentahafu	isentahhafu
3	left back	linksagter	mohlabanedinngeleng	mosireletsi ka leqeleng	motshamekamorago wa molema	ileftibhekhi	ifulibhekhi yanga-kwesokunxele
2	right back	regsagter	mohlabanedigojeng	mosireletsi ho le letona	motshamekamorago wa moja	irayithibhekhi	ifulibhekhi yanga-kwesokudla
	midfielders:	middelveldspelers:	baralokagare:	dibapalahare:	batshamekigare:	abadlala esiswini:	abadlali basesiswini:
7	centre	middelspeler	moropi	sebapalasetsing	motshamekigare	isenta	isenta
8	left half	linkerskakel	motlemaganyinngeleng	sebapalahare ka leqeleng	motshamekakopanyo wa molema	ileftihafu	ihhafu yanga-kwesokunxele
6	right half	regterskakel	motlemaganyigojeng	sebapalahare ho le letona	motshamekakopanyo wa moja	irayithihafu	ihhafu yanga-kwesokudla
	forwards:	voorspelers:	baralokapele:	dibapalapele:	motshamekapele:	abadlali abaphambili:	amafolosi:
9	centre forward	middelvoor	monoši	sebapalapele se mahareng	motshamekapelegare	isentafowadi	isentafowadi
11	left wing	linkervleuel	morapinngeleng	sebapalapele ka leqeleng	motshamekathoko wa molema	iphiko lasekhohlo	iwingi yanga-kwesokunxele
10	right wing	regtervleuel	morapigojeng	sebapalapele ho le letona	motshamekathoko wa moja	iphiko lasekunene	iwingi yangakwesokudla
	formation 4:4:2	formasie 4:4:2	tlhamo 4:4:2	tlhaphiso 4:4:2	tshameko ya 4:4:2	ukuma 4:4:2	iphethini elingu 4:4:2
	(defensive)	(verdedigend)	(ya phemelo)	(tshireletso)	(tshireletso)	(-khuselayo)	(nokuyikela)
1	goalkeeper (goalie)	doelwagter	radino	sethibathibane	motshwaradino	umgcini-pali	unozinti
	defenders:	verdedigers:	bahlabanedi:	basireletsi:	basireletsi:	abakhuseli:	amadifenda:
4	centreback	middelagter	mothušabahlabanedi	mosireletsi ya mahareng	motshamekagaremorago	isentabhekhi	isentabhekhi
5	centrehalf	middelskakel	motlemaganyi	motlatsamosireletsi ya mahareng	mothusa-motshamekagare	isentahafu	isentahhafu
3	left back	linksagter	mohlabanedinngeleng	mosireletsi ka leqeleng	motshamekamorago wa molema	ileftibhekhi	ifulibhekhi yanga-kwesokunxele
2	right back	regsagter	mohlabanedigojeng	mosireletsi ho le letona	motshamekamorago wa moja	irayithibhekhi	ifulibhekhi yanga-kwesokudla
	midfielders:	middelveldspelers:	baralokagare:	dibapalahare:	batshamekigare:	abadlala esiswini:	abadlali basesiswini:
7	inside left	linksbinne	morapšananngeleng	sebapalahare se leqeleng ka hare	motshamekigare wa molema	i-insayidilefti	i-ina yanga-kwesokunxele
6	inside right	regsbinne	morapšanagojeng	sebapalahare ho le letona ka hare	motshamekigare wa moja	i-insayidi rayithi	i-ina yangakwesokudla
8	outside left	linksbuite	morapinngeleng	sebapalahare se leqeleng ka ntle	motshamekintle wa molema	iawuthisayidi lefti	umdlali wasophondweni
10	outside right	regsbuite	morapigojeng	sebapalahare ho le letona ka ntle	motshamekintle wa moja	iawuthisayidi rayithi	umdlali wasophondweni
	forwards:	voorspelers:	baralokapele:	dibapalapele:	motshamekipele:	abadlala phambili:	amafolosi:
9,11	striker (x2)	aanvalsvoorspeler (x2)		mohlasedi (x2)	motshamekipele yo o tlhaselang (x2)	istrayikha (x2)	umgadli (x2)

Sport: soccer

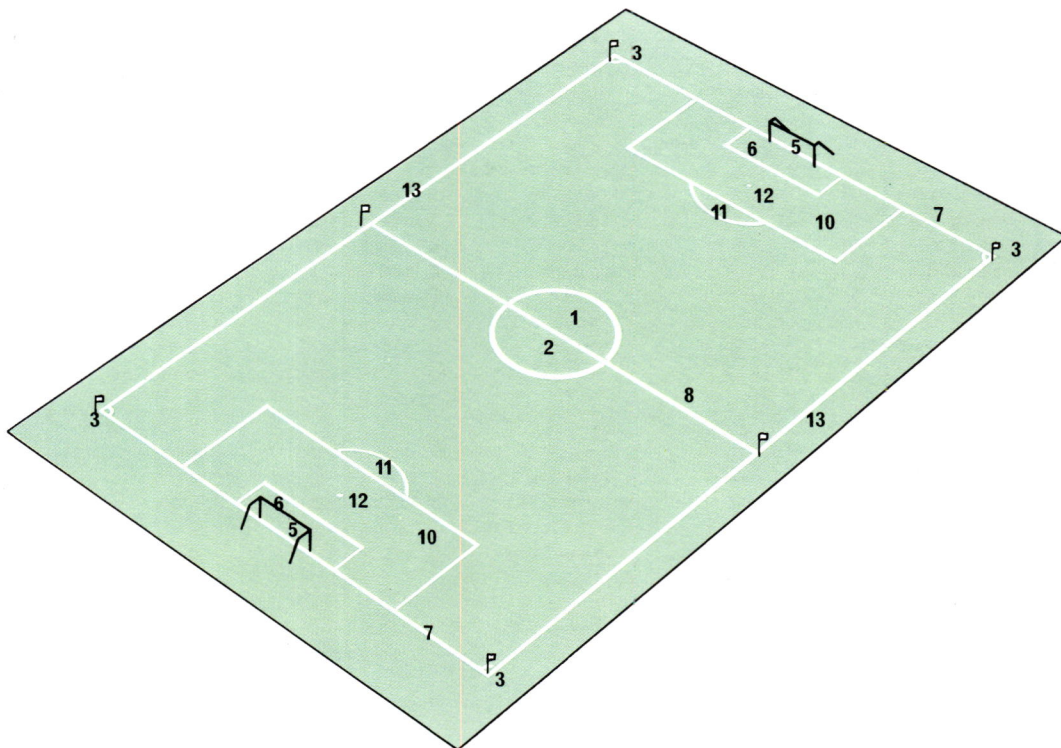

English	Afrikaans	N Sotho	Sesotho	Tswana	Xhosa	Zulu
The field	**Die veld**	**Lebala**	**Lebala**	**Lefelo la motshameko**	**Ibala**	**Inkundla**
1 centre circle	middelsirkel	sedikwadikweng	sedikadikwesetsing	sedikogare	isangqa esisembindini	isiyingi sasesenta
2 centre spot	middelkolletjie	mokhubong	setsi	bogare	ichaphaza elisembindini	isenta
3 corner flag	hoekvlag	folaga ya khutlong	folaga ya hukung	folaga ya khutlo	iflegi esekoneni	ikhonaflegi
4 crossbar	dwarsbalk	lepheko	palo e tshekalletseng	lephakaro	ipali enqamlezileyo	ikhrosibha
5 goal	doel	koulo	ntlha	nno	inqaku	igoli
6 goal area	doelgebied	dikoulong	sebaka sa dintlha	lefelo la dino	umhlaba kafayayo	emagoli
7 goal line	doellyn	moladino	mola wa dintlha	mothaledi wa dino	igowuli layini	ulayini wamapali
8 halfway line	middellyn	molagare	molahare	mothaledigare	umgca osesazulwini	ulayini omaphakathi
linesman	grensregter	mothušamalokwane	ramola	ramola	ilayinzmeni	usomugqa
9 net	net	lelokwa	letlowa	letlowa	umnatha	inethi
10 penalty area	strafskopgebied	phenalething	sebaka sa penele	lefelokotlhao	umhlaba kafayayo	indawo yephenalthi
11 penalty circle	strafskopsirkel	sedikwadikweng sa phenale	sedikadikwe sa penele	sedikokotlhao	isangqa sesohlwayo	isiyingi sephenalthi
12 penalty spot	strafskopmerk	mokhubong wa phenale	letheba la penele	bokotlhao	ibala lesohlwayo	emlotheni
referee	skeidsregter	malokwane	moletsaphala	motsereganyi	usompempe	unompempe
13 touchline	kantlyn	molathoko	moedi wa lebala	mothaledintle	umgca osecaleni	uthashilanyini
14 upright	regop paal	lefata le te tsepamego	palo e tsepameng ya makwallo	pale e e tsepameng	ipali	ipali elimile
Terms	**Terme**	**Mareo**	**Mantswe**	**Mareo**	**Amagama**	**Amagama**
caution	waarskuwing	kgalemo	tlhokomediso	kgalemo	isilumkiso	isexwayiso
corner (kick)	hoek (skop)	go ropa hukung	huku	sekhutlo (thago)	ikona (ukukhaba)	ikhona
foul	vuil spel	papadi ya makgwakgwa	ho bapala hampe	motshameko o o bosula	umdlalo omdaka	ukufonka
free kick	vryskop	thagotokologo	thaho ntle le tshitiso	thagoesi	ifrikhiki	elibekwe phansi
handball	handbal	hentepolo	ho tshwara bolo	kgwele ya seatla	ibhola ebanjiweyo	ukulibamba ngesandla
header	kopbal	kgwele ya go iteiwa ka hlogo	bolo e thulwang ka hlooho	kgwele ya tlhogo	ibhola engeniswe ngentloko	ukulishaya ngekhanda
injury time	beseringstyd	nako ya dikgobalo	nako ya dikotsi	nako ya kemiso	ixesha lengozi	isikhathi sokulimala
kickoff	afskop	-ropa	qalo ya papadi	mathomo	isiqalo	ukulisusa
obstruction	obstruksie	tšhitišo	tshitiso	kgoreletso	uthintelo	ukuvimbela
offside	onkant	ka motswetšing	ho ba lehlakoreng lesele	kemophoso	icala elingelolakho	endaweni engavunyelwe
pass	aangee	-neeletša	ho neheletsa	neeletsa	pasa	-phasa
15 penalty (kick)	strafskop	phenale	penele	thago ya kotlhao	isohlwayo	iphenalthi
save	keer	-kgesa	-thiba	thiba	nqanda	ukuvimba
score	telling	dino	dintlha	dino	iskora	amaphuzu
send off	afstuur	-hlaša	-leleka papading	koba	gxotha	-khiphela ngaphandle
substitute (player)	plaasvervanger	mothibakgala	sebapadi se kenelang se seng	kemedi	ibamba	ongena endaweni yomunye

Sport: rugby

17

2

18 27

19

26

23

25

20

3

2

17

7

5

1

17

11

8

16

24

9

22

10

24

12

26

21 15

25

13

23

14

19

20

17

English	Afrikaans	N Sotho	Sesotho	Tswana	Xhosa	Zulu
Rugby	**Rugby**	**Rugby**	**Rakebi**	**Rakabi**	**Umbhoxo**	**Iragbhi**
The players	**Die spelers**	**Baraloki**	**Dibapadi**	**Batshameki**	**Abadlali**	**Abadlali**
12 centre (centre-threequarter, left centre)	senter (binnesenter)	monošinngeleng	sebapalasetsing (sa ka hare)	sentere ya ka fa teng	isenta (isenta-emtyeni, isenta yasekhohlo)	isenta (yangaphakathi)
13 centre (centre-threequarter, right centre)	senter (buitesenter)	monošigojeng	sebapalasetsing (sa ka ntle)	sentere ya ka fa ntle	isenta (isenta-emtyeni, isenta yakunene)	isenta (yangaphandle)
8 eighth man	agsteman	monna wa boseswai	monna wa borobedi	morobedi	idoda yesibhozo	unamba-8
6 flank forward (loose-head flank)	flank (loskopflank)	morapinngeleng sekramong	sebapalapele leh-lakoreng (se lokolo-hileng)	mofolanka	iflenki	ifolosi langasophikweni
7 flank forward (tighthead flank)	flank (vaskopflank)	morapigojeng sekramong	sebapalapele lehla-koreng (se sitiswang)	mofolanka	iflenki	ifolosi langasophikweni
10 flyhalf (standoff half)	losskakel	morapšana	sebapalahare	folaihalofo	iflayihafu	iflayihhafu
15 fullback	heelagter	moralokamorago	mosireletsi wa ho qetela	fulubeke	umvingci	ifulibhekhi
2 hooker	haker	mokgoetši	hukara	hukere	ihuka	ihhuka
11 left wing	linkervleuel	morapinngeleng wa morago	sebapalaleqeleng	wingi ya molema	iphiko lasekhohlo	iwingi lasokunxele
4 lock forward (loosehead lock)	slot (loskopslot)	mokgonyinngeleng	senotlolo sa kantle	loko	ilokhu	ifolosi eliyingidi
5 lock forward (tighthead lock)	slot (vaskopslot)	mokgonyigojeng	senotlolo sa kahare	loko	ilokhu	ifolosi elingingidi
1 prop forward (loosehead prop)	stut (loskopstut)	mothekginngeleng	motshehetsi wa kantle	poropo	irenka	ifolosi eliyinsika
3 prop forward (tighthead prop)	stut (vaskopstut)	mothekgigojeng	motshehetsi wa kahare	poropo	irenka	ifolosi eliyinsika
14 right wing	regtervleuel	morapigojeng wa morago	sebapala ka ho le letona	wingi ya moja	iphiko lasekunene	iwingi lasokunene
9 scrumhalf	skrumskakel	sekramohafo	sekgotho	sekeramohalofo	isikramhafu	iskramuhhafu
The field	**Die veld**	**Lebala**	**Lebala**	**Botshamokelo**	**Ibala**	**Inkundla**
centrefield	middelveld	bogareng	bohare ba lebala	gareng ga botshamo-kelo	umbindi webala	isisu senkundla
16 centre spot	middelkolletjie	mokhubong	setsi	felo gareng ga bot-shamokelo	ichaphaza embindini	inkaba
17 corner flag	hoekvlag	folaga ya khutlong	folaga ya hukung	folaga ya sekhutlo	iflegi yasekoneni	ikhonaflegi
18 crossbar	dwarslat	lepheko	palo e tshekalletseng	mokgoro	ikhrosbha	ikhrosibha
19 deadline (dead-ball line)	doodlyn	mothalokhweletšo	molamoedi wa papadi	mothaledibofelo	idedilayini	umugqa omgemuva kwamapali
20 goal line	doellyn	mothalodino	mola wa dintlha	mothaledidino	emgceni	ulayini wamapali
21 goal posts	doelpale	mafata a dino	mekwallo	dikgoro	iipali	amapali
22 halfway line	middellyn	molagare	molahare	mothaledigare	usenta	ulayini omaphakathi
23 in goal area	doelgebied	dinong	sebaka sa dintlha	lefelo la dino	umhlaba wokukora	emagoli
24 10-metre line (dotted line)	10-treelyn	mola mitareng tše lesome	mola wa dimetara tse 10	mothaledilesome	iten mitha layini	umugqa ongu-10 mitha
25 22-metre line	kwartlyn	molakotareng	mola wa dimetara tse 22	mothaledikota	i22 mitha layini	umugqa ongo-22 mitha
touch	grens	mollwane	moedi	ntle	uthatshi	umngcele
26 touchline	kantlyn	molathoko	mola wa moedi	mothaledintle	uthatshi layini	ulayini osemaceleni
twenty-two (quarter)	kwartgebied	kotareng	kotara ya lebala	lefelokota	ikota yebala	ikota
27 upright	regop paal	lefata	palo e tsepameng ya mekwallo	pale e e tsepameng	ipali	ipali elimile

Sport: rugby

English	Afrikaans	N Sotho	Sesotho	Tswana	Xhosa	Zulu
Terms	**Terme**	**Mareo**	**Mantswe**	**Mareo**	**Amagama**	**Amagama**
advantage	voordeel	kholego	monyetla	mosola	iadvanteyiji	ilungelo lokwedlula
award a penalty	'n strafskop toeken	-fa phenale	ho nehelana ka penele	go fa thago ya kotlhao	nika isohlwayo	ukunikezwa iphenalthi
backs	agterspelers	baralokamorago	dibapalamorao	motshamekimorago	abadlala emgceni	abadlalemuva
coach	afrigter	mothobodiši	mokwetlisi	mokatisi	umqeqeshi	umlolongi
commentator	kommentator	mogoeledi	mohasi wa papadi	moanedi	umsasazi	umsakazi
conversion	doelskop	ntlha ya poeletso	nno		qabelisa	ikhonveshini
convert (a try)	verdoel ('n drie)	-tshelafatša	ntlha e ntshwang ka mora poeletse	nosa	qabelisa (itrayi)	ukukhonvetha
disallow	nie toelaat	-ganetša	ho hana ntlha	go sa letlelele	sukuvumela	ukungavumeli
dot down, ground	dooddruk	-bolaya kgwele	ho ngola	fosisa	beka phantsi	ukugqoma
dressing room	kleedkamer	boaparelo	phaposi ya ho aparela	boaparelo	indlu yokunxibela	inkamelo lokushintsha
drop (kick)	skepskop	-raga ka go kgelela	bolo e otlangwang pele e rahuwa	thagonno	idropu	umkhahlelo
drop goal	skepdoel	thagokgelelo	ntlha e keneng ka mora ho otlanyo bolo	thagonno	idropu gowuli	idrophugoli
extra time	ekstra tyd	nakokokeletšo	nako e ekeditsweng	nako gape	ixesha elongeziweyo	isikhathi esengeziwe
front rank	voorry	mothalopele wa sekramo	ho itlhoma pele	poropo	irenka	irenki yaphambili
goal kick	doelskop	thagelodinong	thaho ya mekwallong	thagonno	umqabeliso	igoli
halftime	rustyd	nako ya go khutša	kgefutso	boikhutso	ikhefu	isikhathi sekhefu
injury time	beseringstyd	nako ya dikgobalo	nako ya dikotsi	nako ya dikgobalo	ixesha lengozi	isikhathi sokulimala
kick a goal	'n doel skop	-noša ka go raga	ho ntsha ntlha	go nosa	qabelisa ibhola	-khahlela igoli
kickoff	afskop	-ropa	ho qala ha papadi	mathomo	kuyaqalwa	ukukhahlela kokuqala
line-out	lynstaan	tokologano	-fola	thulaganyokolopelo	umgca wokuxhumela ibhola	ilayini-awuthi
linesman, touch judge	grensregter	mothušamalokwane	ramola	ramola	ilinesman	usomugqa
offside	onkant	ka motswetšing	ho ba lehlakoreng lesele	kemophoso	icala elingelolakho	endaweni engavunyelwe
onside	speelkant	e sego ka motswetšing	ho ba lehlakoreng la hao	kemopila	icala elilungileyo	endaweni evunyelwe
order off, send off	afstuur	-hlaša	ho leleka papading	tsamaisa	gxotha	ukukhiphela ngaphandle
1 pass	aangee	-neeletša	ho neheletsa	neeletsa	pasa	-phasa
penalise	straf	-otla	ho otla	-otlhaa	ohlwaya	ukujezisa
penalty kick	strafskop	thagokotlo	thaho ya penele	thagokotlhao	umohlwayo	iphenalthi
referee	skeidsregter	malokwane	moletsaphala	motsereganyi	usompempe	unompempe
rough play	ruwe spel	papadi ya makgwakgwa	papadi e mpe	motshamekomagwata	umdlalo oqatha	ukudlalisana kabi
score	puntetelling	dino	ntlha	dino	isikora	amaphuzu
score a try	'n drie druk	-noša tharo	no ntsha dintlha tse tharo	nosa	beka itrayi	ukufaka ithrayi
scrum	skrum	sekramo	sekgotho	thulaganyo	isikramu	iskramu
2 tackle	doodvat	-phothoma	ho thiba sebapadi	-tshwara	wisa	ukuhlasela
touch kick	buiteskop	thagelontle	thaho moeding wa lebala	thagontle	khabela ngaphandle	ukukhahlela ngaphandle

Sport: cricket

English	Afrikaans	N Sotho	Sesotho	Tswana	Xhosa	Zulu
Cricket	**Krieket**	**Khrikhete**	**Kerikete**	**Kerikete**	**Iqakamba**	**iKhilikithi**
The players	**Die spelers**	**Baraloki**	**Dibapadi**	**Batshameki**	**Abadlali**	**Abadlali**
2 batsman (nonstriker)	kolwer	mmethi	ramolamu (ya sa otleng bolo)	mmetsi	umbethi (ongabholelwayo)	umbhethi(ongagadli)
1 batsman (striker)	medekolwer	motudikayena	ramolamu (ya otlang bolo)	mmetsi (yo o amogelang)	umbethi (obholelwayo)	umbhethi (ongumgadli)
3 bowler	bouler	mopoudi	mmetsi wa bolo	mokolopedi	umjiji	umbhawuli
4 umpire	skeidsregter	malokwane	molaolapapadi	motsereganyi	uampaya	unompempe
fielding positions	veldwerkposisies	maemo a bakgesi	maemo a dibapadi	maemo	iindawo zokuchola	izindawo zabadlali
5 wicketkeeper	paaltjiewagter	mohlapetšadino	mosireletsi	mothibedimorago	umgcini-pali	unomawikhethi
The pitch (the wicket)	**Die kolfblad**	**Bopoulelo**	**Sebaka se kgutlonne pakeng tsa dipalo**	**Lefelo la wikete**	**Ibala**	**Iwikhethi**
bails	dwarsbalkies	maphekwana	thutswana e tshekaletswang hodima dipalo	dikotana	iibheyile	amabheyili
6 bat	kolf	-tula	molamu	sebetsa	ibhadi	ibhethi
7 batting crease	kolfstreep	mola wa tulo	mola wa ramolamu	mothaledi wa mmetsi	umhlaba wokubhetisha	umhlaba wokubhetha
8 boundary	grens	mollwane	moedi	molelwane	ibhawundri	umngcele
9 bowling crease	boulstreep	mola wa poula	mola wa mmetsi	mothaledi wa mokolopedi	umhlaba wokubhowula	umhlaba wokubhawula
10 stumps	penne	dikotana	dipalo	dikota	iipali	amapali
Terms	**Terme**	**Mareo**	**Mantswe**	**Mareo**	**Amagama**	**Amagama**
appeal	appél	boipeletšo	boipiletso	kopo	aphilisha	-khalela
bye	loslopie	kiti ya leoto	bolo e iphetelang	dilatlhwa	ibhayi	ibhayi
duck	nul	lefeela	ntlha ya mahala	sepe	iqanda	iqanda
fielder	veldwerker	mokgesi	sebapadi se ka legoleng	mothibedi	umcholi	umcoshi-bhola
innings	kolfbeurt	sebaka sa go tula	phapanyetsano ya makgetlo	sebaka	amangeno	amangeno
leg before wicket	been voor paaltjie	leoto pele ga dikotana	monyetla wa ho fumana ntlha	leoto pele ga kota	umlenze osithileyo	ukusitha ngomlenze
no ball	foutbal	kgwele ya go fošagala	bolo e se nang ntlha	sekolopelo se se sa dumelwang	ibhola ekwenziwe impazamo kuyo	ibhola eliyiphutha
offside	wegkant	thokong ya hlogo ya motudi	ho ba lehlakoreng lesele		icala elingelolakho	icala elingaphandle
over	boulbeurt	tsenopoulo	sete ya dibata tse tsheletseng ho tswa lehlakoreng le le leng	sebaka sa dikolopelo	iowuva	i-ova
run out	uitgehardloop	-thakeditšwa	ho siya	tabogophoso	irani awuthi	ukukhishelwa ngaphandle
runs	lopies	dikiti	makgetlo a ho matha	ditabogo	imitsi	amarani
stumped	gestonk	-kgesitšwe	ho ntsha ramolamu ka ho tshwara bolo	thutswe	stantshisiwe	ukustampa

Sport: cricket

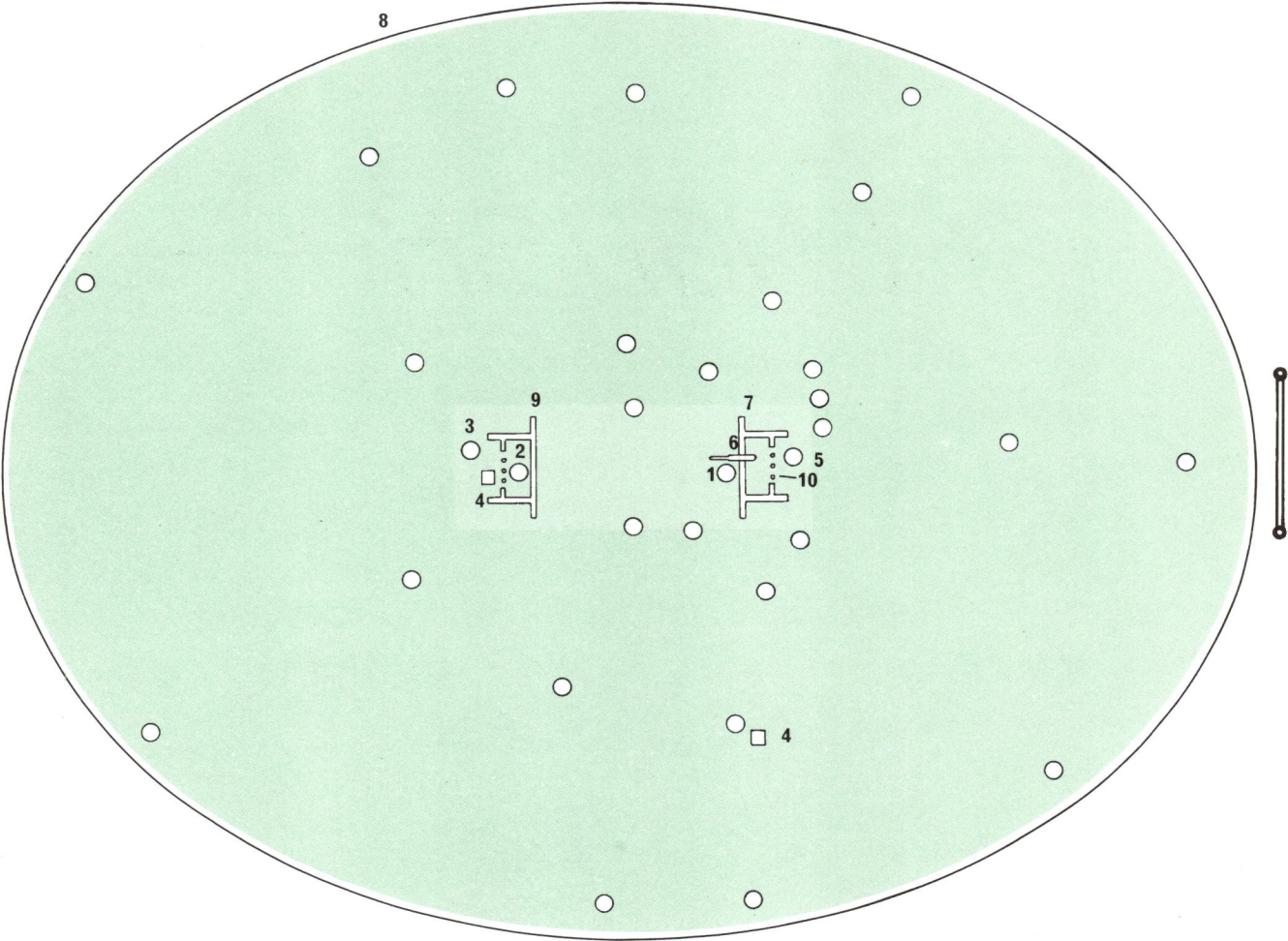

ENGLISH

English	Afrikaans	N Sotho	Sesotho	Tswana	Xhosa	Zulu	A
abacus (n)	telraam	mmadiphetana	mmadibolwana	kgatlhatalama	isibali	i-abakhusi	
abandon (v)	verlaat	-tlogela	-nyahlatsa	-tlogela	-ncama	-yeka	
abattoir (n)	slagplaas	bohlabelo	selagapalo	botlhabelo	isilarha	amadela	
abdomen (n)	buik	mpa	mpa	mpa	isisu	isisu	
abduct (v)	ontvoer	-thopa	-kwetela	-utswa	-thwala	-thwala	
ability (n)	bekwaamheid	bokgoni	bokgoni	kgono	ubuchule	ukwazi	
able (a)	bekwaam	-kgona	-kgona	-kgonang	-kwazi	-nokwazi	
abnormal (a)	abnormaal	-sa tlwaelegago	-sa tlwaelehang	-sa tlwaegang	-ngaqhelekanga	-ngavamile	
aboard (adv)	aan boord	ka gare ga	-palame	-palameng	-ngaphezulu	emkhunjini	
abode (n)	woonplek	bodulo	bodulo	legae	indawo	isikhundla	
abolish (v)	afskaf	-fediša	-fedisa	-khutlisa	-bhangisa	-susa	
aboriginal (n)	oorspronklike inwoner	semelafa	motala	monnafa	inzalelwane	umuntu womdabu	
abort (v)	aborteer	-nyopisa	-senyega	-phanza	-khipha isisu	
abortion (n)	aborsie		nyopiso	tshenyegelo ya mpa	impanza	ukuphuphuma isisu	
abortive (a)	misluk		-nyopileng	-senyegetsweng	-phanzileyo	-gejile	
about (adv)	rond	mo le mola	ka-	gomela	-ngokujikeleyo	nga-	
about (prep)	oor		ka-	ka ga	nga-	phezu kwa-	
above (prep)	bo	godimo ga	-hodima	mo godimo	-phezulu	enhla kwa-	
abscess (n)	verswering	sekaku	seso	sekaku	igqitha	ithumba	
absence (n)	afwesigheid	tlhokego	bosiyo	tlhokafalo	ubungabikho	ukungabikho	
absent (a)	afwesig	-hlokega	-ba siyo	-se yong	-ngekhoyo	-ngekho	
absent-minded (a)	ingedagte	-ya le megopolo	-bua ka pelo	-bua ka pelo	-zungubala	-alukile	
absolute (a)	absoluut		-hle	tota	kanye	ngempela	
absolutely (adv)	absoluut	ruri	ho hang	tota	-ngenene	ngempela	
absorb (v)	absorbeer	-hupa	-monya	-monyela	-funxa	-munca	
abstain (v)	onthou	-ila	-sesefa	-ila	-yeka	-yeka	
abstract (a)	afgetrokke		-sa bonweng	-kgopolo	-ngaphathekiyo	-okusengqondweni kuphela	
absurd (a)	onsinnig	-segišago	-hloka kelello	mo go se nang tlhaloganyo	-nobuhiba	-ngasile	
abundance (n)	oorvloed	bontši	nala	monono	ubuninzi	isibhidli	
abundant (a)	oorvloedig	-ntši	-ngata	-tlalatlalo	-ninzi	-xhaphakile	
abuse (n)	misbruik		tlatlapo	tiriso e e sa siamang	ukusebenzisa kakubi	ukoniwa	
abuse (v)	misbruik	-senya	-tlatlapa	-dirisa e seng ka fa siamong	-sebenzisa kakubi	-ona	
acacia (n)	akasia	mohlare wa akasia	leoka	mmafu	umnga	umkhamba	
academy (n)	akademie	aketemi	akhademi	maithuto	isikolo senkcubeko	imfundo ephakeme	
accelerate (v)	versnel	-fa makhura	-akofisa	-okofatsa	-khawulezisa	-sheshisa	
accelerator (n)	brandstofpedaal	sefamakhura	seakofisi	seokofatso	umcephe	isipuni	
accent (n)	aksent	tobeletšo	tokodiso	kgateletso	uhlobo lokuthetha	isigcizelelo	
accept (v)	aanvaar	-amogela	-amohela	-amogela	-amkela	-amukela	
acceptable (a)	aanvaarbaar	-amogelega	-amoheleha	-amogelesegang	-amkelekileyo	-amukelekayo	
acceptance (n)	aanvaarding	kamogelo	kamohelo	kamogelo	ulwamkelo	ukwamukela	
accident (n)	ongeluk	kotsi	kotsi	kotsi	ingozi	ingozi	
accidental (a)	toevallig	-sewelo	ka tshohanyetso	-go sa nagangweng	-ngobungozi	-ngenomkhuba	
accidentally (adv)	toevallig	ka sewelo	ka tshohanyetso	ka tshoganyo	-ngengozi	ngengozi	
acclaim (n)	toejuiging	magoswi	ditlatse	-nesa pula	ukubonga	ukuhlokoma	
accommodate (v)	huisves	-fa marobalo	-amohela	-tshola	-hlalisa	-nika indawo	
accommodation (n)	huisvesting	marobalo	bodulo	bonno	indawo yokuhlala	indawo yokuhlala nokulala	
accompany (v)	begelei	-felegetša	-felehetsa	-buledisa	-khapha	-phelezela	
accomplice (n)	medepligtige	mosenyiši	motlatsi	mosenyammogo	ihlakani	umlekeleli	
accordion (n)	trekklavier	pianotamolwa	koriana	akordiono	ikhodiyani	inkonsitini esalupiyani	
account (n)	rekening	tšhupaletlotlo	akhaonte	tshupatlotlo	iakhawunti	i-akhawunti	
account (v)	rekenskap gee	-anegela	-seka	-supa tlotlo	-cacisa	-balisisa	
accountant (n)	rekenmeester	mošupatlotlo	akhaontente	mmaditlotlo	umbhali-mali	umbhali wamakhawunti	
accuracy (n)	noukeurigheid	nepo	nepo	nepo	ukuchaneka	ukucophelela	
accurate (a)	noukeurig	-nepegilego	-nepahetseng	-maroka	-chanekileyo	-qonde ngqo	
accusation (n)	beskuldiging	pego	-qoso	tatofatso	isityholo	icala elibekwayo	

51

A	English	Afrikaans	N Sotho	Sesotho	Tswana	Xhosa	Zulu
	accuse (v)	beskuldig	-bega	-qosa	-latofatsa	-tyhola	-beka icala
	accused (n)	beskuldigde	mmegiwa	moqosuwa	mosekisiwa	ummangalelwa	ummangalelwa
	accuser (n)	beskuldiger	mmegi	moqosi	moseki	ummangali	ummangali
	ache (n)	pyn	bohloko	bohloko	setlhabi	ingqaqambo	ubuhlungu
	ache (v)	pyn	-opa	-opa	-opa	-qaqamba	-njunjuza
	achieve (v)	presteer	-phetha	-atleha	-atlanega	-zuza	-feza
	achievement (n)	prestasie	phetho	katleho	katlanego	impumelelo	impumelelo
	acid (a)	suur	-bodila	-bodila	-esete	-muncu	-muncu
	acid (n)	suur	esiti	esiti	esete	ubumuncu	i-asidi
	acknowledge (v)	erken	-dumela	-dumela	-naya motho seditse	-vuma	-vuma
	acne (n)	aknee	thala	sehloba	seso	ukhuphu	izinsunsu
	acoustic (a)	akoesties	-kwalago	-thibela modumo	ka kutlo ya tsebe	-vakalayo	-kwemisindo
	acquaint (v)	bekend wees	-tsebega	tsebisa	-tlwaetse	-azisa	-azisa
	acquaint (v)	bekend wees	-tsebega	-tlwaela	-tlwaela	-aziswa	-azisa
	acquaintance (n)	kennis	motswalle	motswalle	kitso	ulwazano	isazani
	acquaintance (n)	kennismaking	molekane	ho tseba	kitsiso	ulwazano	ukwazana
	acquire (v)	aanskaf	-hwetša	-fumana	-bapala	-zuza	-zuza
	acquisition (n)	aanskaffing	khwetšo	phumano	papadi	inzuzo	ukuzuza
	acquit (v)	vryspreek	-lokolla	-lokolla	-golola	-khulula	-khulula
	acquittal (n)	vryspraak	tokollo	tokollo	kgololo	ugwetyelo	ukukhululwa
	across (adv)	dwars		-rapalletse	rapalala	-ngokuxwesa	phambana na-
	across (prep)	oor		-rapalla	-feteletsa	ngaphaya	phesheya
	active (a)	aktief	-mahlahla	-mafolofolo	-matlhagatlhaga	-sebenzayo	-khuthele
	activist (n)	aktivis	mohlohleletši	ramafolofolo	motlhotlheletsi	ufunzeweni	umkhuthazi
	activity (n)	bedrywigheid	mahlahlo	tshebetso	modiro	unsebenzi	ubukhuphekhuphe
	actor (n)	akteur	sebapadi	sebapadi	moetsi	umdlali	umdlali
	actress (n)	aktrise	moralokigadi	sebapadi	moetsigadi	umdlali	umdlalikazi
	actually (adv)	eintlik		hantlentle	ruri	-ngokwenene	ngempela
	acute (a)	skerp	-bogale	-bohale	-bogale	-bukhali	-cijile
	adamant (a)	onwrikbaar	-ikemišeditše	-manganga	-gwatalalang	-ngenkani	-yitshe
	adapt (v)	aanpas	-amantša	-tjhorisa	-tlwaela	-lungiselela	-vumelanisa
	add (v)	byvoeg	-oketša	-eketsa	-oketsa	-ongeza	-enezela
	addict (n)	verslaafde	mohlankiša	lekgoba	motlwaetsi	ingedle	umlutha
	addiction (n)	verslaafdheid	tlhankišitšo	bokgoba	botlwaelo	ubungedle	ukulutha
	addition (n)	toevoeging	koketšo	keketso	koketso	isongezelelo	ukuhlanganiswa
	additional (a)	bykomend	-oketšago	-eketsang	-oketsang	-ongezelelweyo	-ethasiselayo
	address (n)	adres	atrese	aterese	aterese	iadresi	ikheli
	address (v)	toespreek	-bolela le	-buisa	-buisa	-enza intetho	-khuluma
	adequate (a)	voldoende	-lekanego	-lekaneng	-lekanang	-aneleyo	-anele
	adhere (v)	kleef	-kgomara	-mamarela	-kgomarela	ncamathela	-namathela
	adhesive (a)	klewerig	-kgomarelago	-mamarelang	-kgomarelang	-ncamathelayo	-namathelayo
	adjacent (a)	aangrensend	-bataganego	-bapileng	-bapang	-gudlene	-sondelene
	adjective (n)	byvoeglike naamwoord	lehlaodi	lekgethi	letlhaodi	isiphawuli	isiphawulo
	adjourn (v)	verdaag	-phatlalala	-qhalana	-phatlhalala	-misela ixesha elizayo	-hlehlisa
	adjudicator (n)	beoordelaar	malokwane	moahlodi	moatlhodi	umchongi	umahluli
	admirable (a)	bewonderendswaardig	-rategago	-ratehang	-kgatlhang	-ncomekayo	-babazekile
	admiration (n)	bewondering	tumišo	ho rata	kgatlhego	uncomo	ukubabaza
	admire (v)	bewonder	-duma	-rata	-kgatlha	-buka	-babaza
	admission (n)	toelating	tumelelo	tumello	tumelelo	ulwamkelo	ukwamukelwa
	admit (v)	toelaat	-dumelela	-dumela	-dumelela	-yamkela	-mukela
	admonish (v)	vermaan	-kgala	-kgalema	-kgala	-lumkisa	-khuza
	adolescence (n)	adolessensie	bofsa	ho kena boholo	bosima	ixesha ebomini lokufikisa	ibanga lokukhula
	adolescent (n)	jeugdige	mofsa	mokenaboholo	mosima	umntu ofikisayo	intsha
	adopt (v)	aanneem	-amogela	-amohela	-amogela	-amkela	-thola
	adoption (n)	aanneming	kamogelo	kamohelo	kamogelo	ukwamkela	ukuthola
	adore (v)	aanbid	-rata kudu	-kgahlwa	-rapela	-thanda	-khulekela
	adult (a)	volwasse	-godilego	-holo	-godileng	-dala	-osekhulile
	adult (n)	volwassene	mogolo	moholo	mogolo	umntu omdala	umuntu osekhulile
	adulterer (n)	owerspeler	seotswa	seotswa	sefefe	umkrexezi	isiphingi

English	Afrikaans	N Sotho	Sesotho	Tswana	Xhosa	Zulu	A
adultery (n)	owerspel	bootswa	bootswa	boaka	ukrexezo	uphingo	
adulthood (n)	volwassenheid	bogolo	boholo	bogolo	ubudala	ukukhula	
advance (n)	vooruitgang	tšwelopele	tswelopele	tswelelopele	inkqubela-phambili	ukuqhubeka	
advancement (n)	vordering	tlhabologo	tswelopele	botswelelopele	inyathelo	inqubekela-phambili	
advantage (n)	voordeel	mohola	monyetla	mosola	uncedo	inzuzo	
adverb (n)	bywoord	lehlathi	lehlalosi	letlhalosi	isihlomelo	isandiso	
advertise (v)	adverteer	-tsebiša	-bapatsa	phasalatsa	-thengisa	-azisa	
advertisement (n)	advertensie	tsebiši	papatso	phasalatso	intengiso	isaziso	
advice (n)	raad	keletšo	keletso	kgakololo	icebo	iseluleko	
advise (v)	raad gee	-eletša	-eletsa	-gakolola	-cebisa	-lulekayo	
adviser (n)	raadgewer	moeletši	moeletsi	mogakolodi	umcebisi	umluleki	
advisory (a)	raadgewend	-eletšago	-eletsang	-gakololang	-cebisayo	-lulekayo	
advocate (n)	advokaat	mmoleledi	mmuelli	mmueledi	igqwetha	ummeli	
aerial (n)	lugdraad	eriele	eriale	eriele	ieriyali	ucingo lwewayilense	
aeroplane (n)	vliegtuig	sefofane	sefofane	sefofane	inqwelomoya	indizamshini	
affair (n)	saak	taba	taba	taba	inyewe	udaba	
affect (v)	raak	-ama	-ama	-ama	-bangela	-thinta	
affection (n)	toegeneentheid	lerato	lerato	lorato	umsa	uthando	
affectionate (a)	toegeneë	-ratago	-ratehang	-rategang	-nomsa	-thandekayo	
affidavit (n)	beëdigde verklaring	kenelwa	bopaki bo ngotsweng	pego e e ikanetsweng	isigqibo esifungelweyo	incwadi efungelwe	
affliction (n)	beproewing	pelaelo	tlatlapo	pogisego	imbandezelo	inhlupheko	
afford (v)	bekostig	-kgona go lefa	-kgona	-kgona	-banako	-veza	
afraid (a)	bang	-boifa	-tshaba	-tshabang	-oyikayo	-novalo	
African (a)	Afrika	-Afrika	-Seaforika	-Seafrika	-ongumAfrika	-kwase-Afrika	
African (n)	Afrikaan	Moafrika	Moafrika	Moafrika	umAfrika	umAfrika	
Afrikaner (n)	Afrikaner	Leafrikanere	Leaforikanere	Leaforekannere	iBhulu	iBhunu	
after (place) (prep)	agter	morago ga	ka mora	morago	emva	emuva kwa-	
after (time) (prep)	na	morago ga	ka mora	sena	emva	emuva kwa-	
afterbirth (n)	nageboorte	mohlana	mohlana	motlhala	umkhaya	umhlapho	
afternoon (n)	middag	thapama	thapama	tshokologo	emva kwemini	intambama	
afterwards (adv)	agterna	ka morago	ha morao	kgabagare	-emva koko	kamuva	
again (adv)	weer	gape	hape	gape	kwakhona	futhi	
against (prep)	teen		kgahlanong le-	kgatlhanong le-	-ngqiyama	-phambene na-	
age (n)	ouderdom	bogolo	boholo	bogologolo	ubudala	ubudala	
age (v)	verouder	-tšofala	-tsofala	-tsofala	-aluphala	-guga	
aged (a)	oud	-tšofetšego	-tsofetseng	-tsofetseng	-dala	-gugile	
agenda (n)	agenda	lenanethero	lanane la ditaba	lenanetema	iajenda	i-ajenda	
agent (n)	agent	morekišetši	moemedi	moemedi	iarhente	umenzeli	
aggressive (a)	aanvallend	-hlaselago	-kgopo	bosilo	-olwayo	-hlaselayo	
agile (a)	rats	-tshelago matšato	-matjato	majato	-thambileyo	-lula	
agitator (n)	opstoker	mohlohleletši	mohlohli	motlhotlheletsi	umqhwayi	umhlubukisi	
agree (v)	ooreenstem	-kwana	-dumela	-dumelana	-vuma	-vumelana	
agreeable (a)	aangenaam	-go iketla	-bonolo	-isegang	-vumelanayo	-mnandi	
agreement (n)	ooreenkoms	kwano	tumellano	kutlwano	-imvumelwano	isivumelwano	
agricultural (a)	landboukundig	-temo	-temothuo	-bolemi	-olimo	-zokulima	
agriculture (n)	landbou	bolemi	temothuo	bolemi	ulimo	ulimo	
ahead (adv)	vooruit	pele	ka pele	pele	-ngaphambili	ngaphambili	
aid (n)	hulp	thušo	thuso	thusego	uncedo	usizo	
aid (v)	help	-thuša	-thusa	-thusa	-nceda	-siza	
aim (n)	doel	nepo	sepheo	maikaelelo	injongo	inhloso	
aim (v)	mik	-tšea maleba	-lebisa	-kwaisa	-jolisa	-khomba	
air (n)	lug	moya	moya	mowa	umoya	umoya	
aircraft (n)	vliegtuig	sefofane	sefofane	sefofane	inqwelomoya	indiza	
airmail (n)	lugpos	posomoya	poso ya moya	poso ya mowa	iposi ehamba ngomoya	iposi elihamba ngezindiza	
airport (n)	lughawe	boemelafofane	boemeladifofane	boemeladifofane	isikhululo senqwelomoya	inkundla yezindiza	
alarm (n)	alarm	mokgoši	setsosa	sekuamokgosi	into eyothusayo	imvuso	
albino (n)	albino	lešwefe	lesofe	leswafe	inkawu	umuntu oyinkawu	
alcohol (n)	alkohol	tagi	tahi	tagi	isinxilisi	ugologo	

A	English	Afrikaans	N Sotho	Sesotho	Tswana	Xhosa	Zulu
	alcoholic (a)	alkoholies	-tagišago	-tahang	-tagisang	-nxilisayo	-dakisayo
	alcoholic (n)	alkoholis	setagwa	letahwa	letagwa	inxila	isidakwa
	alert (a)	waaksaam	-phakgamego	-sedi	-nthsa matlho dinameng	-phaphamileyo	-xwayile
	alga (n)	alg	dimelameetseng	lehola la metsing	bolele	ubulembu	i-algi
	alias (n)	alias	-reetšwego la	lebitso le leng	itsegeng le ka la	igama lobuqhetseba	igama mbumbulu
	alibi (n)	alibi	boitatolo	maitatolo	alibi	indlela yokuzikhusela	i-alibi
	alight (a)	aan die brand	-swago	-tuka	-tlhosetsang	-tshayo	-okhele
	alike (a)	gelyk	-swanago	-tshwana	-tshwanang	-fanayo	-fanayo
	alive (a)	lewend	-phelago	-phela	-phelang	-philileyo	-philile
	all (a)	alle	ka moka	-hle	-tlhe	-onke	-nke
	all (beings) (pron)	almal	bohle	-hle	-tlhe	-onke	sonke
	all (things) (pron)	alles	tšohle	-hle	-tlhe	-onke	konke
	allege (v)	beweer	-re	-bolela	-kaya	-banga	-sho
	allergy (n)	allergie	kutlwišišo	aleji	boletswe	ukungalungelani nempilo	i-aleji
	allocate (v)	toewys	-abela	-aba	-aba	-abela	-abela
	allow (v)	toestaan	-dumelela	-dumella	-letla	-vumela	-vumela
	Almighty (n)	Almagtige	Yomaatlaohle	Ya matla ohle	Mothatiyotlhe	Somandla	uSomandla
	almost (adv)	amper	-nyakile	-batlile	-ratile	-phantse	-cishe
	aloe (n)	aalwyn	mokgopha	lekgala	mokgopha	ikhala	umhlaba
	alone (a)	alleen	noši	-mong	-nosi	-dwa	-dwa
	along (prep)	langs	hleng	-pela	ela	ecaleni ku-	ngokulinganise
	aloud (adv)	hardop	-boelela godimo	-tlerola	godimo	-ngokukhwaza	nomsindo
	alphabet (n)	alfabet	alfabete	alfabete	alfabete	ialfabhethi	i-alfabhethi
	also (adv)	ook	gape	le-	gape	na-	futhi
	altar (n)	altaar	altare	aletare	aletare	isibingelelo	ilathi
	alternate (v)	afwissel	-hlatlolana	-tjhentjhana	-refosana	-bolekisana	-phambanisiweyo
	although (conj)	al	le ge	le ha	le fa	nangona	nokuba
	always (adv)	gedurig	ka mehla	ka mehla	tlhola	-soloko	njalo
	amateur (n)	amateur	yo mofsa	moithutwana	magogorwane	irhawu	imfunda-makhwele
	amaze (v)	verbaas	-makatša	-makatsa	-makatsa	-mangalisa	-mangalisa
	amazement (n)	verbasing	makalo	makatso	makatso	ummangaliso	ukumangala
	amazing (a)	verbasend	-makatšago	-makatsang	-makatsang	-mangalisayo	-mangalisayo
	ambassador (n)	ambassadeur	motseta	lenqosa	moemedi	nozakuzaku	inxusa
	ambiguous (a)	dubbelsinnig	-belaetšago	-habedi	-sa tlhalosang	-mbolombini	-fithizile
	ambition (n)	ambisie	tumo	maikemisetso	maikaelelo	ibhongo	ukulangazela
	ambulance (n)	ambulans	koloi ya balwetši	ambulanse	ambilansa	iambulensi	i-ambulense
	ambush (n)	hinderlaag	bolalelo	tallo	talelo	ukulalela	umlalelo
	amendment (n)	wysiging	phetošo	phetolo	tlhabololo	isilungiso	umbandela
	amid (prep)	tussen	gare ga	-hara	gare	phakathi kwa-izidubuli	phakathi kwa-izindubulo
	ammunition (n)	ammunisie	dibetša	dibetsa	marumo		
	amputate (v)	afsit	-kgaola	-poma	-kgaola	-shunqula	-nquma
	amuse (v)	vermaak	-thabiša	-qabola	tlhaletsa	-yolisa	-thokozisa
	amusement (n)	vermaaklikheid	maipshino	boithabiso	tlhaletso	isiyolisi	ukuthokozisa
	amusing (a)	vermaaklik	-thabišago	-qabolang	-tlhaletsang	-yolisayo	-thokozisayo
	anaemia (n)	bloedarmoede	tlhokamadi	phokolo ya madi	tlhokamadi	umlambo	ukuphaphatheka kwegazi
	analogy (n)	analogie	tshwano	papiso	tshwano	imfano	isifanelisano
	analyse (v)	ontleed	-fetleka	-hlopholla	-lokolola	-hlalutya	-hlahlela
	analysis (n)	ontleding	phetleko	mohlophollo	bolokololo	uhlalutyo	umhlahlelo
	ancestor (n)	voorouer	mogologolo	modimo	mogologolo	isinyanya	ukhokho
	ancestral (a)	voorvaderlik	-badimo	-badimo	-sedimo	-yezinyanya	-okhokho
	ancient (a)	antiek	-kgale	-boholoholo	-bogologolo	-mandulo	-okwasendulo
	and (conj)	en	le/gomme	le	le	kunye, na-	na-
	angel (n)	engel	morongwa	lengeloi	moengele	ingelosi	ingelosi
	anger (n)	kwaadheid	pefelo	kgalefo	bojarara	umsindo	ulaka
	anger (v)	kwaad maak	-befediša	-halefisa	-ngadisa	-enza umsindo	-thukuthelisa
	angle (n)	hoek	khutlo	sekgutlo	sekhutlo	igophe	i-engele
	angry (a)	kwaad	-befetšwego	-halefile	-ngadileng	-nomsindo	-thukuthele

English	Afrikaans	N Sotho	Sesotho	Tswana	Xhosa	Zulu	A
animal (n)	dier	phoofolo	phoofolo	phologolo	isilo	isilwane	
ankle (n)	enkel	kgokgoilane	leqaqailana	legwejana	iqatha	iqakala	
anklet (n)	enkelring	mpshiri	boseka	leseka	inqashela	isigqizo	
announce (v)	aankondig	-tsebiša	-tsebisa	-goeletsa	-azisa	-memezela	
announcement (n)	aankondiging	tsebišo	tsebiso	kgoeletso	isaziso	isimemezelo	
annoy (v)	vies maak	-hlopha	-tena	-tena	-caphukisa	-casula	
annoyance (n)	ergernis	tlhophego	ho tena	manga	inkathazo	isinengiso	
annoying (a)	ergerlik	-hlophago	-tenang	-kgwisa manga	-caphukisayo	-canulayo	
annual (a)	jaarliks	ka ngwaga	ka selemo	-ngwaga	-ngonyaka	konyaka	
anoint (v)	salf	-tlola	-tlotsa	-tlola	qhola	-gcoba	
another (a)	'n ander	-ngwe	-ng; -nngwe	-ngwe	-nye	-nye	
another (a)	nog 'n	-ngwe	-ng; -nngwe	-ngwe	-nye	nokunye	
answer (n)	antwoord	karabo	karabo	karabo	impendulo	impendulo	
answer (v)	antwoord	-araba	-araba	-araba	-phendula	-phendula	
ant (n)	mier	tšhošwane	bohlwa	tshoswane	imbovane	intuthwane	
antagonise (v)	vyandig maak	-lwantšha	-tlatlapa	-lotlhanya	-enza ubutshaba	phambana na-	
antagonist (n)	teenstander	molwantšhi	motlatlapi	moidi	umchasi	imbangi	
antelope (n)	wildsbok	phoofolo	nyamatsana	phologolo	iliza	inyamazane	
antenna (n)	lugdraad	eriele	eriale	eriele	iimpondo zewayilesi	i-antena	
anthem (n)	volkslied	mmino wa setšhaba	pina ya setjhaba	pina ya bosetshaba	umhobe	ihubo lesizwe	
antibody (n)	teenliggaam	twantšhi	sehananalemmele	twantshi	isikhuseli-buhlungu	isinqandakufa egazini	
antidote (n)	teengif	tšhitampholo	sebolayatjhefo	tshitabotlhole	isinqandi-sifo	isibiba	
anus (n)	anus	mogwete	sebono	sebono	indutsu	ingquza	
anxiety (n)	kommer	pelaelo	ngongoreho	tlhobaelo	unxunguphalo	imbandezeka	
anxious (a)	bekommerd	-belaelago	-ngongorehile	-tlhobaelang	-nxungupheleyo	-khathazekile	
any (a)	enige	-ngwe le -ngwe	-ng le -ng	-ngwe le -ngwe	-nayiphi	noma	
anybody (pron)	elkeen	mang le mang	mang le mang	mang le mang	-nabani	noma ubani	
anyhow (adv)	hoe dan ook	bjang le bjang	jwang kapa jwang	le gale	-nanjani	noma kunjani	
anyhow (conj)	in elk geval	le ge go le bjalo	feela	mme	kambe	nokho	
anything (pron)	enigiets	eng le eng	-ng le -ng	sengwe le sengwe	nantoni	noma yini	
anywhere (adv)	enige plek	gongwe le gongwe	kae kapa kae	gongwe le gongwe	naphi	nakuphi	
ape (n)	aap	kgabo	kgabo	kgabo	inkawu	uhlobo lwenkawu engenamsila	
ape (v)	na-aap	-ekiša	-etsisa	-etsa	-linganisa	-lingisa	
apex (n)	spits	ntlha	sehlohlolo	setlhoa	incam	isiqongo	
apologise (v)	verskoning vra	-kgopela tshwarelo	-kopa tshwarelo	-kopa boitshwarelo	-cela uxolo	-xolisa	
apology (n)	verskoning	tshwarelo	tshwarelo	boitshwarelo	ungxengxezo	isixoliso	
apostle (n)	apostel	moapostola	moapostola	moaposetolo	umpostile	umphostoli	
apparatus (n)	apparaat	sehlamo	disebediswa	aparata	isixhobo	amalungiselelo	
appeal (n)	beroep	boipiletšo	boipiletso	boikuelo	isibheno	isikhalo	
appeal (v)	beroep doen op	-dira boipiletšo	-ipiletsa	-ipiletsa	-bhena	-khala	
appeal court (n)	appélhof	lekgotla la boipiletšo	lekgotla la boipiletso	lekgotla la boipiletso	inkundla yezibheno	amajaji okugcina	
appear (v)	verskyn	-tšwelela	-hlaha	-tlhaga	-vela	-bonakala	
appearance (n)	verskyning	tšwelelo	ho hlaha	ponalo	imbonakalo	ukubonakala	
appease (v)	bevredig	-kgotsofatša	-kokobetsa	-tlakisa	-xolisa	-duduza	
appendix (n)	aanhangsel	seoketša	sehlomathiso	mametlelelo	umqukumbelo	isithasiselo	
appetite (n)	eetlus	kganyogo ya dijo	takatso ya dijo	keletso ya dijo	umkra	inkanuko	
applaud (v)	toejuig	-opela magoswi	-tlotlisa	-kuelela	-qhwabela	-halalisa	
apple (n)	appel	apola	apole	apole	iapile	i-apula	
applicant (n)	aansoeker	mokgopedi	mokopamosebetsi	mokopi	umceli	umceli	
application (n)	aansoek	kgopelo	kopo ya mosebeti	kopo	isicelo	isicelo	
apply (v)	aansoek doen	-kgopela	-kopa mosebetsi	-kopa	-enza isicelo	-cela	
apply (v)	toepas	-diriša	-sebedisa	tiriso	-sebenzisa	-sebenzisa	
appoint (v)	aanstel	-bea	-hira	-tlhoma	-tyumba	-qasha	
appointment (n)	aanstelling	peo	kgiro	peelano	ukutyumba	ukuqashwa	
appointment (n)	afspraak	kwano	lebaka	kopanyo	idinga	ukunqumelana isikhathi	
appreciate (v)	waardeer	-lekanyetša	-ananela	-anaanela	-ncoma	-ncoma	
apprehensive (a)	bang	-boifago	-tshaba	-tshabegang	-oyikisayo	-novalo	
approach (n)	nadering	tebelego	katamelo	itlhagiso	indlela yokuvelela	ukuvelela	
approach (v)	benader	-bona	-atamela	-tlhagisa	-cothela	-velela	

A	English	Afrikaans	N Sotho	Sesotho	Tswana	Xhosa	Zulu
	appropriate (a)	geskik	-lebanego	-lokelang	-siameng	-lungileyo	-okufanele
	approval (n)	goedkeuring	tumelelo	tumello	thebolo	imvumelwano	imvume
	approve (v)	goedkeur	-dumelela	-dumela	-rebola	-vumelana	-vumela
	approximate (a)	geskat	e ka bago	-akanyang	-ka ne	-kangaka	-linganiselwe
	apricot (n)	appelkoos	apolekose	apolekose	apolekosi	iaprikoso	ibhilikosi
	April (n)	April	Aprele	Mmesa	Moranang	Apreli	u-Aprili
	apron (n)	voorskoot	thetho	forosekoto	khiba	ifaskoti	isibhaxelo
	arbiter (n)	arbiter	moahloledi	moahlodi	motsereganyi	umlamli	umlamuli
	arbitrary (a)	willekeurig	-lamolwago	-hloka leeme	-letlanyang	-zifunelayo	-nganaki umthetho
	arbitrate (v)	arbitreer	-lamola	-ahlola	-letlanya	-ngenelela	-lamula
	archbishop (n)	aartsbiskop	mopišopo pharephare	moatjhebishopo	mobishopomogolo	ibhishophu enkulu	umbhishobhi omkhulu
	architect (n)	argitek	mothadi wa dipolane	moakhiteke	moagi	umcebi wezakhiwo	umklami wezindlu
	area (n)	oppervlakte	naga	sebaka	kgaolo	ummandla	i-eriya
	arena (n)	arena	arena	arena	botlhabanelo	iqonga	inkundla
	argue (v)	stry	-phega kgang	-nganga	ganetsana	-xoxa	-phikisana
	argument (n)	argument	kgang	ngangisano	kgang	ingxoxo	ukuphikisana
	arid (a)	dor	-omilego	-sebataola	-omeletseng	-bharhileyo	-omile
	arise (v)	opstaan	-emelela	-phahama	-tsoga	-vuka	-vuka
	aristocrat (n)	edelman	mokgomana	seithati	kgosana	isihandiba	isilomo
	arithmetic (n)	rekenkunde	thutapalo	dipalo	dipalo	ezobalo	izibalo
	arm (n)	arm	letsogo	letsoho	lebogo	ingalo	ingalo
	arm (v)	bewapen	-itlhama ka dibetša	-hlomela	tlhomelela	-xhoba	-hloma
	armpit (n)	armholte	lehwafa	lehafi	legwafa	ikhwapha	ikhwapha
	arms (n)	wapens	dibetša	dibetsa	dibetsa	izixhobo	izikhali
	army (n)	leër	madira	lebotho	masole	umkhosi	impi
	around (adv)	rond	kua le kua	ka hohle	khadia	-ngokujikelezayo	ngokuzungezile
	arouse (v)	opwek	-tsoša	-tsosa	-tsibosa	-vusa	-vusa
	arrange (v)	skik	-rulaganya	-hlopha	-rulaganya	cwangcisa	-hlela
	arrangement (n)	skikking	thulaganyo	hlophiso	thulaganyo	isicwangciso	uhlelo
	arrest (n)	inhegtenisneming	tshwaro	ho tshwara	kgolego	ukufaka etrongweni	ukuboshwa
	arrest (v)	in hegtenis neem	-swara	-tshwara	-tshwara	-bamba	-bopha
	arrival (n)	aankoms	kgorogo	ho fihla	kgorogo	ukufika	ukufika
	arrive (v)	aankom	-goroga	-fihla	-goroga	-fika	-fika
	arrow (n)	pyl	mosebe	motsu	motsu	utolo	umcibisholo
	arson (n)	brandstigting	tšhumo	tjhesetso	tshubo	utshiso	icala lokushisa
	art (n)	kuns	bokgabo	mokgabo	botswerere	ubugcisa	ubuciko
	artery (n)	slagaar	seišamadi	mothapo	tshika	umthambo	umthambo
	art gallery (n)	kunsgalery	ntlo ya bokgabo	tulo ya mokgabo	bokgabisong	igumbi le zobugcisa	igalari yokobuciko
	article (n)	artikel	setlo	sesebediswa	setlo	inqaku	into
	artificial (a)	kunsmatig	-maitirelo	-maiketsetso	maitirelo	-ngadalwanga	-enziweyo nje
	artificial insemination (n)	kunsmatige inseminasie	kemarišo ya maitirelo	kemariso ya maike-tsetso	kemariso ya maitirelo	uzaliso	ukukhulelisa ngokujova
	artificial respiration (n)	kunsmatige asemhaling	khemišo	phefumoloho ya maiketsetso	khemiso ya maitirelo	impefumlelo	ukuphefumulisa
	arum lily (n)	varkoor	mogaladitwe	tsebe-ya-kolobe		inyibiba	intebe
	ascend (v)	styg	-namela	-nyoloha	-tlhatloga	-nyuka	-enyuka
	ascertain (v)	vasstel	-kgonthiša	-nnetefatsa	-lebelela	qinisekisa	-azisisa
	ash (n)	as	molora	molora	molora	uthuthu	umlotha
	ashamed (a)	skaam	-lewa ke dihlong	-swabile	-jewa ke tlhong	-ba neentloni	-namahloni
	aside (adv)	opsy	ka thoko	ka thoko	sejaro	-ngasecaleni	ngasese
	ask (v)	vra	-kgopela	-botsa	-botsa	-buza	-buza
	asleep (a)	aan die slaap	-ile le boroko	-robetse	-robalang	leleyo	-lele
	asphyxia (n)	versmoring	kgamo	pipelano	khupelo	ufuthaniselo	ukugwaliza
	aspire (v)	streef	-ikemišeditše	-labalabela	-eletsa	-langazelela	-langazela
	ass (n)	donkie	tonki	esele	esele	idonki	imbongolo
	assault (n)	aanranding	kgobatšo	kotlo	moteketo	uhlaselo	uhlaselo
	assault (v)	aanrand	-gobatša	-otla	-teketa	-hlasela	-hlasela
	assegai (n)	assegaai	lerumo	lerumo	segae	umkhonto	umkhonto
	assembly (n)	vergadering	kgobokano	kopano	phuthego	intlanganiso	ibandla
	assess (v)	skat	-lekanya	-akanya	-atlhola	-misa	-nquma

English	Afrikaans	N Sotho	Sesotho	Tswana	Xhosa	Zulu	B
assessor (n)	skatter	moahlodiši	moakanyi	moatlhodi	ummisi	umnqumi wenani	
assist (v)	bystaan	-thuša	-thusa	-thusa	-nceda	-sekela	
assistance (n)	bystand	thušo	thuso	thuso	uncedo	iselekelelo	
assistant (n)	helper	mothuši	mothusi	letsogo	umncedi	umsizi	
assurance (n)	versekering	tšhireletšo	ashorense	asorense	ingqiniseko	umshuwalense	
asthma (n)	asma	asma	lefuba	khupelo	umbefu	umbefu	
astrology (n)	astrologie	astrolotši	bolepi ba dinaledi	bolepinaledi	ufundo ngeenkwenkwezi	ukufundwa kwezinkanyezi	
astronomy (n)	sterrekunde	bonepanaledi	thuto ya dinaledi	bolepanaledi	inzululwazi ngeenkwenkwezi	ukwazi ngezinkanyezi	
astute (a)	slim	-tsarogile	-masene	botlhale	-lumkileyo	-hlakaniphile	
asylum (n)	skuilplaas	botšhabelo	botshabelo	botshabelo	indawo yokubalekela	inqaba	
at (prep)	op	mo	ha-/ho-	go-	phezu; kwa- e-	e-, kwa-	
athletics (n)	atletiek	diatletiki	diatletiki	atletiki	umdlalo wobaleko	i-athletiki	
atlas (n)	atlas	atlase	atlelase	atlelase	iatlasi	incwadi yamabalazwe	
atmosphere (n)	atmosfeer	atemosfere	moya	lefaufau	iatmosfera	i-atmosfiye	
attach (v)	aanheg	-swaragantša	-momahanya	gokelela	-bophelela	-hlanganisa	
attachment (n)	gehegtheid	seswaragantšhi	momahano	kgokelelo	ukubophelela	ukunamathelana	
attack (v)	aanval	-hlasela	-hlasela	tlhaselo	-hlasela	-hlasela	
attain (v)	bereik	-phetha	-fihlela	-fitlha	-fikelela	-zuza	
attempt (n)	poging	teko	teko	boiteko	umzamo	umzamo	
attendance (n)	bywoning	tseno	boteng	tseno	ubukho	ukubakhona	
attitude (n)	houding	boitshwaro	moya	boitshwaro	uluvo	isimo	
attorney (n)	prokureur	ramolao	mmuelli	mmueledi	igqwetha	ummeli	
attract (v)	aantrek	-gogela	-hohela	-ngoka	-tsala	-heha	
attraction (n)	aantrekking	maatlakgogedi	kgohelo	kgogedi	umtsalane	ukuheha	
attractive (a)	aantreklik	-kgahlišago	-hohelang	-ntle	-nomtsalane	-okhangayo	
auction (n)	veiling	fantisi	fantisi	fantisi	intengiso	indali	
auctioneer (n)	afslaer	mofantisi	mofantisi	mofantisi	umthengisi	umdayisi endalini	
audible (a)	hoorbaar	-kwagala	-utlwahala	-utlwalang	-vakalayo	-zwakalayo	
auditor (n)	ouditeur	mohlakiši	mohlahlobaditjhelete	motlhatlhobatlotlo	umhloli-ncwadi	umcwaningi wezimali	
August (n)	Augustus	Agostos	Phato	Phatwe	Agasti	uMandulo	
aunt (n)	tante	rakgadi	mmangwane	mme	anti	umamncane	
author (n)	skrywer	mongwadi	mongodi	mokwadi	umbhali	umbhali	
authorise (v)	magtig	-dumelela	-dumella	-dumelela	-gunyazisa	-pha amandla	
authority (n)	gesag	maatla	matla	bolaodi	igunya	igunya	
autumn (n)	herfs	seregana	hwetla	letlhafula	ukwindla	ukwindla	
available (a)	beskikbaar	-hwetšegago	-fumaneha	teng	-fumaneka	-tholakalayo	
avenge (v)	wreek	-lefeletša	-iphetetsa	-busolosetsa	-phindezela	-phindisela	
average (a)	gemiddeld	-palogare	-mahareng	palogare	-myinga	-okulingene	
avert (v)	keer	-thiba	-kgelosa	-fema	-nqanda	-vika	
avocado pear (n)	avokadopeer	abokato	avokhado	pere ya obokado	iavokhado	ukwatapeya	
avoid (v)	vermy	-ila	-phema	-dikologa	-khwebula	-gwema	
await (v)	wag op	-letela	-emela	-emela	-lindela	-lindela	
awake (v)	ontwaak	-phafoga	-tsosa	-thanya	-phaphamisa	-vuka	
awe (n)	eerbied	tlhompho	tshisimoso	boikokobetso	uloyiko	uvalo	
axe (n)	byl	selepe	selepe	selepe	izembe	imbazo	
axle (n)	as	ase	ase	ase	iasi	i-ekseli	
babble (v)	babbel	-ratharatha	-bebera	-buabua	-bhibhidla	-mpompa	
baboon (n)	bobbejaan	tšhwene	tshwene	tshwene	imfene	imfene	
baby (n)	baba	lesea	lesea	lesea	umntwana	umntwana	
bachelor (n)	jongkêrel	kgope	lesoha	kgope	isoka	impohlo	
back (adv)	terug	morago	-morao	morago	-buya	emuva	
back (n)	rug	mokokotlo	mokokotlo	mokwatla	umqolo	umhlane	
back (v)	steun	-emela	-tshehetsa	-tshegetsa	xhasa	-sekela	
background (n)	agtergrond	boithekgo	tikoloho	lemorago	ikamva	isizinda	
backwash (n)	terugspoeling	kgogelomorago ya meetse	maqhububoelamorao	puseletso	umsinga	ibuya	
bacon (n)	spek	sepeke	nama ya kolobe	nama ya kolobe	isipeke	ubhekeni	

B	English	Afrikaans	N Sotho	Sesotho	Tswana	Xhosa	Zulu
	bacteria (n)	bakterie	dipakteria	kokwana	dibaketeria	intsholongwane	ibhakthiriya
	bad (a)	sleg	-be	-be	-be	-bi	-bi
	badly (adv)	sleg	gampe	hampe	mo go maswe	-kakubi	kabi
	baffle (v)	verbyster	-tlaba	-hlolla	-tsietsa	-dida	-ahlula
	bag (n)	sak	mokotla	mokotla	kgetsi	ingxowa	isaka
	bail (n)	borg	peile	beile	topololo	ibheyile	ibheyili
	bail (v)	borg staan	-beila	-beila	-emela topololo	-bheyila	-bheyila
	bake (v)	bak	-paka	-baka	-besa	-bhaka	-bhaka
	baker (n)	bakker	mopaki	mobaki	mmesi	unobhaka	umbhaki
	bakery (n)	bakkery	lepaka	lebaka	lebaka	ibhaka	ibhikawozi
	balance (n)	balans	tekanetšo	botsitso	seelamaleka	ibhalansi	ukuzimelela
	bald (a)	bles	lefatla	-lefatla	-lefatla	inkqayi	-yimpandla
	ball (n)	bal	kgwele	bolo	kgwele	ibhola	ibhola
	ballad (n)	ballade	balate	balate	balate	ibhaladi	ingoma
	balloon (n)	ballon	palune	balunu	balono	ibhaloni	ibhamuza
	bamboo (n)	bamboes	pampu	leqala	bambusu	umthi webhambu	uqalo
	ban (people) (v)	inperk	-ganetša	-thibela	-iletsa	-gxotha	-valwa umlomo
	ban (things) (v)	verbied	-ganetša	-thibela	-iletsa	-alela	-ngavunyelwa
	banana (n)	piesang	panana	panana	panana	ibhanana	ubhanana
	band (n)	groep	sehlopha	sehlopha	banta	iqela	ibutho
	band (n)	orkes	sehlopha sa baletši	baletsi	okese	iqela lomculo	ibhendi
	bandage (n)	verband	pantetši	banteje	sefapo	ibhandeji	umdweshu
	bangle (n)	armband	leseka	sepetja	leseka	isacholo	isigqizo
	banjo (n)	banjo	pentšu	banjo	banjo	umrhubhe	ibhenjo
	bank (n)	bank	panka	banka	polokelo	ibhanki	ibhange
	banknote (n)	banknoot	lehlare	tjhelete ya pampiri	madi	imali eliphepha	imali yephepha
	banned (people) (a)	ingeperk	-ganetšwago	-thibetse	-iletsweng	-gxothiweyo	abavalelwe umlomo
	banned (things) (a)	verbode	-ganetšwago	-thibetse	-iletsweng	-alelwayo	ezingavunyelwa
	banns (n)	gebooie	ditaelo	dikgaboi	digaboi	isaziso somtshato	izimemezelo zomshado
	baptise (v)	doop	-kolobetša	-kolobetsa	-kolobetsa	-phehlelela	-bhabhadisa
	baptism (n)	doop	kolobetšo	kolobetso	kolobetso	uphehlelelo	umbhabhadiso
	bar (n)	kroeg	para	bara	bara	inkanti	inkantini
	bar (v)	uitsluit	-thibela	-kotela	-tlogela kwa ntle	-nqanda	-vimbela
	barbarian (n)	barbaar	motala	leqaba	motala	indlavini	isidlwabidlwabi
	barbed wire (n)	doringdraad	terata ya meetlwa	terata e metsu	terata ya mebitlwa	ucingo olunameva	ucingo olunameva
	barber (n)	haarsnyer	mmeodi	mokuti	mmeodi	umchebi	umphuci
	bare (a)	kaal	-hlobotšego	-feela	-gotlhegileng	-ze	-nqunu
	bare (v)	ontbloot	-hlobola	-senola	-gotlha	-hlubula	-veza
	bark (n)	bas	sekgamati	lekgapetla	lekwati	ixolo	ixolo
	bark (v)	blaf	-bogola	-bohola	bogola	-khonkotha	-khonkotha
	barrel (n)	vat	faki	faki	faki	ifatyi	umphongolo
	barrier (n)	versperring	lepheko	sethibelo	legora	umqobo	isithiyo
	barter (v)	ruil	-gweba	-ananya	-ananya	-nanisa	-hweba
	basic (a)	basies	-motheo	-motheo	-theo	-sisiseko	-yisisekelo
	basin (n)	kom	sehlapelo	basekomo	tidima	isitya	isitsha
	basis (n)	basis	motheo	motheo	theo	isiseko	isisekelo
	bask (v)	koester	-ora	-athamela	-ora	-gcakamela	-otha
	basket (n)	mandjie	seroto	mmanki	seroto	umnyazi	ubhasikidi
	bat (n)	kolf	mmopu	bete	kolofo	iphini	iphini
	bat (n)	vlermuis	mmankgagane	mmankgane	mmamathwane	ilulwane	ilulwane
	bath (n)	bad	pafo	bate	bata	ibhafu	ubhavu
	bath (v)	bad	-hlapa	-tola	-bata	-bhafa	ukubhava
	bathroom (n)	badkamer	bohlapelo	batekamore	botlhapelo	igumbi lokuhlambela	ibhavulumu
	battery (n)	battery	peteri	beteri	lelatlha	ibhetri	ibhethili
	battle (n)	geveg	ntwa	ntwa	ntwa	umlo	impi
	battle (v)	veg	-lwa	-lwana	-lwa	-lwa	-lwa
	battle-axe (n)	strydbyl	tsaka	kwakwa	magagana	ucelemba	imbemba
	battlefield (n)	slagveld	bohlabanelo	ntweng	ntwa	ithafa leduli	inkundla yempi
	bawdy (a)	onkuis	-otswetšago	tlhapa	-maswe	-nobuhenyu	-enhlamba
	bay (n)	baai	kou	kou	kgogomelo	itheku	itheku

English	Afrikaans	N Sotho	Sesotho	Tswana	Xhosa	Zulu	B
be (v)	wees	-ba	-ba	-ke	-ba	-ba	
beach (n)	strand	khwiti ya lewatle	lewatleng	losi	unxweme	usebe lolwandle	
beacon (n)	baken	pakane	mokolokotwane	bakene	ibhakana	isikhonkwane somdabuli	
bead (n)	kraal	pheta	sefaha	sebaga	amaso	ubuhlalu	
beadwork (n)	kraalwerk	dipheta	difaha	dibaga	amaso	ukuthungwa kobuhlalu	
beak (n)	snawel	molomo wa nonyana	molomo	molomo	umlomo wentaka	umlomo wenyoni	
bean (n)	boontjie	nawa	nawa	nawa	imbotyi	ubhontshisi	
bear (n)	beer	bere	bere	bera	ibhere	ibheja	
bear (v)	duld	-kgotlelela	-mamella	-tshola	-thwala	-bekezela	
beard (n)	baard	seledu	ditedu	tedu	udevu	isilevu	
beast (n)	dier	phoofolo	phoofolo	kgomo	isilo	isilwane	
beat (n)	ritme	mošito	morethetho	kgato	isingqisho	ibhithi	
beautiful (a)	pragtig	-botse	-tle	-ntle	-hle	-bukekayo	
beauty (n)	skoonheid	botse	botle	bontle	ubuhle	ubuhle	
because (conj)	omdat	ka gobane	hobane	gore	ngokuba	ngoba	
beckon (v)	wink	-gwehla	-hwehla	-gwetlha	-khweba	-khweba	
bed (n)	bed	bolao	bethe	bolao	umandlalo	umbhede	
bedbug (n)	weeluis	tšhikidi	tshitshidi	tshitshiri	incukuthu	imbungulu	
bedclothes (n)	beddegoed	malao	diphate	dikobo	iingubo	izingubo zokulala	
bedpan (n)	bedpan	sebjana sa mohla-pologo	thuana	sekotleleithusetso	isitya sokuchamela	isikigi	
bedroom (n)	slaapkamer	borobalelo	kamore	kamore	igumbi lokulala	ikamelo lokulala	
bee (n)	by	nose	notshi	notshe	inyosi	inyosi	
beef (n)	beesvleis	nama ya kgomo	nama ya kgomo	nama ya kgomo	inyama yenkomo	inyama yenkomo	
beer (n)	bier	bjalwa	jwala	bojalwa	utywala	utshwala	
beetle (n)	kewer	khunkhwane	kgolabolokwe	khukhwane	uqongqothwane	ibhungane	
beetroot (n)	beet	pete	bete	bete	ibhitruthi	ibhithrudi	
before (prep)	voor	pele	-pele	pele	-phambi	phambi kwa-	
beg (v)	bedel	-kgopela	-kopa	-kopa	-cenga	-nxiba	
beggar (n)	bedelaar	mokgopedi	mokopi	mokopi	umngqibi	isinxibi	
begin (v)	begin	-thoma	-qala	-thobolola	-qala	-qala	
beginner (n)	beginner	mothomi	moqadi	magogorwane	umqali	inyuwane	
beginning (n)	begin	mathomo	qalo	tshimologo	isiqalo	ukuqala	
behave (v)	jou gedra	-itshwara	-itshwara	-itshola setho	-ziphathe	-zimisa	
behaviour (n)	gedrag	boitshwaro	boitshwaro	boitshwaro	ukuziphatha	ukuziphatha	
behind (prep)	agter	morago	-morao	morago	-ngemva	emuva	
beige (a)	beige	-šwaana	beije	-setlha	-lubhelu-mdaka	-liphuzana	
belch (v)	wind opbreek	-kgeba	-bohla	-kgobola	-bhodla	-bhodla	
believe (v)	glo	-dumela	-dumela	-dumela	-kholelwa	-kholwa	
believer (n)	gelowige	modumedi	modumedi	modumedi	ikholwa	ikholwa	
belittle (v)	verkleineer	-nyatša	-nyenyefatsa	-nyatsa	-delela	-dika	
bell (n)	klok	tshipi	tshepe	tshipi	intsimbi	insimbi	
belly (n)	pens	mogodu	mpa	mpa	umkhaba	isisu	
belong (v)	behoort	-ya	-ya	-wa	-ba	-kwa-	
beloved (a)	bemind	-rategago	-moratuwa	-ratiwa	-thandekayo	-thandiwe	
below (prep)	onder	fase	-tlase	tlase	-ngaphantsi	phansi kwa-	
belt (n)	gordel	lepanta	lebanta	lebanta	ibhanti	ibhande	
bench (n)	bank	panka	banka	banka	ibhanka	ibhentshi	
bend (n)	buiging	kobamo	mothinya	khona	igophe	isigwegwe	
bend (v)	buig	-oba	-koba	-oba	-goba	-goba	
beneficial (a)	voordelig	-holago	-molemo	-mosola	ncedayo	-sizayo	
beside (prep)	langs	hleng ga	-pela	thoko	-caleni kwa-	ohlangothini lwa-	
besides (prep)	buiten	ka ntle le	-ntle le	kwa ntle ga	-ngele kwa-	phandle kwa-	
best (a)	beste	-palago ka moka	-molemo	-ntsha ga tshwene	-ncomekayo	-dlulayo konke	
bet (n)	weddenskap	peelano	mobetjho	peelano	iqashiso	ukubheja	
bet (v)	wed	-beelana	-betjha	-beelana	-qashisa	-bheja	
betray (v)	verraai	-eka	-eka	-eka	-ngcatsha	-khaphela	
better (a)	beter	kaone	-betere	botoka	-phucukileyo	-ngcono	
between (prep)	tussen	gare ga	-hara	gare	-phakathi	ngaphakathi	

B English	Afrikaans	N Sotho	Sesotho	Tswana	Xhosa	Zulu
beware (v)	oppas	-hlokomela	-hlokomela	-tlhokomela	-lumka	-qaphela
bewitch (v)	toor	-loya	-loya	-loa	-thakatha	-thakathela
beyond (prep)	oorkant	mošola wa	-nqane	moseja	-ngaphaya	-phesheya
Bible (n)	Bybel	Bibele	Bebele	Beibele	iBhayibhile	iBhayibheli
biceps (n)	biseps	mošifa wa paesepe	dipotongwane	lerudi	amandla	izinkonyane
bicycle (n)	fiets	paesekela	baesekele	baesekele	ibhayisikili	ibhayisikili
big (a)	groot	-golo	-holo	-tona	-khulu	-khulu
bile (n)	gal	nyoko	nyooko	seumaka	inyongo	inyongo
bilharzia (n)	bilharzia	bilhazia	bilehasia	thotamadi	ibhilhazia	ibhilihaziya
biltong (n)	biltong	mogwapa	sehwapa	segwapa	umqwayito	umqwayiba
binoculars (n)	verkyker	ferekekere	ferekekere	ferekekere	umabonakude	izingilazi zokubuka kude
biology (n)	biologie	payolotši	bayoloji	thutatshelo	ibhayoloji	ibhayoloji
bird (n)	voël	nonyana	nonyana	nonyane	intaka	inyoni
birth (n)	geboorte	pelego	tswalo	pelegi	ukuzala	ukuzalwa
birthday (n)	verjaarsdag	letšatši la matswalo	letsatsi la tswalo	botsalo	umhla wokuzalwa	usuku lokuzalwa
birthmark (n)	moedervlek	lebadi la matswalo	letshwao la tswalo	sematla	umkhango	icasha
birthplace (n)	geboorteplek	botswalelo	tulo ya tswalo	botsholong	isinqe	indawo yokuzalwa
biscuit (n)	koekie	piskiti	basekeite	bisikiti	iqebengwana	ibhiskidi
bishop (n)	biskop	mopišapo	mobishopo	bishopo	ibhishophu	umbhishobhi
bit (n)	bietjie	bonnyane	bonyenyane	bonnyane	intwana	isihlephu
bitch (n)	teef	mpša ya tshadi	ntja	ntswagadi	injakazi	injakazi
bite (n)	hap	kgemo	ho loma	molomo	umthamo	ukuluma
bite (v)	byt	-loma	-loma	-loma	-luma	-luma
bitter (a)	bitter	-babago	-baba	-botlhoko	-krakra	-muncu
black (a)	swart	-so	-tsho	-ntsho	-mnyama	-mnyama
bladder (n)	blaas	sebudula	senya	setlha	isinyi	isinye
blade (n)	blad	bogale	lehare	ntshane	ukutya	ucezu
blame (n)	blaam	molato	phoso	tatofatso	isityholo	isolo
blame (v)	blameer	-bea molato	-bona phoso	-baya molato	-tyhola	-sola
blank (a)	leeg	-se nago selo	-feela	-sepe	-ze	-okungenalutho
blanket (n)	kombers	kobo	kobo	kobo	ingubo	ingubo
bleach (v)	bleik	-šweufatša	-sweufatsa	-tswapola	-khucula	-cacisa umbalo omhlophe
bleed (v)	bloei	-tšwa madi	-tswa madi	-tswa madi	-opha	-opha
bless (v)	seën	-šegofatša	-hlohonolofatsa	-tshegofatsa	sikelela	-busisa
blessing (n)	seëning	lehlogonolo	mahlohonolo	lesego	intsikelelo	isibusiso
blind (a)	blind	-foufetšego	-foufetse	-foufetseng	-ngaboniyo	-yimpumputhe
blind (n)	blinding	seširo	dikgaretene	disiralesedi	ubumfama	ibhulayindi
blink (v)	knipoog	-panya leihlo	-panya	-panya	-qhwanyaza	-phazima
blinkers (n)	oogklappe	dithibelagolebele-lathoko	ditlelapa	diogotlelapa	isikhusi-mehlo	insithamehlo
blister (n)	blaar	lephone	letswabadi	lerophi	idyungudyungu	ibhamuza
block (n)	blok	kota	kutu	mokasa	isiqobo	isigaxa
block (v)	blokkeer	-thiba	-thibela	-thiba	-vingca	-vimbela
blood (n)	bloed	madi	madi	madi	igazi	igazi
blood pressure (n)	bloeddruk	kgatelelo ya madi	kgatello ya madi	kgatelelo ya madi	uxinzelelo lwegazi	umfutho wegazi
blood transfusion (n)	bloedoortapping	tlhabelomadi	phepelo ya madi	tsenyo ya madi	ufunxo-gazi	ukuthasiselwa igazi
blood vessel (n)	bloedvat	tselamadi	mothapo	tshika	umthambo wegazi	umthambo wegazi
bloom (v)	blom	-thunya	-thunya	-thunya	-dubula	-qhakaza
blot (n)	klad	setswata	letheba	kwaba	ichaphaza	ichaphazela
blouse (n)	bloes	polause	bolouso	bolaose	iblawuzi	ibhulawozi
blow (n)	hou	titio	kotlo	petso	isithonga	isigalelo
blow (v)	waai	-foka	-fefola	-foka	-vuthela	-phephetha
blue (a)	blou	botala bja leratadima	-tala; -putswa	-tala	-luhlaza	-zulucwathile
bluebottle (n)	bloublasie	senanawatle	boloubolasie		uhodoshe	isilokazana zolwandle
bluegum (n)	bloekomboom	mopulukomo	boloukomo	leblukomo	umgamtriya	umgathini
blunder (n)	flater	phošo	phoso	tshenyo	imposiso	isiphambeko
blunt (a)	stomp	-kubegilego	-nthithi	-boi	-buthuntu	-buthuntu
board (n)	bord	papetla	boroto	letlapa	ibhodi	ibhodi

English	Afrikaans	N Sotho	Sesotho	Tswana	Xhosa	Zulu	B
boast (v)	spog	-ikgodiša	-ithorisa	-koma	-gwagwisa	-bhamuza	
boastful (a)	spoggerig	-ikgodišago	-ithorisang	-belafalang	-gwagwisayo	-qholoshile	
boat (n)	boot	sekepe	seketswana	mokoro	iphenyane	umkhumbi	
body (n)	liggaam	mmele	mmele	mmele	umzima	umzimba	
boil (n)	bloedvint	sekaku	lethopa	modingwana	ithumba	ithumba	
boil (v)	kook	-bela	-bela	-bela	-bila	-bilisa	
bolt (n)	bout	pouto	boutu	boutu	ibholiti	ibhawodi	
bomb (n)	bom	pomo	bomo	bomo	isiqhushumbisi	ibhomu	
bond (n)	band	setlamo	tlamo	tlamo	ikhonkco	ubudlewane	
bondage (n)	knegskap	bohlanka	bohlanka	botlamo	ubukhoboka	ukuthumbeka	
bone (n)	been	lerapo	lesapo	lerapo	ithambo	ithambo	
book (n)	boek	puku	buka	buka	incwadi	incwadi	
boot (n)	stewel	putsu	butshi	setlhako	isihlangu	isihlangu	
boot (v)	skop	-raga	-raha	-raga	-khaba	-khahlela	
border (n)	grens	mollwane	moedi	molelwane	umda	umncele	
border (v)	grens	-bea mellwane	-sika	-thetha	-enza umda	-phethela	
bore (n)	vervelige mens	moteni	setenane	molapisi	umsinandozele	umuntu odinisayo	
bore (v)	verveel	-tena	-tena	-tena	-dika	-dinisayo	
borrow (v)	leen	-adima	-adima	-adima	-boleka	-boleka	
bosom (n)	boesem	sehuba	sefuba	phega	umxhelo	isifuba	
both (a)	albei	bobedi	-bobedi	-oobedi	-bini	bobabili	
bother (v)	lastig wees	-tshwenya	-kgathatsa	-tshwenya	-khathaza	-khathaza	
bottle (n)	bottel	lepotlelo	botlolo	lebotlolo	ibhotile	ibhodlela	
bottom (n)	bodem	bofase	botlase	botlase	umzantsi	ingaphansi	
bounce (v)	opspring	-tlola	-tlola	-tlola	-qakathisa	-xhuma	
boundary (n)	grenslyn	mollwane	moedi	molelwane	ibhawundri	umncele	
boundless (a)	grensloos	-sa felego	-saballetse	-sakhutleng	-ngenabhawundri	-ngenamkhawulo	
bow (n)	boog	bora	seqha	bora	isaphetha	inkumbela	
bow (n)	strik	lehuto		sethaiso	umphambili-nqanawa	inkintshela yokuhlobisa	
bow (v)	buk	-inama	-inama	-obama	-goba	-goba	
bowels (n)	ingewande	mala	dikahare	mateng	amathumbu	amathumbu	
bowl (n)	bak	mogopo	morifi	mogopo	isitya	isitsha	
bowls (n)	rolbal	kgwele ya go kgokološa	rolobolo	dibaole	ibhola eqengqwayo	amabholi	
box (n)	doos	lepokisi	lebokose	lepokoso	ibhokisi	ibhokisi	
box (v)	boks	-itia ka matswele	-tebela	-ratha	-betha amanqindi	-bhakela	
boxing (n)	boks	dintwa tša matswele	ditebele	mabole	imbethi-manqindi	isibhakela	
box office (n)	kaartjieloket	ofisi ya dithekethe	ntlwana ya ditekete	kantoro ya dikaraki	iofisi yokuthenga itiki	indawo yokuthenga amathikithi	
boy (n)	seun	mošemane	moshanyana	mosimane	inkwenkwe	umfana	
boyfriend (n)	kêrel	moratiwa	mohlankana	lekau	isinqandamathe	isoka	
brackets (n)	hakies	mašakana	masakana	masakana	isibiyeli	izibiyelo	
brag (v)	grootpraat	-ikgodiša	-ikgantsha	-thetha	-qhayisa	-gabaza	
brain (n)	brein	bjoko	booko	boboko	ubuchopho	ubuchopho	
brake (n)	rem	poriki	boriki	-rema	ibreki	ibhuliki	
bran (n)	semels	disemala	ditlhoka	moroko	isemilisi	amakhoba	
branch (n)	tak	lekala	lekala	kala	isebe	igatsha	
brand (n)	handelsmerk	tshwaokgwebo	letshwao la kgwebo	letshwaokgwebo	uphawu	uphawu	
brass (n)	geelkoper	porase	borase	kgotlho	ibrasi	ithusi	
brassière (n)	bra	semmejana	bodise	bra	ibra	ingutshana yokubopha amabele	
brave (a)	dapper	-nago le sebete	-sebete	bogale	-khaliphileyo	-nobuqhawe	
bravery (n)	dapperheid	bogale	sebete	bopelokgale	ubukhalipha	ubuqhawe	
bread (n)	brood	borotho	borotho	borotho	isonka	isinkwa	
breadth (n)	breedte	bophara	bophara	bophaphathi	ububanzi	ububanzi	
break (v)	breek	-roba	-pshatla	-roba	-aphula	-ephuka	
breakfast (n)	ontbyt	sefihlolo	borakefese	sefitlholo	isidlo sakusasa	ibhulakufesi	
breast (n)	bors	sehuba	sefuba	lebele	isifuba	isifuba	
breastbone (n)	borsbeen	kgara	lesapo la sefuba	kgara	ingqoba	ithambo lesifuba	
breath (n)	asem	moya	moya	mowa	umphefumlo	umphefumulo	

B	English	Afrikaans	N Sotho	Sesotho	Tswana	Xhosa	Zulu
	breathe (v)	asemhaal	-buša moya	-phefumoloha	-hema	-phefumla	-phefumula
	breathless (a)	uitasem	-fegelwago	-fehelwa	-kabalanang	-ngaphefumliyo	-khefuzelayo
	breed (v)	teel	-rua	-rua	-rua	-zalisa	-fuya
	breeze (n)	bries	phefšana	moya	pheswana	impepho	unyele
	brew (n)	brousel	pedišo	moritelo	motswako	utywala	okuqungiwe
	brew (v)	brou	-bediša	-ritela	-apaya	-didiyela	-qunga
	bribe (n)	omkoopprys	pipamolomo	tjotjo	pipamolomo	isinyobo	ukufumbathiswa
	bribe (v)	omkoop	-reka	-ntsha tjotjo	-reka	-nyoba	-fumbathisa
	bribery (n)	omkopery	seatlakobong	ho ntsha tjotjo	theko	unyobo	imvalamlomo
	brick (n)	baksteen	setena	setene	setena	isitena	isitini
	bride (n)	bruid	ngwetši	monyaduwa	monyadiwa	umtshakazi	umakoti
	bridegroom (n)	bruidegom	monyadi	monyadi	monyadi	umyeni	umyeni
	bridesmaid (n)	strooimeisie	lekgetla	moetsana	moetsana	abakhaphi	impelesi
	bridge (n)	brug	leporogo	borokgo	moratho	ibhulorho	ibhuloho
	bridle (n)	toom	tomo	tomo	tomo	umkhala	itomu
	brief (a)	beknop	-kopana	-kgutshwane	-khutswafaditsweng	-futshane	-fushane
	briefly (adv)	kortliks	ka bokopana	hakgutshwane	-khutswafatso	-ngokufutshane	kafushane
	bright (a)	helder	-kganyago	-hlakile	-kganyang	qaqambileyo	-khazimulayo
	brilliance (n)	helderheid	kganya	ho hlaka	botlhaletlhale	ukuqaqamba	ubucwazicwazi
	bring (v)	bring	-tliša	-tlisa	-tlisa	-zisa	-letha
	bristle (n)	steekhaar	boditsi	boditse	boditse	unwele	ingqangasi
	British (a)	Brits	-Seisimane	-Manyesemane	-Seesimane	-aseNgilane	-emaNgisi
	broad (a)	breed	-phaphathi	-sephara	-phaphati	-phangaleleyo	-banzi
	broadcast (v)	uitsaai	-gaša	-hasa	-gasa	-sasaza	-sakaza
	broken (a)	stukkend	-robegilego	-pshatlehile	-senyegileng	-aphukileyo	-file
	brood (v)	broei	-alama	-alama	-ilama	-cinga	-fukama
	broom (n)	besem	leswielo	lefielo	lefeelo	umtshayelo	umshanelo
	broomstick (n)	besemstok	kota ya leswielo	mofeng	kota ya lefeelo	intonga yomtshayelo	uthi lomshanelo
	brother (n)	broer	morwarra	moreso	lekaulengwe	umnakwethu	umfowethu
	brother-in-law (n)	swaer	sebara	sware	molangwa	sibali	umlamu
	brown (a)	bruin	-tsothwa	-sootho	-rokwa	-mdaka	-nsundu
	bruise (n)	kneusplek	kgobogo	letetetso	letsadi	umgruzulo	isisihla
	bruise (v)	kneus	-kgoboga	-tetetsa	-tetea	-gruzula	-sicila
	brush (n)	borsel	porosolo	borosolo	borosolo	ibrashi	ibhulashi
	brush (v)	borsel	-porosola	-borosola	-sutlha	brasha	-bhulasha
	brutal (a)	dierlik	-šoro	-soro	-bophologolo	-burhalarhume	-khuhlumezayo
	bubble (n)	borrel	pue	pudula	pudula	iqamza	-bhadla
	buck (n)	bok	phoofolo	nyamatsane	podi	inyamakazi	inyamazane
	bucket (n)	emmer	kgamelo	kgamelo	kgamelo	iemere	ibhakede
	bud (n)	botsel	khukhuša	phupu	letswela	ingcinga	umqumbe
	bug (n)	gogga	khunkhwane	kokwanyana	khukhwane	irhorho	isilwanyakazane
	build (v)	bou	-aga	-(h)aha	-aga	-akha	-akha
	building (n)	gebou	moago	moaho	moago	isakhiwo	isakhiwo
	bulb (n)	bol	segwere	kotola	segwere	ibhalbhu	ibhalbhu
	bulge (v)	uitbult	-kokomoga	-kokomoha	-kokorala	-khukhumala	-dumba
	bull (n)	bul	poo	poho	poo	inkunzi	inkunzi
	bulldog (n)	bulhond	mpša ya lepultoko	pofa	phontshi	unomasinana	ubhova
	bullet (n)	koeël	kolo	kulo	lerumo	imbumbulu	inhlamvu
	bump (v)	stamp	-thula	-thesela	-thula	-nguba	-dubhuza
	bunch (n)	tros	sehlopha	lesihla	seako	isihlahla	isihleke
	bundle (n)	bondel	ngata	seshoba	ngata	umbhumbutho	umqulu
	bunion (n)	knokkeleelt	letšwabadi	torong	dinata	ikhwiniba	inhlumba
	burden (n)	las	morwalo	morwalo	mokgweleo	umthwalo	umthwalo
	burglar (n)	inbreker	mothubi	mothuhi	leepantlo	umqhekezi	umgqekezi
	burgle (v)	inbreek	-thuba	-thuha	-thuba	-qhekeza	-gqekeza
	burial (n)	begrafnis	poloko	poloko	phitlho	umngcwabo	umngcwabo
	burn (n)	brandplek	lebadi la mollo	leqeba la mollo	seso	umtshiso	isibashu
	burn (v)	brand	-swa	-besa	-swa	-tshisa	-shisa
	burst (v)	bars	-pharoga	-phatloha	-phanyega	-gqabhuka	-qhuma
	bury (v)	begrawe	-boloka	-epela	-fitlha	-ngcwaba	-ngcwaba

English	Afrikaans	N Sotho	Sesotho	Tswana	Xhosa	Zulu	C
bus (n)	bus	pese	bese	bese	ibhasi	ibhasi	
bus stop (n)	bushalte	boemapese	setopo sa dibese	maemo a bese	istop sebhasi	isitobhi	
bush (n)	bos	sethokgwa	moru	sekgwa	ityholo	ihlathi	
bushbuck (n)	bosbok	tšhošo	nyamatsane	serolobotlhoko	imbabala	umdaka	
bushveld (n)	bosveld	dikgweng	merung	naga e e lesuthu	idobo	ihlanze	
but (conj)	maar	eupša	empa	mme	kodwa	kodwa	
butcher (n)	slagter	radinama	raselaga	raselaga	unosilarha	ubhusha	
butchery (n)	slagtery	leselaga	selaga	selaga	isilarha	isilaha	
butter (n)	botter	leredi	botoro	serethe	ibhotolo	ibhotela	
butterfly (n)	skoenlapper	serurubele	serurubele	serurubele	ibhabhathane	uvemvane	
buttermilk (n)	karringmelk	motsaro	mofehlo	mokaro	ixibhiya	umbhobe	
butternut (n)	botterskorsie	lefodi	solotsi	lephutshana	usenza	ibhathanathi	
buttock (n)	boud	lerago	lerao	lerago	intsula	isinqe	
button (n)	knoop	konope	konopo	kopela	iqhosha	inkinobho	
buttonhole (n)	knoopsgat	lešoba la konope	lesoba la konopo	leroba la kopela	umngxuma weqhosha	imbobo yenkinobho	
buy (v)	koop	-reka	-reka	-reka	-thenga	-thenga	
buyer (n)	koper	moreki	moreki	moreki	umthengi	umthengi	
by (prep)	by	go	ka-	ke-	-ngase	nga-	
by (prep)	by	go	ka-	ka-	-nga	nga-	
bystander (n)	omstander	moemakgauswi	mobohi	babogedi	ilalela	isibukeli	
cabbage (n)	kool	khabetšhe	khabetjhe	khabetshe	ikhaphetshu	ikhabishi	
cabinet (n)	kabinet	kabinete	kabinete	kabinete	ikhabhinethi	isigungu sikahulumeni	
cable (n)	kabel	mogala	mohala	kabele	intambo	indophi enohlonze	
cactus (n)	kaktus	kaktuse	torofeie	kaketese	ikhala	isihlehle	
café (n)	kafee	khefi	khefi	khefi	ikhefi	ikhefi	
cake (n)	koek	kuku	kuku	kuku	iqebengwana	ikhekhe	
calabash (n)	kalbas	kgapa	mohope	moduto	iselwa	iselwa	
calculate (v)	reken	-bala	-bala	-balela	-bala	-balisisa	
calculator (n)	rekenaar	komphuta	sebadi	komputara	umashini wokubala	umshini wokubala	
calendar (n)	kalender	kalentara	almanaka	alemanaka	ikhalenda	ikhalenda	
calf (n)	kalf	namane	namane	namane	ithole	inkonyane	
call (v)	besoek	-etela	-etela	-etela	-tyelela	-vakasha	
call (v)	roep	-bitša	-bitsa	-bitsa	-biza	-biza	
caller (n)	besoeker	moeng	moeti	moeti	undwendwe	isivakashi	
caller (n)	roeper	mmitši	mmitsi	mmitsi	umbizi	umuntu obizayo	
calm (a)	kalm	-homotšego	-kgutsitse	-kokobelang	-zolileyo	-thulile	
camel (n)	kameel	kamela	kamele	kamela	inkamela	ikhamela	
camera (n)	kamera	khamera	khemera	kamera	ikhamera	ikhamera	
camp (n)	kamp	kampa	kampo	kampa	ikampu	inkambu	
camp (v)	kampeer	-kampa	-kampa	-thibelela	-misa intente	-misa inkambu	
camping (n)	kampering	go kampa	ho kampa	bothibelelo	ukumisa intente	ukukampa	
camp site (n)	kampeerterrein	lefelo la go kampela	setsha sa ho kampa	lefelo la kampa	indawo yokumisa intente	isiza sekambu	
can (n)	kan	kane	kanekane	kane	-kwazi	ithunga	
canal (n)	kanaal	mokero	kanale	kanale	inyoba	umselekazi wamanzi	
cancel (v)	kanselleer	-phumola	-khansela	-sutlha	-rhoxisa	-kansela	
cancer (n)	kanker	bolwetši bja kankere	kankere	kwatsi	umhlaza	umdlavuza	
candle (n)	kers	khantlela	kerese	kerese	ikhandlela	ikhandlela	
cannabis (n)	dagga	patše	matekwane	motokwane	intsangu	insangu	
cannibal (n)	mensvreter	lekgema	ledimo	mojabatho	izim	izimu	
cannon (n)	kanon	kanono	kanono	kanono	inkanunu	umbayimbayi	
canvas (n)	seil	seila	seile	seile	iseyile	useyili	
cap (n)	deksel	sekhurumelo	sekwahelo	sekhurumelo	ityepusi	isivalo	
capillary (n)	haarvat	kapilari	methatswana	tshika	umthanjana	umthanjana	
capital (a)	hoof	-golo	-holo	-golo	ikomkhulu	-khulu	
capsize (v)	omkantel	-thenkgoga	-phethoha	-menoga	-bhukuqa	-gumbeqeka	
captain (n)	kaptein	moetapele	kapotene	molaodi	inkokeli yeqela	ukaputeni	
capture (v)	vang	-swara	-hapa	-thopa	-thimba	-bamba	
car (n)	motor	mmotoro	mmotokara	mmotorokara	imoto	imoto	

C	English	Afrikaans	N Sotho	Sesotho	Tswana	Xhosa	Zulu
	caravan (n)	karavaan	kharabane	kharavane	karafane	ikharavani	ikharavani
	carcass (n)	karkas	setoto	sefifi	setoto	inyamakazi ebuleweyo	isidumbu sesilwane
	card (n)	kaart	karata	karete	karata	ikhadi	ikhadi
	cardboard (n)	karton	khatepoto	khateboto	khateboto	ikhadibhodi	ikhadibhodi
	care (v)	omgee	-hlokomela	-kgathalla	-tlhokomela	-khathalela	ukunakelela
	careful (a)	versigtig	-hlokomelago	-hlokomelang	-kelotlhoko	-lumkileyo	-nakekele
	careless (a)	nalatig	-šaetšago	-bohlaswa	-boatla	-ngakhathaliyo	-nganaki
	caretaker (n)	opsigter	molebeledi	mohlokomedi	molebeledi	umgcinindawo	umbheki
	carpenter (n)	timmerman	mmetli	mmetli	mmetli	umchweli	umbazi
	carrot (n)	wortel	borotlolo	sehwete	segwete	umrqathe	ikhalothi
	carry (v)	dra	-rwala	-rwala	-tshola	-thwala	-thwala
	cart (n)	kar	kariki	kariki	karaki	inqwelo	ikalishi
	cart (v)	karwei	-thotha	-thotha	-tsholela	-thutha	-thutha
	cartilage (n)	kraakbeen	lešetla	lefufuro	lehihiri	intlala	uqwanga
	carve (v)	sny	-ripa	-seta	-seta	-sika	-sika
	case (n)	saak	taba	molato	taba	ingxowa	indaba
	cash (n)	kontant	kheše	tjhelete	madi	imali	ukheshe
	cast (v)	werp	-betša	-akgela	-latlha	-phosa	-phonsa
	castor oil (n)	kasterolie	kasteroli	kasteroli	mokure	ikastoli	ukhasitowela
	castrate (v)	kastreer	-fagola	-fa(h)ola	-fagola	-thena	-phakula
	casualty (n)	ongeval	kotsi	lehlatsipa	kgobadi	ingxwelerha	ingozi
	cat (n)	kat	katse	katse	katse	ikati	ikati
	catalogue (n)	katalogus	kataloko	khataloko	kataloko	ikhathalogu	ikhathalogi
	catch (v)	vang	-swara	-tshwara	-tshwara	-bamba	-bamba
	caterpillar (n)	ruspe	seboko	seboko	nato	umbungu	icimbi
	cattle (n)	vee	diruiwa	dikgomo	dikgomo	iinkomo	izinkomo
	cauliflower (n)	blomkool	kholifolawa	kholifolawa	kholifolawa	ikholiflawa	ukhalifulawa
	cause (n)	oorsaak	lebaka	sesosa	lebaka	imbangi	isisusa
	cause (v)	veroorsaak	-baka	-baka	-baka	-enza	-enza
	caution (n)	versigtigheid	tlhokomelo	tlhokomelo	boipabalelo	umgqalisela	isiqapheliso
	cave (n)	grot	legaga	lehaha	legaga	umqolomba	umgede
	cease (v)	ophou	-fela	-kgaotsa	-khutla	-pheza	-khawula
	ceasefire (n)	skietstilstand	marumofase	ho lala ha ntwa	khutlo ya ntwa	umayime	ukunqamuka kokudubula
	ceiling (n)	plafon	siling	siling	siling	intungo	isilingi
	celebrate (v)	vier	-keteka	-keteka	-keteka	-vuyela	-gubha umkhosi
	celebration (n)	viering	monyanya	mokete	keteko	imivuyo	umkhosi
	celery (n)	seldery	seleri	seleri	morogo wa seleri	iseleri	useleri
	cell (n)	sel	sele	sele	sele	iseli	iseli
	cellist (n)	tjellis	moletši wa tšhelo	motjhelo	moietsi wa tshelo	umclalimrhubhe	umshayi-vayolina
	cello (n)	tjello	tšhelo	tjhelo	tshelo	umrhubhe	ishelo
	cement (n)	sement	samente	samente	samente	isamente	usemende
	cemetery (n)	begraafplaas	mabitleng	mabitleng	mabitleng	emangcwabeni	indawo yamathuna
	censor (v)	sensor	-ganetša	-nyakurela	-sensara	umhluzi weendaba	umbonisici
	census (n)	sensus	palo	palo ya batho	palo ya batho	ubalo lwabantu	ukubalwa kwabantu
	cent (n)	sent	sente	sente	sente	isenti	isenti
	centenary (n)	eeufees	mokete wa ngwagakgolo	mokete wa dilemokgolo	ngwagakgolo wa keteko	ikhulu leminyaka	umkhosi wekhulu leminyaka
	centipede (n)	honderdpoot	legokolodi	lefokolodi	sebokolodi	isongololo	inkume
	centre (n)	middel	bogare	setsing	tikatikwe	isenza	isenta
	centre (n)	middel	bogare	setsi	bogare	umbindi	isenta
	century (n)	eeu	ngwagakgolo	senturu	ngwagakgolo	ikhulu	ikhulu leminyaka
	century (sport) (n)	honderdtal	lekgolo	dilemokgolo	lekgolo	inkulungwane	ikhulu
	ceremony (n)	seremonie	moletlo	mokete	modiro	inkonzo ethile	umgidi
	certificate (n)	sertifikaat	lengwalo la bopaki	lengolo	sethifikheiti	isetifiketi	isetifikethi
	chafe (v)	skaaf	-khumola	-hohla	-gotlha	-khuthula	-gudleka
	chain (n)	ketting	ketane	ketane	keetane	ityathanga	iketanga
	chain (v)	vasketting	-bofa	-tlama	-bofelela ka keetane	-bopha ngetyathanga	-bopha
	chair (n)	stoel	setulo	setulo	setulo	isihlalo	isihlalo
	chair (v)	voorsit	-swara setulo	-dulasetulo	-dula setulo	-chophela	-ongamela

English	Afrikaans	N Sotho	Sesotho	Tswana	Xhosa	Zulu	C
chairman (n)	voorsitter	modulasetulo	modulasetulo	modulasetulo	umhlali-ngaphambili	usihlalo	
chalk (n)	kryt	tšhoko	tjhoko	tshoko	itshokhwe	ushoki	
challenge (n)	uitdaging	tlhohlo	phepetso	kgwetlho	umngeni	inselele	
challenge (v)	uitdaag	-hlohla	-phepetsa	-kgwetlha	-cela umngeni	-cela inselele	
chameleon (n)	verkleurmannetjie	leobu	lenwabo	lelobu	ilovane	unwabu	
champion (n)	kampioen	kgoroto	mmampodi	mmampodi	intshatsheli	ingqwele	
chance (n)	kans	sebaka	sebaka	lobaka	ithuba	ithuba	
change (n)	verandering	phetogo	phetoho	phetogo	utshintsho	inguquko	
change (v)	verander	-fetoga	-fetola	-fetoga	-tshintsha	-shintsha	
chapter (n)	hoofstuk	kgaolo	kgaolo	kgaolo	isahluko	isahluko	
character (n)	karakter	semelo	semelo	moanelwa	umlinganiswa	umlingiswa	
characteristic (a)	kenmerkend	-kgethologanyago	-tsebahala	-tlhagang	-luphawu	-okomkhuba	
charge (law) (v)	aankla	-bega	-qosa	-latofatsa	-mangalelwa	-beka icala	
charge (n)	aanklag	pego	qoso	molato	isimangalo	icala	
charge (price) (v)	vra	-bitša	-bitsa	-kopa	-xabisa	-biza	
charity (n)	liefdadigheid	lerato	lerato	bopelonomi	isisa	umhawu	
charm (n)	sjarme	borategi	mofuthu	mmitsa	umtsalane	ubuhle	
chat (v)	gesels	-boledišana	-qoqa	-tlotla	-ncokola	-xoxa	
chatter (n)	gebabbel	polabolo	lehehle	palabalo	intshwaqane	ubugevugevu	
cheap (a)	goedkoop	-tšhipilego	-sesolo	sesolo	-dla kancinci	-shibhile	
cheat (v)	kul	-fora	-qhekanyetsa	-tsietsa	qhatha	-khohlisa	
check (v)	nagaan	-kgonthiša	-hlahloba	-lekola	-khangela	-hlolisisa	
cheek (n)	wang	lerama	lerama	lesama	isidlele	isihlathi	
cheekbone (n)	wangbeen	lerapothama	lesapo la lerama	phone	isandundu	isiqhoma	
cheerful (a)	vrolik	-thabilego	-nyakalletseng	-thabang	-onwabileyo	-thokozile	
cheese (n)	kaas	tšhese	tjhese	kase	itshizi	ushisi	
cheetah (n)	jagluiperd	lepogo	lengau	lengau	ihlosi	ingulule	
chemist (n)	apteker	mokhemisi	mokhemise	moapoteke	ikhemesti	umkhemisi	
cheque (n)	tjek	tšheke	tjheke	tsheke	itsheke	isheki	
chest (n)	borskas	sehuba	sefuba	sehuba	isifuba	isifuba	
chew (v)	kou	-hlahuna	-hlafuna	-tlhafuna	-hlafuna	-hlafuna	
chicken (n)	hoender	kgogo	tsuonyana	koko	inkuku	inkukhu	
chickenpox (n)	waterpokkies	mabora	baterepokise	thutlwa	irhashalala	inqubulunjwana	
chief (a)	hoof	-golo	-hlooho	bokgosi	-yintloko	-khulu	
chief (n)	hoofman	kgoši	ramohlongwana	kgosi	inkosi	induna	
child (n)	kind	ngwana	ngwana	ngwana	umntwana	umntwana	
childbirth (n)	kindergeboorte	pelego	pelehi	botsholo	ukubeleka	ukubeletha	
childhood (n)	kinderjare	bjana	bongwana	bonyana	ubuntwana	ubuntwana	
chilli (n)	brandrissie	pherefere	tjhilise	thobega	itshilisi	upelepele	
chimney (n)	skoorsteen	setupamuši	tjhemele	sentshamosi	itshimini	ushimula	
chin (n)	ken	seledu	seledu	seledu	isilevu	isilevu	
chip (computer) (n)	vlokkie	sedirišwana sa komphuta	phatsa	lephatlo	icwecwe	ishiphu	
chip (potato) (n)	skyfie	ditšhipisi	tjhipise	tshipisi	itshipsi	ucezu	
chip (v)	'n hap kry	-kgetloga	-shemola	-ketla	-cebula	-qhephula	
chocolate (n)	sjokolade	tšhokolete	tjhokolete	tshokolete	itshokoleti	ushokolethe	
choice (n)	keuse	kgetho	boikgetheto	tlhopo	ukhetho	ukukhetha	
choir (n)	koor	khwaere	khwaere	khwaere	ikwayala	ikwaya	
choke (v)	verstik	-betwa	-qhwela	-kgama	-miwa	-binda	
choose (v)	kies	-kgetha	-kgetha	-tlhopa	-khetha	-khetha	
chop (n)	tjop	kgotswana	tjhopose	-kgotswana	itshopsi	ishobhisi	
chop (v)	kap	-rema	-ratha	-rema	-canda	-gawula	
Christ (n)	Christus	Kriste	Kreste	Keresete	uKrestu	uKrestu	
Christian (a)	Christelik	-Sekriste	-Sekreste	-sekeresete	-obuKrestu	-liKrestu	
Christian (n)	Christen	Mokriste	Mokreste	mokeresete	umKrestu	iKrestu	
Christmas (n)	Kersfees	Keresemose	Keresemese	Keresemose	iKrismesi	uKhisimusi	
chronological (a)	chronologies	ka tlhatlamanomehla	-tatelano	-tlhatlhamano	-landelelana ngamaxesha	-ehlelo lezikhathi zemilando	
church (n)	kerk	kereke	kereke	kereke	icawa	isonto	

C	English	Afrikaans	N Sotho	Sesotho	Tswana	Xhosa	Zulu
	churn (n)	karring	sefehlo	phehlo	-fetlha	inkonkxa yokwenza ibhotolo	-phehla
	chutney (n)	blatjang	dikhanakhana	tjhatene	tshateni	itshatini	ishatini
	cigar (n)	sigaar	sikara	sikara	sikara	isiga	usigazi
	cigarette (n)	sigaret	sekerete	sakarete	sekerete	umdiza	usikilidi
	cinder (n)	sintel	mošidi	molora	legalanyana	ilahle	ilahle
	cinema (n)	bioskoop	paesekopo	baesekopo	baesekopo	umboniso bhanya-bhanya	ibhayisikobho
	circle (n)	sirkel	sediko	sedikadikwe	sediko	isangqa	isiyingi
	circulate (v)	rondgaan	-dikologa	-potoloha	-dikologa	-jikeleza	-zungeleza
	circulation (n)	omloop	tikologo	potoloho	tikologo	umjikelezo	ukuzungeleza
	circumcise (v)	besny	-bolotša	-bolotsa	-rupisa	-alusa	-soka
	circumcision (n)	besnydenis	lebollo	polotso	thupiso	ulwaluko	ukusoka
	circumference (n)	omtrek	sedika	sedika	modiko	umjikelo	umjikelezo wesiyingi
	circus (n)	sirkus	sorokisi	serekise	sorokisi	iserityisi	isekisi
	cistern (n)	waterbak	sehlapelo	sisetene	mokoro	inkonkxa	itangi
	citizen (n)	burger	moagi	moahi	moagi	ummi	isakhamuzi
	citrus (a)	sitrus	-monamune	-molamunu	-monamune	-esitrasi	isithrasi
	city (n)	stad	motsemogolo	motse	motse	isixeko	idolobha
	civil (a)	burgerlik	-segae	-lehae	-gae	-oluntu	-kwezakhamuzi
	civilisation (n)	beskawing	tlhabologo	tswelopele	tlhabologo	impucuko	impucuko
	civilise (v)	beskaaf	-hlabologa	-ntshetsa pele	-tlhabolola	-phucula	-phucuza
	claim (v)	eis	-tsoma tefo	-nqosa	-lopa	-banga	-biza
	clarinet (n)	klarinet	klarinete	tlelarinete	tlelarinete	ixilongo	iklarinethi
	clasp (n)	klem	sepate	letlao	khuparelo	isibambi	isixhakathisi
	clasp (v)	vasklem	-patana	-tseparela	-kopela	-bamba nkqi	-xhakathisa
	class (n)	klas	mphato	tlelase	setlhopa	iklasi	iklasi
	classify (v)	klassifiseer	-hlopha	-hlophisa	-tlhopa	-hlela	-ahlukanisa
	claw (n)	klou	monotlo	ngwaparelo	lonala	uzipho lwentaka	uzipho
	claw (v)	klou	-ngaparela	-ngwaparela	-ngapa	-krwempa	-nwepha
	clay (n)	klei	letsopa	letsopa	mmopa	udongwe	ubumba
	clean (a)	skoon	-hlwekilego	-hlwekile	-phepa	-cocekileyo	-hlanzekile
	clean (v)	skoonmaak	-hlwekiša	-hlwekisa	-phephafatsa	-coca	-hlanza
	cleanliness (n)	sindelikheid	tlhweko	tlhweko	bophepa	ucoceko	ubonono
	cleanse (v)	skoonmaak	-hlwekiša	-hlwekisa	-forola	-hlambulula	-hlanza
	clear (a)	helder	-bonagalago	-hlakile	-bonalang	-mhlophe	-chachile
	clergy (n)	geestelikes	semoya	seruti	boruti	umfundisi	abefundisi
	clerk (n)	klerk	mapalane	tlelereke	tleereke	unobhala	umabhalana
	client (n)	kliënt	modirelwa	moreki	modirelwa	umxhasi	ikhasimende
	cliff (n)	krans	legaga	sephoko	maaka	iliwa	iwa
	climate (n)	klimaat	klimate	tlelaemete	tlilemate	iklameti	iklayimethi
	climb (v)	klim	-namela	-hlwella	-palama	-khwela	-khwela
	cling (v)	klou	-kgomarela	-mamarela	-ngaparela	-bambelela	-nombela
	clinic (n)	kliniek	kliniki	tlelenike	tleniki	ikliniki	ikliniki
	clock (n)	horlosie	sešupanako	tleloko	sesupanako	ixesha	iklogo
	close (a)	naby	kgauswi	-haufi	gaufi	-kufutshane	eduze
	clot (n)	klont	lehlwele	lehlwele	letlhole	ihlwili	isigaxa
	cloth (n)	doek	lešela	lesela	khai	ilaphu	indwangu
	clothe (v)	aantrek	-apara	-apesa	-apara	-nxiba	-embesa
	clothes (n)	klere	diaparo	diaparo	diaparo	iimpahla	izingubo
	cloud (n)	wolk	leru	leru	leru	ilifu	ifu
	club (n)	klub	mokgatlo	mokgatlo	mokgatlho	iklabhu	ikilobhu
	clumsy (a)	lomp	-nokologago	-monyebe	-boatla	-nobuxelegu	-ndaxandaxa
	clutch (n)	koppelaar	klatše	tlelatjhe	tleatshe	iklatshi	iklashi
	coach (n)	afrigter	mothobodiši	mokwetlise	mokatisi	umqeqeshi	umqeqeshi
	coach (v)	afrig	-thobolla	-kwetlisa	-katisa	-qeqesha	-fundisa
	coal (n)	steenkool	malahla	leshala	lelatlha	ilahle	amalahle
	coast (n)	kus	lebopo	lebopo	losi	unxweme	ugu
	coat (n)	jas	jase	jase	jase	idyasi	ibhantshi
	cobra (n)	kobra	peetla	moswa	kake	isikhotsholo	uphempethwane

English	Afrikaans	N Sotho	Sesotho	Tswana	Xhosa	Zulu	C
cobweb (n)	spinnerak	bobi	bolepo	bobi	indlu yesigcawu	ubulembu	
coccyx (n)	stuitjiebeen	setonwana	mankatapa	mokutu	umsintsila	umsinsila	
cock (n)	haan	mogogonope	mokoko	mokoko	umqhagi	iqhude	
cockroach (n)	kakkerlak	lefele	lephele	lefele	iphela	iphela	
cocoa (n)	kakao	khoukhou	khoukhou	khoukhou	ikoko	ukhokho	
cocoon (n)	kokon	khukhune	mokone	mokone	iqombolosha	umfece	
coffee (n)	koffie	kofi	kofi	kofi	ikofu	ikhofi	
coffin (n)	doodskis	lepokisi la bahu	lekase	lekese	umkhumbi	ikhofini	
coin (n)	muntstuk	tšheletetshipi	lewana	ledi	ukhozo lwemali	uhlamvu lwemali	
cold (a)	koud	-tonyago	-bata	-tsididi	-bandayo	-makhaza	
collar (n)	kraag	kholoro	lepetu	kholoro	ikhola	ukhola	
collarbone (n)	sleutelbeen	kgetlane	lesapo la lepetu	kgetlane	ingqosha	ingqwababa	
collect (v)	versamel	-kgobokana	-kgobokanya	-phutha	-qokelela	-qoqa	
college (n)	kollege	kholetšhe	kholetjhe	kholetšhe	ikholeji	ikholiji	
collide (v)	bots	-thula	-thulana	-thulana	-ngqubana	-shayana	
collision (n)	botsing	thulo	thulano	thulano	ungqubano	ukushayisana	
colon (n)	dikderm	lelakgolo	moqopo	telele	undloku	upopopo	
colon (n)	dubbelpunt	kgorwana	kgutlwana	khutlwana	ikholoni	ikholoni	
colour (n)	kleur	mmala	mmala	mmala	umbala	umbala	
coloured (a)	gekleur	-mmala	-mmala	-mmala	-nombala	-okumbala	
comb (n)	kam	kamo	kama	kamo	inkcaza	ikamu	
comb (v)	kam	-kama	-kama	-kama	-chaza	-kama	
combine (v)	kombineer	-kopanya	-kopanya	-kopanya	-dibanisa	-hlanganisa	
come (v)	kom	-tla	-tlo	-tla	-iza	-za	
comedy (n)	komedie	tiragatšo ya metlae	motlae	metlae	ikhomedi	ikhomedi	
comfort (n)	troos	khomotšo	kgothatso	kgomotso	intuthuzelo	induduzo	
comfort (v)	troos	-homotša	-kgothatsa	-gomotsa	-thuthuzela	-duduza	
comfortable (a)	gemaklik	-boiketlo	-iketlileng	-manobonobo	-tofotofo	-nethezekile	
comic (a)	kømies	-segišago	-qabolang	-botshego	-hlekisayo	-hlekisayo	
comic (n)	komiek	moswaswi	qabolo	setshego	isihlekisi	okuhlekisayo	
comma (n)	komma	feelwana	feelwana	phegelwana	ikoma	ikhefana	
commandment (n)	gebod	molao	molao	taolo	umyalelo	umyalo	
commerce (n)	handel	kgwebo	kgwebo	papatso	uqoqosho	uhwebo	
commercial (a)	kommersieel	-kgwebo	-kgwebo	-kgwebo	-ngoqoqosho	-ezohwebo	
commission (n)	kommissie	komisi	khomishene	thwaiso	ikhomishini	ikhomishani	
commissioner of oaths (n)	kommissaris van ede	moeniši	khomishenare wa boikano	moikanisi	umfungi	umfungisi	
committee (n)	komitee	komiti	komiti	khuduthamaga	ikomiti	ikomiti	
common (a)	gewoon	-ka mehla	-tlwaelehileng	-gale	-qhelekileyo	-vamile	
companion (n)	metgesel	mofelegetši	molekane	molekane	iqabane	umhlanganyeli	
companionship (n)	kameraadskap	bonkane	selekane	bolekane	ubuqabane	ubungane	
compare (v)	vergelyk	-bapiša	-bapisa	-bapisa	-thelekisa	-qhathanisa	
comparison (n)	vergelyking	papišo	papiso	papiso	uthelekiso	ukuqhathanisa	
compass (n)	kompas	tšhupakhutlo	kompase	tshupantla	ikhampasi	ikhompasi	
compel (v)	dwing	-gapeletša	-qobella	-gapeletsa	-nyanzela	-phoqa	
compete (v)	wedywer	-phadišana	-hlodisana	-phadisana	-khuphisana	-qhudelana	
competition (n)	wedstryd	phadišaňo	tlhodisano	phadisano	ukhuphiswano	umqhudelwano	
complain (v)	kla	-ngongorega	-tletleba	-ngongorega	-khalaza	-khala	
complainant (n)	klaer	mongongoregi	motletlebi	moseki	ummangali	ummangaleli	
complaint (n)	klagte	ngongorego	tletlebo	dingongora	isikhalazo	insolo	
complete (a)	volledig	-feletšego	-felletseng	-botlalo	-gqibeleyo	-pheleleyo	
complete (v)	voltooi	-fetša	-qetella	-fetsa	-gqibezela	-qedela	
compose (v)	komponeer	-hlama	-qapa	tlhama	-qamba	-qamba	
composer (n)	komponis	mohlami	moqapi	motlhami	umqambi	umqambi	
composition (n)	komposisie	tlhamo ya dikoša	qapo	tlhamo	ukuqamba	ukwakha	
compost (n)	kompos	podišwa	kompose	monontsha	ikhomposi	umquba	
compound (n)	kampong	kompo	kompone	kompone	ubumbaxa	inkomponi	
compress (v)	saampers	-pataganya	-patisa	-tshwaka	-xinzelela	-cindezela	
compulsion (n)	dwang	kgapeletšo	qobello	pateletso	isinyanzelo	isificezelo	
computer (n)	rekenaar	komphuta	khompiuta	komputara	ikompiyuta	ikhomputha	

C	English	Afrikaans	N Sotho	Sesotho	Tswana	Xhosa	Zulu
	conceal (v)	verberg	-fihla	-kwahela	-bitala	-gusha	-fihla
	conceited (a)	verwaand	-ikgogomošago	-ikgohomosa	-boikgantsho	-nekratshi	-ziqhayisa
	conceive (v)	opvat	-bona	-emola	-ima	-qonda	-mitha
	concert (n)	konsert	khonsata	konsarete	khoserete	ikonsathi	ikhonsathi
	concertina (n)	konsertina	krostina	korosetina	korosetina	ikostina	inkositini
	conclusion (n)	gevolgtrekking	phetho	qeto	phetso	umqukumbelo	isiphetho
	concrete (a)	konkreet	-sa popego	-nnete	-bonegang	-bambekayo	-okungaphatheka
	concrete (n)	beton	khonkriti	konkereite	konkreite	into ebambekayo	ukhonkolo
	condemn (v)	veroordeel	-ahlola	-ahlola	-atlhola	-gweba	-sola
	condition (n)	toestand	boemo	boemo	maemo	imeko	ubunjani
	condition (n)	voorwaarde	peelano	peelano	maemo	imfuneko	isimiselo
	conduct (v)	gedra	-itshwara	-itshwara	-itsaya	isimilo	-ziphatha kahle
	conductor (n)	kondukteur	kontae	motsamaisi	kontai	umbhexeshi	ukhondakta
	confer (v)	toeken	-abela	-fana	-fa	-nika	-nika
	conference (n)	konferensie	therišano	seboka	konferense	inkomfa	umhlangano
	confess (v)	bely	-ipobola	-ipolela	-ipobola	-vuma	-vuma
	confession (n)	belydenis	boipobolo	boipolelo	boipobolo	ukuvuma	ukuvuma
	confide (v)	vertroulik meedeel	-loma tsebe	-amela	-bulela mafatlha	-thembela	-hlebela
	confident (a)	vol vertroue	-itshepago	-itshepa	-khupamarama	-zithembileyo	-thembayo
	confidential (a)	vertroulik	-sephiri	-lekunutu	-khupamarama	-lihlebo	-yisifuba
	confiscate (v)	beslag lê op	-amoga	-amoha	-amoga	-thimba	-dla
	conflict (n)	konflik	phapano	kgohlano	kgotlhang	ungquzulwano	udweshu
	conflict (v)	bots	-fapana	-hohlana	-gotlha	-ngquzulana	-phambana
	confuse (v)	verwar	-gakantša	-ferekanya	-tlaetsa	-bhidanisa	-dida
	congeal (v)	stol	-kgahla	-hwama	-gatsela	-jiyisa	-shuba
	congratulate (v)	gelukwens	-lakaletša mahlogonolo	-lebohela	-akgola	-vuyisana	-halalisela
	congregate (v)	vergader	-kgobokana	-phutheha	-phuthega	-hlangana	-buthana
	congregation (n)	gemeente	phuthego	phutheho	phuthego	ibandla	ibandla
	congress (n)	kongres	kopano	seboka	kongrese	inkongolo	inhlangano
	connect (v)	verbind	-kopanya	-hokahanya	-lomagana	-dibanisa	-hlanganisa
	connection (n)	verbinding	kopanyo	kamano	kgolagano	uqhagamshelo	ukuhlangana
	conquer (v)	verower	-fenya	-fenya	-fenya	-oyisa	-ahlula
	conscience (n)	gewete	letswalo	letswalo	segakolodi	isazela	unembeza
	conscious (a)	bewus	-lemogago	-ikutlwang	-utlwa	-sezingqondweni	-zwile
	consciousness (n)	bewussyn	boitemogo	boikutlo	segakolodi	ukuba sezingqondweni	ukwazi
	consent (n)	instemming	kwano	tumelo	tumelo	imvume	ukuvuma
	consent (v)	instem	-kwana	-dumela	-dumela	-vuma	-vuma
	consequence (n)	gevolg	pheletšo	ditholwana	pheletso	isiphumo	umphumela
	conservative (a)	konserwatief	-bolokago	-hananang le phetoho	segologolo	-cinga ngendlela yakudala	-ngadlulisiyo
	conserve (v)	bewaar	-boloka	-boloka	-babalela	-londoloza	-onga
	consider (v)	oorweeg	-akanya	-nahana	-akanya	-cinga	-cabanga
	considerate (a)	bedagsaam	-hlokomelago	-nahanelang	-akanyang	-novelwano	-cabangelayo
	consist (v)	bestaan	-bopilwe ka	-na le	-na le	-enziwe nge-	-bunjwa
	console (v)	opbeur	-kgothatša	-tshedisa	gomotsa	-thuthuzela	-khuza
	consonant (n)	medeklinker	tumammogo	sedumammoho	tumammogo	iqabane	ungwaqa
	conspicuous (a)	opvallend	-bonagalago	-totobetse	-itshupang	-bonakalayo	-qhamile
	conspiracy (n)	sameswering	morero wa ka thoko	mmomori	thero	iyelenqe	uzungu
	constable (n)	konstabel	lephodisa	lepolesa	lepodisi	ipolisa	iphoyisa
	constipation (n)	konstipasie	pipelo	ho sokela	pipelo	ukuqhina	ukuqumba
	constitution (n)	grondwet	molaotheo	molao wa motheo	molaotheo	umgaqo-siseko	ukumisa
	construction (n)	konstruksie	kago	mohaho	kago	isakhiwo	ukwakha
	consult (v)	raadpleeg	-kgopela keletšo	-botsa	-rerisana	-dlana indlebe	-xoxisana
	consumption (n)	verbruik	tirišo	tshebediso	djego	into esetyenzisiweyo	ukudliwa
	contact lens (n)	kontaklens	galasanakaleihlong	lense ya pono	galase ya diporele	ikhontakthi lensi	ingilazi yezibuko
	contact (v)	in aanraking kom	-kopana	-amana	-tlhaeletsa	-hlangana	-thinthana
	contagious (a)	aansteeklik	-fetetšago	-tshwaetsang	-fetelang	-sulelayo	-memethekayo
	contain (v)	bevat	-na le	-tshwara	-tshola	-qulatha	-phatha

English	Afrikaans	N Sotho	Sesotho	Tswana	Xhosa	Zulu	C
container (n)	houer	setšhelo	pitso	setshelo	isikhongozelo	idlelo	
contempt (n)	veragting	lenyatšo	nyedisa	lenyatso	indelo	indelelo	
content (a)	tevrede	-kgotsofetšego	-kgodisang	-tlhatswega ngati	-anelisekile	-enamile	
contentment (n)	tevredenheid	kgotsofalo	kgodiso	go tlhatswega ngati	ukwaneliseka	ukwenama	
contents (n)	inhoud	diteng	dikahare	diteng	umthamo	okuqukethwe	
contest (n)	wedstryd	phadišano	tseko	bapololano	ukhuphiswano	umbango	
continent (n)	vasteland	kontinente	kontinente	kontinente	ilizwe	izwekazi	
continue (v)	vervolg	-tšwetša pele	-tswela pele	-letela	-qhubeka	-qhubisa	
contour (n)	kontoer	mothapalalo	thapallo	konturu	ikhonto	ukunquma nentaba	
contraception (n)	voorbehoeding	thibelapelegi	thibelo ya pelehi	thibela pelego	ukukhusela	ukuzivala	
contract (n)	kontrak	kontraka	kontraka	konteraka	ukurhwaqela	imvumelano	
contract (v)	inkrimp	-hunyela	-finahanya	-funega	-rhwaqela	-fingqana	
contraction (n)	inkrimping	khunyelo	phinahano	khunyelo	urhwaqelo	ukufinyeza	
contradict (v)	weerspreek	-ganetša	-ngangisa	-ganetsa	-ziphikise	-phikisa	
contradiction (n)	weerspreking	kganetšo	ngangisano	kganetso	ukuziphikisa	ukuphikisa	
control (v)	beheer	-laola	-tsamaisa	-laola	-lawula	-phatha	
controversy (n)	twispunt	phapano	tsekiso	kgang e e gotlhang	impikiswano	ukuphikisana	
convalesce (v)	aansterk	-fola	-nonopela	-thamogelwa	-chacha	-lulama	
convene (v)	byeenroep	-bitša	-bokanya	-epa	-biza imbizo	-hlangana	
convenient (a)	gerieflik	-swanelago	-tshwanelang	-siametseng	-lungeleyo	-vumekayo	
conversation (n)	gesprek	poledišano	moqoqo	kgang	incoko	inkulumo	
conversion (n)	omsetting	tshokologo	tshokoloho	tshokologo	uguqulo	impenduko	
convert (n)	bekeerling	mosokologi	mosokolohi	mosokologi	umguquki	umphenduki	
convert (v)	omsit	-sokologa	-sokolla	-sokolola	-guqula	-phendukisa	
convict (n)	gevangene	mogolegwa	motshwaruwa	seboswa	ibanjwa	isiboshwa	
convict (v)	skuldig bevind	-ahlola	-ahlola	-bona molato	-beka ityala	-lahla ngecala	
convince (v)	oortuig	-kgodiša	-kgodisa	-koloba	-qinisekisa	-gculisa	
convulsion (n)	rukking	kikontwane	tshisinyeho	kgaro	umxhuzulo	ukudikiza	
cook (n)	kok	moapei	moapehi	moapei	isipheko	umpheki	
cook (v)	kook	-apea	-apeha	-apaya	-pheka	-pheka	
cool (a)	koel	-fodilego	-phodileng	-tsiditsana	-pholileyo	-pholile	
cool (v)	afkoel	-fola	-fodisa	-tsidifala	-phola	-phola	
co-operate (v)	saamwerk	-dirišana	-sebedisana	-dirisana	-sebenzisana	-sizana	
co-operation (n)	koöperasie	koporasi	koporasi	mokgatlho	iqumrhu la-	inhlangano yobambiswano	
co-operation (n)	samewerking	tirišano	tshebedisano	tirisano	intsebenziswano	ukusizana	
copper (n)	koper	koporo	koporo	kgotlho	ikopolo	ithusi	
copulate (v)	kopuleer	-feka	-robalana	-gwela	-zeka	-hlangana	
copy (book) (n)	eksemplaar	kopi ya puku	buka	seetsi	ikopi	ikhophi	
copy (document) (n)	afskrif	kopi	kopi	seetsi	ikopi	ikhophi	
cord (n)	koord	thapu	kgole	mogala	intambo	umchilo	
cork (n)	kurk	poropo	sepako	poropo	isivingco	ukhokho	
corner (n)	hoek	sekhutlo	sekgutlo	khona	umgwejelo	ikhona	
coronation (n)	kroning	peo ya kgoši	ho beha borena	peo	uthweso	ukugcotshwa	
corpse (n)	lyk	setopo	setopo	setopo	umzimba	isidumbu	
correct (a)	korrek	-nepagetšego	-nepahetse	-nepagetseng	-lungileyo	-lungile	
correct (v)	korrigeer	-phošolla	-nepisa	-siamisa	-lungisa	-lungisa	
corrupt (a)	bedorwe	-senyegilego	-senyehile	-senyegang	-ngcolileyo	-onakele	
corrupt (v)	bederf	-senya	-senya	-senya	-ngcolisa	-bolile	
corruption (n)	bedorwenheid	tshenyego	tshenyo	tshenyego	isingcolo	ukonakala	
costly (a)	kosbaar	-bohlokwa	-turang	-tlhwatlhwa	-xabisayo	-dulile	
costume (n)	kostuum	khosetšhumo	khosetjhumo	paka	isinxibo	ikhositshumu	
cottage (n)	kothuis	ngwakwana	ntlwana	ntlwana	indlwana	indlwana	
cotton wool (n)	watte	wulu ya leokodi	boya ba tshwele	leloba	umqhaphu	uvolo	
cotton (n)	katoen	leokodi	tshwele	letseta	irhali	ukotini	
cough (n)	hoes	kgohlolo	mokgohlane	kgotlholo	ukhohlokhohlo	ukukhwehlela	
cough (v)	hoes	-gohlola	-hohlola	-gotlhola	-khohlela	-khwehlela	
council (n)	raad	lekgotla	lekgotla	lekgotla	ibhunga	ibandla	
councillor (n)	raadslid	mokgomana	letona	molekgotla	ilungu lebhunga	ilungu lasebandla	
count (v)	tel	-bala	-bala	-bala	-bala	-bala	

C English	Afrikaans	N Sotho	Sesotho	Tswana	Xhosa	Zulu
courage (n)	moed	sebete	tiisetso	bopelokgale	isibindi	isibindi
courageous (a)	moedig	-nago le sebete	-tiisetsang	-pelokgale	-nesibindi	-nesibindi
court (n)	hof	kgoro	lekgotla	kgotla	inkundla	inkantolo
cover (n)	deksel	sekhurumelo	sekwahelo	sebipo	iqweqwe	isivalo
cover (v)	dek	-khupetša	-kwahela	-bipa	-gquma	-vala
cow (n)	koei	kgomogadi	kgomo	kgomogadi	inkomo	inkomazi
coward (n)	lafaard	lefšega	lekwala	legatlapa	igwala	igwala
cowardice (n)	lafhartigheid	bofšega	bokwala	boboi	ubugwala	ubugwala
cowardly (a)	lafhartig	-lefšega	-bokwala	-boi	-ngobugwala	-nobugwala
crab (n)	krap	kgenkgerepe	lekgala	lekakauwe	unonkala	inkalankala
crack (a)	puik	-makgethe	-tsebang	-ntlentle	-ngobuncutshe	-ngqazukayo
crack (n)	kraak	monga	lepetso	lenga	uthanda	umnkenke
crack (v)	kraak	-palega	-petsoha	-phanya	-qhekeza	-klewuka
cramp (n)	kramp	bogatšu	kgonyelo	kudupanyo ya tshika	inkantsi	inkwantshu
crawl (v)	kruip	-abula	-kgasa	-abula	-rhubuluza	-khasa
cream (n)	room	lebebe	lebejana	lebebe	ucwambu	ulaza
crease (n)	kreukel	tšhošobano	tshosobano	letsutsuba	amanya	ikhilisi
crease (v)	kreukel	-šošobana	-sosobana	-sosobana	-shwabanisa	-shwabana
create (v)	skep	-bopa	-hlola	-bopa	-dala	-dala
Creator (n)	Skepper	Mmopi	Mohlodi	Mmopi	umDali	uMdali
creature (n)	wese	sebopiwa	sebopuwa	sebopiwa	isidalwa	isidalwa
credit card (n)	kredietkaart	karatakhodi	karete ya molato	karata ya mojela	ikhredithi khadi	ikhadi lokukweleta
credit (n)	krediet	khodi	molato	mojela	ityala	okukweletwayo
credit (v)	krediteer	-nea khodi	-leballa molato	-jela	-bonelela nge-	ukukweletisa
creeper (n)	klimop	senami	morarane	morara	isinaba	intandela
cricket (n)	krieket	khrikhete	seqhomelankong	kerikete	iqakamba	ikhilikithi
cricketer (n)	krieketspeler	mmapadi wa khrikhete	mokerikete	motshamiki wa kerikete	umdlali weqakamba	umdlali wekhilikithi
crime (n)	misdaad	tshenyo	molato	molato	ulwaphulo-mthetho	ubugebengu
criminal (n)	misdadiger	sesenyi	sesenyi	modiramolato	isaphuli-mthetho	isigebengu
cripple (n)	kreupele	segole	seritsa	setlhotsa	isiqhwala	unyonga
cripple (v)	kreupel maak	-hlotša	-holofatsa	-golafatsa	-enzakalisa	-goga
criticise (v)	kritiseer	-swaya phošo	-ntsha diphoso	-kgala	-gxeka	-hlaba
crockery (n)	breekware	dibjana	dijana	dithubegi	izitya	izitsha
crocodile (n)	krokodil	kwena	kwena	kwena	ingwenya	ingwenya
crooked (a)	krom	-kgopamego	-kgopo	-sokameng	-goso	-magwegwe
cross examine (v)	kruisvra	-botšišiša	-fatisisa	-botsolotsa	-buza	-buzisisa
cross (v)	kruis	-fapana	-tshela	-fapaana	umnqamlezo	-dabula
crouch (v)	buk	-kotama	-botha	batalala	-chopha	-gogobala
crow (n)	kraai	legokobu	lekgwaba	legakabe	unomyayi	igwababa
crowbar (n)	koevoet	kepi	moqala	kepu	ikhrowubha	umgxala
crowd (n)	skare	lešaba	matshwele	kokoano	isihlwele	isiqumbi
crowded (a)	propvol	-tletšego phare phare	-qhobellane	-pitlaganeng	-xineneyo	-minyene
crown (n)	kroon	mphapahlogo	mofapahloho	serwalo	isithsaba	umqhele
crucify (v)	kruisig	-bapola	-thakgisa sefapanong	-bapola	-xhoma	-nqamuleza
cruel (a)	wreed	-šoro	-sehloho	-pelompe	-khohlakeleyo	-nonya
cruelty (n)	wreedheid	bošoro	sehloho	bopelompe	inkohlakalo	unya
crumb (n)	krummel	lerathana	lekumane	lefofora	imvuthuluka	imvuthu
crumble (v)	verkrummel	-ratha	-kuma	-fofora	-cukuceza	-bhuduza
crust (n)	korsie	legogo	bohoho	legogo	ukhoko	ukhokho
cry (n)	kreet	mogoo	sello	kgoo	isikhalo	isikhalo
cry (v)	huil	-lla	-lla	-lla	-khala	-khala
cub (n)	welpie	ngwana wa tau	ledinyane	tawana	igoba	iwundlu
cucumber (n)	komkommer	phara	komokomore	phare	ikomkomire	ikhukhamba
culprit (n)	skuldige	mosenyi	ya molato	yo o molato	umoni	umoni
cultivate (v)	bewerk	-lema	-lema	-lema	-lima	-lima
culture (n)	kultuur	setho	setho	setso	inkqubo yesizwe	isimo sempucuko
cunning (a)	slu	-nago le mahlajana	-mano	-boferefere	-nobuqhokolo	-nobuqili
cup (n)	koppie	komiki	komiki	kopi	ikopi	inkomishi
cupboard (n)	kas	khapoto	khabete	raka	ikhabhathi	ikhabethe

English	Afrikaans	N Sotho	Sesotho	Tswana	Xhosa	Zulu	D
curb (v)	inhou	-thiba	-hanela	-ganela	-nqanda	-khuza	
curdle (v)	klonter	-kgahla	-hwama	-rema	-hloba	-jiya	
cure (n)	genesing	kalafo	phodiso	kalafo	isiphilisi	ukuphilisa	
curl (n)	krul	laetse	matsetlela	-gogoropa	umjiko	insonge	
current (a)	huidige	-elehono	-jwale	-segompieno	-eqhubekayo	-amanje	
current (n)	stroom	moela	phula	moela	umsinga	umsinga	
curse (n)	vloek	madimabe	tlhapa	thogo	intshwabulo	isiqalekiso	
curtain (n)	gordyn	garateine	kgaretene	sesiro	ikhetini	ikhethini	
cushion (n)	kussing	mosamelo	mosamo	mosamo	umqamelo	umqamelo	
cut (n)	sny	mosego	leqeba	tshego	inxeba	umsiko	
cut (v)	sny	-sega	-seha	-sega	-sika	-sika	
cutlery (n)	eetgerei	dithipa	dikgaba	maswana	amacephe nezitya	izinto okudliwa ngazo	
cycle (n)	siklus	leboyo	sedikadikwe	tsheko	umjikelo	ukuyingiliza	
cymbal (n)	simbaal	simpale	simbale	simbala	ixina	isimbali	
daily (a)	daagliks	letšatši ka letšatši	ka mehla	-motlha le motlha	-mihla yonke	izinsuko zonke	
dam (n)	dam	letamo	letamo	tamo	idama	idamu	
damage (n)	skade	tshenyego	tshenyo	tshenyegelo	umonakalo	ukulimaza	
damage (v)	beskadig	-senya	-senya	-senya	-onakalisa	-limaza	
damp (a)	vogtig	-monola	-mongobo	-seola	-fumile	-manzana	
damp (n)	vogtigheid	monola	mongobo	bongola	ukufuma	ubumanzi	
dance (n)	dans	go bina	motjeko	pino	umdaniso	ukusina	
dance (v)	dans	-bina	-tjeka	-bina	-danisa	-sina	
dandruff (n)	skilfers	dikelefere	sekerefe	sekgamatha	inkwethu	intuva	
danger (n)	gevaar	kotsi	kotsi	kotsi	ingozi	ingozi	
dangerous (a)	gevaarlik	-kotsi	-kotsi	-kotsi	-nengozi	-nengozi	
dare (n)	uitdaging	tlhohlo	sebete	tlhotlheletso	ubugagu	umlokothi	
dare (v)	uitdaag	-hlohla	-beta pelo	-tlhotlheletsa	-ba ligagu	-lokotha	
dark (a)	donker	-fifetšego	-lefifi	-fitshwa	-mnyama	-fiphele	
darkness (n)	donker	leswiswi	lefifi	lefifi	ubumnyama	ubumnyama	
darn (v)	stop	-thiba	-topa	-topa	-thunga	-dana	
dassie (n)	dassie	pela	pela	pela	imbila	imbila	
date (n)	datum	tšatšikgwedi	mohla	letlha	umhla	idethi	
daughter (n)	dogter	morwedi	moradi	morwadi	intombi	intombi	
daughter-in-law (n)	skoondogter	ngwetši	ngwetsi	ngwetsi	umolokazana	umakoti	
dawn (n)	dagbreek	masa	mafube	bosa	isifingo	ukusa	
day (n)	dag	letšatši	letsatsi	letsatsi	imini	usuku	
daybreak (n)	dagbreek	mahube	mafube	bosa	ubusa	ukusa	
daze (n)	bedwelming	go dikwelela	kidibanyo	kgamorego	ukudideka	ukuphuphutheka	
dazed (a)	bedwelmd	-dikweletšego	-idibane	-dimokanyang	-didekileyo	-phuphuthekisa	
dead (a)	dood	-hwilego	-shweleng	-suleng	-fileyo	-file	
deaf (a)	doof	-sefoa	-tsebetutu	-boshushu	-ngevayo	-ngenakuzwa	
dear (a)	dierbaar	-rategago	-ratehang	-botlhokwatlhokwa	-thandekayo	-thandiwe	
death (n)	dood	lehu	lefu	leso	ukufa	ukufa	
debt (n)	skuld	molato	molato	molato	ityala	isikwenetu	
decade (n)	dekade	ngwagasome	dilemo tse leshome	ngwagasome	inkulungwane	iminyaka eyishumi	
decay (v)	verrot	-bola	-bola	-bola	-buna	-bola	
deceased (a)	oorlede	-hlokafetšego	-shweleng	-suleng	-swelekileyo	-shonileyo	
deceit (n)	bedrog	bofora	thetso	boferefere	inkohliso	inkhohliso	
deceive (v)	bedrieg	-fora	-thetsa	-fora	-khohlisa	-khohlisa	
December (n)	Desember	Desemere	Tshitwe	Sedimonthole	Disemba	uDisemba	
decide (v)	besluit	-phetha	-rera	-atlhola	-enza isigqibo	-nquma	
decision (n)	besluit	phetho	morero	phetso	isigqibo	isinqumo	
declare (v)	verklaar	-bega	-bolela	-bolotsa	-bhengeza	-bika	
decline (v)	afwys	-gana	-hana	-gana	-yala	-ncipha	
decompose (v)	ontbind	-bola	-bola	-bola	-vunda	-bola	
decorate (v)	versier	-kgabiša	-kgabisa	-kgabisa	-hombisa	-hlobisa	
decoration (n)	versiering	kgabišo	mokgabiso	lekgabisa	umhombiso	umhlobiso	
decrease (v)	verminder	-fokotša	-fokotsa	-fokotsa	-nciphisa	-ncipha	
decree (n)	verordening	molao	taelo ya lekgotla	molao	ummiselo	isimemezelo	

D	English	Afrikaans	N Sotho	Sesotho	Tswana	Xhosa	Zulu
	deed (n)	daad	tiro	ketso	tiro	isenzo	isenzo
	deep (a)	diep	-tebilego	-tebileng	-boteng	-nzulu	-shonile
	defamation (n)	belastering	tshenyoina	ketselletso	kgobololo	unyeliso	isihlebo
	defeat (n)	nederlaag	go fenywa	tlholo	phenyo	uloyiso	ukwahluleka
	defeat (v)	verslaan	-fenya	-hlola	-fenya	-oyisa	-hlula
	defecate (v)	ontlas	-nya	-nya	nnyela	-ya endle	-bhosha
	defect (v)	oorloop na	-falala	-fanya	-thobela go	-kreqa	-qembuka
	defence (n)	verdediging	phemelo	tshireletso	phemelo	ukhuselo	ukuvikelwa
	defend (v)	verdedig	-phemela	-sireletsa	-femela	-khusela	-vikela
	defendant (n)	verweerder	moiphemedi	mosireletsi	mosekisiwa	ummangalelwa	umvikeli
	defensive (a)	verdedigend	-phemelago	-sireletsang	-femelang	-khuselayo	-vikelayo
	define (v)	bepaal	-hlatholla	-hlalosa	-ranola	-chaza	-nquma
	deform (v)	vervorm	-senya	-sotha	-golafatsa	limaza	-ona isimo
	defy (v)	trotseer	-hlohla	-hanyetsa	-nyatsa	-dela	-dlelezela
	degree (n)	graad	kgato	degri	dekrii	iqondo	isiqu
	delay (n)	vertraging	tiego	tieho	tiego	ulibaziso	isilibaziso
	delay (v)	vertraag	-diegiša	-dieha	-dia	-libazisa	-libazisa
	delegate (v)	afvaardig	-romela	-laela	-gobelela	-gunyazisa	-thuma
	delete (v)	skrap	-phumola	-phumola	-phimola	-cima	-susa
	deliberate (a)	opsetlik	-boomo	ka boomo	ka bomo	-ngabom	-etshisa
	delicious (a)	heerlik	-bose	-hlabosang	-monate	-mnandi	-mnandi
	delight (n)	blydskap	lethabo	nyakallo	boitumelo	ulonwabo	injabulo
	delight (v)	bly maak	-thabiša	-nyakalatsa	-jesa monate	-onwabisayo	-jabulisa
	delirium (n)	ylhoofdigheid	phafatlo	bohlanya	bogorogoro	impambano	amathezane
	deliver (v)	aflewer	-fihliša	-tsamaisa	-pholosa	-hambisa	-nikeza
	demand (v)	eis	-nyaka	-tseka	-lopa	-banga	-biza
	democracy (n)	demokrasie	temokrasi	demokerasi	pusano	idemokhrasi	ukubusa ngentando yabantu
	demolish (v)	afbreek	-phušula	-heletsa	-senya	-diliza	-diliza
	demon (n)	bose gees	motemone	modemone	satane	idemoni	idimoni
	demonstrate (v)	betoog	-šupetša	-bontsha	-supetsa	-qhankqalaza	-bhikisha
	demonstration (n)	betoging	tšhupetšo	pontsho	tshupetso	uqhankqalazo	ukubhikisha
	dense (a)	dig	-kitlaganego	-teteaneng	-lesuthu	-xineneyo	-minyene
	dent (v)	duik	-phobela	-bothetsa	-pobetsa	-bothoza	-bocoza
	dentist (n)	tandarts	rameno	ngaka ya meno	rameno	ugqirha wamazinyo	inyanga yamazinyo
	dentures (n)	vals tande	meno a sekgowa	meno a maiketsetso	meno a maitirelo	izinxonxo	isethi lamazinyo afakwayo
	deny (v)	ontken	-latola	-hana	-ganela	-khanyela	-phika
	deodorant (n)	reukweermiddel	polayamonkgo	setebelamonko	senkgamonate	isiqholo	umuthi wokuqeda iphunga elibi
	depart (v)	vertrek	-tloga	-falla	-tloga	-nduluka	-emuka
	department (n)	departement	kgoro	lefapha	lefapha	isebe	isigaba
	departure (n)	vertrek	tlogo	phallo	tlogo	unduluko	ukwemuka
	depend (on) (v)	afhang (van)	-ithekgile ka	-itshwarella ka	-ikanya	-xhomekeka	-eyama
	dependant (n)	afhanklike	mofepiwa	mohloki	moikanyi	-umntu oxhomeke-kileyo	isikhonzi
	dependent (a)	afhanklik	-ithekgilego ka	-hlokang	-ikanyang	-xhomekekileyo	-phethwe
	deposit (n)	deposito	peeletšo	peeletso	peeletso	idipozithi	isibeko
	deposit (v)	deponeer	-beeletša	-beeletsa	-bolokela	-dipozitha	-beka
	depress (v)	neerdruk	-nyamiša	-tepeletsa	-gatelela	-cinezela	-cindezela
	depression (n)	bedruktheid	manyami	tepeletso	sekuti	ucinezelo	umnyinyitheko
	deprive (v)	ontneem	-amoga	-hlokisa	-tseela	-alela	-aphuca
	depth (n)	diepte	botebo	botebo	boteng	ubunzulu	ukujula
	deputy (n)	plaasvervanger	motseta	motlatsi	moemedi	isekela	impakatha
	descend (v)	daal	-theoga	-theoha	-fologa	-ihla	-ehla
	descent (n)	daling	theogo	theoho	phologo	ithambeka	ukwehla
	describe (v)	beskrywe	-laodiša	-hlalosa	-tlhalosa	-chaza	-landa
	description (n)	beskrywing	tlhalošo	tlhaloso	tlhaloso	inkcazo	ukulanda
	desert (n)	woestyn	leganata	lefeella	sekaka	intlango	umqothu
	desert (v)	dros	-ngwega	-ngala	-ngala	-qhwesha	-mbuka

English	Afrikaans	N Sotho	Sesotho	Tswana	Xhosa	Zulu	D
deserter (n)	droster	mongwegi	mongadi	mongwegi	umqhweshi	imbuki	
deserve (v)	verdien	-swanelwa	-tshwanelwa	-tshwanelwa	-fanela	-fanela	
desire (n)	begeerte	ledumo	takatso	keletso	umnqweno	inkanuko	
desire (v)	begeer	-duma	-lakatsa	-eletsa	-nqwena	-khanuka	
desk (n)	lessenaar	panka	deseke	banka	idesika	idesiki	
despair (n)	wanhoop	-hloboga	ho nyahama	tsholofologo	ukulahla ithemba	ukuphela ithemba	
desperate (a)	wanhopig	-hlobogilego	-nyahameng	-solofologang	-phelelwe lithemba	-phelelwe yithemba	
dessert (n)	nagereg	phuting	phuting	phuting	isimuncumuncu	ukudla okugcinwa ngakho	
destroy (v)	vernietig	-fediša	-ripitla	-senya	-tshabalalisa	-bhuqa	
detain (v)	aanhou	-golega	-tshwara	-dia	-gcina eluvalelweni	-bopha	
detainee (n)	aangehoudene	mogolegwa	motshwaruwa	motshwarwa	umbanjwa	isiboshwa	
detective (n)	speurder	letseka	lefokisi	letseka	umcuphi	umseshi	
detention (n)	aanhouding	mogolego	tshwaro	tiego	uvalelo	ukuboshwa	
determination (n)	vasberadenheid	phegelelo	morero o tiileng	maikaelelo	ukuzimisela	ukuzimisela	
detest (v)	verafsku	-hlaswa	-hloya	-tlhoa	-caphukela	-enyanya	
detour (n)	omweg	tsela ya moralela	tsela e potolohang	phapogo	umgwegwelezo	umshekelelo	
detribalise (v)	ontstam	-kgokgofala	-kgokgotsa	-kurukurega	-thithisa ubuhlanga	-bhungula	
devastate (v)	verwoes	-fediša	-ripitla	-senya	-tshabalalisa	-bhuqa	
deviate (v)	afwyk	-fapoga	-kgeloha	-fapoga	-phambuka	-ahluka	
deviation (n)	ompad	phapogo	tsela e potolohang	phapogo	uphambuko	ukuphambuka	
devil (n)	duiwel	diabolo	diabolose	satane	umtyholi	uSathane	
devote (v)	toewy	-ikgafa	-ineela	-ineela	-nikela	-zinikela ku-	
dew (n)	dou	phoka	phoka	monyo	umbethe	amazolo	
diabetes (n)	suikersiekte	twetšiswikiri	lefu la tswekere	bolwetse jwa sukiri	isifo seswekile	idayabhithizi	
diagram (n)	diagram	tshwantšho	setshwantsho	tshwantsho	umzobo	isifanekiso esidwe-tshiweyo	
dialect (n)	dialek	mmolelo	mmuo	teme	intetho yesizwana	ulimi lwesigodi	
diamond (n)	diamant	taemane	taemane	teemane	idayimani	idayimani	
diaphragm (n)	diafragma	letswalo	letswalo	letswalo	idayafram	inhlonhla	
diarrhoea (n)	diarree	letšhollo	letshollo	letsholola	urhudo	uhudu	
dictate (v)	voorskrywe	-biletša	-susutlella	-biletsa	-bizela	-bizela	
dictator (n)	diktator	mmušanoši	mosusutlelli	mmusaesi	uzwilakhe	umashiqela	
dictionary (n)	woordeboek	pukuntšu	bukantswe	bukantswe	isichazi-magama	isichazimazwi	
die (v)	doodgaan	-hwa	-shwa	-swa	-fa	-fa	
differ (v)	verskil	-fapana	-fapana	-fapaana	-ahluka	-ahlukana	
difference (n)	verskil	phapano	phapano	pharologano	umahluko	umahluka	
different (a)	verskillend	-fapanego	-fapaneng	-sele	-ahlukileyo	-ahlukile	
difficult (a)	moeilik	-thata	-thata	-thata	-nzima	-nzima	
difficulty (n)	moeilikheid	bothata	bothata	bothata	inzima	ubunzima	
dig (v)	spit	-epa	-tjheka	-epa	-omba	-mba	
dignified (a)	waardig	-hlomphegago	-hlomphehang	-seriti	-ndilekileyo	-nesithunzi	
dignity (n)	waardigheid	tlhompho	hlompho	seriti	undiliseko	isizotha	
diligence (n)	fluksheid	mafolofolo	mafolofolo	bonatla	inkuthalo	inkuthalo	
diligent (a)	fluks	-mafolofolo	-mafolofolo	-manontlhotlho	-khutheleyo	-khuthele	
dilute (v)	verdun	-hlaphola	-hlapholla	-rarolosa	-xuba	-hlambulula	
dim (a)	dof	-sa bonagalego gabotse	-lerotho	-letobo	-luzizi	-fiphele	
dimple (n)	kuiltjie	sesegišabaeng	sebotjhe	pobe	isinxonxo	inkonyane	
dine (v)	hoofmaaltyd eet	-ja letena	-ja	-ja	-dinala	-dla idina	
dining room (n)	eetkamer	bojelo	daenengrumo	bojelo	igumbi lokutyela	ikamelo lokudlela	
dinner (n)	hoofmaal	letena	tinare	tinara	idinala	idina	
dip (v)	insteek	-tipa	-ina	-ina	-thi nkxu	-cwilisa	
diphtheria (n)	witseerkeel	difteria	mmetso o mosweu	mometso-o-mosweu	isifo somqala	isifo esivimbanisa umphimbo	
direct (a)	direk	-lebanego	-tobileng	-maleba	-the nqo	-qondile	
direct (v)	beveel	-laela	-laela	-laola	-yalela	-layeza	
direct (v)	rig	-lebiša	-lebisa	-supetsa	-alatha	-nemba	
direction (n)	rigting	thoko	nnqa	ntlha	icala	ukukhombisa	
directions (n)	aanwysings	ditaetšo	ditaelo	tshupatiriso	izalathisi	iseluleko	

D	**English**	**Afrikaans**	**N Sotho**	**Sesotho**	**Tswana**	**Xhosa**	**Zulu**
	dirty (a)	vuil	-nago le ditšhila	-ditshila	-leswe	-mdaka	-ngcolile
	disability (n)	gebrek	tšhitego	sekodi	bokao	ubulelwe	ukujiyelwa
	disabled (a)	gebreklik	-segole	-holofetse	-segole	-limeleyo	-jiyelwe
	disagree (v)	verskil	-fapana	-fapana	-ganetsa	-ngavumelani	-phambana
	disagreement (n)	meningsverskil	phapano	ho se dumellane	kganetsanyo	intlaba zahlukane	impambano
	disappear (v)	verdwyn	-nyamalela	-nyamela	-nyelela	-sithela	-nyamalala
	disappearance (n)	verdwyning	nyamalelo	nyamelo	nyelelo	ukusithela	ukunyamalala
	disappoint (v)	teleurstel	-nyamiša pelo	-swetsa	-swabisa	-danisa	-dumaza
	disappointment (n)	teleurstelling	monyamišo	tshwetso	maswabi	ukudanisa	indumalo
	disaster (n)	ramp	kotsi	kodua	leralalo	intlekele	isidumo
	disciple (n)	dissipel	morutiwa	morutuwa	molatedi	umdisipile	umlandeli
	discipline (n)	dissipline	thupišo	thapiso	pipelo	imbeko	impatho eqinileyo
	disclose (v)	openbaar	-utolla	-senola	-itsisi	-diza	-veza
	disconnect (v)	losmaak	-lomolla	-fasolla	-bofolola	-khulula	-ahlukanisa
	discount (n)	afslag	phokoletšo	theolelo	phokoletso	isaphulelo	isephulelo emalini
	discount (v)	aftrek	fokoletša	-theolela	-fokoletsa	-aphulela	-nciphisa
	discourage (v)	ontmoedig	-nyemiša pelo	-nyahamisa	-titina	-tyhafisa	-khubeza
	discover (v)	ontdek	-ribolla	-sibolla	-ribolola	-bhaqa	-fumanisa
	discriminate (v)	diskrimineer	-kgetholla	-kgetholla	-tlhotlholola	-calula	-khetha
	discrimination (n)	diskriminasie	kgethollo	kgethollo	letlhotlho	ucalulo	ukukhetha
	discuss (v)	bespreek	-ahlaahla	-buisana	-sekaseka	-xoxa	-xoxisana nga-
	discussion (n)	bespreking	kahlaahlo	puisano	kgang	ingxoxo	ingxoxo
	disease (n)	siekte	bolwetši	lefu	bolwetse	isifo	isifo
	disgrace (n)	skande	dihlong	hlomphollo	botlhabisa ditlhong	ihlazo	ihlazo
	disgust (n)	afkeer	lehloyo	ho nyonya	-ferosa sebete	ucekiseko	isicasulo
	dish (n)	skottel	sebjana	sejana	sejana	isitya	indishi
	dishonest (a)	oneerlik	-sa tshephegego	-sa tshepeheng	-se ikanyegeng	-ngathembekanga	-khohlisayo
	dishonesty (n)	oneerlikheid	bofora	ho hloka botshepehi	go se ikanyege	ubumenemene	inkohliso
	disinfect (v)	ontsmet	-hlwekiša	-hlwekisa	-bolaya ditwatsi	-bulala iintsholong-wane	-bulala imbewu yokufa
	disinfectant (n)	ontsmettingsmiddel	sehlwekiši	sehlwekisi	sebolayaditwatsi	isibulala-ntsholong-wane	umphungo
	disloyalty (n)	dislojaliteit	kgelogo	bokwenehi	bosaikanyegang	ukunganyaniseki	ukuhlubuka
	dismiss (v)	ontslaan	-lokolla	-tebela	-belesetsa	-gxotha	-mukisa
	dismissal (n)	ontslag	tokollo	tebelo	teleko	ugxotho	ukumukiswa
	disobedience (n)	ongehoorsaamheid	go se kwe	kgano	boganana	ukungathobeli	ukungalaleli
	disobey (v)	ongehoorsaam wees	-gana go kwa	-hana	-gana	-sukuthobela	-ngalaleli
	disperse (v)	verstrooi	-phatlalatša	-hasa	-phatlalala	-chitha-chitha	-hlakaza
	dispute (n)	onenigheid	phapang	tsekisano	kganetsano	impikiswano	umbango
	dispute (v)	betwis	-phegišana	-tsekisana	-ganetsa	-phikisana	-banga
	disregard (v)	verontagsaam	-hlokomologa	-hlokomoloha	-tlhokomologa	-sukuhoya	-delela
	dissatisfaction (n)	ontevredenheid	ngongorego	pelaelo	dingongora	ukunganeliseki	ukhonondo
	dissatisfied (a)	ontevrede	-ngongoregago	-belaela	-ngongoregang	-nganelisekanga	-khonondayo
	dissolve (v)	oplos	-tologa	-qhibidiha	-tlhaologa	-nyibilika	-ncibilikisa
	distance (n)	afstand	bokgole	bohole	bokgakala	umgama	ibanga
	distinct (a)	afsonderlik	-kgethologilego	-ikgethang	-gongwe	-cacileyo	-ahlukene
	distinguish (v)	onderskei	-kgethologanya	-kgetha	-farologanya	-ahlula	-ahlukanisa
	distinguished (a)	vooraanstaande	-tsebalegago	bohlokwa	-itshupang	-balulekileyo	-phakeme
	distribute (v)	versprei	-abaganya	-aba	-rathabolola	-aba	-amukezela
	district (n)	distrik	selete	setereke	kgaolo	isithili	ihlelo
	district surgeon (n)	distriksgeneesheer	ngaka ya selete	ngaka ya setereke	ngaka ya kgaolo	ugqirha wesithili	udokotela kahulumeni
	distrust (n)	wantroue	kgonono	pelaelo	pelaelo	ukungathembi	ukungathembi
	distrust (v)	wantrou	-gonona	-belaela	-belaela	-ngathembi	-ngathembi
	disturb (v)	pla	-tshwenya	-ferehla	-feretlha	-phazamisa	-nyakazisa
	disturbance (n)	oproer	mpherefere	pherehlo	pheretlhego	isiphazamiso	ukunyakaza
	ditch (n)	sloot	leope	lengope	lemena	umsele	umsele
	dive (v)	duik	-phonkgela	-qwela	-nwela	-ntywila	-cwila
	diving (n)	duikery	phonkgelo	qwelo	bonwelo	untywilo	ukucwila
	diving board (n)	duikplank	lepolanka la go phonkgela	boroto ya ho qwela	polanka ya bonwelo	iplanga lokuntywila	icwecwe lepulangwe lokucwila

English	Afrikaans	N Sotho	Sesotho	Tswana	Xhosa	Zulu	D
divorce (n)	egskeiding	tlhalo	tlhalo	tlhalo	uqhawulo-mtshato	idivosi	
divorce (v)	skei	-hlala	-hlala	-tlhala	-qhawula umtshato	-divosa	
dizziness (n)	duiseligheid	matladima	modikwadikwane	modikologo	isizunguzane	inzululwane	
do (v)	doen	-dira	-etsa	-dira	-enza	-enza	
doctor (n)	dokter	ngaka	ngaka	ngaka	ugqirha	udokotela	
document (n)	dokument	lengwalo	lengolo	setlankama	uxwebhu	umbhalo	
dog (n)	hond	mpša	ntja	ntšwa	inja	inja	
doll (n)	pop	popi	popi	popo	unopopi	udoli	
domestic (a)	huishoudelik	-legae	-lehae	-legae	-asekhaya	-asendlini	
dominate (v)	oorheers	-buša	-busa	-gagapa	-velela	-busa	
donate (v)	skenk	-fa	-fana	-aba	-nikela ngesisa	-nika	
donation (n)	skenking	mpho	mpho	sehuba	isisa	umnikelo	
done (v)	gedoen	-dirile	-entse	-dirile	-enzile	-enziwe	
donkey (n)	donkie	tonki	tonki	tumuga	imbongolo	imbongolo	
door (n)	deur	lemati	monyako	lebati	ucango	umnyango	
dose (n)	dosis	kelo ya sehlare	tekanyo ya sehlare	selekanyo	ithamo	ithamo elilinganisiweyo	
double (a)	dubbele	gabedi	-habedi	-futaganeng	-phindeneyo	-phindiwe	
double (n)	dubbel	bobedi	bobedi	bobedi	umphindwa	okuphindiweyo	
doubt (n)	twyfel	-pelaelo	pelaelo	pelaelo	intandabuzo	ukusola	
doubt (v)	twyfel	-belaela	-belaela	-belaela	-thandabuza	-sola	
dough (n)	deeg	tege	hlama	leribi	intlama	inhlama	
down (prep)	af	fase	-tlase	tlase	-phantsi	phansi	
doze (v)	sluimer	-potuma	-otsela	-otsela	-lala	-ozela	
dozen (n)	dosyn	tosene	tosene	tosene	idazini	idazini	
drag (v)	sleep	-goga	-hulanya	-gogoba	-rhuqa	-hudula	
drainpipe (n)	rioolpyp	phaephe ya kelatšhila	foro ya ho tlosa metsi	leela la mesele	umbhobho	ipayipi	
draw (v)	sleep	-goga	-hula	-goga	-rhuqa	-donsa	
draw (v)	teken	-thala	-tshwantsha	-tshwantsha	-zoba	-dweba	
drawing (n)	tekening	seswantšho	setshwantsho	setshwantsho	umzobo	umfanekiso	
dread (v)	vrees	-boifa	-tshaba	-boifa	-oyika	uvalo	
dream (n)	droom	toro	toro	toro	iphupha	iphupho	
dream (v)	droom	-lora	-lora	-lora	-phupha	-phupha	
dress (n)	rok	roko	mose	mosese	ilokhwe	ilokwe	
dress (v)	aantrek	-apara	-apara	-apara	-nxiba	-gqokisa	
drink (n)	drankie	seno	seno	seno	isiselo	isiphuzo	
drink (v)	drink	-nwa	-nwa	-nwa	-sela	-phuza	
drip (n)	drup	tripi	lerothodi	lerothodi	ithontsi	iconsi	
drip (v)	drup	-rotha	-rotha	-rotha	-thontsiza	-consa	
drive (v)	bestuur	-otlela	-kganna	-tsamaisa	-qhuba	-shayela	
driver (n)	bestuurder	mootledi	mokganni	mokgweetsi	umqhubi	umshayeli	
driveway (n)	inrit	mokgotha	tselana e kenang	tsela e e tsenang	indledlana	umgwaqo oya endlini	
drizzle (v)	motreën	-sarasara	lefafatsane	-na medupe	umkhumezelo	-khiza	
droop (v)	neerhang	-lepelela	-lepella	-ribama	-jinga	-yenda	
drop (v)	laat val	-weša	-rotha	-usa	-wisa	-wisa	
drought (n)	droogte	komelelo	komello	komelelo	imbalela	ukomisa kwezulu	
drown (v)	verdrink	-kgangwa ke meetse	-kgangwa ke metsi	-beta	-rhaxwa	-minza	
drowse (v)	dommel	-otsela	-otsela	-otsela	-ozela	-ozela	
drug (n)	dwelm	seokobatši	thethefatsi	seritibatsi	iyeza	isidakamizwa	
drug addict (n)	dwelmslaaf	moineedi diokobatšing	lekgoba la dithethefatsi	moritibatsi	umyotywa	isigqili sesidakamizwa	
drugs (n)	dwelms	diokobatši	dithethefatsi	ditaga	amayeza	izidakamizwa	
drum (n)	trom	moropa	moropa	moropa	igubu	isigubhu	
drummer (n)	tromspeler	moletšamoropa	moletsamoropa	motshamiki wa moropa	umbethi-gubu	umshayi wesigubhu	
drunk (a)	dronk	-tagilwego	-tahilwe	-tlhapedisang	-nxilile	-dakiwe	
drunkard (n)	dronklap	setagwa	letahwa	letagwa	inxila	isidakwa	
dry (a)	droog	-omilego	-omme	-omileng	-omileyo	-omile	
dry (v)	droogmaak	-oma	-oma	-oma	-omisa	-omisa	
dryclean (v)	droogskoonmaak	-hlwekišaoma	-hlwekisa ntle ho metsi	-tlhatswa	-drayiklina	-drayiklina	
drycleaner (n)	droogskoonmakery	mohlwekišaoma	mohlwekisa ntle ho metsi	teraetlelini	idrayiklina	umdrayiklini	

D	English	Afrikaans	N Sotho	Sesotho	Tswana	Xhosa	Zulu
	duck (n)	eend	lepidipidi	letata	pidipidi	idada	idada
	duiker (n)	duiker	phuti	phuthi	photi	impunzi	impunzi
	dumb (a)	stom	-semumu	-semumu	-mumu	-sisimumu	-yisimungulu
	dune (n)	duin	mmoto wa mohlaba	totomana	popoma	indunduma	igquma
	dusk (n)	skemer	phirimane	shwalane	letlatlana	urhatya	ukuhwalala
	dust (n)	stof	lerole	lerole	lerole	uthuli	uthuli
	dust (v)	afstof	-phumula lerole	-hlakola	-phimola lerole	-vuthulula	-sula
	duster (n)	stoflap	sephumudi sa lerole	lesela la ho hlakola lerole	sephimodi	ilaphu lokususa uthuli	isesulo
	duty (n)	plig	tshwanelo	tshwanelo	tiro	umsebenzi	imfanelo
	dwarf (n)	dwerg	mponempone	qokofana	lemponempone	uhili	isichwe
	dwelling (n)	woning	bodulo	ntlo	ntlo	indawo yokuhlala	ikhaya
	dynamite (n)	dinamiet	tanamaete	denamaete	talameiti	idamanethi	udalimede
	dysentery (n)	disenterie	tengkhubedu	letshollo le lefubedu	letshololo	isisu segazi	isihudo
	each (pron)	elk(e)	mang le mang	-ng le -ng	ngwe le ngwe	nga(m)nye	yilowo
	eager (a)	gretig	-dumago	-mafolofolo	-gakalelang	-ngokungxamela	-nkamunkamu
	eagle (n)	arend	ntšhu	ntsu	ntsu	ukhozi	ukhozi
	ear (n)	oor	tsebe	tsebe	tsebe	indlebe	indlebe
	earache (n)	oorpyn	bohloko bja ditsebe	bohloko ba tsebe	setlhabi sa tsebe	ukuqaqamba kwendlebe	ubuhlungu bendlebe
	early (a)	vroeg	ka masa	hoseng	-phakela	-kusasa	-masisha
	earn (v)	verdien	-gola	-sebeletsa moputso	-amogela	-zuza	-zuza
	earnings (n)	loon	moputso	moputso	tuelo	umvuzo	imali eholwayo
	earring (n)	oorring	lengina	lesale	lengena	icici	icici
	earth (n)	aarde	lefase	lefatshe	lefatshe	umhlaba	umhlaba
	earthquake (n)	aardbewing	tšhišinyego ya lefase	tshisinyeho ya lefatshe	thoromo ya lefatshe	inyikima	indudumela yomhlaba
	earthworm (n)	erdwurm	nogametsana	nonometsane	monopi	umsundululu	umsundu
	east (adv)	oos	bohlabela	botjhabela	kwa botlhabatsatsi	-mpuma	-sempumalanga
	east (n)	ooste	Bohlabela	botjhabela	botlhabatsatsi	impuma	impumalanga
	eastern (a)	oostelik	-bohlabela	-botjhabela	-botlhabatsatsi	-mpuma	-kwasempumalanga
	easy (a)	maklik	bonolo	-bonolo	-bonolo	-lula	-lula
	eat (v)	eet	-ja	-ja	-ja	-tya	-dla
	echo (n)	weerklank	kgalagalo	modumela	mareetsane	intlokoma	ummemo
	echo (v)	weerklink	-galagala	-dumela	-araba	-hlokoma	-enanela
	eclipse (n)	verduistering	phifalo	phifalo	phifalo	umnyama	ukusithibala
	economise (v)	besuinig	-seketša	-baballa	-papana	-qoqosha	-onga
	economy (n)	ekonomie	ekonomi	paballo	pabalelo	uqoqosho	umnotho
	eczema (n)	ekseem	sekgalaka	lekgopho	mosweswe	umrhawuzelelane	utwayi
	edge (n)	rand	morumo	qophelo	losi	uhlangothi	icala
	edible (a)	eetbaar	-lewago	-jehang	-jewang	-tyekayo	-dlekayo
	edit (v)	redigeer	-rulaganya	-hlophisa	-rulaganya	-hlela	-hlela
	editor (n)	redakteur	morulaganyi	mohlophisi	morulaganyi	umhleli	umhleli
	educate (v)	opvoed	-ruta	-ruta	-ruta	-fundisa	-fundisa
	education (n)	opvoeding	thuto	thuto	thuto	imfundo	imfundo
	eel (n)	paling	paleng	tlhapinohana	tlhapisekanoga	ipalanga	umbokwane
	effect (n)	uitwerking	sephetho	tholwana	sephetho	isiphumo	umphumela
	effect (v)	bewerk	-phetha	-sebetsa	-diragatsa	-phumezo	-feza
	efficiency (n)	doeltreffendheid	bokgoni	bokgoni	bokgoni	inkuthalo	ukuqeqesheka
	efficient (a)	doeltreffend	-kgonago	-kgonang	-kgonang	-khutheleyo	-qeqeshekile
	effort (n)	inspanning	teko	boikgathatso	matsapa	umzamo	umzamo
	effortless (a)	met gemak	ka boiketlo	-bonolo	ka bonolo	-lula	kalula
	egg (n)	eier	lee	lehe	lee	iqanda	iqanda
	eggshell (n)	eierdop	kgapetla ya lee	kgaketlana	kgapa	iqokobhe	igobolondo leqanda
	eight (n)	agt	seswai	robedi	robedi	isibhozo	isishiyagalombili
	eighteen (n)	agtien	lesomeseswai	leshome le borobedi	some robedi	ishumi elinesibhozo	ishumi-nesishiyagalombili
	eighty (n)	tagtig	masomeseswai	mashome a robedi	somaarobedi	amashumi asibhozo	amashumi ayisishiyagalombili
	either (pron)	een van beide	-fe goba -fe	kapa	kana	-nokuba nguwuphi	-kokubili

English	Afrikaans	N Sotho	Sesotho	Tswana	Xhosa	Zulu
either...or (conj)	òf...òf	goba	kapa	kgotsa	nokuba okanye	noma muphi
eject (v)	uitskiet	-ragela ntle	-ntsha	-thunsetsa ntle	-khupha	-potshoza
eland (n)	eland	phohu	phofu	phofu	impofu	impofu
elastic (a)	rekbaar	-raramologago	-tamolohang	-taologo	-ntwebekayo	-jobulukayo
elastic (n)	rek	rekere	tamoloho	rekere	ilastiki	injoloba
elbow (n)	elmboog	setšu	setswe	sekgono	ingqiniba	indololwane
eldest (a)	oudste	-golo	-holo	-mogolo	-dala	-dala kakhulu
elect (v)	verkies	-kgetha	-kgetha	-tlhopha	-nyula	-khethiwe
election (n)	verkiesing	kgetho	kgetho	tlhopho	unyulo	ukhetho
electric (a)	elektries	-mohlagase	-motlakase	-motlakase	-ombane	-kagesi
electricity (n)	elektrisiteit	mohlagase	motlakase	motlakase	umbane	ugesi
element (n)	element	elemente	setho	tlholego	into	ilungu
elephant (n)	olifant	tlou	tlou	tlou	indlovu	indlovu
eleven (n)	elf	lesometee	leshome le motso	some nngwe	ishumi elinanye	ishumi nanye
eligible (a)	geskik	-go kgethega	-lokelang	-siameng	-nokunyulwa	-fanelekile
eliminate (v)	verwyder	-tloša	-ntsha	-tlosa	-denda	-susa
elongate (v)	verleng	-lelefatša	-lelefatsa	-lelefatsa	-olula	-elula
elope (v)	weglooop	-ngwega	-shobela	-thoba	-gcagca	-baleka
eloquence (n)	welsprekendheid	go bolela gabotse	bokgeleke	seshwiri mo puong	ubuciko	ubuqaphuqaphu
else (adv)	anders	-fapanago	-ng	-sele	-nye	-kungenjalo
elsewhere (adv)	elders	mo gongwe	kaekae	gosele	kwenye indawo	kwenye indawo
emaciated (a)	uitgeteer	-otilego	-otileng	-mokodue	-nqinileyo	-nciphile
emancipate (v)	vrymaak	-lokolla	-lokolla bokgobeng	-golola	-khulula	-khulula
embarrass (v)	verleë maak	-leša dihlong	-tsietsa	-akabatsa	-enza iintloni	-finyanisa
embrace (n)	omhelsing	kgokarelo	kopo	kamatlelo	ukwanga	ukugona
embrace (v)	omhels	-gokarela	-kopa	-kamatlela	-anga	-gona
embryo (n)	embrio	pelwana	pelwana	pelwana	isihluma esizalweni	umbungu
emerge (v)	verrys	-tšwa	-phahama	-inoga	-vela	-phuma
emergency (n)	noodgeval	tšhoganetšo	tlokotsi	tshoganyetso	ithuba lokuxakeka	ingozi
emigrate (v)	emigreer	-falala	-falla	-falala	-fuduka	-thuthela kwelinye izwe
eminent (a)	vooraanstaande	-hlomphegago	-konokono	-itsegeng	-balaseleyo	-phakeme
emotion (n)	gevoel	khuduego	phudueho	maikutlo	uluvo	umzwelo
emphasis (n)	klem	kgatelelo	toboketso	kgatelelo	ugxininiso	ukugcizelela
emphasise (v)	beklemtoon	-gatelela	-toboketsa	-gatelela	-gxininisa	-gcizelela
employ (v)	in diens neem	-thwala	-hira	-thapa	-qesha	-qasha
employee (n)	werknemer	modiredi	mohiruwa	modiri	umqeshwa	isisebenzi
employer (n)	werkgewer	mothwadi	mohiri	mohiri	umqeshi	umqashi
employment (n)	werk	mošomo	mosebetsi	tiro	umsebenzi	umsebenzi
empty (a)	leeg	-se nago selo	-feela	-lolea	-ze	-ngenalutho
enclose (v)	insluit	-akaretša	-kenya	-thekeletsa	-valela	-zungezeleka
encourage (v)	aanmoedig	-tutuetša	-kgothaletsa	-nametsa	-khuthaza	-khuthaza
end (n)	einde	bofelo	phetho	bokhutlo	isiphelo	ukugcina
end (v)	eindig	-fela	-phetha	-khutla	-phela	-gcina
endanger (v)	in gevaar stel	-tsenya kotsing	-kenya tsietsing	-tsenya mo kotsing	-faka engozini	-faka engozini
endear (v)	bemind maak	-ratiša	-ratisa	-ratega	-thandisa	-thandekisa
enema (n)	enema	enema	enema	mothulego	ivenge	uchatho
enemy (n)	vyand	lenaba	sera	mmaba	utshaba	isitha
energetic (a)	energiek	-mafolofolo	-matla	-mojato	-namandla	-khuthele
energy (n)	energie	mafolofolo	matla	thata	amandla	umfutho
enforce (v)	afdwing	-gapeletša	-qobella	-gagapa	-nyanzelisa	-phoqa
engaged (a)	beset	-dirišwago	-tshwarehileng	-dirisiwa	-xakekile	-bambekile
engine (n)	enjin	entšene	enjene	enjene	injini	injini
English (a)	Engels	-Seisemane	-Senyesemane	Seesemane	isi Ngesi	isiNgisi
enjoy (v)	geniet	-ipshina ka	-natefelwa	-ja monate	-onwabela	-jabulela
enlarge (v)	vergroot	-godiša	-hodisa	-katolosa	-andisa	-andisa
enlighten (v)	inlig	-tsebiša	-qaqisetsa	-fatlhosa	-khanyisela	-khanyisela
enormous (a)	tamaai	-golo ka maatla	-tonanahadi	-tona	-khulu	-khulukazi
enough (a)	genoeg	-lekanego	-lekaneng	-lekanang	-aneleyo	-anele
enrich (v)	verryk	-humiša	-ruisa	-nontsha	-tyebisa	-cebisa
enrol (v)	inskryf	-ngwadiša	-ngodisa	-kwadisa	-bhalisa	-joyina

E English	Afrikaans	N Sotho	Sesotho	Tswana	Xhosa	Zulu
ensure (v)	verseker	-kgonthiša	-tiisetsa	-tlhomamisa	-qinisekisa	-qiniseka
enter (v)	binnegaan	-tsena	-kena	-tsena	-ngena	-ngena
enthusiasm (n)	geesdrif	phišego	tjheseho	mafolofolo	umdla	ubunkamunkamu
enthusiastic (a)	geesdriftig	-phišego	-tjhesehelang	-mafolofolo	-nomdla	-nkamunkamu
entire (a)	hele	ka moka	-hle	-otlhe	-nke	-phelayo
entrails (n)	ingewande	dikateng	mala	mateng	izibilini	amathumbu
entry (n)	binnekoms	go tsena	kenello	matseno	isango lokungena	ukungena
envelope (n)	koevert	enfelopo	omfolopo	enfelopo	imvulophu	imvilophu
envious (a)	jaloers	-nago le tseba	-mohono	-fufegang	-nomona	-hawukelayo
environment (n)	omgewing	tikologo	tikoloho	tikologo	ubume bendawo	ubunjalo bendawo
envy (n)	naywer	mona	mohono	keletso	umona	umhawu
envy (v)	beny	-duma	-lakatsa	-eletsa	-monela	-hawukela
epidemic (n)	epidemie	leuba	sewa	leroborobo	isifo esosulelayo	isibhadalala
epilepsy (n)	vallende siekte	dihwahwa	sethwathwa	leebana	isifo sokuwa	isithuthwane
equal (a)	gelyk	-lekanago	-lekanang	-lekanang	-linganayo	-lingene
equal (n)	gelyke	molekane	molekane	molekane	ulingano	olingene na-
equal (v)	gelyk wees aan	-lekana	-lekana	-lekana	-linganisa	-lingana na-
equator (n)	ewenaar	mogarafase	ekhweita	mogaralefatshe	ikweyita	inkabazwe
erase (v)	uitvee	-phumola	-hlakola	-phimola	-cima	-sula
eraser (n)	uitveër	sephumodi	sehlakodi	sephimodi	isicimi	isesulo
erect (v)	oprig	-aga	-thea	-aga	-misa	-akha
erosion (n)	wegvreting	kgogolego	kgoholeho	kgogolego	ukhukuliseko	ukuhebhuka
err (v)	fouteer	-dira phošo	-fosa	-fosa	-phazama	-phosisa
error (n)	fout	phošo	phoso	phoso	impazamo	isiphosiso
erupt (v)	uitbars	-thunya	-qhashoha	-ropologa	-gqabhuka	-qhuma
escape (n)	ontsnapping	phonyokgo	phonyoho	phalolo	uqhwesho	ukweqa
escape (v)	ontsnap	-phonyokga	-phonyoha	-falola	-qhwesha	-baleka
escort (n)	metgesel	mofelegetši	mofelehetsi	mmuledisi	ukukhapha	umphelezeli
escort (v)	vergesel	-felegetša	-felehetsa	-buledisa	-khapha	-phelezela
essay (n)	opstel	taodišo	moqoqo	tlhamo	isincoko	indaba elotshiweyo
essence (n)	essensie	bokgonthe	tabataba	tlhokego	ubunto	ingqikithi
essential (a)	essensieel	-nyakegago	-bohlokwa	-tlhokegang	-funekayo	-funekayo
establish (v)	vestig	-hloma	-hloma	-setlela	-zinzisa	-misa
eternal (a)	ewig	-sa felego	-sa feleng	-bosakhuteng	-ngaphakathi	-naphakade
eternity (n)	ewigheid	bosafeleng	bosafeleng	bosayenkae	iphakade	ubuphakade
ethnic (a)	etnies	-serafe		-setso	-buhlanga	-kohlobo lobuzwe
etiquette (n)	etiket	boitshwaro	hlomphano	maitseo	ukuziphatha	usikothi
evangelist (n)	evangelis	moebangedi	Moefangedi	moefanggele	umvangeli	umvangeli
evaporate (v)	verdamp	-moyafala	-moyafala	-mowafala	-ba ngumphunga	-hwamuka
even (adv)	selfs	le ge	-esita	le fa	-ngckulingana	na-
even (a)	gelykmatig	-lekanetšego	-lekana	-lekalekanang	-linganayo	-lingene
evening (n)	aand	mantšiboa	mantsiboya	maitseboa	ngokuhlwa	ukuhlwa
event (n)	gebeurtenis	tiragalo	ketsahalo	tiragalo	isiganeko	isehlakalo
ever (adv)	ooit	-kile	le kgale	kile	wakha	nanini
evergreen (a)	bladhoudend	-talamehleng	-tala selemo sohle	-talafeletseng ruri	-luhlaza njalo	-ngawohlokisi amakhasi
everlasting (a)	ewigdurend	-go sa felego	-sa feleng	-ruri	-ngapheliyo	-ngunaphakade
every (a)	elke	-ngwe le -ngwe	-ng le -ng	-otlhe	-nke	-nke
evict (v)	uitsit	-leleka	-falatsa	-ntsha	-khuphe endlwini	-xosha
evidence (n)	getuienis	bohlatse	bopaki	bopaki	ubungqina	ubufakazi
evil (a)	boos	-be	-kgopo	-bosula	-ngcolile (yo)	-bi
evolution (n)	evolusie	ebolusi	ebolusi	tlhagelelo	ukudaleka	ukusombuluka kwendalo
exact (a)	presies	-nepagetšego	-nepileng	gone jaana	-kanye	-qinisile
exaggerate (v)	oordryf	-feteletša	-feteletsa	-feteletsa	-baxa	-andisa
examination (n)	eksamen	tlhahlobo	hlahlobo	tlhatlhobo	uvavanyo	ukuhlolwa
examine (v)	ondersoek	-hlahloba	-hlahloba	-tlhatlhoba	-vavanya	-phenya
example (n)	voorbeeld	mohlala	mohlala	sekao	umzekelo	isibonelo
exceed (v)	oorskry	-feta	-feta	-gaisa	-gqithisa	-dlula
excel (v)	uitblink	-phala	-kganya	-phala	-gqwesa	-ahlula
excellent (a)	uitmuntend	-phalago	-kganyang	-maatlametlo	-balaseleyo	-hle kakhulu

English	Afrikaans	N Sotho	Sesotho	Tswana	Xhosa	Zulu	**F**
except (prep)	behalwe	ka ntle le	-ntle ho	le fela	ngaphandle	ngaphandle kwa-	
excite (v)	opwind	-hlohleletša	-nyakalatsa	-gakala	-vuyisa	-vusa	
excitement (n)	opwinding	khuduego	-nyakallo	tlhagafatso	uvuyo	umesaso	
exclaim (v)	uitroep	-goa	-hoa	-tsibisa	-khwaza	-memeza	
exclude (v)	uitsluit	-tlogela	-qhela	-tlogela	-nxwema	-valela ngaphandle	
excreta (n)	uitwerpsel	mantle	mantle	lesepa	izibi zomzimba	amasimba	
excuse (n)	ekskuus	tshwarelo	tshwarelo	seipato	ukuzigwebela	izaba	
excuse (v)	verontskuldig	-lebalela	-tshwarela	-itoka	-xolela	-xolela	
execute (v)	teregstel	-bolaya	-fanyeha	-bolaya	-enza	-bulala ngomthetho	
exercise (n)	oefening	kotlollo	thapollo	thobololo	ukuziqhelisa	umsebenzi	
exercise (v)	oefen	-otlolla	-ithapolla	-thobolola	-qhelisa	-sebenza	
exhale (v)	uitasem	-huetša	-phefumoloha	-hemela ntle	-phefumla	-khipha umoya	
exhibit (v)	uitstal	-bontšha	-bontsha	-bontsha	-bonisa	-bukisa	
exhibition (n)	uitstalling	pontšho	pontsho	pontsho	umboniso	umbukiso	
exile (n)	verbanning	teleko	teleko	tshedisomelolwane	ugxotho	ukudingiswa	
exile (v)	verban	-leleka	-leleka	-tshedisa melolwane	-gxotha	-dingisa	
exist (v)	bestaan	-gona	-ba teng	-nna teng	-bakho	-khona	
existence (n)	bestaan	boleng	ho ba teng	boleyo	ubukho	ubukhona	
exit (n)	uitgang	botšo	kgoro	botso	isango lokuphuma	ukuphuma	
exit (v)	uitgaan	-tšwa	-tswa	-tswa	-phuma	-phuma	
exotic (a)	eksoties	-šele	-ditjhabeng	-sa bonweng fela	-ngaqhelekanga	-vele kwelinye izwe	
expand (v)	uitbrei	-godiša	-atolosa	-ngangabolola	-andisa	-khulisa	
expect (v)	verwag	-letela	-lebella	-solofela	-lindela	-ethemba	
expenses (n)	onkoste	ditshenyegelo	ditshenyehelo	tshenyegelo	iindleko	izindleko	
expensive (a)	duur	-turago	-turu	-turang	-dla	-dulile	
experience (n)	ervaring	boitemogelo	boiphihlelo	boitemogelo	amava	ulwazi	
experiment (n)	proefneming	boitekelo	ekseperimente	tekelelo	ilinge	ukulinga	
expert (n)	deskundige	setsebi	kgeleke	setswerere	incutshe	isazi	
explain (v)	verduidelik	-hlaloša	-hlalosa	-tlhalosa	cacisa	-chaza	
explanation (n)	verduideliking	tlhalošo	hlaloso	tlhaloso	ingcaciso	incasiselo	
explode (v)	ontplof	-thunya	-qhoma	-thunya	-gqabhuka	-qhuma	
explore (v)	verken	-hlohlomiša	-utulla	-utulola	-hlola	-hlola	
explosion (n)	ontploffing	go thunya	qhomo	go thunya	ugqabhuko-dubulo	ukuqhuma	
export (n)	uitvoer	kišontle	seyantle	seyantle	umthumeli	-thekelisa	
export (v)	uitvoer	-iša ntle	-kgwebela	-isa ntle	uthumelo kwelinye ilizwe	ukuthekelisa	
expose (v)	blootlê	-utolla	-hlahatsa	-senola	-tyhila	-veza	
express (a)	uitdruklik	-gateletšwego	-totobetseng	-thadisang	-khawulezayo	-khangayo	
express (n)	sneltrein	setimela sa mafofonyane	terene e lebelo	setimelasegaodi	uloliwe okhawulezayo	ushikishi	
express (v)	uitdruk	-hlagiša	-hlahisa	-thadisa	-thumela ngendlela ekhawulezayo	-sho	
extend (v)	uitstrek	-otlolla	-otlolla	-golola	-andisa	-dephisa	
exterminate (v)	uitroei	-fediša	-ripitla	-nyeletsa	-tshabalalisa	-shabalalisa	
extinguish (v)	blus	-tima	-tima	-tima	-cima	-cima	
extra (a)	ekstra	godimo ga	-fetang	-gape	-ongezelelweyo	-ngaphezulu	
extravagance (n)	buitensporigheid	tlopelo	kgalala	bosutlha	inkcitho	ukuhlaphaza	
extravagant (a)	buitensporig	-tlopetšego	-kgalala	-nna bosutlha	-nenkcitho	-hlaphazayo	
eye (n)	oog	leihlo	leihlo	leitlho	iliso	iso	
eyebrow (n)	winkbrou	ntšhikgolo	dintshi	losi	ushiyi	ishiya	
eyelash (n)	wimper	ntšhi	dintshi	ntshi	umsebe	ukhophe	
eyelid (n)	ooglid	phuphu	dintshi	lesi	inkophe	ijwabu lehlo	
eyewitness (n)	ooggetuie	hlatse ya leihlo	paki e boneng	mmoni	ingqina	isibukeli	
fable (n)	fabel	nonwane	tshomo	leinane	intsomi	insumo	
fabric (n)	tekstielstof	lešela	lesela	lesasupa	ilaphu	into ephothwe yabayingubo	
face (n)	gesig	sefahlego	sefahleho	sefatlhego	ubuso	ubuso	
fact (n)	feit	nnete	nnete	ntlha	inqaku	iqiniso	
faction (n)	faksie	lekoko	mokga	mophato	imbambano	isixexelegu	

English	**Afrikaans**	**N Sotho**	**Sesotho**	**Tswana**	**Xhosa**	**Zulu**
factory (n)	fabriek	faporiki	feme	faboriki	iziko-mveliso	ifektri
faculty (n)	fakulteit	lefapha	lekala	lefapha	isebe lemfundo	isigaba
fade (v)	verbleik	-galoga	-thunya	-tswapoga	-sithela	-fiphala
faeces (n)	uitwerpsel	mantle	mantle	mantle	ithafa	amasimba
fail (v)	misluk	-palelwa	-hloleha	-retelelwa	-ngaphumeleli	-hluleka
failure (n)	mislukking	tšhitego	-tlholeho	thetelelo	ukuwa	ukwahluleka
faint (v)	flou word	-idibala	-akgeha	-idibala	-feyinta	-quleka
fair (a)	billik	-lokilego	-tle	-tolamo	-lungile (yo)	-hle
faith (n)	geloof	tumelo	tumelo	tumelo	ukholo	ithemba
faithful (a)	getrou	-botegago	-tshepahalang	-ikanyegang	-thobileyo	-thembekile
fake (a)	vals	-bofora	-lefeela	-phora	-buxoki	-yinkohliso
fall (v)	val	-wa	-wa	-wa	-wa	-wa
false (a)	vals	-bofora	-leshano	sa ikanyegang	-buxoki	-khohlisayo
falsehood (n)	onwaarheid	maaka	leshano	maaka	ubuxoki	amanga
fame (n)	roem	tumo	botumo	tumo	ukubaluleka	udumo
family (n)	familie	leloko	lesika	balelapa	usapho	inzalo
famine (n)	hongersnood	tlala	tlala	lesekere	indlala	indlala
famous (a)	beroemd	-tumilego	-tumileng	-itsegeng	-aziwayo	-dumile
fan (n)	bewonderaar	motumiši	mothahaselli	molatedi	umxhasi	umncomeli
fan (n)	waaier	sefokišamoya	fene	leubelo	isiniki-moya	isephephezelo
fang (n)	slagtand	polai	leino la noha	lebolai	izinyo	inzawu
far (adv)	ver	kgole	-hole	kgakala	-kude	kude
fare (n)	reisgeld	tefo ya leeto	tefello ya leeto	tuelo	imali yokuhamba	imali yokukhwela
farm (n)	plaas	polase	polasi	polase	ifama	ipulazi
farm (v)	boer	-rua	-lema	-rua	-famisha	-lima
farmer (n)	boer	morui	rapolasi	molemirui	umfama	umlimi
fashion (n)	mode	moaparo	mokgwa	moaparo	ifashoni	imfeshini
fast (a)	vinnig	-nago le lebelo	-phakisang	ka bonako	-khawulezayo	-masinyane
fasten (v)	vasmaak	-tlema	-tiisa	-bofa	-bopha	-bopha
fat (a)	vet	-nonnego	-mafura	-nonneng	-tyebileyo	-khuluphele
fat (n)	vet	makhura	mafura	mafura	amafutha	amafutha
fate (n)	lot	boyo	kabelo	ntle ga taolo	ummiselo	isimiselo
father (n)	vader	tata	ntate	rra	utata	ubaba
father-in-law (n)	skoonvader	ratswale	mohwe	ratsale	ubawozala	ubabezala
fatigue (n)	vermoeienis	tapo	mokgathala	tapisego	udino	ukukhathala
fault (n)	fout	phošo	phoso	phoso	imposiso	iphosiso
fauna (n)	fauna	diphedi	diphedi	ditshedi	izilo	izilwane
favour (n)	guns	thušo	molemo	molemo	uncedo	umusa
favour (v)	begunstig	-rata	-rata	-rata	-enzelela	-khetha
favourite (a)	gunsteling	-ratwago go feta	moratuwa	-mmamoratwa	-enzelelayo	-khethekayo
fear (n)	vrees	poifo	tshabo	poifo	uloyiko	ukwesaba
fear (v)	vrees	-boifa	-tshaba	-boifa	-oyika	-esaba
feast (n)	fees	mokete	mokete	moletlo	umsitho	idili
feast (v)	feesvier	-ja mokete	-keteka	-ja moletlo	-bhiyoza	-dikiza
feather (n)	veer	lefofa	lesiba	lefofa	usiba	uphaphe
February (n)	Februarie	Feberware	Hlakola	Tlhakole	Febhuwari	uFebhuwali
feed (v)	voer	-fepa	-fepa	-fepa	-tyisa	-phakela
feel (v)	voel	-kwa	-ama	-utlwa	-vakalelwa	-zwa
feint (v)	voorgee	-ometša	-iketsisa	-oma	-lingisa	-zenzisa
female (a)	vroulik	-tshadi	-tshehadi	-namagadi	-khomokazi	-owesifazane
female (n)	vrou	mosadi	mosadi	namagadi	umfazi	isifazane
fence (n)	draad	legora	terata	legora	ucingo	ucingo
ferment (v)	gis	-bela	-lomosa	-bela	-bilisa	-bila
fern (n)	varing	mmalewaneng	palesa	phatadikgagane	umfisi	isikhomane
fertile (a)	vrugbaar	-nonnego	-nonne	-nonneng	-chumileyo	-vundile
fertilise (v)	bevrug	-nontšha	-nontsha	-ungwisa	-chumisa	-zalisa
fertilise (v)	kunsmis gee	-nontšha mmu	-nontsha	-nontsha	-chumisa	-thela umanyolo
fertiliser (n)	kunsmis	monontšha	monontsha	monontsha	isichumiso	umanyolo
fester (v)	sweer	-tutela	-ikana	-tutela	-funga	-vunda
festival (n)	fees	monyanya	mokete	moletlo	umnyadala	umkhasi

English	Afrikaans	N Sotho	Sesotho	Tswana	Xhosa	Zulu	F
fetch (v)	haal	-lata	-lata	-tsaya	-phuthuma	-landa	
fever (n)	koors	letadi	feberu	letshoroma	ifiva	imfiva	
few (a)	min	-sego kae	-mmalwa	-mmalwa	-mbalwa	-ncane	
fibre (n)	vesel	tlhale	tlhale	tlhale	usinga	uzi	
fiction (n)	fiksie	kanegelogopolwa	tshomo	maitlhamelwa	intsomi	okuqanjiwe	
fidelity (n)	getrouheid	potego	botshepehi	boikanyo	intembeko	ukwethembeka	
field (n)	veld	naga	tshimo	tshimo	ibala	indawo yasendle	
fierce (a)	woes	-šoro	-bohale	-bogale	-oyikeka(yo)	-nolaka	
fifteen (n)	vyftien	lesomehlano	leshome le metso e mehlano	some tlhano	ishumi elinesihlanu	ishumi nesihlanu	
fifty (n)	vyftig	masomehlano	mashome a mahlano	somamatlhano	amashumi amahlanu	amashumi amahlanu	
fig (n)	vy	feiye	feiye	feie	ikhiwane	ikhiwane	
fight (n)	geveg	ntwa	ntwa	ntwa	umlo	ukulwa	
fight (v)	veg	-lwa	-lwana	-lwa	-yilwa	-lwa	
figtree (n)	vyeboom	mofeiye	sefate sa feiye	feie	umthi wekhiwane	umkhiwane	
figure (n)	figuur	sethalwa	setshwantsho	thwadi	umfanekiso	ukulinganisa	
file (n)	leêr	faela	faele	faele	ifayile	isihlabo	
file (n)	vyl	feila	feile	feile	ifila	ifayili	
fill (v)	vol maak	-tlatša	-tlatsa	-tlatsa	-gcwalisa	-gcwalisa	
fillet (n)	filet	filete	tshutshu	thupa	isihlunu	inyama ethambileyo	
filling (n)	stopsel	sešunetšwa	mokato	tlatso	umhlohlo	okugcwalisayo	
film (n)	film	filimi	fileme	setshwantsho	ifilimu	ifilimu	
filter (v)	filtreer	-hlotla	-hlotla	-tlhotlha	-hluza	-vova	
filth (n)	vuilgoed	tšhila	tshila	leswe	ubumdaka	udoti	
fin (n)	vin	lephegwana la hlapi	lepheo la tlhapi	lefafa	iphiko lentlanzi	iphiko lenhlanzi	
final (a)	finaal	-mafelelo	-bofelo	-bofelo	-okugqibela	isigcino	
find (v)	vind	-hwetša	-fumana	-bona	-fumana	-thola	
fine (a)	fyn	-tshesane	-thumisehileng	-boleta	-colekileyo	-coliweyo	
fine (n)	boete	tefišo	tefiso	tefiso	isohlwayo	inhlawulo	
fine (v)	beboet	-lefiša	-lefisa	-duedisa	-ohlwaya	-hlawula	
finger (n)	vinger	monwana	monwana	monwana	umnwe	umunwe	
fingernail (n)	vingernael	lenala	lenala	lenala	uzipho	uzipho lomunwe	
fingerprint (n)	vingerafdruk	kgatišo ya monwana	kgatiso ya monwana	motlhala wa monwana	umnwe	isithupha	
finish (n)	einde	mafelelo	qetelo	khutlo	isiphelo	ukuphela	
finish (v)	klaarmaak	-fetša	-qeta	-fetsa	-phela	-phelisa	
fire brigade (n)	brandweer	batimamollo	setimamollo	batimamolelo	isicima-mlilo	abacimimlilo	
fire (n)	vuur	mollo	mollo	molelo	umlilo	umlilo	
fireplace (n)	vuurherd	sebešo	leifo	leiso	iziko	iziko	
firewood (n)	brandhout	dikgong	patsi	legong	iinkuni	izinkuni	
firm (a)	ferm	-tiilego	-tiileng	-tlhomameng	-zinzile(yo)	-qinile	
first (a)	eerste	-pele	-pele	-ntlha	-kuqala	-okuqala	
first aid (n)	noodhulp	thušo ya potlako	thuso ya pele	thuso ya potlako	uncedo lokuqala	usizo lokuqala	
firstborn (n)	eersgeborene	leitšibulo	letsibolo	leitibolo	inkulu	izibulo	
fish (n)	vis	hlapi	tlhapi	tlhapi	intlanzi	inhlanzi	
fish (v)	visvang	-rea dihlapi	-tshwasa	-thaisa ditlhapi	-bamba intlanzi	-doba	
fish-hook (n)	vishoek	huku ya go rea dihlapi	selope	huku	ihuku yokuloba	udobo	
fishing (n)	visvang	go rea dihlapi	tshwaso ya ditlhapi	go tshwara ditlhapi	ukuloba	ukudoba	
fishing rod (n)	visstok	kobihlapi	leqala la ditlhapi	setshwaro sa ditlhapi	intonga yokuloba	uthi lokudoba	
fishmoth (n)	vismot	mmoto	tshwele	motoutwane	isithiyiseli	umvunya	
fist (n)	vuis	letswele	setebele	lebole	inqindi	inqindi	
fit (v)	pas	-lekana	-lekana	-lekanya	-lungileyo	-lingana	
fits (n)	stuipe	dikontwane	kgonyelo ya mesifa	tatanyane	isifo sokuxhuzula	isithuthwane	
five (n)	vyf	-hlano	hlano	tlhano	isihlanu	isihlanu	
fix (v)	regmaak	-lokiša	-lokisa	-baakanya	-lungisa	-lungisa	
fizz (v)	bruis	-fufula	-kokomoha	-bela	-thi tshu	-hlihla	
flag (n)	vlag	folaga	folakga	folaga	iflegi	ifulagi	
flake (n)	vlokkie	kgapetlana	pudulana	makakaba	ikhitha	ucwecwana	
flame (n)	vlam	kgabo ya mollo	lelakabe	kgabo	idangatye	ilangabi	
flamingo (n)	flamink	tladi	folaminko		ikholwase	umakholwase	
flannel (n)	flanel	folene	folene	folene	ifleni	ifulanela	

F English	Afrikaans	N Sotho	Sesotho	Tswana	Xhosa	Zulu
flap (v)	fladder	-phaphasela	-fosa	-phaphasela	-bhenguza	-bhabhazisa
flash (n)	flits	kgadimo	mmane	legadima	umenye	umbani
flashlight (n)	flitslig	panyepanye	sekammane	kganya	umbane	ithoshi
flat (a)	plat	-phaphathi	-sephara	-phaphathi	-mcaba	-yisicaba
flatter (v)	vlei	-phapea	-thetsa	-baya bubi	-khohlisa	-babaza
flatulent (a)	winderig	-bipetšwego	-pipitletswe	-gogoralang	-qumbelayo	-qumbile
flautist (n)	fluitspeler	moletšanaka	mmapalafoleite	moletsaphala	umdlali-fluti	umshayi-mitshingo
flavour (n)	geur	mohlodi	tatso	moutlwano	isinongo	isinandisi
flavour (v)	geur	-fa mohlodi	-noka	-tswaisa	-nonga	-nandisa
flavouring (n)	geursel	mohlodi	senoko	motswaiso	unongo	ukunandisa
flea (n)	vlooi	letsetse	letsetse	letsetse	intakumba	izeze
flee (v)	vlug	-tšhaba	-baleha	-sia	-bhabha	-baleka
flesh (n)	vleis	nama	nama	nama	inyama	inyama
flicker (v)	flikker	-benyabenya	-panyapanya	-benyabenya	-qhwanyaza	-lontoza
flight (n)	vlug	tšhabo	paleho	tshabo	uhambo ngomoya	ukubaleka
flirt (v)	flirteer	-kalatša	-feba	-fefa	-ncokolisa	-gemenca
float (v)	drywe	-phaphamala	-phaphamala	-kokobala	-dada	-ntanta
flock (n)	trop	mohlape	mohlape	motlhape	umhlambi	umhlambi
flood (n)	vloed	lefula	morwallo	morwalela	isikhukula	isikhukhula
flood (v)	oorstroom	-tlala meetse	-rwalella	-rwalela	-zalisa ngamanzi	-khukhula
floor (n)	verdieping	lebato	mokato	bodilo	umgangatho	isitezi
floor (n)	vloer	lebato	fuluru	bodilo	umgangatho	iphansi
flora (n)	flora	dimedi	dimedi	dimedi	isihluma	izinhlobo zemithi
flour (n)	meel	folouru	phofo	boupe jwa borotho	umgubo	ufulawa
flout (v)	hoon	-kwera	-phaphamala	-nyatsa	-chaza	-hleka uzulu
flow (v)	vloei	-ela	-phalla	-elela	-qukuqela	-gobhoza
flower (n)	blom	letšoba	palesa	sethunya	intyatyambo	imbali
fluent (a)	vlot	-elago	-kgeleke	-thelelelo	-nobuciko	-yingqamundi
fluid (a)	vloeibaar	-seela	-phallang	-elelang	-ngamanzi	-ngamanzi
fluid (n)	vloeistof	seela	sephalli	seedi	ubuyengeyenge	into engamanzi
flute (n)	fluit	naka	foleite	phala	umtshingo	umtshingo
fly (n)	vlieg	ntši	ntsintsi	ntsi	umtnika	impukane
fly (v)	vlieg	-fofa	-fofa	-fofa	-bhabha	-ndiza
foal (n)	vulletjie	pešana	petsana	petsana	inkonyana yehashe	inkonyane yehhashi
foe (n)	vyand	lenaba	sera	mmaba	utshaba	isitha
foetus (n)	fetus	serapolotšwana	fetase	namane	into engekazalwa	umbungu
fog (n)	mis	mouwane	mohodi	mouwane	inkungu	inkunga
fold (n)	vou	momeno	lemeno	lemeno	umgqwetho	umpheco
fold (v)	vou	-mena	-mena	-mena	-songa	-pheca
folklore (n)	volksoorleweringe	dinonwane	tshomo	dikinane	uncwadi lomlomo	amasiko nezi-nganekwane
follow (v)	volg	-latela	-latela	-latela	-landela	-landela
follower (n)	volgeling	molatedi	molatedi	molatedi	umlandeli	umlandeli
food (n)	kos	dijo	dijo	dijo	ukutya	ukudla
fool (n)	dwaas	setlaela	sethoto	lesilo	isibhanxa	isilima
foolishness (n)	dwaasheid	botlaela	bothoto	boeleele	ububhanxa	ubulima
foot (n)	voet	leoto	leoto	lenao	unyawo	unyawo
football (n)	voetbal	kgwele ya maoto	bolo	mosito	ibhola	unobhutshuzwayo
footprint (n)	voetspoor	mohlala	bohato	motlhala	unyawo	unyawo
footstep (n)	voetstap	kgato	mohlala	mosepele	inyathelo	isinyathelo
for (prep)	vir	-el-	bakeng sa-	go	-ya	nga-
forbid (v)	verbied	-iletša	-hanela	-itsa	-alela	-ala
force (n)	krag	maatla	matla	kgapeletso	unyanzelo	amandla
force (v)	forseer	-gapeletša	-susumetsa	-gapeletsa	-nyanzela	-cindezela
forearm (n)	voorarm	sefaka	letsoho	mokgono	ingalo	ingalo
forehead (n)	voorhoof	phatla	phatla	phatla	ibunzi	ibunzi
foreign (a)	vreemd	-šele	-sele	-selabe	-asemzini	-kwezizwe ezinye
forest (n)	bos	sethokgwa	moru	sekgwa	ihlathi	ihlathi
forget (v)	vergeet	-lebala	-lebala	-lebala	-libala	-khohlwa
forgive (v)	vergewe	-lebalela	-tshwarela	-itshwarela	-xolela	-xolela

English	Afrikaans	N Sotho	Sesotho	Tswana	Xhosa	Zulu	F
forgiveness (n)	vergifnis	tebalelo	tshwarelo	boitshwarelo	uxolo	uxolo	
fork (n)	vurk	foroko	fereko	foroko	ifolokhwe	imfologo	
form (n)	vorm	sebopego	sebopeho	foromo	isakhiwo	isimo	
form (v)	vorm	-bopa	-bopa	-bopa	-akha	-bumba	
fornicate (v)	hoereer	-otswa	-hlola	-gokafala	-feba	-feba	
fort (n)	fort	sebo	qhobosheane	ntlo ya phemelo	inqaba	isikaniso	
fortnight (n)	twee weke	bekepedi	beke tse pedi	bekepedi	iiveki ezimbini	amasonto amabili	
fortunate (a)	gelukkig	-mahlatse	-lehloohonolo	-tshego	-nethamsanqa	-nenhlanhla	
fortune (n)	fortuin	lehumo	letlotlo	letlhogonolo	ithamsanqa	umnotho	
forty (n)	veertig	masomenne	mashome a mane	somaamane	amashumi amane	amashumi amane	
forward (adv)	vooruit	pele	-pele	pele	phambili	ngaphambili	
fountain (n)	fontein	sediba	sediba	motswedi	umthombo	umthombo	
four (n)	vier	-ne	nne	nne	isine	okune	
fourteen (n)	veertien	lesomenne	leshome le metso e mene	some nne	ishumi elinesine	ishumi nane	
fowl (n)	hoender	kgogo	kgoho	kgogo	inkuku	inkukhu	
fraction (n)	fraksie	karolo	seabelo	palophatlo	iqhekeza	iqhezu	
fractions (n)	breuke	diabelo	diabelo	dipalophatlo	amaqhekeza	amaqhezu	
fracture (n)	breuk	thobego	thobeho	thobego	-candeka	ukwaphuka	
fragment (n)	brokstuk	seripana	sekoto	kapetla	iqhekeza	ucezwana	
fragrance (n)	geur	monko	monko o monate	lenko	ivumba	amakha	
franchise (n)	kiesreg	tokelo ya go kgetha	boikgethelo	botlhophi	ilungelo lokuvota	ilungelo lokuvota	
fraud (n)	bedrog	bofora	thetso	tsietso	ubuqhetseba	inkohliso	
free (a)	vry	-lokologilego	-lokolohileng	-gololosegileng	-khululekileyo	-khululekile	
free (v)	bevry	-lokolla	-lokolla	-golola	-khulula	-khulula	
freedom (n)	vryheid	tokologo	tokoloho	kgololesego	inkululeko	inkululeko	
freeze (v)	vries	-kgahla	-hwama	-gatsela	-khenkca	-qandisa	
freezer (n)	vrieskas	setšidifatši	sehatsetsi	setsidifatsi	isikhenkcisi	isiqandisi	
freezing point (n)	vriespunt	bokgahlo	ntlha ya leqhweng	boswakgapetla	iqondo lomkhenkce	izinga-qhwa	
fresh (a)	vars	-fsa	-tjha	-swa	-tsha	-sha	
Friday (n)	Vrydag	Labohlano	Labohlano	Labotlhano	ulwesi Hlanu	uLwesihlanu	
friend (n)	vriend	mogwera	motswalle	tsala	umhlobo	umngane	
friendship (n)	vriendskap	bogwera	setswalle	botsalano	ubuhlobo	ubungane	
frighten (v)	skrikmaak	-tšhoša	-tshosa	-tshosa	-oyikisa	-ethusa	
frog (n)	padda	segwagwa	senqanqane	segwagwa	isele	isele	
from (prep)	van	go tšwa go	ho-	go-	ku-	kusuka ku-	
front (a)	voor	-pele	-pele	-pele	phambi	phambili	
frost (n)	ryp	tšhwaane	serame	serame	iqabaka	isithwathwa	
frostbite (n)	vriesbrand	kgatselo	lebabo	go swa bokidi	umtshaza	umshazo	
frown (n)	frons	tšhošobanyo ya phatla	kgwapo	sosobanyo	ukujala	ukuhwaqabala	
frown (v)	frons	-šošobanya phatla	-hwapa	-sosobanya	-finga iintshiyi	-hwaqabala	
fruit (n)	vrug	seenywa	tholwana	leungo	isiqhamo	isithelo	
frustrate (v)	frustreer	-nola moko	-nyahamisa	-bolaya pelo	-danisa	-dikibalisa	
fry (v)	bak	-gadika	-hadika	-gadika	-qhotsa	-thosa	
fuel (n)	brandstof	sebešwa	dibeso	mafura	ipetroli	isibasi	
full (a)	vol	-tletšego	-tletse	-tletseng	-zeleyo	-gcwele	
fullstop (n)	punt	khutlo	kgutlo	khutlo	isingxi	ungqi	
fun (n)	pret	lethabo	monyaka	tlhapedi	isiyolo	ukudlala	
funeral (n)	begrafnis	poloko	phupu	phitlho	umngcwabo	umngcwabo	
fungus (n)	swam	mouta	mokgwabo	mothuthuntshwane	ikhowa	isikhunta	
funnel (n)	tregter	mojagobedi	fanele	setshedi	ifanela	isetho	
funny (a)	snaaks	-segišago	-makatsang	-mabela	-ngaqhelekanga	-hlekisayo	
fur (n)	pels	boya	boya	bowa	ufele	uboya	
furniture (n)	meubels	fenitšhara	thepa ya ntlo	fenitšhara	ifenitshala	ifenisha	
further (a)	verder	-ngwe	-pele	-pele	-phambili	phambili	
fuse (n)	sekering	fiuse	nyalano	fiose	isilumeki	ifiyuzi	
fuse (v)	uitbrand	-swa	-thunya	-swa	-tshisa	-fiyuza	
future (n)	toekoms	bokamoso	bokamoso	isago	ikamva	ikusasa	

G	English	Afrikaans	N Sotho	Sesotho	Tswana	Xhosa	Zulu
	gadget (n)	toestelletjie	tlabele	mokgabiso	sengwenyana	isixhobo	isikhaxelisi
	gain (n)	wins	poelo	phaello	poelo	inzuzo	inzuzo
	gain (v)	wen	-holega	-phaella	-sola	-zuza	-zuza
	gale (n)	stormwind	ledimo	sefefo	phefo ya ledimo	uqhwithela	isiphepho
	gall (n)	gal	nyooko	nyooko	gaumakwe	inyongo	inyongo
	gallbladder (n)	galblaas	santlhoko	mokotlana wa nyooko	santlhoko	inyongo	inyongo
	gallery (n)	galery	sethala	galari	bosupaditshwantsho	iqonga	igalari
	gallop (v)	galop	-kgatha	-kgema	-potokela	-phala	-holobha
	gamble (v)	dobbel	-ralokiša tšhelete	-ananya	-iteka lesego	-bheja	-gembula
	game (n)	spel	papadi	papadi	motshameko	umdlalo	umdlalo
	gang (n)	bende	sehlopha sa dikebeke	sehlopha	mophato	iqela	igengi
	gap (n)	opening	mphatšana	phahla	phatlha	isithuba	isikhala
	garage (n)	motorhawe	karatšhe	karatjhe	karaje	igaraji	igalaji
	garden (n)	tuin	serapa	seratswana	tshingwana	isitiya	ingadi
	gargle (v)	gorrel	-kgakgametša	-kgakgatsa	-gagasetsa	-rhazhaza	-hahaza
	garlic (n)	knoffel	konofele	konofole	konofole	ikonofile	ugaliki
	gas (n)	gas	gase	gase	gase	igesi	igesi
	gasp (v)	snak	-fegelwa	-fehelwa	-goga mowa	-khefuza	-befuzela
	gastric (a)	maag	-mogodu	-letshollo	-mogodu	-esisu	okusesiswini
	gate (n)	hek	sefero	heke	kgoro	isango	isango
	gather (v)	byeenkom	-kgobokana	-bokana	-kgobokana	-hlangana	-hlangana
	gathering (n)	byeenkoms	kgobokano	pokano	phuthego	umhlangano	umhlangano
	gauge (n)	meter	kelo	metara	selekanyi	umlinganiso	igeji
	gaze (v)	staar	-lebelela	-tadima	-leba	-jonga	-jolozela
	gear (n)	rat	kere	kere	kere	igiyeri	igeli
	gender (n)	geslag	bong	bong	bong	isini	ubulili
	general (a)	algemeen	-akaretšago	-akaretsang	-kakaretso	-jikelele	-vamile
	generous (a)	vrygewig	-mabobo	-fanang	-pelotshweu	-ophayo	-nokuphana
	genitals (n)	geslagsorgane	dithobong	marete	mapele	umphantsi	izitho zobulili
	gentle (a)	sagmoedig	-bonolo	bonolo	-bonolo	-zolile (yo)	-mnene
	gently (adv)	saggies	gabonolo	-bonolo	ka bonolo	ngokuzolile yo	ngobunono
	geography (n)	aardrykskunde	thutafase	thuto ya lefatshe	thutafatshe	ijografi	umumo womhlaba
	germ (n)	kiem	twatši	kokwana	mogare	intsholongwane	ijemu
	get (v)	kry	-hwetša	-fumana	-amogela	-fumana	-thola
	ghastly (a)	aaklig	-be	-tshabehang	-be	-oyikeka (yo)	-esabekayo
	ghost (n)	gees	moya	sethotsela	sedimo	isiporho	isipoki
	giant (a)	reuse	-gologolo	-senatla	-tonatona	-gantsontso	-sidlakela
	giant (n)	reus	tšitširipa	senatla	rintlhwe	isigantsontso	umdondoshiya
	giddy (a)	duiselig	-šiišago	-tsekela	-sedidi	-nencilikithi	-nesizunguzane
	gifted (a)	begaaf	-filwego	-bohlale	-botlhale	-nesiphiwo	-nobungcweti
	giggle (v)	giggel	-sega	-keketeha	-tshegatshega	-gigitheka	-gigitheka
	gill (n)	kieu	leswafohlapi	letlopo	kgwafo	indawo yokuphefumla yentlanzi	isiphefumulo
	giraffe (n)	kameelperd	thutlwa	thuhlo	thutlwa	indlulamthi	indlulamithi
	girl (n)	meisie	mosetsana	ngwanana	mosetsana	intombi	intombazane
	girlfriend (n)	nooi	moratiwa	kgarebe	kgarebe	umhlobokazi	intombi
	give (v)	gee	-fa	-fa	-fa	-nika	-pha
	glad (a)	bly	-thabišago	-thabile	-itumelang	-vuya	-jabulile
	glamorous (a)	bekoorlik	-rategago	-hlamatsehang	-ntle	-hle	-khangayo
	glance (v)	vlugtig kyk	-gadima	-thalatsa	-gebenya	-krwaqula	-jantiza
	gland (n)	klier	thaka	pudula	kgeleswa	idlala	idlala
	glass (n)	glas	galase	kgalase	galase	iglasi	ingilazi
	gleam (v)	straal	-kganya	-benya	-benya	-khazimla	-khazimula
	glitter (v)	skitter	-phadima	-phatsima	-phatsima	-bengezela	-benyezela
	glory (n)	glorie	letago	kgalalelo	kgalalelo	uzuko	inkazimulo
	glove (n)	handskoen	tlelafo	hansekunu	hanasekhune	iglavu	igilavu
	glovebox (n)	mossienes	sebolokelo	sehlaha	kgetsi ya ga dimo	isigcini-sandla	isigcini-magilavu
	glow (v)	gloei	-pepenya	-laima	-galalela	-qaqamba	-nkemuzela
	glue (n)	gom	segomaretši	boka	sekgomaretsi	isincamathelisi	-namathelisa
	glue (v)	gom	-gomaretša	-ho tlotsa ka boka	-mametlelela	-ncamathelisa	isinamathelisi

English	Afrikaans	N Sotho	Sesotho	Tswana	Xhosa	Zulu	G
glutton (n)	vraat	sejato	monyollo	legodu	isirhovu	isiminzi	
gnash (v)	kners	-tsikitla meno	-tsikitlanya meno	-huranya	-tshixizisa	-gedla	
gnaw (v)	knaag	-kokona	-kuma	-kokona	-grenya	-gegedla	
go (v)	gaan	-ya	-ya	-ya	-hamba	-ya	
goal (n)	doel	koulo	ntlha	maitlhomo	inqaku	injongo	
goat (n)	bok	pudi	podi	podi	ibhokhwe	imbuzi	
god (n)	god	modimo	modimo	ledimo	isithixo	isithixo	
God (n)	God	Modimo	Modimo	Modimo	uThixo	uNkulunkulu	
gold (n)	goud	gauta	kgauta	gouta	igolide	igolide	
good (a)	goed	-botse	-lokile	-molemo	-lungile	-hle	
goods (n)	goedere	diphahlo	diphahlo	dithoto	iimpahla	izimpahla	
goose (n)	gans	leganse	lekgansi	ganse	irhanisi	ihansi	
gooseberry (n)	appelliefie	mommodi	mokutsuberi	thamme	igusbhere	ugqumgqumu	
gossip (n)	skinderpraatjies	mabarebare	ditshebo	ditshebo	intlebendwane	amahemuhemu	
gossip (v)	skinder	-seba	-seba	-seba	-hleba	-hemuza	
govern (v)	regeer	-buša	-busa	-busa	-lawula	-busa	
government (n)	regering	mmušo	mmuso	mmuso	urhulumente	uhulumeni	
gradually (adv)	geleidelik	ka bonya	-butle	monokela	-kancinci	ngokuya-ngokuya	
grain (n)	graan	mabele	thollo	seako	ukhozo	uhlamvu	
grammar (n)	grammatika	popopolelo	thuto ya puo	gerama	igrama	igrama	
granadilla (n)	granadilla	koronatela	keranatela	granadilla	igranadila	uginindela	
granary (n)	graanskuur	sešego	sekiri sa dithollo	sefala	udladla	inqolobane	
grandchild (n)	kleinkind	motlogolo	setloholo	ngwanaangwanaka	umzukulwana	umzukulu	
granddaughter (n)	kleindogter	motlogolo	setloholo	setlogolwana	umzukulwana	umzukulu wesifazane	
grandfather (n)	oupa	rrakgolo	ntatemoholo	ntatemogolo	ubawomkhulu	ubabamkhulu	
grandmother (n)	ouma	koko	nkgono	mmemogolo	umakhulu	ugogo	
grandson (n)	kleinseun	motlogolo	setloholo	setlogolwana	umzukulwana	umzukulu wesilisa	
grape (n)	druiwe	diterebe	morara	terebe	idiliya	amagrebhisi	
grapefruit (n)	pomelo	pomelo	pomelo	pampalamusu	imbambusi	igilibhufuluthi	
grasp (v)	gryp	-swara	-tshwara	-kakara	-bamba	-bamba	
grass (n)	gras	bjang	jwang	tlhaga	ingca	utshani	
grasshopper (n)	sprinkaan	tšie	bookgolane	tsie	intethe	intethe	
grate (v)	rasper	-gohla	-kuma	-gotlha	-khuhla	-khuhla	
grateful (a)	dankbaar	-lebogilego	-lebohang	-lebogang	-nombulelo	-bongayo	
gratitude (n)	dankbaarheid	tebogo	teboho	tebogo	umbulelo	ukubonga	
grave (a)	gewigtig	-bohlokwa	-boima	-mena phatla	-qingqiweyo	-nzima	
grave (n)	graf	lebitla	lebitla	phupu	ingcwaba	ithuna	
gravel (n)	gruis	lekgwara	kerabole	kgwarapana	igrabile	ugedla	
gravy (n)	sous	moro	moro	moro	umhluzi	umhluzi	
grease (n)	ghries	kirisi	kerisi	kerise	igrisi	igrisi	
grease (v)	smeer	-kirisa	tlotsa ka kerisi	-tshasa	-grisa	-gcoba	
greedy (a)	gulsig	-megabaru	-meharo	-megagaru	-bawayo	-phangayo	
green (n)	groen	-tala	botala	tala	uhlaza	-luhlaza	
green pepper (n)	soetrissie	pherefere ye tala	pepere e tala	pherefere	igrinpepa	upelepele oluhlaza	
greet (v)	groet	-dumediša	-dumedisa	-dumedisa	-bulisa	-bingelela	
grey (n)	grys	-putswa	boputswa	-setlha	hobe	-mpunga	
grief (n)	leed	manyami	mahlomola	botlhoko	intlungu	usizi	
grievance (n)	grief	pelaelo	tletlebo	ngongorego	isikhalo	isikhalo	
grill (v)	rooster	-beša	-hadika	-besa	irostile	insimbi yokosa	
grin (n)	grynslag	tšhinyalalo	tsitlamo	motseno	intsinekana	ukusineka	
grin (v)	gryns	-šinyalala	-tsitlama	-tsena	-sineka	-sineka	
grind (v)	maal	-šila	-sila	-sila	-sila	-gaya	
groan (n)	kreun	tsetlo	pobolo	modumo	umncwino	umbhongo	
groan (v)	kreun	-tsetla	-bobola	-duma	-ncwina	-bubula	
groceries (n)	kruideniersware	dikrosari	kerosari	kerousara	ukutya	igilosa	
groin (n)	lies	lengamu	tshwelesa	lengami	umphakatho	imbilapho	
groove (n)	groef	moseto	sekgetshe	mosetlho	umgca okroliweyo	isisele	
ground (a)	gemaal	-šitšwego	-sitsweng	-sidilweng	-siliweyo	-gayiweyo	
ground (n)	grond	mobu	mobu	mmu	umhlaba	umhlabathi	
group (n)	groep	sehlopha	sehlopha	lesomo	iqela	isiqumbi	

G	English	Afrikaans	N Sotho	Sesotho	Tswana	Xhosa	Zulu
	grow (v)	groei	-mela	-mela	-gola	-khula	-mila
	growl (v)	knor	-bopa	-rora	-kurutla	-vungama	-bhovumula
	grudge (n)	wrok	sekgopi	sekgopi	tshele	inzondo	igqubu
	grumble (v)	brom	-ngunanguna	korotla	-ngongorega	-mbombozela	-khononda
	guarantee (n)	waarborg	tiišetšo	ho ema paneng	netefaletso	isiqinisekiso	isiqinisekiso
	guarantee (v)	waarborg	-tiišetša	-ema pane	-netefatsa	-qinisekisa	-qinisekisa
	guard (n)	wag	moleti	molebedi	modisa	igadi	ugadi
	guard (v)	bewaak	-leta	-lebela	-disa	-gada	-gada
	guardian (n)	voog	mofepi	mohlokomedi	motlamedi	ikhankatha	umondli
	guava (n)	koejawel	kwaba	kwaba	kwaba	igwava	ugwavu
	guerrilla (n)	guerrilla	motšhošetši	raqhwe	belerutwane	igorila	igorila
	guess (n)	raaiskoot	kakanyo	kakanyo	kabelelo	iqashiso	umqandelo
	guess (v)	raai	-akanya	-akanya	-abelela	-qashela	-qandela
	guest (n)	gas	moeng	moeti	moeti	undwendwe	isimenywa
	guide (n)	gids	mohlahli	motataisi	mosupatsela	isikhokelo	igayidi
	guilt (n)	skuld	molato	molato	molato	ityala	icala
	guilty (a)	skuldig	-nago le molato	-molato	-molato	-netyala	-necala
	guineafowl (n)	tarentaal	kgaka	kgaka	kgaka	impangele	impangele
	guitar (n)	kitaar	katara	katara	katara	ikatali	isiginxi
	gull (n)	meeu	mohuta wa nonyana ya lewatle	ledinyane la sephooko		ingabangaba	inyoni-yolwandle
	gullet (n)	slukderm	mometšo	mmetso	mometso	ummizo	umphimbo
	gum (n)	tandvleis	marinini	lerenene	marinini	intsini	insini
	gun (n)	geweer	sethunya	sethunya	tlhobolo	umpu	isibhamu
	gutter (n)	geut	kathara	foro	moedi	igatha	igatha
	gymnastics (n)	gimnastiek	dithobollo	ho tswedipanya mmele	jiminastiki	imithambo	imigilingwane yokuzivivinya
	habit (n)	gewoonte	tlwaelo	tlwaelo	mokgwa	isiqhelo	injwayelo
	haemorrhage (n)	bloeding	go dutla madi	ho dutla madi	tutlamadi	ukopha	umopho
	haemorrhoids (n)	aambeie	matšala	ho petsoha ha sebono	tutlamadi	izikhala	imizoko
	hail (n)	hael	sefako	sefako	sefako	isichotho	isiqhotho
	hair (n)	hare	moriri	boya	moriri	iinwele	izinwele
	hairdresser (n)	haarkapper	mokoti wa moriri	mokuti	mopomi	umchebi	umcwali
	hairy (a)	harig	-meriri ye men-tšimmeleng	-boya	-mariri	-noboya	-noboya
	half (n)	helfte	seripagare	halofo	sephatlo	isiqingatha	uhhafu
	hall (n)	saal	holo	holo	ntlolehalahala	iholo	ihholo
	halt (v)	stop	-emiša	-kgefutsa	-kgonya	-ma	-ma
	halve (v)	halveer	-ripa ka bogare	-fokotsa ka lehare	-halofa	-canda kubini	-caza kabili
	ham (n)	ham	nama ya serope sa kolobe	hemo	nama ya kolobe	isihlunu sehagu	uhemu
	hamburger (n)	hamburger	hampeka	hambekara	hambeka	ihambhega	ihemubhega
	hammer (n)	hamer	hamola	noto	hamore	ihamile	isando
	hammer (v)	hamer	-kokotela	-mula	-touta	-bethelela	-bethela
	hand (n)	hand	seatla	letsoho	seatla	isandla	isandla
	handcuff (n)	boei	tshipiphodisa	lehlaahlela	-golega	ikhamandela	-faka uzankosi
	handkerchief (n)	sakdoek	sakatuku	sakatuku	sakatuku	itshefu	iduku
	handle (n)	handvatsel	mokgoko	mohwele	mofinyana	isiphatho	isibambo
	handle (v)	hanteer	-swara	-tshwara	-tshwara ka matsogo	-phatha	-phatha
	handsome (a)	aantreklik	-bogegago	-tle	-ntle	-nomkhitha	-bukekayo
	handwork (n)	handewerk	modiro wa diatla	mosebetsi wa matsoho	tiro ya diatla	umsebenzi wezandla	izinto ezenziwe ngezandla
	handwriting (n)	handskrif	mongwalo	mongolo	mokwalo	ukubhala	isandla
	hang (v)	hang	-fega	-fanyeha	-kalela	-xhoma	-lengisa
	happen (v)	gebeur	-diragala	-etsahala	-direga	-enzeka	-vela
	happiness (n)	geluk	lethabo	nyakallo	boitumelo	uvuyo	injabulo
	happy (a)	gelukkig	-lethabo	-nyakalletseng	-itumelang	-vuyayo	-thokozile
	harbour (n)	hawe	boemakepe	kou	boemakepe	izibuko	itheku
	hard (a)	hard	-thata	-thata	-thata	-lukhuni	-lukhuni

English	Afrikaans	N Sotho	Sesotho	Tswana	Xhosa	Zulu	**H**
hard (a)	moeilik	-boima	-boima	-thata	-nzima	-nzima	
harm (n)	skade	tshenyegelo	tshenyo	tsenyo	umonakalo	ukulimala	
harmful (a)	skadelik	-kotsi	-senyang	-kotsi	-onakalisayo	-nengozi	
harmless (a)	onskadelik	-se nago kotsi	-se nang tshenyo	-seng kotsi	-nabungozi	-ngenangozi	
harmonica (n)	harmonika	seletšo sa hamonika	haremonika	foleiki	ifleyiti	uhlobo logubhu	
harmony (n)	harmonie	kwanadumo	kutlwano	kutlwano	imvisiswano	ukuzwana	
harp (n)	harp	harepa	harepa	harapa	ugwali	uhabhu	
harvest (n)	oes	puno	kotulo	thobo	isivuno	isivuno	
harvest (v)	oes	-buna	-kotula	-roba	-vuna	-vuna	
haste (n)	haas	lebelo	mojaho	boitlhaganelo	ukungxama	ukusheshisa	
hasty (a)	haastig	-lebelo	-jahileng	-boitlhaganelo	-ngxamileyo	-sheshisa	
hat (n)	hoed	kefa	katiba	futshe	umnqwazi	isigqoko	
hate (v)	haat	-hloya	-hloya	-tlhoa	-thiya	-zonda	
hateful (a)	haatlik	-hloiwago	-hloyang	-ilwang	-thiyileyo	-zondekayo	
hatred (n)	haat	lehloyo	lehloyo	letlhoo	intiyo	inzondo	
haughty (a)	hoogmoedig	-ikgogomošago	-ikgohomosang	-ikgodisang	-ziphakamisileyo	-thwele ikhanda	
have (v)	hê	-na	-ba	-nna le	-ba na-	(-ba-) na-	
hawk (n)	valk	sepekwa	phakwe	nkgodi	ukhetshe	uhele	
haze (n)	waas	mogodi	mohodi	mouwane	inkungu	ufasimbe	
he (pron)	hy	yena	yena	ene	yena	yena	
head (n)	kop	hlogo	hlooho	tlhogo	intloko	ikhanda	
headache (n)	hoofpyn	go rengwa ke hlogo	hlooho e opang	go opa ga tlhogo	intloko ebuhlungu	ukuphathwa ikhanda	
headline (n)	opskrif	hlogo	sehlooho	setlhogo	intloko yomhlathi	isihloko	
heal (v)	genees	-alafa	-phekola	-fodisa	-phila	-elapha	
health (n)	gesondheid	pholo	bophelo bo botle	boitekanelo	impilo	impilo	
healthy (a)	gesond	-phelago gabotse	-phetseng hantle	-itekanelang	-philile	-philile	
heap (n)	hoop	mokgobo	qubu	mokgobe	imfumba	inqwaba	
heap (v)	ophoop	-kgoba	-bokella	-kgobela	-fumba	-nqwabela	
hear (v)	hoor	-kwa	-utlwa	-utlwa	-va	-zwa	
hearsay (n)	hoorsê	mabarebare	bobare	magatwe	undiva	inzwabethi	
heart (n)	hart	pelo	pelo	pelo	intliziyo	inhliziyo	
heartbeat (n)	hartklop	morethetho wa pelo	ho uba ha pelo	mokibo wa pelo	ukungongoza	ukushaya kwenhliziyo	
heartburn (n)	sooibrand	seokolela	lesokolla	lesokolela	isitshisa	isilungulela	
hearth (n)	haard	sebešo	leifo	leiso	iziko	iziko	
heat (n)	hitte	phišo	motjheso	mogote	ubushushu	ukushisa	
heat (v)	warm maak	-ruthetša	-futhumatsa	-gotela	-shushubeza	-fudumeza	
heathen (n)	heiden	moheitene	mohetene	moheitene	ubuhedeni	umhedeni	
heaven (n)	hemel	legodimo	lehodimo	legodimo	izulu	izulu	
heavy (a)	swaar	-boima	-boima	-boima	-nzima	-sinda	
hedge (n)	heining	legora	seotlwana	legora	intendelezo	uthango	
heed (v)	in ag neem	-hlokomela	-ela tlhoko	-tsaya tsia	-lumka	-naka	
heel (n)	hak	serethe	serethe	serethe	isithende	isithende	
heifer (n)	vers	sethole	sethole	moroba	ithokazi	isithole	
height (n)	hoogte	bogodimo	bophahamo	bogodimo	ukuphakama	ukuphakama	
heir (n)	erfgenaam	mojalefa	mojalefa	mojaboswa	indlalifa	indlalifa	
hell (n)	hel	hele	dihele	molete wa molelo	isihogo	kwalasha	
help (n)	hulp	thušo	thuso	thusego	unceda	usizo	
help (v)	help	-thuša	-thusa	-thusa	-nceda	-siza	
helpful (a)	behulpsaam	-thušago	-thusang	-thusang	-ncedayo	-sizayo	
helpless (a)	hulpeloos	-hlokago	-hlokang thuso	-naya pelo	-ngenaluncedo	-thithibele	
hem (n)	soom	lemeno	momeno	lemeno	umgobo	umthungo	
hen (n)	hen	kgogotshadi	sethole	kgogo	isikhukukazi	isikhukhukazi	
her (pron)	haar	-mo-	yena	ene	yena	yena	
herbalist (n)	kruiekenner	ramešunkwane	ramethokgo	ngaka	ixhwele	inyanga yamakhambi	
herbs (n)	kruie	mošunkwane	methokgo	setlama	iyeza	ikhambi	
herd (n)	kudde	mohlape	mohlape	motlhape	umhlambi	umhlambi	
here (adv)	hier	mo	mona	fa	apha	lapha	
heritage (n)	erfenis	bohwa	lefa	boswa	ilifa	ifa	
hero (n)	held	senatla	mohale	mogaka	iqhawe	iqhawe	
heron (n)	reier	kokolohute	seotsanyana	kokolohutwe	ukhwalimanzi	indwandwe	

H	English	Afrikaans	N Sotho	Sesotho	Tswana	Xhosa	Zulu
	hers (pron)	hare	-gagwe	-hae	-gagwe	-khe	okwakhe
	hesitate (v)	aarsel	-dikadika	-tsilatsila	-kabakanya	-thandabuza	-zindela
	hesitation (n)	aarseling	tikadiko	-tsilatsilo	kabakanyo	intandabuzo	ukuzindela
	hiccough (n)	hik	sethekhu	thaabe	kgodisa	ukukhutywa	intwabi
	hidden (a)	versteek	-utilwego	-patilweng	-fitlhilweng	-fihlakeleyo	-fihliwe
	hide (v)	wegsteek	-uta	-pata	-fitlha	-fihla	-fihla
	high (a)	hoog	-godimo	-phahameng	godimo	-phakamile(yo)	-phakeme
	higher (a)	hoër	-godingwana	-phahameng ho feta	godimodimo	-phakamile(yo)	-phakeme kakhudlwana
	highveld (n)	hoëveld	nagadimo	naha e phahameng	nagadimo	ummandla omathafa	inkangala
	hijack (v)	skaak	-tšea ka dikgoka	-kgelosa ka dikgoka	-utswa	qweqwedisa	ukubamba inkunzi
	hill (n)	heuwel	mmoto	leralla	lekgaba	induli	igquma
	him (pron)	hom	-mo-	yena	ene	yena	yena
	hinder (v)	hinder	-thibela	-kgathatsa	-fera	-khathaza	-thiya
	hindrance (n)	hindernis	sekgopi	-tshitiso	kgoreletso	inkathazo	isithiyo
	hinge (n)	hingsel	mokgoko	sekanire	sekaniri	ihenjisi	ihinji
	hip (n)	heup	letheka	noka	noka	ihleza	inqulu
	hippopotamus (n)	seekoei	kubu	kubu	kubu	imvubu	imvubu
	hire (v)	huur	-hira	-hira	-hira	qesha	-qasha
	his (pron)	sy	-gagwe	-hae	ene	-khe	okwakhe
	his (pron)	syne	-gagwe	-hae	-gagwe	-khe	okwakhe
	hiss (v)	sis	-huetša	-letsa molodi	-suma	-futha	-khisila
	history (n)	geskiedenis	histori	nalane	ditiragalo	imbali	umlando
	hit (v)	slaan	-itia	-otla	-itaya	-betha	-shaya
	hoarse (a)	hees	-makgwakgwa	-makgerehlwa	-magweregwere	-rhabaxa	-hoshozile
	hobby (n)	stokperdjie	boitiša	ho itlosa bodutu	tiro ya maitiso	ihobhil isidlalo	umsebenzana wokuzilibazisa
	hoe (v)	skoffel	-hlagola	-hlahola	-tlhagola	-hlakula	-hlakula
	hold (n)	vat	moswaro	tshwaro	seduti	ukubamba	ukubamba
	hold (v)	hou	-swara	-tshwara	-tshwara	-bamba	-bamba
	hole (n)	gat	molete	mokoti	mosima	umngxuma	umgodi
	holiday (n)	vakansie	maikhutšo	phomolo	boikhutso	ikhefu	iholide
	hollow (a)	hol	-gorutšwego	-mohohoma	-lehuti	-ze	-ligobongo
	holy (a)	heilig	-kgethwa	-halalelang	-boitshepo	-ngcwele	-ngcwele
	home (n)	tuiste	legae	lapeng	legae	ikhaya	ikhaya
	homework (n)	huiswerk	modiro wa gae	mosebetsi wa lapeng	tirolegae	umsebenzi wasekhaya	umsebenzi wasekhaya
	homosexual (n)	homoseksueel		-rata wa bong ba hao		italasi	isitabane
	honest (a)	eerlik	-tshepegago	-tshepahalang	-boikanyo	-msulwa	-qotho
	honesty (n)	eerlikheid	botshepegi	botshepehi	boikanyo	ubumsulwa	ubuqotho
	honey (n)	heuning	tswina	mahe a dinotshi	tswine ya dinotshe	ubusi	uju
	honeymoon (n)	wittebrood	hanimunu	hanimunu	madilotsana	ixesha lobumnandi emvakomtshato	ihanimuni
	honour (n)	eer	tlhompho	tlhompho	tlotlego	imbeko	inhlonipho
	honour (v)	eer	-hlompha	-hlompha	-tlotla	-nika imbeko	-hlonipha
	hoof (n)	hoef	tlhako	tlhako	tlhako	uphuphu	isondo
	hook (n)	haak	kobi	huku	sekgwage	igwegwe	ihhuku
	hook (v)	haak	-haka	-haka	-kgogetsa	-gwegwa	-hhuka
	hooligan (n)	skollie	tsotsi	setlokotsebe	sekebekwa	indlavini	isichwensi
	hoot (v)	toet	-letša nakana ya mmotoro	-letsa phala	-letsa lenaka	-khalisa uphondo	-popoza
	hop (v)	hop	-taboga	-tlolatlola	-kopakopa	-tsiba	-kheleza
	hope (n)	hoop	kholofelo	tshepo	tsholofelo	ithemba	ithemba
	hope (v)	hoop	-holofela	-tshepa	-solofela	-themba	-ethemba
	horizon (n)	horison	bogomapono	pheletsong ya lefatshe	khutlopono	ulundi	impelamehlo
	horizontal (a)	horisontaal	-rapamego	-tshekalletseng	-rapameng	-mtyaba	-thwishikile
	horn (n)	horing	lenaka	lenaka	lenaka	uphondo	uphondo
	horror (n)	afsku	tšhiišo	masisapelo	tsitsibanyo	uloyiko	okwesabekayo
	horse (n)	perd	pere	pere	pitse	ihashe	ihhashi
	horserace (n)	perdewedren	mokato wa dipere	reisisi ya dipere	lebelo la dipitse	umdyarho	umjaho wamahhashi
	horseshoe (n)	hoefyster	seeta sa pere	tshepe ya pere	tlhako ya pitse	isiporo	isipolo sehhashi
	hose (n)	tuinslang	lethopo	housephaephe	lethompo	umbhobho	ithumbu

English	Afrikaans	N Sotho	Sesotho	Tswana	Xhosa	Zulu I
hospital (n)	hospitaal	sepetlele	sepetlele	bookelo	isibhedlele	isibhedlela
host (n)	gasheer	monggae	moamohelabaeti	mong-gae	umndwendwelwa	umninindlu
host (v)	gasheer wees	-tlametla	-ho amohela baeti	-nna mong-gae	-amkela iindwendwe	ukubungaza izivakashi
hot dog (n)	worsbroodjie	senkgwanaboroso	hotedoko	hotdog	ihotdogi	ihodogi
hot (a)	warm	-borutho	-tjhesa	-bolelo	-shushu	-fudumele
hotel (n)	hotel	hotele	hotele	hotele	ihotele	ihhotela
hour (n)	uur	iri	hora	ura	iyure	i-awa
house (n)	huis	ngwako	ntlo	ntlo	indlu	indlu
house (v)	huisves	-fa marobalo	-amohela tlung	-nnisa	-qulatha	-hlalisa
household (n)	huishouding	lapa	lelapa	motse	indlu	abomuzi bonke
hovel (n)	pondok	mošašana	mokgoro	ntlwana	ixhobongwana	ifuku
how (adv)	hoe	bjang	jwang	jang	njani	kanjani
however (conj)	maar	eupša	empa	le gale	kodwa	nokho
howl (v)	tjank	-golola	-ngaya	-kua	-khonkotha	-hhewula
huge (a)	reusagtig	-gologolo	-kgolohadi	-tona	-khulu	-yisibhidli
human (a)	menslik	-botho	-botho	-setho	-omntu	-obuntu
humane (a)	mensliewend	-botho	-botho	-setho	-nobuntu	-nomusa
humble (a)	nederig	-ikokobetšago	-ikokobeditseng	-boikokobetso	-lulamile(yo)	-thobile
humid (a)	klam	-monola	-leswe	-bokgola	-fumile	-manzana
humiliate (v)	verneder	-kokobetša	-nyenyefatsa	-nyenyefatsa	phoxa	-dumaza
humility (n)	nederigheid	boikokobetšo	boikokobetso	boikokobetso	ubuntu	intobeko
humour (n)	humor	tshegišo	qabolo	metlae	uburharha	inhliziyo
hunchback (n)	boggelrug	lehutlo	kgirimpana	thotane	isifombo	isifumbu
hundred (n)	honderd	lekgolo	lekgolo	lekgolo	ikhulu	ikhulu
hunger (n)	honger	tlala	tlala	tlala	indlala	ukulamba
hungry (a)	honger	-swerwego ke tlala	-lapileng	-tshwerweng ke tlala	-lambile(yo)	-lambile
hunt (v)	jag	-tsoma	-tsoma	-tsoma	-zingela	-zingela
hunter (n)	jagter	motsomi	setsomi	motsomi	umzingeli	umzingeli
hurry (v)	jaag	-phakiša	-phalla	-potlaka	-ngxama	-phangisa
hurt (v)	seermaak	-gobatša	-ntsha kotsi	-bolaya	-enzakala	-limaza
husband (n)	man	monna	mohatsa	monona	indoda- umyeni	umyeni
husk (n)	skil	lekgapetla	sekgapetla	letlapi	umququ	amahluba
hut (n)	hut	ntlo	mokgoro	mogope	inqugwala	iqhugwane
hyena (n)	hiëna	phiri	lefiritshwane	phiri-e-thamaga	ixhwili	impisi
hygiene (n)	higiëne	maphelo	paballo ya mmele	boitekanelo	impilo	inhlanzeko
hymn (n)	gesang	sefela	sefela	sefala	iculo	ihubo
hyphen (n)	koppelteken	tlami	tlami	tlamanyi	iqhagamshela	ihayifini
hypocrite (n)	skynheilige	moikaketši	moikaketsi	moitimokanyi	umhanahanisi	umzenzisi
hysterics (n)	histerie	mafofonyane	lehabea	mafofonyane	isiphoso	umhayizo
I (pron)	ek	nna	nna/ke-	nna	ndi-	ngi-
ice (n)	ys	lehlwa	leqhwa	kgapetla	umkhenkce	iqhwa
ice cream (n)	roomys	aesekherimi	aesekerimi	bebetsididi	iayiskrim	u-ayisikhilimu
icing (n)	versiersuiker	swikirikgabiša	tswekeresekgabisi	sukiri	isihombisi-keyiki	i-ayisingi
idea (n)	idee	kgopolo	kgopolo	kgopolo	ingcinga	umcabango
ideal (a)	ideaal	maikemišetšo	-hlamatsehang	-maikaelelo	-sengqondweni	-hle
identify (v)	identifiseer	-hlaola	-tseba	-bontsha	-alatha	-khomba
identity (n)	identiteit	boitšhupo	boitsebiso	temogo	ukufana	uqobo lwa-
idiom (n)	idioom	seka	maelana	leele	isaci	isisho
idiot (n)	idioot	setlaela	sethoto	sematla	isitunxa	isilima
idle (a)	ledig	-dutšego ka matsogo	-botswa	-thuba kobo segole	-nqenayo	-ngenzi lutho
idol (n)	afgod	modingwana	modingwana	seseto	intandane	isithixo
if (conj)	as	ge	ha	fa	ukuba	uma
ignite (v)	aansteek	-gotetša	-hotetsa	-gotsa	-lumeka	-okhela
ignition (n)	ontsteking	kgotelo	kgotetso	kgotso	ukulumeka	ukokheleka
ignorance (n)	onkunde	bothotho	ho hloka tsebo	go ikapaya mokatse	intswelo-kwazi	ukungazi
ignore (v)	ignoreer	-hlokomologa	-lala ka mmele	-tlhodisa matlho	-sukunaka	-nganaki
ill (a)	siek	-lwalago	-kula	-bobolang	-gula(yo)	-gula
illegal (a)	onwettig	-ganwago ke molao	-sa yeng ka molao	-e seng ka fa molaong	-ngekho mthethweni	-phambene nomthetho
illegitimate (a)	buite-egtelik	-ka ntle ga lenyalo	letla-le-pepilwe	-wa dikgora	-mgqakhwe	ngaphandle komthetho

English	Afrikaans	N Sotho	Sesotho	Tswana	Xhosa	Zulu
illness (n)	siekte	bolwetši	lefu	bolwetse	isigulo	ukugula
illuminate (v)	verlig	-bonegela	-kgantsha	-sedifatsa	-cacisa	-khanyisa
illustrate (v)	illustreer	-šupetša	-tshwantsha	-tshwantsha	-bonisa	-veza iziboniso
illustration (n)	illustrasie	seswantšho	setshwantsho	tshwantsho	umboniso	isiboniso
ill-mannered (a)	onmanierlik	-sa itshwarego	-mekgwa e mebe	-se nang maitseo	-ngenambeko	-ngahloniphi
ill-treat (v)	mishandel	-tlaiša	-tlatlapa	-kgokgontsha	-phatha kakubi	-phatha kabi
image (n)	beeld	tshwantšho	setshwantsho	setshwano	umfanekiso-ntelekelelo	isithombe
imagine (v)	verbeel	-nagana	-akanya	-tshwantsha	-thelekelela	-cabanga
imitate (v)	namaak	-ekiša	-etsisa	-etsa	-linganisa	-fanisa
immature (a)	onvolwasse	-sa golago	-sa butswang	-tala	-ngekakhuli	-luhlaza
immediate (a)	onmiddellik	-semeetseng	hanghang	-akofa	-kwamsinya	manje
immerse (v)	indompel	-inela	-ina	-ina	-ntywilisa	-cwilisa
immigrate (v)	immigreer	-falala	-falla	-fudugela	-ba ngummi kwelinye ilizwe	-fika ezweni
immodest (a)	onbeskeie	-hlabišago dihlong	-tala	-maikgantsho	-sileyo	-ngenazinhloni
immoral (a)	onsedelik	-bootswa	-be	-bosenabotho	-nyala	-ngcolile
immune (a)	onvatbaar	-soutilwego	-tshwaedisitswe	-tlhabetsweng	-gonyekileyo	-gonyiwe
immunise (v)	immuniseer	-soutiša	-tshwaedisa	-tlhabela	-gonya	-goma
impatient (a)	ongeduldig	-felago pelo	-fela pelo	-felang pelo	-tshiseka(yo)	-xhamazele
imperfect (a)	onvolmaak	-sa phethegago	-sa phethehang	-seng botlalo	-ngagqibelelanga	-ngaphelele
impersonal (a)	onpersoonlik	-hlokago botho	-hloka botho	-sa ipeeng	-ngabhekisi mntwini	-ngaphathelene nabantu
impertinence (n)	astrantheid	moreba	botlokotsebe	bokgwafo	-secaleni	ukweyisa
impolite (a)	onbeleef	-hlokago tlhompho	-sa hlompheng	-makgakga	-ngenambeko	-ngahloniphi
import (n)	invoer	ditšwantle	kgwebiso	seraopo	impahla ethengwe kwelinye ilizwe	impahla engeniswayo
import (v)	invoer	-tliša go tšwa ntle	-hwebisa	-raopa	-thenga kwelinye ilizwe	-ngenisa
important (a)	belangrik	-bohlokwa	-bohlokwa	-botlhokwa	-balulekile(yo)	qavile
impossible (a)	onmoontlik	-sa kgonegego	-sitang	-tata	-ngenakwenzeka	-ngenakwenzeka
impoverish (v)	verarm	-diitša	-fumanehisa	-didisa	-hlwempuza	-phofisa
impress (v)	beïndruk	-khahla	-kgahla	-kgatla	-thabathekisa	-zwisisa
improper (a)	onfatsoenlik	-sa swanelago	-fosahetse	-molema	-ngafanelekanga	-ngafanele
improve (v)	verbeter	-kaonafatša	-lokisa	-tlhabolola	-phucula	-enza kubengcono
improvement (n)	verbetering	kaonafatšo	tokiso	tlhabologo	impucuko	ubungcono
in (prep)	in	-(e)ng	ho/ka/ka hara	mo teng	phakathi	phakathi kwa-
inanimate (a)	leweloos	-sa phelego	-sa pheleng	-sa pheleng	-ngaphiliyo	-ngezwayo
inattentive (a)	onoplettend	-sa hlokomelego	-sa eleng hloko	-sa tlhokomelang	-ngamameli(yo)	-ngalaleli
inaudible (a)	onhoorbaar	-sa kwagalego	-sa utlwahaleng	-sa utlwang	-ngavakali(yo)	-ngezwakali
inch (n)	duim	noko	senoko	noko	i-intshi	iyintshi
incident (n)	voorval	tiragalo	ketsahalo	tiragalo	ingczi isehlo	isigameko
include (v)	insluit	-akaretša	-kenya	-akaretsa	-qukanisa	-faka
inclusive (a)	inklusief	-akaretšago	-kenyang	-akaretsang	-qukile(yo)	-phakathi
income (n)	inkomste	puno	moputso	lotseno	umamkelo	iholo
incomplete (a)	onvolledig	-sa felelago	-sa phethehang	-sa felang	-ngagqibekanga	-ngaphelele
incorrect (a)	onjuis	-fošagetšego	-phoso	-maaka	-ngalunganga	-ngalungile
increase (n)	verhoging	koketšo	keketso	koketso	isongezelelo	ukukhula
increase (v)	vermeerder	-oketša	-eketsa	-oketsa	-ongeza	-khula
increment (n)	verhoging	kokeletšo	kekeletso	koketso	uchatha	ukuqhutshwa kweholo
incurable (a)	ongeneeslik	-sa alafegego	-sa phekoleheng	-seemera	-nganyangekiyo	-ngenakwelashwa
indeed (adv)	werklik	ka kgonthe	ka nnete	tota	kanye	impela
independent (a)	onafhanklik	-ipušago	-lokolohileng	-boipuso	-ngaxhomekekanga	-zimele
index (n)	indeks	tšhupane	tsekahare	dikaelo	uluhlu lwamagama	inkomba
indigenous (a)	inheems	-semelafa	-setala	-tlholegileng	-nkulelane	-kwemvelo
indigestion (n)	slegte spysvertering	tšhilegompe	pipitlelo	mogosane	ukungetyisi	unjongwe
indirect (a)	indirek	-sa lebanyago	-kwekwetlang	-motsopodia	-ngokungathanga ngqo	-zombelezayo
individual (n)	individu	motho	mong	bonosi	umntu	umuntu munye
indoctrinate (v)	indoktrineer	-laela	-hlohlelletsa	-tsenya kakanyo	-hlohla	-funza ngemfundiso ethile
indolent (a)	traag	-tšwafago	-botswa	-botshwakga	-nqenayo	-yivila
industrial (a)	industrieel	-intasteri	-matsoho	-sa diatla	-yoshishino	okomsebenzi wohwebo

English	Afrikaans	N Sotho	Sesotho	Tswana	Xhosa	Zulu	I
industrious (a)	vlytig	-mafolofolo	-kgothetseng	-senatla	-khutheleyo	-khuthele	
inevitable (a)	onvermydelik	-sa phemegego	-ke keng ya phengwa	-sa thibelegeng	-za kwenzeka	-ngenakuvinjelwa	
infancy (n)	kleintyd	bosea	bosea	bongwana	ubuntwana	ubungane	
infant (n)	suigeling	lesea	lesea	ngwanyana	umntwana	ingane esancelayo	
infect (v)	besmet	-fetetša	-tshwaetsa	-fetetsa	-sulela	-thelela	
infectious (a)	besmetlik	-fetelago	-tshwaetsang	-fetelelang	-sulelayo	okuthathelwanayo	
inflamed (a)	onsteek	-kekago	-petlileng	-gotetseng	-tshileyo	-okudumbile	
inflammation (n)	ontsteking	keko	petlo	kgotelo	ukukrala	ukudumba	
inflate (v)	opblaas	-budulela	-butswela	-budulela	-vuthela	-futha	
inflation (n)	inflasie	infleišene	infoleishene	puduloso	i-infleyishini	isivuthela	
influence (n)	invloed	tutuetšo	matla	tlhotlheletso	ifuthe	ithonya	
influence (v)	beïnvloed	-tutuetša	-susumetsa	-tlhotlheletsa	-ba nefuthe	-thonya	
influenza (n)	griep	fulu	mokakallane	letshoroma	umkhuhlane	imfuluyenza	
influx (n)	instroming	tšhologelo	tshubuhlellano	thologelo	ukungena	ukuthutheleka	
inform (v)	meedeel	-tsebiša	-tsebisa	-bega	-azisa	-azisa	
information (n)	inligting	tsebo	tsebiso	tshedimosetso	ulwazi	umbiko	
informer (n)	verklikker	molomatsebe	lehlabaphio	molomatsebe	umazisi	umcebi	
infuriate (v)	woedend maak	-galefiša	-halefisa	-galetsha	-banga umsindo	-thukuthelisa	
inherit (v)	erf	-ja lefa	-ja lefa	-ja boswa	-fumana ilifa	-thola njengefa	
inheritance (n)	erfenis	lefa	lefa	boswa	ilifa	ifa	
initial (n)	voorletter	tlhakapele	enisheale	tlhakaina	unobumba	iletha lokuqala	
inject (v)	inspuit	-hlabela	-hlaba	-tlhaba	-tofa	-hlaba	
injection (n)	inspuiting	tlhabelo	tlhabo	lemao	utofo	uhlabo	
injury (n)	besering	kgobalo	leqeba	ntho	ukwenzakala	ingozi	
ink (n)	ink	enke	enke	enke	i-inki	uyinki	
inland (a)	binnelands	-nagagare	-hare ha naha	nagagare	-ngaphakathi	-phakathi nezwe	
innocent (a)	onskuldig	-hlokago molato	-hloka molato	se nang molato	-msulwa	-msulwa	
inoculate (v)	inent	-hlabela	-enta	enta	-hlaba	-jova	
inoculation (n)	inenting	tlhabelo	moento	mokento	utofo	umjovo	
inquest (n)	doodsondersoek	tlhahlobo ya mohu	patlisiso ya lekgotla	patlisiso ya loso	uphando	ukuhlolwa kwe-mbangela yokufa	
inquire (v)	navraag doen	-nyakišiša	-botsa	-botsa	-buzisa	-buza	
inquiry (n)	navraag	nyakišišo	potso	potso	ukubuza	ukubuza	
inquisitive (a)	nuuskierig	-nyakago go tseba ditaba	-ratang ditaba	-swegaswega	-qavileyo	-nenhlazane	
insane (a)	kranksinnig	-gafago	-hlanya	-tsenwang	-phambeneyo	-hlanyayo	
insanity (n)	kranksinnigheid	bogafa	bohlanya	botseno	impambano	ukuhlanya	
insect (n)	insek	khunkhwane	kokwanyana	tshenekegi	isinambuzane	isinambuzane	
inside (adv)	binne	ka gare	ka hare	teng	ngaphakathi	phakathi	
insist (v)	aandring	-phegelela	-pheella	-tswetelela	-nyanzelisa	-gcizelela	
insistence (n)	aandrang	phegelelo	pheello	tswetelelo	unyanzelo	isigcizelelo	
insolence (n)	parmantigheid	kgang	manganga	makgakga	isigezo	ukungahloniphi	
insomnia (n)	slaaploosheid	tlhobaelo	tlhobaelo	tlhobaelo	isifo sokungalali	ukuqwasha	
inspect (v)	inspekteer	-hlahloba	-hlahloba	-lebaleba	-hlola	-hlola	
inspection (n)	inspeksie	tlhahlobo	hlahlobo	tekolo	uhlolo	ukuhlola	
inspector (n)	inspekteur	mohlahlobi	mohlahlobi	motlhatlhobi	umhloli	umhloli	
instantly (adv)	oombliklik	ka ponyo ya leihlo	-hanghang	ka nakonyana	ngokukhawuleza	khona-manje	
instep (n)	boog	boraoto	mokokotlo wa leoto	khubu	umphezulu wonyawo	amathe onyawo	
instinct (n)	instink	tlhago	sehlaho	tlhago	ithuku	isazela	
instruct (v)	onderrig	-ruta	-rupela	-kaela	-yalela	-fundisa	
instruction (n)	onderrig	thuto	thupelo	kaelo	umyalelo	umyalo	
instructor (n)	instrukteur	molaedi	morupedi	mokaedi	umyaleli	umfundisi	
instrument (n)	instrument	sedirišwa	sesebediswa	sediriswa	isixhobo	isikhali somsebenzi	
insubordinate (a)	ongehoorsaam	-sa kwego	-tellang	-gananang	-ngevayo	-delela	
insult (n)	belediging	kgobošo	tlhapa	sekgopi	isithuko	inhlamba	
insult (v)	beledig	-goboša	-hlapaola	-tlhapatsa	-thuka	-thuka	
insurance (n)	versekering	tšhireletšo	enshorense	putlelelo	i-inshorensi	inshuwarensi	
integrity (n)	integriteit	potego	bokgabane	thokgamo	ingqiqo	ubuqotho	
intelligence (n)	intelligensie	bohlale	hlalefo	botlhale	ubukrele-krele	inhlakanipho	
intelligent (a)	intelligent	-bohlale	-bohlale	-tlhogo	-krele-krele	-khaliphile	

English	Afrikaans	N Sotho	Sesotho	Tswana	Xhosa	Zulu
intend (v)	van plan wees	-ikemišetša	-rera	-ikaelela	-funa	-hlosa
interest (n)	belang	kgahlego	tjheseho	kgatlhego	umdla	umnako
interest (v)	interesseer	-kgahla	-kgahla	-kgatlhega	-enza umdla	-thatheka
interesting (a)	interessant	-kgahlišago	-kgahlisang	-kgatlhang	-nomdla	okunakisayo
interior (n)	binneste	bokateng	bohare	leteng	umphakathi	ingaphakathi
internal (a)	intern	-ka gare	-ka hare	-selegae	-ngaphakathi	ngaphakathi
international (a)	internasionaal	-ditšhaba	-matjhaba	-ditšhaba	-kazwelonke	-ezizwe ngezizwe
interpret (v)	vertolk	-hlatholla	-toloka	-phutholola	-toloka	-humusha
interpreter (n)	tolk	mofetoledi	toloko	mofetoledi	itoliki	umhumushi
interrogate (v)	ondervra	-botšišiša	-botsa	-kolotisa	-buza	-buzisisa
interrupt (v)	onderbreek	-tsena ganong	-sitisa	-kgaolela	-phazamisa	-thikameza
interruption (n)	onderbreking	kgaotšo	tshitiso	kgaolelo	isiphazamiso	isilibazisi
interval (n)	pouse	khutšo	kgefutso	kgaotso	ikhefu	ikhefu
interview (n)	onderhoud	morero	tlhahlobo	go tshwara ditherisano	udliwano-ndlebe	ingxoxo
intestine (n)	derm	lela	lela	lela	ithumbu	ithumbu
intoxicate (v)	bedwelm	-taga	-taha	-tagisa	-nxilisa	-daka
introduce (v)	voorstel	-tsebiša	-tsebisa	-itsise	-azisa	-ethula
introduction (n)	voorstelling	tsebišo	tsebiso	ketelelopele	ukwazisa	isingeniso
invade (v)	inval	-šwahlela	-hlasela	-tlhasela	-ngenela	-hlasela
invalid (a)	ongeldig	-sa šomego	-fokolang	-se kae sepe	-ngumlwelwe	-ngenamandla
invalid (n)	invalide	sekoka	mofokodi	sekoka	umlwelwe	isilinda
invasion (n)	inval	tšhwahlelo	tlhaselo	tlhaselo	uhlaselo	inhlaselo
invent (v)	uitvind	-hlama	-qapa	-ribolola	-bhaqa	-qamba
invention (n)	uitvinding	tlhamo	qapo	tlhamo	ukufunyanwa	ukuqanjwa
investigate (v)	ondersoek	-nyakišiša	-batlisisa	-tlhotlhomisa	-phanda	-hlola
investigation (n)	ondersoek	nyakišišo	patlisiso	tlhotlhomiso	uphando	ukuhlola
invisible (a)	onsigbaar	-sa bonwego	-sa bonahaleng	-sa bonweng	-ngabonakali(yo)	okungabonakali
invitation (n)	uitnodiging	taletšo	memo	taletso	isimemo	isimemo
invite (v)	uitnooi	-laletša	-mema	-laletsa	-mema	-mema
involve (v)	betrek	-ama	-kenya	-ntsenya	-faka	-zongolozela
iris (n)	iris	leratladi la leihlo	thaka ya leihlo	aerisi	umnyama	isiyingi seso
iron (n)	yster	tshipi	tshepe	tshipi	intsimbi	insimbi
iron (v)	stryk	-aena	-sidila	-gatisa	-ayina	ayina
ironwood (n)	ysterhout	legongtshipi	lehongtshepe	motswere	umkhombe	umsimbithi
irony (n)	ironie	kgegeo	makatso	kobiso	isigqebelo	isibhinqo
irrigate (v)	besproei	-nošetša	-nosetsa	-nosa	-nkcenkceshela	-chela ngenkhasa
irrigation (n)	besproeiing	nošetšo	nosetso	nosetso	unkcenkcesho	inkasa
irritate (v)	irriteer	-seleka	-halefisa	-baba	-caphukisa	-casula
island (n)	eiland	sehlakahlaka	sehlekehleke	setlhaketlhake	isiqithi	isiqhingi
issue (n)	kwessie	taba	taba	tema	umba	udaba
issue (v)	uitreik	-hlagiša	-phatlalatsa	-tlhomaganya	-khupha	-phumisa
it (pron)	dit	yona	-na	yone	yona	lokhu
itch (v)	jeuk	-hlohlona	-hlohlona	-baba	-rhawuzela	-lunywa
item (n)	item	ntlha	ntho	ntlhana	into	umcimbi
its (pron)	sy	-yona	ya-	gagwe	-khe	-alo
ivory (n)	ivoor	leino la tlou	lenaka la tlou	lonaka	uphondo lwendlovu	izinyo lendlovu
jackal (n)	jakkals	phukubje	mopheme	phokojwe	udyakalashe	impungushe
jacket (n)	baadjie	baki	baki	baki	ibhatyi	ibhantshi
jail (n)	tronk	kgolego	tjhankane	kgolegelo	itrongo	ijele
jail (v)	opsluit	-golega	-hlahlela	-golega	-valela	-bopha
jam (n)	konfyt	kgotla-o-mone	jeme	jeme	ijem	ujamu
January (n)	Januarie	Janaware	Pherekgong	Ferikgong	eyomQungu	uJanuwari
jar (n)	fles	moruswi	jara	morufa	ingqayi	imbizana
jaw (n)	kaak	mohlagare	mohlahare	letlhaa	umhlathi	umhlathi
jealous (a)	jaloers	-nago le mona	-lefufa	-lefufa	-nomona	-khwelezayo
jealousy (n)	jaloesie	lehufa	lefufa	lefufa	umona	isikhwele
jelly (n)	jellie	jeli	jeli	marere	ijeli	ujeli
jerk (v)	ruk	-utla	-tutla	-kgotha	-xhuzula	-dlukuza
jersey (n)	trui	jeresi	jeresi	jeresi	ijezi	ijezi

English	Afrikaans	N Sotho	Sesotho	Tswana	Xhosa	Zulu	K
Jesus (n)	Jesus	Jesu	Jeso	Jesu	uYesu	uJesu	
jewel (n)	juweel	sebenyabje	lehakwe	lebenya	ilitye lexabiso	itshana eliyigugu	
jilt (v)	afsê	-radia	-nyahlatsa	-koba	-ala	-ala	
jingle (v)	klingel	-tsirinya	-tjhwehletsa	-tsirimana	-khenkceza	-ncenceza	
job (n)	werk	modiro	mosebetsi	tiro	umsebenzi	umsebenzi	
jockey (n)	jokkie	mokatiši	joki	mopalami	inkweli	ujoki	
jog (v)	draf	-kitima	-hlehla	tlhetlha	-ntyuntya	-dledlezela	
join (n)	lasplek	kopantšho	momahatso	kgatlhanyo	ijoyini	indawo ehlanganisiweyo	
join (v)	las	-kopanya	-momahatsa	-kopanya	-joyina	-hlanganisa	
joint (n)	gewrig	noko	lenonyetso	lelokololo	umdibano	inhlangano yamathambo	
joke (n)	grap	motlae	motlae	motlae	isiqhulo	ihlaya	
joke (v)	gekskeer	-swaswa	-swaswa	-tlae	-hlekisa	-tekula	
journey (n)	reis	leeto	leeto	mosepele	uhambo	uhambo	
joy (n)	vreugde	lethabo	nyakallo	boitumelo	uvuyo	injabulo	
judge (n)	regter	moahlodi	moahlodi	moatlhodi	ijaji	ijaji	
judge (v)	oordeel	-ahlola	-ahlola	-atlhola	-gweba	-ehlulela	
judgment (n)	oordeel	kahlolo	kahlolo	katlholo	isigwebo	isinqumo	
judicial (a)	regterlik	-boahlodi	-molao	-bokgaolakgang	-semthethweni	-omsebenzi wamajaji	
judiciary (n)	regbank	lekgotla la toka	baahlodi	bokgaolakgang	ijaji zelizwe jikelele	amajaji	
jug (n)	beker	lebekere	jeke	jeke	inkonkxa	ujeke	
juice (n)	sap	meetsana	lero	matute	incindi	ijusi	
July (n)	Julie	Julae	Phupu	Phukwi	eyeKhala	uJulayi	
jump (n)	sprong	go taboga	tlolo	go tlola	umtsi	ukuxhuma	
jump (v)	spring	-taboga	-tlola	-tlola	-tsiba	-xhuma	
June (n)	Junie	June	Phupjane	Seetebosigo	eyeSilimela	uJuni	
jungle (n)	oerwoud	sethokgwa	mofidibithi	sekgwa	ihlathi	ihlathi	
junior (a)	junior	-nyane	-nyenyane	-botlana	-ncinci	-ncane	
jury (n)	jurie	juri	baahlodi	kgotla	iqumrhu labagwebi	ibandla labasizi bejaji	
just (adv)	net	fela	feela	fela	kanje	-sanda	
just (a)	regverdig	-lokilego	-toka	ka tolamo	nje	-fanele	
justice (n)	geregtigheid	toka	toka	tolamo	ubulungisa	ubulungisa	
justify (v)	regverdig	-lokafatša	-tiisa	-lolamise	-lungisa	-vumela	
keen (a)	toegewyd	-mafolofolo	-thahasellang	-tlhwatlhwa	-nomdla	-cijile	
keep (v)	hou	-swara	-boloka	-boloka	-gcina	-gcina	
kennel (n)	hondehok	serobe sa mpša	ntlwana ya ntja	tshireletso ya dintšwa	indlu yenja	indlu yenja	
kettle (n)	ketel	ketlele	ketlele	ketlele	iketile	igedlela	
key (n)	sleutel	senotlelo	senotlolo	senotlolo	isitshixo	ukhiye	
keyboard (n)	klawerbord	khiipoto	boto ya dinoto	khiboto	amathambo epiyano	ugqoko	
keyhole (n)	sleutelgat	lešobana la senotlelo	lesobana la senotlolo	thobasenotlolo	umngxuma wesitshixo	imbobo kakhiye	
khaki (n)	kakie	khaki	khaki	khaki	ikaki	ukhakhi	
kick (n)	skop	thago	thaho	thago	ukukhaba	ukukhahlela	
kick (v)	skop	-raga	-raha	-raga	-khapa	-khahlela	
kid (n)	bokkie	putšana	potsanyane	potsane	itakane	izinyane	
kidney (n)	nier	pshio	phio	philo	intso	inso	
kill (v)	doodmaak	-bolaya	-bolaya	-bolaya	-bulala	-bulala	
kind (a)	goedhartig	-botho	-mosa	-pelonomi	-nobubele	-nomusa	
kind (n)	soort	mohuta	mofuta	mofuta	uhlobo	uhlobo	
kindness (n)	goedheid	botho	mosa	bopelonomi	ububele	umusa	
king (n)	koning	kgoši	morena	kgosi	ukumkani	inkosi	
kingdom (n)	koninkryk	mmušo	mmuso	bogosi	ubukumkani	ubukhosi	
kiss (n)	soen	katlo	kako	katlo	ukuphuza	ukuqabula	
kiss (v)	soen	-atla	-aka	-atla	-phuza	-qabula	
kitchen (n)	kombuis	khitšhi	kitjhene	boapeelo	ikhitshi	ikhishi	
kite (n)	vlieër	khaete	khaete	sefofi	ikayiti	ikhayithi	
kitten (n)	katjie	katsana	ledinyane la katse	katsana	ikatana	izinyane lekati	
knead (v)	knie	-duba	-duba	-duba	-xovula	-xova	
knee (n)	knie	khuru	lengole	lengole	idolo	idolo	
kneecap (n)	knieskyf	khurumelakhuru	theledi	theledi	idolo	ivi	

K	English	Afrikaans	N Sotho	Sesotho	Tswana	Xhosa	Zulu
	kneel (v)	kniel	-khunama	-kgumama	-khubama	-guqa	-guqa
	knife (n)	mes	thipa	thipa	thipa	imela	umese
	knit (v)	brei	-loga	-loha	-loga	-nita	-nitha
	knitting needle (n)	breinaald	lemao la go loga	lemao la ho loha	lemao	inaliti yokunita	inalidi yokunitha
	knitting (n)	breiwerk	go loga	moloho	selogo	umthungo	ukunitha
	knob (n)	knop	hlogwana	lekuru	makukunopu	igqudu	isikhanda
	knock (n)	klop	kokoto	ho kokota	go kokota	ukunkqonkqoza	-ngqongqoza
	knock (v)	klop	-kokota	-kokota	-kokota	-nkqonkqoza	ukungqongqoza
	knot (n)	knoop	lehuto	lefito	lefunelo	iqhina	ifindo
	knot (v)	knoop	-huna	-fina	-funela	-qhina	-bopha ifindo
	know (v)	weet	-tseba	-tseba	-itse	-azi	-azi
	knowledge (n)	kennis	tsebo	tsebo	kitso	ulwazi	ulwazi
	knuckle (n)	kneukel	senoko	senoko	noko	iquphe	iqupha
	kudu (n)	koedoe	tholo	tholo	tholo	iqhude	umgankla
	label (n)	etiket	sešupo	letshwao	setshwao	ileyibhile	ilebula
	labour (n)	arbeid	mošomo	mosebetsi	tiro	umsebenzi	umsebenzi
	labour (v)	arbei	-šoma	-sebetsa	-dira	-sebenza	-sebenza
	labourer (n)	arbeider	mošomi	mosebeletsi	modiredi	umsebenzi	isisebenzi
	lace (n)	kant	kanta	kanta	kanta	umqukumbelo	uleyisi
	lack (n)	gebrek	tlhokego	tlhoko	go tlhoka	intswelo	ukuhlonga
	lad (n)	knaap	moesa	letlamorwana	mosimane	igatya	umfana
	ladder (n)	leer	lleri	lere	llere	ileri	isikhwelo
	ladle (n)	skeplepel	leho	mpshane	thoka	umcephe	indebe
	lady (n)	dame	mohumagadi	mofumahadi	mme	inenekazi	inkosikazi
	ladybird (n)	lieweheersbesie	podilekgwana	maleshwane	podilekgwana	ubhantom	umanqulwane
	lagoon (n)	strandmeer	letshanatswai	letsha la lewatle	letshanatswai	idike	ichweba
	lair (n)	lêplek	segola	sebaka	kutla	isikhundla	isikhundla
	lake (n)	meer	letsha	letsha	letsha	ichibi	ichibi
	lamb (n)	lam	kwana	konyana	konyana	itakane	izinyane
	lame (a)	mank	-segole	-holofetseng	-tlhotsang	-qhwalela (yo)	-qhugayo
	lament (n)	weeklag	sello	kodiamalla	dikhutsafalo	-khala	isililo
	lamp (n)	lamp	lebone	lebone	lebone	isibane	isibani
	land (n)	land	lefase	naha	lefatshe	umhlaba	umhlaba
	land (v)	land	-kotama	-kotsama	-tsurama	-hlala	-ethula emkhunjini
	landlord (n)	verhuurder	mohiriši	mohirisi	mong	umrini-ndlu	umqashisi
	landmine (n)	landmyn	pomo ya naga	bomo	bomo ya mo mmung	ibhombu	ibhomu eligqitshwayo
	language (n)	taal	polelo	puo	puo	ulwimi	ulimi
	lantern (n)	lantern	lanterene	lantere	lebone	ilanteri	isiketekete
	lard (n)	varkvet	makhura a kolobe	mafura a kolobe	mafura a kolobe	amafutha ehagu	amafutha engulube
	large (a)	groot	-golo	-holo	-tona	-khulu	-khulu
	larva (n)	larwe	seboko	seboko	seboko	umbungu	isibungu
	larynx (n)	larinks	kodu	qoqothwane	kgokgotso	ingqula	umphimbo
	lash (v)	gesel	-otla	-hlasela ka mantswe	-šapa	-betha	-thwibila
	last (a)	laaste	-mafelelo	-qetelang	-bofelo	-gqibela (yo)	-gcinayo
	last (v)	voortduur	-swarelela	-tswela pele	-tshwarelela	-hlala	-hlala isikhathi
	lasting (a)	voortdurend	-sa felego	-tswelang pele	-tlhola	-hlalayo	-hlalayo
	late (a)	laat	-morago ga nako	-morao	-tla thari	-kade	-phuzile
	late (a)	oorlede	hlokafetšego	-hlokahetseng	-moso	-swelekile (yo)	-shonile
	laugh (n)	lag	ditshego	setsheho	setshego	ukuhleka	ukuhleka
	laugh (v)	lag	-sega	-tsheha	-tshega	-hleka	-hleka
	laughter (n)	gelag	ditshego	setsheho	ditshego	intsini	insini
	laundry (n)	wassery	bohlatswetšo	tlhatsuong	botlhatswetso	indawo yokuhlamba impahla	ilondolo
	lavatory (n)	toilet	boithomelo	ntlwana	boithomelo	indlu yangasese	itholethe
	law (n)	wet	molao	molao	molao	umthetho	umthetho
	lawful (a)	wettig	-dumeletšwego	-molao	-molao	-se mthethweni	-njengomthetho
	lawn (n)	grasperk	lapanabjang	mohlwa	bojang	ibala lengca	ungwengwe
	lawnmower (n)	grassnyer	sesegabjang	sekutamohlwa	sesegabojang	umatshini wokucheba ingca	umshini wokusika utshani

English	Afrikaans	N Sotho	Sesotho	Tswana	Xhosa	Zulu	L
lawyer (n)	prokureur	agente	akgente	mmueledi	igqwetha	ummeli	
laxative (n)	lakseermiddel	sehlare sa go gofiša	sehlephisi	setabogisa mala	iyeza lokuhambisa	umuthi wokuhlam-bulula isisu	
lay (v)	dek	-teka	-teka	-baya	-beka	-deka	
laziness (n)	luiheid	botšwafi	botswa	botlapa	ubuvila	ubuvila	
lazy (a)	lui	-tšwafago	-botswa	-setshwakga	-vilaphayo	-livila	
lead (n)	lood	morodi	loto	lerumo	isinyithi	umthofu	
lead (v)	lei	-eta pele	-etella pele	-etelela	-khokela	-hamba phambili	
leader (n)	leier	moetapele	moetapele	moeteledipele	inkokeli	umholi	
leaf (n)	blaar	letlakala	lehlaku	letlhare	igqabi	ikhasi	
leak (n)	lek	modutlo	lesoba	go dutla	uthanda	imbobo	
leak (v)	lek	-dutla	-dutla	-dutla	-vusa	-vuza	
lean (a)	maer	-otilego	-otileng	-bopameng	-bhityile(yo)	-zacile	
lean (v)	leun	-ithekga	-itshetleha	-sekama	-ngqiyama	-ncamasha	
leap year (n)	skrikkeljaar	ngwagamotelele	selemo setshelapalo-matsatsi	ngwagamoleele	unyakande	unyaka onezinsuku ezingu-	
learn (v)	leer	-ithuta	-ithuta	-ruta	-funda	-funda	
least (a)	minste	-nyenyane	-bonyane	-bogolo bogolo	-ncinci	-ncane kakhulu	
leather (n)	leer	letlalo	letlalo	letlalo	ufele	isikhumba	
leave (n)	verlof	khunollo	lefi	khunologo	ikhefu	ilivi	
leave (v)	laat	-tlogela	-tlohela	-tloga	-nduluka	-shiya	
lecture (n)	lesing	thuto	thuto	thuto	isifundo	isifundo	
lecture (v)	doseer	-ruta	-rupela	-ruta	-fundisa	-fundisa	
lecturer (n)	dosent	mofahloši	morupedi	moruti	umhlohli	umfundisi	
ledge (n)	rotslys		mothati	leriba	ungqameko	unqenqema	
left (a)	links	-nngele	-letshehadi	-molema	-khohlo	-bunxele	
left (n)	linkerkant	ka go la nngele	leqele	molema	ikhohlo	ubunxele	
leg (n)	been	leoto	moomo	leoto	umlenze	umlenze	
legal (a)	wetlik	-molao	-molao	-molao	-semthethweni	-omthetho	
legitimate (a)	wettige	-dumeletšwego	-molao	-molao	-semthethweni	-vunyelwe ngumthetho	
lemon (n)	suurlemoen	swiri	sirilamunu	ratsuru	ilamuni	ulamula	
lend (v)	leen	-adima	-adima	-adima	-boleka	-bolekisa	
length (n)	lengte	botelele	bolelele	boleele	ubude	ubude	
leopard (n)	luiperd	nkwe	lengau	nkwe	ihlosi	ingwe	
leper (n)	melaatse	molephera	lepera	molepera	isilephere	umlephero	
less (a)	minder	-fokodiтšwego	-nyenyane	-nnye	-ncinci	-ncane kuna-	
lessen (v)	verminder	-fokotša	-nyenyefatsa	-fokotsa	-nciphisa	-nciphisa	
lesson (n)	les	thuto	thuto	thuto	isifundo	isifundo	
letter (n)	brief	lengwalo	lengolo	lekwalo	incwadi	incwadi	
lettuce (n)	blaarslaai	selae	selae	selae	iletusi	uletisi	
level (a)	gelyk	-lekantšwego	-lekanang	-lekalekaneng	-lingana(yo)	-lingene	
level (n)	vlak	tekanetšo	mokato	bogodimo	umgangatho	ileveli	
lewd (a)	ontugtig	-otswago	-sekgobo		-ngaphucukanga	-nesigweba	
liar (n)	leuenaar	moakedi	ramashano	moaki	ixoki	umqambi-manga	
liberal (a)	liberaal	-gololago	-lokolohileng		-nesisa	-phanayo	
librarian (n)	bibliotekaris	ramapuku	molaeborari	rramabuka	unoncwadi	umphathi welabhulali	
library (n)	biblioteek	bokgobapuku	laeborari	mabuka	ithala leencwadi	ilabhulali	
licence (n)	lisensie	laesense	laesense	lekwalotetla	imvume	ilayisense	
license (v)	lisensieer	-fa laesense	-fana ka laesense	-tetla	-nika iphepha-mvume	-nika ilayisense	
lick (v)	lek	-latswa	-leka	-latswa	-khotha	-khotha	
lid (n)	deksel	sekhurumelo	sekwahelo	sekhurumelo	isiciko	isivalo	
lie (n)	leuen	maaka	leshano	maaka	ubuxoki	amanga	
lie (v)	lê	-lala	-botha	-robala	-lala	-lala	
lie (v)	lieg	-bolela maaka	-bua leshano	-aketsa	-xoka	-qamba amanga	
life (n)	lewe	bophelo	bophelo	bophelo	ubomi	impilo	
lift (n)	hyser	sekuki	lefite	sekuka	ilifti	ilifi	
lift (v)	oplig	-kuka	-phahamisa	-kuka	-phakamisa	-phakamisa	
ligament (n)	ligament	mošifa	lera	ntha	umsipha	umsipha	
light (a)	lig	-bofefo	-bobebo	-lesedi	-baneka	-khanyayo	
light (n)	lig	seetša	kganya	lebone	ukukhanya	ukukhanya	

L	English	Afrikaans	N Sotho	Sesotho	Tswana	Xhosa	Zulu
	lighthouse (n)	vuurtoring	ntloseetša	molollope wa mollo	ntlwana kganya	indlu ekhanyisela inqanawa	isibubulungu
	lightning (n)	weerlig	legadima	letolo	tlhadi	umbane	umbani
	like (prep)	soos	bjalo ka	jwalo ka	jaaka	njenga	-njenga-
	like (v)	hou van	-rata	-rata	-rata	-kholwa	-thanda
	likeable (a)	beminlik	-rategago	-ratehang	-rategwang	-thandekayo	-thandekayo
	likeness (n)	ooreenkoms	tshwano	tshwano	setshwano	imfuzo	ukufana
	lily (n)	lelie	llili	shweshwe	mogaga	inyibiba	umnduze
	limb (n)	ledemaat	setho	setho	mokgono	ilungu	isitho
	lime (n)	kalk	motaga	kalaka	kalaka	ikalika	umcako
	limp (n)	mankheid	mohlotšo	kgolofalo	go tlhotsa	ubuqhwala	ukuxhuga
	limp (v)	mank loop	-hlotša	-qhiletsa	-tlhotsa	-qhwalela	-xhuga
	line (n)	lyn	mothaladi	kgwele	mothalo	umzya	intambo
	linen (n)	linne	lene	masela	llene	ilineni	ulineni
	lining (n)	voering	bokagare	furu	furu	ifuringi	imfulomu
	lion (n)	leeu	tau	tau	tau	ingonyama	ibhubesi
	lioness (n)	leeuwyfie	taugadi	tawana	taugadi	imazi yengonyama	ibhubesi lensikazi
	lip (n)	lip	molomo	pounama	pounama	umlebe	udebe
	liqueur (n)	likeur	senotagi sa sekgowa	lekere	senwamaphodi	utywala	izithako zikagologo
	liquid (a)	vloeibaar	-elago	-mokedikedi	-elelang	-lulwelo	-manzi
	liquid (n)	vloeistof	seela	mokedikedi	seela	ulwelo	uketshezi
	liquor (n)	drank	senotagi	tahi	bojalwa	utywala	ugologo
	lisp (n)	gelispel	go ba le diteme	lehwelea	seleme	ukuteketa	ukufefeza
	lisp (v)	lispel	go ba le diteme	-hwelea	-go nna seleme	-teketa	-fefeza
	listen (v)	luister	-theetša	-mamela	-utlwelela	-mamela	-lalela
	literary (a)	letterkundig	-dingwalo	-sengolwa	-bokwadi	-ngoncwadi	-kwemibhalo
	literature (n)	letterkunde	dingwalo	sengolwa	dikwalo	uncwadi	imibhalo
	little (a)	klein	-nyane	-nyenyane	-nnye	-ncinci	-ncane
	live (v)	leef	-phela	-phela	-phela	-phila	-phila
	lively (a)	lewendig	-mafolofolo	-phelang	-phelang	-phila(yo)	-phekuzayo
	liver (n)	lewer	sebete	sebete	sebete	isibindi	isibindi
	lizard (n)	akkedis	mokgaritswane	mokgodutswane	mokgatitswane	iciklishe	umbankwa
	load (n)	vrag	morwalo	morwalo	morwalo	umthwalo	umthwalo
	load (v)	laai	-laiša	laetjha	-pega	-thwalisa	-thwala
	loaf (n)	brood	borotho	borotho	borotho	isonka	isinkwa
	loan (n)	lening	kadimo	kadimo	kadimo	imboleka	isikwenethu
	loathe (v)	verafsku	-hloya	-hloya	-nyatsa	-caphukela	-enyanya
	local (a)	plaaslik	-gae	-selehae	-selegae	-ale ndawo	-akhona
	lock (n)	slot	sekgonyo	senotlolo	selotlele	isitshixo	isihluthulelo
	lock (v)	sluit	-notlela	-notlela	-lotlela	-tshixa	-hluthulela
	locust (n)	sprinkaan	tšie	lerutle	tsie	intethe	intethe
	lodger (n)	loseerder	mohiri	mohiri	mohiri	umhlaliswa	umqashi
	log (n)	blok	kota	lehong	kota	isigodo	ugodo
	logic (n)	logika	kwagalo	lojiki	kakanyo	ingqiqo	ilojiki
	loin (n)	lende	letheka	noka	noka	isinqe	ukhalo
	loiter (v)	rondslenter	-sesella	-tsekela	-ebaeba	-yatula	-libala
	loneliness (n)	eensaamheid	bodutu	bodutu	bodutu	ubulolo	isizungu
	lonely (a)	eensaam	-jewago ke bodutu	-hlorileng	-bodutu	-dwa	-nesizungu
	long (a)	lang	-telele	-lelele	-leele	-de	-de
	long (v)	verlang	-hlologela	-hlora	-tlhoafala	-khumbula	-langazela
	look (n)	blik	tebelelo	tjhadimo	tebo	inkangeleko	ukubheka
	look (v)	kyk	-lebelela	-tadima	-leba	-jonga	-bheka
	loose (a)	los	-tlemologilego	-lokolohileng	-bolea	-khululekile(yo)	-xegezela
	loot (n)	buit	dithebola	sehohedi	dikgapo	intimbo	umphango
	loot (v)	plunder	-thopa	-utswa	-gapa	-phanga	-phanga
	Lord (n)	Here	Modimo	Morena	Morena	iNkosi	iNkosi
	lorry (n)	vragmotor	lori	lori	llori	ilori	iloli
	lose (v)	verloor	-timetša	-lahleha	-latlha	-lahlekelwa	-lahlekelwa
	loss (n)	verlies	tahlegelo	tahlehelo	tatlhegelo	ilahleko	ukulahlekelwa
	lost (a)	verdwaal	-timetšego	-lahlehileng	-timelang	-lahleka (yo)	-lahlekelwe

English	Afrikaans	N Sotho	Sesotho	Tswana	Xhosa	Zulu	M
lost (a)	verlore	-timeditšwego	-lahlehileng	-timetseng	lahlekile (yo)	-lahlekelwe	
loud (a)	hard	-kwagalago	-hodimo	-thata	-ngxola (yo)	-nomsindo	
lounge (n)	sitkamer	bodulelo	lontjhe	kamore ya boitapoloso	igumbi lokuhlala	ilawunji	
lout (n)	takhaar	tsweya	rametlae	lesutlha	ixuxu	impubumpubu	
lovable (a)	dierbaar	-rategago	-ratehang	-rategwang	-thandekayo	-thandekayo	
love (n)	liefde	lerato	lerato	lerato	uthando	uthando	
lover (n)	minnaar	morati	moratuwa	morati	isithandwa	isithandwa	
low (a)	laag	-fase	-tlase	-fatshe	-zantsi	-ehlile	
lower (a)	laer	-fasana	-tlase hofeta	-fatshefatshe	-zantsana	-ngaphansana	
lowveld (n)	laeveld	nagatlase	naha e tlase	nagatlase	isithabazi	ihlanze	
loyal (a)	lojaal	-botegago	-tshepehang	-ikanyegang	-nyanisekile(yo)	-thembekile	
loyalty (n)	lojaliteit	bogwerano	tshepahalo	boikanyego	ukunyaniseka	ukuthembeka	
luck (n)	geluk	mahlatse	lehloohonolo	lesego	ithamsanqa	inhlanhla	
lucky (a)	gelukkig	-nago le mahlatse	-lehloohonolo	-tshego	-nethamsanqa	-nenhlanhla	
luggage (n)	bagasie	thoto	thoto	dithoto	umthwalo	impahla yendlela	
lullaby (n)	wiegelied	kunkurobala	koeetso	pinanyana	ingoma yosana	umlolozelo	
lump (n)	klont	lekwate	lehlwele	kgwethe	ingongoma	isigaxa	
lunatic (n)	waansinnige	segafa	lehlanya	setseno	igeza	uhlanya	
lunch (n)	middagete	letena	dijo tsa motsheare	dijotshegare	isidlo sasemini	idina	
lung (n)	long	leswafo	letshwafo	lekgwafo	umphunga	iphaphu	
lure (v)	aanlok	-goketša	-hohela	-okisa	umbizane	-yenga	
lust (n)	wellus	kganyogo	meharo	maikaelelo	inkanuko	inkanuko	
luxury (n)	luukse	lehumo	majabajaba	manobonobo	ubumnandi	ubukhizikhizi	
machine (n)	masjien	motšhene	motjhine	motšhini	umashini	umshini	
mad (a)	gek	-gafago	-hlanya	-tsenwang	-phambene (yo)	-luhlanya	
maggot (n)	maaier	seboko	seboko	lenyenye	impethu	isibungu	
magic (n)	towerkuns	boloi	boloi	boloi	ubugqi	umlingo	
magical (a)	magies	-boloi	-boloi	-boloi	-nobugqi	-nomlingo	
magistrate (n)	landdros	maseterata	mmaseterata	magiseterata	umantyi	umantshi	
magnet (n)	magneet	kgogedi	makenete	kgogedi	isitsalane	uzibuthe	
magnetism (n)	magnetisme	bogogedi	bomakenete	bokgogedi	ubutsalane	amandla kazibuthe	
magnify (v)	vergroot	-godiša	-hodisa	-godisa	-andisa	-khulisa	
mail (n)	pos	poso	poso	poso	iposi	iposi	
maim (v)	vermink	-golofatša	-holofatsa	-golafatsa	-limaza	-limaza	
main (a)	vernaamste	-golo	-holo	-golo	-eyona	-khulu	
maintain (v)	handhaaf	-tiiša	-boloka	-tshegetsa	-xhasa	-ondla	
maintenance (n)	onderhoud	phepo	tlhokomelo	tlamelo	inkxaso	isondlo	
maize (n)	mielies	mahea	poone	mmidi	umbona	ummbila	
make (n)	soort	mohuta	mofuta	mofuta	uhlobo	uhlobo	
make (v)	maak	-dira	-etsa	-dira	-enza -qingqa	-enza	
malaria (n)	malaria	letadi	malaria	letshoroma	icesina	uqhuqho	
male (a)	manlik	-tona	-monna	-tonanyana	-nobudoda	-esilisa	
male (n)	man	monna	monna	monna	indoda	isilisa	
malice (n)	boosaardigheid	bobe	lonya	bogale	ulunya	izondo	
malt (n)	mout	mohlaba	mmela	momela	imithombo	imithombo	
mammal (n)	soogdier	seamuši	mamale	seamusi	isidalwa esanyisayo	isilwane esincelisayo	
man (n)	man	monna	monna	monna	indoda	indoda	
manage (v)	bestuur	-laola	laola	-laola	-lawula	-phatha	
management (n)	bestuur	taolo	balaodi	bolaodi	ulawulo	ukuphathwa	
manager (n)	bestuurder	molaodi	molaodi	molaodi	umlawuli	umphathi	
mane (n)	maanhare	mariri	moetse	seriri	isingci	umhlwenga	
mango (n)	mango	manko	mengo	menku	imengo	umango	
manhood (n)	manlikheid	bonna	bonna	bonna	ubudoda	ubudoda	
manner (n)	manier	mokgwa	mokgwa	mokgwa	ukuziphatha	uhlobo	
manure (n)	mis	mmutedi	manyolo	letshotelo	umgquba	umqubo	
many (a)	baie	-ntši	-ngata	-ntsi	-ninzi	-ningi	
map (n)	landkaart	mmepe	mmapa	mmepe	imephu	imephu	
March (n)	Maart	Matšhe	Tlhakubele	Mopitlwe	uMatshi	uMashi	
march (n)	mars	momatšho	motsamao	mogato	ukumatsha	imashi	

M English	Afrikaans	N Sotho	Sesotho	Tswana	Xhosa	Zulu
march (v)	marsjeer	-matšha	-tsamaya	-gata	-matsha	-masha
mare (n)	merrie	pere ya tshadi	mmeri	pitsenamagadi	imazi yehashe	imeli
margin (n)	kantlyn	mollwane	moedi	morato	udini	usebe
mark (n)	merk	leswao	letshwao	letshwao	uphawu	isici
mark (v)	merk	-swaya	-tshwaya	-tshwaya	-phawula	-maka
market (n)	mark	mmaraka	mmaraka	mmaraka	imarike	imakethe
marriage (n)	huwelik	lenyalo	lenyalo	lenyalo	umtshato	umshado
marrow (n)	murg	moko	moko	moko	umongo	umnkantsha
marry (v)	trou	-nyala	-nyala	-nyala	-tshata	-shadisa
martyr (n)	martelaar	motlaišwa	motlatlapuwa wa tumelo	moreswedi	umfelakholo	umfelukholo
marvel (v)	wonder	-makala	-makalla	-makala	-mangalisa	-mangalisa
marvellous (a)	wonderbaarlik	-makatšago	-makatsang	-makatsang	-mangalisa(yo)	-mangalisayo
masculine (a)	manlik	-tona	-bonna	-tonanyana	-nobudoda	-endoda
mason (n)	messelaar	moagi	sehahi	moagi	umakhi	umeselane
master (v)	bemeester	-kgona	-hlola	-kgona	-lawula	-ahlula
mat (n)	mat	moseme	moseme	mmetšhe	ukhuko	icansi
match (n)	vuurhoutjie	lehlokwana la mollo	thutswana mollo	letlhokwa	imatshisi	umentshisi
material (n)	lap	lešela	lesela	khai	ilaphu	indwangu
mathematics (n)	wiskunde	mathematiki	metse	matesisi	imathematika	imathimathiki
mattress (n)	matras	mantarase	materase	bolao	umandlalo	umatilasi
mature (a)	volwasse	-godilego	-hodileng	-godileng	-khulile(yo)	-khulile
maul (v)	kneus	-kgobola	-kgobola	-teteya	-qwenga	-shikashika
maximum (n)	maksimum	botlalokgolo	pheletsong	botlalogolo	iqondo eliphezulu	-khulu kakhulu
May (n)	Mei	Mei	Motsheanong	Mothseganong	uMeyi	uMeyi
may (v)	mag	-ka-	-ka	-ka nna	-nga	-nga-
maybe (adv)	miskien	mohlamong	mohlomong	gongwe	mhlawumbi	mhlawumbe
mayor (n)	burgemeester	ramotse	ramotse	meiyara	isibonda	imeya
me (pron)	my	n-	nna	nna	mna	mina
meal (n)	maal	dijo	dijo	dijo	isidlo	isidlo
mean (a)	gemeen	-be	-be	-maswe	-nentsingiselo	-ncishanayo
mean (v)	bedoel	-ra	-re	-kaya	-singisela	-qonda
meaning (n)	bedoeling	maikemišetšo	hobolelwang	kakanyo	injongo	ingqondo
meaning (n)	betekenis	tlhološo	moelelo	bokao	intsingiselo	incazelo
measles (n)	masels	mooko	mmoko	mmokwana	imasisi	isimungumungwane
measure (n)	maat	tekanyo	tekanyo	seelo	umlinganiselo	isilinganiso
measure (v)	meet	-lekanya	-lekanya	-lekanya	-linganisa	-linganisa
meat (n)	vleis	nama	nama	nama	inyama	inyama
mechanic (n)	werktuigkundige	makhanekhe	motehi	mothudi	umkhandi	umakheniki
mechanical (a)	meganies	-semotšhene	-ka boyona	-bothudi	-ngokomatshini	-omshini
medal (n)	medalje	mentlele	kgau	mentlele	imbasa	imendlela
mediate (v)	bemiddel	-lamola	-emela	-tsereganya	-lamla	-lamula
mediator (n)	bemiddelaar	molamodi	moemedi	motsereganyi	umlamli	umlamuli
medical (a)	medies	-bongaka	-meriana	-bongaka	-obugqirha	-elaphayo
medicine (n)	medisyne	sehlare	meriana	molemo	iyeza	umuthi
meek (a)	gedwee	-ikokobetšego	-ikokobeditseng	-pelonolo	-lulamile(yo)	-bekile
meercat (n)	meerkat	moswe	mosha	mošwe	igala	ububhibhi
meet (v)	ontmoet	-kopana le	-teana	-kopana	-dibana	-hlangana na-
meeting (n)	ontmoeting	kopano	teano	kgatlhano	indibano	ukuhlangana
meeting (n)	vergadering	kopano	kopano	kopano	intlanganiso	umhlangano
melon (n)	meloen	phara ya sekgowa	lehapu	mokate	ivatala	ikhabe
melt (v)	smelt	-tologa	-qhibidiha	-gakologa	-nyibilika	-ncibilika
member (n)	lid	leloko	setho	tokololo	ilungu	ilunga
membership (n)	lidmaatskap	boloko	botho	botokololo	ubulungu	ubulunga
memorial (a)	herdenking	-segopotšo	sehopotso	-kgakologelo	-nesikhumbuzo	isikhumbuzo
mend (v)	heelmaak	-lokišo	-lokisa	-baakanya	-ngciba	-lungisa
menstruate (v)	menstrueer	-hlapa	-ya kgweding	-bona kgwedi	-hlamba	-qaka
menstruation (n)	menstruasie	lehlapo	ho ya kgweding	tlhatswo	ukuhlamba	iqako
menu (n)	spyskaart	lenaneo la dijo	lenane la dijo	buka ya dijo	izipheko imenyu	imenyu
merciful (a)	genadig	-kgaugelo	-mohau	-pelotlhomogi	-nenceba	-nesihawu

English	Afrikaans	N Sotho	Sesotho	Tswana	Xhosa	Zulu	M
mercury (n)	kwik	mekhuri	metjhuri	mekhuri	imetyhuri	ummpunyumpunyu	
mercy (n)	genade	kgaugelo	mohau	bopelotlhomogi	inceba	isihawu	
mess (n)	gemors	bošaedi	bohlaswa	makgaphila	ubumdaka	isibhixi	
mess (v)	bemors	-tšhilafatša	-silafatsa	-senya	-enza mdaka	-bhixiza	
message (n)	boodskap	molaetša	molaetsa	molaetsa	umyalezo	umbiko	
messenger (n)	bode	morongwa	moromuwa	morongwa	isigidimi	isithunywa	
messy (a)	morsig	-ditšhila	-ditshila	-makgaphila	-onakeleyo	-nesibhixi	
metal (n)	metaal	metale	tshepe	tshipi	isinyithi	insimbi	
method (n)	metode	mokgwa	mokgwa	mokgwa	umgaqo	umkhuba	
metre (n)	meter	metara	metara	metara	imitha	imitha	
microscope (n)	mikroskoop	maekrosekopo	maekorosekoupo	maekorosekopo	imakroskopu	umasikilopu	
microwave (n)	mikrogolf	maekroweife	leqhubu la maekoro	maekorowafe	amazanana	imakhroweyivi	
midday (n)	middag	mosegare wa sekgalela	motsheare	sethoboloko	iminenkulu	imini	
midnight (n)	middernag	bošegogare	kgitla	bosigogare	ezinzulwini zobusuku	phakathi kwamabili	
midwife (n)	vroedvrou	mmelegiši	mobelehisi	mmelegisi	umbelekisikazi	umbelethisi	
migrant (a)	swerwend	-kobakobanago	-molakolako	-hudugang	-fudukayo	-thuthela kwelinye izwe	
migrate (v)	migreer	-huduga	-falla	-huduga	-fuduka	-akha kwelinye izwe	
migration (n)	migrasie	khudugo	phallo	khudugo	imfuduko	ukuya kwelinye izwe	
mild (a)	matig	-lekanetšego	-phodileng	-bonolo	-lungile (yo)	-bekile	
mildew (n)	muf	nyakgahlo	poya	mouta	ukungunda	isikhunta	
mile (n)	myl	maele	maele	mmaele	imayile	imayela	
military (a)	militêre	-bohlabani	-sesole	-sesole	-omkhosi	-empi	
milk (n)	melk	maswi	lebese	mašwi	ubisi	ubisi	
million (n)	miljoen	milione	milijone	mileone	isigidi	isigidi	
millipede (n)	duisendpoot	legokolodi	lefokolodi	sebokolodi	isongololo	ishongololo	
mimosa (n)	mimosa	mooka	mimosa	mookana	umnga	umunga	
mince (n)	maalvleis	nama ye e šitšwego	nama e sitsweng	nama e e sitsweng	inyama esiliweyo	inyama egayiweyo	
mind (n)	verstand	mogopolo	kelello	tlhaloganyo	ingqondo	umqondo	
mind (v)	omgee	-hlokomela	-kgathalla	-kgathala	-khathalela	-khathala nga-	
mine (pron)	myne	-ka	-ka	-me	yam	-ami	
mineral (n)	mineraal	minerale	minerale	serašwa	isimbiwa	isansimbi	
minimum (n)	minimum	botlalonyane	bonyane	bobotlana	ubuncinane	-ncane kakhulu	
minister (n)	minister	tona	letona	tona	umphathiswa	isikhonzi	
minister (n)	predikant	moruti	moruti	moruti	umfundisi	umfundisi	
minute (a)	heel klein	-nyennyane	-nyenyane hahole	-nnyenye	-ncinane	-ncane	
minute (n)	minuut	motsotso	motsotso	motsotso	umzuzu	iminithi	
miracle (n)	wonderwerk	mohlolo	mohlolo	motlholo	ummangaliso	isimangaliso	
mirror (n)	spieël	seipone	seipone	seipone	isipili	isibuko	
misbehave (v)	jou swak gedra	-lebala go itshwara	-itshwara hampe	-itlontlolola	-ziphatha kakubi	-ziphatha kabi	
miscellaneous (a)	allerlei	-mehutahuta	-tsohletsohle	-tsele le tsele	-ngxubevange	-yinhlanganisela	
mischief (n)	kattekwaad	makokwana	botlokotsebe	letshwenyo	intlondi	ukuklina	
mischievous (a)	ondeund	-selekago	-botlokotsebe	-letshwenyo	-nentlondi	-klinile	
miser (n)	vrek	ngame	lekgonatha	ngame	igogotya	iqonqela	
miserly (a)	vrekkerig	-ngame	-bokgonatha	-ngame	-ngobugogotya	-mbanyile	
misery (n)	ellende	mathatha	bosisapelo	tshotlego	ubugogotya	ukuhlupheka	
misfortune (n)	teenspoed	madimabe	bomadimabe	kgaba	ilishwa	ishwa	
mislead (v)	mislei	-foraforetša	-kgelosa	-digela ka lemena	-lukuhla	-dukisa	
misleading (a)	misleidend	-foraforetšago	-kgelosang	-digela ka lemena	-lukuhla(yo)	-dukisayo	
miss (v)	mis	-foša	-fosa	-fosa	-phosa	-geja	
mission (n)	sending	thomo	thomo	borongwa	ubizo	ukuthunywa	
missionary (n)	sendeling	moruti	moromuwa	morongwa	umthunywa umfundisi	umfundisi	
mist (n)	mis	mouwane	mohodi	mouwane	inkungu	inkungu	
mistake (n)	fout	phošo	phoso	phoso	impazamo	isiphosiso	
misunderstand (v)	misverstaan	-sa kwišiše	-se utlwisise	-utlwela	-ngaqondi kakuhle	-ngezwa	
misunderstanding (n)	misverstand	go se kwišiše	ho se utlwisise	se nang kutlwisiso	ukungaqondani	ukungezwani	
mix (v)	meng	-tswaka	-kopanya	-tswaka	-xuba	-xubana	
mixture (n)	mengsel	motswako	kopanyo	motswako	umxube	ixube	
moan (n)	gekerm	tsetlo	pelaelo	tuma	ukugcuma	imbubuzi	
moan (v)	kerm	-tsetla	-belaela	-duma	-gcuma	-bubuza	
mock (v)	bespot	-kwera	-soma	-sotla	-phoxa	-kloloda	

99

M	English	Afrikaans	N Sotho	Sesotho	Tswana	Xhosa	Zulu
	modern (a)	modern	-sebjalebjale	-sejwalejwale	-sešwa	-ntsha	-yesimanje
	modest (a)	beskeie	-sa ikgantšhego	-imametseng	-boingotlo	-lulamile(yo)	-namahloni
	mohair (n)	sybokhaar	boya bja lesaepoko	boya ba podi	boboa jwa podi	uboya beseyibhokhwe	uboya bembuzi yaseAngora
	moist (a)	vogtig	-monola	-mongobo	-ngolang	-fumile	-manzana
	moisten (v)	natmaak	-thapiša	-kolobisa	-ngodisa	-manzisa	-manzisa
	moisture (n)	vog	monola	mongobo	bokgola	ukufuma	ubumanzi
	molar (n)	kiestand	leino la mohlagare	mohlahare	leino	umhlathi	izinyo lomhlathi
	mole (n)	mol	khwiti	mokunyane	serunya	intuku	ivukusi
	moment (n)	oomblik	motsotso	motsotso	nakonyana	ithuba	umzuzu
	Monday (n)	Maandag	Mošupologo	Mantaha	Mosupologo	uMvulo	uMsombuluko
	money (n)	geld	tšhelete	tjhelete	madi	imali	imali
	monkey (n)	aap	kgabo	tshwene	kgabo	inkawu	inkawu
	month (n)	maand	kgwedi	kgwedi	kgwedi	inyanga	inyanga
	monument (n)	monument	monyumente	sefika	sefikantswe	ilitye lesikhumbuzo	itshe lesikhumbuzo
	mood (n)	bui	maikutlo	moya	maikutlo	imeko	ukuma kwenhliziyo
	moon (n)	maan	kgwedi	kgwedi	ngwedi	inyanga	inyanga
	moonlight (n)	maanlig	seetša sa kgwedi	ngwedi	lesedi la ngwedi	inyanga	unyezi
	more (a)	meer	-go feta fao	-hape	gape	-ngaphezulu	-ningi ngokudlula
	morning (n)	oggend	moswana	hoseng	phakela	intsasa	ekuseni
	mosquito (n)	muskiet	monang	monwang	monang	ingcongconi	umiyane
	motel (n)	motel	motele	motele	motele	ihotele	imothela
	moth (n)	mot	mmoto	mmoto	serurubele	uvivingane	ibhu
	mother (n)	moeder	mma	mme	mme	umama	umama
	mother-in-law (n)	skoonmoeder	mmatswale	matsale	matsale	uninazala	umamezala
	motive (n)	beweegrede	lebaka	morero	boitlhomo	isizathu	isisusa
	motorcar (n)	motor	mmotoro	koloi	mmotorokara	imoto	imoto
	motorcycle (n)	motorfiets	thuthuthu	sethuthuthu	sethuthuthu	isithuthuthu	isithuthuthu
	mould (n)	vorm	sebopi	popo	sebopelo	ubumbeko	isikhutha
	mould (v)	vorm	-bopa	-bopa	-bopa	-bumba	-khutha
	moult (v)	verhaar	-sola	-sola	-tlhobega	-obuza	-hluba
	mount (v)	opklim	-namela	-hlwella	-pagama	-qabela	-khwela
	mount (v)	vassit	-momaganya	-kgomaretsa	-tshwarwa	-qinisa	-misa
	mountain (n)	berg	thaba	thaba	thaba	intaba	intaba
	mourn (v)	rou	-lla	-lla	-roula	-zila	-lilela
	mourning (n)	rou	sello	sello	boroulo	izila	isililo
	mouse (n)	muis	legotlo	tweba	peba	impuku	igundane
	moustache (n)	snor	maledu a ka godima ga molomo	matshwala	tedu	amabhovu	amadevu
	mouth (n)	mond	molomo	molomo	molomo	umlomo	umlomo
	mouth organ (n)	mondfluitjie	foleitši	foleiti	foleiki	ifleyiti	imfiliji
	mouthful (n)	mondvol	tekanyo ye e tlalago molomo	mothamo	mothama	umthamo	umthamo
	move (v)	beweeg	-šutha	-sisinyeha	-tshikinya	-shukuma	-nyakazisa
	move (v)	skuif	-šuthiša	-suthisa	-sutisa	-shenxa	-nyukuza
	move (v)	trek	-huduga	-tsamaya	-goga	-hamba	-emuka
	moving (a)	bewegend	-sepelago	-tsamayang	-sutang	-hambayo	-nomhawu
	moving (a)	roerend	-ka šuthišwago	-sisinyehang	-tshikinyang	shukumayo	-nyakazayo
	much (a)	veel	-ntši	-ngata	-ntsi	-kanga	-ningi
	mucus (n)	slym	mamina	mamina	mamina	uxakaxa	isikhwehlela
	mud (n)	modder	leraga	seretse	seretse	udaka	udaka
	muddy (a)	modderig	-leraga	-seretse	-matlepetlepe	-nodaka	-nodaka
	mug (n)	beker	pekere	lebekere	lebekere	imagi	imagi
	mule (n)	muil	meila	mmoulo	mmoulo	imeyile	umnyuzi
	multiply (v)	vermenigvuldig	-atiša	-atisa	-ata	-phinda-phinda	-phinda
	multiracial (a)	veelrassig	-boditšhaba	-matjhaba	-ditšhabatšhaba	umxube weentlanga	-zinhlangangezinhlanga
	multitude (n)	menigte	lešabašaba	matshwele	boidiidi	isihlwele	isizuku
	mumps (n)	pampoentjies	mauwe	pampunkisi	makidiane	uqwilikane	uzagiga
	municipal (a)	munisipaal	-mmasepala	-mmasepala	-mmasepala	-edolophu	-kamasipalati
	municipality (n)	munisipaliteit	mmasepala	mmasepala	mmasepala	ibhunga ledolophu	umasipalati

English	Afrikaans	N Sotho	Sesotho	Tswana	Xhosa	Zulu	N
murder (n)	moord	polao	polao	polao	ubugebenga	ukubulala umuntu	
murder (v)	vermoor	-bolaya	-bolaya	-bolaya	-bulala	-bulala	
murderer (n)	moordenaar	mmolai	mmolai	mmolai	isigebenga	umbulali	
murmur (n)	gemurmel	pobolo	tumaelo	go ngunanguna	ukudumzela	-hlokoma	
muscle (n)	spier	mošifa	mosifa	mosifa	isihlunu	umsipha	
museum (n)	museum	musiamo	musiamo	musiamo	imuziyam	imnyuziyamu	
mushroom (n)	sampioen	tokwane	letswalo	leboa	ikhowa	ikhowe	
music (n)	musiek	moopelo	mmino	mmino	umculo	umculo	
musical (a)	musikaal	-moopelo	-mmino	-mmino	-nomculo	-mculo	
musician (n)	musikant	ramelodi	sebini	rammino	umculi	isazi somculo	
mussel (n)	mossel	mohuta wa kgopa ya lewatle	mosele		imbaza	imbaza	
must (v)	moet	-swanetše	-tlamehile	-tshwanetse	-mele	-bo-	
mustard (n)	mosterd	mostara	mosetareta	masetete	imostade	umasitadi	
mutilate (v)	skend	-senya	-tamukanya	-senya	-limaza	-nqumanquma	
mutter (v)	mompel	-bobola	-honotha	-mumura	-mbombozela	-munqazela	
mutton (n)	skaapvleis	nama ya nku	nama ya nku	nama ya nku	inyama yegusha	inyama yemvu	
muzzle (n)	snoet	molomo	molomo o motsu	nko	umlomo wesilwanyana	impumulo	
my (pron)	my	-ka/n-	-ka	-ka	yam	-mi	
mysterious (a)	geheimsinnig	-khupamarama	-mohlolo	-bosaitseweng	-mangalisayo	-fihlakele	
mystery (n)	misterie	khupamarama	mohlolo	bosaitseweng	ummangaliso	imfihlakalo	
myth (n)	mite	nonwane	tshomo	naane	intsomi	insumo	
naartjie (n)	nartjie	nariki	narike	nariki	inartyisi	inantshi	
nail (n)	spyker	sepekere	sepekere	sepekere	isikhonkwane	isipikili	
nail (v)	spyker	-kokotela	-kokotela	-kokotela	-bethelela	-bethela	
naked (a)	kaal	-hlobotšego	-hlobotseng	-lepono	-ze	-nqunu	
name (n)	naam	leina	lebitso	leina	igama	igama	
name (v)	noem	-rea leina	-bitsa	-taya	-biza	-biza	
nappy (n)	babadoek	leiri	leleire	mongato	ilaphu	inephi	
narrate (v)	vertel	-anegela	-qoqela	-anela	-balisa	-landa	
narrow (a)	smal	-sese	-tshesane	-tshesane	-mxinwa	-mcingo	
nasal (a)	nasaal	-nko	-nko	-nkong	-mpumlo	-ekhala	
nasty (a)	gemeen	-be	-ditshila	-bosula	-bi	-bi	
nation (n)	nasie	setšhaba	setjhaba	setšhaba	isizwe	isizwe	
national (a)	nasionaal	-setšhaba	-setjhaba	-bosetšhaba	-nobuzwe	-esizwe	
nationalism (n)	nasionalisme	bosetšhaba	botjhaba	bosetšhaba	ubuzwe	ubuzwe	
natural (a)	natuurlik	-tlhago	-hlaho	-tlhaga	-endalo	-yimvelo	
nature reserve (n)	natuurreservaat	nagatšhireletšo	poloko ya tsa hlaho	bosireletso jwa tlholego	iziko logcino-ndalo	isiqiwu	
nature (n)	natuur	tlhago	hlaho	tlholego	indalo	imvelo	
naughty (a)	stout	-selekago	-thibaneng ditsebe	-bosilo	-gezayo	-delela	
nausea (n)	naarheid	go feroga dibete	ho feroha	go tlhatsa	isizothezothe	isicanucanu	
nauseate (v)	naar maak	-feroša dibete	-ferola	tlhatsisa	-zotha	-canula	
navel (n)	naeltjie	mokhubu	mokguba	khubu	inkaba	inkaba	
navy (n)	vloot	kgoro ya dikepe	dikepe tsa ntwa	lefapha la dikepe	iinqanawa	amasotsha asemkhunjini	
near (adv)	naby	kgauswi	haufi	-gaufi	kufutshane	-eduze	
nearly (adv)	byna	-nyakile go-	-batlile	-batla	phantse	-cishe	
neat (a)	netjies	-bothakga	makgethe	-sethakga	-cocekile (yo)	-nobunono	
necessary (a)	noodsaaklik	-nyakegago	-hlokahang	-tlhokegang	-mfuneko	-dingekile	
necessity (n)	noodsaaklikheid	nyakego	tlhokeho	tlhokafalo	imfuneko	isidingo	
neck (n)	nek	molala	molala	molala	intamo	intamo	
necklace (n)	halssnoer	pheta	sefaha	ditalama	intsimbi yomqala	umgaxo	
nectar (n)	nektar	manopi	lero	botshe	incindi	uju	
need (n)	behoefte	nyakego	bohloki	setlhokwa	imfuneko	inswelo	
need (v)	nodig hê	-hloka	-hloka	-tlhoka	-funa	-swela	
needle (n)	naald	nalete	nale	lemao	inaliti	inaliti	
neglect (v)	verwaarloos	-hlokomologa	-hlokomoloha	-tlhokomologa	-ngakhathaleli	-debeselwe	
negligence (n)	nalatigheid	tlhokomologo	bohlaswa	tlhokomologo	ukungakhathali	ukunganaki	
negligent (a)	nalatig	-sa hlokomelego	-bohlaswa	-tlhokomologo	-khathali(yo)	-nganaki	

N	**English**	**Afrikaans**	**N Sotho**	**Sesotho**	**Tswana**	**Xhosa**	**Zulu**
	negotiate (v)	onderhandel	-rerišana	-buisana	-buisanya	-thethathethana	-xoxisana
	neighbour (n)	buurman	moagišani	moahisane	moagisani	ummelwane	umakhelwane
	nephew (n)	neef	setlogolo	motjhana	ntsala	umtshana	umshana
	nerve (n)	senuwee	mothapo	mothapo	lesika	umthambo-luvo	umuzwa
	nervous (a)	senuweeagtig	-tšhogatšhogago	-letswalo	-mafafa	-phakuzela(yo)	-namatata
	nervousness (n)	senuweeagtigheid	go tšhogatšhoga	letswalo	mafafa	ubuphaku-phaku	amatata
	nest (n)	nes	sehlaga	sehlaha	sentlhaga	indlwane	isidleke
	nestle (v)	nestel	-dula ka go iketla	-baballa	-aga	-quthuma	-khosela
	never (adv)	nooit	le gatee	le kgale	-e seng	soze	-ngeke
	new (a)	nuut	-fsa	-tjha	-swa	-tsha	-sha
	newcomer (n)	nuweling	yo mofsa	mofihli	moswa	umfiki	inyuwane
	newly (adv)	onlangs	malobanyana	-haufi	seswa	-sandula	kabusha
	news (n)	nuus	ditaba	ditaba	kgang	iindaba	izindaba
	newspaper (n)	koerant	kuranta	koranta	kuranta	iphephandaba	iphephandaba
	next to (prep)	langs	hleng ga-	haufi le-	-thoko ga	-caleni kwa-	-seceleni kwa-
	next (a)	volgende	-latelago	-latelang	-latelang	-landelayo	-landelayo
	nice (a)	aangenaam	-bose	-hlabosang	-monate	-mnandi	-mnandi
	niece (n)	niggie	setlogolo	motjhana	ntsala	umtshana	umshanakazi
	night (n)	nag	bošego	bosiu	bosigo	ubusuku	ubusuku
	nightmare (n)	nagmerrie	segateledi	ho phofa	toro e maswe	iphupha elibi	iphupho elesabisayo
	nightwatchman (n)	nagwag	moletabošego	matjekelane	matshinkilane	umantshingilane	ugadi
	nine (n)	nege	senyane	robong	robongwe	ithoba	isishiyagalolunye
	nineteen (n)	neëntien	lesomesenyane	leshome le metso e robo	some robongwe	ishumi elinethoba	ishumi nesishiyagalolunye
	ninety (n)	neëntig	masomesenyane	mashome a robong	somaarobongwe	amashumi alithoba	amashumi ayishiyagalolunye
	nipple (n)	tepel	tlhoko	tlhoko	tlhoko	ingono	ingono
	nobody (pron)	niemand	e sego motho	ha ho motho	ope	akamntu	akukho-muntu
	nod (n)	knik	go dumela ka hlogo	ho oma ka hloho	-othuma	ukunqwala	ukunqekuza
	nod (v)	knik	-dumela ka hlogo	-oma ka hloho	-koma	-nqwala	-nqekuza
	noise (n)	geraas	lešata	lerata	leratla	ingxolo	umsindo
	noisy (a)	raserig	-lešata	-lerata	-leratla	-ngxolayo	-nomsindo
	nonsense (n)	onsin	ditšiebadimo	lefeela	matlhapolosa	ubuvuvu	umbhedo
	noon (n)	middag	mosegare wa sekgalela	motshehare	motshegare	iminemaqanda	imini
	nor (conj)	nòg	le ge e ka ba	kapa	le fa e le	okanye	noma
	north (a)	noord	-leboa	-Leboya	-bokone	-ntla	-asenyakatho
	north (n)	noorde	leboa	Leboya	bokone	umntla	inyakatho
	nose (n)	neus	nko	nko	nko	impumlo	ikhala
	nostril (n)	neusgat	kgalananko	lesoba la nko	lerobananko	iphumlo	ikhala
	nothing (n)	niks	selo	letho	-pe	ubungabikho	ize
	notice (n)	kennisgewing	tsebišo	tsebiso	kitsiso	isaziso	umnako
	notice (v)	opmerk	-lemoga	-elellwa	-lemoga	-qaphela	-naka
	notify (v)	kennis gee	-tsebiša	-tsebisa	-itsise	-azisa	-azisa
	notoriety (n)	berugtheid	bosehlogo	botumo	tumo	ukuduma	udumo olubi
	noun (n)	selfstandige naamwoord	leina	lebitso	leina	isibizo	ibizo
	novel (n)	roman	padi	pale	padi	inoveli	inoveli
	November (n)	November	Nofemere	Pudungwana	Ngwanatseele	uNcvemba	uNovemba
	now (adv)	nou	bjale	jwale	-jaanong	ngoku	manje
	nuisance (n)	steurnis	matshwenyego	kgathatso	letshwenyo	inkathazo	inkathazo
	numb (a)	dood	-hwilego bogatšo	-sa utlweng	-bosisi	-fileyo	-ngasezwa
	number (n)	nommer	nomoro	palo	palo	inani	inombolo
	nun (n)	non	moitlamigadi	moitlami	moitlami	unongendi	isisitela
	nurse (n)	verpleegster	mooki	nese	mooki	umongikazi	unesi
	nurse (v)	verpleeg	-oka	-oka	-oka	-onga	-nesa
	nut (n)	neut	koko	tholwana	thamane	inqoba	inhlamvu yomuthi eqathwayo
	nutrition (n)	voeding	phepo	phepo	dijo	isondlo	ukondliwa komzimba

English	Afrikaans	N Sotho	Sesotho	Tswana	Xhosa	Zulu	O
oak (n)	eikeboom	moeike	eike	oak	umoki	i-oki	
oar (n)	roeispaan	lehuduo	lesokwana	selabo	iphini	umgwedli	
oath (n)	eed	kano	kano	kano	isifungo	isifungo	
oats (n)	hawer	outse	habore	habore	iowutsi	ifoliji	
obedience (n)	gehoorsaamheid	go kwa	boikokobetso	kutlo	intobeko	ukulalela	
obedient (a)	gehoorsaam	-kwago	-ikokobeditse	-kutlo	-thobekile(yo)	-lalelayo	
obey (v)	gehoorsaam wees	-kwa	-ikokobetsa	-utlwa	-thobela	-lalela	
object (n)	voorwerp	selo	ntho	selo	injongo senzi	into	
object (v)	beswaar maak	-gana	-hana	-gana	-ala	-phikisa	
objectionable (a)	aanstootlik	-kgopišago	-hanwang	-kgopisang	aleka(yo)	-ngathandeki	
obligation (n)	verpligting	tshwanelo	tlamo	mokgaphe	imfanelo	isibopho	
obscene (a)	onbetaamlik	-be	-hlabisang dihlong	-tlhokang botho	-ngcolileyo	-nenhlamba	
obscenity (n)	onbetaamlikheid	bobe	manyala	botlhokabotho	ukungcola	inhlamba	
observant (a)	oplettend	-hlokomelago	-sedi	-elang tlhoko	-qaphelayo	-qaphelayo	
observe (v)	waarneem	-lemoga	-ela hloko	-lepa	-qaphela	-qaphela	
observer (n)	waarnemer	molemogi	molemohi	molepi	umqapheli	ingqapheli	
obstacle (n)	hindernis	lepheko	tshito	kgoreletso	umqobo	isivimbelo	
obstinate (a)	hardkoppig	-ngangelago	-manganga	-kgopo	-ngevayo	-nenkani	
obstruct (v)	belemmer	-šitiša	-sitisa	-kgoreletsa	-thintela	-vimbela	
obstruction (n)	belemmernis	tšhitišo	tshitiso	kgoreletso	uthintelo	ukuvimbela	
obtain (v)	bekom	-humana	-fumana	-bona	-zuza	-zuza	
obvious (a)	vanselfsprekend	-molaleng	-totobetse	mo pepeneneng	-cacile(yo)	-bonakele	
occasion (n)	geleentheid	lebaka	sebaka	motlha	ithuba	umkhosi	
occur (v)	voorkom	-diragala	-etsahala	-nna teng	-enzeka	-vela	
ocean (n)	oseaan	lewatle	lewatle	lewatle	ulwandle	ulwandle	
ochre (n)	oker	letsoku	letsoku	letsoku	imbola	uhlobo lwebumba	
October (n)	Oktober	Oktobore	Mphalane	Diphalane	Oktobha	u-Okthoba	
odd (a)	onewe	-sa lekanelego	ntho esele	-setlholo	-ngumnqakathi	-dwa-nje	
oesophagus (n)	slukderm	mometšo	mmetso	mometso	ummizo	umminzo	
of (prep)	van	ya-	ya-	wa, a, tsa,…	ya-	-a-	
offence (n)	oortreding	molato	tshitelo	sekgopi	ityala	isicunulo	
offend (v)	aanstoot gee	-kgopiša	-sitelwa	-kgopa	-khubekisa	-cunula	
offensive (a)	aanstootlik	-kgopišago	-hlokofatsang	-tlhokang botho	-khubekisayo	-cunulayo	
offer (n)	aanbod	tšhišinyo	mpho	kabelo	umnikelo	isithembiso	
offer (v)	aanbied	-šišinya	-fa	-naya	-nikela	-thembisa	
office (n)	kantoor	ofisi	kantoro	ofisi	iofisi	ihhovisi	
official (a)	amptelik	-semmušo	-mmuso	semmuso	-burhulumente	-esikhundla	
official (n)	amptenaar	mohlankedi	mohlanka wa mmuso	mosimegi	igosa	isiphathimandla	
often (adv)	dikwels	gantši	kgafetsa	atisa	njalo	kaningi	
oil (n)	olie	oli	oli	ole	ioli	i-oyili	
old (a)	oud	-tala	-holo	-gologolo	-dala	-dala	
olive (n)	olyf	mohlware	tholwana ya mohlware	motlhware	umnquma	i-olivi	
omen (n)	voorteken	tlholo	pontsho	sekai	umhlola	ibika	
ominous (a)	onheilspellend	-tšhošago	-tshabehang	-botlhodi	-omhlola	-nemihlola	
omission (n)	weglating	tlogelo	sekgeo	tlhokomologo	ushiyo	ukushiya	
omit (v)	weglaat	-tlogela	-tlohela	-lesa	-shiya	-shiya	
on (prep)	op	godimo ga	ho-	ka	phezu	phezu kwa-	
once (adv)	een maal	gatee	hang	gangwe	kanye	kanye	
one (n)	een	tee	nngwe	nngwe	inye	ukunye	
onion (n)	ui	eie	eie	eie	itswele	u-anyanisi	
only (adv)	slegs	fela	feela	fela	kuphela	kuphela	
only (a)	enigste	nnoši	feela	-nosi	-kuphela	-dwa	
onward (adv)	voorwaarts	pele	pele	pele	phambili	phambili	
ooze (v)	sypel	-tshotshoma	-dutla	-tsimoga	-thululeka	-bhicika	
open (a)	oop	-butšwego	-bulehile	-bulegileng	-vulekile(yo)	-vuliwe	
open (v)	oopmaak	-bula	-bula	-bula	-vula	-vula	
opening (n)	opening	pulo	boahlamo	phatlha	intunja	ukuvula	
openly (a)	openlik	-molaleng	-pontsheng	mo pepeneneng	-phandle	-obala	
operate (v)	opereer	-bua	-bua	-ara	-qhaqha	-hlinza	
operation (n)	operasie	puo	puo	karo	uqhaqho	ukuhlinza	

O	English	Afrikaans	N Sotho	Sesotho	Tswana	Xhosa	Zulu
	operator (n)	operateur	modiriši	sebui	modiri	umqhaqhi	umqhubi-msebenzi
	opinion (n)	mening	kgopolo	kgopolo	kakanyo	uluvo	umbono
	opportunity (n)	geleentheid	sebaka	monyetla	tshiamelo	ithuba	ithuba
	oppose (v)	opponeer	-ganetša	-hanyetsa	-ganetsa	-chasa	-melana na-
	opposition (n)	opposisie	kganetšo	kganyetso	kganetso	inkcaso	ukumelana
	oppress (v)	onderdruk	-gatelela	-tuba	-gatelela	-cinezela	-cindezela
	oppression (n)	onderdrukking	kgatelelo	botubo	kgatelelo	ingcinezelo	ukucindezela
	oppressor (n)	onderdrukker	mogateledi	motubi	mogateledi	umcinezeli	umcindezeli
	or (conj)	of	goba	kapa	ampo	okanye	noma
	orange juice (n)	lemoensap	todi ya dinamune	lero la lamunu	matute a namune	incindi yeorenji	ujusi kawolintshi
	orange (a)	oranje	-modipa	-lamunu	-bonamune	-orenji	umbala wewolintshi
	orange (n)	lemoen	namune	lamunu	namune	iorenji	iwolintshi
	orchestra (n)	orkes	okese	diletsi	okesetera	iokhestra	i-okhestra
	order (n)	bevel	taelo	taelo	tao	umyalelo	umyalezo
	order (v)	beveel	-laela	-laela	-laela	-yalela	-layeza
	ordinary (a)	gewoon	-ka mehla	-ka mehla	-itsegeng	-qhelekile(yo)	-vamile
	organ (n)	orrel	okane	thomo	letlole	uhadi	i-ogani
	organisation (n)	organisasie	peakanyo	mokgatlo	thulaganyo	umbutho	inhlangano
	organise (v)	reël	-beakanya	-hlophisa	-rulaganya	-ququzelela	-hlela
	organist (n)	orrelis	moletšaokane	rathomo	moletsiletlole	umdlali -hadi	umdlali we-ogani
	origin (n)	oorsprong	mathomo	tlhaho	tshimologo	imvelo	umdabu
	ornament (n)	ornament	sekgabišo	mokgabiso	kgabiso	umhombiso	umhlobiso
	orphan (n)	weeskind	tšhuana	kgutsana	khutsana	inkedama	intandane
	orphanage (n)	weeshuis	ditšhuaneng	dikgutsaneng	dikhutsaneng	umzi weenkedama	ikhaya lezintandane
	ostrich (n)	volstruis	mpšhe	mpjhe	ntshwe	inciniba	intshe
	other (a)	ander	-ngwe	-ng	-sele	-nye	-nye
	otherwise (adv)	anders	ge go se bjalo	ka hosele	ka go sele	kungenjalo	ngokunye
	our (pron)	ons	-rena	-rona	rona	-ithu	-ithu
	ours (pron)	ons s'n	-rena	-rona	-rona	-ithu	abethu
	ourselves (pron)	onsself	-i-	rona	rona	thina	thina
	out (prep)	uit		ka ntle	ntle	phandle	phandle
	outbreak (n)	uitbreking	go wa (ga bolwetši)	qhomo	tshimologo	uqhambuko	ukuqhamuka
	outcome (n)	uitkoms	pheletšo	pheletso	botsho	isiphumo	umphumela
	outside (n)	buitekant	ka ntle	ka ntle	lentle	umphandle	umphandle
	ovary (n)	eierstok	popelo	popelo	tsala	isiyilelo -qanda	izizalo
	oven (n)	oond	onto	onto	bobesetso	iontu	uhhavini
	over (prep)	oor	godimo ga	(ka)hodima	fa godimo	ngaphezulu	phesheya
	overalls (n)	oorpak	obarolo	obarolo	obarolo	iovaroli	i-ovaloli
	overcast (a)	bewolk	-nago le maru	-maru a thibile	-maruru	-sibekele	-buyisile
	overcoat (n)	oorjas	jase	jase	jase	idyasi	ijazi
	overcome (v)	te bowe kom	-fenya	-hlola	-fenya	-oyisa	-ahlula
	overcrowd (v)	oorvol wees	-tlala batho	-subuhlellana	-betagana	-xinanisa	-butheleka
	overflow (v)	oorloop	-falala	-kgaphatseha	-tshologa	-phuphuma	-chichima
	overgrown (a)	toegegroei	-medilego	-pupeditsweng	-sekgwa	-khule gqitha	-enile
	overpower (v)	oorweldig	-fenya	-fekisa	-fekeetsa	-oyisa	-ahlula
	overseas (n)	oorsee	mošola wa mawatle	mose ho mawatle	moseja	phesheya	phesheya
	overshadow (v)	oorskadu	-phala	-sira	-khurumetsa	-sitha	-engama
	overtake (v)	verbysteek	-feta	-feta	-feta	-dlula	-edlula
	overthrow (v)	omvergooi	-menola	diha	-diga	-bhukuqa	-wisa
	owe (v)	skuld	-kolota	-kolota	-kolota	-tyala	-kweleta
	owl (n)	uil	leribiši	sephooko	morubisi	isikhova	isikhova
	own (a)	eie	-ka	-ka	-ga-	yam	-a-
	own (v)	besit	-na le	-rua	-na le	-banayo	-ba- na-
	owner (n)	eienaar	mong	monga	mong	umnini	umnikazi
	ox (n)	os	pholo	pholo	pholo	inkabi yenkomo	inkabi
	oxygen (n)	suurstof	oksitšene	okosejene	okosijene	umongomoya	i-oksijini
	oyster (n)	oester	kgopa ya lewatle	oesetere		imbatyisi	ukhwathu
	pack (v)	pak	-paka	-pakela	-paka	-bekelela	-hlanganisa
	pact (n)	verdrag	kgwerano	tumellano	tumalano	umnqophiso	isivumelwano

English	Afrikaans	N Sotho	Sesotho	Tswana	Xhosa	Zulu
paddock (n)	veekampie	kampana	lekgulo	kampa	idlelo	inkambu
padlock (n)	hangslot	sekgonyo	seloto	lloko	iqhaga	ingide
pagan (a)	heidens	-boheitene	-bohedene	-moheitene	-obuhedeni	-obuhedeni
pagan (n)	heiden	moheitene	mohedene	moheitene	umhedeni	umhedeni
page (n)	bladsy	letlakala	leqephe	tsebe	iphepha	ikhasi
pail (n)	emmer	kgamelo	kgamelo	kgamelo	iemele	ithunga
pain (n)	pyn	bohloko	lehlaba	botlhoko	iintlungu	ubuhlungu
paint (n)	verf	pente	pente	pente	ipeyinti	upende
paint (v)	verf	-penta	-penta	-penta	-qaba	-penda
pair (n)	paar	bobedi	bobedi	bobedi	isibini	amaphahla
palace (n)	paleis	mošate	ntlo ya borena	ntlo ya segosi	ibhotwe	iphalasi
palate (n)	verhemelte	magalapa	lehalapa	magalapa	inkalakahla	ulwanga
pale (a)	bleek	-galogilego	-retetseng	-setlha	-mthuzubala	-mhloshana
palm (n)	palm	legoswi	seatla	legofi	intende yesandla	intende yesandla
pamphlet (n)	pamflet	pukwana	bukana	lokwalonyana	incwadana	iphamfulethe
pan (n)	pan	pane	pane	mogobe	ipani	ipani
pancreas (n)	pankreas	pankarea	manyeme	marakanamantsi	amasi	amanyikwe
pane (n)	ruit	galase ya lefasetere	kgalase ya fensetere	reite	iglasi yefestile	iwindi
panel van (n)	paneelwa	bene	panelevena	bene	iveni yokusebenza	iveni
panic (n)	paniek	letšhogo	letshoho	letshogo	ukuphaphazela	ukuphaphazela
panic (v)	paniekerig wees	-tšhogile	-tshoha	-tshoga	-phaphazela	-phaphazela
pant (v)	hyg	-fegelwa	-fehelwa	-fegelwa	-khefuzela	-phefuzela
pantihose (n)	kousbroekie	phenthihouse	phenthihouse	makusa	ipentihowusi	amasokisi abesifazane
pantry (n)	spens	bobolokelo bja dijo	sepense	polokelo ya dijo	ipentri	iphandolo
paper (n)	papier	pampiri	pampiri	pampiri	iphepha	iphepha
parable (n)	gelykenis	seswantšho	setshwantsho	setshwantsho	umzekeliso	umzekeliso
paraffin (n)	paraffien	parafene	parafini	parafene	iparafini	uphalafini
paragraph (n)	paragraaf	temana	tema	tema	umhlathi	isigaba
parallel (n)	parallel	mmapano	thapallo	papo	isinxusi	-hambisanayo
paralyse (v)	verlam	-rephiša	-holofatsa	-bolaya mfama	-bulala imithambo	-thwebula
paralysis (n)	verlamming	morepho	kgolofalo	go swa mfama	ukungasebenzi kwe-lungu lomzimba	umthwebulo
paramount (a)	hoogste	-gologolo	-holo	-godimodimo	-ongamele(yo)	-khulu kunakho konke
parcel (n)	pakket	phasela	seshoba	phasele	ipasile	iphakethe
pardon (v)	vergewe	-lebalela	-tshwarela	-itshwarela	-xolela	-xolela
parent (n)	ouer	motswadi	motswadi	motsadi	umzali	umzali
park (n)	park	phaka	paka	phaka	ipaka	ipaki
park (v)	parkeer	-phaka	-emisa	-emisa	-misa	-paka
parking ticket (n)	parkeerkaartjie	thekete ya molato wa go phaka	tekete ya ho paka	thekete ya go phaka	itikiti lokumisa	ithikithi lokupaka
parking (n)	parkering	lefelo la go phaka	kemong ya dipalangwang	lefelo la go phaka	indawo yokumisa	ukupaka
parliament (n)	parlement	kgotlakgolo	kgotlakgolo	palamente	ipalamente	iphalamende
parole (n)	parool	tokollo ka kwelobohloko	parole	paroule	isithembiso sokungabaleki	isithembiso sokungabaleki
parsley (n)	pietersielie	pareseli	sehwete se sesweu	paresele	umfuno	ipasili
part (n)	deel	seripa	karolo	kaba	isahlulo	umunxa
part (v)	skei	-kgaogana	-arola	-kgaogana	-ahlukana	-ahlukananisa
particular (a)	besonder	-itšego	-ikgethang	-segolo	-thile	-thile
parting (n)	paadjie	tselana	karohano	kgaogano	indledlana	ukwahlukana
partner (n)	vennoot	modirišani	mohwebisani	mogwebisani	iqabane	umata
party (n)	party	phathi	mokga	setlhopa	iqela	umcimbi
pass (n)	pas	pasa	kgoro	pasa	ipasi	ipasi
pass (v)	verbygaan	-feta	-feta	-feta	-dlula	-dlula
passenger (n)	passasier	monamedi	mopalami	mopalami	umhambi	umgibeli
past (n)	verlede	lefetile	nako e fetileng	segologolo	ixesha eladlulayo	isikhathi esidlulileyo
paste (n)	pasta	sekgomaretši	sekgomaretsi	bogobe	intlama	ubundubundu
paste (v)	plak	-gomaretša	-kgomaretsa	-kgomaretsa	-ncamathisela	-namathelisa
pastry (n)	pastei	kukunama	hlama	phae	intlama yekeyiki	uqweqwe lukaphayi
pasture (n)	weiveld	mafulo	makgulo	mafulo	idelo	idlelo

P	English	Afrikaans	N Sotho	Sesotho	Tswana	Xhosa	Zulu
	patch (n)	lappie	segaswa	petjhe	sebata	isiziba	isibheqe
	path (n)	pad	tsela	tselanyana	tsela	indledlana	indlela
	patience (n)	geduld	bopelotelele	mamello	boitshoko	umonde	ukubekezela
	patient (a)	geduldig	-bopelotelele	-mamellang	-pelotelele	-nomonde	-bekile
	patient (n)	pasiënt	molwetši	mokudi	mmobodi	isigulana	isiguli
	pattern (n)	patroon	sekaelo	paterone	paterone	isizeko	iphethini
	paunch (n)	boepmaag	mogodu	lekuka	lebotsane	intesha	umkhaba
	pauper (n)	behoeftige	mohloki	mofutsana	modidi	udwayi	uphanqu
	pavement (n)	sypaadjie	tselathokwana	tselathoko	mokwakwa	indledlana yeenyawo	iphevumente
	paw (n)	poot	borofa	maro	leroo	ithupha	isidladla
	pawpaw (n)	papaja	phopho	phopho	phoophoo	ipopo	upopo
	pay (n)	betaling	tefo	moputso	tuelo	intlawulo	inkokhelo
	pay (v)	betaal	-lefa	-putsa	-duela	-hlawula	-khokha
	payer (n)	betaler	molefi	molefi	moduedi	umhlawuli	umkhokhi
	payment (n)	betaling	tefo	tefo	tuelo	intlawulo	inkokhelo
	pea (n)	ertjie	erekisi	erekisi	erekisi	ierityisi	inhlamvu kaphizi
	peace (n)	vrede	khutšo	kgotso	kagiso	uxolo	ukuthula
	peach (n)	perske	perekisi	perekisi	perekisi	ipesika	ipetshisi
	peak (n)	piek	ntlhora	tlhoro	setlhora	incopho	isihloko
	peanut (n)	grondboontjie	tokomane	letokomane	letonkomane	indongomane	intongomane
	pear (n)	peer	piere	pere	pere	ipere	ipheya
	peck (v)	pik	-kobola	-kota	-kopa	-nqola	-ngawuza
	peculiar (a)	eienaardig	-makatšago	-ikgethileng	-sele	-ngaqhelekanga	-mangalisayo
	pedal (n)	pedaal	petala	bohato	setlhako	isinyathelo	isinyathelo
	pedestrian (n)	voetganger	mosepelakamaoto	ya tsamayang ka maoto	motsamayi	umhambi ngeenyawo	umhambiphansi
	peel (n)	skil	lekgephola	lekgapetla	letlape	uqweqwe	ikhasi
	peel (v)	skil	-kgephola	-ebola	-obola	-chuba	-hluba
	peep (v)	loer	-hlodimela	-nyarela	-okomela	-kroba	-lunguza
	peg (n)	pen	kokontwane	thakgisa	lemapo	isikhonkwane	isikhonkwane
	peg (v)	vaspen	-kokotela	-thakgisa	-tlapisa	-bethelela	-bethela
	pelvis (n)	bekken	letheka	noka	setlhana	ihleza	ithebe
	pen (n)	pen	pene	pene	pene	usiba	ipeni
	penalise (v)	straf	-otla	-otla	-otlhaa	-ohlwaya	-hlawulisa
	penalty (n)	straf	kotlo	kotlo	kotlhao	isohlwayo	ihlawulo
	pencil (n)	potlood	phensele	pensele	phensele	ipensile	ipensele
	penetrate (v)	binnedring	-tsenelela	-phunyeletsa	-nanganela	-tyhutyha	-ngena
	peninsula (n)	skiereiland	sekasehlakahlaka	peninsula	sekasetlhake	usingasiqithi	inhlonhlo
	penis (n)	penis	ntoto	ntoto	lepele	umthondo	umthondo
	penknife (n)	knipmes	thipana	thipa	kopelwane	umgotywana	igotshwa
	pennywhistle (n)	kwêlafluitjie	fulutu	foleiti	folutu	impentshana	imfengwane
	pension (n)	pensioen	phenšene	phenshene	phenšene	umhlalaphantsi	impesheni
	people (n)	mense	batho	batho	batho	abantu	abantu
	pepper (n)	peper	pepere	pepere	pherefere	ipepile	upelepele
	percent (n)	persent	phesente	phesente	phesente	ipesenti	iphesenti
	percolate (v)	perkoleer	-hlotla	-monyela	-dutla	-bilisa	-chinineka
	perfect (a)	volmaak	-phethegilego	-phethahetseng	-itekanela	-gqibelele(yo)	-gweda
	perform (v)	uitvoer	-phetha	-etsa	-dira	-enza	-enza
	performance (n)	uitvoering	mophetho	ketso	diaba	ukwenza	ukwenza
	performer (n)	uitvoerder	mophethi	moetsi	modiri	umenzi	umenzi
	perfume (n)	parfuum	monko	senoko	monko	isiqholo	usende
	perhaps (adv)	miskien	mohlamongwe	mohlomong	gongwe	mhlawumbi	mhlawumbe
	peril (n)	gevaar	kotsi	kotsi	bobe	ingozi	ingozi
	perish (v)	omkom	-bola	-shwa	-swa	-nyamalala	-bhubha
	perjure (v)	meineed pleeg	-enolla	-bua leshano kgotla	-senya maikano	-funga ubuxoki	-fungela amanga
	perjury (n)	meineed	kenollo	bopaki ba leshano	tshenyo ya maikano	ukufunga ubuxoki	ukufungela amanga
	permanent (a)	permanent	-mmaruri	-tsitsitseng	-ruri	-sigxina	-hlalayo
	permission (n)	toestemming	tumelo	tumello	tetla	imvume	imvume
	permit (n)	permit	tumelo	tumello	tetla	imvume	iphomende
	permit (v)	toelaat	-dumelela	-dumella	-letla	-vumela	-vumela

English	Afrikaans	N Sotho	Sesotho	Tswana	Xhosa	Zulu	P
persevere (v)	volhard	-kgotlelela	-qhophella	-itshoka	-zingisa	-khuthazela	
person (n)	persoon	motho	motho	motho	umntu	umuntu	
personal (a)	persoonlik	-motho	-ka nama	-sebele	-akho	-komuntu uqobo lwakhe	
perspiration (n)	perspirasie	sethitho	mofufutso	mofufutso	umbilo	umjuluko	
perspire (v)	perspireer	-tšwa sethitho	-fufulelwa	-fufula	-bila	-juluka	
persuade (v)	oorreed	-kgodiša	-qophella	-sokasoka	-cenga	-bonisa	
persuasion (n)	oorreding	kgodišo	qophello	kgono	ukucenga	ukubonisa	
perturb (v)	verontrus	-tšhoša	-kgathatsa	-ferekana	-khathaza	-ethusa	
pest (n)	pes	leuba	phehli	sesenyi	ubhubhane	inkathazo	
pester (v)	pla	-tshwenya	-kgathatsa	-tshwenya	-khathaza	-khathaza	
pet (n)	troeteldier	seruiwaseratwa	phoofolo e ratwang	seotlwana	isilo-qabane	ukuntoko	
petal (n)	kroonblaar	petala ya letšoba	petale	letlharelegolo	igqabi	isigcebe sembali	
petrol (n)	petrol	peterolo	peterole	peterolo	ipetroli	upetroli	
petticoat (n)	onderrok	onoroko	onnoroko	mosese	unomtidili	ipitikoti	
petty (a)	kleinlik	-nyatšegago	-sa tsebisahaleng	-nyenyane	-ncinane	-ncinyane	
pharmacist (n)	apteker	mokhemisi	mokhemise	moapoteke	unokhemesti	umkhemisi	
phenomenon (n)	verskynsel	ponagalo	ketsahalo	ponagalo	into	isenzeko	
phlegm (n)	fleim	mamina	sehohlola	sehuba	isikhohlela	isikhwehlela	
photograph (n)	foto	seswantšho	setshwantsho	setshwantsho	ifoto	isithombe	
photograph (v)	fotografeer	-swantša	-tshwantsha	-tshwantsha	-fota	-thatha isithombe	
phrase (n)	sinsnede	sekafoko	sekapolelo	ntlha	ibinzana	isigejane samazwi	
physique (n)	liggaamsbou	popego	seemo sa mmele	popego	ukwakhiwa komzimba	umzimba	
pianist (n)	klavierspeler	moraloki wa piano	moletsathomo	moletsi wa piano	umdlalihadi	umshayi wopiyane	
piano (n)	klavier	piano	thomo	piano	uhadi	upiyane	
pick (v)	uitkies	-kgetha	-thonya	-tlhopa	-khetha	-khetha	
pickpocket (n)	sakkeroller	lehodu	mosetjhi	senakgodi	umkhuthuzi	umkhuthuzi	
picnic (n)	piekniek	pikiniki	pikinike	pikiniki	ipikiniki	ipikiniki	
picnic (v)	piekniek hou	-dira pikiniki	-ho tshwara pikinike	-ja pikiniki	-bamba ipikniki	-phuma ipikiniki	
picture (n)	prent	seswantšho	setshwantsho	setshwantsho	umfanekiso	umfanekiso	
piece (n)	stuk	seripa	sekotwana	semika	isijungqe	isiqephu	
pierce (v)	deursteek	-phunya	-phunya	-tlhaba	-hlaba	-bhoboza	
pig (n)	vark	kolobe	kolobe	kolobe	ihagu	ingulube	
pigeon (n)	duif	leeba	leeba	leeba	ihobe	ijuba	
pile (n)	stapel	ngata	pokello	tlhatlaganyo	-fumba	isitaki	
pile (v)	stapel	-hlophela	-bokella	-tlhatlaganya	imfumba	-taka	
pill (n)	pil	pilisi	pilisi	pilisi	ipilisi	iphilisi	
pillow (n)	kussing	mosamelo	mosamo	mosamo	umqamelo	umcamelo	
pimple (n)	puisie	kemola	sehloba	kuruga	iqhakuva	insunsumba	
pin (n)	speld	sepalete	sepelete	kgokelo	isipeliti	isipeleti	
pin (v)	vasspeld	-bofa ka sepalete	-ngomela ka sepelete	-kgokela	-qhobosha	-bopha ngesipeleti	
pinch (v)	knyp	-soba	-tsipa	-nota	-tswikila	-ncweba	
pineapple (n)	pynappel	phaeneapole	peineapole	peinapole	ipayinapile	uphayinaphu	
pink (n)	pienk	pinki	pinke	pinki	ipinki	umbala wesiphofu	
pip (n)	pit	thaka	tlhodiso	thapo	ipete	uhlamvu	
pipe (n)	pyp	peipi	peipe	kakana	umbhobho	ipipi	
pit (n)	gat	petse	sekoti	lemena	umngxuma	umgodi	
pitchfork (n)	gaffel	leselo	foroko	gafole	ifolokhwe yokulayisha	imfologo yotshani	
pith (n)	pit	moko	kgafole	moko	umongo, ipete	umongo	
pitiful (a)	jammerlik	-nyamišago	-haulang	-tlhomolang pelo	-novelwano	-nomhawu	
pity (n)	jammerte	manyami	mohau	go tlhomola pelo	usizi	umhawu	
place (n)	plek	felo	tulo	felo	indawo	indawo	
plague (n)	plaag	matshwenyego	sewa	leroborobo	isigulo	inkathazo	
plain (a)	gewoon	-ka mehla	-tlwaelehileng	-komota	-cacile(yo)	-ngafekethisiwe	
plaintiff (n)	eiser	mmelaedi	moqosi	moseki	ummangali	ummangali	
plait (n)	vlegsel	leetse	thapo	leetse	umphotho	iqakathi	
plan (n)	plan	maano	leqheka	leano	icebo	isu	
plan (v)	beplan	-loga maano	-hlopha	-loga leano	-ceba	-klama	
planet (n)	planeet	polanete	polanete	naledi	iplanethi	iplanethi	
plank (n)	plank	lepolanka	lepolanka	lebatsana	iplanga	ipulangwe	
plant (n)	plant	semela	sejalo	semela	isityalo	isithombo	

P English	Afrikaans	N Sotho	Sesotho	Tswana	Xhosa	Zulu
plant (v)	plant	-bjala	-jala	-jwala	-tyala	-tshala
plastic (n)	plastiek	plastiki	polasetike	polasetiki	iplastiki	ipulastiki
plate (n)	bord	poroto	poleiti	boroto	ipleyiti	isitsha
platform (n)	platform	polatefomo	sebae	serala	iqonga	ipulatifomu
play (n)	toneelstuk	tiragatšo	tshwantshiso	motshameko	umdlalo	umdlalo
play (v)	speel	-bapala	-bapala	-tshameka	-dlala	-dlala
plea (n)	pleidooi	thapelo	thapedi	go ala diatla	isicelo	ukuphendula ecaleni
plead (n)	pleit	thapeletšo	-rapela	go ala diatla	ukuzithethela	-phendula ecaleni
pleasure (n)	plesier	lethabo	thabo	monate	ubumnandi	injabulo
plentiful (a)	talryk	-atilego	-ngata	-tlalatlalang	-ninzi	-ningi
plenty (a)	volop	-atilego	-tletsetletse	-ntsi	-zele	-ningi
pleurisy (n)	borsvliesontsteking	ploresi	ho ruruha ka sefubeng	boletswe jwa letha la makgwa	ukralo lwenwebu-miphunga	amahlaba
pliers (n)	knyptang	kinipitane	letlao	tang	itanka	udlawu
plot (n)	komplot	bolotšana	mmomori	morero	iyelenqe	icebo
plot (v)	saamsweer	-rera ka sephiri	-etsa mmomori	-sokela motho pelo	-bhunga	-ceba
plough (n)	ploeg	mogoma	mohoma	mogoma	ikhuba	igeja
plough (v)	ploeg	-lema	-lema	-lema	-lima	-lima
pluck (v)	pluk	-kga	-kgola	-fula	-xhwitha	-kha
plug (n)	prop	sethibo	sekwahelo	sethibo	isivingco	isivimbo
plug (v)	toestop	-poropela	-kwala	-kaba	-vingca	-vimba
plum (n)	pruim	poreimi	poraema	poreimi	iplamu	ipulamu
plural (n)	meervoud	bontšhi	bongata	bontsi	isininzi	ubuningi
pneumonia (n)	longontsteking	nyumonia	nyomonia	nyumonia	inyumoniya	izibhobo
pocket (n)	sak	mokotla	pokotho	potla	ipokotho	isikhwama
pockmark (n)	pokmerk	lebadi la sekobonyane	kgwadiamaoma	leroba	irhongo	imfoloko
pod (n)	peul	sephotlwa	monawa	mhure	umdumba	umdumba
poem (n)	gedig	sereto	thothokiso	leboko	isibongo	inkondlo
poet (n)	digter	sereti	sethothokisi	mmoki	imbongi	imbongi
point (n)	punt	ntlha	ntlha	ntlha	iqondo	isihloko
poison (n)	gif	mpholo	tjhefo	more	ityhefu	isihlungu
poison (v)	vergiftig	-ješa mpholo	-fa tjhefo	-bolaya	-tyhefa	-faka isihlungu
pole (n)	paal	kota	palo	sesana	isibonda	isigxobo
polecat (n)	muishond	nakedi	nakedi	nakedi	iqaqa	iqaqa
police (n)	polisie	maphodisa	lepolesa	mapodisa	ipolisa	amaphoyisa
policeman (n)	polisieman	lephodisa	lepolesa	lepodisa	ipolisa	iphoyisa
police station (n)	polisiekantoor	seteišene sa maphodisa	seteishene sa sepolesa	lefelo la mapodisa	isikhululo samapolisa	ipholisiteshi
policy (n)	beleid	maikemišetšo	leano	maikemisetso	umgaqo	umgomo
polish (n)	politoer	pholiši	poleshe	pholetšhe	amafutha	upholishi
polish (v)	poleer	-pholiša	-polesha	-poletšha	-qaba	-pholisha
polite (a)	hoflik	-botho	-ikokobeditseng	-bonolo	-mbeko	-thobekile
political (a)	polities	-politiki	-politike	-sepoletiki	-nobupolitika	-nobupoliti
politics (n)	politiek	politiki	dipolitike	poletiki	iipolitiki	ipolitiki
pollen (n)	stuifmeel	modula	modula	mmudula	ipoleni	impova
pollution (n)	besoedeling	tšhilafatšo	tshilafatso	kgotlelo	ukungcoliseka	ukungcolisa
polygamy (n)	poligamie	go nyala basadi ba bantši	sethepu	bogadikane	isithembu	isithembu
ponder (v)	bepeins	-akanya	-lohotha	-akanya	-zikisa	-cabanga
pool (n)	poel	sediba	letamo	letlodi	ichibi	ichibi
poor (a)	arm	-diilago	-futsanehileng	-humanegileng	-lihlwempu	-mpofu
poor (n)	armes	badiidi	mafutsana	bahumanegi	ihlwempu	abampofu
pope (n)	pous	mopapa	mopapa	mopapa	ipowupu	uPhapha
poplar (n)	populier	mopopoliri	populiri	popoleri	umthi wepampiri	ubhabhulini
popular (a)	gewild	-tumilego	-tumileng	-rategang	-aziwayo	-akubantu
population (n)	bevolking	baagi	baahi	baagi	uluntu	inani labantu
porcupine (n)	ystervark	noko	noko	noko	incanda	ingungumbane
pork (n)	varkvleis	nama ya kolobe	nama ya kolobe	nama ya kolobe	inyama yehagu	inyama yengulube
porridge (n)	pap	bogobe	papa	bogobe	isidudu	iphalishi
portion (n)	gedeelte	kabelo	karolo	kaba	isabelo	inxenye

English	Afrikaans	N Sotho	Sesotho	Tswana	Xhosa	Zulu	P
position (n)	posisie	leemo	boemo	maemo	indawo	isimo	
positive (a)	positief	-nyakegago	-dumelang	-ruri	-qinisekile(yo)	-gamele	
possible (a)	moontlik	-kgonegago	-etsahalang	-gongwe	-ngenzeka	-enzekayo	
post (n)	pos	poso	poso	poso	iposi	iposi	
post (v)	pos	-posa	-posa	-romela	-posa	-posa	
postage stamp (n)	posseël	setempe	setempe	setempe	istampu sokuposa	isitembu	
postal order (n)	posorder	posotere	posetaleota	poseotore	ipostal-oda	iposoda	
postcard (n)	poskaart	poskarata	posekarete	posokarata	iposi-khadi	iposikhadi	
posterity (n)	nageslag	leloko	leloko	bana	isizukulwana	izizukulwane ezizayo	
postman (n)	posbode	morwalaposo	raposo	ramakwalo	unoposi	umuntu weposi	
post office (n)	poskantoor	posong	posong	posong	iposofisi	iposi	
postpone (v)	uitstel	-thiša	-suthisetsa morao	-beisa pelo	-hlehlisa	-hlehlisa	
pot (n)	pot	pitša	pitsa	pitsa	imbiza	ibhodwe	
potato (n)	aartappel	letapola	tapole	lekwele	itapile	izambane	
pottery (n)	pottebakkery	bobopapitša	bobopi	popo ya dinkgo	umsebenzi wodongwe	umsebenzi wokubumba	
pound (v)	fynstamp	-thuma	-tula	-touta	-cola	-gxoba	
pour (v)	skink	-tšhela	-tshela	-tshela	-galela	-thela	
pout (v)	pruil	-hlonama	-petlekisa melomo	-betolola	-jala	-phukula umlomo	
poverty (n)	armoede	bodiidi	bofutsana	bohumanegi	ubuhlwempu	ubumpofu	
power (n)	mag	maatla	matla	maatla	amandla	amandla	
powerful (a)	magtig	-nago le maatla	-matla	-maatla	-namandla	-namandla	
practical (a)	prakties	-tirišo	-ka etswang	-tiriso	-ngenzeka	-nokwenzeka	
practise (v)	oefen	-tlwaetša	-hlakisa	-katisa	qhelisa	-zijwayeza	
praise (n)	lof	moreto	thoriso	pako	uncomo	ukubonga	
praise (v)	loof	-reta	-rorisa	-boka	-ncoma	-bonga	
praiseworthy (a)	lofwaardig	-retegago	-lokelwang ho roriswa	-bokwang	-ncomeka(yo)	-bongekayo	
pray (v)	bid	-rapela	-rapela	-rapela	-thandaza	-thandaza	
prayer (n)	gebed	thapelo	thapelo	thapelo	umthandazo	umthandazo	
preach (v)	preek	-rera	-ruta	-rera	-shumayela	-shumayela	
preacher (n)	predikant	moruti	moruti	moreri	umshumayeli	umshumayeli	
precede (v)	voorafgaan	-eta pele	-etella pele	-etelela	-khokela	-andulela	
precious (a)	kosbaar	-bohlokwa	-bohlokwa	-tlhokegang	-xabisekile (yo)	-nqabile	
predator (n)	roofdier	sebata	sebata	sebata	irhamncwa	isilwane esiphangayo	
predict (v)	voorspel	-laola	-porofeta	-supetsa	-xela	-bikezela	
prediction (n)	voorspelling	taolo	boporofeta	tshupetso	isiprofeto	umbiko	
preface (n)	voorwoord	ketapele	ketapele	ketapele	imbulambethe	isanduleliso	
prefer (v)	verkies	-rata	-kgetha	-rata	-khetha	-enyula	
pregnant (a)	swanger	-imilego	-emere	-merwalo	-nzima	-khulelwe	
prejudice (n)	vooroordeel	tshekamo	leeme	katlholelopele	ukuqale ugwebe	ukulimaza	
preparation (n)	voorbereiding	boitokišetšo	tokisetso	paakanyetso	amalungiselelo	ukulungisela	
prepare (v)	voorberei	-lokišetša	-lokis(ets)a	-baakanya	-lungiselela	-lungisa	
prescribe (v)	voorskryf	-kgethela	-balla	-laetsa	-alatha	-layeza	
prescribed (a)	voorgeskrewe	-kgethetšwego	-baletsweng	-beilweng	-alathelwe(yo)	-qokiwe	
prescription (n)	voorskrif	taelelo	taelo	taetso	umyalelo	isithako	
present (n)	geskenk	mpho	mpho	mpho	isipho	isipho	
present (v)	skenk	-fa	-fa	-fa	-pha	-pha	
preserve (v)	bewaar	-boloka	-boloka	-boloka	-londoloza	-londoloza	
president (n)	president	mopresidente	moporesidente	poresidente	umongameli	umongameli	
press (n)	pers	kgatišo	kgatiso	kgatiso	abashicileli	into yokucindizela	
press (v)	pers	-gatiša	-hatisa	-gatisa	-cudisa	-cindizela	
pressure (n)	druk	kgatelelo	kgatello	kgatelelo	uxinzelelo	ukucindizela	
presume (v)	veronderstel	-hloma	-lekanya	-tseela gore	-zindla	-xhomondela	
pretence (n)	skyn	boikgakantšho	boikaketsi	boitimokanyo	ukuzenzisa	ukuzenzisa	
pretend (v)	voorgee	-ikgakantša	-ikaketsa	-konkometsa	-zenzisa	-zenzisa	
pretext (n)	voorwendsel	boikgakantšho	thetso	seipato	amampunge	icebo	
pretty (a)	mooi	-botse	-tle	-ntle	-hle	-hle	
prevent (v)	voorkom	-thibela	-thibela	-kganna	-nqaba	-vimbela	
prevention (n)	voorkoming	thibelo	thibelo	kganelo	unqando	ukuvimbela	
prey (n)	prooi	sebolawa	nyamatsane	sebolawa	ixhoba	inyamazane edliwayo	
prey (v)	aas	-ja	selope	-ja	-zingela	-phanga	

P	English	Afrikaans	N Sotho	Sesotho	Tswana	Xhosa	Zulu
	price (n)	prys	theko	theko	tlhotlhwa	ixabiso	intengo
	prickly pear (n)	turksvy	foiye	torofeie	mokgopha	itolofiya	isihlehle
	pride (n)	trots	boikgogomošo	boikgohomoso	boikgodiso	ikratshi	ukuzidla
	priest (n)	priester	moprista	moprista	moruti	umbingeleli	umpristi
	primitive (a)	primitief	-segologolo	-seholoholo	-bogologolo	-ndala	-asendulo
	prince (n)	prins	kgošana	kgosana	kgosana	inkosana	uprinsi
	princess (n)	prinses	kgošigatšana	kgosatsana	morwadiaakgosi	inkosazana	uprinsesi
	principal (n)	hoof	hlogo	hlooho	mogokgo	inqununu	unhloko
	principle (n)	beginsel	theo	theo	theo	inqobo	umthetho
	print (v)	druk	-gatiša	-hatisa	-gatisa	-shicilela	-cindizela
	prison (n)	gevangenis	kgolego	tjhankane	kgolegelo	itolongo itrongo	ijele
	prisoner (n)	gevangene	mogolegwa	motshwaruwa	mogolegwa	umbanjwa	isiboshwa
	prisoner-of-war (n)	krygsgevangene	lethopša	motshwaruwa wa ntweng	setshwarwa-sa-ntwa	umbanjwa wemfazwe	umthunjwa
	private (a)	privaat	-motho a nnoši	poraefete	-sephiri	-angasese	-akhe yedwa
	prize (n)	prys	sefoka	moputso	sekgele	ibhaso	umklomelo
	prize (v)	op prys stel	-lebogela	-rorisa	-akgola	-xabisa	-klomela
	problem (n)	probleem	bothata	qaka	bothata	ingxaki	inkinga
	procedure (n)	prosedure	tshepedišo	tsamaiso	tsamaiso	inkqubo	indlela yenqubo
	proceed (v)	voortgaan	-tšwela pele	-tswela pele	-tswelela pele	-qhuba	-qhubeka
	proceedings (n)	verrigtinge	ditiro	diketsahalo	ditiragalo	inkqubo	ukuthethwa kwecala
	produce (v)	produseer	-tšweletša	-hlahisa	-uma	-velisa	-thela
	product (n)	produk	setšweletšo	sebewa	kumo	imveliso	isithelo
	professor (n)	professor	moprofesa	moporofesa	moporofesara	injingalwazi	uprofesa
	profit (n)	wins	poelo	phaello	morokotso	ingeniso	inzuzo
	profit (v)	wins maak	-boelwa	-fumana phaello	-busetsa	-zuza	-zuza
	profitable (a)	lonend	-hodišago	-putsang	-busetsang	-nengeniso	-zuzisayo
	program (n)	program	lenaneo	lenane	lenaneo	inkqubo	iprogramu
	programme (n)	program	lenaneo	lenaneo	lenaneo	inkqubo	iprogramu
	progress (n)	vooruitgang	tšwelopele	tswelopele	tswelelopele	inkqubela	inqubeko
	progress (v)	vooruitgaan	-tšwela pele	-tswela pele	-tswelela pele	-qhubela phambili	-qhubeka
	progressive (a)	progressief	-tšwelago pele	-tswelang pele	-gatelelang pele	-nenkqubela	-qhubekelayo
	prohibit (v)	verbied	-ganetša	-thibela	-itsa	-alela	-nqabela
	prolong (v)	verleng	-lelefatša	-lelefatsa	-golola	-olula	-dephisa
	prominent (a)	prominent	-bohlokwa	-tsebahalang	-itshupileng	-dandalaza(yo)	-dumileyo
	promise (n)	belofte	kholofetšo	tshepiso	tsholofetso	isithembiso	isithembiso
	promise (v)	belowe	-holofetša	-tshepisa	-solofetsa	-thembisa	-thembisa
	promote (v)	bevorder	-tšwetša pele	-phahamisa	-tsweletsa	-nyusela	-enyusa
	promotion (n)	bevordering	tšweletšopele	phahamiso	tlhatloso	unyuselo	ukwenyuswa
	pronoun (n)	voornaamwoord	lešala	leemedi	leemedi	isimelabizo	isabizwana
	pronounce (v)	uitspreek	-kwagatša	-utlwahatsa	-kapodisa	-biza	-phumisela
	pronunciation (n)	uitspraak	kwagatšo	qapodiso	kapodiso	ubizo	ukuphumisela
	proof (n)	bewys	bohlatse	bopaki	bosupi	ubungqina	ubufakazi
	property (n)	eiendom	thoto	leruo	thoto	impahla	impahla
	prophet (n)	profeet	moprofeta	moporofeta	moporofiti	umprofeti	umprofethi
	proposal (n)	voorstel	tšhišinyo	tlhahiso	tlhagiso	isincululo	isongozo
	propose (v)	voorstel	-šišinya	-hlahisa	-tlhagisa	-ndulula	-songoza
	prosecute (v)	vervolg	-sekiša	-nqosa	-sekisa	-tshutshisa	-mangalela
	prosecution (n)	vervolging	tshekišo	ho nqosa	tshekiso	utshutshiso	ukumangalelwa
	prosecutor (n)	aanklaer	mosekiši	motjhotjhisi	mosekisi	umtshutshisi	ummangaleli
	prosper (v)	floreer	-atlega	-atleha	-tswelela pele	-chuma	-chuma
	prosperous (a)	florerend	-atlegilego	-atlehileng	-tswelelang pele	-nempumelelo	-chumile
	prostitute (n)	prostituut	kgeke	seotswa	sefefe	ihenyukazi	isifebe
	protect (v)	beskerm	-šireletša	-sireletsa	-babalela	-khusela	-vikela
	protest (v)	protesteer	-kgokgona	-hanyetsa	-ganana	-chasa	-nqaba
	proud (a)	trots	-ikgogomošago	-ikgohomosang	-mabela	-zidla(yo)	-zidlayo
	prove (v)	bewys	-kgonthišiša	-bontsha	-supa	-ngqina	-bonisa
	proverb (n)	spreekwoord	seema	maele	seane	iqhalo	isaga
	provide (v)	voorsien	-fa	-fa	-tlamela	-bonelela	-nika
	prune (v)	snoei	-poma	-faola	-poma	-thena	-nquma

English	Afrikaans	N Sotho	Sesotho	Tswana	Xhosa	Zulu	R
psalm (n)	psalm	pesaleme	pesaleme	pesaleme	indumiso	ihubo	
puberty (n)	puberteit	bofsa	ho kena boholo	bokau/boroba	ukufikisa	isikhathi sokuthomba	
public (a)	openbaar	-setšhaba	-pontsheng	-bathong	-kawonke-wonke	-ephabhuliki	
public (n)	publiek	batho	batho bohle	batho	uwonke-wonke	iphabhuliki	
publish (v)	uitgee	-phatlalatša	-phatlalatsa	-phasalala	-papasha	-shicilela	
pull (v)	trek	-goga	-hula	-goga	-tsala	-donsa	
pulse (n)	pols	morethetho	ho uba ha pelo	kubakubo	umbilini	isikhupha	
pump (n)	pomp	pompo	pompo	pompo	impopo	iphampu	
pump (v)	pomp	-pompa	-pompa	-pompa	-mpompa	-futha	
pumpkin (n)	pampoen	lefodi	mokopu	lephutshe	ithanga	ithanga	
punch (v)	slaan	-nganka	-otla	-betsa	-betha	-bhakela	
puncture (n)	lekplek	lešoba	pantjhara	phantšhara	umngxunyana	imbobo	
punish (v)	straf	-otla	-otla	-otlhaya	-ohlwaya	-jezisa	
punishment (n)	straf	kotlo	kotlo	kotlhao	isohlwayo	isijeziso	
pupil (n)	leerling	morutiwa	morutwana	morutwana	umntwana	umfundi	
puppy (n)	klein hondjie	mpšanyana	ntjanyana	ntšwanyana	injana	umdlwane	
pure (a)	suiwer	-hlwekilego	-hlwekileng	phepa	-cwengileyo	-msulwa	
purgative (n)	purgeermiddel	segofiši	sehlare sa ho tshollisa	mothubiso	iyeza lokuhambisa	umuthi wokuhudisa	
purge (v)	skoonmaak	-gofa	-hlwekisa	phukutsa	-coca	-hlanza	
purify (v)	suiwer	-hlwekiša	-hlwekisa	-phepafatsa	-cwenga	-hlanza	
purity (n)	suiwerheid	tlhwekišo	hlweko	boitsheko	ukucwenga	ukuhlanzeka	
purple (a)	pers	perese	perese	perese	-mfusa	ubunsomi	
purpose (n)	oogmerk	maikemišetšo	morero	tebo	injongo	ingqondo	
purse (n)	beursie	sekgwama	sekgwama	kgwatlha	isipaji	isikhwama semali	
pursue (v)	najaag	-rakadiša	-lelekisa	-leleka	-landela	-landelisa	
pus (n)	etter	maladu	boladu	boladu	ubovu	ubovu	
push (v)	stoot	-kgorometša	-susumetsa	-kgarametsa	-tyhala	-sunduza	
put (v)	sit	-bea fase	-bea	-baya	-beka	-beka	
puzzle (n)	legkaart	mantharane	malepa	malepa	ukudideka	indida	
puzzle (n)	raaisel	marara	selotho	malea	iqashiso	isiphicaphicwano	
puzzle (v)	verwar	-gakantša	-lotha	-tlhakanya tlhogo	-dida	-dida	
pyjamas (n)	pajamas	ditšwarwamalaong	dipejama	pejama	ingutyana yokulala	amaphijama	
python (n)	luislang	hlware	tlhware	tlhware	ugqoloma	inhlwathi	
qualification (n)	kwalifikasie	thuto	boithutelo	borutegi	inkcazo	ilungelo	
qualified (a)	gekwalifiseerd	-rutegilego	-rutehileng	-rutegileng	-fanelekileyo	-nelungelo	
quality (n)	kwaliteit	khwaliti	bonono	boleng	umgangatho	ubunjani	
quantity (n)	hoeveelheid	bokaakang	bokaakang	selekano	ubungakanani	ubungako	
quarrel (n)	twis	phapano	qabang	kgotlhang	ingxabano	ukuxabana	
quarrel (v)	twis	-fapana	-qabana	-omana	-xabana	-xabana	
quarter (n)	kwart	kwarata	kotara	kota	isahlulo	ikwata	
queen (n)	koningin	kgošigadi	mofumahadi	kgosigadi	ikumkanikazi	indlovukazi	
queer (a)	snaaks	-makatšago	-makatsang	-sa itsegeng	-ngaqhelekanga	-mangalisayo	
quell (v)	demp	-thiba	-kokobetsa	-okobatsa	-bhangisa	-thulisa	
quench (v)	les	thuto	-nyorolla	-nyorolola	-phelisa unxano	-qeda ukoma	
question (n)	vraag	potšišo	potso	potso	umbuzo	umbuzo	
question (v)	vra	-botšiša	-botsa	-botsa	-buza	-buza	
queue (n)	tou	molokoloko	mola	mola	umtya	ihele	
queue (v)	toustaan	-lokologana	-koloka	-tlhomagana	-ma umtya	-hlaba ihele	
quick (a)	gou	-ka pela	ka pele	-bofefo	-khawuleza(yo)	-sheshayo	
quickly (adv)	gou	ka pela	ka pele	ka bonako	ngokukhawuleza	ngokushesha	
quiet (a)	stil	-homotšego	-thotseng	-didimetseng	-cwaka	-thulile	
quilt (n)	verekombers	kobo ya mafofa	kobo ya masiba	kobo ya diphofa	ikwiliti	ikhwilithi	
quince (n)	kweper	kwepere	kwepere	kopere	ikwepile	ukwipili	
quite (a)	taamlik	-tloga e le	-haholoholo	-ruri	noko	impela	
quotation (n)	aanhaling	khoutho	qotso	nopolo	ukucaphula	ukucaphuna	
quote (v)	aanhaal	-khoutha	-qotsa	-nopola	-caphula	-caphuna	
rabbit (n)	konyn	mmutla	mmutlanyana	mmutla	uhlobo lomvundla	unogwaja	
race (n)	wedren	tšhiano	peiso	lebelo	umdyarho	umjaho	

R	English	Afrikaans	N Sotho	Sesotho	Tswana	Xhosa	Zulu
	race (v)	resies ja	-šiana	-beisa	ja -siana	-ngenela umdyarho	-jaha
	racehorse (n)	renperd	pere ya mokato	pere ya peiso	pitse ya lebelo	ihashe lomdyarho	ihhashi lomjaho
	racial (a)	rasse	-merafe	-semorabe	ya semorafe	-nobuhlanga	-ngokwezinhlanga
	racist (a)	rassisties	-kgethollago	-mohloyamerabe	-bomorafe	-nobuhlanga	-bandlululayo ngokwezinhlanga
	radiator (n)	verkoeler	radietere	radietare	setsidifatsi	iradiyeyitha	iradiyetha
	radical (a)	radikaal	-tšwelego tseleng	-haholoholo	-gakgamatsang	-noluvo lotshintsho olugqibeleleyo	-empela
	radicle (n)	wortel	modu	motswana	modinyana	ingcambu	impande
	radio (n)	radio	radio	radio	seromamowa	unomathotholo	iwayalense
	radish (n)	radys	rateise	rateise	radisi	umfuno onegaqa	uradishi
	raft (n)	vlot	sephaphami	pholletso	moratho	isihlenga	isihlenga
	rafter (n)	dakbalk	kota ya go rulela	leballo	kapa	iplanga lophahla	umjibe
	rag (n)	lap	lenkgeretla	sekatana	lesela	ilaphu	isidwedwe
	rage (n)	woede	pefelo	kgalefo	bogale	ingqumbo	ulaka
	ragged (a)	verflenterd	-mankgeretla	-dikatana	-makgasa	-dlakadlaka	-manikiniki
	raid (n)	strooptog	thopo	phutuhelo	thopo	uhlaselo	ukuhlasela
	raid (v)	stroop	-thopa	-futuhela	-thopa	-hlasela	-hlasela
	rail (n)	staaf	seporo	setshehetso	seporo	intonga	umshayo
	railway (n)	spoorweg	seporo sa ditimela	seporo	seporo	isiporo	uloliwe
	rain (n)	reën	pula	pula	pula	imvula	imvula
	rain (v)	reën	-na	-na	-na	-na	-na
	rainbow (n)	reënboog	molalatladi	mookodi	motshewabadimo	umnyama	uthingo lwenkosazane
	raincoat (n)	reënjas	jase ya pula	jase ya pula	jase ya pula	idyasi yemvula	ijazi lemvula
	raindrop (n)	reëndruppel	lerothodi	lerothodi la pula	lerothodi	iqabaza lemvula	iconsi
	rain gauge (n)	reënmeter	kelapula	semethapula	metere ya pula	isilinganisi semvula	isilinganiso semvula
	raise (v)	ophef	-phagamiša	-phahamisa	-tlhatlosa	-nyusa	-phakamisa
	raisin (n)	rosyntjie	makwapi a diterebe	dirasenkise	moretlwa	irasentyisi	urezini
	rake (n)	hark	hareka	haraka	haraka	iharika	ihhala
	rake (v)	hark	-hareka	-haraka	-haraka	-harika	-hhala
	ram (n)	ram	phooko	pheleu	phelefu	inkunz'egusha	inqama
	ramshackle (a)	bouvallig	-lerope	-helehang	-letlotla	-bobosi, -dilikayo	-khehlezelayo
	rape (n)	verkragting	kato	peto	petelelo	udlwengulo	ukudlwengula
	rape (v)	verkrag	-kata	-beta	-betelela	-dlwengula	-dlwengula
	rapid (a)	vlugtig	lebelo	-ka pele	-bonako	-khawulezayo	-ngejubane
	rare (a)	seldsaam	-bohlokwa	-sewelo	-tlhokegang	-nqabile(yo)	-ngavamile
	rash (n)	veluitslag	mogorogo	kgophole	bogwata	irhashalala	umqubuko
	rat (n)	rot	peba	kgoto	legotlo	ibuzi	igundane
	ration (n)	rantsoen	kabelo	reshene	kabelo	umxhesho	ilesheni
	rattle (n)	ratel	segwaši	tjhwehletjhwehle	letlhao	ingxolo	igenqeza
	rattle (v)	ratel	-gwaša	-tjhwehletsa	-kgorotlha	-kroxoma	-gunquza
	ravine (n)	kloof	legaga	kgohlo	molatswana	ingxondorha	isihosha
	raw (a)	rou	-tala	-tala	-tala	-krwada	-luhlaza
	ray (n)	straal	lehlasedi	lehlasedi	lerang	ilitha	umsebe
	razor (n)	skeermes	sebeolo	lehare	legare	ireyiza	ireza
	reach (v)	bereik	-fihlela	-fihlela	-fitlha	-fikelela	-fica
	read (v)	lees	-bala	-bala	-bala	-funda	-funda
	ready (a)	gereed	-itokišeditšego	-lokileng	-baakantsweng	-lunga	-lungile
	real (a)	werklik	-nnete	-nnete	-tota	-yinyani, -nene	-liqiniso
	really (adv)	werklik	ruri	ka nnete	-tota	ngokwenyani	-ngempela
	reap (v)	oes	-buna	-kotula	-kotula	-vuna	-vuna
	rear (a)	agterste	-morago	-morao	-morago	-semva	-ngemuva
	rear (v)	grootmaak	-godiša	-otla	-rua	-khulisa	-khulisa
	reason (n)	rede	lebaka	lebaka	lebaka	isizathu	isizathu
	reason (v)	redeneer	-tšea kgang	-nahana	-akanya	-cinga	-cabanga
	reasonable (a)	redelik	-sa belaetšago	-utlwahalang	-utlwagalang	-nengqondo	-faneleyo
	rebel (n)	rebel	lerabela	lerabele	morukutlhi	umnxaxhi	imbuka
	rebel (v)	rebelleer	-rabela	-rabela	-tsuolola	-qharkqalaza	-embuka
	rebellion (n)	opstand	borabela	borabele	borukutlhi	uvukelo	ukwambuka
	receipt (n)	kwitansie	rasiti	rasite	tshupatefo	irisiti	irisidi

English	Afrikaans	N Sotho	Sesotho	Tswana	Xhosa	Zulu	R
receive (v)	ontvang	-amogela	-amohela	-amogela	-fumana	-amukela	
reception (n)	ontvangs	kamogelo	kamohelo(ng)	kamogelo	ulwamkelo	ukwamukelwa	
receptionist (n)	ontvangsklerk	moamogedi	moamohedi	telereke ya kamogelo	umamkeli	umemukeli-bahambeli	
recipe (n)	resep	tšhupetšo ya go tswaka	resepe	theo ya kapeo	iresiphi	isu lokupheka	
recite (v)	opsê	-reta	-thothokisa	-boka	-cengceleza	-landa	
recognise (v)	herken	-lemoga	-tseba	-lemoga	-nakana	-bona	
recognition (n)	herkenning	temogo	ho tseba	temogo	unakano	ukubona	
recollect (v)	onthou	-gopola	-hopola	-gopola	-khumbula	-khumbula	
recommend (v)	aanbeveel	-digela	-kgothalletsa	-atlanegisa	-ncoma	-ncoma	
recommendation (n)	aanbeveling	tigelo	kgothalletso	katlanegiso	uncomo	ukuncoma	
record (n)	rekord	pego	rekoto	rekoto	ubungqina	irekhodi	
record (v)	opteken	-ngwala	-rekota	-kwala	-bhala	-qopha	
recover (v)	herstel	-tielela	-hlaphohelwa	-fola	-fumana	-sinda	
recovery (n)	herstel	tielelo	tlhaphohelo	pholo	ukufumana	ukusinda	
rectangle (n)	reghoek	khutlonnethwi	kgutlonne	khutlonne	uxande	unxande	
rectum (n)	rektum	motsila	mohlamu	lela-la-sebi	undloku, undonci	umdidi	
red (a)	rooi	-hubedu	-fubedu	-hibidu	-bomvu	-bomvu	
redeem (v)	goedmaak	-phološa	-lopolla	-rekolola	-sindisa	-hlenga	
reduce (v)	verminder	-fokotša	-fokotsa	-ngotla	-nciphisa	-nciphisa	
reed (n)	riet	lehlakanoka	lehlaka	letlhaka	ingcongolo	umhlanga	
reef (n)	rif	mokekema	mokokotlo	lekekema	iseyile	uthunge lwamatshe	
refer (v)	verwys	-ra	-lebisa	-umaka	-bhekisa	-dlulisela	
referee (n)	skeidsregter	moahloledi	moletsaphala	motsereganyi	usompempe	unompempe	
reference (n)	verwysing	lengwalo la bohlatse	lengolo la bopaki	tshupetso	ukukhangela	ireferense	
reference (n)	getuigskrif	tšhupetšo	tebiso	kumako	ukubhekisa	ukudlulisela	
refinement (n)	verfyndheid	tshekišo	botho bo felletseng	bophepafatso	ukucokisa	ukuphucuka	
reflection (n)	weerkaatsing	pekenyo	seipone	tshupatshwano	umenyezelo	ukubuyiswa	
reflex (n)	refleks	tiragalo yeo e sa laolwego	ho nyaroha	kutlo	ukuzenzekela	ukugwenguka	
reform (n)	hervorming	mpshafatšo	tshokoloho	phetolo	uhlaziyo	ukuguquka	
refrigerator (n)	yskas	setšidifatši	forije	setsidifatsi	ifriji	ifriji	
refuge (n)	skuiling	botšhabelo	botshabelo	botshabelo	ikhusi	isiphephelo	
refund (v)	terugbetaal	-bušetša tšhelete	-buseletsa	-busetsa	-hlawula	-buyisela	
refuse (n)	vullis	tšhila	dithole	matlakala	inkunkuma	izibi	
refuse (v)	weier	-gana	-hana	-gana	-ala	-ala	
region (n)	streek	selete	setereke	kgaolo	inqila	isifunda	
register (n)	register	rejistara	rejisetara	rejisetara	irejista	irejista	
regret (n)	spyt	tshwabo	boinyatso	boikotlhao	ukuzisola	ukudabukela	
regret (v)	spyt hê	-swaba	-inyatsa	-otlhaya	-zisole	-dabukela	
regulation (n)	regulasie	molawana	molao	molao	umthetho	umthetho	
reign (n)	bewind	pušo	mmuso	puso	ulawulo	ukubusa	
reign (v)	heers	-buša	-busa	-busa	-lawula	-busa	
rein (n)	leisel	tomo	leleisele	lerapa	intambo	itomu	
reject (v)	verwerp	-gana	-nyahlatsa	-gana	-gxotha	-enqaba	
rejection (n)	verwerping	kgano	nyahlatso	kgano	ukulahla	ukwenqaba	
relation (n)	familielid	moloko	leloko	tsala ya madi	isizalwana	isihlobo	
relation (n)	verhouding	kamano	setswalle	kutlwano	unxulumano	ukuphathana	
relationship (n)	verhouding	kamano	setswalle	tsalano	unxulumano	ukuhambelana	
release (n)	loslating	tokollo	tokollo	kgololo	ukhululo	inkululeko	
release (v)	loslaat	-lokolla	-lokolla	-golola	-khulula	-khulula	
reliable (a)	betroubaar	-botegago	-tshepahalang	-boikanyego	-thembekile(yo)	-thembekile	
relief (n)	verligting	kimollo	thuso	go ikutlwa o le motho	isiqabu	usizo	
relieve (v)	verlig	-imolla	-thusa	-wela makgwafo	-qabula	-siza	
religion (n)	godsdiens	bodumedi	tumelo	bodumedi	inkolo	inkolo	
religious (a)	godsdienstig	-bodumedi	-dumelang	-sedumedi	-kholiwe(yo)	-kholiwe	
reluctant (a)	teensinnig	-sa ratego	-monyebe	-itsemeletsang	-nqenayo	-ngathandi	
rely (v)	staatmaak	-tshepha	-tshepa	-ikanya	-thembela	-themba	
remain (v)	agterbly	-šala	-sala	-sala	-sala	-sala	
remainder (n)	oorblyfsel	mašaledi	ho setseng	lesalela	intsalela	insalela	

R	English	Afrikaans	N Sotho	Sesotho	Tswana	Xhosa	Zulu
	remember (v)	onthou	-gopola	-hopola	-gakologelwa	-khumbula	-khumbula
	remind (v)	herinner	-gopotša	-hopotsa	-gopotsa	-khumbuza	-khumbuza
	reminder (n)	herinnering	kgopotšo	kgopotso	kgakololo	isikhumbuzo	isikhumbuzo
	remote (a)	afgeleë	-kgole	-hole	-gole	-kude	-kude
	removal (n)	trek	khudugo	ho falla	tshuto	imfuduko	ukuthutha
	removal (n)	verwydering	tlošo	tshuthiso	tloso	ushenxiso	ukususa
	remove (v)	verwyder	-tloša	-suthisa	-tlosa	-shenxisa	-susa
	renown (n)	beroemdheid	setumo	setumo	kitsego	indumasi	udumo
	rent (n)	huur	rente	rente	legago	ingqesho	intela
	rent (v)	huur	-hira	-hira	-hira	qesha	qasha
	repeat (v)	herhaal	-boeletša	-pheta	-boelela	-phinda	-phinda
	repent (v)	berou hê	-itshola	-sokoloha	-ikotlhaya	zoh waya	-guquka
	reply (n)	antwoord	karabo	karabo	karabo	impendulo	impendulo
	reply (v)	antwoord gee	-araba	-araba	-araba	-phendula	-phendula
	report (n)	verslag	pego	tlaleho	polelo	ingxelo	umbiko
	report (v)	berig	-bega	-tlaleha	-bolela	-nika ingxelo	-bika
	reporter (n)	verslaggewer	mmegi	motlalehi	mmegi	umniki-ngxelo	umbiki
	represent (v)	verteenwoordig	-emela	-emela	-emela	-mela	-mela
	representative (n)	verteenwoordiger	moemedi	moemedi	moemedi	ummeli	ummeli
	repulsive (a)	walglik	-ferošago dibete	-nyonyehang	-sisimosang	-gxothayo	-enyanyekayo
	request (n)	versoek	kgopelo	kopo	kopo	isicelo	isicelo
	request (v)	versoek	-kgopela	-kopa	-kopa	-cela	-cela
	rescue (n)	redding	phološo	pholoso	phaloso	uncedo	ukusindisa
	rescue (v)	red	-phološa	-pholosa	-namola	-nceda	-sindisa
	resemble (v)	aard na	-swana	-futsa	-tshwana	-fana na-	-fana
	reserve (n)	reserwe	motlatši	poloko	namaoeme	umbeko	isabelo
	reserve (v)	reserveer	-beeletša	-boloka	-dibeletsa	-bekela	-bambela
	residence (n)	verblyfplek	modulo	bodulo	bonno	indawo	umuzi
	resign (v)	bedank	-itlamolla	-dihela marapo	-itlamolola	-rhoxa	-shiya
	resist (v)	weerstaan	-ganetša	-hana	-swedietega	-xhathisa	-zabalaza
	resistance (n)	weerstand	kganetšo	matla	twantsho	ukuxhathisa	ukuzabalaza
	respect (n)	respek	tlhompho	tlhompho	tlotlego	imbeko	ukuhlonipha
	respect (v)	respekteer	-hlompha	hlompha	-tlotla	-ba nembeko	-hlonipha
	respectable (a)	fatsoenlik	-hlomphegago	-hlomphehang	-tlotlegang	-hlcniphekile(yo)	-nesithunzi
	respiration (n)	asemhaling	khemo	phefumoloho	khemo	ukuphefumla	ukuphefumula
	respond (v)	respondeer	-araba	-arabela	-tsiboga	-phendula	-phendula
	rest (n)	rus	khutšo	phomolo	boikhutso	ubilo	ukuphumula
	rest (v)	rus	-khutša	-phomola	-lapolosa	-phumla	-phumula
	restaurant (n)	restaurant	restorante	resetjhurente	resetshurente	indawo yokutyela	indlu yokudlela
	restless (a)	rusteloos	-sa iketlego	-kgathatsehileng	-tlhorang	-ngonwabanga	-yaluzayo
	restrain (v)	beperk	-iletša	-thibela	-kganna	-thintela	-khuza
	restrict (v)	inperk	-beela mellwane	-hanela	-kganna	-thintela	-nqanda
	restriction (n)	inperking	go beela mellwane	kganelo	kganno	isithintelo	ukunqanda
	result (n)	uitslag	sephetho	ditholwana	dipholo	ingxelo	umphumela
	result (v)	volg	-tšwa	-latela	-latela	-phuma ku-	-landela
	retaliate (v)	vergeld	-lefeletša	-itwanela	-iposolosetsa	-phindisa	-phindisa
	retire (v)	aftree	-rola modiro	-phomola	-rola tiro	-beka phantsi iintambo	-hlala phansi
	retreat (n)	terugtog	katogo	ho tjhetjha	go ikutla	inguqu	ukuhlehlela
	return (v)	terugkeer	-boa	-kgutla	-boela	-buya	-goduka
	reveal (v)	openbaar	-bonagatša	-senola	-senola	-tyhila	-seza
	revise (v)	wysig	-fetoša	-pheta	boelela	-phengulula	-bukeza
	revolt (n)	opstand	mpherefere	kweneho	tsuololo	uvukelo	ukuvukela
	revolution (n)	revolusie	mpherefere	phetohelo	botsuolodi	uvukelo	ukuvukela umbuso
	revolve (v)	draai	-dikologa	-potoloha	dikologa	-jikeleza	-zungeza
	revolver (n)	rewolwer	raboloro	rabolloro	raborolo	umpu	ivolovolo
	reward (n)	beloning	tefo	moputso	tuelo	umvuzo	umklomelo
	reward (v)	beloon	-lefa	-putsa	-duela	-vuza	-klomela
	rhetoric (n)	retoriek	makgethe a polelo	bokgeleke	kgelekiso	ubuciko	ubuciko
	rheumatic (a)	rumaties	-bonyelele	-ramathesele	-bonyelele	-tyatyamba(yo)	-ofehlane
	rheumatism (n)	rumatiek	bonyelele	ramathesele	bonyelele	isifo samathambo	ikhunkulo

English	Afrikaans	N Sotho	Sesotho	Tswana	Xhosa	Zulu	**R**
rhinoceros (n)	renoster	tšhukudu	tshukudu	tshukudu	umkhombe	ubhejane	
rhyme (n)	rym	morumokwano	morumo	morumo	imfano-ziphelo	imvumelwano	
rhyme (v)	rym	-ruma	-ruma	-ruma	-rayima	-vumelana	
rhythm (n)	ritme	mošito	morethetho	mosito	isingqisho	isigqi	
rib (n)	rib	kgopo	kgopo	logopo	ubambo	ubambo	
ribbon (n)	lint	lente	lelente	lente	ibhanti	iribhini	
rice (n)	rys	reise	reise	reisi	irayisi	irayisi	
rich (a)	ryk	-humilego	-ruileng	-humileng	-tyebile (yo)	-nothile	
ride (n)	rit	go namela	palama	makoko	ireyi	ukugibela	
ride (v)	ry	-sepela ka	-palama	-pagama	-reya	-gibela	
ridge (n)	rug	mopopotlo	mokokotlo	lekhubu	umqolo	unqenqema	
ridicule (n)	spottery	kwero	tshomo	losotlo	intlekisa	ukuhleka	
ridicule (v)	bespot	-kwera	-soma	-sotla	-hlekisa	-hleka	
rifle (n)	geweer	sethunya	sethunya	tlhobolo	umbaxa	isibhamu	
right (a)	reg	-lokilego	-nepileng	-siame	-lungile(yo)	-qondile	
right (n)	regterkant	la go ja	letsohong le letona	moja	ukunene	ubunene	
ring (n)	ring	palamonwana	reng	mhiri	iringi	indandatho	
ring (v)	lui	-lla	-letsa	-lela	-khalisa	-khala	
ringworm (n)	ringwurm	pudutša	setlapedi	sephinyasapodi	isitshanguba	umbandamu	
rinse (v)	uitspoel	-tšokotša	-tsokotsa	-tsokotsa	-pula	-yakaza	
riot (n)	onlus	mpherefere	morusu	moferefere	isidubedube	isidumo	
riot (v)	oproer maak	-tsoša mpherefere	-etsa morusu	-feretlha	-gwayimba	-banga isidumo	
riotous (a)	wanordelik	-mpherefere	-morusu	-khuduego	-gwayimbile (yo)	-nodweshu	
ripe (a)	ryp	-budulego	-butswitseng	-budule	-vuthiwe (yo)	-vuthiwe	
rise (n)	styging	thotogo	bophahamo	tlhatloso	unyusa	ukukhuphuka	
rise (v)	styg	-rotoga	-phahama	-tlhatlosa	-nyusa	-khuphuka	
risk (n)	risiko	moleko	qomatsi	diphatsa	ingozi	ingozi	
risk (v)	waag	-phonkgela	-baka qomatsi	-tsena diphatsa	-faka engozini	-zifaka engozini	
rival (n)	mededinger	mophegišani	mohanyetsi	moselammapa	umchasi	imbangi	
river (n)	rivier	noka	noka	noka	umlambo	umfula	
road (n)	pad	tsela	tsela	tsela	indlela	umgwaqo	
roar (n)	brul	mororo	mororo	modumo	umgqumo	ukubhadla	
roar (v)	brul	-rora	-rora	-rora	-gquma	-bhadla	
roast (v)	oondbraai	-beša	-hadika	-gadika	-oja	-osa	
rob (v)	beroof	-hula	-tlatlapa	-thukhutha	-khuthuza	-phanga	
robber (n)	rower	mohudi	motlatlapi	senokwane	umkhuthuzi	umphangi	
robot (n)	robot	roboto	roboto	roboto	irobhothi	irobhothi	
rock (n)	rots	leswika	lefika	lefika	imbokotho iliwa	idwala	
roll (n)	rol	rolo	rolo	momenagano	irolo	ukugingqika	
roll (v)	rol	-kgokološa	-theteha	-pitika	-phethula	-gingqika	
roof (n)	dak	tlhaka	marulelo	borulelo	uphahla	uphahla	
room (n)	kamer	phapoši	kamore	phaposi	igumbi	ikamelo	
rooster (n)	hoenderhaan	mogogonope	mokoko	mokoko	umqhagi	iqhude	
root (n)	wortel	modu	motso	modi	umnqathe	impande	
rope (n)	tou	thapo	mohala	mogala	intambo	indophi	
rose (n)	roos	rosi	rouse	rouse	irowuzi	iroza	
rot (v)	verrot	-bola	-bola	-bola	-bola	-bola	
rotten (a)	verrot	-bodilwego	-bodileng	-bodileng	-bolile (yo)	-bolile	
rough (a)	ru	-makgwakgwa	-soro	-magotsane	-rhabaxa	-mahhadla	
roughage (n)	vesel	tlhale	tshwele	ditlhotlhori	isintlakantlakiso	umhhadlazo	
round (a)	rond	-nkgokolo	-tjhitja	-potokwe	-ngqukuva	-yindilinga	
row (n)	ry	mothaladi	mola	mola	umgca	uhlu	
row (v)	roei	-hudua	-soka	-kgaphela metsi	-bhexa	-gwedla	
rub (v)	vryf	-gohla	-pikitla	-gotlha	-hlikihla	-hlikihla	
rubber (n)	rubber	raba	raba	rekere	irabha	irabha	
rubber (n)	wisser	sephumodi	raba	sephimola	irabha	injoloba	
rubbish (n)	vuilgoed	matlakala	ditshila	malele	inkunkuma	izibi	
rubbish bin (n)	vullisblik	thini ya matlakala	motou wa ditshila	selatlhelamalele	umgqomo	umgqomo wezibi	
rubbish heap (n)	vullishoop	thothobolo	qubu ya ditshila	thuthubudu	izala	inqumbi yezibi	
rude (a)	onbeskof	-hlokago mekgwa	-tala	-mafega	-krwada	-ngahloniphi	

115

R	English	Afrikaans	N Sotho	Sesotho	Tswana	Xhosa	Zulu
	rugby (n)	rugby	rugby	rakebi	rakabi	umboxo	iragbhi
	rule (n)	reël	molao	molao	molao	umthetho	umthetho
	rule (v)	regeer	-buša	-busa	-busa	-lawula	-busa
	ruler (n)	liniaal	rula	rula	rula	irula	irula
	ruler (n)	regeerder	mmuši	mmusi	mmusi	umlawuli	umbusi
	rumour (n)	gerug	mabarebare	bobare	mokgwasa	umingimingi	amahemuhemu
	rump (n)	kruis	noka	noka	mokuane	ithebe	isinqe
	run (v)	hardloop	-kitima	-matha	-taboga	-baleka	-gijima
	rupture (v)	skeur	-gagoga	-tabola	-phanya	-gqabhuka	-gqabuka
	rural (a)	plattelands	-nageng	-mahae	-metsesegae	-maphandleni	-maphandleni
	rush (v)	haas	-phakiša	-potlaka	-itlhaganela	-ngxama	-sheshisa
	rust (n)	roes	rusi	mafome	morodu	umhlwa	ukuthomba
	rust (v)	roes	-rusa	-ba le mafome	-rusa	-ba nomhlwa	-thomba
	sack (n)	sak	mokotla	mokotla	kgetsi	ingxowa	isaka
	sack (v)	afdank	-leleka	-tebela	-koba	-gxotha	-xosha
	sacred (a)	heilig	-kgethwa	-halalelang	-boitshepo	-ngcwele	-ngcwele
	sacrifice (n)	offerande	sehlabelo	sehlabelo	setlhabelo	idini	umnikelo
	sacrifice (v)	opoffer	-itapiša	-hlabela	-tlhabela	-nikezela	-dela
	sad (a)	treurig	-maswabi	-hlomohileng	-hutsafetseng	-lusizi	-dabukile
	saddle (n)	saal	sala	qhana	sale	isali	isihlalo
	sadness (n)	droefheid	manyami	maswabi	khutsafalo	usizi	ukudabuka
	safe (a)	veilig	-lotegilego	-bolokehileng	-bolokegileng	-ngenangozi	-londekile
	safe (n)	brandkluis	seife	polokelo	letlole	isefu	isisefo
	safety pin (n)	haakspeld	sepalete	sepelete	kgokelo	isipeliti	isipelete
	safety (n)	veiligheid	boiphemelo	polokeho	polokesego	ukhuseleko	ukulondeka
	sail (n)	seil	seila	seile	seile	iseyile	useyili
	sail (v)	seil	-thala	-sesa	-thala	-hamba ngenqanawa	-ntweza
	saint (n)	heilige	mokgethwa	mohalaledi	moitshepi	ingcwele	ongcwele
	salad (n)	slaai	selae	selae	salata	isaladi	isaladi
	salary (n)	salaris	moputso	moputso	tuelo	umvuzo	iholo
	sale (n)	uitverkoping	thekišo	thekiso	thekiso	iseyile	indali
	saliva (n)	speeksel	mare	mathe	mathe	amathe	amathe
	salt (n)	sout	letswai	letswai	letswai	ityuwa	itswayi
	salute (n)	saluut	tumedišo	tumediso	go rolela hutshe	ukhahlelo	indesheni
	salute (v)	salueer	-dumediša	-dumedisa	-rolela hutshe	-khahlela	-shaya indesheni
	salvation (n)	verlossing	phološo	pholoho	pholoso	usindiso	usindiso
	same (a)	dieselfde	-swanago	-tshwanang	-tshwana le	-nye	-fanayo
	samp (n)	stampmielies	setampa	setampo	setampa	umngqusho	isitambu
	sample (n)	monster	sešupo	sesupo	sesupo	isampulu	isampula
	sanction (n)	sanksie	kotlo ya ekonomi	tumello	dikiletsokotlhao	imvume	ukukhinyabeza
	sand (n)	sand	lešabašaba	lehlabathe	motlhaba	intlabathi	isihlabathi
	sandal (n)	sandaal	ramphašane	moqathatso	mpheetšhane	imbadada	ingxabulela
	sandwich (n)	toebroodjie	sangwetšhi	semeje	borothopate	iqebengwana	isenwishi
	sane (a)	verstandig	-bohlale	-kutlwisiso	-fodileng tlhogo	-nengqondo	-hlakaniphile
	sanitary towel (n)	sanitêre doekie	tukwana ya bosadi	phete	phete	iphedi	ithawula lokusubela
	sarcasm (n)	sarkasme	kodutlo	sesomo	ditshotlo	impoxo	umbhuqo
	satisfaction (n)	bevrediging	kgotsofalo	kgotsofalo	kgotsofalo	ulwaneliseko	isaneliso
	satisfy (v)	bevredig	-kgotsofatša	-kgotsofatsa	-kgora	-anelisa	-anelisa
	Saturday (n)	Saterdag	Mokibelo	Moqebelo	Matlhatso	uMgqibelo	uMgqibelo
	sauce (n)	sous	souso	souso	moro	umhluzi	umhluzi
	saucepan (n)	kastrol	kastrolo	pitsa	pitsanyana	imbiza	ipani
	sausage (n)	wors	boroso	soseje	boroso	isoseji	isositshi
	save (v)	red	-phološa	-pholosa	pholosa	-sindisa	-sindisa
	savings (n)	spaargeld	dipolokelo	tjhelete e bolokilweng	poloko	imali egciniweyo	imali elondoloziwe
	savour (v)	geniet	-ipshina	-natefelwa	-ja monate	-nambitha	-zwa
	savoury (a)	smaaklik	-bose	-monate	-monate	-nencasa	-mnandi
	saw (n)	saag	saga	saga	šage	isarha	isaha
	saw (v)	saag	-saga	-saga	-šaga	-sarha	-saha
	saxophone (n)	saxofoon	seksafone	sekesofoune	terompeta	ixilongo	iseksafoni

116

English	Afrikaans	N Sotho	Sesotho	Tswana	Xhosa	Zulu	S
say (v)	sê	-re	-bolela	-re	-thi	-sho	
scab (n)	rofie	legogo	lekgwekgwe	lepalo	ukhoko	uqweqwe	
scald (v)	skroei	-babola	-photjhola	-fisa	-tyabula	-shisa	
scale (n)	skaal	sekala	sekala	sekale	isikali	isikali	
scalp (n)	kopvel	letlalo la hlogo	letlalo la hlooho	letlalo la tlhogo	ufele lwentloko	isikhumba sekhanda	
scandal (n)	skandaal	selešadihlong	maswabi	kgopiso	ihlazo	ichilo	
scar (n)	litteken	lebadi	lebadi	lebadi	isiva	isibanda	
scarf (n)	serp	sekhafo	sekhafo	sekafo	isikhafu	isikhafu	
scarlet (n)	helderrooi	bohubedu bja madi	mmala o mofubedu	bohibiduhibidu	ububomvu	-bomvu klebhu	
scatter (v)	strooi	-phatlalatša	-qhala	-falatsa	-sasaza	-sakaza	
scene (n)	toneel	temana	sebaka	felo	umbono	indawo	
scheme (n)	skema	peakanyo	morero	thulaganyo	isikimu	uhlelo	
school (n)	skool	sekolo	sekolo	sekolo	isikolo	isikole	
science (n)	wetenskap	thutamahlale	mahlale	boitseanape	inzululwazi	isayensi	
scissors (n)	skêr	sekero	sekere	sekere	isikere	isikelo	
scold (v)	uitskel	-roga	-kgalemela	-omanya	-ngxolisa	-thethisa	
scoop (v)	skep	-ga	-kga	-gaba	-kha	-kha	
scorch (v)	skroei	-babola	-tlabola	-babola	-tshisa	-shisa	
score (n)	telling	palo	ntlha	sekoro	amanqaku	isikolo	
score (v)	punte aanteken	-noša	-tshwaya dintlha	-nosa	-fumana inqaku	-nqoba	
scorn (n)	veragting	lenyatšo	nyediso	losotlo	ugxeko	ukweyisa	
scorn (v)	verag	-nyatša	-nyedisa	-sotla	-gxeka	-eyisa	
scorpion (n)	skerpioen	phepheng	phepheng	phepheng	unomadudwane	ufezela	
scoundrel (n)	skobbejak	sekebeka	molotsana	legwaragwara	ixoki	ihilikiqi	
scour (v)	skuur	-gohla	-hohla	-gotlha	-khuhla	-khuhla	
scout (n)	verkenner	hlodi	sehlwela	lesupatsela	intlola	inhloli	
scout (v)	rondkyk	-hlola	-hlwela	-lebaleba	-zingela	-hlola	
scowl (n)	suur gesig	mongongoregi	lonya	modilolo	ukujama	ukuhwaqabala	
scowl (v)	suur kyk	-gerula	-nyemotsa	-dilola	-jamela	-hwaqabala	
scramble (v)	klouter	-namela	-ngwangwarela	-palama	-sikremblisha	-phangelana	
scrap (v)	skrap	-khantshela	-kgehlemanya	-ngapa	-susa	-yeka	
scrape (v)	skraap	-fala	-ngwapa	-fala	-krwela	-phala	
scratch (n)	krap	mongwao	mongwapo	ntho	umkrwelo	umudwa	
scratch (v)	krap	-ngwaya	-ngwapa	-ngapa	-krwela	-klwebha	
scream (n)	gil	legoo	mohoo	kgoo	isikhalo	ukuklabalasa	
scream (v)	gil	-goa	-hoa	-kua	-khala	-klabalasa	
screen (n)	skerm	seširo	lehlafi	sesiro	isikhuseli	isisitho	
screw (n)	skroef	sekurufi	sekurufu	sekurufu	isikrufu	isikulufo	
screw (v)	skroef	-kurufela	-kurufella	-tantela	-skrufela	-kulufa	
scrub (v)	skrop	-gohla	-koropa	-koropa	-khuhla	-khuhla	
sculpt (v)	beeldhou	-betla	-betla ditshwantsho	-betla	-qingqa	-qopha amatshe	
sculptor (n)	beeldhouer	mmetli wa diswantšho	mmetladitshwantsho	mmetli	umqingqi	umqophi	
sea (n)	see	lewatle	lewatle	lewatle	ulwandle	ulwandle	
seam (n)	naat	moroko	moroko	moroko	umthungo	umthungo	
search (n)	soektog	monyako	patlo	patlo	ukufuna	ukucinga	
search (v)	soek	-nyaka	-batla	-batla	-funa	-cinga	
season (n)	seisoen	sehla	nako ya selemo	setlha	ixesha lonyaka	isikhathi sonyaka	
seat (n)	sitplek	bodulo	bodulo	manno	isihlalo	isihlalo	
seatbelt (n)	sitplekgordel	lepanta la boitšhireletšo	lebanta la setulo	lebanta la tshireletso	ibhanti yesinqe	ibhande lemoto	
secluded (a)	afgesonderd	-hlaotšwego	-kgethetsweng	-botlhaolelong	-nxwema	-sithekile	
second (a)	tweede	-bobedi	-bobedi	-bobedi	-bini	-esibili	
second (n)	sekonde	motsotswana	motsotswana	motsotswana	umzuzwana	isekeni	
second (v)	sekondeer	-tlatša	-tlatsa	-tlatsa	-xhasa	-sekela	
secrecy (n)	geheimhouding	sephiri	bokunutu	bosaitseweng	imfihlo	ukufihleka	
secret (n)	geheim	sephiri	lekunutu	khupamarama	ihlebo	imfihlo	
secretary (n)	sekretaris	mongwaledi	mongodi	mokwaledi	unobhala	unobhala	
secretary bird (n)	sekretarisvoël	tlhame	mmamolangwane	ramolongwana	ingxangxosi	intinginono	
section (n)	afdeling	karolo	karolo	karolo	icandelo	isigaba	
secure (a)	veilig	-lotegilego	-bolokehileng	-babalelang	-khuselekileyo	-londekile	

	English	Afrikaans	N Sotho	Sesotho	Tswana	Xhosa	Zulu
S	secure (v)	beveilig	-šireletša	-boloka	-babalesega	-khusela	-londoloza
	sediment (n)	sediment	kgaširiri	ditshifa	leraga	intlenga	inzika
	sedition (n)	opruiing	moferefere	phetohelo	tsuololo	isiphendu	ukuvukela umbuso
	see (v)	sien	-bona	-bona	-bona	-bona	-bona
	seed (n)	saad	peu	peo	peo	imbewu	imbewu
	seem (v)	skyn	-bonagala	-tadimeha	-kete	-bonakala	kungathi
	segment (n)	segment	mosehlwana	mosehlo	seripa	isuntsu	izenge
	segregate (v)	segregeer	-kgetholla	-arola	-kgaoganya	ahlula	-ahlukanisa
	seize (v)	gryp	-swara	-tshwara	-tshwara	-bamba	-bamba
	seldom (adv)	selde	go sego kae	ka sewelo	mokabagangwe	ngafane	kancane
	self (n)	self	i-	motho ka sebele	nna	mna	ubumina
	self-confidence (n)	selfvertroue	boitshepo	boitshepo	boitshepo	ukuzithemba	ukuzithemba
	selfish (a)	selfsugtig	-lejelathoko	-inahanelang	-pelotshetlha	-cingela(yo)	-nomhawu
	sell (v)	verkoop	-rekiša	-rekisa	-rekisa	-thengisa	-thengisa
	senate (n)	senaat	senate	senate	senate	isenethi	isenethe
	send (v)	stuur	-roma	-roma	-roma	-thuma	-thuma
	senior (a)	senior	-golo	-holo	-golwane	-dala	-dala
	sense (n)	sin	sekwi	kelello	tlhaloganyo	ingqondo	ingqondo
	sensitive (a)	gevoelig	-kgwathegago maikutlo	-utlwang	-sisimogang	-vakalela(yo)	-nozwela
	sentence (n)	sin	lefoko	polelo	polelo	isivakalisi	umusho
	separate (a)	afsonderlik	-aroganego	-arohaneng	-kgaoganngweng	-ahlula	-ahlukene
	September (n)	September	Setemere	Loetse	Lwetse	uSeptemba	uSepthemba
	sequel (n)	gevolg	pheletšo	se hlahlamang	tatelo	isiqhamo	impumelelo
	sequence (n)	reeks	tatelano	tatelano	tatelano	ulandelelwano	ukulandelana
	sergeant (n)	sersant	satšene	sajene	seresanta	isajini	usayitsheni
	serious (a)	ernstig	-šoro	-hlokofetseng	-tlhonamang	-xhalisekile(yo)	-qukethe
	sermon (n)	preek	thero	thuto	thero	intshumayelo	intshumayelo
	servant (n)	bediende	mohlanka	mohlanka	motlhanka	isicaka	isisebenzi
	serve (v)	dien	-direla	-sebeletsa	-direla	-khonza	-sebenzela
	serviette (n)	servet	sebiete	seviete	seiphimodi	ilatshana lezandla	iseviyethe
	set (n)	stel	sehlopha	sete	thaiso	iseti	isethi
	set (v)	stel	-rea	-tjheha	-thaya	-seta	-beka
	seven (n)	sewe	šupa	supa	-supa	isixhenxe	isikhombisa
	seventeen (n)	sewentien	lesomešupa	leshome le metso e supileng	some supa	ishumi elinesixhenxe	ishumi nesikhombisa
	seventy (n)	sewentig	masomešupa	mashome a supileng	somaasupa	amashumi asixhenxe	amashumi ayisikhombisa
	several (a)	verskeie	-mehutahuta	-tse itseng	-mmalwa	-qela	-ningana
	sew (v)	naaldwerk doen	-roka	-roka	-roka	-thunga	-thunga
	sewerage (n)	riolering	tsela ya kelatšhila	thothomantle	kgogoleloleswe	umjelo wezibi	ipayipi lendle
	sewing (n)	naaldwerk	moroko	moroko	thoko	umthungo	umthungo
	sewing machine (n)	naaimasjien	motšhene wa go roka	motjhine o rokang	motšhene wa go roka	umatshini wokuthunga	umshini wokuthunga
	shade (n)	skadu	moriti	moriti	moriti	umthunzi	umthunzi
	shadow (n)	skaduwee	moriti	moriti	moriti	umthunzi	isithunzi
	shaft (n)	skag	mokoti	tjhafo	motlhoboloko	umphini	umgodi
	shaft (n)	steel	mpheng	mofeng	mfinyane	intsimbi	umphini
	shake (v)	skud	-šišinya	-tsukutla	-reketla	-hlukuhla	-nyakazisa
	shallow (a)	vlak	-sa išego	-sa tebang	-maphara	-nobudibi	-ngashonile
	shame (n)	skaamte	dihlong	dihlong	tlhong	ihlazo	amahloni
	share (n)	deel	kabelo	karolo	kabelo	isahlulo	isabelo
	share (v)	deel	-abela	-arola	-kgaogana	-ahlulelana	-cazelana
	shark (n)	haai	šaka	shake	šaka	ukrebe	imfingo
	sharp (a)	skerp	-bogale	-bohale	-bogale	-bukhali	-bukhali
	shave (v)	skeer	-beola	-beola	-beola	-tsheva	-shefa
	shaving cream (n)	skeerroom	sešepe sa go beola	sesepa sa ho beola	sesepa sa go beola	ikhrim yokutsheva	ukhilimu wokushefa
	shawl (n)	tjalie	tšale	tjale	mogagolwane	ityali	itshali
	she (pron)	sy	yena	yena	ene	yena	yena
	sheaf (n)	gerf	ngata	ngata	ngata	isithungu	isithungu
	sheath (n)	skede	segatla	selata	kgwatlha	isingxobo	umgodlo

English	Afrikaans	N Sotho	Sesotho	Tswana	Xhosa	Zulu	S
sheep (n)	skaap	nku	nku	nku	igusha	imvu	
sheet (n)	laken	lakane	lakane	phephenene	ishiti	ishidi	
shelf (n)	rak	raka	raka	raka	ishelufu	ishalofu	
shell (n)	skulp	kgopa	kgetla	legapa	iqokobhe	igobolondo	
shepherd (n)	skaapwagter	modiši	modisa	modisa	umalusi	umalusi wezimvu	
shield (n)	skild	kotse	thebe	thebe	ikhaka	ihawa	
shield (v)	beskerm	-šireletša	-sireletsa	-sireletsa	-khusela	-vikela	
shin (n)	skeen	moomo	moomo	motwane	uxhongo	umbala	
shine (v)	skyn	-kganya	-benya	-phatsima	-khanya	-khanya	
shiny (a)	blink	-phadimago	-benyang	-phatsimang	-khanyayo	-khanyayo	
ship (n)	skip	sekepe	sekepe	sekepe	inqanawa	umkhumbi	
shirt (n)	hemp	hempe	hempe	hempe	ihempe	ihembe	
shiver (v)	bewe	-roromela	-thothomela	-roroma	-ngcangcazela	-qhaqhazela	
shoe (n)	skoen	seeta	seeta	setlhako	isihlangu	isicathulo	
shoelace (n)	skoenveter	lerala la dieta	leqhwele	thapo ya setlhako	umtya wesihlangu	intambo yesicathulo	
shoot (v)	skiet	-thunya	-thunya	-thuntsha	-dubula	-dubula	
shop (n)	winkel	lebenkele	lebenkele	lebenkele	ivenkile	isitolo	
shop (v)	inkopies doen	-reka	-reka	-reka	-thenga	-thenga	
shop steward (n)	segsman	mmaditsela	molaodi lebenkeleng	mmueledi	ummeli	ummeli-zisebenzi	
short (a)	kort	-kopana	-kgutshwane	-khutswane	-futshane	-fushane	
shorten (v)	verkort	-khutsofatša	-kgutsufatsa	khutshwafatsa	-enza mfutshane	-fushanisa	
shorts (n)	kortbroek	marokgo a dišothi	borikgwe bo bokgutshwane	mankopa	ushoti	isikhindi	
shot (n)	skoot	thunyo	thunyo	thunyo	isithonga	ukudubula	
shoulder (n)	skouer	legetla	lehetla	legetla	iligxa	ihlombe	
shoulderblade (n)	skouerblad	segetla	lesapo la lehetla	legope	igxalaba	isiphanga	
shovel (n)	skoppie	sekopogarafo	garafu	sekopo	isikophu	ifosholo	
show (n)	skou	pontšho	pontsho	pontsho	umboniso	umbukiso	
show (n)	vertoning	pontšho	pontsho	pontsho	umboniso	ukubukisa	
show (v)	wys	-bontšha	-bontsha	-bontsha	-bonisa	-khombisa	
shower (n)	stortbad	šawara	shaware	šawara	ishawa	ishawa	
shower (v)	stort	-šawara	-tola	-tlhapa	-shawarisha	-shawa	
shred (v)	snipper	-ripaganya	-ranthanya	-gabela	isiqwenga	-sika	
shrill (a)	skerp	-thibago ditsebe	-bohale	-itayang tsebe	-bukhali	-ntontolozayo	
shrink (v)	krimp	-hunyela	-honyela	-gonega	-shwabana	-shwabana	
shrivel (v)	verskrompel	-šošobanya	-finahana	-kokoropana	-shwabanisa	-shwabana	
shrub (n)	struik	sehlašana	sehlahla	setlhatsana	ityholo	isihlahlana	
shrug (n)	skouerophaling	go emiša magetla	ho sihletsa mahetla	khutlolo	unyuso-magxa	ukuqhikiza	
shudder (v)	sidder	-thothomela	tlakasela	-tsipoga	-hlasimla	-hlakanyeka	
shuffle (v)	skuifel	-ritša	-fetola	-kgosoba	-shixiza	-shudula	
shun (v)	vermy	-ila	-phema	-sisimoga	-dedela	-balekela	
shut (a)	toe	-tswaletšwego	-kwetsweng	-tswetswe	-valile(yo)	-valiweyo	
shut (v)	toemaak	-tswalela	-kwala	-tswala	-vala	-vala	
shy (a)	skugter	-dihlong	ditlhong	-tlhabiwang ke kgala	-neentloni	-namahloni	
sick (a)	siek	-lwalago	-kulang	-lwalang	-gula(yo)	-gulayo	
sicken (v)	siek word	-lwala	-kudisa	-lwala	-gulisa	-gulisa	
sickle (n)	sekel	sekele	sekele	sekele	irhengqe	isikela	
sickly (a)	sieklik	-segwahla	-bokoa	-bokoa	-gulayo	-xhwalile	
sickness (n)	siekte	bolwetši	bolwetse	bolwetse	isigulo	ukugula	
side (n)	sy	lehlakore	lehlakore	boseja	icala	icala	
sieve (n)	sif	sefo	sefe	sefo	intluzo	isisefo	
sift (v)	sif	-sefa	-sefa	-sefa	-hluza	-sefa	
sight (n)	sig	pono	pono	pono	ukubona	ukubuka	
sign (n)	teken	tšhupo	letshwao	sekai	uphawu	isibonakaliso	
sign (v)	teken	-saena	-saena	-saena	-tyikitya	-sayina	
signal (n)	sinjaal	temoši	temoso	sekai	umqondiso	isiginali	
signature (n)	handtekening	tshaeno	tshaeno	tshaeno	umtyikityo	ukusayina	
silence (n)	stilte	setu	kgutso	tidimalo	ucwaka	ukuthula	
silence (v)	stilmaak	-homotša	-kgutsisa	didimatsa	-thulisa	-thulisa	
silk (n)	sy	sei	selika	sei	isilika	usilika	

S	**English**	**Afrikaans**	**N Sotho**	**Sesotho**	**Tswana**	**Xhosa**	**Zulu**
	silver (n)	silwer	silibera	silefera	selefera	isilivere	isilivə
	similar (a)	eenders	-swanago	-tshwanang	-tshwanang	-fana(yo)	-fanayo
	simple (a)	eenvoudig	-bonolo	-bonolo	-nolo	-lula	-sobala
	sin (n)	sonde	sebe	sebe	sebe	isono	isono
	since (adv)	sedert	go tloga	ho tloha-	ka gonne	ukusukela	ukusukela kwa-
	sincere (a)	opreg	-kgonthe	-nnete	-tota	-thembekile(yo)	-qotho
	sinew (n)	sening	mošifa	lesika	lesika	iintsinga	umsipha
	sing (v)	sing	-opela	-bina	-opela	-cula	-cula
	singe (v)	skroei	-babola	-tlabola	-babola	-rhawula	-hanguza
	single (a)	enkel	-tee	-ng	-ngwe	-nye	-nye
	sink (n)	opwasbak	sehlapelo	sinki	setlhatswelo	isinki	usinki
	sink (v)	sink	-sobela	-tetebela	-nwela	-tshona	-shona
	sip (n)	slukkie	tshoro	kotjelo	mothangwana	ukurhabula	umhabulo
	sip (v)	slurp	-sora	-habola	-gobola	-rhabula	-habula
	sirloin (n)	lendestuk	nama ya kgomo ya mokokotlong	noka	setlhana	isinqe	isinqe
	sister (n)	suster	kgaetšedi	kgaitsedi	kgaitsadi	udade	udade
	sister-in-law (n)	skoonsuster	mogadibo	ngwetsi	mogadibo	umlanyakazi	umlamu
	sit (v)	sit	-dula	-dula	-nna	-hlala	-hlala
	six (n)	ses	tshela	tshelela	borataro	isithandathu	isithupha
	sixteen (n)	sestien	lesometshela	leshome le metso e tsheletseng	some thataro	ishumi elinesithandathu	ishumi nesithupha
	sixty (n)	sestig	masometshela	mashome a tsheletseng	somaamarataro	amashumi amathandathu	amashumi ayisithupha
	size (n)	grootte	bogolo	boholo	saese	isayizi	ubukhulu
	skeleton (n)	geraamte	marapo a mmele	mohlolohlolo	letlhotlholo	uphahla	ugobhozi
	skim (v)	afskep	-okola	-okola	-kokola	-ongula	-cwenga
	skin (n)	vel	letlalo	letlalo	letlalo	ufelə	isikhumba
	skip (v)	oorslaan	-tshela	-tlola	-tlola	-gqabada	-eqa
	skip (v)	touspring	-sela kgati	-tlola	-tlola kgati	-tsiba	-ngqatha
	skirt (n)	romp	sekhethe	sekhete	mosese	umbhinqo	isiketi
	skull (n)	skedel	legata	lehata	legata	ukhakayi	ithambo lekhanda
	skunk (n)	muishond	nakedi	nakedi	nakedi	iqaqa	iqaqa
	sky (n)	lug	leratadimo	lehodimo	loapi	isibhakabhaka	isibhakabhaka
	slander (n)	laster	kgobošo	ketselletso	-fala	isityholo	-hleba
	slang (n)	sleng	sempara	seleng	puotlaopo	isithetho	isidolobha
	slant (v)	skuins loop	-sekama	-sekama	-sekama	-kekela	-tsheka
	slap (n)	klap	phasolo	tjabelo	tlelapa	ukuqhwaba	impama
	slap (v)	klap	-phasola	-jabela	-bata	-qhwaba	-mukula
	slaughter (n)	slagting	polao	polao	polao	ukuxhela	ukuhlaba
	slaughter (v)	slag	-hlaba	-bolaya	-tlhaba	-xhela	-hlaba
	slave (n)	slaaf	lekgoba	lekgoba	lekgoba	ikhoboka	isigqila
	slavery (n)	slawerny	bokgoba	bokgoba	bokgoba	ubukhoboka	ubugqila
	sleep (n)	slaap	boroko	boroko	boroko	ukulala	ubuthongo
	sleep (v)	slaap	-robala	-robala	-robala	-lala	-lala
	sleepless (a)	slapeloos	-hlobaelago	-hlobaelang	-tlhobaelang	-qwayitekile	-ngenabuthongo
	sleepy (a)	vaak	-swerwego ke boroko	-otselang	-otselang	-ozelayo	-nobuthongo
	sleet (n)	ysreën	lehlwapula	tsheola	sefokabolea	iliqhwa	ingele
	sleeve (n)	mou	letsogo la seaparo	letsoho	letsogo	umkhono	umkhono
	slender (a)	tingerig	-otilego	-tshesane	-motsotsoropa	-cuthene (yo)	-cuthene
	slice (n)	sny	selai	sengwathwana	pharo	isilayi	ucezu
	slice (v)	skywe sny	-sega selai	-ngwatha	-farola	-sika	-sika
	slide (v)	gly	-thelela	-thella	-relela	-tyibilika	-shelela
	slim (a)	skraal	-sese	-tshesane	-bopameng	-bhityile(yo)	-nesimo esincane
	slippery (a)	glibberig	-boreledi	-thellang	-relelang	-mtyibilizi	-bushelelezi
	slope (n)	helling	tshekamo	motheo	mothulama	ithambeka	iqele
	slow (a)	stadig	-nanyago	butle	-bonya	-cothayo	kancane
	slum (n)	krotbuurt	mekutwaneng	mekhukhu	mathikithwane	ubuxhifilili	indawo engenampilo
	small (a)	klein	-nyane	-nyenyane	-nnye	-ncinci	-ncane

English	Afrikaans	N Sotho	Sesotho	Tswana	Xhosa	Zulu	S
smallpox (n)	waterpokkies	sekobonyane	sekgolopane	sekokonyane	ingqakaqha	ingxibongo	
smell (n)	reuk	monkgo	monko	monkgo	ivumba	iphunga	
smell (v)	ruik	-dupa	-nkga	-nkga	-nukisa	-nuka	
smile (n)	glimlag	monywanyo	lebonyo	mongebo	uncumo	ukumamatheka	
smile (v)	glimlag	-nywanywa	-bonya	-ngeba	-ncuma	-mamatheka	
smirk (v)	grynslag	-šunyalala	-tsillama	-senama	-sineka	-sineka	
smoke (n)	rook	muši	mosi	mosi	umsi	intuthu	
smoke (v)	rook	-kgoga	-tsuba	-goga	qhuma	-bhema	
smooth (a)	glad	-boreledi	-boreledi	-borethe	-gudile (yo)	-bushelezi	
snail (n)	slak	kgopa	kgofu	kgopa	usinyeke	umnenke	
snake (n)	slang	noga	noha	noga	inyoka	inyoka	
snare (n)	strik	molaba	sefi	segole	isabatha	ugibe	
snatch (v)	gaps	-phamola	-phamola	-phamola	-xhwila	-hlwitha	
sneeze (n)	nies	moethimolo	moethimolo	mofikela	ukuthimla	isithimuka	
sneeze (v)	nies	-ethimola	-ethimola	-ethimola	-thimla	-thimula	
sniff (v)	snuif	-fola	-fofonela	-sunetsa	-rhogola	-hela	
snore (n)	snork	moono	mohono	mogono	ukurhona	ukuhona	
snore (v)	snork	-ona	-hona	-gona	-rhona	-hona	
snow (n)	sneeu	lehlwa	lehlwa	letlhwa	ikhephu	iqhwa	
snow (v)	sneeu	-na lehlwa	-kgetheha	-go wa ga letlhwa	-khephuza	-khithika	
soak (v)	week	-ina	-ina	-inela	-anya	-cwilisa	
soap (n)	seep	sešepe	sesepa	molora	isepha	insipho	
soapstone (n)	seepsteen	monoto	sesepa	tootso	umgudlo	umgudlo	
soccer (n)	sokker	kgwele ya maoto	bolo	sokere	isoka	unobhutshuzwayo	
society (n)	samelewing	phedišanommogo	batho	loago	uluntu	ukuhlangana	
society (n)	vereniging	kopano	mokgatlo	mokgatlho	umbutho	inhlangano	
sock (n)	sokkie	sokisi	kauso	kausu	ikawusi	isokisi	
soft (a)	sag	-boleta	-bonolo	-boleta	-thambile(yo)	-thambile	
softly (adv)	saggies	gannyane	ha bonolo	ka bonolo	ngokuthamba	kancane	
soil (n)	grond	mmu	mobu	mmu	umhlaba	umhlabathi	
soldier (n)	soldaat	mohlabani	lesole	lesole	ijoni	isotsha	
solicitor (n)	prokureur	ramolao	mmuelli	mmueledi	igqwetha	ummeli	
solid (a)	vas	-thata	-thata	-kgotlhaganeng	-qinile(yo)	-qinile	
solve (v)	oplos	-rarolla	-rarolla	-rarabolola	-xazulula	-qaqa	
some (a)	sommige	-ngwe	-ng	-ngwe	-nye	-thize	
son (n)	seun	morwa	mora	morwa	unyana	indodana	
song (n)	liedjie	košana	pina	kopelo	ingoma	iculo	
son-in-law (n)	skoonseun	mokgonyana	mokgwenyana	mogwe	umkhwenyana	umkhwenyana	
soon (adv)	binnekort	ka pela	-haufinyane	tloga	kungekudala	masinyane	
soothe (v)	kalmeer	-okobatša	-kgutsisa	-tlakisa	-thomalalisa	-duduza	
sore (a)	seer	-bohloko	-bohloko	-botlhoko	-buhlungu	-buhlungu	
sore (n)	seer	ntho	seso	seso	isilonda	isilonda	
sorghum (n)	sorghum	mabele	mabele	lebele	amazimba	amabele	
sorrow (n)	smart	mahlomola	maswabi	kutlobotlhoko	usizi	usizi	
soul (n)	siel	moya	moya	mowa	umphefumlo	umphefumulo	
sound (n)	klank	modumo	modumo	modumo	isandi	umsindo	
soup (n)	sop	sopo	sopho	sopo	umhluzi	isobho	
sour (a)	suur	-bodila	-bodila	-botlha	-muncu	-munya	
source (n)	bron	mohlodi	mohlodi	motswedi	imvelaphi	umthombo	
south (a)	suid	-borwa	-borwa	-borwa	-zantsi	-aseningizimu	
south (n)	suide	borwa	borwa	borwa	umzantsi	iningizimu	
southern (a)	suidelik	-borwa	-borwa	-borwa	-zantsi	-kwaseningizimu	
Southern Cross (n)	Suiderkruis	Sefapanaledi sa Borwa	Sefapano sa Borwa	Dithutlwa	uMnqamlezo wase-mZantsi	iSouthern Cross	
souvenir (n)	aandenking	segopotšo	sehopotso	segopotsi	isikhumbuzo	isikhumbuziso	
sow (n)	sog	kolobe ya tshadi	kolobe e tshehadi	kolobe e namagadi	imazi yehagu	ingulube yensikazi	
sow (v)	saai	-gaša	-jala	-jwala	-hlwayela	-tshala	
space (n)	ruimte	sebakabaka	sebaka	sebaka	isithuba	isikhala	
spade (n)	graaf	garafo	garafu	garawe	umhlakulo	ihalavu	
spanner (n)	moersleutel	sepanere	sepanere	tshoko	inkunzana	isipanela	

English	Afrikaans	N Sotho	Sesotho	Tswana	Xhosa	Zulu
spare (v)	spaar	-boloka	-boloka	-boloka	-gcina	-onga
spark (n)	vonk	hlase	tlhase	tlhase	intlantsi	inhlansi
sparkle (v)	vonkel	-benyabenya	-benya	-lakasela	-khazimla	-khazimula
spasm (n)	spasma	bogatšu	kgonyelo ya mesifa	kudupanyo	inkantsi	ukugongobala
spawn (v)	uitbroei	-beela mae	-qhotsa	-thuba	-zala	-zalela
speak (v)	praat	-bolela	-bua	-bua	-thetha	-khuluma
spear (n)	spies	lerumo	lerumo	lerumo	umkhonto	umkhonto
special (a)	spesiaal	-itšego	-ikgethileng	-tlhaolegileng	-odwa	-ngavamile
speck (n)	stippel	ntlhana	letheba	tlhaka	isibi	ibalana
spectacles (n)	bril	dipaketsane	diborele	borele	iindondo	izibuko
spectator (n)	toeskouer	mmogedi	mmohi	mmogedi	umbukeli	isibukeli
speed (n)	spoed	lebelo	lebelo	lebelo	isantya	ijubane
spell (v)	spel	-peleta	-peleta	-peleta	-isihlandlo	-pela
spend (v)	bestee	-šomiša tšhelete	-sebedisa	-tlhola	-chitha	-khokha
spice (n)	spesery	senoko	dinoko	seloki	isiqholo	isipayisi
spider (n)	spinnekop	segokgo	sekgo	segokgo	isigcawu	ulwembu
spill (v)	mors	-falatša	-tsholla	-tsholola	-chitha	-chitha
spinal cord (n)	rugmurg	moko wa mokokotlo	mokolla	mokolela	umnqonqo	umfunkulu
spine (n)	ruggraat	mokokotlo	mokokotlo	mokokotlo	umchachazo	umgogodla
spirit (n)	gees	moya	moya	mowa	umphefumlo	umphefumulo
spirits (n)	spiritus	seporitšhi	sepiriti	segwai	imimoya	isipirithi
spit (v)	spoeg	-tshwa	-tshwela	-kgwa	-tshica	-khafula
spleen (n)	milt	lebete	lebete	lebete	udakada	ubende
split (v)	splits	-pharola	-petsola	-phatloga	-canda	-qanda
sponge (n)	spons	sepontšhe	seponse	ngami	imfunxa	isipanji
spoon (n)	lepel	leho	kgaba	loswana	icephe	ukhezo
sport (n)	sport	papadi	papadi	motshameko	umdlalo	umdlalo
spot (n)	kol	patso	letheba	ngwato	ibala	ibala
spotted (a)	gekol	-nago le dipatso	-rolo	-maronthotho	-ngqoqo	-mabalabala
sprain (n)	verstuiting	thinyego	nonyetseho	phetsego	ukukruneka	isenyelo
sprain (v)	verstuit	-thinya	-nonyetseha	-phetsega	-kruneka	-enyelisa
spread (v)	versprei	-fetetša	-hasa	-phasalatsa	-sasaza	-sakaza
spring (n)	lente	seruthwana	selemo	dikgakologo	intwasahlobo	intwasahlobo
spring (v)	spring	-hlaga	-tlola	-tsipoga	-tsiba	-eqa
springbok (n)	springbok	tshephe	tshepe	tshephe	ibhadi	insephe
sprinkle (v)	sprinkel	-šašetša	-fafatsa	kgatsha	-fefa	-fafaza
sprinkler (n)	sprinkelaar	sešašetši	sefafatsi	sekgatshi	isifefi	isifafazo
sprout (v)	uitloop	-hloga	-hloma	-tlhoga	-ntshula	-hluma
spy (n)	spioen	hlodi	sehlwela	setlhodi	ungcothoza	inhloli
spy (v)	spioeneer	-hlola	-hlwela	-tlhola	-ngcothoza	-hlola
square (a)	vierkantig	-khutlonne	-kgutlonne	-bentlelaka	-xande	-yisikwele
square (n)	vierkant	khutlonne	kgutlonnetsepa	bentlelaka	uxande	isikwele
squash (n)	muurbal	sekwaše	sekwashe	sekwašhe	iskwashi	isikwashi
squash (v)	platdruk	-pinya	-buretsa	-tlhantlha	-cumza	-pitshiza
squat (v)	hurk	-kotama	-qotama	-kotama	-chopha	-qoshama
squeeze (v)	druk	-pitla	-tlhotla	-beleatanya	-cudisa	-cindezela
squint (v)	skeel	-leana	-pelekana	-pelekanya	-fifithekisa	-nxwema
stab (v)	steek	-hlaba	-hlaba	-tlhaba	-hlaba	-hlaba
stable (a)	stabiel	-sa fetogego	-tiileng	-tlhomameng	-zinzile(yo)	-qinile mbe
stable (n)	stal	setala	lesaka	setale	isitali	isitebele
stagger (v)	slinger	-tlhatlharega	-thekesela	-thetheekela	-gxadazela	-bhadazela
stagnant (a)	stagnant	-emego	-emeng	-emeng	-mileyo	-mi ndawonye
stain (n)	vlek	setaki	letheba	sebala	isitshele	ibala
stain (v)	bevlek	-tšhilafatša	-etsa letheba	-timpatsa	-dyobha	-ninda
stairs (n)	trappe	menamelo	diterapa	ditepese	izitepu	isitezi
stale (a)	oud	-kgale	-kgale	-tsofetseng	-dala	-duvile
stalk (n)	stingel	lenono	lehlaka	motang	umnyiki	ugaba
stalk (v)	bekruip	-khukhunela	-nanara	-ratela	-landela	-nyonyobela
stallion (n)	hings	pere ya tona	poho ya pere	pheke	inkunzi yehashe	inkunzi yehhashi
stammer (n)	gehakkel	kgamakgametšo	bohwelea	go kwakwaetsa	ithintitha	ukungingiza

English	Afrikaans	N Sotho	Sesotho	Tswana	Xhosa	Zulu	S
stammer (v)	hakkel	-kgamakgametša	-hwelea	-kwakwaetsa	-thintitha	-ngingiza	
stamp (n)	seël	setempe	setempe	setempe	istampu	isitembu	
stamp (v)	bestempel	-tempa	-tempa	-kiba	-gximfiza	-sicilela	
stand (n)	stand	kemo	tsetsepelo	setlhomo	isikhundla	ukuma	
stand (v)	staan	-ema	-ema	-ema	-ma	-ma	
standard (a)	standaard	-leemo	-boemo	-tlhomamo	-mgangatho	-lunge nomthetho	
standard (n)	standaard	leemo	boemo	kemo	umgangatho	umgomo	
star (n)	ster	naledi	naledi	naledi	inkwenkwezi	inkanyezi	
starch (n)	stysel	setatšhe	seteisele	seteisele	isitatshi	isitashi	
starch (v)	styf	-tatšha	-teisela	-teisela	-qina	-tasha	
stare (n)	gestaar	tebelelo	tjamelo	go lebelela	undwanya	ukugqoloza	
stare (v)	staar	-lebelela	-tjamela	-lebelela	-thi ndwanya	-gqoloza	
start (n)	begin	mathomo	qalo	bothomo	isiqalo	ekuqaleni	
start (v)	begin	-thoma	-qala	-thoma	-qala	-qala	
starve (v)	honger ly	-bolawa ke tlala	-lapa	-bolawa ke tlala	-lamba	-lamba	
state (n)	staat	naga	naha	naga	imeko	uhulumeni	
state (v)	vermeld	-bega	-hlahisa	-bolela	-xela	-sho	
statement (n)	verklaring	pego	tokodiso	polelo	ingxelo	isitetimente	
station (n)	stasie	seteišene	seteishene	seteišene	isikhululo	isiteshi	
stationary (a)	stilstaande	-emego	-emeng	-emeng	-mileyo	-mi ndawonye	
stationery (n)	skryfbehoeftes	dingwalelo	tsa ho ngola	dikwalelo	iincwadi zokubhalela	izimpahla zokubhala	
statue (n)	beeld	seswantšho	seemahale	sefikantswe	umfanekiso oqingqiweyo	isifanekiso	
steak (n)	biefstuk	nama ya kgomo	tshutshu	nama ya kgomo	isihlunu	isiteki	
steal (v)	steel	-utswa	-utswa	-utswa	-ba	-eba	
steam (n)	stoom	mušimeetse	phufodi	phufudi	umphunga	isitimu	
steep (a)	steil	-rotogago	moepa	-mokong	-mqengqelezi	-nommango	
stem (n)	stam	kutu	kutu	kutu	isiqu	isiqu	
stem (v)	voortspruit	-hlaga	-hloma	-tswa	-vuma	-khalima	
step (n)	tree	kgato	mohato	kgato	inyathela	isinyathelo	
step (v)	trap	-gatela pele	-hata	-gata	-nyathela	-hamba	
stepladder (n)	trapleer	lleri	lere	lere	ileri	isitebhisi	
sterile (a)	steriel	-hlwekišitšwego ditwatši	-hlwekileng	-opafetseng	-ngenazintsholo-ngwane	-ngenamagciwane	
sterilise (v)	steriliseer	-hlwekiša	-hlwekisa	-opafatsa	-bulala iintsholo-ngwane	-thena	
stethoscope (n)	stetoskoop	seteteskopo	setetesekoupo	sethetosekoupo	isixilongi	izipopolo	
stew (n)	bredie	setšhuu	setjhu	setshuu	isityu	isitshulu	
stick (n)	stok	patla	molamu	thobane	intonga	induku	
stick (v)	vasplak	-gomaretša	-kgomaretsa	-ngaparetsa	-ncamathela	-namathela	
stiff (a)	styf	-gwagwaladitšwego	-tsitsipaneng	-tshume	-qinileyo	-lukhuni	
still (adv)	nog	-sa-	-sa	-sa	kwakhona	-sa-	
stimulus (n)	stimulus	sematlafatši	motsosa	setsibosi	isivuseleli	imbangela	
sting (n)	steek	tomo	sehlabi	lebolela	ulwamvila	ukuhlaba	
sting (v)	steek	-loma	-hlaba	-loma	-hlaba	-hlaba	
stink (n)	stank	monkgo	monko o mobe	monkgo	ivumba	iphunga elibi	
stink (v)	stink	-nkga	-nkga hampe	-nkga	-nuka	-nuka kabi	
stir (v)	roer	-hudua	-fudua	-fudua	-zamisa	-bonda	
stirrup (n)	stiebeuel	bogato bja sala	moraho	tlhatlosi	istibili	isitibili	
stock (n)	voorraad	phahlo	thepa	mmudungwana	umlibo	impahla	
stockings (n)	kouse	dikauso	dikauso	kausu	iikawusi	amasokisi amade	
stomach (n)	maag	mpa	mohodu	mpa	isisu	isisu	
stone (n)	klip	leswika	lejwe	letlapa	ilitye	ilitshe	
stone (v)	met klippe gooi	-foša ka maswika	-tlepetsa	-kolopa ka matlapa	-gibisela	-gxoba ngamatshe	
stoop (v)	buk	-inama	-inama	-obama	-goba	-khothama	
stop (v)	stop	-emiša	-ema	-ema	-ima	-vimba	
stopper (n)	stopprop	sethibo	poropo	sethibo	isivingco	isivimbo	
store (n)	winkel	lebenkele	lebenkele	setoro	ivenkile	isitolo	
store (v)	bêre	-boloka	-boloka	-boloka	-gcina	-beka	
stork (n)	ooievaar	mantlopodi	mokotatsie	lekollwane	ingwamza	unogolantethe	

English	Afrikaans	N Sotho	Sesotho	Tswana	Xhosa	Zulu
storm (n)	storm	ledimo	sefefo	kgwanyape	isiphango	isivunguvungu
story (n)	verhaal	kanegelo	pale	kgang	ibali	indaba
stout (a)	geset	-nonnego	-tenya	-kima	-omeleleyo	-khuluphele
stove (n)	stoof	setofo	setofo	setofo	isitofu	isitofu
straight (a)	reguit	-rego thwi	-otlolohileng	-motwenene	-the tse	-qondile
strange (a)	vreemd	-šele	-sele	-sele	-ngaqhelekanga	-ngaziwa
stranger (n)	vreemdeling	moeng	moditjhaba	moditšhaba	umrtu wasemzini	umfokazi
strangle (v)	verwurg	-kgama	-kgama	-beta	-krwitsha	-khama
straw (n)	strooi	ditlhoka	mmoko	letlhaka	udiza	utshani obomileyo
strawberry (n)	aarbei	arapei	monokotshwai	seterooberi	iqurube	isitrobheli
stray (v)	afdwaal	-timetšego	-kgelohileng	-timela	-lahlekayo	-eduka
stream (n)	stroom	moela	noka	moedi	umlambo	umfudlana
street (n)	straat	mokgotha	seterata	mmila	isitalato	isitaladi
strength (n)	sterkte	maatla	matla	bothata	amandla	amandla
stress (n)	spanningsdruk	go lapa mmele le moya	kgatello	mathata	ugxininiso	ukucindizelwa
strike (n)	staking	seteraeke	seteraeke	go ngala	uqhushululu	isiteleka
strike (v)	staak	-teraeka	-teraeka	-ngala	enza uqhushululu	-teleka
string (n)	tou	thapo	kgole	thapo	umtya	intambo
strip (n)	strook	moseto	sekgetjhana	moreto	umcu	umdweshu
strip (v)	ontbloot	-apola	-hlobola	-apola	-bhunya	-hluba
stripe (n)	streep	mothalo	moreto	mothalo	umgca	umushu
strive (v)	strewe	-katana	-labalabela	-leka	-zabalaza	-zama
strong (a)	sterk	-maatla	-matla	-maatla	-namandla	-namandla
stubborn (a)	koppig	-manganga	-manganga	-bodipa	-nenkani	-nenkani
stud (n)	stoetery	botswadišakgomo	mohlape	thuo	amanashe	isitadi
student (n)	student	moithuti	moithuti	moithuti	umfundi	isitshudeni
study (v)	studeer	-ithuta	-ithuta	-ithuta	-funda	-funda
stumble (v)	struikel	-thetšega	-kgetshemela	-kgokgoetsega	-khubeka	-khubeka
stump (n)	stomp	kota	kutu	sesana	isiphunzi	isiphunzi
stun (v)	verstom	-tlaba	-makatsa	-makatsa	-khwankqisa	-ndiyazisa
stupid (a)	onnosel	-sethotho	-sethoto	-seeleele	-bhanxa(yo)	-phukuzekile
stutter (n)	gestotter	kgamakgametšo	bohwelea	go kwakwaetsa	ubuthintitha	ukungingiza
stutter (v)	stotter	-kgamakgametša	-hwelea	-kwakwaetsa	-thintitha	-ngingiza
subdue (v)	onderwerp	-fenya	-hatella	-gatelela	-oyisa	-ahlula
subject (n)	onderwerp	sediri	taba	sediri	intloko	isimemela
submerge (v)	onderdompel	-inela	-qwedisa	-nwela	-ntywilisa	-cwilisa
subpoena (n)	dagvaarding	piletšotshekong	samane	piletsatshekong	isamani	isamaniso
substance (n)	stof	selo	ntho	sere	into	isiqa
subtract (v)	aftrek	-ntšha	-tlosa	-ntsha	-thabatha	-susa
suburb (n)	voorstad	karolwana ya toropo	motsana	motsana wa dintlha	ihlonyelwa	isabhebhe
suburban (a)	voorstedelik	-karolwana ya toropo	-motsana	-motsana wa dintlha	-ehlomela ledolophu	-pathelene nesabhebhe
succeed (v)	slaag	-atlega	-atleha	-tlhatlhama	-phumelela	-phumelela
success (n)	sukses	katlego	katleho	katlego	impumelelo	impumelelo
such (a)	sulke	-bjalo	-jwalo	-sekete	njenga	-nje
suck (v)	suig	-mona	-monya	-mona	-ncanca	-munya
sudden (a)	skielik	-ka pela	ka tshohanyetso	ka tshoganyetso	-khawulezile(yo)	masinya
suffer (v)	ly	-hlokofala	-utlwa bohloko	-boga	-gula	-hlupheka
sugar (n)	suiker	swikiri	tswekere	sukiri	iswekile	ushukela
suicide (n)	selfmoord	boipolao	boipolao	boipolao	ukuzibulala	ukuzibulala
suit (n)	pak	sutu	sutu	sutu	isuti	isudi
sulk (v)	dikmond wees	-hlonama	-ngala	-tsupa	-qumba	-khunsa
sullen (a)	nors	-hlonamago	-lonya	-ngomaelang	-lushwaca	-luhlwibi
sulphur (n)	swawel	sebabole	sebabole	sebabole	isalfure	isalufa
summary (n)	opsomming	kakaretšo	kakaretso	khutshwafatso	isishwankathelo	iqoqo
summer (n)	somer	selemo	lehlabula	selemo	ihlobo	ihlobo
summit (n)	kruin	tlhora	tlhoro	tlhora	incopho	isiqongo
summon (v)	ontbied	-bitša	-bitsa	-bitsa	-bizela enkundleni	-biza
summons (n)	dagvaarding	tagafara	samane	tagafara	isamani	isamaniso
sun (n)	son	letšatši	letsatsi	letsatsi	ilanga	ilanga
sunbeam (n)	sonstraal	lehlasedi	lehlasedi	lerang la letsatsi	ilitha	umsebe welanga

English	Afrikaans	N Sotho	Sesotho	Tswana	Xhosa	Zulu	S
Sunday (n)	Sondag	Sontaga	Sontaha	Latshipi	iCawa	iSonto	
sundown (n)	sononder	phirimo	madikelo	mampa-a-kolobe	ukuhlwa	ukushona kwelanga	
sunflower (n)	sonneblom	sonopolomo	sonobolomo	sonobolomo	ujongilanga	ujikanelanga	
sunglasses (n)	sonbril	dipaketsane tša letšatši	disonoborele	diporele tsa letsatsi	iindondo	amagogolosi	
sunlight (n)	sonlig	seetša sa letšatši	kganya ya letsatsi	lesedi la letsatsi	ilanga	ukukhanya kwelanga	
sunrise (n)	sonop	tlhabo	tjhabo ya letsatsi	tlhabo ya letsatsi	ukuphuma kwelanga	ukuphuma kwelanga	
sunset (n)	sononder	phirimo	madikelo	phirimo ya letsatsi	ukutshona kwelanga	ukushona kwelanga	
suntan (n)	sonbruin		ho tjheswa ke letsatsi	go fiswa ke letsatsi	ubuntsundu	ukugqunqa	
supermarket (n)	supermark	supamakete	supamakete	lebenkele	untozonke	isuphamakethe	
supper (n)	aandete	dijo tša selalelo	dijo tsa mantsiboya	selalelo	isophoro	isapha	
supply (v)	verskaf	-neela	-fa	-fa	-bonelela	-nika	
support (v)	ondersteun	-thuša	-tshehetsa	-tshegetsa	-xhasa	-sekela	
suppose (v)	veronderstel	-hloma	-lekanya	-itlhoma	-cinga	-cabanga	
supreme court (n)	hooggeregshof	kgotlakgolo	lekgotla le phahameng	kgotla ya bogaolakgang	inkundla ephakamileyo	inkantolo yamaJaji	
sure (a)	seker	-nnete	-tiileng	-ruri	-qinisekile(yo)	-qinisekile	
surgeon (n)	chirurg	ngaka ya go bua	ngaka	ngaka ya karo	ugqirha	udokotela ohlinzayo	
surgery (n)	chirurgie	bobui	bongaka ba thipa	karo	ubugqirha	ukuhlinzwa	
surname (n)	van	sefane	fane	sefane	ifani	isibongo	
surprise (n)	verrassing	makatšo	makatso	kgakgamalo	isothuso	isimangaliso	
surprise (v)	verras	-makatša	-makatsa	-makatsa	-othusa	-mangalisa	
surrender (n)	oorgawe	boineelo	boineelo	boineelo	ukunikezela	ukuthela	
surrender (v)	oorgee	-ineela	-ineela	-ineela	-nikezela	-thela	
surround (v)	omring	-dika	-bokanela	-dikanyetsa	-rhangqa	-zungeza	
suspect (n)	verdagte	mogopolelwa	mmelaelwa	mmelaelwa	umrhanelwa	osolwayo	
suspect (v)	verdink	-gopolela	-belaela	-belaela	-rhanela	-sola	
suspend (v)	opskort	-fega	-behela ka thoko	-lepeletsa	-xhoma	-hlehlisa	
suspended sentence (n)	opgeskorte vonnis	kahlolo ye e fegilwego	ho ahlolelwa ka ntle	kotlhao e e beetsweng thoko	isigwebo esixhonyiweyo	isijeziso esilengisiwe	
suspicion (n)	agterdog	kgonono	pelaelo	pelaelo	urhano	insolo	
swallow (v)	sluk	-metša	-kwenya	-metsa	-ginya	-gwinya	
swamp (n)	moeras	mohlaka	mohlaka	motsitlana	umgxobhozo	ixhaphozi	
swarm (n)	swerm	motšhitšhi	mohlape	segopa	ibubu	ibololwane	
swear (v)	vloek	-roga	-hlapaola	-roga	-thuka	-thuka	
sweat (n)	sweet	mphufutšo	mofufutso	mofufutso	umbilo	umjuluko	
sweat (v)	sweet	-fufulelwa	-fufulelwa	-fufula	-bila	-juluka	
sweep (v)	vee	-swiela	-fiela	-feela	-tshayela	-shanela	
sweet (a)	soet	-bose	-monate	-botshe	-sutu	-mtoti	
sweet (n)	lekker	dipompong	pompong	semonamone	ilekese	iswidi	
sweet potato (n)	patat	morepa	patata	potata	ibhatata	ubhatata	
swell (v)	swel	-roroga	-ruruha	-ruruga	-dumba	-vuvuka	
swelling (n)	swelsel	mororogo	ho ruruha	thurugo	ukudumba	ithubulela	
swim (v)	swem	-rutha	-sesa	-thuma	-dada	-bhukuda	
swimmer (n)	swemmer	moruthi	sesesi	mothumi	indadi	inhlambi	
swimming (n)	swem	go rutha	ho sesa	go thuma	ukudada	ukubhukuda	
swimming pool (n)	swembad	boruthelo	letsha la ho sesa	bothumelo	ichibi lokuqubha	ichibi lokuhlamba	
switch (n)	skakelaar	switšhi	sewitjhe	switšhi	iswitshi	iswitshi	
switch (v)	oorskakel	-foša dithapo	-kgeloha	-tshuba	-switsha	-shintsha	
sword (n)	swaard	tšhoša	sabole	sabole	isabile	inkemba	
syllable (n)	lettergreep	noko	senoko	noko	ilungu	ilunga	
syllabus (n)	leerplan	lenaneothuto	lenanethuto	lenanethuto	isilabhasi	uhlelo lwezifundo	
symbol (n)	simbool	sešupo	sesupo	sekai	isimboli	uphawu	
sympathetic (a)	simpatiek	-kwelanobohloko	-mohau	-boutlwelobotlhoko	-novelwano	-zwelayo	
sympathy (n)	simpatie	kwelanobohloko	kutlwelobohloko	boutlwelobotlhoko	uvelwano	uzwelo	
symptom (n)	simptoom	sebontšhi	letshwao	sesupo	uphawu	isibonakaliso	
synthetic (a)	sinteties	-maitirelo	-tswakaneng	-se nang boleng	-dityanisiwe(yo)	-qanjiwe	
syphilis (n)	sifilis	thosola	mokaola	thosola	ihash'elingewu	ugcunsula	
syringe (n)	spuit	kurumane	sepeiti	sepeiti	inaliti	isirinji	
system (n)	stelsel	peakanyo	tsela	thulaganyo	umiso	ihlelo	

T	English	Afrikaans	N Sotho	Sesotho	Tswana	Xhosa	Zulu
	table (n)	tafel	tafola	tafole	tafole	itafile	itafula
	tablecloth (n)	tafeldoek	tafoletuku	lesela la tafole	tafoletuku	ilaphu letafile	indwangu yetafula
	tablet (n)	tablet	pilisi	pilisi	pilisi	itafilana	iphilisi
	tabulate (v)	tabuleer	-hlopha	-hlohlomisa	-rulaganya	-chaka	-loba ngezinhla
	tackle (v)	aanpak	-thoma	-hlasela	-thoma	-hlasela	-qala
	tadpole (n)	paddavissie	kolopisane	bokudubete	koduntwane	isabonkolo	ushobishobi
	tail (n)	stert	mosela	mohatla	mogatla	umsila	umsila
	tailor (n)	kleremaker	moroki	seroki	mosegi	umsiki wempahla	umthungi
	take (v)	neem	-tšea	-nka	-tsaya	-thatha	-thatha
	tale (n)	storie	nonwane	pale	motlotlo	ibali	inganekwane
	talent (n)	talent	talente	talente	neo	italente	ukuhlakanipha
	talented (a)	talentvol	-atetšwego ke ditalente	-nang le talente	-neo	-netalente	-hlakaniphile
	talk (n)	praatjie	polelwana	puo	polelo	incoko	ingxoxo
	talk (v)	praat	-bolela	-bua	-bua	-thetha	-khuluma
	talkative (a)	spraaksaam	-bolelago kudu	-lehehle	-buabuang	-thethayo	-ngundabeni
	tall (a)	lang	-telele	-lelele	-leele	-de	-de
	tambourine (n)	tamboeryn	moropana	moropana	moropana	igutyana elikhenkcezayo	ithamborini
	tame (a)	mak	-tlwaetšego	-thapileng	-bokgwafo	-mbuna	-thambile
	tame (v)	tem	-tapiša	-thapisa	-katisa	-lulamisa	-thambisa
	tampon (n)	tampon	sethibo	thempone	tampone	isivingco	ithemponi
	tan (v)	bruin brand	go ora letšatši	-suha	-suga	mthubi bomvu	-nsundu
	tank (n)	tenk	tanka	tanka	tanka	-itanki	ithangi
	tap (n)	kraan	pompi	thepe	thepe	itepu	umpompi
	tape measure (n)	maatband	lentitekanya	tekanyi	theipi	ulutya	ithephu
	tapeworm (n)	lintwurm	nogana ya mala	manyowa	mphe	intshulube	ingcili
	tar (n)	teer	sekontiri	sekontiri	sekontere	itha	itiyela
	tar (v)	teer	-tšhela sekontini	-tshela sekontiri	-tshasa sekontere	-qaba itha	-faka itiyela
	tariff (n)	tarief	tefo	tefello	tuelo	uluhlu lwamaxabiso	ihlelo lemali
	tarpaulin (n)	seil	seila	seile	seile	iseyile	useyili
	tart (n)	tert	terete	terete	kuku	ikeyiki ethile	ikhekhe
	task (n)	taak	modiro	mosebetsi	tema	umsebenzi	umsebenzi
	taste (n)	smaak	mohlodi	tatso	moutlwalo	incasa	ukuzwangomlomo
	taste (v)	proe	-kwa ka leleme	-latswa	-utlwa	-ngcamla	-zwa
	tasteless (a)	smaakloos	-hlokago mohlodi	bosula	-bosula	-javujavu	-duma
	tattered (a)	toiingrig	-kgeretlanego	-maharaswa	-lekgasa	-jacekileyo	-manikiniki
	taunt (v)	uitlok	-rumula	-soma	-okisa	-cunukisa	-chukuluza
	tax (n)	belasting	motšhelo	lekgetho	lekgetho	irhafu	intela
	tax (v)	belas	-lefiša	-kgafisa	-kgetha	-rhafisa	-thelisa
	taxi (n)	taxi	thekisi	tekesi	thekesi	iteksi	ithekisi
	tea (n)	tee	teye	tee	tee	iti	itiye
	teacher (n)	onderwyser	morutiši	titjhere	morutabana	ititshala	uthisha
	team (n)	span	sepane	sehlopha	setlhopa	iqela	ithimu
	teapot (n)	teepot	pitšana ya teye	pitsa ya tee	ketlele ya tee	imbiza yeti	ithiphothi
	tear (v)	skeur	-kgeila	-tabola	-gagola	-krazula	-dabula
	tears (n)	trane	megokgo	dikeledi	dikeledi	iinyembezi	izinyembezi
	tease (v)	terg	-hlohla	-hlohla	-rumola	-qhula	-gcona
	teat (n)	tepel	tlhoko	tlhoko	letsele	ingono	ibele
	technical (a)	tegnies	-botsebi	-tegeniki	-thekeniki	-bugcisa	-nobuthekiniki
	technikon (n)	tegnikon	theknikone	tekenikone	thekenikono	iziko lobugcisa	ithekinikhoni
	technique (n)	tegniek	thekeniki	botsebi	thekeniki	isixhobo	ithekiniki
	technology (n)	tegnologie	theknolotši	tekenoloji	thekenoloji	ulwazi ngobugcisa	itheknoloji
	teeth (n)	tande	meno	meno	meno	amazinyo	amazinyo
	telegram (n)	telegram	thelekramo	mohala	mogala	ucingo	ithelegrama
	telephone (n)	telefoon	thelefomo	thelefone	mogala	ifoni	ithelefoni
	telephone booth (n)	telefoonhokkie	ntlwanathelefomo	ntlwana ya thelefone	ntlwana ya mogala	indlwana yefoni	ingosi yethelefoni
	telephone directory (n)	telefoongids	puku ya thelefomo	tataiso ya thelefone	buka ya dinomoro tsa mogala	isalathisi-foni	inkomba yethelefoni
	telescope (n)	teleskoop	theleskopo	ferekekere	thelesekopo	umabonakude	ithelisikobho
	television (n)	televisie	thelebišene	thelebeshene	thelefišene	ithelevizhini	ithelevishini

English	Afrikaans	N Sotho	Sesotho	Tswana	Xhosa	Zulu	T
tell (v)	vertel	-laodiša	-bolela	-bolela	-xela	-landa	
temper (n)	humeur	maikutlo	-boitshwaro	bobetwapelo	umsindo	ulaka	
temperature (n)	temperatuur	themperetša	temperetjha	themperetša	ubushushu	ukushisa	
temptation (n)	verleiding	moleko	moleko	thaelo	ulingo	isiyengo	
ten (n)	tien	lesome	leshome	some	ishumi	ishumi	
tenant (n)	bewoner	moagi	mohiri	mohiri	umqeshi	umqashi	
tender (a)	teer	-nanana	-bonolo	-nana	-thambile (yo)	-thambile	
tender (n)	tender	tentere	tentere	bonana	umongameli	ithenda	
tendon (n)	sening	mošifa	mosifa	mosifa	umsipha	umsipha	
tendril (n)	rankie	motlang	tatamolebo	molebo	isibambelelo	umliba	
tennis (n)	tennis	thenese	tenese	thenese	intenetya	ithenisi	
tense (a)	gespanne	-ngangegilego	-sataletseng	-gagametseng	-xhalile (yo)	-shaqekile	
tent (n)	tent	tente	tente	tente	intente	ithende	
tepid (a)	lou	-boruthwana	-foofo	-bothitonyana	-dikidiki	-fudumele	
term (n)	term	lebaka	nako	lereo	iseshini	ibizo	
term (n)	termyn	lebaka	nako	kgweditharo	isigqibo	ithemu	
terrace (n)	terras	terase	mothati	sebopelo	ithala	itheresi	
terrible (a)	vreeslik	-tšhošago	-tshabehang	-mpe	-oyikekayo	-esabekayo	
terrify (v)	verskrik	-tšhoša	-tshosa haholo	-tshosa	-oyikisa	-ethusa	
terror (n)	terreur	tšhošetšo	tshoho	borukutlhi	uloyiko	ukwesabisa	
terrorism (n)	terrorisme	botšhošetši	boferekanyi	borukutlhi	ubunqolobi	impoqa	
test (n)	toets	teko	teko	teko	uvavanyo	inhlolo	
test (v)	toets	-leka	-leka	-leka	-vavanya	-hlola	
testicle (n)	teelbal	lerete	lerete	thala	isende	isende	
testify (v)	getuig	-hlatsela	-paka	-paka	-ngqina	-fakaza	
testimony (n)	getuienis	bohlatse	bopaki	bosupi	ubungqina	ubufakazi	
tetanus (n)	klem in die kake	tetanose	tsitsipano ya mohlahare	kitlano ya meno	uqino-mihlathi	ithethanusi	
than (conj)	as		ho feta	go	kuna-	na-	
thank (v)	bedank	-leboga	-leboha	-leboga	-bulela	-bonga	
thanks (n)	dank	tebogo	diteboho	tebogo	umbulelo	ukubonga	
that (pron)	dat	gore	eo	gore	ukuba	ukuze	
thatch (n)	dekgras	bjang bja go rulela	marulelo a jwang	maragomagolo	ufulelo	utshani bokufulela	
thatch (v)	dek	-rulela	-rulela ka jwang	-rulela	-fulela	-fulela	
theatre (n)	teater	teatere	thietha	teatere	iqonga	ithiyetha	
their (pron)	hulle	-bona	-bona	bona	-bo	bona	
theirs (pron)	hulle s'n	-bona	-bona	-bona	-bo	okwabo	
them (pron)	hulle	-ba-	bona	bona	bona	bona	
theme (n)	tema	kgwekgwe	mokotaba	morero	umxholo	indikimba	
then (adv)	dan		jwale	jaale	kwaza	lapho	
then (adv)	toe		jwale	ke fa	kwaza	ngesikhathi	
there (adv)	daar	gona	moo	foo	phaya	lapho	
they (pron)	hulle	bona	bona	bona	ba-	bona	
thick (a)	dik	-koto	-tenya	-kima	-khulu	-nohlonze	
thicken (v)	dik maak	-kotofatša	-teteanya	loa	-enza nkulu	-enza kubeluhlonzi	
thief (n)	dief	lehodu	leshodu	legodu	isela	isela	
thigh (n)	dy	serope	serope	serope	ithanga	ithanga	
thin (a)	dun	-sesane	-sesane	-sesane	-nciphile(yo)	-zacile	
thing (n)	ding	selo	ntho	selo	into	into	
think (v)	dink	-gopola	-nahana	-akanya	-cinga	-cabanga	
third (a)	derde	-boraro	-raro	-nngwe-tharong	-thathu	-esithathu	
thirst (n)	dors	lenyora	lenyora	lenyora	unxano	ukoma	
thirsty (a)	dorstig	-nyorilwego	-nyorilwe	-nyorilweng	-nxaniwe (yo)	-omile	
this (pron)	dit	ye	-na	tse	le	lokhu	
thong (n)	riem	lebja	lerapo	kgole	intambo	intambo	
thorax (n)	borskas	sehuba	sefuba	sehuba	isifuba	isifuba	
thorn (n)	doring	mootlwa	moutla	mmitlwa	iliva	iva	
those (pron)	daardie	tšeo	-no	tsele	leya	lokho	
though (conj)	hoewel	le ge	le ha	le mororo	naxa	nokho	
thought (n)	gedagte	kgopolo	kgopolo	kakanyo	ingcinga	umcabanago	

English	Afrikaans	N Sotho	Sesotho	Tswana	Xhosa	Zulu
thousand (n)	duisend	sekete	sekete	sekete	iwaka	inkulungwane
thrash (v)	uitklop	-fenya	-pola	-setla	-bhula	-dinda
thread (n)	draad	tlhale	tshwele	tlhale	umtya	ucingo
threat (n)	dreigement	tšhošetšo	tshokelo	setshoso	intsongelo	usongo
three (n)	drie	tharo	tharo	tharo	ntathu	kuthathu
thrift (n)	spaarsaamheid	go seketša	paballo	tshomarelo	ukugcisa	isineke sokonga
throat (n)	keel	mogolo	mmetso	mometso	umqala	umphimbo
throb (n)	klopping	go opa	ho uba	moubo	undondozelo	ukufutha
throttle (v)	wurg	-kgama	-kgama	-kgama	-krwitsha	-khama
through (prep)	deur	ka-	ka-	ke	-nga	nga-
throw (v)	gooi	-betša	-akgela	-kolopa	-gibisela	-phonsa
thumb (n)	duim	nkgogorupa	monwana o motona	kgonotswe	ubhontsi	isithupha
thunder (n)	donder	modumo	seaduma	modumo	iindudumo	ukuduma
Thursday (n)	Donderdag	Labone	Labone	Labone	uLwesine	uLwesine
tick (n)	luis	kgofa	kgofa	kgofa	indlanga	umkhaza
tick (v)	tik	-bethabetha	-tshwaya	-thobola	-krwela	-ncenceza
ticket (n)	kaartjie	thekethe	tekete	thekethe	itikiti	ithikithi
ticket office (n)	kaartjieskantoor	ofisi ya dithekethe	ofisi ya ditekete	kantoro ya dithekethe	iofisi yamatikiti	ihhovisilamathikithi
tickle (v)	kielie	-tsikinya	-tsikinya	-tsikitla	-nyumbaza	-kitaza
tide (n)	gety	phulawatle	leqhubu	nako	umsinga	ibuya
tidy (a)	netjies	-bothakga	-makgethe	-bothakga	-cocekile (yo)	-lungisiwe
tie (n)	das	thai	tae	thae	iqhina	uthayi
tie (v)	bind	-bofa	-tlama	-tlama	-bopha	-bopha
tight (a)	styf	-tiilego	-tiileng	-gagametseng	-qinile(yo)	-qinile
tighten (v)	span	-nganga	-tiisa	-gagamatsa	-qinisa	-qinisa
time (n)	tyd	nako	nako	nako	ixesha	isikhathi
timetable (n)	rooster	tšhupapaka	tshupapaka	lenanatiro	ithayimtheyibhili	uhlelo lwesikhathi
timid (a)	skugter	-dihlong	-boi	-boi	-nkwantya (yo)	-ethukayo
tip (n)	punt	ntlha	ntlha	ntlha	incam	isihloko
tiptoe (v)	op die tone loop	-nanabela	-tsamaya ka ditsetsekwame	-nangasela	-hamba ngoobhontsi	-hamba ngamazwani
tire (v)	moeg word	-lapa	-kgathala	-lapa	-dinwa	-khathala
tired (a)	moeg	-lapilego	-kgathetseng	-lapileng	-dinayo	-khathele
tissue (n)	weefsel	tlhalenama	popeho	thogwa	ulucu	isicubu
title (n)	titel	thaetlele	sehlooho	setlhogo	isihloko	ibizo
to (prep)	na	go-	ho-	go	ku-	ku-
toad (n)	brulpadda	letlametlo	latlametlu	segwagwa	indubula	isele
tobacco (n)	tabak	motšoko	kwae	motsoko	icuba	ugwayi
today (n)	vandag	lehono	kajeno	gompieno	namhlanje	namuhla
toddler (n)	peuter	mapimpana	mokgasi	ngwana	isibothwana	ingane
toe (n)	toon	monwana wa leoto	monwana wa leoto	monwana	uzwane	uzwani
toenail (n)	toonnael	lenala la monwana wa leoto	lenala la monwana	lonala lwa leoto	uziphe	izipho lozwani
together (adv)	saam	gammogo	hammoho (le)	mmogo	sonke	-hlangene
toilet (n)	toilet	boithomelo	ntlwana	boithomelo	indlu yangasese	itholethe
toilet paper (n)	toiletpapier	pampiri ya go itlhakola	pampiri ya ntlwana	pampiri ya boithomelo	iphepha lokusula	iphepha lasetholethe
toiletries (n)	toiletware	ditlabakelo tša boitlhwekĭ	tsa ho itlhatswa	tsa go tlhapa	iimpahlana zokuzicoca	okokuzimotonga
tomato (n)	tamatie	tamati	tamati	tamati	itumata	utamatisi
tomb (n)	graf	lebitla	lebitla	lebitla	ingcwaba	ithuna
tombstone (n)	grafsteen	letlapa la lebitla	lejwe la sehopotso	letlapa la phupu	ilitye	itshe lethuna
tomorrow (n)	môre	gosasa	hosane	ka moso	ngomso	kusasa
tongue (n)	tong	leleme	leleme	leleme	ulwimi	ulimi
tonsils (n)	mangels	dithaka	ditemetwane	dikodu	indimla	amadlala asemphinjweni
too (adv)	ook	le	hape	le	na-	futhi
tool (n)	werktuig	thulusi	thulosi	sediriswa	isixhobo	ithulusi
tooth (n)	tand	leino	leino	leino	izinyo	izinyo
toothache (n)	tandpyn	go thunya ga leino	leino le opang	motlhagare	izinyo	ubuhlungu bezinyo
toothpaste (n)	tandepasta	mogohlo wa meno	sesepa sa meno	sesepa sa meno	intlama yamazinyo	umuthi wamazinyo

English	Afrikaans	N Sotho	Sesotho	Tswana	Xhosa	Zulu	T
top (n)	top	godimo	hodimo	bogodimo	umphezulu	isihloko	
torch (n)	flitslig	panyepanye	serumola	lobone	itotshi	ithoshi	
tortoise (n)	skilpad	khudu	kgudu	khudu	ufudo	ufudu	
total (n)	totaal	palomoka	kakaretso	tsotlhe	iyonke	isamba	
touch (n)	aanraking	kgwatho	kamo	kamo	uchukumiso	ukuthinta	
touch (v)	raak	-kgwatha	-ama	-kgoma	-chukumisa	-thinta	
tough (a)	taai	-tiilego	-thata	-ntha	-omelele(yo)	-lukhuni	
tour (n)	rondreis	leeto	leeto	go ja nala	ukhenketho	uhambo	
tour (v)	rondreis	-eta	-eta	-ja nala	-khenketha	-hamba	
tourist (n)	toeris	moeti	moeti	mojanala	umkhenkethi	isihambi	
tow (v)	sleep	-goga	-hula	-goga	-rhuqa	-donsa	
towel (n)	handdoek	toulo	thaole	toulo	itawuli	ithawula	
town (n)	dorp	toropo	toropo	motse	idolophu	idolobha	
tow rope (n)	sleeptou	thapo ya go goga	ropo ya ho hula	thapo ya go goga	intambo yokurhuqa	intambo yokudonsa	
toy (n)	speelding	sebapadišwa	nthwa ho bapala	setshamekiso	into yokudlala	into yokudlala	
track (n)	spoor	mohlala	mohlala	motlhala	umzila	isipolo	
track (v)	opspoor	-lata mohlala	-nka mohlala	-batla	-landela	-landela isipolo	
tracksuit (n)	sweetpak	sutu ya boitšhidillo	terekesutu	terekesutu	itreksutu	itrekisudi	
trade (n)	handel	kgwebo	kgwebo	kgwebo	urhwebo	ukuhweba	
trade (v)	handel dryf	-gweba	-hweba	-rekisa	-rhweba	-hweba	
trade union (n)	vakbond	mokgatlo wa bašomi	kopano ya basebetsi	teradeyuniene	umanyano lwabase-benzi	inyonyana yezisebenzi	
tradition (n)	tradisie	tlwaelo	moetlo	tlhago	isithethe	isiko lezizukulwane	
traditional (a)	tradisioneel	-tlwaelo	-moetlo	-tlhago	ngokwesithethe	ngokwesiko	
traffic (n)	verkeer	therafiki	sephethephethe	pharakano	izithuthi	itrefiki	
tragedy (n)	tragedie	masetlapelo	masetlapelo	ditlhomolapelo	intlekele	umbangalusizi	
tragic (a)	tragies	-masetlapelo	-sehloho	-tlhomolang pelo	-nobuntlekele	-nosizi	
train (n)	trein	setimela	terene	setimela	uloliwe	isitimela	
train (v)	afrig	-ruta	-ruta	-katisa	-qeqesha	-fundisa	
traitor (n)	verraaier	moeki	moeki	motsietsi	umngcatshi	imbuka	
translate (v)	vertaal	-fetolela	-fetolela	-fetola	-guqulela	-humusha	
translator (n)	vertaler	mofetoledi	mofetoledi	mofetoledi	umguquli	umhumushi	
transparent (a)	deurskynend	-bonagatšago	-bonaletsang	-bonalatsang	-krelekrele	-khanyayo	
trap (n)	strik	molaba	sefi	serai	isigu	isicupho	
travel (v)	reis	-eta	-eta	-kgabaganya	-thabatha uhambo	-hamba	
traveller (n)	reisiger	moeti	moeti	moetedi	umhambi	isihambi	
tray (n)	skinkbord	therei	sekenkeboroto	terei	itreyi	ithreyi	
tread (v)	trap	-gata	-hata	-gata	-nyathela	-nyathela	
treason (n)	verraad	boepi	keko	boepapuso	ungcatsho	ukwambuka	
treasure (n)	skat	lehumo	letlotlo	ramatlotlo	ubutyebi	igugu	
treat (v)	behandel	-alafa	-tshwara	-tshola	-phatha	-elapha	
treatment (n)	behandeling	kalafo	tshwaro	tsholo	impatho	ukwelapha	
tree (n)	boom	sehlare	sefate	setlhare	umthi	umuthi	
tremble (v)	bewe	-roromela	-thothomela	-roroma	-ngcangcazela	-qhaqhazela	
trespass (v)	oortree	-tshela molao	-tlola	-sutlha	-ophula umthetho	-eqa umthetho	
trespasser (n)	oortreder	mosenyi	motlodi	motlodi	umaphuli-mthetho	umeqi	
trial (n)	verhoor	tsheko	teko	tshekiso	ityala	ukuthethwa kwecala	
triangle (n)	driehoek	khutlotharo	kgutlotharo	khutlotharo	unxantathu	unxantathu	
tributary (n)	takrivier	nokakeledi	lekala la noka	modutela	isebe	umngenela	
trick (n)	skelmstreek	bofora	mano	malepa	iqhinga	inkohliso	
trip (n)	reis	leeto	leeto	loeto	uhambo	uhambo	
trip (v)	struikel	-kgopša	-kgopa	-kgopa	-khubeka	-khubeka	
triumph (n)	triomf	phenyo	tlholo	phenyo	uloyiso	ukunqoba	
trivial (a)	niksbeduidend	-lefela	-sa tsebisahaleng	-sepe	-ngenamsebenzi	-yimfeketho	
trouble (n)	moeite	boitapišo	matsapa	molato	ingxaki	inkathazo	
trouble (v)	kwel	-tshwenya	-kgathatsa	-tshwenya	-khathaza	-khathaza	
trousers (n)	langbroek	borokgo bjo botelele	borikgwe	phase	ibrukhwe	ibhulukwe	
truck (n)	trok	letorokisi	leteroko	koloi	itroko	itologo	
true (a)	waar	-makgonthe	-nnete	-tota	-nyanisile(yo)	-qinisile	
trumpet (n)	trompet	porompeta	terompeta	phala	ixilongo	icilongo	

T	**English**	**Afrikaans**	**N Sotho**	**Sesotho**	**Tswana**	**Xhosa**	**Zulu**
	trumpeter (n)	trompetblaser	moletšaporompeta	moletsaterompeta	moletsi wa phala	umdlali-xilongo	umfuthi wecilongo
	trustworthy (a)	betroubaar	-botegago	-tshepahalang	-boikanyo	-thembekile(yo)	-thembekile
	truth (n)	waarheid	nnete	nnete	nnete	inyani	iqiniso
	try (v)	probeer	-leka	-leka	-leka	-zama	-zama
	tsetse fly (n)	tsetsevlieg	ntšhitsetse	seboba	tsetse	ingcongconi	itsetse
	tuberculosis (n)	tuberkulose	bolwetši bja mafahla	lefuba	lehuba	isifo sephepha	ufuba
	Tuesday (n)	Dinsdag	Labobedi	Labobedi	Labobedi	ulwesiBini	uLwesibili
	tumour (n)	gewas	sešo	tlhahala	tlhagala	ithumba	ithumba
	tune (n)	wysie	molodi	modumo	pina	ingonyana	ivumo
	tunnel (n)	tonnel	thanele	mohohoma	mogogoro	itonela	ithonela
	turkey (n)	kalkoen	kalakune	kalekune	kalakune	ikalkuni	ikalikuni
	turn (n)	beurt	lebaka	lekgetlo	sebaka	ithuba	ithuba
	turn (v)	draai	-dikologa	-fapoha	-tshika	-jika	-jika
	turnip (n)	raap	rapa	rapa	thenipe	ithenephu	utheniphu
	turquoise (n)	turkoois	thekoise	thekoise	botala	ilitye lexabiso	itshe eliluhlaza
	twelve (n)	twaalf	lesomepedi	leshome le metso e mmedi	some pedi	ishumi elinesibini	ishumi nambili
	twenty (n)	twintig	masomepedi	mashome a mabedi	somaamabedi	amashumi amabini	amashumi amabili
	twice (n)	twee maal	gabedi	habedi	ga bedi	isibini	kabili
	twig (n)	takkie	lekalana	lekala	kala	isetyana	igatshana
	twin (n)	tweeling	mafahla	mafahla	lefatlha	iwele	iwele
	two (n)	twee	pedi	pedi	bobedi	isibini	isibili
	type (n)	tipe	mohuta	mofuta	mofuta	uhlobo	uhlobo
	type (v)	tik	-tlanya	-tlanya	-thaepa	-chwetheza	-thayipha ngomshini
	typewriter (n)	tikmasjien	setlanyi	motjhene wa ho tlanya	setlanyi	umashini wokuchwetheza	umshini wokuthayipha
	typhoid (n)	ingewandskoors	tengkgolo	lefu la letshollo	letshoroma la mala	icesina	interika
	typist (n)	tikster	motlanyi	motlanyi	motlanyi	umchwethezi	ithayiphisi
	tyre (n)	buiteband	thaere	thaere	thaere	itayala	ithaya
	udder (n)	uier	mokaka	letswele	thele	ibele	umbele
	ugly (a)	lelik	-be	-be	-maswe	-bi	-bi
	ulcer (n)	ulkus	sešo	seso	tlhagala	isilonda	isilonda
	ultimate (a)	uiterste	-fetišago	-qetellong	-bofelong	-okugqibela	-kokugcina
	umbrella (n)	sambreel	samporele	samporele	sekhukhu	isambuleni	isambulela
	unaccustomed (a)	ongewoond	-sa tlwaelago	-sa tlwaelehang	-sa tlwaelwang	-ngaqhelanga	-ngajwayele
	unafraid (a)	onbevrees	-sa boifego	-sa tshabeng	-sa tshabeng	-ngoyikiyo	-ngesabi
	unalterable (a)	onveranderlik	-sa fetogego	-sa fetoheng	-sa fetogeng	-ngajikiyo	-ngaguquki
	unanimous (a)	eenstemmig	-botee	-ntsweleng	-bongwefela	-omxhelomnye	-vumelene
	unarmed (a)	ongewapend	-sa itlhamago ka dibetša	-sa hlomelang	-se nang dibetsa	-ngaxhobanga	-ngahlomile
	unauthorised (a)	ongemagtig	-se nago tokelo	-se nang tokelo	-se nang tumelelo	-ngagunyaziswanga	-ngagunyaziwe
	unavailable (a)	onverkrygbaar	-sa hwetšagalago	-sa fumaneheng	-tlhokegang	-ngafumanekiyo	-ngatholakali
	unaware (a)	onbewus	-sa tsebego	-sa elellweng	-sa itseng	-ngaqondanga	-nganaki
	unbeliever (n)	ongelowige	moditšhaba	mohetene	moheitene	umntu ongakholwayo	ongakholiwe
	unborn (a)	ongebore	-sego ya tswalwa	-sa tswalwang	-sa tsalweng	-ngazelwanga	-ngakazalwa
	uncertain (a)	onseker	-belaetšago	-sa tsebeng hantle	-belaelang	-ngaqinisekanga	-ngabaza
	uncharitable (a)	onbarmhartig	-hlokago botho	-se nang mohau	-se nang pelo	-ngenamfesane	-ngenamhawu
	uncivilised (a)	onbeskaaf	-hlokago setho	-tala	-tala	-ngaphucukanga	-ngaphucuzekile
	uncle (n)	oom	malome	malome	malome	umalume	umalume
	unclean (a)	onrein	-sa hlwekago	-ditshila	-maswe	-mdaka	-ngcolile
	uncomfortable (a)	ongemaklik	-go se iketle	-sa tsitsang	-tlhoatlhoegang	-ngekho mfumamfuma	-nganethezekile
	uncommon (a)	ongewoon	-sa tlwaelwago	-sa tlwaelehang	-sa tlwaelwang	-ngaqhelekanga	-ngavamile
	unconscious (a)	bewusteloos	-idibetšego	-akgehileng	-idibetseng	-lahlekelwe ziingqondo	-qalekile
	uncooked (a)	ongaar	-tala	-tala	-korobetseng	-ngaphekwanga	-luhlaza
	undamaged (a)	onbeskadig	-sego -senyega	-sa senyehang	-sa senyegang	-ngonakelanga	-ngalimalanga
	undecided (a)	onbeslis	-sego wa ahlolwa	-sa tsitsang	-sa atlholwang	-ngenasigqibo	-nhliziyombili
	undependable (a)	onbetroubaar	-sa botegego	-sa tshepahaleng	-sa tshepiwang	-ngathembakalanga	-ngathembeki
	under (prep)	onder	fase	tlasa	tlhase	ngaphantsi	phansi

English	Afrikaans	N Sotho	Sesotho	Tswana	Xhosa	Zulu	U
underdeveloped (a)	onderontwikkeld	-nago le tlhabologo ye nnyane	-sa tswelang pele	-sa tlhabololwang	-ngakhulanga gqibi	-ngathuthukisiwe	
understand (v)	verstaan	-kwišiša	-utlwisisa	-tlhaloganya	qonda	qonda	
undeserved (a)	onverdiend	-sa swanelego	-sa elellwang	-sa tshwanelwang	-ngafanelanga	-ngafanele	
undesirable (a)	ongewens	-sa nyakegego	-sa hlokahaleng	-ditsatsa	-nganqwenelekiyo	-ngafuneki	
undeveloped (a)	onontwikkeld	-hlokago tlhabologo	-sa ntshetswang pele	-sa tlhabololwang	-ngekasetyenziswa	-ngathuthukile	
undignified (a)	onwaardig	-hlokago maemo	-tellehang	-seng maemo	-ngenasithozela	-ngenasithunzi	
undisciplined (a)	ongedissiplineerd	-hlokago boitshwaro	-se nang mekgwa	-sa rutwang	-ngaqeqeshekanga	-ngenamthetho	
undisclosed (a)	onvermeld	-sa tšweletšwago	-sa bolelwang	-sa senolwang	-ngatyhilwanga	-ngavezwanga	
undisputed (a)	onbetwis	-sa ganetšwego	-sa phehisweng kgang	-sa ganelwang	-ngaphikiswa(yo)	-ngenakuphikiswa	
undo (v)	losmaak	-bofolla	-lokolla	-tlhatlhamolola	-khulula	-qaqa	
undoubted (a)	ongetwyfeld	-sa belaetšego	-sa belaetseng	-tota	-ngenakuthanda-tyuzwa	-sobala	
undress (v)	uittrek	-apola	-hlobola	-apola	-khulula	-khumula	
unearth (v)	opgrawe	-epolla	-tjhekolla	-epolola	-vumbulula	-vumbulula	
uneasy (a)	ongerus	-sa iketlego	-sa tsitsang	-kokonetseng	-ngonwabanga	-novalo	
uneducated (a)	ongeleerd	-go se rutege	-sa rutehang	-tala	-ngafundanga	-ngafundile	
unemployed (a)	werkloos	-hlokago mošomo	-sa sebetseng	-se nang tiro	-ngaqeshwanga	-ngenamsebenzi	
unequal (a)	ongelyk	-sa lekanego	-sa lekaneng	-sa lekaneng	-ngalinganiyo	-ngalingene	
uneven (a)	ongelyk	-sa lekanego	-sa lekaneng	-makgawekgawe	-ngalinganiyo	-namaduma	
unexpected (a)	onverwag	-sewelo	-sa lebellwang	-tshoganyetso	-ngalindelekanga	-zumayo	
unexpectedly (adv)	onverwags	ka sewelo	-sa lebellwang	ka tshoganyetso	ngokungalindelekanga	ngokuzuma	
unfaithful (a)	ontrou	-go se botege	-sa tshepahaleng	-sa ikanyegwang	-ngathembekanga	-ngathembekile	
unfinished (a)	onvoltooid	-sa phethagago	-sa phethahalang	-sa felang	-ngagqitywanga	-ngaqediwe	
unfit (a)	ongeskik	-sa lokelago	-sa lokelang	-siameng	-ngafanelekanga	-ngalungele	
unforgettable (a)	onvergeetlik	-go se lebalege	-sa lebaleheng	-sa lebalweng	-ngalibalekiyo	-ngakhohlwa	
unforgivable (a)	onvergeeflik	-go se swarelege	-sa tshwarelweng	-sa itshwarelweng	-ngaxolelekiyo	-ngathethelelwa	
unfortunately (adv)	ongelukkig	ka maswabi	-madimabe	-e seng sego	ngelishwa	-ngelishwa	
unfulfilled (a)	onvervuld	-sa phethagago	-sa phethahatswang	-sa tlhomamiswang	-ngazalisekanga	-ngafeziwe	
unfurnished (a)	ongemeubileerd	-se nago fenišara	-se nang thepa	-se nang fenitšhara	-ngenafenitshala	-ngenayo ifenisha	
ungrateful (a)	ondankbaar	-sa lebogego	-se nang teboho	-se nang tebogo	-ngenambulelo	-ngabongi	
unhappy (a)	ongelukkig	-nyamilego	-sa thabang	-bosula	-ngonwabanga	-hluphekile	
unhealthy (a)	ongesond	tše di sa agego mmele	-se nang bophelo	-lwalang	-ngaphilanga	-ngaphilile	
unhygienic (a)	onhigiënies	-ditšhila	-sa hlwekang	-maswe	-ngenampilo	-ngenanhlanzeko	
uniform (n)	uniform	yunifomo	yunifomo	semphato	ukufana	inyufomu	
unimportant (a)	onbelangrik	-sego bohlokwa	-seng ya bohlokwa	-sa tlhokegwang	umdibaniso	-ncane	
union (n)	unie	kopano	kopano	kopano	ubunye	inyunyana	
unit (n)	eenheid	botee	bonngwe	seelo	manya	uhlamvu	
unite (v)	verenig	-kopanya	-kopanya	-kopana	umanyano	-hlanganisa	
unity (n)	eenheid	botee	bonngwe	seoposengwe	umanyano	ubunye	
university (n)	universiteit	yunibesiti	yunibesithi	yunibeseti	iyunivesithi	iyunivesiti	
unjust (a)	onregverdig	-sa lokago	-se nang toka	-tshiamololo	-ngenabulungisa	-ngalungile	
unkind (a)	onvriendelik	-hlokago botho	-lonya	-seng bopelonomi	-ngenabubele	-ngenamusa	
unknowingly (adv)	onwetend	ka go se tsebe	-sa tsebe	-sa itse	ngokungazi	ngokungazi	
unload (v)	aflaai	-laolla	-laolla	-folosa	-thula	-ethula	
unlucky (a)	ongelukkig	-nago le madimabe	-madimabe	-bosula	-ngenathamsanqa	nebhadi	
unmarried (a)	ongetroud	-sego a nyala	-sa nyalwang	-kgope	-ngatshatanga	-ngaganile	
unmerciful (a)	ongenadig	-hlokago kguagelo	-se nang mohau	-se nang maitshwarelo	-ngenanceba	-ngenamhawu	
unplanned (a)	onbedoeld	-sa akanywago	-sa hlophuwang	-seng loano	-ngacetywanga	-ngahleliwe	
unpunctual (a)	nie stip nie	-go se be nakong	-sa bolokeng nako	-e seng ka nako	-ngagcini xesha	-ngagcinisikhathi	
unravel (v)	ontrafel	-hlahlamolla	-qhaqholla	-rarabolola	-combulula	-qaqa	
unrewarded (a)	onbeloond	-go se lefše	-sa lefuweng	-sa duelwang	-ngavuzwanga	-ngabongwanga	
unsafe (a)	onveilig	-kotsi	-se nang tshireletso	-sa bolokegwang	-nobungozi	-nengozi	
unselfish (a)	onselfsugtig	-hlokago mona	-sa ikgopoleng	-boitebalo	-ngazicingeliyo	-nomhawu	
unsuccessful (a)	onvoorspoedig	-hlokago katlego	-madimabe	-sa kgonegwang	-ngaphumelelanga	-ngaphumelelanga	
untidy (a)	slordig	-bošaedi	-bohlaswa	-boatla	-mdaka	-mahlikihliki	
until (conj)	tot	go fihlela	ho fihlela	go fitlhelela	kude	kuze	
unwary (a)	onbehoedsaam	-sa hlokomelego	-sa kgathalleng	-se na tlhaga	-ngaphaphamanga	-ngaxwayile	
unwilling (a)	onwillig	-go se rate	-sa rateng	-boitsemeletso	-ngafuniyo	-ngathandi	
up (prep)	op	godimo	hodima	mo	phezulu	phezulu	

131

U

English	Afrikaans	N Sotho	Sesotho	Tswana	Xhosa	Zulu
uphold (v)	hoog hou	-boloka	-phahamisa	-tshegetsa	-xhasa	-phakamisa
uproar (n)	lawaai	lešata	lerata	magawegawe	ingxolo	umsindo
upset (a)	ontsteld	-tshwenyegilego moyeng	-kgathatseha	-tsuololang	-phazamisekile(yo)	-thunukele
upset (v)	ontstel	-nyamiša	-kgathatsa	-tsuolola	-phazamisa	-thunukalisa
urban (a)	stedelik	-toropong	-metseng e meholo	-semotseng	-asezidolophini	-semadolobheni
urbanisation (n)	verstedeliking	toropofatšo	tokisetso ya metse e meholo	go tlwaetsa setoropo	isimo sedolophu	ukuphila isidolobha
urge (n)	drang	kganyogo	takatso	maikutlo	uthundezo	ukuphokophela
urge (v)	aanspoor	-hlohleletša	-kgothaletsa	-kurusa	-thundeza	-gqugquzela
urinate (v)	urineer	-rota	-rota	-rota	-chama	-chama
urine (n)	urine	moroto	moroto	moroto	umchamo	umchamo
us (pron)	ons	-re-	rona	rona	-ethu	thina
use (n)	gebruik	tirišo	tshebediso	mosola	intsebenziso	umsebenzi
use (v)	gebruik	-diriša	-sebedisa	-dirisa	-sebenzisa	-sebenzisa
useful (a)	nuttig	-mohola	-bohlokwa	-mosola	-nokusetyenziswa	-nomsebenzi
useless (a)	nutteloos	-hlokago mohola	-se nang thuso	-sepe	-ngenamsebenzi	-ngasizi
usually (adv)	gewoonlik	ka mehla	-atisa	tlhola	ngokuqhelekileyo	ngokuvamileyo
uvula (n)	kleintongetjie	lelengwana	lelengwana	lelengwana	incakancaka	ugovane
vacancy (n)	vakature	sebaka	sekgeo	phatlhatiro	isithuba	isikhala
vacant (a)	vakant	-bulegilego	-sekgeo	-phatlhatiro	-ngenanto	-ngenalutho
vacate (v)	uittrek	-tloga	-ikgula	-ntsha	-enza ingabi nanto	-thutha
vaccinate (v)	inent	-enta	enta	-enta	-gonya	-gcaba
vaccination (n)	inenting	kento	kento	mokento	ugonyo	umgcabo
vacuum (n)	lugleegte	-hlokago moya	sebaka se feela	lephaka	ihamte	isikhala esingenamoya
vagrant (n)	rondloper	moneneri	molakolako	sengae	ihilihili	uzulane
vague (a)	vaag	-go se kwišišege	-sa utlwahaleng	-mathaithai	-ngacacanga	-ngezwakali kahle
vain (a)	ydel	-lefela	-lefeela	-lefela	-lambathayo	-ziqhenya
valid (a)	geldig	-yago ka molao	-nnete	-nnete	-xabisekile(yo)	-lungile
valley (n)	vallei	moedi	phula	mogorogoro	intlambo	isigodi
valuable (a)	waardevol	-bohlokwa	-bohlokwa	-botlhokwa	-nexabiso	nenani eliphakeme
value (n)	waarde	mohola	bohlokwa	tlhotlhwa	ixabiso	inani
value (v)	waardeer	-lekanyetša	-rata	-phophotha legetla	-xabisa	-beka inani
valve (n)	klep	belefe	belofo	belefo	isivalo	ivalfu
vapour (n)	wasem	moyameetse	mouwane	phufudi	umphunga	umhwamuko
varied (a)	gevarieerd	-fapafapanago	-fapaneng	-mofutafuta	-ahluka-hlukene(yo)	-nhlobonhlobo
variety (n)	verskeidenheid	mehutahuta	bongata	mofutafuta	iintlobo ngeentlobo	izinhlobonhlobo
vary (v)	varieer	-fapanatsopa	-fapanya	-fetola	-ahluka	-hlukana
vase (n)	vaas	sebjanatsopa	bolompoto	morufadišeše	ivazi	ivazi
veal (n)	kalfsvleis	nama ya namane	nama ya namane	nama ya namane	inyama yethole	inyama yenkonyane
vegetable (n)	groente	morogo	meroho	morogo	imifuno	uhlaza
veil (n)	sluier	seširo	lesira	lesire	isigqubuthelo	iveli
vein (n)	aar	setlišamadi	mothapo	lesika	umthambo	umthambo
veld (n)	veld	naga	naha	naga	ilindle	indle
vengeance (n)	wraak	tefeletšo	boiphetetso	pusoloso	impindezelo	impindiselo
venison (n)	wildsvleis	nama ya phoofolo	nama ya nyamatsane	nama ya diphologolo	inyama yenyamakazi	inyama yenyamazane
venom (n)	venyn	bohloko	tjhefo	botlhole	intiyo	isihlungu
verb (n)	werkwoord	lediri	leetsi	lediri	isenzi	isenzo
verbal (a)	mondeling	-molomo	-molomo	ka puo	-omlomo	-ngomlomo
verdict (n)	uitspraak	kahlolo	kahlolo	katlholo	isigwebo	isinqumo
vernacular (n)	volkstaal	leleme la setšhaba	puo ya lapeng	segae	ulwimi lwemveli	ulimi
verse (n)	vers	temana	temana	tema	ivesi	indima
vertebra (n)	werwel	mokolo	lesapo la mokokotlo	letlhotlholo	umqolo	izongwe lomhlandla
vertebrate (n)	werweldier	phoofolo ya mokokotlo	phoofolo e nang le lesapo la moko kotlo	phologolo ya mokokotlo	isilwanyana esinomqolo	isilwane esinomhlandla
vertical (a)	vertikaal	-tsepamego	-otlolohileng	-tsepameng	-nkqo	-qonde phezulu
very (a)	heel	kudu	-hle	-thata	-khulu	kakhulu
vest (n)	onderhemp	penehempe	besete	besete	ivesti	ivesti

132

English	Afrikaans	N Sotho	Sesotho	Tswana	Xhosa	Zulu	W
vice (n)	ondeug	bošula	bobe	bosula	umkhuba	umkhuba omubi	
vice-chairman (n)	ondervoorsitter	seatla sa modulasetulo	motlatsi wa modulasetulo	modulasetilo wa bobedi	usekela-sihlalo	usekelasihlalo	
victim (n)	slagoffer	sehlabelo	phofu	sebolaiwa	ixhoba	umhlatshelo	
video recorder (n)	videokassetopnemer	segatiši sa video	motjhine wa vidio		ividiyo	isiqophi sezwi nezithombe	
view (n)	uitsig	pono	tjhadimo	pono	umbono	umbukiso	
view (v)	bekyk	-bogela	-tadima	-leba	-jonga	-buka	
vigilance (n)	waaksaamheid	phakgamo	tebelo	botlhaga	ukuphaphama	ukuqaphela	
vigorous (a)	kragtig	-maatla	-matla	-maatla	-ngamandla	-ngamandla	
village (n)	dorpie	motse	motsana	motse	isixeko	idolobhana	
villain (n)	skurk	sekebeka	motlatlapi	molotsana	itshivela	isigebengu	
vine (n)	wingerdstok	morara	sefate sa morara	terebe	umdiliya	isivini	
vinegar (n)	asyn	binika	asene	aseine	ivinika	uvinika	
violence (n)	geweld	bošoro	pefo	boganka	ububhovubhovu	isidlakadlaka	
violin (n)	viool	fiolo	violene	baeyolene	ifidyoli	ivayolini	
violinist (n)	vioolspeler	moletšafiolo	mmapalaviolene	moletsi wa baeyolene	umdlali-fidyoli	umshayivayolini	
virgin (n)	maagd	ngwanenyana	morwetsana	bokgarebe	idlolo	intombi emsulwa	
visa (n)	visum	bisa	visa	tumelelo	ivisa	ivisa	
visible (a)	sigbaar	-bonagalago	-bonahalang	-bonala	-bonakalayo	-bonakala	
vision (n)	gesigsvermoë	pono	pono	pono	umbono	ukubona	
visit (n)	besoek	ketelo	ketelo	leeto	utyelelo	ukuvakashela	
visit (v)	besoek	-etela	-etela	-etela	-tyelela	-vakashela	
visitor (n)	besoeker	moeng	moeti	moeti	undwendwe	isivakashi	
vocabulary (n)	woordeskat	tlotlontšu	letlotlo la mantswe	mafoko	isigama	amagama	
voice (n)	stem	lentšu	lentswe	lentswe	ilizwi	izwi	
volcano (n)	vulkaan	bolkano	bolekano	lekgwamolelo	intabamlilo	intabamlilo	
volume (n)	volume	bolumo	mothamo	mothama	umthamo	ubukhulu ba-	
voluntary (a)	vrywillig	-go se gapeletšwe	ka boithatelo	-ithaopang	-zithandelayo	-ngentando	
volunteer (n)	vrywilliger	moithapi	mothahaselli	moithaopa	ivolontiya	uvolontiya	
volunteer (v)	vrywillig onderneem	-ithaopa	-thahasella	-ithaopa	-zithandele	-volontiya	
vomit (n)	vomeersel	mahlatša	mahlatsa	matlhatsa	ukugabha	ubuhlanzo	
vomit (v)	vomeer	-hlatša	-hlatsa	-tlhatsa	-gabha	-hlanza	
vote (n)	stem	bouto	bouto	kgetho	ivoti	ukuvota	
vote (v)	stem	-kgetha	-bouta	-kgetha	-vota	-vota	
vow (n)	gelofte	keno	kano	maikano	-funga	isifungo	
vowel (n)	klinker	tumanoši	tumannotshi	tumanosi	isikhamiso	unkamisa	
vulgar (a)	vulgêr	-mahlapa	-tlhapa	-maswe	-thukayo	-ngenamahloni	
vulture (n)	aasvoël	lenong	lenong	lenong	ixhalanga	inqe	
wade (v)	waad	-tsena	-phoka	-gobua	-nyovula	-bhoxoza	
wafer (n)	wafel	kuku ya weifere	bohobe	sepapetlanyana	isonka somthendeleko	ucwecwane	
wag (v)	swaai	-hwidinya	-tsoka	-tsokotsa	-jiwula	-tshikizisa	
wagon (n)	wa	koloi	koloi	koloi	inqwelo	inqola	
wail (v)	weeklaag	-golola	-bohola	-bokolela	-enza isijwili	-khala	
waist (n)	middel	letheka	letheka	letheka	isinqe	iguma	
waistcoat (n)	onderbaadjie	onoropaki	onnorobaki	baaki ya tlase	indulubhatyi	intolibhantshi	
wait (v)	wag	-leta	-leta	-leta	-linda	-linda	
waiter (n)	kelner	weitara	mofepi	modigedi	iweyitara	uweta	
wake (v)	wakker word	-phafoga	-phaphama	-tsoga	-vuka	-phaphama	
walk (n)	wandeling	mosepelo	ho tsamaya	motsamao	umhambo	ukuhamba	
walk (v)	loop	-sepela	-tsamaya	-tsamaya	-hamba	-hamba	
wall (n)	muur	leboto	lebota	lebota	udonga	udonga	
wallet (n)	notetas	sepatšhe	walete	khuana	iwolethi	iwalethi	
wallow (v)	wentel	-dikologa	-potoloha	-bidikama	ukuzibhijabhija	-huquza	
wander (v)	dwaal	-tlaruma	-tsekela	-teatea	-bhadula	-zula	
want (v)	wil hê	-nyaka	-batla	-batla	-funa	-funa	
war (n)	oorlog	ntwa	ntwa	ntwa	imfazwe	impi	
warm (a)	warm	-borutho	-tjhesang	-bolelo	-shushu	-fudumele	
warn (v)	waarsku	-lemoša	-eletsa	-tlhagisa	-lumkisa	-qaphisa	

	English	Afrikaans	N Sotho	Sesotho	Tswana	Xhosa	Zulu
W	warning (n)	waarskuwing	temošo	keletso	kgalemo	isilumkiso	isiqapheliso
	wart (n)	vrat	tlhokofele	monyollo	kakana	intsumpa	insumpa
	wash (v)	was	-hlapa	-hlatswa	-tlhatswa	-hlamba	-geza
	wasp (n)	perdeby	mobu	seboba	mofu	unomeva	umuvi
	waste (n)	afval	tšhila	dithole	tshenyego	inkcitho	izibi
	waste (v)	vermors	-senya	-senya	-senya	-chitha	-lahla
	watch (n)	horlosie	sešupanako	watjhe	sesupanako	ixesha	iwashi
	watch (v)	dophou	-hlokomela	-disa	-lepa	-qwalasela	-bheka
	water (n)	water	meetse	metsi	metsi	amanzi	amanzi
	water (v)	natgooi	-nošetša	-nwesetsa	-nosa	-manzisa	-chelela
	waterfall (n)	waterval	phororo	phororo	lephothoselo	ingxangxasi	impophoma
	watermelon (n)	waatlemoen	legapu	lehapu	legapu	ivatala	ikhabe
	wave (n)	brander	lephoto	leqhubu	lekhubu	amaza	igagasi
	wax (n)	was	motu	dikonokono	boka	umphula	ingcino
	way (n)	pad	tsela	tsela	tsela	indlela	indlela
	we (pron)	ons	rena	rona	rona	thina	thina
	weak (a)	swak	-fokolago	-fokolang	-bokoa	-buthathaka	-ngenamandla
	weakness (n)	swakheid	bofokodi	bofokodi	bokoa	ubuthathaka	ukungaqini
	wealth (n)	rykdom	khumo	leruo	lehumo	ubutyebi	umnotho
	wean (v)	speen	-lomolla	-kgwesa	-alosa	-lumla	-lumula
	weapon (n)	wapen	sebetša	sebetsa	sebetsa	isixhobo	isikhali
	wear (v)	dra	-apara	-apara	-rwala	-nxiba	-gqoka
	weariness (n)	moegheid	tapo	mokgathala	letsapa	ukudinwa	ukukhathala
	weary (a)	vermoeid	-lapilego	-kgathetseng	-lapileng	-diniwe(yo)	-khathele
	weather (n)	weer	boso	bosa ba lehodimo	bosa	imozulu	izulu
	weave (v)	weef	-loga	-loha	-loga	-photha	-aluka
	weaving (n)	wewery	mologo	moloho	go loga	ukuphotha	ukwaluka
	wed (v)	trou	-nyala	-nyala	-nyala	-tshata	-shada
	wedding (n)	bruilof	monyanya wa lenyalo	lenyalo	lenyalo	umtshato	umshado
	Wednesday (n)	Woensdag	Laboraro	Laboraro	Laboraro	uLwesithathu	ulwesithathu
	weed (n)	onkruid	sekoro	lehola	mofero	ukhula	ukhula
	weed (v)	onkruid uittrek	-hlogola	-hlaola	-tlhagola	-susa ukhula	-hlakula
	week (n)	week	beke	beke	beke	iveki	iviki
	weekly (a)	weekliks	-beke	ka beke	ka beke	-ngeveki	ngeviki
	weep (v)	huil	-lla	-lla	-lela	-lila	-khala
	weevil (n)	kalander	tšhupa	tshupa	motoutwana	ingqokoqwane	indudwane
	weigh (v)	weeg	-kala	-bekga	-kala	-linganisela	-kala
	weight (n)	gewig	boima	boima	boima	ubunzima	isisindo
	welcome (n)	welkom	kamogelo	kamohelo	kamogelo	ulwamkelo	ukwemukela
	welcome (v)	verwelkom	-amogela ka lethabo	-amohela	-amogela	-amkela	-emukela
	welfare (n)	welsyn	boiphedišo	katleho	kagiso	intlalo-ntle	inhlalakahle
	well (a)	goed	gabotse	hantle	pila	kakuhle	kahle
	well (n)	put	petse	sediba	sediba	iqula	umgodi onomthombo
	well-known (a)	welbekend	-tumilego	-tsebahalang	-itsegeng	-aziwayo	-dumileyo
	west (adv)	wes	bodikela	-bophirima	bophirima	ntshona	entshonalanga
	west (n)	weste	bodikela	Bophirima	bophirima	intshonalanga	intshonalanga
	western (a)	westelik	-bodikela	-bophirima	-bophirima	-asentshona	-ntshonalanga
	wet (a)	nat	-kolobilego	-metsi	-metsi	-manzi	-manzi
	whale (n)	walvis	leruarua	leruarua	leruarua	umnenga	umkhoma
	what (pron)	wat	eng	eng	eng	ntoni	yini
	wheat (n)	koring	korong	koro	korong	ingqolowa	ukolo
	wheel (n)	wiel	leotwana	lebidi	leotwana	ivili	isondo
	wheelbarrow (n)	kruiwa	kiribane	kereibaya	kiriba	ikiriva	ibhala
	wheeze (v)	hyg	-buša moya ka bothata	-fehelwa	-hupela	-tswina	-bhohoza
	when (adv)	wanneer	neng	neng	leng	nini	nini
	where (adv)	waar	kae	kae	kae	phi	-phi
	whether (conj)	of	goba	kapa	fa	ukuba	noma
	which (pron)	watter	-fe	-fe	-fe	yiphi	-phi
	while (conj)	terwyl	mola	ha	-ntse	ngelixa	ngenkathi

English	Afrikaans	N Sotho	Sesotho	Tswana	Xhosa	Zulu
whimper (v)	sanik	-lla	-lla	-kuruetsa	-khwina	-bibitheka
whip (n)	sweep	sefepi	sephadi	seme	isabhokhwe	isiswebhu
whip (v)	raps	-itia	-shapa	-setla	-nqasha	-thwisha
whirlpool (n)	maalstroom	moelaphirihlwa	metsi a ferellang	kgogela	iqula elibizelayo	isiphethu
whiskers (n)	snor	maledu a ka godimo ga molomo	matshwala	tedu	amabhovu	amadevu
whisper (n)	gefluister	go sebaseba	nyenyeletso	mosebo	usebezo	ukuhleba
whisper (v)	fluister	-sebaseba	-hweshetsa	-seba	-sebeza	-hleba
whistle (n)	fluit	nakana	phala	molodi	impempe	ikhwelo
whistle (v)	fluit	-letša molodi	-letsa molodi	-tswirinya	-betha impempe	-shaya ikhwelo
white (n)	wit	tšhweu	bosweu	bosweu	ubumhlophe	-mhlophe
whitewash (n)	witkalk	kalaka ye tšhweu	kalaka e tshweu	kalaka	ikalika	umcako
who (pron)	wie	mang	mang	mang	ubani	ubani
whole (a)	heel	-ohle	-felletseng	-tlhe	yonke	-philile
wholesome (a)	heilsaam	-lokilego	-molemo	-bokompa	-philile(yo)	-philisayo
whooping cough (n)	kinkhoes	lethakgo	mokgokgothwane	kgookgoo	unkonkonko	ukhohlokhohlo
whore (n)	hoer	sefebe	sefebe	sefefe	ihenyukazi	isifebe
whose (pron)	wie se	-mang	-mang	mang	kabani	-kabani
why (adv)	waarom	ka lebaka lang	hobaneng	go reng	ngokuba	ngani
wide (a)	wyd	-phaphathi	batsi	-phaphathi	-banzi	-banzi
widow (n)	weduwee	mohlologadi	mohlolohadi	motlholagadi	umhlolokazi	umfelokazi
widower (n)	wewenaar	mohlologadi wa monna	mohlolohadi wa monna	moswagadi	umhlolo	umfelwa
wife (n)	vrou	mogatša	mosadi	mosadi	umfazi	unkosikazi
wild (a)	wild	-naga	-hlaha	-tlhaga	-ndwebile (yo)	-asendle
wilderness (n)	wildernis	lešoka	lehwatateng	sekgwa	ilindle	indle
wildlife (n)	natuurlewe	bophelolešokeng	bophelo bo hlaha	bophelonageng	ubomi basendle	impilo yasendle
wilful (a)	moedswillig	-matepe	ka boomo	-boitaolo	-nenkani	ngamabomu
will (n)	wil	thato	thato	thato	intando	intando
will (v)	sal	-tlo-	-tla	-tla	-za	-zo-
willow (n)	wilgerboom	moduwane	moduwane	modibonoka	umngcunube	umnyezane
wilt (v)	kwyn	-pona	-pona	-otobala	-buna	-fehleka
win (v)	wen	-fenya	-hlola	-sia	-zuza	-wina
wind (n)	wind	phefo	moya	phefo	umoya	umoya
window (n)	venster	lefastere	fensetere	fensetere	ifestile	ifasitela
windpipe (n)	gorrelpyp	mogolo	qoqotho	kgokgotsho	umqala	uqhoqhoqho
windscreen (n)	voorruit	seširaphefo	fensetere ya moya	sesiraphefo	ifestile engaphambili emotweni	ifasitela lemoto langaphambili
wine (n)	wyn	beine	beine	beine	iwayini	iwayini
wineglass (n)	wynkelkie	senwelwana	kgalase ya beine	galase ya beine	iglasi yokusela iwayini	ingilazi yewayini
winelist (n)	wynkaart	lenaneo la dibeine	lenane la beine	thulaganyo ya beine	uluhlu lweentlobo zewayini	uhla lwamawayini
wing (n)	vlerk	lefego	lepheo	lefuka	iphiko	iphiko
wink (n)	knipogie	ponyo ya leihlo	panyo	go panya	uqhwanyazo	ukucwayiza
wink (v)	knipoog	-nyabetša leihlo	-panya	-panya	-qoba iliso	-cwayiza
winter (n)	winter	marega	mariha	mariga	ubusika	ubusika
wipe (v)	afvee	-phumola	-phumola	-phimola	-sula	-sula
wire (n)	draad	motato	terata	bothale	ucingo	ucingo
wire (v)	bedraad	-tsenya mathale	-tlama terata	-lokela bothale	-faka ucingo	-faka ucingo
wisdom (n)	wysheid	bohlale	bohlale	botlhale	ubulumko	inhlakanipho
wise (a)	wys	-bohlale	-bohlale	-botlhale	-lumkile (yo)	-hlakaniphile
wish (n)	wens	kganyogo	takatso	keletso	umnqweno	isifiso
wish (v)	wens	-kganyoga	-lakatsa	-eletsa	-nqwena	-fisa
witchcraft (n)	toorkuns	boloi	boloi	boloi	ubugqwirha	ubuthakathi
witchdoctor (n)	toordokter	moloi	ramethokgo	ngaka	igqirha	umthakathi
with (prep)	met	le	le	ka	nga-	nga-
withdraw (v)	terugtrek	-katoga	-hula	-funyetsa	-rhoxa	-khipha
wither (v)	verlep	-pona	-pona	-swaba	-bunisa	-oma
within (adv)	binne	ka gare	ka hare	teng	ngaphakathi	ngaphakathi
without (adv)	buite	ka ntle	ka ntle	bisa	ngaphandle	ngaphandle

W

English	Afrikaans	N Sotho	Sesotho	Tswana	Xhosa	Zulu
witness (n)	getuie	paki	paki	mosupi	ingqina	ufakazi
woman (n)	vrou	mosadi	mosadi	mosadi	umfazi	umfazi
womb (n)	baarmoeder	popelo	popelo	popelo	isizalo	isibeletho
wonder (n)	wonder	mohlolo	mohlolo	motlholo	ummangaliso	isimangaliso
wonder (v)	wonder	-makala	-hlolla	-gakgamala	-mangalisa	-mangala
wonderful (a)	wonderlik	-makatšago	-makatsang	-ntle	-mangalisa (yo)	-mangalisayo
wood (n)	hout	kota	lehong	legong	iinkuni	ukhuni
wool (n)	wol	boya	boya	boboa	uboya	uvolo
word (n)	woord	lentšu	lentswe	lefoko	igama	igama
work (n)	werk	modiro	mosebetsi	tiro	umsebenzi	umsebenzi
work (v)	werk	-dira	-sebetsa	-dira	-sebenza	-sebenza
worker (n)	werker	modiri	mosebetsi	modiri	umsebenzi	isisebenzi
world (n)	wêreld	lefase	lefatshe	lefatshe	ilizwe	umhlaba
worm (n)	wurm	seboko	seboko	seboko	impethu	impethu
worry (v)	bekommer	-belaela	-kgathatseha	-tshwenya	-hlupha	-khathazeka
wound (n)	wond	ntho	leqeba	ntho	inxeba	inxeba
wound (v)	wond	-gobatša	-ntsha kotsi	-ntsha ntho	-enzakalisa	-limaza
wrap (v)	toedraai	-phuthela	-phuthela	-phutela	-bhijela	-songa
wreck (n)	wrak	matlhenkge	moswahla	thubego	ubutyobo	umbhabhalala
wriggle (v)	wriemel	-širašira	-sosobanya	-menekana	-jubalaza	-shobashoba
wring (v)	wring	-phetla	-sotha	-soka	-jija	-sontiza
wrinkle (n)	plooi	mašošo	maswebe	letsuba	umbimbi	umfingcizo
wrinkle (v)	plooi	-šošobanya	-sosobanya	-tsutsubanya	-shwabanisa	-fingciza
wrist (n)	pols	senoko so seatla	lenonyeletso	letlhalela	isihlahla	isihlakala
write (v)	skryf	-ngwala	-ngola	-kwala	-bhala	-bhala
writing (n)	skrif	mongwalo	mongolo	mokwalo	umbhalo	umbhalo
writing paper (n)	skryfpapier	pampiri ya go ngwalela	pampiri ya ho ngolla	pampiri	iphepha lokubhala	iphepha lokubhala
wrong (a)	verkeerd	-phošo	-phoso	-phoso	-ngalunganga	-ngalungile
x-ray (n)	x-straal	eksrei	x-rei	ekeserei	ugesi	iX-reyi
xylophone (n)	xilofoon	silofone	zaelofone	saelefono	isiginci samagqudwana	izayilofoni
yacht (n)	seiljag	seketswana	seketswana sa seile	seketswana	isikhephe sogqatso	umkhumbi
yard (n)	werf	jarata	jarete	jarata	ibala	iyadi
yawn (n)	gaap	kedimolo	kedimolo	edimolo	ukuzamla	ukuzamula
yawn (v)	gaap	-edimola	-edimola	-edimola	-zamla	-zamula
year (n)	jaar	ngwaga	selemo	ngwaga	unyaka	unyaka
yearly (a)	jaarliks	ka ngwaga	selemo le selemo	-ngwaga le ngwaga	-omnyaka	ngeminyaka
yearn (v)	hunker	-hlologela	-labalabela	-eletsa	-langazelela	-langazela
yeast (n)	gis	mahlabego	tomoso	sebidiso	igwele	imvubelo
yellow (n)	geel	serolane	tshehla	bosetlha	ibala elimthubi	-liphuzi
yesterday (n)	gister	maabane	maobane	maabane	izolo	izolo
yoke (n)	juk	joko	joko	joko	idyokhwe	ijoka
yolk (n)	eiergeel	mothobe	mothwebe	boe	umthubi	isikhupha seqanda
you (pron)	julle	lena	lona	lona	nina	nina
you (pron)	jy	wena	wena	wena	wena	wena
young (a)	jong	-fsa	-motjha	-nana	-tsha	-ncane
young (n)	kleintjie	ngwana	ledinyane	ngwana	umntwana	isiyayo
your (pron)	jou	-gago	-hao	-gago	-akho	-kho
your (pron)	julle	-lena	-lona	-lona	-enu	-inu
yours (pron)	joune	-gago	-hao	-gago	-akho	okwakho
yours (pron)	julle s'n	-lena	-lona	-lona	-enu	okwenu
youth (n)	jeug	bafsa	motjha	bošwa	ulutsha	ubusha
zebra (n)	sebra	pitsi ya naga	qwaha	pitse-ya-naga	iqwarhashe	idube
zero (n)	nul	lefeela	noto	lefelo	unothi	iqanda
zigzag (n)	sigsag	manyokenyoke	matswedintsweke	manyokenyoke	ujikojiko	igwinci
zipper (n)	ritssluiter	sengamedi	zipo	sekonopelo sa sipi	iziphu	iziphu
zone (n)	sone	karolo	lebatowa	kgaolo	ummandla	isifunda
zoo (n)	dieretuin	serapa sa diphoofolo	zuu	zuu	iziko lezilwanyana	izu

AFRIKAANS

PRONUNCIATION

Afrikaans uses the typical guttural sounds of Germanic languages, particularly the hard **g**, the rolling **r** and the **t** sound for the **d**. Similarly, **w** may be pronounced as **v**, while **v** is pronounced with an **f** sound.

The following table is based on English pronunciation; letters not listed are the same in English.

Letter (group)	in Afrikaans	as in the English
a	kap	*u* in *cup*
a(a)u	gemia(a)u	*ow* in *cow*
aa	daad	*u* in *cup* but longer like *ah*
aai	paai	*y* in *why*
ae	dae	*u* in *dust* but longer like *ah* followed by article *a*
c	Calvinis	*k* in *kitten*
c	celsius	*s* in *size*
ch	chemie	guttural like *ch* in *loch*
ch	chloor	*k* in *kitten*
ch/sj	China	*sh* in *shot*
d	bed	*t* in *tart*
e	edel	*ee* in *deer*
ê	hê	*ai* in *hair*
e	ken	*e* in *hen*
e	bevat	*e* in *angel*
ee	een	*ee* in *deer*
eë/ië	leë/skiër	*ea* in *fear* (two sounds)
eeu	eeufees	*ew* in *few*
ei	bleik	*ay* in *play*
eu	deur	*ee* in *deer* with lips pouted
eu	euforie	*ew* in *few* but shorter
g	groot	guttural like *ch* in *loch*
gh	gholf	*g* in *golf*
i	sit	*e* in *angel*
ie	dier	*ee* in *breed*
ie	siek	*i* in *sick*
j	jammer	*y* in *you*
kn	knoop	*c* in *cat* followed by *n* in *no* with rapidly spoken *â* sound between

Letter (group)	in Afrikaans	as in the English
ng	bang	*ng* in *sing*
o	bode	*oo* in *loot* followed by rapid *w* with pouted lips
o	euforie	*oo* in *loot* but shorter
ô	môre	*au* in *cause*
o	oggend	*o* in *fort* but shorter
o	potjie	*oy* in *boy*
oe	voer	*oo* in *loot*
oe	voet	*oo* in *loot* but shorter
oë	vermoë	*oe* in *doer*
oei	koei	*ooey* in *phooey* but preceded by rapid *w*
oo	soom	*oo* in *loot* followed by rapid *w* with pouted lips
ooi	sooi	*oi* in *oil* but preceded by rapid *w*
ou	bout	*oa* in *coat*
r	duiker	*r* in *very* (lightly rolled)
r	rond	strongly rolled – almost Scots
tj	tjank	*ch* in *chunk*
u	put	*e* in *angel* but with lips pouted
u	u	*i* in *sick* but with lips pouted
ui	lui	*ay* in *play* but longer with pouted lips
uie	beduie	*aye* in *player* but longer and with pouted lips
uu	duur	*ee* in *breed* but with lips pouted
v	vul	*f* in *fun*
w	swem	*w* in *sweep*
w	water	*v* in *visit*
y	yster	*ay* in *play*

Afrikaans	English	N Sotho	Sesotho	Tswana	Xhosa	Zulu	A
aaklig	ghastly (a)	-be	-tshabehang	-be	-oyikeka (yo)	-esabekayo	
aalwyn	aloe (n)	mokgopha	lekgala	mokgopha	ikhala	umhlaba	
aambeie	haemorrhoids (n)	matšala	ho petsoha ha sebono	tutlamadi	izikhala	imizoko	
aanbeveel	recommend (v)	-digela	-kgothalletsa	-atlanegisa	-ncoma	-ncoma	
aanbeveling	recommendation (n)	tigelo	kgothalletso	katlanegiso	uncomo	ukuncoma	
aanbid	adore (v)	-rata kudu	-kgahlwa	-rapela	-thanda	-khulekela	
aanbied	offer (v)	-šišinya	-fa	-naya	-nikela	-thembisa	
aanbod	offer (n)	tšhišinyo	mpho	kabelo	umnikelo	isithembiso	
aan boord	aboard (adv)	ka gare ga	-palame	-palameng	-ngaphezulu	emkhunjini	
aand	evening (n)	mantšiboa	mantsiboya	maitseboa	ngokuhlwa	ukuhlwa	
aandenking	souvenir (n)	segopotšo	sehopotso	segopotsi	isikhumbuzo	isikhumbuziso	
aandete	supper (n)	dijo tša selalelo	dijo tsa mantsiboya	selalelo	isophoro	isapha	
aan die brand	alight (a)	-swago	-tuka	-tlhosetsang	-tshayo	-okhele	
aan die slaap	asleep (a)	-ile le boroko	-robetse	-robalang	-leleyo	-lele	
aandrang	insistence (n)	phegelelo	pheello	tswetelelo	unyanzelo	isigcizelelo	
aandring	insist (v)	-phegelela	-pheella	-tswetelela	-nyanzelisa	-gcizelela	
aangehoudene	detainee (n)	mogolegwa	motshwaruwa	motshwarwa	umbanjwa	isiboshwa	
aangenaam	nice (a)	-bose	-hlabosang	-monate	-mnandi	-mnandi	
aangenaam	agreeable (a)	-go iketla	-bonolo	-isegang	-vumelanayo	-mnandi	
aangrensend	adjacent (a)	-bataganego	-bapileng	-bapang	-gudlene	-sondelene	
aanhaal	quote (v)	-khoutha	-qotsa	-nopola	-caphula	-caphuna	
aanhaling	quotation (n)	khoutho	qotso	nopolo	ukucaphula	ukucaphuna	
aanhangsel	appendix (n)	seoketša	sehlomathiso	mametlelelo	umqukumbelo	isithasiselo	
aanheg	attach (v)	-swaragantšha	-momahanya	gokelela	-bophelela	-hlanganisa	
aanhou	detain (v)	-golega	-tshwara	-dia	-gcina eluvalelweni	-bopha	
aanhouding	detention (n)	mogolego	tshwaro	tiego	uvalelo	ukuboshwa	
aankla	charge (law) (v)	-bega	-qosa	-latofatsa	-mangalelwa	-beka icala	
aanklaer	prosecutor (n)	mosekiši	motjhotjhisi	mosekisi	umtshutshisi	ummangaleli	
aanklag	charge (n)	pego	qoso	molato	isimangalo	icala	
aankom	arrive (v)	-goroga	-fihla	-goroga	-fika	-fika	
aankoms	arrival (n)	kgorogo	ho fihla	kgorogo	ukufika	ukufika	
aankondig	announce (v)	-tsebiša	-tsebisa	-goeletsa	-azisa	-memezela	
aankondiging	announcement (n)	tsebišo	tsebiso	kgoeletso	isaziso	isimemezelo	
aanlok	lure (v)	-goketša	-hohela	-okisa	umbizane	-yenga	
aanmoedig	encourage (v)	-tutuetša	-kgothaletsa	-nametsa	-khuthaza	-khuthaza	
aanneem	adopt (v)	-amogela	-amohela	-amogela	-amkela	-thola	
aanneming	adoption (n)	kamogelo	kamohelo	kamogelo	ukwamkela	ukuthola	
aanpak	tackle (v)	-thoma	-hlasela	-thoma	-hlasela	-qala	
aanpas	adapt (v)	-amantša	-tjhorisa	-tlwaela	-lungiselela	-vumelanisa	
aanraking	touch (n)	kgwatho	kamo	kamo	uchukumiso	ukuthinta	
aanrand	assault (v)	-gobatša	-otla	-teketa	-hlasela	-hlasela	
aanranding	assault (n)	kgobatšo	kotlo	moteketo	uhlaselo	uhlaselo	
aanskaf	acquire (v)	-hwetša	-fumana	-bapala	-zuza	-zuza	
aanskaffing	acquisition (n)	khwetšo	phumano	papadi	inzuzo	ukuzuza	
aansoek	application (n)	kgopelo	kopo ya mosebeti	kopo	isicelo	isicelo	
aansoek doen	apply (v)	-kgopela	-kopa mosebeti	-kopa	-enza isicelo	-cela	
aansoeker	applicant (n)	mokgopedi	mokopamosebetsi	mokopi	umceli	umceli	
aanspoor	urge (v)	-hlohleletša	-kgothaletsa	-kurusa	-thundeza	-gqugquzela	
aansteek	ignite (v)	-gotetša	-hotetsa	-gotsa	-lumeka	-okhela	
aansteeklik	contagious (a)	-fetetšago	-tshwaetsang	-fetelang	-sulelayo	-memethekayo	
aanstel	appoint (v)	-bea	-hira	-tlhoma	-tyumba	-qasha	
aanstelling	appointment (n)	peo	kgiro	peelano	ukutyumba	ukuqashwa	
aansterk	convalesce (v)	-fola	-nonopela	-thamogelwa	-chacha	-lulama	
aanstoot gee	offend (v)	-kgopiša	-sitelwa	-kgopa	-khubekisa	-cunula	
aanstootlik	offensive (a)	-kgopišago	-hlokofatsang	-tlhokang botho	-khubekisayo	-cunulayo	
aanstootlik	objectionable (a)	-kgopišago	-hanwang	-kgopisang	aleka(yo)	-ngathandeki	
aantrek	attract (v)	-gogela	-hohela	-ngoka	-tsala	-heha	
aantrek	clothe (v)	-apara	-apesa	-apara	-nxiba	-embesa	
aantrek	dress (v)	-apara	-apara	-apara	-nxiba	-gqokisa	
aantrekking	attraction (n)	maatlakgogedi	kgohelo	kgogedi	umtsalane	ukuheha	

A	Afrikaans	English	N Sotho	Sesotho	Tswana	Xhosa	Zulu
	aantreklik	attractive (a)	-kgahlišago	-hohelang	-ntle	-nomtsalane	-okhangayo
	aantreklik	handsome (a)	-bogegago	-tle	-ntle	-nomkhitha	-bukekayo
	aanvaar	accept (v)	-amogela	-amohela	-amogela	-amkela	-amukela
	aanvaarbaar	acceptable (a)	-amogelega	-amoheleha	-amogelesegang	-amkelekileyo	-amukelekayo
	aanvaarding	acceptance (n)	kamogelo	kamohelo	kamogelo	ulwamkelo	ukwamukela
	aanval	attack (v)	-hlasela	-hlasela	tlhaselo	-hlasela	-hlasela
	aanvallend	aggressive (a)	-hlaselago	-kgopo	bosilo	-olwayo	-hlaselayo
	aanwysings	directions (n)	ditaetšo	ditaelo	tshupatiriso	izalathisi	iseluleko
	aap	ape (n)	kgabo	kgabo	kgabo	inkawu	uhlobo lwenkawu engenamsila
	aap	monkey (n)	kgabo	tshwene	kgabo	inkawu	inkawu
	aar	vein (n)	setlišamadi	mothapo	lesika	umthambo	umthambo
	aarbei	strawberry (n)	arapei	monokotshwai	seterooberi	iqunube	isitrobheli
	aardbewing	earthquake (n)	tšhišinyego ya lefase	tshisinyeho ya lefatshe	thoromo ya lefatshe	inyikima	indudumela yomhlaba
	aarde	earth (n)	lefase	lefatshe	lefatshe	umhlaba	umhlaba
	aard na	resemble (v)	-swana	-futsa	-tshwana	-fana na-	-fana
	aardrykskunde	geography (n)	thutafase	thuto ya lefatshe	thutafatshe	ijografi	umumo womhlaba
	aarsel	hesitate (v)	-dikadika	-tsilatsila	-kabakanya	-thandabuza	-zindela
	aarseling	hesitation (n)	tikadiko	-tsilatsilo	kabakanyo	intandabuzo	ukuzindela
	aartappel	potato (n)	letapola	tapole	lekwele	itapile	izambane
	aartsbiskop	archbishop (n)	mopišopo pharephare	moatjhebishopo	mobishopomogolo	ibhishophu enkulu	umbhishobhi omkhulu
	aas	prey (v)	-ja	selope	-ja	-zingela	-phanga
	aasvoël	vulture (n)	lenong	lenong	lenong	ixhalanga	inqe
	abnormaal	abnormal (a)	-sa tlwaelegago	-sa tlwaelehang	-sa tlwaegang	-ngaqhelekanga	-ngavamile
	aborsie	abortion (n)		nyopiso	tshenyegelo ya mpa	impanza	ukuphuphuma isisu
	aborteer	abort (v)		-nyopisa	-senyega	-phanza	-khipha isisu
	absoluut	absolute (a)		-hle	tota	kanye	ngempela
	absoluut	absolutely (adv)	ruri	ho hang	tota	-ngenene	ngempela
	absorbeer	absorb (v)	-hupa	-monya	-monyela	-furxa	-munca
	adolessensie	adolescence (n)	bofsa	ho kena boholo	bosima	ixesha ebomini lokufikisa	ibanga lokukhula
	adres	address (n)	atrese	aterese	aterese	iadresi	ikheli
	adverteer	advertise (v)	-tsebiša	-bapatsa	phasalatsa	-thengisa	-azisa
	advertensie	advertisement (n)	tsebiši	papatso	phasalatso	intengiso	isaziso
	advokaat	advocate (n)	mmoleledi	mmuelli	mmueledi	igqwetha	ummeli
	af	down (prep)	fase	-tlase	tlase	-phantsi	phansi
	afbreek	demolish (v)	-phušula	-heletsa	-senya	-diliza	-diliza
	afdank	sack (v)	-leleka	-tebela	-koba	-gxotha	-xosha
	afdeling	section (n)	karolo	karolo	karolo	icandelo	isigaba
	afdwaal	stray (v)	-timetšego	-kgelohileng	-timela	-lahlekayo	-eduka
	afdwing	enforce (v)	-gapeletša	-qobella	-gagapa	-nyanzelisa	-phoqa
	afgeleë	remote (a)	-kgole	-hole	-gole	-kude	-kude
	afgesonderd	secluded (a)	-hlaotšwego	-kgethetsweng	-botlhaolelong	-nxwema	-sithekile
	afgetrokke	abstract (a)		-sa bonweng	-kgopolo	-ngaphathekiyo	-okusengqondweni kuphela
	afgod	idol (n)	modingwana	modingwana	seseto	intandane	isithixo
	afhang (van)	depend (on) (v)	-ithekgile ka	-itshwarella ka	-ikanya	-xhomekeka	-eyama
	afhanklik	dependent (a)	-ithekgilego ka	-hlokang	-ikanyang	-xhomekekileyo	-phethwe
	afhanklike	dependant (n)	mofepiwa	mohloki	moikanyi	umntu oxhomeke-kileyo	isikhonzi
	afkeer	disgust (n)	lehloyo	ho nyonya	-ferosa sebete	ucekiseko	isicasulo
	afkoel	cool (v)	-fola	-fodisa	-tsidifala	-phola	-phola
	aflaai	unload (v)	-laolla	-laolla	-folosa	-thula	-ethula
	aflewer	deliver (v)	-fihliša	-tsamaisa	-pholosa	-hambisa	-nikeza
	afrig	coach (v)	-thobolla	-kwetlisa	-katisa	-qeqesha	-fundisa
	afrig	train (v)	-ruta	-ruta	-katisa	-qeqesha	-fundisa
	afrigter	coach (n)	mothobodiši	mokwetlise	mokatisi	umqeqeshi	umqeqeshi
	Afrika	African (a)	-Afrika	-Seaforika	-Seafrika	-ongumAfrika	-kwase-Afrika
	Afrikaan	African (n)	Moafrika	Moaforika	Moafrika	umAfrika	umAfrika
	Afrikaner	Afrikaner (n)	Leafrikanere	Leaforikanere	Leaforekannere	iBhulu	iBhunu

Afrikaans	English	N Sotho	Sesotho	Tswana	Xhosa	Zulu	A
afsê	jilt (v)	-radia	-nyahlatsa	-koba	-ala	-ala	
afsit	amputate (v)	-kgaola	-poma	-kgaola	-shunqula	-nquma	
afskaf	abolish (v)	-fediša	-fedisa	-khutlisa	-bhangisa	-susa	
afskep	skim (v)	-okola	-okola	-kokola	-ongula	-cwenga	
afskrif	copy (document) (n)	kopi	kopi	seetsi	ikopi	ikhophi	
afsku	horror (n)	tšhiišo	masisapelo	tsitsibanyo	uloyiko	okwesabekayo	
afslaer	auctioneer (n)	mofantisi	mofantisi	mofantisi	umthengisi	umdayisi endalini	
afslag	discount (n)	phokoletšo	theolelo	phokoletso	isaphulelo	isephulelo emalini	
afsonderlik	separate (a)	-aroganego	-arohaneng	-kgaoganngweng	-ahlula	-ahlukene	
afsonderlik	distinct (a)	-kgethologilego	-ikgethang	-gongwe	-cacileyo	-ahlukene	
afspraak	appointment (n)	kwano	lebaka	kopanyo	idinga	ukunqumelana isikhathi	
afstand	distance (n)	bokgole	bohole	bokgakala	umgama	ibanga	
afstof	dust (v)	-phumula lerole	-hlakola	-phimola lerole	-vuthulula	-sula	
aftree	retire (v)	-rola modiro	-phomola	-rola tiro	-beka phantsi iintambo	-hlala phansi	
aftrek	subtract (v)	-ntšha	-tlosa	-ntsha	-thabatha	-susa	
aftrek	discount (v)	fokoletša	-theolela	-fokoletsa	-aphulela	-nciphisa	
afvaardig	delegate (v)	-romela	-laela	-gobelela	-gunyazisa	-thuma	
afval	waste (n)	tšhila	dithole	tshenyego	inkcitho	izibi	
afvee	wipe (v)	-phumola	-phumola	-phimola	-sula	-sula	
afwesig	absent (a)	-hlokega	-ba siyo	-se yong	-ngekhoyo	-ngekho	
afwesigheid	absence (n)	tlhokego	bosiyo	tlhokafalo	ubungabikho	ukungabikho	
afwissel	alternate (v)	-hlatlolana	-tjhentjhana	-refosana	-bolekisana	-phambanisiweyo	
afwyk	deviate (v)	-fapoga	-kgeloha	-fapoga	-phambuka	-ahluka	
afwys	decline (v)	-gana	-hana	-gana	-yala	-ncipha	
agenda	agenda (n)	lenanethero	lanane la ditaba	lenanetema	iajenda	i-ajenda	
agent	agent (n)	morekišetši	moemedi	moemedi	iarhente	umenzeli	
agt	eight (n)	seswai	robedi	robedi	isibhozo	isishiyagalombili	
agter	after (place) (prep)	morago ga	ka mora	morago	emva	emuva kwa-	
agter	behind (prep)	morago	-morao	morago	-ngemva	emuva	
agterbly	remain (v)	-šala	-sala	-sala	-sala	-sala	
agterdog	suspicion (n)	kgonono	pelaelo	pelaelo	urhano	insolo	
agtergrond	background (n)	boithekgo	tikoloho	lemorago	ikamva	isizinda	
agterna	afterwards (adv)	ka morago	ha morao	kgabagare	-emva koko	kamuva	
agterste	rear (a)	-morago	-morao	-morago	-semva	-ngemuva	
agtien	eighteen (n)	lesomeseswai	leshome le borobedi	some robedi	ishumi elinesibhozo	ishumi-nesishiyagalombili	
akademie	academy (n)	aketemi	akhademi	maithuto	isikolo senkcubeko	imfundo ephakeme	
akasia	acacia (n)	mohlare wa akasia	leoka	mmafu	umnga	umkhamba	
akkedis	lizard (n)	mokgaritswane	mokgodutswane	mokgatitswane	icikilishe	umbankwa	
aknee	acne (n)	thala	sehloba	seso	ukhuphu	izinsunsu	
akoesties	acoustic (a)	-kwalago	-thibela modumo	ka kutlo ya tsebe	-vakalayo	-kwemisindo	
aksent	accent (n)	tobeletšo	tokodiso	kgateletso	uhlobo lokuthetha	isigcizelelo	
akteur	actor (n)	sebapadi	sebapadi	moetsi	umdlali	umdlali	
aktief	active (a)	-mahlahla	-mafolofolo	-matlhagatlhaga	-sebenzayo	-khuthele	
aktivis	activist (n)	mohlohleletši	ramafolofolo	motlhotlheletsi	ufunzeweni	umkhuthazi	
aktrise	actress (n)	moralokigadi	sebapadi	moetsigadi	umdlali	umdlalikazi	
al	although (conj)	le ge	le ha	le fa	nangona	nokuba	
alarm	alarm (n)	mokgoši	setsosa	sekuamokgosi	into eyothusayo	imvuso	
albei	both (a)	bobedi	-bobedi	-oobedi	-bini	bobabili	
albino	albino (n)	lešwefe	lesofe	leswafe	inkawu	umuntu oyinkawu	
alfabet	alphabet (n)	alafabete	alafabete	alafabete	ialfabhethi	i-alfabhethi	
alg	alga (n)	dimelameetseng	lehola la metsing	bolele	ubulembu	i-algi	
algemeen	general (a)	-akaretšago	-akaretsang	-kakaretso	-jikelele	-vamile	
alias	alias (n)	-reetšwego la	lebitso le leng	itsegeng le ka la	igama lobuqhetseba	igama mbumbulu	
alibi	alibi (n)	boitatolo	maitatolo	alibi	indlela yokuzikhusela	i-alibi	
alkohol	alcohol (n)	tagi	tahi	tagi	isinxilisi	ugologo	
alkoholies	alcoholic (a)	-tagišago	-tahang	-tagisang	-nxilisayo	-dakisayo	
alkoholis	alcoholic (n)	setagwa	letahwa	letagwa	inxila	isidakwa	
alle	all (a)	ka moka	-hle	-tlhe	-onke	-nke	
alleen	alone (a)	noši	-mong	-nosi	-dwa	-dwa	

A	Afrikaans	English	N Sotho	Sesotho	Tswana	Xhosa	Zulu
	allergie	allergy (n)	kutlwišišo	aleji	boletswe	ukungalungelani nempilo	i-aleji
	allerlei	miscellaneous (a)	-mehutahuta	-tsohletsohle	-tsele le tsele	-ngxubevange	-yinhlanganisela
	alles	all (things) (pron)	tšohle	-hle	-tlhe	-onke	konke
	Almagtige	Almighty (n)	Yomaatlaohle	Ya matla ohle	Mothatiyotlhe	Somandla	uSomandla
	almal	all (beings) (pron)	bohle	-hle	-tlhe	-onke	sonke
	altaar	altar (n)	altare	aletare	aletare	isibingelelo	ilathi
	amateur	amateur (n)	yo mofsa	moithutwana	magogorwane	irhawu	imfunda-makhwele
	ambassadeur	ambassador (n)	motseta	lenqosa	moemedi	nozakuzaku	inxusa
	ambisie	ambition (n)	tumo	maikemisetso	maikaelelo	ibhongo	ukulangazela
	ambulans	ambulance (n)	koloi ya balwetši	ambulanse	ambilansa	iambulensi	i-ambulense
	ammunisie	ammunition (n)	dibetsa	dibetša	marumo	izidubuli	izindubulo
	amper	almost (adv)	-nyakile	-batlile	-ratile	-phantse	-cishe
	amptelik	official (a)	-semmušo	-mmuso	semmuso	-burhulumente	-esikhundla
	amptenaar	official (n)	mohlankedi	mohlanka wa mmuso	mosimegi	igosa	isiphathimandla
	analogie	analogy (n)	tshwano	papiso	tshwano	imfano	isifanelisano
	ander	other (a)	-ngwe	-ng	-sele	-nye	-nye
	anders	otherwise (adv)	ge go se bjalo	ka hosele	ka go sele	kungenjalo	ngokunye
	anders	else (adv)	-fapanago	-ng	-sele	-nye	-kungenjalo
	antiek	ancient (a)	-kgale	-boholoholo	-bogologolo	-mandulo	-okwasendulo
	antwoord	answer (v)	-araba	-araba	-araba	-phendula	-phendula
	antwoord	answer (n)	karabo	karabo	karabo	impendulo	impendulo
	antwoord	reply (n)	karabo	karabo	karabo	impendulo	impendulo
	antwoord gee	reply (v)	-araba	-araba	-araba	-phendula	-phendula
	anus	anus (n)	mogwete	sebono	sebono	indutsi	ingquza
	apostel	apostle (n)	moapostola	moapostola	moaposetolo	umpostile	umphostoli
	apparaat	apparatus (n)	sehlamo	disebediswa	aparata	isixhobo	amalungiselelo
	appel	apple (n)	apola	apole	apole	iapile	i-apula
	appélhof	appeal court (n)	lekgotla la boipiletšo	lekgotla la boipiletso	lekgotla la boipiletso	inkundla yezibheno	amajaji okugcina
	appelkoos	apricot (n)	apolekose	apolekose	apolekosi	iaprikoso	ibhilikosi
	appelliefie	gooseberry (n)	mommodi	mokutsuberi	thamme	igusbhere	ugqumgqumu
	April	April (n)	Aprele	Mmesa	Moranang	Apreli	u-Aprili
	apteker	pharmacist (n)	mokhemisi	mokhemise	moapoteke	unokhemesti	umkhemisi
	apteker	chemist (n)	mokhemisi	mokhemise	moapoteke	ikhemesti	umkhemisi
	arbei	labour (v)	-šoma	-sebetsa	-dira	-sebenza	-sebenza
	arbeid	labour (n)	mošomo	mosebetsi	tiro	umsebenzi	umsebenzi
	arbeider	labourer (n)	mošomi	mosebeletsi	modiredi	umsebenzi	isisebenzi
	arbiter	arbiter (n)	moahloledi	moahlodi	motsereganyi	umlamli	umlamuli
	arbitreer	arbitrate (v)	-lamola	-ahlola	-letlanya	-ngenelela	-lamula
	arena	arena (n)	arena	arena	botlhabanelo	iqonga	inkundla
	arend	eagle (n)	ntšhu	ntsu	ntsu	ukhozi	ukhozi
	argitek	architect (n)	mothadi wa dipolane	moakhiteke	moagi	umcebi wezakhiwo	umklami wezindlu
	argument	argument (n)	kgang	ngangisano	kgang	ingxoxo	ukuphikisana
	arm	poor (a)	-diilago	-futsanehileng	-humanegileng	-lihlwempu	-mpofu
	arm	arm (n)	letsogo	letsoho	lebogo	ingalo	ingalo
	armband	bangle (n)	leseka	sepetja	leseka	isacholo	isigqizo
	armes	poor (n)	badiidi	mafutsana	bahumanegi	ihlwempu	abampofu
	armholte	armpit (n)	lehwafa	lehafi	legwafa	ikhwapha	ikhwapha
	armoede	poverty (n)	bodiidi	bofutsana	bohumanegi	ubuhlwempu	ubumpofu
	artikel	article (n)	setlo	sesebediswa	setlo	inqaku	into
	as	than (conj)		ho feta	go	kuna-	na-
	as	axle (n)	ase	ase	ase	iasi	i-ekseli
	as	ash (n)	molora	molora	molora	uthuthu	umlotha
	as	if (conj)	ge	ha	fa	ukuba	uma
	asem	breath (n)	moya	moya	mowa	umphefumlo	umphefumulo
	asemhaal	breathe (v)	-buša moya	-phefumoloha	-hema	-phefumla	-phefumula
	asemhaling	respiration (n)	khemo	phefumoloho	khemo	ukuphefumla	ukuphefumula
	asma	asthma (n)	asma	lefuba	khupelo	umbefu	umbefu
	assegaai	assegai (n)	lerumo	lerumo	segae	umkhonto	umkhonto
	astrantheid	impertinence (n)	moreba	botlokotsebe	bokgwafo	-secaleni	ukweyisa

Afrikaans	English	N Sotho	Sesotho	Tswana	Xhosa	Zulu	B
astrologie	astrology (n)	astrolotši	bolepi ba dinaledi	bolepinaledi	ufundo ngeenkwenkwezi	ukufundwa kwezinkanyezi	
asyn	vinegar (n)	binika	asene	aseine	ivinika	uvinika	
atlas	atlas (n)	atlase	atlelase	atlelase	iatlasi	incwadi yamabalazwe	
atletiek	athletics (n)	diatletiki	diatletiki	atletiki	umdlalo wobaleko	i-athletiki	
atmosfeer	atmosphere (n)	atemosfere	moya	lefaufau	iatmosfera	i-atmosfiye	
Augustus	August (n)	Agostos	Phato	Phatwe	Agasti	uMandulo	
avokadopeer	avocado pear (n)	abokato	avokhado	pere ya obokado	iavokhado	ukwatapeya	
baadjie	jacket (n)	baki	baki	baki	ibhatyi	ibhantshi	
baai	bay (n)	kou	kou	kgogomelo	itheku	itheku	
baard	beard (n)	seledu	ditedu	tedu	udevu	isilevu	
baarmoeder	womb (n)	popelo	popelo	popelo	isizalo	isibeletho	
baba	baby (n)	lesea	lesea	lesea	umntwana	umntwana	
babadoek	nappy (n)	leiri	leleire	mongato	ilaphu	inephi	
babbel	babble (v)	-ratharatha	-bebera	-buabua	-bhibhidla	-mpompa	
bad	bath (v)	-hlapa	-tola	-bata	-bhafa	ukubhava	
bad	bath (n)	pafo	bate	bata	ibhafu	ubhavu	
badkamer	bathroom (n)	bohlapelo	batekamore	botlhapelo	igumbi lokuhlambela	ibhavulumu	
bagasie	luggage (n)	thoto	thoto	dithoto	umthwalo	impahla yendlela	
baie	many (a)	-ntši	-ngata	-ntsi	-ninzi	-ningi	
bak	bowl (n)	mogopo	morifi	mogopo	isitya	isitsha	
bak	bake (v)	-paka	-baka	-besa	-bhaka	-bhaka	
bak	fry (v)	-gadika	-hadika	-gadika	-qhotsa	-thosa	
baken	beacon (n)	pakane	mokolokotwane	bakene	ibhakana	isikhonkwane somdabuli	
bakker	baker (n)	mopaki	mobaki	mmesi	unobhaka	umbhaki	
bakkery	bakery (n)	lepaka	lebaka	lebaka	ibhaka	ibhikawozi	
baksteen	brick (n)	setena	setene	setena	isitena	isitini	
bakterie	bacteria (n)	dipakteria	kokwana	dibakeria	intsholongwane	ibhakthiriya	
bal	ball (n)	kgwele	bolo	kgwele	ibhola	ibhola	
balans	balance (n)	tekanetšo	botsitso	seelamaleka	ibhalansi	ukuzimelela	
ballade	ballad (n)	balate	balate	balate	ibhaladi	ingoma	
ballon	balloon (n)	palune	balunu	balono	ibhaloni	ibhamuza	
bamboes	bamboo (n)	pampu	leqala	bambusu	umthi webhambu	uqalo	
band	bond (n)	setlamo	tlamo	tlamo	ikhonkco	ubudlewane	
bang	afraid (a)	-boifa	-tshaba	-tshabang	-oyikayo	-novalo	
bang	apprehensive (a)	-boifago	-tshaba	-tshabegang	-oyikisayo	-novalo	
banjo	banjo (n)	pentšu	banjo	banjo	umrhubhe	ibhenjo	
bank	bench (n)	panka	banka	banka	ibhanka	ibhentshi	
bank	bank (n)	panka	banka	polokelo	ibhanki	ibhange	
banknoot	banknote (n)	lehlare	tjhelete ya pampiri	madi	imali eliphepha	imali yephepha	
barbaar	barbarian (n)	motala	leqaba	motala	indlavini	isidlwabidlwabi	
bars	burst (v)	-pharoga	-phatloha	-phanyega	-gqabhuka	-qhuma	
bas	bark (n)	sekgamati	lekgapetla	lekwati	ixolo	ixolo	
basies	basic (a)	-motheo	-motheo	-theo	-sisiseko	-yisisekelo	
basis	basis (n)	motheo	motheo	theo	isiseko	isisekelo	
battery	battery (n)	peteri	beteri	lelatlha	ibhetri	ibhethili	
beboet	fine (v)	-lefiša	-lefisa	-duedisa	-ohlwaya	-hlawula	
bed	bed (n)	bolao	bethe	bolao	umandlalo	umbhede	
bedagsaam	considerate (a)	-hlokomelago	-nahanelang	-akanyang	-novelwano	-cabangelayo	
bedank	resign (v)	-itlamolla	-dihela marapo	-itlamolola	-rhoxa	-shiya	
bedank	thank (v)	-leboga	-leboha	-leboga	-bulela	-bonga	
beddegoed	bedclothes (n)	malao	diphate	dikobo	iingubo	izingubo zokulala	
bedel	beg (v)	-kgopela	-kopa	-kopa	-cenga	-nxiba	
bedelaar	beggar (n)	mokgopedi	mokopi	mokopi	umngqibi	isinxibi	
bederf	corrupt (v)	-senya	-senya	-senya	-ngcolisa	-bolile	
bediende	servant (n)	mohlanka	mohlanka	motlhanka	isicaka	isisebenzi	
bedoel	mean (v)	-ra	-re	-kaya	-singisela	-qonda	
bedoeling	meaning (n)	maikemišetšo	hobolelwang	kakanyo	injongo	ingqondo	

143

B	**Afrikaans**	**English**	**N Sotho**	**Sesotho**	**Tswana**	**Xhosa**	**Zulu**
	bedorwe	corrupt (a)	-senyegilego	-senyehile	-senyegang	-ngcolileyo	-onakele
	bedorwenheid	corruption (n)	tshenyego	tshenyo	tshenyego	isingcolo	ukonakala
	bedpan	bedpan (n)	sebjana sa mohlapologo	thuana	sekotleleithusetso	isitya sokuchamela	isikigi
	bedraad	wire (v)	-tsenya mathale	-tlama terata	-lokela bothale	-faka ucingo	-faka ucingo
	bedrieg	deceive (v)	-fora	-thetsa	-fora	-khohlisa	-khohlisa
	bedrog	fraud (n)	bofora	thetso	tsietso	ubuqhetseba	inkohliso
	bedrog	deceit (n)	bofora	thetso	boferefere	inkchliso	inkhohliso
	bedruktheid	depression (n)	manyami	tepeletso	sekuti	ucinezelo	umnyinyitheko
	bedrywigheid	activity (n)	mahlahlo	tshebetso	modiro	unsebenzi	ubukhuphekhuphe
	bedwelm	intoxicate (v)	-taga	-taha	-tagisa	-nxilisa	-daka
	bedwelmd	dazed (a)	-dikweletšego	-idibane	-dimokanyang	-didekileyo	-phuphuthekisa
	bedwelming	daze (n)	go dikwelela	kidibanyo	kgamorego	ukudideka	ukuphuphutheka
	beëdigde verklaring	affidavit (n)	kenelwa	bopaki bo ngotsweng	pego e e ikanetsweng	isigqibo esifungelweyo	incwadi efungelwe
	beeld	statue (n)	seswantšho	seemahale	sefikantswe	umfanekiso oqingqiweyo	isifanekiso
	beeld	image (n)	tshwantšho	setshwantsho	setshwano	umfanekiso-ntelekelelo	isithombe
	beeldhou	sculpt (v)	-betla	-betla ditshwantsho	-betla	-qingqa	-qopha amatshe
	beeldhouer	sculptor (n)	mmetli wa diswantšho	mmetladitshwantsho	mmetli	umqingqi	umqophi
	been	leg (n)	leoto	moomo	leoto	umlenze	umlenze
	been	bone (n)	lerapo	lesapo	lerapo	ithambo	ithambo
	beer	bear (n)	bere	bere	bera	ibhere	ibheja
	beesvleis	beef (n)	nama ya kgomo	nama ya kgomo	nama ya kgomo	inyama yenkomo	inyama yenkomo
	beet	beetroot (n)	pete	bete	bete	ibhitruthi	ibhithrudi
	begaaf	gifted (a)	-filwego	-bohlale	-botlhale	-nesiphiwo	-nobungcweti
	begeer	desire (v)	-duma	-lakatsa	-eletsa	-nqwena	-khanuka
	begeerte	desire (n)	ledumo	takatso	keletso	umnqweno	inkanuko
	begelei	accompany (v)	-felegetša	-felehetsa	-buledisa	-khapha	-phelezela
	begin	start (v)	-thoma	-qala	-thoma	-qala	-qala
	begin	start (n)	mathomo	qalo	bothomo	isiqalo	ekuqaleni
	begin	begin (v)	-thoma	-qala	-thobolola	-qala	-qala
	begin	beginning (n)	mathomo	qalo	tshimologo	isiqalo	ukuqala
	beginner	beginner (n)	mothomi	moqadi	magogorwane	umqali	inyuwane
	beginsel	principle (n)	theo	theo	theo	inqobo	umthetho
	begraafplaas	cemetery (n)	mabitleng	mabitleng	mabitleng	emangcwabeni	indawo yamathuna
	begrafnis	funeral (n)	poloko	phupu	phitlho	umngcwabo	umngcwabo
	begrafnis	burial (n)	poloko	poloko	phitlho	umngcwabo	umngcwabo
	begrawe	bury (v)	-boloka	-epela	-fitlha	-ngcwaba	-ngcwaba
	begunstig	favour (v)	-rata	-rata	-rata	-enzelela	-khetha
	behalwe	except (prep)	ka ntle le	-ntle ho	le fela	ngaphandle	ngaphandle kwa-
	behandel	treat (v)	-alafa	-tshwara	-tshola	-phatha	-elapha
	behandeling	treatment (n)	kalafo	tshwaro	tsholo	impatho	ukwelapha
	beheer	control (v)	-laola	-tsamaisa	-laola	-lawula	-phatha
	behoefte	need (n)	nyakego	bohloki	setlhokwa	imfuneko	inswelo
	behoeftige	pauper (n)	mohloki	mofutsana	modidi	udwayi	uphanqu
	behoort	belong (v)	-ya	-ya	-wa	-ba	-kwa-
	behulpsaam	helpful (a)	-thušago	-thusang	-thusang	-ncedayo	-sizayo
	beige	beige (a)	-šwaana	beije	-setlha	-lubhelu-mdaka	-liphuzana
	beïndruk	impress (v)	-khahla	-kgahla	-kgatla	-thabathekisa	-zwisisa
	beïnvloed	influence (v)	-tutuetša	-susumetsa	-tlhotlheletsa	-ba nefuthe	-thonya
	bekeerling	convert (n)	mosokologi	mosokolohi	mosokologi	umguquki	umphenduki
	bekend wees	acquaint (v)	-tsebega	-tsebisa	-tlwaetse	-azisa	-azisa
	beker	jug (n)	lebekere	jeke	jeke	inkonkxa	ujeke
	beker	mug (n)	pekere	lebekere	lebekere	imagi	imagi
	bekken	pelvis (n)	letheka	noka	setlhana	ihleza	ithebe
	beklemtoon	emphasise (v)	-gatelela	-toboketsa	-gatelela	-gxininisa	-gcizelela
	beknop	brief (a)	-kopana	-kgutshwane	-khutswafaditsweng	-futshane	-fushane
	bekom	obtain (v)	-humana	-fumana	-bona	-zuza	-zuza
	bekommer	worry (v)	-belaela	-kgathatseha	-tshwenya	-hlupha	-khathazeka

Afrikaans	English	N Sotho	Sesotho	Tswana	Xhosa	Zulu
bekommerd	anxious (a)	-belaelago	-ngongorehile	-tlhobaelang	-nxungupheleyo	-khathazekile
bekoorlik	glamorous (a)	-rategago	-hlamatsehang	ntle	-hle	-khangayo
bekostig	afford (v)	-kgona go lefa	-kgona	-kgona	-banako	-veza
bekruip	stalk (v)	-khukhunela	-nanara	-ratela	-landela	-nyonyobela
bekwaam	able (a)	-kgona	-kgona	-kgonang	-kwazi	-nokwazi
bekwaamheid	ability (n)	bokgoni	bokgoni	kgono	ubuchule	ukwazi
bekyk	view (v)	-bogela	-tadima	-leba	-jonga	-buka
belang	interest (n)	kgahlego	tjheseho	kgatlhego	umdla	umnako
belangrik	important (a)	-bohlokwa	-bohlokwa	-botlhokwa	-balulekile(yo)	-qavile
belas	tax (v)	-lefiša	-kgafisa	-kgetha	-rhafisa	-thelisa
belastering	defamation (n)	tshenyoina	ketselletso	kgobololo	unyeliso	isihlebo
belasting	tax (n)	motšhelo	lekgetho	lekgetho	irhafu	intela
beledig	insult (v)	-goboša	-hlapaola	-tlhapatsa	-thuka	-thuka
belediging	insult (n)	kgobošo	tlhapa	sekgopi	isithuko	inhlamba
beleid	policy (n)	maikemišetšo	leano	maikemisetso	umgaqo	umgomo
belemmer	obstruct (v)	-šitiša	-sitisa	-kgoreletsa	-thintela	-vimbela
belemmernis	obstruction (n)	tšhitišo	tshitiso	kgoreletso	uthintelo	ukuvimbela
belofte	promise (n)	kholofetšo	tshepiso	tsholofetso	isithembiso	isithembiso
beloning	reward (n)	tefo	moputso	tuelo	umvuzo	umklomelo
beloon	reward (v)	-lefa	-putsa	-duela	-vuza	-klomela
belowe	promise (v)	-holofetša	-tshepisa	-solofetsa	-thembisa	-thembisa
bely	confess (v)	-ipobola	-ipolela	-ipobola	-vuma	-vuma
belydenis	confession (n)	boipobolo	boipolelo	boipobolo	ukuvuma	ukuvuma
bemeester	master (v)	-kgona	-hlola	-kgona	-lawula	-ahlula
bemiddel	mediate (v)	-lamola	-emela	-tsereganya	-lamla	-lamula
bemiddelaar	mediator (n)	molamodi	moemedi	motsereganyi	umlamli	umlamuli
bemind	beloved (a)	-rategago	-moratuwa	-ratiwa	-thandekayo	-thandiwe
bemind maak	endear (v)	-ratiša	-ratisa	-ratega	-thandisa	-thandekisa
beminlik	likeable (a)	-rategago	-ratehang	-rategwang	-thandekayo	-thandekayo
bemors	mess (v)	-tšhilafatša	-silafatsa	-senya	-enza mdaka	-bhixiza
benader	approach (v)	-bona	-atamela	-tlhagisa	-cothela	-velela
bende	gang (n)	sehlopha sa dikebeke	sehlopha	mophato	iqela	igengi
beny	envy (v)	-duma	-lakatsa	-eletsa	-monela	-hawukela
beoordelaar	adjudicator (n)	malokwane	moahlodi	moatlhodi	umchongi	umahluli
bepaal	define (v)	-hlatholla	-hlalosa	-ranola	-chaza	-nquma
bepeins	ponder (v)	-akanya	-lohotha	-akanya	-zikisa	-cabanga
beperk	restrain (v)	-iletša	-thibela	-kganna	-thintela	-khuza
beplan	plan (v)	-loga maano	-hlopha	-loga leano	-ceba	-klama
beproewing	affliction (n)	pelaelo	tlatlapo	pogisego	imbandezelo	inhlupheko
bêre	store (v)	-boloka	-boloka	-boloka	-gcina	-beka
bereik	reach (v)	-fihlela	-fihlela	-fitlha	-fikelela	-fica
bereik	attain (v)	-phetha	-fihlela	-fitlha	-fikelela	-zuza
berg	mountain (n)	thaba	thaba	thaba	intaba	intaba
berig	report (v)	-bega	-tlaleha	-bolela	-nika ingxelo	-bika
beroemd	famous (a)	-tumilego	-tumileng	-itsegeng	-aziwayo	-dumile
beroemdheid	renown (n)	setumo	setumo	kitsego	indumasi	udumo
beroep	appeal (n)	boipiletšo	boipiletso	boikuelo	isibheno	isikhalo
beroep doen op	appeal (v)	-dira boipiletšo	-ipiletsa	-ipiletsa	-bhena	-khala
beroof	rob (v)	-hula	-tlatlapa	-thukhutha	-khuthuza	-phanga
berou hê	repent (v)	-itshola	-sokoloha	-ikotlhaya	zohlwaya	-guquka
berugtheid	notoriety (n)	bosehlogo	botumo	tumo	ukuduma	udumo olubi
besem	broom (n)	leswielo	lefielo	lefeelo	umtshayelo	umshanelo
besemstok	broomstick (n)	kota ya leswielo	mofeng	kota ya lefeelo	intonga yomtshayelo	uthi lomshanelo
besering	injury (n)	kgobalo	leqeba	ntho	ukwenzakala	ingozi
beset	engaged (a)	-dirišwago	-tshwarehileng	-dirisiwa	-xakekile	-bambekile
besit	own (v)	-na le	-rua	-na le	-banayo	-ba- na-
beskaaf	civilise (v)	-hlabologa	-ntshetsa pele	-tlhabolola	-phucula	-phucuza
beskadig	damage (v)	-senya	-senya	-senya	-onakalisa	-limaza
beskawing	civilisation (n)	tlhabologo	tswelopele	tlhabologo	impucuko	impucuko
beskeie	modest (a)	-sa ikgantšhego	-imametseng	-boingotlo	-lulamile(yo)	-namahloni

B

Afrikaans	English	N Sotho	Sesotho	Tswana	Xhosa	Zulu
beskerm	protect (v)	-šireletša	-sireletsa	-babalela	-khusela	-vikela
beskerm	shield (v)	-šireletša	-sireletsa	-sireletsa	-khusela	-vikela
beskikbaar	available (a)	-hwetšegago	-fumaneha	teng	-fumaneka	-tholakalayo
beskrywe	describe (v)	-laodiša	-hlalosa	-tlhalosa	-chaza	-landa
beskrywing	description (n)	tlhalošo	tlhaloso	tlhaloso	inkcazo	ukulanda
beskuldig	accuse (v)	-bega	-qosa	-latofatsa	-tyhola	-beka icala
beskuldigde	accused (n)	mmegiwa	moqosuwa	mosekisiwa	ummangalelwa	ummangalelwa
beskuldiger	accuser (n)	mmegi	moqosi	moseki	ummangali	ummangali
beskuldiging	accusation (n)	pego	-qoso	tatofatso	isityholo	icala elibekwayo
beslag lê op	confiscate (v)	-amoga	-amoha	-amoga	-thimba	-dla
besluit	decision (n)	phetho	morero	phetso	isigqibo	isinqumo
besluit	decide (v)	-phetha	-rera	-atlhola	-enza isigqibo	-nquma
besmet	infect (v)	-fetetša	-tshwaetsa	-fetetsa	-sulela	-thelela
besmetlik	infectious (a)	-fetelago	-tshwaetsang	-fetelelang	-sulelayo	okuthathelwanayo
besny	circumcise (v)	-bolotša	-bolotsa	-rupisa	-alusa	-soka
besnydenis	circumcision (n)	lebollo	polotso	thupiso	ulwaluko	ukusoka
besoedeling	pollution (n)	tšhilafatšo	tshilafatso	kgotlelo	ukungcoliseka	ukungcolisa
besoek	visit (v)	-etela	-etela	-etela	-tyelela	-vakashela
besoek	visit (n)	ketelo	ketelo	leeto	utyelelo	ukuvakashela
besoek	call (v)	-etela	-etela	-etela	-tyelela	-vakasha
besoeker	visitor (n)	moeng	moeti	moeti	undwendwe	isivakashi
besoeker	caller (n)	moeng	moeti	moeti	undwendwe	isivakashi
besonder	particular (a)	-itšego	-ikgethang	-segolo	-thile	-thile
bespot	ridicule (v)	-kwera	-soma	-sotla	-hlekisa	-hleka
bespot	mock (v)	-kwera	-soma	-sotla	-phoxa	-kloloda
bespreek	discuss (v)	-ahlaahla	-buisana	-sekaseka	-xoxa	-xoxisana nga-
bespreking	discussion (n)	kahlaahlo	puisano	kgang	ingxoxo	ingxoxo
besproei	irrigate (v)	-nošetša	-nosetsa	-nosa	-nkcenkceshela	-chela ngenkhasa
besproeiing	irrigation (n)	nošetšo	nosetso	nosetso	unkcenkcesho	inkasa
bestaan	consist (v)	-bopilwe ka	-na le	-na le	-enziwe nge-	-bunjwa
bestaan	existence (n)	boleng	ho ba teng	boleyo	ubukho	ubukhona
bestaan	exist (v)	-gona	-ba teng	-nna teng	-bakho	-khona
beste	best (a)	-palago ka moka	-molemo	-ntsha ga tshwene	-ncomekayo	-dlulayo konke
bestee	spend (v)	-šomiša tšhelete	-sebedisa	-tlhola	-chitha	-khokha
bestempel	stamp (v)	-tempa	-tempa	-kiba	-gximfiza	-sicilela
bestuur	manage (v)	-laola	laola	-laola	-lawula	-phatha
bestuur	management (n)	taolo	balaodi	bolaodi	ulawulo	ukuphathwa
bestuur	drive (v)	-otlela	-kganna	-tsamaisa	-qhuba	-shayela
bestuurder	manager (n)	molaodi	molaodi	molaodi	umlawuli	umphathi
bestuurder	driver (n)	mootledi	mokganni	mokgweetsi	umqhubi	umshayeli
besuinig	economise (v)	-seketša	-baballa	-papana	-qoqosha	-onga
beswaar maak	object (v)	-gana	-hana	-gana	-ala	-phikisa
betaal	pay (v)	-lefa	-putsa	-duela	-hlawula	-khokha
betaler	payer (n)	molefi	molefi	moduedi	umhlawuli	umkhokhi
betaling	payment (n)	tefo	tefo	tuelo	intlawulo	inkokhelo
betaling	pay (n)	tefo	moputso	tuelo	intlawulo	inkokhelo
betekenis	meaning (n)	tlhalošo	moelelo	bokao	intsingiselo	incazelo
beter	better (a)	kaone	-betere	botoka	-phucukileyo	-ngcono
betoging	demonstration (n)	tšhupetšo	pontsho	tshupetso	uqhankqalazo	ukubhikisha
beton	concrete (n)	khonkriti	konkereite	konkreite	into ebambekayo	ukhonkolo
betoog	demonstrate (v)	-šupetša	-bontsha	-supetsa	-qhankqalaza	-bhikisha
betrek	involve (v)	-ama	-kenya	-ntsenya	-faka	-zongolozela
betroubaar	reliable (a)	-botegago	-tshepahalang	-boikanyego	-thembekile(yo)	-thembekile
betroubaar	trustworthy (a)	-botegago	-tshepahalang	-boikanyo	-thembekile(yo)	-thembekile
betwis	dispute (v)	-phegišana	-tsekisana	-ganetsa	-phikisana	-banga
beursie	purse (n)	sekgwama	sekgwama	kgwatlha	isipaji	isikhwama semali
beurt	turn (n)	lebaka	lekgetlo	sebaka	ithuba	ithuba
bevat	contain (v)	-na le	-tshwara	-tshola	-qulatha	-phatha
beveel	order (v)	-laela	-laela	-laela	-yalela	-layeza
beveel	direct (v)	-laela	-laela	-laola	-yalela	-layeza

Afrikaans	English	N Sotho	Sesotho	Tswana	Xhosa	Zulu	B
beveilig	secure (v)	-šireletša	-boloka	-babalesega	-khusela	-londoloza	
bevel	order (n)	taelo	taelo	tao	umyalelo	umyalezo	
bevlek	stain (v)	-tšhilafatša	-etsa letheba	-timpatsa	-dyobha	-ninda	
bevolking	population (n)	baagi	baahi	baagi	uluntu	inani labantu	
bevorder	promote (v)	-tšwetša pele	-phahamisa	-tsweletsa	-nyusela	-enyusa	
bevordering	promotion (n)	tšweletšopele	phahamiso	tlhatloso	unyuselo	ukwenyuswa	
bevredig	satisfy (v)	-kgotsofatša	-kgotsofatsa	-kgora	-anelisa	-anelisa	
bevredig	appease (v)	-kgotsofatša	-kokobetsa	-tlakisa	-xolisa	-duduza	
bevrediging	satisfaction (n)	kgotsofalo	kgotsofalo	kgotsofalo	ulwaneliseko	isaneliso	
bevrug	fertilise (v)	-nontša	-nontsha	-ungwisa	-chumisa	-zalisa	
bevry	free (v)	-lokolla	-lokolla	-golola	-khulula	-khulula	
bewaak	guard (v)	-leta	-lebela	-disa	-gada	-gada	
bewaar	preserve (v)	-boloka	-boloka	-boloka	-londoloza	-londoloza	
bewaar	conserve (v)	-boloka	-boloka	-babalela	-londoloza	-onga	
bewapen	arm (v)	-itlhama ka dibetša	-hlomela	tlhomela	-xhoba	-hloma	
bewe	shiver (v)	-roromela	-thothomela	-roroma	-ngcangcazela	qhaqhazela	
bewe	tremble (v)	-roromela	-thothomela	-roroma	-ngcangcazela	qhaqhazela	
beweeg	move (v)	-šutha	-sisinyeha	-tshikinya	-shukuma	-nyakazisa	
beweegrede	motive (n)	lebaka	morero	boitlhomo	isizathu	isisusa	
beweer	allege (v)	-re	-bolela	-kaya	-banga	-sho	
bewegend	moving (a)	-sepelago	-tsamayang	-sutang	-hambayo	-nomhawu	
bewerk	cultivate (v)	-lema	-lema	-lema	-lima	-lima	
bewerk	effect (v)	-phetha	-sebetsa	-diragatsa	-phumezo	-feza	
bewind	reign (n)	pušo	mmuso	puso	ulawulo	ukubusa	
bewolk	overcast (a)	-nago le maru	-maru a thibile	-maruru	-sibekele	-buyisile	
bewonder	admire (v)	-duma	-rata	-kgatlha	-buka	-babaza	
bewonderaar	fan (n)	motumiši	mothahaselli	molatedi	umxhasi	umncomeli	
bewonderendswaardig	admirable (a)	-rategago	-ratehang	-kgatlhang	-ncomekayo	-babazekile	
bewondering	admiration (n)	tumišo	ho rata	kgatlhego	uncomo	ukubabaza	
bewoner	tenant (n)	moagi	mohiri	mohiri	umqeshi	umqashi	
bewus	conscious (a)	-lemogago	-ikutlwang	-utlwa	-sezingqondweni	-zwile	
bewussyn	consciousness (n)	boitemogo	boikutlo	segakolodi	ukuba sezingqondweni	ukwazi	
bewusteloos	unconscious (a)	-idibetšego	-akgehileng	-idibetseng	-lahlekelwe ziingqondo	-qalekile	
bewys	prove (v)	-kgonthišiša	-bontsha	-supa	-ngqina	-bonisa	
bewys	proof (n)	bohlatse	bopaki	bosupi	ubungqina	ubufakazi	
biblioteek	library (n)	bokgobapuku	laeborari	mabuka	ithala leencwadi	ilabhulali	
bibliotekaris	librarian (n)	ramapuku	molaeborari	rramabuka	unoncwadi	umphathi welabhulali	
bid	pray (v)	-rapela	-rapela	-rapela	-thandaza	-thandaza	
biefstuk	steak (n)	nama ya kgomo	tshutshu	nama ya kgomo	isihlunu	isiteki	
bier	beer (n)	bjalwa	jwala	bojalwa	utywala	utshwala	
bietjie	bit (n)	bonnyane	bonyenyane	bonnyane	intwana	isihlephu	
bilharzia	bilharzia (n)	bilhazia	bilehasia	thotamadi	ibhilhazia	ibhilihaziya	
billik	fair (a)	-lokilego	-tle	-tolamo	-lungile (yo)	-hle	
biltong	biltong (n)	mogwapa	sehwapa	segwapa	umqwayito	umqwayiba	
bind	tie (v)	-bofa	-tlama	-tlama	-bopha	-bopha	
binne	within (adv)	ka gare	ka hare	teng	ngaphakathi	ngaphakathi	
binne	inside (adv)	ka gare	ka hare	teng	ngaphakathi	phakathi	
binnedring	penetrate (v)	-tsenelela	-phunyeletsa	-nanganela	-tyhutyha	-ngena	
binnegaan	enter (v)	-tsena	-kena	-tsena	-ngena	-ngena	
binnekoms	entry (n)	go tsena	kenello	matseno	isango lokungena	ukungena	
binnekort	soon (adv)	ka pela	-haufinyane	tloga	kungekudala	masinyane	
binnelands	inland (a)	-nagagare	-hare ha naha	nagagare	-ngaphakathi	-phakathi nezwe	
binneste	interior (n)	bokateng	bohare	leteng	umphakathi	ingaphakathi	
biologie	biology (n)	payolotši	bayoloji	thutatshelo	ibhayoloji	ibhayoloji	
bioskoop	cinema (n)	paesekopo	baesekopo	baesekopo	umboniso bhanya-bhanya	ibhayisikobho	
biseps	biceps (n)	mošifa wa paesepe	dipotongwane	lerudi	amandla	izinkonyane	
biskop	bishop (n)	mopišapo	mobishopo	bishopo	ibhishophu	umbhishobhi	

B	Afrikaans	English	N Sotho	Sesotho	Tswana	Xhosa	Zulu
	bitter	bitter (a)	-babago	-baba	-botlhoko	-krakra	-muncu
	blaam	blame (n)	molato	phoso	tatofatso	isityholo	isolo
	blaar	leaf (n)	letlakala	lehlaku	letlhare	igqabi	ikhasi
	blaar	blister (n)	lephone	letswabadi	lerophi	idyungudyungu	ibhamuza
	blaarslaai	lettuce (n)	selae	selae	selae	iletusi	uletisi
	blaas	bladder (n)	sebudula	senya	setlha	isinyi	isinye
	blad	blade (n)	bogale	lehare	ntshane	ukutya	ucezu
	bladhoudend	evergreen (a)	-talamehleng	-tala selemo sohle	-talafeletseng ruri	-luhlaza njalo	-ngawohlokisi amakhasi
	bladsy	page (n)	letlakala	leqephe	tsebe	iphepha	ikhasi
	blaf	bark (v)	-bogola	-bohola	bogola	-khonkotha	-khonkotha
	blameer	blame (v)	-bea molato	-bona phoso	-baya molato	-tyhola	-sola
	blatjang	chutney (n)	dikhanakhana	tjhatene	tshateni	itshatini	ishatini
	bleek	pale (a)	-galogilego	-retetseng	-setlha	-mthuzubala	-mhloshana
	bleik	bleach (v)	-šweufatša	-sweufatsa	-tswapola	-khucula	-cacisa umbalo omhlophe
	bles	bald (a)	lefatla	-lefatla	-lefatla	inkqayi	-yimpandla
	blik	look (n)	tebelelo	tjhadimo	tebo	inkangeleko	ukubheka
	blind	blind (a)	-foufetšego	-foufetse	-foufetseng	-ngaboniyo	-yimpumputhe
	blinding	blind (v)	seširo	dikgaretene	disiralesedi	ubumfama	ibhulayindi
	blink	shiny (a)	-phadimago	-benyang	-phatsimang	-khanyayo	-khanyayo
	bloed	blood (n)	madi	madi	madi	igazi	igazi
	bloedarmoede	anaemia (n)	tlhokamadi	phokolo ya madi	tlhokamadi	umlambo	ukuphaphatheka kwegazi
	bloeddruk	blood pressure (n)	kgatelelo ya madi	kgatello ya madi	kgatelelo ya madi	uxinzelelo lwegazi	umfutho wegazi
	bloeding	haemorrhage (n)	go dutla madi	ho dutla madi	tutlamadi	ukopha	umopho
	bloedoortapping	blood transfusion (n)	tlhabelomadi	phepelo ya madi	tsenyo ya madi	ufunxo-gazi	ukuthasiselwa igazi
	bloedvat	blood vessel (n)	tselamadi	mothapo	tshika	umthambo wegazi	umthambo wegazi
	bloedvint	boil (n)	sekaku	lethopa	modingwana	ithumba	ithumba
	bloei	bleed (v)	-tšwa madi	-tswa madi	-tswa madi	-opha	-opha
	bloekomboom	bluegum (n)	mopulukomo	boloukomo	leblukomo	umgamtriya	umgathini
	bloes	blouse (n)	polause	bolouso	bolaose	iblawuzi	ibhulawozi
	blok	log (n)	kota	lehong	kota	isigodo	ugodo
	blok	block (n)	kota	kutu	mokasa	isiqobo	isigaxa
	blokkeer	block (v)	-thiba	-thibela	-thiba	-vingca	-vimbela
	blom	flower (n)	letšoba	palesa	sethunya	intyatyambo	imbali
	blom	bloom (v)	-thunya	-thunya	-thunya	-dubula	-qhakaza
	blomkool	cauliflower (n)	kholifolawa	kholifolawa	kholifolawa	ikholiflawa	ukhalifulawa
	blootlê	expose (v)	-utolla	-hlahatsa	-senola	-tyhila	-veza
	blou	blue (a)	botala bja leratadima	-tala; -putswa	-tala	-luhlaza	-zulucwathile
	bloublasie	bluebottle (n)	senanawatle	boloubolasie		uhocoshe	isilokazana zolwandle
	blus	extinguish (v)	-tima	-tima	-itumelang	-cima	-cima
	bly	glad (a)	-thabišago	-thabile	-itumelang	-vuya	-jabulile
	blydskap	delight (n)	lethabo	nyakallo	boitumelo	ulonwabo	injabulo
	bly maak	delight (v)	-thabiša	-nyakalatsa	-jesa monate	-onwabisayo	-jabulisa
	bo	above (prep)	godimo ga	-hodima	mo godimo	-phezulu	enhla kwa-
	bobbejaan	baboon (n)	tšhwene	tshwene	tshwene	imfene	imfene
	bode	messenger (n)	morongwa	moromuwa	morongwa	isigicimi	isithunywa
	bodem	bottom (n)	bofase	botlase	botlase	umzantsi	ingaphansi
	boei	handcuff (n)	tshipiphodisa	lehlaahlela	-golega	ikhamandela	-faka uzankosi
	boek	book (n)	puku	buka	buka	incwadi	incwadi
	boepmaag	paunch (n)	mogodu	lekuka	lebotsane	intesha	umkhaba
	boer	farm (v)	-rua	-lema	-rua	-famsha	-lima
	boer	farmer (n)	morui	rapolasi	molemirui	umfama	umlimi
	boesem	bosom (n)	sehuba	sefuba	phega	umxhelo	isifuba
	boete	fine (n)	tefišo	tefiso	tefiso	isohlwayo	inhlawulo
	boggelrug	hunchback (n)	lehutlo	kgirimpana	thotane	isifombo	isifumbu
	bok	goat (n)	pudi	podi	podi	ibhokhwe	imbuzi
	bok	buck (n)	phoofolo	nyamatsane	podi	inyamakazi	inyamazane
	bokkie	kid (n)	putšana	potsanyane	potsane	itakane	izinyane
	boks	box (v)	-itia ka matswele	-tebela	-ratha	-betha amanqindi	-bhakela

Afrikaans	English	N Sotho	Sesotho	Tswana	Xhosa	Zulu	B
boks	boxing (n)	dintwa tša matswele	ditebele	mabole	imbethi-manqindi	isibhakela	
bol	bulb (n)	segwere	kotola	segwere	ibhalbhu	ibhalbhu	
bom	bomb (n)	pomo	bomo	bomo	isiqhushumbisi	ibhomu	
bondel	bundle (n)	ngata	seshoba	ngata	umbhumbutho	umqulu	
boodskap	message (n)	molaetša	molaetsa	molaetsa	umyalezo	umbiko	
boog	instep (n)	boraoto	mokokotlo wa leoto	khubu	umphezulu wonyawo	amathe onyawo	
boog	bow (n)	bora	seqha	bora	isaphetha	inkumbela	
boom	tree (n)	sehlare	sefate	setlhare	umthi	umuthi	
boontjie	bean (n)	nawa	nawa	nawa	imbotyi	ubhontshisi	
boos	evil (a)	-be	-kgopo	-bosula	-ngcolile (yo)	-bi	
boosaardigheid	malice (n)	bobe	lonya	bogale	ulunya	izondo	
boot	boat (n)	sekepe	seketswana	mokoro	iphenyane	umkhumbi	
bord	plate (n)	poroto	poleiti	boroto	ipleyiti	isitsha	
bord	board (n)	papetla	boroto	letlapa	ibhodi	ibhodi	
borg	bail (n)	peile	beile	topololo	ibheyile	ibheyili	
borg staan	bail (v)	-beila	-beila	-emela topololo	-bheyila	-bheyila	
borrel	bubble (n)	pue	pudula	pudula	iqamza	-bhadla	
bors	breast (n)	sehuba	sefuba	lebele	isifuba	isifuba	
borsbeen	breastbone (n)	kgara	lesapo la sefuba	kgara	ingqoba	ithambo lesifuba	
borsel	brush (v)	-porosola	-borosola	-sutlha	brasha	-bhulasha	
borsel	brush (n)	porosolo	borosolo	borosolo	ibrashi	ibhulashi	
borskas	thorax (n)	sehuba	sefuba	sehuba	isifuba	isifuba	
borskas	chest (n)	sehuba	sefuba	sehuba	isifuba	isifuba	
borsvliesontsteking	pleurisy (n)	ploresi	ho ruruha ka sefubeng	boletswe jwa letha la makgwa	ukralo lwenwebu-miphunga	amahlaba	
bos	forest (n)	sethokgwa	moru	sekgwa	ihlathi	ihlathi	
bos	bush (n)	sethokgwa	moru	sekgwa	ityholo	ihlathi	
bosbok	bushbuck (n)	tšhošo	nyamatsane	serolobotlhoko	imbabala	umdaka	
bose gees	demon (n)	motemone	modemone	satane	idemoni	idimoni	
bosveld	bushveld (n)	dikgweng	merung	naga e e lesuthu	idobo	ihlanze	
bots	collide (v)	-thula	-thulana	-thulana	-ngqubana	-shayana	
bots	conflict (v)	-fapana	-hohlana	-gotlha	-ngquzulana	-phambana	
botsel	bud (n)	khukhuša	phupu	letswela	ingcinga	umqumbe	
botsing	collision (n)	thulo	thulano	thulano	ungqubano	ukushayisana	
bottel	bottle (n)	lepotlelo	botlolo	lebotlolo	ibhotile	ibhodlela	
botter	butter (n)	leredi	botoro	serethe	ibhotolo	ibhotela	
botterskorsie	butternut (n)	lefodi	solotsi	lephutshana	usenza	ibhathanathi	
bou	build (v)	-aga	-(h)aha	-aga	-akha	-akha	
boud	buttock (n)	lerago	lerao	lerago	intsula	isinqe	
bout	bolt (n)	pouto	boutu	boutu	ibholiti	ibhawodi	
bouvallig	ramshackle (a)	-lerope	-helehang	-letlotla	-bobosi,-dilikayo	-khehlezelayo	
bra	brassière (n)	semmejane	bodise	bra	ibra	ingutshana yokubopha amabele	
brand	burn (v)	-swa	-besa	-swa	-tshisa	-shisa	
brander	wave (n)	lephoto	leqhubu	lekhubu	amaza	igagasi	
brandhout	firewood (n)	dikgong	patsi	legong	iinkuni	izinkuni	
brandkluis	safe (n)	seife	polokelo	letlole	isefu	isisefo	
brandplek	burn (n)	lebadi la mollo	leqeba la mollo	seso	umtshiso	isibashu	
brandrissie	chilli (n)	pherefere	tjhilise	thobega	itshilisi	upelepele	
brandstigting	arson (n)	tšhumo	tjhesetso	tshubo	utshiso	icala lokushisa	
brandstof	fuel (n)	sebešwa	dibeso	mafura	ipetroli	isibasi	
brandstofpedaal	accelerator (n)	sefamakhura	seakofisi	seokofatso	umcephe	isipuni	
brandweer	fire brigade (n)	batimamollo	setimamollo	batimamolelo	isicima-mlilo	abacimimlilo	
bredie	stew (n)	setšhuu	setjhu	setshuu	isityu	isitshulu	
breed	broad (a)	-phaphathi	-sephara	-phaphati	-phangaleleyo	-banzi	
breedte	breadth (n)	bophara	bophara	bophaphathi	ububanzi	ububanzi	
breek	break (v)	-roba	-pshatla	-roba	-aphula	-ephuka	
breekware	crockery (n)	dibjana	dijana	dithubegi	izitya	izitsha	
brei	knit (v)	-loga	-loha	-loga	-nita	-nitha	
brein	brain (n)	bjoko	booko	boboko	ubuchopho	ubuchopho	

B

Afrikaans	English	N Sotho	Sesotho	Tswana	Xhosa	Zulu
breinaald	knitting needle (n)	lemao la go loga	lemao la ho loha	lemao	inaliti yokunita	inalidi yokunitha
breiwerk	knitting (n)	go loga	moloho	selogo	umthungo	ukunitha
breuk	fracture (n)	thobego	thobeho	thobego	-candeka	ukwaphuka
breuke	fractions (n)	diabelo	diabelo	dipalophatlo	amaqhekeza	amaqhezu
brief	letter (n)	lengwalo	lengolo	lekwalo	incwadi	incwadi
bries	breeze (n)	phefšana	moya	pheswana	impepho	unyele
bril	spectacles (n)	dipaketsane	diborele	borele	iindondo	izibuko
bring	bring (v)	-tliša	-tlisa	-tlisa	-zisa	-letha
Brits	British (a)	-Seisimane	-Manyesemane	-Seesimane	-aseNgilane	-emaNgisi
broei	brood (v)	-alama	-alama	-ilama	-cinga	-fukama
broer	brother (n)	morwarra	moreso	lekaulengwe	umnakwethu	umfowethu
brokstuk	fragment (n)	seripana	sekoto	kapetla	iqhekeza	ucezwana
brom	grumble (v)	-ngunanguna	korotla	-ngongorega	-mbombozela	-khononda
bron	source (n)	mohlodi	mohlodi	motswedi	imve_aphi	umthombo
brood	loaf (n)	borotho	borotho	borotho	isonka	isinkwa
brood	bread (n)	borotho	borotho	borotho	isonka	isinkwa
brou	brew (v)	-bediša	-ritela	-apaya	-didiyela	-qunga
brousel	brew (n)	pedišo	moritelo	motswako	utywala	okuqungiwe
brug	bridge (n)	leporogo	borokgo	moratho	ibhulorho	ibhuloho
bruid	bride (n)	ngwetši	monyaduwa	monyadiwa	umtshakazi	umakoti
bruidegom	bridegroom (n)	monyadi	monyadi	monyadi	umyeni	umyeni
bruilof	wedding (n)	monyanya wa lenyalo	lenyalo	lenyalo	umtshato	umshado
bruin	brown (a)	-tsothwa	-sootho	-rokwa	-mdaka	-nsundu
bruin brand	tan (v)	go ora letšatši	-suha	-suga	mthubi bomvu	-nsundu
bruis	fizz (v)	-fufula	-kokomoha	-bela	-thi tshu	-hlihla
brul	roar (v)	-rora	-rora	-rora	-gquma	-bhadla
brul	roar (n)	mororo	mororo	modumo	umgqumo	ukubhadla
brulpadda	toad (n)	letlametlo	latlametlu	segwagwa	indubula	isele
bui	mood (n)	maikutlo	moya	maikutlo	imeko	ukuma kwenhliziyo
buig	bend (v)	-oba	-koba	-oba	-goba	-goba
buiging	bend (n)	kobamo	mothinya	khona	igophe	isigwegwe
buik	abdomen (n)	mpa	mpa	mpa	isisu	isisu
buit	loot (n)	dithebola	sehohedi	dikgapo	intimbo	umphango
buite	without (adv)	ka ntle	ka ntle	bisa	ngaphandle	ngaphandle
buiteband	tyre (n)	thaere	thaere	thaere	itayala	ithaya
buite-egtelik	illegitimate (a)	-ka ntle ga lenyalo	letla-le-pepilwe	-wa dikgora	-mgqakhwe	ngaphandle komthetho
buitekant	outside (n)	ka ntle	ka ntle	lentle	umphandle	umphandle
buiten	besides (prep)	ka ntle le	-ntle le	kwa ntle ga	-ngele kwa-	phandle kwa-
buitensporig	extravagant (a)	-tlopetšego	-kgalala	-nna bosutlha	-nenkcitho	-hlaphazayo
buitensporigheid	extravagance (n)	tlopelo	kgalala	bosutlha	inkcitho	ukuhlaphaza
buk	stoop (v)	-inama	-inama	-obama	-goba	-khothama
buk	bow (v)	-inama	-inama	-obama	-goba	-goba
buk	crouch (v)	-kotama	-botha	batalala	-chopha	-gogobala
bul	bull (n)	poo	poho	poo	inkunzi	inkunzi
bulhond	bulldog (n)	mpša ya lepultoko	pofa	phontshi	unomasinana	ubhova
burgemeester	mayor (n)	ramotse	ramotse	meiyara	isibonda	imeya
burger	citizen (n)	moagi	moahi	moagi	ummi	isakhamuzi
burgerlik	civil (a)	-segae	-lehae	-gae	-oluntu	-kwezakhamizi
bus	bus (n)	pese	bese	bese	ibhasi	ibhasi
bushalte	bus stop (n)	boemapese	setopo sa dibese	maemo a bese	istop sebhasi	isitobhi
buurman	neighbour (n)	moagišani	moahisane	moagisani	ummelwane	umakhelwane
by	bee (n)	nose	notshi	notshe	inyosi	inyosi
by	by (prep)	go	ka-	ke-	-ngase	nga-
by	by (prep)	go	ka-	ka-	-nga	nga-
Bybel	Bible (n)	Bibele	Bebele	Beibele	iBhayibhile	iBhayibheli
byeenkom	gather (v)	-kgobokana	-bokana	-kgobokana	-hlangana	-hlangana
byeenkoms	gathering (n)	kgobokano	pokano	phuthego	umhlangano	umhlangano
byeenroep	convene (v)	-bitša	-bokanya	-epa	-biza imbizo	-hlangana
bykomend	additional (a)	-oketšago	-eketsang	-oketsang	-ongezelelweyo	-ethasiselayo
byl	axe (n)	selepe	selepe	selepe	izembe	imbazo

Afrikaans	English	N Sotho	Sesotho	Tswana	Xhosa	Zulu	D
byna	nearly (adv)	-nyakile go-	-batlile	-batla	phantse	-cishe	
bystaan	assist (v)	-thuša	-thusa	-thusa	-nceda	-sekela	
bystand	assistance (n)	thušo	thuso	thuso	uncedo	iselekelelo	
byt	bite (v)	-loma	-loma	-loma	-luma	-luma	
byvoeg	add (v)	-oketša	-eketsa	-oketsa	-ongeza	-enezela	
byvoeglike naamwoord	adjective (n)	lehlaodi	lekgethi	letlhaodi	isiphawuli	isiphawulo	
bywoning	attendance (n)	tseno	boteng	tseno	ubukho	ukubakhona	
bywoord	adverb (n)	lehlathi	lehlalosi	letlhalosi	isihlomelo	isandiso	
chirurg	surgeon (n)	ngaka ya go bua	ngaka	ngaka ya karo	ugqirha	udokotela ohlinzayo	
chirurgie	surgery (n)	bobui	bongaka ba thipa	karo	ubugqirha	ukuhlinzwa	
Christelik	Christian (a)	-Sekriste	-Sekreste	-sekeresete	-obuKrestu	-liKrestu	
Christen	Christian (n)	Mokriste	Mokreste	mokeresete	umKrestu	iKrestu	
Christus	Christ (n)	Kriste	Kreste	Keresete	uKrestu	uKrestu	
chronologies	chronological (a)	ka tlhatlamanomehla	-tatelano	-tlhatlhamano	-landelelana ngamaxesha	-ehlelo lezikhathi zemilando	
daad	deed (n)	tiro	ketso	tiro	isenzo	isenzo	
daagliks	daily (a)	letšatši ka letšatši	ka mehla	-motlha le motlha	-mihla yonke	izinsuko zonke	
daal	descend (v)	-theoga	-theoha	-fologa	-ihla	-ehla	
daar	there (adv)	gona	moo	foo	phaya	lapho	
daardie	those (pron)	tšeo	-no	tsele	leya	lokho	
dag	day (n)	letšatši	letsatsi	letsatsi	imini	usuku	
dagbreek	dawn (n)	masa	mafube	bosa	isifingo	ukusa	
dagbreek	daybreak (n)	mahube	mafube	bosa	ubusa	ukusa	
dagga	cannabis (n)	patše	matekwane	motokwane	intsangu	insangu	
dagvaarding	subpoena (n)	piletšotshekong	samane	piletsatshekong	isamani	isamaniso	
dagvaarding	summons (n)	tagafara	samane	tagafara	isamani	isamaniso	
dak	roof (n)	tlhaka	marulelo	borulelo	uphahla	uphahla	
dakbalk	rafter (n)	kota ya go rulela	leballo	kapa	iplanga lophahla	umjibe	
daling	descent (n)	theogo	theoho	phologo	ithambeka	ukwehla	
dam	dam (n)	letamo	letamo	tamo	idama	idamu	
dame	lady (n)	mohumagadi	mofumahadi	mme	inenekazi	inkosikazi	
dan	then (adv)		jwale	jaale	kwaza	lapho	
dank	thanks (n)	tebogo	diteboho	tebogo	umbulelo	ukubonga	
dankbaar	grateful (a)	-lebogilego	-lebohang	-lebogang	-nombulelo	-bongayo	
dankbaarheid	gratitude (n)	tebogo	teboho	tebogo	umbulelo	ukubonga	
dans	dance (n)	go bina	motjeko	pino	umdaniso	ukusina	
dans	dance (v)	-bina	-tjeka	-bina	-danisa	-sina	
dapper	brave (a)	-nago le sebete	-sebete	bogale	-khaliphileyo	-nobuqhawe	
dapperheid	bravery (n)	bogale	sebete	bopelokgale	ubukhalipha	ubuqhawe	
das	tie (n)	thai	tae	thae	iqhina	uthayi	
dassie	dassie (n)	pela	pela	pela	imbila	imbila	
dat	that (pron)	gore	eo	gore	ukuba	ukuze	
datum	date (n)	tšatšikgwedi	mohla	letlha	umhla	idethi	
deeg	dough (n)	tege	hlama	leribi	intlama	inhlama	
deel	share (v)	-abela	-arola	-kgaogana	-ahlulelana	-cazelana	
deel	share (n)	kabelo	karolo	kabelo	isahlulo	isabelo	
deel	part (n)	seripa	karolo	kaba	isahlulo	umunxa	
dek	thatch (v)	-rulela	-rulela ka jwang	-rulela	-fulela	-fulela	
dek	lay (v)	-teka	-teka	-baya	-beka	-deka	
dek	cover (v)	-khupetša	-kwahela	-bipa	-gquma	-vala	
dekade	decade (n)	ngwagasome	dilemo tse leshome	ngwagasome	inkulungwane	iminyaka eyishumi	
dekgras	thatch (n)	bjang bja go rulela	marulelo a jwang	maragomagolo	ufulelo	utshani bokufulela	
deksel	lid (n)	sekhurumelo	sekwahelo	sekhurumelo	isiciko	isivalo	
deksel	cap (n)	sekhurumelo	sekwahelo	sekhurumelo	ityepusi	isivalo	
deksel	cover (n)	sekhurumelo	sekwahelo	sebipo	iqweqwe	isivalo	
demokrasie	democracy (n)	temokrasi	demokerasi	pusano	idemokhrasi	ukubusa ngentando yabantu	

D	Afrikaans	English	N Sotho	Sesotho	Tswana	Xhosa	Zulu
	demp	quell (v)	-thiba	-kokobetsa	-okobatsa	-bhangisa	-thulisa
	departement	department (n)	kgoro	lefapha	lefapha	isebe	isigaba
	deponeer	deposit (v)	-beeletša	-beeletsa	-bolokela	-dipczitha	-beka
	deposito	deposit (n)	peeletšo	peeletso	peeletso	idipozithi	isibeko
	derde	third (a)	-boraro	-raro	-nngwe-tharong	-thathu	-esithathu
	derm	intestine (n)	lela	lela	lela	ithumbu	ithumbu
	Desember	December (n)	Desemere	Tshitwe	Sedimonthole	Disemba	uDisemba
	deskundige	expert (n)	setsebi	kgeleke	setswerere	incutshe	isazi
	deur	through (prep)	ka-	ka-	ke	-nga	nga-
	deur	door (n)	lemati	monyako	lebati	ucanzo	umnyango
	deurskynend	transparent (a)	-bonagatšago	-bonaletsang	-bonalatsang	-krelekrele	-khanyayo
	deursteek	pierce (v)	-phunya	-phunya	-tlhaba	-hlaba	-bhoboza
	diafragma	diaphragm (n)	letswalo	letswalo	letswalo	idayafram	inhlonhla
	diagram	diagram (n)	tshwantšho	setshwantsho	tshwantsho	umzobo	isifanekiso esidwe-tshiweyo
	dialek	dialect (n)	mmolelo	mmuo	teme	intetho yesizwana	ulimi lwesigodi
	diamant	diamond (n)	taemane	taemane	teemane	idayimani	idayimani
	diarree	diarrhoea (n)	letšhollo	letshollo	letsholola	urhudo	uhudu
	dief	thief (n)	lehodu	leshodu	legodu	isela	isela
	dien	serve (v)	-direla	-sebeletsa	-direla	-khonza	-sebenzela
	diep	deep (a)	-tebilego	-tebileng	-boteng	-nzulu	-shonile
	diepte	depth (n)	botebo	botebo	boteng	ubunzulu	ukujula
	dier	animal (n)	phoofolo	phoofolo	phologolo	isilo	isilwane
	dier	beast (n)	phoofolo	phoofolo	kgomo	isilo	isilwane
	dierbaar	lovable (a)	-rategago	-ratehang	-rategwang	-thandekayo	-thandekayo
	dierbaar	dear (a)	-rategago	-ratehang	-botlhokwatlhokwa	-thandekayo	-thandiwe
	dieretuin	zoo (n)	serapa sa diphoofolo	zuu	zuu	iziko lezilwanyana	izu
	dierlik	brutal (a)	-šoro	-soro	-bophologolo	-burhalarhume	-khuhlumezayo
	dieselfde	same (a)	-swanago	-tshwanang	-tshwana le	-nye	-fanayo
	dig	dense (a)	-kitlaganego	-teteaneng	-lesuthu	-xineneyo	-minyene
	digter	poet (n)	sereti	sethothokisi	mmoki	imbcngi	imbongi
	dik	thick (a)	-koto	-tenya	-kima	-khu u	-nohlonze
	dikderm	colon (n)	lelakgolo	moqopo	telele	undloku	upopopo
	dik maak	thicken (v)	-kotofatša	-teteanya	loa	-enza nkulu	-enza kubeluhlonzi
	dikmond wees	sulk (v)	-hlonama	-ngala	-tsupa	-qumba	-khunsa
	diktator	dictator (n)	mmušanoši	mosusutlelli	mmusaesi	uzwi akhe	umashiqela
	dikwels	often (adv)	gantši	kgafetsa	atisa	njalo	kaningi
	dinamiet	dynamite (n)	tanamaete	denamaete	talameiti	idamanethi	udalimede
	ding	thing (n)	selo	ntho	selo	into	into
	dink	think (v)	-gopola	-nahana	-akanya	-cinga	-cabanga
	Dinsdag	Tuesday (n)	Labobedi	Labobedi	Labobedi	ulwesiBini	uLwesibili
	direk	direct (a)	-lebanego	-tobileng	-maleba	-thenqo	-qondile
	disenterie	dysentery (n)	tengkhubedu	letshollo le lefubedu	letsholola	isisu segazi	isihudo
	diskriminasie	discrimination (n)	kgethollo	kgethollo	letlhotlho	ucalulo	ukukhetha
	diskrimineer	discriminate (v)	-kgetholla	-kgetholla	-tlhotlholola	-calula	-khetha
	dislojaliteit	disloyalty (n)	kgelogo	bokwenehi	bosaikanyegang	ukunganyaniseki	ukuhlubuka
	dissipel	disciple (n)	morutiwa	morutuwa	molatedi	umdisipile	umlandeli
	dissipline	discipline (n)	thupišo	thapiso	pipelo	imbeko	impatho eqinileyo
	distrik	district (n)	selete	setereke	kgaolo	isithili	ihlelo
	distriksgeneesheer	district surgeon (n)	ngaka ya selete	ngaka ya setereke	ngaka ya kgaolo	ugqirha wesithili	udokotela kahulumeni
	dit	this (pron)	ye	-na	tse	le	lokhu
	dit	it (pron)	yona	-na	yone	yona	lokhu
	dobbel	gamble (v)	-ralokiša tšhelete	-ananya	-iteka lesego	-bheja	-gembula
	doek	cloth (n)	lešela	lesela	khai	ilaphu	indwangu
	doel	goal (n)	koulo	ntlha	maitlhomo	inqaku	injongo
	doel	aim (n)	nepo	sepheo	maikaelelo	injongo	inhloso
	doeltreffend	efficient (a)	-kgonago	-kgonang	-kgonang	-khutheleyo	-qeqeshekile
	doeltreffendheid	efficiency (n)	bokgoni	bokgoni	bokgoni	inkuthalo	ukuqeqesheka
	doen	do (v)	-dira	-etsa	-dira	-enza	-enza
	dof	dim (a)	-sa bonagalego gabotse	-lerotho	-letobo	-luzizi	-fiphele

Afrikaans	English	N Sotho	Sesotho	Tswana	Xhosa	Zulu	D
dogter	daughter (n)	morwedi	moradi	morwadi	intombi	intombi	
dokter	doctor (n)	ngaka	ngaka	ngaka	ugqirha	udokotela	
dokument	document (n)	lengwalo	lengolo	setlankama	uxwebhu	umbhalo	
dommel	drowse (v)	-otsela	-otsela	-otsela	-ozela	-ozela	
donder	thunder (n)	modumo	seaduma	modumo	iindudumo	ukuduma	
Donderdag	Thursday (n)	Labone	Labone	Labone	uLwesine	uLwesine	
donker	darkness (n)	leswiswi	lefifi	lefifi	ubumnyama	ubumnyama	
donker	dark (a)	-fifetšego	-lefifi	-fitshwa	-mnyama	-fiphele	
donkie	ass (n)	tonki	esele	esele	idonki	imbongolo	
donkie	donkey (n)	tonki	tonki	tumuga	imbongolo	imbongolo	
dood	numb (a)	-hwilego bogatšo	-sa utlweng	-bosisi	-fileyo	-ngasezwa	
dood	dead (a)	-hwilego	-shweleng	-suleng	-fileyo	-file	
dood	death (n)	lehu	lefu	leso	ukufa	ukufa	
doodgaan	die (v)	-hwa	-shwa	-swa	-fa	-fa	
doodmaak	kill (v)	-bolaya	-bolaya	-bolaya	-bulala	-bulala	
doodskis	coffin (n)	lepokisi la bahu	lekase	lekese	umkhumbi	ikhofini	
doodsondersoek	inquest (n)	tlhahlobo ya mohu	patlisiso ya lekgotla	patlisiso ya loso	uphando	ukuhlolwa kwembangela yokufa	
doof	deaf (a)	-sefoa	-tsebetutu	-boshushu	-ngevayo	-ngenakuzwa	
doop	baptise (v)	-kolobetša	-kolobetsa	-kolobetsa	-phehlelela	-bhabhadisa	
doop	baptism (n)	kolobetšo	kolobetso	kolobetso	uphehlelelo	umbhabhadiso	
doos	box (n)	lepokisi	lebokose	lepokoso	ibhokisi	ibhokisi	
dophou	watch (v)	-hlokomela	-disa	-lepa	-qwalasela	-bheka	
dor	arid (a)	-omilego	-sebataola	-omeletseng	-bharhileyo	-omile	
doring	thorn (n)	mootlwa	moutla	mmitlwa	iliva	iva	
doringdraad	barbed wire (n)	terata ya meetlwa	terata e metsu	terata ya mebitlwa	ucingo olunameva	ucingo olunameva	
dorp	town (n)	toropo	toropo	motse	idolophu	idolobha	
dorpie	village (n)	motse	motsana	motse	isixeko	idolobhana	
dors	thirst (n)	lenyora	lenyora	lenyora	unxano	ukoma	
dorstig	thirsty (a)	-nyorilwego	-nyorilwe	-nyorilweng	-nxaniwe (yo)	-omile	
doseer	lecture (v)	-ruta	-rupela	-ruta	-fundisa	-fundisa	
dosent	lecturer (n)	mofahloši	morupedi	moruti	umhlohli	umfundisi	
dosis	dose (n)	kelo ya sehlare	tekanyo ya sehlare	selekanyo	ithamo	ithamo elilinganisiweyo	
dosyn	dozen (n)	tosene	tosene	tosene	idazini	idazini	
dou	dew (n)	phoka	phoka	monyo	umbethe	amazolo	
dra	wear (v)	-apara	-apara	-rwala	-nxiba	-gqoka	
dra	carry (v)	-rwala	-rwala	-tshola	-thwala	-thwala	
draad	thread (n)	tlhale	tshwele	tlhale	umtya	ucingo	
draad	wire (n)	motato	terata	bothale	ucingo	ucingo	
draad	fence (n)	legora	terata	legora	ucingo	ucingo	
draai	revolve (v)	-dikologa	-potoloha	dikologa	-jikeleza	-zungeza	
draai	turn (v)	-dikologa	-fapoha	-tshika	-jika	-jika	
draf	jog (v)	-kitima	-hlehla	tlhetlha	-ntyuntya	-dledlezela	
drang	urge (n)	kganyogo	takatso	maikutlo	uthundezo	ukuphokophela	
drank	liquor (n)	senotagi	tahi	bojalwa	utywala	ugologo	
drankie	drink (n)	seno	seno	seno	isiselo	isiphuzo	
dreigement	threat (n)	tšhošetšo	tshokelo	setshoso	intsongelo	usongo	
drie	three (n)	tharo	tharo	tharo	ntathu	kuthathu	
driehoek	triangle (n)	khutlotharo	kgutlotharo	khutlotharo	unxantathu	unxantathu	
drink	drink (v)	-nwa	-nwa	-nwa	-sela	-phuza	
droefheid	sadness (n)	manyami	maswabi	khutsafalo	usizi	ukudabuka	
dronk	drunk (a)	-tagilwego	-tahilwe	-tlhapedisang	-nxilile	-dakiwe	
dronklap	drunkard (n)	setagwa	letahwa	letagwa	inxila	isidakwa	
droog	dry (a)	-omilego	-omme	-omileng	-omileyo	-omile	
droogmaak	dry (v)	-oma	-oma	-oma	-omisa	-omisa	
droogskoonmaak	dryclean (v)	-hlwekišaoma	-hlwekisa ntle ho metsi	-tlhatswa	-drayiklina	-drayiklina	
droogskoonmakery	drycleaner (n)	mohlwekišaoma	mohlwekisa ntle ho metsi	teraetlelini	idrayiklina	umdrayiklini	
droogte	drought (n)	komelelo	komello	komelelo	imbalela	ukomisa kwezulu	

D	Afrikaans	English	N Sotho	Sesotho	Tswana	Xhosa	Zulu
	droom	dream (v)	-lora	-lora	-lora	-phupha	-phupha
	droom	dream (n)	toro	toro	toro	iphupha	iphupho
	dros	desert (v)	-ngwega	-ngala	-ngala	-qhwesha	-mbuka
	droster	deserter (n)	mongwegi	mongadi	mongwegi	umqhweshi	imbuki
	druiwe	grape (n)	diterebe	morara	terebe	idiliya	amagrebhisi
	druk	pressure (n)	kgatelelo	kgatello	kgatelelo	uxinzelelo	ukucindizela
	druk	print (v)	-gatiša	-hatisa	-gatisa	-shicilela	-cindizela
	druk	squeeze (v)	-pitla	-tlhotla	-beleatanya	-cudisa	-cindezela
	drup	drip (n)	tripi	lerothodi	lerothodi	ithontsi	iconsi
	drup	drip (v)	-rotha	-rotha	-rotha	-thontsiza	-consa
	drywe	float (v)	-phaphamala	-phaphamala	-kokobala	-dada	-ntanta
	dubbel	double (n)	bobedi	bobedi	bobedi	umphindwa	okuphindiweyo
	dubbele	double (a)	gabedi	-habedi	-futaganeng	-phindeneyo	-phindiwe
	dubbelpunt	colon (n)	kgorwana	kgutlwana	khutlwana	ikholoni	ikholoni
	dubbelsinnig	ambiguous (a)	-belaetšago	-habedi	-sa tlhalosang	-mbolombini	-fithizile
	duif	pigeon (n)	leeba	leeba	leeba	ihobe	ijuba
	duik	dent (v)	-phobela	-bothetsa	-pobetsa	-bothoza	-bocoza
	duik	dive (v)	-phonkgela	-qwela	-nwela	-ntywila	-cwila
	duiker	duiker (n)	phuti	phuthi	photi	impunzi	impunzi
	duikery	diving (n)	phonkgelo	qwelo	bonwelo	untywilo	ukucwila
	duikplank	diving board (n)	lepolanka la go phonkgela	boroto ya ho qwela	polanka ya bonwelo	iplanga lokuntywila	icwecwe lepulangwe lokucwila
	duim	thumb (n)	nkgogorupa	monwana o motona	kgonotswe	ubhontsi	isithupha
	duim	inch (n)	noko	senoko	noko	i-intshi	iyintshi
	duin	dune (n)	mmoto wa mohlaba	totomana	popoma	indunduma	igquma
	duiselig	giddy (a)	-šiišago	-tsekela	-sedidi	-nenzilikithi	-nesizunguzane
	duiseligheid	dizziness (n)	matladima	modikwadikwane	modikologo	isizunguzane	inzululwane
	duisend	thousand (n)	sekete	sekete	sekete	iwaka	inkulungwane
	duisendpoot	millipede (n)	legokolodi	lefokolodi	sebokolodi	isongololo	ishongololo
	duiwel	devil (n)	diabolo	diabolose	satane	umtyholi	uSathane
	duld	bear (v)	-kgotlelela	-mamella	-tshola	-thwala	-bekezela
	dun	thin (a)	-sesane	-sesane	-sesane	-nciphile(yo)	-zacile
	duur	expensive (a)	-turago	-turu	-turang	-dla	-dulile
	dwaal	wander (v)	-tlaruma	-tsekela	-teatea	-bhadula	-zula
	dwaas	fool (n)	setlaela	sethoto	lesilo	isibhanxa	isilima
	dwaasheid	foolishness (n)	botlaela	bothoto	boeleele	ububhanxa	ubulima
	dwang	compulsion (n)	kgapeletšo	qobello	pateletso	isinyanzelo	isificezelo
	dwars	across (adv)		-rapalletse	rapalala	-ngoxuxwesa	phambana na-
	dwelm	drug (n)	seokobatši	thethefatsi	seritibatsi	iyeza	isidakamizwa
	dwelms	drugs (n)	diokobatši	dithethefatsi	ditaga	amayeza	izidakamizwa
	dwelmslaaf	drug addict (n)	moineedi diokobatšing	lekgoba la dithethefatsi	moritibatsi	umyotywa	isigqili sesidakamizwa
	dwerg	dwarf (n)	mponempone	qokofana	lemponempone	uhili	isichwe
	dwing	compel (v)	-gapeletša	-qobella	-gapeletsa	-nyanzela	-phoqa
	dy	thigh (n)	serope	serope	serope	ithanga	ithanga
	edelman	aristocrat (n)	mokgomana	seithati	kgosana	isihandiba	isilomo
	eed	oath (n)	kano	kano	kano	isifungo	isifungo
	een	one (n)	tee	nngwe	nngwe	inye	ukunye
	eend	duck (n)	lepidipidi	letata	pidipidi	idada	idada
	eenders	similar (a)	-swanago	-tshwanang	-tshwanang	-fana(yo)	-fanayo
	eenheid	unit (n)	botee	bonngwe	seelo	-manya	uhlamvu
	eenheid	unity (n)	botee	bonngwe	seoposengwe	umanyano	ubunye
	een maal	once (adv)	gatee	hang	gangwe	kanye	kanye
	eensaam	lonely (a)	-jewago ke bodutu	-hlorileng	-bodutu	-dwa	-nesizungu
	eensaamheid	loneliness (n)	bodutu	bodutu	bodutu	ubulolo	isizungu
	eenstemmig	unanimous (a)	-botee	-ntsweleng	-bongwefela	-omxhelomnye	-vumelene
	een van beide	either (pron)	-fe goba -fe	kapa	kana	-nokuba nguwuphi	-kokubili
	eenvoudig	simple (a)	-bonolo	-bonolo	-nolo	-lula	-sobala
	eer	honour (n)	tlhompho	tlhompho	tlotlego	imbeko	inhlonipho
	eer	honour (v)	-hlompha	-hlompha	-tlotla	-nika imbeko	-hlonipha

Afrikaans	English	N Sotho	Sesotho	Tswana	Xhosa	Zulu	E
eerbied	awe (n)	tlhompho	tshisimoso	boikokobetso	uloyiko	uvalo	
eerlik	honest (a)	-tshepegago	-tshepahalang	-boikanyo	-msulwa	-qotho	
eerlikheid	honesty (n)	botshepegi	botshepehi	boikanyo	ubumsulwa	ubuqotho	
eersgeborene	firstborn (n)	leitšibulo	letsibolo	leitibolo	inkulu	izibulo	
eerste	first (a)	-pele	-pele	-ntlha	-kuqala	-okuqala	
eet	eat (v)	-ja	-ja	-ja	-tya	-dla	
eetbaar	edible (a)	-lewago	-jehang	-jewang	-tyekayo	-dlekayo	
eetgerei	cutlery (n)	dithipa	dikgaba	maswana	amacephe nezitya	izinto okudliwa ngazo	
eetkamer	dining room (n)	bojelo	daenengrumo	bojelo	igumbi lokutyela	ikamelo lokudlela	
eetlus	appetite (n)	kganyogo ya dijo	takatso ya dijo	keletso ya dijo	umkra	inkanuko	
eeu	century (n)	ngwagakgolo	senturu	ngwagakgolo	ikhulu	ikhulu leminyaka	
eeufees	centenary (n)	mokete wa ngwagakgolo	mokete wa dilemokgolo	ngwagakgolo wa keteko	ikhulu leminyaka	umkhosi wekhulu leminyaka	
egskeiding	divorce (n)	tlhalo	tlhalo	tlhalo	uqhawulo-mtshato	idivosi	
eie	own (a)	-ka	-ka	-ga-	yam	-a-	
eienaar	owner (n)	mong	monga	mong	umnini	umnikazi	
eienaardig	peculiar (a)	-makatšago	-ikgethileng	-sele	-ngaqhelekanga	-mangalisayo	
eiendom	property (n)	thoto	leruo	thoto	impahla	impahla	
eier	egg (n)	lee	lehe	lee	iqanda	iqanda	
eierdop	eggshell (n)	kgapetla ya lee	kgaketlana	kgapa	iqokobhe	igobolondo leqanda	
eiergeel	yolk (n)	mothobe	mothwebe	boe	umthubi	isikhupha seqanda	
eierstok	ovary (n)	popelo	popelo	tsala	isiyilelo -qanda	izizalo	
eikeboom	oak (n)	moeike	eike	oak	umoki	i-oki	
eiland	island (n)	sehlakahlaka	sehlekehleke	setlhaketlhake	isiqithi	isiqhingi	
einde	finish (n)	mafelelo	qetelo	khutlo	isiphelo	ukuphela	
einde	end (n)	bofelo	phetho	bokhutlo	isiphelo	ukugcina	
eindig	end (v)	-fela	-phetha	-khutla	-phela	-gcina	
eintlik	actually (adv)		hantlentle	ruri	-ngokwenene	ngempela	
eis	claim (v)	-tsoma tefo	-nqosa	-lopa	-banga	-biza	
eis	demand (v)	-nyaka	-tseka	-lopa	-banga	-biza	
eiser	plaintiff (n)	mmelaedi	moqosi	moseki	ummangali	ummangali	
ek	I (pron)	nna	nna/ke-	nna	ndi-	ngi-	
ekonomie	economy (n)	ekonomi	paballo	pabalelo	uqoqosho	umnotho	
eksamen	examination (n)	tlhahlobo	hlahlobo	tlhatlhobo	uvavanyo	ukuhlolwa	
ekseem	eczema (n)	sekgalaka	lekgopho	moswewe	umrhawuzelelane	utwayi	
eksemplaar	copy (book) (n)	kopi ya puku	buka	seetsi	ikopi	ikhophi	
ekskuus	excuse (n)	tshwarelo	tshwarelo	seipato	ukuzigwebela	izaba	
eksoties	exotic (a)	-šele	-ditjhabeng	-sa bonweng fela	-ngaqhelekanga	-vele kwelinye izwe	
ekstra	extra (a)	godimo ga	-fetang	-gape	-ongezelelweyo	-ngaphezulu	
eland	eland (n)	phohu	phofu	phofu	impofu	impofu	
elders	elsewhere (adv)	mo gongwe	kaekae	gosele	kwenye indawo	-kwenye indawo	
elektries	electric (a)	-mohlagase	-motlakase	-motlakase	-ombane	-kagesi	
elektrisiteit	electricity (n)	mohlagase	motlakase	motlakase	umbane	ugesi	
element	element (n)	elemente	setho	tlholego	into	ilungu	
elf	eleven (n)	lesometee	leshome le motso	some nngwe	ishumi elinanye	ishumi nanye	
elk(e)	each (pron)	mang le mang	-ng le -ng	ngwe le ngwe	nga(m)nye	yilowo	
elke	every (a)	-ngwe le -ngwe	-ng le -ng	-otlhe	-nke	-nke	
elkeen	anybody (pron)	mang le mang	mang le mang	mang le mang	-nabani	noma ubani	
ellende	misery (n)	mathatha	bosisapelo	tshotlego	ubugogotya	ukuhlupheka	
elmboog	elbow (n)	setšu	setswe	sekgono	ingqiniba	indololwane	
embrio	embryo (n)	pelwana	pelwana	pelwana	isihluma esizalweni	umbungu	
emigreer	emigrate (v)	-falala	-falla	-falala	-fuduka	-thuthela kwelinye izwe	
emmer	pail (n)	kgamelo	kgamelo	kgamelo	iemele	ithunga	
emmer	bucket (n)	kgamelo	kgamelo	kgamelo	iemere	ibhakede	
en	and (conj)	le/gomme	le	le	kunye, na-	na-	
enema	enema (n)	enema	enema	mothulego	ivenge	uchatho	
energie	energy (n)	mafolofolo	matla	thata	amandla	umfutho	
energiek	energetic (a)	-mafolofolo	-matla	-mojato	-namandla	-khuthele	
engel	angel (n)	morongwa	lengeloi	moengele	ingelosi	ingelosi	
Engels	English (a)	-Seisemane	-Senyesemane	Seesemane	isi Ngesi	isiNgisi	

E	Afrikaans	English	N Sotho	Sesotho	Tswana	Xhosa	Zulu
	enige	any (a)	-ngwe le -ngwe	-ng le -ng	-ngwe le -ngwe	-nayiphi	noma
	enige plek	anywhere (adv)	gongwe le gongwe	kae kapa kae	gongwe le gongwe	naphi	nakuphi
	enigiets	anything (pron)	eng le eng	-ng le -ng	sengwe le sengwe	nantoni	noma yini
	enigste	only (a)	nnoši	feela	-nosi	-kuphela	-dwa
	enjin	engine (n)	entšene	enjene	enjene	injini	injini
	enkel	single (a)	-tee	-ng	-ngwe	-nye	-nye
	enkel	ankle (n)	kgokgoilane	leqaqailana	legwejana	iqatha	iqakala
	enkelring	anklet (n)	mpshiri	boseka	leseka	inqashela	isigqizo
	epidemie	epidemic (n)	leuba	sewa	leroborobo	isifo esosulelayo	isibhadalala
	erdwurm	earthworm (n)	nogametsana	nonometsane	monopi	umsundululu	umsundu
	erf	inherit (v)	-ja lefa	-ja lefa	-ja boswa	-fumana ilifa	-thola njengefa
	erfenis	heritage (n)	bohwa	lefa	boswa	ilifa	ifa
	erfenis	inheritance (n)	lefa	lefa	boswa	ilifa	ifa
	erfgenaam	heir (n)	mojalefa	mojalefa	mojaboswa	indlalifa	indlalifa
	ergerlik	annoying (a)	-hlophago	-tenang	-kgwisa manga	-caphukisayo	-canulayo
	ergernis	annoyance (n)	tlhophego	ho tena	manga	inkathazo	isinengiso
	erken	acknowledge (v)	-dumela	-dumela	-naya motho seditse	-vuma	-vuma
	ernstig	serious (a)	-šoro	-hlokofetseng	-tlhonamang	-xhalisekile(yo)	-qukethe
	ertjie	pea (n)	erekisi	erekisi	erekisi	ierityisi	inhlamvu kaphizi
	ervaring	experience (n)	boitemogelo	boiphihlelo	boitemogelo	amava	ulwazi
	essensie	essence (n)	bokgonthe	tabataba	tlhokego	ubunto	ingqikithi
	essensieel	essential (a)	-nyakegago	-bohlokwa	-tlhokegang	-funekayo	-funekayo
	etiket	label (n)	sešupo	letshwao	setshwao	ileyibhile	ilebula
	etiket	etiquette (n)	boitshwaro	hlomphano	maitseo	ukuziphatha	usikothi
	etnies	ethnic (a)	-serafe		-setso	-buhlanga	-kohlobo lobuzwe
	etter	pus (n)	maladu	boladu	boladu	ubovu	ubovu
	evangelis	evangelist (n)	moebangedi	Moefangedi	moefanggele	umvangeli	umvangeli
	evolusie	evolution (n)	ebolusi	ebolusi	tlhagelelo	ukudaleka	ukusombuluka kwendalo
	ewenaar	equator (n)	mogarafase	ekhweita	mogaralefatshe	ikweyita	inkabazwe
	ewig	eternal (a)	-sa felego	-sa feleng	-bosakhuteng	-ngaphakathi	-naphakade
	ewigdurend	everlasting (a)	-go sa felego	-sa feleng	-ruri	-ngapheliyo	-ngunaphakade
	ewigheid	eternity (n)	bosafeleng	bosafeleng	bosayenkae	iphakade	ubuphakade
	fabel	fable (n)	nonwane	tshomo	leinane	intsomi	insumo
	fabriek	factory (n)	faporiki	feme	faboriki	iziko-mveliso	ifektri
	faksie	faction (n)	lekoko	mokga	mophato	imbambano	isixexelegu
	fakulteit	faculty (n)	lefapha	lekala	lefapha	isebe lemfundo	isigaba
	familie	family (n)	leloko	lesika	balelapa	usapho	inzalo
	familielid	relation (n)	moloko	leloko	tsala ya madi	isizalwana	isihlobo
	fatsoenlik	respectable (a)	-hlomphegago	-hlomphehang	-tlotlegang	-hloniphekile(yo)	-nesithunzi
	fauna	fauna (n)	diphedi	diphedi	ditshedi	izilo	izilwane
	Februarie	February (n)	Feberware	Hlakola	Tlhakole	Febhuwari	uFebhuwali
	fees	feast (n)	mokete	mokete	moletlo	umsitho	idili
	fees	festival (n)	monyanya	mokete	moletlo	umnyadala	umkhasi
	feesvier	feast (v)	-ja mokete	-keteka	-ja moletlo	-bhiyoza	-dikiza
	feit	fact (n)	nnete	nnete	ntlha	inqaku	iqiniso
	ferm	firm (a)	-tiilego	-tiileng	-tlhomameng	-zinzile(yo)	-qinile
	fetus	foetus (n)	serapolotšwana	fetase	namane	into engekazalwa	umbungu
	fiets	bicycle (n)	paesekela	baesekele	baesekele	ibhayisikili	ibhayisikili
	figuur	figure (n)	sethalwa	setshwantsho	thwadi	umfanekiso	ukulinganisa
	fiksie	fiction (n)	kanegelogopolwa	tshomo	maitlhamelwa	intsomi	okuqanjiwe
	filet	fillet (n)	filete	tshutshu	thupa	isihlunu	inyama ethambileyo
	film	film (n)	filimi	fileme	setshwantsho	ifilimu	ifilimu
	filtreer	filter (v)	-hlotla	-hlotla	-tlhotlha	-hluza	-vova
	finaal	final (a)	-mafelelo	-bofelo	-bofelo	-okugqibela	isigcino
	fladder	flap (v)	-phaphasela	-fosa	-phaphasela	-bhenguza	-bhabhazisa
	flamink	flamingo (n)	tladi	folaminko		ikholwase	umakholwase
	flanel	flannel (n)	folene	folene	folene	ifleni	ifulanela
	flater	blunder (n)	phošo	phoso	tshenyo	impcsiso	isiphambeko

Afrikaans	English	N Sotho	Sesotho	Tswana	Xhosa	Zulu	**G**
fleim	phlegm (n)	mamina	sehohlola	sehuba	isikhohlela	isikhwehlela	
fles	jar (n)	moruswi	jara	morufa	ingqayi	imbizana	
flikker	flicker (v)	-benyabenya	-panyapanya	-benyabenya	-qhwanyaza	-lontoza	
flirteer	flirt (v)	-kalatša	-feba	-fefa	-ncokolisa	-gemenca	
flits	flash (n)	kgadimo	mmane	legadima	umenye	umbani	
flitslig	torch (n)	panyepanye	serumola	lobone	itotshi	ithoshi	
flitslig	flashlight (n)	panyepanye	sekammane	kganya	umbane	ithoshi	
flora	flora (n)	dimedi	dimedi	dimedi	isihluma	izinhlobo zemithi	
floreer	prosper (v)	-atlega	-atleha	-tswelela pele	-chuma	-chuma	
florerend	prosperous (a)	-atlegilego	-atlehileng	-tswelelang pele	-nempumelelo	-chumile	
flou word	faint (v)	-idibala	-akgeha	-idibala	-feyinta	-quleka	
fluister	whisper (v)	-sebaseba	-hweshetsa	-seba	-sebeza	-hleba	
fluit	whistle (n)	nakana	phala	molodi	impempe	ikhwelo	
fluit	whistle (v)	-letša molodi	-letsa molodi	-tswirinya	-betha impempe	-shaya ikhwelo	
fluit	flute (n)	naka	foleite	phala	umtshingo	umtshingo	
fluitspeler	flautist (n)	moletšanaka	mmapalafoleite	moletsaphala	umdlali-fluti	umshayi-mitshingo	
fluks	diligent (a)	-mafolofolo	-mafolofolo	-manontlhotlho	-khutheleyo	-khuthele	
fluksheid	diligence (n)	mafolofolo	mafolofolo	bonatla	inkuthalo	inkuthalo	
fontein	fountain (n)	sediba	sediba	motswedi	umthombo	umthombo	
forseer	force (v)	-gapeletša	-susumetsa	-gapeletsa	-nyanzela	-cindezela	
fort	fort (n)	sebo	qhobosheane	ntlo ya phemelo	inqaba	isikaniso	
fortuin	fortune (n)	lehumo	letlotlo	letlhogonolo	ithamsanqa	umnotho	
foto	photograph (n)	seswantšho	setshwantsho	setshwantsho	ifoto	isithombe	
fotografeer	photograph (v)	-swantša	-tshwantsha	-tshwantsa	-fota	-thatha isithombe	
fout	fault (n)	phošo	phoso	phoso	imposiso	iphosiso	
fout	mistake (n)	phošo	phoso	phoso	impazamo	isiphosiso	
fout	error (n)	phošo	phoso	phoso	impazamo	isiphosiso	
fouteer	err (v)	-dira phošo	-fosa	-fosa	-phazama	-phosisa	
fraksie	fraction (n)	karolo	seabelo	palophatlo	iqhekeza	iqhezu	
frons	frown (v)	-šošobanya phatla	-hwapa	-sosobanya	-finga iintshiyi	-hwaqabala	
frons	frown (n)	tšhošobanyo ya phatla	kgwapo	sosobanyo	ukujala	ukuhwaqabala	
frustreer	frustrate (v)	-nola moko	-nyahamisa	-bolaya pelo	-danisa	-dikibalisa	
fyn	fine (a)	-tshesane	-thumisehileng	-boleta	-colekileyo	-coliweyo	
fynstamp	pound (v)	-thuma	-tula	-touta	-cola	-gxoba	
gaan	go (v)	-ya	-ya	-ya	-hamba	-ya	
gaap	yawn (v)	-edimola	-edimola	-edimola	-zamla	-zamula	
gaap	yawn (n)	kedimolo	kedimolo	edimolo	ukuzamla	ukuzamula	
gaffel	pitchfork (n)	leselo	foroko	gafole	ifolokhwe yokulayisha	imfologo yotshani	
gal	gall (n)	nyooko	nyooko	gaumakwe	inyongo	inyongo	
gal	bile (n)	nyoko	nyooko	seumaka	inyongo	inyongo	
galblaas	gallbladder (n)	santlhoko	mokotlana wa nyooko	santlhoko	inyongo	inyongo	
galery	gallery (n)	sethala	galari	bosupaditshwantsho	iqonga	igalari	
galop	gallop (v)	-kgatha	-kgema	-potokela	-phala	-holobha	
gans	goose (n)	leganse	lekgansi	ganse	irhanisi	ihansi	
gaps	snatch (v)	-phamola	-phamola	-phamola	-xhwila	-hlwitha	
gas	gas (n)	gase	gase	gase	igesi	igesi	
gas	guest (n)	moeng	moeti	moeti	undwendwe	isimenywa	
gasheer	host (n)	monggae	moamohelabaeti	mong-gae	umndwendwelwa	umninindlu	
gasheer wees	host (v)	-tlametla	-ho amohela baeti	-nna mong-gae	-amkela iindwendwe	ukubungaza izivakashi	
gat	hole (n)	molete	mokoti	mosima	umngxuma	umgodi	
gat	pit (n)	petse	sekoti	lemena	umngxuma	umgodi	
gebabbel	chatter (n)	polabolo	lehehle	palabalo	intshwaqane	ubugevugevu	
gebed	prayer (n)	thapelo	thapelo	thapelo	umthandazo	umthandazo	
gebeur	happen (v)	-diragala	-etsahala	-direga	-enzeka	-vela	
gebeurtenis	event (n)	tiragalo	ketsahalo	tiragalo	isiganeko	isehlakalo	
gebod	commandment (n)	molao	molao	taolo	umyalelo	umyalo	
gebooie	banns (n)	ditaelo	dikgaboi	digaboi	isaziso somtshato	izimemezelo zomshadu	
geboorte	birth (n)	pelego	tswalo	pelegi	ukuzala	ukuzalwa	
geboorteplek	birthplace (n)	botswalelo	tulo ya tswalo	botsholong	isinqe	indawo yokuzalwa	

G	Afrikaans	English	N Sotho	Sesotho	Tswana	Xhosa	Zulu
	gebou	building (n)	moago	moaho	moago	isakhiwo	isakhiwo
	gebrek	lack (n)	tlhokego	tlhoko	go tlhoka	intswelo	ukuhlonga
	gebrek	disability (n)	tšhitego	sekodi	bokao	ubulelwe	ukujiyelwa
	gebreklik	disabled (a)	-segole	-holofetse	-segole	-limeleyo	-jiyelwe
	gebruik	use (v)	-diriša	-sebedisa	-dirisa	-sebenzisa	-sebenzisa
	gebruik	use (n)	tirišo	tshebediso	mosola	intsebenziso	umsebenzi
	gedagte	thought (n)	kgopolo	kgopolo	kakanyo	ingcinga	umcabanago
	gedeelte	portion (n)	kabelo	karolo	kaba	isabelo	inxenye
	gedig	poem (n)	sereto	thothokiso	leboko	isibongo	inkondlo
	gedoen	done (v)	-dirile	-entse	-dirile	-enzile	-enziwe
	gedra	conduct (v)	-itshwara	-itshwara	-itsaya	isimilo	-ziphatha kahle
	gedrag	behaviour (n)	boitshwaro	boitshwaro	boitshwaro	ukuziphatha	ukuziphatha
	geduld	patience (n)	bopelotelele	mamello	boitshoko	umonde	ukubekezela
	geduldig	patient (a)	-bopelotelele	-mamellang	-pelotelele	-nomonde	-bekile
	gedurig	always (adv)	ka mehla	ka mehla	tlhola	-soloko	njalo
	gedwee	meek (a)	-ikokobetšego	-ikokobeditseng	-pelonolo	-lulamile(yo)	-bekile
	gee	give (v)	-fa	-fa	-fa	-nika	-pha
	geel	yellow (n)	serolane	tshehla	bosetlha	ibala elimthubi	
	geelkoper	brass (n)	porase	borase	kgotlho	ibrasi	ithusi
	gees	spirit (n)	moya	moya	mowa	umphefumlo	umphefumulo
	gees	ghost (n)	moya	sethotsela	sedimo	isiporho	isipoki
	geesdrif	enthusiasm (n)	phišego	tjheseho	mafolofolo	umdla	ubunkamunkamu
	geesdriftig	enthusiastic (a)	-phišego	-tjhesehelang	-mafolofolo	-nomdla	-nkamunkamu
	geestelikes	clergy (n)	semoya	seruti	boruti	umfundisi	abefundisi
	gefluister	whisper (n)	go sebaseba	nyenyeletso	mosebo	usebezo	ukuhleba
	gehakkel	stammer (n)	kgamakgametšo	bohwelea	go kwakwaetsa	ithintitha	ukungingiza
	gehegtheid	attachment (n)	seswaragantšhi	momahano	kgokelelo	ukubophelela	ukunamathelana
	geheim	secret (n)	sephiri	lekunutu	khupamarama	ihlebo	imfihlo
	geheimhouding	secrecy (n)	sephiri	bokunutu	bosaitseweng	imfihlo	ukufihleka
	geheimsinnig	mysterious (a)	-khupamarama	-mohlolo	-bosaitseweng	-mangalisayo	-fihlakele
	gehoorsaam	obedient (a)	-kwago	-ikokobeditse	-kutlo	-thobekile(yo)	-lalelayo
	gehoorsaamheid	obedience (n)	go kwa	boikokobetso	kutlo	intobeko	ukulalela
	gehoorsaam wees	obey (v)	-kwa	-ikokobetsa	-utlwa	-thobela	-lalela
	gek	mad (a)	-gafago	-hlanya	-tsenwang	-phambene (yo)	-luhlanya
	gekerm	moan (n)	tsetlo	pelaelo	tuma	ukugcuma	imbubuzi
	gekleur	coloured (a)	-mmala	-mmala	-mmala	-nombala	-okumbala
	gekol	spotted (a)	-nago le dipatso	-rolo	-maronthotho	-ngqoqo	-mabalabala
	gekskeer	joke (v)	-swaswa	-swaswa	-tlae	-hlekisa	-tekula
	gekwalifiseerd	qualified (a)	-rutegilego	-rutehileng	-rutegileng	-fanelekileyo	-nelungelo
	gelag	laughter (n)	ditshego	setsheho	ditshego	intsini	insini
	geld	money (n)	tšhelete	tjhelete	madi	imali	imali
	geldig	valid (a)	-yago ka molao	-nnete	-nnete	-xabisekile(yo)	-lungile
	geleentheid	occasion (n)	lebaka	sebaka	motlha	ithuba	umkhosi
	geleentheid	opportunity (n)	sebaka	monyetla	tshiamelo	ithuba	ithuba
	geleidelik	gradually (adv)	ka bonya	-butle	monokela	-kancinci	ngokuya-ngokuya
	gelispel	lisp (n)	go ba le diteme	lehwelea	seleme	ukuteketa	ukufefeza
	gelofte	vow (n)	keno	kano	maikano	-funga	isifungo
	geloof	faith (n)	tumelo	tumelo	tumelo	ukholo	ithemba
	gelowige	believer (n)	modumedi	modumedi	modumedi	ikholwa	ikholwa
	geluk	happiness (n)	lethabo	nyakallo	boitumelo	uvuyo	injabulo
	geluk	luck (n)	mahlatse	lehloohonolo	lesego	ithamsanqa	inhlanhla
	gelukkig	fortunate (a)	-mahlatse	-lehloohonolo	-tshego	-nethamsanqa	-nenhlanhla
	gelukkig	happy (a)	-lethabo	-nyakalletseng	-itumelang	-vuyayo	-thokozile
	gelukkig	lucky (a)	-nago le mahlatse	-lehloohonolo	-tshego	-nethamsanqa	-nenhlanhla
	gelukwens	congratulate (v)	-lakaletša mahlogonolo	-lebohela	-akgola	-vuyisana	-halalisela
	gelyk	level (a)	-lekantšwego	-lekanang	-lekalekaneng	-lingana(yo)	-lingene
	gelyk	alike (a)	-swanago	-tshwana	-tshwanang	fanayo	-fanayo
	gelyk	equal (a)	-lekanago	-lekanang	-lekanang	-linganayo	-lingene
	gelyke	equal (n)	molekane	molekane	molekane	ulingano	olingene na-

Afrikaans	English	N Sotho	Sesotho	Tswana	Xhosa	Zulu	G
gelykenis	parable (n)	seswantšho	setshwantsho	setshwantsho	umzekeliso	umzekeliso	
gelykmatig	even (a)	-lekanetšego	-lekana	-lekalekanang	-linganayo	-lingene	
gelyk wees aan	equal (v)	-lekana	-lekana	-lekana	-linganisa	-lingana na-	
gemaal	ground (a)	-šitšwego	-sitsweng	-sidilweng	-siliweyo	-gayiweyo	
gemaklik	comfortable (a)	-boiketlo	-iketlileng	-manobonobo	-tofotofo	-nethezekile	
gemeen	mean (a)	-be	-be	-maswe	-nentsingiselo	-ncishanayo	
gemeen	nasty (a)	-be	-ditshila	-bosula	-bi	-bi	
gemeente	congregation (n)	phuthego	phutheho	phuthego	ibandla	ibandla	
gemiddeld	average (a)	-palogare	-mahareng	palogare	-myinga	-okulingene	
gemors	mess (n)	bošaedi	bohlaswa	makgaphila	ubumdaka	isibhixi	
gemurmel	murmur (n)	pobolo	tumaelo	go ngunanguna	ukudumzela	-hlokoma	
genade	mercy (n)	kgaugelo	mohau	bopelotlhomogi	inceba	isihawu	
genadig	merciful (a)	-kgaugelo	-mohau	-pelotlhomogi	-nenceba	-nesihawu	
genees	heal (v)	-alafa	-phekola	-fodisa	-phila	-elapha	
genesing	cure (n)	kalafo	phodiso	kalafo	isiphilisi	ukuphilisa	
geniet	savour (v)	-ipshina	-natefelwa	-ja monate	-nambitha	-zwa	
geniet	enjoy (v)	-ipshina ka	-natefelwa	-ja monate	-onwabela	-jabulela	
genoeg	enough (a)	-lekanego	-lekaneng	-lekanang	-aneleyo	-anele	
geraamte	skeleton (n)	marapo a mmele	mohlolohlolo	letlhotlholo	uphahla	ugobhozi	
geraas	noise (n)	lešata	lerata	leratla	ingxolo	umsindo	
gereed	ready (a)	-itokišeditšego	-lokileng	-baakantsweng	-lunga	-lungile	
geregtigheid	justice (n)	toka	toka	tolamo	ubulungisa	ubulungisa	
gerf	sheaf (n)	ngata	ngata	ngata	isithungu	isithungu	
gerieflik	convenient (a)	-swanelago	-tshwanelang	-siametseng	-lungeleyo	-vumekayo	
gerug	rumour (n)	mabarebare	bobare	mokgwasa	umingimingi	amahemuhemu	
gesag	authority (n)	maatla	matla	bolaodi	igunya	igunya	
gesang	hymn (n)	sefela	sefela	sefala	iculo	ihubo	
gesel	lash (v)	-otla	-hlasela ka mantswe	-šapa	-betha	-thwibila	
gesels	chat (v)	-boledišana	-qoqa	-tlotla	ncokola	-xoxa	
geset	stout (a)	-nonnego	-tenya	-kima	-omeleleyo	-khuluphele	
gesig	face (n)	sefahlego	sefahleho	sefatlhego	ubuso	ubuso	
gesigsvermoë	vision (n)	pono	pono	pono	umbono	ukubona	
geskat	approximate (a)	e ka bago	-akanyang	-ka ne	-kangaka	-linganiselwe	
geskenk	present (n)	mpho	mpho	mpho	isipho	isipho	
geskiedenis	history (n)	histori	nalane	ditiragalo	imbali	umlando	
geskik	appropriate (a)	-lebanego	-lokelang	-siameng	-lungileyo	-okufanele	
geskik	eligible (a)	-go kgethega	-lokelang	-siameng	-nokunyulwa	-fanelekile	
geslag	gender (n)	bong	bong	bong	isini	ubulili	
geslagsorgane	genitals (n)	dithobong	marete	mapele	umphantsi	izitho zobulili	
gesond	healthy (a)	-phelago gabotse	-phetseng hantle	-itekanelang	-philile	-philile	
gesondheid	health (n)	pholo	bophelo bo botle	boitekanelo	impilo	impilo	
gespanne	tense (a)	-ngangegilego	-sataletseng	-gagametseng	-xhalile (yo)	-shaqekile	
gesprek	conversation (n)	poledišano	moqoqo	kgang	incoko	inkulumo	
gestaar	stare (n)	tebelelo	tjamelo	go lebelela	undwanya	ukugqoloza	
gestotter	stutter (n)	kgamakgametšo	bohwelea	go kwakwaetsa	ubuthintitha	ukungingiza	
getrou	faithful (a)	-botegago	-tshepahalang	-ikanyegang	-thobileyo	-thembekile	
getrouheid	fidelity (n)	potego	botshepehi	boikanyo	intembeko	ukwethembeka	
getuie	witness (n)	paki	paki	mosupi	ingqina	ufakazi	
getuienis	testimony (n)	bohlatse	bopaki	bosupi	ubungqina	ubufakazi	
getuienis	evidence (n)	bohlatse	bopaki	bopaki	ubungqina	ubufakazi	
getuig	testify (v)	-hlatsela	-paka	-paka	-ngqina	-fakaza	
getuigskrif	reference (n)	lengwalo la bohlatse	lengolo la bopaki	tshupetso	ukukhangela	ireferense	
gety	tide (n)	phulawatle	leqhubu	nako	umsinga	ibuya	
geur	fragrance (n)	monko	monko o monate	lenko	ivumba	amakha	
geur	flavour (n)	mohlodi	tatso	moutlwano	isinongo	isinandisi	
geur	flavour (v)	-fa mohlodi	-noka	-tswaisa	-nonga	-nandisa	
geursel	flavouring (n)	mohlodi	senoko	motswaiso	unongo	ukunandisa	
geut	gutter (n)	kathara	foro	moedi	igatha	igatha	
gevaar	peril (n)	kotsi	kotsi	bobe	ingozi	ingozi	
gevaar	danger (n)	kotsi	kotsi	kotsi	ingozi	ingozi	

G Afrikaans	English	N Sotho	Sesotho	Tswana	Xhosa	Zulu
gevaarlik	dangerous (a)	-kotsi	-kotsi	-kotsi	-nengozi	-nengozi
gevangene	prisoner (n)	mogolegwa	motshwaruwa	mogolegwa	umbanjwa	isiboshwa
gevangene	convict (n)	mogolegwa	motshwaruwa	seboswa	ibanjwa	isiboshwa
gevangenis	prison (n)	kgolego	tjhankane	kgolegelo	itolongo itrongo	ijele
gevarieerd	varied (a)	-fapafapanago	-fapaneng	-mofutafuta	-ahluka-hlukene(yo)	-nhlobonhlobo
geveg	fight (n)	ntwa	ntwa	ntwa	umlo	ukulwa
geveg	battle (n)	ntwa	ntwa	ntwa	umlo	impi
gevoel	emotion (n)	khuduego	phudueho	maikutlo	uluvo	umzwelo
gevoelig	sensitive (a)	-kgwathegago maikutlo	-utlwang	-sisimogang	-vakalela(yo)	-nozwela
gevolg	sequel (n)	pheletšo	se hlahlamang	tatelo	isiqhamo	impumelelo
gevolg	consequence (n)	pheletšo	ditholwana	pheletso	isiphumo	umphumela
gevolgtrekking	conclusion (n)	phetho	qeto	phetso	umqukumbelo	isiphetho
gewas	tumour (n)	sešo	tlhahala	tlhagala	ithumba	ithumba
geweer	rifle (n)	sethunya	sethunya	tlhobolo	umbaxa	isibhamu
geweer	gun (n)	sethunya	sethunya	tlhobolo	umpu	isibhamu
geweld	violence (n)	bošoro	pefo	boganka	ububhovubhovu	isidlakadlaka
gewete	conscience (n)	letswalo	letswalo	segakolodi	isazela	unembeza
gewig	weight (n)	boima	boima	boima	ubunzima	isisindo
gewigtig	grave (a)	-bohlokwa	-boima	-mena phatla	-qingqiweyo	-nzima
gewild	popular (a)	-tumilego	-tumileng	-rategang	-aziwayo	-akubantu
gewoon	ordinary (a)	-ka mehla	-ka mehla	-itsegeng	qhelekile(yo)	-vamile
gewoon	plain (a)	-ka mehla	-tlwaelehileng	-komota	-cacile(yo)	-ngafekethisiwe
gewoon	common (a)	-ka mehla	-tlwaelehileng	-gale	qhelekileyo	-vamile
gewoonlik	usually (adv)	ka mehla	-atisa	tlhola	ngoxuqhelekileyo	ngokuvamileyo
gewoonte	habit (n)	tlwaelo	tlwaelo	mokgwa	isiqhelo	injwayelo
gewrig	joint (n)	noko	lenonyetso	lelokololo	umdibano	inhlangano yamathambo
ghries	grease (n)	kirisi	kerisi	kerise	igrisi	igrisi
gids	guide (n)	mohlahli	motataisi	mosupatsela	isikhokelo	igayidi
gif	poison (n)	mpholo	tjhefo	more	ityhefu	isihlungu
giggel	giggle (v)	-sega	-keketeha	-tshegatshega	-gigitheka	-gigitheka
gil	scream (n)	legoo	mohoo	kgoo	isikhalo	ukuklabalasa
gil	scream (v)	-goa	-hoa	-kua	-khala	-klabalasa
gimnastiek	gymnastics (n)	dithobollo	ho tswedipanya mmele	jiminastiki	imithambo	imigilingwane yokuzivivinya
gis	ferment (v)	-bela	-lomosa	-bela	-bilisa	-bila
gis	yeast (n)	mahlabego	tomoso	sebidiso	igwele	imvubelo
gister	yesterday (n)	maabane	maobane	maabane	izolo	izolo
glad	smooth (a)	-boreledi	-boreledi	-borethe	-gucile (yo)	-bushelezi
glas	glass (n)	galase	kgalase	galase	iglasi	ingilazi
glibberig	slippery (a)	-boreledi	-thellang	-relelang	-mtyibilizi	-bushelelezi
glimlag	smile (n)	monywanyo	lebonyo	mongebo	uncumo	ukumamatheka
glimlag	smile (v)	-nywanywa	-bonya	-ngeba	-ncuma	-mamatheka
glo	believe (v)	-dumela	-dumela	-dumela	-kholelwa	-kholwa
gloei	glow (v)	-pepenya	-laima	-galalela	-qacamba	-nkemuzela
glorie	glory (n)	letago	kgalalelo	kgalalelo	uzuko	inkazimulo
gly	slide (v)	-thelela	-thella	-relela	-tyibilika	-shelela
God	God (n)	Modimo	Modimo	Modimo	uThixo	uNkulunkulu
god	god (n)	modimo	modimo	ledimo	isithixo	isithixo
godsdiens	religion (n)	bodumedi	tumelo	bodumedi	inkolo	inkolo
godsdienstig	religious (a)	-bodumedi	-dumelang	-sedumedi	-kholiwe(yo)	-kholiwe
goed	well (a)	gabotse	hantle	pila	kakuhle	kahle
goed	good (a)	-botse	-lokile	-molemo	-lungile	-hle
goedere	goods (n)	diphahlo	diphahlo	dithoto	iimpahla	izimpahla
goedhartig	kind (a)	-botho	-mosa	-pelonomi	-nobubele	-nomusa
goedheid	kindness (n)	botho	mosa	bopelonomi	ububele	umusa
goedkeur	approve (v)	-dumelela	-dumela	-rebola	-vumelana	-vumela
goedkeuring	approval (n)	tumelelo	tumello	thebolo	imvumelwano	imvume
goedkoop	cheap (a)	-tšhipilego	-sesolo	sesolo	-dla kancinci	-shibhile

Afrikaans	English	N Sotho	Sesotho	Tswana	Xhosa	Zulu
goedmaak	redeem (v)	-phološa	-lopolla	-rekolola	-sindisa	-hlenga
gogga	bug (n)	khunkhwane	kokwanyana	khukhwane	irhorho	isilwanyakazane
gom	glue (v)	-gomaretša	-ho tlotsa ka boka	-mametlelela	-ncamathelisa	isinamathelisi
gom	glue (n)	segomaretši	boka	sekgomaretsi	isincamathelisi	-namathelisa
gooi	throw (v)	-betša	-akgela	-kolopa	-gibisela	-phonsa
gordel	belt (n)	lepanta	lebanta	lebanta	ibhanti	ibhande
gordyn	curtain (n)	garateine	kgaretene	sesiro	ikhetini	ikhethini
gorrel	gargle (v)	-kgakgametša	-kgakgatsa	-gagasetsa	-rharhaza	-hahaza
gorrelpyp	windpipe (n)	mogolo	qoqotho	kgokgotsho	umqala	uqhoqhoqho
gou	quickly (adv)	ka pela	ka pele	ka bonako	ngokukhawuleza	ngokushesha
gou	quick (a)	-ka pela	ka pele	-bofefo	-khawuleza(yo)	-sheshayo
goud	gold (n)	gauta	kgauta	gouta	igolide	igolide
graad	degree (n)	kgato	degri	dekrii	iqondo	isiqu
graaf	spade (n)	garafo	garafu	garawe	umhlakulo	ihalavu
graan	grain (n)	mabele	thollo	seako	ukhozo	uhlamvu
graanskuur	granary (n)	sešego	sekiri sa dithollo	sefala	udladla	inqolobane
graf	tomb (n)	lebitla	lebitla	lebitla	ingcwaba	ithuna
graf	grave (n)	lebitla	lebitla	phupu	ingcwaba	ithuna
grafsteen	tombstone (n)	letlapa la lebitla	lejwe la sehopotso	letlapa la phupu	ilitye	itshe lethuna
grammatika	grammar (n)	popopolelo	thuto ya puo	gerama	igrama	igrama
granadilla	granadilla (n)	koronatela	keranatela	granadilla	igranadila	uginindela
grap	joke (n)	motlae	motlae	motlae	isiqhulo	ihlaya
gras	grass (n)	bjang	jwang	tlhaga	ingca	utshani
grasperk	lawn (n)	lapanabjang	mohlwa	bojang	ibala lengca	ungwengwe
grassnyer	lawnmower (n)	sesegabjang	sekutamohlwa	sesegabojang	umatshini wokucheba ingca	umshini wokusika utshani
grens	border (n)	mollwane	moedi	molelwane	umda	umncele
grens	border (v)	-bea mellwane	-sika	-thetha	-enza umda	-phethela
grensloos	boundless (a)	-sa felego	-saballetse	-sakhutleng	-ngenabhawundri	-ngenamkhawulo
grenslyn	boundary (n)	mollwane	moedi	molelwane	ibhawundri	umncele
gretig	eager (a)	-dumago	-mafolofolo	-gakalelang	-ngokungxamela	-nkamunkamu
grief	grievance (n)	pelaelo	tletlebo	ngongorego	isikhalo	isikhalo
griep	influenza (n)	fulu	mokakallane	letshoroma	umkhuhlane	imfuluyenza
groef	groove (n)	moseto	sekgetshe	mosetlho	umgca okroliweyo	isisele
groei	grow (v)	-mela	-mela	-gola	-khula	-mila
groen	green (n)	-tala	botala	tala	uhlaza	-luhlaza
groente	vegetable (n)	morogo	meroho	morogo	imifuno	uhlaza
groep	group (n)	sehlopha	sehlopha	lesomo	iqela	isiqumbi
groep	band (n)	sehlopha	sehlopha	banta	iqela	ibutho
groet	greet (v)	-dumediša	-dumedisa	-dumedisa	-bulisa	-bingelela
grond	soil (n)	mmu	mobu	mmu	umhlaba	umhlabathi
grond	ground (n)	mobu	mobu	mmu	umhlaba	umhlabathi
grondboontjie	peanut (n)	tokomane	letokomane	letonkomane	indongomane	intongomane
grondwet	constitution (n)	molaotheo	molao wa motheo	molaotheo	umgaqo-siseko	ukumisa
groot	large (a)	-golo	-holo	-tona	-khulu	-khulu
groot	big (a)	-golo	-holo	-tona	-khulu	-khulu
grootmaak	rear (v)	-godiša	-otla	-rua	-khulisa	-khulisa
grootpraat	brag (v)	-ikgodiša	-ikgantsha	-thetha	-qhayisa	-gabaza
grootte	size (n)	bogolo	boholo	saese	isayizi	ubukhulu
grot	cave (n)	legaga	lehaha	legaga	umqolomba	umgede
gruis	gravel (n)	lekgwara	kerabole	kgwarapana	igrabile	ugedla
gryns	grin (v)	-šinyalala	-tsitlama	-tsena	-sineka	-sineka
grynslag	smirk (v)	-šunyalala	-tsillama	-senama	-sineka	-sineka
grynslag	grin (n)	tšhinyalalo	tsitlamo	motseno	intsinekana	ukusineka
gryp	seize (v)	-swara	-tshwara	-tshwara	-bamba	-bamba
gryp	grasp (v)	-swara	-tshwara	-kakara	-bamba	-bamba
grys	grey (n)	-putswa	boputswa	-setlha	hobe	-mpunga
guerrilla	guerrilla (n)	motšhošetši	raqhwe	belerutwane	igorila	igorila
gulsig	greedy (a)	-megabaru	-meharo	-megagaru	-bawayo	-phangayo

G

Afrikaans	English	N Sotho	Sesotho	Tswana	Xhosa	Zulu
guns	favour (n)	thušo	molemo	molemo	uncedo	umusa
gunsteling	favourite (a)	-ratwago go feta	moratuwa	-mmamoratwa	-enzelelayo	-khethekayo
haai	shark (n)	šaka	shake	šaka	ukrebe	imfingo
haak	hook (v)	-haka	-haka	-kgogetsa	-gwegwa	-hhuka
haak	hook (n)	kobi	huku	sekgwage	igwegwe	ihhuku
haakspeld	safety pin (n)	sepalete	sepelete	kgokelo	isipeliti	isipelete
haal	fetch (v)	-lata	-lata	-tsaya	-phuthuma	-landa
haan	cock (n)	mogogonope	mokoko	mokoko	umqhagi	iqhude
haar	her (pron)	-mo-	yena	ene	yena	yena
haard	hearth (n)	sebešo	leifo	leiso	iziko	iziko
haarkapper	hairdresser (n)	mokoti wa moriri	mokuti	mopomi	umchebi	umcwali
haarsnyer	barber (n)	mmeodi	mokuti	mmeodi	umchebi	umphuci
haarvat	capillary (n)	kapilari	methatswana	tshika	umthanjana	umthanjana
haas	rush (v)	-phakiša	-potlaka	-itlhaganela	-ngxama	-sheshisa
haas	haste (n)	lebelo	mojaho	boitlhaganelo	ukungxama	ukusheshisa
haastig	hasty (a)	-lebelo	-jahileng	-boitlhaganelo	-ngxamileyo	-sheshisa
haat	hate (v)	-hloya	-hloya	-tlhoa	-thiya	-zonda
haat	hatred (n)	lehloyo	lehloyo	letlhoo	intiyo	inzondo
haatlik	hateful (a)	-hloiwago	-hloyang	-ilwang	-thiyileyo	-zondekayo
hael	hail (n)	sefako	sefako	sefako	isichotho	isiqhotho
hak	heel (n)	serethe	serethe	serethe	isithende	isithende
hakies	brackets (n)	mašakana	masakana	masakana	isibiyeli	izibiyelo
hakkel	stammer (v)	-kgamakgametša	-hwelea	-kwakwaetsa	-thintitha	-ngingiza
halssnoer	necklace (n)	pheta	sefaha	ditalama	intsimbi yomqala	umgaxo
halveer'	halve (v)	-ripa ka bogare	-fokotsa ka lehare	-halofa	-canda kubini	-caza kabili
ham	ham (n)	nama ya serope sa kolobe	hemo	nama ya kolobe	isihlunu sehagu	uhemu
hamburger	hamburger (n)	hampeka	hambekara	hambeka	ihambhega	ihemubhega
hamer	hammer (n)	hamola	noto	hamore	ihamile	isando
hamer	hammer (v)	-kokotela	-mula	-touta	-bethelela	-bethela
hand	hand (n)	seatla	letsoho	seatla	isancla	isandla
handdoek	towel (n)	toulo	thaole	toulo	itawuli	ithawula
handel	trade (n)	kgwebo	kgwebo	kgwebo	urhwebo	ukuhweba
handel	commerce (n)	kgwebo	kgwebo	papatso	uqoqosho	uhwebo
handel dryf	trade (v)	-gweba	-hweba	-rekisa	-rhweba	-hweba
handelsmerk	brand (n)	tshwaokgwebo	letshwao la kgwebo	letshwaokgwebo	uphawu	uphawu
handewerk	handwork (n)	modiro wa diatla	mosebetsi wa matsoho	tiro ya diatla	umsebenzi wezandla	izinto ezenziwe ngezandla
handhaaf	maintain (v)	-tiiša	-boloka	-tshegetsa	-xhasa	-ondla
handskoen	glove (n)	tlelafo	hansekunu	hanasekhune	iglavu	igilavu
handskrif	handwriting (n)	mongwalo	mongolo	mokwalo	ukubhala	isandla
handtekening	signature (n)	tshaeno	tshaeno	tshaeno	umtyikityo	ukusayina
handvatsel	handle (n)	mokgoko	mohwele	mofinyana	isiphatho	isibambo
hang	hang (v)	-fega	-fanyeha	-kalela	-xhoma	-lengisa
hangslot	padlock (n)	sekgonyo	seloto	lloko	iqhaga	ingide
hanteer	handle (v)	-swara	-tshwara	-tshwara ka matsogo	-phatha	-phatha
hap	bite (n)	kgemo	ho loma	molomo	umthamo	ukuluma
hard	hard (a)	-thata	-thata	-thata	-lukhuni	-lukhuni
hard	loud (a)	-kwagalago	-hodimo	-thata	-ngxola (yo)	-nomsindo
hardkoppig	obstinate (a)	-ngangelago	-manganga	-kgopo	-ngevayo	-nenkani
hardloop	run (v)	-kitima	-matha	-taboga	-baleka	-gijima
hardop	aloud (adv)	-boelela godimo	-tlerola	godimo	-ngokukhwaza	nomsindo
hare	hair (n)	moriri	boya	moriri	iinwele	izinwele
hare	hers (pron)	-gagwe	-hae	-gagwe	-khe	okwakhe
harig	hairy (a)	-meriri ye mentšimmeleng	-boya	-mariri	-noboya	-noboya
hark	rake (n)	hareka	haraka	haraka	iharika	ihhala
hark	rake (v)	-hareka	-haraka	-haraka	-harika	-hhala
harmonie	harmony (n)	kwanadumo	kutlwano	kutlwano	imvisiswano	ukuzwana

Afrikaans	English	N Sotho	Sesotho	Tswana	Xhosa	Zulu	H
harmonika	harmonica (n)	seletšo sa hamonika	haremonika	foleiki	ifleyiti	uhlobo logubhu	
harp	harp (n)	harepa	harepa	harapa	ugwali	uhabhu	
hart	heart (n)	pelo	pelo	pelo	intliziyo	inhliziyo	
hartklop	heartbeat (n)	morethetho wa pelo	ho uba ha pelo	mokibo wa pelo	ukungongoza	ukushaya kwenhliziyo	
hawe	harbour (n)	boemakepe	kou	boemakepe	izibuko	itheku	
hawer	oats (n)	outse	habore	habore	iowutsi	ifoliji	
hê	have (v)	-na	-ba	-nna le	-ba na-	(-ba-) na-	
heel	very (a)	kudu	-hle	-thata	-khulu	kakhulu	
heel	whole (a)	-ohle	-felletseng	-tlhe	yonke	-philile	
heel klein	minute (a)	-nyennyane	-nyenyane hahole	-nnyennye	-ncinane	-ncane	
heelmaak	mend (v)	-lokišo	-lokisa	-baakanya	-ngciba	-lungisa	
heerlik	delicious (a)	-bose	-hlabosang	-monate	-mnandi	-mnandi	
heers	reign (v)	-buša	-busa	-busa	-lawula	-busa	
hees	hoarse (a)	-makgwakgwa	-makgerehlwa	-magweregwere	-rhabaxa	-hoshozile	
heiden	heathen (n)	moheitene	mohetene	moheitene	ubuhedeni	umhedeni	
heiden	pagan (n)	moheitene	mohedene	moheitene	umhedeni	umhedeni	
heidens	pagan (a)	-boheitene	-bohedene	-moheitene	-obuhedeni	-obuhedeni	
heilig	sacred (a)	-kgethwa	-halalelang	-boitshepo	-ngcwele	-ngcwele	
heilig	holy (a)	-kgethwa	-halalelang	-boitshepo	-ngcwele	-ngcwele	
heilige	saint (n)	mokgethwa	mohalaledi	moitshepi	ingcwele	ongcwele	
heilsaam	wholesome (a)	-lokilego	-molemo	-bokompa	-philile(yo)	-philisayo	
heining	hedge (n)	legora	seotlwana	legora	intendelezo	uthango	
hek	gate (n)	sefero	heke	kgoro	isango	isango	
hel	hell (n)	hele	dihele	molete wa molelo	isihogo	kwalasha	
held	hero (n)	senatla	mohale	mogaka	iqhawe	iqhawe	
helder	bright (a)	-kganyago	-hlakile	-kganyang	-qaqambileyo	-khazimulayo	
helder	clear (a)	-bonagalago	-hlakile	-bonalang	-mhlophe	-chachile	
helderheid	brilliance (n)	kganya	ho hlaka	botlhaletlhale	ukuqaqamba	ubucwazicwazi	
helderrooi	scarlet (n)	bohubedu bja madi	mmala o mofubedu	bohibiduhibidu	ububomvu	-bomvu klebhu	
hele	entire (a)	ka moka	-hle	-otlhe	-nke	-phelayo	
helfte	half (n)	seripagare	halofo	sephatlo	isiqingatha	uhhafu	
helling	slope (n)	tshekamo	motheo	mothulama	ithambeka	iqele	
help	help (v)	-thuša	-thusa	-thusa	-nceda	-siza	
help	aid (v)	-thuša	-thusa	-thusa	-nceda	-siza	
helper	assistant (n)	mothuši	mothusi	letsogo	umncedi	umsizi	
hemel	heaven (n)	legodimo	lehodimo	legodimo	izulu	izulu	
hemp	shirt (n)	hempe	hempe	hempe	ihempe	ihembe	
hen	hen (n)	kgogotshadi	sethole	kgogo	isikhukukazi	isikhukhukazi	
herdenking	memorial (a)	-segopotšo	sehopotso	-kgakologelo	-nesikhumbuzo	isikhumbuzo	
Here	Lord (n)	Modimo	Morena	Morena	iNkosi	iNkosi	
herfs	autumn (n)	seregana	hwetla	letlhafula	ukwindla	ukwindla	
herhaal	repeat (v)	-boeletša	-pheta	-boelela	-phinda	-phinda	
herinner	remind (v)	-gopotša	-hopotsa	-gopotsa	-khumbuza	-khumbuza	
herinnering	reminder (n)	kgopotšo	kgopotso	kgakololo	isikhumbuzo	isikhumbuzo	
herken	recognise (v)	-lemoga	-tseba	-lemoga	-nakana	-bona	
herkenning	recognition (n)	temogo	ho tseba	temogo	unakano	ukubona	
herstel	recover (v)	-tielela	-hlaphohelwa	-fola	-fumana	-sinda	
herstel	recovery (n)	tielelo	tlhaphohelo	pholo	ukufumana	ukusinda	
hervorming	reform (n)	mpshafatšo	tshokoloho	phetolo	uhlaziyo	ukuguquka	
heuning	honey (n)	tswina	mahe a dinotshi	tswine ya dinotshe	ubusi	uju	
heup	hip (n)	letheka	noka	noka	ihleza	inqulu	
heuwel	hill (n)	mmoto	leralla	lekgaba	induli	igquma	
hiëna	hyena (n)	phiri	lefiritshwane	phiri-e-thamaga	ixhwili	impisi	
hier	here (adv)	mo	mona	fa	apha	lapha	
higiëne	hygiene (n)	maphelo	paballo ya mmele	boitekanelo	impilo	inhlanzeko	
hik	hiccough (n)	sethekhu	thaabe	kgodisa	ukukhutywa	intwabi	
hinder	hinder (v)	-thibela	-kgathatsa	-fera	-khathaza	-thiya	
hinderlaag	ambush (n)	bolalelo	tallo	talelo	ukulalela	umlalelo	
hindernis	hindrance (n)	sekgopi	-tshitiso	kgoreletso	inkathazo	isithiyo	
hindernis	obstacle (n)	lepheko	tshito	kgoreletso	umqobo	isivimbelo	

	Afrikaans	English	N Sotho	Sesotho	Tswana	Xhosa	Zulu
	hings	stallion (n)	pere ya tona	poho ya pere	pheke	inkunzi yehashe	inkunzi yehhashi
	hingsel	hinge (n)	mokgoko	sekanire	sekaniri	ihenqisi	ihinji
	histerie	hysterics (n)	mafofonyane	lehabea	mafofonyane	isiphoso	umhayizo
	hitte	heat (n)	phišo	motjheso	mogote	ubushushu	ukushisa
	hoe	how (adv)	bjang	jwang	jang	njani	kanjani
	hoed	hat (n)	kefa	katiba	futshe	umnqwazi	isigqoko
	hoe dan ook	anyhow (adv)	bjang le bjang	jwang kapa jwang	le gale	-nanjani	noma kunjani
	hoef	hoof (n)	tlhako	tlhako	tlhako	uphuphu	isondo
	hoefyster	horseshoe (n)	seeta sa pere	tshepe ya pere	tlhako ya pitse	isiporo	isipolo sehhashi
	hoek	angle (n)	khutlo	sekgutlo	sekhutlo	igophe	i-engele
	hoek	corner (n)	sekhutlo	sekgutlo	khona	umgwejelo	ikhona
	hoender	chicken (n)	kgogo	tsuonyana	koko	inkuku	inkukhu
	hoender	fowl (n)	kgogo	kgoho	kgogo	inkuku	inkukhu
	hoenderhaan	rooster (n)	mogogonope	mokoko	mokoko	umqhagi	iqhude
	hoër	higher (a)	-godingwana	-phahameng ho feta	godimodimo	-phakamile(yo)	-phakeme kakhudlwana
	hoer	whore (n)	sefebe	sefebe	sefefe	ihenyukazi	isifebe
	hoereer	fornicate (v)	-otswa	-hlola	-gokafala	-feba	-feba
	hoes	cough (n)	kgohlolo	mokgohlane	kgotlholo	ukhohlokhohlo	ukukhwehlela
	hoes	cough (v)	-gohlola	-hohlola	-gotlhola	-khohlela	-khwehlela
	hoeveelheid	quantity (n)	bokaakang	bokaakang	selekano	ubungakanani	ubungako
	hoëveld	highveld (n)	nagadimo	naha e phahameng	nagadimo	ummandla omathafa	inkangala
	hoewel	though (conj)	le ge	le ha	le mororo	naxa	nokho
	hof	court (n)	kgoro	lekgotla	kgotla	inkundla	inkantolo
	hoflik	polite (a)	-botho	-ikokobeditseng	-bonolo	-mbeko	-thobekile
	hol	hollow (a)	-gorutšwego	-mohohoma	-lehuti	-ze	-ligobongo
	hom	him (pron)	-mo-	yena	ene	yena	yena
	homoseksueel	homosexual (n)		-rata wa bong ba hao		italasi	isitabane
	hond	dog (n)	mpša	ntja	ntšwa	inja	inja
	hondehok	kennel (n)	serobe sa mpša	ntlwana ya ntja	tshireletso ya dintšwa	indlu yenja	indlu yenja
	honderd	hundred (n)	lekgolo	lekgolo	lekgolo	ikhulu	ikhulu
	honderdpoot	centipede (n)	legokolodi	lefokolodi	sebokolodi	isongololo	inkume
	honderdtal	century (sport) (n)	lekgolo	dilemokgolo	lekgolo	inkulungwane	ikhulu
	honger	hungry (a)	-swerwego ke tlala	-lapileng	-tshwerweng ke tlala	-lambile(yo)	-lambile
	honger	hunger (n)	tlala	tlala	tlala	indlala	ukulamba
	honger ly	starve (v)	-bolawa ke tlala	-lapa	-bolawa ke tlala	-lamba	-lamba
	hongersnood	famine (n)	tlala	tlala	lesekere	indlala	indlala
	hoof	capital (a)	-golo	-holo	-golo	ikomkhulu	-khulu
	hoof	chief (a)	-golo	-hlooho	bokgosi	-yintloko	-khulu
	hoof	principal (n)	hlogo	hlooho	mogokgo	inqununu	unhloko
	hoofmaal	dinner (n)	letena	tinare	tinara	idinala	idina
	hoofmaaltyd eet	dine (v)	-ja letena	-ja	-ja	-dinala	-dla idina
	hoofman	chief (n)	kgoši	ramohlongwana	kgosi	inkosi	induna
	hoofpyn	headache (n)	go rengwa ke hlogo	hlooho e opang	go opa ga tlhogo	intloko ebuhlungu	ukuphathwa ikhanda
	hoofstuk	chapter (n)	kgaolo	kgaolo	kgaolo	isahluko	isahluko
	hoog	high (a)	-godimo	-phahameng	godimo	-phakamile(yo)	-phakeme
	hooggeregshof	supreme court (n)	kgotlakgolo	lekgotla le phahameng	kgotla ya bogaolakgang	inkundla ephakamileyo	inkantolo yamaJaji
	hoog hou	uphold (v)	-boloka	-phahamisa	-tshegetsa	-xhasa	-phakamisa
	hoogmoedig	haughty (a)	-ikgogomošago	-ikgohomosang	-ikgodisang	-ziphakamisileyo	-thwele ikhanda
	hoogste	paramount (a)	-gologolo	-holo	-godimodimo	-ongamele(yo)	-khulu kunakho konke
	hoogte	height (n)	bogodimo	bophahamo	bogodimo	ukuphakama	ukuphakama
	hoon	flout (v)	-kwera	-phaphamala	-nyatsa	-chaza	-hleka uzulu
	hoop	heap (n)	mokgobo	qubu	mokgobe	imfumba	inqwaba
	hoop	hope (n)	kholofelo	tshepo	tsholofelo	ithemba	ithemba
	hoop	hope (v)	-holofela	-tshepa	-solofela	-themba	-ethemba
	hoor	hear (v)	-kwa	-utlwa	-utlwa	-va	-zwa
	hoorbaar	audible (a)	-kwagala	-utlwahala	-utlwalang	-vakalayo	-zwakalayo
	hoorsê	hearsay (n)	mabarebare	bobare	magatwe	undiva	inzwabethi
	hop	hop (v)	-taboga	-tlolatlola	-kopakopa	-tsiba	-kheleza
	horing	horn (n)	lenaka	lenaka	lenaka	uphondo	uphondo

Afrikaans	English	N Sotho	Sesotho	Tswana	Xhosa	Zulu	I
horison	horizon (n)	bogomapono	pheletsong ya lefatshe	khutlopono	ulundi	impelamehlo	
horisontaal	horizontal (a)	-rapamego	-tshekalletseng	-rapameng	-mtyaba	-thwishikile	
horlosie	clock (n)	sešupanako	tleloko	sesupanako	ixesha	iklogo	
horlosie	watch (n)	sešupanako	watjhe	sesupanako	ixesha	iwashi	
hospitaal	hospital (n)	sepetlele	sepetlele	bookelo	isibhedlele	isibhedlela	
hotel	hotel (n)	hotele	hotele	hotele	ihotele	ihhotela	
hou	hold (v)	-swara	-tshwara	-tshwara	-bamba	-bamba	
hou	keep (v)	-swara	-boloka	-boloka	-gcina	-gcina	
hou	blow (n)	titio	kotlo	petso	isithonga	isigalelo	
houding	attitude (n)	boitshwaro	moya	boitshwaro	uluvo	isimo	
houer	container (n)	setšhelo	pitso	setshelo	isikhongozelo	idlelo	
hout	wood (n)	kota	lehong	legong	iinkuni	ukhuni	
hou van	like (v)	-rata	-rata	-rata	-kholwa	-thanda	
huidige	current (a)	-elehono	-jwale	-segompieno	-eqhubekayo	-amanje	
huil	weep (v)	-lla	-lla	-lela	-lila	-khala	
huil	cry (v)	-lla	-lla	-lla	-khala	-khala	
huis	house (n)	ngwako	ntlo	ntlo	indlu	indlu	
huishoudelik	domestic (a)	-legae	-lehae	-legae	-asekhaya	-asendlini	
huishouding	household (n)	lapa	lelapa	motse	indlu	abomuzi bonke	
huisves	house (v)	-fa marobalo	-amohela tlung	-nnisa	-qulatha	-hlalisa	
huisves	accommodate (v)	-fa marobalo	-amohela	-tshola	-hlalisa	-nika indawo	
huisvesting	accommodation (n)	marobalo	bodulo	bonno	indawo yokuhlala	indawo yokuhlala nokulala	
huiswerk	homework (n)	modiro wa gae	mosebetsi wa lapeng	tirolegae	umsebenzi wasekhaya	umsebenzi wasekhaya	
hulle	their (pron)	-bona	-bona	bona	-bo	bona	
hulle	them (pron)	-ba-	bona	bona	bona	bona	
hulle	they (pron)	bona	bona	bona	ba-	bona	
hulle s'n	theirs (pron)	-bona	-bona	-bona	-bo	okwabo	
hulp	help (n)	thušo	thuso	thusego	unceda	usizo	
hulp	aid (n)	thušo	thuso	thusego	uncedo	usizo	
hulpeloos	helpless (a)	-hlokago	-hlokang thuso	-naya pelo	-ngenaluncedo	-thithibele	
humeur	temper (n)	maikutlo	-boitshwaro	bobetwapelo	umsindo	ulaka	
humor	humour (n)	tshegišo	qabolo	metlae	uburharha	inhliziyo	
hunker	yearn (v)	-hlologela	-labalabela	-eletsa	-langazelela	-langazela	
hurk	squat (v)	-kotama	-qotama	-kotama	-chopha	-qoshama	
hut	hut (n)	ntlo	mokgoro	mogope	inqugwala	iqhugwane	
huur	rent (v)	-hira	-hira	-hira	-qesha	-qasha	
huur	rent (n)	rente	rente	legago	ingqesho	intela	
huur	hire (v)	-hira	-hira	-hira	-qesha	-qasha	
huwelik	marriage (n)	lenyalo	lenyalo	lenyalo	umtshato	umshado	
hy	he (pron)	yena	yena	ene	yena	yena	
hyg	wheeze (v)	-buša moya ka bothata	-fehelwa	-hupela	-tswina	-bhohoza	
hyg	pant (v)	-fegelwa	-fehelwa	-fegelwa	-khefuzela	-phefuzela	
hyser	lift (n)	sekuki	lefite	sekuka	ilifti	ilifi	
ideaal	ideal (a)	maikemišetšo	-hlamatsehang	-maikaelelo	-sengqondweni	-hle	
idee	idea (n)	kgopolo	kgopolo	kgopolo	ingcinga	umcabango	
identifiseer	identify (v)	-hlaola	-tseba	-bontsha	-alatha	-khomba	
identiteit	identity (n)	boitšhupo	boitsebiso	temogo	ukufana	uqobo lwa-	
idioom	idiom (n)	seka	maelana	leele	isaci	isisho	
idioot	idiot (n)	setlaela	sethoto	sematla	isitunxa	isilima	
ignoreer	ignore (v)	-hlokomologa	-lala ka mmele	-tlhodisa matlho	-sukunaka	-nganaki	
illustrasie	illustration (n)	seswantšho	setshwantsho	tshwantsho	umboniso	isiboniso	
illustreer	illustrate (v)	-šupetša	-tshwantsha	-tshwantsha	-bonisa	-veza iziboniso	
immigreer	immigrate (v)	-falala	-falla	-fudugela	-ba ngummi kwelinye ilizwe	-fika ezweni	
immuniseer	immunise (v)	-soutiša	-tshwaedisa	-tlhabela	-gonya	-goma	
in	in (prep)	-(e)ng	ho/ka/ka hara	mo teng	phakathi	phakathi kwa-	
in aanraking kom	contact (v)	-kopana	-amana	-tlhaeletsa	-hlangana	-thinthana	

Afrikaans	English	N Sotho	Sesotho	Tswana	Xhosa	Zulu
in ag neem	heed (v)	-hlokomela	-ela tlhoko	-tsaya tsia	-lumka	-naka
inbreek	burgle (v)	-thuba	-thuha	-thuba	-qhekeza	-gqekeza
inbreker	burglar (n)	mothubi	mothuhi	leepantlo	umqhekezi	umgqekezi
indeks	index (n)	tšhupane	tsekahare	dikaelo	uluhlu lwamagama	inkomba
in diens neem	employ (v)	-thwala	-hira	-thapa	-qesha	-qasha
indirek	indirect (a)	-sa lebanyago	-kwekwetlang	-motsopodia	-ngokungathanga ngqo	-zombelezayo
individu	individual (n)	motho	mong	bonosi	umntu	umuntu munye
indoktrineer	indoctrinate (v)	-laela	-hlohlelletsa	-tsenya kakanyo	-hlohla	-funza ngemfundiso ethile
indompel	immerse (v)	-inela	-ina	-ina	-ntywilisa	-cwilisa
industrieel	industrial (a)	-intasteri	-matsoho	-sa diatla	-yoshishino	okomsebenzi wohwebo
in elk geval	anyhow (conj)	le ge go le bjalo	feela	mme	kambe	nokho
inent	vaccinate (v)	-enta	enta	-enta	-gonya	-gcaba
inent	inoculate (v)	-hlabela	-enta	enta	-hlaba	-jova
inenting	vaccination (n)	kento	kento	mokento	ugonyo	umgcabo
inenting	inoculation (n)	tlhabelo	moento	mokento	utofo	umjovo
inflasie	inflation (n)	infleišene	infoleishene	puduloso	i-infleyishini	isivuthela
ingedagte	absent-minded (a)	-ya le megopolo	-bua ka pelo	-bua ka pelo	-zungubala	-alukile
ingeperk	banned (people) (a)	-ganetšwago	-thibetse	-iletsweng	-gxcthiweyo	abavalelwe umlomo
in gevaar stel	endanger (v)	-tsenya kotsing	-kenya tsietsing	-tsenya mo kotsing	-faka engozini	-faka engozini
ingewande	bowels (n)	mala	dikahare	mateng	amathumbu	amathumbu
ingewande	entrails (n)	dikateng	mala	mateng	izibilini	amathumbu
ingewandskoors	typhoid (n)	tengkgolo	lefu la letshollo	letshoroma la mala	icesina	interika
inheems	indigenous (a)	-semelafa	-setala	-tlholegileng	-nkulelane	-kwemvelo
in hegtenis neem	arrest (v)	-swara	-tshwara	-tshwara	-bamba	-bopha
inhegtenisneming	arrest (n)	tshwaro	ho tshwara	kgolego	ukufaka etrongweni	ukuboshwa
inhou	curb (v)	-thiba	-hanela	-ganela	-nqanda	-khuza
inhoud	contents (n)	diteng	dikahare	diteng	umthamo	okuqukethwe
ink	ink (n)	enke	enke	enke	i-inki	uyinki
inklusief	inclusive (a)	-akaretšago	-kenyang	-akaretsang	-qukile(yo)	-phakathi
inkomste	income (n)	puno	moputso	lotseno	umamkelo	iholo
inkopies doen	shop (v)	-reka	-reka	-reka	-thenga	-thenga
inkrimp	contract (v)	-hunyela	-finahanya	-funega	-rhwaqela	-fingqana
inkrimping	contraction (n)	khunyelo	phinahano	khunyelo	urhwaqelo	ukufinyeza
inlig	enlighten (v)	-tsebiša	-qaqisetsa	-fatlhosa	-khanyisela	-khanyisela
inligting	information (n)	tsebo	tsebiso	tshedimosetso	ulwazi	umbiko
inperk	restrict (v)	-beela mellwane	-hanela	-kganna	-thintela	-nqanda
inperk	ban (people) (v)	-ganetša	-thibela	-iletsa	-gxctha	-valwa umlomo
inperking	restriction (n)	go beela mellwane	kganelo	kganno	isithintelo	ukunqanda
inrit	driveway (n)	mokgotha	tselana e kenang	tsela e e tsenang	indledlana	umgwaqo oya endlini
insek	insect (n)	khunkhwane	kokwanyana	tshenekegi	isinambuzane	isinambuzane
inskryf	enrol (v)	-ngwadiša	-ngodisa	-kwadisa	-bhalisa	-joyina
insluit	include (v)	-akaretša	-kenya	-akaretsa	-qukanisa	-faka
insluit	enclose (v)	-akaretša	-kenya	-thekeletsa	-valela	-zungezeleka
inspanning	effort (n)	teko	boikgathatso	matsapa	umzamo	umzamo
inspeksie	inspection (n)	tlhahlobo	hlahlobo	tekolo	uhlolo	ukuhlola
inspekteer	inspect (v)	-hlahloba	-hlahloba	-lebaleba	-hlola	-hlola
inspekteur	inspector (n)	mohlahlobi	mohlahlobi	motlhatlhobi	umhloli	umhloli
inspuit	inject (v)	-hlabela	-hlaba	-tlhaba	-tofa	-hlaba
inspuiting	injection (n)	tlhabelo	tlhabo	lemao	utofo	uhlabo
insteek	dip (v)	-tipa	-ina	-ina	-thi nkxu	-cwilisa
instem	consent (v)	-kwana	-dumela	-dumela	-vuma	-vuma
instemming	consent (n)	kwano	tumelo	tumelo	imvume	ukuvuma
instink	instinct (n)	tlhago	sehlaho	tlhago	ithuku	isazela
instroming	influx (n)	tšhologelo	tshubuhlellano	thologelo	ukungena	ukuthutheleka
instrukteur	instructor (n)	molaedi	morupedi	mokaedi	umyaleli	umfundisi
instrument	instrument (n)	sedirišwa	sesebediswa	sediriswa	isixhobo	isikhali somsebenzi
integriteit	integrity (n)	potego	bokgabane	thokgamo	ingqiqo	ubuqotho
intelligensie	intelligence (n)	bohlale	hlalefo	botlhale	ubuxrele-krele	inhlakanipho
intelligent	intelligent (a)	-bohlale	-bohlale	-tlhogo	-krele-krele	-khaliphile

Afrikaans	English	N Sotho	Sesotho	Tswana	Xhosa	Zulu	K
interessant	interesting (a)	-kgahlišago	-kgahlisang	-kgatlhang	-nomdla	okunakisayo	
interesseer	interest (v)	-kgahla	-kgahla	-kgatlhega	-enza umdla	-thatheka	
intern	internal (a)	-ka gare	-ka hare	-selegae	-ngaphakathi	ngaphakathi	
internasionaal	international (a)	-ditšhaba	-matjhaba	-ditšhaba	-kazwelonke	-ezizwe ngezizwe	
inval	invasion (n)	tšhwahlelo	tlhaselo	tlhaselo	uhlaselo	inhlaselo	
inval	invade (v)	-šwahlela	-hlasela	-tlhasela	-ngenela	-hlasela	
invalide	invalid (n)	sekoka	mofokodi	sekoka	umlwelwe	isilinda	
invloed	influence (n)	tutuetšo	matla	tlhotlheletso	ifuthe	ithonya	
invoer	import (n)	ditšwantle	kgwebiso	seraopo	impahla ethengwe kwelinye ilizwe	impahla engeniswayo	
invoer	import (v)	-tliša go tšwa ntle	-hwebisa	-raopa	-thenga kwelinye ilizwe	-ngenisa	
iris	iris (n)	leratladi la leihlo	thaka ya leihlo	aerisi	umnyama	isiyingi seso	
ironie	irony (n)	kgegeo	makatso	kobiso	isigqebelo	isibhinqo	
irriteer	irritate (v)	-seleka	-halefisa	-baba	-caphukisa	-casula	
item	item (n)	ntlha	ntho	ntlhana	into	umcimbi	
ivoor	ivory (n)	leino la tlou	lenaka la tlou	lonaka	uphondo lwendlovu	izinyo lendlovu	
jaag	hurry (v)	-phakiša	-phalla	-potlaka	-ngxama	-phangisa	
jaar	year (n)	ngwaga	selemo	ngwaga	unyaka	unyaka	
jaarliks	yearly (a)	ka ngwaga	selemo le selemo	-ngwaga le ngwaga	-omnyaka	ngeminyaka	
jaarliks	annual (a)	ka ngwaga	ka selemo	-ngwaga	-ngonyaka	konyaka	
jag	hunt (v)	-tsoma	-tsoma	-tsoma	-zingela	-zingela	
jagluiperd	cheetah (n)	lepogo	lengau	lengau	ihlosi	ingulule	
jagter	hunter (n)	motsomi	setsomi	motsomi	umzingeli	umzingeli	
jakkals	jackal (n)	phukubje	mopheme	phokojwe	udyakalashe	impungushe	
jaloers	jealous (a)	-nago le mona	-lefufa	-lefufa	-nomona	-khwelezayo	
jaloers	envious (a)	-nago le tseba	-mohono	-fufegang	-nomona	-hawukelayo	
jaloesie	jealousy (n)	lehufa	lefufa	lefufa	umona	isikhwele	
jammerlik	pitiful (a)	-nyamišago	-haulang	-tlhomolang pelo	-novelwano	-nomhawu	
jammerte	pity (n)	manyami	mohau	go tlhomola pelo	usizi	umhawu	
Januarie	January (n)	Janaware	Pherekgong	Ferikgong	eyomQungu	uJanuwari	
jas	coat (n)	jase	jase	jase	idyasi	ibhantshi	
jellie	jelly (n)	jeli	jeli	marere	ijeli	ujeli	
Jesus	Jesus (n)	Jesu	Jeso	Jesu	uYesu	uJesu	
jeug	youth (n)	bafsa	motjha	bošwa	ulutsha	ubusha	
jeugdige	adolescent (n)	mofsa	mokenaboholo	mosima	umntu ofikisayo	intsha	
jeuk	itch (v)	-hlohlona	-hlohlona	-baba	-rhawuzela	-lunywa	
jokkie	jockey (n)	mokatiši	joki	mopalami	inkweli	ujoki	
jong	young (a)	-fsa	-motjha	-nana	-tsha	-ncane	
jongkêrel	bachelor (n)	kgope	lesoha	kgope	isoka	impohlo	
jou	your (pron)	-gago	-hao	-gago	-akho	-kho	
jou gedra	behave (v)	-itshwara	-itshwara	-itshola setho	-ziphathe	-zimisa	
joune	yours (pron)	-gago	-hao	-gago	-akho	okwakho	
jou swak gedra	misbehave (v)	-lebala go itshwara	-itshwara hampe	-itlontlolola	-ziphatha kakubi	-ziphatha kabi	
juk	yoke (n)	joko	joko	joko	idyokhwe	ijoka	
Julie	July (n)	Julae	Phupu	Phukwi	eyeKhala	uJulayi	
julle	you (pron)	lena	lona	lona	nina	nina	
julle	your (pron)	-lena	-lona	-lona	-enu	-inu	
julle s'n	yours (pron)	-lena	-lona	-lona	-enu	okwenu	
Junie	June (n)	June	Phupjane	Seetebosigo	eyeSilimela	uJuni	
junior	junior (a)	-nyane	-nyenyane	-botlana	-ncinci	-ncane	
jurie	jury (n)	juri	baahlodi	kgotla	iqumrhu labagwebi	ibandla labasizi bejaji	
juweel	jewel (n)	sebenyabje	lehakwe	lebenya	ilitye lexabiso	itshana eliyigugu	
jy	you (pron)	wena	wena	wena	wena	wena	
kaak	jaw (n)	mohlagare	mohlahare	letlhaa	umhlathi	umhlathi	
kaal	bare (a)	-hlobotšego	-feela	-gotlhegileng	-ze	-nqunu	
kaal	naked (a)	-hlobotšego	-hlobotseng	-lepono	-ze	-nqunu	
kaart	card (n)	karata	karete	karata	ikhadi	ikhadi	
kaartjie	ticket (n)	thekethe	tekete	thekethe	itikiti	ithikithi	

K	Afrikaans	English	N Sotho	Sesotho	Tswana	Xhosa	Zulu
	kaartjieloket	box office (n)	ofisi ya dithekethe	ntlwana ya ditekete	kantoro ya dikaraki	iofisi yokuthenga itiki	indawo yokuthenga amathikithi
	kaartjieskantoor	ticket office (n)	ofisi ya dithekethe	ofisi ya kitekete	kantoro ya dithekethe	iofisi yamatiki	ihhovisilamathikithi
	kaas	cheese (n)	tsĕse	tjhese	kase	itshizi	ushishi
	kabel	cable (n)	mogala	mohala	kabele	intambo	indophi enohlonze
	kabinet	cabinet (n)	kabinete	kabinete	kabinete	ikhabhinethi	isigungu sikahulumeni
	kafee	café (n)	khefi	khefi	khefi	ikhefi	ikhefi
	kakao	cocoa (n)	khoukhou	khoukhou	khoukhou	ikoko	ukhokho
	kakie	khaki (n)	khaki	khaki	khaki	ikaki	ukhakhi
	kakkerlak	cockroach (n)	lefele	lephele	lefele	iphela	iphela
	kaktus	cactus (n)	kaktuse	torofeie	kaketese	ikhala	isihlehle
	kalander	weevil (n)	tšhupa	tshupa	motoutwana	ingqokoqwane	indudwane
	kalbas	calabash (n)	kgapa	mohope	moduto	iselwa	iselwa
	kalender	calendar (n)	kalentara	almanaka	alemanaka	ikhalenda	ikhalenda
	kalf	calf (n)	namane	namane	namane	ithole	inkonyane
	kalfsvleis	veal (n)	nama ya namane	nama ya namane	nama ya namane	inyama yethole	inyama yenkonyane
	kalk	lime (n)	motaga	kalaka	kalaka	ikalika	umcako
	kalkoen	turkey (n)	kalakune	kalakune	kalakune	ikalkuni	ikalikuni
	kalm	calm (a)	-homotšego	-kgutsitse	-kokobelang	-zolileyo	-thulile
	kalmeer	soothe (v)	-okobatša	-kgutsisa	-tlakisa	-thomalalisa	-duduza
	kam	comb (n)	kamo	kama	kamo	inkcaza	ikamu
	kam	comb (v)	-kama	-kama	-kama	-chaza	-kama
	kameel	camel (n)	kamela	kamele	kamela	inkamela	ikhamela
	kameelperd	giraffe (n)	thutlwa	thuhlo	thutlwa	indlulamthi	indlulamithi
	kamer	room (n)	phapoši	kamore	phaposi	igumbi	ikamelo
	kamera	camera (n)	khamera	khemera	kamera	ikhamera	ikhamera
	kameraadskap	companionship (n)	bonkane	selekane	bolekane	ubuqabane	ubungane
	kamp	camp (n)	kampa	kampo	kampa	ikampu	inkambu
	kampeer	camp (v)	-kampa	-kampa	-thibelela	-misa intente	-misa inkambu
	kampeerterrein	camp site (n)	lefelo la go kampela	setsha sa ho kampa	lefelo la kampa	indawo yokumisa intente	isiza sekambu
	kampering	camping (n)	go kampa	ho kampa	bothibelelo	ukumisa intente	ukukampa
	kampioen	champion (n)	kgoroto	mmampodi	mmampodi	intshatsheli	ingqwele
	kampong	compound (n)	kompo	kompone	kompone	ubumbaxa	inkomponi
	kan	can (n)	kane	kanekane	kane	-kwazi	ithunga
	kanaal	canal (n)	mokero	kanale	kanale	inyoba	umselekazi wamanzi
	kanker	cancer (n)	bolwetši bja kankere	kankere	kwatsi	umhlaza	umdlavuza
	kanon	cannon (n)	kanono	kanono	kanono	inkanunu	umbayimbayi
	kans	chance (n)	sebaka	sebaka	lobaka	ithuba	ithuba
	kanselleer	cancel (v)	-phumola	-khansela	-sutlha	-rhoxisa	-kansela
	kant	lace (n)	kanta	kanta	kanta	umqukumbelo	uleyisi
	kantlyn	margin (n)	mollwane	moedi	morato	udini	usebe
	kantoor	office (n)	ofisi	kantoro	ofisi	iofisi	ihhovisi
	kap	chop (v)	-rema	-ratha	-rema	-canda	-gawula
	kaptein	captain (n)	moetapele	kapotene	molaodi	inkokeli yeqela	ukaputeni
	kar	cart (n)	kariki	kariki	karaki	inqwelo	ikalishi
	karakter	character (n)	semelo	semelo	moanelwa	umlinganiswa	umlingiswa
	karavaan	caravan (n)	kharabane	kharavane	karafane	ikharavani	ikharavani
	karkas	carcass (n)	setoto	sefifi	setoto	inyamakazi ebuleweyo	isidumbu sesilwane
	karring	churn (n)	sefehlo	phehlo	-fetlha	inkonkxa yokwenza ibhotolo	-phehla
	karringmelk	buttermilk (n)	motsaro	mofehlo	mokaro	ixibhiya	umbhobe
	karton	cardboard (n)	khatepoto	khateboto	khateboto	ikhadibhodi	ikhadibhodi
	karwei	cart (v)	-thotha	-thotha	-tsholela	-thutha	-thutha
	kas	cupboard (n)	khapoto	khabete	raka	ikhabhathi	ikhabethe
	kasterolie	castor oil (n)	kasteroli	kasteroli	mokure	ikastoli	ukhasitowela
	kastreer	castrate (v)	-fagola	-fa(h)ola	-fagola	-thena	-phakula
	kastrol	saucepan (n)	kastrolo	pitsa	pitsanyana	imbiza	ipani
	kat	cat (n)	katse	katse	katse	ikati	ikati
	katalogus	catalogue (n)	kataloko	khataloko	kataloko	ikhathalogu	ikhathalogi

Afrikaans	English	N Sotho	Sesotho	Tswana	Xhosa	Zulu	K
katjie	kitten (n)	katsana	ledinyane la katse	katsana	ikatana	izinyane lekati	
katoen	cotton (n)	leokodi	tshwele	letseta	irhali	ukotini	
kattekwaad	mischief (n)	makokwana	botlokotsebe	letshwenyo	intlondi	ukuklina	
keel	throat (n)	mogolo	mmetso	mometso	umqala	umphimbo	
keer	avert (v)	-thiba	-kgelosa	-fema	-nqanda	-vika	
kelner	waiter (n)	weitara	mofepi	modigedi	iweyitara	uweta	
ken	chin (n)	seledu	seledu	seledu	isilevu	isilevu	
kenmerkend	characteristic (a)	-kgethologanyago	-tsebahala	-tlhagang	-luphawu	-okomkhuba	
kennis	knowledge (n)	tsebo	tsebo	kitso	ulwazi	ulwazi	
kennis	acquaintance (n)	motswalle	motswalle	kitso	ulwazano	isazani	
kennis gee	notify (v)	-tsebiša	-tsebisa	-itsise	-azisa	-azisa	
kennisgewing	notice (n)	tsebišo	tsebiso	kitsiso	isaziso	umnako	
kennismaking	acquaintance (n)	molekane	ho tseba	kitsiso	ulwazano	ukwazana	
kêrel	boyfriend (n)	moratiwa	mohlankana	lekau	isinqandamathe	isoka	
kerk	church (n)	kereke	kereke	kereke	icawa	isonto	
kerm	moan (v)	-tsetla	-belaela	-duma	-gcuma	-bubuza	
kers	candle (n)	khantlela	kerese	kerese	ikhandlela	ikhandlela	
Kersfees	Christmas (n)	Keresemose	Keresemese	Keresemose	iKrismesi	uKhisimusi	
ketel	kettle (n)	ketlele	ketlele	ketlele	iketile	igedlela	
ketting	chain (n)	ketane	ketane	keetane	ityathanga	iketanga	
keuse	choice (n)	kgetho	boikgetheto	tlhopo	ukhetho	ukukhetha	
kewer	beetle (n)	khunkhwane	kgolabolokwe	khukhwane	uqongqothwane	ibhungane	
kielie	tickle (v)	-tsikinya	-tsikinya	-tsikitla	-nyumbaza	-kitaza	
kiem	germ (n)	twatši	kokwana	mogare	intsholongwane	ijemu	
kies	choose (v)	-kgetha	-kgetha	-tlhopa	-khetha	-khetha	
kiesreg	franchise (n)	tokelo ya go kgetha	boikgethelo	botlhophi	ilungelo lokuvota	ilungelo lokuvota	
kiestand	molar (n)	leino la mohlagare	mohlahare	leino	umhlathi	izinyo lomhlathi	
kieu	gill (n)	leswafohlapi	letlopo	kgwafo	indawo yokuphefumla yentlanzi	isiphefumulo	
kind	child (n)	ngwana	ngwana	ngwana	umntwana	umntwana	
kindergeboorte	childbirth (n)	pelego	pelehi	botsholo	ukubeleka	ukubeletha	
kinderjare	childhood (n)	bjana	bongwana	bonyana	ubuntwana	ubuntwana	
kinkhoes	whooping cough (n)	lethakgo	mokgokgothwane	kgookgoo	unkonkonko	ukhohlokhohlo	
kitaar	guitar (n)	katara	katara	katara	ikatali	isiginxi	
kla	complain (v)	-ngongorega	-tletleba	-ngongorega	-khalaza	-khala	
klaarmaak	finish (v)	-fetša	-qeta	-fetsa	-phela	-phelisa	
klad	blot (n)	setswata	letheba	kwaba	ichaphaza	ichaphazela	
klaer	complainant (n)	mongongoregi	motletlebi	moseki	ummangali	ummangaleli	
klagte	complaint (n)	ngongorego	tletlebo	dingongora	isikhalazo	insolo	
klam	humid (a)	-monola	-leswe	-bokgola	-fumile	-manzana	
klank	sound (n)	modumo	modumo	modumo	isandi	umsindo	
klap	slap (n)	phasolo	tjabelo	tlelapa	ukuqhwaba	impama	
klap	slap (v)	-phasola	-jabela	-bata	-qhwaba	-mukula	
klarinet	clarinet (n)	klarinete	tlelarinete	tlelarinete	ixilongo	iklarinethi	
klas	class (n)	mphato	tlelase	setlhopa	iklasi	iklasi	
klassifiseer	classify (v)	-hlopha	-hlophisa	-tlhopa	-hlela	-ahlukanisa	
klavier	piano (n)	piano	thomo	piano	uhadi	upiyane	
klavierspeler	pianist (n)	moraloki wa piano	moletsathomo	moletsi wa piano	umdlalihadi	umshayi wopiyane	
klawerbord	keyboard (n)	khiipoto	boto ya dinoto	khiboto	amathambo epiyano	ugqoko	
kleef	adhere (v)	-kgomara	-mamarela	-kgomarela	-ncamathela	-namathela	
klei	clay (n)	letsopa	letsopa	mmopa	udongwe	ubumba	
klein	small (a)	-nyane	-nyenyane	-nnye	-ncinci	-ncane	
klein	little (a)	-nyane	-nyenyane	-nnye	-ncinci	-ncane	
kleindogter	granddaughter (n)	motlogolo	setloholo	setlogolwana	umzukulwana	umzukulu wesifazane	
klein hondjie	puppy (n)	mpšanyana	ntjanyana	ntšwanyana	injana	umdlwane	
kleinkind	grandchild (n)	motlogolo	setloholo	ngwanaangwanaka	umzukulwana	umzukulu	
kleinlik	petty (a)	-nyatšegago	-sa tsebisahaleng	-nyenyane	-ncinane	-ncinyane	
kleinseun	grandson (n)	motlogolo	setloholo	setlogolwana	umzukulwana	umzukulu wesilisa	
kleintjie	young (n)	ngwana	ledinyane	ngwana	umntwana	isiyayo	
kleintongetjie	uvula (n)	lelengwana	lelengwana	lelengwana	incakancaka	ugovane	

K	Afrikaans	English	N Sotho	Sesotho	Tswana	Xhosa	Zulu
	kleintyd	infancy (n)	bosea	bosea	bongwana	ubuntwana	ubungane
	klem	clasp (n)	sepate	letlao	khuparelo	isibambi	isixhakathisi
	klem	emphasis (n)	kgatelelo	toboketso	kgatelelo	ugxininiso	ukugcizelela
	klem in die kake	tetanus (n)	tetanose	tsitsipano ya mohlahare	kitlano ya meno	uqino-mihlathi	ithethanusi
	klep	valve (n)	belefe	belofo	belefo	isivalo	ivalfu
	klere	clothes (n)	diaparo	diaparo	diaparo	iimpahla	izingubo
	kleremaker	tailor (n)	moroki	seroki	mosegi	umsski wempahla	umthungi
	klerk	clerk (n)	mapalane	tlelereke	tleereke	unobhala	umabhalana
	kleur	colour (n)	mmala	mmala	mmala	umbala	umbala
	klewerig	adhesive (a)	-kgomarelago	-mamarelang	-kgomarelang	-ncamathelayo	-namathelayo
	kliënt	client (n)	modirelwa	moreki	modirelwa	umxhasi	ikhasimende
	klier	gland (n)	thaka	pudula	kgeleswa	idlala	idlala
	klim	climb (v)	-namela	-hlwella	-palama	-khwela	-khwela
	klimaat	climate (n)	klimate	tlelaemete	tlilemate	iklameti	iklayimethi
	klimop	creeper (n)	senami	morarane	morara	isinaba	intandela
	klingel	jingle (v)	-tsirinya	-tjhwehletsa	-tsirimana	-khenkceza	-ncenceza
	kliniek	clinic (n)	kliniki	tlelenike	tleniki	ikliniki	ikliniki
	klinker	vowel (n)	tumanoši	tumannotshi	tumanosi	isikhamiso	unkamisa
	klip	stone (n)	leswika	lejwe	letlapa	ilitye	ilitshe
	klok	bell (n)	tshipi	tshepe	tshipi	intsimbi	insimbi
	klont	lump (n)	lekwate	lehlwele	kgwethe	ingongoma	isigaxa
	klont	clot (n)	lehlwele	lehlwele	letlhole	ihlwili	isigaxa
	klonter	curdle (v)	-kgahla	-hwama	-rema	-hloba	-jiya
	kloof	ravine (n)	legaga	kgohlo	molatswana	ingxondorha	isihosha
	klop	knock (n)	kokoto	ho kokota	go kokota	ukunkqonkqoza	-ngqongqoza
	klop	knock (v)	-kokota	-kokota	-kokota	-nkqonkqoza	ukungqongqoza
	klopping	throb (n)	go opa	ho uba	moubo	undondozelo	ukufutha
	klou	cling (v)	-kgomarela	-mamarela	-ngaparela	-bambelela	-nombela
	klou	claw (v)	-ngaparela	-ngwaparela	-ngapa	-krwempa	-nwepha
	klou	claw (n)	monotlo	ngwaparelo	lonala	uzipho lwentaka	uzipho
	klouter	scramble (v)	-namela	-ngwangwarela	-palama	-sikremblisha	-phangelana
	klub	club (n)	mokgatlo	mokgatlo	mokgatlho	iklabhu	ikilobhu
	knaag	gnaw (v)	-kokona	-kuma	-kokona	-grenya	-gegedla
	knaap	lad (n)	moesa	letlamorwana	mosimane	igatya	umfana
	knegskap	bondage (n)	bohlanka	bohlanka	botlamo	ubukhoboka	ukuthumbeka
	kners	gnash (v)	-tsikitla meno	-tsikitlanya meno	-huranya	-tshixizisa	-gedla
	kneukel	knuckle (n)	senoko	senoko	noko	iquphe	iqupha
	kneus	maul (v)	-kgobola	-kgobola	-teteya	-qwenga	-shikashika
	kneus	bruise (v)	-kgoboga	-tetetsa	-tetea	-gruzula	-sicila
	kneusplek	bruise (n)	kgobogo	letetetso	letsadi	umgruzulo	isisihla
	knie	knead (v)	-duba	-duba	-duba	-xovula	-xova
	knie	knee (n)	khuru	lengole	lengole	idolo	idolo
	kniel	kneel (v)	-khunama	-kgumama	-khubama	-guqa	-guqa
	knieskyf	kneecap (n)	khurumelakhuru	theledi	theledi	idolo	ivi
	knik	nod (v)	-dumela ka hlogo	-oma ka hloho	-koma	-nqwala	-nqekuza
	knik	nod (n)	go dumela ka hlogo	ho oma ka hloho	-othuma	ukunqwala	ukunqekuza
	knipmes	penknife (n)	thipana	thipa	kopelwane	umgotywana	igotshwa
	knipogie	wink (n)	ponyo ya leihlo	panyo	go panya	uqhwanyazo	ukucwayiza
	knipoog	wink (v)	-nyabetša leihlo	-panya	-panya	-qoba iliso	-cwayiza
	knipoog	blink (v)	-panya leihlo	-panya	-panya	-qhwanyaza	-phazima
	knoffel	garlic (n)	konofele	konofole	konofole	ikonofile	ugaliki
	knokkeleelt	bunion (n)	letšwabadi	torong	dinata	ikhwiniba	inhlumba
	knoop	knot (v)	-huna	-fina	-funela	-qhina	-bopha ifindo
	knoop	knot (n)	lehuto	lefito	lefunelo	iqhina	ifindo
	knoop	button (n)	konope	konopo	kopela	iqhosha	inkinobho
	knoopsgat	buttonhole (n)	lešoba la konope	lesoba la konopo	leroba la kopela	umngxuma weqhosha	imbobo yenkinobho
	knop	knob (n)	hlogwana	lekuru	makukunopu	igqudu	isikhanda
	knor	growl (v)	-bopa	-rora	-kurutla	-vungama	-bhovumula
	knyp	pinch (v)	-soba	-tsipa	-nota	-tswkila	-ncweba

Afrikaans	English	N Sotho	Sesotho	Tswana	Xhosa	Zulu	K
knyptang	pliers (n)	kinipitane	letlao	tang	itanka	udlawu	
kobra	cobra (n)	peetla	moswa	kake	isikhotsholo	uphempethwane	
koedoe	kudu (n)	tholo	tholo	tholo	iqhude	umgankla	
koeël	bullet (n)	kolo	kulo	lerumo	imbumbulu	inhlamvu	
koei	cow (n)	kgomogadi	kgomo	kgomogadi	inkomo	inkomazi	
koejawel	guava (n)	kwaba	kwaba	kwaba	igwava	ugwavu	
koek	cake (n)	kuku	kuku	kuku	iqebengwana	ikhekhe	
koekie	biscuit (n)	piskiti	basekeite	bisikiti	iqebengwana	ibhiskidi	
koel	cool (a)	-fodilego	-phodileng	-tsiditsana	-pholileyo	-pholile	
koerant	newspaper (n)	kuranta	koranta	kuranta	iphephandaba	iphephandaba	
koester	bask (v)	-ora	-athamela	-ora	-gcakamela	-otha	
koevert	envelope (n)	enfelopo	omfolopo	enfelopo	imvulophu	imvilophu	
koevoet	crowbar (n)	kepi	moqala	kepu	ikhrowubha	umgxala	
koffie	coffee (n)	kofi	kofi	kofi	ikofu	ikhofi	
kok	cook (n)	moapei	moapehi	moapei	isipheko	umpheki	
kokon	cocoon (n)	khukhune	mokone	mokone	iqombolosha	umfece	
kol	spot (n)	patso	letheba	ngwato	ibala	ibala	
kolf	bat (n)	mmopu	bete	kolofo	iphini	iphini	
kollege	college (n)	kholetšhe	kholetjhe	kholetšhe	ikholeji	ikholiji	
kom	basin (n)	sehlapelo	basekomo	tidima	isitya	isitsha	
kom	come (v)	-tla	-tlo	-tla	-iza	-za	
kombers	blanket (n)	kobo	kobo	kobo	ingubo	ingubo	
kombineer	combine (v)	-kopanya	-kopanya	-kopanya	-dibanisa	-hlanganisa	
kombuis	kitchen (n)	khitšhi	kitjhene	boapeelo	ikhitshi	ikhishi	
komedie	comedy (n)	tiragatšo ya metlae	motlae	metlae	ikhomedi	ikhomedi	
komiek	comic (n)	moswaswi	qabolo	setshego	isihlekisi	okuhlekisayo	
komies	comic (a)	-segišago	-qabolang	-botshego	-hlekisayo	-hlekisayo	
komitee	committee (n)	komiti	komiti	khuduthamaga	ikomiti	ikomiti	
komkommer	cucumber (n)	phara	komokomore	phare	ikomkomire	ikhukhamba	
komma	comma (n)	feelwana	feelwana	phegelwana	ikoma	ikhefana	
kommer	anxiety (n)	pelaelo	ngongoreho	tlhobaelo	unxunguphalo	imbandezeka	
kommersieel	commercial (a)	-kgwebo	-kgwebo	-kgwebo	-ngoqoqosho	-ezohwebo	
kommissaris van ede	commissioner of oaths (n)	moeniši	khomishenare wa boikano	moikanisi	umfungi	umfungisi	
kommissie	commission (n)	komisi	khomishene	thwaiso	ikhomishini	ikhomishani	
kompas	compass (n)	tšhupakhutlo	kompase	tshupantla	ikhampasi	ikhompasi	
komplot	plot (n)	bolotšana	mmomori	morero	iyelenqe	icebo	
komponeer	compose (v)	-hlama	-qapa	tlhama	-qamba	-qamba	
komponis	composer (n)	mohlami	moqapi	motlhami	umqambi	umqambi	
kompos	compost (n)	podišwa	kompose	monontsha	ikhomposi	umquba	
komposisie	composition (n)	tlhamo ya dikoša	qapo	tlhamo	ukuqamba	ukwakha	
kondukteur	conductor (n)	kontae	motsamaisi	kontai	umbhexeshi	ukhondakta	
konferensie	conference (n)	therišano	seboka	konferense	inkomfa	umhlangano	
konflik	conflict (n)	phapano	kgohlano	kgotlhang	ungquzulwano	udweshu	
konfyt	jam (n)	kgotla-o-mone	jeme	jeme	ijem	ujamu	
kongres	congress (n)	kopano	seboka	kongrese	inkongolo	inhlangano	
koning	king (n)	kgoši	morena	kgosi	ukumkani	inkosi	
koningin	queen (n)	kgošigadi	mofumahadi	kgosigadi	ikumkanikazi	indlovukazi	
koninkryk	kingdom (n)	mmušo	mmuso	bogosi	ubukumkani	ubukhosi	
konkreet	concrete (a)	-sa popego	-nnete	-bonegang	-bambekayo	-okungaphatheka	
konsert	concert (n)	khonsata	konsarete	khoserete	ikonsathi	ikhonsathi	
konsertina	concertina (n)	krostina	korosetina	korosetina	ikostina	inkositini	
konserwatief	conservative (a)	-bolokago	-hananang le phetoho	segologolo	-cinga ngendlela yakudala	-ngadlulisiyo	
konstabel	constable (n)	lephodisa	lepolesa	lepodisi	ipolisa	iphoyisa	
konstipasie	constipation (n)	pipelo	ho sokela	pipelo	ukuqhina	ukuqumba	
konstruksie	construction (n)	kago	mohaho	kago	isakhiwo	ukwakha	
kontaklens	contact lens (n)	galasanakaleihlong	lense ya pono	galase ya diporele	ikhontakthi lensi	ingilazi yezibuko	
kontant	cash (n)	kheše	tjhelete	madi	imali	ukheshe	
kontoer	contour (n)	mothapalalo	thapallo	konturu	ikhonto	ukunquma nentaba	

K

Afrikaans	English	N Sotho	Sesotho	Tswana	Xhosa	Zulu
kontrak	contract (n)	kontraka	kontraka	konteraka	ukurhwaqela	imvumelano
konyn	rabbit (n)	mmutla	mmutlanyana	mmutla	uhlobo lomvundla	unogwaja
kook	boil (v)	-bela	-bela	-bela	-bila	-bilisa
kook	cook (v)	-apea	-apeha	-apaya	-pheka	-pheka
kool	cabbage (n)	khabetše	khabetjhe	khabetshe	ikhaphetshu	ikhabishi
koop	buy (v)	-reka	-reka	-reka	-thenga	-thenga
koöperasie	co-operation (n)	koporasi	koporasi	mokgatlho	iqumrhu la-	inhlangano yobambiswano
koor	choir (n)	khwaere	khwaere	khwaere	ikwayala	ikwaya
koord	cord (n)	thapu	kgole	mogala	intambo	umchilo
koors	fever (n)	letadi	feberu	letshoroma	ifiva	imfiva
kop	head (n)	hlogo	hlooho	tlhogo	intloko	ikhanda
koper	buyer (n)	moreki	moreki	moreki	umthengi	umthengi
koper	copper (n)	koporo	koporo	kgotlho	ikopolo	ithusi
koppelaar	clutch (n)	klatše	tlelatjhe	tleatshe	iklatshi	iklashi
koppelteken	hyphen (n)	tlami	tlami	tlamanyi	iqhagamshela	ihayifini
koppie	cup (n)	komiki	komiki	kopi	ikopi	inkomishi
koppig	stubborn (a)	-manganga	-manganga	-bodipa	-nenkani	-nenkani
kopuleer	copulate (v)	-feka	-robalana	-gwela	-zeka	-hlangana
kopvel	scalp (n)	letlalo la hlogo	letlalo la hlooho	letlalo la tlhogo	ufele lwentloko	isikhumba sekhanda
koring	wheat (n)	korong	koro	korong	ingqolowa	ukolo
korrek	correct (a)	-nepagetšego	-nepahetse	-nepagetseng	-lungileyo	-lungile
korrigeer	correct (v)	-phošolla	-nepisa	-siamisa	-lungisa	-lungisa
korsie	crust (n)	legogo	bohoho	legogo	ukhoko	ukhokho
kort	short (a)	-kopana	-kgutshwane	-khutswane	-futshane	-fushane
kortbroek	shorts (n)	marokgo a dišothi	borikgwe bo bokgutshwane	mankopa	ushoti	isikhindi
kortliks	briefly (adv)	ka bokopana	hakgutshwane	-khutswafatso	-ngokufutshane	kafushane
kos	food (n)	dijo	dijo	dijo	ukutya	ukudla
kosbaar	precious (a)	-bohlokwa	-bohlokwa	-tlhokegang	-xabisekile (yo)	-nqabile
kosbaar	costly (a)	-bohlokwa	-turang	-tlhwatlhwa	-xabisayo	-dulile
kostuum	costume (n)	khosetšhumo	khosetjhumo	paka	isinxibo	ikhositshumu
kothuis	cottage (n)	ngwakwana	ntlwana	ntlwana	indlwana	indlwana
kou	chew (v)	-hlahuna	-hlafuna	-tlhafuna	-hlafuna	-hlafuna
koud	cold (a)	-tonyago	-bata	-tsididi	-bandayo	-makhaza
kousbroekie	pantihose (n)	phenthihouse	phentihouse	makusa	ipentihowusi	amasokisi abesifazane
kouse	stockings (n)	dikauso	dikauso	kausu	iikawusi	amasokisi amade
kraag	collar (n)	kholoro	lepetu	kholoro	ikhola	ukhola
kraai	crow (n)	legokobu	lekgwaba	legakabe	unomyayi	igwababa
kraak	crack (n)	monga	lepetso	lenga	uthanda	umnkenke
kraak	crack (v)	-palega	-petsoha	-phanya	-qhekeza	-klewuka
kraakbeen	cartilage (n)	lešetla	lefufuro	lehihiri	intlala	uqwanga
kraal	bead (n)	pheta	sefaha	sebaga	amaso	ubuhlalu
kraalwerk	beadwork (n)	dipheta	difaha	dibaga	amaso	ukuthungwa kobuhlalu
kraan	tap (n)	pompi	thepe	thepe	itepu	umpompi
krag	force (n)	maatla	matla	kgapeletso	unyanzelo	amandla
kragtig	vigorous (a)	-maatla	-matla	-maatla	-ngamandla	-ngamandla
kramp	cramp (n)	bogatšu	kgonyelo	kudupanyo ya tshika	inkantsi	inkwantshu
kranksinnig	insane (a)	-gafago	-hlanya	-tsenwang	-phambeneyo	-hlanyayo
kranksinnigheid	insanity (n)	bogafa	bohlanya	botseno	impambano	ukuhlanya
krans	cliff (n)	legaga	sephoko	maaka	iliwa	iwa
krap	scratch (n)	mongwao	mongwapo	ntho	umkrwelo	umudwa
krap	scratch (v)	-ngwaya	-ngwapa	-ngapa	-krwela	-klwebha
krap	crab (n)	kgenkgerepe	lekgala	lekakauwe	unonkala	inkalankala
krediet	credit (n)	khodi	molato	mojela	ityala	okukweletwayo
kredietkaart	credit card (n)	karatakhodi	karete ya molato	karata ya mojela	ikhredithi khadi	ikhadi lokukweleta
krediteer	credit (v)	-nea khodi	-leballa molato	-jela	-bonelela nge-	ukukweletisa
kreet	cry (n)	mogoo	sello	kgoo	isikhalo	isikhalo
kreukel	crease (n)	tšhošobano	tshosobano	letsutsuba	amarhya	ikhilisi
kreukel	crease (v)	-šošobana	-sosobana	-sosobana	-shwabanisa	-shwabana

Afrikaans	English	N Sotho	Sesotho	Tswana	Xhosa	Zulu	K
kreun	groan (n)	tsetlo	pobolo	modumo	umncwino	umbhongo	
kreun	groan (v)	-tsetla	-bobola	-duma	-ncwina	-bubula	
kreupele	cripple (n)	segole	seritsa	setlhotsa	isiqhwala	unyonga	
kreupel maak	cripple (v)	-hlotša	-holofatsa	-golafatsa	-enzakalisa	-goga	
krieket	cricket (n)	khrikhete	seqhomelankong	kerikete	iqakamba	ikhilikithi	
krieketspeler	cricketer (n)	mmapadi wa khrikhete	mokerikete	motshamiki wa kerikete	umdlali weqakamba	umdlali wekhilikithi	
krimp	shrink (v)	-hunyela	-honyela	-gonega	-shwabana	-shwabana	
kritiseer	criticise (v)	-swaya phošo	-ntsha diphoso	-kgala	-gxeka	-hlaba	
kroeg	bar (n)	para	bara	bara	inkanti	inkantini	
krokodil	crocodile (n)	kwena	kwena	kwena	ingwenya	ingwenya	
krom	crooked (a)	-kgopamego	-kgopo	-sokameng	-goso	-magwegwe	
kroning	coronation (n)	peo ya kgoši	ho beha borena	peo	uthweso	ukugcotshwa	
kroon	crown (n)	mphapahlogo	mofapahloho	serwalo	isithaba	umqhele	
kroonblaar	petal (n)	petala ya letšoba	petale	letlharelegolo	igqabi	isigcebe sembali	
krotbuurt	slum (n)	mekutwaneng	mekhukhu	mathikithwane	ubuxhifilili	indawo engenampilo	
kruideniersware	groceries (n)	dikrosari	kerosari	kerousara	ukutya	igilosa	
kruie	herbs (n)	mošunkwane	methokgo	setlama	iyeza	ikhambi	
kruiekenner	herbalist (n)	ramešunkwane	ramethokgo	ngaka	ixhwele	inyanga yamakhambi	
kruin	summit (n)	tlhora	tlhoro	tlhora	incopho	isiqongo	
kruip	crawl (v)	-abula	-kgasa	-abula	-rhubuluza	-khasa	
kruis	rump (n)	noka	noka	mokuane	ithebe	isinqe	
kruis	cross (v)	-fapana	-tshela	-fapaana	umnqamlezo	-dabula	
kruisig	crucify (v)	-bapola	-thakgisa sefapanong	-bapola	-xhoma	-nqamuleza	
kruisvra	cross examine (v)	-botšišiša	-fatisisa	-botsolotsa	-buza	-buzisisa	
kruiwa	wheelbarrow (n)	kiribane	kereibaya	kiriba	ikiriva	ibhala	
krul	curl (v)	laetse	matsetlela	-gogoropa	umjiko	insonge	
krummel	crumb (n)	lerathana	lekumane	lefofora	imvuthuluka	imvuthu	
kry	get (v)	-hwetša	-fumana	-amogela	-fumana	-thola	
krygsgevangene	prisoner-of-war (n)	lethopša	motshwaruwa wa ntweng	setshwarwa-sa-ntwa	umbanjwa wemfazwe	umthunjwa	
kryt	chalk (n)	tšhoko	tjhoko	tshoko	itshokhwe	ushoki	
kudde	herd (n)	mohlape	mohlape	motlhape	umhlambi	umhlambi	
kuiltjie	dimple (n)	sesegišabaeng	sebotjhe	pobe	isinxonxo	inkonyane	
kul	cheat (v)	-fora	-qhekanyetsa	-tsietsa	-qhatha	-khohlisa	
kultuur	culture (n)	setho	setho	setso	inkqubo yesizwe	isimo sempucuko	
kuns	art (n)	bokgabo	mokgabo	botswerere	ubugcisa	ubuciko	
kunsgalery	art gallery (n)	ntlo ya bokgabo	tulo ya mokgabo	bokgabisong	igumbi le zobugcisa	igalari yokobuciko	
kunsmatig	artificial (a)	-maitirelo	-maiketsetso	maitirelo	-ngadalwanga	-enziweyo nje	
kunsmatige asemhaling	artificial respiration (n)	khemišo	phefumoloho ya maiketsetso	khemiso ya maitirelo	impefumlelo	ukuphefumulisa	
kunsmatige inseminasie	artificial insemination (n)	kemarišo ya maitirelo	kemariso ya maiketsetso	kemariso ya maitirelo	uzaliso	ukukhulelisa ngokujova	
kunsmis	fertiliser (n)	monontšha	monontsha	monontsha	isichumiso	umanyolo	
kunsmis gee	fertilise (v)	-nontšha mmu	-nontsha	-nontsha	-chumisa	-thela umanyolo	
kurk	cork (n)	poropo	sepako	poropo	isivingco	ukhokho	
kus	coast (n)	lebopo	lebopo	losi	unxweme	ugu	
kussing	pillow (n)	mosamelo	mosamo	mosamo	umqamelo	umcamelo	
kussing	cushion (n)	mosamelo	mosamo	mosamo	umqamelo	umqamelo	
kwaad	angry (a)	-befetšwego	-halefile	-ngadileng	-nomsindo	-thukuthele	
kwaadheid	anger (n)	pefelo	kgalefo	bojarara	umsindo	ulaka	
kwaad maak	anger (v)	-befediša	-halefisa	-ngadisa	-enza umsindo	-thukuthelisa	
kwalifikasie	qualification (n)	thuto	boithutelo	borutegi	inkcazo	ilungelo	
kwaliteit	quality (n)	khwaliti	bonono	boleng	umgangatho	ubunjani	
kwart	quarter (n)	kwarata	kotara	kota	isahlulo	ikwata	
kwel	trouble (v)	-tshwenya	-kgathatsa	-tshwenya	-khathaza	-khathaza	
kwêlafluitjie	pennywhistle (n)	fulutu	foleiti	folutu	impentshana	imfengwane	
kweper	quince (n)	kwepere	kwepere	kopere	ikwepile	ukwipili	
kwessie	issue (n)	taba	taba	tema	umba	udaba	
kwik	mercury (n)	mekhuri	metjhuri	mekhuri	imetyhuri	ummpunyumpunyu	

K	Afrikaans	English	N Sotho	Sesotho	Tswana	Xhosa	Zulu
	kwitansie	receipt (n)	rasiti	rasite	tshupatefo	irisiti	irisidi
	kwyn	wilt (v)	-pona	-pona	-otobala	-buna	-fehleka
	kyk	look (v)	-lebelela	-tadima	-leba	-jonga	-bheka
	laag	low (a)	-fase	-tlase	-fatshe	-zantsi	-ehlile
	laai	load (v)	-laiša	laetjha	-pega	-thwalisa	-thwala
	laaste	last (a)	-mafelelo	-qetelang	-bofelo	-gqibela (yo)	-gcinayo
	laat	leave (v)	-tlogela	-tlohela	-tloga	-nduluka	-shiya
	laat	late (a)	-morago ga nako	-morao	-tla thari	-kade	-phuzile
	laat val	drop (v)	-weša	-rotha	-usa	-wisa	-wisa
	laer	lower (a)	-fasana	-tlase hofeta	-fatshefatshe	-zantsana	-ngaphansana
	laeveld	lowveld (n)	nagatlase	naha e tlase	nagatlase	isithabazi	ihlanze
	lafaard	coward (n)	lefšega	lekwala	legatlapa	igwala	igwala
	lafhartig	cowardly (a)	-lefšega	-bokwala	-boi	-ngobugwala	-nobugwala
	lafhartigheid	cowardice (n)	bofšega	bokwala	boboi	ubugwala	ubugwala
	lag	laugh (v)	-sega	-tsheha	-tshega	-hleka	-hleka
	lag	laugh (n)	ditshego	setsheho	setshego	ukuhleka	ukuhleka
	laken	sheet (n)	lakane	lakane	phephenene	ishiti	ishidi
	lakseermiddel	laxative (n)	sehlare sa go gofiša	sehlephisi	setabogisa mala	iyeza lokuhambisa	umuthi wokuhlambulula isisu
	lam	lamb (n)	kwana	konyana	konyana	itakane	izinyane
	lamp	lamp (n)	lebone	lebone	lebone	isibane	isibani
	land	land (n)	lefase	naha	lefatshe	umhlaba	umhlaba
	land	land (v)	-kotama	-kotsama	-tsurama	-hlala	-ethula emkhunjini
	landbou	agriculture (n)	bolemi	temothuo	bolemi	ulimo	ulimo
	landboukundig	agricultural (a)	-temo	-temothuo	-bolemi	-olimo	-zokulima
	landdros	magistrate (n)	maseterata	mmaseterata	magiseterata	umantyi	umantshi
	landkaart	map (n)	mmepe	mmapa	mmepe	imephu	imephu
	landmyn	landmine (n)	pomo ya naga	bomo	bomo ya mo mmung	ibhombu	ibhomu eligqitshwayo
	lang	tall (a)	-telele	-lelele	-leele	-de	-de
	lang	long (a)	-telele	-lelele	-leele	-de	-de
	langbroek	trousers (n)	borokgo bjo botelele	borikgwe	phase	ibrukhwe	ibhulukwe
	langs	next to (prep)	hleng ga-	haufi le-	-thoko ga	-caleni kwa-	-seceleni kwa-
	langs	along (prep)	hleng	-pela	ela	ecaleni ku-	ngokulinganisene
	langs	beside (prep)	hleng ga	-pela	thoko	-caleni kwa-	ohlangothini lwa-
	lantern	lantern (n)	lanterene	lantere	lebone	ilanteri	isiketekete
	lap	rag (n)	lenkgeretla	sekatana	lesela	ilaphu	isidwedwe
	lap	material (n)	lešela	lesela	khai	ilaphu	indwangu
	lappie	patch (n)	segaswa	petjhe	sebata	isiziba	isibheqe
	larinks	larynx (n)	kodu	qoqothwane	kgokgotso	ingqula	umphimbo
	larwe	larva (n)	seboko	seboko	seboko	umbungu	isibungu
	las	join (v)	-kopanya	-momahatsa	-kopanya	-joyina	-hlanganisa
	las	burden (n)	morwalo	morwalo	mokgweleo	umthwalo	umthwalo
	lasplek	join (n)	kopantšho	momahatso	kgatlhanyo	ijoyini	indawo ehlanganisiweyo
	laster	slander (n)	kgobošo	ketselletso	-fala	isityholo	-hleba
	lastig wees	bother (v)	-tshwenya	-kgathatsa	-tshwenya	-khathaza	-khathaza
	lawaai	uproar (n)	lešata	lerata	magawegawe	ingxolo	umsindo
	lê	lie (v)	-lala	-botha	-robala	-lala	-lala
	ledemaat	limb (n)	setho	setho	mokgono	ilungu	isitho
	ledig	idle (a)	-dutšego ka matsogo	-botswa	-thuba kobo segole	-nqenayo	-ngenzi lutho
	leed	grief (n)	manyami	mahlomola	botlhoko	intlungu	usizi
	leef	live (v)	-phela	-phela	-phela	-phila	-phila
	leeg	blank (a)	-se nago selo	-feela	-sepe	-ze	-okungenalutho
	leeg	empty (a)	-se nago selo	-feela	-lolea	-ze	-ngenalutho
	leen	lend (v)	-adima	-adima	-adima	-boleka	-bolekisa
	leen	borrow (v)	-adima	-adima	-adima	-boleka	-boleka
	leër	army (n)	madira	lebotho	masole	umkhosi	impi
	lêer	file (n)	faela	faele	faele	ifayile	isihlabo
	leer	leather (n)	letlalo	letlalo	letlalo	ufele	isikhumba
	leer	learn (v)	-ithuta	-ithuta	-ruta	-funda	-funda

Afrikaans	English	N Sotho	Sesotho	Tswana	Xhosa	Zulu	L
leer	ladder (n)	lleri	lere	llere	ileri	isikhwelo	
leerling	pupil (n)	morutiwa	morutwana	morutwana	umntwana	umfundi	
leerplan	syllabus (n)	lenaneothuto	lenanethuto	lenanethuto	isilabhasi	uhlelo lwezifundo	
lees	read (v)	-bala	-bala	-bala	-funda	-funda	
leeu	lion (n)	tau	tau	tau	ingonyama	ibhubesi	
leeuwyfie	lioness (n)	taugadi	tawana	taugadi	imazi yengonyama	ibhubesi lensikazi	
legkaart	puzzle (n)	mantharane	malepa	malepa	ukudideka	indida	
lei	lead (v)	-eta pele	-etella pele	-etelela	-khokela	-hamba phambili	
leier	leader (n)	moetapele	moetapele	moeteledipele	inkokeli	umholi	
leisel	rein (n)	tomo	leleisele	lerapa	intambo	itomu	
lek	lick (v)	-latswa	-leka	-latswa	-khotha	-khotha	
lek	leak (v)	-dutla	-dutla	-dutla	-vusa	-vuza	
lek	leak (n)	modutlo	lesoba	go dutla	uthanda	imbobo	
lekker	sweet (n)	dipompong	pompong	semonamone	ilekese	iswidi	
lekplek	puncture (n)	lešoba	pantjhara	phantšhara	umngxunyana	imbobo	
lelie	lily (n)	llili	shweshwe	mogaga	inyibiba	umnduze	
lelik	ugly (a)	-be	-be	-maswe	-bi	-bi	
lemoen	orange (n)	namune	lamunu	namune	iorenji	iwolintshi	
lemoensap	orange juice (n)	todi ya dinamune	lero la lamunu	matute a namune	incindi yeorenji	ujusi kawolintshi	
lende	loin (n)	letheka	noka	noka	isinqe	ukhalo	
lendestuk	sirloin (n)	nama ya kgomo ya mokokotlong	noka	setlhana	isinqe	isinqe	
lengte	length (n)	botelele	bolelele	boleele	ubude	ubude	
lening	loan (n)	kadimo	kadimo	kadimo	imboleka	isikwenethu	
lente	spring (n)	seruthwana	selemo	dikgakologo	intwasahlobo	intwasahlobo	
lepel	spoon (n)	leho	kgaba	loswana	icephe	ukhezo	
lêplek	lair (n)	segola	sebaka	kutla	isikhundla	isikhundla	
les	quench (v)	thuto	-nyorolla	-nyorolola	-phelisa unxano	-qeda ukoma	
les	lesson (n)	thuto	thuto	thuto	isifundo	isifundo	
lesing	lecture (n)	thuto	thuto	thuto	isifundo	isifundo	
lessenaar	desk (n)	panka	deseke	banka	idesika	idesiki	
lettergreep	syllable (n)	noko	senoko	noko	ilungu	ilunga	
letterkunde	literature (n)	dingwalo	sengolwa	dikwalo	uncwadi	imibhalo	
letterkundig	literary (a)	-dingwalo	-sengolwa	-bokwadi	-ngoncwadi	-kwemibhalo	
leuen	lie (n)	maaka	leshano	maaka	ubuxoki	amanga	
leuenaar	liar (n)	moakedi	ramashano	moaki	ixoki	umqambi-manga	
leun	lean (v)	-ithekga	-itshetleha	-sekama	-ngqiyama	-ncamasha	
lewe	life (n)	bophelo	bophelo	bophelo	ubomi	impilo	
leweloos	inanimate (a)	-sa phelego	-sa pheleng	-sa pheleng	-ngaphiliyo	-ngezwayo	
lewend	alive (a)	-phelago	-phela	-phelang	-philileyo	-philile	
lewendig	lively (a)	-mafolofolo	-phelang	-phelang	-phila(yo)	-phekuzayo	
lewer	liver (n)	sebete	sebete	sebete	isibindi	isibindi	
liberaal	liberal (a)	-gololago	-lokolohileng		-nesisa	-phanayo	
lid	member (n)	leloko	setho	tokololo	ilungu	ilunga	
lidmaatskap	membership (n)	boloko	botho	botokololo	ubulungu	ubulunga	
liedjie	song (n)	košana	pina	kopelo	ingoma	iculo	
liefdadigheid	charity (n)	lerato	lerato	bopelonomi	isisa	umhawu	
liefde	love (n)	lerato	lerato	lerato	uthando	uthando	
lieg	lie (v)	-bolela maaka	-bua leshano	-aketsa	-xoka	-qamba amanga	
lies	groin (n)	lengamu	tshwelesa	lengami	umphakatho	imbilapho	
lieweheersbesie	ladybird (n)	podilekgwana	maleshwane	podilekgwana	ubhantom	umanqulwane	
lig	light (a)	-bofefo	-bobebo	-lesedi	-baneka	-khanyayo	
lig	light (n)	seetša	kganya	lebone	ukukhanya	ukukhanya	
ligament	ligament (n)	mošifa	lera	ntha	umsipha	umsipha	
liggaam	body (n)	mmele	mmele	mmele	umzima	umzimba	
liggaamsbou	physique (n)	popego	seemo sa mmele	popego	ukwakhiwa komzimba	umzimba	
likeur	liqueur (n)	senotagi sa sekgowa	lekere	senwamaphodi	utywala	izithako zikagologo	
liniaal	ruler (n)	rula	rula	rula	irula	irula	
linkerkant	left (n)	ka go la nngele	leqele	molema	ikhohlo	ubunxele	
links	left (a)	-nngele	-letshehadi	-molema	-khohlo	-bunxele	

L	Afrikaans	English	N Sotho	Sesotho	Tswana	Xhosa	Zulu
	linne	linen (n)	lene	masela	llene	ilineni	ulineni
	lint	ribbon (n)	lente	lelente	lente	ibhanti	iribhini
	lintwurm	tapeworm (n)	nogana ya mala	manyowa	mphe	intshulube	ingcili
	lip	lip (n)	molomo	pounama	pounama	umlebe	udebe
	lisensie	licence (n)	laesense	laesense	lekwalotetla	imvume	ilayisense
	lisensieer	license (v)	-fa laesense	-fana ka laesense	-tetla	-nika iphepha-mvume	-nika ilayisense
	lispel	lisp (v)	go ba le diteme	-hwelea	-go nna seleme	-teketa	-fefeza
	litteken	scar (n)	lebadi	lebadi	lebadi	isiva	isibanda
	loer	peep (v)	-hlodimela	-nyarela	-okomela	-kroba	-lunguza
	lof	praise (n)	moreto	thoriso	pako	uncomo	ukubonga
	lofwaardig	praiseworthy (a)	-retegago	-lokelwang ho roriswa	-bokwang	-ncomeka(yo)	-bongekayo
	logika	logic (n)	kwagalo	lojiki	kakanyo	ingqiqo	ilojiki
	lojaal	loyal (a)	-botegago	-tshepehang	-ikanyegang	-nyanisekile(yo)	-thembekile
	lojaliteit	loyalty (n)	bogwerano	tshepahalo	boikanyego	ukunyaniseka	ukuthembeka
	lomp	clumsy (a)	-nokologago	-monyebe	-boatla	-nobuxelegu	-ndaxandaxa
	lonend	profitable (a)	-hodišago	-putsang	-busetsang	-nengeniso	-zuzisayo
	long	lung (n)	leswafo	letshwafo	lekgwafo	umphunga	iphaphu
	longontsteking	pneumonia (n)	nyumonia	nyomonia	nyumonia	inyumoniya	izibhobo
	lood	lead (n)	morodi	loto	lerumo	isinyithi	umthofu
	loof	praise (v)	-reta	-rorisa	-boka	-ncoma	-bonga
	loon	earnings (n)	moputso	moputso	tuelo	umvuzo	imali eholwayo
	loop	walk (v)	-sepela	-tsamaya	-tsamaya	-hamba	-hamba
	los	loose (a)	-tlemologilego	-lokolohileng	-bolea	-khululekile(yo)	-xegezela
	loseerder	lodger (n)	mohiri	mohiri	mohiri	umhlaliswa	umqashi
	loslaat	release (v)	-lokolla	-lokolla	-golola	-khulula	-khulula
	loslating	release (n)	tokollo	tokollo	kgololo	ukhululo	inkululeko
	losmaak	undo (v)	-bofolla	-lokolla	-tlhatlhamolola	-khulula	-qaqa
	losmaak	disconnect (v)	-lomolla	-fasolla	-bofolola	-khulula	-ahlukanisa
	lot	fate (n)	boyo	kabelo	ntle ga taolo	ummiselo	isimiselo
	lou	tepid (a)	-boruthwana	-foofo	-bothitonyana	-dikidiki	-fudumele
	lug	sky (n)	leratadimo	lehodimo	loapi	isibhakabhaka	isibhakabhaka
	lug	air (n)	moya	moya	mowa	umoya	umoya
	lugdraad	antenna (n)	eriele	eriale	eriele	iimpondo zewayilesi	i-antena
	lugdraad	aerial (n)	eriele	eriale	eriele	ieriyali	ucingo lwewayilense
	lughawe	airport (n)	boemelafofane	boemeladifofane	boemeladifofane	isikhululo senqwelomoya	inkundla yezindiza
	lugleegte	vacuum (n)	-hlokago moya	sebaka se feela	lephaka	ihamte	isikhala esingenamoya
	lugpos	airmail (n)	posomoya	poso ya moya	poso ya mowa	iposi ehamba ngomoya	iposi elihamba ngezindiza
	lui	ring (v)	-lla	-letsa	-lela	-khalisa	-khala
	lui	lazy (a)	-tšwafago	-botswa	-setshwakga	-vilaphayo	-livila
	luiheid	laziness (n)	botšwafi	botswa	botlapa	ubuvila	ubuvila
	luiperd	leopard (n)	nkwe	lengau	nkwe	ihlosi	ingwe
	luis	tick (n)	kgofa	kgofa	kgofa	indlanga	umkhaza
	luislang	python (n)	hlware	tlhware	tlhware	ugqoloma	inhlwathi
	luister	listen (v)	-theetša	-mamela	-utlwelela	-mamela	-lalela
	luukse	luxury (n)	lehumo	majabajaba	manobonobo	ubumnandi	ubukhizikhizi
	ly	suffer (v)	-hlokofala	-utlwa bohloko	-boga	-gula	-hlupheka
	lyk	corpse (n)	setopo	setopo	setopo	umzimba	isidumbu
	lyn	line (n)	mothaladi	kgwele	mothalo	umtya	intambo
	maag	gastric (a)	-mogodu	-letshollo	-mogodu	-esisu	okusesiswini
	maag	stomach (n)	mpa	mohodu	mpa	isisu	isisu
	maagd	virgin (n)	ngwanenyana	morwetsana	bokgarebe	idlolo	intombi emsulwa
	maaier	maggot (n)	seboko	seboko	lenyenye	impethu	isibungu
	maak	make (v)	-dira	-etsa	-dira	-enza -qingqa	-enza
	maal	grind (v)	-šila	-sila	-sila	-sila	-gaya
	maal	meal (n)	dijo	dijo	dijo	isidlo	isidlo
	maalstroom	whirlpool (n)	moelaphirihlwa	metsi a ferellang	kgogela	iqula elibizelayo	isiphethu
	maalvleis	mince (n)	nama ye e šitšwego	nama e sitsweng	nama e e sitsweng	inyama esiliweyo	inyama egayiweyo

Afrikaans	English	N Sotho	Sesotho	Tswana	Xhosa	Zulu	M
maan	moon (n)	kgwedi	kgwedi	ngwedi	inyanga	inyanga	
maand	month (n)	kgwedi	kgwedi	kgwedi	inyanga	inyanga	
Maandag	Monday (n)	Mošupologo	Mantaha	Mosupologo	uMvulo	uMsombuluko	
maanhare	mane (n)	mariri	moetse	seriri	isingci	umhlwenga	
maanlig	moonlight (n)	seetša sa kgwedi	ngwedi	lesedi la ngwedi	inyanga	unyezi	
maar	however (conj)	eupša	empa	le gale	kodwa	nokho	
maar	but (conj)	eupša	empa	mme	kodwa	kodwa	
Maart	March (n)	Matšhe	Tlhakubele	Mopitlwe	uMatshi	uMashi	
maat	measure (n)	tekanyo	tekanyo	seelo	umlinganiselo	isilinganiso	
maatband	tape measure (n)	lentitekanya	tekanyi	theipi	ulutya	ithephu	
maer	lean (a)	-otilego	-otileng	-bopameng	-bhityile(yo)	-zacile	
mag	may (v)	-ka-	-ka	-ka nna	-nga	-nga-	
mag	power (n)	maatla	matla	maatla	amandla	amandla	
magies	magical (a)	-boloi	-boloi	-boloi	-nobuqqi	-nomlingo	
magneet	magnet (n)	kgogedi	makenete	kgogedi	isitsalane	uzibuthe	
magnetisme	magnetism (n)	bogogedi	bomakenete	bokgogedi	ubutsalane	amandla kazibuthe	
magtig	powerful (a)	-nago le maatla	-matla	-maatla	-namandla	-namandla	
magtig	authorise (v)	-dumelela	-dumella	-dumelela	-gunyazisa	-pha amandla	
mak	tame (a)	-tlwaetšego	-thapileng	-bokgwafo	-mbuna	-thambile	
maklik	easy (a)	bonolo	-bonolo	-bonolo	-lula	-lula	
maksimum	maximum (n)	botlalokgolo	pheletsong	botlalogolo	iqondo eliphezulu	-khulu kakhulu	
malaria	malaria (n)	letadi	malaria	letshoroma	icesina	uqhuqho	
man	husband (n)	monna	mohatsa	monona	indoda- umyeni	umyeni	
man	male (n)	monna	monna	monna	indoda	isilisa	
man	man (n)	monna	monna	monna	indoda	indoda	
mandjie	basket (n)	seroto	mmanki	seroto	umnyazi	ubhasikidi	
mangels	tonsils (n)	dithaka	ditemetwane	dikodu	indimla	amadlala asemphinjweni	
mango	mango (n)	manko	mengo	menku	imengo	umango	
manier	manner (n)	mokgwa	mokgwa	mokgwa	ukuziphatha	uhlobo	
mank	lame (a)	-segole	-holofetseng	-tlhotsang	-qhwalela (yo)	-qhugayo	
mankheid	limp (n)	mohlotšo	kgolofalo	go tlhotsa	ubuqhwala	ukuxhuga	
mank loop	limp (v)	-hlotša	-qhiletsa	-tlhotsa	-qhwalela	-xhuga	
manlik	male (a)	-tona	-monna	-tonanyana	-nobudoda	-esilisa	
manlik	masculine (a)	-tona	-bonna	-tonanyana	-nobudoda	-endoda	
manlikheid	manhood (n)	bonna	bonna	bonna	ubudoda	ubudoda	
mark	market (n)	mmaraka	mmaraka	mmaraka	imarike	imakethe	
mars	march (n)	momatšho	motsamao	mogato	ukumatsha	imashi	
marsjeer	march (v)	-matša	-tsamaya	-gata	-matsha	-masha	
martelaar	martyr (n)	motlaišwa	motlatlapuwa wa tumelo	moreswedi	umfelakholo	umfelukholo	
masels	measles (n)	mooko	mmoko	mmokwana	imasisi	isimungumungwane	
masjien	machine (n)	motšhene	motjhine	motšhini	umashini	umshini	
mat	mat (n)	moseme	moseme	mmetšhe	ukhuko	icansi	
matig	mild (a)	-lekanetšego	-phodileng	-bonolo	-lungile (yo)	-bekile	
matras	mattress (n)	mantarase	materase	bolao	umandlalo	umatilasi	
medalje	medal (n)	mentlele	kgau	mentlele	imbasa	imendlela	
mededinger	rival (n)	mophegišani	mohanyetsi	moselammapa	umchasi	imbangi	
medeklinker	consonant (n)	tumammogo	sedumammoho	tumammogo	iqabane	ungwaqa	
medepligtige	accomplice (n)	mosenyiši	motlatsi	mosenyammogo	ihlakani	umlekeleli	
medies	medical (a)	-bongaka	-meriana	-bongaka	-obugqirha	-elaphayo	
medisyne	medicine (n)	sehlare	meriana	molemo	iyeza	umuthi	
meedeel	inform (v)	-tsebiša	-tsebisa	-bega	-azisa	-azisa	
meel	flour (n)	folouru	phofo	boupe jwa borotho	umgubo	ufulawa	
meer	lake (n)	letsha	letsha	letsha	ichibi	ichibi	
meer	more (a)	-go feta fao	-hape	gape	-ngaphezulu	-ningi ngokudlula	
meerkat	meercat (n)	moswe	mosha	mošwe	igala	ububhibhi	
meervoud	plural (n)	bontšhi	bongata	bontsi	isininzi	ubuningi	
meet	measure (v)	-lekanya	-lekanya	-lekanya	-linganisa	-linganisa	
meeu	gull (n)	mohuta wa nonyana ya lewatle	ledinyane la sephooko		ingabangaba	inyoni-yolwandle	

M	Afrikaans	English	N Sotho	Sesotho	Tswana	Xhosa	Zulu
	meganies	mechanical (a)	-semotšhene	-ka boyona	-bothudi	-ngokomatshini	-omshini
	Mei	May (n)	Mei	Motsheanong	Mothseganong	uMeyi	uMeyi
	meineed	perjury (n)	kenollo	bopaki ba leshano	tshenyo ya maikano	ukufunga ubuxoki	ukufungela amanga
	meineed pleeg	perjure (v)	-enolla	-bua leshano kgotla	-senya maikano	-funga ubuxoki	-fungela amanga
	meisie	girl (n)	mosetsana	ngwanana	mosetsana	intombi	intombazane
	melaatse	leper (n)	molephera	lepera	molepera	isilephere	umlephero
	melk	milk (n)	maswi	lebese	mašwi	ubisi	ubisi
	meloen	melon (n)	phara ya sekgowa	lehapu	mokate	ivatala	ikhabe
	meng	mix (v)	-tswaka	-kopanya	-tswaka	-xuba	-xubana
	mengsel	mixture (n)	motswako	kopanyo	motswako	umxube	ixube
	menigte	multitude (n)	lešabašaba	matshwele	boidiidi	isihlwele	isizuku
	mening	opinion (n)	kgopolo	kgopolo	kakanyo	uluvo	umbono
	meningsverskil	disagreement (n)	phapano	ho se dumellane	kganetsanyo	intlaba zahlukane	impambano
	mense	people (n)	batho	batho	batho	abantu	abantu
	mensliewend	humane (a)	-botho	-botho	-setho	-nobuntu	-nomusa
	menslik	human (a)	-botho	-botho	-setho	-omntu	-obuntu
	menstruasie	menstruation (n)	lehlapo	ho ya kgweding	tlhatswo	ukuhlamba	iqako
	menstrueer	menstruate (v)	-hlapa	-ya kgweding	-bona kgwedi	-hlamba	-qaka
	mensvreter	cannibal (n)	lekgema	ledimo	mojabatho	izim	izimu
	merk	mark (n)	leswao	letshwao	letshwao	uphawu	isici
	merk	mark (v)	-swaya	-tshwaya	-tshwaya	-phawula	-maka
	merrie	mare (n)	pere ya tshadi	mmeri	pitsenamagadi	imazi yehashe	imeli
	mes	knife (n)	thipa	thipa	thipa	imela	umese
	messelaar	mason (n)	moagi	sehahi	moagi	umakhi	umeselane
	met	with (prep)	le	le	ka	nga-	nga-
	metaal	metal (n)	metale	tshepe	tshipi	isinyithi	insimbi
	meter	gauge (n)	kelo	metara	selekanyi	umlinganiso	igeji
	meter	metre (n)	metara	metara	metara	imitha	imitha
	met gemak	effortless (a)	ka boiketlo	-bonolo	ka bonolo	-lula	kalula
	metgesel	companion (n)	mofelegetši	molekane	molekane	iqabane	umhlanganyeli
	metgesel	escort (n)	mofelegetši	mofelehetsi	mmuledisi	ukukhapha	umphelezeli
	met klippe gooi	stone (v)	-foša ka maswika	-tlepetsa	-kolopa ka matlapa	-gibisela	-gxoba ngamatshe
	metode	method (n)	mokgwa	mokgwa	mokgwa	umgaqo	umkhuba
	meubels	furniture (n)	fenitšhara	thepa ya ntlo	fenitšhara	ifenitshala	ifenisha
	middag	midday (n)	mosegare wa sekgalela	motsheare	sethoboloko	iminenkulu	imini
	middag	noon (n)	mosegare wa sekgalela	motshehare	motshegare	iminemaqanda	imini
	middag	afternoon (n)	thapama	thapama	tshokologo	emva kwemini	intambama
	middagete	lunch (n)	letena	dijo tsa motsheare	dijotshegare	isidlo sasemini	idina
	middel	waist (n)	letheka	letheka	letheka	isinqe	iguma
	middel	centre (n)	bogare	setsing	tikatikwe	isenta	isenta
	middel	centre (n)	bogare	setsi	bogare	umbindi	isenta
	middernag	midnight (n)	bošegogare	kgitla	bosigogare	ezinzulwini zobusuku	phakathi kwamabili
	mielies	maize (n)	mahea	poone	mmidi	umbona	ummbila
	mier	ant (n)	tšhošwane	bohlwa	tshoswane	imbovane	intuthwane
	migrasie	migration (n)	khudugo	phallo	khudugo	imfuduko	ukuya kwelinye izwe
	migreer	migrate (v)	-huduga	-falla	-huduga	-fuduka	-akha kwelinye izwe
	mik	aim (v)	-tšea maleba	-lebisa	-kwaisa	-jolisa	-khomba
	mikrogolf	microwave (n)	maekroweife	leqhubu la maekoro	maekorowafe	amazanana	imakhroweyivi
	mikroskoop	microscope (n)	maekrosekopo	maekorosekoupo	maekorosekopo	imakroskopu	umasikilopu
	militêre	military (a)	-bohlabani	-sesole	-sesole	-omkhosi	-empi
	miljoen	million (n)	milione	milijone	mileone	isigidi	isigidi
	milt	spleen (n)	lebete	lebete	lebete	udakada	ubende
	mimosa	mimosa (n)	mooka	mimosa	mookana	umnga	umunga
	min	few (a)	-sego kae	-mmalwa	-mmalwa	-mbalwa	-ncane
	minder	less (a)	-fokoditšwego	-nyenyane	-nnye	-ncinci	-ncane kuna-
	mineraal	mineral (n)	minerale	minerale	serašwa	isimbiwa	isansimbi
	minimum	minimum (n)	botlalonyane	bonyane	bobotlana	ubuncinane	-ncane kakhulu
	minister	minister (n)	tona	letona	tona	umphathiswa	isikhonzi
	minnaar	lover (n)	morati	moratuwa	morati	isithandwa	isithandwa
	minste	least (a)	-nyenyane	-bonyane	-bogolo bogolo	-ncinci	-ncane kakhulu

Afrikaans	English	N Sotho	Sesotho	Tswana	Xhosa	Zulu	M
minuut	minute (n)	motsotso	motsotso	motsotso	umzuzu	iminithi	
mis	fog (n)	mouwane	mohodi	mouwane	inkungu	inkunga	
mis	manure (n)	mmutedi	manyolo	letshotelo	umgquba	umqubo	
mis	miss (v)	-foša	-fosa	-fosa	-phosa	-geja	
mis	mist (n)	mouwane	mohodi	mouwane	inkungu	inkungu	
misbruik	abuse (n)		tlatlapo	tiriso e e sa siamang	ukusebenzisa kakubi	ukoniwa	
misbruik	abuse (v)	-senya	-tlatlapa	-dirisa e seng ka fa siamong	-sebenzisa kakubi	-ona	
misdaad	crime (n)	tšhenyo	molato	molato	ulwaphulo-mthetho	ubugebengu	
misdadiger	criminal (n)	sesenyi	sesenyi	modiramolato	isaphuli-mthetho	isigebengu	
mishandel	ill-treat (v)	-tlaiša	-tlatlapa	-kgokgontsha	-phatha kakubi	-phatha kabi	
miskien	maybe (adv)	mohlamong	mohlomong	gongwe	mhlawumbi	mhlawumbe	
miskien	perhaps (adv)	mohlamongwe	mohlomong	gongwe	mhlawumbi	mhlawumbe	
mislei	mislead (v)	-foraforetša	-kgelosa	-digela ka lemena	-lukuhla	-dukisa	
misleidend	misleading (a)	-foraforetšago	-kgelosang	-digela ka lemena	-lukuhla(yo)	-dukisayo	
misluk	abortive (a)		-nyopileng	-senyegetsweng	-phanzileyo	-gejile	
misluk	fail (v)	-palelwa	-hloleha	-retelelwa	-ngaphumeleli	-hluleka	
mislukking	failure (n)	tšhitego	-tlholeho	thetelelo	ukuwa	ukwahluleka	
misterie	mystery (n)	khupamarama	mohlolo	bosaitseweng	ummangaliso	imfihlakalo	
misverstaan	misunderstand (v)	-sa kwišiše	-se utlwisise	-utlwela	-ngaqondi kakuhle	-ngezwa	
misverstand	misunderstanding (n)	go se kwišiše	ho se utlwisise	se nang kutlwisiso	ukungaqondani	ukungezwani	
mite	myth (n)	nonwane	tshomo	naane	intsomi	insumo	
modder	mud (n)	leraga	seretse	seretse	udaka	udaka	
modderig	muddy (a)	-leraga	-seretse	-matlepetlepe	-nodaka	-nodaka	
mode	fashion (n)	moaparo	mokgwa	moaparo	ifashoni	imfeshini	
modern	modern (a)	-sebjalebjale	-sejwalejwale	-sešwa	-ntsha	-yesimanje	
moed	courage (n)	sebete	tiisetso	bopelokgale	isibindi	isibindi	
moeder	mother (n)	mma	mme	mme	umama	umama	
moedervlek	birthmark (n)	lebadi la matswalo	letshwao la tswalo	sematla	umkhango	icasha	
moedig	courageous (a)	-nago le sebete	-tiisetsang	-pelokgale	-nesibindi	-nesibindi	
moedswillig	wilful (a)	-matepe	ka boomo	-boitaolo	-nenkani	ngamabomu	
moeg	tired (a)	-lapilego	-kgathetseng	-lapileng	-dinayo	-khathele	
moegheid	weariness (n)	tapo	mokgathala	letsapa	ukudinwa	ukukhathala	
moeg word	tire (v)	-lapa	-kgathala	-lapa	-dinwa	-khathala	
moeilik	hard (a)	-boima	-boima	-thata	-nzima	-nzima	
moeilik	difficult (a)	-thata	-thata	-thata	-nzima	-nzima	
moeilikheid	difficulty (n)	bothata	bothata	bothata	inzima	ubunzima	
moeite	trouble (n)	boitapišo	matsapa	molato	ingxaki	inkathazo	
moeras	swamp (n)	mohlaka	mohlaka	motsitlana	umgxobhozo	ixhaphozi	
moersleutel	spanner (n)	sepanere	sepanere	tshoko	inkunzana	isipanela	
moet	must (v)	-swanetše	-tlamehile	-tshwanetse	-mele	-bo-	
mol	mole (n)	khwiti	mokunyane	serunya	intuku	ivukusi	
mompel	mutter (v)	-bobola	-honotha	-mumura	-mbombozela	-munqazela	
mond	mouth (n)	molomo	molomo	molomo	umlomo	umlomo	
mondeling	verbal (a)	-molomo	-molomo	ka puo	-omlomo	-ngomlomo	
mondfluitjie	mouth organ (n)	foleitši	foleiti	foleiki	ifleyiti	imfiliji	
mondvol	mouthful (n)	tekanyo ye e tlalago molomo	mothamo	mothama	umthamo	umthamo	
monster	sample (n)	sešupo	sesupo	sesupo	isampulu	isampula	
monument	monument (n)	monyumente	sefika	sefikantswe	ilitye lesikhumbuzo	itshe lesikhumbuzo	
mooi	pretty (a)	-botse	-tle	-ntle	-hle	-hle	
moontlik	possible (a)	-kgonegago	-etsahalang	-gongwe	-ngenzeka	-enzekayo	
moord	murder (n)	polao	polao	polao	ubugebenga	ukubulala umuntu	
moordenaar	murderer (n)	mmolai	mmolai	mmolai	isigebenga	umbulali	
môre	tomorrow (n)	gosasa	hosane	ka moso	ngomso	kusasa	
mors	spill (v)	-falatša	-tsholla	-tsholola	-chitha	-chitha	
morsig	messy (a)	-ditšhila	-ditshila	-makgaphila	-onakeleyo	-nesibhixi	
mossel	mussel (n)	mohuta wa kgopa ya lewatle	mosele		imbaza	imbaza	
mossienes	glovebox (n)	sebolokelo	sehlaha	kgetsi ya ga dimo	isigcini-sandla	isigcini-magilavu	

179

M	Afrikaans	English	N Sotho	Sesotho	Tswana	Xhosa	Zulu
	mosterd	mustard (n)	mostara	mosetareta	masetete	imostade	umasitadi
	mot	moth (n)	mmoto	mmoto	serurubele	uvivingane	ibhu
	motel	motel (n)	motele	motele	motele	ihotele	imothela
	motor	motorcar (n)	mmotoro	koloi	mmotorokara	imotɔ	imoto
	motor	car (n)	mmotoro	mmotokara	mmotorokara	imotɔ	imoto
	motorfiets	motorcycle (n)	thuthuthu	sethuthuthu	sethuthuthu	isithuthuthu	isithuthuthu
	motorhawe	garage (n)	karatše	karatjhe	karaje	igaraji	igalaji
	motreën	drizzle (v)	-sarasara	lefafatsane	-na medupe	umkhumezelo	-khiza
	mou	sleeve (n)	letsogo la seaparo	letsoho	letsogo	umkhono	umkhono
	mout	malt (n)	mohlaba	mmela	momela	imithombo	imithombo
	muf	mildew (n)	nyakgahlo	poya	mouta	ukungunda	isikhunta
	muil	mule (n)	meila	mmoulo	mmoulo	imeyile	umnyuzi
	muis	mouse (n)	legotlo	tweba	peba	impuku	igundane
	muishond	skunk (n)	nakedi	nakedi	nakedi	iqaqa	iqaqa
	muishond	polecat (n)	nakedi	nakedi	nakedi	iqaqa	iqaqa
	munisipaal	municipal (a)	-mmasepala	-mmasepala	-mmasepala	-edolophu	-kamasipalati
	munisipaliteit	municipality (n)	mmasepala	mmasepala	mmasepala	ibhunga ledolophu	umasipalati
	muntstuk	coin (n)	tšheletetshipi	lewana	ledi	ukhɔzo lwemali	uhlamvu lwemali
	murg	marrow (n)	moko	moko	moko	umoɔngo	umnkantsha
	museum	museum (n)	musiamo	musiamo	musiamo	imuziyam	imnyuziyamu
	musiek	music (n)	moopelo	mmino	mmino	umculo	umculo
	musikaal	musical (a)	-moopelo	-mmino	-mmino	-nomculo	-mculo
	musikant	musician (n)	ramelodi	sebini	rammino	umculi	isazi somculo
	muskiet	mosquito (n)	monang	monwang	monang	ingcongconi	umiyane
	muur	wall (n)	leboto	lebota	lebota	udonga	udonga
	muurbal	squash (n)	sekwaše	sekwashe	sekwaše	iskwashi	isikwashi
	my	me (pron)	n-	nna	nna	mna	mina
	my	my (pron)	-ka/n-	-ka	-ka	yam	-mi
	myl	mile (n)	maele	maele	mmaele	imayile	imayela
	myne	mine (pron)	-ka	-ka	-me	yam	-ami
	na	to (prep)	go-	ho-	go	ku-	ku-
	na	after (time) (prep)	morago ga	ka mora	sena	emva	emuva kwa-
	na-aap	ape (v)	-ekiša	-etsisa	-etsa	-linganisa	-lingisa
	naaimasjien	sewing machine (n)	motšhene wa go roka	motjhine o rokang	motšhene wa go roka	umatshini wokuthunga	umshini wokuthunga
	naald	needle (n)	nalete	nale	lemao	inaliti	inaliti
	naaldwerk	sewing (n)	moroko	moroko	thoko	umthungo	umthungo
	naaldwerk doen	sew (v)	-roka	-roka	-roka	-thunga	-thunga
	naam	name (n)	leina	lebitso	leina	igama	igama
	naarheid	nausea (n)	go feroga dibete	ho feroha	go tlhatsa	isizothezothe	isicanucanu
	naar maak	nauseate (v)	-feroša dibete	-ferola	tlhatsisa	-zotha	-canula
	naat	seam (n)	moroko	moroko	moroko	umthungo	umthungo
	naby	near (adv)	kgauswi	haufi	-gaufi	kufutshane	-eduze
	naby	close (a)	kgauswi	-haufi	gaufi	-kufutshane	eduze
	nadering	approach (n)	tebelego	katamelo	itlhagiso	indlela yokuvelela	ukuvelela
	naeltjie	navel (n)	mokhubu	mokguba	khubu	inkaba	inkaba
	nag	night (n)	bošego	bosiu	bosigo	ubusuku	ubusuku
	nagaan	check (v)	-kgonthiša	-hlahloba	-lekola	-khangela	-hlolisisa
	nageboorte	afterbirth (n)	mohlana	mohlana	motlhala	umkhaya	umhlapho
	nagereg	dessert (n)	phuting	phuting	phuting	isimuncumuncu	ukudla okugcinwa ngakho
	nageslag	posterity (n)	leloko	leloko	bana	isizukulwana	izizukulwane ezizayo
	nagmerrie	nightmare (n)	segateledi	ho phofa	toro e maswe	iphupha elibi	iphupho elesabisayo
	nagwag	nightwatchman (n)	moletabošego	matjekelane	matshinkilane	umantshingilane	ugadi
	najaag	pursue (v)	-rakadiša	-lelekisa	-leleka	-landela	-landelisa
	nalatig	negligent (a)	-sa hlokomelego	-bohlaswa	-tlhokomologo	-khathali(yo)	-nganaki
	nalatig	careless (a)	-šaetšago	-bohlaswa	-boatla	-ngakhathaliyo	-nganaki
	nalatigheid	negligence (n)	tlhokomologo	bohlaswa	tlhokomologo	ukungakhathali	ukunganaki
	namaak	imitate (v)	-ekiša	-etsisa	-etsa	-linganisa	-fanisa
	'n ander	another (a)	-ngwe	-ngi-nngwe	-nye	-nye	-nye

Afrikaans	English	N Sotho	Sesotho	Tswana	Xhosa	Zulu
nartjie	naartjie (n)	nariki	narike	nariki	inartyisi	inantshi
nasaal	nasal (a)	-nko	-nko	-nkong	-mpumlo	-ekhala
nasie	nation (n)	setšhaba	setjhaba	setšhaba	isizwe	isizwe
nasionaal	national (a)	-setšhaba	-setjhaba	-bosetšhaba	-nobuzwe	-esizwe
nasionalisme	nationalism (n)	bosetšhaba	botjhaba	bosetšhaba	ubuzwe	ubuzwe
nat	wet (a)	-kolobilego	-metsi	-metsi	-manzi	-manzi
natgooi	water (v)	-nošetša	-nwesetsa	-nosa	-manzisa	-chelela
natmaak	moisten (v)	-thapiša	-kolobisa	-ngodisa	-manzisa	-manzisa
natuur	nature (n)	tlhago	hlaho	tlholego	indalo	imvelo
natuurlewe	wildlife (n)	bophelolešokeng	bophelo bo hlaha	bophelonageng	ubomi basendle	impilo yasendle
natuurlik	natural (a)	-tlhago	-hlaho	-tlhaga	-endalo	-yimvelo
natuurreservaat	nature reserve (n)	nagatšhireletšo	poloko ya tsa hlaho	bosireletso jwa tlholego	iziko logcino-ndalo	isiqiwu
navraag	inquiry (n)	nyakišišo	potso	potso	ukubuza	ukubuza
navraag doen	inquire (v)	-nyakišiša	-botsa	-botsa	-buzisa	-buza
naywer	envy (n)	mona	mohono	keletso	umona	umhawu
nederig	humble (a)	-ikokobetšago	-ikokobeditseng	-boikokobetso	-lulamile(yo)	-thobile
nederigheid	humility (n)	boikokobetšo	boikokobetso	boikokobetso	ubuntu	intobeko
nederlaag	defeat (n)	go fenywa	tlholo	phenyo	uloyiso	ukwahluleka
neef	nephew (n)	setlogolo	motjhana	ntsala	umtshana	umshana
neem	take (v)	-tšea	-nka	-tsaya	-thatha	-thatha
neëntien	nineteen (n)	lesomesenyane	leshome le metso e robo	some robongwe	ishumi elinethoba	ishumi nesishiyagalolunye
neëntig	ninety (n)	masomesenyane	mashome a robong	somaarobongwe	amashumi alithoba	amashumi ayishiyagalolunye
neerdruk	depress (v)	-nyamiša	-tepeletsa	-gatelela	-cinezela	-cindezela
neerhang	droop (v)	-lepelela	-lepella	-ribama	-jinga	-yenda
nege	nine (n)	senyane	robong	robongwe	ithoba	isishiyagalolunye
nek	neck (n)	molala	molala	molala	intamo	intamo
nektar	nectar (n)	manopi	lero	botshe	incindi	uju
nes	nest (n)	sehlaga	sehlaha	sentlhaga	indlwane	isidleke
nestel	nestle (v)	-dula ka go iketla	-baballa	-aga	-quthuma	-khosela
net	just (adv)	fela	feela	fela	kanje	-sanda
netjies	tidy (a)	-bothakga	-makgethe	-bothakga	-cocekile (yo)	-lungisiwe
netjies	neat (a)	-bothakga	makgethe	-sethakga	-cocekile (yo)	-nobunono
neus	nose (n)	nko	nko	nko	impumlo	ikhala
neusgat	nostril (n)	kgalananko	lesoba la nko	lerobananko	iphumlo	ikhala
neut	nut (n)	koko	tholwana	thamane	inqoba	inhlamvu yomuthi eqathwayo
niemand	nobody (pron)	e sego motho	ha ho motho	ope	akamntu	akukho-muntu
nier	kidney (n)	pshio	phio	philo	intso	inso
nies	sneeze (v)	-ethimola	-ethimola	-ethimola	-thimla	-thimula
nies	sneeze (n)	moethimolo	moethimolo	mofikela	ukuthimla	isithimuka
nie stip nie	unpunctual (a)	-go se be nakong	-sa bolokeng nako	-e seng ka nako	-ngagcini xesha	-ngagcinisikhathi
niggie	niece (n)	setlogolo	motjhana	ntsala	umtshana	umshanakazi
niks	nothing (n)	selo	letho	-pe	ubungabikho	ize
niksbeduidend	trivial (a)	-lefela	-sa tsebisahaleng	-sepe	-ngenamsebenzi	-yimfeketho
nodig hê	need (v)	-hloka	-hloka	-tlhoka	-funa	-swela
noem	name (v)	-rea leina	-bitsa	-taya	-biza	-biza
nòg	nor (conj)	le ge e ka ba	kapa	le fa e le	okanye	noma
nog	still (adv)	-sa-	-sa	-sa	kwakhona	-sa-
nog 'n	another (a)	-ngwe	-ng; -nngwe	-ngwe	-nye	nokunye
nommer	number (n)	nomoro	palo	palo	inani	inombolo
non	nun (n)	moitlamigadi	moitlami	moitlami	unongendi	isisitela
noodgeval	emergency (n)	tšhoganetšo	tlokotsi	tshoganyetso	ithuba lokuxakeka	ingozi
noodhulp	first aid (n)	thušo ya potlako	thuso ya pele	thuso ya potlako	uncedo lokuqala	usizo lokuqala
noodsaaklik	necessary (a)	-nyakegago	-hlokehang	-tlhokegang	-mfuneko	-dingekile
noodsaaklikheid	necessity (n)	nyakego	tlhokeho	tlhokafalo	imfuneko	isidingo
nooi	girlfriend (n)	moratiwa	kgarebe	kgarebe	umhlobokazi	intombi
nooit	never (adv)	le gatee	le kgale	-e seng	soze	-ngeke

181

N	Afrikaans	English	N Sotho	Sesotho	Tswana	Xhosa	Zulu
	noord	north (a)	-leboa	-Leboya	-bokone	-ntla	-asenyakatho
	noorde	north (n)	leboa	Leboya	bokone	umntla	inyakatho
	nors	sullen (a)	-hlonamago	-lonya	-ngomaelang	-lushwaca	-luhlwibi
	notetas	wallet (n)	sepatše	walete	khuana	iwolethi	iwalethi
	nou	now (adv)	bjale	jwale	-jaanong	ngoku	manje
	noukeurig	accurate (a)	-nepegilego	-nepahetseng	-maroka	-chanekileyo	-qonde ngqo
	noukeurigheid	accuracy (n)	nepo	nepo	nepo	ukuchaneka	ukucophelela
	November	November (n)	Nofemere	Pudungwana	Ngwanatseele	uNovemba	uNovemba
	nul	zero (n)	lefeela	noto	lefelo	unothi	iqanda
	nutteloos	useless (a)	-hlokago mohola	-se nang thuso	-sepe	-ngenamsebenzi	-ngasizi
	nuttig	useful (a)	-mohola	-bohlokwa	-mosola	-nokusetyenziswa	-nomsebenzi
	nuus	news (n)	ditaba	ditaba	kgang	iindaba	izindaba
	nuuskierig	inquisitive (a)	-nyakago go tseba ditaba	-ratang ditaba	-swegaswega	qavileyo	-nenhlazane
	nuut	new (a)	-fsa	-tjha	-swa	-tsha	-sha
	nuweling	newcomer (n)	yo mofsa	mofihli	moswa	umfiki	inyuwane
	oefen	practise (v)	-tlwaetša	-hlakisa	-katisa	qhelisa	-zijwayeza
	oefen	exercise (v)	-otlolla	-ithapolla	-thobolola	-qhelisa	-sebenza
	oefening	exercise (n)	kotlollo	thapollo	thobololo	ukuziqhelisa	umsebenzi
	oerwoud	jungle (n)	sethokgwa	mofidibithi	sekgwa	ihlathi	ihlathi
	oes	reap (v)	-buna	-kotula	-kotula	-vuna	-vuna
	oes	harvest (n)	puno	kotulo	thobo	isivuno	isivuno
	oes	harvest (v)	-buna	-kotula	-roba	-vuna	-vuna
	oester	oyster (n)	kgopa ya lewatle	oesetere		imbatyisi	ukhwathu
	of	or (conj)	goba	kapa	ampo	okanye	noma
	of	whether (conj)	goba	kapa	fa	ukuba	noma
	offerande	sacrifice (n)	sehlabelo	sehlabelo	setlhabelo	idini	umnikelo
	òf…òf	either…or (conj)	goba	kapa	kgotsa	nokuba okanye	noma muphi
	oggend	morning (n)	moswana	hoseng	phakela	intsasa	ekuseni
	oker	ochre (n)	letsoku	letsoku	letsoku	imbola	uhlobo lwebumba
	Oktober	October (n)	Oktobore	Mphalane	Diphalane	Oktobha	u-Okthoba
	olie	oil (n)	oli	oli	ole	ioli	i-oyili
	olifant	elephant (n)	tlou	tlou	tlou	indlovu	indlovu
	olyf	olive (n)	mohlware	tholwana ya mohlware	motlhware	umnquma	i-olivi
	omdat	because (conj)	ka gobane	hobane	gore	ngokuba	ngoba
	omgee	mind (v)	-hlokomela	-kgathalla	-kgathala	-khathalela	-khathala nga-
	omgee	care (v)	-hlokomela	-kgathalla	-tlhokomela	-khathalela	ukunakelela
	omgewing	environment (n)	tikologo	tikoloho	tikologo	ubume bendawo	ubunjalo bendawo
	omhels	embrace (v)	-gokarela	-kopa	-kamatlela	-anga	-gona
	omhelsing	embrace (n)	kgokarelo	kopo	kamatlelo	ukwanga	ukugona
	omkantel	capsize (v)	-thenkgoga	-phethoha	-menoga	-bhukuqa	-gumbeqeka
	omkom	perish (v)	-bola	-shwa	-swa	-nyamalala	-bhubha
	omkoop	bribe (v)	-reka	-ntsha tjotjo	-reka	-nyoba	-fumbathisa
	omkoopprys	bribe (n)	pipamolomo	tjotjo	pipamolomo	isinyobo	ukufumbathiswa
	omkopery	bribery (n)	seatlakobong	ho ntsha tjotjo	theko	unyobo	imvalamlomo
	omloop	circulation (n)	tikologo	potoloho	tikologo	umjikelezo	ukuzungeleza
	ompad	deviation (n)	phapogo	tsela e potolohang	phapogo	uphambuko	ukuphambuka
	omring	surround (v)	-dika	-bokanela	-dikanyetsa	-rhangqa	-zungeza
	omsetting	conversion (n)	tshokologo	tshokoloho	tshokologo	uguqulo	impenduko
	omsit	convert (v)	-sokologa	-sokolla	-sokolola	-guqula	-phendukisa
	omstander	bystander (n)	moemakgauswi	mobohi	babogedi	ilalela	isibukeli
	omtrek	circumference (n)	sedika	sedika	modiko	umjikelo	umjikelezo wesiyingi
	omvergooi	overthrow (v)	-menola	diha	-diga	-bhukuqa	-wisa
	omweg	detour (n)	tsela ya moralela	tsela e potolohang	phapogo	umgwegwelezo	umshekelelo
	onafhanklik	independent (a)	-ipušago	-lokolohileng	-boipuso	-ngaxhomekekanga	-zimele
	onbarmhartig	uncharitable (a)	-hlokago botho	-se nang mohau	-se nang pelo	-ngenamfesane	-ngenamhawu
	onbedoeld	unplanned (a)	-sa akanywago	-sa hlophuwang	-seng loano	-ngacetywanga	-ngahleliwe
	onbehoedsaam	unwary (a)	-sa hlokomelego	-sa kgathalleng	-se na tlhaga	-ngaphaphamanga	-ngaxwayile
	onbelangrik	unimportant (a)	-sego bohlokwa	-seng ya bohlokwa	-sa tlhokegwang	umdibaniso	-ncane

Afrikaans	English	N Sotho	Sesotho	Tswana	Xhosa	Zulu	O
onbeleef	impolite (a)	-hlokago tlhompho	-sa hlompheng	-makgakga	-ngenambeko	-ngahloniphi	
onbeloond	unrewarded (a)	-go se lefše	-sa lefuweng	-sa duelwang	-ngavuzwanga	-ngabongwanga	
onbeskaaf	uncivilised (a)	-hlokago setho	-tala	-tala	-ngaphucukanga	-ngaphucuzekile	
onbeskadig	undamaged (a)	-sego -senyega	-sa senyehang	-sa senyegang	-ngonakelanga	-ngalimalanga	
onbeskeie	immodest (a)	-hlabišago dihlong	-tala	-maikgantsho	-sileyo	-ngenazinhloni	
onbeskof	rude (a)	-hlokago mekgwa	-tala	-mafega	-krwada	-ngahloniphi	
onbeslis	undecided (a)	-sego wa ahlolwa	-sa tsitsang	-sa atlholwang	-ngenasigqibo	-nhliziyombili	
onbetaamlik	obscene (a)	-be	-hlabisang dihlong	-tlhokang botho	-ngcolileyo	-nenhlamba	
onbetaamlikheid	obscenity (n)	bobe	manyala	botlhokabotho	ukungcola	inhlamba	
onbetroubaar	undependable (a)	-sa botegego	-sa tshepahaleng	-sa tshepiwang	-ngathembakalanga	-ngathembeki	
onbetwis	undisputed (a)	-sa ganetšwego	-sa phehisweng kgang	-sa ganelwang	-ngaphikiswa(yo)	-ngenakuphikiswa	
onbevrees	unafraid (a)	-sa boifego	-sa tshabeng	-sa tshabeng	-ngoyikiyo	-ngesabi	
onbewus	unaware (a)	-sa tsebego	-sa elellweng	-sa itseng	-ngaqondanga	-nganaki	
ondankbaar	ungrateful (a)	-sa lebogego	-se nang teboho	-se nang tebogo	-ngenambulelo	-ngabongi	
onder	under (prep)	fase	tlasa	tlhase	ngaphantsi	phansi	
onder	below (prep)	fase	-tlase	tlase	-ngaphantsi	phansi kwa-	
onderbaadjie	waistcoat (n)	onoropaki	onnorobaki	baaki ya tlase	indulubhatyi	intolibhantshi	
onderbreek	interrupt (v)	-tsena ganong	-sitisa	-kgaolela	-phazamisa	-thikameza	
onderbreking	interruption (n)	kgaotšo	tshitiso	kgaolelo	isiphazamiso	isilibazisi	
onderdompel	submerge (v)	-inela	-qwedisa	-nwela	-ntywilisa	-cwilisa	
onderdruk	oppress (v)	-gatelela	-tuba	-gatelela	-cinezela	-cindezela	
onderdrukker	oppressor (n)	mogateledi	motubi	mogateledi	umcinezeli	umcindezeli	
onderdrukking	oppression (n)	kgatelelo	botubo	kgatelelo	ingcinezelo	ukucindezela	
onderhandel	negotiate (v)	-rerišana	-buisana	-buisanya	-thethathethana	-xoxisana	
onderhemp	vest (n)	penehempe	besete	besete	ivesti	ivesti	
onderhoud	interview (n)	morero	tlhahlobo	go tshwara ditherisano	udliwano-ndlebe	ingxoxo	
onderhoud	maintenance (n)	phepo	tlhokomelo	tlamelo	inkxaso	isondlo	
onderontwikkeld	underdeveloped (a)	-nago le tlhabologo ye nnyane	-sa tswelang pele	-sa tlhabololwang	-ngakhulanga gqibi	-ngathu	
onderrig	instruct (v)	-ruta	-rupela	-kaela	-yalela	-fundisa	
onderrig	instruction (n)	thuto	thupelo	kaelo	umyalelo	umyalo	
onderrok	petticoat (n)	onoroko	onnoroko	mosese	unomtidili	ipitikoti	
onderskei	distinguish (v)	-kgethologanya	-kgetha	-farologanya	-ahlula	-ahlukanisa	
ondersoek	investigate (v)	-nyakišiša	-batlisisa	-tlhotlhomisa	-phanda	-hlola	
ondersoek	investigation (n)	nyakišišo	patlisiso	tlhotlhomiso	uphando	ukuhlola	
ondersoek	examine (v)	-hlahloba	-hlahloba	-tlhatlhoba	-vavanya	-phenya	
ondersteun	support (v)	-thuša	-tshehetsa	-tshegetsa	-xhasa	-sekela	
ondervoorsitter	vice-chairman (n)	seatla sa modulasetulo	motlatsi wa modulasetulo	modulasetilo wa bobedi	usekela-sihlalo	usekelasihlalo	
ondervra	interrogate (v)	-botšišiša	-botsa	-kolotisa	-buza	-buzisisa	
onderwerp	subject (n)	sediri	taba	sediri	intloko	isimemela	
onderwerp	subdue (v)	-fenya	-hatella	-gatelela	-oyisa	-ahlula	
onderwyser	teacher (n)	morutiši	titjhere	morutabana	ititshala	uthisha	
ondeug	vice (n)	bošula	bobe	bosula	umkhuba	umkhuba omubi	
ondeund	mischievous (a)	-selekago	-botlokotsebe	-letshwenyo	-nentlondi	-klinile	
oneerlik	dishonest (a)	-sa tshephegego	-sa tshepeheng	-se ikanyegeng	-ngathembekanga	-khohlisayo	
oneerlikheid	dishonesty (n)	bofora	ho hloka botshepehi	go se ikanyege	ubumenemene	inkohliso	
onenigheid	dispute (n)	phapang	tsekisano	kganetsano	impikiswano	umbango	
onewe	odd (a)	-sa lekanelego	ntho esele	-setlholo	-ngumnqakathi	-dwa-nje	
onfatsoenlik	improper (a)	-sa swanelago	-fosahetse	-molema	-ngafanelekanga	-ngafanele	
ongaar	uncooked (a)	-tala	-tala	-korobetseng	-ngaphekwanga	-luhlaza	
ongebore	unborn (a)	-sego ya tswalwa	-sa tswalwang	-sa tsalweng	-ngazelwanga	-ngakazalwa	
ongedissiplineerd	undisciplined (a)	-hlokago boitshwaro	-se nang mekgwa	-sa rutwang	-ngaqeqeshekanga	-ngenamthetho	
ongeduldig	impatient (a)	-felago pelo	-fela pelo	-felang pelo	-tshiseka(yo)	-xhamazele	
ongehoorsaam	insubordinate (a)	-sa kwego	-tellang	-gananang	-ngevayo	-delela	
ongehoorsaamheid	disobedience (n)	go se kwe	kgano	boganana	ukungathobeli	ukungalaleli	
ongehoorsaam wees	disobey (v)	-gana go kwa	-hana	-gana	-sukuthobela	-ngalaleli	
ongeldig	invalid (a)	-sa šomego	-fokolang	-se kae sepe	-ngumlwelwe	-ngenamandla	
ongeleerd	uneducated (a)	-go se rutege	-sa rutehang	-tala	-ngafundanga	-ngafundile	
ongelowige	unbeliever (n)	moditšhaba	mohetene	moheitene	umntu ongakholwayo	ongakholiwe	

O

Afrikaans	English	N Sotho	Sesotho	Tswana	Xhosa	Zulu
ongeluk	accident (n)	kotsi	kotsi	kotsi	ingozi	ingozi
ongelukkig	unfortunately (adv)	ka maswabi	-madimabe	-e seng sego	ngelishwa	-ngelishwa
ongelukkig	unlucky (a)	-nago le madimabe	-madimabe	-bosula	-ngenathamsanqa	nebhadi
ongelukkig	unhappy (a)	-nyamilego	-sa thabang	-bosula	-ngonwabanga	-hluphekile
ongelyk	unequal (a)	-sa lekanego	-sa lekaneng	-sa lekaneng	-ngalinganiyo	-ngalingene
ongelyk	uneven (a)	-sa lekanego	-sa lekaneng	-makgawekgawe	-ngalinganiyo	-namaduma
ongemagtig	unauthorised (a)	-se nago tokelo	-se nang tokelo	-se nang tumelelo	ngagunyaziswanga	-ngagunyaziwe
ongemaklik	uncomfortable (a)	-go se iketle	-sa tsitsang	-tlhoatlhoegang	-ngekho mfumamfuma	-nganethezekile
ongemeubileerd	unfurnished (a)	-se nang fenišara	-se nang thepa	-se nang fenitšhara	-ngenafenitshala	-ngenayo ifenisha
ongenadig	unmerciful (a)	-hlokago kguagelo	-se nang mohau	-se nang maitshwarelo	-ngenanceba	-ngenamhawu
ongeneeslik	incurable (a)	-sa alafegego	-sa phekoleheng	-seemera	-nganyangekiyo	-ngenakwelashwa
ongerus	uneasy (a)	-sa iketlego	-sa tsitsang	-kokonetseng	-ngonwabanga	-novalo
ongeskik	unfit (a)	-sa lokelego	-sa lokelang	-sa siameng	-ngafanelekanga	-ngalungele
ongesond	unhealthy (a)	tše di sa agego mmele	-se nang bophelo	-lwalang	ngaphilanga	-ngaphilile
ongetroud	unmarried (a)	-sego a nyala	-sa nyalwang	-kgope	-ngatshatanga	-ngaganile
ongetwyfeld	undoubted (a)	-sa belaetšego	-sa belaetseng	-tota	-ngenakuthanda-tyuzwa	-sobala
ongeval	casualty (n)	kotsi	lehlatsipa	kgobadi	ingxwelerha	ingozi
ongewapend	unarmed (a)	-sa itlhamago ka dibetša	-sa hlomelang	-se nang dibetsa	-ngaxhobanga	-ngahlomile
ongewens	undesirable (a)	-sa nyakegego	-sa hlokahaleng	-ditsatsa	-nganqwenelekiyo	-ngafuneki
ongewoon	uncommon (a)	-sa tlwaelwago	-sa tlwaelehang	-sa tlwaelwang	-ngaqhelekanga	-ngavamile
ongewoond	unaccustomed (a)	-sa tlwaelago	-sa tlwaelehang	-sa tlwaelwang	-ngaqhelanga	-ngajwayele
onheilspellend	ominous (a)	-tšhošago	-tshabehang	-botlhodi	-omhlola	-nemihlola
onhigiënies	unhygienic (a)	-ditšhila	-sa hlwekang	-maswe	-ngenampilo	-ngenanhlanzeko
onhoorbaar	inaudible (a)	-sa kwagalego	-sa utlwahaleng	-sa utlwang	-ngavakali(yo)	-ngezwakali
onjuis	incorrect (a)	-fošagetšego	-phoso	-maaka	-ngalunganga	-ngalungile
onkoste	expenses (n)	ditshenyegelo	ditshenyehelo	tshenyegelo	iindleko	izindleko
onkruid	weed (n)	sekoro	lehola	mofero	ukhula	ukhula
onkruid uittrek	weed (v)	-hlogola	-hlaola	-tlhagola	-susa ukhula	-hlakula
onkuis	bawdy (a)	-otswetšago	tlhapa	-maswe	-nobuhenyu	-enhlamba
onkunde	ignorance (n)	bothotho	ho hloka tsebo	go ikapaya mokatse	intswelo-kwazi	ukungazi
onlangs	newly (adv)	malobanyana	-haufi	seswa	-sandula	kabusha
onlus	riot (n)	mpherefere	morusu	moferefere	isidubedube	isidumo
onmanierlik	ill-mannered (a)	-sa itshwarego	-mekgwa e mebe	-se nang maitseo	-ngenambeko	-ngahloniphi
onmiddellik	immediate (a)	-semeetseng	hanghang	-akofa	-kwamsinya	manje
onmoontlik	impossible (a)	-sa kgonegego	-sitang	-tata	-ngenakwenzeka	-ngenakwenzeka
onnosel	stupid (a)	-sethotho	-sethoto	-seeleele	-bhanxa(yo)	-phukuzekile
onontwikkeld	undeveloped (a)	-hlokago tlhabologo	-sa ntshetswang pele	-sa tlhabololwang	-ngekasetyenziswa	-ngathuthukile
onoplettend	inattentive (a)	-sa hlokomelego	-sa eleng hloko	-sa tlhokomelang	-ngamameli(yo)	-ngalaleli
onpersoonlik	impersonal (a)	-hlokago botho	-hloka botho	-sa ipeeng	-ngabhekisi mntwini	-ngaphathelene nabantu
onregverdig	unjust (a)	-sa lokago	-se nang toka	-tshiamololo	-ngenabulungisa	-ngalungile
onrein	unclean (a)	-sa hlwekago	-ditshila	-maswe	-mdaka	-ngcolile
ons	us (pron)	-re-	rona	rona	-ethu	thina
ons	we (pron)	rena	rona	rona	thina	thina
ons	our (pron)	-rena	-rona	rona	-ithu	-ithu
onsedelik	immoral (a)	-bootswa	-be	-bosenabotho	-nyala	-ngcolile
onseker	uncertain (a)	-belaetšago	-sa tsebeng hantle	-belaelang	-ngaqinisekanga	-ngabaza
onselfsugtig	unselfish (a)	-hlokago mona	-sa ikgopoleng	-boitebalo	-ngazicingeliyo	-nomhawu
onsigbaar	invisible (a)	-sa bonwego	-sa bonahaleng	-sa bonweng	-ngabonakali(yo)	okungabonakali
onsin	nonsense (n)	ditšiebadimo	lefeela	matlhapolosa	ubuvuvu	umbhedo
onsinnig	absurd (a)	-segišago	-hloka kelello	mo go se nang tlhaloganyo	-nobuhiba	-ngasile
onskadelik	harmless (a)	-se nago kotsi	-se nang tshenyo	-seng kotsi	-nabungozi	-ngenangozi
onskuldig	innocent (a)	-hlokago molato	-hloka molato	se nang molato	-msulwa	-msulwa
onsself	ourselves (pron)	-i-	rona	rona	thina	thina
ons s'n	ours (pron)	-rena	-rona	-rona	-ithu	abethu
onsteek	inflamed (a)	-kekago	-petlileng	-gotetseng	-tshileyo	-okudumbile
ontbied	summon (v)	-bitša	-bitsa	-bitsa	-bizela enkundleni	-biza
ontbind	decompose (v)	-bola	-bola	-bola	-vunda	-bola

Afrikaans	English	N Sotho	Sesotho	Tswana	Xhosa	Zulu	O
ontbloot	strip (v)	-apola	-hlobola	-apola	-bhunya	-hluba	
ontbloot	bare (v)	-hlobola	-senola	-gotlha	-hlubula	-veza	
ontbyt	breakfast (n)	sefihlolo	borakefese	sefitlholo	isidlo sakusasa	ibhulakufesi	
ontdek	discover (v)	-ribolla	-sibolla	-ribolola	-bhaqa	-fumanisa	
ontevrede	dissatisfied (a)	-ngongoregago	-belaela	-ngongoregang	-nganelisekanga	-khonondayo	
ontevredenheid	dissatisfaction (n)	ngongorego	pelaelo	dingongora	ukunganeliseki	ukhonondo	
onthou	recollect (v)	-gopola	-hopola	-gopola	-khumbula	-khumbula	
onthou	remember (v)	-gopola	-hopola	-gakologelwa	-khumbula	-khumbula	
onthou	abstain (v)	-ila	-sesefa	-ila	-yeka	-yeka	
ontken	deny (v)	-latola	-hana	-ganela	-khanyela	-phika	
ontlas	defecate (v)	-nya	-nya	-nnyela	-ya endle	-bhosha	
ontleding	analysis (n)	phetleko	mohlophollo	bolokololo	uhlalutyo	umhlahlelo	
ontleed	analyse (v)	-fetleka	-hlopholla	-lokolola	-hlalutya	-hlahlela	
ontmoedig	discourage (v)	-nyemiša pelo	-nyahamisa	-titina	-tyhafisa	-khubeza	
ontmoet	meet (v)	-kopana le	-teana	-kopana	-dibana	-hlangana na-	
ontmoeting	meeting (n)	kopano	teano	kgatlhano	indibano	ukuhlangana	
ontneem	deprive (v)	-amoga	-hlokisa	-tseela	-alela	-aphuca	
ontplof	explode (v)	-thunya	-qhoma	-thunya	-gqabhuka	-qhuma	
ontploffing	explosion (n)	go thunya	qhomo	go thunya	ugqabhuko-dubulo	ukuqhuma	
ontrafel	unravel (v)	-hlahlamolla	-qhaqholla	-rarabolola	-combulula	-qaqa	
ontrou	unfaithful (a)	-go se botege	-sa tshepahaleng	-sa ikanyegwang	-ngathembekanga	-ngathembekile	
ontslaan	dismiss (v)	-lokolla	-tebela	-belesetsa	-gxotha	-mukisa	
ontslag	dismissal (n)	tokollo	tebelo	teleko	ugxotho	ukumukiswa	
ontsmet	disinfect (v)	-hlwekiša	-hlwekisa	-bolaya ditwatsi	-bulala iintsholong-wane	-bulala imbewu yokufa	
ontsmettingsmiddel	disinfectant (n)	sehlwekiši	sehlwekisi	sebolayaditwatsi	isibulala-ntsholong-wane	umphungo	
ontsnap	escape (v)	-phonyokga	-phonyoha	-falola	-qhwesha	-baleka	
ontsnapping	escape (n)	phonyokgo	phonyoho	phalolo	uqhwesho	ukweqa	
ontstam	detribalise (v)	-kgokgofala	-kgokgotsa	-kurukurega	-thitshisa ubuhlanga	-bhungula	
ontsteking	ignition (n)	kgotelo	kgotetso	kgotso	ukulumeka	ukokheleka	
ontsteking	inflammation (n)	keko	petlo	kgotelo	ukukrala	ukudumba	
ontstel	upset (v)	-nyamiša	-kgathatsa	-tsuolola	-phazamisa	-thunukalisa	
ontsteld	upset (a)	-tshwenyegilego moyeng	-kgathatseha	-tsuololang	-phazamisekile(yo)	-thunukele	
ontugtig	lewd (a)	-otswago	-sekgobo		-ngaphucukanga	-nesigweba	
ontvang	receive (v)	-amogela	-amohela	-amogela	-fumana	-amukela	
ontvangs	reception (n)	kamogelo	kamohelo(ng)	kamogelo	ulwamkelo	ukwamukelwa	
ontvangsklerk	receptionist (n)	moamogedi	moamohedi	telereke ya kamogelo	umamkeli	umemukeli-bahambeli	
ontvoer	abduct (v)	-thopa	-kwetela	-utswa	-thwala	-thwala	
ontwaak	awake (v)	-phafoga	-tsosa	-thanya	-phaphamisa	-vuka	
onvatbaar	immune (a)	-soutilwego	-tshwaedisitswe	-tlhabetsweng	-gonyekileyo	-gonyiwe	
onveilig	unsafe (a)	-kotsi	-se nang tshireletso	-sa bolokegwang	-nobungozi	-nengozi	
onveranderlik	unalterable (a)	-sa fetogego	-sa fetoheng	-sa fetogeng	-ngajikiyo	-ngaguquki	
onverdiend	undeserved (a)	-sa swanelego	-sa elellwang	-sa tshwanelwang	-ngafanelanga	-ngafanele	
onvergeeflik	unforgivable (a)	-go se swarelege	-sa tshwarelweng	-sa itshwarelweng	-ngaxolelekiyo	-ngathethelelwa	
onvergeetlik	unforgettable (a)	-go se lebalege	-sa lebaleheng	-sa lebalweng	-ngalibalekiyo	-ngakhohlwa	
onverkrygbaar	unavailable (a)	-sa hwetšagalago	-sa fumaneheng	-tlhokegang	-ngafumanekiyo	-ngatholakali	
onvermeld	undisclosed (a)	-sa tšweletšwago	-sa bolelwang	-sa senolwang	-ngatyhilwanga	-ngavezwanga	
onvermydelik	inevitable (a)	-sa phemegego	-ke keng ya phengwa	-sa thibelegeng	-za kwenzeka	-ngenakuvinjelwa	
onvervuld	unfulfilled (a)	-sa phethegago	-sa phethahatswang	-sa tlhomamiswang	-ngazalisekanga	-ngafeziwe	
onverwag	unexpected (a)	-sewelo	-sa lebellwang	-tshoganyetso	-ngalindelekanga	-zumayo	
onverwags	unexpectedly (adv)	ka sewelo	-sa lebellwang	ka tshoganyetso	ngokungalindelekanga	ngokuzuma	
onvolledig	incomplete (a)	-sa felelago	-sa phethang	-sa felang	-ngagqibekanga	-ngaphelele	
onvolmaak	imperfect (a)	-sa phethegago	-sa phethehang	-seng botlalo	-ngagqibelelanga	-ngaphelele	
onvoltooid	unfinished (a)	-sa phethegago	-sa phethahalang	-sa felang	-ngagqitywanga	-ngaqediwe	
onvolwasse	immature (a)	-sa golago	-sa butswang	-tala	-ngekakhuli	-luhlaza	
onvoorspoedig	unsuccessful (a)	-hlokago katlego	-madimabe	-sa kgonegwang	-ngaphumelelanga	-ngaphumelelanga	
onvriendelik	unkind (a)	-hlokago botho	-lonya	-seng bopelonomi	-ngenabubele	-ngenamusa	
onwaardig	undignified (a)	-hlokago maemo	-tellehang	-seng maemo	-ngenasithozela	-ngenasithunzi	

O

Afrikaans	English	N Sotho	Sesotho	Tswana	Xhosa	Zulu
onwaarheid	falsehood (n)	maaka	leshano	maaka	ubuxoki	amanga
onwetend	unknowingly (adv)	ka go se tsebe	-sa tsebe	-sa itse	ngokungazi	ngokungazi
onwettig	illegal (a)	-ganwago ke molao	-sa yeng ka molao	-e seng ka fa molaong	-ngekho mthethweni	-phambene nomthetho
onwillig	unwilling (a)	-go se rate	-sa rateng	-boitsemeletso	-ngafuniyo	-ngathandi
onwrikbaar	adamant (a)	-ikemišeditše	-manganga	-gwatalalang	-ngenkani	-yitshe
oog	eye (n)	leihlo	leihlo	leitlho	iliso	iso
ooggetuie	eyewitness (n)	hlatse ya leihlo	paki e boneng	mmoni	ingqina	isibukeli
oogklappe	blinkers (n)	dithibelagolebele-lathoko	ditlelapa	diogotlelapa	isikhusi-mehlo	insithamehlo
ooglid	eyelid (n)	phuphu	dintshi	lesi	inkophe	ijwabu lehlo
oogmerk	purpose (n)	maikemišetšo	morero	tebo	injongo	ingqondo
ooievaar	stork (n)	mantlopodi	mokotatsie	lekollwane	ingwamza	unogolantethe
ooit	ever (adv)	-kile	le kgale	kile	wakha	nanini
ook	too (adv)	le	hape	le	na-	futhi
ook	also (adv)	gape	le-	gape	na-	futhi
oom	uncle (n)	malome	malome	malome	umalume	umalume
oomblik	moment (n)	motsotso	motsotso	nakonyana	ithuba	umzuzu
oombliklik	instantly (adv)	ka ponyo ya leihlo	-hanghang	ka nakonyana	ngokukhawuleza	khona-manje
oond	oven (n)	onto	onto	bobesetso	ionti	uhhavini
oondbraai	roast (v)	-beša	-hadika	-gadika	-oja	-osa
oop	open (a)	-butšwego	-bulehile	-bulegileng	-vulekile(yo)	-vuliwe
oopmaak	open (v)	-bula	-bula	-bula	-vula	-vula
oor	over (prep)	godimo ga	(ka)hodima	fa godimo	ngaphezulu	phesheya
oor	across (prep)		-rapalla	-feteletsa	ngaphaya	phesheya
oor	about (prep)		ka-	ka ga	nga-	phezu kwa-
oor	ear (n)	tsebe	tsebe	tsebe	indlebe	indlebe
oorblyfsel	remainder (n)	mašaledi	ho setseng	lesalela	intsalela	insalela
oordeel	judge (v)	-ahlola	-ahlola	-atlhola	-gweba	-ehlulela
oordeel	judgment (n)	kahlolo	kahlolo	katlholo	isigwebo	isinqumo
oordryf	exaggerate (v)	-feteletša	-feteletsa	-feteletsa	-baxa	-andisa
ooreenkoms	likeness (n)	tshwano	tshwano	setshwano	imfuzo	ukufana
ooreenkoms	agreement (n)	kwano	tumellano	kutlwano	-imvumelwano	isivumelwano
ooreenstem	agree (v)	-kwana	-dumela	-dumelana	-vuma	-vumelana
oorgawe	surrender (n)	boineelo	boineelo	boineelo	ukunikezela	ukuthela
oorgee	surrender (v)	-ineela	-ineela	-ineela	-nikezela	-thela
oorheers	dominate (v)	-buša	-busa	-gagapa	-velela	-busa
oorjas	overcoat (n)	jase	jase	jase	idyasi	ijazi
oorkant	beyond (prep)	mošola wa	-nqane	moseja	ngaphaya	-phesheya
oorlede	late (a)	hlokafetšego	-hlokahetseng	-moso	-swelekile (yo)	-shonile
oorlede	deceased (n)	-hlokafetšego	-shweleng	-suleng	-swelekileyo	-shonileyo
oorlog	war (n)	ntwa	ntwa	ntwa	imfazwe	impi
oorloop	overflow (v)	-falala	-kgaphatseha	-tshologa	-phuphuma	-chichima
oorloop na	defect (v)	-falala	-fanya	-thobela go	-kreqa	-qembuka
oorpak	overalls (n)	obarolo	obarolo	obarolo	iovaroli	i-ovaloli
oorpyn	earache (n)	bohloko bja ditsebe	bohloko ba tsebe	setlhabi sa tsebe	ukuqaqamba kwendlebe	ubuhlungu bendlebe
oorreding	persuasion (n)	kgodišo	qophello	kgono	ukucenga	ukubonisa
oorreed	persuade (v)	-kgodiša	-qophella	-sokasoka	-cenga	-bonisa
oorring	earring (n)	lengina	lesale	lengena	icici	icici
oorsaak	cause (n)	lebaka	sesosa	lebaka	imbangi	isisusa
oorsee	overseas (n)	mošola wa mawatle	mose ho mawatle	moseja	phesheya	phesheya
oorskadu	overshadow (v)	-phala	-sira	-khurumetsa	-sitha	-engama
oorskakel	switch (v)	-foša dithapo	-kgeloha	-tshuba	-switsha	-shintsha
oorskry	exceed (v)	-feta	-feta	-gaisa	-gqithisa	-dlula
oorslaan	skip (v)	-tshela	-tlola	-tlola	-gqabada	-eqa
oorsprong	origin (n)	mathomo	tlhaho	tshimologo	imvelo	umdabu
oorspronklike inwoner	aboriginal (n)	semelafa	motala	monnafa	inzalelwane	umuntu womdabu
oorstroom	flood (v)	-tlala meetse	-rwalella	-rwalela	-zalisa ngamanzi	-khukhula
oortreder	trespasser (n)	mosenyi	motlodi	motlodi	umaphuli-mthetho	umeqi
oortreding	offence (n)	molato	tshitelo	sekgopi	ityala	isicunulo
oortree	trespass (v)	-tshela molao	-tlola	-sutlha	-ophula umthetho	-eqa umthetho

Afrikaans	English	N Sotho	Sesotho	Tswana	Xhosa	Zulu	O
oortuig	convince (v)	-kgodiša	-kgodisa	-koloba	-qinisekisa	-gculisa	
oorvloed	abundance (n)	bontši	nala	monono	ubuninzi	isibhidli	
oorvloedig	abundant (a)	-ntši	-ngata	-tlalatlalo	-ninzi	-xhaphakile	
oorvol wees	overcrowd (v)	-tlala batho	-subuhlellana	-betagana	-xinanisa	-butheleka	
oorweeg	consider (v)	-akanya	-nahana	-akanya	-cinga	-cabanga	
oorweldig	overpower (v)	-fenya	-fekisa	-fekeetsa	-oyisa	-ahlula	
oos	east (adv)	bohlabela	botjhabela	kwa botlhabatsatsi	-mpuma	-sempumalanga	
ooste	east (n)	Bohlabela	botjhabela	botlhabatsatsi	impuma	impumalanga	
oostelik	eastern (a)	-bohlabela	-botjhabela	-botlhabatsatsi	-mpuma	-kwasempumalanga	
op	up (prep)	godimo	hodima	mo	phezulu	phezulu	
op	on (prep)	godimo ga	ho-	ka	phezu	phezu kwa-	
op	at (prep)	mo	ha-/ho-ditsetsekwame	go-	phezu; kwa- e-	e-, kwa-	
opbeur	console (v)	-kgothatša	-tshedisa	gomotsa	-thuthuzela	-khuza	
opblaas	inflate (v)	-budulela	-butswela	-budulela	-vuthela	-futha	
op die tone loop	tiptoe (v)	-nanabela	-tsamaya ka	-nangasela	-hamba ngoobhontsi	-hamba ngamazwani	
openbaar	public (a)	-setšhaba	-pontsheng	-bathong	-kawonke-wonke	-ephabhuliki	
openbaar	reveal (v)	-bonagatša	-senola	-senola	-tyhila	-seza	
openbaar	disclose (v)	-utolla	-senola	-itsisi	-diza	-veza	
opening	gap (n)	mphatšana	phahla	phatlha	isithuba	isikhala	
opening	opening (n)	pulo	boahlamo	phatlha	intunja	ukuvula	
openlik	openly (a)	-molaleng	-pontsheng	mo pepeneneng	-phandle	-obala	
operasie	operation (n)	puo	puo	karo	uqhaqho	ukuhlinza	
operateur	operator (n)	modiriši	sebui	modiri	umqhaqhi	umqhubi-msebenzi	
opereer	operate (v)	-bua	-bua	-ara	-qhaqha	-hlinza	
opgeskorte vonnis	suspended sentence (n)	kahlolo ye e fegilwego	ho ahlolelwa ka ntle	kotlhao e e beetsweng thoko	isigwebo esixho-nyiweyo	isijeziso esilengisiwe	
opgrawe	unearth (v)	-epolla	-tjhekolla	-epolola	-vumbulula	-vumbulula	
ophef	raise (v)	-phagamiša	-phahamisa	-tlhatlosa	-nyusa	-phakamisa	
ophoop	heap (v)	-kgoba	-bokella	-kgobela	-fumba	-nqwabela	
ophou	cease (v)	-fela	-kgaotsa	-khutla	-pheza	-khawula	
opklim	mount (v)	-namela	-hlwella	-pagama	-qabela	-khwela	
oplettend	observant (a)	-hlokomelago	-sedi	-elang tlhoko	-qaphelayo	-qaphelayo	
oplig	lift (v)	-kuka	-phahamisa	-kuka	-phakamisa	-phakamisa	
oplos	solve (v)	-rarolla	-rarolla	-rarabolola	-xazulula	-qaqa	
oplos	dissolve (v)	-tologa	-qhibidiha	-tlhaologa	-nyibilika	-ncibilikisa	
opmerk	notice (v)	-lemoga	-elellwa	-lemoga	-qaphela	-naka	
opoffer	sacrifice (v)	-itapiša	-hlabela	-tlhabela	-nikezela	-dela	
oppas	beware (v)	-hlokomela	-hlokomela	-tlhokomela	-lumka	-qaphela	
oppervlakte	area (n)	naga	sebaka	kgaolo	ummandla	i-eriya	
opponeer	oppose (v)	-ganetša	-hanyetsa	-ganetsa	-chasa	-melana na-	
opposisie	opposition (n)	kganetšo	kganyetso	kganetso	inkcaso	ukumelana	
op prys stel	prize (v)	-lebogela	-rorisa	-akgola	-xabisa	-klomela	
opreg	sincere (a)	-kgonthe	-nnete	-tota	-thembekile(yo)	-qotho	
oprig	erect (v)	-aga	-thea	-aga	-misa	-akha	
oproer	disturbance (n)	mpherefere	pherehlo	pheretlhego	isiphazamiso	ukunyakaza	
oproer maak	riot (v)	-tsoša mpherefere	-etsa morusu	-feretlha	-gwayimba	-banga isidumo	
opruiing	sedition (n)	moferefere	phetohelo	tsuololo	isiphendu	ukuvukela umbuso	
opsê	recite (v)	-reta	-thothokisa	-boka	-cengceleza	-landa	
opsetlik	deliberate (a)	-boomo	ka boomo	ka bomo	-ngabom	-etshisa	
opsigter	caretaker (n)	molebeledi	mohlokomedi	molebeledi	umgcinindawo	umbheki	
opskort	suspend (v)	-fega	-behela ka thoko	-lepeletsa	-xhoma	-hlehlisa	
opskrif	headline (n)	hlogo	sehlooho	setlhogo	intloko yomhlathi	isihloko	
opsluit	jail (v)	-golega	-hlahlela	-golega	-valela	-bopha	
opsomming	summary (n)	kakaretšo	kakaretso	khutshwafatso	isishwankathelo	iqoqo	
opspoor	track (v)	-lata mohlala	-nka mohlala	-batla	-landela	-landela isipolo	
opspring	bounce (v)	-tlola	-tlola	-tlola	-qakathisa	-xhuma	
opstaan	arise (v)	-emelela	-phahama	-tsoga	-vuka	-vuka	
opstand	rebellion (n)	borabela	borabele	borukutlhi	uvukelo	ukwambuka	
opstand	revolt (n)	mpherefere	kweneho	tsuololo	uvukelo	ukuvukela	

187

Afrikaans	English	N Sotho	Sesotho	Tswana	Xhosa	Zulu
opstel	essay (n)	taodišo	moqoqo	tlhamo	isincoko	indaba elotshiweyo
opstoker	agitator (n)	mohlohleletši	mohlohli	motlhotlheletsi	umchwayi	umhlubukisi
opsy	aside (adv)	ka thoko	ka thoko	sejaro	-ngasecaleni	ngasese
opteken	record (v)	-ngwala	-rekota	-kwala	-bhala	-qopha
opvallend	conspicuous (a)	-bonagalago	-totobetse	-itshupang	-bonakalayo	-qhamile
opvat	conceive (v)	-bona	-emola	-ima	-qonda	-mitha
opvoed	educate (v)	-ruta	-ruta	-ruta	-fundisa	-fundisa
opvoeding	education (n)	thuto	thuto	thuto	imfundo	imfundo
opwasbak	sink (n)	sehlapelo	sinki	setlhatswelo	isinki	usinki
opwek	arouse (v)	-tsoša	-tsosa	-tsibosa	-vusa	-vusa
opwind	excite (v)	-hlohleletša	-nyakalatsa	-gakala	-vuyisa	-vusa
opwinding	excitement (n)	khuduego	-nyakallo	tlhagafatso	uvuyo	umesaso
oranje	orange (a)	-modipa	-lamunu	-bonamune	-orenji	umbala wewolintshi
organisasie	organisation (n)	peakanyo	mokgatlo	thulaganyo	umbutho	inhlangano
orkes	orchestra (n)	okese	diletsi	okesetera	iokhestra	i-okhestra
orkes	band (n)	sehlopha sa baletši	baletsi	okese	iqela lomculo	ibhendi
ornament	ornament (n)	sekgabišo	mokgabiso	kgabiso	umhombiso	umhlobiso
orrel	organ (n)	okane	thomo	letlole	uhadi	i-ogani
orrelis	organist (n)	moletšaokane	rathomo	moletsiletlole	umdlali -hadi	umdlali we-ogani
os	ox (n)	pholo	pholo	pholo	inkabi yenkomo	inkabi
oseaan	ocean (n)	lewatle	lewatle	lewatle	ulwandle	ulwandle
oud	stale (a)	-kgale	-kgale	-tsofetseng	-dala	-duvile
oud	old (a)	-tala	-holo	-gologolo	-dala	-dala
oud	aged (a)	-tšofetšego	-tsofetseng	-tsofetseng	-dala	-gugile
ouderdom	age (n)	bogolo	boholo	bogologolo	ubudala	ubudala
ouditeur	auditor (n)	mohlakiši	mohlahlobaditjhelete	motlhatlhobatlotlo	umhloli-ncwadi	umcwaningi wezimali
oudste	eldest (a)	-golo	-holo	-mogolo	-dala	-dala kakhulu
ouer	parent (n)	motswadi	motswadi	motsadi	umzali	umzali
ouma	grandmother (n)	koko	nkgono	mmemogolo	umakhulu	ugogo
oupa	grandfather (n)	rrakgolo	ntatemoholo	ntatemogolo	ubawomkhulu	ubabamkhulu
owerspel	adultery (n)	bootswa	bootswa	boaka	ukrexezo	uphingo
owerspeler	adulterer (n)	seotswa	seotswa	sefefe	umkrexezi	isiphingi
paadjie	parting (n)	tselana	karohano	kgaogano	indledlana	ukwahlukana
paal	pole (n)	kota	palo	sesana	isibonda	isigxobo
paar	pair (n)	bobedi	bobedi	bobedi	isibini	amaphahla
pad	road (n)	tsela	tsela	tsela	indlela	umgwaqo
pad	way (n)	tsela	tsela	tsela	indlela	indlela
pad	path (n)	tsela	tselanyana	tsela	indledlana	indlela
padda	frog (n)	segwagwa	senqanqane	segwagwa	isele	isele
paddavissie	tadpole (n)	kolopisane	bokudubete	koduntwane	isabonkolo	ushobishobi
pajamas	pyjamas (n)	ditšwarwamalaong	dipejama	pejama	ingutyana yokulala	amaphijama
pak	suit (n)	sutu	sutu	sutu	isuti	isudi
pak	pack (v)	-paka	-pakela	-paka	-bekelela	-hlanganisa
pakket	parcel (n)	phasela	seshoba	phasele	ipasile	iphakethe
paleis	palace (n)	mošate	ntlo ya borena	ntlo ya segosi	ibhotwe	iphalasi
paling	eel (n)	paleng	tlhapinohana	tlhapisekanoga	ipalanga	umbokwane
palm	palm (n)	legoswi	seatla	legofi	intende yesandla	intende yesandla
pamflet	pamphlet (n)	pukwana	bukana	lokwalonyana	incwadana	iphamfulethe
pampoen	pumpkin (n)	lefodi	mokopu	lephutshe	ithanga	ithanga
pampoentjies	mumps (n)	mauwe	pampunkisi	makidiane	uqwilikane	uzagiga
pan	pan (n)	pane	pane	mogobe	ipani	ipani
paneelwa	panel van (n)	bene	panelevena	bene	iveni yokusebenza	iveni
paniek	panic (n)	letšhogo	letshoho	letshogo	ukuphaphazela	ukuphaphazela
paniekerig wees	panic (v)	-tšhogile	-tshoha	-tshoga	-phaphazela	-phaphazela
pankreas	pancreas (n)	pankarea	manyeme	marakanamantsi	amasi	amanyikwe
pap	porridge (n)	bogobe	papa	bogobe	isidudu	iphalishi
papaja	pawpaw (n)	phopho	phopho	phoophoo	ipopo	upopo
papier	paper (n)	pampiri	pampiri	pampiri	iphepha	iphepha
paraffien	paraffin (n)	parafene	parafini	parafene	iparafini	uphalafini

Afrikaans	English	N Sotho	Sesotho	Tswana	Xhosa	Zulu	P
paragraaf	paragraph (n)	temana	tema	tema	umhlathi	isigaba	
parallel	parallel (n)	mmapano	thapallo	papo	isinxusi	-hambisanayo	
parfuum	perfume (n)	monko	senoko	monko	isiqholo	usende	
park	park (n)	phaka	paka	phaka	ipaka	ipaki	
parkeer	park (v)	-phaka	-emisa	-emisa	-misa	-paka	
parkeerkaartjie	parking ticket (n)	thekete ya molato wa go phaka	tekete ya ho paka	thekete ya go phaka	itikiti lokumisa	ithikithi	
parkering	parking (n)	lefelo la go phaka	kemong ya dipalangwang	lefelo la go phaka	indawo yokumisa	ukupaka	
parlement	parliament (n)	kgotlakgolo	kgotlakgolo	palamente	ipalamente	iphalamende	
parmantigheid	insolence (n)	kgang	manganga	makgakga	isigezo	ukungahloniphi	
parool	parole (n)	tokollo ka kwelobohloko	parole	paroule	isithembiso sokungabaleki	isithembiso sokungabaleki	
party	party (n)	phathi	mokga	setlhopa	iqela	umcimbi	
pas	fit (v)	-lekana	-lekana	-lekanya	-lungileyo	-lingana	
pas	pass (n)	pasa	kgoro	pasa	ipasi	ipasi	
pasiënt	patient (n)	molwetši	mokudi	mmobodi	isigulana	isiguli	
passasier	passenger (n)	monamedi	mopalami	mopalami	umhambi	umgibeli	
pasta	paste (n)	sekgomaretši	sekgomaretsi	bogobe	intlama	ubundubundu	
pastei	pastry (n)	kukunama	hlama	phae	intlama yekeyiki	uqweqwe lukaphayi	
patat	sweet potato (n)	morepa	patata	potata	ibhatata	ubhatata	
patroon	pattern (n)	sekaelo	paterone	paterone	isizeko	iphethini	
pedaal	pedal (n)	petala	bohato	setlhako	isinyathelo	isinyathelo	
peer	pear (n)	piere	pere	pere	ipere	ipheya	
pels	fur (n)	boya	boya	bowa	ufele	uboya	
pen	peg (n)	kokontwane	thakgisa	lemapo	isikhonkwane	isikhonkwane	
pen	pen (n)	pene	pene	pene	usiba	ipeni	
penis	penis (n)	ntoto	ntoto	lepele	umthondo	umthondo	
pens	belly (n)	mogodu	mpa	mpa	umkhaba	isisu	
pensioen	pension (n)	phenšene	phenshene	phenšene	umhlalaphantsi	impesheni	
peper	pepper (n)	pepere	pepere	pherefere	ipepile	upelepele	
perd	horse (n)	pere	pere	pitse	ihashe	ihhashi	
perdeby	wasp (n)	mobu	seboba	mofu	unomeva	umuvi	
perdewedren	horserace (n)	mokato wa dipere	reisisi ya dipere	lebelo la dipitse	umdyarho	umjaho wamahhashi	
perkoleer	percolate (v)	-hlotla	-monyela	-dutla	-bilisa	-chinineka	
permanent	permanent (a)	-mmaruri	-tsitsitseng	-ruri	-sigxina	-hlalayo	
permit	permit (n)	tumelo	tumello	tetla	imvume	iphomende	
pers	press (n)	kgatišo	kgatiso	kgatiso	abashicileli	into yokucindizela	
pers	press (v)	-gatiša	-hatisa	-gatisa	-cudisa	-cindizela	
pers	purple (a)	perese	perese	perese	-mfusa	ubunsomi	
persent	percent (n)	phesente	phesente	phesente	ipesenti	iphesenti	
perske	peach (n)	perekisi	perekisi	perekisi	ipesika	ipetshisi	
persoon	person (n)	motho	motho	motho	umntu	umuntu	
persoonlik	personal (a)	-motho	-ka nama	-sebele	-akho	-komuntu uqobo lwakhe	
perspirasie	perspiration (n)	sethitho	mofufutso	mofufutso	umbilo	umjuluko	
perspireer	perspire (v)	-tšwa sethitho	-fufulelwa	-fufula	-bila	-juluka	
pes	pest (n)	leuba	phehli	sesenyi	ubhubhane	inkathazo	
petrol	petrol (n)	peterolo	peterole	peterolo	ipetroli	upetroli	
peul	pod (n)	sephotlwa	monawa	mhure	umdumba	umdumba	
peuter	toddler (n)	mapimpana	mokgasi	ngwana	isibothwana	ingane	
piek	peak (n)	ntlhora	tlhoro	setlhora	incopho	isihloko	
piekniek	picnic (n)	pikiniki	pikinike	pikiniki	ipikiniki	ipikiniki	
piekniek hou	picnic (v)	-dira pikiniki	-ho tshwara pikinike	-ja pikiniki	-bamba ipiknki	-phuma ipikiniki	
pienk	pink (n)	pinki	pinke	pinki	ipinki	umbala wesiphofu	
piesang	banana (n)	panana	panana	panana	ibhanana	ubhanana	
pietersielie	parsley (n)	pareseli	sehwete se sesweu	paresele	umfuno	ipasili	
pik	peck (v)	-kobola	-kota	-kopa	-nqola	-ngawuza	
pil	pill (n)	pilisi	pilisi	pilisi	ipilisi	iphilisi	
pit	pith (n)	moko	kgafole	moko	umongo, ipete	umongo	
pit	pip (n)	thaka	tlhodiso	thapo	ipete	uhlamvu	

P	Afrikaans	English	N Sotho	Sesotho	Tswana	Xhosa	Zulu
	pla	pester (v)	-tshwenya	-kgathatsa	-tshwenya	-khathaza	-khathaza
	pla	disturb (v)	-tshwenya	-ferehla	-feretlha	-phazamisa	-nyakazisa
	plaag	plague (n)	matshwenyego	sewa	leroborobo	isigulo	inkathazo
	plaas	farm (n)	polase	polasi	polase	ifama	ipulazi
	plaaslik	local (a)	-gae	-selehae	-selegae	-ale ndawo	-akhona
	plaasvervanger	deputy (n)	motseta	motlatsi	moemedi	isekela	impakatha
	plafon	ceiling (n)	siling	siling	siling	intungo	isilingi
	plak	paste (v)	-gomaretša	-kgomaretsa	-kgomaretsa	-ncamathisela	-namathelisa
	plan	plan (n)	maano	leqheka	leano	icebo	isu
	planeet	planet (n)	polanete	polanete	naledi	iplanethi	iplanethi
	plank	plank (n)	lepolanka	lepolanka	lebatsana	iplanga	ipulangwe
	plant	plant (v)	-bjala	-jala	-jwala	-tyala	-tshala
	plant	plant (n)	semela	sejalo	semela	isityalo	isithombo
	plastiek	plastic (n)	plastiki	polasetike	polasetiki	iplastiki	ipulastiki
	plat	flat (a)	-phaphathi	-sephara	-phaphathi	-mcaba	-yisicaba
	platdruk	squash (v)	-pinya	-buretsa	-tlhantlha	-cumza	-pitshiza
	platform	platform (n)	polatefomo	sebae	serala	iqonga	ipulatifomu
	plattelands	rural (a)	-nageng	-mahae	-metsesegae	-maphandleni	-maphandleni
	pleidooi	plea (n)	thapelo	thapedi	go ala diatla	isicelo	ukuphendula ecaleni
	pleit	plead (n)	thapeletšo	-rapela	go ala diatla	ukuzithethela	-phendula ecaleni
	plek	place (n)	felo	tulo	felo	indawo	indawo
	plesier	pleasure (n)	lethabo	thabo	monate	ubumnandi	injabulo
	plig	duty (n)	tshwanelo	tshwanelo	tiro	umsebenzi	imfanelo
	ploeg	plough (v)	-lema	-lema	-lema	-lima	-lima
	ploeg	plough (n)	mogoma	mohoma	mogoma	ikhuba	igeja
	plooi	wrinkle (v)	-šošobanya	-sosobanya	-tsutsubanya	-shwabanisa	-fingciza
	plooi	wrinkle (n)	mašošo	maswebe	letsuba	umbimbi	umfingcizo
	pluk	pluck (v)	-kga	-kgola	-fula	-xhwitha	-kha
	plunder	loot (v)	-thopa	-utswa	-gapa	-phanga	-phanga
	poel	pool (n)	sediba	letamo	letlodi	ichibi	ichibi
	poging	attempt (n)	teko	teko	boiteko	umzamo	umzamo
	pokmerk	pockmark (n)	lebadi la sekobonyane	kgwadiamaoma	leroba	irhongo	imfoloko
	poleer	polish (v)	-pholiša	-polesha	-poletša	-qaba	-pholisha
	poligamie	polygamy (n)	go nyala basadi ba bantši	sethepu	bogadikane	isithembu	isithembu
	polisie	police (n)	maphodisa	lepolesa	mapodisa	ipolisa	amaphoyisa
	polisiekantoor	police station (n)	seteišene sa maphodisa	seteishene sa sepolesa	lefelo la mapodisa	isikhululo samapolisa	ipholisiteshi
	polisieman	policeman (n)	lephodisa	lepolesa	lepodisa	ipolisa	iphoyisa
	politiek	politics (n)	politiki	dipolitike	poletiki	iipolitiki	ipolitiki
	polities	political (a)	-politiki	-politike	-sepoletiki	-nobupolitika	-nobupolitiki
	politoer	polish (n)	pholiši	poleshe	pholetšhe	amafutha	upholishi
	pols	pulse (n)	morethetho	ho uba ha pelo	kubakubo	umbilini	isikhupha
	pols	wrist (n)	senoko so seatla	lenonyeletso	letlhalela	isihlahla	isihlakala
	pomelo	grapefruit (n)	pomelo	pomelo	pampalamusu	imbambusi	igilibhufuluthi
	pomp	pump (v)	-pompa	-pompa	-pompa	-mpompa	-futha
	pomp	pump (n)	pompo	pompo	pompo	impopo	iphampu
	pondok	hovel (n)	mošašana	mokgoro	ntlwana	ixhobongwana	ifuku
	poot	paw (n)	borofa	maro	leroo	ithupha	isidladla
	pop	doll (n)	popi	popi	popo	unopopi	udoli
	populier	poplar (n)	mopopoliri	populiri	popoleri	umthi wepampiri	ubhabhulini
	pos	mail (n)	poso	poso	poso	iposi	iposi
	pos	post (n)	poso	poso	poso	iposi	iposi
	pos	post (v)	-posa	-posa	-romela	-posa	-posa
	posbode	postman (n)	morwalaposo	raposo	ramakwalo	unoposi	umuntu weposi
	posisie	position (n)	leemo	boemo	maemo	indawo	isimo
	positief	positive (a)	-nyakegago	-dumelang	-ruri	-qinisekile(yo)	-gamele
	poskaart	postcard (n)	poskarata	posekarete	posokarata	iposi-khadi	iposikhadi
	poskantoor	post office (n)	posong	posong	posong	iposofisi	iposi
	posorder	postal order (n)	posotere	posetaleota	poseotore	ipostal-oda	iposoda

Afrikaans	English	N Sotho	Sesotho	Tswana	Xhosa	Zulu	P
posseël	postage stamp (n)	setempe	setempe	setempe	istampu sokuposa	isitembu	
pot	pot (n)	pitša	pitsa	pitsa	imbiza	ibhodwe	
potlood	pencil (n)	phensele	pensele	phensele	ipensile	ipensele	
pottebakkery	pottery (n)	bobopapitša	bobopi	popo ya dinkgo	umsebenzi wodongwe	umsebenzi wokubumba	
pous	pope (n)	mopapa	mopapa	mopapa	ipowupu	uPhapha	
pouse	interval (n)	khutšo	kgefutso	kgaotso	ikhefu	ikhefu	
praat	speak (v)	-bolela	-bua	-bua	-thetha	-khuluma	
praat	talk (v)	-bolela	-bua	-bua	-thetha	-khuluma	
praatjie	talk (n)	polelwana	puo	polelo	incoko	ingxoxo	
pragtig	beautiful (a)	-botse	-tle	-ntle	-hle	-bukekayo	
prakties	practical (a)	-tirišo	-ka etswang	-tiriso	-ngenzeka	-nokwenzeka	
predikant	minister (n)	moruti	moruti	moruti	umfundisi	umfundisi	
predikant	preacher (n)	moruti	moruti	moreri	umshumayeli	umshumayeli	
preek	sermon (n)	thero	thuto	thero	intshumayelo	intshumayelo	
preek	preach (v)	-rera	-ruta	-rera	-shumayela	-shumayela	
prent	picture (n)	seswantšho	setshwantsho	setshwantsho	umfanekiso	umfanekiso	
president	president (n)	mopresidente	moporesidente	poresidente	umongameli	umongameli	
presies	exact (a)	-nepagetšego	-nepileng	gone jaana	-kanye	-qinisile	
prestasie	achievement (n)	phetho	katleho	katlanego	impumelelo	impumelelo	
presteer	achieve (v)	-phetha	-atleha	-atlanega	-zuza	-feza	
pret	fun (n)	lethabo	monyaka	tlhapedi	isiyolo	ukudlala	
priester	priest (n)	moprista	moprista	moruti	umbingeleli	umpristi	
primitief	primitive (a)	-segologolo	-seholoholo	-bogologolo	-ndala	-asendulo	
prins	prince (n)	kgošana	kgosana	kgosana	inkosana	uprinsi	
prinses	princess (n)	kgošigatšana	kgosatsana	morwadiaakgosi	inkosazana	uprinsesi	
privaat	private (a)	-motho a nnoši	poraefete	-sephiri	-angasese	-akhe yedwa	
probeer	try (v)	-leka	-leka	-leka	-zama	-zama	
probleem	problem (n)	bothata	qaka	bothata	ingxaki	inkinga	
produk	product (n)	setšweletšo	sebewa	kumo	imveliso	isithelo	
produseer	produce (v)	-tšweletša	-hlahisa	-uma	-velisa	-thela	
proe	taste (v)	-kwa ka leleme	-latswa	-utlwa	-ngcamla	-zwa	
proefneming	experiment (n)	boitekelo	ekseperimente	tekelelo	ilinge	ukulinga	
profeet	prophet (n)	moprofeta	moporofeta	moporofiti	umprofeti	umprofethi	
professor	professor (n)	moprofesa	moporofesa	moporofesara	injingalwazi	uprofesa	
program	programme (n)	lenaneo	lenaneo	lenaneo	inkqubo	iprogramu	
program	program (n)	lenaneo	lenane	lenaneo	inkqubo	iprogramu	
progressief	progressive (a)	-tšwelago pele	-tswelang pele	-gatelelang pele	-nenkqubela	-qhubekelayo	
prokureur	solicitor (n)	ramolao	mmuelli	mmueledi	igqwetha	ummeli	
prokureur	lawyer (n)	agente	akgente	mmueledi	igqwetha	ummeli	
prokureur	attorney (n)	ramolao	mmuelli	mmueledi	igqwetha	ummeli	
prominent	prominent (a)	-bohlokwa	-tsebahalang	-itshupileng	-dandalaza(yo)	-dumileyo	
prooi	prey (n)	sebolawa	nyamatsane	sebolawa	ixhoba	inyamazane edliwayo	
prop	plug (n)	sethibo	sekwahelo	sethibo	isivingco	isivimbo	
propvol	crowded (a)	-tletšego phare phare	-qhobellane	-pitlaganeng	-xineneyo	-minyene	
prosedure	procedure (n)	tshepedišo	tsamaiso	tsamaiso	inkqubo	indlela yenqubo	
prostituut	prostitute (n)	kgeke	seotswa	sefefe	ihenyukazi	isifebe	
protesteer	protest (v)	-kgokgona	-hanyetsa	-ganana	-chasa	-nqaba	
pruil	pout (v)	-hlonama	-petlekisa melomo	-betolola	-jala	-phukula umlomo	
pruim	plum (n)	poreimi	poraema	poreimi	iplamu	ipulamu	
prys	prize (n)	sefoka	moputso	sekgele	ibhaso	umklomelo	
prys	price (n)	theko	theko	tlhotlhwa	ixabiso	intengo	
psalm	psalm (n)	pesaleme	pesaleme	pesaleme	indumiso	ihubo	
puberteit	puberty (n)	bofsa	ho kena boholo	bokau/boroba	ukufikisa	isikhathi sokuthomba	
publiek	public (n)	batho	batho bohle	batho	uwonke-wonke	iphabhuliki	
puik	crack (a)	-makgethe	-tsebang	-ntlentle	-ngobuncutshe	-ngqazukayo	
puisie	pimple (n)	kemola	sehloba	kuruga	iqhakuva	insunsumba	
punt	tip (n)	ntlha	ntlha	ntlha	incam	isihloko	
punt	fullstop (n)	khutlo	kgutlo	khutlo	isingxi	ungqi	
punt	point (n)	ntlha	ntlha	ntlha	iqondo	isihloko	

P	Afrikaans	English	N Sotho	Sesotho	Tswana	Xhosa	Zulu
	punte aanteken	score (v)	-noša	-tshwaya dintlha	-nosa	-fumana inqaku	-nqoba
	purgeermiddel	purgative (n)	segofiši	sehlare sa ho tshollisa	mothubiso	iyeza lokuhambisa	umuthi wokuhudisa
	put	well (n)	petse	sediba	sediba	iqula	umgodi onomthombo
	pyl	arrow (n)	mosebe	motsu	motsu	utolo	umcibisholo
	pyn	ache (n)	bohloko	bohloko	setlhabi	ingcaqambo	ubuhlungu
	pyn	ache (v)	-opa	-opa	-opa	-qaqamba	-njunjuza
	pyn	pain (n)	bohloko	lehlaba	botlhoko	iintlungu	ubuhlungu
	pynappel	pineapple (n)	phaeneapole	peineapole	peinapole	ipayinapile	uphayinaphu
	pyp	pipe (n)	peipi	peipe	kakana	umbhobho	ipipi
	raad	advice (n)	keletšo	keletso	kgakololo	icebo	iseluleko
	raad	council (n)	lekgotla	lekgotla	lekgotla	ibhunga	ibandla
	raad gee	advise (v)	-eletša	-eletsa	-gakolola	-cebisa	-lulekayo
	raadgewend	advisory (a)	-eletšago	-eletsang	-gakololang	-cebisayo	-lulekayo
	raadgewer	adviser (n)	moeletši	moeletsi	mogakolodi	umcebisi	umluleki
	raadpleeg	consult (v)	-kgopela keletšo	-botsa	-rerisana	-dlana indlebe	-xoxisana
	raadslid	councillor (n)	mokgomana	letona	molekgotla	ilungu lebhunga	ilungu lasebandla
	raai	guess (v)	-akanya	-akanya	-abelela	-qashela	-qandela
	raaisel	puzzle (n)	marara	selotho	malea	iqashiso	isiphicaphicwano
	raaiskoot	guess (n)	kakanyo	kakanyo	kabelelo	iqashiso	umqandelo
	raak	touch (v)	-kgwatha	-ama	-kgoma	-chukumisa	-thinta
	raak	affect (v)	-ama	-ama	-ama	-bangela	-thinta
	raap	turnip (n)	rapa	rapa	thenipe	ithenephu	utheniphu
	radikaal	radical (a)	-tšwelego tseleng	-haholoholo	-gakgamatsang	-noluvo lotshintsho olugqibeleleyo	-empela
	radio	radio (n)	radio	radio	seromamowa	unomathotholo	iwayalense
	radys	radish (n)	rateise	rateise	radisi	umfuno onegaqa	uradishi
	rak	shelf (n)	raka	raka	raka	ishelufu	ishalofu
	ram	ram (n)	phooko	pheleu	phelefu	inkunz'egusha	inqama
	ramp	disaster (n)	kotsi	kodua	leralalo	intlekele	isidumo
	rand	edge (n)	morumo	qophelo	losi	uhlangothi	icala
	rankie	tendril (n)	motlang	tatamolebo	molebo	isibambelelo	umliba
	rantsoen	ration (n)	kabelo	reshene	kabelo	umxhesho	ilesheni
	raps	whip (v)	-itia	-shapa	-setla	-nqasha	-thwisha
	raserig	noisy (a)	-lešata	-lerata	-leratla	-ngxolayo	-nomsindo
	rasper	grate (v)	-gohla	-kuma	-gotlha	-khuhla	-khuhla
	rasse	racial (a)	-merafe	-semorabe	ya semorafe	-nobuhlanga	-ngokwezinhlanga
	rassisties	racist (a)	-kgethollago	-mohloyamerabe	-bomorafe	-nobuhlanga	-bandlululayo ngokwezinhlanga
	rat	gear (n)	kere	kere	kere	igiyeri	igeli
	ratel	rattle (n)	segwaši	tjhwehletjhwehle	letlhao	ingxolo	igenqeza
	ratel	rattle (v)	-gwaša	-tjhwehletsa	-kgorotlha	-kroxoma	-gunquza
	rats	agile (a)	-tshelago matšato	-matjato	majato	-thambileyo	-lula
	rebel	rebel (n)	lerabela	lerabele	morukutlhi	umnxaxhi	imbuka
	rebelleer	rebel (v)	-rabela	-rabela	-tsuolola	-qhankqalaza	-embuka
	red	save (v)	-phološa	-pholosa	pholosa	-sindisa	-sindisa
	red	rescue (v)	-phološa	-pholosa	-namola	-nceda	-sindisa
	redakteur	editor (n)	morulaganyi	mohlophisi	morulaganyi	umhleli	umhleli
	redding	rescue (n)	phološo	pholoso	phaloso	uncedo	ukusindisa
	rede	reason (n)	lebaka	lebaka	lebaka	isizathu	isizathu
	redelik	reasonable (a)	-sa belaetšago	-utlwahalang	-utlwagalang	-nengqondo	-faneleyo
	redeneer	reason (v)	-tšea kgang	-nahana	-akanya	-cinga	-cabanga
	redigeer	edit (v)	-rulaganya	-hlophisa	-rulaganya	-hlela	-hlela
	reeks	sequence (n)	tatelano	tatelano	tatelano	ulandelelwano	ukulandelana
	reël	rule (n)	molao	molao	molao	umthetho	umthetho
	reël	organise (v)	-beakanya	-hlophisa	-rulaganya	-ququzelela	-hlela
	reën	rain (n)	pula	pula	pula	imvula	imvula
	reën	rain (v)	-na	-na	-na	-na	-na
	reënboog	rainbow (n)	molalatladi	mookodi	motshewabadimo	umnyama	uthingo lwenkosazane
	reëndruppel	raindrop (n)	lerothodi	lerothodi la pula	lerothodi	iqabaza lemvula	iconsi

Afrikaans	English	N Sotho	Sesotho	Tswana	Xhosa	Zulu	R
reënjas	raincoat (n)	jase ya pula	jase ya pula	jase ya pula	idyasi yemvula	ijazi lemvula	
reënmeter	rain gauge (n)	kelapula	semethapula	metere ya pula	isilinganisi semvula	isilinganiso semvula	
refleks	reflex (n)	tiragalo yeo e sa laolwego	ho nyaroha	kutlo	ukuzenzekela	ukugwenguka	
reg	right (a)	-lokilego	-nepileng	-siame	-lungile(yo)	-qondile	
regbank	judiciary (n)	lekgotla la toka	baahlodi	bokgaolakgang	ijaji zelizwe jikelele	amajaji	
regeer	rule (v)	-buša	-busa	-busa	-lawula	-busa	
regeer	govern (v)	-buša	-busa	-busa	-lawula	-busa	
regeerder	ruler (n)	mmuši	mmusi	mmusi	umlawuli	umbusi	
regering	government (n)	mmušo	mmuso	mmuso	urhulumente	uhulumeni	
reghoek	rectangle (n)	khutlonnethwi	kgutlonne	khutlonne	uxande	unxande	
register	register (n)	rejistara	rejisetara	rejisetara	irejista	irejista	
regmaak	fix (v)	-lokiša	-lokisa	-baakanya	-lungisa	-lungisa	
regter	judge (n)	moahlodi	moahlodi	moatlhodi	ijaji	ijaji	
regterkant	right (n)	la go ja	letsohong le letona	moja	ukunene	ubunene	
regterlik	judicial (a)	-boahlodi	-molao	-bokgaolakgang	-semthethweni	-omsebenzi wamajaji	
reguit	straight (a)	-rego thwi	-otlolohileng	-motwenene	-the tse	-qondile	
regulasie	regulation (n)	molawana	molao	molao	umthetho	umthetho	
regverdig	justify (v)	-lokafatša	-liisa	-lolamise	-lungisa	-vumela	
regverdig	just (a)	-lokilego	-toka	ka tolamo	nje	-fanele	
reier	heron (n)	kokolohute	seotsanyana	kokolohutwe	ukhwalimanzi	indwandwe	
reis	travel (v)	-eta	-eta	-kgabaganya	-thabatha uhambo	-hamba	
reis	trip (n)	leeto	leeto	loeto	uhambo	uhambo	
reis	journey (n)	leeto	leeto	mosepele	uhambo	uhambo	
reisgeld	fare (n)	tefo ya leeto	tefello ya leeto	tuelo	imali yokuhamba	imali yokukhwela	
reisiger	traveller (n)	moeti	moeti	moetedi	umhambi	isihambi	
rek	elastic (n)	rekere	tamoloho	rekere	ilastiki	injoloba	
rekbaar	elastic (a)	-raramologago	-tamolohang	-taologo	-ntwebekayo	-jobulukayo	
reken	calculate (v)	-bala	-bala	-balela	-bala	-balisisa	
rekenaar	calculator (n)	komphuta	sebadi	komputara	umashini wokubala	umshini wokubala	
rekenaar	computer (n)	komphuta	khompiuta	komputara	ikompiyuta	ikhomputha	
rekening	account (n)	tšhupaletlotlo	akhaonte	tshupatlotlo	iakhawunti	i-akhawunti	
rekenkunde	arithmetic (n)	thutapalo	dipalo	dipalo	ezobalo	izibalo	
rekenmeester	accountant (n)	mošupatlotlo	akhaontente	mmaditlotlo	umbhali-mali	umbhali wamakhawunti	
rekenskap gee	account (v)	-anegela	-seka	-supa tlotlo	-cacisa	-balisisa	
rekord	record (n)	pego	rekoto	rekoto	ubungqina	irekhodi	
rektum	rectum (n)	motsila	mohlamu	lela-la-sebi	undloku, undonci	umdidi	
rem	brake (n)	poriki	boriki	-rema	ibreki	ibhuliki	
renoster	rhinoceros (n)	tšhukudu	tshukudu	tshukudu	umkhombe	ubhejane	
renperd	racehorse (n)	pere ya mokato	pere ya peiso	pitse ya lebelo	ihashe lomdyarho	ihhashi lomjaho	
resep	recipe (n)	tšhupetšo ya go tswaka	resepe	theo ya kapeo	iresiphi	isu lokupheka	
reserveer	reserve (v)	-beeletša	-boloka	-dibeletsa	-bekela	-bambela	
reserwe	reserve (n)	motlatši	poloko	namaoeme	umbeko	isabelo	
resies ja	race (v)	-šiana	-beisa	ja -siana	-ngenela umdyarho	-jaha	
respek	respect (n)	tlhompho	tlhompho	tlotlego	imbeko	ukuhlonipha	
respekteer	respect (v)	-hlompha	hlompha	-tlotla	-ba nembeko	-hlonipha	
respondeer	respond (v)	-araba	-arabela	-tsiboga	-phendula	-phendula	
restaurant	restaurant (n)	restorante	resetjhurente	resetshurente	indawo yokutyela	indlu yokudlela	
retoriek	rhetoric (n)	makgethe a polelo	bokgeleke	kgelekiso	ubuciko	ubuciko	
reuk	smell (n)	monkgo	monko	monkgo	ivumba	iphunga	
reukweermiddel	deodorant (n)	polayamonkgo	setebelamonko	senkgamonate	isiqholo	umuthi wokuqeda iphunga elibi	
reus	giant (n)	tšitširipa	senatla	rintlhwe	isigantsontso	umdondoshiya	
reusagtig	huge (a)	-gologolo	-kgolohadi	-tona	-khulu	-yisibhidli	
reuse	giant (a)	-gologolo	-senatla	-tonatona	-gantsontso	-sidlakela	
revolusie	revolution (n)	mpherefere	phetohelo	botsuolodi	uvukelo	ukuvukela umbuso	
rewolwer	revolver (n)	raboloro	rabolloro	raborolo	umpu	ivolovolo	
rib	rib (n)	kgopo	kgopo	logopo	ubambo	ubambo	

R

Afrikaans	English	N Sotho	Sesotho	Tswana	Xhosa	Zulu
riem	thong (n)	lebja	lerapo	kgole	intambo	intambo
riet	reed (n)	lehlakanoka	lehlaka	letlhaka	ingcongolo	umhlanga
rif	reef (n)	mokekema	mokokotlo	lekekema	iseyile	uthunge lwamatshe
rig	direct (v)	-lebiša	-lebisa	-supetsa	-alatha	-nemba
rigting	direction (n)	thoko	nnqa	ntlha	icala	ukukhombisa
ring	ring (n)	palamonwana	reng	mhiri	iringi	indandatho
ringwurm	ringworm (n)	pudutša	setlapedi	sephinyasapodi	isitshanguba	umbandamu
riolering	sewerage (n)	tsela ya kelatšhila	thothomantle	kgogoleloleswe	umjelo wezibi	ipayipi lendle
rioolpyp	drainpipe (n)	phaephe ya kelatšhila	foro ya ho tlosa metsi	leela la mesele	umthobho	ipayipi
risiko	risk (n)	moleko	qomatsi	diphatsa	ingozi	ingozi
rit	ride (n)	go namela	palama	makoko	ireyi	ukugibela
ritme	rhythm (n)	mošito	morethetho	mosito	isingqisho	isigqi
ritme	beat (n)	mošito	morethetho	kgato	isingqisho	ibhithi
ritssluiter	zipper (n)	sengamedi	zipo	sekonopelo sa sipi	iziphu	iziphu
rivier	river (n)	noka	noka	noka	umlambo	umfula
robot	robot (n)	roboto	roboto	roboto	irobhothi	irobhothi
roei	row (v)	-hudua	-soka	-kgaphela metsi	-bhexa	-gwedla
roeispaan	oar (n)	lehuduo	lesokwana	selabo	iphini	umgwedli
roem	fame (n)	tumo	botumo	tumo	ukubaluleka	udumo
roep	call (v)	-bitša	-bitsa	-bitsa	-biza	-biza
roeper	caller (n)	mmitši	mmitsi	mmitsi	umbizi	umuntu obizayo
roer	stir (v)	-hudua	-fudua	-fudua	-zamisa	-bonda
roerend	moving (a)	-ka šuthišwago	-sisinyehang	-tshikinyang	shukumayo	-nyakazayo
roes	rust (n)	rusi	mafome	morodu	umhlwa	ukuthomba
roes	rust (v)	-rusa	-ba le mafome	-rusa	-ba nomhlwa	-thomba
rofie	scab (n)	legogo	lekgwekgwe	lepalo	ukhoko	uqweqwe
rok	dress (n)	roko	mose	mosese	ilokhwe	ilokwe
rol	roll (n)	rolo	rolo	momenagano	irolo	ukugingqika
rol	roll (v)	-kgokološa	-theteha	-pitika	-phethula	-gingqika
rolbal	bowls (n)	kgwele ya go kgokološa	rolobolo	dibaole	ibhola eqengqwayo	amabholi
roman	novel (n)	padi	pale	padi	inoveli	inoveli
romp	skirt (n)	sekhethe	sekhete	mosese	umbhinqo	isiketi
rond	round (a)	-nkgokolo	-tjhitja	-potokwe	-ngqukuva	-yindilinga
rond	about (adv)	mo le mola	ka-	gomela	-ngokujikeleyo	nga-
rond	around (adv)	kua le kua	ka hohle	khadia	-ngokujikelezayo	ngokuzungezile
rondgaan	circulate (v)	-dikologa	-potoloha	-dikologa	-jikelezisa	-zungeleza
rondkyk	scout (v)	-hlola	-hlwela	-lebaleba	-zingela	-hlola
rondloper	vagrant (n)	moneneri	molakolako	sengae	ihilihili	uzulane
rondreis	tour (v)	-eta	-eta	-ja nala	-khenketha	-hamba
rondreis	tour (n)	leeto	leeto	go ja nala	ukhenketho	uhambo
rondslenter	loiter (v)	-sesella	-tsekela	-ebaeba	-yabula	-libala
roofdier	predator (n)	sebata	sebata	sebata	irhamncwa	isilwane esiphangayo
rooi	red (a)	-hubedu	-fubedu	-hibidu	-bomvu	-bomvu
rook	smoke (v)	-kgoga	-tsuba	-goga	-qhuma	-bhema
rook	smoke (n)	muši	mosi	mosi	umsi	intuthu
room	cream (n)	lebebe	lebejana	lebebe	ucwambu	ulaza
roomys	ice cream (n)	aesekherimi	aesekerimi	bebetsididi	iayiskrim	u-ayisikhilimu
roos	rose (n)	rosi	rouse	rouse	irowuzi	iroza
rooster	timetable (n)	tšhupapaka	tshupapaka	lenanatiro	ithayimtheyibhili	uhlelo lwesikhathi
rooster	grill (v)	-beša	-hadika	-besa	irostile	insimbi yokosa
rosyntjie	raisin (n)	makwapi a diterebe	dirasenkise	moretlwa	irasentyisi	urezini
rot	rat (n)	peba	kgoto	legotlo	ibuzi	igundane
rots	rock (n)	leswika	lefika	lefika	imbokotho iliwa	idwala
rotslys	ledge (n)		mothati	leriba	ungqameko	unqenqema
rou	raw (a)	-tala	-tala	-tala	-krwada	-luhlaza
rou	mourning (n)	sello	sello	boroulo	izila	isililo
rou	mourn (v)	-lla	-lla	-roula	-zila	-lilela
rower	robber (n)	mohudi	motlatlapi	senokwane	umkhuthuzi	umphangi
ru	rough (a)	-makgwakgwa	-soro	-magotsane	-rhabaxa	-mahhadla

Afrikaans	English	N Sotho	Sesotho	Tswana	Xhosa	Zulu	S
rubber	rubber (n)	raba	raba	rekere	irabha	irabha	
rug	ridge (n)	mopopotlo	mokokotlo	lekhubu	umqolo	unqenqema	
rug	back (n)	mokokotlo	mokokotlo	mokwatla	umqolo	umhlane	
rugby	rugby (n)	rugby	rakebi	rakabi	umboxo	iragbhi	
ruggraat	spine (n)	mokokotlo	mokokotlo	mokokotlo	umchachazo	umgogodla	
rugmurg	spinal cord (n)	moko wa mokokotlo	mokolla	mokolela	umnqonqo	umfunkulu	
ruik	smell (v)	-dupa	-nkga	-nkga	-nukisa	-nuka	
ruil	barter (v)	-gweba	-ananya	-ananya	-nanisa	-hweba	
ruimte	space (n)	sebakabaka	sebaka	sebaka	isithuba	isikhala	
ruit	pane (n)	galase ya lefasetere	kgalase ya fensetere	reite	iglasi yefestile	iwindi	
ruk	jerk (v)	-utla	-tutla	-kgotha	-xhuzula	-dlukuza	
rukking	convulsion (n)	kikontwane	tshisinyeho	kgaro	umxhuzulo	ukudikiza	
rumatiek	rheumatism (n)	bonyelele	ramathesele	bonyelele	isifo samathambo	ikhunkulo	
rumaties	rheumatic (a)	-bonyelele	-ramathesele	-bonyelele	-tyatyamba(yo)	-ofehlane	
rus	rest (n)	khutšo	phomolo	boikhutso	ubilo	ukuphumula	
rus	rest (v)	-khutša	-phomola	-lapolosa	-phumla	-phumula	
ruspe	caterpillar (n)	seboko	seboko	nato	umbungu	icimbi	
rusteloos	restless (a)	-sa iketlego	-kgathatsehileng	-tlhorang	-ngonwabanga	-yaluzayo	
ry	row (n)	mothaladi	mola	mola	umgca	uhlu	
ry	ride (v)	-sepela ka	-palama	-pagama	-reya	-gibela	
ryk	rich (a)	-humilego	-ruileng	-humileng	-tyebile (yo)	-nothile	
rykdom	wealth (n)	khumo	leruo	lehumo	ubutyebi	umnotho	
rym	rhyme (n)	morumokwano	morumo	morumo	imfano-ziphelo	imvumelwano	
rym	rhyme (v)	-ruma	-ruma	-ruma	rayima	-vumelana	
ryp	ripe (a)	-budulego	-butswitseng	-budule	-vuthiwe (yo)	-vuthiwe	
ryp	frost (n)	tšhwaane	serame	serame	iqabaka	isithwathwa	
rys	rice (n)	reise	reise	reisi	irayisi	irayisi	
saad	seed (n)	peu	peo	peo	imbewu	imbewu	
saag	saw (n)	saga	saga	šage	isarha	isaha	
saag	saw (v)	-saga	-saga	-šaga	-sarha	-saha	
saai	sow (v)	-gaša	-jala	-jwala	-hlwayela	-tshala	
saak	affair (n)	taba	taba	taba	inyewe	udaba	
saak	case (n)	taba	molato	taba	ingxowa	indaba	
saal	saddle (n)	sala	qhana	sale	isali	isihlalo	
saal	hall (n)	holo	holo	ntlolehalahala	iholo	ihholo	
saam	together (adv)	gammogo	hammoho (le)	mmogo	sonke	-hlangene	
saampers	compress (v)	-pataganya	-patisa	-tshwaka	-xinzelela	-cindezela	
saamsweer	plot (v)	-rera ka sephiri	-etsa mmomori	-sokela motho pelo	-bhunga	-ceba	
saamwerk	co-operate (v)	-dirišana	-sebedisana	-dirisana	-sebenzisana	-sizana	
sag	soft (a)	-boleta	-bonolo	-boleta	-thambile(yo)	-thambile	
saggies	softly (adv)	gannyane	ha bonolo	ka bonolo	ngokuthamba	kancane	
saggies	gently (adv)	gabonolo	-bonolo	ka bonolo	ngokuzolile yo	ngobunono	
sagmoedig	gentle (a)	-bonolo	bonolo	-bonolo	-zolile (yo)	-mnene	
sak	sack (n)	mokotla	mokotla	kgetsi	ingxowa	isaka	
sak	pocket (n)	mokotla	pokotho	potla	ipokotho	isikhwama	
sak	bag (n)	mokotla	mokotla	kgetsi	ingxowa	isaka	
sakdoek	handkerchief (n)	sakatuku	sakatuku	sakatuku	itshefu	iduku	
sakkeroller	pickpocket (n)	lehodu	mosetjhi	senakgodi	umkhuthuzi	umkhuthuzi	
sal	will (v)	-tlo-	-tla	-tla	-za	-zo-	
salaris	salary (n)	moputso	moputso	tuelo	umvuzo	iholo	
salf	anoint (v)	-tlola	-tlotsa	-tlola	-qhola	-gcoba	
salueer	salute (v)	-dumediša	-dumedisa	-rolela hutshe	-khahlela	-shaya indesheni	
saluut	salute (n)	tumedišo	tumediso	go rolela hutshe	ukhahlelo	indesheni	
sambreel	umbrella (n)	samporele	samporele	sekhukhu	isambuleni	isambulela	
samelewing	society (n)	phedišanommogo	batho	loago	uluntu	ukuhlangana	
sameswering	conspiracy (n)	morero wa ka thoko	mmomori	thero	iyelenqe	uzungu	
samewerking	co-operation (n)	tirišano	tshebedisano	tirisano	intsebenziswano	ukusizana	
sampioen	mushroom (n)	tokwane	letswalo	leboa	ikhowa	ikhowe	
sand	sand (n)	lešabašaba	lehlabathe	motlhaba	intlabathi	isihlabathi	

S	Afrikaans	English	N Sotho	Sesotho	Tswana	Xhosa	Zulu
	sandaal	sandal (n)	ramphašane	moqathatso	mpheetšhane	imbadada	ingxabulela
	sanik	whimper (v)	-lla	-lla	-kuruetsa	-khwina	-bibitheka
	sanitêre doekie	sanitary towel (n)	tukwana ya bosadi	phete	phete	iphedi	ithawula lokusubela
	sanksie	sanction (n)	kotlo ya ekonomi	tumello	dikiletsokotlhao	imvume	ukukhinyabeza
	sap	juice (n)	meetsana	lero	matute	incindi	ijusi
	sarkasme	sarcasm (n)	kodutlo	sesomo	ditshotlo	impoxo	umbhuqo
	Saterdag	Saturday (n)	Mokibelo	Moqebelo	Matlhatso	uMgqibelo	uMgqibelo
	saxofoon	saxophone (n)	seksafone	sekesofoune	terompeta	ixilongo	iseksafoni
	sê	say (v)	-re	-bolela	-re	-thi	-sho
	sebra	zebra (n)	pitsi ya naga	qwaha	pitse-ya-naga	iqwarhashe	idube
	sedert	since (adv)	go tloga	ho tloha-	ka gonne	ukusukela	ukusukela kwa-
	sediment	sediment (n)	kgaširiri	ditshifa	leraga	intlenga	inzika
	see	sea (n)	lewatle	lewatle	lewatle	ulwandle	ulwandle
	seekoei	hippopotamus (n)	kubu	kubu	kubu	imvubu	imvubu
	seël	stamp (n)	setempe	setempe	setempe	istampu	isitembu
	seën	bless (v)	-šegofatša	-hlohonolofatsa	-tshegofatsa	sikelela	-busisa
	seëning	blessing (n)	lehlogonolo	mahlohonolo	lesego	intsikelelo	isibusiso
	seep	soap (n)	sešepe	sesepa	molora	isepha	insipho
	seepsteen	soapstone (n)	monoto	sesepa	tootso	umgudlo	umgudlo
	seer	sore (a)	-bohloko	-bohloko	-botlhoko	-buhlungu	-buhlungu
	seer	sore (n)	ntho	seso	seso	isilonda	isilonda
	seermaak	hurt (v)	-gobatša	-ntsha kotsi	-bolaya	-enzakala	-limaza
	segment	segment (n)	mosehlwana	mosehlo	seripa	isuntsu	izenge
	segregeer	segregate (v)	-kgetholla	-arola	-kgaoganya	-ahlula	-ahlukanisa
	segsman	shop steward (n)	mmaditsela	molaodi lebenkeleng	mmueledi	ummeli	ummeli-zisebenzi
	seil	sail (n)	seila	seile	seile	iseyile	useyili
	seil	sail (v)	-thala	-sesa	-thala	-hamba ngenqanawa	-ntweza
	seil	tarpaulin (n)	seila	seile	seile	iseyile	useyili
	seil	canvas (n)	seila	seile	seile	iseyile	useyili
	seiljag	yacht (n)	seketswana	seketswana sa seile	seketswana	isikhephe sogqatso	umkhumbi
	seisoen	season (n)	sehla	nako ya selemo	setlha	ixesha lonyaka	isikhathi sonyaka
	sekel	sickle (n)	sekele	sekele	sekele	irhengqe	isikela
	seker	sure (a)	-nnete	-tiileng	-ruri	-qinisekile(yo)	-qinisekile
	sekering	fuse (n)	fiuse	nyalano	fiose	isilumeki	ifiyuzi
	sekonde	second (n)	motsotswana	motsotswana	motsotswana	umzuzwana	isekeni
	sekondeer	second (v)	-tlatša	-tlatsa	-tlatsa	-xhasa	-sekela
	sekretaris	secretary (n)	mongwaledi	mongodi	mokwaledi	unobhala	unobhala
	sekretarisvoël	secretary bird (n)	tlhame	mmamolangwane	ramolongwana	ingxangxosi	intinginono
	sel	cell (n)	sele	sele	sele	iseli	iseli
	selde	seldom (adv)	go sego kae	ka sewelo	mokabagangwe	ngafane	kancane
	seldery	celery (n)	seleri	seleri	morogo wa seleri	iseleri	useleri
	seldsaam	rare (a)	-bohlokwa	-sewelo	-tlhokegang	-nqabile(yo)	-ngavamile
	self	self (n)	i-	motho ka sebele	nna	mna	ubumina
	selfmoord	suicide (n)	boipolao	boipolao	boipolao	ukuzibulala	ukuzibulala
	selfs	even (adv)	le ge	-esita	le fa	-ngokulingana	na-
	selfstandige naamwoord	noun (n)	leina	lebitso	leina	isibizo	ibizo
	selfsugtig	selfish (a)	-lejelathoko	-inahanelang	-pelotshetlha	-cingela(yo)	-nomhawu
	selfvertroue	self-confidence (n)	boitshepo	boitshepo	boitshepo	ukuzithemba	ukuzithemba
	semels	bran (n)	disemala	ditlhoka	moroko	isemilisi	amakhoba
	sement	cement (n)	samente	samente	samente	isamente	usemende
	senaat	senate (n)	senate	senate	senate	isenethi	isenethe
	sendeling	missionary (n)	moruti	moromuwa	morongwa	umthunywa umfundisi	umfundisi
	sending	mission (n)	thomo	thomo	borongwa	ubizo	ukuthunywa
	sening	sinew (n)	mošifa	lesika	lesika	iintsinga	umsipha
	sening	tendon (n)	mošifa	mosifa	mosifa	umsipha	umsipha
	senior	senior (a)	-golo	-holo	-golwane	-dala	-dala
	sensor	censor (v)	-ganetša	-nyakurela	-sensara	umhluzi weendaba	umbonisici
	sensus	census (n)	palo	palo ya batho	palo ya batho	ubalo lwabantu	ukubalwa kwabantu
	sent	cent (n)	sente	sente	sente	isenti	isenti

Afrikaans	English	N Sotho	Sesotho	Tswana	Xhosa	Zulu	S
senuwee	nerve (n)	mothapo	mothapo	lesika	umthambo-luvo	umuzwa	
senuweeagtig	nervous (a)	-tšhogatšhogago	-letswalo	-mafafa	-phakuzela(yo)	-namatata	
senuweeagtigheid	nervousness (n)	go tšhogatšhoga	letswalo	mafafa	ubuphaku-phaku	amatata	
September	September (n)	Setemere	Loetse	Lwetse	uSeptemba	uSepthemba	
seremonie	ceremony (n)	moletlo	mokete	modiro	inkonzo ethile	umgidi	
serp	scarf (n)	sekhafo	sekhafo	sekafo	isikhafu	isikhafu	
sersant	sergeant (n)	satšene	sajene	seresanta	isajini	usayitsheni	
sertifikaat	certificate (n)	lengwalo la bopaki	lengolo	sethifikheiti	isetifiketi	isetifikethi	
servet	serviette (n)	sebiete	seviete	seiphimodi	ilatshana lezandla	iseviyethe	
ses	six (n)	tshela	tshelela	borataro	isithandathu	isithupha	
sestien	sixteen (n)	lesometshela	leshome le metso e tsheletseng	some thataro	ishumi elinesithandathu	ishumi nesithupha	
sestig	sixty (n)	masometshela	mashome a tsheletseng	somaamarataro	amashumi amathandathu	amashumi ayisithupha	
seun	son (n)	morwa	mora	morwa	unyana	indodana	
seun	boy (n)	mošemane	moshanyana	mosimane	inkwenkwe	umfana	
sewe	seven (n)	šupa	supa	-supa	isixhenxe	isikhombisa	
sewentien	seventeen (n)	lesomešupa	leshome le metso e supileng	some supa	ishumi elinesixhenxe	ishumi nesikhombisa	
sewentig	seventy (n)	masomešupa	mashome a supileng	somaasupa	amashumi asixhenxe	amashumi ayisikhombisa	
sidder	shudder (v)	-thothomela	tlakasela	-tsipoga	-hlasimla	-hlakanyeka	
siek	sick (a)	-lwalago	-kulang	-lwalang	-gula(yo)	-gulayo	
siek	ill (a)	-lwalago	-kula	-bobolang	-gula(yo)	-gula	
sieklik	sickly (a)	-segwahla	-bokoa	-bokoa	-gulayo	-xhwalile	
siekte	sickness (n)	bolwetši	bolwetse	bolwetse	isigulo	ukugula	
siekte	illness (n)	bolwetši	lefu	bolwetse	isigulo	ukugula	
siekte	disease (n)	bolwetši	lefu	bolwetse	isifo	isifo	
siek word	sicken (v)	-lwala	-kudisa	-lwala	-gulisa	-gulisa	
siel	soul (n)	moya	moya	mowa	umphefumlo	umphefumulo	
sien	see (v)	-bona	-bona	-bona	-bona	-bona	
sif	sieve (n)	sefo	sefe	sefo	intluzo	isisefo	
sif	sift (v)	-sefa	-sefa	-sefa	-hluza	-sefa	
sifilis	syphilis (n)	thosola	mokaola	thosola	ihash'elingwevu	ugcunsula	
sig	sight (n)	pono	pono	pono	ukubona	ukubuka	
sigaar	cigar (n)	sikara	sikara	sikara	isiga	usigazi	
sigaret	cigarette (n)	sekerete	sakarete	sekerete	umdiza	usikilidi	
sigbaar	visible (a)	-bonagalago	-bonahalang	-bonala	-bonakalayo	-bonakala	
sigsag	zigzag (n)	manyokenyoke	matswedintsweke	manyokenyoke	ujikojiko	igwinci	
siklus	cycle (n)	leboyo	sedikadikwe	tsheko	umjikelo	ukuyingiliza	
silwer	silver (n)	silibera	silefera	selefera	isilivere	isiliva	
simbaal	cymbal (n)	simpale	simbale	simbala	ixina	isimbali	
simbool	symbol (n)	sešupo	sesupo	sekai	isimboli	uphawu	
simpatie	sympathy (n)	kwelanobohloko	kutlwelobohloko	boutlwelobotlhoko	uvelwano	uzwelo	
simpatiek	sympathetic (a)	-kwelanobohloko	-mohau	-boutlwelobotlhoko	-novelwano	-zwelayo	
simptoom	symptom (n)	sebontšhi	letshwao	sesupo	uphawu	isibonakaliso	
sin	sentence (n)	lefoko	polelo	polelo	isivakalisi	umusho	
sin	sense (n)	sekwi	kelello	tlhaloganyo	ingqondo	ingqondo	
sindelikheid	cleanliness (n)	tlhweko	tlhweko	bophepa	ucoceko	ubonono	
sing	sing (v)	-opela	-bina	-opela	-cula	-cula	
sinjaal	signal (n)	temoši	temoso	sekai	umqondiso	isiginali	
sink	sink (v)	-sobela	-tetebela	-nwela	-tshona	-shona	
sinsnede	phrase (n)	sekafoko	sekapolelo	ntlha	ibinzana	isigejane samazwi	
sintel	cinder (n)	mošidi	molora	legalanyana	ilahle	ilahle	
sinteties	synthetic (a)	-maitirelo	-tswakaneng	-se nang boleng	-dityanisiwe(yo)	-qanjiwe	
sirkel	circle (n)	sediko	sedikadikwe	sediko	isangqa	isiyingi	
sirkus	circus (n)	sorokisi	serekise	sorokisi	iserityisi	isekisi	
sis	hiss (v)	-huetša	-letsa molodi	-suma	-futha	-khisila	
sit	put (v)	-bea fase	-bea	-baya	-beka	-beka	
sit	sit (v)	-dula	-dula	-nna	-hlala	-hlala	

S	Afrikaans	English	N Sotho	Sesotho	Tswana	Xhosa	Zulu
	sitkamer	lounge (n)	bodulelo	lontjhe	kamore ya boitapoloso	igumbi lokuhlala	ilawunji
	sitplek	seat (n)	bodulo	bodulo	manno	isihlalo	isihlalo
	sitplekgordel	seatbelt (n)	lepanta la boitšhireletšo	lebanta la setulo	lebanta la tshireletso	ibhanti yesinqe	ibhande lemoto
	sitrus	citrus (a)	-monamune	-molamunu	-monamune	-esitrasi	isithrasi
	sjarme	charm (n)	borategi	mofuthu	mmitsa	umtsalane	ubuhle
	sjokolade	chocolate (n)	tšhokolete	tjhokolete	tshokolete	itshokoleti	ushokolethe
	skaaf	chafe (v)	-khumola	-hohla	-gotlha	-khuthula	-gudleka
	skaak	hijack (v)	-tšea ka dikgoka	-kgelosa ka dikgoka	-utswa	-qweqwedisa	ukubamba inkunzi
	skaal	scale (n)	sekala	sekala	sekale	isikali	isikali
	skaam	ashamed (a)	-lewa ke dihlong	-swabile	-jewa ke tlhong	-ba neentloni	-namahloni
	skaamte	shame (n)	dihlong	dihlong	tlhong	ihlazo	amahloni
	skaap	sheep (n)	nku	nku	nku	igusha	imvu
	skaapvleis	mutton (n)	nama ya nku	nama ya nku	nama ya nku	inyama yegusha	inyama yemvu
	skaapwagter	shepherd (n)	modiši	modisa	modisa	umalusi	umalusi wezimvu
	skade	harm (n)	tshenyegelo	tshenyo	tsenyo	umonakalo	ukulimala
	skade	damage (n)	tshenyego	tshenyo	tshenyegelo	umonakalo	ukulimaza
	skadelik	harmful (a)	-kotsi	-senyang	-kotsi	-onakalisayo	-nengozi
	skadu	shade (n)	moriti	moriti	moriti	umthunzi	umthunzi
	skaduwee	shadow (n)	moriti	moriti	moriti	umthunzi	isithunzi
	skag	shaft (n)	mokoti	tjhafo	motlhoboloko	umphini	umgodi
	skakelaar	switch (n)	switšhi	sewitjhe	switšhi	iswitshi	iswitshi
	skandaal	scandal (n)	selešadihlong	maswabi	kgopiso	ihlazo	ichilo
	skande	disgrace (n)	dihlong	hlomphollo	botlhabisa ditlhong	ihlazo	ihlazo
	skare	crowd (n)	lešaba	matshwele	kokoano	isihlwele	isiqumbi
	skat	treasure (n)	lehumo	letlotlo	ramatlotlo	ubutyebi	igugu
	skat	assess (v)	-lekanya	-akanya	-atlhola	-misa	-nquma
	skatter	assessor (n)	moahlodiši	moakanyi	moatlhodi	ummisi	umnqumi wenani
	skede	sheath (n)	segatla	selata	kgwatlha	isingxobo	umgodlo
	skedel	skull (n)	legata	lehata	legata	ukhakayi	ithambo lekhanda
	skeel	squint (v)	-leana	-pelekana	-pelekanya	-fifithekisa	-nxwema
	skeen	shin (n)	moomo	moomo	motwane	uxhongo	umbala
	skeer	shave (v)	-beola	-beola	-beola	-tsheva	-shefa
	skeermes	razor (n)	sebeolo	lehare	legare	ireyiza	ireza
	skeerroom	shaving cream (n)	sešepe sa go beola	sesepa sa ho beola	sesepa sa go beola	ikhrim yokutsheva	ukhilimu wokushefa
	skei	part (v)	-kgaogana	-arola	-kgaogana	-ahlukana	-ahlukananisa
	skei	divorce (v)	-hlala	-hlala	-tlhala	-qhawula umtshato	-divosa
	skeidsregter	referee (n)	moahloledi	moletsaphala	motsereganyi	usompempe	unompempe
	skelmstreek	trick (n)	bofora	mano	malepa	iqhinga	inkohliso
	skema	scheme (n)	peakanyo	morero	thulaganyo	isikimu	uhlelo
	skemer	dusk (n)	phirimane	shwalane	letlatlana	urhatya	ukuhwalala
	skend	mutilate (v)	-senya	-tamukanya	-senya	-limaza	-nqumanquma
	skenk	present (v)	-fa	-fa	-fa	-pha	-pha
	skenk	donate (v)	-fa	-fana	-aba	-nikela ngesisa	-nika
	skenking	donation (n)	mpho	mpho	sehuba	isisa	umnikelo
	skep	scoop (v)	-ga	-kga	-gaba	-kha	-kha
	skep	create (v)	-bopa	-hlola	-bopa	-dala	-dala
	skeplepel	ladle (n)	leho	mpshane	thoka	umcephe	indebe
	Skepper	Creator (n)	Mmopi	Mohlodi	Mmopi	umDali	uMdali
	skêr	scissors (n)	sekero	sekere	sekere	isikere	isikelo
	skerm	screen (n)	seširo	lehlafi	sesiro	isikhuseli	isisitho
	skerp	shrill (a)	-thibago ditsebe	-bohale	-itayang tsebe	-bukhali	-ntontolozayo
	skerp	sharp (a)	-bogale	-bohale	-bogale	-bukhali	-bukhali
	skerp	acute (a)	-bogale	-bohale	-bogale	-bukhali	-cijile
	skerpioen	scorpion (n)	phepheng	phepheng	phepheng	unomadudwane	ufezela
	skeur	rupture (v)	-gagoga	-tabola	-phanya	-gqabhuka	-gqabuka
	skeur	tear (v)	-kgeila	-tabola	-gagola	-krazula	-dabula
	skielik	sudden (a)	-ka pela	ka tshohanyetso	ka tshoganyetso	-khawulezile(yo)	masinya
	skiereiland	peninsula (n)	sekasehlakahlaka	peninsula	sekasetlhake	usingasiqithi	inhlonhlo
	skiet	shoot (v)	-thunya	-thunya	-thuntsha	-dubula	-dubula

Afrikaans	English	N Sotho	Sesotho	Tswana	Xhosa	Zulu	S
skietstilstand	ceasefire (n)	marumofase	ho lala ha ntwa	khutlo ya ntwa	umayime	ukunqamuka kokudubula	
skik	arrange (v)	-rulaganya	-hlopha	-rulaganya	cwangcisa	-hlela	
skikking	arrangement (n)	thulaganyo	hlophiso	thulaganyo	isicwangciso	uhlelo	
skil	husk (n)	lekgapetla	sekgapetla	letlapi	umququ	amahluba	
skil	peel (n)	lekgephola	lekgapetla	letlape	uqweqwe	ikhasi	
skil	peel (v)	-kgephola	-ebola	-obola	-chuba	-hluba	
skild	shield (n)	kotse	thebe	thebe	ikhaka	ihawu	
skilfers	dandruff (n)	dikelfere	sekerefe	sekgamatha	inkwethu	intuva	
skilpad	tortoise (n)	khudu	kgudu	khudu	ufudo	ufudo	
skinder	gossip (v)	-seba	-seba	-seba	-hleba	-hemuza	
skinderpraatjies	gossip (n)	mabarebare	ditshebo	ditshebo	intlebendwane	amahemuhemu	
skink	pour (v)	-tšhela	-tshela	-tshela	-galela	-thela	
skinkbord	tray (n)	therei	sekenkeboroto	terei	itreyi	ithreyi	
skip	ship (n)	sekepe	sekepe	sekepe	inqanawa	umkhumbi	
skitter	glitter (v)	-phadima	-phatsima	-phatsima	-bengezela	-benyezela	
skobbejak	scoundrel (n)	sekebeka	molotsana	legwaragwara	ixoki	ihilikiqi	
skoen	shoe (n)	seeta	seeta	setlhako	isihlangu	isicathulo	
skoenlapper	butterfly (n)	serurubele	serurubele	serurubele	ibhabhathane	uvemvane	
skoenveter	shoelace (n)	lerala la dieta	leqhwele	thapo ya setlhako	umtya wesihlangu	intambo yesicathulo	
skoffel	hoe (v)	-hlagola	-hlahola	-tlhagola	-hlakula	-hlakula	
skollie	hooligan (n)	tsotsi	setlokotsebe	sekebekwa	indlavini	isichwensi	
skool	school (n)	sekolo	sekolo	sekolo	isikolo	isikole	
skoon	clean (a)	-hlwekilego	-hlwekile	-phepa	-cocekileyo	-hlanzekile	
skoondogter	daughter-in-law (n)	ngwetši	ngwetsi	ngwetsi	umolokazana	umakoti	
skoonheid	beauty (n)	botse	botle	bontle	ubuhle	ubuhle	
skoonmaak	purge (v)	-gofa	-hlwekisa	phukutsa	-coca	-hlanza	
skoonmaak	clean (v)	-hlwekiša	-hlwekisa	-phephafatsa	-coca	-hlanza	
skoonmaak	cleanse (v)	-hlwekiša	-hlwekisa	-forola	-hlambulula	-hlanza	
skoonmoeder	mother-in-law (n)	mmatswale	matsale	matsale	uninazala	umamezala	
skoonseun	son-in-law (n)	mokgonyana	mokgwenyana	mogwe	umkhwenyana	umkhwenyana	
skoonsuster	sister-in-law (n)	mogadibo	ngwetši	mogadibo	umlanyakazi	umlamu	
skoonvader	father-in-law (n)	ratswale	mohwe	ratsale	ubawozala	ubabezala	
skoorsteen	chimney (n)	setupamuši	tjhemele	sentshamosi	itshimini	ushimula	
skoot	shot (n)	thunyo	thunyo	thunyo	isithonga	ukudubula	
skop	kick (n)	thago	thaho	thago	ukukhaba	ukukhahlela	
skop	kick (v)	-raga	-raha	-raga	-khapa	-khahlela	
skop	boot (v)	-raga	-raha	-raga	-khaba	-khahlela	
skoppie	shovel (n)	sekopogarafo	garafu	sekopo	isikophu	ifosholo	
skottel	dish (n)	sebjana	sejana	sejana	isitya	indishi	
skou	show (n)	pontšho	pontsho	pontsho	umboniso	umbukiso	
skouer	shoulder (n)	legetla	lehetla	legetla	iligxa	ihlombe	
skouerblad	shoulderblade (n)	segetla	lesapo la lehetla	legope	igxalaba	isiphanga	
skouerophaling	shrug (n)	go emiša magetla	ho sihletsa mahetla	khutlolo	unyuso-magxa	ukuqhikiza	
skraal	slim (a)	-sese	-tshesane	-bopameng	-bhityile(yo)	-nesimo esincane	
skraap	scrape (v)	-fala	-ngwapa	-fala	-krwela	-phala	
skrap	scrap (v)	-khantshela	-kgehlemanya	-ngapa	-susa	-yeka	
skrap	delete (v)	-phumola	-phumola	-phimola	-cima	-susa	
skrif	writing (n)	mongwalo	mongolo	mokwalo	umbhalo	umbhalo	
skrikkeljaar	leap year (n)	ngwagamotelele	selemo setshelapalo-matsatsi	ngwagamoleele	unyakande	unyaka onezinsuku ezingu-	
skrikmaak	frighten (v)	-tšhoša	-tshosa	-tshosa	-oyikisa	-ethusa	
skroef	screw (n)	sekurufi	sekurufu	sekurufu	isikrufu	isikulufo	
skroef	screw (v)	-kurufela	-kurufella	-tantela	-skrufela	-kulufa	
skroei	scorch (v)	-babola	-tlabola	-babola	-tshisa	-shisa	
skroei	scald (v)	-babola	-photjhola	-fisa	-tyabula	-shisa	
skroei	singe (v)	-babola	-tlabola	-babola	-rhawula	-hanguza	
skrop	scrub (v)	-gohla	-koropa	-koropa	-khuhla	-khuhla	
skryf	write (v)	-ngwala	-ngola	-kwala	-bhala	-bhala	
skryfbehoeftes	stationery (n)	dingwalelo	tsa ho ngola	dikwalelo	iincwadi zokubhalela	izimpahla zokubhala	

S	Afrikaans	English	N Sotho	Sesotho	Tswana	Xhosa	Zulu
	skryfpapier	writing paper (n)	pampiri ya go ngwalela	pampiri ya ho ngolla	pampiri	iphepha lokubhala	iphepha lokubhala
	skrywer	author (n)	mongwadi	mongodi	mokwadi	umbhali	umbhali
	skud	shake (v)	-šišinya	-tsukutla	-reketla	-hlukuhla	-nyakazisa
	skugter	shy (a)	-dihlong	ditlhong	-tlhabiwang ke kgala	-neentloni	-namahloni
	skugter	timid (a)	-dihlong	-boi	-boi	-nkwantya (yo)	-ethukayo
	skuif	move (v)	-šuthiša	-suthisa	-sutisa	-shenxa	-nyukuza
	skuifel	shuffle (v)	-ritša	-fetola	-kgosoba	-shixiza	-shudula
	skuiling	refuge (n)	botšhabelo	botshabelo	botshabelo	ikhusi	isiphephelo
	skuilplaas	asylum (n)	botšhabelo	botshabelo	botshabelo	indawo yokubalekela	inqaba
	skuins loop	slant (v)	-sekama	-sekama	-sekama	-kekela	-tsheka
	skuld	guilt (n)	molato	molato	molato	ityala	icala
	skuld	owe (v)	-kolota	-kolota	-kolota	-tyala	-kweleta
	skuld	debt (n)	molato	molato	molato	ityala	isikwenetu
	skuldig	guilty (a)	-nago le molato	-molato	-molato	-netyala	-necala
	skuldig bevind	convict (v)	-ahlola	-ahlola	-bona molato	-beka ityala	-lahla ngecala
	skuldige	culprit (n)	mosenyi	ya molato	yo o molato	umoni	umoni
	skulp	shell (n)	kgopa	kgetla	legapa	iqokobhe	igobolondo
	skurk	villain (n)	sekebeka	motlatlapi	molotsana	itshivela	isigebengu
	skuur	scour (v)	-gohla	-hohla	-gotlha	-khuhla	-khuhla
	skyfie	chip (potato) (n)	ditšhipisi	tjhipise	tshipisi	itshipsi	ucezu
	skyn	pretence (n)	boikgakantšho	boikaketsi	boitimokanyo	ukuzenzisa	ukuzenzisa
	skyn	seem (v)	-bonagala	-tadimeha	-kete	-bonakala	kungathi
	skyn	shine (v)	-kganya	-benya	-phatsima	-khanya	-khanya
	skynheilige	hypocrite (n)	moikaketši	moikaketsi	moitimokanyi	umhanahanisi	umzenzisi
	skywe sny	slice (v)	-sega selai	-ngwatha	-farola	-sika	-sika
	slaaf	slave (n)	lekgoba	lekgoba	lekgoba	ikhoboka	isigqila
	slaag	succeed (v)	-atlega	-atleha	-tlhatlhama	-phumelela	-phumelela
	slaai	salad (n)	selae	selae	salata	isaladi	isaladi
	slaan	punch (v)	-nganka	-otla	-betsa	-betha	-bhakela
	slaan	hit (v)	-itia	-otla	-itaya	-betha	-shaya
	slaap	sleep (n)	boroko	boroko	boroko	ukulala	ubuthongo
	slaap	sleep (v)	-robala	-robala	-robala	-lala	-lala
	slaapkamer	bedroom (n)	borobalelo	kamore	kamore	igumbi lokulala	ikamelo lokulala
	slaaploosheid	insomnia (n)	tlhobaelo	tlhobaelo	tlhobaelo	isifo sokungalali	ukuqwasha
	slag	slaughter (v)	-hlaba	-bolaya	-tlhaba	-xhela	-hlaba
	slagaar	artery (n)	seišamadi	mothapo	tshika	umthambo	umthambo
	slagoffer	victim (n)	sehlabelo	phofu	sebolaiwa	ixhoba	umhlatshelo
	slagplaas	abattoir (n)	bohlabelo	selagapalo	botlhabelo	isilarha	amadela
	slagtand	fang (n)	polai	leino la noha	lebolai	izinyo	inzawu
	slagter	butcher (n)	radinama	raselaga	raselaga	unosilarha	ubhusha
	slagtery	butchery (n)	leselaga	selaga	selaga	isilarha	isilaha
	slagting	slaughter (n)	polao	polao	polao	ukuxhela	ukuhlaba
	slagveld	battlefield (n)	bohlabanelo	ntweng	ntwa	ithafa leduli	inkundla yempi
	slak	snail (n)	kgopa	kgofu	kgopa	usinyeke	umnenke
	slang	snake (n)	noga	noha	noga	inyoka	inyoka
	slapeloos	sleepless (a)	-hlobaelago	-hlobaelang	-tlhobaelang	-qwayitekile	-ngenabuthongo
	slawerny	slavery (n)	bokgoba	bokgoba	bokgoba	ubukhoboka	ubugqila
	sleep	tow (v)	-goga	-hula	-goga	-rhuqa	-donsa
	sleep	drag (v)	-goga	-hulanya	-gogoba	-rhuqa	-hudula
	sleep	draw (v)	-goga	-hula	-goga	-rhuqa	-donsa
	sleeptou	tow rope (n)	thapo ya go goga	ropo ya ho hula	thapo ya go goga	intambo yokurhuqa	intambo yokudonsa
	sleg	bad (a)	-be	-be	-be	-bi	-bi
	sleg	badly (adv)	gampe	hampe	mo go maswe	-kakubi	kabi
	slegs	only (adv)	fela	feela	fela	kuphela	kuphela
	slegte spysvertering	indigestion (n)	tšhilegompe	pipitlelo	mogosane	ukungetyisi	unjongwe
	sleng	slang (n)	sempara	seleng	puotlaopo	isithetho	isidolobha
	sleutel	key (n)	senotlelo	senotlolo	senotlolo	isitshixo	ukhiye
	sleutelbeen	collarbone (n)	kgetlane	lesapo la lepetu	kgetlane	ingqosha	ingqwababa
	sleutelgat	keyhole (n)	lešobana la senotlelo	lesobana la senotlolo	thobasenotlolo	umngxuma wesitshixo	imbobo kakhiye
	slim	astute (a)	-tsarogile	-masene	botlhale	-lumkileyo	-hlakaniphile

Afrikaans	English	N Sotho	Sesotho	Tswana	Xhosa	Zulu	S
slinger	stagger (v)	-tlhatlharega	-thekesela	-thetheekela	-gxadazela	-bhadazela	
sloot	ditch (n)	leope	lengope	lemena	umsele	umsele	
slordig	untidy (a)	-bošaedi	-bohlaswa	-boatla	-mdaka	-mahlikihliki	
slot	lock (n)	sekgonyo	senotlolo	selotlele	isitshixo	isihluthulelo	
slu	cunning (a)	-nago le mahlajana	-mano	-boferefere	-nobuqhokolo	-nobuqili	
sluier	veil (n)	seširo	lesira	lesire	isigqubuthelo	iveli	
sluimer	doze (v)	-potuma	-otsela	-otsela	-lala	-ozela	
sluit	lock (v)	-notlela	-notlela	-lotlela	-tshixa	-hluthulela	
sluk	swallow (v)	-metša	-kwenya	-metsa	-ginya	-gwinya	
slukderm	gullet (n)	mometšo	mmetso	mometso	ummizo	umphimbo	
slukderm	oesophagus (n)	mometšo	mmetso	mometso	ummizo	umminzo	
slukkie	sip (n)	tshoro	kotjelo	mothangwana	ukurhabula	umhabulo	
slurp	sip (v)	-sora	-habola	-gobola	-rhabula	-habula	
slym	mucus (n)	mamina	mamina	mamina	uxakaxa	isikhwehlela	
smaak	taste (n)	mohlodi	tatso	moutlwalo	incasa	ukuzwangomlomo	
smaaklik	savoury (a)	-bose	-monate	-monate	-nencasa	-mnandi	
smaakloos	tasteless (a)	-hlokago mohlodi	bosula	-bosula	-javujavu	-duma	
smal	narrow (a)	-sese	-tshesane	-tshesane	-mxinwa	-mcingo	
smart	sorrow (n)	mahlomola	maswabi	kutlobotlhoko	usizi	usizi	
smeer	grease (v)	-kirisa	tlotsa ka kerisi	-tshasa	-grisa	-gcoba	
smelt	melt (v)	-tologa	-qhibidiha	-gakologa	-nyibilika	-ncibilika	
snaaks	queer (a)	-makatšago	-makatsang	-sa itsegeng	-ngaqhelekanga	-mangalisayo	
snaaks	funny (a)	-segišago	-makatsang	-mabela	-ngaqhelekanga	-hlekisayo	
snak	gasp (v)	-fegelwa	-fehelwa	-goga mowa	-khefuza	-befuzela	
snawel	beak (n)	molomo wa nonyana	molomo	molomo	umlomo wentaka	umlomo wenyoni	
sneeu	snow (n)	lehlwa	lehlwa	letlhwa	ikhephu	iqhwa	
sneeu	snow (v)	-na lehlwa	-kgetheha	-go wa ga letlhwa	-khephuza	-khithika	
sneltrein	express (n)	setimela sa mafofonyane	terene e lebelo	setimelasegaodi	uloliwe okhawulezayo	ushikishi	
snipper	shred (v)	-ripaganya	-ranthanya	-gabela	isiqwenga	-sika	
snoei	prune (v)	-poma	-faola	-poma	-thena	-nquma	
snoet	muzzle (n)	molomo	molomo o motsu	nko	umlomo wesilwanyana	impumulo	
snor	whiskers (n)	maledu a ka godimo	matshwala ga molomo	tedu	amabhovu	amadevu	
snor	moustache (n)	maledu a ka godima ga molomo	matshwala	tedu	amabhovu	amadevu	
snork	snore (n)	moono	mohono	mogono	ukurhona	ukuhona	
snork	snore (v)	-ona	-hona	-gona	-rhona	-hona	
snuif	sniff (v)	-fola	-fofonela	-sunetsa	-rhogola	-hela	
sny	slice (n)	selai	sengwathwana	pharo	isilayi	ucezu	
sny	carve (v)	-ripa	-seta	-seta	-sika	-sika	
sny	cut (n)	mosego	leqeba	tshego	inxeba	umsiko	
sny	cut (v)	-sega	-seha	-sega	-sika	-sika	
soek	search (v)	-nyaka	-batla	-batla	-funa	-cinga	
soektog	search (n)	monyako	patlo	patlo	ukufuna	ukucinga	
soen	kiss (n)	katlo	kako	katlo	ukuphuza	ukuqabula	
soen	kiss (v)	-atla	-aka	-atla	-phuza	-qabula	
soet	sweet (a)	-bose	-monate	-botshe	-sutu	-mtoti	
soetrissie	green pepper (n)	pherefere ye tala	pepere e tala	pherefere	igrinpepa	upelepele oluhlaza	
sog	sow (n)	kolobe ya tshadi	kolobe e tshehadi	kolobe e namagadi	imazi yehagu	ingulube yensikazi	
sokker	soccer (n)	kgwele ya maoto	bolo	sokere	isoka	unobhutshuzwayo	
sokkie	sock (n)	sokisi	kauso	kausu	ikawusi	isokisi	
soldaat	soldier (n)	mohlabani	lesole	lesole	ijoni	isotsha	
somer	summer (n)	selemo	lehlabula	selemo	ihlobo	ihlobo	
sommige	some (a)	-ngwe	-ng	-ngwe	-nye	-thize	
son	sun (n)	letšatši	letsatsi	letsatsi	ilanga	ilanga	
sonbril	sunglasses (n)	dipaketsane tša letšatši	disonoborele	diporele tsa letsatsi	iindondo	amagogolosi	
sonbruin	suntan (n)		ho tjheswa ke letsatsi	go fiswa ke letsatsi	ubuntsundu	ukugqunqa	
Sondag	Sunday (n)	Sontaga	Sontaha	Latshipi	iCawa	iSonto	
sonde	sin (n)	sebe	sebe	sebe	isono	isono	

S	Afrikaans	English	N Sotho	Sesotho	Tswana	Xhosa	Zulu
	sone	zone (n)	karolo	lebatowa	kgaolo	ummandla	isifunda
	sonlig	sunlight (n)	seetša sa letšatši	kganya ya letsatsi	lesedi la letsatsi	ilanga	ukukhanya kwelanga
	sonneblom	sunflower (n)	sonopolomo	sonobolomo	sonobolomo	ujongilanga	ujikanelanga
	sononder	sunset (n)	phirimo	madikelo	phirimo ya letsatsi	ukutshona kwelanga	ukushona kwelanga
	sononder	sundown (n)	phirimo	madikelo	mampa-a-kolobe	ukuhlwa	ukushona kwelanga
	sonop	sunrise (n)	tlhabo	tjhabo ya letsatsi	tlhabo ya letsatsi	ukuphuma kwelanga	ukuphuma kwelanga
	sonstraal	sunbeam (n)	lehlasedi	lehlasedi	lerang la letsatsi	ilitha	umsebe welanga
	soogdier	mammal (n)	seamuši	mamale	seamusi	isidalwa esanyisayo	isilwane esincelisayo
	sooibrand	heartburn (n)	seokolela	lesokolla	lesokolela	isitshisa	isilungulela
	soom	hem (n)	lemeno	momeno	lemeno	umgobo	umthungo
	soort	kind (n)	mohuta	mofuta	mofuta	uhlobo	uhlobo
	soort	make (n)	mohuta	mofuta	mofuta	uhlobo	uhlobo
	soos	like (prep)	bjalo ka	jwalo ka	jaaka	njenga	-njenga-
	sop	soup (n)	sopo	sopho	sopo	umhluzi	isobho
	sorghum	sorghum (n)	mabele	mabele	lebele	amazimba	amabele
	sous	sauce (n)	souso	souso	moro	umhluzi	umhluzi
	sous	gravy (n)	moro	moro	moro	umhluzi	umhluzi
	sout	salt (n)	letswai	letswai	letswai	ityuwa	itswayi
	spaar	spare (v)	-boloka	-boloka	-boloka	-gcina	-onga
	spaargeld	savings (n)	dipolokelo	tjhelete e bolokilweng	poloko	imali egciniweyo	imali elondoloziwe
	spaarsaamheid	thrift (n)	go seketša	paballo	tshomarelo	ukugcisa	isineke sokonga
	span	team (n)	sepane	sehlopha	setlhopa	iqela	ithimu
	span	tighten (v)	-nganga	-tiisa	-gagamatsa	-qinisa	-qinisa
	spanningsdruk	stress (n)	go lapa mmele le moya	kgatello	mathata	ugxininiso	ukucindizelwa
	spasma	spasm (n)	bogatšu	kgonyelo ya mesifa	kudupanyo	inkantsi	ukugongobala
	speeksel	saliva (n)	mare	mathe	mathe	amathe	amathe
	speel	play (v)	-bapala	-bapala	-tshameka	-dlala	-dlala
	speelding	toy (n)	sebapadišwa	nthwa ho bapala	setshamekiso	into yokudlala	into yokudlala
	speen	wean (v)	-lomolla	-kgwesa	-alosa	-lumla	-lumula
	spek	bacon (n)	sepeke	nama ya kolobe	nama ya kolobe	isipeke	ubhekeni
	spel	spell (v)	-peleta	-peleta	-peleta	-isihlandlo	-pela
	spel	game (n)	papadi	papadi	motshameko	umclalo	umdlalo
	speld	pin (n)	sepalete	sepelete	kgokelo	isipeliti	isipeleti
	spens	pantry (n)	bobolokelo bja dijo	sepense	polokelo ya dijo	ipentri	iphandolo
	spesery	spice (n)	senoko	dinoko	seloki	isiqholo	isipayisi
	spesiaal	special (a)	-itšego	-ikgethileng	-tlhaolegileng	-odwa	-ngavamile
	speurder	detective (n)	letseka	lefokisi	letseka	umcuphi	umseshi
	spieël	mirror (n)	seipone	seipone	seipone	isipili	isibuko
	spier	muscle (n)	mošifa	mosifa	mosifa	isihlunu	umsipha
	spies	spear (n)	lerumo	lerumo	lerumo	umkhonto	umkhonto
	spinnekop	spider (n)	segokgo	sekgo	segokgo	isigcawu	ulwembu
	spinnerak	cobweb (n)	bobi	bolepo	bobi	indlu yesigcawu	ubulembu
	spioen	spy (n)	hlodi	sehlwela	setlhodi	ungcothoza	inhloli
	spioeneer	spy (v)	-hlola	-hlwela	-tlhola	-ngcothoza	-hlola
	spiritus	spirits (n)	seporitši	sepiriti	segwai	imimoya	isipirithi
	spit	dig (v)	-epa	-tjheka	-epa	-omba	-mba
	spits	apex (n)	ntlha	sehlohlolo	setlhoa	incam	isiqongo
	splits	split (v)	-pharola	-petsola	-phatloga	-canda	-qanda
	spoed	speed (n)	lebelo	lebelo	lebelo	isantya	ijubane
	spoeg	spit (v)	-tshwa	-tshwela	-kgwa	-tshica	-khafula
	spog	boast (v)	-ikgodiša	-ithorisa	-koma	-gwagwisa	-bhamuza
	spoggerig	boastful (a)	-ikgodišago	-ithorisang	-belafalang	-gwagwisayo	-qholoshile
	spons	sponge (n)	sepontše	seponse	ngami	imfunxa	isipanji
	spoor	track (n)	mohlala	mohlala	motlhala	umzila	isipolo
	spoorweg	railway (n)	seporo sa ditimela	seporo	seporo	isiporo	uloliwe
	sport	sport (n)	papadi	papadi	motshameko	umdlalo	umdlalo
	spottery	ridicule (n)	kwero	tshomo	losotlo	intlekisa	ukuhleka
	spraaksaam	talkative (a)	-bolelago kudu	-lehehle	-buabuang	-thethayo	-ngundabeni
	spreekwoord	proverb (n)	seema	maele	seane	iqhalo	isaga
	spring	spring (v)	-hlaga	-tlola	-tsipoga	-tsiba	-eqa

Afrikaans	English	N Sotho	Sesotho	Tswana	Xhosa	Zulu	S
spring	jump (v)	-taboga	-tlola	-tlola	-tsiba	-xhuma	
springbok	springbok (n)	tshephe	tshepe	tshephe	ibhadi	insephe	
sprinkaan	grasshopper (n)	tšie	bookgolane	tsie	intethe	intethe	
sprinkaan	locust (n)	tšie	lerutle	tsie	intethe	intethe	
sprinkel	sprinkle (v)	-šašetša	-fafatsa	kgatsha	-fefa	-fafaza	
sprinkelaar	sprinkler (n)	sešašetši	sefafatsi	sekgatshi	isifefi	isifafazo	
sprong	jump (n)	go taboga	tlolo	go tlola	umtsi	ukuxhuma	
spuit	syringe (n)	kurumane	sepeiti	sepeiti	inaliti	isirinji	
spyker	nail (n)	sepekere	sepekere	sepekere	isikhonkwane	isipikili	
spyker	nail (v)	-kokotela	-kokotela	-kokotela	-bethelela	-bethela	
spyskaart	menu (n)	lenaneo la dijo	lenane la dijo	buka ya dijo	izipheko imenyu	imenyu	
spyt	regret (n)	tshwabo	boinyatso	boikotlhao	ukuzisola	ukudabukela	
spyt hê	regret (v)	-swaba	-inyatsa	-otlhaya	-zisole	-dabukela	
staaf	rail (n)	seporo	setshehetso	seporo	intonga	umshayo	
staak	strike (v)	-teraeka	-teraeka	-ngala	enza uqhushululu	-teleka	
staan	stand (v)	-ema	-ema	-ema	-ma	-ma	
staar	stare (v)	-lebelela	-tjamela	-lebelela	-thi ndwanya	-gqoloza	
staar	gaze (v)	-lebelela	-tadima	-leba	-jonga	-jolozela	
staat	state (n)	naga	naha	naga	imeko	uhulumeni	
staatmaak	rely (v)	-tshepha	-tshepa	-ikanya	-thembela	-themba	
stabiel	stable (a)	-sa fetogego	-tiileng	-tlhomameng	-zinzile(yo)	-qinile mbe	
stad	city (n)	motsemogolo	motse	motse	isixeko	idolobha	
stadig	slow (a)	inanyago	butle	-bonya	-cothayo	kancane	
stagnant	stagnant (a)	-emego	-emeng	-emeng	-mileyo	-mi ndawonye	
staking	strike (n)	seteraeke	seteraeke	go ngala	uqhushululu	isiteleka	
stal	stable (n)	setala	lesaka	setale	isitali	isitebele	
stam	stem (n)	kutu	kutu	kutu	isiqu	isiqu	
stamp	bump (v)	-thula	-thesela	-thula	-ngquba	-dubhuza	
stampmielies	samp (n)	setampa	setampo	setampa	umngqusho	isitambu	
stand	stand (n)	kemo	tsetsepelo	setlhomo	isikhundla	ukuma	
standaard	standard (a)	-leemo	-boemo	-tlhomamo	-mgangatho	-lunge nomthetho	
standaard	standard (n)	leemo	boemo	kemo	umgangatho	umgomo	
stank	stink (n)	monkgo	monko o mobe	monkgo	ivumba	iphunga elibi	
stapel	pile (n)	ngata	pokello	tlhatlaganyo	-fumba	isitaki	
stapel	pile (v)	-hlophela	-bokella	-tlhatlaganya	imfumba	-taka	
stasie	station (n)	seteišene	seteishene	seteišene	isikhululo	isiteshi	
stedelik	urban (a)	-toropong	-metseng e meholo	-semotseng	-asezidolophini	-semadolobheni	
steek	stab (v)	-hlaba	-hlaba	-tlhaba	-hlaba	-hlaba	
steek	sting (v)	-loma	-hlaba	-loma	-hlaba	-hlaba	
steek	sting (n)	tomo	sehlabi	lebolela	ulwamvila	ukuhlaba	
steekhaar	bristle (n)	boditsi	boditse	boditse	unwele	ingqangasi	
steel	shaft (n)	mpheng	mofeng	mfinyane	intsimbi	umphini	
steel	steal (v)	-utswa	-utswa	-utswa	-ba	-eba	
steenkool	coal (n)	malahla	leshala	lelatlha	ilahle	amalahle	
steil	steep (a)	-rotogago	moepa	-mokong	-mqengqelezi	-nommango	
stel	set (v)	-rea	-tjheha	-thaya	-seta	-beka	
stel	set (n)	sehlopha	sete	thaiso	iseti	isethi	
stelsel	system (n)	peakanyo	tsela	thulaganyo	umiso	ihlelo	
stem	voice (n)	lentšu	lentswe	lentswe	ilizwi	izwi	
stem	vote (v)	-kgetha	-bouta	-kgetha	-vota	-vota	
stem	vote (n)	bouto	bouto	kgetho	ivoti	ukuvota	
ster	star (n)	naledi	naledi	naledi	inkwenkwezi	inkanyezi	
steriel	sterile (a)	-hlwekišitšwego ditwatši	-hlwekileng	-opafetseng	-ngenazintsholo-ngwane	-ngenamagciwane	
steriliseer	sterilise (v)	-hlwekiša	-hlwekisa	-opafatsa	-bulala iintsholo-longwane	-thena	
sterk	strong (a)	-maatla	-matla	-maatla	-namandla	-namandla	
sterkte	strength (n)	maatla	matla	bothata	amandla	amandla	
sterrekunde	astronomy (n)	bonepanaledi	thuto ya dinaledi	bolepanaledi	inzululwazi ngeenkwenkwezi	ukwazi ngezinkanyezi	

Afrikaans	English	N Sotho	Sesotho	Tswana	Xhosa	Zulu
stert	tail (n)	mosela	mohatla	mogatla	umsila	umsila
stetoskoop	stethoscope (n)	seteteskopo	setetesekoupo	sethetosekoupo	isixilongi	izipopolo
steun	back (v)	-emela	-tshehetsa	-tshegetsa	xhasa	-sekela
steurnis	nuisance (n)	matshwenyego	kgathatso	letshwenyo	inkathazo	inkathazo
stewel	boot (n)	putsu	butshi	setlhako	isihlangu	isihlangu
stiebeuel	stirrup (n)	bogato bja sala	moraho	tlhatlosi	istibili	isitibili
stil	quiet (a)	-homotšego	-thotseng	-didimetseng	-cwaka	-thulile
stilmaak	silence (v)	-homotša	-kgutsisa	didimatsa	-thulisa	-thulisa
stilstaande	stationary (a)	-emego	-emeng	-emeng	-mileyo	-mi ndawonye
stilte	silence (n)	setu	kgutso	tidimalo	ucwaka	ukuthula
stimulus	stimulus (n)	sematlafatši	motsosa	setsibosi	isivuseleli	imbangela
stingel	stalk (n)	lenono	lehlaka	motang	umnyiki	ugaba
stink	stink (v)	-nkga	-nkga hampe	-nkga	-nuka	-nuka kabi
stippel	speck (n)	ntlhana	letheba	tlhaka	isibi	ibalana
stoel	chair (n)	setulo	setulo	setulo	isihlalo	isihlalo
stoetery	stud (n)	botswadišakgomo	mohlape	thuo	amahashe	isitadi
stof	substance (n)	selo	ntho	sere	into	isiqa
stof	dust (n)	lerole	lerole	lerole	uthuli	uthuli
stoflap	duster (n)	sephumudi sa lerole	lesela la ho hlakola lerole	sephimodi	ilaphu lokususa uthuli	isesulo
stok	stick (n)	patla	molamu	thobane	intonga	induku
stokperdjie	hobby (n)	boitiša	ho itlosa bodutu	tiro ya maitiso	ihobhil isidlalo	umsebenzana wokuzilibazisa
stol	congeal (v)	-kgahla	-hwama	-gatsela	-jiyisa	-shuba
stom	dumb (a)	-semumu	-semumu	-mumu	-sisimumu	-yisimungulu
stomp	stump (n)	kota	kutu	sesana	isiphunzi	isiphunzi
stomp	blunt (a)	-kubegilego	-nthithi	-boi	-buthuntu	-buthuntu
stoof	stove (n)	setofo	setofo	setofo	isitofu	isitofu
stoom	steam (n)	mušimeetse	phufodi	phufudi	umphunga	isitimu
stoot	push (v)	-kgorometša	-susumetsa	-kgarametsa	-tyhala	-sunduza
stop	stop (v)	-emiša	-ema	-ema	-ima	-vimba
stop	halt (v)	-emiša	-kgefutsa	-kgonya	-ma	-ma
stop	darn (v)	-thiba	-topa	-topa	-thunga	-dana
stopprop	stopper (n)	sethibo	poropo	sethibo	isivingco	isivimbo
stopsel	filling (n)	sešunetšwa	mokato	tlatso	umhlohlo	okugcwalisayo
storie	tale (n)	nonwane	pale	motlotlo	ibali	inganekwane
storm	storm (n)	ledimo	sefefo	kgwanyape	isiphango	isivunguvungu
stormwind	gale (n)	ledimo	sefefo	phefo ya ledimo	uqhwithela	isiphepho
stort	shower (v)	-šawara	-tola	-tlhapa	-shawarisha	-shawa
stortbad	shower (n)	šawara	shaware	šawara	ishawa	ishawa
stotter	stutter (v)	-kgamakgametša	-hwelea	-kwakwaetsa	-thintitha	-ngingiza
stout	naughty (a)	-selekago	-thibaneng ditsebe	-bosilo	-gezayo	-delela
straal	ray (n)	lehlasedi	lehlasedi	lerang	ilitha	umsebe
straal	gleam (v)	-kganya	-benya	-benya	-khazimla	-khazimula
straat	street (n)	mokgotha	seterata	mmila	isitalato	isitaladi
straf	punish (v)	-otla	-otla	-otlhaya	-ohlwaya	-jezisa
straf	punishment (n)	kotlo	kotlo	kotlhao	isohlwayo	isijeziso
straf	penalty (n)	kotlo	kotlo	kotlhao	isohlwayo	ihlawulo
straf	penalise (v)	-otla	-otla	-otlhaa	-ohlwaya	-hlawulisa
strand	beach (n)	khwiti ya lewatle	lewatleng	losi	unxweme	usebe lolwandle
strandmeer	lagoon (n)	letshanatswai	letsha la lewatle	letshanatswai	idike	ichweba
streef	aspire (v)	-ikemišeditše	-labalabela	-eletsa	-langazelela	-langazela
streek	region (n)	selete	setereke	kgaolo	inqila	isifunda
streep	stripe (n)	mothalo	moreto	mothalo	umgca	umushu
strewe	strive (v)	-katana	-labalabela	-leka	-zabalaza	-zama
strik	snare (n)	molaba	sefi	segole	isabatha	ugibe
strik	trap (n)	molaba	sefi	serai	isigu	isicupho
strik	bow (n)	lehuto		sethaiso	umphambili-nqanawa	inkintshela yokuhlobisa
strooi	scatter (v)	-phatlalatša	-qhala	-falatsa	-sasaza	-sakaza
strooi	straw (n)	ditlhoka	mmoko	letlhaka	udiza	utshani obomileyo

Afrikaans	English	N Sotho	Sesotho	Tswana	Xhosa	Zulu	S
strooimeisie	bridesmaid (n)	lekgetla	moetsana	moetsana	abakhaphi	impelesi	
strook	strip (n)	moseto	sekgetjhana	moreto	umcu	umdweshu	
stroom	stream (n)	moela	noka	moedi	umlambo	umfudlana	
stroom	current (n)	moela	phula	moela	umsinga	umsinga	
stroop	raid (v)	-thopa	-futuhela	-thopa	-hlasela	-hlasela	
strooptog	raid (n)	thopo	phutuhelo	thopo	uhlaselo	ukuhlasela	
struik	shrub (n)	sehlašana	sehlahla	setlhatsana	ityholo	isihlahlana	
struikel	stumble (v)	-thetšega	-kgetshemela	-kgokgoetsega	-khubeka	-khubeka	
struikel	trip (v)	-kgopša	-kgopa	-kgopa	-khubeka	-khubeka	
stry	argue (v)	-phega kgang	-nganga	ganetsana	-xoxa	-phikisana	
strydbyl	battle-axe (n)	tsaka	kwakwa	magagana	ucelemba	imbemba	
stryk	iron (v)	-aena	-sidila	-gatisa	-ayina	ayina	
studeer	study (v)	-ithuta	-ithuta	-ithuta	-funda	-funda	
student	student (n)	moithuti	moithuti	moithuti	umfundi	isitshudeni	
stuifmeel	pollen (n)	modula	modula	mmudula	ipoleni	impova	
stuipe	fits (n)	dikontwane	kgonyelo ya mesifa	tatanyane	isifo sokuxhuzula	isithuthwane	
stuitjiebeen	coccyx (n)	setonwana	mankatapa	mokutu	umsintsila	umsinsila	
stuk	piece (n)	seripa	sekotwana	semika	isijungqe	isiqhephu	
stukkend	broken (a)	-robegilego	-pshatlehile	-senyegileng	-aphukileyo	-file	
stuur	send (v)	-roma	-roma	-roma	-thuma	-thuma	
styf	stiff (a)	-gwagwaladitšwego	-tsitsipaneng	-tshume	qinileyo	-lukhuni	
styf	starch (v)	-tatšha	-teisela	-teisela	-qina	-tasha	
styf	tight (a)	-tiilego	-tiileng	-gagametseng	-qinile(yo)	-qinile	
styg	rise (v)	-rotoga	-phahama	-tlhatlosa	-nyusa	-khuphuka	
styg	ascend (v)	-namela	-nyoloha	-tlhatloga	-nyuka	-enyuka	
styging	rise (n)	thotogo	bophahamo	tlhatloso	unyuso	ukukhuphuka	
stysel	starch (n)	setatšhe	seteisele	seteisele	isitatshi	isitashi	
suid	south (a)	-borwa	-borwa	-borwa	-zantsi	-aseningizimu	
suide	south (n)	borwa	borwa	borwa	umzantsi	iningizimu	
suidelik	southern (a)	-borwa	-borwa	-borwa	-zantsi	-kwaseningizimu	
Suiderkruis	Southern Cross (n)	Sefapanaledi sa Borwa	Sefapano sa Borwa	Dithutlwa	uMnqamlezo wase-mZantsi	iSouthern Cross	
suig	suck (v)	-mona	-monya	-mona	-ncanca	-munya	
suigeling	infant (n)	lesea	lesea	ngwanyana	umntwana	ingane esancelayo	
suiker	sugar (n)	swikiri	tswekere	sukiri	iswekile	ushukela	
suikersiekte	diabetes (n)	twetšiswikiri	lefu la tswekere	bolwetse jwa sukiri	isifo seswekile	idayabhithizi	
suiwer	pure (a)	-hlwekilego	-hlwekileng	phepa	-cwengileyo	-msulwa	
suiwer	purify (v)	-hlwekiša	-hlwekisa	-phepafatsa	-cwenga	-hlanza	
suiwerheid	purity (n)	tlhwekišo	hlweko	boitsheko	ukucwenga	ukuhlanzeka	
sukses	success (n)	katlego	katleho	katlego	impumelelo	impumelelo	
sulke	such (a)	-bjalo	-jwalo	-sekete	njenga	-nje	
supermark	supermarket (n)	supamakete	supamakete	lebenkele	untozonke	isuphamakethe	
suster	sister (n)	kgaetšedi	kgaitsedi	kgaitsadi	udade	udade	
suur	sour (a)	-bodila	-bodila	-botlha	-muncu	-munya	
suur	acid (a)	-bodila	-bodila	-esete	-muncu	-muncu	
suur	acid (n)	esiti	esiti	esete	ubumuncu	i-asidi	
suur gesig	scowl (n)	mongongoregi	lonya	modilolo	ukujama	ukuhwaqabala	
suur kyk	scowl (v)	-gerula	-nyemotsa	-dilola	-jamela	-hwaqabala	
suurlemoen	lemon (n)	swiri	sirilamunu	ratsuru	ilamuni	ulamula	
suurstof	oxygen (n)	oksitšene	okosejene	okosijene	umongomoya	i-oksijini	
swaai	wag (v)	-hwidinya	-tsoka	-tsokotsa	-jiwula	-tshikizisa	
swaar	heavy (a)	-boima	-boima	-boima	-nzima	-sinda	
swaard	sword (n)	tšhoša	sabole	sabole	isabile	inkemba	
swaer	brother-in-law (n)	sebara	sware	molangwa	sibali	umlamu	
swak	weak (a)	-fokolago	-fokolang	-bokoa	-buthathaka	-ngenamandla	
swakheid	weakness (n)	bofokodi	bofokodi	bokoa	ubuthathaka	ukungaqini	
swam	fungus (n)	mouta	mokgwabo	mothuthuntshwane	ikhowa	isikhunta	
swanger	pregnant (a)	-imilego	-emere	-merwalo	-nzima	-khulelwe	
swart	black (a)	-so	-tsho	-ntsho	-mnyama	-mnyama	
swawel	sulphur (n)	sebabole	sebabole	sebabole	isalfure	isalufa	

S	Afrikaans	English	N Sotho	Sesotho	Tswana	Xhosa	Zulu
	sweep	whip (n)	sefepi	sephadi	seme	isabhokhwe	isiswebhu
	sweer	fester (v)	-tutela	-ikana	-tutela	-funga	-vunda
	sweet	sweat (v)	-fufulelwa	-fufulelwa	-fufula	-bila	-juluka
	sweet	sweat (n)	mphufutšo	mofufutso	mofufutso	umbilo	umjuluko
	sweetpak	tracksuit (n)	sutu ya boitšhidillo	terekesutu	terekesutu	itreksutu	itrekisudi
	swel	swell (v)	-roroga	-ruruha	-ruruga	-dumba	-vuvuka
	swelsel	swelling (n)	mororogo	ho ruruha	thurugo	ukudumba	ithubulela
	swem	swimming (n)	go rutha	ho sesa	go thuma	ukudada	ukubhukuda
	swem	swim (v)	-rutha	-sesa	-thuma	-dada	-bhukuda
	swembad	swimming pool (n)	boruthelo	letsha la ho sesa	bothumelo	ichibi lokuqubha	ichibi lokuhlamba
	swemmer	swimmer (n)	moruthi	sesesi	mothumi	indadi	inhlambi
	swerm	swarm (n)	motšhitši	mohlape	segopa	ibubu	ibololwane
	swerwend	migrant (a)	-kobakobanago	-molakolako	-hudugang	-fudukayo	-thuthela kwelinye izwe
	sy	his (pron)	-gagwe	-hae	ene	-khe	okwakhe
	sy	its (pron)	-yona	ya-	gagwe	-khe	-alo
	sy	she (pron)	yena	yena	ene	yena	yena
	sy	side (n)	lehlakore	lehlakore	boseja	icala	icala
	sy	silk (n)	sei	selika	sei	isilika	usilika
	sybokhaar	mohair (n)	boya bja lesaepoko	boya ba podi	boboa jwa podi	uboya beseyibhokhwe	uboya bembuzi yaseAngora
	syne	his (pron)	-gagwe	-hae	-gagwe	-khe	okwakhe
	sypaadjie	pavement (n)	tselathokwana	tselathoko	mokwakwa	indledlana yeenyawo	iphevumente
	sypel	ooze (v)	-tshotshoma	-dutla	-tsimoga	-thululeka	-bhicika
	taai	tough (a)	-tiilego	-thata	-ntha	-omelele(yo)	-lukhuni
	taak	task (n)	modiro	mosebetsi	tema	umsebenzi	umsebenzi
	taal	language (n)	polelo	puo	puo	ulwimi	ulimi
	taamlik	quite (a)	-tloga e le	-haholoholo	-ruri	noko	impela
	tabak	tobacco (n)	motšoko	kwae	motsoko	icuba	ugwayi
	tablet	tablet (n)	pilisi	pilisi	pilisi	itafilana	iphilisi
	tabuleer	tabulate (v)	-hlopha	-hlohlomisa	-rulaganya	-chaka	-loba ngezinhla
	tafel	table (n)	tafola	tafole	tafole	itafile	itafula
	tafeldoek	tablecloth (n)	tafoletuku	lesela la tafole	tafoletuku	ilaphu letafile	indwangu yetafula
	tagtig	eighty (n)	masomeseswai	mashome a robedi	somaarobedi	amashumi asibhozo	amashumi ayisishiyagalombili
	tak	branch (n)	lekala	lekala	kala	isebe	igatsha
	takhaar	lout (n)	tsweya	rametlae	lesutlha	ixuxu	impubumpubu
	takkie	twig (n)	lekalana	lekala	kala	isetyana	igatshana
	takrivier	tributary (n)	nokakeledi	lekala la noka	modutela	isebe	umngenela
	talent	talent (n)	talente	talente	neo	italente	ukuhlakanipha
	talentvol	talented (a)	-atetšwego ke ditalente	-nang le talente	-neo	-netalente	-hlakaniphile
	talryk	plentiful (a)	-atilego	-ngata	-tlalatlalang	-ninzi	-ningi
	tamaai	enormous (a)	-golo ka maatla	-tonanahadi	-tona	-khulu	-khulukazi
	tamatie	tomato (n)	tamati	tamati	tamati	itumata	utamatisi
	tamboeryn	tambourine (n)	moropana	moropana	moropana	igutyana elikhenkcezayo	ithamborini
	tampon	tampon (n)	sethibo	thempone	tampone	isivingco	ithemponi
	tand	tooth (n)	leino	leino	leino	izinyo	izinyo
	tandarts	dentist (n)	rameno	ngaka ya meno	rameno	ugqirha wamazinyo	inyanga yamazinyo
	tande	teeth (n)	meno	meno	meno	amazinyo	amazinyo
	tandepasta	toothpaste (n)	mogohlo wa meno	sesepa sa meno	sesepa sa meno	intlama yamazinyo	umuthi wamazinyo
	tandpyn	toothache (n)	go thunya ga leino	leino le opang	motlhagare	izinyo	ubuhlungu bezinyo
	tandvleis	gum (n)	marinini	lerenene	marinini	intsini	insini
	tante	aunt (n)	rakgadi	mmangwane	mme	anti	umamncane
	tarentaal	guineafowl (n)	kgaka	kgaka	kgaka	impangele	impangele
	tarief	tariff (n)	tefo	tefello	tuelo	uluhlu lwamaxabiso	ihlelo lemali
	taxi	taxi (n)	thekisi	tekesi	thekesi	iteksi	ithekisi
	teater	theatre (n)	teatere	thietha	teatere	iqonga	ithiyetha
	te bowe kom	overcome (v)	-fenya	-hlola	-fenya	-oyisa	-ahlula
	tee	tea (n)	teye	tee	tee	iti	itiye

Afrikaans	English	N Sotho	Sesotho	Tswana	Xhosa	Zulu	T
teef	bitch (n)	mpša ya tshadi	ntja	ntswagadi	injakazi	injakazi	
teel	breed (v)	-rua	-rua	-rua	-zalisa	-fuya	
teelbal	testicle (n)	lerete	lerete	thala	isende	isende	
teen	against (prep)		kgahlanong le-	kgatlhanong le-	-ngqiyama	-phambene na-	
teengif	antidote (n)	tšhitampholo	sebolayatjhefo	tshitabotlhole	isinqandi-sifo	isibiba	
teenliggaam	antibody (n)	twantšhi	sehananalemmele	twantshi	isikhuseli-buhlungu	isinqandakufa egazini	
teensinnig	reluctant (a)	-sa ratego	-monyebe	-itsemeletsang	-nqenayo	-ngathandi	
teenspoed	misfortune (n)	madimabe	bomadimabe	kgaba	ilishwa	ishwa	
teenstander	antagonist (n)	molwantšhi	motlatlapi	moidi	umchasi	imbangi	
teepot	teapot (n)	pitšana ya teye	pitsa ya tee	ketlele ya tee	imbiza yeti	ithiphothi	
teer	tar (n)	sekontiri	sekontiri	sekontere	itha	itiyela	
teer	tar (v)	-tšhela sekontini	-tshela sekontiri	-tshasa sekontere	-qaba itha	-faka itiyela	
teer	tender (a)	-nanana	-bonolo	-nana	-thambile (yo)	-thambile	
tegniek	technique (n)	thekeniki	botsebi	thekeniki	isixhobo	ithekiniki	
tegnies	technical (a)	-botsebi	-tegeniki	-thekeniki	-bugcisa	-nobuthekiniki	
tegnikon	technikon (n)	theknikone	tekenikone	thekenikono	iziko lobugcisa	ithekinikhoni	
tegnologie	technology (n)	theknolotši	tekenoloji	thekenoloji	ulwazi ngobugcisa	itheknoloji	
teken	sign (v)	-saena	-saena	-saena	-tyikitya	-sayina	
teken	sign (n)	tšhupo	letshwao	sekai	uphawu	isibonakaliso	
teken	draw (v)	-thala	-tshwantsha	-tshwantsha	-zoba	-dweba	
tekening	drawing (n)	seswantšho	setshwantsho	setshwantsho	umzobo	umfanekiso	
tekstielstof	fabric (n)	lešela	lesela	lesasupa	ilaphu	into ephothwe yabayingubo	
tel	count (v)	-bala	-bala	-bala	-bala	-bala	
telefoon	telephone (n)	thelefomo	thelefone	mogala	ifoni	ithelefoni	
telefoongids	telephone directory (n)	puku ya thelefomo	tataiso ya thelefone	buka ya dinomoro tsa mogala	isalathsi-foni	inkomba yet	
telefoonhokkie	telephone booth (n)	ntlwanathelefomo	ntlwana ya thelefone	ntlwana ya mogala	indlwana yefoni	ingosi yethelefoni	
telegram	telegram (n)	thelekramo	mohala	mogala	ucingo	ithelegrama	
teleskoop	telescope (n)	theleskopo	ferekekere	thelesekopo	umabonakude	ithelisikobho	
teleurstel	disappoint (v)	-nyamiša pelo	-swetsa	-swabisa	-danisa	-dumaza	
teleurstelling	disappointment (n)	monyamišo	tshwetso	maswabi	ukudanisa	indumalo	
televisie	television (n)	thelebišene	thelebeshene	thelefišene	ithelevizhini	ithelevishini	
telling	score (n)	palo	ntlha	sekoro	amanqaku	isikolo	
telraam	abacus (n)	mmadiphetana	mmadibolwana	kgatlhatalama	isibali	i-abakhusi	
tem	tame (v)	-tapiša	-thapisa	-katisa	-lulamisa	-thambisa	
tema	theme (n)	kgwekgwe	mokotaba	morero	umxholo	indikimba	
temperatuur	temperature (n)	themperetša	temperetjha	themperetša	ubushushu	ukushisa	
tender	tender (n)	tentere	tentere	bonana	umongameli	ithenda	
tenk	tank (n)	tanka	tanka	tanka	-itanki	ithangi	
tennis	tennis (n)	thenese	tenese	thenese	intenetya	ithenisi	
tent	tent (n)	tente	tente	tente	intente	ithende	
tepel	teat (n)	tlhoko	tlhoko	letsele	ingono	ibele	
tepel	nipple (n)	tlhoko	tlhoko	tlhoko	ingono	ingono	
teregstel	execute (v)	-bolaya	-fanyeha	-bolaya	-enza	-bulala ngomthetho	
terg	tease (v)	-hlohla	-hlohla	-rumola	-qhula	-gcona	
term	term (n)	lebaka	nako	lereo	iseshini	ibizo	
termyn	term (n)	lebaka	nako	kgweditharo	isigqibo	ithemu	
terras	terrace (n)	terase	mothati	sebopelo	ithala	itheresi	
terreur	terror (n)	tšhošetšo	tshoho	borukutlhi	uloyiko	ukwesabisa	
terrorisme	terrorism (n)	botšhošetši	boferekanyi	borukutlhi	ubunqolobi	impoqa	
tert	tart (n)	terete	terete	kuku	ikeyiki ethile	ikhekhe	
terug	back (adv)	morago	-morao	morago	-buya	emuva	
terugbetaal	refund (v)	-bušetša tšhelete	-buseletsa	-busetsa	-hlawula	-buyisela	
terugkeer	return (v)	-boa	-kgutla	-boela	-buya	-goduka	
terugspoeling	backwash (n)	kgogelomorago ya meetse	maqhububoelamorao	puseletso	umsinga	ibuya	
terugtog	retreat (n)	katogo	ho tjhetjha	go ikutla	inguqu	ukuhlehlela	
terugtrek	withdraw (v)	-katoga	-hula	-funyetsa	-rhoxa	-khipha	
terwyl	while (conj)	mola	ha	-ntse	ngelixa	ngenkathi	

T	Afrikaans	English	N Sotho	Sesotho	Tswana	Xhosa	Zulu
	tevrede	content (a)	-kgotsofetšego	-kgodisang	-tlhatswega ngati	-anelisekile	-enamile
	tevredenheid	contentment (n)	kgotsofalo	kgodiso	go tlhatswega ngati	ukwaneliseka	ukwenama
	tien	ten (n)	lesome	leshome	some	ishumi	ishumi
	tik	type (v)	-tlanya	-tlanya	-thaepa	-chwetheza	-thayipha ngomshini
	tik	tick (v)	-bethabetha	-tshwaya	-thobola	-krwela	-ncenceza
	tikmasjien	typewriter (n)	setlanyi	motjhene wa ho tlanya	setlanyi	umashini wokuchwetheza	umshini wokuthayipha
	tikster	typist (n)	motlanyi	motlanyi	motlanyi	umchwethezi	ithayiphisi
	timmerman	carpenter (n)	mmetli	mmetli	mmetli	umchweli	umbazi
	tingerig	slender (a)	-otilego	-tshesane	-motsotsoropa	-cuthene (yo)	-cuthene
	tipe	type (n)	mohuta	mofuta	mofuta	uhlobo	uhlobo
	titel	title (n)	thaetlele	sehlooho	setlhogo	isihloko	ibizo
	tjalie	shawl (n)	tšale	tjale	mogagolwane	ityali	itshali
	tjank	howl (v)	-golola	-ngaya	-kua	-khonkotha	-hhewula
	tjek	cheque (n)	tšheke	tjheke	tsheke	itsheke	isheki
	tjellis	cellist (n)	moletši wa tšhelo	motjhelo	moietsi wa tshelo	umdlalimrhubhe	umshayi-vayolina
	tjello	cello (n)	tšhelo	tjhelo	tshelo	umrhubhe	ishelo
	tjop	chop (n)	kgotswana	tjhopose	-kgotswana	itshopsi	ishobhisi
	toe	shut (a)	-tswaletšwego	-kwetsweng	-tswetswe	-valile(yo)	-valiweyo
	toe	then (adv)		jwale	ke fa	kwaza	ngesikhathi
	toebroodjie	sandwich (n)	sangwetši	semeje	borothopate	iqebengwana	isenwishi
	toedraai	wrap (v)	-phuthela	-phuthela	-phutela	-bhijela	-songa
	toegegroei	overgrown (a)	-medilego	-pupeditsweng	-sekgwa	-khule gqitha	-enile
	toegeneentheid	affection (n)	lerato	lerato	lorato	umsa	uthando
	toegeneë	affectionate (a)	-ratago	-ratahang	-rategang	-nomsa	-thandekayo
	toegewyd	keen (a)	-mafolofolo	-thahasellang	-tlhwatlhwa	-nomdla	-cijile
	toejuig	applaud (v)	-opela magoswi	-tlotlisa	-kuelela	-qhwabela	-halalisa
	toejuiging	acclaim (n)	magoswi	ditlatse	-nesa pula	ukubonga	ukuhlokoma
	toeken	confer (v)	-abela	-fana	-fa	-nika	-nika
	toekoms	future (n)	bokamoso	bokamoso	isago	ikamva	ikusasa
	toelaat	permit (v)	-dumelela	-dumella	-letla	-vumela	-vumela
	toelaat	admit (v)	-dumelela	-dumela	-dumelela	-yamkela	-mukela
	toelating	admission (n)	tumelelo	tumello	tumelelo	ulwamkelo	ukwamukelwa
	toemaak	shut (v)	-tswalela	-kwala	-tswala	-vala	-vala
	toepas	apply (v)	-diriša	-sebedisa	tiriso	-sebenzisa	-sebenzisa
	toeris	tourist (n)	moeti	moeti	mojanala	umkhenkethi	isihambi
	toeskouer	spectator (n)	mmogedi	mmohi	mmogedi	umbukeli	isibukeli
	toespreek	address (v)	-bolela le	-buisa	-buisa	-enza intetho	-khuluma
	toestaan	allow (v)	-dumelela	-dumella	-letla	-vumela	-vumela
	toestand	condition (n)	boemo	boemo	maemo	imeko	ubunjani
	toestelletjie	gadget (n)	tlabele	mokgabiso	sengwenyana	isixhobo	isikhaxelisi
	toestemming	permission (n)	tumelo	tumello	tetla	imvume	imvume
	toestop	plug (v)	-poropela	-kwala	-kaba	-vingca	-vimba
	toet	hoot (v)	-letša nakana ya mmotoro	-letsa phala	-letsa lenaka	-khalisa uphondo	-popoza
	toets	test (v)	-leka	-leka	-leka	-vavanya	-hlola
	toets	test (n)	teko	teko	teko	uvavanyo	inhlolo
	toevallig	accidental (a)	-sewelo	ka tshohanyetso	-go sa nagangweng	-ngobungozi	-ngenomkhuba
	toevallig	accidentally (adv)	ka sewelo	ka tshohanyetso	ka tshoganyo	-ngengozi	ngengozi
	toevoeging	addition (n)	koketšo	keketso	koketso	isongezelelo	ukuhlanganiswa
	toewy	devote (v)	-ikgafa	-ineela	-ineela	-nikela	-zinikela ku-
	toewys	allocate (v)	-abela	-aba	-aba	-abela	-abela
	toiingrig	tattered (a)	-kgeretlanego	-maharaswa	-lekgasa	-jacekileyo	-manikiniki
	toilet	toilet (n)	boithomelo	ntlwana	boithomelo	indlu yangasese	itholethe
	toilet	lavatory (n)	boithomelo	ntlwana	boithomelo	indlu yangasese	itholethe
	toiletpapier	toilet paper (n)	pampiri ya go itlhakola	pampiri ya ntlwana	pampiri ya boithomelo	iphepha lokusula	iphepha lasetholethe
	toiletware	toiletries (n)	ditlabakelo tša boitlhweki	tša ho itlhatswa	tsa go tlhapa	iimpahlana zokuzicoca	okok
	tolk	interpreter (n)	mofetoledi	toloko	mofetoledi	itoloki	umhumushi
	toneel	scene (n)	temana	sebaka	felo	umbono	indawo

Afrikaans	English	N Sotho	Sesotho	Tswana	Xhosa	Zulu	T
toneelstuk	play (n)	tiragatšo	tshwantshiso	motshameko	umdlalo	umdlalo	
tong	tongue (n)	leleme	leleme	leleme	ulwimi	ulimi	
tonnel	tunnel (n)	thanele	mohohoma	mogogoro	itonela	ithonela	
toom	bridle (n)	tomo	tomo	tomo	umkhala	itomu	
toon	toe (n)	monwana wa leoto	monwana wa leoto	monwana	uzwane	uzwani	
toonnael	toenail (n)	lenala la monwana wa leoto	lenala la monwana	lonala lwa leoto	uzipho	izipho lozwani	
toor	bewitch (v)	-loya	-loya	-loa	-thakatha	-thakathela	
toordokter	witchdoctor (n)	moloi	ramethokgo	ngaka	igqirha	umthakathi	
toorkuns	witchcraft (n)	boloi	boloi	boloi	ubugqwirha	ubuthakathi	
top	top (n)	godimo	hodimo	bogodimo	umphezulu	isihloko	
tot	until (conj)	go fihlela	ho fihlela	go fitlhelela	kude	kuze	
totaal	total (n)	palomoka	kakaretso	tsotlhe	iyonke	isamba	
tou	queue (n)	molokoloko	mola	mola	umtya	ihele	
tou	rope (n)	thapo	mohala	mogala	intambo	indophi	
tou	string (n)	thapo	kgole	thapo	umtya	intambo	
touspring	skip (v)	-sela kgati	-tlola	-tlola kgati	-tsiba	-ngqatha	
toustaan	queue (v)	-lokologana	-koloka	-tlhomagana	-ma umtya	-hlaba ihele	
towerkuns	magic (n)	boloi	boloi	boloi	ubugqi	umlingo	
traag	indolent (a)	-tšwafago	-botswa	-botshwakga	-nqenayo	-yivila	
tradisie	tradition (n)	tlwaelo	moetlo	tlhago	isithethe	isiko lezizukulwane	
tradisioneel	traditional (a)	-tlwaelo	-moetlo	-tlhago	ngokwesithethe	ngokwesiko	
tragedie	tragedy (n)	masetlapelo	masetlapelo	ditlhomolapelo	intlekele	umbangalusizi	
tragies	tragic (a)	-masetlapelo	-sehloho	-tlhomolang pelo	-nobuntlekele	-nosizi	
trane	tears (n)	megokgo	dikeledi	dikeledi	iinyembezi	izinyembezi	
trap	step (v)	-gatela pele	-hata	-gata	-nyathela	-hamba	
trap	tread (v)	-gata	-hata	-gata	-nyathela	-nyathela	
trapleer	stepladder (n)	lleri	lere	lere	ileri	isitebhisi	
trappe	stairs (n)	menamelo	diterapa	ditepese	izitepu	isitezi	
tree	step (n)	kgato	mohato	kgato	inyathela	isinyathelo	
tregter	funnel (n)	mojagobedi	fanele	setshedi	ifanela	isetho	
trein	train (n)	setimela	terene	setimela	uloliwe	isitimela	
trek	pull (v)	-goga	-hula	-goga	-tsala	-donsa	
trek	removal (n)	khudugo	ho falla	tshuto	imfuduko	ukuthutha	
trek	move (v)	-huduga	-tsamaya	-goga	-hamba	-emuka	
trekklavier	accordion (n)	pianotamolwa	koriana	akordiono	ikhodiyani	inkonsitini esalupiyani	
treurig	sad (a)	-maswabi	-hlomohileng	-hutsafetseng	-lusizi	-dabukile	
triomf	triumph (n)	phenyo	tlholo	phenyo	uloyiso	ukunqoba	
troeteldier	pet (n)	seruiwaseratwa	phoofolo e ratwang	seotlwana	isilo-qabane	ukuntoko	
trok	truck (n)	letorokisi	leteroko	koloi	itroko	itologo	
trom	drum (n)	moropa	moropa	moropa	igubu	isigubhu	
trompet	trumpet (n)	porompeta	terompeta	phala	ixilongo	icilongo	
trompetblaser	trumpeter (n)	moletšaporompeta	moletsaterompeta	moletsi wa phala	umdlali-xilongo	umfuthi wecilongo	
tromspeler	drummer (n)	moletšamoropa	moletsamoropa	motshamiki wa moropa	umbethi-gubu	umshayi wesigubhu	
tronk	jail (n)	kgolego	tjhankane	kgolegelo	itrongo	ijele	
troos	comfort (n)	khomotšo	kgothatso	kgomotso	intuthuzelo	induduzo	
troos	comfort (v)	-homotša	-kgothatsa	-gomotsa	-thuthuzela	-duduza	
trop	flock (n)	mohlape	mohlape	motlhape	umhlambi	umhlambi	
tros	bunch (n)	sehlopha	lesihla	seako	isihlahla	isihleke	
trots	pride (n)	boikgogomošo	boikgohomoso	boikgodiso	ikratshi	ukuzidla	
trots	proud (a)	-ikgogomošago	-ikgohomosang	-mabela	-zidla(yo)	-zidlayo	
trotseer	defy (v)	-hlohla	-hanyetsa	-nyatsa	-dela	-dlelezela	
trou	wed (v)	-nyala	-nyala	-nyala	-tshata	-shada	
trou	marry (v)	-nyala	-nyala	-nyala	-tshata	-shadisa	
trui	jersey (n)	jeresi	jeresi	jeresi	ijezi	ijezi	
tsetsevlieg	tsetse fly (n)	ntšhitsetse	seboba	tsetse	ingcongconi	itsetse	
tuberkulose	tuberculosis (n)	bolwetši bja mafahla	lefuba	lehuba	isifo sephepha	ufuba	
tuin	garden (n)	serapa	seratswana	tshingwana	isitiya	ingadi	
tuinslang	hose (n)	lethopo	housephaephe	lethompo	umbhobho	ithumbu	

T	Afrikaans	English	N Sotho	Sesotho	Tswana	Xhosa	Zulu
	tuiste	home (n)	legae	lapeng	legae	ikhaya	ikhaya
	turkoois	turquoise (n)	thekoise	thekoise	botala	ilitye lexabiso	itshe eliluhlaza
	turksvy	prickly pear (n)	foiye	torofeie	mokgopha	itolofiya	isihlehle
	tussen	amid (prep)	gare ga	-hara	gare	phakathi kwa-	phakathi kwa-
	tussen	between (prep)	gare ga	-hara	gare	-phakathi	ngaphakathi
	twaalf	twelve (n)	lesomepedi	leshome le metso e mmedi	some pedi	ishumi elinesibini	ishumi nambili
	twee	two (n)	pedi	pedi	bobedi	isibini	isibili
	tweede	second (a)	-bobedi	-bobedi	-bobedi	-bini	-esibili
	tweeling	twin (n)	mafahla	mafahla	lefatlha	iwele	iwele
	twee maal	twice (n)	gabedi	habedi	ga bedi	isibini	kabili
	twee weke	fortnight (n)	bekepedi	beke tse pedi	bekepedi	iiveki ezimbini	amasonto amabili
	twintig	twenty (n)	masomepedi	mashome a mabedi	somaamabedi	amashumi amabini	amashumi amabili
	twis	quarrel (n)	phapano	qabang	kgotlhang	ingxabano	ukuxabana
	twis	quarrel (v)	-fapana	-qabana	-omana	-xabana	-xabana
	twispunt	controversy (n)	phapano	tsekiso	kgang e e gotlhang	impikiswano	ukuphikisana
	twyfel	doubt (n)	-pelaelo	pelaelo	pelaelo	intandabuzo	ukusola
	twyfel	doubt (v)	-belaela	-belaela	-belaela	-thandabuza	-sola
	tyd	time (n)	nako	nako	nako	ixesha	isikhathi
	ui	onion (n)	eie	eie	eie	itswele	u-anyanisi
	uier	udder (n)	mokaka	letswele	thele	ibele	umbele
	uil	owl (n)	leribiši	sephooko	morubisi	isikhova	isikhova
	uit	out (prep)		ka ntle	ntle	phandle	phandle
	uitasem	breathless (a)	-fegelwago	-fehelwa	-kabalanang	-ngaphefumliyo	-khefuzelayo
	uitasem	exhale (v)	-huetša	-phefumoloha	-hemela ntle	-phefumla	-khipha umoya
	uitbars	erupt (v)	-thunya	-qhashoha	-ropologa	-gqabhuka	-qhuma
	uitblink	excel (v)	-phala	-kganya	-phala	-gqwesa	-ahlula
	uitbrand	fuse (v)	-swa	-thunya	-swa	-tshisa	-fiyuza
	uitbrei	expand (v)	-godiša	-atolosa	-ngangabolola	-andisa	-khulisa
	uitbreking	outbreak (n)	go wa (ga bolwetši)	qhomo	tshimologo	uqhambuko	ukuqhamuka
	uitbroei	spawn (v)	-beela mae	-qhotsa	-thuba	-zala	-zalela
	uitbult	bulge (v)	-kokomoga	-kokomoha	-kokorala	-khukhumala	-dumba
	uitdaag	challenge (v)	-hlohla	-phepetsa	-kgwetlha	-cela umngeni	-cela inselele
	uitdaag	dare (v)	-hlohla	-beta pelo	-tlhotlheletsa	-ba ligagu	-lokotha
	uitdaging	challenge (n)	tlhohlo	phepetso	kgwetlho	umngeni	inselele
	uitdaging	dare (n)	tlhohlo	sebete	tlhotlheletso	ubugagu	umlokothi
	uitdruk	express (v)	-hlagiša	-hlahisa	-thadisa	-thumela ngendlela ekhawulezayo	-sho
	uitdruklik	express (a)	-gateletšwego	-totobetseng	-thadisang	-khawulezayo	-khangayo
	uiterste	ultimate (a)	-fetišago	-qetellong	-bofelong	-okugqibela	-kokugcina
	uitgaan	exit (v)	-tšwa	-tswa	-tswa	-phuma	-phuma
	uitgang	exit (n)	botšo	kgoro	botso	isango lokuphuma	ukuphuma
	uitgee	publish (v)	-phatlalatša	-phatlalatsa	-phasalala	-papasha	-shicilela
	uitgeteer	emaciated (a)	-otilego	-otileng	-mokodue	-nqinileyo	-nciphile
	uitkies	pick (v)	-kgetha	-thonya	-tlhopa	-khetha	-khetha
	uitklop	thrash (v)	-fenya	-pola	-setla	-bhula	-dinda
	uitkoms	outcome (n)	pheletšo	pheletso	botsho	isiphumo	umphumela
	uitlok	taunt (v)	-rumula	-soma	okisa	-cunukisa	-chukuluza
	uitloop	sprout (v)	-hloga	-hloma	-tlhoga	-ntshula	-hluma
	uitmuntend	excellent (a)	-phalago	-kganyang	-maatlametlo	-balaseleyo	-hle kakhulu
	uitnodiging	invitation (n)	taletšo	memo	taletso	isimemo	isimemo
	uitnooi	invite (v)	-laletša	-mema	-laletsa	-mema	-mema
	uitreik	issue (v)	-hlagiša	-phatlalatsa	-tlhomaganya	-khupha	-phumisa
	uitroei	exterminate (v)	-fediša	-ripitla	-nyeletsa	-tshabalalisa	-shabalalisa
	uitroep	exclaim (v)	-goa	-hoa	-tsibisa	-khwaza	-memeza
	uitsaai	broadcast (v)	-gaša	-hasa	-gasa	-sasaza	-sakaza
	uitsig	view (n)	pono	tjhadimo	pono	umbono	umbukiso
	uitsit	evict (v)	-leleka	-falatsa	-ntsha	-khuphe endlwini	-xosha
	uitskel	scold (v)	-roga	-kgalemela	-omanya	-ngxolisa	-thethisa

Afrikaans	English	N Sotho	Sesotho	Tswana	Xhosa	Zulu	V
uitskiet	eject (v)	-ragela ntle	-ntsha	-thunsetsa ntle	-khupha	-potshoza	
uitslag	result (n)	sephetho	ditholwana	dipholo	ingxelo	umphumela	
uitsluit	bar (v)	-thibela	-kotela	-tlogela kwa ntle	-nqanda	-vimbela	
uitsluit	exclude (v)	-tlogela	-qhela	-tlogela	-nxwema	-valela ngaphandle	
uitspoel	rinse (v)	-tšokotša	-tsokotsa	-tsokotsa	-pula	-yakaza	
uitspraak	pronunciation (n)	kwagatšo	qapodiso	kapodiso	ubizo	ukuphumisela	
uitspraak	verdict (n)	kahlolo	kahlolo	katlholo	isigwebo	isinqumo	
uitspreek	pronounce (v)	-kwagatša	-utlwahatsa	-kapodisa	-biza	-phumisela	
uitstal	exhibit (v)	-bontšha	-bontsha	-bontsha	-bonisa	-bukisa	
uitstalling	exhibition (n)	pontšho	pontsho	pontsho	umboniso	umbukiso	
uitstel	postpone (v)	-thiša	-suthisetsa morao	-beisa pelo	-hlehlisa	-hlehlisa	
uitstrek	extend (v)	-otlolla	-otlolla	-golola	-andisa	-dephisa	
uittrek	undress (v)	-apola	-hlobola	-apola	-khulula	-khumula	
uittrek	vacate (v)	-tloga	-ikgula	-ntsha	-enza ingabi nanto	-thutha	
uitvee	erase (v)	-phumola	-hlakola	-phimola	-cima	-sula	
uitveër	eraser (n)	sephumodi	sehlakodi	sephimodi	isicimi	isesulo	
uitverkoping	sale (n)	thekišo	thekiso	thekiso	iseyile	indali	
uitvind	invent (v)	-hlama	-qapa	-ribolola	-bhaqa	-qamba	
uitvinding	invention (n)	tlhamo	qapo	tlhamo	ukufunyanwa	ukuqanjwa	
uitvoer	perform (v)	-phetha	-etsa	-dira	-enza	-enza	
uitvoer	export (v)	-iša ntle	-kgwebela	-isa ntle	uthumelo kwelinye ilizwe	ukuthekelisa	
uitvoer	export (n)	kišontle	seyantle	seyantle	umthumeli	-thekelisa	
uitvoerder	performer (n)	mophethi	moetsi	modiri	umenzi	umenzi	
uitvoering	performance (n)	mophetho	ketso	diaba	ukwenza	ukwenza	
uitwerking	effect (n)	sephetho	tholwana	sephetho	isiphumo	umphumela	
uitwerpsel	excreta (n)	mantle	mantle	lesepa	izibi zomzimba	amasimba	
uitwerpsel	faeces (n)	mantle	mantle	mantle	ithafa	amasimba	
ulkus	ulcer (n)	sešo	seso	tlhagala	isilonda	isilonda	
unie	union (n)	kopano	kopano	kopano	ubunye	inyunyana	
uniform	uniform (n)	yunifomo	yunifomo	semphato	ukufana	inyufomu	
universiteit	university (n)	yunibesiti	yunibesithi	yunibeseti	iyunivesithi	iyunivesiti	
urine	urine (n)	moroto	moroto	moroto	umchamo	umchamo	
urineer	urinate (v)	-rota	-rota	-rota	-chama	-chama	
uur	hour (n)	iri	hora	ura	iyure	i-awa	
vaag	vague (a)	-go se kwišišege	-sa utlwahaleng	-mathaithai	-ngacacanga	-ngezwakali kahle	
vaak	sleepy (a)	-swerwego ke boroko	-otselang	-otselang	-ozelayo	-nobuthongo	
vaas	vase (n)	sebjanatsopa	bolompoto	morufadišeše	ivazi	ivazi	
vader	father (n)	tata	ntate	rra	utata	ubaba	
vakansie	holiday (n)	maikhutšo	phomolo	boikhutso	ikhefu	iholide	
vakant	vacant (a)	-bulegilego	-sekgeo	-phatlhatiro	-ngenanto	-ngenalutho	
vakature	vacancy (n)	sebaka	sekgeo	phatlhatiro	isithuba	isikhala	
vakbond	trade union (n)	mokgatlo wa bašomi	kopano ya basebetsi	teradeyuniene	umanyano lwabase-benzi	inyonyana yezisebenzi	
val	fall (v)	-wa	-wa	-wa	-wa	-wa	
valk	hawk (n)	sepekwa	phakwe	nkgodi	ukhetshe	uhele	
vallei	valley (n)	moedi	phula	mogorogoro	intlambo	isigodi	
vallende siekte	epilepsy (n)	dihwahwa	sethwathwa	leebana	isifo sokuwa	isithuthwane	
vals	fake (a)	-bofora	-lefeela	-phora	-buxoki	-yinkohliso	
vals	false (a)	-bofora	-leshano	sa ikanyegang	-buxoki	-khohlisayo	
vals tande	dentures (n)	meno a sekgowa	meno a maiketsetso	meno a maitirelo	izinxonxo	isethi lamazinyo afakwayo	
van	surname (n)	sefane	fane	sefane	ifani	isibongo	
van	from (prep)	go tšwa go	ho-	go-	ku-ya	kusuka ku-	
van	of (prep)	ya-	ya-	wa, a, tsa,...	ya-	-a-	
vandag	today (n)	lehono	kajeno	gompieno	namhlanje	namuhla	
vang	capture (v)	-swara	-hapa	-thopa	-thimba	-bamba	
vang	catch (v)	-swara	-tshwara	-tshwara	-bamba	-bamba	
van plan wees	intend (v)	-ikemišetša	-rera	-ikaelela	-funa	-hlosa	

V	Afrikaans	English	N Sotho	Sesotho	Tswana	Xhosa	Zulu
	vanselfsprekend	obvious (a)	-molaleng	-totobetse	mo pepeneneng	-cacile(yo)	-bonakele
	varieer	vary (v)	-fapanya	-fapanya	-fetola	-ahluka	-hlukana
	varing	fern (n)	mmalewaneng	palesa	phatadikgagane	umfisi	isikhomane
	vark	pig (n)	kolobe	kolobe	kolobe	ihagu	ingulube
	varkoor	arum lily (n)	mogaladitwe	tsebe-ya-kolobe		inyibiba	intebe
	varkvet	lard (n)	makhura a kolobe	mafura a kolobe	mafura a kolobe	amafutha ehagu	amafutha engulube
	varkvleis	pork (n)	nama ya kolobe	nama ya kolobe	nama ya kolobe	inyama yehagu	inyama yengulube
	vars	fresh (a)	-fsa	-tjha	-swa	-tsha	-sha
	vas	solid (a)	-thata	-thata	-kgotlhaganeng	qinile(yo)	-qinile
	vasberadenheid	determination (n)	phegelelo	morero o tiileng	maikaelelo	ukuzimisela	ukuzimisela
	vasketting	chain (v)	-bofa	-tlama	-bofelela ka keetane	-bopha ngetyathanga	-bopha
	vasklem	clasp (v)	-patana	-tseparela	-kopela	-bamba nkqi	-xhakathisa
	vasmaak	fasten (v)	-tlema	-tiisa	-bofa	-bopha	-bopha
	vaspen	peg (v)	-kokotela	-thakgisa	-tlapisa	-bethelela	-bethela
	vasplak	stick (v)	-gomaretša	-kgomaretsa	-ngaparetsa	-ncamathela	-namathela
	vassit	mount (v)	-momaganya	-kgomaretsa	-tshwarwa	-qinisa	-misa
	vasspeld	pin (v)	-bofa ka sepalete	-ngomela ka sepelete	-kgokela	-qhobosha	-bopha ngesipeleti
	vasstel	ascertain (v)	-kgonthiša	-nnetefatsa	-lebelela	qinisekisa	-azisisa
	vasteland	continent (n)	kontinente	kontinente	kontinente	ilizwe	izwekazi
	vat	hold (n)	moswaro	tshwaro	seduti	ukubamba	ukubamba
	vat	barrel (n)	faki	faki	faki	ifatyi	umphongolo
	vee	sweep (v)	-swiela	-fiela	-feela	-tshayela	-shanela
	vee	cattle (n)	diruiwa	dikgomo	dikgomo	iinkomo	izinkomo
	veekampie	paddock (n)	kampana	lekgulo	kampa	idlelo	inkambu
	veel	much (a)	-ntši	-ngata	-ntsi	-kanga	-ningi
	veelrassig	multiracial (a)	-boditšhaba	-matjhaba	-ditšhabatšhaba	umxube weentlanga	-zinhlangangezinhlanga
	veer	feather (n)	lefofa	lesiba	lefofa	usiba	uphaphe
	veertien	fourteen (n)	lesomenne	leshome le metso e mene	some nne	ishumi elinesine	ishumi nane
	veertig	forty (n)	masomenne	mashome a mane	somaamane	amashumi amane	amashumi amane
	veg	fight (v)	-lwa	-lwana	-lwa	-yilwa	-lwa
	veg	battle (v)	-lwa	-lwana	-lwa	-lwa	-lwa
	veilig	secure (a)	-lotegilego	-bolokehileng	-babalelang	-khuselekileyo	-londekile
	veilig	safe (a)	-lotegilego	-bolokehileng	-bolokegileng	-ngenangozi	-londekile
	veiligheid	safety (n)	boiphemelo	polokeho	polokesego	ukhuseleko	ukulondeka
	veiling	auction (n)	fantisi	fantisi	fantisi	intengiso	indali
	vel	skin (n)	letlalo	letlalo	letlalo	ufele	isikhumba
	veld	veld (n)	naga	naha	naga	ilindle	indle
	veld	field (n)	naga	tshimo	tshimo	ibala	indawo yasendle
	veluitslag	rash (n)	mogorogo	kgophole	bogwata	irhashalala	umqubuko
	vennoot	partner (n)	modirišani	mohwebisani	mogwebisani	iqabane	umata
	venster	window (n)	lefastere	fensetere	fensetere	ifestile	ifasitela
	venyn	venom (n)	bohloko	tjhefo	botlhole	intiyo	isihlungu
	ver	far (adv)	kgole	-hole	kgakala	-kude	kude
	verafsku	loathe (v)	-hloya	-hloya	-nyatsa	-caphukela	-enyanya
	verafsku	detest (v)	-hlaswa	-hloya	-tlhoa	-caphukela	-enyanya
	verag	scorn (v)	-nyatša	-nyedisa	-sotla	-gxeka	-eyisa
	veragting	scorn (n)	lenyatšo	nyediso	losotlo	ugxeko	ukweyisa
	veragting	contempt (n)	lenyatšo	nyedisa	lenyatso	indelo	indelelo
	verander	change (v)	-fetoga	-fetola	-fetoga	-tshintsha	-shintsha
	verandering	change (n)	phetogo	phetoho	phetogo	utshintsho	inguquko
	verarm	impoverish (v)	-diitša	-fumanehisa	-didisa	-hlwempuza	-phofisa
	verbaas	amaze (v)	-makatša	-makatsa	-makatsa	-mangalisa	-mangalisa
	verban	exile (v)	-leleka	-leleka	-tshedisa melolwane	-gxotha	-dingisa
	verband	bandage (n)	pantetši	banteje	sefapo	ibhandeji	umdweshu
	verbanning	exile (n)	teleko	teleko	tshedisomelolwane	ugxotho	ukudingiswa
	verbasend	amazing (a)	-makatšago	-makatsang	-makatsang	-mangalisayo	-mangalisayo
	verbasing	amazement (n)	makalo	makatso	makatso	ummangaliso	ukumangala
	verbeel	imagine (v)	-nagana	-akanya	-tshwantsha	-thelekelela	-cabanga
	verberg	conceal (v)	-fihla	-kwahela	-bitala	-gusha	-fihla

Afrikaans	English	N Sotho	Sesotho	Tswana	Xhosa	Zulu	V
verbeter	improve (v)	-kaonafatša	-lokisa	-tlhabolola	-phucula	-enza kubengcono	
verbetering	improvement (n)	kaonafatšo	tokiso	tlhabologo	impucuko	ubungcono	
verbied	prohibit (v)	-ganetša	-thibela	-itsa	-alela	-nqabela	
verbied	forbid (v)	-iletša	-hanela	-itsa	-alela	-nqabela	
verbied	ban (things) (v)	-ganetša	-thibela	-iletsa	-alela	-ngavunyelwa	
verbind	connect (v)	-kopanya	-hokahanya	-lomagana	-dibanisa	-hlanganisa	
verbinding	connection (n)	kopanyo	kamano	kgolagano	uqhagamshelo	ukuhlangana	
verbleik	fade (v)	-galoga	-thunya	-tswapoga	-sithela	-fiphala	
verblyfplek	residence (n)	modulo	bodulo	bonno	indawo	umuzi	
verbode	banned (things) (a)	-ganetšwago	-thibetse	-iletsweng	-alelwayo	ezingavunyelwa	
verbruik	consumption (n)	tirišo	tshebediso	dijego	into esetyenzisiweyo	ukudliwa	
verbygaan	pass (v)	-feta	-feta	-feta	-dlula	-dlula	
verbysteek	overtake (v)	-feta	-feta	-feta	-dlula	-edlula	
verbyster	baffle (v)	-tlaba	-hlolla	-tsietsa	-dida	-ahlula	
verdaag	adjourn (v)	-phatlalala	-qhalana	-phatlhalala	-misela ixesha elizayo	-hlehlisa	
verdagte	suspect (n)	mogopolelwa	mmelaelwa	mmelaelwa	umrhanelwa	osolwayo	
verdamp	evaporate (v)	-moyafala	-moyafala	-mowafala	-ba ngumphunga	-hwamuka	
verdedig	defend (v)	-phemela	-sireletsa	-femela	-khusela	-vikela	
verdedigend	defensive (a)	-phemelago	-sireletsang	-femelang	-khuselayo	-vikelayo	
verdediging	defence (n)	phemelo	tshireletso	phemelo	ukhuselo	ukuvikelwa	
verder	further (a)	-ngwe	-pele	-pele	-phambili	phambili	
verdien	earn (v)	-gola	-sebeletsa moputso	-amogela	-zuza	-zuza	
verdien	deserve (v)	-swanelwa	-tshwanelwa	-tshwanelwa	-fanela	-fanela	
verdieping	floor (n)	lebato	mokato	bodilo	umgangatho	isitezi	
verdink	suspect (v)	-gopolela	-belaela	-belaela	-rhanela	-sola	
verdrag	pact (n)	kgwerano	tumellano	tumalano	umnqophiso	isivumelwano	
verdrink	drown (v)	-kgangwa ke meetse	-kgangwa ke metsi	-beta	-rhaxwa	-minza	
verduidelik	explain (v)	-hlaloša	-hlalosa	-tlhalosa	cacisa	-chaza	
verduideliking	explanation (n)	tlhalošo	hlaloso	tlhaloso	ingcaciso	incasiselo	
verduistering	eclipse (n)	phifalo	phifalo	phifalo	umnyama	ukusithibala	
verdun	dilute (v)	-hlaphola	-hlapholla	-rarolosa	-xuba	-hlambulula	
verdwaal	lost (a)	-timetšego	-lahlehileng	-timelang	-lahleka (yo)	-lahlekelwe	
verdwyn	disappear (v)	-nyamalela	-nyamela	-nyelela	-sithela	-nyamalala	
verdwyning	disappearance (n)	nyamalelo	nyamelo	nyelelo	ukusithela	ukunyamalala	
verekombers	quilt (n)	kobo ya mafofa	kobo ya masiba	kobo ya diphofa	ikwiliti	ikhwilithi	
verenig	unite (v)	-kopanya	-kopanya	-kopana	umanyano	-hlanganisa	
vereniging	society (n)	kopano	mokgatlo	mokgatlho	umbutho	inhlangano	
verf	paint (n)	pente	pente	pente	ipeyinti	upende	
verf	paint (v)	-penta	-penta	-penta	-qaba	-penda	
verflenterd	ragged (a)	-mankgeretla	-dikatana	-makgasa	-dlakadlaka	-manikiniki	
verfyndheid	refinement (n)	tshekišo	botho bo felletseng	bophepafatso	ukucokisa	ukuphucuka	
vergader	congregate (v)	-kgobokana	-phutheha	-phuthega	-hlangana	-buthana	
vergadering	meeting (n)	kopano	kopano	kopano	intlanganiso	umhlangano	
vergadering	assembly (n)	kgobokano	kopano	phuthego	intlanganiso	ibandla	
vergeet	forget (v)	-lebala	-lebala	-lebala	-libala	-khohlwa	
vergeld	retaliate (v)	-lefeletša	-itwanela	-iposolosetsa	-phindisa	-phindisa	
vergelyk	compare (v)	-bapiša	-bapisa	-bapisa	-thelekisa	-qhathanisa	
vergelyking	comparison (n)	papišo	papiso	papiso	uthelekiso	ukuqhathanisa	
vergesel	escort (v)	-felegetša	-felehetsa	-buledisa	-khapha	-phelezela	
vergewe	forgive (v)	-lebalela	-tshwarela	-itshwarela	-xolela	-xolela	
vergewe	pardon (v)	-lebalela	-tshwarela	-itshwarela	-xolela	-xolela	
vergifnis	forgiveness (n)	tebalelo	tshwarelo	boitshwarelo	uxolo	uxolo	
vergiftig	poison (v)	-ješa mpholo	-fa tjhefo	-bolaya	-tyhefa	-faka isihlungu	
vergroot	magnify (v)	-godiša	-hodisa	-godisa	-andisa	-khulisa	
vergroot	enlarge (v)	-godiša	-hodisa	-katolosa	-andisa	-andisa	
verhaal	story (n)	kanegelo	pale	kgang	ibali	indaba	
verhaar	moult (v)	-sola	-sola	-tlhobega	-obuza	-hluba	
verhemelte	palate (n)	magalapa	lehalapa	magalapa	inkalakahla	ulwanga	
verhoging	increment (n)	kokeletšo	kekeletso	koketso	uchatha	ukuqhutshwa kweholo	
verhoging	increase (n)	koketšo	keketso	koketso	isongezelelo	ukukhula	

V	Afrikaans	English	N Sotho	Sesotho	Tswana	Xhosa	Zulu
	verhoor	trial (n)	tsheko	teko	tshekiso	ityala	ukuthethwa kwecala
	verhouding	relation (n)	kamano	setswalle	kutlwano	unxulumano	ukuphathana
	verhouding	relationship (n)	kamano	setswalle	tsalano	unxulumano	ukuhambelana
	verhuurder	landlord (n)	mohiriši	mohirisi	mong	umnini-ndlu	umqashisi
	verjaarsdag	birthday (n)	letšatši la matswalo	letsatsi la tswalo	botsalo	umhla wokuzalwa	usuku lokuzalwa
	verkeer	traffic (n)	therafiki	sephethephethe	pharakano	izithuthi	itrefiki
	verkeerd	wrong (a)	-phošo	-phoso	-phoso	-ngalunganga	-ngalungile
	verken	explore (v)	-hlohlomiša	-utulla	-utulola	-hlola	-hlola
	verkenner	scout (n)	hlodi	sehlwela	lesupatsela	intlola	inhloli
	verkies	prefer (v)	-rata	-kgetha	-rata	-khetha	-enyula
	verkies	elect (v)	-kgetha	-kgetha	-tlhopha	-nyula	-khethiwe
	verkiesing	election (n)	kgetho	kgetho	tlhopho	unyulo	ukhetho
	verklaar	declare (v)	-bega	-bolela	-bolotsa	-bhengeza	-bika
	verklaring	statement (n)	pego	tokodiso	polelo	ingxelo	isitetimente
	verkleineer	belittle (v)	-nyatša	-nyenyefatsa	-nyatsa	-delela	-dika
	verkleurmannetjie	chameleon (n)	leobu	lenwabo	lelobu	ilovane	unwabu
	verklikker	informer (n)	molomatsebe	lehlabaphio	molomatsebe	umazisi	umcebi
	verkoeler	radiator (n)	radietere	radietare	setsidifatsi	iradiyeyitha	iradiyetha
	verkoop	sell (v)	-rekiša	-rekisa	-rekisa	-thengisa	-thengisa
	verkort	shorten (v)	-khutsofatša	-kgutsufatsa	khutshwafatsa	-enza mfutshane	-fushanisa
	verkrag	rape (v)	-kata	-beta	-betelela	-dlwengula	-dlwengula
	verkragting	rape (n)	kato	peto	petelelo	udlwengulo	ukudlwengula
	verkrummel	crumble (v)	-ratha	-kuma	-fofora	-cukuceza	-bhuduza
	verkyker	binoculars (n)	ferekekere	ferekekere	ferekekere	umabonakude	izingilazi zokubuka kude
	verlaat	abandon (v)	-tlogela	-nyahlatsa	-tlogela	-ncama	-yeka
	verlam	paralyse (v)	-rephiša	-holofatsa	-bolaya mfama	-bulala imithambo	-thwebula
	verlamming	paralysis (n)	morepho	kgolofalo	go swa mfama	ukungasebenzi kwelungu lomzimba	umthwebulo
	verlang	long (v)	-hlologela	-hlora	-tlhoafala	-khumbula	-langazela
	verlede	past (n)	lefetile	nako e fetileng	segologolo	ixesha eladlulayo	isikhathi esidlulileyo
	verleë maak	embarrass (v)	-leša dihlong	-tsietsa	-akabatsa	-enza iintloni	-finyanisa
	verleiding	temptation (n)	moleko	moleko	thaelo	ulingo	isiyengo
	verleng	prolong (v)	-lelefatša	-lelefatsa	-golola	-olula	-dephisa
	verleng	elongate (v)	-lelefatša	-lelefatsa	-lelefatsa	-olula	-elula
	verlep	wither (v)	-pona	-pona	-swaba	-bunisa	-oma
	verlies	loss (n)	tahlegelo	tahlehelo	tatlhegelo	ilahleko	ukulahlekelwa
	verlig	relieve (v)	-imolla	-thusa	-wela makgwafo	-qabula	-siza
	verlig	illuminate (v)	-bonegela	-kgantsha	-sedifatsa	-cacisa	-khanyisa
	verligting	relief (n)	kimollo	thuso	go ikutlwa o le motho	isiqabu	usizo
	verlof	leave (n)	khunollo	lefi	khunologo	ikhefu	ilivi
	verloor	lose (v)	-timetša	-lahleha	-latlha	-lahlekelwa	-lahlekelwa
	verlore	lost (a)	-timeditšwego	-lahlehileng	-timetseng	lahlekile (yo)	-lahlekelwe
	verlossing	salvation (n)	phološo	pholoho	pholoso	usindiso	usindiso
	vermaak	amuse (v)	-thabiša	-qabola	tlhaletsa	-yolisa	-thokozisa
	vermaaklik	amusing (a)	-thabišago	-qabolang	-tlhaletsang	-yolisayo	-thokozisayo
	vermaaklikheid	amusement (n)	maipshino	boithabiso	tlhaletso	isiyolisi	ukuthokozisa
	vermaan	admonish (v)	-kgala	-kgalema	-kgala	-lumkisa	-khuza
	vermeerder	increase (v)	-oketša	-eketsa	-oketsa	-ongeza	-khula
	vermeld	state (v)	-bega	-hlahisa	-bolela	-xela	-sho
	vermenigvuldig	multiply (v)	-atiša	-atisa	-ata	-phinda-phinda	-phinda
	verminder	reduce (v)	-fokotša	-fokotsa	-ngotla	-nciphisa	-nciphisa
	verminder	lessen (v)	-fokotša	-nyenyefatsa	-fokotsa	-nciphisa	-nciphisa
	verminder	decrease (v)	-fokotša	-fokotsa	-fokotsa	-nciphisa	-ncipha
	vermink	maim (v)	-golofatša	-holofatsa	-golafatsa	-limaza	-limaza
	vermoeid	weary (a)	-lapilego	-kgathetseng	-lapileng	-dinwe(yo)	-khathele
	vermoeienis	fatigue (n)	tapo	mokgathala	tapisego	udino	ukukhathala
	vermoor	murder (v)	-bolaya	-bolaya	-bolaya	-bulala	-bulala
	vermors	waste (v)	-senya	-senya	-senya	-chitha	-lahla
	vermy	shun (v)	-ila	-phema	-sisimoga	-dedela	-balekela

Afrikaans	English	N Sotho	Sesotho	Tswana	Xhosa	Zulu
vermy	avoid (v)	-ila	-phema	-dikologa	-khwebula	-gwema
vernaamste	main (a)	-golo	-holo	-golo	-eyona	-khulu
verneder	humiliate (v)	-kokobetša	-nyenyefatsa	-nyenyefatsa	phoxa	-dumaza
vernietig	destroy (v)	-fediša	-ripitla	-senya	-tshabalalisa	-bhuqa
veronderstel	presume (v)	-hloma	-lekanya	-tseela gore	-zindla	-xhomondela
veronderstel	suppose (v)	-hloma	-lekanya	-itlhoma	-cinga	-cabanga
verontagsaam	disregard (v)	-hlokomologa	-hlokomoloha	-tlhokomologa	-sukuhoya	-delela
verontrus	perturb (v)	-tšhoša	-kgathatsa	-ferekana	-khathaza	-ethusa
verontskuldig	excuse (v)	-lebalela	-tshwarela	-itoka	-xolela	-xolela
veroordeel	condemn (v)	-ahlola	-ahlola	-atlhola	-gweba	-sola
veroorsaak	cause (v)	-baka	-baka	-baka	-enza	-enza
verordening	decree (n)	molao	taelo ya lekgotla	molao	ummiselo	isimemezelo
verouder	age (v)	-tšofala	-tsofala	-tsofala	-aluphala	-guga
verower	conquer (v)	-fenya	-fenya	-fenya	-oyisa	-ahlula
verpleeg	nurse (v)	-oka	-oka	-oka	-onga	-nesa
verpleegster	nurse (n)	mooki	nese	mooki	umongikazi	unesi
verpligting	obligation (n)	tshwanelo	tlamo	mokgaphe	imfanelo	isibopho
verraad	treason (n)	boepi	keko	boepapuso	ungcatsho	ukwambuka
verraai	betray (v)	-eka	-eka	-eka	-ngcatsha	-khaphela
verraaier	traitor (n)	moeki	moeki	motsietsi	umngcatshi	imbuka
verras	surprise (v)	-makatša	-makatsa	-makatsa	-othusa	-mangalisa
verrassing	surprise (n)	makatšo	makatso	kgakgamalo	isothuso	isimangaliso
verrigtinge	proceedings (n)	ditiro	diketsahalo	ditiragalo	inkqubo	ukuthethwa kwecala
verrot	rot (v)	-bola	-bola	-bola	-bola	-bola
verrot	rotten (a)	-bodilwego	-bodileng	-bodileng	-bolile (yo)	-bolile
verrot	decay (v)	-bola	-bola	-bola	-buna	-bola
verryk	enrich (v)	-humiša	-ruisa	-nontsha	-tyebisa	-cebisa
verrys	emerge (v)	-tšwa	-phahama	-inoga	-vela	-phuma
vers	verse (n)	temana	temana	tema	ivesi	indima
vers	heifer (n)	sethole	sethole	moroba	ithokazi	isithole
versamel	collect (v)	-kgobokana	-kgobokanya	-phutha	-qokelela	-qoqa
verseker	ensure (v)	-kgonthiša	-tiisetsa	-tlhomamisa	-qinisekisa	-qiniseka
versekering	insurance (n)	tšhireletšo	enshorense	putlelelo	i-inshorensi	inshuwarensi
versekering	assurance (n)	tšhireletšo	ashorense	asorense	ingqiniseko	umshuwalense
versier	decorate (v)	-kgabiša	-kgabisa	-kgabisa	-hombisa	-hlobisa
versiering	decoration (n)	kgabišo	mokgabiso	lekgabisa	umhombiso	umhlobiso
versiersuiker	icing (n)	swikirikgabiša	tswekeresekgabisi	sukiri	isihombisi-keyiki	i-ayisingi
versigtig	careful (a)	-hlokomelago	-hlokomelang	-kelotlhoko	-lumkileyo	-nakekele
versigtigheid	caution (n)	tlhokomelo	tlhokomelo	boipabalelo	umgqalisela	isiqapheliso
verskaf	supply (v)	-neela	-fa	-fa	-bonelela	-nika
verskeidenheid	variety (n)	mehutahuta	bongata	mofutafuta	iintlobo ngeentlobo	izinhlobonhlobo
verskeie	several (a)	-mehutahuta	-tse itseng	-mmalwa	-qela	-ningana
verskil	difference (n)	phapano	phapano	pharologano	umahluko	umahluka
verskil	differ (v)	-fapana	-fapana	-fapaana	-ahluka	-ahlukana
verskil	disagree (v)	-fapana	-fapana	-ganetsa	-ngavumelani	-phambana
verskillend	different (a)	-fapanego	-fapaneng	-sele	-ahlukileyo	-ahlukile
verskoning	apology (n)	tshwarelo	tshwarelo	boitshwarelo	ungxengxezo	isixoliso
verskoning vra	apologise (v)	-kgopela tshwarelo	-kopa tshwarelo	-kopa boitshwarelo	-cela uxolo	-xolisa
verskrik	terrify (v)	-tšhoša	-tshosa haholo	-tshosa	-oyikisa	-ethusa
verskrompel	shrivel (v)	-šošobanya	-finahana	-kokoropana	-shwabanisa	-shwabana
verskyn	appear (v)	-tšwelela	-hlaha	-tlhaga	-vela	-bonakala
verskyning	appearance (n)	tšwelelo	ho hlaha	ponalo	imbonakalo	ukubonakala
verskynsel	phenomenon (n)	ponagalo	ketsahalo	ponagalo	into	isenzeko
verslaafde	addict (n)	mohlankiša	lekgoba	motlwaetsi	ingedle	umlutha
verslaafdheid	addiction (n)	tlhankišitšo	bokgoba	botlwaelo	ubungedle	ukulutha
verslaan	defeat (v)	-fenya	-hlola	-fenya	-oyisa	-hlula
verslag	report (n)	pego	tlaleho	polelo	ingxelo	umbiko
verslaggewer	reporter (n)	mmegi	motlalehi	mmegi	umniki-ngxelo	umbiki
versmoring	asphyxia (n)	kgamo	pipelano	khupelo	ufuthaniselo	ukugwaliza
versnel	accelerate (v)	-fa makhura	-akofisa	-okofatsa	-khawulezisa	-sheshisa

V	Afrikaans	English	N Sotho	Sesotho	Tswana	Xhosa	Zulu
	versoek	request (v)	-kgopela	-kopa	-kopa	-cela	-cela
	versoek	request (n)	kgopelo	kopo	kopo	isicelo	isicelo
	versperring	barrier (n)	lepheko	sethibelo	legora	umqobo	isithiyo
	versprei	spread (v)	-fetetša	-hasa	-phasalatsa	-sasaza	-sakaza
	versprei	distribute (v)	-abaganya	-aba	-rathabolola	-aba	-amukezela
	verstaan	understand (v)	-kwišiša	-utlwisisa	-tlhaloganya	-qonda	-qonda
	verstand	mind (n)	mogopolo	kelello	tlhaloganyo	ingqondo	umqondo
	verstandig	sane (a)	-bohlale	-kutlwisiso	-fodileng tlhogo	-nengqondo	-hlakaniphile
	verstedeliking	urbanisation (n)	toropofatšo	tokisetso ya metse e meholo	go tlwaetsa setoropo	isimo sedolophu	ukuphila isidolobha
	versteek	hidden (a)	-utilwego	-patilweng	-fitlhilweng	-fihlakeleyo	-fihliwe
	verstik	choke (v)	-betwa	-qhwela	-kgama	-miwa	-binda
	verstom	stun (v)	-tlaba	-makatsa	-makatsa	-khwankqisa	-ndiyazisa
	verstrooi	disperse (v)	-phatlalatša	-hasa	-phatlalala	-chitha-chitha	-hlakaza
	verstuit	sprain (v)	-thinya	-nonyetseha	-phetsega	-kruneka	-enyelisa
	verstuiting	sprain (n)	thinyego	nonyetseho	phetsego	ukukruneka	isenyelo
	verswering	abscess (n)	sekaku	seso	sekaku	igqitha	ithumba
	vertaal	translate (v)	-fetolela	-fetolela	-fetola	-guqulela	-humusha
	vertaler	translator (n)	mofetoledi	mofetoledi	mofetoledi	umguquli	umhumushi
	verteenwoordig	represent (v)	-emela	-emela	-emela	-mela	-mela
	verteenwoordiger	representative (n)	moemedi	moemedi	moemedi	ummeli	ummeli
	vertel	tell (v)	-laodiša	-bolela	-bolela	-xela	-landa
	vertel	narrate (v)	-anegela	-qoqela	-anela	-balisa	-landa
	vertikaal	vertical (a)	-tsepamego	-otlolohileng	-tsepameng	-nkqo	-qonde phezulu
	vertolk	interpret (v)	-hlatholla	-toloka	-phutholola	-tolika	-humusha
	vertoning	show (n)	pontšho	pontsho	pontsho	umboniso	ukubukisa
	vertraag	delay (v)	-diegiša	-dieha	-dia	-libazisa	-libazisa
	vertraging	delay (n)	tiego	tieho	tiego	ulibaziso	isilibaziso
	vertrek	departure (n)	tlogo	phallo	tlogo	unduluko	ukwemuka
	vertrek	depart (v)	-tloga	-falla	-tloga	-nduluka	-emuka
	vertroulik	confidential (a)	-sephiri	-lekunutu	-khupamarama	-lihlebo	-yisifuba
	vertroulik meedeel	confide (v)	-loma tsebe	-amela	-bulela mafatlha	-thembela	-hlebela
	verveel	bore (v)	-tena	-tena	-tena	-dika	-dinisayo
	vervelige mens	bore (n)	moteni	setenane	molapisi	umsimandozele	umuntu odinisayo
	vervolg	prosecute (v)	-sekiša	-nqosa	-sekisa	-tshutshisa	-mangalela
	vervolg	continue (v)	-tšwetša pele	-tswela pele	-letela	-qhubeka	-qhubisa
	vervolging	prosecution (n)	tshekišo	ho nqosa	tshekiso	utshutshiso	ukumangalelwa
	vervorm	deform (v)	-senya	-sotha	-golafatsa	-limaza	-ona isimo
	verwaand	conceited (a)	-ikgogomošago	-ikgohomosa	-boikgantsho	-nekratshi	-ziqhayisa
	verwaarloos	neglect (v)	-hlokomologa	-hlokomoloha	-tlhokomologa	-ngakhathaleli	-debeselwe
	verwag	expect (v)	-letela	-lebella	-solofela	-lindela	-ethemba
	verwar	puzzle (v)	-gakantša	-lotha	-tlhakanya tlhogo	-dida	-dida
	verwar	confuse (v)	-gakantšha	-ferekanya	-tlaetsa	-bhidanisa	-dida
	verweerder	defendant (n)	moiphemedi	mosireletsi	mosekisiwa	ummangalelwa	umvikeli
	verwelkom	welcome (v)	-amogela ka lethabo	-amohela	-amogela	-amkela	-emukela
	verwerp	reject (v)	-gana	-nyahlatsa	-gana	-gxotha	-enqaba
	verwerping	rejection (n)	kgano	nyahlatso	kgano	ukulahla	ukwenqaba
	verwoes	devastate (v)	-fediša	-ripitla	-senya	-tshabalalisa	-bhuqa
	verwurg	strangle (v)	-kgama	-kgama	-beta	-krwitsha	-khama
	verwyder	remove (v)	-tloša	-suthisa	-tlosa	-shenxisa	-susa
	verwyder	eliminate (v)	-tloša	-ntsha	-tlosa	-denca	-susa
	verwydering	removal (n)	tlošo	tshuthiso	tloso	ushenxiso	ukususa
	verwys	refer (v)	-ra	-lebisa	-umaka	-bhekisa	-dlulisela
	verwysing	reference (n)	tšhupetšo	tebiso	kumako	ukubhekisa	ukudlulisela
	vesel	roughage (n)	tlhale	tshwele	ditlhotlhori	isintlakantlakiso	umhhadlazo
	vesel	fibre (n)	tlhale	tlhale	tlhale	usinga	uzi
	vestig	establish (v)	-hloma	-hloma	-setlela	-zinzisa	-misa
	vet	fat (n)	makhura	mafura	mafura	amafutha	amafutha
	vet	fat (a)	-nonnego	-mafura	-nonneng	-tyebileyo	-khuluphele

Afrikaans	English	N Sotho	Sesotho	Tswana	Xhosa	Zulu	V
videokassetopnemer	video recorder (n)	segatiši sa video	motjhine wa vidio		ividiyo	isiqophi sezwi nezithombe	
vier	four (n)	-ne	nne	nne	isine	okune	
vier	celebrate (v)	-keteka	-keteka	-keteka	-vuyela	-gubha umkhosi	
viering	celebration (n)	monyanya	mokete	keteko	imivuyo	umkhosi	
vierkant	square (n)	khutlonne	kgutlonnetsepa	bentlelaka	uxande	isikwele	
vierkantig	square (a)	-khutlonne	-kgutlonne	-bentlelaka	-xande	-yisikwele	
vies maak	annoy (v)	-hlopha	-tena	-tena	-caphukisa	-casula	
vin	fin (n)	lephegwana la hlapi	lepheo la tlhapi	lefafa	iphiko lentlanzi	iphiko lenhlanzi	
vind	find (v)	-hwetša	-fumana	-bona	-fumana	-thola	
vinger	finger (n)	monwana	monwana	monwana	umnwe	umunwe	
vingerafdruk	fingerprint (n)	kgatišo ya monwana	kgatiso ya monwana	motlhala wa monwana	umnwe	isithupha	
vingernael	fingernail (n)	lenala	lenala	lenala	uzipho	uzipho lomunwe	
vinnig	fast (a)	-nago le lebelo	-phakisang	ka bonako	-khawulezayo	-masinyane	
viool	violin (n)	fiolo	violene	baeyolene	ifidyoli	ivayolini	
vioolspeler	violinist (n)	moletšafiolo	mmapalaviolene	moletsi wa baeyolene	umdlali-fidyoli	umshayivayolini	
vir	for (prep)	-el-	bakeng sa-	go	-ya	nga-	
vis	fish (n)	hlapi	tlhapi	tlhapi	intlanzi	inhlanzi	
vishoek	fish-hook (n)	huku ya go rea dihlapi	selope	huku	ihuku yokuloba	udobo	
vismot	fishmoth (n)	mmoto	tshwele	motoutwane	isithiyiseli	umvunya	
visstok	fishing rod (n)	kobihlapi	leqala la ditlhapi	setshwaro sa ditlhapi	intonga yokuloba	uthi lokudoba	
visum	visa (n)	bisa	visa	tumelelo	ivisa	ivisa	
visvang	fishing (n)	go rea dihlapi	tshwaso ya ditlhapi	go tshwara ditlhapi	ukuloba	ukudoba	
visvang	fish (v)	-rea dihlapi	-tshwasa	-thaisa ditlhapi	-bamba intlanzi	-doba	
vlag	flag (n)	folaga	folakga	folaga	iflegi	ifulagi	
vlak	shallow (a)	-sa išego	-sa tebang	-maphara	-nobudibi	-ngashonile	
vlak	level (n)	tekanetšo	mokato	bogodimo	umgangatho	ileveli	
vlam	flame (n)	kgabo ya mollo	lelakabe	kgabo	idangatye	ilangabi	
vlegsel	plait (n)	leetse	thapo	leetse	umphotho	iqakathi	
vlei	flatter (v)	-phapea	-thetsa	-baya bubi	-khohlisa	-babaza	
vleis	flesh (n)	nama	nama	nama	inyama	inyama	
vleis	meat (n)	nama	nama	nama	inyama	inyama	
vlek	stain (n)	setaki	letheba	sebala	isitshele	ibala	
vlerk	wing (n)	lefego	lepheo	lefuka	iphiko	iphiko	
vlermuis	bat (n)	mmankgagane	mmankgane	mmamathwane	ilulwane	ilulwane	
vlieër	kite (n)	khaete	khaete	sefofi	ikayiti	ikhayithi	
vlieg	fly (v)	-fofa	-fofa	-fofa	-bhabha	-ndiza	
vlieg	fly (n)	ntši	ntsintsi	ntsi	umthika	impukane	
vliegtuig	aircraft (n)	sefofane	sefofane	sefofane	inqwelomoya	indiza	
vliegtuig	aeroplane (n)	sefofane	sefofane	sefofane	inqwelomoya	indizamshini	
vloed	flood (n)	lefula	morwallo	morwalela	isikhukula	isikhukhula	
vloei	flow (v)	-ela	-phalla	-elela	-qukuqela	-gobhoza	
vloeibaar	fluid (a)	-seela	-phallang	-elelang	-ngamanzi	-ngamanzi	
vloeibaar	liquid (a)	-elago	-mokedikedi	-elelang	-lulwelo	-manzi	
vloeistof	fluid (n)	seela	sephalli	seedi	ubuyengeyenge	into engamanzi	
vloeistof	liquid (n)	seela	mokedikedi	seela	ulwelo	uketshezi	
vloek	swear (v)	-roga	-hlapaola	-roga	-thuka	-thuka	
vloek	curse (n)	madimabe	tlhapa	thogo	intshwabulo	isiqalekiso	
vloer	floor (n)	lebato	fuluru	bodilo	umgangatho	iphansi	
vlokkie	flake (n)	kgapetlana	pudulana	makakaba	ikhitha	ucwecwana	
vlokkie	chip (computer) (n)	sedirišwana sa komphuta	phatsa	lephatlo	icwecwe	ishiphu	
vlooi	flea (n)	letsetse	letsetse	letsetse	intakumba	izeze	
vloot	navy (n)	kgoro ya dikepe	dikepe tsa ntwa	lefapha la dikepe	iinqanawa	amasotsha asemkhunjini	
vlot	raft (n)	sephaphami	pholletso	moratho	isihlenga	isihlenga	
vlot	fluent (a)	-elago	-kgeleke	-thelelelo	-nobuciko	-yingqamundi	
vlug	flight (n)	tšhabo	paleho	tshabo	uhambo ngomoya	ukubaleka	
vlug	flee (v)	-tšhaba	-baleha	-sia	-bhabha	-baleka	
vlugtig	rapid (a)	lebelo	-ka pele	-bonako	-khawulezayo	-ngejubane	
vlugtig kyk	glance (v)	-gadima	-thalatsa	-gebenya	-krwaqula	-jantiza	

V Afrikaans	English	N Sotho	Sesotho	Tswana	Xhosa	Zulu
vlytig	industrious (a)	-mafolofolo	-kgothetseng	-senatla	-khutheleyo	-khuthele
voeding	nutrition (n)	phepo	phepo	dijo	isondlo	ukondliwa komzimba
voël	bird (n)	nonyana	nonyana	nonyane	intaka	inyoni
voel	feel (v)	-kwa	-ama	-utlwa	-vakalelwa	-zwa
voer	feed (v)	-fepa	-fepa	-fepa	-tyisa	-phakela
voering	lining (n)	bokagare	furu	furu	ifuringi	imfulomu
voet	foot (n)	leoto	leoto	lenao	unyawo	unyawo
voetbal	football (n)	kgwele ya maoto	bolo	mosito	ibhola	unobhutshuzwayo
voetganger	pedestrian (n)	mosepelakamaoto	ya tsamayang ka maoto	motsamayi	umhambi ngeenyawo	umhambiphansi
voetspoor	footprint (n)	mohlala	bohato	motlhala	unyawo	unyawo
voetstap	footstep (n)	kgato	mohlala	mosepele	inyathelo	isinyathelo
vog	moisture (n)	monola	mongobo	bokgola	ukufuma	ubumanzi
vogtig	moist (a)	-monola	-mongobo	-ngolang	-fumile	-manzana
vogtig	damp (a)	-monola	-mongobo	-seola	-fumile	-manzana
vogtigheid	damp (n)	monola	mongobo	bongola	ukufuma	ubumanzi
vol	full (a)	-tletšego	-tletse	-tletseng	-zeleyo	-gcwele
voldoende	adequate (a)	-lekanego	-lekaneng	-lekanang	-aneleyo	-anele
volg	result (v)	-tšwa	-latela	-latela	-phuma ku-	-landela
volg	follow (v)	-latela	-latela	-latela	-landela	-landela
volgeling	follower (n)	molatedi	molatedi	molatedi	umlandeli	umlandeli
volgende	next (a)	-latelago	-latelang	-latelang	-landelayo	-landelayo
volhard	persevere (v)	-kgotlelela	-qhophella	-itshoka	-zingisa	-khuthazela
volkslied	anthem (n)	mmino wa setšhaba	pina ya setjhaba	pina ya bosetshaba	umhobe	ihubo lesizwe
volksoorleweringe	folklore (n)	dinonwane	tshomo	dikinane	uncwadi lomlomo	amasiko nezinganekwane
volkstaal	vernacular (n)	leleme la setšhaba	puo ya lapeng	segae	ulwimi lwemveli	ulimi
volledig	complete (a)	-feletšego	-felletseng	-botlalo	-gqibeleyo	-pheleleyo
vol maak	fill (v)	-tlatša	-tlatsa	-tlatsa	-gcwalisa	-gcwalisa
volmaak	perfect (a)	-phethegilego	-phethahetseng	-itekanela	-gqibelele(yo)	-gweda
volop	plenty (a)	-atilego	-tletsetletse	-ntsi	-zele	-ningi
volstruis	ostrich (n)	mpšhe	mpjhe	ntshwe	inciniba	intshe
voltooi	complete (v)	-fetša	-qetella	-fetsa	-gqibezela	-qedela
volume	volume (n)	bolumo	mothamo	mothama	umthamo	ubukhulu ba-
vol vertroue	confident (a)	-itshepago	-itshepa	-khupamarama	-zithembileyo	-thembayo
volwasse	mature (a)	-godilego	-hodileng	-godileng	-khulile(yo)	-khulile
volwasse	adult (a)	-godilego	-holo	-godileng	-dala	-osekhulile
volwassene	adult (n)	mogolo	moholo	mogolo	umntu omdala	umuntu osekhulile
volwassenheid	adulthood (n)	bogolo	boholo	bogolo	ubudala	ukukhula
vomeer	vomit (v)	-hlatša	-hlatsa	-tlhatsa	-gabha	-hlanza
vomeersel	vomit (n)	mahlatša	mahlatsa	matlhatsa	ukugabha	ubuhlanzo
vonk	spark (n)	hlase	tlhase	tlhase	intlantsi	inhlansi
vonkel	sparkle (v)	-benyabenya	-benya	-lakasela	-khazimla	-khazimula
voog	guardian (n)	mofepi	mohlokomedi	motlamedi	ikhankatha	umondli
voor	front (a)	-pele	-pele	-pele	phambi	phambili
voor	before (prep)	pele	-pele	pele	-phambi	phambi kwa-
vooraanstaande	distinguished (a)	-tsebalegago	bohlokwa	-itshupang	-balulekileyo	-phakeme
vooraanstaande	eminent (a)	-hlomphegago	-konokono	-itsegeng	-balaseleyo	-phakeme
voorafgaan	precede (v)	-eta pele	-etella pele	-etelela	-khokela	-andulela
voorarm	forearm (n)	sefaka	letsoho	mokgono	ingalo	ingalo
voorbeeld	example (n)	mohlala	mohlala	sekao	umzekelo	isibonelo
voorbehoeding	contraception (n)	thibelapelegi	thibelo ya pelehi	thibela pelego	ukukhusela	ukuzivala
voorberei	prepare (v)	-lokišetša	-lokis(ets)a	-baakanya	-lungiselela	-lungisa
voorbereiding	preparation (n)	boitokišetšo	tokisetso	paakanyetso	amalungiselelo	ukulungisela
voordeel	advantage (n)	mohola	monyetla	mosola	uncedo	inzuzo
voordelig	beneficial (a)	-holago	-molemo	-mosola	-ncedayo	-sizayo
voorgee	pretend (v)	-ikgakantšha	-ikaketsa	-konkometsa	-zenzisa	-zenzisa
voorgee	feint (v)	-ometša	-iketsisa	-oma	-lingisa	-zenzisa
voorgeskrewe	prescribed (a)	-kgethetšwego	-baletsweng	-beilweng	-alathelwe(yo)	-qokiwe
voorhoof	forehead (n)	phatla	phatla	phatla	ibunzi	ibunzi

218

Afrikaans	English	N Sotho	Sesotho	Tswana	Xhosa	Zulu	V
voorkom	prevent (v)	-thibela	-thibela	-kganna	-nqaba	-vimbela	
voorkom	occur (v)	-diragala	-etsahala	-nna teng	-enzeka	-vela	
voorkoming	prevention (n)	thibelo	thibelo	kganelo	unqando	ukuvimbela	
voorletter	initial (n)	tlhakapele	enisheale	tlhakaina	unobumba	iletha lokuqala	
voornaamwoord	pronoun (n)	lešala	leemedi	leemedi	isimelabizo	isabizwana	
vooroordeel	prejudice (n)	tshekamo	leeme	katlholelopele	ukuqale ugwebe	ukulimaza	
voorouer	ancestor (n)	mogologolo	modimo	mogologolo	isinyanya	ukhokho	
voorraad	stock (n)	phahlo	thepa	mmudungwana	umlibo	impahla	
voorruit	windscreen (n)	seširaphefo	fensetere ya moya	sesiraphefo	ifestile engaphambili emotweni	ifasitela lemoto langaphambili	
voorsien	provide (v)	-fa	-fa	-tlamela	-bonelela	-nika	
voorsit	chair (v)	-swara setulo	-dulasetulo	-dula setulo	-chophela	-ongamela	
voorsitter	chairman (n)	modulasetulo	modulasetulo	modulasetulo	umhlali-ngaphambili	usihlalo	
voorskoot	apron (n)	thetho	forosekoto	khiba	ifaskoti	isibhaxelo	
voorskrif	prescription (n)	taelelo	taelo	taetso	umyalelo	isithako	
voorskryf	prescribe (v)	-kgethela	-balla	-laetsa	-alatha	-layeza	
voorskrywe	dictate (v)	-biletša	-susutlella	-biletsa	-bizela	-bizela	
voorspel	predict (v)	-laola	-porofeta	-supetsa	-xela	-bikezela	
voorspelling	prediction (n)	taolo	boporofeta	tshupetso	isiprofeto	umbiko	
voorstad	suburb (n)	karolwana ya toropo	motsana	motsana wa dintlha	ihlonyelwa	isabhebhe	
voorstedelik	suburban (a)	-karolwana ya toropo	-motsana	-motsana wa dintlha	-ehlomela ledolophu	-pathelene nesabhebhe	
voorstel	proposal (n)	tšhišinyo	tlhahiso	tlhagiso	isindululo	isongozo	
voorstel	propose (v)	-šišinya	-hlahisa	-tlhagisa	-ndulula	-songoza	
voorstel	introduce (v)	-tsebiša	-tsebisa	-itsise	-azisa	-ethula	
voorstelling	introduction (n)	tsebišo	tsebiso	ketelelopele	ukwazisa	isingeniso	
voortdurend	lasting (a)	-sa felego	-tswelang pele	-tlhola	-hlalayo	-hlalayo	
voortduur	last (v)	-swarelela	-tswela pele	-tshwarelela	-hlala	-hlala isikhathi	
voorteken	omen (n)	tlholo	pontsho	sekai	umhlola	ibika	
voortgaan	proceed (v)	-tšwela pele	-tswela pele	-tswelela pele	-qhuba	-qhubeka	
voortspruit	stem (v)	-hlaga	-hloma	-tswa	-vuma	-khalima	
vooruit	forward (adv)	pele	-pele	pele	phambili	ngaphambili	
vooruit	ahead (adv)	pele	ka pele	pele	-ngaphambili	ngaphambili	
vooruitgaan	progress (v)	-tšwela pele	-tswela pele	-tswelela pele	-qhubela phambili	-qhubeka	
vooruitgang	progress (n)	tšwelopele	tswelopele	tswelelopele	inkqubela	inqubeko	
vooruitgang	advance (n)	tšwelopele	tswelopele	tswelelopele	inkqubela-phambili	ukuqhubeka	
voorvaderlik	ancestral (a)	-badimo	-badimo	-sedimo	-yezinyanya	-okhokho	
voorval	incident (n)	tiragalo	ketsahalo	tiragalo	ingozi isehlo	isigameko	
voorwaarde	condition (n)	peelano	peelano	maemo	imfuneko	isimiselo	
voorwaarts	onward (adv)	pele	pele	pele	phambili	phambili	
voorwendsel	pretext (n)	boikgakantšho	thetso	seipato	amampunge	icebo	
voorwerp	object (n)	selo	ntho	selo	injongo senzi	into	
voorwoord	preface (n)	ketapele	ketapele	ketapele	imbulambethe	isanduleliso	
vordering	advancement (n)	tlhabologo	tswelopele	botswelelopele	inyathelo	inqubekela-phambili	
vorm	form (v)	-bopa	-bopa	-bopa	-akha	-bumba	
vorm	form (n)	sebopego	sebopeho	foromo	isakhiwo	isimo	
vorm	mould (v)	-bopa	-bopa	-bopa	-bumba	-khutha	
vorm	mould (n)	sebopi	popo	sebopelo	ubumbeko	isikhutha	
vou	fold (v)	-mena	-mena	-mena	-songa	-pheca	
vou	fold (n)	momeno	lemeno	lemeno	umgqwetho	umpheco	
vra	question (v)	-botšiša	-botsa	-botsa	-buza	-buza	
vra	ask (v)	-kgopela	-botsa	-botsa	-buza	-buza	
vra	charge (price) (v)	-bitša	-bitsa	-kopa	-xabisa	-biza	
vraag	question (n)	potšišo	potso	potso	umbuzo	umbuzo	
vraat	glutton (n)	sejato	monyollo	legodu	isirhovu	isiminzi	
vrag	load (n)	morwalo	morwalo	morwalo	umthwalo	umthwalo	
vragmotor	lorry (n)	lori	lori	llori	ilori	iloli	
vrat	wart (n)	tlhokofele	monyollo	kakana	intsumpa	insumpa	
vrede	peace (n)	khutšo	kgotso	kagiso	uxolo	ukuthula	
vreemd	strange (a)	-šele	-sele	-sele	-ngaqhelekanga	-ngaziwa	

V	Afrikaans	English	N Sotho	Sesotho	Tswana	Xhosa	Zulu
	vreemd	foreign (a)	-šele	-sele	-selabe	-asemzini	-kwezizwe ezinye
	vreemdeling	stranger (n)	moeng	moditjhaba	moditšhaba	umntu wasemzini	umfokazi
	vrees	fear (n)	poifo	tshabo	poifo	uloyiko	ukwesaba
	vrees	fear (v)	-boifa	-tshaba	-boifa	-oyika	-esaba
	vrees	dread (v)	-boifa	-tshaba	-boifa	-oyika	uvalo
	vreeslik	terrible (a)	-tšhošago	-tshabehang	-mpe	-oyikekayo	-esabekayo
	vrek	miser (n)	ngame	lekgonatha	ngame	igogotya	iqonqela
	vrekkerig	miserly (a)	-ngame	-bokgonatha	-ngame	-ngobugogotya	-mbanyile
	vreugde	joy (n)	lethabo	nyakallo	boitumelo	uvuyo	injabulo
	vriend	friend (n)	mogwera	motswalle	tsala	umhlobo	umngane
	vriendskap	friendship (n)	bogwera	setswalle	botsalano	ubuhlobo	ubungane
	vries	freeze (v)	-kgahla	-hwama	-gatsela	-khenkca	-qandisa
	vriesbrand	frostbite (n)	kgatselo	lebabo	go swa bokidi	umtshaza	umshazo
	vrieskas	freezer (n)	setšidifatši	sehatsetsi	setsidifatsi	isikhenkcisi	isiqandisi
	vriespunt	freezing point (n)	bokgahlo	ntlha ya leqhweng	boswakgapetla	iqondo lomkhenkce	izinga-qhwa
	vroedvrou	midwife (n)	mmelegiši	mobelehisi	mmelegisi	umbelekisikazi	umbelethisi
	vroeg	early (a)	ka masa	hoseng	-phakela	-kusasa	-masisha
	vrolik	cheerful (a)	-thabilego	-nyakalletseng	-thabang	-onwabileyo	-thokozile
	vrou	wife (n)	mogatša	mosadi	mosadi	umfazi	unkosikazi
	vrou	female (n)	mosadi	mosadi	namagadi	umfazi	isifazane
	vrou	woman (n)	mosadi	mosadi	mosadi	umfazi	umfazi
	vroulik	female (a)	-tshadi	-tshehadi	-namagadi	-khomokazi	-owesifazane
	vrug	fruit (n)	seenywa	tholwana	leungo	isiqhamo	isithelo
	vrugbaar	fertile (a)	-nonnego	-nonne	-nonneng	-chumileyo	-vundile
	vry	free (a)	-lokologilego	-lokolohileng	-gololosegileng	-khululekileyo	-khululekile
	Vrydag	Friday (n)	Labohlano	Labohlano	Labotlhano	ulwesi Hlanu	uLwesihlanu
	vryf	rub (v)	-gohla	-pikitla	-gotlha	-hlikihla	-hlikihla
	vrygewig	generous (a)	-mabobo	-fanang	-pelotshweu	-ophayo	-nokuphana
	vryheid	freedom (n)	tokologo	tokoloho	kgololesego	inkululeko	inkululeko
	vrymaak	emancipate (v)	-lokolla	-lokolla bokgobeng	-golola	-khulula	-khulula
	vryspraak	acquittal (n)	tokollo	tokollo	kgololo	ugwetyelo	ukukhululwa
	vryspreek	acquit (v)	-lokolla	-lokolla	-golola	-khulula	-khulula
	vrywillig	voluntary (a)	-go se gapeletšwe	ka boithatelo	-ithaopang	-zithandelayo	-ngentando
	vrywilliger	volunteer (n)	moithapi	mothahaselli	moithaopa	ivolontiya	uvolontiya
	vrywillig onderneem	volunteer (v)	-ithaopa	-thahasella	-ithaopa	-zithandele	-volontiya
	vuil	dirty (a)	-nago le ditšhila	-ditshila	-leswe	-mdaka	-ngcolile
	vuilgoed	rubbish (n)	matlakala	ditshila	malele	inkunkuma	izibi
	vuilgoed	filth (n)	tšhila	tshila	leswe	ubumdaka	udoti
	vuis	fist (n)	letswele	setebele	lebole	inqindi	inqindi
	vulgêr	vulgar (a)	-mahlapa	-tlhapa	-maswe	-thukayo	-ngenamahloni
	vulkaan	volcano (n)	bolkano	bolekano	lekgwamolelo	intabamlilo	intabamlilo
	vulletjie	foal (n)	pešana	petsana	petsana	inkonyana yehashe	inkonyane yehhashi
	vullis	refuse (n)	tšhila	dithole	matlakala	inkunkuma	izibi
	vullisblik	rubbish bin (n)	thini ya matlakala	motou wa ditshila	selatlhelamalele	umgqomo	umgqomo wezibi
	vullishoop	rubbish heap (n)	thothobolo	qubu ya ditshila	thuthubudu	izala	inqumbi yezibi
	vurk	fork (n)	foroko	fereko	foroko	ifolokhwe	imfologo
	vuur	fire (n)	mollo	mollo	molelo	umlilo	umlilo
	vuurherd	fireplace (n)	sebešo	leifo	leiso	iziko	iziko
	vuurhoutjie	match (n)	lehlokwana la mollo	thutswana mollo	letlhokwa	imatshisi	umentshisi
	vuurtoring	lighthouse (n)	ntloseetša	molollope wa mollo	ntlwana kganya	indlu ekhanyisela inqanawa	isibubulungu
	vy	fig (n)	feiye	feiye	feie	ikhiwane	ikhiwane
	vyand	foe (n)	lenaba	sera	mmaba	utshaba	isitha
	vyand	enemy (n)	lenaba	sera	mmaba	utshaba	isitha
	vyandig maak	antagonise (v)	-lwantšha	-tlatlapa	-lotlhanya	-enza ubutshaba	phambana na-
	vyeboom	figtree (n)	mofeiye	sefate sa feiye	feie	umthi wekhiwane	umkhiwane
	vyf	five (n)	-hlano	hlano	tlhano	isihlanu	isihlanu
	vyftien	fifteen (n)	lesomehlano	leshome le metso e mehlano	some tlhano	ishumi elinesihlanu	ishumi nesihlanu

Afrikaans	English	N Sotho	Sesotho	Tswana	Xhosa	Zulu
vyftig	fifty (n)	masomehlano	mashome a mahlano	somamatlhano	amashumi amahlanu	amashumi amahlanu
vyl	file (n)	feila	feile	feile	ifila	ifayili
wa	wagon (n)	koloi	koloi	koloi	inqwelo	inqola
waad	wade (v)	-tsena	-phoka	-gobua	-nyovula	-bhoxoza
waag	risk (v)	-phonkgela	-baka qomatsi	-tsena diphatsa	-faka engozini	-zifaka engozini
waai	blow (v)	-foka	-fefola	-foka	-vuthela	-phephetha
waaier	fan (n)	sefokišamoya	fene	leubelo	isiniki-moya	isephephezelɔ
waaksaam	alert (a)	-phakgamego	-sedi	-nthsa matlho dinameng	-phaphamileyo	-xwayile
waaksaamheid	vigilance (n)	phakgamo	tebelo	botlhaga	ukuphaphama	ukuqaphela
waansinnige	lunatic (n)	segafa	lehlanya	setseno	igeza	uhlanya
waar	true (a)	-makgonthe	-nnete	-tota	-nyanisile(yo)	-qinisile
waar	where (adv)	kae	kae	kae	phi	-phi
waarborg	guarantee (v)	-tiišetša	-ema pane	-netefatsa	-qinisekisa	-qinisekisa
waarborg	guarantee (n)	tiišetšo	ho ema paneng	netefaletso	isiqinisekiso	isiqinisekiso
waarde	value (n)	mohola	bohlokwa	tlhotlhwa	ixabiso	inani
waardeer	value (v)	-lekanyetša	-rata	-phophotha legetla	-xabisa	-beka inani
waardeer	appreciate (v)	-lekanyetša	-ananela	-anaanela	-ncoma	-ncoma
waardevol	valuable (a)	-bohlokwa	-bohlokwa	-botlhokwa	-nexabiso	nenani eliphakeme
waardig	dignified (a)	-hlomphegago	-hlomphehang	-seriti	-ndilekileyo	-nesithunzi
waardigheid	dignity (n)	tlhompho	hlompho	seriti	undiliseko	isizotha
waarheid	truth (n)	nnete	nnete	nnete	inyani	iqiniso
waarneem	observe (v)	-lemoga	-ela hloko	-lepa	-qaphela	-qaphela
waarnemer	observer (n)	molemogi	molemohi	molepi	umqapheli	ingqapheli
waarom	why (adv)	ka lebaka lang	hobaneng	go reng	ngokuba	ngani
waarsku	warn (v)	-lemoša	-eletsa	-tlhagisa	-lumkisa	-qaphisa
waarskuwing	warning (n)	temošo	keletso	kgalemo	isilumkiso	isiqapheliso
waas	haze (n)	mogodi	mohodi	mouwane	inkungu	ufasimbe
waatlemoen	watermelon (n)	legapu	lehapu	legapu	ivatala	ikhabe
wafel	wafer (n)	kuku ya weifere	bohobe	sepapetlanyana	isonka somthendeleko	ucwecwane
wag	wait (v)	-leta	-leta	-leta	-linda	-linda
wag	guard (n)	moleti	molebedi	modisa	igadi	ugadi
wag op	await (v)	-letela	-emela	-emela	-lindela	-lindela
wakker word	wake (v)	-phafoga	-phaphama	-tsoga	-vuka	-phaphama
walglik	repulsive (a)	-ferošago dibete	-nyonyehang	-sisimosang	-gxothayo	-enyanyekayo
walvis	whale (n)	leruarua	leruarua	leruarua	umnenga	umkhoma
wandeling	walk (n)	mosepelo	ho tsamaya	motsamao	umhambo	ukuhamba
wang	cheek (n)	lerama	lerama	lesama	isidlele	isihlathi
wangbeen	cheekbone (n)	lerapothama	lesapo la lerama	phone	isandundu	isiqhoma
wanhoop	despair (n)	-hloboga	ho nyahama	tsholofologo	ukulahla ithemba	ukuphela ithemba
wanhopig	desperate (a)	-hlobogilego	-nyahameng	-solofologang	-phelelwe lithemba	-phelelwe yithemba
wanneer	when (adv)	neng	neng	leng	nini	nini
wanordelik	riotous (a)	-mpherefere	-morusu	-khuduego	-gwayimbile (yo)	-nodweshu
wantrou	distrust (v)	-gonona	-belaela	-belaela	-ngathembi	-ngathembi
wantroue	distrust (n)	kgonono	pelaelo	pelaelo	ukungathembi	ukungathembi
wapen	weapon (n)	sebetša	sebetsa	sebetsa	isixhobo	isikhali
wapens	arms (n)	dibetša	dibetsa	dibetsa	izixhobo	izikhali
warm	warm (a)	-borutho	-tjhesang	-bolelo	-shushu	-fudumele
warm	hot (a)	-borutho	-tjhesa	-bolelo	-shushu	-fudumele
warm maak	heat (v)	-ruthetša	-futhumatsa	-gotela	-shushubeza	-fudumeza
was	wax (n)	motu	dikonokono	boka	umphula	ingcino
was	wash (v)	-hlapa	-hlatswa	-tlhatswa	-hlamba	-geza
wasem	vapour (n)	moyameetse	mouwane	phufudi	umphunga	umhwamuko
wassery	laundry (n)	bohlatswetšo	tlhatsuong	botlhatswetso	indawo yokuhlamba impahla	ilondolo
wat	what (pron)	eng	eng	eng	ntoni	yini
water	water (n)	meetse	metsi	metsi	amanzi	amanzi
waterbak	cistern (n)	sehlapelo	sisetene	mokoro	inkonkxa	itangi
waterpokkies	smallpox (n)	sekobonyane	sekgolopane	sekokonyane	ingqakaqha	ingxibongo

W	**Afrikaans**	**English**	**N Sotho**	**Sesotho**	**Tswana**	**Xhosa**	**Zulu**
	waterpokkies	chickenpox (n)	mabora	baterepokise	thutlwa	irhashalala	inqubulunjwana
	waterval	waterfall (n)	phororo	phororo	lephothoselo	ingxangxasi	impophoma
	watte	cotton wool (n)	wulu ya leokodi	boya ba tshwele	leloba	umqhaphu	uvolo
	watter	which (pron)	-fe	-fe	-fe	yiphi	-phi
	wed	bet (v)	-beelana	-betjha	-beelana	-qashisa	-bheja
	weddenskap	bet (n)	peelano	mobetjho	peelano	iqashiso	ukubheja
	wedren	race (n)	tšhiano	peiso	lebelo	umdyarho	umjaho
	wedstryd	competition (n)	phadišano	tlhodisano	phadisano	ukhuphiswano	umqhudelwano
	wedstryd	contest (n)	phadišano	tseko	bapololano	ukhuphiswano	umbango
	weduwee	widow (n)	mohlologadi	mohlolohadi	motlholagadi	umhlolokazi	umfelokazi
	wedywer	compete (v)	-phadišana	-hlodisana	-phadisana	-khuphisana	-qhudelana
	weef	weave (v)	-loga	-loha	-loga	-photha	-aluka
	weefsel	tissue (n)	tlhalenama	popeho	thogwa	ulucu	isicubu
	weeg	weigh (v)	-kala	-bekga	-kala	-linganisela	-kala
	week	soak (v)	-ina	-ina	-inela	-anya	-cwilisa
	week	week (n)	beke	beke	beke	iveki	iviki
	weeklaag	wail (v)	-golola	-bohola	-bokolela	-enza isijwili	-khala
	weeklag	lament (n)	sello	kodiamalla	dikhutsafalo	-khala	isililo
	weekliks	weekly (a)	-beke	ka beke	ka beke	-ngeveki	ngeviki
	weeluis	bedbug (n)	tšhikidi	tshitshidi	tshitshiri	incukuthu	imbungulu
	weer	weather (n)	boso	bosa ba lehodimo	bosa	imozulu	izulu
	weer	again (adv)	gape	hape	gape	kwakhona	futhi
	weerkaatsing	reflection (n)	pekenyo	seipone	tshupatshwano	umenyezelo	ukubuyiswa
	weerklank	echo (n)	kgalagalo	modumela	mareetsane	intlokoma	ummemo
	weerklink	echo (v)	-galagala	-dumela	-araba	-hlokoma	-enanela
	weerlig	lightning (n)	legadima	letolo	tlhadi	umbane	umbani
	weerspreek	contradict (v)	-ganetša	-ngangisa	-ganetsa	-ziphikise	-phikisa
	weerspreking	contradiction (n)	kganetšo	ngangisano	kganetso	ukuziphikisa	ukuphikisa
	weerstaan	resist (v)	-ganetša	-hana	-swedietega	-xhathisa	-zabalaza
	weerstand	resistance (n)	kganetšo	matla	twantsho	ukuxhathisa	ukuzabalaza
	wees	be (v)	-ba	-ba	-ke	-ba	-ba
	weeshuis	orphanage (n)	ditšhuaneng	dikgutsaneng	dikhutsaneng	umzi weenkedama	ikhaya lezintandane
	weeskind	orphan (n)	tšhuana	kgutsana	khutsana	inkedama	intandane
	weet	know (v)	-tseba	-tseba	-itse	-azi	-azi
	weglaat	omit (v)	-tlogela	-tlohela	-lesa	-shiya	-shiya
	weglating	omission (n)	tlogelo	sekgeo	tlhokomologo	ushiyo	ukushiya
	wegloop	elope (v)	-ngwega	-shobela	-thoba	-gcagca	-baleka
	wegsteek	hide (v)	-uta	-pata	-fitlha	-fihla	-fihla
	wegvreting	erosion (n)	kgogolego	kgoholeho	kgogolego	ukhukuliseko	ukuhebhuka
	weier	refuse (v)	-gana	-hana	-gana	-ala	-ala
	weiveld	pasture (n)	mafulo	makgulo	mafulo	idelo	idlelo
	welbekend	well-known (a)	-tumilego	-tsebahalang	-itsegeng	-aziwayo	-dumileyo
	welkom	welcome (n)	kamogelo	kamohelo	kamogelo	ulwamkelo	ukwemukela
	wellus	lust (n)	kganyogo	meharo	maikaelelo	inkanuko	inkanuko
	welpie	cub (n)	ngwana wa tau	ledinyane	tawana	igoba	iwundlu
	welsprekendheid	eloquence (n)	go bolela gabotse	bokgeleke	seshwiri mo puong	ubuciko	ubuqaphuqaphu
	welsyn	welfare (n)	boiphedišo	katleho	kagiso	intlalo-ntle	inhlalakahle
	wen	win (v)	-fenya	-hlola	-sia	-zuza	-wina
	wen	gain (v)	-holega	-phaella	-sola	-zuza	-zuza
	wens	wish (v)	-kganyoga	-lakatsa	-eletsa	-noqwena	-fisa
	wens	wish (n)	kganyogo	takatso	keletso	umnqweno	isifiso
	wentel	wallow (v)	-dikologa	-potoloha	-bidikama	ukuzibhijabhija	-huquza
	wêreld	world (n)	lefase	lefatshe	lefatshe	ilizwe	umhlaba
	werf	yard (n)	jarata	jarete	jarata	ibala	iyadi
	werk	work (v)	-dira	-sebetsa	-dira	-sebenza	-sebenza
	werk	work (n)	modiro	mosebetsi	tiro	umsebenzi	umsebenzi
	werk	job (n)	modiro	mosebetsi	tiro	umsebenzi	umsebenzi
	werk	employment (n)	mošomo	mosebetsi	tiro	umsebenzi	umsebenzi
	werker	worker (n)	modiri	mosebetsi	modiri	umsebenzi	isisebenzi
	werkgewer	employer (n)	mothwadi	mohiri	mohiri	umqeshi	umqashi

Afrikaans	English	N Sotho	Sesotho	Tswana	Xhosa	Zulu
werklik	really (adv)	ruri	ka nnete	-tota	ngokwenyani	-ngempela
werklik	real (a)	-nnete	-nnete	-tota	-yinyani, -nene	-liqiniso
werklik	indeed (adv)	ka kgonthe	ka nnete	tota	kanye	impela
werkloos	unemployed (a)	-hlokago mošomo	-sa sebetseng	-se nang tiro	-ngaqeshwanga	-ngenamsebenzi
werknemer	employee (n)	modiredi	mohiruwa	modiri	umqeshwa	isisebenzi
werktuig	tool (n)	thulusi	thulosi	sediriswa	isixhobo	ithulusi
werktuigkundige	mechanic (n)	makhanekhe	motehi	mothudi	umkhandi	umakheniki
werkwoord	verb (n)	lediri	leetsi	lediri	isenzi	isenzo
werp	cast (v)	-betša	-akgela	-latlha	-phosa	-phonsa
werwel	vertebra (n)	mokolo	lesapo la mokokotlo	letlhotlholo	umqolo	izongwe lomhlandla
werweldier	vertebrate (n)	phoofolo ya mokokotlo	phoofolo e nang le lesapo la moko kotlo	phologolo ya mokokotlo	isilwanyana esinomqolo	isilwane esinomhlandla
wes	west (adv)	bodikela	-bophirima	bophirima	ntshona	entshonalanga
wese	creature (n)	sebopiwa	sebopuwa	sebopiwa	isidalwa	isidalwa
weste	west (n)	bodikela	Bophirima	bophirima	intshonalanga	intshonalanga
westelik	western (a)	-bodikela	-bophirima	-bophirima	-asentshona	-ntshonalanga
wet	law (n)	molao	molao	molao	umthetho	umthetho
wetenskap	science (n)	thutamahlale	mahlale	boitseanape	inzululwazi	isayensi
wetlik	legal (a)	-molao	-molao	-molao	-semthethweni	-omthetho
wettig	lawful (a)	-dumeletšwego	-molao	-molao	-se mthethweni	-njengomthetho
wettige	legitimate (a)	-dumeletšwego	-molao	-molao	-semthethweni	-vunyelwe ngumthetho
wewenaar	widower (n)	mohlologadi wa monna	mohlolohadi wa monna	moswagadi	umhlolo	umfelwa
wewery	weaving (n)	mologo	moloho	go loga	ukuphotha	ukwaluka
wie	who (pron)	mang	mang	mang	ubani	ubani
wiegelied	lullaby (n)	kunkurobala	koeetso	pinanyana	ingoma yosana	umlolozelo
wiel	wheel (n)	leotwana	lebidi	leotwana	ivili	isondo
wie se	whose (pron)	-mang	-mang	mang	kabani	-kabani
wil	will (n)	thato	thato	thato	intando	intando
wild	wild (a)	-naga	-hlaha	-tlhaga	-ndwebile (yo)	-asendle
wildernis	wilderness (n)	lešoka	lehwatateng	sekgwa	ilindle	indle
wildsbok	antelope (n)	phoofolo	nyamatsana	phologolo	iliza	inyamazane
wildsvleis	venison (n)	nama ya phoofolo	nama ya nyamatsane	nama ya diphologolo	inyama yenyamakazi	inyama yenyamazane
wilgerboom	willow (n)	moduwane	moduwane	modibonoka	umngcunube	umnyezane
wil hê	want (v)	-nyaka	-batla	-batla	-funa	-funa
willekeurig	arbitrary (a)	-lamolwago	-hloka leeme	-letlanyang	-zifunelayo	-nganaki umthetho
wimper	eyelash (n)	ntšhi	dintshi	ntshi	umsebe	ukhophe
wind	wind (n)	phefo	moya	phefo	umoya	umoya
winderig	flatulent (a)	-bipetšwego	-pipitletswe	-gogoralang	-qumbelayo	-qumbile
wind opbreek	belch (v)	-kgeba	-bohla	-kgobola	-bhodla	-bhodla
wingerdstok	vine (n)	morara	sefate sa morara	terebe	umdiliya	isivini
wink	beckon (v)	-gwehla	-hwehla	-gwetlha	-khweba	-khweba
winkbrou	eyebrow (n)	ntšhikgolo	dintshi	losi	ushiyi	ishiya
winkel	shop (n)	lebenkele	lebenkele	lebenkele	ivenkile	isitolo
winkel	store (n)	lebenkele	lebenkele	setoro	ivenkile	isitolo
wins	profit (n)	poelo	phaello	morokotso	ingeniso	inzuzo
wins	gain (n)	poelo	phaello	poelo	inzuzo	inzuzo
wins maak	profit (v)	-boelwa	-fumana phaello	-busetsa	-zuza	-zuza
winter	winter (n)	marega	mariha	mariga	ubusika	ubusika
wiskunde	mathematics (n)	mathematiki	metse	matesisi	imathematika	imathimathiki
wisser	rubber (n)	sephumodi	raba	sephimola	irabha	injoloba
wit	white (n)	tšhweu	bosweu	bosweu	ubumhlophe	-mhlophe
witkalk	whitewash (n)	kalaka ye tšhweu	kalaka e tshweu	kalaka	ikalika	umcako
witseerkeel	diphtheria (n)	difteria	mmetso o mosweu	mometso-o-mosweu	isifo somqala	isifo esivimbanisa umphimbo
wittebrood	honeymoon (n)	hanimunu	hanimunu	madilotsana	ixesha lobumnandi emvakomtshato	ihanimuni
woede	rage (n)	pefelo	kgalefo	bogale	ingqumbo	ulaka
woedend maak	infuriate (v)	-galefiša	-halefisa	-galetsha	-banga umsindo	-thukuthelisa

Y	Afrikaans	English	N Sotho	Sesotho	Tswana	Xhosa	Zulu
	Woensdag	Wednesday (n)	Laboraro	Laboraro	Laboraro	uLwesithathu	ulwesithathu
	woes	fierce (a)	-šoro	-bohale	-bogale	-oyikeka(yo)	-nolaka
	woestyn	desert (n)	leganata	lefeella	sekaka	intlango	umqothu
	wol	wool (n)	boya	boya	boboa	uboya	uvolo
	wolk	cloud (n)	leru	leru	leru	ilifu	ifu
	wond	wound (n)	ntho	leqeba	ntho	inxeba	inxeba
	wond	wound (v)	-gobatša	-ntsha kotsi	-ntsha ntho	-enzakalisa	-limaza
	wonder	wonder (n)	mohlolo	mohlolo	motlholo	ummangaliso	isimangaliso
	wonder	wonder (v)	-makala	-hlolla	-gakgamala	-mangalisa	-mangala
	wonder	marvel (v)	-makala	-makalla	-makala	-mangalisa	-mangalisa
	wonderbaarlik	marvellous (a)	-makatšago	-makatsang	-makatsang	-mangalisa(yo)	-mangalisayo
	wonderlik	wonderful (a)	-makatšago	-makatsang	-ntle	-mangalisa (yo)	-mangalisayo
	wonderwerk	miracle (n)	mohlolo	mohlolo	motlholo	ummangaliso	isimangaliso
	woning	dwelling (n)	bodulo	ntlo	ntlo	indawo yokuhlala	ikhaya
	woonplek	abode (n)	bodulo	bodulo	legae	indawo	isikhundla
	woord	word (n)	lentšu	lentswe	lefoko	igama	igama
	woordeboek	dictionary (n)	pukuntšu	bukantswe	bukantswe	isichazi-magama	isichazimazwi
	woordeskat	vocabulary (n)	tlotlontšu	letlotlo la mantswe	mafoko	isigama	amagama
	wors	sausage (n)	boroso	soseje	boroso	isoseji	isositshi
	worsbroodjie	hot dog (n)	senkgwanaboroso	hotedoko	hotdog	ihotdogi	ihodogi
	wortel	radicle (n)	modu	motswana	modinyana	ingcambu	impande
	wortel	root (n)	modu	motso	modi	umnqathe	impande
	wortel	carrot (n)	borotlolo	sehwete	segwete	umnqathe	ikhalothi
	wraak	vengeance (n)	tefeletšo	boiphetetso	pusoloso	impindezelo	impindiselo
	wrak	wreck (n)	matlhenkge	moswahla	thubego	ubutyobo	umbhabhalala
	wreed	cruel (a)	-šoro	-sehloho	-pelompe	-khohlakeleyo	-nonya
	wreedheid	cruelty (n)	bošoro	sehloho	bopelompe	inkohlakalo	unya
	wreek	avenge (v)	-lefeletša	-iphetetsa	-busolosetsa	-phindezela	-phindisela
	wriemel	wriggle (v)	-širašira	-sosobanya	-menekana	-jubalaza	-shobashoba
	wring	wring (v)	-phetla	-sotha	-soka	-jija	-sontiza
	wrok	grudge (n)	sekgopi	sekgopi	tshele	inzondo	igqubu
	wurg	throttle (v)	-kgama	-kgama	-kgama	-krwitsha	-khama
	wurm	worm (n)	seboko	seboko	seboko	impethu	impethu
	wyd	wide (a)	-phaphathi	batsi	-phaphathi	-banzi	-banzi
	wyn	wine (n)	beine	beine	beine	iwayini	iwayini
	wynkaart	winelist (n)	lenaneo la dibeine	lenane la beine	thulaganyo ya beine	uluhlu lweentlobo zewayini	uhla lwamawayini
	wynkelkie	wineglass (n)	senwelwana	kgalase ya beine	galase ya beine	iglasi yokusela iwayini	ingilazi yewayini
	wys	show (v)	-bontša	-bontsha	-bontsha	-bonisa	-khombisa
	wys	wise (a)	-bohlale	-bohlale	-botlhale	-lumkile (yo)	-hlakaniphile
	wysheid	wisdom (n)	bohlale	bohlale	botlhale	ubulumko	inhlakanipho
	wysie	tune (n)	molodi	modumo	pina	ingonyana	ivumo
	wysig	revise (v)	-fetoša	-pheta	boelela	-phengulula	-bukeza
	wysiging	amendment (n)	phetošo	phetolo	tlhabololo	isilungiso	umbandela
	xilofoon	xylophone (n)	silofone	zaelofone	saelefono	isiginci samagqudwana	izayilofoni
	x-straal	x-ray (n)	eksrei	x-rei	ekeserei	ugesi	iX-reyi
	ydel	vain (a)	-lefela	-lefeela	-lefela	-lambathayo	-ziqhenya
	ylhoofdigheid	delirium (n)	phafatlo	bohlanya	bogorogoro	impambano	amathezane
	ys	ice (n)	lehlwa	leqhwa	kgapetla	umkhenkce	iqhwa
	yskas	refrigerator (n)	setšidifatši	forije	setsidifatsi	ifriji	ifriji
	ysreën	sleet (n)	lehlwapula	tsheola	sefokabolea	ilichwa	ingele
	yster	iron (n)	tshipi	tshepe	tshipi	intsimbi	insimbi
	ysterhout	ironwood (n)	legongtshipi	lehongtshepe	motswere	umkhombe	umsimbithi
	ystervark	porcupine (n)	noko	noko	noko	incanda	ingungumbane

— NORTHERN SOTHO —

Northern Sotho is spoken by approximately 2,5-million people in the northern areas of the Transvaal. It is a member of the Sotho language group of the southeastern zone of Bantu languages. The other members of the Sotho language group are Sesotho, Tswana and Rotse. Historical and geographical reasons and not linguistic ones are responsible for the subdivision of Northern Sotho, Sesotho and Tswana. Members of some Northern Sotho dialects can converse with speakers of certain Tswana dialects more easily than with speakers of some Northern Sotho dialects.

Geographically, Northern Sotho is confined to the northern and eastern Transvaal. The boundary of the Northern Sotho speaking area may be drawn by an imaginary line from Pretoria through Middelburg, Groblersdal and Lydenburg to Sabie. From Sabie the line runs along the Sabie River and then north through Bushbuckridge and Klaserie, across the Olifants River, then westwards as far as Louis Trichardt, and northwards again as far as Messina. From there it moves westwards to the Botswana border and then southwards through the Potgietersrus district, through Warmbad and back to Pretoria.

Different dialect clusters are found in the Northern Sotho speaking area. The most important dialects in the south-central dialect cluster are Kopa and Ndebele-Sotho. The dialects of the central district are Pedi, Tau and Kone. Northern Sotho as a written language was based originally on this cluster. The main dialects of the northwestern cluster are Tlokwa, Hananwa, Matlala, Moletši and Mamabolo; of the northeastern cluster they are Lobedu, Phalaborwa, Khaga and Dzwabo; the eastern cluster is equated with the Pai dialect; and the east-central cluster with the Pulana and Kutswe dialects.

It is important to remember that, in common with other southern African indigenous languages, the structure of Northern Sotho — a tonal language — is very different to Western languages. Northern Sotho is governed by the noun, which is split into various classes. It is what is known as an agglutinating language, with the many suffixes and prefixes used in word construction causing sound changes.

PRONUNCIATION

Four factors govern the correct pronunciation of Northern Sotho: speech sounds, syllable structure, tone and length.

SPEECH SOUNDS

The speech sounds here are the official ones, and make no mention of the variants found in dialect. They can be divided into two main categories: vowels and consonants.

Vowels in Northern Sotho are all voiced. The vowels − and their approximate sounds − are:

a as in **nama** (*meat*), similar to the English *far*
i as in **moriri** (*hair*), similar to the English *it*
e as in **pele** (*in front*), similar to the English *we*
ê as in **selêpê** (*axe*), similar to the Afrikaans *sê*
o as in **noko** (*porcupine*), similar to the Afrikaans *lojaal*
ô as in **tôrô** (*dream*), similar to the Afrikaans *môre*
u as in **kutu** (*stem*), similar to the English *bull*

An important phenomenon of the vowels is that those pronounced with a higher tongue position may influence the pronunciation of those vowels (usually preceding) with a lower tongue position, causing a raising of the tongue in the pronunciation of the latter; **a,** however, is not affected by this.

Consonants are characterised by a complete or partial obstruction of the air current at the place of articulation. They may be classified according to the place and manner of articulation. The following consonants − and their approximate sounds − may be distinguished in Northern Sotho:

b as in **bana** (*children*), similar to the English *able*
bj as in **bjang** (*grass*), no equivalent
d as in **madi** (*blood*), no equivalent
f as in **lefofa** (*feather*), similar to the English *suffer*
fs as in **bofsa** (*youth*), both sounds pronounced (no equivalent)
fš as in **lefšega** (*coward*), no equivalent
g as in **segagabi** (*reptile*), no equivalent
h as in **mohumi** (*rich man*), no equivalent
h as in **sehebehebe** (*whisper*), similar to the English *have*
hl as in **sehlare** (*tree*), no equivalent, but similar to the Welsh *Llewellyn*
j as in **sejo** (*food*), similar to the English *azure*
k as in **phoka** (*dew*), roughly similar to the English *back*
kg as in **kgomo** (*head of cattle*), aspirated, both sounds pronounced (no equivalent)
kh as in **khudu** (*tortoise*), aspirated, similar to the English *kindle*
l as in **molala** (*neck*), similar to the English *lay*
m as in **meetse** (*water*), similar to the English *him*

my as in **go-myemyela** (*to smile*), similar to the English sound *miaow*
n as in **namane** (*calf*), similar to the English *now*
ng as in **ngaka** (*doctor*), similar to the English *sing*
ny as in **monyadi** (*bridegroom*), no equivalent
p as in **pula** (*rain*), roughly similar to the English *lip*
ph as in **phala** (*impala*), aspirated, similar to the English *pull*
pš as in **mpša** (*dog*), no equivalent
psh as in **pshio** (*kidney*), aspirated, similar to the English *pss* in the sound *psst*
pšh as in **pšha** (*evaporate*), aspirated (no equivalent)
r as in **lerapo** (*bone*), no equivalent
s as in **mosese** (*dress*), similar to the English *dress*
š as in **lešata** (*noise*), similar to the English *shilling*
t as in **tau** (*lion*), roughly similar to the English *at*
th as in **thipa** (*knife*), aspirated, similar to the English *till*
tl as in **tladi** (*lightning*), no equivalent
tlh as in **tlhako** (*hoof*), aspirated (no equivalent)
ts as in **motse** (*village*), roughly similar to the English *sits*
tš as in **letšatši** (*sun*), roughly similar to the English *chirp*
tsh as in **ntsha** (*duiker ram*), aspirated, no equivalent
tšh as in **tšhemo** (*land for sowing*), aspirated, similar to the first *ch* in the English *church*
w as in **nawa** (*bean*), similar to the English *wet*
y as in **bolaya** (*kill*), similar to the English *yet*

It is of the utmost importance to distinguish between aspirated (pronounced with a rush of air following) and unaspirated consonants in Northern Sotho as they may be regarded as different speech sounds and have different meanings, for example:
phalo (*scrapings from a skin*)
palo (*beginning*)

Take note also that the [w] sound may be used with many of the above sounds. When it follows a speech sound in which the lips are not involved, the sound should be pronounced with rounded lips; the [w] should not be pronounced as a separate sound.
gw as in **segwagwa** (*frog*), which approximates the Malmesbury Afrikaans [r]

SYLLABLE STRUCTURE

In most instances, the syllable in Northern Sotho ends in a vowel, e.g.:
se-ru-ru-be-le (*butterfly*)

In those instances where syllabic consonants occur, elision of a vowel has historically taken place or the syllabic consonant developed from a consonant and a following vowel, e.g.:
mo-le-lo: mo-l-lo (*fire*)
nuni: nong (*vulture*)

The following types of syllables occur in Northern Sotho (where C indicates consonant and V vowel):

-CV- syllables, e.g.:

le-tša-tši (*sun*)

mo-sa-di (*woman*)

-V- syllables, e.g.:

le-e (*egg*)

le-i-no (*tooth*)

-CCV- syllables, e.g.:

thwa-lo (*hire*)

ngwa-na (*child*)

-C- syllables, e.g.:

m-ma-la (*colour*)

go-l-la (*to cry*)

mo-n-na (*man*)

ba-a-n-nya-tša (*they despise me*)

TONE

In Northern Sotho each syllable of a word has a specific tone, i.e. a specific pitch of voice with which it is pronounced. A number of absolute pitches can be observed but these can be reduced to two distinctive pitches: high and low. This is one of the most important factors governing correct pronunciation, and carelessness in its application leads to misunderstandings. The entire meaning of a word can be changed by the mere tone pattern with which it is pronounced, e.g.:

legaga (*cliff*), compared with

legaga (*sloughed skin*)

where the first syllable **ga** of the first word is pronounced with a high pitch and the same syllable in the second word with a low pitch.

Numerous rules govern the tone of Northern Sotho words, and anyone interested in the correct pronunciation will have to rely on hearing the words being pronounced by a mother tongue speaker.

LENGTH

This is another very important factor to be considered in pronunciation. Length refers to the lengthened pronunciation of a specific syllable in a word. It is indicated phonetically by a colon after the long syllable. In Northern Sotho, the penultimate (second last) syllable of a word is pronounced with length, e.g.:

Se:ga (*Cut*)

Sega na:ma (*Cut the meat*)

Bana bale ba nyaka mon:na (*Those children are looking for the man*)

NORTHERN SOTHO WORDS

Northern Sotho uses a method known to linguists as 'disjunctive', which means that a word consists of several units. For example, the conjugated verb, **ke a sapela** (*I am going*) consists of three different segments. So, in the example

Monna o ja bogobe (*The man eats porridge*)

four orthographic (or practical) words are discernible. However, all the units in the practical orthography of Northern Sotho that are written as separate 'words' cannot be scientifically proven to be linguistic words, which consist at least of a root or a root plus other constituent parts (prefixes and/or suffixes).

The root denotes the basic meaning of the word. The most effective way to explain this is to compare a series of words related to the same central concept, e.g. 'human'. Such examples are:

motho (*person*)

batho (*people*)

setho (*humanely*)

botho (*humanity*)

mothofatša (*humanise*)

mothonyana (*insignificant person*)

Here the part of the words that conveys the reference to 'person' is **-tho-** and this is thus the root of each word. The additional elements, prefixes and suffixes added before or after the root, extend the scope of the root.

The following word categories exist in Northern Sotho: nouns, pronouns, verbs, demonstrative-copulatives, adverbs, particles, conjunctions, ideophones, interjections. These are classified into the following main and sub-categories, depending on their morphological, syntactical, semantic and phonological similarities:

Substantives: nouns and pronouns

Predicatives: verbs and demonstrative-copulatives

Morphologically heterogeneous words: adverbs, particles, conjunctions

Plus the following two that do not follow the normal form of Northern Sotho words:

Ideophones

Interjections

NOUNS

The main principles on which Northern Sotho is based are:
The system of noun classes; and
The system of concords.

With some exceptions, nouns in Northern Sotho are composed of two parts in their basic form, viz. the prefix and the root:

motho: mo- + **-tho** (*person*)

The noun may also be composed of a class prefix plus a stem. The stem includes a root plus one or more suffixes, e.g.:

morwalo: mo- + **-rwal-** + **-ô** (*a load*)

morwalelo: mo- + **-rwal-** + **-êl-** + **-ô** (*a flood*)

Noun prefixes have three major functions:
They are used to distinguish between different classes of nouns;
They are used to distinguish between singular and plural; and
They determine the form of the corresponding pronouns and qualificative and predicative concords.

Because of the different noun prefixes, all nouns in Northern Sotho are grouped into the following 17 classes:

In most of the examples given, the prefix of one class indicates the singular and the prefix of the following class the plural. For class 14 this is not the case: it makes use of the prefix of class 6 in the plural. The prefix of class 15 is detached from the stem but this does not mean it is not a prefix, just like those of the other classes. Nouns in classes 16, 17 and 18 are locative (expressing whereabouts) and do not indicate singular or plural. And finally, the class prefix of class 9 is present only in monosyllabic stems.

The prefixes of the noun classes determine the form of the corresponding qualificative and predicative concords as well as the form of the pronouns. Thus

bôna: ba- + **-ô-** + **-na** (*they*)

where the **ba-** functions as a concordial prefix in the construction of the absolute pronoun **bôna**, referring to a noun from class 2, e.g.:

Banna ba a ja (*The men are eating*)

Bôna ba a ja (*They are eating*)

Class	Prefix	Northern Sotho	English equivalent
1	**mo-**	**motho**	*person*
2	**ba-**	**batho**	*people*
1a	**-**	**malome**	*uncle (maternal)*
1b	**bo-**	**bomalome**	*uncles (uncle and company)*
3	**mo-**	**molomo**	*mouth*
4	**me-**	**melomo**	*mouths*
5	**le-**	**lerumo**	*spear*
6	**ma-**	**marumo**	*spears*
7	**se-**	**selêpe**	*axe*
8	**di-**	**dilepe**	*axes*
9	**N-**	**ntwa**	*war*
10	**diN-**	**dintwa**	*wars*
14	**bo-**	**bogobe**	*porridge*
15	**go-**	**go bona**	*seeing*
16	**fa-**	**fase**	*on the ground*
17	**go-**	**godimo**	*on top of*
18	**mo-**	**morago**	*behind*

THE PREDICATIVE

The predicative is a word which expresses the action performed by the substantive (noun or pronoun) or describes some aspect pertaining to it.

For example:

The child **drinks** water; or

The cattle, **there they are**

There are two types of predicative words:

Verbs, which include mostly verbal roots that are intrinsically predicative in force, plus one or more verbal prefixes and suffixes, as in

Ngwana o nwa meetsi (*The child drinks water*)

Demonstrative-copulatives, which consist of a root together with a morpheme (small sections of words) and a suffix with a pronominal (demonstrative) meaning, which must agree concordially. For example:

Dikgomo šidio! (*The cattle, there they are!*)

The verbal root is the most important part of the verb. It is the part of the verb around which the other verbal elements are arranged. If we look at the sentence

Monna o a thuša (*The man helps*)

we see that the **o-** can be replaced with **ba-** without changing the intrinsic meaning of 'help'. The **-a-** can also be replaced, for instance with **-tla-** without changing the intrinsic meaning. The sentence now becomes

Ba tla thuša (*They will help*)

The ending **-thusa** (-a) can also be changed, for instance to **ga ba thuše** (*they do not help*) without changing the intrinsic meaning of 'help'. However, as soon as one replaces **-thuš-**, the verb loses its meaning. Thus **-thuš-** is the verbal root.

In the word list given in this book, the Northern Sotho equivalents of the English verbs are verbal stems and not fully fledged verbs, e.g.:

-sepela (*go/walk*)

Users of the word list should bear in mind that a verbal stem can be used only with its concord(s) in actual speech, unless when used as an imperative:

Batho ba a sepela (*The people go/walk*)

Sepela! (*Go!*)

The subject must be represented in the verb by a subjectival concord, e.g.:

Monna o a ja (*The man is eating*)

O a ja (*He is eating*)

This concord is in most cases identical to the class prefix of the noun, except when a nasal sound appears in a class prefix and the nasal sound is dropped, e.g.:

Banna ba a ja (*The men are eating*)

Selêpê se a rema (*The axe is chopping*)

but

Motse o a tuka (*The village is burning*)

Verbal forms are morphologically, semantically and syntactically complicated by sub-categories of the verb known as mood, tense and actually. These cannot be dealt with here due to limited space.

CONCORDS

The first and second person subject concords (I/we and you/you) are:

1st person singular (I): **-ke-** as in **Nna ke a ja** (*I am eating*)

1st person plural (we): **-re-** as in **Rena re a ja** (*We are eating*)

2nd person singular (you): **-o-** as in **Wena o a ja** (*You are eating*)

2nd person plural (you): **-le-** as in **Lena le a ja** (*You are eating*)

The object may also be represented in the verb by means of an object concord, for example:

Monna o ja nama (*The man is eating meat*)

can be represented as

Monna o a e ja (*The man eats it*)

The objectival concord is identical in form with the subjectival concord except for class 1 nouns where it is **mo**, for example:

Re thusa monna (*We help/are helping the man*)

Re a mo thusa (*We help/are helping him*)

The object concords for the first and second person are:

1st person singular (me): **-N-** as in **E a ntoma** (*It is biting me*)

1st person plural (us): **-re-** as in **Ba a re bona** (*They are seeing us*)

2nd person singular (you): **-go-** as in **Ke a go bona** (*I am seeing you*)

2nd person plural (you): **-le-** as in **Re a le bona** (*We are seeing you*)

The object concord is usually used when the object is known and is not repeated after the predicate, for example:

Monna o ja nama (*The man eats meat*)

Monna o a e ja (*The man eats it*)

However, when the object is present in a sentence and its object concord is also used in the predicate, the object is emphasised, for example:

Ke bitša lesogana (*I am calling the young man*)

Ke e le bitša, lesogana (*I am calling him, the young man*)

THE COPULATIVE WORD GROUP

Copulatives reflect a relationship of 'to be' between a subject and the complement. Thus, copulatives consist of the

1. Copula: the verb that identifies the predicate with the subject, for example: The man **is** a preacher; followed by the

2. Complement: the word or words used after the copula to complete a predicate construction, for example

The man is a **preacher**.

The nature of the expressed relationship between the subject and the complement gives rise to identifying, descriptive and associative copulatives, for example:

Identifying: Monna (subject) **ke** (copula) **moruti** (complement) (*The man is a preacher*)

Descriptive: Selêpê (subject) **se** (copula) **bogale** (complement) (*The axe is sharp*)

Associative: Mosadi (subject) **o na le** (copula) **bana** (complement) (*The woman has children*)

Although the copula conveys a verbal meaning (to be) it cannot be treated as a verb because all copulas are not verbs. However, as in the case of verbs, the form and meaning of the copula is influenced by mood, tense and actuality.

N Sotho	English	Afrikaans	N Sotho	English	Afrikaans
-abaganya	distribute (v)	versprei	asma	asthma (n)	asma
-abela	share (v)	deel	astrolotši	astrology (n)	astrologie
-abela	confer (v)	toeken	atemosfere	atmosphere (n)	atmosfeer
-abela	allocate (v)	toewys	-atetšwego ke ditalente	talented (a)	talentvol
abokato	avocado pear (n)	avokadopeer	-atilego	plenty (a)	volop
-abula	crawl (v)	kruip	-atilego	plentiful (a)	talryk
-adima	borrow (v)	leen	-atiša	multiply (v)	vermenigvuldig
-adima	lend (v)	leen	-atla	kiss (v)	soen
-aena	iron (v)	stryk	atlase	atlas (n)	atlas
aesekherimi	ice cream (n)	roomys	-atlega	succeed (v)	slaag
-Afrika	African (a)	Afrika	-atlega	prosper (v)	floreer
-aga	erect (v)	oprig	-atlegilego	prosperous (a)	florerend
-aga	build (v)	bou	atrese	address (n)	adres
agente	lawyer (n)	prokureur			
Agostos	August (n)	Augustus	-ba	be (v)	wees
-ahlaahla	discuss (v)	bespreek	-ba-	them (pron)	hulle
-ahlola	condemn (v)	veroordeel	baagi	population (n)	bevolking
-ahlola	convict (v)	skuldig bevind	-babago	bitter (a)	bitter
-ahlola	judge (v)	oordeel	-babola	scald (v)	skroei
-akanya	consider (v)	oorweeg	-babola	singe (v)	skroei
-akanya	guess (v)	raai	-babola	scorch (v)	skroei
-akanya	ponder (v)	bepeins	badiidi	poor (n)	armes
-akaretša	include (v)	insluit	-badimo	ancestral (a)	voorvaderlik
-akaretša	enclose (v)	insluit	bafsa	youth (n)	jeug
-akaretšago	inclusive (a)	inklusief	-baka	cause (v)	veroorsaak
-akaretšago	general (a)	algemeen	baki	jacket (n)	baadjie
aketemi	academy (n)	akademie	-bala	read (v)	lees
-alafa	heal (v)	genees	-bala	calculate (v)	reken
-alafa	treat (v)	behandel	-bala	count (v)	tel
-alama	brood (v)	broei	balate	ballad (n)	ballade
alfabete	alphabet (n)	alfabet	-bapala	play (v)	speel
altare	altar (n)	altaar	-bapiša	compare (v)	vergelyk
-ama	involve (v)	betrek	-bapola	crucify (v)	kruisig
-ama	affect (v)	raak	-bataganego	adjacent (a)	aangrensend
-amantšha	adapt (v)	aanpas	batho	people (n)	mense
-amoga	confiscate (v)	beslag lê op	batho	public (n)	publiek
-amoga	deprive (v)	ontneem	batimamollo	fire brigade (n)	brandweer
-amogela	adopt (v)	aanneem	-be	bad (a)	sleg
-amogela	receive (v)	ontvang	-be	evil (a)	boos
-amogela	accept (v)	aanvaar	-be	ghastly (a)	aaklig
-amogela ka lethabo	welcome (v)	verwelkom	-be	mean (a)	gemeen
-amogelega	acceptable (a)	aanvaarbaar	-be	nasty (a)	gemeen
-anegela	account (v)	rekenskap gee	-be	obscene (a)	onbetaamlik
-anegela	narrate (v)	vertel	-be	ugly (a)	lelik
-apara	wear (v)	dra	-bea	appoint (v)	aanstel
-apara	dress (v)	aantrek	-bea fase	put (v)	sit
-apara	clothe (v)	aantrek	-beakanya	organise (v)	reël
-apea	cook (v)	kook	-bea mellwane	border (v)	grens
apola	apple (n)	appel	-bea molato	blame (v)	blameer
-apola	strip (v)	ontbloot	-bediša	brew (v)	brou
-apola	undress (v)	uittrek	-beela mae	spawn (v)	uitbroei
apolekose	apricot (n)	appelkoos	-beela mellwane	restrict (v)	inperk
Aprele	April (n)	April	-beelana	bet (v)	wed
-araba	respond (v)	respondeer	-beeletša	reserve (v)	reserveer
-araba	reply (v)	antwoord gee	-beeletša	deposit (v)	deponeer
-araba	answer (v)	antwoord	-befediša	anger (v)	kwaad maak
arapei	strawberry (n)	aarbei	-befetšwego	angry (a)	kwaad
arena	arena (n)	arena	-bega	declare (v)	verklaar
-aroganego	separate (a)	afsonderlik	-bega	accuse (v)	beskuldig
ase	axle (n)	as	-bega	charge (law) (v)	aankla

B	N Sotho	English	Afrikaans		N Sotho	English	Afrikaans
	-bega	report (v)	berig		bobopapitša	pottery (n)	pottebakkery
	-bega	state (v)	vermeld		bobui	surgery (n)	chirurgie
	-beila	bail (v)	borg staan		bodiidi	poverty (n)	armoede
	beine	wine (n)	wyn		-bodikela	western (a)	westelik
	-beke	weekly (a)	weekliks		bodikela	west (n)	weste
	beke	week (n)	week		bodikela	west (adv)	wes
	bekepedi	fortnight (n)	twee weke		-bodila	acid (a)	suur
	-bela	boil (v)	kook		-bodila	sour (a)	suur
	-bela	ferment (v)	gis		-bodilwego	rotten (a)	verrot
	-belaela	doubt (v)	twyfel		-boditšhaba	multiracial (a)	veelrassig
	-belaela	worry (v)	bekommer		boditsi	bristle (n)	steekhaar
	-belaelago	anxious (a)	bekommerd		bodulelo	lounge (n)	sitkamer
	-belaetšago	uncertain (a)	onseker		bodulo	abode (n)	woonplek
	-belaetšago	ambiguous (a)	dubbelsinnig		bodulo	dwelling (n)	woning
	belefe	valve (n)	klep		bodulo	seat (n)	sitplek
	bene	panel van (n)	paneelwa		bodumedi	religion (n)	godsdiens
	-benyabenya	flicker (v)	flikker		-bodumedi	religious (a)	godsdienstig
	-benyabenya	sparkle (v)	vonkel		bodutu	loneliness (n)	eensaamheid
	-beola	shave (v)	skeer		-boelela godimo	aloud (adv)	hardop
	bere	bear (n)	beer		-boeletša	repeat (v)	herhaal
	-beša	grill (v)	rooster		-boelwa	profit (v)	wins maak
	-beša	roast (v)	oondbraai		boemakepe	harbour (n)	hawe
	-bethabetha	tick (v)	tik		boemapese	bus stop (n)	bushalte
	-betla	sculpt (v)	beeldhou		boemelafofane	airport (n)	lughawe
	-betša	cast (v)	werp		boemo	condition (n)	toestand
	-betša	throw (v)	gooi		boepi	treason (n)	verraad
	-betwa	choke (v)	verstik		-bofa	chain (v)	vasketting
	Bibele	Bible (n)	Bybel		-bofa	tie (v)	bind
	-biletša	dictate (v)	voorskrywe		-bofa ka sepalete	pin (v)	vasspeld
	bilhazia	bilharzia (n)	bilharzia		bofase	bottom (n)	bodem
	-bina	dance (v)	dans		-bofefo	light (a)	lig
	binika	vinegar (n)	asyn		bofelo	end (n)	einde
	-bipetšwego	flatulent (a)	winderig		bofokodi	weakness (n)	swakheid
	bisa	visa (n)	visum		-bofolla	undo (v)	losmaak
	-bitša	call (v)	roep		bofora	fraud (n)	bedrog
	-bitša	charge (price) (v)	vra		bofora	deceit (n)	bedrog
	-bitša	convene (v)	byeenroep		bofora	dishonesty (n)	oneerlikheid
	-bitša	summon (v)	ontbied		bofora	trick (n)	skelmstreek
	-bjala	plant (v)	plant		-bofora	fake (a)	vals
	bjale	now (adv)	nou		-bofora	false (a)	vals
	-bjalo	such (a)	sulke		bofsa	adolescence (n)	adolessensie
	bjalo ka	like (prep)	soos		bofsa	puberty (n)	puberteit
	bjalwa	beer (n)	bier		bofšega	cowardice (n)	lafhartigheid
	bjana	childhood (n)	kinderjare		bogafa	insanity (n)	kranksinnigheid
	bjang	grass (n)	gras		-bogale	acute (a)	skerp
	bjang	how (adv)	hoe		bogale	blade (n)	blad
	bjang bja go rulela	thatch (n)	dekgras		bogale	bravery (n)	dapperheid
	bjang le bjang	anyhow (adv)	hoe dan ook		-bogale	sharp (a)	skerp
	bjoko	brain (n)	brein		bogare	centre (n)	middel
	-boa	return (v)	terugkeer		bogare	centre (n)	middel
	-boahlodi	judicial (a)	regterlik		bogato bja sala	stirrup (n)	stiebeuel
	bobe	malice (n)	boosaardigheid		bogatšu	cramp (n)	kramp
	bobe	obscenity (n)	onbetaamlikheid		bogatšu	spasm (n)	spasma
	bobedi	both (a)	albei		-bogegago	handsome (a)	aantreklik
	bobedi	double (n)	dubbel		-bogela	view (v)	bekyk
	bobedi	pair (n)	paar		bogobe	porridge (n)	pap
	-bobedi	second (a)	tweede		bogodimo	height (n)	hoogte
	bobi	cobweb (n)	spinnerak		bogogedi	magnetism (n)	magnetisme
	-bobola	mutter (v)	mompel		-bogola	bark (v)	blaf
	bobolokelo bja dijo	pantry (n)	spens		bogolo	adulthood (n)	volwassenheid

N Sotho	English	Afrikaans	N Sotho	English	Afrikaans	B
bogolo	age (n)	ouderdom	boitemogo	consciousness (n)	bewussyn	
bogolo	size (n)	grootte	boithekgo	background (n)	agtergrond	
bogomapono	horizon (n)	horison	boithomelo	lavatory (n)	toilet	
bogwera	friendship (n)	vriendskap	boithomelo	toilet (n)	toilet	
bogwerano	loyalty (n)	lojaliteit	boitiša	hobby (n)	stokperdjie	
-boheitene	pagan (a)	heidens	boitokišetšo	preparation (n)	voorbereiding	
bohlabanelo	battlefield (n)	slagveld	boitshepo	self-confidence (n)	selfvertroue	
-bohlabani	military (a)	militêre	boitšhupo	identity (n)	identiteit	
-bohlabela	eastern (a)	oostelik	boitshwaro	etiquette (n)	etiket	
Bohlabela	east (n)	ooste	boitshwaro	behaviour (n)	gedrag	
bohlabela	east (adv)	oos	boitshwaro	attitude (n)	houding	
bohlabelo	abattoir (n)	slagplaas	bojelo	dining room (n)	eetkamer	
-bohlale	intelligent (a)	intelligent	bokaakang	quantity (n)	hoeveelheid	
bohlale	intelligence (n)	intelligensie	bokagare	lining (n)	voering	
-bohlale	sane (a)	verstandig	bokamoso	future (n)	toekoms	
-bohlale	wise (a)	wys	bokateng	interior (n)	binneste	
bohlale	wisdom (n)	wysheid	bokgabo	art (n)	kuns	
bohlanka	bondage (n)	knegskap	bokgahlo	freezing point (n)	vriespunt	
bohlapelo	bathroom (n)	badkamer	bokgoba	slavery (n)	slawerny	
bohlatse	proof (n)	bewys	bokgobapuku	library (n)	biblioteek	
bohlatse	evidence (n)	getuienis	bokgole	distance (n)	afstand	
bohlatse	testimony (n)	getuienis	bokgoni	ability (n)	bekwaamheid	
bohlatswetšo	laundry (n)	wassery	bokgoni	efficiency (n)	doeltreffendheid	
bohle	all (beings) (pron)	almal	bokgonthe	essence (n)	essensie	
bohloko	ache (n)	pyn	-bola	decay (v)	verrot	
bohloko	pain (n)	pyn	-bola	decompose (v)	ontbind	
-bohloko	sore (a)	seer	-bola	perish (v)	omkom	
bohloko	venom (n)	venyn	-bola	rot (v)	verrot	
bohloko bja ditsebe	earache (n)	oorpyn	bolalelo	ambush (n)	hinderlaag	
-bohlokwa	costly (a)	kosbaar	bolao	bed (n)	bed	
-bohlokwa	grave (a)	gewigtig	-bolawa ke tlala	starve (v)	honger ly	
-bohlokwa	important (a)	belangrik	-bolaya	execute (v)	teregstel	
-bohlokwa	precious (a)	kosbaar	-bolaya	kill (v)	doodmaak	
-bohlokwa	prominent (a)	prominent	-bolaya	murder (v)	vermoor	
-bohlokwa	rare (a)	seldsaam	-boledišana	chat (v)	gesels	
-bohlokwa	valuable (a)	waardevol	-bolela	speak (v)	praat	
bohubedu bja madi	scarlet (n)	helderrooi	-bolela	talk (v)	praat	
bohwa	heritage (n)	erfenis	-bolelago kudu	talkative (a)	spraaksaam	
-boifa	afraid (a)	bang	-bolela le	address (v)	toespreek	
-boifa	fear (v)	vrees	-bolela maaka	lie (v)	lieg	
-boifa	dread (v)	vrees	bolemi	agriculture (n)	landbou	
-boifago	apprehensive (a)	bang	boleng	existence (n)	bestaan	
-boiketlo	comfortable (a)	gemaklik	-boleta	soft (a)	sag	
boikgakantšho	pretence (n)	skyn	bolkano	volcano (n)	vulkaan	
boikgakantšho	pretext (n)	voorwendsel	-boloi	magical (a)	magies	
boikgogomošo	pride (n)	trots	boloi	magic (n)	towerkuns	
boikokobetšo	humility (n)	nederigheid	boloi	witchcraft (n)	toorkuns	
boima	weight (n)	gewig	-boloka	bury (v)	begrawe	
-boima	hard (a)	moeilik	-boloka	conserve (v)	bewaar	
-boima	heavy (a)	swaar	-boloka	preserve (v)	bewaar	
boineelo	surrender (n)	oorgawe	-boloka	spare (v)	spaar	
boiphedišo	welfare (n)	welsyn	-boloka	store (v)	bêre	
boiphemelo	safety (n)	veiligheid	-boloka	uphold (v)	hoog hou	
boipiletšo	appeal (n)	beroep	-bolokago	conservative (a)	konserwatief	
boipobolo	confession (n)	belydenis	boloko	membership (n)	lidmaatskap	
boipolao	suicide (n)	selfmoord	-bolotša	circumcise (v)	besny	
boitapišo	trouble (n)	moeite	bolotšana	plot (n)	komplot	
boitatolo	alibi (n)	alibi	bolumo	volume (n)	volume	
boitekelo	experiment (n)	proefneming	bolwetši	disease (n)	siekte	
boitemogelo	experience (n)	ervaring	bolwetši	illness (n)	siekte	

B

N Sotho	English	Afrikaans
bolwetši	sickness (n)	siekte
bolwetši bja kankere	cancer (n)	kanker
bolwetši bja mafahla	tuberculosis (n)	tuberkulose
-bona	approach (v)	benader
-bona	conceive (v)	opvat
-bona	see (v)	sien
-bona	their (pron)	hulle
-bona	theirs (pron)	hulle s'n
bona	they (pron)	hulle
-bonagala	seem (v)	skyn
-bonagalago	clear (a)	helder
-bonagalago	conspicuous (a)	opvallend
-bonagalago	visible (a)	sigbaar
-bonagatša	reveal (v)	openbaar
-bonagatšago	transparent (a)	deurskynend
-bonegela	illuminate (v)	verlig
bonepanaledi	astronomy (n)	sterrekunde
bong	gender (n)	geslag
-bongaka	medical (a)	medies
bonkane	companionship (n)	kameraadskap
bonna	manhood (n)	manlikheid
bonnyane	bit (n)	bietjie
-bonolo	simple (a)	eenvoudig
bonolo	easy (a)	maklik
-bonolo	gentle (a)	sagmoedig
-bontšha	exhibit (v)	uitstal
-bontšha	show (v)	wys
bontšhi	plural (n)	meervoud
bontši	abundance (n)	oorvloed
bonyelele	rheumatism (n)	rumatiek
-bonyelele	rheumatic (a)	rumaties
-boomo	deliberate (a)	opsetlik
-bootswa	immoral (a)	onsedelik
bootswa	adultery (n)	owerspel
-bopa	create (v)	skep
-bopa	form (v)	vorm
-bopa	growl (v)	knor
-bopa	mould (v)	vorm
bopelotelele	patience (n)	geduld
-bopelotelele	patient (a)	geduldig
bophara	breadth (n)	breedte
bophelo	life (n)	lewe
bophelolešokeng	wildlife (n)	natuurlewe
-bopilwe ka	consist (v)	bestaan
bora	bow (n)	boog van voet
borabela	rebellion (n)	opstand
boraoto	instep (n)	boog van voet
-boraro	third (a)	derde
borategi	charm (n)	sjarme
-boreledi	slippery (a)	glibberig
-boreledi	smooth (a)	glad
borobalelo	bedroom (n)	slaapkamer
borofa	paw (n)	poot
borokgo bjo botelele	trousers (n)	langbroek
boroko	sleep (n)	slaap
boroso	sausage (n)	wors
borotho	bread (n)	brood
borotho	loaf (n)	brood
borotlolo	carrot (n)	wortel
boruthelo	swimming pool (n)	swembad

N Sotho	English	Afrikaans
-borutho	hot (a)	warm
-borutho	warm (a)	warm
-boruthwana	tepid (a)	lou
-borwa	south (a)	suid
borwa	south (n)	suide
-borwa	southern (a)	suidelik
bošaedi	mess (n)	gemors
-bošaedi	untidy (a)	slordig
bosafeleng	eternity (n)	ewigheid
-bose	delicious (a)	heerlik
-bose	nice (a)	aangenaam
-bose	savoury (a)	smaaklik
-bose	sweet (a)	soet
bosea	infancy (n)	kleintyd
bošego	night (n)	nag
bošegogare	midnight (n)	middernag
bosehlogo	notoriety (n)	berugtheid
bosetšhaba	nationalism (n)	nasionalisme
boso	weather (n)	weer
bošoro	cruelty (n)	wreedheid
bošoro	violence (n)	geweld
bošula	vice (n)	ondeug
botala bja leratadima	blue (a)	blou
botebo	depth (n)	diepte
-botee	unanimous (a)	eenstemmig
botee	unit (n)	eenheid
botee	unity (n)	eenheid
-botegago	faithful (a)	getrou
-botegago	loyal (a)	lojaal
-botegago	reliable (a)	betroubaar
-botegago	trustworthy (a)	betroubaar
botelele	length (n)	lengte
-bothakga	neat (a)	netjies
-bothakga	tidy (a)	netjies
bothata	difficulty (n)	moeilikheid
bothata	problem (n)	probleem
-botho	human (a)	menslik
-botho	humane (a)	mensliewend
-botho	kind (a)	goedhartig
botho	kindness (n)	goedheid
-botho	polite (a)	hoflik
bothotho	ignorance (n)	onkunde
botlaela	foolishness (n)	dwaasheid
botlalokgolo	maximum (n)	maksimum
botlalonyane	minimum (n)	minimum
-botse	beautiful (a)	pragtig
botse	beauty (n)	skoonheid
-botse	good (a)	goed
-botse	pretty (a)	mooi
-botsebi	technical (a)	tegnies
botšhabelo	asylum (n)	skuilplaas
botšhabelo	refuge (n)	skuiling
botshepegi	honesty (n)	eerlikheid
botšhošetši	terrorism (n)	terrorisme
-botšiša	question (v)	vra
-botšišiša	cross examine (v)	kruisvra
-botšišiša	interrogate (v)	ondervra
botšo	exit (n)	uitgang
botswadišakgomo	stud (n)	stoetery
botšwafi	laziness (n)	luiheid

43

N Sotho	English	Afrikaans	N Sotho	English	Afrikaans
botswalelo	birthplace (n)	geboorteplek	dimelameetseng	alga (n)	alg
bouto	vote (n)	stem	dingwalelo	stationery (n)	skryfbehoeftes
boya	fur (n)	pels	-dingwalo	literary (a)	letterkundig
boya	wool (n)	wol	dingwalo	literature (n)	letterkunde
boya bja lesaepoko	mohair (n)	sybokhaar	dinonwane	folklore (n)	volksoorleweringe
boyo	fate (n)	lot	dintwa tša matswele	boxing (n)	boks
-bua	operate (v)	opereer	diokobatši	drugs (n)	dwelms
-budulego	ripe (a)	ryp	dipaketsane	spectacles (n)	bril
-budulela	inflate (v)	opblaas	dipaketsane tša letšatši	sunglasses (n)	sonbril
-bula	open (v)	oopmaak	dipakteria	bacteria (n)	bakterie
-bulegilego	vacant (a)	vakant	diphahlo	goods (n)	goedere
-buša	dominate (v)	oorheers	diphedi	fauna (n)	fauna
-buša	govern (v)	regeer	dipheta	beadwork (n)	kraalwerk
-buna	harvest (v)	oes	dipolokelo	savings (n)	spaargeld
-buna	reap (v)	oes	dipompong	sweet (n)	lekker
-buša	reign (v)	heers	-dira	do (v)	doen
-buša	rule (v)	regeer	-dira	make (v)	maak
-buša moya	breathe (v)	asemhaal	-dira	work (v)	werk
-buša moya ka bothata	wheeze (v)	hyg	-dira boipiletšo	appeal (v)	beroep doen op
-bušetša tšhelete	refund (v)	terugbetaal	-diragala	happen (v)	gebeur
-butšwego	open (a)	oop	-diragala	occur (v)	voorkom
			-dira phošo	err (v)	fouteer
Desemere	December (n)	Desember	-dira pikiniki	picnic (v)	piekniek hou
diabelo	fractions (n)	breuke	-direla	serve (v)	dien
diabolo	devil (n)	duiwel	-dirile	done (v)	gedoen
diaparo	clothes (n)	klere	-diriša	use (v)	gebruik
diatletiki	athletics (n)	atletiek	-diriša	apply (v)	toepas
dibetša	ammunition (n)	ammunisie	-dirišana	co-operate (v)	saamwerk
dibetša	arms (n)	wapens	-dirišwago	engaged (a)	beset
dibjana	crockery (n)	breekware	diruiwa	cattle (n)	vee
-diegiša	delay (v)	vertraag	disemala	bran (n)	semels
difteria	diphtheria (n)	witseerkeel	ditaba	news (n)	nuus
-digela	recommend (v)	aanbeveel	ditaelo	banns (n)	gebooie
dihlong	disgrace (n)	skande	ditaetšo	directions (n)	aanwysings
dihlong	shame (n)	skaamte	diteng	contents (n)	inhoud
-dihlong	shy (a)	skugter	diterebe	grape (n)	druiwe
-dihlong	timid (a)	skugter	dithaka	tonsils (n)	mangels
dihwahwa	epilepsy (n)	vallende siekte	dithebola	loot (n)	buit
-diilago	poor (a)	arm	dithibelagolebele-lathoko	blinkers (n)	oogklappe
-diitša	impoverish (v)	verarm	dithipa	cutlery (n)	eetgerei
dijo	food (n)	kos	dithobollo	gymnastics (n)	gimnastiek
dijo	meal (n)	maal	dithobong	genitals (n)	geslagsorgane
dijo tša selalelo	supper (n)	aandete	ditiro	proceedings (n)	verrigtinge
-dika	surround (v)	omring	ditlabakelo tša boitlhweki	toiletries (n)	toiletware
-dikadika	hesitate (v)	aarsel	ditlhoka	straw (n)	strooi
dikateng	entrails (n)	ingewande	-ditšhaba	international (a)	internasionaal
dikauso	stockings (n)	kouse	ditshego	laugh (n)	lag
dikelfere	dandruff (n)	skilfers	ditshego	laughter (n)	gelag
dikgong	firewood (n)	brandhout	ditshenyegelo	expenses (n)	onkoste
dikgweng	bushveld (n)	bosveld	-ditšhila	messy (a)	morsig
dikhanakhana	chutney (n)	blatjang	-ditšhila	unhygienic (a)	onhigiënies
-dikologa	circulate (v)	rondgaan	ditšhipisi	chip (potato) (n)	skyfie
-dikologa	revolve (v)	draai	ditšhuaneng	orphanage (n)	weeshuis
-dikologa	turn (v)	draai	ditšiebadimo	nonsense (n)	onsin
-dikologa	wallow (v)	wentel	ditšwantle	import (n)	invoer
dikontwane	fits (n)	stuipe	ditšwarwamalaong	pyjamas (n)	pajamas
dikrosari	groceries (n)	kruideniersware	-duba	knead (v)	knie
-dikweletšego	dazed (a)	bedwelmd	-dula	sit (v)	sit
dimedi	flora (n)	flora			

D	N Sotho	English	Afrikaans		N Sotho	English	Afrikaans
	-dula ka go iketla	nestle (v)	nestel		e sego motho	nobody (pron)	niemand
	-duma	admire (v)	bewonder		esiti	acid (n)	suur
	-duma	desire (v)	begeer		-eta	tour (v)	rondreis
	-duma	envy (v)	beny		-eta	travel (v)	reis
	-dumago	eager (a)	gretig		-eta pele	lead (v)	lei
	-dumediša	greet (v)	groet		-eta pele	precede (v)	voorafgaan
	-dumediša	salute (v)	salueer		-etela	call (v)	besoek
	-dumela	acknowledge (v)	erken		-etela	visit (v)	besoek
	-dumela	believe (v)	glo		-ethimola	sneeze (v)	nies
	-dumela ka hlogo	nod (v)	knik		eupša	but (conj)	maar
	-dumelela	admit (v)	toelaat		eupša	however (conj)	maar
	-dumelela	allow (v)	toestaan				
	-dumelela	approve (v)	goedkeur		-fa	donate (v)	skenk
	-dumelela	authorise (v)	magtig		-fa	give (v)	gee
	-dumelela	permit (v)	toelaat		-fa	provide (v)	voorsien
	-dumeletšwego	lawful (a)	wettig		-fa	present (v)	skenk
	-dumeletšwego	legitimate (a)	wettige		faela	file (n)	leêr
	-dupa	smell (v)	ruik		-fagola	castrate (v)	kastreer
	-dutla	leak (v)	lek		faki	barrel (n)	vat
	-dutšego ka matsogo	idle (a)	ledig		-fala	scrape (v)	skraap
					-fa laesense	license (v)	lisensieer
	ebolusi	evolution (n)	evolusie		-falala	defect (v)	oorloop na
	-edimola	yawn (v)	gaap		-falala	emigrate (v)	emigreer
	eie	onion (n)	ui		-falala	immigrate (v)	immigreer
	-eka	betray (v)	verraai		-falala	overflow (v)	oorloop
	e ka bago	approximate (a)	geskat		-falatša	spill (v)	mors
	-ekiša	ape (v)	na-aap		-fa makhura	accelerate (v)	versnel
	-ekiša	imitate (v)	namaak		-fa marobalo	house (v)	huisves
	ekonomi	economy (n)	ekonomie		-fa marobalo	accommodate (v)	huisves
	eksrei	x-ray (n)	x-straal		-fa mohlodi	flavour (v)	geur
	-el-	for (prep)	vir		fantisi	auction (n)	veiling
	-ela	flow (v)	vloei		-fapafapanago	varied (a)	gevarieerd
	-elago	fluent (a)	vlot		-fapana	conflict (v)	bots
	-elago	liquid (a)	vloeibaar		-fapana	cross (v)	kruis
	-elehono	current (a)	huidige		-fapana	differ (v)	verskil
	elemente	element (n)	element		-fapana	disagree (v)	verskil
	-eletša	advise (v)	raad gee		-fapana	quarrel (v)	twis
	-eletšago	advisory (a)	raadgewend		-fapanago	else (adv)	anders
	-ema	stand (v)	staan		-fapanego	different (a)	verskillend
	-emego	stagnant (a)	stagnant		-fapanya	vary (v)	varieer
	-emego	stationary (a)	stilstaande		-fapoga	deviate (v)	afwyk
	-emela	back (v)	steun		faporiki	factory (n)	fabriek
	-emela	represent (v)	verteenwoordig		-fasana	lower (a)	laer
	-emelela	arise (v)	opstaan		fase	below (prep)	onder
	-emiša	halt (v)	stop		-fase	low (a)	laag
	-emiša	stop (v)	stop		fase	under (prep)	onder
	enema	enema (n)	enema		fase	down (prep)	af
	enfelopo	envelope (n)	koevert		-fe	which (pron)	watter
	-(e)ng	in (prep)	in		Feberware	February (n)	Februarie
	eng	what (pron)	wat		-fediša	abolish (v)	afskaf
	eng le eng	anything (pron)	enigiets		-fediša	destroy (v)	vernietig
	enke	ink (n)	ink		-fediša	devastate (v)	verwoes
	-enolla	perjure (v)	meineed pleeg		-fediša	exterminate (v)	uitroei
	-enta	vaccinate (v)	inent		feelwana	comma (n)	komma
	entšene	engine (n)	enjin		-fega	hang (v)	hang
	-epa	dig (v)	spit		-fega	suspend (v)	opskort
	-epolla	unearth (v)	opgrawe		-fegelwa	pant (v)	hyg
	erekisi	pea (n)	ertjie		-fegelwa	gasp (v)	snak
	eriele	aerial (n)	lugdraad		-fegelwago	breathless (a)	uitasem
	eriele	antenna (n)	lugdraad		-fe goba -fe	either (pron)	een van beide

N Sotho	English	Afrikaans	N Sotho	English	Afrikaans	**G**
feila	file (n)	vyl	-fola	convalesce (v)	aansterk	
feiye	fig (n)	vy	folaga	flag (n)	vlag	
-feka	copulate (v)	kopuleer	foleitši	mouth organ (n)	mondfluitjie	
fela	just (adv)	net	folene	flannel (n)	flanel	
fela	only (adv)	slegs	folouru	flour (n)	meel	
-fela	end (v)	eindig	-fora	cheat (v)	kul	
-fela	cease (v)	ophou	-fora	deceive (v)	bedrieg	
-felago pelo	impatient (a)	ongeduldig	-foraforetša	mislead (v)	mislei	
-felegetša	escort (v)	vergesel	-foraforetšago	misleading (a)	misleidend	
-felegetša	accompany (v)	begelei	foroko	fork (n)	vurk	
-feletšego	complete (a)	volledig	-foša	miss (v)	mis	
felo	place (n)	plek	-foša dithapo	switch (v)	oorskakel	
fenitšhara	furniture (n)	meubels	-fošagetšego	incorrect (a)	onjuis	
-fenya	conquer (v)	verower	-foša ka maswika	stone (v)	met klippe gooi	
-fenya	defeat (v)	verslaan	-foufetšego	blind (a)	blind	
-fenya	overcome (v)	te bowe kom	-fsa	young (a)	jong	
-fenya	overpower (v)	oorweldig	-fsa	new (a)	nuut	
-fenya	subdue (v)	onderwerp	-fsa	fresh (a)	vars	
-fenya	thrash (v)	uitklop	-fufula	fizz (v)	bruis	
-fenya	win (v)	wen	-fufulelwa	sweat (v)	sweet	
-fepa	feed (v)	voer	fulu	influenza (n)	griep	
ferekekere	binoculars (n)	verkyker	fulutu	pennywhistle (n)	kwêlafluitjie	
-feroša dibete	nauseate (v)	naar maak				
-ferošago dibete	repulsive (a)	walglik	-ga	scoop (v)	skep	
-feta	exceed (v)	oorskry	gabedi	double (a)	dubbele	
-feta	overtake (v)	verbysteek	gabedi	twice (n)	twee maal	
-feta	pass (v)	verbygaan	gabonolo	gently (adv)	saggies	
-fetelago	infectious (a)	besmetlik	gabotse	well (a)	goed	
-feteletša	exaggerate (v)	oordryf	-gadika	fry (v)	bak	
-fetetša	infect (v)	besmet	-gadima	glance (v)	vlugtig kyk	
-fetetša	spread (v)	versprei	-gae	local (a)	plaaslik	
-fetetšago	contagious (a)	aansteeklik	-gafago	mad (a)	gek	
-fetišago	ultimate (a)	uiterste	-gafago	insane (a)	kranksinnig	
-fetleka	analyse (v)	ontleed	-gago	your (pron)	jou	
-fetoga	change (v)	verander	-gago	yours (pron)	joune	
-fetolela	translate (v)	vertaal	-gagoga	rupture (v)	skeur	
-fetoša	revise (v)	wysig	-gagwe	hers (pron)	hare	
-fetša	complete (v)	voltooi	-gagwe	his (pron)	syne	
-fetša	finish (v)	klaarmaak	-gagwe	his (pron)	sy	
-fifetšego	dark (a)	donker	-gakantša	puzzle (v)	verwar	
-fihla	conceal (v)	verberg	-gakantšha	confuse (v)	verwar	
-fihlela	reach (v)	bereik	-galagala	echo (v)	weerklink	
-fihliša	deliver (v)	aflewer	galasanakaleihlong	contact lens (n)	kontaklens	
filete	fillet (n)	filet	galase	glass (n)	glas	
filimi	film (n)	film	galase ya lefasetere	pane (n)	ruit	
-filwego	gifted (a)	begaaf	-galefiša	infuriate (v)	woedend maak	
fiolo	violin (n)	viool	-galoga	fade (v)	verbleik	
fiuse	fuse (n)	sekering	-galogilego	pale (a)	bleek	
-fodilego	cool (a)	koel	gammogo	together (adv)	saam	
-fofa	fly (v)	vlieg	gampe	badly (adv)	sleg	
foiye	prickly pear (n)	turksvy	-gana	against (prep)	teen	
-foka	blow (v)	waai	-gana	decline (v)	afwys	
-fokoditšwego	less (a)	minder	-gana	object (v)	beswaar maak	
-fokolago	weak (a)	swak	-gana	refuse (v)	weier	
fokoletša	discount (v)	aftrek	-gana	reject (v)	verwerp	
-fokotša	reduce (v)	verminder	-gana go kwa	disobey (v)	ongehoorsaam wees	
-fokotša	decrease (v)	verminder	-ganetša	ban (people) (v)	inperk	
-fokotša	lessen (v)	verminder	-ganetša	ban (things) (v)	verbied	
-fola	sniff (v)	snuif	-ganetša	censor (v)	sensor	
-fola	cool (v)	afkoel	-ganetša	contradict (v)	weerspreek	

G	N Sotho	English	Afrikaans	N Sotho	English	Afrikaans
	-ganetša	oppose (v)	opponeer	-godiša	expand (v)	uitbrei
	-ganetša	prohibit (v)	verbied	-godiša	magnify (v)	vergroot
	-ganetša	resist (v)	weerstaan	-godiša	rear (v)	grootmaak
	-ganetšwago	banned (people) (a)	ingeperk	go dumela ka hlogo	nod (n)	knik
	-ganetšwago	banned (things) (a)	verbode	go dutla madi	haemorrhage (n)	bloeding
	gannyane	softly (adv)	saggies	go emiša magetla	shrug (n)	skouerophaling
	gantši	often (adv)	dikwels	-gofa	purge (v)	skoonmaak
	-ganwago ke molao	illegal (a)	onwettig	go fenywa	defeat (n)	nederlaag
	gape	again (adv)	weer	go feroga dibete	nausea (n)	naarheid
	gape	also (adv)	ook	-go feta fao	more (a)	meer
	-gapeletša	compel (v)	dwing	go fihlela	until (conj)	tot
	-gapeletša	enforce (v)	afdwing	-goga	drag (v)	sleep
	-gapeletša	force (v)	forseer	-goga	draw (v)	sleep
	garafo	spade (n)	graaf	-goga	pull (v)	trek
	garateine	curtain (n)	gordyn	-goga	tow (v)	sleep
	gare ga	amid (prep)	tussen	-gogela	attract (v)	aantrek
	gare ga	between (prep)	tussen	-gohla	grate (v)	rasper
	-gaša	broadcast (v)	uitsaai	-gohla	rub (v)	vryf
	-gaša	sow (v)	saai	-gohla	scour (v)	skuur
	gase	gas (n)	gas	-gohla	scrub (v)	skrop
	-gata	tread (v)	trap	-gohlola	cough (v)	hoes
	gatee	once (adv)	een maal	-go iketla	agreeable (a)	aangenaam
	-gatela pele	step (v)	trap	go kampa	camping (n)	kampering
	-gatelela	emphasise (v)	beklemtoon	-gokarela	embrace (v)	omhels
	-gatelela	oppress (v)	onderdruk	-goketša	lure (v)	aanlok
	-gateletšwego	express (a)	uitdruklik	-go kgethega	eligible (a)	geskik
	-gatiša	press (v)	pers	go kwa	obedience (n)	gehoorsaamheid
	-gatiša	print (v)	druk	-gola	earn (v)	verdien
	gauta	gold (n)	goud	go lapa mmele le moya	stress (n)	spanningsdruk
	ge	if (conj)	as	-golega	detain (v)	aanhou
	ge go se bjalo	otherwise (adv)	anders	-golega	jail (v)	opsluit
	-gerula	scowl (v)	suur kyk	-golo	big (a)	groot
	go-	to (prep)	na	-golo	capital (a)	hoof
	go	by (prep)	by	-golo	chief (a)	hoof
	-goa	exclaim (v)	uitroep	-golo	eldest (a)	oudste
	-goa	scream (v)	gil	-golo	large (a)	groot
	goba	either...or (conj)	òf...òf	-golo	main (a)	vernaamste
	goba	or (conj)	of	-golo	senior (a)	senior
	goba	whether (conj)	of	-golofatša	maim (v)	vermink
	go ba le diteme	lisp (n)	gelispel	go loga	knitting (n)	breiwerk
	go ba le diteme	lisp (v)	lispel	-gologolo	giant (a)	reuse
	-gobatša	wound (v)	wond	-gologolo	huge (a)	reusagtig
	-gobatša	hurt (v)	seermaak	-gologolo	paramount (a)	hoogste
	-gobatša	assault (v)	aanrand	-golo ka maatla	enormous (a)	tamaai
	go beela mellwane	restriction (n)	inperking	-golola	howl (v)	tjank
	go bina	dance (n)	dans	-golola	wail (v)	weeklaag
	go bolela gabotse	eloquence (n)	welsprekendheid	-gololago	liberal (a)	liberaal
	-goboša	insult (v)	beledig	-gomaretša	paste (v)	plak
	go dikwelela	daze (n)	bedwelming	-gomaretša	glue (v)	gom
	-godilego	adult (a)	volwasse	-gomaretša	stick (v)	vasplak
	-godilego	mature (a)	volwasse	-gona	exist (v)	bestaan
	-godimo	high (a)	hoog	gona	there (adv)	daar
	godimo	top (n)	top	go namela	ride (n)	rit
	godimo	up (prep)	op	gongwe le gongwe	anywhere (adv)	enige plek
	godimo ga	above (prep)	bo	-gonona	distrust (v)	wantrou
	godimo ga	extra (a)	ekstra	go nyala basadi ba bantši	polygamy (n)	poligamie
	godimo ga	on (prep)	op			
	godimo ga	over (prep)	oor	go opa	throb (n)	klopping
	-godingwana	higher (a)	hoër	go ora letšatši	tan (v)	bruin brand
	-godiša	enlarge (v)	vergroot	-gopola	recollect (v)	onthou

N Sotho	English	Afrikaans	N Sotho	English	Afrikaans	H
-gopola	remember (v)	onthou	-hlaga	spring (v)	spring	
-gopola	think (v)	dink	-hlaga	stem (v)	voortspruit	
-gopolela	suspect (v)	verdink	-hlagiša	express (v)	uitdruk	
-gopotša	remind (v)	herinner	-hlagiša	issue (v)	uitreik	
gore	that (pron)	dat	-hlagola	hoe (v)	skoffel	
go rea dihlapi	fishing (n)	visvang	-hlahlamolla	unravel (v)	ontrafel	
go rengwa ke hlogo	headache (n)	hoofpyn	-hlahloba	inspect (v)	inspekteer	
-goroga	arrive (v)	aankom	-hlahloba	examine (v)	ondersoek	
go rutha	swimming (n)	swem	-hlahuna	chew (v)	kou	
-gorutšwego	hollow (a)	hol	-hlala	divorce (v)	skei	
-go sa felego	everlasting (a)	ewigdurend	-hlaloša	explain (v)	verduidelik	
gosasa	tomorrow (n)	môre	-hlama	compose (v)	komponeer	
go sebaseba	whisper (n)	gefluister	-hlama	invent (v)	uitvind	
-go se be nakong	unpunctual (a)	nie stip nie	-hlano	five (n)	vyf	
-go se botege	unfaithful (a)	ontrou	-hlaola	identify (v)	identifiseer	
-go se gapeletšwe	voluntary (a)	vrywillig	-hlaotšwego	secluded (a)	afgesonderd	
go sego kae	seldom (adv)	selde	-hlapa	bath (v)	bad	
-go se iketle	uncomfortable (a)	ongemaklik	-hlapa	menstruate (v)	menstrueer	
go seketša	thrift (n)	spaarsaamheid	-hlapa	wash (v)	was	
go se kwe	disobedience (n)	ongehoorsaamheid	-hlaphola	dilute (v)	verdun	
go se kwišiše	misunderstanding (n)	misverstand	hlapi	fish (n)	vis	
-go se kwišišege	vague (a)	vaag	hlase	spark (n)	vonk	
-go se lebalege	unforgettable (a)	onvergeetlik	-hlasela	attack (v)	aanval	
-go se lefše	unrewarded (a)	onbeloond	-hlaselago	aggressive (a)	aanvallend	
-go se rate	unwilling (a)	onwillig	-hlaswa	detest (v)	verafsku	
-go se rutege	uneducated (a)	ongeleerd	-hlatholla	define (v)	bepaal	
-go se swarelege	unforgivable (a)	onvergeeflik	-hlatholla	interpret (v)	vertolk	
go taboga	jump (n)	sprong	-hlatlolana	alternate (v)	afwissel	
-gotetša	ignite (v)	aansteek	-hlatša	vomit (v)	vomeer	
go thunya	explosion (n)	ontploffing	-hlatsela	testify (v)	getuig	
go thunya ga leino	toothache (n)	tandpyn	hlatse ya leihlo	eyewitness (n)	ooggetuie	
go tloga	since (adv)	sedert	hleng	along (prep)	langs	
go tsena	entry (n)	binnekoms	hleng ga	beside (prep)	langs	
go tšhogatšhoga	nervousness (n)	senuweeagtigheid	hleng ga-	next to (prep)	langs	
go tšwa go	from (prep)	van	-hlobaelago	sleepless (a)	slapeloos	
go wa (ga bolwetši)	outbreak (n)	uitbreking	-hloboga	despair (n)	wanhoop	
-gwagwaladitšwego	stiff (a)	styf	-hlobogilego	desperate (a)	wanhopig	
-gwaša	rattle (v)	ratel	-hlobola	bare (v)	ontbloot	
-gweba	barter (v)	ruil	-hlobotšego	bare (a)	kaal	
-gweba	trade (v)	handel dryf	-hlobotšego	naked (a)	kaal	
-gwehla	beckon (v)	wink	hlodi	scout (n)	verkenner	
			hlodi	spy (n)	spioen	
-haka	hook (v)	haak	-hlodimela	peep (v)	loer	
hamola	hammer (n)	hamer	-hloga	sprout (v)	uitloop	
hampeka	hamburger (n)	hamburger	hlogo	head (n)	kop	
hanimunu	honeymoon (n)	wittebrood	hlogo	headline (n)	opskrif	
hareka	rake (n)	hark	hlogo	principal (n)	hoof	
-hareka	rake (v)	hark	-hlogola	weed (v)	onkruid uittrek	
harepa	harp (n)	harp	hlogwana	knob (n)	knop	
hele	hell (n)	hel	-hlohla	tease (v)	terg	
hempe	shirt (n)	hemp	-hlohla	dare (v)	uitdaag	
-hira	hire (v)	huur	-hlohla	challenge (v)	uitdaag	
-hira	rent (v)	huur	-hlohla	defy (v)	trotseer	
histori	history (n)	geskiedenis	-hlohleletša	excite (v)	opwind	
-hlaba	slaughter (v)	slag	-hlohleletša	urge (v)	aanspoor	
-hlaba	stab (v)	steek	-hlohlomiša	explore (v)	verken	
-hlabela	inject (v)	inspuit	-hlohlona	itch (v)	jeuk	
-hlabela	inoculate (v)	inent	-hloiwago	hateful (a)	haatlik	
-hlabišago dihlong	immodest (a)	onbeskeie	-hloka	need (v)	nodig hê	
-hlabologa	civilise (v)	beskaaf	hlokafetšego	late (a)	oorlede	

H	N Sotho	English	Afrikaans	N Sotho	English	Afrikaans
	-hlokafetšego	deceased (a)	oorlede	-hlwekilego	pure (a)	suiwer
	-hlokago	helpless (a)	hulpeloos	-hlwekiša	disinfect (v)	ontsmet
	-hlokago boitshwaro	undisciplined (a)	ongedissiplineerd	-hlwekiša	clean (v)	skoonmaak
	-hlokago botho	impersonal (a)	onpersoonlik	-hlwekiša	cleanse (v)	skoonmaak
	-hlokago botho	uncharitable (a)	onbarmhartig	-hlwekiša	purify (v)	suiwer
	-hlokago botho	unkind (a)	onvriendelik	-hlwekiša	sterilise (v)	steriliseer
	-hlokago katlego	unsuccessful (a)	onvoorspoedig	-hlwekišaoma	dryclean (v)	droogskoonmaak
	-hlokago kguagelo	unmerciful (a)	ongenadig	-hlwekišitšwego	sterile (a)	steriel
	-hlokago maemo	undignified (a)	onwaardig	ditwatši		
	-hlokago mekgwa	rude (a)	onbeskof	-hodišago	profitable (a)	lonend
	-hlokago mohlodi	tasteless (a)	smaakloos	-holago	beneficial (a)	voordelig
	-hlokago mohola	useless (a)	nutteloos	-holega	gain (v)	wen
	-hlokago molato	innocent (a)	onskuldig	holo	hall (n)	saal
	-hlokago mona	unselfish (a)	onselfsugtig	-holofela	hope (v)	hoop
	-hlokago mošomo	unemployed (a)	werkloos	-holofetša	promise (v)	belowe
	-hlokago moya	vacuum (n)	lugleegte	-homotša	comfort (v)	troos
	-hlokago setho	uncivilised (a)	onbeskaaf	-homotša	silence (v)	stilmaak
	-hlokago tlhabologo	undeveloped (a)	onontwikkeld	-homotšego	calm (a)	kalm
	-hlokago tlhompho	impolite (a)	onbeleef	-homotšego	quiet (a)	stil
	-hlokega	absent (a)	afwesig	hotele	hotel (n)	hotel
	-hlokofala	suffer (v)	ly	-hubedu	red (a)	rooi
	-hlokomela	beware (v)	oppas	-hudua	row (v)	roei
	-hlokomela	care (v)	omgee	-hudua	stir (v)	roer
	-hlokomela	heed (v)	in ag neem	-huduga	migrate (v)	migreer
	-hlokomela	mind (v)	omgee	-huduga	move (v)	trek
	-hlokomela	watch (v)	dophou	-huetša	exhale (v)	uitasem
	-hlokomelago	careful (a)	versigtig	-huetša	hiss (v)	sis
	-hlokomelago	considerate (a)	bedagsaam	huku ya go rea dihlapi	fish-hook (n)	vishoek
	-hlokomelago	observant (a)	oplettend	-hula	rob (v)	beroof
	-hlokomologa	disregard (v)	verontagsaam	-humana	obtain (v)	bekom
	-hlokomologa	ignore (v)	ignoreer	-humilego	rich (a)	ryk
	-hlokomologa	neglect (v)	verwaarloos	-humiša	enrich (v)	verryk
	-hlola	scout (v)	rondkyk	-huna	knot (v)	knoop
	-hlola	spy (v)	spioeneer	-hunyela	contract (v)	inkrimp
	-hlologela	long (v)	verlang	-hunyela	shrink (v)	krimp
	-hlologela	yearn (v)	hunker	-hupa	absorb (v)	absorbeer
	-hloma	suppose (v)	veronderstel	-hwa	die (v)	doodgaan
	-hloma	presume (v)	veronderstel	-hwetša	acquire (v)	aanskaf
	-hloma	establish (v)	vestig	-hwetša	find (v)	vind
	-hlompha	respect (v)	respekteer	-hwetša	get (v)	kry
	-hlompha	honour (v)	eer	-hwetšegago	available (a)	beskikbaar
	-hlomphegago	dignified (a)	waardig	-hwidinya	wag (v)	swaai
	-hlomphegago	eminent (a)	vooraanstaande	-hwilego	dead (a)	dood
	-hlomphegago	respectable (a)	fatsoenlik	-hwilego bogatšo	numb (a)	dood
	-hlonama	sulk (v)	dikmond wees			
	-hlonama	pout (v)	pruil	-i-	ourselves (pron)	onsself
	-hlonamago	sullen (a)	nors	i-	self (n)	self
	-hlopha	tabulate (v)	tabuleer	-idibala	faint (v)	flou word
	-hlopha	classify (v)	klassifiseer	-idibetšego	unconscious (a)	bewusteloos
	-hlopha	annoy (v)	vies maak	-ikemišeditše	adamant (a)	onwrikbaar
	-hlophago	annoying (a)	ergerlik	-ikemišeditše	aspire (v)	streef
	-hlophela	pile (v)	stapel	-ikemišetša	intend (v)	van plan wees
	-hlotla	percolate (v)	perkoleer	-ikgafa	devote (v)	toewy
	-hlotla	filter (v)	filtreer	-ikgakantšha	pretend (v)	voorgee
	-hlotša	cripple (v)	kreupel maak	-ikgodiša	boast (v)	spog
	-hlotša	limp (v)	mank loop	-ikgodiša	brag (v)	grootpraat
	-hloya	loathe (v)	verafsku	-ikgodišago	boastful (a)	spoggerig
	-hloya	hate (v)	haat	-ikgogomošago	conceited (a)	verwaand
	hlware	python (n)	luislang	-ikgogomošago	haughty (a)	hoogmoedig
	-hlwekilego	clean (a)	skoon	-ikgogomošago	proud (a)	trots

N Sotho	English	Afrikaans	N Sotho	English	Afrikaans	K
-ikokobetšago	humble (a)	nederig	Julae	July (n)	Julie	
-ikokobetšego	meek (a)	gedwee	June	June (n)	Junie	
-ila	abstain (v)	onthou	juri	jury (n)	jurie	
-ila	avoid (v)	vermy				
-ila	shun (v)	vermy	-ka-	may (v)	mag	
-ile le boroko	asleep (a)	aan die slaap	-ka	mine (pron)	myne	
-iletša	forbid (v)	verbied	-ka	own (a)	eie	
-iletša	restrain (v)	beperk	kabelo	portion (n)	gedeelte	
-imilego	pregnant (a)	swanger	kabelo	ration (n)	rantsoen	
-imolla	relieve (v)	verlig	kabelo	share (n)	deel	
-ina	soak (v)	week	kabinete	cabinet (n)	kabinet	
-inama	bow (v)	buk	ka boiketlo	effortless (a)	met gemak	
-inama	stoop (v)	buk	ka bokopana	briefly (adv)	kortliks	
-ineela	surrender (v)	oorgee	ka bonya	gradually (adv)	geleidelik	
-inela	immerse (v)	indompel	kadimo	loan (n)	lening	
-inela	submerge (v)	onderdompel	kae	where (adv)	waar	
infleišene	inflation (n)	inflasie	ka gare	inside (adv)	binne	
-intasteri	industrial (a)	industrieel	-ka gare	internal (a)	intern	
-ipobola	confess (v)	bely	ka gare	within (adv)	binne	
-ipshina	savour (v)	geniet	ka gare ga	aboard (adv)	aan boord	
-ipshina ka	enjoy (v)	geniet	kago	construction (n)	konstruksie	
-ipušago	independent (a)	onafhanklik	ka gobane	because (conj)	omdat	
iri	hour (n)	uur	ka go la nngele	left (n)	linkerkant	
-iša ntle	export (v)	uitvoer	ka go se tsebe	unknowingly (adv)	onwetend	
-itapiša	sacrifice (v)	opoffer	kahlaahlo	discussion (n)	bespreking	
-ithaopa	volunteer (v)	vrywillig onderneem	kahlolo	judgment (n)	oordeel	
-ithekga	lean (v)	leun	kahlolo	verdict (n)	uitspraak	
-ithekgilego ka	dependent (a)	afhanklik	kahlolo ye e fegilwego	suspended sentence (n)	opgeskorte vonnis	
-ithekgile ka	depend (on) (v)	afhang (van)	kakanyo	guess (n)	raaiskoot	
-ithuta	learn (v)	leer	kakaretšo	summary (n)	opsomming	
-ithuta	study (v)	studeer	ka kgonthe	indeed (adv)	werklik	
-itia	hit (v)	slaan	kaktuse	cactus (n)	kaktus	
-itia	whip (v)	raps	-kala	weigh (v)	weeg	
-itia ka matswele	box (v)	boks	kalafo	cure (n)	genesing	
-itlamolla	resign (v)	bedank	kalafo	treatment (n)	behandeling	
-itlhama ka dibetša	arm (v)	bewapen	kalaka ye tšhweu	whitewash (n)	witkalk	
-itokišeditšego	ready (a)	gereed	kalakune	turkey (n)	kalkoen	
-itšego	particular (a)	besonder	-kalatša	flirt (v)	flirteer	
-itšego	special (a)	spesiaal	ka lebaka lang	why (adv)	waarom	
-itshepago	confident (a)	vol vertroue	kalentara	calendar (n)	kalender	
-itshola	repent (v)	berou hê	-kama	comb (v)	kam	
-itshwara	behave (v)	jou gedra	kamano	relation (n)	verhouding	
-itshwara	conduct (v)	gedra	kamano	relationship (n)	verhouding	
			ka masa	early (a)	vroeg	
-ja	eat (v)	eet	ka maswabi	unfortunately (adv)	ongelukkig	
-ja	prey (v)	aas	ka mehla	always (adv)	gedurig	
-ja lefa	inherit (v)	erf	-ka mehla	common (a)	gewoon	
-ja letena	dine (v)	hoofmaaltyd eet	-ka mehla	ordinary (a)	gewoon	
-ja mokete	feast (v)	feesvier	-ka mehla	plain (a)	gewoon	
Janaware	January (n)	Januarie	ka mehla	usually (adv)	gewoonlik	
jarata	yard (n)	werf	kamela	camel (n)	kameel	
jase	coat (n)	jas	kamo	comb (n)	kam	
jase	overcoat (n)	oorjas	kamogelo	adoption (n)	aanneming	
jase ya pula	raincoat (n)	reënjas	kamogelo	acceptance (n)	aanvaarding	
jeli	jelly (n)	jellie	kamogelo	reception (n)	ontvangs	
jeresi	jersey (n)	trui	kamogelo	welcome (n)	welkom	
-ješa mpholo	poison (v)	vergiftig	ka moka	all (a)	alle	
Jesu	Jesus (n)	Jesus	ka moka	entire (a)	hele	
-jewago ke bodutu	lonely (a)	eensaam	ka morago	afterwards (adv)	agterna	
joko	yoke (n)	juk	kampa	camp (n)	kamp	

K

N Sotho	English	Afrikaans	N Sotho	English	Afrikaans
-kampa	camp (v)	kampeer	keletšo	advice (n)	raad
kampana	paddock (n)	veekampie	kelo	gauge (n)	meter
-ka/n-	my (pron)	my	kelo ya sehlare	dose (n)	dosis
kane	can (n)	kan	kemarišo ya	artificial	kunsmatige
kanegelo	story (n)	verhaal	maitirelo	insemination (n)	inseminasie
kanegelogopolwa	fiction (n)	fiksie	kemo	stand (n)	stand
ka ngwaga	annual (a)	jaarliks	kemola	pimple (n)	puisie
kano	oath (n)	eed	kenelwa	affidavit (n)	beëdigde verklaring
kanono	cannon (n)	kanon	keno	vow (n)	gelofte
kanta	lace (n)	kant	kenollo	perjury (n)	meineed
ka ntle	outside (n)	buitekant	kento	vaccination (n)	inenting
ka ntle	without (adv)	buite	kepi	crowbar (n)	koevoet
-ka ntle ga lenyalo	illegitimate (a)	buite-egtelik	kere	gear (n)	rat
ka ntle le	except (prep)	behalwe	kereke	church (n)	kerk
ka ntle le	besides (prep)	buiten	Keresemose	Christmas (n)	Kersfees
-kaonafatša	improve (v)	verbeter	ketane	chain (n)	ketting
kaonafatšo	improvement (n)	verbetering	ketapele	preface (n)	voorwoord
kaone	better (a)	beter	-keteka	celebrate (v)	vier
-ka pela	quick (a)	gou	ketelo	visit (n)	besoek
ka pela	quickly (adv)	gou	ketlele	kettle (n)	ketel
ka pela	soon (adv)	binnekort	-kga	pluck (v)	pluk
-ka pela	sudden (a)	skielik	-kgabiša	decorate (v)	versier
kapilari	capillary (n)	haarvat	kgabišo	decoration (n)	versiering
ka ponyo ya leihlo	instantly (adv)	oombliklik	kgabo	monkey (n)	aap
karabo	answer (n)	antwoord	kgabo	ape (n)	aap
karabo	reply (n)	antwoord	kgabo ya mollo	flame (n)	vlam
karata	card (n)	kaart	kgadimo	flash (n)	flits
karatakhodi	credit card (n)	kredietkaart	kgaetšedi	sister (n)	suster
karatšhe	garage (n)	motorhawe	-kgahla	congeal (v)	stol
kariki	cart (n)	kar	-kgahla	curdle (v)	klonter
karolo	fraction (n)	fraksie	-kgahla	freeze (v)	vries
karolo	section (n)	afdeling	-kgahla	interest (v)	interesseer
karolo	zone (n)	sone	kgahlego	interest (n)	belang
karolwana ya toropo	suburb (n)	voorstad	-kgahlišago	attractive (a)	aantreklik
-karolwana ya toropo	suburban (a)	voorstedelik	-kgahlišago	interesting (a)	interessant
ka sewelo	accidentally (adv)	toevallig	kgaka	guineafowl (n)	tarentaal
ka sewelo	unexpectedly (adv)	onverwags	-kgakgametša	gargle (v)	gorrel
kasteroli	castor oil (n)	kasterolie	-kgala	admonish (v)	vermaan
kastrolo	saucepan (n)	kastrol	kgalagalo	echo (n)	weerklank
-ka šuthišwago	moving (a)	roerend	kgalananko	nostril (n)	neusgat
-kata	rape (v)	verkrag	-kgale	ancient (a)	antiek
kataloko	catalogue (n)	katalogus	-kgale	stale (a)	oud
-katana	strive (v)	strewe	-kgama	strangle (v)	verwurg
katara	guitar (n)	kitaar	-kgama	throttle (v)	wurg
kathara	gutter (n)	geut	-kgamakgametša	stammer (v)	hakkel
ka thoko	aside (adv)	opsy	-kgamakgametša	stutter (v)	stotter
katlego	success (n)	sukses	kgamakgametšo	stammer (n)	gehakkel
ka tlhatlamanomehla	chronological (a)	chronologies	kgamakgametšo	stutter (n)	gestotter
katlo	kiss (n)	soen	kgamelo	bucket (n)	emmer
kato	rape (n)	verkragting	kgamelo	pail (n)	emmer
-katoga	withdraw (v)	terugtrek	kgamo	asphyxia (n)	versmoring
katogo	retreat (n)	terugtog	kganetšo	contradiction (n)	weerspreking
katsana	kitten (n)	katjie	kganetšo	opposition (n)	opposisie
katse	cat (n)	kat	kganetšo	resistance (n)	weerstand
ke	by (prep)	deur	kgang	argument (n)	argument
kedimolo	yawn (n)	gaap	kgang	insolence (n)	parmantigheid
kefa	hat (n)	hoed	-kgangwa ke meetse	drown (v)	verdrink
-kekago	inflamed (a)	ontsteek	kgano	rejection (n)	verwerping
keko	inflammation (n)	ontsteking	kganya	brilliance (n)	helderheid
kelapula	rain gauge (n)	reënmeter	-kganya	gleam (v)	straal

N Sotho	English	Afrikaans	N Sotho	English	Afrikaans	K
-kganya	shine (v)	skyn	-kgoba	heap (v)	ophoop	
-kganyago	bright (a)	helder	kgobalo	injury (n)	besering	
-kganyoga	wish (v)	wens	kgobatšo	assault (n)	aanranding	
kganyogo	lust (n)	wellus	-kgoboga	bruise (v)	kneus	
kganyogo	urge (n)	drang	kgobogo	bruise (n)	kneusplek	
kganyogo	wish (n)	wens	-kgobokana	gather (v)	byeenkom	
kganyogo ya dijo	appetite (n)	eetlus	-kgobokana	congregate (v)	vergader	
-kgaogana	part (v)	skei	-kgobokana	collect (v)	versamel	
-kgaola	amputate (v)	afsit	kgobokano	gathering (n)	byeenkoms	
kgaolo	chapter (n)	hoofstuk	kgobokano	assembly (n)	vergadering	
kgaotšo	interruption (n)	onderbreking	-kgobola	maul (v)	kneus	
kgapa	calabash (n)	kalbas	kgobošo	insult (n)	belediging	
kgapeletšo	compulsion (n)	dwang	kgobošo	slander (n)	laster	
kgapetlana	flake (n)	vlokkie	-kgodiša	convince (v)	oortuig	
kgapetla ya lee	eggshell (n)	eierdop	-kgodiša	persuade (v)	oorreed	
kgara	breastbone (n)	borsbeen	kgodišo	persuasion (n)	oorreding	
kgaširiri	sediment (n)	sediment	kgofa	tick (n)	luis	
kgatelelo	pressure (n)	druk	-kgoga	smoke (v)	rook	
kgatelelo	emphasis (n)	klem	kgogedi	magnet (n)	magneet	
kgatelelo	oppression (n)	onderdrukking	kgogelomorago ya	backwash (n)	terugspoeling	
kgatelelo ya madi	blood pressure (n)	bloeddruk	meetse			
-kgatha	gallop (v)	galop	kgogo	chicken (n)	hoender	
kgatišo	press (n)	pers	kgogo	fowl (n)	hoender	
kgatišo ya monwana	fingerprint (n)	vingerafdruk	kgogolego	erosion (n)	wegvreting	
kgato	degree (n)	graad	kgogotshadi	hen (n)	hen	
kgato	step (n)	tree	kgohlolo	cough (n)	hoes	
kgato	footstep (n)	voetstap	kgokarelo	embrace (n)	omhelsing	
kgatselo	frostbite (n)	vriesbrand	-kgokgofala	detribalise (v)	ontstam	
kgaugelo	mercy (n)	genade	kgokgoilane	ankle (n)	enkel	
-kgaugelo	merciful (a)	genadig	-kgokgona	protest (v)	protesteer	
kgauswi	near (adv)	naby	-kgokološa	roll (v)	rol	
kgauswi	close (a)	naby	kgole	far (adv)	ver	
-kgeba	belch (v)	wind opbreek	-kgole	remote (a)	afgeleë	
kgegeo	irony (n)	ironie	kgolego	jail (n)	tronk	
-kgeila	tear (v)	skeur	kgolego	prison (n)	gevangenis	
kgeke	prostitute (n)	prostituut	-kgomara	adhere (v)	kleef	
kgelogo	disloyalty (n)	dislojaliteit	-kgomarela	cling (v)	klou	
kgemo	bite (n)	hap	-kgomarelago	adhesive (a)	klewerig	
kgenkgerepe	crab (n)	krap	kgomogadi	cow (n)	koei	
-kgephola	peel (v)	skil	-kgona	able (a)	bekwaam	
-kgeretlanego	tattered (a)	toiingrig	-kgona	master (v)	bemeester	
-kgetha	choose (v)	kies	-kgonago	efficient (a)	doeltreffend	
-kgetha	elect (v)	verkies	-kgona go lefa	afford (v)	bekostig	
-kgetha	pick (v)	uitkies	-kgonegago	possible (a)	moontlik	
-kgetha	vote (v)	stem	kgonono	distrust (n)	wantroue	
-kgethela	prescribe (v)	voorskryf	kgonono	suspicion (n)	agterdog	
-kgethetšwego	prescribed (a)	voorgeskrewe	-kgonthe	sincere (a)	opreg	
kgetho	choice (n)	keuse	-kgonthiša	ascertain (v)	vasstel	
kgetho	election (n)	verkiesing	-kgonthiša	check (v)	nagaan	
-kgetholla	discriminate (v)	diskrimineer	-kgonthiša	ensure (v)	verseker	
-kgetholla	segregate (v)	segregeer	-kgonthišiša	prove (v)	bewys	
-kgethollago	racist (a)	rassisties	kgopa	shell (n)	skulp	
kgethollo	discrimination (n)	diskriminasie	kgopa	snail (n)	slak	
-kgethologanya	distinguish (v)	onderskei	-kgopamego	crooked (a)	krom	
-kgethologanyago	characteristic (a)	kenmerkend	kgopa ya lewatle	oyster (n)	oester	
-kgethologilego	distinct (a)	afsonderlik	kgope	bachelor (n)	jongkêrel	
-kgethwa	holy (a)	heilig	-kgopela	apply (v)	aansoek doen	
-kgethwa	sacred (a)	heilig	-kgopela	ask (v)	vra	
kgetlane	collarbone (n)	sleutelbeen	-kgopela	beg (v)	bedel	
-kgetloga	chip (v)	'n hap kry	-kgopela	request (v)	versoek	

K

N Sotho	English	Afrikaans
-kgopela keletšo	consult (v)	raadpleeg
-kgopela tshwarelo	apologise (v)	verskoning vra
kgopelo	application (n)	aansoek
kgopelo	request (n)	versoek
-kgopiša	offend (v)	aanstoot gee
-kgopišago	objectionable (a)	aanstootlik
-kgopišago	offensive (a)	aanstootlik
kgopo	rib (n)	rib
kgopolo	idea (n)	idee
kgopolo	thought (n)	gedagte
kgopolo	opinion (n)	mening
kgopotšo	reminder (n)	herinnering
-kgopša	trip (v)	struikel
kgoro	department (n)	departement
kgoro	court (n)	hof
kgorogo	arrival (n)	aankoms
-kgorometša	push (v)	stoot
kgoroto	champion (n)	kampioen
kgoro ya dikepe	navy (n)	vloot
kgorwana	colon (n)	dubbelpunt
kgošana	prince (n)	prins
kgoši	chief (n)	hoofman
kgoši	king (n)	koning
kgošigadi	queen (n)	koningin
kgošigatšana	princess (n)	prinses
kgotelo	ignition (n)	ontsteking
-kgothatša	console (v)	opbeur
kgotlakgolo	parliament (n)	parlement
kgotlakgolo	supreme court (n)	hooggeregshof
kgotla-o-mone	jam (n)	konfyt
-kgotlelela	persevere (v)	volhard
-kgotlelela	bear (v)	duld
kgotsofalo	contentment (n)	tevredenheid
kgotsofalo	satisfaction (n)	bevrediging
-kgotsofatša	appease (v)	bevredig
-kgotsofatša	satisfy (v)	bevredig
-kgotsofetšego	content (a)	tevrede
kgotswana	chop (n)	tjop
-kgwatha	touch (v)	raak
-kgwathegago maikutlo	sensitive (a)	gevoelig
kgwatho	touch (n)	aanraking
kgwebo	commerce (n)	handel
-kgwebo	commercial (a)	kommersieel
kgwebo	trade (n)	handel
kgwedi	month (n)	maand
kgwedi	moon (n)	maan
kgwekgwe	theme (n)	tema
kgwele	ball (n)	bal
kgwele ya go kgokološa	bowls (n)	rolbal
kgwele ya maoto	football (n)	voetbal
kgwele ya maoto	soccer (n)	sokker
kgwerano	pact (n)	verdrag
khabetšhe	cabbage (n)	kool
khaete	kite (n)	vlieër
-khahla	impress (v)	beïndruk
khaki	khaki (n)	kakie
khamera	camera (n)	kamera
khantlela	candle (n)	kers

N Sotho	English	Afrikaans
-khantshela	scrap (v)	skrap
khapoto	cupboard (n)	kas
kharabane	caravan (n)	karavaan
khatepoto	cardboard (n)	karton
khefi	café (n)	kafee
khemišo	artificial respiration (n)	kunsmatige asemhaling
khemo	respiration (n)	asemhaling
kheše	cash (n)	kontant
khiipoto	keyboard (n)	klawerbord
khitšhi	kitchen (n)	kombuis
khodi	credit (n)	krediet
kholetšhe	college (n)	kollege
kholifolawa	cauliflower (n)	blomkool
kholofelo	hope (n)	hoop
kholofetšo	promise (n)	belofte
kholoro	collar (n)	kraag
khomotšo	comfort (n)	troos
khonkriti	concrete (n)	beton
khonsata	concert (n)	konsert
khosetšhumo	costume (n)	kostuum
khoukhou	cocoa (n)	kakao
-khoutha	quote (v)	aanhaal
khoutho	quotation (n)	aanhaling
khrikhete	cricket (n)	krieket
khudu	tortoise (n)	skilpad
khuduego	emotion (n)	gevoel
khuduego	excitement (n)	opwinding
khudugo	migration (n)	migrasie
khudugo	removal (n)	trek
khukhune	cocoon (n)	kokon
-khukhunela	stalk (v)	bekruip
khukhuša	bud (n)	botsel
khumo	wealth (n)	rykdom
-khumola	chafe (v)	skaaf
-khunama	kneel (v)	kniel
khunkhwane	beetle (n)	kewer
khunkhwane	bug (n)	gogga
khunkhwane	insect (n)	insek
khunollo	leave (n)	verlof
khunyelo	contraction (n)	inkrimping
-khupamarama	mysterious (a)	geheimsinnig
khupamarama	mystery (n)	misterie
-khupetša	cover (v)	dek
khuru	knee (n)	knie
khurumelakhuru	kneecap (n)	knieskyf
khutlo	angle (n)	hoek
khutlo	fullstop (n)	punt
-khutlonne	square (a)	vierkantig
khutlonne	square (n)	vierkant
khutlonnethwi	rectangle (n)	reghoek
khutlotharo	triangle (n)	driehoek
-khutša	rest (v)	rus
khutšo	interval (n)	pouse
khutšo	peace (n)	vrede
khutšo	rest (n)	rus
-khutsofatša	shorten (v)	verkort
khwaere	choir (n)	koor
khwaliti	quality (n)	kwaliteit
khwetšo	acquisition (n)	aanskaffing

N Sotho	English	Afrikaans	N Sotho	English	Afrikaans	K
khwiti	mole (n)	mol	konope	button (n)	knoop	
khwiti ya lewatle	beach (n)	strand	kontae	conductor (n)	kondukteur	
kikontwane	convulsion (n)	rukking	kontinente	continent (n)	vasteland	
-kile	ever (adv)	ooit	kontraka	contract (n)	kontrak	
kimollo	relief (n)	verligting	-kopana	brief (a)	beknop	
kinipitane	pliers (n)	knyptang	-kopana	contact (v)	in aanraking kom	
kiribane	wheelbarrow (n)	kruiwa	-kopana	short (a)	kort	
kirisi	grease (n)	ghries	-kopana le	meet (v)	ontmoet	
-kirisa	grease (v)	smeer	kopano	congress (n)	kongres	
kišontle	export (n)	uitvoer	kopano	meeting (n)	vergadering	
-kitima	jog (v)	draf	kopano	meeting (n)	ontmoeting	
-kitima	run (v)	hardloop	kopano	society (n)	vereniging	
-kitlaganego	dense (a)	dig	kopano	union (n)	unie	
klarinete	clarinet (n)	klarinet	kopantšho	join (n)	lasplek	
klatše	clutch (n)	koppelaar	-kopanya	combine (v)	kombineer	
klimate	climate (n)	klimaat	-kopanya	connect (v)	verbind	
kliniki	clinic (n)	kliniek	-kopanya	join (v)	las	
-kobakobanago	migrant (a)	swerwend	-kopanya	unite (v)	verenig	
kobamo	bend (n)	buiging	kopanyo	connection (n)	verbinding	
kobi	hook (n)	haak	kopi	copy (document) (n)	afskrif	
kobihlapi	fishing rod (n)	visstok	kopi ya puku	copy (book) (n)	eksemplaar	
kobo	blanket (n)	kombers	koporasi	co-operation (n)	koöperasie	
-kobola	peck (v)	pik	koporo	copper (n)	koper	
kobo ya mafofa	quilt (n)	verekombers	koronatela	granadilla (n)	granadilla	
kodu	larynx (n)	larinks	korong	wheat (n)	koring	
kodutlo	sarcasm (n)	sarkasme	košana	song (n)	liedjie	
kofi	coffee (n)	koffie	kota	block (n)	blok	
kokeletšo	increment (n)	verhoging	kota	log (n)	blok	
koketšo	addition (n)	toevoeging	kota	pole (n)	paal	
koketšo	increase (n)	verhoging	kota	stump (n)	stomp	
koko	grandmother (n)	ouma	kota	wood (n)	hout	
koko	nut (n)	neut	-kotama	crouch (v)	buk	
-kokobetša	humiliate (v)	verneder	-kotama	land (v)	land	
kokolohute	heron (n)	reier	-kotama	squat (v)	hurk	
-kokomoga	bulge (v)	uitbult	kota ya go rulela	rafter (n)	dakbalk	
-kokona	gnaw (v)	knaag	kota ya leswielo	broomstick (n)	besemstok	
kokontwane	peg (n)	pen	kotlo	penalty (n)	straf	
-kokota	knock (v)	klop	kotlo	punishment (n)	straf	
-kokotela	hammer (v)	hamer	kotlollo	exercise (n)	oefening	
-kokotela	nail (v)	spyker	kotlo ya ekonomi	sanction (n)	sanksie	
-kokotela	peg (v)	vaspen	-koto	thick (a)	dik	
kokoto	knock (n)	klop	-kotofatša	thicken (v)	dik maak	
kolo	bullet (n)	koeël	kotse	shield (n)	skild	
kolobe	pig (n)	vark	kotsi	accident (n)	ongeluk	
-kolobetša	baptise (v)	doop	kotsi	casualty (n)	ongeval	
kolobetšo	baptism (n)	doop	kotsi	danger (n)	gevaar	
kolobe ya tshadi	sow (n)	sog	-kotsi	dangerous (a)	gevaarlik	
-kolobilego	wet (a)	nat	kotsi	disaster (n)	ramp	
koloi	wagon (n)	wa	-kotsi	harmful (a)	skadelik	
koloi ya balwetši	ambulance (n)	ambulans	kotsi	peril (n)	gevaar	
kolopisane	tadpole (n)	paddavissie	-kotsi	unsafe (a)	onveilig	
-kolota	owe (v)	skuld	kou	bay (n)	baai	
komelelo	drought (n)	droogte	koulo	goal (n)	doel	
komiki	cup (n)	koppie	Kriste	Christ (n)	Christus	
komisi	commission (n)	kommissie	krostina	concertina (n)	konsertina	
komiti	committee (n)	komitee	kua le kua	around (adv)	rond	
komphuta	calculator (n)	rekenaar	-kubegilego	blunt (a)	stomp	
komphuta	computer (n)	rekenaar	kubu	hippopotamus (n)	seekoei	
kompo	compound (n)	kampong	kudu	very (a)	heel	
konofele	garlic (n)	knoffel	-kuka	lift (v)	oplig	

K

N Sotho	English	Afrikaans	N Sotho	English	Afrikaans
kuku	cake (n)	koek	-laodiša	tell (v)	vertel
kukunama	pastry (n)	pastei	-laola	control (v)	beheer
kuku ya weifere	wafer (n)	wafel	-laola	manage (v)	bestuur
kunkurobala	lullaby (n)	wiegelied	-laola	predict (v)	voorspel
kuranta	newspaper (n)	koerant	-laolla	unload (v)	aflaai
-kurufela	screw (v)	skroef	lapa	household (n)	huishouding
kurumane	syringe (n)	spuit	-lapa	tire (v)	moeg word
kutlwišišo	allergy (n)	allergie	lapanabjang	lawn (n)	grasperk
kutu	stem (n)	stam	-lapilego	tired (a)	moeg
-kwa	feel (v)	voel	-lapilego	weary (a)	vermoeid
-kwa	hear (v)	hoor	-lata	fetch (v)	haal
-kwa	obey (v)	gehoorsaam wees	-lata mohlala	track (v)	opspoor
kwaba	guava (n)	koejawel	-latela	follow (v)	volg
-kwagala	audible (a)	hoorbaar	-latelago	next (a)	volgende
-kwagalago	loud (a)	hard	-latola	deny (v)	ontken
kwagalo	logic (n)	logika	-latswa	lick (v)	lek
-kwagatša	pronounce (v)	uitspreek	le	too (adv)	ook
kwagatšo	pronunciation (n)	uitspraak	le	with (prep)	met
-kwago	obedient (a)	gehoorsaam	le/gomme	and (conj)	en
-kwa ka leleme	taste (v)	proe	Leafrikanere	Afrikaner (n)	Afrikaner
-kwalago	acoustic (a)	akoesties	-leana	squint (v)	skeel
-kwana	consent (v)	instem	lebadi	scar (n)	litteken
-kwana	agree (v)	ooreenstem	lebadi la matswalo	birthmark (n)	moedervlek
kwana	lamb (n)	lam	lebadi la mollo	burn (n)	brandplek
kwanadumo	harmony (n)	harmonie	lebadi la sekobonyane	pockmark (n)	pokmerk
kwano	agreement (n)	ooreenkoms	lebaka	cause (n)	oorsaak
kwano	appointment (n)	afspraak	lebaka	motive (n)	beweegrede
kwano	consent (n)	instemming	lebaka	occasion (n)	geleentheid
kwarata	quarter (n)	kwart	lebaka	reason (n)	rede
-kwelanobohloko	sympathetic (a)	simpatiek	lebaka	term (n)	termyn
kwelanobohloko	sympathy (n)	simpatie	lebaka	term (n)	term
kwena	crocodile (n)	krokodil	lebaka	turn (n)	beurt
kwepere	quince (n)	kweper	-lebala	forget (v)	vergeet
-kwera	flout (v)	hoon	-lebala go itshwara	misbehave (v)	jou swak gedra
-kwera	ridicule (v)	bespot	-lebalela	excuse (v)	verontskuldig
-kwera	mock (v)	bespot	-lebalela	forgive (v)	vergewe
kwero	ridicule (n)	spottery	-lebalela	pardon (v)	vergewe
-kwišiša	understand (v)	verstaan	-lebanego	appropriate (a)	geskik
			-lebanego	direct (a)	direk
Labobedi	Tuesday (n)	Dinsdag	lebato	floor (n)	vloer
Labohlano	Friday (n)	Vrydag	lebato	floor (n)	verdieping
Labone	Thursday (n)	Donderdag	lebebe	cream (n)	room
Laboraro	Wednesday (n)	Woensdag	lebekere	jug (n)	beker
-laela	direct (v)	beveel	-lebelela	gaze (v)	staar
-laela	indoctrinate (v)	indoktrineer	-lebelela	look (v)	kyk
-laela	order (v)	beveel	-lebelela	stare (v)	staar
laesense	licence (n)	lisensie	-lebelo	hasty (a)	haastig
laetse	curl (n)	krul	lebelo	haste (n)	haas
la go ja	right (n)	regterkant	lebelo	rapid (a)	vlugtig
-laiša	load (v)	laai	lebelo	speed (n)	spoed
-lakaletša	congratulate (v)	gelukwens	lebenkele	store (n)	winkel
mahlogonolo			lebenkele	shop (n)	winkel
lakane	sheet (n)	laken	lebete	spleen (n)	milt
-lala	lie (v)	lê	-lebiša	direct (v)	rig
-laletša	invite (v)	uitnooi	lebitla	grave (n)	graf
-lamola	arbitrate (v)	arbitreer	lebitla	tomb (n)	graf
-lamola	mediate (v)	bemiddel	lebja	thong (n)	riem
-lamolwago	arbitrary (a)	willekeurig	-leboa	north (a)	noord
lanterene	lantern (n)	lantern	leboa	north (n)	noorde
-laodiša	describe (v)	beskrywe	-leboga	thank (v)	bedank

N Sotho	English	Afrikaans	N Sotho	English	Afrikaans
lebogela	prize (v)	op prys stel	le ge	even (adv)	selfs
-lebogilego	grateful (a)	dankbaar	le ge	though (conj)	hoewel
lebollo	circumcision (n)	besnydenis	le ge e ka ba	nor (conj)	nòg
lebone	lamp (n)	lamp	le ge go le bjalo	anyhow (conj)	in elk geval
lebopo	coast (n)	kus	legetla	shoulder (n)	skouer
leboto	wall (n)	muur	legodimo	heaven (n)	hemel
leboyo	cycle (n)	siklus	legogo	crust (n)	korsie
ledimo	gale (n)	stormwind	legogo	scab (n)	rofie
ledimo	storm (n)	storm	legokobu	crow (n)	kraai
lediri	verb (n)	werkwoord	legokolodi	centipede (n)	honderdpoot
ledumo	desire (n)	begeerte	legokolodi	millipede (n)	duisendpoot
lee	egg (n)	eier	legongtshipi	ironwood (n)	ysterhout
leeba	pigeon (n)	duif	legoo	scream (n)	gil
leemo	position (n)	posisie	legora	fence (n)	draad
-leemo	standard (a)	standaard	legora	hedge (n)	heining
leemo	standard (n)	standaard	legoswi	palm (n)	palm
leeto	journey (n)	reis	legotlo	mouse (n)	muis
leeto	tour (n)	rondreis	lehlakanoka	reed (n)	riet
leeto	trip (n)	reis	lehlakore	side (n)	sy
leetse	plait (n)	vlegsel	lehlaodi	adjective (n)	byvoeglike naamwoord
lefa	inheritance (n)	erfenis	lehlapo	menstruation (n)	menstruasie
-lefa	pay (v)	betaal	lehlare	banknote (n)	banknoot
-lefa	reward (v)	beloon	lehlasedi	sunbeam (n)	sonstraal
lefapha	faculty (n)	fakulteit	lehlasedi	ray (n)	straal
lefase	earth (n)	aarde	lehlathi	adverb (n)	bywoord
lefase	land (n)	land	lehlogonolo	blessing (n)	seëning
lefase	world (n)	wêreld	lehlokwana la mollo	match (n)	vuurhoutjie
lefastere	window (n)	venster	lehloyo	disgust (n)	afkeer
lefatla	bald (a)	bles	lehloyo	hatred (n)	haat
lefeela	zero (n)	nul	lehlwa	snow (n)	sneeu
lefego	wing (n)	vlerk	lehlwa	ice (n)	ys
-lefela	trivial (a)	niksbeduidend	lehlwapula	sleet (n)	ysreën
-lefela	vain (a)	ydel	lehlwele	clot (n)	klont
lefele	cockroach (n)	kakkerlak	leho	spoon (n)	lepel
-lefeletša	avenge (v)	wreek	leho	ladle (n)	skeplepel
-lefeletša	retaliate (v)	vergeld	lehodu	thief (n)	dief
lefelo la go kampela	camp site (n)	kampeerterrein	lehodu	pickpocket (n)	sakkeroller
lefelo la go phaka	parking (n)	parkering	lehono	today (n)	vandag
lefetile	past (n)	verlede	lehu	death (n)	dood
-lefiša	fine (v)	beboet	lehuduo	oar (n)	roeispaan
-lefiša	tax (v)	belas	lehufa	jealousy (n)	jaloesie
lefodi	butternut (n)	botterskorsie	lehumo	fortune (n)	fortuin
lefodi	pumpkin (n)	pampoen	lehumo	luxury (n)	luukse
lefofa	feather (n)	veer	lehumo	treasure (n)	skat
lefoko	sentence (n)	sin	lehutlo	hunchback (n)	boggelrug
lefšega	coward (n)	lafaard	lehuto	knot (n)	knoop
-lefšega	cowardly (a)	lafhartig	lehuto	bow (n)	strik
lefula	flood (n)	vloed	lehwafa	armpit (n)	armholte
legadima	lightning (n)	weerlig	leihlo	eye (n)	oog
-legae	domestic (a)	huishoudelik	leina	name (n)	naam
legae	home (n)	tuiste	leina	noun (n)	selfstandige naamwoord
legaga	cave (n)	grot			
legaga	cliff (n)	krans	leino	tooth (n)	tand
legaga	ravine (n)	kloof	leino la mohlagare	molar (n)	kiestand
leganata	desert (n)	woestyn	leino la tlou	ivory (n)	ivoor
leganse	goose (n)	gans	leiri	nappy (n)	babadoek
legapu	watermelon (n)	waatlemoen	leitšibulo	firstborn (n)	eersgeborene
legata	skull (n)	skedel	-lejelathoko	selfish (a)	selfsugtig
le gatee	never (adv)	nooit	-leka	test (v)	toets
le ge	although (conj)	al	-leka	try (v)	probeer

L	N Sotho	English	Afrikaans	N Sotho	English	Afrikaans
	lekala	branch (n)	tak	lenaneo	programme (n)	program
	lekalana	twig (n)	takkie	lenaneo la dibeine	winelist (n)	wynkaart
	-lekana	equal (v)	gelyk wees aan	lenaneo la dijo	menu (n)	spyskaart
	-lekana	fit (v)	pas	lenaneothuto	syllabus (n)	leerplan
	-lekanago	equal (a)	gelyk	lenanethero	agenda (n)	agenda
	-lekanego	adequate (a)	voldoende	lene	linen (n)	linne
	-lekanego	enough (a)	genoeg	lengamu	groin (n)	lies
	-lekanetšego	even (a)	gelykmatig	lengina	earring (n)	oorring
	-lekanetšego	mild (a)	matig	lengwalo	document (n)	dokument
	-lekantšwego	level (a)	gelyk	lengwalo	letter (n)	brief
	-lekanya	measure (v)	meet	lengwalo la bohlatse	reference (n)	getuigskrif
	-lekanya	assess (v)	skat	lengwalo la bopaki	certificate (n)	sertifikaat
	-lekanyetša	appreciate (v)	waardeer	lenkgeretla	rag (n)	lap
	-lekanyetša	value (v)	waardeer	lenong	vulture (n)	aasvoël
	lekgapetla	husk (n)	skil	lenono	stalk (n)	stingel
	lekgema	cannibal (n)	mensvreter	lente	ribbon (n)	lint
	lekgephola	peel (n)	skil	lentitekanya	tape measure (n)	maatband
	lekgetla	bridesmaid (n)	strooimeisie	lentšu	word (n)	woord
	lekgoba	slave (n)	slaaf	lentšu	voice (n)	stem
	lekgolo	century (sport) (n)	honderdtal	lenyalo	marriage (n)	huwelik
	lekgolo	hundred (n)	honderd	lenyatšo	contempt (n)	veragting
	lekgotla	council (n)	raad	lenyatšo	scorn (n)	veragting
	lekgotla la boipiletšo	appeal court (n)	appélhof	lenyora	thirst (n)	dors
	lekgotla la toka	judiciary (n)	regbank	leobu	chameleon (n)	verkleurmannetjie
	lekgwara	gravel (n)	gruis	leokodi	cotton (n)	katoen
	lekoko	faction (n)	faksie	leope	ditch (n)	sloot
	lekwate	lump (n)	klont	leoto	foot (n)	voet
	lela	intestine (n)	derm	leoto	leg (n)	been
	lelakgolo	colon (n)	dikderm	leotwana	wheel (n)	wiel
	-lelefatša	elongate (v)	verleng	lepaka	bakery (n)	bakkery
	-lelefatša	prolong (v)	verleng	lepanta	belt (n)	gordel
	-leleka	evict (v)	uitsit	lepanta la boitšhireletšo	seatbelt (n)	sitplekgordel
	-leleka	exile (v)	verban			
	-leleka	sack (v)	afdank	-lepelela	droop (v)	neerhang
	leleme	tongue (n)	tong	lephegwana la hlapi	fin (n)	vin
	leleme la setšhaba	vernacular (n)	volkstaal	lepheko	barrier (n)	versperring
	lelengwana	uvula (n)	kleintongetjie	lepheko	obstacle (n)	hindernis
	leloko	family (n)	familie	lephodisa	constable (n)	konstabel
	leloko	member (n)	lid	lephodisa	policeman (n)	polisieman
	leloko	posterity (n)	nageslag	lephone	blister (n)	blaar
	-lema	cultivate (v)	bewerk	lephoto	wave (n)	brander
	-lema	plough (v)	ploeg	lepidipidi	duck (n)	eend
	lemao la go loga	knitting needle (n)	breinaald	lepogo	cheetah (n)	jagluiperd
	lemati	door (n)	deur	lepokisi	box (n)	doos
	lemeno	hem (n)	soom	lepokisi la bahu	coffin (n)	doodskis
	-lemoga	notice (v)	opmerk	lepolanka	plank (n)	plank
	-lemoga	observe (v)	waarneem	lepolanka la go phonkgela	diving board (n)	duikplank
	-lemoga	recognise (v)	herken			
	-lemogago	conscious (a)	bewus	leporogo	bridge (n)	brug
	-lemoša	warn (v)	waarsku	lepotlelo	bottle (n)	bottel
	lena	you (pron)	julle	lerabela	rebel (n)	rebel
	-lena	your (pron)	julle	leraga	mud (n)	modder
	-lena	yours (pron)	julle s'n	-leraga	muddy (a)	modderig
	lenaba	enemy (n)	vyand	lerago	buttock (n)	boud
	lenaba	foe (n)	vyand	lerala la dieta	shoelace (n)	skoenveter
	lenaka	horn (n)	horing	lerama	cheek (n)	wang
	lenala	fingernail (n)	vingernael	lerapo	bone (n)	been
	lenala la monwana wa leoto	toenail (n)	toonnael	lerapothama	cheekbone (n)	wangbeen
				leratadimo	sky (n)	lug
	lenaneo	program (n)	program	lerathana	crumb (n)	krummel

N Sotho	English	Afrikaans	N Sotho	English	Afrikaans	L
leratladi la leihlo	iris (n)	iris	-letela	expect (v)	verwag	
lerato	affection (n)	toegeneentheid	letena	dinner (n)	hoofmaal	
lerato	charity (n)	liefdadigheid	letena	lunch (n)	middagete	
lerato	love (n)	liefde	lethabo	fun (n)	pret	
leredi	butter (n)	botter	-lethabo	happy (a)	gelukkig	
lerete	testicle (n)	teelbal	lethabo	delight (n)	blydskap	
leribiši	owl (n)	uil	lethabo	happiness (n)	geluk	
lerole	dust (n)	stof	lethabo	joy (n)	vreugde	
-lerope	ramshackle (a)	bouvallig	lethabo	pleasure (n)	plesier	
lerothodi	raindrop (n)	reëndruppel	lethakgo	whooping cough (n)	kinkhoes	
leru	cloud (n)	wolk	letheka	hip (n)	heup	
leruarua	whale (n)	walvis	letheka	loin (n)	lende	
lerumo	assegai (n)	assegaai	letheka	pelvis (n)	bekken	
lerumo	spear (n)	spies	letheka	waist (n)	middel	
lešaba	crowd (n)	skare	lethopo	hose (n)	tuinslang	
lešabašaba	multitude (n)	menigte	lethopša	prisoner-of-war (n)	krygsgevangene	
lešabašaba	sand (n)	sand	letlakala	leaf (n)	blaar	
-leša dihlong	embarrass (v)	verleë maak	letlakala	page (n)	bladsy	
lešala	pronoun (n)	voornaamwoord	letlalo	leather (n)	leer	
lešata	noise (n)	geraas	letlalo	skin (n)	vel	
-lešata	noisy (a)	raserig	letlalo la hlogo	scalp (n)	kopvel	
lešata	uproar (n)	lawaai	letlametlo	toad (n)	brulpadda	
lesea	baby (n)	baba	letlapa la lebitla	tombstone (n)	grafsteen	
lesea	infant (n)	suigeling	letorokisi	truck (n)	trok	
leseka	bangle (n)	armband	-letša molodi	whistle (v)	fluit	
lešela	fabric (n)	tekstielstof	-letša nakana ya	hoot (v)	toet	
lešela	material (n)	lap	mmotoro			
lešela	cloth (n)	doek	letšatši	day (n)	dag	
leselaga	butchery (n)	slagtery	letšatši	sun (n)	son	
leselo	pitchfork (n)	gaffel	letšatši ka letšatši	daily (a)	daagliks	
lešetla	cartilage (n)	kraakbeen	letšatši la matswalo	birthday (n)	verjaarsdag	
lešoba	puncture (n)	lekplek	letseka	detective (n)	speurder	
lešoba la konope	buttonhole (n)	knoopsgat	letsetse	flea (n)	vlooi	
lešobana la senotlelo	keyhole (n)	sleutelgat	letsha	lake (n)	meer	
lešoka	wilderness (n)	wildernis	letshanatswai	lagoon (n)	strandmeer	
lesome	ten (n)	tien	letšhogo	panic (n)	paniek	
lesomehlano	fifteen (n)	vyftien	letšhollo	diarrhoea (n)	diarree	
lesomenne	fourteen (n)	veertien	letšoba	flower (n)	blom	
lesomepedi	twelve (n)	twaalf	letsogo	arm (n)	arm	
lesomesenyane	nineteen (n)	neëntien	letsogo la seaparo	sleeve (n)	mou	
lesomeseswai	eighteen (n)	agtien	letsoku	ochre (n)	oker	
lesomešupa	seventeen (n)	sewentien	letsopa	clay (n)	klei	
lesometee	eleven (n)	elf	letšwabadi	bunion (n)	knokkeleelt	
lesometshela	sixteen (n)	sestien	letswai	salt (n)	sout	
leswafo	lung (n)	long	letswalo	conscience (n)	gewete	
leswafohlapi	gill (n)	kieu	letswalo	diaphragm (n)	diafragma	
leswao	mark (n)	merk	letswele	fist (n)	vuis	
lešwefe	albino (n)	albino	leuba	epidemic (n)	epidemie	
leswielo	broom (n)	besem	leuba	pest (n)	pes	
leswika	rock (n)	rots	-lewago	edible (a)	eetbaar	
leswika	stone (n)	klip	-lewa ke dihlong	ashamed (a)	skaam	
leswiswi	darkness (n)	donker	lewatle	ocean (n)	oseaan	
-leta	guard (v)	bewaak	lewatle	sea (n)	see	
-leta	wait (v)	wag	-lla	cry (v)	huil	
letadi	fever (n)	koors	-lla	mourn (v)	rou	
letadi	malaria (n)	malaria	-lla	ring (v)	lui	
letago	glory (n)	glorie	-lla	weep (v)	huil	
letamo	dam (n)	dam	-lla	whimper (v)	sanik	
letapola	potato (n)	aartappel	lleri	ladder (n)	leer	
-letela	await (v)	wag op	lleri	stepladder (n)	trapleer	

L	N Sotho	English	Afrikaans	N Sotho	English	Afrikaans
	llili	lily (n)	lelie	maekroweife	microwave (n)	mikrogolf
	-loga	knit (v)	brei	maele	mile (n)	myl
	-loga	weave (v)	weef	mafahla	twin (n)	tweeling
	-loga maano	plan (v)	beplan	-mafelelo	final (a)	finaal
	-lokafatša	justify (v)	regverdig	mafelelo	finish (n)	einde
	-lokilego	fair (a)	billik	-mafelelo	last (a)	laaste
	-lokilego	just (a)	regverdig	mafofonyane	hysterics (n)	histerie
	-lokilego	right (a)	reg	mafolofolo	diligence (n)	fluksheid
	-lokilego	wholesome (a)	heilsaam	-mafolofolo	diligent (a)	fluks
	-lokiša	fix (v)	regmaak	-mafolofolo	energetic (a)	energiek
	-lokišetša	prepare (v)	voorberei	mafolofolo	energy (n)	energie
	-lokišo	mend (v)	heelmaak	-mafolofolo	industrious (a)	vlytig
	-lokolla	dismiss (v)	ontslaan	-mafolofolo	keen (a)	toegewyd
	-lokolla	emancipate (v)	vrymaak	-mafolofolo	lively (a)	lewendig
	-lokolla	free (v)	bevry	mafulo	pasture (n)	weiveld
	-lokolla	release (v)	loslaat	magalapa	palate (n)	verhemelte
	-lokolla	acquit (v)	vryspreek	magoswi	acclaim (n)	toejuiging
	-lokologana	queue (v)	toustaan	mahea	maize (n)	mielies
	-lokologilego	free (a)	vry	mahlabego	yeast (n)	gis
	-loma	bite (v)	byt	-mahlahla	active (a)	aktief
	-loma	sting (v)	steek	mahlahlo	activity (n)	bedrywigheid
	-loma tsebe	confide (v)	vertroulik meedeel	-mahlapa	vulgar (a)	vulgêr
	-lomolla	disconnect (v)	losmaak	-mahlatša	vomit (n)	vomeersel
	-lomolla	wean (v)	speen	-mahlatse	fortunate (a)	gelukkig
	-lora	dream (v)	droom	mahlatse	luck (n)	geluk
	lori	lorry (n)	vragmotor	mahlomola	sorrow (n)	smart
	-lotegilego	safe (a)	veilig	mahube	daybreak (n)	dagbreek
	-lotegilego	secure (a)	veilig	maikemišetšo	ideal (a)	ideaal
	-loya	bewitch (v)	toor	maikemišetšo	meaning (n)	bedoeling
	-lwa	battle (v)	veg	maikemišetšo	policy (n)	beleid
	-lwa	fight (v)	veg	maikemišetšo	purpose (n)	oogmerk
	-lwala	sicken (v)	siek word	maikhutšo	holiday (n)	vakansie
	-lwalago	ill (a)	siek	maikutlo	mood (n)	bui
	-lwalago	sick (a)	siek	maikutlo	temper (n)	humeur
	-lwantšha	antagonise (v)	vyandig maak	maipshino	amusement (n)	vermaaklikheid
				-maitirelo	artificial (a)	kunsmatig
	maabane	yesterday (n)	gister	-maitirelo	synthetic (a)	sinteties
	maaka	falsehood (n)	onwaarheid	-makala	marvel (v)	wonder
	maaka	lie (n)	leuen	-makala	wonder (v)	wonder
	maano	plan (n)	plan	makalo	amazement (n)	verbasing
	maatla	authority (n)	gesag	-makatša	amaze (v)	verbaas
	maatla	force (n)	krag	-makatša	surprise (v)	verras
	maatla	power (n)	mag	-makatšago	amazing (a)	verbasend
	maatla	strength (n)	sterkte	-makatšago	marvellous (a)	wonderbaarlik
	-maatla	strong (a)	sterk	-makatšago	peculiar (a)	eienaardig
	-maatla	vigorous (a)	kragtig	-makatšago	queer (a)	snaaks
	maatlakgogedi	attraction (n)	aantrekking	-makatšago	wonderful (a)	wonderlik
	mabarebare	gossip (n)	skinderpraatjies	makatšo	surprise (n)	verrassing
	mabarebare	hearsay (n)	hoorsê	-makgethe	crack (a)	puik
	mabarebare	rumour (n)	gerug	makgethe a polelo	rhetoric (n)	retoriek
	mabele	grain (n)	graan	-makgonthe	true (a)	waar
	mabele	sorghum (n)	sorghum	-makgwakgwa	hoarse (a)	hees
	mabitleng	cemetery (n)	begraafplaas	-makgwakgwa	rough (a)	ru
	-mabobo	generous (a)	vrygewig	makhanekhe	mechanic (n)	werktuigkundige
	mabora	chickenpox (n)	waterpokkies	makhura	fat (n)	vet
	madi	blood (n)	bloed	makhura a kolobe	lard (n)	varkvet
	madimabe	curse (n)	vloek	makokwana	mischief (n)	kattekwaad
	madimabe	misfortune (n)	teenspoed	makwapi a diterebe	raisin (n)	rosyntjie
	madira	army (n)	leër	mala	bowels (n)	ingewande
	maekrosekopo	microscope (n)	mikroskoop	maladu	pus (n)	etter

N Sotho	English	Afrikaans	N Sotho	English	Afrikaans	M
malahla	coal (n)	steenkool	mathatha	misery (n)	ellende	
malao	bedclothes (n)	beddegoed	mathematiki	mathematics (n)	wiskunde	
maledu a ka godima ga molomo	moustache (n)	snor	mathomo	beginning (n)	begin	
			mathomo	origin (n)	oorsprong	
maledu a ka godimo ga molomo	whiskers (n)	snor	mathomo	start (n)	begin	
			matladima	dizziness (n)	duiseligheid	
malobanyana	newly (adv)	onlangs	matlakala	rubbish (n)	vuilgoed	
malokwane	adjudicator (n)	beoordelaar	matlhenkge	wreck (n)	wrak	
malome	uncle (n)	oom	matšala	haemorrhoids (n)	aambeie	
mamina	mucus (n)	slym	-matšha	march (v)	marsjeer	
mamina	phlegm (n)	fleim	Matšhe	March (n)	Maart	
mang	who (pron)	wie	matshwenyego	nuisance (n)	steurnis	
-mang	whose (pron)	wie se	matshwenyego	plague (n)	plaag	
-manganga	stubborn (a)	koppig	mauwe	mumps (n)	pampoentjies	
mang le mang	anybody (pron)	elkeen	-medilego	overgrown (a)	toegegroei	
mang le mang	each (pron)	elk(e)	meetsana	juice (n)	sap	
-mankgeretla	ragged (a)	verflenterd	meetse	water (n)	water	
manko	mango (n)	mango	-megabaru	greedy (a)	gulsig	
manopi	nectar (n)	nektar	megokgo	tears (n)	trane	
mantarase	mattress (n)	matras	-mehutahuta	miscellaneous (a)	allerlei	
mantharane	puzzle (n)	legkaart	-mehutahuta	several (a)	verskeie	
mantle	excreta (n)	uitwerpsel	mehutahuta	variety (n)	verskeidenheid	
mantle	faeces (n)	uitwerpsel	Mei	May (n)	Mei	
mantlopodi	stork (n)	ooievaar	meila	mule (n)	muil	
mantšiboa	evening (n)	aand	mekhuri	mercury (n)	kwik	
manyami	depression (n)	bedruktheid	mekutwaneng	slum (n)	krotbuurt	
manyami	grief (n)	leed	-mela	grow (v)	groei	
manyami	pity (n)	jammerte	-mena	fold (v)	vou	
manyami	sadness (n)	droefheid	menamelo	stairs (n)	trappe	
manyokenyoke	zigzag (n)	sigsag	meno	teeth (n)	tande	
mapalane	clerk (n)	klerk	meno a sekgowa	dentures (n)	vals tande	
maphelo	hygiene (n)	higiëne	-menola	overthrow (v)	omvergooi	
maphodisa	police (n)	polisie	mentlele	medal (n)	medalje	
mapimpana	toddler (n)	kleuter	-merafe	racial (a)	rasse	
marapo a mmele	skeleton (n)	geraamte	-meriri ye	hairy (a)	harig	
marara	puzzle (n)	raaisel	mentšimmeleng			
mare	saliva (n)	speeksel	metale	metal (n)	metaal	
marega	winter (n)	winter	metara	metre (n)	meter	
marinini	gum (n)	tandvleis	-metša	swallow (v)	sluk	
mariri	mane (n)	maanhare	milione	million (n)	miljoen	
marobalo	accommodation (n)	huisvesting	minerale	mineral (n)	mineraal	
marokgo a dišothi	shorts (n)	kortbroek	mma	mother (n)	moeder	
marumofase	ceasefire (n)	skietstilstand	mmadiphetana	abacus (n)	telraam	
masa	dawn (n)	dagbreek	mmaditsela	shop steward (n)	segsman	
mašakana	brackets (n)	hakies	mmala	colour (n)	kleur	
mašaledi	remainder (n)	oorblyfsel	-mmala	coloured (a)	gekleur	
maseterata	magistrate (n)	landdros	mmalewaneng	fern (n)	varing	
masetlapelo	tragedy (n)	tragedie	mmankgagane	bat (n)	vlermuis	
-masetlapelo	tragic (a)	tragies	mmapadi wa khrikhete	cricketer (n)	krieketspeler	
masomehlano	fifty (n)	vyftig	mmapano	parallel (n)	parallel	
masomenne	forty (n)	veertig	mmaraka	market (n)	mark	
masomepedi	twenty (n)	twintig	-mmaruri	permanent (a)	permanent	
masomesenyane	ninety (n)	neëntig	mmasepala	municipality (n)	munisipaliteit	
masomeseswai	eighty (n)	tagtig	-mmasepala	municipal (a)	munisipaal	
masomešupa	seventy (n)	sewentig	mmatswale	mother-in-law (n)	skoonmoeder	
masometshela	sixty (n)	sestig	mmegi	accuser (n)	beskuldiger	
mašošo	wrinkle (n)	plooi	mmegi	reporter (n)	verslaggewer	
-maswabi	sad (a)	treurig	mmegiwa	accused (n)	beskuldigde	
maswi	milk (n)	melk	mmelaedi	plaintiff (n)	eiser	
-matepe	wilful (a)	moedswillig	mmele	body (n)	liggaam	

M	N Sotho	English	Afrikaans	N Sotho	English	Afrikaans
	mmelegiši	midwife (n)	vroedvrou	modiro wa diatla	handwork (n)	handewerk
	mmeodi	barber (n)	haarsnyer	modiro wa gae	homework (n)	huiswerk
	mmepe	map (n)	landkaart	modiši	shepherd (n)	skaapwagter
	mmetli	carpenter (n)	timmerman	moditšhaba	unbeliever (n)	ongelowige
	mmetli wa diswantšho	sculptor (n)	beeldhouer	modu	radicle (n)	wortel
	mmino wa setšhaba	anthem (n)	volkslied	modu	root (n)	wortel
	mmitši	caller (n)	roeper	modula	pollen (n)	stuifmeel
	mmogedi	spectator (n)	toeskouer	modulasetulo	chairman (n)	voorsitter
	mmolai	murderer (n)	moordenaar	modulo	residence (n)	verblyfplek
	mmoleledi	advocate (n)	advokaat	modumedi	believer (n)	gelowige
	mmolelo	dialect (n)	dialek	modumo	sound (n)	klank
	Mmopi	Creator (n)	Skepper	modumo	thunder (n)	donder
	mmopu	bat (n)	kolf	modutlo	leak (n)	lek
	mmoto	fishmoth (n)	vismot	moduwane	willow (n)	wilgerboom
	mmoto	hill (n)	heuwel	moebangedi	evangelist (n)	evangelis
	mmoto	moth (n)	mot	moedi	valley (n)	vallei
	mmotoro	motorcar (n)	motor	moeike	oak (n)	eikeboom
	mmotoro	car (n)	motor	moeki	traitor (n)	verraaier
	mmoto wa mohlaba	dune (n)	duin	moela	current (n)	stroom
	mmu	soil (n)	grond	moela	stream (n)	stroom
	mmušanoši	dictator (n)	diktator	moelaphirihlwa	whirlpool (n)	maalstroom
	mmuši	ruler (n)	regeerder	moeletši	adviser (n)	raadgewer
	mmušo	government (n)	regering	moemakgauswi	bystander (n)	omstander
	mmušo	kingdom (n)	koninkryk	moemedi	representative (n)	verteenwoordiger
	mmutedi	manure (n)	mis	moeng	caller (n)	besoeker
	mmutla	rabbit (n)	konyn	moeng	guest (n)	gas
	mo	at (prep)	op	moeng	stranger (n)	vreemdeling
	-mo-	her (pron)	haar	moeng	visitor (n)	besoeker
	mo	here (adv)	hier	moeniši	commissioner of oaths (n)	kommissaris van ede
	-mo-	him (pron)	hom			
	Moafrika	African (n)	Afrikaan	moesa	lad (n)	knaap
	moagi	citizen (n)	burger	moetapele	captain (n)	kaptein
	moagi	tenant (n)	bewoner	moetapele	leader (n)	leier
	moagi	mason (n)	messelaar	moethimolo	sneeze (n)	nies
	moagišani	neighbour (n)	buurman	moeti	traveller (n)	reisiger
	moago	building (n)	gebou	moeti	tourist (n)	toeris
	moahlodi	judge (n)	regter	mofahloši	lecturer (n)	dosent
	moahlodiši	assessor (n)	skatter	mofantisi	auctioneer (n)	afslaer
	moahloledi	arbiter (n)	arbiter	mofeiye	figtree (n)	vyeboom
	moahloledi	referee (n)	skeidsregter	mofelegetši	companion (n)	metgesel
	moakedi	liar (n)	leuenaar	mofelegetši	escort (n)	metgesel
	moamogedi	receptionist (n)	ontvangsklerk	mofepi	guardian (n)	voog
	moaparo	fashion (n)	mode	mofepiwa	dependant (n)	afhanklike
	moapei	cook (n)	kok	moferefere	sedition (n)	opruiing
	moapostola	apostle (n)	apostel	mofetoledi	interpreter (n)	tolk
	mobu	ground (n)	grond	mofetoledi	translator (n)	vertaler
	mobu	wasp (n)	perdeby	mofsa	adolescent (n)	jeugdige
	Modimo	God (n)	God	mogadibo	sister-in-law (n)	skoonsuster
	modimo	god (n)	god	mogala	cable (n)	kabel
	Modimo	Lord (n)	Here	mogaladitwe	arum lily (n)	varkoor
	modingwana	idol (n)	afgod	mogarafase	equator (n)	ewenaar
	-modipa	orange (a)	oranje	mogateledi	oppressor (n)	onderdrukker
	modiredi	employee (n)	werknemer	mogatša	wife (n)	vrou
	modirelwa	client (n)	kliënt	mogodi	haze (n)	waas
	modiri	worker (n)	werker	mogodu	paunch (n)	boepmaag
	modirišani	partner (n)	vennoot	-mogodu	gastric (a)	maag
	modiriši	operator (n)	operateur	mogodu	belly (n)	pens
	modiro	job (n)	werk	mogogonope	cock (n)	haan
	modiro	task (n)	taak	mogogonope	rooster (n)	hoenderhaan
	modiro	work (n)	werk	mogohlo wa meno	toothpaste (n)	tandepasta

252

N Sotho	English	Afrikaans	N Sotho	English	Afrikaans
mogolego	detention (n)	aanhouding	-mohola	useful (a)	nuttig
mogolegwa	detainee (n)	aangehoudene	mohola	value (n)	waarde
mogolegwa	convict (n)	gevangene	mohudi	robber (n)	rower
mogolegwa	prisoner (n)	gevangene	mohumagadi	lady (n)	dame
mogolo	adult (n)	volwassene	mohuta	kind (n)	soort
mogolo	throat (n)	keel	mohuta	make (n)	soort
mogolo	windpipe (n)	gorrelpyp	mohuta	type (n)	tipe
mogologolo	ancestor (n)	voorouer	mohuta wa kgopa ya lewatle	mussel (n)	mossel
mogoma	plough (n)	ploeg			
mo gongwe	elsewhere (adv)	elders	mohuta wa nonyana ya lewatle	gull (n)	meeu
mogoo	cry (n)	kreet			
mogopo	bowl (n)	bak	moikaketši	hypocrite (n)	skynheilige
mogopolelwa	suspect (n)	verdagte	moineedi diokobatšing	drug addict (n)	dwelmslaaf
mogopolo	mind (n)	verstand	moiphemedi	defendant (n)	verweerder
mogorogo	rash (n)	veluitslag	moithapi	volunteer (n)	vrywilliger
mogwapa	biltong (n)	biltong	moithuti	student (n)	student
mogwera	friend (n)	vriend	moitlamigadi	nun (n)	non
mogwete	anus (n)	anus	mojagobedi	funnel (n)	tregter
moheitene	heathen (n)	heiden	mojalefa	heir (n)	erfgenaam
moheitene	pagan (n)	heiden	mokaka	udder (n)	uier
mohiri	lodger (n)	loseerder	mokatiši	jockey (n)	jokkie
mohiriši	landlord (n)	verhuurder	mokato wa dipere	horserace (n)	perdewedren
mohlaba	malt (n)	mout	mokekema	reef (n)	rif
mohlabani	soldier (n)	soldaat	mokero	canal (n)	kanaal
mohlagare	jaw (n)	kaak	mokete	feast (n)	fees
-mohlagase	electric (a)	elektries	mokete wa centenary (n)		eeufees
mohlagase	electricity (n)	elektrisiteit	ngwagakgolo		
mohlahli	guide (n)	gids	mokgaritswane	lizard (n)	akkedis
mohlahlobi	inspector (n)	inspekteur	mokgatlo	club (n)	klub
mohlaka	swamp (n)	moeras	mokgatlo wa bašomi	trade union (n)	vakbond
mohlakiši	auditor (n)	ouditeur	mokgethwa	saint (n)	heilige
mohlala	track (n)	spoor	mokgobo	heap (n)	hoop
mohlala	example (n)	voorbeeld	mokgoko	handle (n)	handvatsel
mohlala	footprint (n)	voetspoor	mokgoko	hinge (n)	hingsel
mohlami	composer (n)	komponis	mokgomana	councillor (n)	raadslid
mohlamong	maybe (adv)	miskien	mokgomana	aristocrat (n)	edelman
mohlamongwe	perhaps (adv)	miskien	mokgonyana	son-in-law (n)	skoonseun
mohlana	afterbirth (n)	nageboorte	mokgopedi	applicant (n)	aansoeker
mohlanka	servant (n)	bediende	mokgopedi	beggar (n)	bedelaar
mohlankedi	official (n)	amptenaar	mokgopha	aloe (n)	aalwyn
mohlankiša	addict (n)	verslaafde	mokgoši	alarm (n)	alarm
mohlape	flock (n)	trop	mokgotha	driveway (n)	inrit
mohlape	herd (n)	kudde	mokgotha	street (n)	straat
mohlare wa akasia	acacia (n)	akasia	mokgwa	manner (n)	manier
mohlodi	flavour (n)	geur	mokgwa	method (n)	metode
mohlodi	flavouring (n)	geursel	mokhemisi	pharmacist (n)	apteker
mohlodi	source (n)	bron	mokhemisi	chemist (n)	apteker
mohlodi	taste (n)	smaak	mokhubu	navel (n)	naeltjie
mohlohleletši	activist (n)	aktivis	Mokibelo	Saturday (n)	Saterdag
mohlohleletši	agitator (n)	opstoker	moko	marrow (n)	murg
mohloki	pauper (n)	behoeftige	moko	pith (n)	pit
mohlolo	miracle (n)	wonderwerk	mokokotlo	back (n)	rug
mohlolo	wonder (n)	wonder	mokokotlo	spine (n)	ruggraat
mohlologadi	widow (n)	weduwee	mokolo	vertebra (n)	werwel
mohlologadi wa monna	widower (n)	wewenaar	mokoti	shaft (n)	skag
			mokoti wa moriri	hairdresser (n)	haarkapper
mohlotšo	limp (n)	mankheid	mokotla	bag (n)	sak
mohlware	olive (n)	olyf	mokotla	pocket (n)	sak
mohlwekišaoma	drycleaner (n)	droogskoonmakery	mokotla	sack (n)	sak
mohola	advantage (n)	voordeel	moko wa mokokotlo	spinal cord (n)	rugmurg

M	N Sotho	English	Afrikaans	N Sotho	English	Afrikaans
	Mokriste	Christian (n)	Christen	molwetši	patient (n)	pasiënt
	mola	while (conj)	terwyl	-momaganya	mount (v)	vassit
	molaba	snare (n)	strik	momatšho	march (n)	mars
	molaba	trap (n)	strik	momeno	fold (n)	vou
	molaedi	instructor (n)	instrukteur	mometšo	gullet (n)	slukderm
	molaetša	message (n)	boodskap	mometšo	oesophagus (n)	slukderm
	molala	neck (n)	nek	mommodi	gooseberry (n)	appelliefie
	molalatladi	rainbow (n)	reënboog	mona	envy (n)	naywer
	-molaleng	obvious (a)	vanselfsprekend	-mona	suck (v)	suig
	-molaleng	openly (a)	openlik	monamedi	passenger (n)	passasier
	molamodi	mediator (n)	bemiddelaar	-monamune	citrus (a)	sitrus
	molao	commandment (n)	gebod	monang	mosquito (n)	muskiet
	molao	decree (n)	verordening	moneneri	vagrant (n)	rondloper
	-molao	legal (a)	wetlik	mong	owner (n)	eienaar
	molao	law (n)	wet	monga	crack (n)	kraak
	molao	rule (n)	reël	monggae	host (n)	gasheer
	molaodi	manager (n)	bestuurder	mongongoregi	complainant (n)	klaer
	molaotheo	constitution (n)	grondwet	mongongoregi	scowl (n)	suur gesig
	molatedi	follower (n)	volgeling	mongwadi	author (n)	skrywer
	molato	blame (n)	blaam	mongwaledi	secretary (n)	sekretaris
	molato	debt (n)	skuld	mongwalo	handwriting (n)	handskrif
	molato	guilt (n)	skuld	mongwalo	writing (n)	skrif
	molato	offence (n)	oortreding	mongwao	scratch (n)	krap
	molawana	regulation (n)	regulasie	mongwegi	deserter (n)	droster
	molebeledi	caretaker (n)	opsigter	monkgo	smell (n)	reuk
	molefi	payer (n)	betaler	monkgo	stink (n)	stank
	molekane	equal (n)	gelyke	monko	fragrance (n)	geur
	molekane	acquaintance (n)	kennismaking	monko	perfume (n)	parfuum
	moleko	risk (n)	risiko	monna	husband (n)	man
	moleko	temptation (n)	verleiding	monna	male (n)	man
	molemogi	observer (n)	waarnemer	monna	man (n)	man
	mo le mola	about (adv)	rond	-monola	damp (a)	vogtig
	molephera	leper (n)	melaatse	monola	damp (n)	vogtigheid
	moletabošego	nightwatchman (n)	nagwag	-monola	humid (a)	klam
	molete	hole (n)	gat	-monola	moist (a)	vogtig
	moleti	guard (n)	wag	monola	moisture (n)	vog
	moletlo	ceremony (n)	seremonie	monontšha	fertiliser (n)	kunsmis
	moletšafiolo	violinist (n)	vioolspeler	monotlo	claw (n)	klou
	moletšamoropa	drummer (n)	tromspeler	monoto	soapstone (n)	seepsteen
	moletšanaka	flautist (n)	fluitspeler	monwana	finger (n)	vinger
	moletšaokane	organist (n)	orrelis	monwana wa leoto	toe (n)	toon
	moletšaporompeta	trumpeter (n)	trompetblaser	monyadi	bridegroom (n)	bruidegom
	moletši wa tšhelo	cellist (n)	tjellis	monyako	search (n)	soektog
	mollo	fire (n)	vuur	monyamišo	disappointment (n)	teleurstelling
	mollwane	border (n)	grens	monyanya	festival (n)	fees
	mollwane	boundary (n)	grenslyn	monyanya	celebration (n)	viering
	mollwane	margin (n)	kantlyn	monyanya wa lenyalo	wedding (n)	bruilof
	molodi	tune (n)	wysie	monyumente	monument (n)	monument
	mologo	weaving (n)	wewery	monywanyo	smile (n)	glimlag
	moloi	witchdoctor (n)	toordokter	mooka	mimosa (n)	mimosa
	moloko	relation (n)	familielid	mooki	nurse (n)	verpleegster
	molokoloko	queue (n)	tou	mooko	measles (n)	masels
	molomatsebe	informer (n)	verklikker	moomo	shin (n)	skeen
	molomo	lip (n)	lip	moono	snore (n)	snork
	-molomo	verbal (a)	mondeling	moopelo	music (n)	musiek
	molomo	mouth (n)	mond	-moopelo	musical (a)	musikaal
	molomo	muzzle (n)	snoet	mootledi	driver (n)	bestuurder
	molomo wa nonyana	beak (n)	snawel	mootlwa	thorn (n)	doring
	molora	ash (n)	as	mopaki	baker (n)	bakker
	molwantšhi	antagonist (n)	teenstander	mopapa	pope (n)	pous

N Sotho	English	Afrikaans	N Sotho	English	Afrikaans	M
mophegišani	rival (n)	mededinger	moruti	preacher (n)	predikant	
mophethi	performer (n)	uitvoerder	morutiši	teacher (n)	onderwyser	
mophetho	performance (n)	uitvoering	morutiwa	disciple (n)	dissipel	
mopišapo	bishop (n)	biskop	morutiwa	pupil (n)	leerling	
mopišopo pharephare	archbishop (n)	aartsbiskop	morwa	son (n)	seun	
mopopoliri	poplar (n)	populier	morwalaposo	postman (n)	posbode	
mopopotlo	ridge (n)	rug	morwalo	burden (n)	las	
mopresidente	president (n)	president	morwalo	load (n)	vrag	
moprista	priest (n)	priester	morwarra	brother (n)	broer	
moprofesa	professor (n)	professor	morwedi	daughter (n)	dogter	
moprofeta	prophet (n)	profeet	mosadi	female (n)	vrou	
mopulukomo	bluegum (n)	bloekomboom	mosadi	woman (n)	vrou	
moputso	earnings (n)	loon	mosamelo	cushion (n)	kussing	
moputso	salary (n)	salaris	mosamelo	pillow (n)	kussing	
morago	back (adv)	terug	mošašana	hovel (n)	pondok	
morago	behind (prep)	agter	mošate	palace (n)	paleis	
-morago	rear (a)	agterste	mosebe	arrow (n)	pyl	
morago ga	after (place) (prep)	agter	mosegare wa sekgalela	noon (n)	middag	
morago ga	after (time) (prep)	na	mosegare wa sekgalela	midday (n)	middag	
-morago ga nako	late (a)	laat	mosego	cut (n)	sny	
moralokigadi	actress (n)	aktrise	mosehlwana	segment (n)	segment	
moraloki wa piano	pianist (n)	klavierspeler	mosekiši	prosecutor (n)	aanklaer	
morara	vine (n)	wingerdstok	mosela	tail (n)	stert	
morati	lover (n)	minnaar	mošemane	boy (n)	seun	
moratiwa	boyfriend (n)	kêrel	moseme	mat (n)	mat	
moratiwa	girlfriend (n)	nooi	mosenyi	trespasser (n)	oortreder	
moreba	impertinence (n)	astrantheid	mosenyi	culprit (n)	skuldige	
moreki	buyer (n)	koper	mosenyiši	accomplice (n)	medepligtige	
morekišetši	agent (n)	agent	mosepelakamaoto	pedestrian (n)	voetganger	
morepa	sweet potato (n)	patat	mosepelo	walk (n)	wandeling	
morepho	paralysis (n)	verlamming	moseto	groove (n)	groef	
morero	interview (n)	onderhoud	moseto	strip (n)	strook	
morero wa ka thoko	conspiracy (n)	sameswering	mosetsana	girl (n)	meisie	
morethetho	pulse (n)	pols	mošidi	cinder (n)	sintel	
morethetho wa pelo	heartbeat (n)	hartklop	mošifa	ligament (n)	ligament	
moreto	praise (n)	lof	mošifa	muscle (n)	spier	
moriri	hair (n)	hare	mošifa	sinew (n)	sening	
moriti	shade (n)	skadu	mošifa	tendon (n)	sening	
moriti	shadow (n)	skaduwee	mošifa wa paesepe	biceps (n)	biseps	
moro	gravy (n)	sous	mošito	rhythm (n)	ritme	
morodi	lead (n)	lood	mošito	beat (n)	ritme	
morogo	vegetable (n)	groente	mosokologi	convert (n)	bekeerling	
moroki	tailor (n)	kleremaker	mošola wa	beyond (prep)	oorkant	
moroko	seam (n)	naat	mošola wa mawatle	overseas (n)	oorsee	
moroko	sewing (n)	naaldwerk	mošomi	labourer (n)	arbeider	
morongwa	angel (n)	engel	mošomo	labour (n)	arbeid	
morongwa	messenger (n)	bode	mošomo	employment (n)	werk	
moropa	drum (n)	trom	mostara	mustard (n)	mosterd	
moropana	tambourine (n)	tamboeryn	mošunkwane	herbs (n)	kruie	
mororo	roar (n)	brul	mošupatlotlo	accountant (n)	rekenmeester	
mororogo	swelling (n)	swelsel	Mošupologo	Monday (n)	Maandag	
moroto	urine (n)	urine	moswana	morning (n)	oggend	
morui	farmer (n)	boer	moswaro	hold (n)	vat	
morulaganyi	editor (n)	redakteur	moswaswi	comic (n)	komiek	
morumo	edge (n)	rand	moswe	meercat (n)	meerkat	
morumokwano	rhyme (n)	rym	motaga	lime (n)	kalk	
moruswi	jar (n)	fles	motala	barbarian (n)	barbaar	
moruthi	swimmer (n)	swemmer	motato	wire (n)	draad	
moruti	missionary (n)	sendeling	motele	motel (n)	motel	
moruti	minister (n)	predikant	motemone	demon (n)	bose gees	

M	N Sotho	English	Afrikaans		N Sotho	English	Afrikaans
	moteni	bore (n)	vervelige mens		mphapahlogo	crown (n)	kroon
	mothadi wa dipolane	architect (n)	argitek		mphato	class (n)	klas
	mothaladi	line (n)	lyn		mphatšana	gap (n)	opening
	mothaladi	row (n)	ry		mpheng	shaft (n)	steel
	mothalo	stripe (n)	streep		mpherefere	disturbance (n)	oproer
	mothapalalo	contour (n)	kontoer		mpherefere	revolt (n)	opstand
	mothapo	nerve (n)	senuwee		mpherefere	revolution (n)	revolusie
	motheo	basis (n)	basis		mpherefere	riot (n)	onlus
	-motheo	basic (a)	basies		-mpherefere	riotous (a)	wanordelik
	motho	individual (n)	individu		mpho	donation (n)	skenking
	motho	person (n)	persoon		mpho	present (n)	geskenk
	-motho	personal (a)	persoonlik		mpholo	poison (n)	gif
	-motho a nnoši	private (a)	privaat		mphufutšo	sweat (n)	sweet
	mothobe	yolk (n)	eiergeel		mponempone	dwarf (n)	dwerg
	mothobodiši	coach (n)	afrigter		mpša	dog (n)	hond
	mothomi	beginner (n)	beginner		mpšanyana	puppy (n)	klein hondjie
	mothubi	burglar (n)	inbreker		mpša ya lepultoko	bulldog (n)	bulhond
	mothuši	assistant (n)	helper		mpša ya tshadi	bitch (n)	teef
	mothwadi	employer (n)	werkgewer		mpshafatšo	reform (n)	hervorming
	motlae	joke (n)	grap		mpšhe	ostrich (n)	volstruis
	motlaišwa	martyr (n)	martelaar		mpshiri	anklet (n)	enkelring
	motlang	tendril (n)	rankie		muši	smoke (n)	rook
	motlanyi	typist (n)	tikster		musiamo	museum (n)	museum
	motlatši	reserve (n)	reserwe		mušimeetse	steam (n)	stoom
	motlogolo	grandchild (n)	kleinkind				
	motlogolo	granddaughter (n)	kleindogter		n-	me (pron)	my
	motlogolo	grandson (n)	kleinseun		-na	have (v)	hê
	motsaro	buttermilk (n)	karringmelk		-na	rain (v)	reën
	motse	village (n)	dorpie		naga	area (n)	oppervlakte
	motsemogolo	city (n)	stad		naga	field (n)	veld
	motseta	ambassador (n)	ambassadeur		naga	state (n)	staat
	motseta	deputy (n)	plaasvervanger		naga	veld (n)	veld
	motšhelo	tax (n)	belasting		-naga	wild (a)	wild
	motšhene	machine (n)	masjien		nagadimo	highveld (n)	hoëveld
	motšhene wa go roka	sewing machine (n)	naaimasjien		-nagagare	inland (a)	binnelands
	motšhitšhi	swarm (n)	swerm		-nagana	imagine (v)	verbeel
	motšhošetši	guerrilla (n)	guerrilla		nagatlase	lowveld (n)	laeveld
	motsila	rectum (n)	rektum		nagatšhireletšo	nature reserve (n)	natuurreservaat
	motšoko	tobacco (n)	tabak		-nageng	rural (a)	plattelands
	motsomi	hunter (n)	jagter		-nago le dipatso	spotted (a)	gekol
	motsotso	minute (n)	minuut		-nago le ditšhila	dirty (a)	vuil
	motsotso	moment (n)	oomblik		-nago le lebelo	fast (a)	vinnig
	motsotswana	second (n)	sekonde		-nago le maatla	powerful (a)	magtig
	motswadi	parent (n)	ouer		-nago le madimabe	unlucky (a)	ongelukkig
	motswako	mixture (n)	mengsel		-nago le mahlajana	cunning (a)	slu
	motswalle	acquaintance (n)	kennis		-nago le mahlatse	lucky (a)	gelukkig
	motu	wax (n)	was		-nago le maru	overcast (a)	bewolk
	motumiši	fan (n)	bewonderaar		-nago le molato	guilty (a)	skuldig
	mouta	fungus (n)	swam		-nago le mona	jealous (a)	jaloers
	mouwane	fog (n)	mis		-nago le sebete	courageous (a)	moedig
	mouwane	mist (n)	mis		-nago le sebete	brave (a)	dapper
	moya	air (n)	lug		-nago le tlhabologo ye nyane	underdeveloped (a)	onderontwikkeld
	moya	breath (n)	asem				
	moya	ghost (n)	gees		-nago le tseba	envious (a)	jaloers
	moya	soul (n)	siel		naka	flute (n)	fluit
	moya	spirit (n)	gees		nakana	whistle (n)	fluit
	-moyafala	evaporate (v)	verdamp		nakedi	polecat (n)	muishond
	moyameetse	vapour (n)	wasem		nakedi	skunk (n)	muishond
	mpa	abdomen (n)	buik		nako	time (n)	tyd
	mpa	stomach (n)	maag		-na le	contain (v)	bevat

N Sotho	English	Afrikaans	N Sotho	English	Afrikaans
-na le	own (v)	besit	ngwako	house (n)	huis
naledi	star (n)	ster	ngwakwana	cottage (n)	kothuis
-na lehlwa	snow (v)	sneeu	-ngwala	record (v)	opteken
nalete	needle (n)	naald	-ngwala	write (v)	skryf
nama	flesh (n)	vleis	ngwana	young (n)	kleintjie
nama	meat (n)	vleis	ngwana	child (n)	kind
namane	calf (n)	kalf	ngwana wa tau	cub (n)	welpie
nama ya kgomo	beef (n)	beesvleis	ngwanenyana	virgin (n)	maagd
nama ya kgomo	steak (n)	biefstuk	-ngwaya	scratch (v)	krap
nama ya kgomo ya mokokotlong	sirloin (n)	lendestuk	-ngwe	another (a)	'n ander
nama ya kolobe	pork (n)	varkvleis	-ngwe	another (a)	nog 'n
nama ya namane	veal (n)	kalfsvleis	-ngwe	further (a)	verder
nama ya nku	mutton (n)	skaapvleis	-ngwe	other (a)	ander
nama ya phoofolo	venison (n)	wildsvleis	-ngwe	some (a)	sommige
nama ya serope sa kolobe	ham (n)	ham	-ngwega	desert (v)	dros
			-ngwega	elope (v)	wegloop
nama ye e šitšwego	mince (n)	maalvleis	-ngwe le -ngwe	every (a)	elke
-namela	ascend (v)	styg	-ngwe le -ngwe	any (a)	enige
-namela	climb (v)	klim	ngwetši	daughter-in-law (n)	skoondogter
-namela	mount (v)	opklim	ngwetši	bride (n)	bruid
-namela	scramble (v)	klouter	-nkga	stink (v)	stink
namune	orange (n)	lemoen	nkgogorupa	thumb (n)	duim
-nanabela	tiptoe (v)	op die tone loop	-nkgokolo	round (a)	rond
-nanana	tender (a)	teer	-nko	nasal (a)	nasaal
-nanyago	slow (a)	stadig	nko	nose (n)	neus
nariki	naartjie (n)	nartjie	nku	sheep (n)	skaap
nawa	bean (n)	boontjie	nkwe	leopard (n)	luiperd
-ne	four (n)	vier	nna	I (pron)	ek
-nea khodi	credit (v)	krediteer	nnete	fact (n)	feit
-neela	supply (v)	verskaf	-nnete	real (a)	werklik
neng	when (adv)	wanneer	-nnete	sure (a)	seker
-nepagetšego	correct (a)	korrek	nnete	truth (n)	waarheid
-nepagetšego	exact (a)	presies	-nngele	left (a)	links
-nepegilego	accurate (a)	noukeurig	nnoši	only (a)	enigste
nepo	accuracy (n)	noukeurigheid	Nofemere	November (n)	November
nepo	aim (n)	doel	noga	snake (n)	slang
ngaka	doctor (n)	dokter	nogametsana	earthworm (n)	erdwurm
ngaka ya go bua	surgeon (n)	chirurg	nogana ya mala	tapeworm (n)	lintwurm
ngaka ya selete	district surgeon (n)	distriksgeneesheer	noka	river (n)	rivier
ngame	miser (n)	vrek	noka	rump (n)	kruis
-ngame	miserly (a)	vrekkerig	nokakeledi	tributary (n)	takrivier
-nganga	tighten (v)	span	noko	inch (n)	duim
-ngangegilego	tense (a)	gespanne	noko	joint (n)	gewrig
-ngangelago	obstinate (a)	hardkoppig	noko	porcupine (n)	ystervark
-nganka	punch (v)	slaan	noko	syllable (n)	lettergreep
-ngaparela	claw (v)	klou	-nokologago	clumsy (a)	lomp
ngata	bundle (n)	bondel	-nola moko	frustrate (v)	frustreer
ngata	pile (n)	stapel	nomoro	number (n)	nommer
ngata	sheaf (n)	gerf	-nonnego	fat (a)	vet
-ngongorega	complain (v)	kla	-nonnego	fertile (a)	vrugbaar
-ngongoregago	dissatisfied (a)	ontevrede	-nonnego	stout (a)	geset
ngongorego	complaint (n)	klagte	-nontšha	fertilise (v)	bevrug
ngongorego	dissatisfaction (n)	ontevredenheid	-nontšha mmu	fertilise (v)	kunsmis gee
-ngunanguna	grumble (v)	brom	nonwane	myth (n)	mite
-ngwadiša	enrol (v)	inskryf	nonwane	fable (n)	fabel
ngwaga	year (n)	jaar	nonwane	tale (n)	storie
ngwagakgolo	century (n)	eeu	nonyana	bird (n)	vol
ngwagamotelele	leap year (n)	skrikkeljaar	-noša	score (v)	punte aanteken
ngwagasome	decade (n)	dekade	nose	bee (n)	by
			-nošetša	water (v)	natgooi

257

N Sotho	English	Afrikaans	N Sotho	English	Afrikaans
-nošetšo	irrigate (v)	besproei	-nyane	small (a)	klein
nošetšo	irrigation (n)	besproeiing	-nyatša	belittle (v)	verkleineer
noši	alone (a)	alleen	-nyatša	scorn (v)	verag
-notlela	lock (v)	sluit	-nyatšegago	petty (a)	kleinlik
ntho	sore (n)	seer	-nyemiša pelo	discourage (v)	ontmoedig
ntho	wound (n)	wond	-nyennyane	minute (a)	heel klein
ntlha	apex (n)	spits	-nyenyane	least (a)	minste
ntlha	item (n)	item	nyoko	bile (n)	gal
ntlha	point (n)	punt	nyooko	gall (n)	gal
ntlha	tip (n)	punt	-nyorilwego	thirsty (a)	dorstig
ntlhana	speck (n)	stippel	nyumonia	pneumonia (n)	longontsteking
ntlhora	peak (n)	piek	-nywanywa	smile (v)	glimlag
ntlo	hut (n)	hut			
ntloseetša	lighthouse (n)	vuurtoring	-oba	bend (v)	buig
ntlo ya bokgabo	art gallery (n)	kunsgalery	obarolo	overalls (n)	oorpak
ntlwanathelefomo	telephone booth (n)	telefoonhokkie	ofisi	office (n)	kantoor
ntoto	penis (n)	penis	ofisi ya dithekethe	ticket office (n)	kaartjieskantoor
-ntšha	subtract (v)	aftrek	ofisi ya dithekethe	box office (n)	kaartjieloket
ntši	eyelash (n)	wimper	-ohle	whole (a)	heel
ntšhikgolo	eyebrow (n)	winkbrou	-oka	nurse (v)	verpleeg
ntšhitsetse	tsetse fly (n)	tsetsevlieg	okane	organ (n)	orrel
ntšhu	eagle (n)	arend	okese	orchestra (n)	orkes
-ntši	abundant (a)	oorvloedig	-oketša	add (v)	byvoeg
ntši	fly (n)	vlieg	-oketša	increase (v)	vermeerder
-ntši	many (a)	baie	-oketšago	additional (a)	bykomend
-ntši	much (a)	veel	-okobatša	soothe (v)	kalmeer
ntwa	war (n)	oorlog	-okola	skim (v)	afskep
ntwa	fight (n)	geveg	oksitšene	oxygen (n)	suurstof
ntwa	battle (n)	geveg	Oktobore	October (n)	Oktober
-nwa	drink (v)	drink	oli	oil (n)	olie
-nya	defecate (v)	ontlas	-oma	dry (v)	droogmaak
-nyabetša leihlo	wink (v)	knipoog	-ometša	feint (v)	voorgee
-nyaka	search (v)	soek	-omilego	arid (a)	dor
-nyaka	want (v)	wil hê	-omilego	dry (a)	droog
-nyaka	demand (v)	eis	-ona	snore (v)	snork
-nyakago go tseba	inquisitive (a)	nuuskierig	onoroko	petticoat (n)	onderrok
ditaba			onoropaki	waistcoat (n)	onderbaadjie
-nyakegago	essential (a)	essensieel	onto	oven (n)	oond
-nyakegago	necessary (a)	noodsaaklik	-opa	ache (v)	pyn
-nyakegago	positive (a)	positief	-opela	sing (v)	sing
nyakego	necessity (n)	noodsaaklikheid	-opela magoswi	applaud (v)	toejuig
nyakego	need (n)	behoefte	-ora	bask (v)	koester
nyakgahlo	mildew (n)	muf	-otilego	emaciated (a)	uitgeteer
-nyakile	almost (adv)	amper	-otilego	lean (a)	maer
-nyakile go-	nearly (adv)	byna	-otilego	slender (a)	tingerig
-nyakišiša	inquire (v)	navraag doen	-otla	lash (v)	gesel
-nyakišiša	investigate (v)	ondersoek	-otla	penalise (v)	straf
nyakišišo	investigation (n)	ondersoek	-otla	punish (v)	straf
nyakišišo	inquiry (n)	navraag	-otlela	drive (v)	bestuur
-nyala	wed (v)	trou	-otlolla	exercise (v)	oefen
-nyala	marry (v)	trou	-otlolla	extend (v)	uitstrek
-nyamalela	disappear (v)	verdwyn	-otsela	drowse (v)	dommel
nyamalelo	disappearance (n)	verdwyning	-otswa	fornicate (v)	hoereer
-nyamilego	unhappy (a)	ongelukkig	-otswago	lewd (a)	ontugtig
-nyamiša	depress (v)	neerdruk	-otswetšago	bawdy (a)	onkuis
-nyamiša	upset (v)	ontstel	outse	oats (n)	hawer
-nyamišago	pitiful (a)	jammerlik			
-nyamiša pelo	disappoint (v)	teleurstel	padi	novel (n)	roman
-nyane	junior (a)	junior	paesekela	bicycle (n)	fiets
-nyane	little (a)	klein	paesekopo	cinema (n)	bioskoop

N Sotho	English	Afrikaans	N Sotho	English	Afrikaans	P
pafo	bath (n)	bad	peile	bail (n)	borg	
-paka	bake (v)	bak	peipi	pipe (n)	pyp	
-paka	pack (v)	pak	pekenyo	reflection (n)	weerkaatsing	
pakane	beacon (n)	baken	pekere	mug (n)	beker	
paki	witness (n)	getuie	pela	dassie (n)	dassie	
-palago ka moka	best (a)	beste	pelaelo	affliction (n)	beproewing	
palamonwana	ring (n)	ring	pelaelo	anxiety (n)	kommer	
-palega	crack (v)	kraak	-pelaelo	doubt (n)	twyfel	
-palelwa	fail (v)	misluk	pelaelo	grievance (n)	grief	
paleng	eel (n)	paling	pele	ahead (adv)	vooruit	
palo	census (n)	sensus	pele	before (prep)	voor	
palo	score (n)	telling	-pele	first (a)	eerste	
-palogare	average (a)	gemiddeld	pele	forward (adv)	vooruit	
palomoka	total (n)	totaal	-pele	front (a)	voor	
palune	balloon (n)	ballon	pele	onward (adv)	voorwaarts	
pampiri	paper (n)	papier	pelego	birth (n)	geboorte	
pampiri ya go itlhakola	toilet paper (n)	toiletpapier	pelego	childbirth (n)	kindergeboorte	
pampiri ya go ngwalela	writing paper (n)	skryfpapier	-peleta	spell (v)	spel	
pampu	bamboo (n)	bamboes	pelo	heart (n)	hart	
panana	banana (n)	piesang	pelwana	embryo (n)	embrio	
pane	pan (n)	pan	pene	pen (n)	pen	
panka	bank (n)	bank	penehempe	vest (n)	onderhemp	
panka	bench (n)	bank	-penta	paint (v)	verf	
panka	desk (n)	lessenaar	pente	paint (n)	verf	
pankarea	pancreas (n)	pankreas	pentšu	banjo (n)	banjo	
pantetši	bandage (n)	verband	peo	appointment (n)	aanstelling	
-panya leihlo	blink (v)	knipoog	peo ya kgoši	coronation (n)	kroning	
panyepanye	flashlight (n)	flitslig	-pepenya	glow (v)	gloei	
panyepanye	torch (n)	flitslig	pepere	pepper (n)	peper	
papadi	game (n)	spel	pere	horse (n)	perd	
papadi	sport (n)	sport	perekisi	peach (n)	perske	
papetla	board (n)	bord	perese	purple (a)	pers	
papišo	comparison (n)	vergelyking	pere ya mokato	racehorse (n)	renperd	
para	bar (n)	kroeg	pere ya tona	stallion (n)	hings	
parafene	paraffin (n)	paraffien	pere ya tshadi	mare (n)	merrie	
pareseli	parsley (n)	pietersielie	pesaleme	psalm (n)	psalm	
pasa	pass (n)	pas	pešana	foal (n)	vulletjie	
-pataganya	compress (v)	saampers	pese	bus (n)	bus	
-patana	clasp (v)	vasklem	petala	pedal (n)	pedaal	
patla	stick (n)	stok	petala ya letšoba	petal (n)	kroonblaar	
patše	cannabis (n)	dagga	pete	beetroot (n)	beet	
patso	spot (n)	kol	peteri	battery (n)	battery	
payolotši	biology (n)	biologie	peterolo	petrol (n)	petrol	
peakanyo	organisation (n)	organisasie	petse	pit (n)	gat	
peakanyo	scheme (n)	skema	petse	well (n)	put	
peakanyo	system (n)	stelsel	peu	seed (n)	saad	
peba	rat (n)	rot	-phadima	glitter (v)	skitter	
pedi	two (n)	twee	-phadimago	shiny (a)	blink	
pedišo	brew (n)	brousel	-phadišana	compete (v)	wedywer	
peelano	bet (n)	weddenskap	phadišano	competition (n)	wedstryd	
peelano	condition (n)	voorwaarde	phadišano	contest (n)	wedstryd	
peeletšo	deposit (n)	deposito	phaeneapole	pineapple (n)	pynappel	
peetla	cobra (n)	kobra	phaephe ya kelatšhila	drainpipe (n)	rioolpyp	
pefelo	anger (n)	kwaadheid	phafatlo	delirium (n)	ylhoofdigheid	
pefelo	rage (n)	woede	-phafoga	awake (v)	ontwaak	
pego	accusation (n)	beskuldiging	-phafoga	wake (v)	wakker word	
pego	charge (n)	aanklag	-phagamiša	raise (v)	ophef	
pego	record (n)	rekord	phahlo	stock (n)	voorraad	
pego	report (n)	verslag	phaka	park (n)	park	
pego	statement (n)	verklaring	-phaka	park (v)	parkeer	

P	N Sotho	English	Afrikaans	N Sotho	English	Afrikaans
	-phakgamego	alert (a)	waaksaam	pherefere ye tala	green pepper (n)	soetrissie
	phakgamo	vigilance (n)	waaksaamheid	phesente	percent (n)	persent
	-phakiša	hurry (v)	jaag	-phetha	achieve (v)	presteer
	-phakiša	rush (v)	haas	-phetha	attain (v)	bereik
	-phala	excel (v)	uitblink	pheta	bead (n)	kraal
	-phala	overshadow (v)	oorskadu	-phetha	decide (v)	besluit
	-phalago	excellent (a)	uitmuntend	-phetha	effect (v)	bewerk
	-phamola	snatch (v)	gaps	pheta	necklace (n)	halssnoer
	phapang	dispute (n)	onenigheid	-phetha	perform (v)	uitvoer
	phapano	conflict (n)	konflik	-phethegilego	perfect (a)	volmaak
	phapano	controversy (n)	twispunt	phetho	achievement (n)	prestasie
	phapano	difference (n)	verskil	phetho	conclusion (n)	gevolgtrekking
	phapano	disagreement (n)	meningsverskil	phetho	decision (n)	besluit
	phapano	quarrel (n)	twis	-phetla	wring (v)	wring
	-phapea	flatter (v)	vlei	phetleko	analysis (n)	ontleding
	-phaphamala	float (v)	drywe	phetogo	change (n)	verandering
	-phaphasela	flap (v)	fladder	phetošo	amendment (n)	wysiging
	-phaphathi	broad (a)	breed	phifalo	eclipse (n)	verduistering
	-phaphathi	flat (a)	plat	phiri	hyena (n)	hiëna
	-phaphathi	wide (a)	wyd	phirimane	dusk (n)	skemer
	phapogo	deviation (n)	ompad	phirimo	sundown (n)	sononder
	phapoši	room (n)	kamer	phirimo	sunset (n)	sononder
	phara	cucumber (n)	komkommer	phišego	enthusiasm (n)	geesdrif
	phara ya sekgowa	melon (n)	meloen	-phišego	enthusiastic (a)	geesdriftig
	-pharoga	burst (v)	bars	phišo	heat (n)	hitte
	-pharola	split (v)	splits	-phobela	dent (v)	duik
	phasela	parcel (n)	pakket	phohu	eland (n)	eland
	-phasola	slap (v)	klap	phoka	dew (n)	dou
	phasolo	slap (n)	klap	phokoletšo	discount (n)	afslag
	phathi	party (n)	party	-pholiša	polish (v)	poleer
	phatla	forehead (n)	voorhoof	pholiši	polish (n)	politoer
	-phatlalala	adjourn (v)	verdaag	pholo	health (n)	gesondheid
	-phatlalatša	disperse (v)	verstrooi	pholo	ox (n)	os
	-phatlalatša	publish (v)	uitgee	-phološa	save (v)	red
	-phatlalatša	scatter (v)	strooi	-phološa	rescue (v)	red
	phedišanommogo	society (n)	samelewing	-phološa	redeem (v)	goedmaak
	phefo	wind (n)	wind	phološo	salvation (n)	verlossing
	phefšana	breeze (n)	bries	phološo	rescue (n)	redding
	-phega kgang	argue (v)	stry	-phonkgela	risk (v)	waag
	-phegelela	insist (v)	aandring	-phonkgela	dive (v)	duik
	phegelelo	insistence (n)	aandrang	phonkgelo	diving (n)	duikery
	phegelelo	determination (n)	vasberadenheid	-phonyokga	escape (v)	ontsnap
	-phegišana	dispute (v)	betwis	phonyokgo	escape (n)	ontsnapping
	-phela	live (v)	leef	phoofolo	animal (n)	dier
	-phelago	alive (a)	lewend	phoofolo	antelope (n)	wildsbok
	-phelago gabotse	healthy (a)	gesond	phoofolo	beast (n)	dier
	pheletšo	consequence (n)	gevolg	phoofolo	buck (n)	bok
	pheletšo	outcome (n)	uitkoms	phoofolo ya	vertebrate (n)	werweldier
	pheletšo	sequel (n)	gevolg	mokokotlo		
	-phemela	defend (v)	verdedig	phooko	ram (n)	ram
	-phemelago	defensive (a)	verdedigend	phopho	pawpaw (n)	papaja
	phemelo	defence (n)	verdediging	phororo	waterfall (n)	waterval
	phensele	pencil (n)	potlood	phošo	blunder (n)	flater
	phenšene	pension (n)	pensioen	phošo	mistake (n)	fout
	phenthihouse	pantihose (n)	kousbroekie	phošo	error (n)	fout
	phenyo	triumph (n)	triomf	phošo	fault (n)	fout
	phepheng	scorpion (n)	skerpioen	-phošo	wrong (a)	verkeerd
	phepo	maintenance (n)	onderhoud	-phošolla	correct (v)	korrigeer
	phepo	nutrition (n)	voeding	phukubje	jackal (n)	jakkals
	pherefere	chilli (n)	brandrissie	phulawatle	tide (n)	gety

N Sotho	English	Afrikaans	N Sotho	English	Afrikaans	R
-phumola	cancel (v)	kanselleer	-pona	wilt (v)	kwyn	
-phumola	delete (v)	skrap	ponagalo	phenomenon (n)	verskynsel	
-phumola	erase (v)	uitvee	pono	sight (n)	sig	
-phumola	wipe (v)	afvee	pono	view (n)	uitsig	
-phumula lerole	dust (v)	afstof	pono	vision (n)	gesigsvermoë	
-phunya	pierce (v)	deursteek	pontšho	exhibition (n)	uitstalling	
phuphu	eyelid (n)	ooglid	pontšho	show (n)	skou	
-phušula	demolish (v)	afbreek	pontšho	show (n)	vertoning	
phuthego	congregation (n)	gemeente	ponyo ya leihlo	wink (n)	knipogie	
-phuthela	wrap (v)	toedraai	poo	bull (n)	bul	
phuti	duiker (n)	duiker	popego	physique (n)	liggaamsbou	
phuting	dessert (n)	nagereg	popelo	ovary (n)	eierstok	
piano	piano (n)	klavier	popelo	womb (n)	baarmoeder	
pianotamolwa	accordion (n)	trekklavier	popi	doll (n)	pop	
piere	pear (n)	peer	popopolelo	grammar (n)	grammatika	
pikiniki	picnic (n)	piekniek	porase	brass (n)	geelkoper	
piletšotshekong	subpoena (n)	dagvaarding	poreimi	plum (n)	pruim	
pilisi	pill (n)	pil	poriki	brake (n)	rem	
pilisi	tablet (n)	tablet	porompeta	trumpet (n)	trompet	
pinki	pink (n)	pienk	-poropela	plug (v)	toestop	
-pinya	squash (v)	platdruk	poropo	cork (n)	kurk	
pipamolomo	bribe (n)	omkoopprys	-porosola	brush (v)	borsel	
pipelo	constipation (n)	konstipasie	porosolo	brush (n)	borsel	
piskiti	biscuit (n)	koekie	poroto	plate (n)	bord	
-pitla	squeeze (v)	druk	-posa	post (v)	pos	
pitša	pot (n)	pot	poskarata	postcard (n)	poskaart	
pitšana ya teye	teapot (n)	teepot	poso	post (n)	pos	
pitsi ya naga	zebra (n)	sebra	poso	mail (n)	pos	
plastiki	plastic (n)	plastiek	posomoya	airmail (n)	lugpos	
ploresi	pleurisy (n)	borsvliesontsteking	posong	post office (n)	poskantoor	
pobolo	murmur (n)	gemurmel	posotere	postal order (n)	posorder	
podilekgwana	ladybird (n)	lieweheersbesie	potego	fidelity (n)	getrouheid	
podišwa	compost (n)	kompos	potego	integrity (n)	integriteit	
poelo	gain (n)	wins	potšišo	question (n)	vraag	
poelo	profit (n)	wins	-potuma	doze (v)	sluimer	
poifo	fear (n)	vrees	pouto	bolt (n)	bout	
polabolo	chatter (n)	gebabbel	pshio	kidney (n)	nier	
polai	fang (n)	slagtand	pudi	goat (n)	bok	
polanete	planet (n)	planeet	pudutša	ringworm (n)	ringwurm	
polao	murder (n)	moord	pue	bubble (n)	borrel	
polao	slaughter (n)	slagting	puku	book (n)	boek	
polase	farm (n)	plaas	pukuntšu	dictionary (n)	woordeboek	
polatefomo	platform (n)	platform	puku ya thelefomo	telephone directory (n)	telefoongids	
polause	blouse (n)	bloes	pukwana	pamphlet (n)	pamflet	
polayamonkgo	deodorant (n)	reukweermiddel	pula	rain (n)	reën	
poledišano	conversation (n)	gesprek	pulo	opening (n)	opening	
polelo	language (n)	taal	puno	harvest (n)	oes	
polelwana	talk (n)	praatjie	puno	income (n)	inkomste	
politiki	politics (n)	politiek	puo	operation (n)	operasie	
-politiki	political (a)	polities	pušo	reign (n)	bewind	
poloko	funeral (n)	begrafnis	putšana	kid (n)	bokkie	
poloko	burial (n)	begrafnis	putsu	boot (n)	stewel	
-poma	prune (v)	snoei	-putswa	grey (n)	grys	
pomelo	grapefruit (n)	pomelo				
pomo	bomb (n)	bom	-ra	mean (v)	bedoel	
pomo ya naga	landmine (n)	landmyn	-ra	refer (v)	verwys	
-pompa	pump (v)	pomp	raba	rubber (n)	rubber	
pompi	tap (n)	kraan	-rabela	rebel (v)	rebelleer	
pompo	pump (n)	pomp	raboloro	revolver (n)	rewolwer	
-pona	wither (v)	verlep	-radia	jilt (v)	afsê	

R	N Sotho	English	Afrikaans
	radietere	radiator (n)	verkoeler
	radinama	butcher (n)	slagter
	radio	radio (n)	radio
	-raga	boot (v)	skop
	-raga	kick (v)	skop
	-ragela ntle	eject (v)	uitskiet
	raka	shelf (n)	rak
	-rakadiša	pursue (v)	najaag
	rakgadi	aunt (n)	tante
	-ralokiša tšhelete	gamble (v)	dobbel
	ramapuku	librarian (n)	bibliotekaris
	ramelodi	musician (n)	musikant
	rameno	dentist (n)	tandarts
	ramešunkwane	herbalist (n)	kruiekenner
	ramolao	attorney (n)	prokureur
	ramolao	solicitor (n)	prokureur
	ramotse	mayor (n)	burgemeester
	ramphašane	sandal (n)	sandaal
	rapa	turnip (n)	raap
	-rapamego	horizontal (a)	horisontaal
	-rapela	pray (v)	bid
	-raramologago	elastic (a)	rekbaar
	-rarolla	solve (v)	oplos
	rasiti	receipt (n)	kwitansie
	-rata	favour (v)	begunstig
	-rata	like (v)	hou van
	-rata	prefer (v)	verkies
	-ratago	affectionate (a)	toegeneë
	-rata kudu	adore (v)	aanbid
	-rategago	admirable (a)	bewonderendswaardig
	-rategago	beloved (a)	bemind
	-rategago	dear (a)	dierbaar
	-rategago	glamorous (a)	bekoorlik
	-rategago	likeable (a)	beminlik
	-rategago	lovable (a)	dierbaar
	rateise	radish (n)	radys
	-ratha	crumble (v)	verkrummel
	-ratharatha	babble (v)	babbel
	-ratiša	endear (v)	bemind maak
	ratswale	father-in-law (n)	skoonvader
	-ratwago go feta	favourite (a)	gunsteling
	-re	allege (v)	beweer
	-re	say (v)	sê
	-re-	us (pron)	ons
	-rea	set (v)	stel
	-rea dihlapi	fish (v)	visvang
	-rea leina	name (v)	noem
	-reetšwego la	alias (n)	alias
	-rego thwi	straight (a)	reguit
	reise	rice (n)	rys
	rejistara	register (n)	register
	-reka	bribe (v)	omkoop
	-reka	buy (v)	koop
	-reka	shop (v)	inkopies doen
	rekere	elastic (n)	rek
	-rekiša	sell (v)	verkoop
	-rema	chop (v)	kap
	-rena	our (pron)	ons
	-rena	ours (pron)	ons s'n
	rena	we (pron)	ons
	rente	rent (n)	huur
	-rephiša	paralyse (v)	verlam
	-rera	preach (v)	preek
	-rera ka sephiri	plot (v)	saamsweer
	-rerišana	negotiate (v)	onderhandel
	restorante	restaurant (n)	restaurant
	-reta	praise (v)	loof
	-reta	recite (v)	opsê
	-retegago	praiseworthy (a)	lofwaardig
	-ribolla	discover (v)	ontdek
	-ripa	carve (v)	sny
	-ripaganya	shred (v)	snipper
	-ripa ka bogare	halve (v)	halveer
	-ritša	shuffle (v)	skuifel
	-roba	break (v)	breek
	-robala	sleep (v)	slaap
	-robegilego	broken (a)	stukkend
	roboto	robot (n)	robot
	-roga	scold (v)	uitskel
	-roga	swear (v)	vloek
	-roka	sew (v)	naaldwerk doen
	roko	dress (n)	rok
	-rola modiro	retire (v)	aftree
	rolo	roll (n)	rol
	-roma	send (v)	stuur
	-romela	delegate (v)	afvaardig
	-rora	roar (v)	brul
	-roroga	swell (v)	swel
	-roromela	shiver (v)	bewe
	-roromela	tremble (v)	bewe
	rosi	rose (n)	roos
	-rota	urinate (v)	urineer
	-rotha	drip (v)	drup
	-rotoga	rise (v)	styg
	-rotogago	steep (a)	steil
	rrakgolo	grandfather (n)	oupa
	-rua	breed (v)	teel
	-rua	farm (v)	boer
	rugby	rugby (n)	rugby
	rula	ruler (n)	liniaal
	-rulaganya	arrange (v)	skik
	-rulaganya	edit (v)	redigeer
	-rulela	thatch (v)	dek
	-ruma	rhyme (v)	rym
	-rumula	taunt (v)	uitlok
	ruri	really (adv)	werklik
	ruri	absolutely (adv)	absoluut
	-rusa	rust (v)	roes
	rusi	rust (n)	roes
	-ruta	educate (v)	opvoed
	-ruta	instruct (v)	onderrig
	-ruta	lecture (v)	doseer
	-ruta	train (v)	afrig
	-rutegilego	qualified (a)	gekwalifiseerd
	-rutha	swim (v)	swem
	-ruthetša	heat (v)	warm maak
	-rwala	carry (v)	dra
	-sa-	still (adv)	nog
	-sa akanywago	unplanned (a)	onbedoeld

N Sotho	English	Afrikaans	N Sotho	English	Afrikaans	S
-sa alafegego	incurable (a)	ongeneeslik	-šašetša	sprinkle (v)	sprinkel	
-sa belaetšago	reasonable (a)	redelik	-sa šomego	invalid (a)	ongeldig	
-sa belaetšego	undoubted (a)	ongetwyfeld	-sa swanelago	improper (a)	onfatsoenlik	
-sa boifego	unafraid (a)	onbevrees	-sa swanelego	undeserved (a)	onverdiend	
-sa bonagalego	dim (a)	dof	-sa tlwaelago	unaccustomed (a)	ongewoond	
gabotse			-sa tlwaelegago	abnormal (a)	abnormaal	
-sa bonwego	invisible (a)	onsigbaar	-sa tlwaelwago	uncommon (a)	ongewoon	
-sa botegego	undependable (a)	onbetroubaar	-sa tsebego	unaware (a)	onbewus	
-saena	sign (v)	teken	satšene	sergeant (n)	sersant	
-šaetšago	careless (a)	nalatig	-sa tshephegego	dishonest (a)	oneerlik	
-sa felego	boundless (a)	grensloos	-sa tšweletšwago	undisclosed (a)	onvermeld	
-sa felego	eternal (a)	ewig	šawara	shower (n)	stortbad	
-sa felego	lasting (a)	voortdurend	-šawara	shower (v)	stort	
-sa felelago	incomplete (a)	onvolledig	seamuši	mammal (n)	soogdier	
-sa fetogego	stable (a)	stabiel	seatla	hand (n)	hand	
-sa fetogego	unalterable (a)	onveranderlik	seatlakobong	bribery (n)	omkopery	
saga	saw (n)	saag	seatla sa modulasetulo	vice-chairman (n)	ondervoorsitter	
-saga	saw (v)	saag	-seba	gossip (v)	skinder	
-sa ganetšwego	undisputed (a)	onbetwis	sebabole	sulphur (n)	swawel	
-sa golago	immature (a)	onvolwasse	sebaka	chance (n)	kans	
-sa hlokomelego	negligent (a)	nalatig	sebaka	opportunity (n)	geleentheid	
-sa hlokomelego	inattentive (a)	onoplettend	sebaka	vacancy (n)	vakature	
-sa hlokomelego	unwary (a)	onbehoedsaam	sebakabaka	space (n)	ruimte	
-sa hlwekago	unclean (a)	onrein	sebapadi	actor (n)	akteur	
-sa hwetšagalago	unavailable (a)	onverkrygbaar	sebapadišwa	toy (n)	speelding	
-sa iketlego	uneasy (a)	ongerus	sebara	brother-in-law (n)	swaer	
-sa iketlego	restless (a)	rusteloos	-sebaseba	whisper (v)	fluister	
-sa ikgantšhego	modest (a)	beskeie	sebata	predator (n)	roofdier	
-sa išego	shallow (a)	vlak	sebe	sin (n)	sonde	
-sa itlhamago ka	unarmed (a)	ongewapend	sebenyabje	jewel (n)	juweel	
dibetša			sebeolo	razor (n)	skeermes	
-sa itshwarego	ill-mannered (a)	onmanierlik	sebešo	fireplace (n)	vuurherd	
šaka	shark (n)	haai	sebešo	hearth (n)	haard	
sakatuku	handkerchief (n)	sakdoek	sebešwa	fuel (n)	brandstof	
-sa kgonegego	impossible (a)	onmoontlik	sebete	courage (n)	moed	
-sa kwagalego	inaudible (a)	onhoorbaar	sebete	liver (n)	lewer	
-sa kwego	insubordinate (a)	ongehoorsaam	sebetša	weapon (n)	wapen	
-sa kwišiše	misunderstand (v)	misverstaan	sebiete	serviette (n)	servet	
-šala	remain (v)	agterbly	-sebjalebjale	modern (a)	modern	
sala	saddle (n)	saal	sebjana	dish (n)	skottel	
-sa lebanyago	indirect (a)	indirek	sebjana sa mohla-	bedpan (n)	bedpan	
-sa lebogego	ungrateful (a)	ondankbaar	pologo			
-sa lekanego	uneven (a)	ongelyk	sebjanatsopa	vase (n)	vaas	
-sa lekanego	unequal (a)	ongelyk	sebo	fort (n)	fort	
-sa lekanelego	odd (a)	onewe	seboko	caterpillar (n)	ruspe	
-sa lokago	unjust (a)	onregverdig	seboko	larva (n)	larwe	
-sa lokelego	unfit (a)	ongeskik	seboko	maggot (n)	maaier	
samente	cement (n)	sement	seboko	worm (n)	wurm	
samporele	umbrella (n)	sambreel	sebolawa	prey (n)	prooi	
sangwetšhi	sandwich (n)	toebroodjie	sebolokelo	glovebox (n)	mossienes	
santlhoko	gallbladder (n)	galblaas	sebontšhi	symptom (n)	simptoom	
-sa nyakegego	undesirable (a)	ongewens	sebopego	form (n)	vorm	
-sa phelego	inanimate (a)	leweloos	sebopi	mould (n)	vorm	
-sa phemegego	inevitable (a)	onvermydelik	sebopiwa	creature (n)	wese	
-sa phethegago	imperfect (a)	onvolmaak	sebudula	bladder (n)	blaas	
-sa phethegago	unfinished (a)	onvoltooid	sediba	fountain (n)	fontein	
-sa phethegago	unfulfilled (a)	onvervuld	sediba	pool (n)	poel	
-sa popego	concrete (a)	konkreet	sedika	circumference (n)	omtrek	
-sarasara	drizzle (v)	motreën	sediko	circle (n)	sirkel	
-sa ratego	reluctant (a)	teensinnig	sediri	subject (n)	onderwerp	

S

N Sotho	English	Afrikaans	N Sotho	English	Afrikaans
sediri**š**wa	instrument (n)	instrument	-sego -senyega	undamaged (a)	onbeskadig
sediri**š**wana sa komphuta	chip (computer) (n)	vlokkie	-sego wa ahlolwa	undecided (a)	onbeslis
-seela	fluid (a)	vloeibaar	-sego ya tswalwa	unborn (a)	ongebore
seela	fluid (n)	vloeistof	segwagwa	frog (n)	padda
seela	liquid (n)	vloeistof	-segwahla	sickly (a)	sieklik
seema	proverb (n)	spreekwoord	segwa**š**i	rattle (n)	ratel
seenywa	fruit (n)	vrug	segwere	bulb (n)	bol
seeta	shoe (n)	skoen	sehla	season (n)	seisoen
seeta sa pere	horseshoe (n)	hoefyster	sehlabelo	victim (n)	slagoffer
seet**š**a	light (n)	lig	sehlabelo	sacrifice (n)	offerande
seet**š**a sa kgwedi	moonlight (n)	maanlig	sehlaga	nest (n)	nes
seet**š**a sa let**š**at**š**i	sunlight (n)	sonlig	sehlakahlaka	island (n)	eiland
-sefa	sift (v)	sif	sehlamo	apparatus (n)	apparaat
sefahlego	face (n)	gesig	sehlapelo	sink (n)	opwasbak
sefaka	forearm (n)	voorarm	sehlapelo	basin (n)	kom
sefako	hail (n)	hael	sehlapelo	cistern (n)	waterbak
sefamakhura	accelerator (n)	brandstofpedaal	sehlare	medicine (n)	medisyne
sefane	surname (n)	van	sehlare	tree (n)	boom
Sefapanaledi sa Borwa	Southern Cross (n)	Suiderkruis	sehlare sa go gofi**š**a	laxative (n)	lakseermiddel
sefebe	whore (n)	hoer	sehla**š**ana	shrub (n)	struik
sefehlo	churn (n)	karring	sehlopha	band (n)	groep
sefela	hymn (n)	gesang	sehlopha	bunch (n)	tros
sefepi	whip (n)	sweep	sehlopha	group (n)	groep
sefero	gate (n)	hek	sehlopha	set (n)	stel
sefihlolo	breakfast (n)	ontbyt	sehlopha sa balet**š**i	band (n)	orkes
sefo	sieve (n)	sif	sehlopha sa dikebeke	gang (n)	bende
-sefoa	deaf (a)	doof	sehlweki**š**i	disinfectant (n)	ontsmettingsmiddel
sefofane	aeroplane (n)	vliegtuig	sehuba	breast (n)	bors
sefofane	aircraft (n)	vliegtuig	sehuba	bosom (n)	boesem
sefoka	prize (n)	prys	sehuba	chest (n)	borskas
sefoki**š**amoya	fan (n)	waaier	sehuba	thorax (n)	borskas
-sega	cut (v)	sny	sei	silk (n)	sy
-sega	giggle (v)	giggel	seife	safe (n)	brandkluis
-sega	laugh (v)	lag	seila	tarpaulin (n)	seil
-segae	civil (a)	burgerlik	seila	canvas (n)	seil
segafa	lunatic (n)	waansinnige	seila	sail (n)	seil
-sega selai	slice (v)	skywe sny	seipone	mirror (n)	spieël
segaswa	patch (n)	lappie	sei**š**amadi	artery (n)	slagaar
segateledi	nightmare (n)	nagmerrie	-Seisemane	English (a)	Engels
segati**š**i sa video	video recorder (n)	videokassetopnemer	-Seisimane	British (a)	Brits
segatla	sheath (n)	skede	sejato	glutton (n)	vraat
segetla	shoulderblade (n)	skouerblad	seka	idiom (n)	idioom
-segi**š**ago	absurd (a)	onsinnig	sekaelo	pattern (n)	patroon
-segi**š**ago	comic (a)	komies	sekafoko	phrase (n)	sinsnede
-segi**š**ago	funny (a)	snaaks	sekaku	abscess (n)	verswering
-sego a nyala	unmarried (a)	ongetroud	sekaku	boil (n)	bloedvint
-sego bohlokwa	unimportant (a)	onbelangrik	sekala	scale (n)	skaal
-**š**egofat**š**a	bless (v)	seën	-sekama	slant (v)	skuins loop
segofi**š**i	purgative (n)	purgeermiddel	sekasehlakahlaka	peninsula (n)	skiereiland
-sego kae	few (a)	min	sekebeka	scoundrel (n)	skobbejak
segokgo	spider (n)	spinnekop	sekebeka	villain (n)	skurk
segola	lair (n)	lêplek	sekele	sickle (n)	sekel
-segole	disabled (a)	gebreklik	sekepe	boat (n)	boot
segole	cripple (n)	kreupele	sekepe	ship (n)	skip
-segole	lame (a)	mank	sekerete	cigarette (n)	sigaret
-segologolo	primitive (a)	primitief	sekero	scissors (n)	skêr
segomaret**š**i	glue (n)	gom	sekete	thousand (n)	duisend
-segopot**š**o	memorial (a)	herdenking	-seket**š**a	economise (v)	besuinig
segopot**š**o	souvenir (n)	aandenking	seketswana	yacht (n)	seiljag
			sekgabi**š**o	ornament (n)	ornament

N Sotho	English	Afrikaans	N Sotho	English	Afrikaans	S
sekgalaka	eczema (n)	ekseem	-semmušo	official (a)	amptelik	
sekgamati	bark (n)	bas	-semotšhene	mechanical (a)	meganies	
sekgomaretši	paste (n)	pasta	semoya	clergy (n)	geesteliks	
sekgonyo	lock (n)	slot	sempara	slang (n)	sleng	
sekgonyo	padlock (n)	hangslot	-semumu	dumb (a)	stom	
sekgopi	grudge (n)	wrok	-se nago fenišara	unfurnished (a)	ongemeubileerd	
sekgopi	hindrance (n)	hindernis	-se nago kotsi	harmless (a)	onskadelik	
sekgwama	purse (n)	beursie	-se nago selo	blank (a)	leeg	
sekhafo	scarf (n)	serp	-se nago selo	empty (a)	leeg	
sekhethe	skirt (n)	romp	-se nago tokelo	unauthorised (a)	ongemagtig	
sekhurumelo	cap (n)	deksel	senami	creeper (n)	klimop	
sekhurumelo	cover (n)	deksel	senanawatle	bluebottle (n)	bloublasie	
sekhurumelo	lid (n)	deksel	senate	senate (n)	senaat	
sekhutlo	corner (n)	hoek	senatla	hero (n)	held	
-sekiša	prosecute (v)	vervolg	sengamedi	zipper (n)	ritssluiter	
sekobonyane	smallpox (n)	waterpokkies	senkgwanaboroso	hot dog (n)	worsbroodjie	
sekoka	invalid (n)	invalide	seno	drink (n)	drankie	
sekolo	school (n)	skool	senoko	knuckle (n)	kneukel	
sekontiri	tar (n)	teer	senoko	spice (n)	spesery	
sekopogarafo	shovel (n)	skoppie	senoko so seatla	wrist (n)	pols	
sekoro	weed (n)	onkruid	senotagi	liquor (n)	drank	
-Sekriste	Christian (a)	Christelik	senotagi sa sekgowa	liqueur (n)	likeur	
seksafone	saxophone (n)	saxofoon	senotlelo	key (n)	sleutel	
sekuki	lift (n)	hyser	sente	cent (n)	sent	
sekurufi	screw (n)	skroef	senwelwana	wineglass (n)	wynkelkie	
sekwaše	squash (n)	muurbal	-senya	abuse (v)	misbruik	
sekwi	sense (n)	sin	-senya	corrupt (v)	bederf	
selae	salad (n)	slaai	-senya	damage (v)	beskadig	
selae	lettuce (n)	blaarslaai	-senya	deform (v)	vervorm	
selai	slice (n)	sny	-senya	mutilate (v)	skend	
-sela kgati	skip (v)	touspring	-senya	waste (v)	vermors	
sele	cell (n)	sel	senyane	nine (n)	nege	
-šele	exotic (a)	eksoties	-senyegilego	corrupt (a)	bedorwe	
-šele	foreign (a)	vreemd	seoketša	appendix (n)	aanhangsel	
-šele	strange (a)	vreemd	seokobatši	drug (n)	dwelm	
seledu	beard (n)	baard	seokolela	heartburn (n)	sooibrand	
seledu	chin (n)	ken	seotswa	adulterer (n)	owerspeler	
-seleka	irritate (v)	irriteer	sepalete	pin (n)	speld	
-selekago	mischievous (a)	ondeund	sepalete	safety pin (n)	haakspeld	
-selekago	naughty (a)	stout	sepane	team (n)	span	
selemo	summer (n)	somer	sepanere	spanner (n)	moersleutel	
selepe	axe (n)	byl	sepate	clasp (n)	klem	
seleri	celery (n)	seldery	sepatšhe	wallet (n)	notetas	
selešadihlong	scandal (n)	skandaal	sepeke	bacon (n)	spek	
selete	district (n)	distrik	sepekere	nail (n)	spyker	
selete	region (n)	streek	sepekwa	hawk (n)	valk	
seletšo sa hamonika	harmonica (n)	harmonika	-sepela	walk (v)	loop	
sello	lament (n)	weeklag	-sepelago	moving (a)	bewegend	
sello	mourning (n)	rou	-sepela ka	ride (v)	ry	
selo	substance (n)	stof	sepetlele	hospital (n)	hospitaal	
selo	thing (n)	ding	sephaphami	raft (n)	vlot	
selo	nothing (n)	niks	sephetho	effect (n)	uitwerking	
selo	object (n)	voorwerp	sephetho	result (n)	uitslag	
sematlafatši	stimulus (n)	stimulus	-sephiri	confidential (a)	vertroulik	
-semeetseng	immediate (a)	onmiddellik	sephiri	secrecy (n)	geheimhouding	
semela	plant (n)	plant	sephiri	secret (n)	geheim	
semelafa	aboriginal (n)	oorspronklike inwoner	sephotlwa	pod (n)	peul	
-semelafa	indigenous (a)	inheems	sephumodi	eraser (n)	uitveër	
semelo	character (n)	karakter	sephumodi	rubber (n)	wisser	
semmejana	brassière (n)	bra	sephumudi sa lerole	duster (n)	stoflap	

S	N Sotho	English	Afrikaans	N Sotho	English	Afrikaans
	sepontšhe	sponge (n)	spons	seteišene sa maphodisa	police station (n)	polisiekantoor
	seporitšhi	spirits (n)	spiritus	Setemere	September (n)	September
	seporo	rail (n)	staaf	setempe	stamp (n)	seël
	seporo sa ditimela	railway (n)	spoorweg	setempe	postage stamp (n)	posseël
	-serafe	ethnic (a)	etnies	setena	brick (n)	baksteen
	serapa	garden (n)	tuin	seteraeke	strike (n)	staking
	serapa sa diphoofolo	zoo (n)	dieretuin	seteteskopo	stethoscope (n)	stetoskoop
	serapolotšwana	foetus (n)	fetus	sethala	gallery (n)	galery
	seregana	autumn (n)	herfs	sethalwa	figure (n)	figuur
	serethe	heel (n)	hak	sethekhu	hiccough (n)	hik
	sereti	poet (n)	digter	sethibo	plug (n)	prop
	sereto	poem (n)	gedig	sethibo	stopper (n)	stopprop
	seripa	part (n)	deel	sethibo	tampon (n)	tampon
	seripa	piece (n)	stuk	sethitho	perspiration (n)	perspirasie
	seripagare	half (n)	helfte	setho	culture (n)	kultuur
	seripana	fragment (n)	brokstuk	setho	limb (n)	ledemaat
	serobe sa mpša	kennel (n)	hondehok	sethokgwa	forest (n)	bos
	serope	thigh (n)	dy	sethokgwa	bush (n)	bos
	seroto	basket (n)	mandjie	sethokgwa	jungle (n)	oerwoud
	seruiwaseratwa	pet (n)	troeteldier	sethole	heifer (n)	vers
	serurubele	butterfly (n)	skoenlapper	-sethotho	stupid (a)	onnosel
	seruthwana	spring (n)	lente	sethunya	rifle (n)	geweer
	-sesane	thin (a)	dun	sethunya	gun (n)	geweer
	sešašetši	sprinkler (n)	sprinkelaar	setimela	train (n)	trein
	-sese	narrow (a)	smal	setimela sa mafofonyane	express (n)	sneltrein
	-sese	slim (a)	skraal	setlaela	fool (n)	dwaas
	sesegabjang	lawnmower (n)	grassnyer	setlaela	idiot (n)	idioot
	sesegišabaeng	dimple (n)	kuiltjie	setlamo	bond (n)	band
	sešego	granary (n)	graanskuur	setlanyi	typewriter (n)	tikmasjien
	-sesella	loiter (v)	rondslenter	setlišamadi	vein (n)	aar
	sesenyi	criminal (n)	misdadiger	setlo	article (n)	artikel
	sešepe	soap (n)	seep	setlogolo	nephew (n)	neef
	sešepe sa go beola	shaving cream (n)	skeerroom	setlogolo	niece (n)	niggie
	seširaphefo	windscreen (n)	voorruit	setofo	stove (n)	stoof
	seširo	blind (n)	blinding	setonwana	coccyx (n)	stuitjiebeen
	seširo	screen (n)	skerm	setopo	corpse (n)	lyk
	seširo	veil (n)	sluier	setoto	carcass (n)	karkas
	sešo	tumour (n)	gewas	setsebi	expert (n)	deskundige
	sešo	ulcer (n)	ulkus	-setšhaba	national (a)	nasionaal
	sešunetšwa	filling (n)	stopsel	-setšhaba	public (a)	openbaar
	sešupanako	clock (n)	horlosie	setšhaba	nation (n)	nasie
	sešupanako	watch (n)	horlosie	setšhelo	container (n)	houer
	sešupo	label (n)	etiket	setšhuu	stew (n)	bredie
	sešupo	sample (n)	monster	setšidifatši	freezer (n)	vrieskas
	sešupo	symbol (n)	simbool	setšidifatši	refrigerator (n)	yskas
	seswai	eight (n)	agt	setšu	elbow (n)	elmboog
	seswantšho	drawing (n)	tekening	setswata	blot (n)	klad
	seswantšho	illustration (n)	illustrasie	setšweletšo	product (n)	produk
	seswantšho	parable (n)	gelykenis	setu	silence (n)	stilte
	seswantšho	photograph (n)	foto	setulo	chair (n)	stoel
	seswantšho	picture (n)	prent	setumo	renown (n)	beroemdheid
	seswantšho	statue (n)	beeld	setupamuši	chimney (n)	skoorsteen
	seswaragantšhi	attachment (n)	gehegtheid	-sewelo	accidental (a)	toevallig
	setagwa	alcoholic (n)	alkoholis	-sewelo	unexpected (a)	onverwag
	setagwa	drunkard (n)	dronklap	-šiana	race (v)	resies ja
	setaki	stain (n)	vlek	-šiišago	giddy (a)	duiselig
	setala	stable (n)	stal	sikara	cigar (n)	sigaar
	setampa	samp (n)	stampmielies	-šila	grind (v)	maal
	setatšhe	starch (n)	stysel			
	seteišene	station (n)	stasie			

N Sotho	English	Afrikaans	N Sotho	English	Afrikaans	**T**
silibera	silver (n)	silwer	-swantšha	photograph (v)	fotografeer	
siling	ceiling (n)	plafon	-swara	arrest (v)	in hegtenis neem	
silofone	xylophone (n)	xilofoon	-swara	capture (v)	vang	
simpale	cymbal (n)	simbaal	-swara	catch (v)	vang	
-šinyalala	grin (v)	gryns	-swara	grasp (v)	gryp	
-širašira	wriggle (v)	wriemel	-swara	handle (v)	hanteer	
-šireletša	protect (v)	beskerm	-swara	hold (v)	hou	
-šireletša	secure (v)	beveilig	-swara	keep (v)	hou	
-šireletša	shield (v)	beskerm	-swara	seize (v)	gryp	
-šišinya	offer (v)	aanbied	-swaragantšha	attach (v)	aanheg	
-šišinya	propose (v)	voorstel	-swara setulo	chair (v)	voorsit	
-šišinya	shake (v)	skud	-swarelela	last (v)	voortduur	
-šitiša	obstruct (v)	belemmer	-swaswa	joke (v)	gekskeer	
-šitšwego	ground (a)	gemaal	-swaya	mark (v)	merk	
-so	black (a)	swart	-swaya phošo	criticise (v)	kritiseer	
-soba	pinch (v)	knyp	-swerwego ke boroko	sleepy (a)	vaak	
-sobela	sink (v)	sink	-swerwego ke tlala	hungry (a)	honger	
sokisi	sock (n)	sokkie	-šweufatša	bleach (v)	bleik	
-sokologa	convert (v)	omsit	-swiela	sweep (v)	vee	
-sola	moult (v)	verhaar	swikiri	sugar (n)	suiker	
-šoma	labour (v)	arbei	swikirikgabiša	icing (n)	versiersuiker	
-šomiša tšhelete	spend (v)	bestee	swiri	lemon (n)	suurlemoen	
sonopolomo	sunflower (n)	sonneblom	switšhi	switch (n)	skakelaar	
Sontaga	Sunday (n)	Sondag				
sopo	soup (n)	sop	taba	affair (n)	saak	
-sora	sip (v)	slurp	taba	case (n)	saak	
-šoro	brutal (a)	dierlik	taba	issue (n)	kwessie	
-šoro	cruel (a)	wreed	-taboga	hop (v)	hop	
-šoro	fierce (a)	woes	-taboga	jump (v)	spring	
-šoro	serious (a)	ernstig	taelelo	prescription (n)	voorskrif	
sorokisi	circus (n)	sirkus	taelo	order (n)	bevel	
-šošobana	crease (v)	kreukel	taemane	diamond (n)	diamant	
-šošobanya	wrinkle (v)	plooi	tafola	table (n)	tafel	
-šošobanya	shrivel (v)	verskrompel	tafoletuku	tablecloth (n)	tafeldoek	
-šošobanya phatla	frown (v)	frons	-taga	intoxicate (v)	bedwelm	
-souso	sauce (n)	sous	tagafara	summons (n)	dagvaarding	
-soutilwego	immune (a)	onvatbaar	tagi	alcohol (n)	alkohol	
-soutiša	immunise (v)	immuniseer	-tagilwego	drunk (a)	dronk	
-šunyalala	smirk (v)	grynslag	-tagišago	alcoholic (a)	alkoholies	
šupa	seven (n)	sewe	tahlegelo	loss (n)	verlies	
supamakete	supermarket (n)	supermark	-tala	green (n)	groen	
-šupetša	illustrate (v)	illustreer	-tala	old (a)	oud	
-šupetša	demonstrate (v)	betoog	-tala	raw (a)	rou	
-šutha	move (v)	beweeg	-tala	uncooked (a)	ongaar	
-šuthiša	move (v)	skuif	-talamehleng	evergreen (a)	bladhoudend	
sutu	suit (n)	pak	talente	talent (n)	talent	
sutu ya boitšhidillo	tracksuit (n)	sweetpak	taletšo	invitation (n)	uitnodiging	
-swa	fuse (v)	uitbrand	tamati	tomato (n)	tamatie	
-swa	burn (v)	brand	tanamaete	dynamite (n)	dinamiet	
-šwaana	beige (a)	beige	tanka	tank (n)	tenk	
-swaba	regret (v)	spyt hê	taodišo	essay (n)	opstel	
-swago	alight (a)	aan die brand	taolo	management (n)	bestuur	
-šwahlela	invade (v)	inval	taolo	prediction (n)	voorspelling	
-swana	resemble (v)	aard na	-tapiša	tame (v)	tem	
-swanago	similar (a)	eenders	tapo	fatigue (n)	vermoeienis	
-swanago	alike (a)	gelyk	tapo	weariness (n)	moegheid	
-swanago	same (a)	dieselfde	tata	father (n)	vader	
-swanelago	convenient (a)	gerieflik	tatelano	sequence (n)	reeks	
-swanelwa	deserve (v)	verdien	-tatšha	starch (v)	styf	
-swanetše	must (v)	moet	tau	lion (n)	leeu	

T	N Sotho	English	Afrikaans	N Sotho	English	Afrikaans
	taugadi	lioness (n)	leeuwyfie	thai	tie (n)	das
	teatere	theatre (n)	teater	thaka	gland (n)	klier
	tebalelo	forgiveness (n)	vergifnis	thaka	pip (n)	pit
	tebelego	approach (n)	nadering	thala	acne (n)	aknee
	tebelelo	look (n)	blik	-thala	draw (v)	teken
	tebelelo	stare (n)	gestaar	-thala	sail (v)	seil
	-tebilego	deep (a)	diep	thanele	tunnel (n)	tonnel
	tebogo	gratitude (n)	dankbaarheid	thapama	afternoon (n)	middag
	tebogo	thanks (n)	dank	thapeletšo	plead (n)	pleit
	tee	one (n)	een	thapelo	plea (n)	pleidooi
	-tee	single (a)	enkel	thapelo	prayer (n)	gebed
	tefeletšo	vengeance (n)	wraak	-thapiša	moisten (v)	natmaak
	tefišo	fine (n)	boete	thapo	rope (n)	tou
	tefo	pay (n)	betaling	thapo	string (n)	tou
	tefo	payment (n)	betaling	thapo ya go goga	tow rope (n)	sleeptou
	tefo	reward (n)	beloning	thapu	cord (n)	koord
	tefo	tariff (n)	tarief	tharo	three (n)	drie
	tefo ya leeto	fare (n)	reisgeld	-thata	difficult (a)	moeilik
	tege	dough (n)	deeg	-thata	hard (a)	hard
	-teka	lay (v)	dek	-thata	solid (a)	vas
	tekanetšo	balance (n)	balans	thato	will (n)	wil
	tekanetšo	level (n)	vlak	-theetša	listen (v)	luister
	tekanyo	measure (n)	maat	thekeniki	technique (n)	tegniek
	tekanyo ye e tlalago molomo	mouthful (n)	mondvol	thekete ya molato wa go phaka	parking ticket (n)	parkeerkaartjie
	teko	attempt (n)	poging	thekethe	ticket (n)	kaartjie
	teko	effort (n)	inspanning	thekisi	taxi (n)	taxi
	teko	test (n)	toets	thekišo	sale (n)	uitverkoping
	teleko	exile (n)	verbanning	theknikone	technikon (n)	tegnikon
	-telele	long (a)	lang	theknolotši	technology (n)	tegnologie
	-telele	tall (a)	lang	theko	price (n)	prys
	temana	paragraph (n)	paragraaf	thekoise	turquoise (n)	turkoois
	temana	scene (n)	toneel	thelebišene	television (n)	televisie
	temana	verse (n)	vers	thelefomo	telephone (n)	telefoon
	-temo	agricultural (a)	landboukundig	thelekramo	telegram (n)	telegram
	temogo	recognition (n)	herkenning	-thelela	slide (v)	gly
	temokrasi	democracy (n)	demokrasie	theleskopo	telescope (n)	teleskoop
	temoši	signal (n)	sinjaal	themperetšha	temperature (n)	temperatuur
	temošo	warning (n)	waarskuwing	thenese	tennis (n)	tennis
	-tempa	stamp (v)	bestempel	-thenkgoga	capsize (v)	omkantel
	-tena	bore (v)	verveel	theo	principle (n)	beginsel
	tengkgolo	typhoid (n)	ingewandskoors	-theoga	descend (v)	daal
	tengkhubedu	dysentery (n)	disenterie	theogo	descent (n)	daling
	tente	tent (n)	tent	therafiki	traffic (n)	verkeer
	tentere	tender (n)	tender	therei	tray (n)	skinkbord
	-teraeka	strike (v)	staak	therišano	conference (n)	konferensie
	terase	terrace (n)	terras	thero	sermon (n)	preek
	terata ya meetlwa	barbed wire (n)	doringdraad	thetho	apron (n)	voorskoot
	terete	tart (n)	tert	-thetšega	stumble (v)	struikel
	tetanose	tetanus (n)	klem in die kake	-thiba	avert (v)	keer
	teye	tea (n)	tee	-thiba	block (v)	blokkeer
	thaba	mountain (n)	berg	-thiba	curb (v)	inhou
	-thabilego	cheerful (a)	vrolik	-thiba	darn (v)	stop
	-thabiša	amuse (v)	vermaak	-thiba	quell (v)	demp
	-thabiša	delight (v)	bly maak	-thibago ditsebe	shrill (a)	skerp
	-thabišago	amusing (a)	vermaaklik	-thibela	bar (v)	uitsluit
	-thabišago	glad (a)	bly	-thibela	hinder (v)	hinder
	thaere	tyre (n)	buiteband	-thibela	prevent (v)	voorkom
	thaetlele	title (n)	titel	thibelapelegi	contraception (n)	voorbehoeding
	thago	kick (n)	skop	thibelo	prevention (n)	voorkoming

N Sotho	English	Afrikaans	N Sotho	English	Afrikaans	T
thini ya matlakala	rubbish bin (n)	vullisblik	tiego	delay (n)	vertraging	
-thinya	sprain (v)	verstuit	-tielela	recover (v)	herstel	
thinyego	sprain (n)	verstuiting	tielelo	recovery (n)	herstel	
thipa	knife (n)	mes	tigelo	recommendation (n)	aanbeveling	
thipana	penknife (n)	knipmes	-tiilego	firm (a)	ferm	
-thiša	postpone (v)	uitstel	-tiilego	tight (a)	styf	
thobego	fracture (n)	breuk	-tiilego	tough (a)	taai	
-thobolla	coach (v)	afrig	-tiiša	maintain (v)	handhaaf	
thoko	direction (n)	rigting	-tiišetša	guarantee (v)	waarborg	
tholo	kudu (n)	koedoe	tiišetšo	guarantee (n)	waarborg	
-thoma	begin (v)	begin	tikadiko	hesitation (n)	aarseling	
-thoma	start (v)	begin	tikologo	circulation (n)	omloop	
-thoma	tackle (v)	aanpak	tikologo	environment (n)	omgewing	
thomo	mission (n)	sending	-tima	extinguish (v)	blus	
-thopa	abduct (v)	ontvoer	-timeditšwego	lost (a)	verlore	
-thopa	loot (v)	plunder	-timetša	lose (v)	verloor	
-thopa	raid (v)	stroop	-timetšego	lost (a)	verdwaal	
thopo	raid (n)	strooptog	-timetšego	stray (a)	afdwaal	
thosola	syphilis (n)	sifilis	-tipa	dip (v)	insteek	
-thotha	cart (v)	karwei	tiragalo	event (n)	gebeurtenis	
thothobolo	rubbish heap (n)	vullishoop	tiragalo	incident (n)	voorval	
-thothomela	shudder (v)	sidder	tiragalo yeo e sa laolwego	reflex (n)	refleks	
thoto	luggage (n)	bagasie				
thoto	property (n)	eiendom	tiragatšo	play (n)	toneelstuk	
thotogo	rise (n)	styging	tiragatšo ya metlae	comedy (n)	komedie	
-thuba	burgle (v)	inbreek	tirišano	co-operation (n)	samewerking	
-thula	bump (v)	stamp	tirišo	consumption (n)	verbruik	
-thula	collide (v)	bots	-tirišo	practical (a)	prakties	
thulaganyo	arrangement (n)	skikking	tirišo	use (n)	gebruik	
thulo	collision (n)	botsing	tiro	deed (n)	daad	
thulusi	tool (n)	werktuig	titio	blow (n)	hou	
-thuma	pound (v)	fynstamp	-tla	come (v)	kom	
-thunya	bloom (v)	blom	-tlaba	baffle (v)	verbyster	
-thunya	erupt (v)	uitbars	-tlaba	stun (v)	verstom	
-thunya	explode (v)	ontplof	tlabele	gadget (n)	toestelletjie	
-thunya	shoot (v)	skiet	tladi	flamingo (n)	flamink	
thunyo	shot (n)	skoot	-tlaiša	ill-treat (v)	mishandel	
thupišo	discipline (n)	dissipline	tlala	famine (n)	hongersnood	
-thuša	aid (v)	help	tlala	hunger (n)	honger	
-thuša	assist (v)	bystaan	-tlala batho	overcrowd (v)	oorvol wees	
-thuša	help (v)	help	-tlala meetse	flood (v)	oorstroom	
-thuša	support (v)	ondersteun	-tlametla	host (v)	gasheer wees	
-thušago	helpful (a)	behulpsaam	tlami	hyphen (n)	koppelteken	
thušo	aid (n)	hulp	-tlanya	type (v)	tik	
thušo	assistance (n)	bystand	-tlaruma	wander (v)	dwaal	
thušo	favour (n)	guns	-tlatša	fill (v)	vol maak	
thušo	help (n)	hulp	-tlatša	second (v)	sekondeer	
thušo ya potlako	first aid (n)	noodhulp	tlelafo	glove (n)	handskoen	
thutafase	geography (n)	aardrykskunde	-tlema	fasten (v)	vasmaak	
thutamahlale	science (n)	wetenskap	-tlemologilego	loose (a)	los	
thutapalo	arithmetic (n)	rekenkunde	-tletšego	full (a)	vol	
thuthuthu	motorcycle (n)	motorfiets	-tletšego phare phare	crowded (a)	propvol	
thutlwa	giraffe (n)	kameelperd	tlhabelo	injection (n)	inspuiting	
thuto	education (n)	opvoeding	tlhabelo	inoculation (n)	inenting	
thuto	instruction (n)	onderrig	tlhabelomadi	blood transfusion (n)	bloedoortapping	
thuto	lecture (n)	lesing	tlhabo	sunrise (n)	sonop	
thuto	lesson (n)	les	tlhabologo	advancement (n)	vordering	
thuto	qualification (n)	kwalifikasie	tlhabologo	civilisation (n)	beskawing	
thuto	quench (v)	les	tlhago	instinct (n)	instink	
-thwala	employ (v)	in diens neem	-tlhago	natural (a)	natuurlik	

T	N Sotho	English	Afrikaans	N Sotho	English	Afrikaans
	tlhago	nature (n)	natuur	tlou	elephant (n)	olifant
	tlhahlobo	examination (n)	eksamen	tlwaelo	habit (n)	gewoonte
	tlhahlobo	inspection (n)	inspeksie	-tlwaelo	traditional (a)	tradisioneel
	tlhahlobo ya mohu	inquest (n)	doodsondersoek	tlwaelo	tradition (n)	tradisie
	tlhaka	roof (n)	dak	-tlwaetša	practise (v)	oefen
	tlhakapele	initial (n)	voorletter	-tlwaetšego	tame (a)	mak
	tlhako	hoof (n)	hoef	tobeletšo	accent (n)	aksent
	tlhale	fibre (n)	vesel	todi ya dinamune	orange juice (n)	lemoensap
	tlhale	roughage (n)	vesel	toka	justice (n)	geregtigheid
	tlhale	thread (n)	draad	tokelo ya go kgetha	franchise (n)	kiesreg
	tlhalenama	tissue (n)	weefsel	tokollo	acquittal (n)	vryspraak
	tlhalo	divorce (n)	egskeiding	tokollo	dismissal (n)	ontslag
	tlhalošo	description (n)	beskrywing	tokollo	release (n)	loslating
	tlhalošo	explanation (n)	verduideliking	tokollo ka	parole (n)	parool
	tlhalošo	meaning (n)	betekenis	kwelobohloko		
	tlhame	secretary bird (n)	sekretarisvoël	tokologo	freedom (n)	vryheid
	tlhamo	invention (n)	uitvinding	tokomane	peanut (n)	grondboontjie
	tlhamo ya dikoša	composition (n)	komposisie	tokwane	mushroom (n)	sampioen
	tlhankišitšo	addiction (n)	verslaafdheid	-tologa	dissolve (v)	oplos
	-tlhatlharega	stagger (v)	slinger	-tologa	melt (v)	smelt
	tlhobaelo	insomnia (n)	slaaploosheid	tomo	bridle (n)	toom
	tlhohlo	challenge (n)	uitdaging	tomo	rein (n)	leisel
	tlhohlo	dare (n)	uitdaging	tomo	sting (n)	steek
	tlhokamadi	anaemia (n)	bloedarmoede	-tona	male (a)	manlik
	tlhokego	absence (n)	afwesigheid	-tona	masculine (a)	manlik
	tlhokego	lack (n)	gebrek	tona	minister (n)	minister
	tlhoko	nipple (n)	tepel	tonki	ass (n)	donkie
	tlhoko	teat (n)	tepel	tonki	donkey (n)	donkie
	tlhokofele	wart (n)	vrat	-tonyago	cold (a)	koud
	tlhokomelo	caution (n)	versigtigheid	toro	dream (n)	droom
	tlhokomologo	negligence (n)	nalatigheid	toropo	town (n)	dorp
	tlholo	omen (n)	voorteken	toropofatšo	urbanisation (n)	verstedeliking
	tlhompho	awe (n)	eerbied	-toropong	urban (a)	stedelik
	tlhompho	dignity (n)	waardigheid	tosene	dozen (n)	dosyn
	tlhompho	honour (n)	eer	toulo	towel (n)	handdoek
	tlhompho	respect (n)	respek	tripi	drip (n)	drup
	tlhophego	annoyance (n)	ergernis	tsaka	battle-axe (n)	strydbyl
	tlhora	summit (n)	kruin	tšale	shawl (n)	tjalie
	tlhwekišo	purity (n)	suiwerheid	-tsarogile	astute (a)	slim
	tlhweko	cleanliness (n)	sindelikheid	tšatšikgwedi	date (n)	datum
	-tliša	bring (v)	bring	-tšea	take (v)	neem
	-tliša go tšwa ntle	import (v)	invoer	-tšea ka dikgoka	hijack (v)	skaak
	-tlo-	will (v)	sal	-tšea kgang	reason (v)	redeneer
	-tloga	vacate (v)	uittrek	-tšea maleba	aim (v)	mik
	-tloga	depart (v)	vertrek	-tseba	know (v)	weet
	-tloga e le	quite (a)	taamlik	-tsebalegago	distinguished (a)	vooraanstaande
	-tlogela	abandon (v)	verlaat	tsebe	ear (n)	oor
	-tlogela	exclude (v)	uitsluit	-tsebega	acquaint (v)	bekend wees
	-tlogela	leave (v)	laat	-tsebega	acquaint (v)	bekend wees
	-tlogela	omit (v)	weglaat	-tsebiša	advertise (v)	adverteer
	tlogelo	omission (n)	weglating	-tsebiša	announce (v)	aankondig
	tlogo	departure (n)	vertrek	-tsebiša	enlighten (v)	inlig
	-tlola	anoint (v)	salf	-tsebiša	inform (v)	meedeel
	-tlola	bounce (v)	opspring	-tsebiša	introduce (v)	voorstel
	tlopelo	extravagance (n)	buitensporigheid	-tsebiša	notify (v)	kennis gee
	-tlopetšego	extravagant (a)	buitensporig	tsebiši	advertisement (n)	advertensie
	-tloša	eliminate (v)	verwyder	tsebišo	announcement (n)	aankondiging
	-tloša	remove (v)	verwyder	tsebišo	introduction (n)	voorstelling
	tlošo	removal (n)	verwydering	tsebišo	notice (n)	kennisgewing
	tlotlontšu	vocabulary (n)	woordeskat	tsebo	information (n)	inligting

N Sotho	English	Afrikaans	N Sotho	English	Afrikaans	**T**
tsebo	knowledge (n)	kennis	-tšhilafatša	stain (v)	bevlek	
tše di sa agego mmele	unhealthy (a)	ongesond	-tšhilafatša	mess (v)	bemors	
tsela	path (n)	pad	tšhilafatšo	pollution (n)	besoedeling	
tsela	road (n)	pad	tšhilegompe	indigestion (n)	slegte spysvertering	
tsela	way (n)	pad	tšhinyalalo	grin (n)	grynslag	
tselamadi	blood vessel (n)	bloedvat	tshipi	iron (n)	yster	
tselana	parting (n)	paadjie	tshipi	bell (n)	klok	
tselathokwana	pavement (n)	sypaadjie	-tšhipilego	cheap (a)	goedkoop	
tsela ya kelatšhila	sewerage (n)	riolering	tshipiphodisa	handcuff (n)	boei	
tsela ya moralela	detour (n)	omweg	tšhireletšo	assurance (n)	versekering	
-tsena	enter (v)	binnegaan	tšhireletšo	insurance (n)	versekering	
-tsena	wade (v)	waad	tšhišinyego ya lefase	earthquake (n)	aardbewing	
-tsena ganong	interrupt (v)	onderbreek	tšhišinyo	proposal (n)	voorstel	
-tsenelela	penetrate (v)	binnedring	tšhišinyo	offer (n)	aanbod	
tseno	attendance (n)	bywoning	tšhitampholo	antidote (n)	teengif	
-tsenya kotsing	endanger (v)	in gevaar stel	tšhitego	disability (n)	gebrek	
-tsenya mathale	wire (v)	bedraad	tšhitego	failure (n)	mislukking	
tšeo	those (pron)	daardie	tšhitišo	obstruction (n)	belemmernis	
-tsepamego	vertical (a)	vertikaal	tšhoganetšo	emergency (n)	noodgeval	
-tsetla	groan (v)	kreun	-tšhogatšhogago	nervous (a)	senuweeagtig	
-tsetla	moan (v)	kerm	-tšhogile	panic (v)	paniekerig wees	
tsetlo	groan (n)	kreun	tšhoko	chalk (n)	kryt	
tsetlo	moan (n)	gekerm	tšhokolete	chocolate (n)	sjokolade	
-tšhaba	flee (v)	vlug	tshokologo	conversion (n)	omsetting	
tšhabo	flight (n)	vlug	tšhologelo	influx (n)	instroming	
-tshadi	female (a)	vroulik	tshoro	sip (n)	slukkie	
tshaeno	signature (n)	handtekening	-tšhoša	terrify (v)	verskrik	
tshegišo	humour (n)	humor	-tšhoša	perturb (v)	verontrus	
tshekamo	slope (n)	helling	-tšhoša	frighten (v)	skrikmaak	
tshekamo	prejudice (n)	vooroordeel	tšhoša	sword (n)	swaard	
tšheke	cheque (n)	tjek	-tšhošago	terrible (a)	vreeslik	
tshekišo	refinement (n)	verfyndheid	-tšhošago	ominous (a)	onheilspellend	
tshekišo	prosecution (n)	vervolging	tšhošetšo	threat (n)	dreigement	
tsheko	trial (n)	verhoor	tšhošetšo	terror (n)	terreur	
-tšhela	pour (v)	skink	tšhošo	bushbuck (n)	bosbok	
tshela	six (n)	ses	tšhošobano	crease (n)	kreukel	
-tshela	skip (v)	oorslaan	tšhošobanyo ya phatla	frown (n)	frons	
-tshelago matšato	agile (a)	rats	tšhošwane	ant (n)	mier	
-tshela molao	trespass (v)	oortree	-tshotshoma	ooze (v)	sypel	
-tshela sekontini	tar (v)	teer	tšhuana	orphan (n)	weeskind	
tšhelete	money (n)	geld	tšhukudu	rhinoceros (n)	renoster	
tšheletetshipi	coin (n)	muntstuk	tšhumo	arson (n)	brandstigting	
tšhelo	cello (n)	tjello	tšhupa	weevil (n)	kalander	
tshenyegelo	harm (n)	skade	tšhupakhutlo	compass (n)	kompas	
tshenyego	corruption (n)	bedorwenheid	tšhupaletlotlo	account (n)	rekening	
tshenyego	damage (n)	skade	tšhupane	index (n)	indeks	
tshenyo	crime (n)	misdaad	tšhupapaka	timetable (n)	rooster	
tshenyoina	defamation (n)	belastering	tšhupetšo	demonstration (n)	betoging	
tshepedišo	procedure (n)	prosedure	tšhupetšo	reference (n)	verwysing	
-tshepegago	honest (a)	eerlik	tšhupetšo ya go	recipe (n)	resep	
-tshepha	rely (v)	staatmaak	tswaka			
tshephe	springbok (n)	springbok	tšhupo	sign (n)	teken	
-tshesane	fine (a)	fyn	-tshwa	spit (v)	spoeg	
tšhese	cheese (n)	kaas	tšhwaane	frost (n)	ryp	
tšhiano	race (n)	wedren	tšhwabo	regret (n)	spyt	
tšhiišo	horror (n)	afsku	tšhwahlelo	invasion (n)	inval	
tšhikidi	bedbug (n)	weeluis	tshwanelo	obligation (n)	verpligting	
tšhila	waste (n)	afval	tshwanelo	duty (n)	plig	
tšhila	filth (n)	vuilgoed	tshwano	likeness (n)	ooreenkoms	
tšhila	refuse (n)	vullis	tshwano	analogy (n)	analogie	

Y

N Sotho	English	Afrikaans	N Sotho	English	Afrikaans
tshwantšho	diagram (n)	diagram	tukwana ya bosadi	sanitary towel (n)	sanitêre doekie
tshwantšho	image (n)	beeld	tumammogo	consonant (n)	medeklinker
tshwaokgwebo	brand (n)	handelsmerk	tumanoši	vowel (n)	klinker
tshwarelo	excuse (n)	ekskuus	tumedišo	salute (n)	saluut
tshwarelo	apology (n)	verskoning	tumelelo	admission (n)	toelating
tshwaro	arrest (n)	inhegtenisneming	tumelelo	approval (n)	goedkeuring
tšhwene	baboon (n)	bobbejaan	tumelo	permission (n)	toestemming
-tshwenya	disturb (v)	pla	tumelo	faith (n)	geloof
-tshwenya	bother (v)	lastig wees	tumelo	permit (n)	permit
-tshwenya	trouble (v)	kwel	-tumilego	well-known (a)	welbekend
-tshwenya	pester (v)	pla	-tumilego	popular (a)	gewild
-tshwenyegilego	upset (a)	ontsteld	-tumilego	famous (a)	beroemd
moyeng			tumišo	admiration (n)	bewondering
tšhweu	white (n)	wit	tumo	ambition (n)	ambisie
tšie	grasshopper (n)	sprinkaan	tumo	fame (n)	roem
tšie	locust (n)	sprinkaan	-turago	expensive (a)	duur
-tsikinya	tickle (v)	kielie	-tutela	fester (v)	sweer
-tsikitla meno	gnash (v)	kners	-tutuetša	influence (v)	beïnvloed
-tsirinya	jingle (v)	klingel	-tutuetša	encourage (v)	aanmoedig
tšitširipa	giant (n)	reus	tutuetšo	influence (n)	invloed
-tšofala	age (v)	verouder	twantšhi	antibody (n)	teenliggaam
-tšofetšego	aged (a)	oud	twatši	germ (n)	kiem
tšohle	all (things) (pron)	alles	twetšiswikiri	diabetes (n)	suikersiekte
-tšokotša	rinse (v)	uitspoel			
-tsoma	hunt (v)	jag	-uta	hide (v)	wegsteek
-tsoma tefo	claim (v)	eis	-utilwego	hidden (a)	versteek
-tsoša	arouse (v)	opwek	-utla	jerk (v)	ruk
-tsoša mpherefere	riot (v)	oproer maak	-utolla	expose (v)	blootlê
-tsothwa	brown (a)	bruin	-utolla	disclose (v)	openbaar
tsotsi	hooligan (n)	skollie	-utswa	steal (v)	steel
-tšwa	emerge (v)	verrys			
-tšwa	exit (v)	uitgaan	-wa	fall (v)	val
-tšwa	result (v)	volg	weitara	waiter (n)	kelner
-tšwafago	indolent (a)	traag	wena	you (pron)	jy
-tšwafago	lazy (a)	lui	-weša	drop (v)	laat val
-tswaka	mix (v)	meng	wulu ya leokodi	cotton wool (n)	watte
-tswalela	shut (v)	toemaak			
-tswaletšwego	shut (a)	toe	ya-	of (prep)	van
-tšwa madi	bleed (v)	bloei	-ya	go (v)	gaan
-tšwa sethitho	perspire (v)	perspireer	-ya	belong (v)	behoort
-tšwelago pele	progressive (a)	progressief	-yago ka molao	valid (a)	geldig
-tšwela pele	proceed (v)	voortgaan	-ya le megopolo	absent-minded (a)	ingedagte
-tšwela pele	progress (v)	vooruitgaan	ye	this (pron)	dit
-tšwelego tseleng	radical (a)	radikaal	yena	he (pron)	hy
-tšwelela	appear (v)	verskyn	yena	she (pron)	sy
tšwelelo	appearance (n)	verskyning	yenayena	very (a)	heel
-tšweletša	produce (v)	produseer	Yomaatlaohle	Almighty (n)	Almagtige
tšweletšopele	promotion (n)	bevordering	yo mofsa	newcomer (n)	nuweling
tšwelopele	advance (n)	vooruitgang	yo mofsa	amateur (n)	amateur
tšwelopele	progress (n)	vooruitgang	yona	it (pron)	dit
-tšwetša pele	promote (v)	bevorder	-yona	its (pron)	sy
-tšwetša pele	continue (v)	vervolg	yunibesiti	university (n)	universiteit
tsweya	lout (n)	takhaar	yunifomo	uniform (n)	uniform
tswina	honey (n)	heuning			

SESOTHO

Sesotho, or Southern Sotho, is spoken in Lesotho, the Free State, QwaQwa, the northern Transkei and the southern Transvaal, especially in the Witwatersrand and the Vaal. It is also spoken in the vicinity of Pretoria and Brits.

Sesotho was one of the first African languages to be reduced to writing, and it has an extensive literature. It is also one of the most uniform of southern Africa's written African languages, so uniform that little is known about its dialects. According to scholars, the written form of Sesotho was originally based on the Tlokwa dialect. Today the written language is mostly based on the Kwena and Fokeng dialects. Although few, there are variations in the spoken form of the language and these alternatives are accepted in the written form.

Although the dictionary contains a fair vocabulary of the Sesotho words in current use, new concepts that have only recently been introduced to the Sesotho culture borrow heavily from the other languages, with Sotho-ised foreign words or phrases.

It is important to remember that, in common with other southern African indigenous languages, the structure of Sesotho – a tonal language – is very different to Western languages. Sesotho is governed by the noun, which is split into various classes. It is what is known as an agglutinating language (a combination of simple word elements to express a specific meaning), with the many suffixes and prefixes used in sentence construction causing sound changes.

PRONUNCIATION

Four factors govern the correct pronunciation of Sesotho: speech sounds, syllable structure, tone and length.

SPEECH SOUNDS

These are divided into two main categories: vowels and consonants, and a minor category of semi-vowels (vocal consonants).

Vowels are spoken with the mouth open and without any obstruction by the tongue. Differences between vowels are caused by the change in the resonance cavity, the position of the tongue and the configuration of the lips. The basic vowels – and their approximate sounds – are:
a in **-araba** (*answer*), similar to the English *far*, but pronounced further forward
e in **lebelo** (*speed*), similar to the English *we*
ê in **-mêma** (*invite*), similar to the Afrikaans *sê*
i in **-bina** (*sing*), similar to the English *it*
o in **noka** (*river*), similar to the Afrikaans *lojaal*
ô in **nôka** (*hip*), similar to the Afrikaans *môre*
u in **-bula** (*open*), similar to the English *bull*

Note that the accents (diacritics) on the ê and ô have not been used in the word lists because they are generally not used in written literature. However, they would be essential to a formal reference book to reflect the correct pronunciation.

Consonants are articulated with a complete or partial obstruction of the air passage at a certain place. They are thus classified according to the manner of breath control and place of articulation.
b in **-bala** (*read*), similar to the English *able*
d in **-duba** (*knead*), similar to the English *doll*
f in **-fofa** (*fly*), similar to the English *after*
g in **galase** (*glass*), similar to the Afrikaans *gaap*. This is a foreign sound to Sesotho, used only in borrowings, mainly from English and Afrikaans.
h in **haholo** (*much*), similar to the English *hand*. Some speakers pronounce this sound without voice.
j in **kajeno** (*today*), similar to the Cape Flats Afrikaans *jy*. Some speakers force out the breath quickly (the fricative).
k in **-kena** (*enter*), similar to the English *back*
l in **-latola** (*deny*), similar to the English *lay*
m in **madi** (*blood*), similar to the English *him*
n in **nama** (*meat*), similar to the English *and*
p in **pula** (*rain*), similar to the English *lip*
q in **-qeta** (*finish*), a click sound, comparable to the sound of a cork being pulled from a bottle
r in **moriri** (*hair*), similar to the English *red*
s in **sefate** (*tree*), similar to the English *dress*
t in **tau** (*lion*), similar to the English *tin*

Pairs of letters that are pronounced quickly to make the same sound (digraphs):
bj in **-bjara** (*crush*), (no equivalent)
fj in **-lefjwa** (*be paid*), (no equivalent)
hl in **-hlahloba** (*examine*), (no local equivalent, but similar to the Welsh *Llewellyn*). This sound interchanges with **tlh** in **hlapi: tlhapi** (*fish*) and **sehlare: setlhare** (*medicine*)
kg in **kgaka** (*guineafowl*), (no equivalent)
ng in **ngwana** (*child*), similar to the English *linger*
ny in **-nyala** (*marry*), similar to the English *Kenya*
nq in **nqalo** (*place*), the same click as before, but nasalised
pj in **-pjatla** (*boil well*), (no equivalent)
sh in **mashala** (*coal*), (no equivalent)
tj in **-tjeka** (*dance*), (no equivalent)
tl in **tlou** (*elephant*), similar to the English *little*
ts in **tsebe** (*ear*), similar to the English *sits*

Aspirated consonants:
kh in **khefi** (*cafe*), similar to the English *kindle*
ph in **phiri** (*hyena*), similar to the English *pull*
pjh in **-pjhatla** (*smash*), (no equivalent)
qh in **qhobosheane** (*fortress*), an aspirated click
th in **thaba** (*mountain*), similar to the English *till*
tjh in **tjhelete** (*money*), (no equivalent)
tlh in **tlhaho** (*origin*), (no local equivalent but similar to the Welsh *Llewellyn*)
tsh as in **tshwene** (*baboon*), similar to the English *change*

Unusual consonants are **c, v, x** and **z**, which represent uncommon and foreign sounds, for example:
nce-nce-nce represents the sound of a clock ticking, while **nxa** is a sound of disgust.

Semi-vowels (vocalic consonants) are:
y in **yunibesithi** (*university*), similar to the English *yes*
w in **wena** (*you*), similar to the English *wet*

SYLLABLE STRUCTURE

In most cases the syllable in Sesotho takes the shape CV (where C indicates consonant and V vowel):
se-fa-te (*tree*)
mo-fe-re-fe-re (*trouble*)
The following types of syllables also occur:
V: **le-i-no** (*tooth*)
C: **mo-l-lo** (*fire*)

TONE

Sesotho and other African languages are generally referred to as tonal languages. Each syllable of a word in these languages has a specific tone — a specific pitch of voice with which it is pronounced. This is one of the most important factors governing pronunciation, and if not used correctly can cause misunderstanding. The entire meaning of a word can change if pronounced with a different tone, for example: **noka** (*river*) but **nôka** (*hip*)

There are unfortunately no rules governing the teaching and learning of tone in Sesotho. The only way to learn is to listen to mother tongue speakers and imitate them.

LENGTH

The length of time taken to pronounce a syllable varies according to the usage. In Sesotho the penultimate (second last) syllable of a word is usually longer (indicated phonetically by a colon after the long syllable), for example:

more:ki (*buyer*)

tsama:ja (*go*)

SESOTHO WORDS

Sesotho uses a method known to linguists as 'disjunctive', which means that a word consists of several units. For example, the conjugated verb, **ke a tsamaya** (*I am going*) consists of three different segments. When you look at the following sentence you see six words, though in fact it consists only of three.

Ka tsatsi le leng ka mmona (*One day I saw him*); the three 'words' being **ka tsatsi**, **le leng** and **ka mmona**.

Sesotho experts call the separate words orthographic (or practical), and the complete words, which consist of at least a root or a root plus other constituent parts (prefix and/or suffix), linguistic.

Each word may be classified into the following word categories, in terms of meaning, structure and usability: noun, pronoun, adjective, quantitative, enumerative, possessive, verb, copulative, adverb, ideophone, conjunctive and interjective.

Most of these categories may be classified into the following bigger units:

Substantives functioning as the subject or object in a sentence (noun, pronoun, possessive, adjective, relative and enumerative);

Predicatives acting as predicates of a sentence (verb, auxiliary, copulative and ideophone);

Qualificatives serving to qualify substantives (adjective, relative, enumerative, possessive, quantitative and demonstrative); and

Descriptives modifying predicatives (adverb and ideophone); **Conjunctives** (conjunctions); and **Interjectives** (interjections).

NOUNS

Nouns consist of a prefix + root + suffix. All of the following words, for example, relate to people (-tho). As the prefix changes, so does the meaning, all of which, however, are linked to the central meaning of 'people'.

motho (*person*)
batho (*people*)
botho (*humanity; kindness*)
setho (*culture; as a human being;* etc.).

The part of the word that conveys the consistent reference to the concept of 'human' is **-tho** – the root in each example. The additional elements are the prefixes and suffixes added to extend the meaning.

The noun prefix (also known as the class prefix) has three major functions:
To distinguish between the different classes of noun;
To distinguish between singular and plural; and
To determine the form of the corresponding pronouns, qualificatives and predicatives.

Because of the different noun prefixes, Sesotho nouns are grouped into various noun classes:

Class	Prefix	Sesotho	English equivalent
1	mo-	monna	man
2	ba-	banna	men
1a	-	malome	uncle (maternal)
1b	bo-	bomalome	uncles
3	mo-	molomo	mouth
4	me-	melomo	mouths
5	le-	lefatshe	country
6	ma-	mafatshe	countries
7	se-	seeta	shoe
8	di-	dieta	shoes
9	N-	podi	goat
10	diN-	dipodi	goats
14	bo-	bohobe	bread
15	ho-	ho ja	to eat
16	fa-	fatshe	on the ground
17	ho-	hodimo	on top
18	mo-	morao	behind

This classification is done also on the basis of the meanings of the words. For instance, classes 1, 2, 1a and 1b contain human beings exclusively. Classes 3 and 4 contain, to a very great extent, trees, plants, natural phenomena and parts of the body. From these examples you can see that the prefixes also serve to distinguish between singular and plural (see classes 2, 1b, 4, 6, 8 and 10).

It is essential that the different parts of a sentence agree with each other grammatically in tense, gender, person or case, etc., known to linguists as 'concord'. This concordial agreement is dependent on the prefix of the noun, determining the form of the corresponding pronominal, qualificative and predicative prefixes.

Word groups, sentences and conversation are structured according to specific rules of the language, which ensure that the sentence agrees with the class prefix in a given word group or sentence:

batho bona: ba- + -o- + -na (*they the people*) (pronominal prefix)
lejwe lona: le- + -o- + -na (*it the stone*) (the pronominal prefix)
batho bohle: ba- + -ohle (*all the people*) (quantitative prefix)
setjhaba sohle: se- + -ohle (*the whole nation*) (quantitative prefix)
sefate se seholo (*a big tree*) (adjectival concord)
lejwe le lenyenyane (*a small stone*) (adjectival concord)
lefatshe la rona (*our country*) (possessive concord)
sejana sa ganta (*a golden dish*) (possessive concord)
sefate se wele (*a tree has fallen*) (subject concord)
lefika le suthisitswe (*a rock has been moved*) (subject concord)
sefate se seholo se setala sa ditholwana se wele (*the big, green fruit tree has fallen*).

For this reason, the Sesotho word list is organised on the word stems, rather than the linguistic words themselves, especially in the case of qualificatives and predicatives. Thus:

big: **-holo**
fallen: **-wele**
moved: **-suthisitswe**
small: **-nyenyane**

THE PREDICATIVE

Predicatives are those parts of a sentence or phrase that either describe an action by the subject or object (as in 'the man ran faster') or its state (as in 'the tree is green'). In the first case they are known as verb predicatives, and in the second as copulative predicatives. Verbs are mainly formed from roots that are intrinsically predicative in force; while copulatives derive from parts of speech with no predicative force, such as substantives, qualificatives and adverbs, for example:

Verb: **Mme o pheha nama** (*mother cooks meat*)

Copulative: **Ntate ke moruti** (*father is a priest*)

Verbs can signify both the action and the state of the subject:

Ntate o a bona (*father is seeing*)

Copulatives, on the other hand, signify only the state of a subject:

Thabiso o bohlale (*Thabiso is clever*).

The verbal root is the most important part of the verb, the part around which the word is built. On examining **o a bona** (*he sees*) closely, we notice that **o-** can be replaced by **ba-**, thus **ba a bona** (*they see*), and the central meaning of *see* is retained. The **-a-** can also be replaced, for example, by **-sa-**, **ba sa bona** (*they are still seeing*) without changing that central meaning of *see*. In the negative **ntate o a bona** (*father sees*) is **ntate ha a bone** (*father does not see*).

From our original example of **o a bona** (*he sees*) we have seen how it is possible to change all the building blocks of the verb, except for **-bon-**. This is the root and it is unchangeable and irreducible. Changing the root would mean changing the entire meaning of the word:

Ntate o a bina (*father is singing*)

In this dictionary, English verbs have been translated into Sesotho with verbal stems:

sing: **-bina**

see: **-bona**

fallen: **-wele**

moved: **-suthisitswe**

The user of this dictionary should thus remember to use the stems with their appropriate prefixes or concords, unless, of course, the verb stems are in the imperative:

sing: **bina!**

see: **bona!**

CONCORDS

The first and second person subject concords (I/we and you/you) are:

1st person singular (I): **-ke-** as in **Nna ke a ja** (*I am eating*)

1st person plural (we): **-re-** as in **Rona re a ja** (*we are eating*)

2nd person singular (you): **-o-** as in **Wena o a ja** (*you are eating*)

2nd person plural (you): **-le-** as in **Lona le a ja** (*you are eating*)

The object concord is included in the verb by adding, for example:

Monna o ja nama (*the man is eating/eats meat*) becomes **Monna o a e ja** (*the man is eating/eats it*)

The object concord is identical in form to the subject concord except for class 1 nouns where it is **mo**, for example:

Re thusa monna (*we help/are helping the man*) becomes **Re a mo thusa** (*we help/are helping him*)

The object concords for the first and second person are:

1st person singular (me): **-N-** as in **E a ntoma** (*it is biting me*)

1st person plural (us): **-re-** as in **Ba a re bona** (*they are seeing us*)

2nd person singular (you): **-o-** as in **Ke a o bona** (*I am seeing you*)

2nd person plural (you): **-le-** as in **Re a le bona** (*we are seeing you*)

The object concord is usually used when the object is known and is not repeated after the object itself, for example:

Monna o ja nama (*the man eats meat*)

Monna o a e ja (*the man eats it*)

However, when the object is expressed and its object concord is also used in the predicate, the object is emphasised, for example:

Ke bitsa mohlankana (*I am calling the young man*)

Ke a mo bitsa, mohlankana (*I am calling him, the young man*).

Sesotho	English	Afrikaans	Sesotho	English	Afrikaans	A
-aba	allocate (v)	toewys	ase	axle (n)	as	
-aba	distribute (v)	versprei	asene	vinegar (n)	asyn	
-adima	borrow (v)	leen	ashorense	assurance (n)	versekering	
-adima	lend (v)	leen	-atamela	approach (v)	benader	
aesekerimi	ice cream (n)	roomys	aterese	address (n)	adres	
-ahlola	arbitrate (v)	arbitreer	-athamela	bask (v)	koester	
-ahlola	condemn (v)	veroordeel	-atisa	multiply (v)	vermenigvuldig	
-ahlola	convict (v)	skuldig bevind	-atisa	usually (adv)	gewoonlik	
-ahlola	judge (v)	oordeel	-atleha	achieve (v)	presteer	
-aka	kiss (v)	soen	-atleha	prosper (v)	floreer	
-akanya	assess (v)	skat	-atleha	succeed (v)	slaag	
-akanya	guess (v)	raai	-atlehileng	prosperous (a)	florerend	
-akanya	imagine (v)	verbeel	atlelase	atlas (n)	atlas	
-akanyang	approximate (a)	geskat	-atolosa	expand (v)	uitbrei	
-akaretsang	general (a)	algemeen	avokhado	avocado (n)	avokado	
-akgeha	faint (v)	flou word				
-akgehileng	unconscious (a)	bewusteloos	-ba	be (v)	wees	
-akgela	cast (v)	werp	-ba	have (v)	hê	
-akgela	throw (v)	gooi	baahi	population (n)	bevolking	
akgente	lawyer (n)	prokureur	baahlodi	jury (n)	jurie	
akhademi	academy (n)	akademie	baahlodi	judiciary (n)	regbank	
akhaonte	account (n)	rekening	-baba	bitter (a)	bitter	
akhaontente	accountant (n)	rekenmeester	-baballa	nestle (v)	nestel	
-akofisa	accelerate (v)	versnel	-baballa	economise (v)	besuinig	
-alama	brood (v)	broei	-badimo	ancestral (a)	voorvaderlik	
aleji	allergy (n)	allergie	baesekele	bicycle (n)	fiets	
aletare	altar (n)	altaar	baesekopo	cinema (n)	bioskoop	
alfabete	alphabet (n)	alfabet	-baka	bake (v)	bak	
almanaka	calendar (n)	kalender	-baka	cause (v)	veroorsaak	
-ama	affect (v)	raak	-baka qomatsi	risk (v)	waag	
-ama	feel (v)	voel	bakeng sa-	for (prep)	vir	
-ama	touch (v)	raak	baki	jacket (n)	baadjie	
-amana	contact (v)	in aanraking kom	-bala	calculate (v)	reken	
ambulanse	ambulance (n)	ambulans	-bala	count (v)	tel	
-amela	confide (v)	vertroulik meedeel	-bala	read (v)	lees	
-amoha	confiscate (v)	beslag lê op	balaodi	management (n)	bestuur	
-amohela	accommodate (v)	huisves	balate	ballad (n)	ballade	
-amohela	welcome (v)	verwelkom	-baleha	flee (v)	vlug	
-amohela	accept (v)	aanvaar	-ba le mafome	rust (v)	roes	
-amohela	adopt (v)	aanneem	baletsi	band (n)	orkes	
-amohela	receive (v)	ontvang	-baletsweng	prescribed (a)	voorgeskrewe	
-amohela tlung	house (v)	huisves	-balla	prescribe (v)	voorskryf	
-amoheleha	acceptable (a)	aanvaarbaar	balunu	balloon (n)	ballon	
-ananela	appreciate (v)	waardeer	banjo	banjo (n)	banjo	
-ananya	barter (v)	ruil	banka	bank (n)	bank	
-ananya	gamble (v)	dobbel	banka	bench (n)	bank	
-apara	dress (v)	aantrek	banteje	bandage (n)	verband	
-apara	wear (v)	dra	-bapala	play (v)	speel	
-apeha	cook (v)	kook	-bapatsa	advertise (v)	adverteer	
-apesa	clothe (v)	aantrek	-bapileng	adjacent (a)	aangrensend	
apole	apple (n)	appel	-bapisa	compare (v)	vergelyk	
apolekose	apricot (n)	appelkoos	bara	bar (n)	kroeg	
-araba	answer (v)	antwoord	basekeite	biscuit (n)	koekie	
-araba	reply (v)	antwoord gee	basekomo	basin (n)	kom	
-arabela	respond (v)	respondeer	-ba siyo	absent (a)	afwesig	
arena	arena (n)	arena	-bata	cold (a)	koud	
-arohaneng	separate (a)	afsonderlik	bate	bath (n)	bad	
-arola	part (v)	skei	batekamore	bathroom (n)	badkamer	
-arola	segregate (v)	segregeer	-ba teng	exist (v)	bestaan	
-arola	share (v)	deel	baterepokise	chickenpox (n)	waterpokkies	

B	Sesotho	English	Afrikaans	Sesotho	English	Afrikaans
	batho	people (n)	mense	bobare	rumour (n)	gerug
	batho	society (n)	samelewing	bobe	vice (n)	ondeug
	batho bohle	public (n)	publiek	-bobebo	light (a)	lig
	-batla	search (v)	soek	-bobedi	both (a)	albei
	-batla	want (v)	wil hê	bobedi	double (n)	dubbel
	-batlile	almost (adv)	amper	bobedi	pair (n)	paar
	-batlile	nearly (adv)	byna	-bobedi	second (a)	tweede
	-batlisisa	investigate (v)	ondersoek	-bobola	groan (v)	kreun
	batsi	wide (a)	wyd	bobopi	pottery (n)	pottebakkery
	bayoloji	biology (n)	biologie	-bodila	acid (a)	suur
	-be	bad (a)	sleg	-bodila	sour (a)	suur
	-be	immoral (a)	onsedelik	-bodileng	rotten (a)	verrot
	-be	mean (a)	gemeen	bodise	brassière (n)	bra
	-be	ugly (a)	lelik	boditse	bristle (n)	steekhaar
	-bea	put (v)	sit	bodulo	accommodation (n)	huisvesting
	Bebele	Bible (n)	Bybel	bodulo	abode (n)	woonplek
	-bebera	babble (v)	babbel	bodulo	residence (n)	verblyfplek
	-beeletsa	deposit (v)	deponeer	bodulo	seat (n)	sitplek
	-behela ka thoko	suspend (v)	opskort	bodutu	loneliness (n)	eensaamheid
	beije	beige (a)	beige	boemeladifofane	airport (n)	lughawe
	-beila	bail (v)	borg staan	boemo	condition (n)	toestand
	beile	bail (n)	borg	boemo	position (n)	posisie
	beine	wine (n)	wyn	-boemo	standard (a)	standaard
	-beisa	race (v)	resies ja	boemo	standard (n)	standaard
	beke	week (n)	week	-bofelo	final (a)	finaal
	beke tse pedi	fortnight (n)	twee weke	boferekanyi	terrorism (n)	terrorisme
	-bekga	weigh (v)	weeg	bofokodi	weakness (n)	swakheid
	-bela	boil (v)	kook	bofutsana	poverty (n)	armoede
	-belaela	moan (v)	kerm	-bohale	acute (a)	skerp
	-belaela	dissatisfied (a)	ontevrede	-bohale	sharp (a)	skerp
	-belaela	doubt (v)	twyfel	-bohale	shrill (a)	skerp
	-belaela	distrust (v)	wantrou	-bohale	fierce (a)	woes
	-belaela	suspect (v)	verdink	bohare	interior (n)	binneste
	belofo	valve (n)	klep	bohato	pedal (n)	pedaal
	-benya	gleam (v)	straal	bohato	footprint (n)	voetspoor
	-benya	shine (v)	skyn	-bohedene	pagan (a)	heidens
	-benya	sparkle (v)	vonkel	-bohla	belch (v)	wind opbreek
	-benyang	shiny (a)	blink	-bohlale	gifted (a)	begaaf
	-beola	shave (v)	skeer	-bohlale	intelligent (a)	intelligent
	bere	bear (n)	beer	-bohlale	wise (a)	wys
	-besa	burn (v)	brand	bohlale	wisdom (n)	wysheid
	bese	bus (n)	bus	bohlanka	bondage (n)	knegskap
	besete	vest (n)	onderhemp	bohlanya	delirium (n)	ylhoofdigheid
	-beta	rape (v)	verkrag	bohlanya	insanity (n)	kranksinnigheid
	-beta pelo	dare (v)	uitdaag	-bohlaswa	careless (a)	nalatig
	bete	beetroot (n)	beet	bohlaswa	mess (n)	gemors
	bete	bat (n)	kolf	bohlaswa	negligence (n)	nalatigheid
	-betere	better (a)	beter	bohlaswa	negligent (a)	nalatig
	beteri	battery (n)	battery	-bohlaswa	untidy (a)	slordig
	bethe	bed (n)	bed	bohloki	need (n)	behoefte
	-betjha	bet (v)	wed	bohloko	ache (n)	pyn
	-betla ditshwantsho	sculpt (v)	beeldhou	-bohloko	sore (a)	seer
	bilehasia	bilharzia (n)	bilharzia	bohloko ba tsebe	earache (n)	oorpyn
	-bina	sing (v)	sing	bohlokwa	distinguished (a)	vooraanstaande
	-bitsa	call (v)	roep	-bohlokwa	essential (a)	essensieel
	-bitsa	charge (price) (v)	vra	-bohlokwa	important (a)	belangrik
	-bitsaa	name (v)	noem	-bohlokwa	precious (a)	kosbaar
	-bitsa	summon (v)	ontbied	-bohlokwa	useful (a)	nuttig
	boahlamo	opening (n)	opening	-bohlokwa	valuable (a)	waardevol
	bobare	hearsay (n)	hoorsê	bohlokwa	value (n)	waarde

Sesotho	English	Afrikaans	Sesotho	English	Afrikaans	B
bohlwa	ant (n)	mier	-bola	decay (v)	verrot	
bohobe	wafer (n)	wafel	-bola	decompose (v)	ontbind	
bohoho	crust (n)	korsie	-bola	rot (v)	verrot	
-bohola	bark (v)	blaf	boladu	pus (n)	etter	
-bohola	wail (v)	weeklaag	-bolaya	kill (v)	doodmaak	
bohole	distance (n)	afstand	-bolaya	murder (v)	vermoor	
boholo	adulthood (n)	volwassenheid	-bolaya	slaughter (v)	slag	
boholo	age (n)	ouderdom	bolekano	volcano (n)	vulkaan	
boholo	size (n)	grootte	-bolela	allege (v)	beweer	
-boholoholo	ancient (a)	antiek	-bolela	declare (v)	verklaar	
bohwelea	stammer (n)	gehakkel	-bolela	say (v)	sê	
bohwelea	stutter (n)	gestotter	-bolela	tell (v)	vertel	
-boi	timid (a)	skugter	bolelele	length (n)	lengte	
boikaketsi	pretence (n)	skyn	bolepi ba dinaledi	astrology (n)	astrologie	
boikgathatso	effort (n)	inspanning	bolepo	cobweb (n)	spinnerak	
boikgethelo	franchise (n)	kiesreg	bolo	ball (n)	bal	
boikgetheto	choice (n)	keuse	bolo	football (n)	voetbal	
boikgohomoso	pride (n)	trots	bolo	soccer (n)	sokker	
boikokobetso	humility (n)	nederigheid	boloi	magic (n)	towerkuns	
boikokobetso	obedience (n)	gehoorsaamheid	-boloi	magical (a)	magies	
boikutlo	consciousness (n)	bewussyn	boloi	witchcraft (n)	toorkuns	
-boima	grave (a)	gewigtig	-boloka	conserve (v)	bewaar	
-boima	hard (a)	moeilik	-boloka	keep (v)	hou	
-boima	heavy (a)	swaar	-boloka	maintain (v)	handhaaf	
boima	weight (n)	gewig	-boloka	preserve (v)	bewaar	
boineelo	surrender (n)	oorgawe	-boloka	reserve (v)	reserveer	
boinyatso	regret (n)	spyt	-boloka	secure (v)	beveilig	
boiphetetso	vengeance (n)	wraak	-boloka	spare (v)	spaar	
boiphihlelo	experience (n)	ervaring	-boloka	store (v)	bêre	
boipiletso	appeal (n)	beroep	-bolokehileng	safe (a)	veilig	
boipolao	suicide (n)	selfmoord	-bolokehileng	secure (a)	veilig	
boipolelo	confession (n)	belydenis	bolompoto	vase (n)	vaas	
boithabiso	amusement (n)	vermaaklikheid	-bolotsa	circumcise (v)	besny	
boithutelo	qualification (n)	kwalifikasie	boloubolasie	bluebottle (n)	bloublasie	
boitsebiso	identity (n)	identiteit	boloukomo	bluegum (n)	bloekomboom	
boitshepo	self-confidence (n)	selfvertroue	bolouso	blouse (n)	bloes	
boitshwaro	behaviour (n)	gedrag	bolwetse	sickness (n)	siekte	
-boitshwaro	temper (n)	humeur	bomadimabe	misfortune (n)	teenspoed	
boka	glue (n)	gom	bomakenete	magnetism (n)	magnetisme	
bokaakang	quantity (n)	hoeveelheid	bomo	bomb (n)	bom	
bokamoso	future (n)	toekoms	bomo	landmine (n)	landmyn	
-bokana	gather (v)	byeenkom	-bona	see (v)	sien	
-bokanela	surround (v)	omring	-bona	their (pron)	hulle	
-bokanya	convene (v)	byeenroep	-bona	theirs (pron)	hulle s'n	
-bokella	heap (v)	ophoop	bona	them (pron)	hulle	
-bokella	pile (v)	stapel	bona	they (pron)	hulle	
bokgabane	integrity (n)	integriteit	-bonahalang	visible (a)	sigbaar	
bokgeleke	eloquence (n)	welsprekendheid	-bonaletsang	transparent (a)	deurskynend	
bokgeleke	rhetoric (n)	retoriek	-bona phoso	blame (v)	blameer	
bokgoba	addiction (n)	verslaafdheid	bong	gender (n)	geslag	
bokgoba	slavery (n)	slawerny	bongaka ba thipa	surgery (n)	chirurgie	
-bokgonatha	miserly (a)	vrekkerig	bongata	plural (n)	meervoud	
bokgoni	ability (n)	bekwaamheid	bongata	variety (n)	verskeidenheid	
bokgoni	efficiency (n)	doeltreffendheid	bongwana	childhood (n)	kinderjare	
-bokoa	sickly (a)	sieklik	-bonna	masculine (a)	manlik	
bokudubete	tadpole (n)	paddavissie	bonna	manhood (n)	manlikheid	
bokunutu	secrecy (n)	geheimhouding	bonngwe	unit (n)	eenheid	
-bokwala	cowardly (a)	lafhartig	bonngwe	unity (n)	eenheid	
bokwala	cowardice (n)	lafhartigheid	-bonolo	agreeable (a)	aangenaam	
bokwenehi	disloyalty (n)	dislojaliteit	-bonolo	simple (a)	eenvoudig	

B	Sesotho	English	Afrikaans	Sesotho	English	Afrikaans
	-bonolo	easy (a)	maklik	bosiu	night (n)	nag
	-bonolo	effortless (a)	met gemak	bosiyo	absence (n)	afwesigheid
	-bonolo	soft (a)	sag	bosula	tasteless (a)	smaakloos
	bonolo	gentle (a)	sagmoedig	bosweu	white (n)	wit
	-bonolo	gently (adv)	saggies	botala	green (n)	groen
	-bonolo	tender (a)	teer	botebo	depth (n)	diepte
	bonono	quality (n)	kwaliteit	boteng	attendance (n)	bywoning
	-bontsha	demonstrate (v)	betoog	-botha	crouch (v)	buk
	-bontsha	prove (v)	bewys	-botha	lie (v)	lê
	-bontsha	exhibit (v)	uitstal	bothata	difficulty (n)	moeilikheid
	-bontsha	show (v)	wys	-bothetsa	dent (v)	duik
	-bonya	smile (v)	glimlag	-botho	human (a)	menslik
	-bonyane	least (a)	minste	-botho	humane (a)	mensliewend
	bonyane	minimum (n)	minimum	botho	membership (n)	lidmaatskap
	bonyenyane	bit (n)	bietjie	botho bo felletseng	refinement (n)	verfyndheid
	bookgolane	grasshopper (n)	sprinkaan	bothoto	foolisaness (n)	dwaasheid
	booko	brain (n)	brein	botjhaba	nationalism (n)	nasionalisme
	bootswa	adultery (n)	owerspel	botjhabela	east (adv)	oos
	-bopa	mould (v)	vorm	-botjhabela	eastern (a)	oostelik
	-bopa	form (v)	vorm	botjhabela	east (n)	ooste
	bopaki	evidence (n)	getuienis	botlase	bottom (n)	bodem
	bopaki	proof (n)	bewys	botle	beauty (n)	skoonheid
	bopaki	testimony (n)	getuienis	botlokotsebe	mischief (n)	kattekwaad
	bopaki ba leshano	perjury (n)	meineed	-botlokotsebe	mischievous (a)	ondeund
	bopaki bo ngotsweng	affidavit (n)	beëdigde verklaring	botlokotsebe	impertinence (n)	astrantheid
	bophahamo	height (n)	hoogte	botlolo	bottle (n)	bottel
	bophahamo	rise (n)	styging	botoro	butter (n)	botter
	bophara	breadth (n)	breedte	boto ya dinoto	keyboard (n)	klawerbord
	bophelo	life (n)	lewe	-botsa	ask (v)	vra
	bophelo bo botle	health (n)	gesondheid	-botsa	consult (v)	raadpleeg
	bophelo bo hlaha	wildlife (n)	natuurlewe	-botsa	interrogate (v)	ondervra
	-bophirima	west (adv)	wes	-botsa	inquire (v)	navraag doen
	bophirima	west (n)	weste	-botsa	question (v)	vra
	-bophirima	western (a)	westelik	botsebi	technique (n)	tegniek
	boporofeta	prediction (n)	voorspelling	botshabelo	asylum (n)	skuilplaas
	boputswa	grey (n)	grys	botshabelo	refuge (n)	skuiling
	borabele	rebellion (n)	opstand	botshepehi	fidelity (n)	getrouheid
	borakefese	breakfast (n)	ontbyt	botshepehi	honesty (n)	eerlikheid
	borase	brass (n)	geelkoper	botsitso	balance (n)	balans
	-boreledi	smooth (a)	glad	-botswa	idle (a)	ledig
	borikgwe	trousers (n)	langbroek	-botswa	indolent (a)	traag
	borikgwe bo	shorts (n)	kortbroek	botswa	laziness (n)	luiheid
	bokgutshwane			-botswa	lazy (a)	lui
	boriki	brake (n)	rem	botubo	oppression (n)	onderdrukking
	borokgo	bridge (n)	brug	botumo	fame (n)	roem
	boroko	sleep (n)	slaap	botumo	notoriety (n)	berugtheid
	-borosola	brush (v)	borsel	-bouta	vote (v)	stem
	borosolo	brush (n)	borsel	bouto	vote (n)	stem
	borotho	bread (n)	brood	boutu	bolt (n)	bout
	borotho	loaf (n)	brood	boya	fur (n)	pels
	boroto	board (n)	bord	boya	hair (n)	hare
	boroto ya ho qwela	diving board (n)	duikplank	-boya	hairy (a)	harig
	-borwa	south (a)	suid	boya	wool (n)	wol
	borwa	south (n)	suide	boya ba podi	mohair (n)	sybokhaar
	-borwa	southern (a)	suidelik	boya ba tshwele	cotton wool (n)	watte
	bosa ba lehodimo	weather (n)	weer	-bua	operate (v)	opereer
	bosafeleng	eternity (n)	ewigheid	-bua	speak (v)	praat
	bosea	infancy (n)	kleintyd	-bua	talk (v)	praat
	boseka	anklet (n)	enkelring	-bua ka pelo	absent-minded (a)	ingedagte
	bosisapelo	misery (n)	ellende	-bua leshano	lie (v)	lieg

Sesotho	English	Afrikaans	Sesotho	English	Afrikaans
-bua leshano kgotla	perjure (v)	meineed pleeg	dilemo tse leshome	decade (n)	dekade
-buisa	address (v)	toespreek	diletsi	orchestra (n)	orkes
-buisana	discuss (v)	bespreek	dimedi	flora (n)	flora
-buisana	negotiate (v)	onderhandel	dinoko	spice (n)	spesery
buka	book (n)	boek	dintshi	eyebrow (n)	winkbrou
buka	copy (book) (n)	eksemplaar	dintshi	eyelash (n)	wimper
bukana	pamphlet (n)	pamflet	dintshi	eyelid (n)	ooglid
bukantswe	dictionary (n)	woordeboek	dipalo	arithmetic (n)	rekenkunde
-bula	open (v)	oopmaak	dipejama	pyjamas (n)	pajamas
-bulehile	open (a)	oop	diphahlo	goods (n)	goedere
-buretsa	squash (v)	platdruk	diphate	bedclothes (n)	beddegoed
-busa	dominate (v)	oorheers	diphedi	fauna (n)	fauna
-busa	govern (v)	regeer	dipolitike	politics (n)	politiek
-busa	reign (v)	heers	dipotongwane	biceps (n)	biseps
-busa	rule (v)	regeer	dirasenkise	raisin (n)	rosyntjie
-buseletsa	refund (v)	terugbetaal	-disa	watch (v)	dophou
-butle	gradually (adv)	geleidelik	disebediswa	apparatus (n)	apparaat
butle	slow (a)	stadig	disonoborele	sunglasses (n)	sonbril
butshi	boot (n)	stewel	ditaba	news (n)	nuus
-butswela	inflate (v)	opblaas	ditaelo	directions (n)	aanwysings
-butswitseng	ripe (a)	ryp	ditebele	boxing (n)	boks
			diteboho	thanks (n)	dank
daenengrumo	dining room (n)	eetkamer	ditedu	beard (n)	baard
degri	degree (n)	graad	ditemetwane	tonsils (n)	mangels
demokerasi	democracy (n)	demokrasie	diterapa	stairs (n)	trappe
denamaete	dynamite (n)	dinamiet	dithethefatsi	drugs (n)	dwelms
deseke	desk (n)	lessenaar	dithole	refuse (n)	vullis
diabelo	fractions (n)	breuke	dithole	waste (n)	afval
diabolose	devil (n)	duiwel	ditholwana	consequence (n)	gevolg
diaparo	clothes (n)	klere	ditholwana	result (n)	uitslag
diatletiki	athletics (n)	atletiek	-ditjhabeng	exotic (a)	eksoties
dibeso	fuel (n)	brandstof	ditlatse	acclaim (n)	toejuiging
dibetsa	ammunition (n)	ammunisie	ditlelapa	blinkers (n)	oogklappe
dibetsa	arms (n)	wapens	ditlhoka	bran (n)	semels
diborele	spectacles (n)	bril	ditlhong	shy (a)	skugter
-dieha	delay (v)	vertraag	ditshebo	gossip (n)	skinderpraatjies
difaha	beadwork (n)	kraalwerk	ditshenyehelo	expenses (n)	onkoste
diha	overthrow (v)	omvergooi	ditshifa	sediment (n)	sediment
-dihela marapo	resign (v)	bedank	-ditshila	unclean (a)	onrein
dihele	hell (n)	hel	ditshila	rubbish (n)	vuilgoed
dihlong	shame (n)	skaamte	-ditshila	dirty (a)	vuil
dijana	crockery (n)	breekware	-ditshila	nasty (a)	gemeen
dijo	food (n)	kos	-ditshila	messy (a)	morsig
dijo	meal (n)	maal	-duba	knead (v)	knie
dijo tsa mantsiboya	supper (n)	aandete	-dula	sit (v)	sit
dijo tsa motsheare	lunch (n)	middagete	-dulasetulo	chair (v)	voorsit
dikahare	bowels (n)	ingewande	-dumedisa	greet (v)	groet
dikahare	contents (n)	inhoud	-dumedisa	salute (v)	salueer
-dikatana	ragged (a)	verflenterd	-dumela	acknowledge (v)	erken
dikauso	stockings (n)	kouse	-dumela	admit (v)	toelaat
dikeledi	tears (n)	trane	-dumela	agree (v)	ooreenstem
dikepe tsa ntwa	navy (n)	vloot	-dumela	approve (v)	goedkeur
diketsahalo	proceedings (n)	verrigtinge	-dumela	believe (v)	glo
dikgaba	cutlery (n)	eetgerei	-dumela	consent (v)	instem
dikgaboi	banns (n)	gebooie	-dumela	echo (v)	weerklink
dikgaretene	blind (n)	blinding	-dumelang	positive (a)	positief
dikgomo	cattle (n)	vee	-dumelang	religious (a)	godsdienstig
dikgutsaneng	orphanage (n)	weeshuis	-dumella	allow (v)	toestaan
dikonokono	wax (n)	was	-dumella	authorise (v)	magtig
dilemokgolo	century (sport) (n)	honderdtal	-dumella	permit (v)	toelaat

D	Sesotho	English	Afrikaans	Sesotho	English	Afrikaans
	-dutla	leak (v)	lek	-etsahala	happen (v)	gebeur
	-dutla	ooze (v)	sypel	-etsahala	occur (v)	voorkom
				-etsahalang	possible (a)	moontlik
	-ebola	peel (v)	skil	-etsa letheba	stain (v)	bevlek
	ebolusi	evolution (n)	evolusie	-etsa mmomori	plot (v)	saamsweer
	-edimola	yawn (v)	gaap	-etsa morusu	riot (v)	oproer maak
	eie	onion (n)	ui	-etsisa	ape (v)	na-aap
	eike	oak (n)	eikeboom	-etsisa	imitate (v)	namaak
	-eka	betray (v)	verraai			
	-eketsa	add (v)	byvoeg	-fa	give (v)	gee
	-eketsa	increase (v)	vermeerder	-fa	offer (v)	aanbied
	-eketsang	additional (a)	bykomend	-fa	present (v)	skenk
	ekhweita	equator (n)	ewenaar	-fa	provide (v)	voorsien
	ekseperimente	experiment (n)	proefneming	-fa	supply (v)	verskaf
	-ela hloko	observe (v)	waarneem	faele	file (n)	leêr
	-ela tlhoko	heed (v)	in ag neem	-fafatsa	sprinkle (v)	sprinkel
	-elellwa	notice (v)	opmerk	-fa(h)ola	castrate (v)	kastreer
	-eletsa	advise (v)	raad gee	faki	barrel (n)	vat
	-eletsa	warn (v)	waarsku	-falatsa	evict (v)	uitsit
	-eletsang	advisory (a)	raadgewend	-falla	depart (v)	vertrek
	-ema	stand (v)	staan	-falla	emigrate (v)	emigreer
	-ema	stop (v)	stop	-falla	immigrate (v)	immigreer
	-ema pane	guarantee (v)	waarborg	-falla	migrate (v)	migreer
	-emela	await (v)	wag op	-fana	confer (v)	toeken
	-emela	mediate (v)	bemiddel	-fana	donate (v)	skenk
	-emela	represent (v)	verteenwoordig	-fana ka laesense	license (v)	lisensieer
	-emeng	stagnant (a)	stagnant	-fanang	generous (a)	vrygewig
	-emeng	stationary (a)	stilstaande	fane	surname (n)	van
	-emere	pregnant (a)	swanger	fanele	funnel (n)	tregter
	-emisa	park (v)	parkeer	fantisi	auction (n)	veiling
	-emola	conceive (v)	opvat	-fanya	defect (v)	oorloop na
	empa	but (conj)	maar	-fanyeha	execute (v)	teregstel
	empa	however (conj)	maar	-fanyeha	hang (v)	hang
	enema	enema (n)	enema	-faola	prune (v)	snoei
	eng	what (pron)	wat	-fapana	differ (v)	verskil
	enisheale	initial (n)	voorletter	-fapana	disagree (v)	verskil
	enjene	engine (n)	enjin	-fapaneng	different (a)	verskillend
	enke	ink (n)	ink	-fapaneng	varied (a)	gevarieerd
	enshorense	insurance (n)	versekering	-fapanya	vary (v)	varieer
	-enta	inoculate (v)	inent	-fapoha	turn (v)	draai
	enta	vaccinate (v)	inent	-fasolla	disconnect (v)	losmaak
	-entse	done (v)	gedoen	-fatisisa	cross examine (v)	kruisvra
	eo	that (pron)	dat	-fa tjhefo	poison (v)	vergiftig
	-epela	bury (v)	begrawe	-fe	which (pron)	watter
	erekisi	pea (n)	ertjie	-feba	flirt (v)	flirteer
	eriale	antenna (n)	lugdraad	feberu	fever (n)	koors
	eriale	aerial (n)	lugdraad	-fedisa	abolish (v)	afskaf
	esele	ass (n)	donkie	feela	anyhow (conj)	in elk geval
	-esita	even (adv)	selfs	-feela	bare (a)	kaal
	esiti	acid (n)	suur	-feela	blank (a)	leeg
	-eta	tour (v)	rondreis	-feela	empty (a)	leeg
	-eta	travel (v)	reis	feela	just (adv)	net
	-etela	call (v)	besoek	feela	only (a)	enigste
	-etela	visit (v)	besoek	feela	only (adv)	slegs
	-etella pele	lead (v)	lei	feelwana	comma (n)	komma
	-etella pele	precede (v)	voorafgaan	-fefola	blow (v)	waai
	-ethimola	sneeze (v)	nies	-fehelwa	breathless (a)	uitasem
	-etsa	do (v)	doen	-fehelwa	gasp (v)	snak
	-etsa	make (v)	maak	-fehelwa	pant (v)	hyg
	-etsa	perform (v)	uitvoer	-fehelwa	wheeze (v)	hyg

Sesotho	English	Afrikaans
feile	file (n)	vyl
feiye	fig (n)	vy
-fekisa	overpower (v)	oorweldig
-fela pelo	impatient (a)	ongeduldig
-felehetsa	accompany (v)	begelei
-felehetsa	escort (v)	vergesel
-felletseng	complete (a)	volledig
-felletseng	whole (a)	heel
feme	factory (n)	fabriek
fene	fan (n)	waaier
fensetere	window (n)	venster
fensetere ya moya	windscreen (n)	voorruit
-fenya	conquer (v)	verower
-fepa	feed (v)	voer
-ferehla	disturb (v)	pla
-ferekanya	confuse (v)	verwar
ferekekere	binoculars (n)	verkyker
ferekekere	telescope (n)	teleskoop
fereko	fork (n)	vurk
-ferola	nauseate (v)	naar maak
-feta	exceed (v)	oorskry
-feta	overtake (v)	verbysteek
-feta	pass (v)	verbygaan
-fetang	extra (a)	ekstra
fetase	foetus (n)	fetus
-feteletsa	exaggerate (v)	oordryf
-fetola	change (v)	verander
-fetola	shuffle (v)	skuifel
-fetolela	translate (v)	vertaal
-fiela	sweep (v)	vee
-fihla	arrive (v)	aankom
-fihlela	reach (v)	bereik
-fihlela	attain (v)	bereik
fileme	film (n)	film
-fina	knot (v)	knoop
-finahana	shrivel (v)	verskrompel
-finahanya	contract (v)	inkrimp
-fodisa	cool (v)	afkoel
-fofa	fly (v)	vlieg
-fofonela	sniff (v)	snuif
-fokolang	invalid (a)	ongeldig
-fokolang	weak (a)	swak
-fokotsa	decrease (v)	verminder
-fokotsa	reduce (v)	verminder
-fokotsa ka lehare	halve (v)	halveer
folakga	flag (n)	vlag
folaminko	flamingo (n)	flamink
foleite	flute (n)	fluit
foleiti	mouth organ (n)	mondfluitjie
foleiti	pennywhistle (n)	kwêlafluitjie
folene	flannel (n)	flanel
-foofo	tepid (a)	lou
forije	refrigerator (n)	yskas
foro	gutter (n)	geut
foroko	pitchfork (n)	gaffel
forosekoto	apron (n)	voorskoot
foro ya ho tlosa metsi	drainpipe (n)	rioolpyp
-fosa	err (v)	fouteer
-fosa	flap (v)	fladder
-fosa	miss (v)	mis

Sesotho	English	Afrikaans
-fosahetse	improper (a)	onfatsoenlik
-foufetse	blind (a)	blind
-fubedu	red (a)	rooi
-fudua	stir (v)	roer
-fufulelwa	perspire (v)	perspireer
-fufulelwa	sweat (v)	sweet
fuluru	floor (n)	vloer
-fumana	acquire (v)	aanskaf
-fumana	find (v)	vind
-fumana	get (v)	kry
-fumana	obtain (v)	bekom
-fumana phaello	profit (v)	wins maak
-fumaneha	available (a)	beskikbaar
-fumanehisa	impoverish (v)	verarm
furu	lining (n)	voering
-futhumatsa	heat (v)	warm maak
-futsa	resemble (v)	aard na
-futsanehileng	poor (a)	arm
-futuhela	raid (v)	stroop
galari	gallery (n)	galery
garafu	shovel (n)	skoppie
garafu	spade (n)	graaf
gase	gas (n)	gas
ha	if (conj)	as
ha	while (conj)	terwyl
habedi	twice (n)	twee maal
-habedi	ambiguous (a)	dubbelsinnig
-habedi	double (a)	dubbele
-habola	sip (v)	slurp
ha bonolo	softly (adv)	saggies
habore	oats (n)	hawer
-hadika	fry (v)	bak
-hadika	grill (v)	rooster
-hadika	roast (v)	oondbraai
-hae	hers (pron)	hare
-hae	his (pron)	sy
-hae	his (pron)	syne
-(h)aha	build (v)	bou
ha-/ho-	at (prep)	op
-haholoholo	radical (a)	radikaal
-haholoholo	quite (a)	taamlik
ha ho motho	nobody (pron)	niemand
-haka	hook (v)	haak
hakgutshwane	briefly (adv)	kortliks
-halalelang	holy (a)	heilig
-halalelang	sacred (a)	heilig
-halefile	angry (a)	kwaad
-halefisa	anger (v)	kwaad maak
-halefisa	infuriate (v)	woedend maak
-halefisa	irritate (v)	irriteer
halofo	half (n)	helfte
hambekara	hamburger (n)	hamburger
hammoho (le)	together (adv)	saam
ha morao	afterwards (adv)	agterna
hampe	badly (adv)	sleg
-hana	object (v)	beswaar maak
-hana	decline (v)	afwys
-hana	deny (v)	ontken

H

Sesotho	English	Afrikaans
-hana	disobey (v)	ongehoorsaam wees
-hana	refuse (v)	weier
-hana	resist (v)	weerstaan
-hananang le phetoho	conservative (a)	konserwatief
-hanela	curb (v)	inhou
-hanela	forbid (v)	verbied
-hanela	restrict (v)	inperk
hang	once (adv)	een maal
hanghang	immediate (a)	onmiddellik
-hanghang	instantly (adv)	oombliklik
hanimunu	honeymoon (n)	wittebrood
hansekunu	glove (n)	handskoen
hantle	well (a)	goed
hantlentle	actually (adv)	eintlik
-hanwang	objectionable (a)	aanstootlik
-hanyetsa	defy (v)	trotseer
-hanyetsa	oppose (v)	opponeer
-hanyetsa	protest (v)	protesteer
-hao	your (pron)	jou
-hao	yours (pron)	joune
-hapa	capture (v)	vang
hape	again (adv)	weer
-hape	more (a)	meer
hape	too (adv)	ook
-hara	amid (prep)	tussen
-hara	between (prep)	tussen
haraka	rake (n)	hark
-haraka	rake (v)	hark
-hare ha naha	inland (a)	binnelands
haremonika	harmonica (n)	harmonika
harepa	harp (n)	harp
-hasa	broadcast (v)	uitsaai
-hasa	disperse (v)	verstrooi
-hasa	spread (v)	versprei
-hata	step (v)	trap
-hata	tread (v)	trap
-hatella	subdue (v)	onderwerp
-hatisa	press (v)	pers
-hatisa	print (v)	druk
-haufi	close (a)	naby
haufi	near (adv)	naby
-haufi	newly (adv)	onlangs
haufi le-	next to (prep)	langs
-haufinyane	soon (adv)	binnekort
-haulang	pitiful (a)	jammerlik
heke	gate (n)	hek
-helehang	ramshackle (a)	bouvallig
-heletsa	demolish (v)	afbreek
hemo	ham (n)	ham
hempe	shirt (n)	hemp
-hira	appoint (v)	aanstel
-hira	employ (v)	in diens neem
-hira	hire (v)	huur
-hira	rent (v)	huur
-hlaba	inject (v)	inspuit
-hlaba	stab (v)	steek
-hlaba	sting (v)	steek
-hlabela	sacrifice (v)	opoffer
-hlabisang dihlong	obscene (a)	onbetaamlik
-hlabosang	delicious (a)	heerlik
-hlabosang	nice (a)	aangenaam
-hlafuna	chew (v)	kou
-hlaha	appear (v)	verskyn
-hlaha	wild (a)	wild
-hlahatsa	expose (v)	blootlê
-hlahisa	express (v)	uitdruk
-hlahisa	produce (v)	produseer
-hlahisa	propose (v)	voorstel
-hlahisa	state (v)	vermeld
-hlahlela	jail (v)	opsluit
-hlahloba	check (v)	nagaan
-hlahloba	examine (v)	ondersoek
-hlahloba	inspect (v)	inspekteer
hlahlobo	examination (n)	eksamen
hlahlobo	inspection (n)	inspeksie
-hlaho	natural (a)	natuurlik
hlaho	nature (n)	natuur
-hlahola	hoe (v)	skoffel
-hlakile	bright (a)	helder
-hlakile	clear (a)	helder
-hlakisa	practise (v)	oefen
-hlakola	dust (v)	afstof
Hlakola	February (n)	Februarie
-hlakola	erase (v)	uitvee
-hlala	divorce (v)	skei
hlalefo	intelligence (n)	intelligensie
-hlalosa	define (v)	bepaal
-hlalosa	describe (v)	beskrywe
-hlalosa	explain (v)	verduidelik
hlaloso	explanation (n)	verduideliking
hlama	dough (n)	deeg
hlama	pastry (n)	pastei
-hlamatsehang	glamorous (a)	bekoorlik
-hlamatsehang	ideal (a)	ideaal
hlano	five (n)	vyf
-hlanya	insane (a)	kranksinnig
-hlanya	mad (a)	gek
-hlaola	weed (v)	onkruid uittrek
-hlapaola	insult (v)	beledig
-hlapaola	swear (v)	vloek
-hlaphohelwa	recover (v)	herstel
-hlapholla	dilute (v)	verdun
-hlasela	attack (v)	aanval
-hlasela	invade (v)	inval
-hlasela	tackle (v)	aanpak
-hlasela ka mantswe	lash (v)	gesel
-hlatsa	vomit (v)	vomeer
-hlatswa	wash (v)	was
-hle	absolute (a)	absoluut
-hle	all (a)	alle
-hle	all (things) (pron)	alles
-hle	all (beings) (pron)	almal
-hle	entire (a)	hele
-hle	very (a)	heel
-hlehla	jog (v)	draf
-hlobaelang	sleepless (a)	slapeloos
-hlobola	strip (v)	ontbloot
-hlobola	undress (v)	uittrek
-hlobotseng	naked (a)	kaal
-hlodisana	compete (v)	wedywer

Sesotho	English	Afrikaans	Sesotho	English	Afrikaans	H
-hlohla	tease (v)	terg	-hlwekile	clean (a)	skoon	
-hlohlelletsa	indoctrinate (v)	indoktrineer	-hlwekileng	pure (a)	suiwer	
-hlohlomisa	tabulate (v)	tabuleer	-hlwekileng	sterile (a)	steriel	
-hlohlona	itch (v)	jeuk	-hlwekisa	clean (v)	skoonmaak	
-hlohonolofatsa	bless (v)	seën	-hlwekisa	cleanse (v)	skoonmaak	
-hloka	need (v)	nodig hê	-hlwekisa	disinfect (v)	ontsmet	
-hloka botho	impersonal (a)	onpersoonlik	-hlwekisa	purify (v)	suiwer	
-hlokahetseng	late (a)	oorlede	-hlwekisa	purge (v)	skoonmaak	
-hloka kelello	absurd (a)	onsinnig	-hlwekisa	sterilise (v)	steriliseer	
-hloka leeme	arbitrary (a)	willekeurig	-hlwekisa ntle ho metsi	dryclean (v)	droogskoonmaak	
-hloka molato	innocent (a)	onskuldig	hlweko	purity (n)	suiwerheid	
-hlokang	dependent (a)	afhanklik	-hlwela	scout (v)	rondkyk	
-hlokang thuso	helpless (a)	hulpeloos	-hlwela	spy (v)	spioeneer	
-hlokehang	necessary (a)	noodsaaklik	-hlwella	climb (v)	klim	
-hlokisa	deprive (v)	ontneem	-hlwella	mount (v)	opklim	
-hlokofatsang	offensive (a)	aanstootlik	ho-	from (prep)	van	
-hlokofetseng	serious (a)	ernstig	ho-	on (prep)	op	
-hlokomela	beware (v)	oppas	ho-	to (prep)	na	
-hlokomelang	careful (a)	versigtig	-hoa	scream (v)	gil	
-hlokomoloha	disregard (v)	verontagsaam	-hoa	exclaim (v)	uitroep	
-hlokomoloha	neglect (v)	verwaarloos	ho ahlolelwa ka ntle	suspended sentence (n)	opgeskorte vonnis	
-hlola	create (v)	skep	-ho amohela baeti	host (v)	gasheer wees	
-hlola	defeat (v)	verslaan	hobane	because (conj)	omdat	
-hlola	fornicate (v)	hoereer	hobaneng	why (adv)	waarom	
-hlola	master (v)	bemeester	ho ba teng	existence (n)	bestaan	
-hlola	overcome (v)	te bowe kom	ho beha borena	coronation (n)	kroning	
-hlola	win (v)	wen	hobolelwang	meaning (n)	bedoeling	
-hloleha	fail (v)	misluk	-hodileng	mature (a)	volwasse	
-hlolla	baffle (v)	verbyster	-hodima	above (prep)	bo	
-hlolla	wonder (v)	wonder	hodima	up (prep)	op	
-hloma	establish (v)	vestig	-hodimo	loud (a)	hard	
-hloma	sprout (v)	uitloop	hodimo	top (n)	top	
-hloma	stem (v)	voortspruit	-hodisa	magnify (v)	vergroot	
-hlomela	arm (v)	bewapen	-hodisa	enlarge (v)	vergroot	
-hlomohileng	sad (a)	treurig	ho dutla madi	haemorrhage (n)	bloeding	
-hlompha	honour (v)	eer	ho ema paneng	guarantee (n)	waarborg	
hlompha	respect (v)	respekteer	ho falla	removal (n)	trek	
hlomphano	etiquette (n)	etiket	ho feroha	nausea (n)	naarheid	
-hlomphehang	dignified (a)	waardig	ho feta	than (conj)	as	
-hlomphehang	respectable (a)	fatsoenlik	ho fihla	arrival (n)	aankoms	
hlompho	dignity (n)	waardigheid	ho fihlela	until (conj)	tot	
hlomphollo	disgrace (n)	skande	ho hang	absolutely (adv)	absoluut	
-hlooho	chief (a)	hoof	-hohela	attract (v)	aantrek	
hlooho	head (n)	kop	-hohela	lure (v)	aanlok	
hlooho	principal (n)	hoof	-hohelang	attractive (a)	aantreklik	
hlooho e opang	headache (n)	hoofpyn	-hohla	chafe (v)	skaaf	
-hlopha	arrange (v)	skik	-hohla	scour (v)	skuur	
-hlopha	plan (v)	beplan	ho hlaha	appearance (n)	verskyning	
-hlophisa	classify (v)	klassifiseer	ho hlaka	brilliance (n)	helderheid	
-hlophisa	edit (v)	redigeer	-hohlana	conflict (v)	bots	
-hlophisa	organise (v)	reël	ho hloka botshepehi	dishonesty (n)	oneerlikheid	
hlophiso	arrangement (n)	skikking	ho hloka tsebo	ignorance (n)	onkunde	
-hlopholla	analyse (v)	ontleed	-hohlola	cough (v)	hoes	
-hlora	long (v)	verlang	ho itlosa bodutu	hobby (n)	stokperdjie	
-hlorileng	lonely (a)	eensaam	-hokahanya	connect (v)	verbind	
-hlotla	filter (v)	filtreer	ho/ka/ka hara	in (prep)	in	
-hloya	detest (v)	verafsku	ho kampa	camping (n)	kampering	
-hloya	hate (v)	haat	ho kena boholo	puberty (n)	puberteit	
-hloya	loathe (v)	verafsku	ho kena boholo	adolescence (n)	adolessensie	
-hloyang	hateful (a)	haatlik	ho kokota	knock (n)	klop	

287

H	Sesotho	English	Afrikaans	Sesotho	English	Afrikaans
	ho lala ha ntwa	ceasefire (n)	skietstilstand	ho tswedipanya	gymnastics (n)	gimnastiek
	-hole	far (adv)	ver	mmele		
	-hole	remote (a)	afgeleë	ho uba	throb (n)	klopping
	-holo	adult (a)	volwasse	ho uba ha pelo	pulse (n)	pols
	-holo	big (a)	groot	ho uba ha pelo	heartbeat (n)	hartklop
	-holo	capital (a)	hoof	housephaephe	hose (n)	tuinslang
	-holo	eldest (a)	oudste	ho ya kgweding	menstruation (n)	menstruasie
	holo	hall (n)	saal	huku	hook (n)	haak
	-holo	large (a)	groot	-hula	draw (v)	sleep
	-holo	main (a)	vernaamste	-hula	pull (v)	trek
	-holo	old (a)	oud	-hula	tow (v)	sleep
	-holo	paramount (a)	hoogste	-hula	withdraw (v)	terugtrek
	-holo	senior (a)	senior	-hulanya	drag (v)	sleep
	-holofatsa	cripple (v)	kreupel maak	-hwama	congeal (v)	stol
	-holofatsa	maim (v)	vermink	-hwama	curdle (v)	klonter
	-holofatsa	paralyse (v)	verlam	-hwama	freeze (v)	vries
	-holofetse	disabled (a)	gebreklik	-hwapa	frown (v)	frons
	-holofetseng	lame (a)	mank	-hweba	trade (v)	handel dryf
	ho loma	bite (n)	hap	-hwebisa	import (v)	invoer
	-hona	snore (v)	snork	-hwehla	beckon (v)	wink
	-honotha	mutter (v)	mompel	-hwelea	lisp (v)	lispel
	ho nqosa	prosecution (n)	vervolging	-hwelea	stammer (v)	hakkel
	ho ntsha tjotjo	bribery (n)	omkopery	-hwelea	stutter (v)	stotter
	ho nyahama	despair (n)	wanhoop	-hweshetsa	whisper (v)	fluister
	ho nyaroha	reflex (n)	refleks	hwetla	autumn (n)	herfs
	-honyela	shrink (v)	krimp			
	ho nyonya	disgust (n)	afkeer	-idibane	dazed (a)	bedwelmd
	ho oma ka hloho	nod (n)	knik	-ikaketsa	pretend (v)	voorgee
	ho petsoha ha sebono	haemorrhoids (n)	aambeie	-ikana	fester (v)	sweer
	ho phofa	nightmare (n)	nagmerrie	-iketlileng	comfortable (a)	gemaklik
	-hopola	recollect (v)	onthou	-iketsisa	feint (v)	voorgee
	-hopola	remember (v)	onthou	-ikgantsha	brag (v)	grootpraat
	-hopotsa	remind (v)	herinner	-ikgethang	distinct (a)	afsonderlik
	hora	hour (n)	uur	-ikgethang	particular (a)	besonder
	ho rata	admiration (n)	bewondering	-ikgethileng	special (a)	spesiaal
	ho ruruha	swelling (n)	swelsel	-ikgethileng	peculiar (a)	eienaardig
	ho ruruha ka	pleurisy (n)	borsvliesontsteking	-ikgohomosa	conceited (a)	verwaand
	sefubeng			-ikgohomosang	proud (a)	trots
	hosane	tomorrow (n)	môre	-ikgohomosang	haughty (a)	hoogmoedig
	ho se dumellane	disagreement (n)	meningsverskil	-ikgula	vacate (v)	uittrek
	hoseng	morning (n)	oggend	-ikokobeditse	obedient (a)	gehoorsaam
	hoseng	early (a)	vroeg	-ikokobeditseng	humble (a)	nederig
	ho sesa	swimming (n)	swem	-ikokobeditseng	polite (a)	hoflik
	ho setseng	remainder (n)	oorblyfsel	-ikokobeditseng	meek (a)	gedwee
	ho se utlwisise	misunderstanding (n)	misverstand	-ikokobetsa	obey (v)	gehoorsaam wees
	ho sihletsa mahetla	shrug (n)	skouerophaling	-ikutlwang	conscious (a)	bewus
	ho sokela	constipation (n)	konstipasie	-imametseng	modest (a)	beskeie
	hotedoko	hot dog (n)	worsbroodjie	-ina	immerse (v)	indompel
	hotele	hotel (n)	hotel	-ina	soak (v)	week
	ho tena	annoyance (n)	ergernis	-ina	dip (v)	insteek
	-hotetsa	ignite (v)	aansteek	-inahanelang	selfish (a)	selfsugtig
	ho tjheswa ke letsatsi	suntan (n)	sonbruin	-inama	stoop (v)	buk
	ho tjhetjha	retreat (v)	terugtog	-inama	bow (v)	buk
	ho tloha-	since (adv)	sedert	-ineela	devote (v)	toewy
	-ho tlotsa ka boka	glue (v)	gom	-ineela	surrender (v)	oorgee
	ho tsamaya	walk (n)	wandeling	infoleishene	inflation (n)	inflasie
	ho tseba	recognition (n)	herkenning	-inyatsa	regret (v)	spyt hê
	ho tseba	acquaintance (n)	kennismaking	-iphetetsa	avenge (v)	wreek
	ho tshwara	arrest (n)	inhegtenisneming	-ipiletsa	appeal (v)	beroep doen op
	-ho tshwara pikinike	picnic (v)	piekniek hou	-ipolela	confess (v)	bely

Sesotho	English	Afrikaans	Sesotho	English	Afrikaans	K
-ithapolla	exercise (v)	oefen	kae	where (adv)	waar	
-ithorisa	boast (v)	spog	kaekae	elsewhere (adv)	elders	
-ithorisang	boastful (a)	spoggerig	kae kapa kae	anywhere (adv)	enige plek	
-ithuta	learn (v)	leer	-ka etswang	practical (a)	prakties	
-ithuta	study (v)	studeer	ka hare	inside (adv)	binne	
-itshepa	confident (a)	vol vertroue	-ka hare	internal (a)	intern	
-itshetleha	lean (v)	leun	ka hare	within (adv)	binne	
-itshwara	behave (v)	jou gedra	(ka)hodima	over (prep)	oor	
-itshwara	conduct (v)	gedra	kahlolo	judgment (n)	oordeel	
-itshwara hampe	misbehave (v)	jou swak gedra	kahlolo	verdict (n)	uitspraak	
-itshwarella ka	depend (on) (v)	afhang (van)	ka hohle	around (adv)	rond	
-itwanela	retaliate (v)	vergeld	ka hosele	otherwise (adv)	anders	
			kajeno	today (n)	vandag	
-ja	dine (v)	hoofmaaltyd eet	kakanyo	guess (n)	raaiskoot	
-ja	eat (v)	eet	kakaretso	summary (n)	opsomming	
-jabela	slap (v)	klap	kakaretso	total (n)	totaal	
-jahileng	hasty (a)	haastig	kako	kiss (n)	soen	
-jala	plant (v)	plant	kalaka	lime (n)	kalk	
-jala	sow (v)	saai	kalaka e tshweu	whitewash (n)	witkalk	
-ja lefa	inherit (v)	erf	kalakune	turkey (n)	kalkoen	
jara	jar (n)	fles	kama	comb (n)	kam	
jarete	yard (n)	werf	-kama	comb (v)	kam	
jase	coat (n)	jas	kamano	connection (n)	verbinding	
jase	overcoat (n)	oorjas	ka mehla	always (adv)	gedurig	
jase ya pula	raincoat (n)	reënjas	ka mehla	daily (a)	daagliks	
-jehang	edible (a)	eetbaar	-ka mehla	ordinary (a)	gewoon	
jeke	jug (n)	beker	kamele	camel (n)	kameel	
jeli	jelly (n)	jellie	kamo	touch (n)	aanraking	
jeme	jam (n)	konfyt	kamohelo	acceptance (n)	aanvaarding	
jeresi	jersey (n)	trui	kamohelo	adoption (n)	aanneming	
Jeso	Jesus (n)	Jesus	kamohelo	welcome (n)	welkom	
joki	jockey (n)	jokkie	kamohelo(ng)	reception (n)	ontvangs	
joko	yoke (n)	juk	ka mora	after (place) (prep)	agter	
jwala	beer (n)	bier	ka mora	after (time) (prep)	na	
-jwale	current (a)	huidige	kamore	bedroom (n)	slaapkamer	
jwale	now (adv)	nou	kamore	room (n)	kamer	
jwale	then (adv)	dan	-kampa	camp (v)	kampeer	
jwale	then (adv)	toe	kampo	camp (n)	kamp	
-jwalo	such (a)	sulke	kanale	canal (n)	kanaal	
jwalo ka	like (prep)	soos	-ka nama	personal (a)	persoonlik	
jwang	grass (n)	gras	kanekane	can (n)	kan	
jwang	how (adv)	hoe	kankere	cancer (n)	kanker	
jwang kapa jwang	anyhow (adv)	hoe dan ook	ka nnete	indeed (adv)	werklik	
			ka nnete	really (adv)	werklik	
ka-	about (prep)	oor	kano	oath (n)	eed	
ka-	about (adv)	rond	kano	vow (n)	gelofte	
ka-	by (prep)	by	kanono	cannon (n)	kanon	
-ka	may (v)	mag	kanta	lace (n)	kant	
-ka	mine (pron)	myne	ka ntle	out (prep)	uit	
-ka	my (pron)	my	ka ntle	outside (n)	buitekant	
-ka	own (a)	eie	ka ntle	without (adv)	buite	
ka-	through (prep)	deur	kantoro	office (n)	kantoor	
ka beke	weekly (a)	weekliks	kapa	either (pron)	een van beide	
kabelo	fate (n)	lot	kapa	either...or (conj)	òf...òf	
kabinete	cabinet (n)	kabinet	kapa	nor (conj)	nòg	
ka boithatelo	voluntary (a)	vrywillig	kapa	or (conj)	of	
ka boomo	deliberate (a)	opsetlik	kapa	whether (conj)	of	
ka boomo	wilful (a)	moedswillig	ka pele	ahead (adv)	vooruit	
-ka boyona	mechanical (a)	meganies	ka pele	quick (a)	gou	
kadimo	loan (n)	lening	ka pele	quickly (adv)	gou	

K

Sesotho	English	Afrikaans	Sesotho	English	Afrikaans
-ka pele	rapid (a)	vlugtig	ketane	chain (n)	ketting
kapotene	captain (n)	kaptein	ketapele	preface (n)	voorwoord
karabo	answer (n)	antwoord	-keteka	feast (v)	feesvier
karabo	reply (n)	antwoord	-keteka	celebrate (v)	vier
karatjhe	garage (n)	motorhawe	ketelo	visit (n)	besoek
karete	card (n)	kaart	ketlele	kettle (n)	ketel
karete ya molato	credit card (n)	kredietkaart	ketsahalo	event (n)	gebeurtenis
kariki	cart (n)	kar	ketsahalo	phenomenon (n)	verskynsel
karohano	parting (n)	paadjie	ketsahalo	incident (n)	voorval
karolo	part (n)	deel	ketselletso	defamation (n)	belastering
karolo	portion (n)	gedeelte	ketselletso	slander (n)	laster
karolo	section (n)	afdeling	ketso	deed (n)	daad
karolo	share (n)	deel	ketso	performance (n)	uitvoering
ka selemo	annual (a)	jaarliks	-kga	scoop (v)	skep
ka sewelo	seldom (adv)	selde	kgaba	spoon (n)	lepel
kasteroli	castor oil (n)	kasterolie	-kgabisa	decorate (v)	versier
katamelo	approach (n)	nadering	kgabo	ape (n)	aap
katara	guitar (n)	kitaar	kgafetsa	often (adv)	dikwels
ka thoko	aside (adv)	opsy	-kgafisa	tax (v)	belas
katiba	hat (n)	hoed	kgafole	pith (n)	pit
katleho	achievement (n)	prestasie	-kgahla	impress (v)	beïndruk
katleho	success (n)	sukses	-kgahla	interest (v)	interesseer
katleho	welfare (n)	welsyn	kgahlanong le-	against (prep)	teen
katse	cat (n)	kat	-kgahlisang	interesting (a)	interessant
ka tshohanyetso	accidental (a)	toevallig	-kgahlwa	adore (v)	aanbid
ka tshohanyetso	accidentally (adv)	toevallig	kgaitsedi	sister (n)	suster
ka tshohanyetso	sudden (a)	skielik	kgaka	guineafowl (n)	tarentaal
kauso	sock (n)	sokkie	kgaketlana	eggshell (n)	eierdop
kedimolo	yawn (n)	gaap	-kgakgatsa	gargle (v)	gorrel
kekeletso	increment (n)	verhoging	-kgalala	extravagant (a)	buitensporig
-ke keng ya phengwa	inevitable (a)	onvermydelik	kgalala	extravagance (n)	buitensporigheid
-keketeha	giggle (v)	giggel	kgalalelo	glory (n)	glorie
keketso	addition (n)	toevoeging	kgalase	glass (n)	glas
keketso	increase (n)	verhoging	kgalase ya beine	wineglass (n)	wynkelkie
keko	treason (n)	verraad	kgalase ya fensetere	pane (n)	ruit
kelello	mind (n)	verstand	-kgale	stale (a)	oud
kelello	sense (n)	sin	kgalefo	anger (n)	kwaadheid
keletso	advice (n)	raad	kgalefo	rage (n)	woede
keletso	warning (n)	waarskuwing	-kgalema	admonish (v)	vermaan
kemariso ya maiketsetso	artificial insemination (n)	kunsmatige inseminasie	-kgalemela	scold (v)	uitskel
			-kgama	strangle (v)	verwurg
kemong ya dipalangwang	parking (n)	parkering	-kgama	throttle (v)	wurg
			kgamelo	bucket (n)	emmer
-kena	enter (v)	binnegaan	kgamelo	pail (n)	emmer
kenello	entry (n)	binnekoms	kganelo	restriction (n)	inperking
kento	vaccination (n)	inenting	-kgangwa ke metsi	drown (v)	verdrink
-kenya	involve (v)	betrek	-kganna	drive (v)	bestuur
-kenya	include (v)	insluit	kgano	disobedience (n)	ongehoorsaamheid
-kenya	enclose (v)	insluit	-kgantsha	illuminate (v)	verlig
-kenyang	inclusive (a)	inklusief	kganya	light (n)	lig
-kenya tsietsing	endanger (v)	in gevaar stel	-kganya	excel (v)	uitblink
kerabole	gravel (n)	gruis	-kganyang	excellent (a)	uitmuntend
keranatela	granadilla (n)	granadilla	kganya ya letsatsi	sunlight (n)	sonlig
kere	gear (n)	rat	kganyetso	opposition (n)	opposisie
kereibaya	wheelbarrow (n)	kruiwa	kgaolo	chapter (n)	hoofstuk
kereke	church (n)	kerk	-kgaotsa	cease (v)	ophou
kerese	candle (n)	kers	-kgaphatseha	overflow (v)	oorloop
Keresemese	Christmas (n)	Kersfees	kgarebe	girlfriend (n)	nooi
kerisi	grease (n)	ghries	kgaretene	curtain (n)	gordyn
kerosari	groceries (n)	kruideniersware	-kgasa	crawl (v)	kruip

Sesotho	English	Afrikaans	Sesotho	English	Afrikaans	K
kgatello	pressure (n)	druk	kgoholeho	erosion (n)	wegvreting	
kgatello	stress (n)	spanningsdruk	-kgokgotsa	detribalise (v)	ontstam	
kgatello ya madi	blood pressure (n)	bloeddruk	-kgola	pluck (v)	pluk	
-kgathala	tire (v)	moeg word	kgolabolokwe	beetle (n)	kewer	
-kgathalla	mind (v)	omgee	kgole	cord (n)	koord	
-kgathalla	care (v)	omgee	kgole	string (n)	tou	
-kgathatsa	hinder (v)	hinder	kgolofalo	limp (n)	mankheid	
-kgathatsa	trouble (v)	kwel	kgolofalo	paralysis (n)	verlamming	
-kgathatsa	bother (v)	lastig wees	-kgolohadi	huge (a)	reusagtig	
-kgathatsa	upset (v)	ontstel	-kgomaretsa	paste (v)	plak	
-kgathatsa	pester (v)	pla	-kgomaretsa	stick (v)	vasplak	
-kgathatsa	perturb (v)	verontrus	-kgomaretsa	mount (v)	vassit	
-kgathatseha	worry (v)	bekommer	kgomo	cow (n)	koei	
-kgathatseha	upset (a)	ontsteld	-kgona	able (a)	bekwaam	
-kgathatsehileng	restless (a)	rusteloos	-kgona	afford (v)	bekostig	
kgathatso	nuisance (n)	steurnis	-kgonang	efficient (a)	doeltreffend	
-kgathetseng	tired (a)	moeg	kgonyelo	cramp (n)	kramp	
-kgathetseng	weary (a)	vermoeid	kgonyelo ya mesifa	fits (n)	stuipe	
kgatiso	press (n)	pers	kgonyelo ya mesifa	spasm (n)	spasma	
kgatiso ya monwana	fingerprint (n)	vingerafdruk	-kgopa	trip (v)	struikel	
kgau	medal (n)	medalje	kgophole	rash (n)	veluitslag	
kgauta	gold (n)	goud	-kgopo	evil (a)	boos	
-kgefutsa	halt (v)	stop	-kgopo	aggressive (a)	aanvallend	
kgefutso	interval (n)	pouse	-kgopo	crooked (a)	krom	
-kgehlemanya	scrap (v)	skrap	kgopo	rib (n)	rib	
kgeleke	expert (n)	deskundige	kgopolo	thought (n)	gedagte	
-kgeleke	fluent (a)	vlot	kgopolo	idea (n)	idee	
-kgeloha	deviate (v)	afwyk	kgopolo	opinion (n)	mening	
-kgeloha	switch (v)	oorskakel	kgopotso	reminder (n)	herinnering	
-kgelohileng	stray (v)	afdwaal	kgoro	pass (n)	pas	
-kgelosa	avert (v)	keer	kgoro	exit (n)	uitgang	
-kgelosa	mislead (v)	mislei	kgosana	prince (n)	prins	
-kgelosa ka dikgoka	hijack (v)	skaak	kgosatsana	princess (n)	prinses	
-kgelosang	misleading (a)	misleidend	kgotetso	ignition (n)	ontsteking	
-kgema	gallop (v)	galop	-kgothaletsa	encourage (v)	aanmoedig	
-kgetha	choose (v)	kies	-kgothaletsa	urge (v)	aanspoor	
-kgetha	distinguish (v)	onderskei	-kgothalletsa	recommend (v)	aanbeveel	
-kgetha	elect (v)	verkies	kgothalletso	recommendation (n)	aanbeveling	
-kgetha	prefer (v)	verkies	-kgothatsa	comfort (v)	troos	
-kgetheha	snow (v)	sneeu	kgothatso	comfort (n)	troos	
-kgethetsweng	secluded (a)	afgesonderd	-kgothetseng	industrious (a)	vlytig	
kgetho	election (n)	verkiesing	kgotlakgolo	parliament (n)	parlement	
-kgetholla	discriminate (v)	diskrimineer	kgoto	rat (n)	rot	
kgethollo	discrimination (n)	diskriminasie	kgotso	peace (n)	vrede	
kgetla	shell (n)	skulp	kgotsofalo	satisfaction (n)	bevrediging	
-kgetshemela	stumble (v)	struikel	-kgotsofatsa	satisfy (v)	bevredig	
kgirimpana	hunchback (n)	boggelrug	kgudu	tortoise (n)	skilpad	
kgiro	appointment (n)	aanstelling	-kgumama	kneel (v)	kniel	
kgitla	midnight (n)	middernag	-kgutla	return (v)	terugkeer	
-kgobokanya	collect (v)	versamel	kgutlo	fullstop (n)	punt	
-kgobola	maul (v)	kneus	kgutlonne	rectangle (n)	reghoek	
-kgodisa	convince (v)	oortuig	-kgutlonne	square (a)	vierkantig	
-kgodisang	content (a)	tevrede	kgutlonnetsepa	square (n)	vierkant	
kgodiso	contentment (n)	tevredenheid	kgutlotharo	triangle (n)	driehoek	
kgofa	tick (n)	luis	kgutlwana	colon (n)	dubbelpunt	
kgofu	snail (n)	slak	kgutsana	orphan (n)	weeskind	
kgohelo	attraction (n)	aantrekking	-kgutshwane	brief (a)	beknop	
kgohlano	conflict (n)	konflik	-kgutshwane	short (a)	kort	
kgohlo	ravine (n)	kloof	-kgutsisa	soothe (v)	kalmeer	
kgoho	fowl (n)	hoender	-kgutsisa	silence (v)	stilmaak	

K

Sesotho	English	Afrikaans
-kgutsitse	calm (a)	kalm
kgutso	silence (n)	stilte
-kgutsufatsa	shorten (v)	verkort
kgwadiamaoma	pockmark (n)	pokmerk
kgwapo	frown (n)	frons
-kgwebela	export (v)	uitvoer
kgwebiso	import (v)	invoer
kgwebo	trade (n)	handel
kgwebo	commerce (n)	handel
-kgwebo	commercial (a)	kommersieel
kgwedi	month (n)	maand
kgwedi	moon (n)	maan
kgwele	line (n)	lyn
-kgwesa	wean (v)	speen
khabete	cupboard (n)	kas
khabetjhe	cabbage (n)	kool
khaete	kite (n)	vlieër
khaki	khaki (n)	kakie
-khansela	cancel (v)	kanselleer
kharavane	caravan (n)	karavaan
khataloko	catalogue (n)	katalogus
khateboto	cardboard (n)	karton
khefi	café (n)	kafee
khemera	camera (n)	kamera
kholetjhe	college (n)	kollege
kholifolawa	cauliflower (n)	blomkool
khomishenare wa boikano	commissioner of oaths (n)	kommissaris van ede
khomishene	commission (n)	kommissie
khompiuta	computer (n)	rekenaar
khosetjhumo	costume (n)	kostuum
khoukhou	cocoa (n)	kakao
khwaere	choir (n)	koor
kidibanyo	daze (n)	bedwelming
kitjhene	kitchen (n)	kombuis
-koba	bend (v)	buig
kobo	blanket (n)	kombers
kobo ya masiba	quilt (n)	verekombers
kodiamalla	lament (n)	weeklag
kodua	disaster (n)	ramp
koeetso	lullaby (n)	wiegelied
kofi	coffee (n)	koffie
-kokobetsa	appease (v)	bevredig
-kokobetsa	quell (v)	demp
-kokomoha	fizz (v)	bruis
-kokomoha	bulge (v)	uitbult
-kokota	knock (v)	klop
-kokotela	nail (v)	spyker
kokwana	bacteria (n)	bakterie
kokwana	germ (n)	kiem
kokwanyana	bug (n)	gogga
kokwanyana	insect (n)	insek
kolobe	pig (n)	vark
kolobe e tshehadi	sow (n)	sog
-kolobetsa	baptise (v)	doop
kolobetso	baptism (n)	doop
-kolobisa	moisten (v)	natmaak
koloi	motorcar (n)	motor
koloi	wagon (n)	wa
-koloka	queue (v)	toustaan

Sesotho	English	Afrikaans
-kolota	owe (v)	skuld
komello	drought (n)	droogte
komiki	cup (n)	koppie
komiti	committee (n)	komitee
komokomore	cucumber (n)	komkommer
kompase	compass (n)	kompas
kompone	compound (n)	kampong
kompose	compost (n)	kompos
konkereite	concrete (n)	beton
konofole	garlic (n)	knoffel
-konokono	eminent (a)	vooraanstaande
konopo	button (n)	knoop
konsarete	concert (n)	konsert
kontinente	continent (n)	vasteland
kontraka	contract (n)	kontrak
konyana	lamb (n)	lam
-kopa	beg (v)	bedel
-kopa	embrace (v)	omhels
-kopa	request (v)	versoek
-kopa mosebetsi	apply (v)	aansoek doen
kopano	meeting (n)	vergadering
kopano	union (n)	unie
kopano	assembly (n)	vergadering
kopano ya basebetsi	trade union (n)	vakbond
-kopanya	unite (v)	verenig
-kopanya	combine (v)	kombineer
-kopanya	mix (v)	meng
kopanyo	mixture (n)	mengsel
-kopa tshwarelo	apologise (v)	verskoning vra
kopi	copy (document) (n)	afskrif
kopo	embrace (n)	omhelsing
kopo	request (n)	versoek
koporasi	co-operation (n)	koöperasie
koporo	copper (n)	koper
kopo ya mosebeti	application (n)	aansoek
koranta	newspaper (n)	koerant
koriana	accordion (n)	trekklavier
koro	wheat (n)	koring
-koropa	scrub (v)	skrop
korosetina	concertina (n)	konsertina
korotla	grumble (v)	brom
-kota	peck (v)	pik
kotara	quarter (n)	kwart
-kotela	bar (v)	uitsluit
kotjelo	sip (n)	slukkie
kotlo	assault (n)	aanranding
kotlo	blow (n)	hou
kotlo	punishment (n)	straf
kotlo	penalty (n)	straf
kotola	bulb (n)	bol
-kotsama	land (v)	land
kotsi	danger (n)	gevaar
kotsi	peril (n)	gevaar
-kotsi	dangerous (a)	gevaarlik
kotsi	accident (n)	ongeluk
-kotula	harvest (v)	oes
-kotula	reap (v)	oes
kotulo	harvest (n)	oes
kou	bay (n)	baai
kou	harbour (n)	hawe

Sesotho	English	Afrikaans	Sesotho	English	Afrikaans	L
Kreste	Christ (n)	Christus	-laolla	unload (v)	aflaai	
kubu	hippopotamus (n)	seekoei	-lapa	starve (v)	honger ly	
-kudisa	sicken (v)	siek word	lapeng	home (n)	tuiste	
kuku	cake (n)	koek	-lapileng	hungry (a)	honger	
-kula	ill (a)	siek	-lata	fetch (v)	haal	
-kulang	sick (a)	siek	-latela	result (v)	volg	
kulo	bullet (n)	koeël	-latela	follow (v)	volg	
-kuma	gnaw (v)	knaag	-latelang	next (a)	volgende	
-kuma	grate (v)	rasper	latlametlu	toad (n)	brulpadda	
-kuma	crumble (v)	verkrummel	-latswa	taste (v)	proe	
-kurufella	screw (v)	skroef	le	and (conj)	en	
kutlwano	harmony (n)	harmonie	le	with (prep)	met	
kutlwelobohloko	sympathy (n)	simpatie	le-	also (adv)	ook	
-kutlwisiso	sane (a)	verstandig	Leaforikanere	Afrikaner (n)	Afrikaner	
kutu	block (n)	blok	leano	policy (n)	beleid	
kutu	stem (n)	stam	lebabo	frostbite (n)	vriesbrand	
kutu	stump (n)	stomp	lebadi	scar (n)	litteken	
kwaba	guava (n)	koejawel	lebaka	reason (n)	rede	
kwae	tobacco (n)	tabak	lebaka	bakery (n)	bakkery	
-kwahela	cover (v)	dek	lebaka	appointment (n)	afspraak	
-kwahela	conceal (v)	verberg	-lebala	forget (v)	vergeet	
kwakwa	battle-axe (n)	strydbyl	-leballa molato	credit (v)	krediteer	
-kwala	plug (v)	toestop	leballo	rafter (n)	dakbalk	
-kwala	shut (v)	toemaak	lebanta	belt (n)	gordel	
-kwekwetlang	indirect (a)	indirek	lebanta la setulo	seatbelt (n)	sitplekgordel	
kwena	crocodile (n)	krokodil	lebatowa	zone (n)	sone	
kweneho	revolt (n)	opstand	lebejana	cream (n)	room	
-kwenya	swallow (v)	sluk	lebekere	mug (n)	beker	
kwepere	quince (n)	kweper	-lebela	guard (v)	bewaak	
-kwetela	abduct (v)	ontvoer	-lebella	expect (v)	verwag	
-kwetlisa	coach (v)	afrig	lebelo	speed (n)	spoed	
-kwetsweng	shut (a)	toe	lebenkele	store (n)	winkel	
			lebenkele	shop (n)	winkel	
-labalabela	aspire (v)	streef	lebese	milk (n)	melk	
-labalabela	strive (v)	strewe	lebete	spleen (n)	milt	
-labalabela	yearn (v)	hunker	lebidi	wheel (n)	wiel	
Labobedi	Tuesday (n)	Dinsdag	-lebisa	aim (v)	mik	
Labohlano	Friday (n)	Vrydag	-lebisa	direct (v)	rig	
Labone	Thursday (n)	Donderdag	-lebisa	refer (v)	verwys	
Laboraro	Wednesday (n)	Woensdag	lebitla	grave (n)	graf	
laeborari	library (n)	biblioteek	lebitla	tomb (n)	graf	
-laela	delegate (v)	afvaardig	lebitso	noun (n)	selfstandige naamwoord	
-laela	direct (v)	beveel				
-laela	order (v)	beveel	lebitso	name (n)	naam	
laesense	licence (n)	lisensie	lebitso le leng	alias (n)	alias	
laetjha	load (v)	laai	-leboha	thank (v)	bedank	
-lahleha	lose (v)	verloor	-lebohang	grateful (a)	dankbaar	
-lahlehileng	lost (a)	verlore	-lebohela	congratulate (v)	gelukwens	
-lahlehileng	lost (a)	verdwaal	lebokose	box (n)	doos	
-laima	glow (v)	gloei	lebone	lamp (n)	lamp	
lakane	sheet (n)	laken	lebonyo	smile (n)	glimlag	
-lakatsa	desire (v)	begeer	lebopo	coast (n)	kus	
-lakatsa	envy (v)	beny	lebota	wall (n)	muur	
-lakatsa	wish (v)	wens	lebotho	army (n)	leër	
-lala ka mmele	ignore (v)	ignoreer	Leboya	north (n)	noorde	
lamunu	orange (n)	lemoen	-Leboya	north (a)	noord	
-lamunu	orange (a)	oranje	ledimo	cannibal (n)	mensvreter	
lanane la ditaba	agenda (n)	agenda	ledinyane	young (n)	kleintjie	
lantere	lantern (n)	lantern	ledinyane	cub (n)	welpie	
laola	manage (v)	bestuur	ledinyane la katse	kitten (n)	katjie	

293

L	Sesotho	English	Afrikaans	Sesotho	English	Afrikaans
	leeba	pigeon (n)	duif	lehlabaphio	informer (n)	verklikker
	leeme	prejudice (n)	vooroordeel	lehlabathe	sand (n)	sand
	leemedi	pronoun (n)	voornaamwoord	lehlabula	summer (n)	somer
	leeto	trip (n)	reis	lehlafi	screen (n)	skerm
	leeto	journey (n)	reis	lehlaka	reed (n)	riet
	leeto	tour (n)	rondreis	lehlaka	stalk (n)	stingel
	leetsi	verb (n)	werkwoord	lehlakore	side (n)	sy
	lefa	inheritance (n)	erfenis	lehlaku	leaf (n)	blaar
	lefa	heritage (n)	erfenis	lehlalosi	adverb (n)	bywoord
	lefafatsane	drizzle (v)	motreën	lehlanya	lunatic (n)	waansinnige
	lefapha	department (n)	departement	lehlasedi	ray (n)	straal
	-lefatla	bald (a)	bles	lehlasedi	sunbeam (n)	sonstraal
	lefatshe	earth (n)	aarde	lehlatsipa	casualty (n)	ongeval
	lefatshe	world (n)	wêreld	-lehloohonolo	lucky (a)	gelukkig
	lefeela	nonsense (n)	onsin	-lehloohonolo	fortunate (a)	gelukkig
	-lefeela	fake (a)	vals	lehloohonolo	luck (n)	geluk
	-lefeela	vain (a)	ydel	lehloyo	hatred (n)	haat
	lefeella	desert (n)	woestyn	lehlwa	snow (n)	sneeu
	lefi	leave (n)	verlof	lehlwele	lump (n)	klont
	lefielo	broom (n)	besem	lehlwele	clot (n)	klont
	lefifi	darkness (n)	donker	lehodimo	sky (n)	lug
	-lefifi	dark (a)	donker	lehodimo	heaven (n)	hemel
	lefika	rock (n)	rots	lehola	weed (n)	onkruid
	lefiritshwane	hyena (n)	hiëna	lehola la metsing	alga (n)	alg
	-lefisa	fine (v)	beboet	lehong	log (n)	blok
	lefite	lift (n)	hyser	lehong	wood (n)	hout
	lefito	knot (n)	knoop	lehongtshepe	ironwood (n)	ysterhout
	lefokisi	detective (n)	speurder	lehwatateng	wilderness (n)	wildernis
	lefokolodi	centipede (n)	honderdpoot	lehwelea	lisp (n)	gelispel
	lefokolodi	millipede (n)	duisendpoot	leifo	fireplace (n)	vuurherd
	lefu	disease (n)	siekte	leifo	hearth (n)	haard
	lefu	illness (n)	siekte	leihlo	eye (n)	oog
	lefu	death (n)	dood	leino	tooth (n)	tand
	lefuba	tuberculosis (n)	tuberkulose	leino la noha	fang (n)	slagtand
	lefuba	asthma (n)	asma	leino le opang	toothache (n)	tandpyn
	-lefufa	jealous (a)	jaloers	lejwe	stone (n)	klip
	lefufa	jealousy (n)	jaloesie	lejwe la sehopotso	tombstone (n)	grafsteen
	lefufuro	cartilage (n)	kraakbeen	-leka	lick (v)	lek
	lefu la letshollo	typhoid (n)	ingewandskoors	-leka	try (v)	probeer
	lefu la tswekere	diabetes (n)	suikersiekte	-leka	test (v)	toets
	le ha	though (conj)	hoewel	lekala	faculty (n)	fakulteit
	le ha	although (conj)	al	lekala	branch (n)	tak
	lehabea	hysterics (n)	histerie	lekala	twig (n)	takkie
	-lehae	civil (a)	burgerlik	lekala la noka	tributary (n)	takrivier
	-lehae	domestic (a)	huishoudelik	-lekana	equal (v)	gelyk wees aan
	lehafi	armpit (n)	armholte	-lekana	even (a)	gelykmatig
	lehaha	cave (n)	grot	-lekana	fit (v)	pas
	lehakwe	jewel (n)	juweel	-lekanang	equal (a)	gelyk
	lehalapa	palate (n)	verhemelte	-lekanang	level (a)	gelyk
	lehapu	melon (n)	meloen	-lekaneng	enough (a)	genoeg
	lehapu	watermelon (n)	waatlemoen	-lekaneng	adequate (a)	voldoende
	lehare	razor (n)	skeermes	-lekanya	measure (v)	meet
	lehare	blade (n)	blad	-lekanya	presume (v)	veronderstel
	lehata	skull (n)	skedel	-lekanya	suppose (v)	veronderstel
	lehe	egg (n)	eier	lekase	coffin (n)	doodskis
	lehehle	chatter (n)	gebabbel	lekere	liqueur (n)	likeur
	-lehehle	talkative (a)	spraaksaam	lekgala	aloe (n)	aalwyn
	lehetla	shoulder (n)	skouer	lekgala	crab (n)	krap
	lehlaahlela	handcuff (n)	boei	le kgale	never (adv)	nooit
	lehlaba	pain (n)	pyn	le kgale	ever (adv)	ooit

Sesotho	English	Afrikaans	Sesotho	English	Afrikaans	L
lekgansi	goose (n)	gans	lengolo	document (n)	dokument	
lekgapetla	bark (n)	bas	lengolo	certificate (n)	sertifikaat	
lekgapetla	peel (n)	skil	lengolo la bopaki	reference (n)	getuigskrif	
lekgethi	adjective (n)	byvoeglike naamwoord	lengope	ditch (n)	sloot	
lekgetho	tax (n)	belasting	lenong	vulture (n)	aasvoël	
lekgetlo	turn (n)	beurt	lenonyeletso	wrist (n)	pols	
lekgoba	slave (n)	slaaf	lenonyetso	joint (n)	gewrig	
lekgoba	addict (n)	verslaafde	lenqosa	ambassador (n)	ambassadeur	
lekgoba la dithethefatsi	drug addict (n)	dwelmslaaf	lense ya pono	contact lens (n)	kontaklens	
lekgolo	hundred (n)	honderd	lentswe	voice (n)	stem	
lekgonatha	miser (n)	vrek	lentswe	word (n)	woord	
lekgopho	eczema (n)	ekseem	lenwabo	chameleon (n)	verkleurmannetjie	
lekgotla	court (n)	hof	lenyalo	wedding (n)	bruilof	
lekgotla	council (n)	raad	lenyalo	marriage (n)	huwelik	
lekgotla la boipiletso	appeal court (n)	appélhof	lenyora	thirst (n)	dors	
lekgotla le phahameng	supreme court (n)	hooggeregshof	leoka	acacia (n)	akasia	
lekgulo	paddock (n)	veekampie	leoto	foot (n)	voet	
lekgwaba	crow (n)	kraai	-lepella	droop (v)	neerhang	
lekgwekgwe	scab (n)	rofie	lepera	leper (n)	melaatse	
lekuka	paunch (n)	boepmaag	lepetso	crack (n)	kraak	
lekumane	crumb (n)	krummel	lepetu	collar (n)	kraag	
lekunutu	secret (n)	geheim	lephele	cockroach (n)	kakkerlak	
-lekunutu	confidential (a)	vertroulik	lepheo	wing (n)	vlerk	
lekuru	knob (n)	knop	lepheo la tlhapi	fin (n)	vin	
lekwala	coward (n)	lafaard	lepolanka	plank (n)	plank	
lela	intestine (n)	derm	lepolesa	constable (n)	konstabel	
lelakabe	flame (n)	vlam	lepolesa	policeman (n)	polisieman	
lelapa	household (n)	huishouding	lepolesa	police (n)	polisie	
-lelefatsa	elongate (v)	verleng	leqaba	barbarian (n)	barbaar	
-lelefatsa	prolong (v)	verleng	leqala	bamboo (n)	bamboes	
leleire	nappy (n)	babadoek	leqala la ditlhapi	fishing rod (n)	visstok	
leleisele	rein (n)	leisel	leqaqailana	ankle (n)	enkel	
-leleka	exile (v)	verban	leqeba	injury (n)	besering	
-lelekisa	pursue (v)	najaag	leqeba	cut (n)	sny	
-lelele	long (a)	lang	leqeba	wound (n)	wond	
-lelele	tall (a)	lang	leqeba la mollo	burn (n)	brandplek	
leleme	tongue (n)	tong	leqele	left (n)	linkerkant	
lelengwana	uvula (n)	kleintongetjie	leqephe	page (n)	bladsy	
lelente	ribbon (n)	lint	leqheka	plan (n)	plan	
leloko	relation (n)	familielid	leqhubu	wave (n)	brander	
leloko	posterity (n)	nageslag	leqhubu	tide (n)	gety	
-lema	farm (v)	boer	leqhubu la maekoro	microwave (n)	mikrogolf	
-lema	cultivate (v)	bewerk	leqhwa	ice (n)	ys	
-lema	plough (v)	ploeg	leqhwele	shoelace (n)	skoenveter	
lemao la ho loha	knitting needle (n)	breinaald	lera	ligament (n)	ligament	
lemeno	fold (n)	vou	lerabele	rebel (n)	rebel	
lenaka	horn (n)	horing	leralla	hill (n)	heuwel	
lenaka la tlou	ivory (n)	ivoor	lerama	cheek (n)	wang	
lenala	fingernail (n)	vingernael	lerao	buttock (n)	boud	
lenala la monwana	toenail (n)	toonnael	lerapo	thong (n)	riem	
lenane	program (n)	program	lerata	noise (n)	geraas	
lenane la beine	winelist (n)	wynkaart	lerata	uproar (n)	lawaai	
lenane la dijo	menu (n)	spyskaart	-lerata	noisy (a)	raserig	
lenaneo	programme (n)	program	lerato	love (n)	liefde	
lenanethuto	syllabus (n)	leerplan	lerato	charity (n)	liefdadigheid	
lengau	cheetah (n)	jagluiperd	lerato	affection (n)	toegeneentheid	
lengau	leopard (n)	luiperd	lere	ladder (n)	leer	
lengeloi	angel (n)	engel	lere	stepladder (n)	trapleer	
lengole	knee (n)	knie	lerenene	gum (n)	tandvleis	
lengolo	letter (n)	brief	lerete	testicle (n)	teelbal	

	Sesotho	English	Afrikaans	Sesotho	English	Afrikaans
L	lero	nectar (n)	nektar	lesoha	bachelor (n)	jongkêrel
	lero	juice (n)	sap	lesokolla	heartburn (n)	sooibrand
	lero la lamunu	orange juice (n)	lemoensap	lesokwana	oar (n)	roeispaan
	lerole	dust (n)	stof	lesole	soldier (n)	soldaat
	-lerotho	dim (a)	dof	-leswe	humid (a)	klam
	lerothodi	drip (n)	drup	-leta	wait (v)	wag
	lerothodi la pula	raindrop (n)	reëndruppel	letahwa	alcoholic (n)	alkoholis
	leru	cloud (n)	wolk	letahwa	drunkard (n)	dronklap
	leruarua	whale (n)	walvis	letamo	dam (n)	dam
	lerumo	assegai (n)	assegaai	letamo	pool (n)	poel
	lerumo	spear (n)	spies	letata	duck (n)	eend
	leruo	property (n)	eiendom	leteroko	truck (n)	trok
	leruo	wealth (n)	rykdom	letetetso	bruise (n)	kneusplek
	lerutle	locust (n)	sprinkaan	letheba	blot (n)	klad
	lesaka	stable (n)	stal	letheba	spot (n)	kol
	lesale	earring (n)	oorring	letheba	speck (n)	stippel
	lesapo	bone (n)	been	letheba	stain (n)	vlek
	lesapo la lehetla	shoulderblade (n)	skouerblad	letheka	waist (n)	middel
	lesapo la lepetu	collarbone (n)	sleutelbeen	letho	nothing (n)	niks
	lesapo la lerama	cheekbone (n)	wangbeen	lethopa	boil (n)	bloedvint
	lesapo la mokokotlo	vertebra (n)	werwel	letla-le-pepilwe	illegitimate (a)	buite-egtelik
	lesapo la sefuba	breastbone (n)	borsbeen	letlalo	leather (n)	leer
	lesea	baby (n)	baba	letlalo	skin (n)	vel
	lesea	infant (n)	suigeling	letlalo la hlooho	scalp (n)	kopvel
	lesela	cloth (n)	doek	letlamorwana	lad (n)	knaap
	lesela	material (n)	lap	letlao	clasp (n)	klem
	lesela	fabric (n)	tekstielstof	letlao	pliers (n)	knyptang
	lesela la ho hlakola lerole	duster (n)	stoflap	letlopo	gill (n)	kieu
				letlotlo	treasure (n)	skat
	lesela la tafole	tablecloth (n)	tafeldoek	letlotlo	fortune (n)	fortuin
	leshala	coal (n)	steenkool	letlotlo la mantswe	vocabulary (n)	woordeskat
	leshano	falsehood (n)	onwaarheid	letokomane	peanut (n)	grondboontjie
	leshano	lie (n)	leuen	letolo	lightning (n)	weerlig
	-leshano	false (a)	vals	letona	councillor (n)	raadslid
	leshodu	thief (n)	dief	letona	minister (n)	minister
	leshome	ten (n)	tien	-letsa	ring (v)	lui
	leshome le borobedi	eighteen (n)	agtien	-letsa molodi	hiss (v)	sis
	leshome le metso e mehlano	fifteen (n)	vyftien	-letsa molodi	whistle (v)	fluit
	leshome le metso e mene	fourteen (n)	veertien	-letsa phala	hoot (v)	toet
				letsatsi	day (n)	dag
	leshome le metso e mmedi	twelve (n)	twaalf	letsatsi	sun (n)	son
				letsatsi la tswalo	birthday (n)	verjaarsdag
	leshome le metso e robo	nineteen (n)	neëntien	letsetse	flea (n)	vlooi
	leshome le metso e supileng	seventeen (n)	sewentien	letsha	lake (n)	meer
				letsha la ho sesa	swimming pool (n)	swembad
	leshome le metso e tsheletseng	sixteen (n)	sestien	letsha la lewatle	lagoon (n)	strandmeer
				-letshehadi	left (a)	links
	leshome le motso	eleven (n)	elf	letshoho	panic (n)	paniek
	lesiba	feather (n)	veer	letshollo	diarrhoea (n)	diarree
	lesihla	bunch (n)	tros	-letshollo	gastric (a)	maag-
	lesika	family (n)	familie	letshollo le lefubedu	dysentery (n)	disenterie
	lesika	sinew (n)	sening	letshwafo	lung (n)	long
	lesira	veil (n)	sluier	letshwao	label (n)	etiket
	lesoba	leak (n)	lek	letshwao	mark (n)	merk
	lesoba la konopo	buttonhole (n)	knoopsgat	letshwao	symptom (n)	simptoom
	lesoba la nko	nostril (n)	neusgat	letshwao	sign (n)	teken
	lesobana la senotlolo	keyhole (n)	sleutelgat	letshwao la kgwebo	brand (n)	handelsmerk
	lesofe	albino (n)	albino	letshwao la tswalo	birthmark (n)	moedervlek
				letsibolo	firstborn (n)	eersgeborene
				letsoho	arm (n)	arm

Sesotho	English	Afrikaans	Sesotho	English	Afrikaans	M
letsoho	hand (n)	hand	-loya	bewitch (v)	toor	
letsoho	forearm (n)	voorarm	-lwana	battle (v)	veg	
letsoho	sleeve (n)	mou	-lwana	fight (v)	veg	
letsohong le letona	right (n)	regterkant				
letsoku	ochre (n)	oker	mabele	sorghum (n)	sorghum	
letsopa	clay (n)	klei	mabitleng	cemetery (n)	begraafplaas	
letswabadi	blister (n)	blaar	madi	blood (n)	bloed	
letswai	salt (n)	sout	madikelo	sundown (n)	sononder	
letswalo	diaphragm (n)	diafragma	madikelo	sunset (n)	sononder	
letswalo	conscience (n)	gewete	-madimabe	unsuccessful (a)	onvoorspoedig	
letswalo	mushroom (n)	sampioen	-madimabe	unfortunately (adv)	ongelukkig	
-letswalo	nervous (a)	senuweeagtig	-madimabe	unlucky (a)	ongelukkig	
letswalo	nervousness (n)	senuweeagtigheid	maekorosekoupo	microscope (n)	mikroskoop	
letswele	udder (n)	uier	maelana	idiom (n)	idioom	
lewana	coin (n)	muntstuk	maele	mile (n)	myl	
lewatle	sea (n)	see	maele	proverb (n)	spreekwoord	
lewatle	ocean (n)	oseaan	mafahla	twin (n)	tweeling	
lewatleng	beach (n)	strand	-mafolofolo	active (a)	aktief	
-lla	cry (v)	huil	mafolofolo	diligence (n)	fluksheid	
-lla	weep (v)	huil	-mafolofolo	diligent (a)	fluks	
-lla	whimper (v)	sanik	-mafolofolo	eager (a)	gretig	
-lla	mourn (v)	rou	mafome	rust (n)	roes	
Loetse	September (n)	September	mafube	daybreak (n)	dagbreek	
-loha	weave (v)	weef	mafube	dawn (n)	dagbreek	
-loha	knit (v)	brei	mafura	fat (n)	vet	
-lohotha	ponder (v)	bepeins	-mafura	fat (a)	vet	
lojiki	logic (n)	logika	mafura a kolobe	lard (n)	varkvet	
-lokelang	eligible (a)	geskik	mafutsana	poor (n)	armes	
-lokelang	appropriate (a)	geskik	-mahae	rural (a)	plattelands	
-lokelwang ho roriswa	praiseworthy (a)	lofwaardig	-maharaswa	tattered (a)	toiingrig	
-lokile	good (a)	goed	-mahareng	average (a)	gemiddeld	
-lokileng	ready (a)	gereed	mahe a dinotshi	honey (n)	heuning	
-lokis(ets)a	prepare (v)	voorberei	mahlale	science (n)	wetenskap	
-lokisa	mend (v)	heelmaak	mahlatsa	vomit (n)	vomeersel	
-lokisa	fix (v)	regmaak	mahlohonolo	blessing (n)	seëning	
-lokisa	improve (v)	verbeter	mahlomola	grief (n)	leed	
-lokolla	release (v)	loslaat	maikemisetso	ambition (n)	ambisie	
-lokolla	undo (v)	losmaak	-maiketsetso	artificial (a)	kunsmatig	
-lokolla	free (v)	bevry	maitatolo	alibi (n)	alibi	
-lokolla	acquit (v)	vryspreek	majabajaba	luxury (n)	luukse	
-lokolla bokgobeng	emancipate (v)	vrymaak	-makalla	marvel (v)	wonder	
-lokolohileng	loose (a)	los	-makatsa	surprise (v)	verras	
-lokolohileng	independent (a)	onafhanklik	-makatsa	stun (v)	verstom	
-lokolohileng	free (a)	vry	-makatsa	amaze (v)	verbaas	
-lokolohileng	liberal (a)	liberaal	-makatsang	queer (a)	snaaks	
-loma	bite (v)	byt	-makatsang	funny (a)	snaaks	
-lomosa	ferment (v)	gis	-makatsang	amazing (a)	verbasend	
-lona	your (pron)	julle	-makatsang	marvellous (a)	wonderbaarlik	
-lona	yours (pron)	julle s'n	-makatsang	wonderful (a)	wonderlik	
lona	you (pron)	julle	makatso	irony (n)	ironie	
lontjhe	lounge (n)	sitkamer	makatso	amazement (n)	verbasing	
lonya	malice (n)	boosaardigheid	makatso	surprise (n)	verrassing	
-lonya	sullen (a)	nors	makenete	magnet (n)	magneet	
lonya	scowl (n)	suur gesig	-makgerehlwa	hoarse (a)	hees	
-lonya	unkind (a)	onvriendelik	makgethe	neat (a)	netjies	
-lopolla	redeem (v)	goedmaak	-makgethe	tidy (a)	netjies	
-lora	dream (v)	droom	makgulo	pasture (n)	weiveld	
lori	lorry (n)	vragmotor	mala	entrails (n)	ingewande	
-lotha	puzzle (v)	verwar	malaria	malaria (n)	malaria	
loto	lead (n)	lood	malepa	puzzle (n)	legkaart	

M	Sesotho	English	Afrikaans	Sesotho	English	Afrikaans
	maleshwane	ladybird (n)	lieweheersbesie	-matjhaba	international (a)	internasionaal
	malome	uncle (n)	oom	-matjhaba	multiracial (a)	veelrassig
	mamale	mammal (n)	soogdier	-matla	energetic (a)	energiek
	-mamarela	cling (v)	klou	matla	authority (n)	gesag
	-mamarela	adhere (v)	kleef	matla	power (n)	mag
	-mamarelang	adhesive (a)	klewerig	matla	strength (n)	sterkte
	-mamela	listen (v)	luister	matla	force (n)	krag
	-mamella	bear (v)	duld	matla	influence (n)	invloed
	-mamellang	patient (a)	geduldig	-matla	powerful (a)	magtig
	mamello	patience (n)	geduld	matla	energy (n)	energie
	mamina	mucus (n)	slym	-matla	vigorous (a)	kragtig
	mang	who (pron)	wie	-matla	strong (a)	sterk
	-mang	whose (pron)	wie se	matla	resistance (n)	weerstand
	manganga	insolence (n)	parmantigheid	matsale	mother-in-law (n)	skoonmoeder
	-manganga	stubborn (a)	koppig	matsapa	trouble (n)	moeite
	-manganga	obstinate (a)	hardkoppig	matsetlela	curl (n)	krul
	-manganga	adamant (a)	onwrikbaar	matshwele	multitude (n)	menigte
	mang le mang	anybody (pron)	elkeen	matshwele	crowd (n)	skare
	mankatapa	coccyx (n)	stuitjiebeen	-matsoho	industrial (a)	industrieel
	mano	trick (n)	skelmstreek	matswedintsweke	zigzag (n)	sigsag
	-mano	cunning (a)	slu	-meharo	greedy (a)	gulsig
	Mantaha	Monday (n)	Maandag	meharo	lust (n)	wellus
	mantle	excreta (n)	uitwerpsel	-mekgwa e mebe	ill-mannered (a)	onmanierlik
	mantle	faeces (n)	uitwerpsel	mekhukhu	slum (n)	krotbuurt
	mantsiboya	evening (n)	aand	-mela	grow (v)	groei
	manyala	obscenity (n)	onbetaamlikheid	-mema	invite (v)	uitnooi
	manyeme	pancreas (n)	pankreas	memo	invitation (n)	uitnodiging
	-Manyesemane	British (a)	Brits	-mena	fold (v)	vou
	manyolo	manure (n)	mis	mengo	mango (n)	mango
	manyowa	tapeworm (n)	lintwurm	meno	teeth (n)	tande
	maobane	yesterday (n)	gister	meno a maiketsetso	dentures (n)	vals tande
	maqhububoelamorao	backwash (n)	terugspoeling	meriana	medicine (n)	medisyne
	marete	genitals (n)	geslagsorgane	-meriana	medical (a)	medies
	mariha	winter (n)	winter	meroho	vegetable (n)	groente
	maro	paw (n)	poot	merung	bushveld (n)	bosveld
	-maru a thibile	overcast (a)	bewolk	metara	gauge (n)	meter
	marulelo	roof (n)	dak	metara	metre (n)	meter
	marulelo a jwang	thatch (n)	dekgras	methatswana	capillary (n)	haarvat
	masakana	brackets (n)	hakies	methokgo	herbs (n)	kruie
	masela	linen (n)	linne	metjhuri	mercury (n)	kwik
	-masene	astute (a)	slim	metse	mathematics (n)	wiskunde
	masetlapelo	tragedy (n)	tragedie	-metseng e meholo	urban (a)	stedelik
	mashome a mabedi	twenty (n)	twintig	-metsi	wet (a)	nat
	mashome a mahlano	fifty (n)	vyftig	metsi	water (n)	water
	mashome a mane	forty (n)	veertig	metsi a ferellang	whirlpool (n)	maalstroom
	mashome a robedi	eighty (n)	tagtig	milijone	million (n)	miljoen
	mashome a robong	ninety (n)	neëntig	mimosa	mimosa (n)	mimosa
	mashome a supileng	seventy (n)	sewentig	minerale	mineral (n)	mineraal
	mashome a tsheletseng	sixty (n)	sestig	mmadibolwana	abacus (n)	telraam
	masisapelo	horror (n)	aïsku	-mmala	coloured (a)	gekleur
	maswabi	sadness (n)	droefheid	mmala	colour (n)	kleur
	maswabi	scandal (n)	skandaal	mmala o mofubedu	scarlet (n)	helderrooi
	maswabi	sorrow (n)	smart	-mmalwa	few (a)	min
	maswebe	wrinkle (n)	plooi	mmamolangwane	secretary bird (n)	sekretarisvoël
	matekwane	cannabis (n)	dagga	mmampodi	champion (n)	kampioen
	materase	mattress (n)	matras	mmane	flash (n)	flits
	-matha	run (v)	hardloop	mmangwane	aunt (n)	tante
	mathe	saliva (n)	speeksel	mmankgane	bat (n)	vlermuis
	-matjato	agile (a)	rats	mmanki	basket (n)	mandjie
	matjekelane	nightwatchman (n)	nagwag	mmapa	map (n)	landkaart

Sesotho	English	Afrikaans	Sesotho	English	Afrikaans	**M**
mmapalafoleite	flautist (n)	fluitspeler	mobu	soil (n)	grond	
mmapalaviolene	violinist (n)	vioolspeler	modemone	demon (n)	bose gees	
mmaraka	market (n)	mark	modikwadikwane	dizziness (n)	duiseligheid	
-mmasepala	municipal (a)	munisipaal	Modimo	God (n)	God	
mmasepala	municipality (n)	munisipaliteit	modimo	god (n)	god	
mmaseterata	magistrate (n)	landdros	modimo	ancestor (n)	voorouer	
mme	mother (n)	moeder	modingwana	idol (n)	afgod	
mmela	malt (n)	mout	modisa	shepherd (n)	skaapwagter	
mmelaelwa	suspect (n)	verdagte	moditjhaba	stranger (n)	vreemdeling	
mmele	body (n)	liggaam	modula	pollen (n)	stuifmeel	
mmeri	mare (n)	merrie	modulasetulo	chairman (n)	voorsitter	
Mmesa	April (n)	April	modumedi	believer (n)	gelowige	
mmetladitshwantsho	sculptor (n)	beeldhouer	modumela	echo (n)	weerklank	
mmetli	carpenter (n)	timmerman	modumo	sound (n)	klank	
mmetso	throat (n)	keel	modumo	tune (n)	wysie	
mmetso	gullet (n)	slukderm	moduwane	willow (n)	wilgerboom	
mmetso	oesophagus (n)	slukderm	moedi	border (n)	grens	
mmetso o mosweu	diphtheria (n)	witseerkeel	moedi	boundary (n)	grenslyn	
-mmino	musical (a)	musikaal	moedi	margin (n)	kantlyn	
mmino	music (n)	musiek	Moefangedi	evangelist (n)	evangelis	
mmitsi	caller (n)	roeper	moeki	traitor (n)	verraaier	
mmohi	spectator (n)	toeskouer	moelelo	meaning (n)	betekenis	
mmoko	measles (n)	masels	moeletsi	adviser (n)	raadgewer	
mmoko	straw (n)	strooi	moemedi	agent (n)	agent	
mmolai	murderer (n)	moordenaar	moemedi	mediator (n)	bemiddelaar	
mmomori	plot (n)	komplot	moemedi	representative (n)	verteenwoordiger	
mmomori	conspiracy (n)	sameswering	moento	inoculation (n)	inenting	
mmoto	moth (n)	mot	moepa	steep (a)	steil	
mmotokara	car (n)	motor	moetapele	leader (n)	leier	
mmoulo	mule (n)	muil	moethimolo	sneeze (n)	nies	
mmuelli	advocate (n)	advokaat	moeti	caller (n)	besoeker	
mmuelli	attorney (n)	prokureur	moeti	visitor (n)	besoeker	
mmuelli	solicitor (n)	prokureur	moeti	guest (n)	gas	
mmuo	dialect (n)	dialek	moeti	traveller (n)	reisiger	
mmusi	ruler (n)	regeerder	moeti	tourist (n)	toeris	
-mmuso	official (a)	amptelik	moetlo	tradition (n)	tradisie	
mmuso	reign (n)	bewind	-moetlo	traditional (a)	tradisioneel	
mmuso	kingdom (n)	koninkryk	moetsana	bridesmaid (n)	strooimeisie	
mmuso	government (n)	regering	moetse	mane (n)	maanhare	
mmutlanyana	rabbit (n)	konyn	moetsi	performer (n)	uitvoerder	
Moaforika	African (n)	Afrikaan	mofantisi	auctioneer (n)	afslaer	
moahi	citizen (n)	burger	mofapahloho	crown (n)	kroon	
moahisane	neighbour (n)	buurman	mofehlo	buttermilk (n)	karringmelk	
moahlodi	arbiter (n)	arbiter	mofelehetsi	escort (n)	metgesel	
moahlodi	adjudicator (n)	beoordelaar	mofeng	broomstick (n)	besemstok	
moahlodi	judge (n)	regter	mofeng	shaft (n)	steel	
moaho	building (n)	gebou	mofepi	waiter (n)	kelner	
moakanyi	assessor (n)	skatter	mofetoledi	translator (n)	vertaler	
moakhiteke	architect (n)	argitek	mofidibithi	jungle (n)	oerwoud	
moamohedi	receptionist (n)	ontvangsklerk	mofihli	newcomer (n)	nuweling	
moamohelabaeti	host (n)	gasheer	mofokodi	invalid (n)	invalide	
moapehi	cook (n)	kok	mofufutso	perspiration (n)	perspirasie	
moapostola	apostle (n)	apostel	mofufutso	sweat (n)	sweet	
moatjhebishopo	archbishop (n)	aartsbiskop	mofumahadi	lady (n)	dame	
mobaki	baker (n)	bakker	mofumahadi	queen (n)	koningin	
mobelehisi	midwife (n)	vroedvrou	mofuta	make (n)	soort	
mobetjho	bet (n)	weddenskap	mofuta	kind (n)	soort	
mobishopo	bishop (n)	biskop	mofuta	type (n)	tipe	
mobohi	bystander (n)	omstander	mofuthu	charm (n)	sjarme	
mobu	ground (n)	grond	mofutsana	pauper (n)	behoeftige	

M	Sesotho	English	Afrikaans	Sesotho	English	Afrikaans
	mohaho	construction (n)	konstruksie	mohlwekisa ntle ho metsi	drycleaner (n)	droogskoonmakery
	mohala	cable (n)	kabel	mohodi	mist (n)	mis
	mohala	telegram (n)	telegram	mohodi	fog (n)	mis
	mohala	rope (n)	tou	mohodi	haze (n)	waas
	mohalaledi	saint (n)	heilige	mohodu	stomach (n)	maag
	mohale	hero (n)	held	-mohohoma	hollow (a)	hol
	mohanyetsi	rival (n)	mededinger	mohohoma	tunnel (n)	tonnel
	mohatla	tail (n)	stert	moholo	adult (n)	volwassene
	mohato	step (n)	tree	mohoma	plough (n)	ploeg
	mohatsa	husband (n)	man	-mohono	envious (a)	jaloers
	-mohau	merciful (a)	genadig	mohono	envy (n)	naywer
	mohau	mercy (n)	genade	mohono	snore (n)	snork
	mohau	pity (n)	jammerte	mohoo	scream (n)	gil
	-mohau	sympathetic (a)	simpatiek	mohope	calabash (n)	kalbas
	mohedene	pagan (n)	heiden	mohwe	father-in-law (n)	skoonvader
	mohetene	heathen (n)	heiden	mohwebisani	partner (n)	vennoot
	mohetene	unbeliever (n)	ongelowige	mohwele	handle (n)	handvatsel
	mohiri	tenant (n)	bewoner	moikaketsi	hypocrite (n)	skynheilige
	mohiri	lodger (n)	loseerder	moithuti	student (n)	student
	mohiri	employer (n)	werkgewer	moithutwana	amateur (n)	amateur
	mohirisi	landlord (n)	verhuurder	moitlami	nun (n)	non
	mohiruwa	employee (n)	werknemer	mojaho	haste (n)	haas
	mohla	date (n)	datum	mojalefa	heir (n)	erfgenaam
	mohlahare	molar (n)	kiestand	mokakallane	influenza (n)	griep
	mohlahare	jaw (n)	kaak	mokaola	syphilis (n)	sifilis
	mohlahlobaditjhelete	auditor (n)	ouditeur	mokato	filling (n)	stopsel
	mohlahlobi	inspector (n)	inspekteur	mokato	level (n)	vlak
	mohlaka	swamp (n)	moeras	mokato	floor (n)	verdieping
	mohlala	track (n)	spoor	mokedikedi	liquid (n)	vloeistof
	mohlala	footstep (n)	voetstap	-mokedikedi	liquid (a)	vloeibaar
	mohlala	example (n)	voorbeeld	mokenaboholo	adolescent (n)	jeugdige
	mohlamu	rectum (n)	rektum	mokerikete	cricketer (n)	krieketspeler
	mohlana	afterbirth (n)	nageboorte	mokete	feast (n)	fees
	mohlanka	servant (n)	bediende	mokete	festival (n)	fees
	mohlankana	boyfriend (n)	kêrel	mokete	ceremony (n)	seremonie
	mohlanka wa mmuso	official (n)	amptenaar	mokete	celebration (n)	viering
	mohlape	herd (n)	kudde	mokete wa dilemokgolo	centenary (n)	eeufees
	mohlape	swarm (n)	swerm	mokga	faction (n)	faksie
	mohlape	flock (n)	trop	mokga	party (n)	party
	mohlape	stud (n)	stoetery	mokgabiso	ornament (n)	ornament
	Mohlodi	Creator (n)	Skepper	mokgabiso	gadget (n)	toestelletjie
	mohlodi	source (n)	bron	mokgabiso	decoration (n)	versiering
	mohlohli	agitator (n)	opstoker	mokgabo	art (n)	kuns
	mohloki	dependant (n)	afhanklike	mokganni	driver (n)	bestuurder
	mohlokomedi	caretaker (n)	opsigter	mokgasi	toddler (n)	peuter
	mohlokomedi	guardian (n)	voog	mokgathala	weariness (n)	moegheid
	-mohlolo	mysterious (a)	geheimsinnig	mokgathala	fatigue (n)	vermoeienis
	mohlolo	mystery (n)	misterie	mokgatlo	club (n)	klub
	mohlolo	wonder (n)	wonder	mokgatlo	organisation (n)	organisasie
	mohlolo	miracle (n)	wonderwerk	mokgatlo	society (n)	vereniging
	mohlolohadi	widow (n)	weduwee	mokgodutswane	lizard (n)	akkedis
	mohlolohadi wa monna	widower (n)	wewenaar	mokgohlane	cough (n)	hoes
	mohlolohlolo	skeleton (n)	geraamte	mokgokgothwane	whooping cough (n)	kinkhoes
	mohlomong	maybe (adv)	miskien	mokgoro	hut (n)	hut
	mohlomong	perhaps (adv)	miskien	mokgoro	hovel (n)	pondok
	mohlophisi	editor (n)	redakteur	mokguba	navel (n)	naeltjie
	mohlophollo	analysis (n)	ontleding	mokgwa	manner (n)	manier
	-mohloyamerabe	racist (a)	rassisties	mokgwa	method (n)	metode
	mohlwa	lawn (n)	grasperk			

Sesotho	English	Afrikaans	Sesotho	English	Afrikaans	M
mokgwa	fashion (n)	mode	molefi	payer (n)	betaler	
mokgwabo	fungus (n)	swam	molekane	equal (n)	gelyke	
mokgwenyana	son-in-law (n)	skoonseun	molekane	companion (n)	metgesel	
mokhemise	chemist (n)	apteker	moleko	temptation (n)	verleiding	
mokhemise	pharmacist (n)	apteker	-molemo	best (a)	beste	
moko	marrow (n)	murg	molemo	favour (n)	guns	
mokoko	cock (n)	haan	-molemo	wholesome (a)	heilsaam	
mokoko	rooster (n)	hoenderhaan	-molemo	beneficial (a)	voordelig	
mokokotlo	back (n)	rug	molemohi	observer (n)	waarnemer	
mokokotlo	ridge (n)	rug	moletsamoropa	drummer (n)	tromspeler	
mokokotlo	reef (n)	rif	moletsaphala	referee (n)	skeidsregter	
mokokotlo	spine (n)	ruggraat	moletsaterompeta	trumpeter (n)	trompetblaser	
mokokotlo wa leoto	instep (n)	boog	moletsathomo	pianist (n)	klavierspeler	
mokolla	spinal cord (n)	rugmurg	mollo	fire (n)	vuur	
mokolokotwane	beacon (n)	baken	moloho	knitting (n)	breiwerk	
mokone	cocoon (n)	kokon	moloho	weaving (n)	wewery	
mokopamosebetsi	applicant (n)	aansoeker	molollope wa mollo	lighthouse (n)	vuurtoring	
mokopi	beggar (n)	bedelaar	-molomo	verbal (a)	mondeling	
mokopu	pumpkin (n)	pampoen	molomo	mouth (n)	mond	
mokotaba	theme (n)	tema	molomo	beak (n)	snawel	
mokotatsie	stork (n)	ooievaar	molomo o motsu	muzzle (n)	snoet	
mokoti	hole (n)	gat	molora	ash (n)	as	
mokotla	bag (n)	sak	molora	cinder (n)	sintel	
mokotla	sack (n)	sak	molotsana	scoundrel (n)	skobbejak	
mokotlana wa nyooko	gallbladder (n)	galblaas	momahano	attachment (n)	gehegtheid	
Mokreste	Christian (n)	Christen	-momahanya	attach (v)	aanheg	
mokudi	patient (n)	pasiënt	-momahatsa	join (v)	las	
mokunyane	mole (n)	mol	momahatso	join (n)	lasplek	
mokuti	hairdresser (n)	haarkapper	momeno	hem (n)	soom	
mokuti	barber (n)	haarsnyer	mona	here (adv)	hier	
mokutsuberi	gooseberry (n)	appelliefie	-monate	savoury (a)	smaaklik	
mokwetlise	coach (n)	afrigter	-monate	sweet (a)	soet	
mola	row (n)	ry	monawa	pod (n)	peul	
mola	queue (n)	tou	-mong	alone (a)	alleen	
molaeborari	librarian (n)	bibliotekaris	mong	individual (n)	individu	
molaetsa	message (n)	boodskap	monga	owner (n)	eienaar	
molakolako	vagrant (n)	rondloper	mongadi	deserter (n)	droster	
-molakolako	migrant (a)	swerwend	-mongobo	damp (a)	vogtig	
molala	neck (n)	nek	mongobo	damp (n)	vogtigheid	
molamu	stick (n)	stok	mongobo	moisture (n)	vog	
-molamunu	citrus (a)	sitrus	-mongobo	moist (a)	vogtig	
molao	commandment (n)	gebod	mongodi	secretary (n)	sekretaris	
molao	rule (n)	reël	mongodi	author (n)	skrywer	
molao	regulation (n)	regulasie	mongolo	handwriting (n)	handskrif	
-molao	judicial (a)	regterlik	mongolo	writing (n)	skrif	
-molao	legal (a)	wetlik	mongwapo	scratch (n)	krap	
-molao	lawful (a)	wettig	monko	smell (n)	reuk	
molao	law (n)	wet	monko o mobe	stink (n)	stank	
-molao	legitimate (a)	wettige	monko o monate	fragrance (n)	geur	
molaodi	manager (n)	bestuurder	-monna	male (a)	manlik	
molaodi lebenkeleng	shop steward (n)	segsman	monna	man (n)	man	
molao wa motheo	constitution (n)	grondwet	monna	male (n)	man	
molatedi	follower (n)	volgeling	monokotshwai	strawberry (n)	aarbei	
molato	credit (n)	krediet	monontsha	fertiliser (n)	kunsmis	
molato	crime (n)	misdaad	monwana	finger (n)	vinger	
molato	case (n)	saak	monwana o motona	thumb (n)	duim	
molato	guilt (n)	skuld	monwana wa leoto	toe (n)	toon	
molato	debt (n)	skuld	monwang	mosquito (n)	muskiet	
-molato	guilty (a)	skuldig	-monya	absorb (v)	absorbeer	
molebedi	guard (n)	wag	-monya	suck (v)	suig	

M

Sesotho	English	Afrikaans	Sesotho	English	Afrikaans
monyadi	bridegroom (n)	bruidegom	moreso	brother (n)	broer
monyaduwa	bride (n)	bruid	morethetho	beat (n)	ritme
monyaka	fun (n)	pret	morethetho	rhythm (n)	ritme
monyako	door (n)	deur	moreto	stripe (n)	streep
-monyebe	clumsy (a)	lomp	morifi	bowl (n)	bak
-monyebe	reluctant (a)	teensinnig	moritelo	brew (n)	brousel
-monyela	percolate (v)	perkoleer	moriti	shadow (n)	skaduwee
monyetla	opportunity (n)	geleentheid	moriti	shade (n)	skadu
monyetla	advantage (n)	voordeel	moro	gravy (n)	sous
monyollo	glutton (n)	vraat	moroko	seam (n)	naat
monyollo	wart (n)	vrat	moroko	sewing (n)	naaldwerk
moo	there (adv)	daar	moromuwa	messenger (n)	bode
mookodi	rainbow (n)	reënboog	moromuwa	missionary (n)	sendeling
moomo	leg (n)	been	moropa	drum (n)	trom
moomo	shin (n)	skeen	moropana	tambourine (n)	tamboeryn
mopalami	passenger (n)	passasier	mororo	roar (n)	brul
mopapa	pope (n)	pous	moroto	urine (n)	urine
mopheme	jackal (n)	jakkals	moru	bush (n)	bos
moporesidente	president (n)	president	moru	forest (n)	bos
moporofesa	professor (n)	professor	morumo	rhyme (n)	rym
moporofeta	prophet (n)	profeet	morupedi	lecturer (n)	dosent
moprista	priest (n)	priester	morupedi	instructor (n)	instrukteur
moputso	pay (n)	betaling	morusu	riot (n)	onlus
moputso	reward (n)	beloning	-morusu	riotous (a)	wanordelik
moputso	income (n)	inkomste	moruti	minister (n)	predikant
moputso	earnings (n)	loon	moruti	preacher (n)	predikant
moputso	salary (n)	salaris	morutuwa	disciple (n)	dissipel
moputso	prize (n)	prys	morutwana	pupil (n)	leerling
moqadi	beginner (n)	beginner	morwallo	flood (n)	vloed
moqala	crowbar (n)	koevoet	morwalo	burden (n)	las
moqapi	composer (n)	komponis	morwalo	load (n)	vrag
moqathatso	sandal (n)	sandaal	morwetsana	virgin (n)	maagd
Moqebelo	Saturday (n)	Saterdag	-mosa	kind (a)	goedhartig
moqopo	colon (n)	dikderm	mosa	kindness (n)	goedheid
moqoqo	conversation (n)	gesprek	mosadi	wife (n)	vrou
moqoqo	essay (n)	opstel	mosadi	female (n)	vrou
moqosi	accuser (n)	beskuldiger	mosadi	woman (n)	vrou
moqosi	plaintiff (n)	eiser	mosamo	pillow (n)	kussing
moqosuwa	accused (n)	beskuldigde	mosamo	cushion (n)	kussing
mora	son (n)	seun	mose	dress (n)	rok
moradi	daughter (n)	dogter	mosebeletsi	labourer (n)	arbeider
moraho	stirrup (n)	stiebeuel	mosebetsi	task (n)	taak
-morao	behind (prep)	agter	mosebetsi	work (n)	werk
-morao	rear (a)	agterste	mosebetsi	labour (n)	arbeid
-morao	late (a)	laat	mosebetsi	job (n)	werk
-morao	back (adv)	terug	mosebetsi	worker (n)	werker
morara	grape (n)	druiwe	mosebetsi	employment (n)	werk
morarane	creeper (n)	klimop	mosebetsi wa lapeng	homework (n)	huiswerk
-moratuwa	beloved (a)	bemind	mosebetsi wa matsoho	handwork (n)	handewerk
moratuwa	favourite (a)	gunsteling	mosehlo	segment (n)	segment
moratuwa	lover (n)	minnaar	mose ho mawatle	overseas (n)	oorsee
moreki	buyer (n)	koper	mosele	mussel (n)	mossel
moreki	client (n)	kliënt	moseme	mat (n)	mat
Morena	Lord (n)	Here	mosetareta	mustard (n)	mosterd
morena	king (n)	koning	mosetjhi	pickpocket (n)	sakkeroller
morero	motive (n)	beweegrede	mosha	meercat (n)	meerkat
morero	decision (n)	besluit	moshanyana	boy (n)	seun
morero	purpose (n)	oogmerk	mosi	smoke (n)	rook
morero	scheme (n)	skema	mosifa	tendon (n)	sening
morero o tiileng	determination (n)	vasberadenheid	mosifa	muscle (n)	spier

Sesotho	English	Afrikaans
mosireletsi	defendant (n)	verweerder
mosokolohi	convert (n)	bekeerling
mosusutlelli	dictator (n)	diktator
moswa	cobra (n)	kobra
moswahla	wreck (n)	wrak
motala	aboriginal (n)	oorspronklike inwoner
motataisi	guide (n)	gids
motehi	mechanic (n)	werktuigkundige
motele	motel (n)	motel
mothahaselli	fan (n)	bewonderaar
mothahaselli	volunteer (n)	vrywilliger
mothamo	mouthful (n)	mondvol
mothamo	volume (n)	volume
mothapo	blood vessel (n)	bloedvat
mothapo	vein (n)	aar
mothapo	nerve (n)	senuwee
mothapo	artery (n)	slagaar
mothati	ledge (n)	rotslys
mothati	terrace (n)	terras
motheo	basis (n)	basis
-motheo	basic (a)	basies
motheo	slope (n)	helling
mothinya	bend (n)	buiging
motho	person (n)	persoon
motho ka sebele	self (n)	self
mothuhi	burglar (n)	inbreker
mothusi	assistant (n)	helper
mothwebe	yolk (n)	eiergeel
motjeko	dance (n)	dans
motjha	youth (n)	jeug
-motjha	young (a)	jong
motjhana	nephew (n)	neef
motjhana	niece (n)	niggie
motjhelo	cellist (n)	tjellis
motjhene wa ho tlanya	typewriter (n)	tikmasjien
motjheso	heat (n)	hitte
motjhine	machine (n)	masjien
motjhine o rokang	sewing machine (n)	naaimasjien
motjhine wa vidio	video recorder (n)	videokassetopnemer
motjhotjhisi	prosecutor (n)	aanklaer
motlae	joke (n)	grap
motlae	comedy (n)	komedie
motlakase	electricity (n)	elektrisiteit
-motlakase	electric (a)	elektries
motlalehi	reporter (n)	verslaggewer
motlanyi	typist (n)	tikster
motlatlapi	robber (n)	rower
motlatlapi	villain (n)	skurk
motlatlapi	antagonist (n)	teenstander
motlatlapuwa wa tumelo	martyr (n)	martelaar
motlatsi	accomplice (n)	medepligtige
motlatsi	deputy (n)	plaasvervanger
motlatsi wa modulasetulo	vice-chairman (n)	ondervoorsitter
motletlebi	complainant (n)	klaer
motlodi	trespasser (n)	oortreder
motou wa ditshila	rubbish bin (n)	vullisblik
motsamaisi	conductor (n)	kondukteur
motsamao	march (n)	mars

Sesotho	English	Afrikaans
motsana	village (n)	dorpie
-motsana	suburban (a)	voorstedelik
motsana	suburb (n)	voorstad
motse	city (n)	stad
Motsheanong	May (n)	Mei
motsheare	midday (n)	middag
motshehare	noon (n)	middag
motshwaruwa	detainee (n)	aangehoudene
motshwaruwa	convict (n)	gevangene
motshwaruwa	prisoner (n)	gevangene
motshwaruwa wa ntweng	prisoner-of-war (n)	krygsgevangene
motso	root (n)	wortel
motsosa	stimulus (n)	stimulus
motsotso	minute (n)	minuut
motsotso	moment (n)	oomblik
motsotswana	second (n)	sekonde
motsu	arrow (n)	pyl
motswadi	parent (n)	ouer
motswalle	acquaintance (n)	kennis
motswalle	friend (n)	vriend
motswana	radicle (n)	wortel
motubi	oppressor (n)	onderdrukker
moutla	thorn (n)	doring
mouwane	vapour (n)	wasem
moya	breeze (n)	bries
moya	atmosphere (n)	atmosfeer
moya	breath (n)	asem
moya	mood (n)	bui
moya	spirit (n)	gees
moya	attitude (n)	houding
moya	air (n)	lug
moya	soul (n)	siel
moya	wind (n)	wind
-moyafala	evaporate (v)	verdamp
mpa	abdomen (n)	buik
mpa	belly (n)	pens
Mphalane	October (n)	Oktober
mpho	present (n)	geskenk
mpho	donation (n)	skenking
mpho	offer (n)	aanbod
mpjhe	ostrich (n)	volstruis
mpshane	ladle (n)	skeplepel
-mula	hammer (v)	hamer
musiamo	museum (n)	museum
-na	this (pron)	dit
-na	it (pron)	dit
-na	rain (v)	reën
naha	land (n)	land
naha	state (n)	staat
naha	veld (n)	veld
naha e phahameng	highveld (n)	hoëveld
naha e tlase	lowveld (n)	laeveld
-nahana	consider (v)	oorweeg
-nahana	think (v)	dink
-nahana	reason (v)	redeneer
-nahanelang	considerate (a)	bedagsaam
nakedi	polecat (n)	muishond
nakedi	skunk (n)	muishond

N	Sesotho	English	Afrikaans	Sesotho	English	Afrikaans
	nako	time (n)	tyd	-ngodisa	enrol (v)	inskryf
	nako	term (n)	termyn	-ngola	write (v)	skryf
	nako	term (n)	term	-ngomela ka sepelete	pin (v)	vasspeld
	nako e fetileng	past (n)	verlede	-ngongorehile	anxious (a)	bekommerd
	nako ya selemo	season (n)	seisoen	ngongoreho	anxiety (n)	kommer
	nala	abundance (n)	oorvloed	ngwana	child (n)	kind
	nalane	history (n)	geskiedenis	ngwanana	girl (n)	meisie
	-na le	consist (v)	bestaan	-ngwangwarela	scramble (v)	klouter
	nale	needle (n)	naald	-ngwapa	scratch (v)	krap
	naledi	star (n)	ster	-ngwapa	scrape (v)	skraap
	nama	flesh (n)	vleis	-ngwaparela	claw (v)	klou
	nama	meat (n)	vleis	ngwaparelo	claw (n)	klou
	nama e sitsweng	mince (n)	maalvleis	-ngwatha	slice (v)	skywe sny
	namane	calf (n)	kalf	ngwedi	moonlight (n)	maanlig
	nama ya kgomo	beef (n)	beesvleis	ngwetsi	sister-in-law (n)	skoonsuster
	nama ya kolobe	bacon (n)	spek	ngwetsi	daughter-in-law (n)	skoondogter
	nama ya kolobe	pork (n)	varkvleis	-nka	take (v)	neem
	nama ya namane	veal (n)	kalfsvleis	-nka mohlala	track (v)	opspoor
	nama ya nku	mutton (n)	skaapvleis	-nkga	smell (v)	ruik
	nama ya nyamatsane	venison (n)	wildsvleis	-nkga hampe	stink (v)	stink
	-nanara	stalk (v)	bekruip	nkgono	grandmother (n)	ouma
	-nang le talente	talented (a)	talentvol	-nko	nasal (a)	nasaal
	narike	naartjie (n)	nartjie	nko	nose (n)	neus
	-natefelwa	enjoy (v)	geniet	nku	sheep (n)	skaap
	-natefelwa	savour (v)	geniet	nna	me (pron)	my
	nawa	bean (n)	boontjie	nna/ke-	I (pron)	ek
	neng	when (adv)	wanneer	nne	four (n)	vier
	-nepahetse	correct (a)	korrek	-nnete	valid (a)	geldig
	-nepahetseng	accurate (a)	noukeurig	nnete	fact (n)	feit
	-nepileng	exact (a)	presies	-nnete	concrete (a)	konkreet
	-nepileng	right (a)	reg	-nnete	sincere (a)	opreg
	-nepisa	correct (v)	korrigeer	nnete	truth (n)	waarheid
	nepo	accuracy (n)	noukeurigheid	-nnete	true (a)	waar
	nese	nurse (n)	verpleegster	-nnete	real (a)	werklik
	-ng	else (adv)	anders	-nnetefatsa	ascertain (v)	vasstel
	-ng	other (a)	ander	nngwe	one (n)	een
	-ng	some (a)	sommige	nnqa	direction (n)	rigting
	-ng	single (a)	enkel	-no	those (pron)	daardie
	-ng; -nngwe	another (a)	nog 'n	noha	snake (n)	slang
	-ng; -nngwe	another (a)	'n ander	noka	pelvis (n)	bekken
	ngaka	surgeon (n)	chirurg	-noka	flavour (v)	geur
	ngaka	doctor (n)	dokter	noka	hip (n)	heup
	ngaka ya meno	dentist (n)	tandarts	noka	rump (n)	kruis
	ngaka ya setereke	district surgeon (n)	distriksgeneesheer	noka	loin (n)	lende
	-ngala	desert (v)	dros	noka	river (n)	rivier
	-ngala	sulk (v)	dikmond wees	noka	stream (n)	stroom
	-nganga	argue (v)	stry	noko	porcupine (n)	ystervark
	-ngangisa	contradict (v)	weerspreek	-nonne	fertile (a)	vrugbaar
	ngangisano	contradiction (n)	weerspreking	nonometsane	earthworm (n)	erdwurm
	ngangisano	argument (n)	argument	-nonopela	convalesce (v)	aansterk
	-ngata	many (a)	baie	-nontsha	fertilise (v)	bevrug
	ngata	sheaf (n)	gerf	-nontsha	fertilise (v)	kunsmis gee
	-ngata	abundant (a)	oorvloedig	nonyana	bird (n)	voël
	-ngata	plentiful (a)	talryk	-nonyetseha	sprain (v)	verstuit
	-ngata	much (a)	veel	nonyetseho	sprain (n)	verstuiting
	-ngaya	howl (v)	tjank	-nosetsa	irrigate (v)	besproei
	-ng le -ng	any (a)	enige	nosetso	irrigation (n)	besproeiing
	-ng le -ng	anything (pron)	enigiets	-notlela	lock (v)	sluit
	-ng le -ng	every (a)	elke	noto	hammer (n)	hamer
	-ng le -ng	each (pron)	elk(e)	noto	zero (n)	nul

Sesotho	English	Afrikaans	Sesotho	English	Afrikaans
notshi	bee (n)	by	-nyakalletseng	cheerful (a)	vrolik
-nqane	beyond (prep)	oorkant	nyakallo	delight (n)	blydskap
-nqosa	claim (v)	eis	nyakallo	happiness (n)	geluk
-nqosa	prosecute (v)	vervolg	-nyakallo	excitement (n)	opwinding
ntate	father (n)	vader	nyakallo	joy (n)	vreugde
ntatemoholo	grandfather (n)	oupa	-nyakurela	censor (v)	sensor
-nthithi	blunt (a)	stomp	-nyala	wed (v)	trou
ntho	thing (n)	ding	-nyala	marry (v)	trou
ntho	item (n)	item	nyalano	fuse (n)	sekering
ntho	substance (n)	stof	nyamatsana	antelope (n)	wildsbok
ntho	object (n)	voorwerp	nyamatsane	prey (n)	prooi
ntho esele	odd (a)	onewe	nyamatsane	bushbuck (n)	bosbok
nthwa ho bapala	toy (n)	speelding	nyamatsane	buck (n)	bok
ntja	dog (n)	hond	-nyamela	disappear (v)	verdwyn
ntja	bitch (n)	teef	nyamelo	disappearance (n)	verdwyning
ntjanyana	puppy (n)	klein hondjie	-nyarela	peep (v)	loer
-ntle ho	except (prep)	behalwe	nyedisa	contempt (n)	veragting
-ntle le	besides (prep)	buiten	-nyedisa	scorn (v)	verag
ntlha	goal (n)	doel	nyediso	scorn (n)	veragting
ntlha	tip (n)	punt	-nyemotsa	scowl (v)	suur kyk
ntlha	point (n)	punt	-nyenyane	little (a)	klein
ntlha	score (n)	telling	-nyenyane	small (a)	klein
ntlha ya leqhweng	freezing point (n)	vriespunt	-nyenyane	less (a)	minder
ntlo	house (n)	huis	-nyenyane	junior (a)	junior
ntlo	dwelling (n)	woning	-nyenyane hahole	minute (a)	heel klein
ntlo ya borena	palace (n)	paleis	-nyenyefatsa	humiliate (v)	verneder
ntlwana	cottage (n)	kothuis	-nyenyefatsa	belittle (v)	verkleineer
ntlwana	toilet (n)	toilet	-nyenyefatsa	lessen (v)	verminder
ntlwana	lavatory (n)	toilet	nyenyeletso	whisper (n)	gefluister
ntlwana ya ditekete	box office (n)	kaartjieloket	-nyoloha	ascend (v)	styg
ntlwana ya ntja	kennel (n)	hondehok	nyomonia	pneumonia (n)	longontsteking
ntlwana ya thelefone	telephone booth (n)	telefoonhokkie	-nyonyehang	repulsive (a)	walglik
ntoto	penis (n)	penis	nyooko	gall (n)	gal
-ntsha	eject (v)	uitskiet	nyooko	bile (n)	gal
-ntsha	eliminate (v)	verwyder	-nyopileng	abortive (a)	misluk
-ntsha diphoso	criticise (v)	kritiseer	-nyopisa	abort (v)	aborteer
-ntsha kotsi	hurt (v)	seermaak	nyopiso	abortion (n)	aborsie
-ntsha kotsi	wound (v)	wond	-nyorilwe	thirsty (a)	dorstig
-ntsha tjotjo	bribe (v)	omkoop	-nyorolla	quench (v)	les
-ntshetsa pele	civilise (v)	beskaaf			
ntsintsi	fly (n)	vlieg	obarolo	overalls (n)	oorpak
ntsu	eagle (n)	arend	oesetere	oyster (n)	oester
-ntsweleng	unanimous (a)	eenstemmig	ofisi ya ditekete	ticket office (n)	kaartjieskantoor
ntwa	battle (n)	geveg	-oka	nurse (v)	verpleeg
ntwa	fight (n)	geveg	-okola	skim (v)	afskep
ntwa	war (n)	oorlog	okosejene	oxygen (n)	suurstof
ntweng	battlefield (n)	slagveld	oli	oil (n)	olie
-nwa	drink (v)	drink	-oma	dry (v)	droogmaak
-nwesetsa	water (v)	natgooi	-oma ka hloho	nod (v)	knik
-nya	defecate (v)	ontlas	omfolopo	envelope (n)	koevert
-nyahameng	desperate (a)	wanhopig	-omme	dry (a)	droog
-nyahamisa	frustrate (v)	frustreer	onnorobaki	waistcoat (n)	onderbaadjie
-nyahamisa	discourage (v)	ontmoedig	onnoroko	petticoat (n)	onderrok
-nyahlatsa	jilt (v)	afsê	onto	oven (n)	oond
-nyahlatsa	abandon (v)	verlaat	-opa	ache (v)	pyn
-nyahlatsa	reject (v)	verwerp	-otileng	emaciated (a)	uitgeteer
nyahlatso	rejection (n)	verwerping	-otileng	lean (a)	maer
-nyakalatsa	delight (v)	bly maak	-otla	assault (v)	aanrand
-nyakalatsa	excite (v)	opwind	-otla	penalise (v)	straf
-nyakalletseng	happy (a)	gelukkig	-otla	hit (v)	slaan

305

O

Sesotho	English	Afrikaans
-otla	punch (v)	slaan
-otla	rear (v)	grootmaak
-otla	punish (v)	straf
-otlolla	extend (v)	uitstrek
-otlolohileng	straight (a)	reguit
-otlolohileng	vertical (a)	vertikaal
-otsela	doze (v)	sluimer
-otsela	drowse (v)	dommel
-otselang	sleepy (a)	vaak
paballo	economy (n)	ekonomie
paballo	thrift (n)	spaarsaamheid
paballo ya mmele	hygiene (n)	higiëne
-paka	testify (v)	getuig
paka	park (n)	park
-pakela	pack (v)	pak
paki	witness (n)	getuie
paki e boneng	eyewitness (n)	ooggetuie
palama	ride (n)	rit
-palama	ride (v)	ry
-palame	aboard (adv)	aan boord
pale	novel (n)	roman
pale	tale (n)	storie
pale	story (n)	verhaal
paleho	flight (n)	vlug
palesa	flower (n)	blom
palesa	fern (n)	varing
palo	number (n)	nommer
palo	pole (n)	paal
palo ya batho	census (n)	sensus
pampiri	paper (n)	papier
pampiri ya ho ngolla	writing paper (n)	skryfpapier
pampiri ya ntlwana	toilet paper (n)	toiletpapier
pampunkisi	mumps (n)	pampoentjies
panana	banana (n)	piesang
pane	pan (n)	pan
panelevena	panel van (n)	paneelwa
pantjhara	puncture (n)	lekplek
-panya	blink (v)	knipoog
-panya	wink (v)	knipoog
-panyapanya	flicker (v)	flikker
panyo	wink (n)	knipogie
papa	porridge (n)	pap
papadi	sport (n)	sport
papadi	game (n)	spel
papatso	advertisement (n)	advertensie
papiso	analogy (n)	analogie
papiso	comparison (n)	vergelyking
parafini	paraffin (n)	paraffien
parole	parole (n)	parool
-pata	hide (v)	wegsteek
patata	sweet potato (n)	patat
paterone	pattern (n)	patroon
-patilweng	hidden (a)	versteek
-patisa	compress (v)	saampers
patlisiso	investigation (n)	ondersoek
patlisiso ya lekgotla	inquest (n)	doodsondersoek
patlo	search (n)	soektog
patsi	firewood (n)	brandhout
pedi	two (n)	twee

Sesotho	English	Afrikaans
peelano	condition (n)	voorwaarde
peeletso	deposit (n)	deposito
pefo	violence (n)	geweld
peineapole	pineapple (n)	pynappel
peipe	pipe (n)	pyp
peiso	race (n)	wedren
pela	dassie (n)	dassie
-pela	along (prep)	langs
-pela	beside (prep)	langs
pelaelo	suspicion (n)	agterdog
pelaelo	moan (n)	gekerm
pelaelo	dissatisfaction (n)	ontevredenheid
pelaelo	doubt (n)	twyfel
pelaelo	distrust (n)	wantroue
-pele	first (a)	eerste
-pele	forward (adv)	vooruit
pele	onward (adv)	voorwaarts
-pele	front (a)	voor
-pele	further (a)	verder
-pele	before (prep)	voor
pelehi	childbirth (n)	kindergeboorte
-pelekana	squint (v)	skeel
-peleta	spell (v)	spel
pelo	heart (n)	hart
pelwana	embryo (n)	embrio
pene	pen (n)	pen
peninsula	peninsula (n)	skiereiland
pensele	pencil (n)	potlood
-penta	paint (v)	verf
pente	paint (n)	verf
peo	seed (n)	saad
pepere	pepper (n)	peper
pepere e tala	green pepper (n)	soetrissie
pere	horse (n)	perd
pere	pear (n)	peer
perekisi	peach (n)	perske
perese	purple (a)	pers
pere ya peiso	racehorse (n)	renperd
pesaleme	psalm (n)	psalm
petale	petal (n)	kroonblaar
peterole	petrol (n)	petrol
petjhe	patch (n)	lappie
-petlekisa melomo	pout (v)	pruil
-petlileng	inflamed (a)	onsteek
petlo	inflammation (n)	ontsteking
peto	rape (n)	verkragting
petsana	foal (n)	vulletjie
-petsoha	crack (v)	kraak
-petsola	split (v)	splits
-phaella	gain (v)	wen
phaello	gain (n)	wins
phaello	profit (n)	wins
-phahama	arise (v)	opstaan
-phahama	rise (v)	styg
-phahama	emerge (v)	verrys
-phahameng	high (a)	hoog
-phahameng ho feta	higher (a)	hoër
-phahamisa	promote (v)	bevorder
-phahamisa	uphold (v)	hoog hou
-phahamisa	lift (v)	oplig

Sesotho	English	Afrikaans	Sesotho	English	Afrikaans	P
-phahamisa	raise (v)	ophef	phetohelo	revolution (n)	revolusie	
phahamiso	promotion (n)	bevordering	phetoho	change (n)	verandering	
phahla	gap (n)	opening	phetolo	amendment (n)	wysiging	
-phakisang	fast (a)	vinnig	-phetseng hantle	healthy (a)	gesond	
phakwe	hawk (n)	valk	phifalo	eclipse (n)	verduistering	
phala	whistle (n)	fluit	phinahano	contraction (n)	inkrimping	
-phalla	hurry (v)	jaag	phio	kidney (n)	nier	
-phalla	flow (v)	vloei	-phodileng	cool (a)	koel	
-phallang	fluid (a)	vloeibaar	-phodileng	mild (a)	matig	
phallo	migration (n)	migrasie	phodiso	cure (n)	genesing	
phallo	departure (n)	vertrek	phofo	flour (n)	meel	
-phamola	snatch (v)	gaps	phofu	victim (n)	slagoffer	
phapano	difference (n)	verskil	phofu	eland (n)	eland	
-phaphama	wake (v)	wakker word	phoka	dew (n)	dou	
-phaphamala	float (v)	drywe	-phoka	wade (v)	waad	
-phaphamala	flout (v)	hoon	phokolo ya madi	anaemia (n)	bloedarmoede	
phatla	forehead (n)	voorhoof	pholletso	raft (n)	vlot	
-phatlalatsa	publish (v)	uitgee	pholo	ox (n)	os	
-phatlalatsa	issue (v)	uitreik	pholoho	salvation (n)	verlossing	
-phatloha	burst (v)	bars	-pholosa	save (v)	red	
Phato	August (n)	Augustus	-pholosa	rescue (v)	red	
phatsa	chip (computer) (n)	vlokkie	pholoso	rescue (n)	redding	
-phatsima	glitter (v)	skitter	-phomola	retire (v)	aftree	
-pheella	insist (v)	aandring	-phomola	rest (v)	rus	
pheello	insistence (n)	aandrang	phomolo	holiday (n)	vakansie	
-phefumoloha	breathe (v)	asemhaal	phomolo	rest (n)	rus	
-phefumoloha	exhale (v)	uitasem	-phonyoha	escape (v)	ontsnap	
phefumoloho	respiration (n)	asemhaling	phonyoho	escape (n)	ontsnapping	
phefumoloho ya	artificial	kunsmatige	phoofolo	animal (n)	dier	
maiketsetso	respiration (n)	asemhaling	phoofolo	beast (n)	dier	
phehli	pest (n)	pes	phoofolo e nang le	vertebrate (n)	werweldier	
phehlo	churn (n)	karring	lesapo la			
-phekola	heal (v)	genees	moko kotlo			
-phela	alive (a)	lewend	phoofolo e ratwang	pet (n)	troeteldier	
-phela	live (v)	leef	phopho	pawpaw (n)	papaja	
-phelang	lively (a)	lewendig	phororo	waterfall (n)	waterval	
pheletso	outcome (n)	uitkoms	phoso	blame (n)	blaam	
pheletsong	maximum (n)	maksimum	phoso	mistake (n)	fout	
pheletsong ya lefatshe	horizon (n)	horison	phoso	fault (n)	fout	
pheleu	ram (n)	ram	-phoso	incorrect (a)	onjuis	
-phema	avoid (v)	vermy	-phoso	wrong (a)	verkeerd	
-phema	shun (v)	vermy	phoso	blunder (n)	flater	
phenshene	pension (n)	pensioen	phoso	error (n)	fout	
phentihouse	pantihose (n)	kousbroekie	-photjhola	scald (v)	skroei	
phepelo ya madi	blood transfusion (n)	bloedoortapping	phudueho	emotion (n)	gevoel	
-phepetsa	challenge (v)	uitdaag	phufodi	steam (n)	stoom	
phepetso	challenge (n)	uitdaging	phula	current (n)	stroom	
phepheng	scorpion (n)	skerpioen	phula	valley (n)	vallei	
phepo	nutrition (n)	voeding	phumano	acquisition (n)	aanskaffing	
pherehlo	disturbance (n)	oproer	-phumola	wipe (v)	afvee	
Pherekgong	January (n)	Januarie	-phumola	delete (v)	skrap	
phesente	percent (n)	persent	-phunya	pierce (v)	deursteek	
-pheta	repeat (v)	herhaal	-phunyeletsa	penetrate (v)	binnedring	
-pheta	revise (v)	wysig	Phupjane	June (n)	Junie	
phete	sanitary towel (n)	sanitêre doekie	phupu	bud (n)	botsel	
-phetha	end (v)	eindig	phupu	funeral (n)	begrafnis	
-phethahetseng	perfect (a)	volmaak	Phupu	July (n)	Julie	
phetho	end (n)	einde	-phutheha	congregate (v)	vergader	
-phethoha	capsize (v)	omkantel	phutheho	congregation (n)	gemeente	
phetohelo	sedition (n)	opruiing	-phuthela	wrap (v)	toedraai	

P	Sesotho	English	Afrikaans	Sesotho	English	Afrikaans
	phuthi	duiker (n)	duiker	popelo	ovary (n)	eierstok
	phuting	dessert (n)	nagereg	popelo	womb (n)	baarmoeder
	phutuhelo	raid (n)	strooptog	popi	doll (n)	pop
	pikinike	picnic (n)	piekniek	popo	mould (n)	vorm
	-pikitla	rub (v)	vryf	populiri	poplar (n)	populier
	pilisi	pill (n)	pil	poraefete	private (a)	privaat
	pilisi	tablet (n)	tablet	poraema	plum (n)	pruim
	pina	song (n)	liedjie	-porofeta	predict (v)	voorspel
	pina ya setjhaba	anthem (n)	volkslied	poropo	stopper (n)	stopprop
	pinke	pink (n)	pienk	-posa	post (v)	pos
	pipelano	asphyxia (n)	versmoring	posekarete	postcard (n)	poskaart
	pipitlelo	indigestion (n)	slegte spysvertering	posetaleota	postal order (n)	posorder
	-pipitletswe	flatulent (a)	winderig	poso	mail (n)	pos
	pitsa	pot (n)	pot	poso	post (n)	pos
	pitsa	saucepan (n)	kastrol	posong	post office (n)	poskantoor
	pitsa ya tee	teapot (n)	teepot	poso ya moya	airmail (n)	lugpos
	pitso	container (n)	houer	-potlaka	rush (v)	haas
	pobolo	groan (n)	kreun	-potoloha	circulate (v)	rondgaan
	podi	goat (n)	bok	-potoloha	wallow (v)	wentel
	pofa	bulldog (n)	bulhond	-potoloha	revolve (v)	draai
	poho	bull (n)	bul	potoloho	circulation (n)	omloop
	poho ya pere	stallion (n)	hings	potsanyane	kid (n)	bokkie
	pokano	gathering (n)	byeenkoms	potso	inquiry (n)	navraag
	pokello	pile (n)	stapel	potso	question (n)	vraag
	pokotho	pocket (n)	sak	pounama	lip (n)	lip
	-pola	thrash (v)	uitklop	poya	mildew (n)	muf
	polanete	planet (n)	planeet	-pshatla	break (v)	breek
	polao	murder (n)	moord	-pshatlehile	broken (a)	stukkend
	polao	slaughter (n)	slagting	pudula	gland (n)	klier
	polasetike	plastic (n)	plastiek	pudula	bubble (n)	borrel
	polasi	farm (n)	plaas	pudulana	flake (n)	vlokkie
	poleiti	plate (n)	bord	Pudungwana	November (n)	November
	polelo	sentence (n)	sin	puisano	discussion (n)	bespreking
	-polesha	polish (v)	poleer	pula	rain (n)	reën
	poleshe	polish (n)	politoer	puo	operation (n)	operasie
	-politike	political (a)	polities	puo	language (n)	taal
	polokeho	safety (n)	veiligheid	puo	talk (n)	praatjie
	polokelo	safe (n)	brandkluis	puo ya lapeng	vernacular (n)	volkstaal
	poloko	burial (n)	begrafnis	-pupeditsweng	overgrown (a)	toegegroei
	poloko	reserve (n)	reserwe	-putsa	pay (v)	betaal
	poloko ya tsa hlaho	nature reserve (n)	natuurreservaat	-putsa	reward (v)	beloon
	polotso	circumcision (n)	besnydenis	-putsang	profitable (a)	lonend
	-poma	amputate (v)	afsit			
	pomelo	grapefruit (n)	pomelo	-qabana	quarrel (v)	twis
	-pompa	pump (v)	pomp	qabang	quarrel (n)	twis
	pompo	pump (n)	pomp	-qabola	amuse (v)	vermaak
	pompong	sweet (n)	lekker	-qabolang	comic (a)	komies
	-pona	wither (v)	verlep	-qabolang	amusing (a)	vermaaklik
	-pona	wilt (v)	kwyn	qabolo	humour (n)	humor
	pono	sight (n)	sig	qabolo	comic (n)	komiek
	pono	vision (n)	gesigsvermoë	qaka	problem (n)	probleem
	-pontsheng	openly (a)	openlik	-qala	begin (v)	begin
	-pontsheng	public (a)	openbaar	-qala	start (v)	begin
	pontsho	show (n)	skou	qalo	start (n)	begin
	pontsho	show (n)	vertoning	qalo	beginning (n)	begin
	pontsho	exhibition (n)	uitstalling	-qapa	compose (v)	komponeer
	pontsho	omen (n)	voorteken	-qapa	invent (v)	uitvind
	pontsho	demonstration (n)	betoging	qapo	composition (n)	komposisie
	poone	maize (n)	mielies	qapo	invention (n)	uitvinding
	popeho	tissue (n)	weefsel	qapodiso	pronunciation (n)	uitspraak

Sesotho	English	Afrikaans	Sesotho	English	Afrikaans
-qaqisetsa	enlighten (v)	inlig	rakebi	rugby (n)	rugby
-qeta	finish (v)	klaarmaak	ramafolofolo	activist (n)	aktivis
-qetelang	last (a)	laaste	ramashano	liar (n)	leuenaar
-qetella	complete (v)	voltooi	ramathesele	rheumatism (n)	rumatiek
-qetellong	ultimate (a)	uiterste	-ramathesele	rheumatic (a)	rumaties
qetelo	finish (n)	einde	ramethokgo	herbalist (n)	kruiekenner
qeto	conclusion (n)	gevolgtrekking	ramethokgo	witchdoctor (n)	toordokter
-qhala	scatter (v)	strooi	rametlae	lout (n)	takhaar
-qhalana	adjourn (v)	verdaag	ramohlongwana	chief (n)	hoofman
qhana	saddle (n)	saal	ramotse	mayor (n)	burgemeester
-qhaqholla	unravel (v)	ontrafel	-ranthanya	shred (v)	snipper
-qhashoha	erupt (v)	uitbars	rapa	turnip (n)	raap
-qhekanyetsa	cheat (v)	kul	-rapalla	across (prep)	oor
-qhela	exclude (v)	uitsluit	-rapalletse	across (adv)	dwars
-qhibidiha	melt (v)	smelt	-rapela	pray (v)	bid
-qhibidiha	dissolve (v)	oplos	-rapela	plead (n)	pleit
-qhiletsa	limp (v)	mank loop	rapolasi	farmer (n)	boer
-qhobellane	crowded (a)	propvol	raposo	postman (n)	posbode
qhobosheane	fort (n)	fort	raqhwe	guerrilla (n)	guerrilla
-qhoma	explode (v)	ontplof	-raro	third (a)	derde
qhomo	outbreak (n)	uitbreking	-rarolla	solve (v)	oplos
qhomo	explosion (n)	ontploffing	raselaga	butcher (n)	slagter
-qhophella	persevere (v)	volhard	rasite	receipt (n)	kwitansie
-qhotsa	spawn (v)	uitbroei	-rata	like (v)	hou van
-qhwela	choke (v)	verstik	-rata	value (v)	waardeer
-qobella	compel (v)	dwing	-rata	admire (v)	bewonder
-qobella	enforce (v)	afdwing	-rata	favour (v)	begunstig
qobello	compulsion (n)	dwang	-ratang ditaba	inquisitive (a)	nuuskierig
qokofana	dwarf (n)	dwerg	-rata wa bong ba hao	homosexual (n)	homoseksueel
qomatsi	risk (n)	risiko	-ratehang	likeable (a)	beminlik
-qophella	persuade (v)	oorreed	-ratehang	lovable (a)	dierbaar
qophello	persuasion (n)	oorreding	-ratehang	affectionate (a)	toegeneë
qophelo	edge (n)	rand	-ratehang	admirable (a)	bewonderendswaardig
-qoqa	chat (v)	gesels	-ratehang	dear (a)	dierbaar
-qoqela	narrate (v)	vertel	rateise	radish (n)	radys
qoqotho	windpipe (n)	gorrelpyp	-ratha	chop (v)	kap
qoqothwane	larynx (n)	larinks	rathomo	organist (n)	orrelis
-qosa	charge (law) (v)	aankla	-ratisa	endear (v)	bemind maak
-qosa	accuse (v)	beskuldig	-re	mean (v)	bedoel
-qoso	accusation (n)	beskuldiging	reise	rice (n)	rys
qoso	charge (n)	aanklag	reisisi ya dipere	horserace (n)	perdewedren
-qotama	squat (v)	hurk	rejisetara	register (n)	register
-qotsa	quote (v)	aanhaal	-reka	buy (v)	koop
qotso	quotation (n)	aanhaling	-reka	shop (v)	inkopies doen
qubu	heap (n)	hoop	-rekisa	sell (v)	verkoop
qubu ya ditshila	rubbish heap (n)	vullishoop	-rekota	record (v)	opteken
qwaha	zebra (n)	sebra	rekoto	record (n)	rekord
-qwedisa	submerge (v)	onderdompel	reng	ring (n)	ring
-qwela	dive (v)	duik	rente	rent (n)	huur
qwelo	diving (n)	duikery	-rera	decide (v)	besluit
			-rera	intend (v)	van plan wees
raba	rubber (n)	wisser	resepe	recipe (n)	resep
raba	rubber (n)	rubber	resetjhurente	restaurant (n)	restaurant
-rabela	rebel (v)	rebelleer	reshene	ration (n)	rantsoen
rabolloro	revolver (n)	rewolwer	-retetseng	pale (a)	bleek
radietare	radiator (n)	verkoeler	-ripitla	devastate (v)	verwoes
radio	radio (n)	radio	-ripitla	exterminate (v)	uitroei
-raha	boot (v)	skop	-ripitla	destroy (v)	vernietig
-raha	kick (v)	skop	-ritela	brew (v)	brou
raka	shelf (n)	rak	-robala	sleep (v)	slaap

R	Sesotho	English	Afrikaans	Sesotho	English	Afrikaans
	-robalana	copulate (v)	kopuleer	-sa hlokahaleng	undesirable (a)	ongewens
	robedi	eight (n)	agt	-sa hlomelang	unarmed (a)	ongewapend
	-robetse	asleep (a)	aan die slaap	-sa hlompheng	impolite (a)	onbeleef
	robong	nine (n)	nege	-sa hlophuwang	unplanned (a)	onbedoeld
	roboto	robot (n)	robot	-sa hlwekang	unhygienic (a)	onhigiënies
	-roka	sew (v)	naaldwerk doen	-sa ikgopoleng	unselfish (a)	onselfsugtig
	-rolo	spotted (a)	gekol	sajene	sergeant (n)	sersant
	rolo	roll (n)	rol	sakarete	cigarette (n)	sigaret
	rolobolo	bowls (n)	rolbal	sakatuku	handkerchief (n)	sakdoek
	-roma	send (v)	stuur	-sa kgathalleng	unwary (a)	onbehoedsaam
	-rona	our (pron)	ons	-sala	remain (v)	agterbly
	rona	we (pron)	ons	-sa lebaleheng	unforgettable (a)	onvergeetlik
	rona	us (pron)	ons	-sa lebellwang	unexpectedly (adv)	onverwags
	rona	ourselves (pron)	onsself	-sa lebellwang	unexpected (a)	onverwag
	-rona	ours (pron)	ons s'n	-sa lefuweng	unrewarded (a)	onbeloond
	ropo ya ho hula	tow rope (n)	sleeptou	-sa lekaneng	unequal (a)	ongelyk
	-rora	growl (v)	knor	-sa lekaneng	uneven (a)	ongelyk
	-rora	roar (v)	brul	-sa lokelang	unfit (a)	ongeskik
	-rorisa	praise (v)	loof	samane	subpoena (n)	dagvaarding
	-rorisa	prize (v)	op prys stel	samane	summons (n)	dagvaarding
	-rota	urinate (v)	urineer	samente	cement (n)	sement
	-rotha	drip (v)	drup	samporele	umbrella (n)	sambreel
	-rotha	drop (v)	laat val	-sa ntshetswang pele	undeveloped (a)	onontwikkeld
	rouse	rose (n)	roos	-sa nyalwang	unmarried (a)	ongetroud
	-rua	own (v)	besit	-sa phehisweng kgang	undisputed (a)	onbetwis
	-rua	breed (v)	teel	-sa phekoleheng	incurable (a)	ongeneeslik
	-ruileng	rich (a)	ryk	-sa pheleng	inanimate (a)	leweloos
	-ruisa	enrich (v)	verryk	-sa phethahalang	unfinished (a)	onvoltooid
	rula	ruler (n)	liniaal	-sa phethahatswang	unfulfilled (a)	onvervuld
	-rulela ka jwang	thatch (v)	dek	-sa phethehang	incomplete (a)	onvolledig
	-ruma	rhyme (v)	rym	-sa phethehang	imperfect (a)	onvolmaak
	-rupela	lecture (v)	doseer	-sa rateng	unwilling (a)	onwillig
	-rupela	instruct (v)	onderrig	-sa rutehang	uneducated (a)	ongeleerd
	-ruruha	swell (v)	swel	-sa sebetseng	unemployed (a)	werkloos
	-ruta	preach (v)	preek	-sa senyehang	undamaged (a)	onbeskadig
	-ruta	educate (v)	opvoed	-sataletseng	tense (a)	gespanne
	-ruta	train (v)	afrig	-sa tebang	shallow (a)	vlak
	-rutehileng	qualified (a)	gekwalifiseerd	-sa thabang	unhappy (a)	ongelukkig
	-rwala	carry (v)	dra	-sa tlwaelehang	abnormal (a)	abnormaal
	-rwalella	flood (v)	oorstroom	-sa tlwaelehang	uncommon (a)	ongewoon
				-sa tlwaelehang	unaccustomed (a)	ongewoond
	-sa	still (adv)	nog	-sa tsebe	unknowingly (adv)	onwetend
	-saballetse	boundless (a)	grensloos	-sa tsebeng hantle	uncertain (a)	onseker
	-sa belaetseng	undoubted (a)	ongetwyfeld	-sa tsebisahaleng	petty (a)	kleinlik
	sabole	sword (n)	swaard	-sa tsebisahaleng	trivial (a)	niksbeduidend
	-sa bolelwang	undisclosed (a)	onvermeld	-sa tshabeng	unafraid (a)	onbevrees
	-sa bolokeng nako	unpunctual (a)	nie stip nie	-sa tshepahaleng	unfaithful (a)	ontrou
	-sa bonahaleng	invisible (a)	onsigbaar	-sa tshepahaleng	undependable (a)	onbetroubaar
	-sa bonweng	abstract (a)	afgetrokke	-sa tshepeheng	dishonest (a)	oneerlik
	-sa butswang	immature (a)	onvolwasse	-sa tshwarelweng	unforgivable (a)	onvergeeflik
	-sa elellwang	undeserved (a)	onverdiend	-sa tsitsang	uncomfortable (a)	ongemaklik
	-sa elellweng	unaware (a)	onbewus	-sa tsitsang	uneasy (a)	ongerus
	-sa eleng hloko	inattentive (a)	onoplettend	-sa tsitsang	undecided (a)	onbeslis
	-saena	sign (v)	teken	-sa tswalwang	unborn (a)	ongebore
	-sa feleng	eternal (a)	ewig	-sa utlwahaleng	inaudible (a)	onhoorbaar
	-sa feleng	everlasting (a)	ewigdurend	-sa utlwahaleng	vague (a)	vaag
	-sa fetoheng	unalterable (a)	onveranderlik	-sa utlweng	numb (a)	dood
	-sa fumaneheng	unavailable (a)	onverkrygbaar	-sa yeng ka molao	illegal (a)	onwettig
	saga	saw (n)	saag	seabelo	fraction (n)	fraksie
	-saga	saw (v)	saag	seaduma	thunder (n)	donder

Sesotho	English	Afrikaans	Sesotho	English	Afrikaans	**S**
-Seaforika	African (a)	Afrika	-sefa	sift (v)	sif	
seakofisi	accelerator (n)	brandstofpedaal	sefafatsi	sprinkler (n)	sprinkelaar	
seatla	palm (n)	palm	sefaha	necklace (n)	halssnoer	
-seba	gossip (v)	skinder	sefaha	bead (n)	kraal	
sebabole	sulphur (n)	swawel	sefahleho	face (n)	gesig	
sebadi	calculator (n)	rekenaar	sefako	hail (n)	hael	
sebae	platform (n)	platform	Sefapano sa Borwa	Southern Cross (n)	Suiderkruis	
sebaka	lair (n)	lêplek	sefate	tree (n)	boom	
sebaka	space (n)	ruimte	sefate sa feiye	figtree (n)	vyeboom	
sebaka	area (n)	oppervlakte	sefate sa morara	vine (n)	wingerdstok	
sebaka	scene (n)	toneel	sefe	sieve (n)	sif	
sebaka	chance (n)	kans	sefebe	whore (n)	hoer	
sebaka	occasion (n)	geleentheid	sefefo	gale (n)	stormwind	
sebaka se feela	vacuum (n)	lugleegte	sefefo	storm (n)	storm	
sebapadi	actress (n)	aktrise	sefela	hymn (n)	gesang	
sebapadi	actor (n)	akteur	sefi	trap (n)	strik	
sebata	predator (n)	roofdier	sefi	snare (n)	strik	
-sebataola	arid (a)	dor	sefifi	carcass (n)	karkas	
sebe	sin (n)	sonde	sefika	monument (n)	monument	
-sebedisa	spend (v)	bestee	sefofane	aircraft (n)	vliegtuig	
-sebedisa	use (v)	gebruik	sefofane	aeroplane (n)	vliegtuig	
-sebedisa	apply (v)	toepas	sefuba	bosom (n)	boesem	
-sebedisana	co-operate (v)	saamwerk	sefuba	thorax (n)	borskas	
-sebeletsa	serve (v)	dien	sefuba	chest (n)	borskas	
-sebeletsa moputso	earn (v)	verdien	sefuba	breast (n)	bors	
-sebete	brave (a)	dapper	-seha	cut (v)	sny	
sebete	dare (n)	uitdaging	sehahi	mason (n)	messelaar	
sebete	liver (n)	lewer	sehananalemmele	antibody (n)	teenliggaam	
sebete	bravery (n)	dapperheid	sehatsetsi	freezer (n)	vrieskas	
-sebetsa	work (v)	werk	sehlabelo	sacrifice (n)	offerande	
sebetsa	weapon (n)	wapen	sehlabi	sting (n)	steek	
-sebetsa	labour (v)	arbei	sehlaha	nest (n)	nes	
-sebetsa	effect (v)	bewerk	sehlaha	glovebox (n)	mossienes	
sebewa	product (n)	produk	sehlahla	shrub (n)	struik	
sebini	musician (n)	musikant	se hlahlamang	sequel (n)	gevolg	
seboba	tsetse fly (n)	tsetsevlieg	sehlaho	instinct (n)	instink	
seboba	wasp (n)	perdeby	sehlakodi	eraser (n)	uitveër	
seboka	congress (n)	kongres	sehlare sa ho tshollisa	purgative (n)	purgeermiddel	
seboka	conference (n)	konferensie	sehlekehleke	island (n)	eiland	
seboko	maggot (n)	maaier	sehlephisi	laxative (n)	lakseermiddel	
seboko	caterpillar (n)	ruspe	sehloba	pimple (n)	puisie	
seboko	worm (n)	wurm	sehloba	acne (n)	aknee	
seboko	larva (n)	larwe	sehlohlolo	apex (n)	spits	
sebolayatjhefo	antidote (n)	teengif	-sehloho	cruel (a)	wreed	
sebono	anus (n)	anus	sehloho	cruelty (n)	wreedheid	
sebopeho	form (n)	vorm	-sehloho	tragic (a)	tragies	
sebopuwa	creature (n)	wese	sehlomathiso	appendix (n)	aanhangsel	
sebotjhe	dimple (n)	kuiltjie	sehlooho	headline (n)	opskrif	
sebui	operator (n)	operateur	sehlooho	title (n)	titel	
-sedi	alert (a)	waaksaam	sehlopha	group (n)	groep	
-sedi	observant (a)	oplettend	sehlopha	team (n)	span	
sediba	fountain (n)	fontein	sehlopha	gang (n)	bende	
sediba	well (n)	put	sehlopha	band (n)	groep	
sedika	circumference (n)	omtrek	sehlwekisi	disinfectant (n)	ontsmettingsmiddel	
sedikadikwe	circle (n)	sirkel	sehlwela	scout (n)	verkenner	
sedikadikwe	cycle (n)	siklus	sehlwela	spy (n)	spioen	
sedumammoho	consonant (n)	medeklinker	sehohedi	loot (n)	buit	
seemahale	statue (n)	beeld	sehohlola	phlegm (n)	fleim	
seemo sa mmele	physique (n)	liggaamsbou	-seholoholo	primitive (a)	primitief	
seeta	shoe (n)	skoen	sehopotso	souvenir (n)	aandenking	

S	Sesotho	English	Afrikaans	Sesotho	English	Afrikaans
	sehopotso	memorial (a)	herdenking	selae	lettuce (n)	blaarslaai
	sehwapa	biltong (n)	biltong	selae	salad (n)	slaai
	sehwete	carrot (n)	wortel	selaga	butchery (n)	slagtery
	sehwete se sesweu	parsley (n)	pietersielie	selagapalo	abattoir (n)	slagplaas
	seile	canvas (n)	seil	selata	sheath (n)	skede
	seile	sail (n)	seil	sele	cell (n)	sel
	seile	tarpaulin (n)	seil	-sele	foreign (a)	vreemd
	seipone	reflection (n)	weerkaatsing	-sele	strange (a)	vreemd
	seipone	mirror (n)	spieël	seledu	chin (n)	ken
	seithati	aristocrat (n)	edelman	-selehae	local (a)	plaaslik
	sejalo	plant (n)	plant	selekane	companionship (n)	kameraadskap
	sejana	dish (n)	skottel	selemo	year (n)	jaar
	-sejwalejwale	modern (a)	modern	selemo	spring (n)	lente
	-seka	account (v)	rekenskap gee	selemo setshelapalo-	leap year (n)	skrikkeljaar
	sekala	scale (n)	skaal	matsatsi		
	-sekama	slant (v)	skuins loop	seleng	slang (n)	sleng
	sekammane	flashlight (n)	flitslig	selepe	axe (n)	byl
	sekanire	hinge (n)	hingsel	seleri	celery (n)	seldery
	sekapolelo	phrase (n)	sinsnede	selika	silk (n)	sy
	sekatana	rag (n)	lap	sello	cry (n)	kreet
	sekele	sickle (n)	sekel	sello	mourning (n)	rou
	sekenkeboroto	tray (n)	skinkbord	selope	prey (v)	aas
	sekepe	ship (n)	skip	selope	fish-hook (n)	vishoek
	sekere	scissors (n)	skêr	selotho	puzzle (n)	raaisel
	sekerefe	dandruff (n)	skilfers	seloto	padlock (n)	hangslot
	sekesofoune	saxophone (n)	saxofoon	semeje	sandwich (n)	toebroodjie
	sekete	thousand (n)	duisend	semelo	character (n)	karakter
	seketswana	boat (n)	boot	semethapula	rain gauge (n)	reënmeter
	seketswana sa seile	yacht (n)	seiljag	-semorabe	racial (a)	rasse
	sekgapetla	husk (n)	skil	-semumu	dumb (a)	stom
	sekgeo	omission (n)	weglating	-se nang bophelo	unhealthy (a)	ongesond
	-sekgeo	vacant (a)	vakant	-se nang mekgwa	undisciplined (a)	ongedissiplineerd
	sekgeo	vacancy (n)	vakature	-se nang mohau	uncharitable (a)	onbarmhartig
	sekgetjhana	strip (n)	strook	-se nang mohau	unmerciful (a)	ongenadig
	sekgetshe	groove (n)	groef	-se nang teboho	ungrateful (a)	ondankbaar
	sekgo	spider (n)	spinnekop	-se nang thepa	unfurnished (a)	ongemeubileerd
	-sekgobo	lewd (a)	ontugtig	-se nang thuso	useless (a)	nutteloos
	sekgolopane	smallpox (n)	waterpokkies	-se nang toka	unjust (a)	onregverdig
	sekgomaretsi	paste (n)	pasta	-se nang tokelo	unauthorised (a)	ongemagtig
	sekgopi	grudge (n)	wrok	-se nang tshenyo	harmless (a)	onskadelik
	sekgutlo	corner (n)	hoek	-se nang tshireletso	unsafe (a)	onveilig
	sekgutlo	angle (n)	hoek	senate	senate (n)	senaat
	sekgwama	purse (n)	beursie	-senatla	giant (a)	reuse
	sekhafo	scarf (n)	serp	senatla	giant (n)	reus
	sekhete	skirt (n)	romp	-sengolwa	literary (a)	letterkundig
	sekiri sa dithollo	granary (n)	graanskuur	sengolwa	literature (n)	letterkunde
	sekodi	disability (n)	gebrek	sengwathwana	slice (n)	sny
	sekolo	school (n)	skool	-seng ya bohlokwa	unimportant (a)	onbelangrik
	sekontiri	tar (n)	teer	seno	drink (n)	drankie
	sekoti	pit (n)	gat	senoko	inch (n)	duim
	sekoto	fragment (n)	brokstuk	senoko	flavouring (n)	geursel
	sekotwana	piece (n)	stuk	senoko	knuckle (n)	kneukel
	-Sekreste	Christian (a)	Christelik	senoko	syllable (n)	lettergreep
	sekurufu	screw (n)	skroef	senoko	perfume (n)	parfuum
	sekutamohlwa	lawnmower (n)	grassnyer	-senola	bare (v)	ontbloot
	sekwahelo	lid (n)	deksel	-senola	reveal (v)	openbaar
	sekwahelo	cap (n)	deksel	-senola	disclose (v)	openbaar
	sekwahelo	cover (n)	deksel	senotlolo	lock (n)	slot
	sekwahelo	plug (n)	prop	senotlolo	key (n)	sleutel
	sekwashe	squash (n)	muurbal	senqanqane	frog (n)	padda

Sesotho	English	Afrikaans
sente	cent (n)	sent
senturu	century (n)	eeu
-senya	damage (v)	beskadig
-senya	corrupt (v)	bederf
senya	bladder (n)	blaas
-senya	waste (v)	vermors
-senyang	harmful (a)	skadelik
-senyehile	corrupt (a)	bedorwe
-Senyesemane	English (a)	Engels
seotlwana	hedge (n)	heining
seotsanyana	heron (n)	reier
seotswa	adulterer (n)	owerspeler
seotswa	prostitute (n)	prostituut
sepako	cork (n)	kurk
sepanere	spanner (n)	moersleutel
sepeiti	syringe (n)	spuit
sepekere	nail (n)	spyker
sepelete	safety pin (n)	haakspeld
sepelete	pin (n)	speld
sepense	pantry (n)	spens
sepetja	bangle (n)	armband
sepetlele	hospital (n)	hospitaal
sephadi	whip (n)	sweep
sephalli	fluid (n)	vloeistof
-sephara	broad (a)	breed
-sephara	flat (a)	plat
sepheo	aim (n)	doel
sephethephethe	traffic (n)	verkeer
sephoko	cliff (n)	krans
sephooko	owl (n)	uil
sepiriti	spirits (n)	spiritus
seponse	sponge (n)	spons
seporo	railway (n)	spoorweg
seqha	bow (n)	boog
seqhomelankong	cricket (n)	krieket
sera	enemy (n)	vyand
sera	foe (n)	vyand
serame	frost (n)	ryp
seratswana	garden (n)	tuin
serekise	circus (n)	sirkus
serethe	heel (n)	hak
-seretse	muddy (a)	modderig
seretse	mud (n)	modder
seritsa	cripple (n)	kreupele
seroki	tailor (n)	kleremaker
serope	thigh (n)	dy
serumola	torch (n)	flitslig
serurubele	butterfly (n)	skoenlapper
seruti	clergy (n)	geestelikes
-sesa	sail (v)	seil
-sesa	swim (v)	swem
-sesane	thin (a)	dun
sesebediswa	article (n)	artikel
sesebediswa	instrument (n)	instrument
-sesefa	abstain (v)	onthou
sesenyi	criminal (n)	misdadiger
sesepa	soap (n)	seep
sesepa	soapstone (n)	seepsteen
sesepa sa ho beola	shaving cream (n)	skeerroom
sesepa sa meno	toothpaste (n)	tandepasta
sesesi	swimmer (n)	swemmer
seshoba	bundle (n)	bondel
seshoba	parcel (n)	pakket
seso	sore (n)	seer
seso	abscess (n)	verswering
seso	ulcer (n)	ulkus
-sesole	military (a)	militêre
-sesolo	cheap (a)	goedkoop
sesomo	sarcasm (n)	sarkasme
sesosa	cause (n)	oorsaak
sesupo	sample (n)	monster
sesupo	symbol (n)	simbool
-seta	carve (v)	sny
-setala	indigenous (a)	inheems
setampo	samp (n)	stampmielies
sete	set (n)	stel
setebelamonko	deodorant (n)	reukweermiddel
setebele	fist (n)	vuis
seteisele	starch (n)	stysel
seteishene	station (n)	stasie
seteishene sa sepolesa	police station (n)	polisiekantoor
setempe	postage stamp (n)	posseël
setempe	stamp (n)	seël
setenane	bore (n)	vervelige mens
setene	brick (n)	baksteen
seteraeke	strike (n)	staking
seterata	street (n)	straat
setereke	district (n)	distrik
setereke	region (n)	streek
setetesekoupo	stethoscope (n)	stetoskoop
sethepu	polygamy (n)	poligamie
sethibelo	barrier (n)	versperring
setho	element (n)	element
setho	culture (n)	kultuur
setho	limb (n)	ledemaat
setho	member (n)	lid
sethole	hen (n)	hen
sethole	heifer (n)	vers
sethothokisi	poet (n)	digter
sethoto	fool (n)	dwaas
sethoto	idiot (n)	idioot
-sethoto	stupid (a)	onnosel
sethotsela	ghost (n)	gees
sethunya	rifle (n)	geweer
sethunya	gun (n)	geweer
sethuthuthu	motorcycle (n)	motorfiets
sethwathwa	epilepsy (n)	vallende siekte
setimamollo	fire brigade (n)	brandweer
setjhaba	nation (n)	nasie
-setjhaba	national (a)	nasionaal
setjhu	stew (n)	bredie
setlapedi	ringworm (n)	ringwurm
setloholo	grandson (n)	kleinseun
setloholo	grandchild (n)	kleinkind
setloholo	granddaughter (n)	kleindogter
setlokotsebe	hooligan (n)	skollie
setofo	stove (n)	stoof
setopo	corpse (n)	lyk
setopo sa dibese	bus stop (n)	bushalte
setsha sa ho kampa	camp site (n)	kampeerterrein

S

Sesotho	English	Afrikaans	Sesotho	English	Afrikaans
setshehetso	rail (n)	staaf	-sitisa	obstruct (v)	belemmer
setsheho	laughter (n)	gelag	-sitisa	interrupt (v)	onderbreek
setsheho	laugh (n)	lag	-sitsweng	ground (a)	gemaal
setshwantsho	image (n)	beeld	-soka	row (v)	roei
setshwantsho	figure (n)	figuur	-sokolla	convert (v)	omsit
setshwantsho	parable (n)	gelykenis	-sokoloha	repent (v)	berou hê
setshwantsho	photograph (n)	foto	-sola	moult (v)	verhaar
setshwantsho	diagram (n)	diagram	solotsi	butternut (n)	botterskorsie
setshwantsho	illustration (n)	illustrasie	-soma	ridicule (v)	bespot
setshwantsho	picture (n)	prent	-soma	taunt (v)	uitlok
setshwantsho	drawing (n)	tekening	-soma	mock (v)	bespot
setsi	centre (n)	middel	sonobolomo	sunflower (n)	sonneblom
setsing	centre (n)	middel	Sontaha	Sunday (n)	Sondag
setsomi	hunter (n)	jagter	-sootho	brown (a)	bruin
setsosa	alarm (n)	alarm	sopho	soup (n)	sop
setswalle	relation (n)	verhouding	-soro	brutal (a)	dierlik
setswalle	relationship (n)	verhouding	-soro	rough (a)	ru
setswalle	friendship (n)	vriendskap	soseje	sausage (n)	wors
setswe	elbow (n)	elmboog	-sosobana	crease (v)	kreukel
setulo	chair (n)	stoel	-sosobanya	wriggle (v)	wriemel
setumo	renown (n)	beroemdheid	-sosobanya	wrinkle (v)	plooi
-se utlwisise	misunderstand (v)	misverstaan	-sotha	wring (v)	wring
seviete	serviette (n)	servet	-sotha	deform (v)	vervorm
sewa	epidemic (n)	epidemie	souso	sauce (n)	sous
sewa	plague (n)	plaag	-subuhlellana	overcrowd (v)	oorvol wees
-sewelo	rare (a)	seldsaam	-suha	tan (v)	bruin brand
sewitjhe	switch (n)	skakelaar	supa	seven (n)	sewe
seyantle	export (n)	uitvoer	supamakete	supermarket (n)	supermark
shake	shark (n)	haai	-susumetsa	influence (v)	beïnvloed
-shapa	whip (v)	raps	-susumetsa	force (v)	forseer
shaware	shower (n)	stortbad	-susumetsa	push (v)	stoot
-shemola	chip (v)	'n hap kry	-susutlella	dictate (v)	voorskrywe
-shobela	elope (v)	wegloop	-suthisa	move (v)	skuif
-shwa	die (v)	doodgaan	-suthisa	remove (v)	verwyder
-shwa	perish (v)	omkom	-suthisetsa morao	postpone (v)	uitstel
shwalane	dusk (n)	skemer	sutu	suit (n)	pak
-shweleng	dead (a)	dood	-swabile	ashamed (a)	skaam
-shweleng	deceased (a)	oorlede	sware	brother-in-law (n)	swaer
shweshwe	lily (n)	lelie	-swaswa	joke (v)	gekskeer
-sibolla	discover (v)	ontdek	-swetsa	disappoint (v)	teleurstel
-sidila	iron (v)	stryk	-sweufatsa	bleach (v)	bleik
-sika	border (v)	grens			
sikara	cigar (n)	sigaar	taba	issue (n)	kwessie
-sila	grind (v)	maal	taba	subject (n)	onderwerp
-silafatsa	mess (v)	bemors	taba	affair (n)	saak
silefera	silver (n)	silwer	tabataba	essence (n)	essensie
siling	ceiling (n)	plafon	-tabola	tear (v)	skeur
simbale	cymbal (n)	simbaal	-tabola	rupture (v)	skeur
sinki	sink (n)	opwasbak	-tadima	view (v)	bekyk
-sira	overshadow (v)	oorskadu	-tadima	look (v)	kyk
-sireletsa	defend (v)	verdedig	-tadima	gaze (v)	staar
-sireletsa	protect (v)	beskerm	-tadimeha	seem (v)	skyn
-sireletsa	shield (v)	beskerm	tae	tie (n)	das
-sireletsang	defensive (a)	verdedigend	taelo	order (n)	bevel
sirilamunu	lemon (n)	suurlemoen	taelo	prescription (n)	voorskrif
sisetene	cistern (n)	waterbak	taelo ya lekgotla	decree (n)	verordening
-sisinyeha	move (v)	beweeg	taemane	diamond (n)	diamant
-sisinyehang	moving (a)	roerend	tafole	table (n)	tafel
-sitang	impossible (a)	onmoontlik	-taha	intoxicate (v)	bedwelm
-sitelwa	offend (v)	aanstoot gee	-tahang	alcoholic (a)	alkoholies

Sesotho	English	Afrikaans	Sesotho	English	Afrikaans
tahi	alcohol (n)	alkohol	teleko	exile (n)	verbanning
tahi	liquor (n)	drank	-tellang	insubordinate (a)	ongehoorsaam
-tahilwe	drunk (a)	dronk	-tellehang	undignified (a)	onwaardig
tahlehelo	loss (n)	verlies	tema	paragraph (n)	paragraaf
takatso	desire (n)	begeerte	temana	verse (n)	vers
takatso	urge (n)	drang	temoso	signal (n)	sinjaal
takatso	wish (n)	wens	-temothuo	agricultural (a)	landboukundig
takatso ya dijo	appetite (n)	eetlus	temothuo	agriculture (n)	landbou
-tala	rude (a)	onbeskof	-tempa	stamp (v)	bestempel
-tala	immodest (a)	onbeskeie	temperetjha	temperature (n)	temperatuur
-tala	uncooked (a)	ongaar	-tena	bore (v)	verveel
-tala	uncivilised (a)	onbeskaaf	-tena	annoy (v)	vies maak
-tala	raw (a)	rou	-tenang	annoying (a)	ergerlik
-tala; -putswa	blue (a)	blou	tenese	tennis (n)	tennis
-tala selemo sohle	evergreen (a)	bladhoudend	tente	tent (n)	tent
talente	talent (n)	talent	tentere	tender (n)	tender
tallo	ambush (n)	hinderlaag	-tenya	stout (a)	geset
tamati	tomato (n)	tamatie	-tenya	thick (a)	dik
-tamolohang	elastic (a)	rekbaar	-tepeletsa	depress (v)	neerdruk
tamoloho	elastic (n)	rek	tepeletso	depression (n)	bedruktheid
-tamukanya	mutilate (v)	skend	-teraeka	strike (v)	staak
tanka	tank (n)	tenk	terata	fence (n)	draad
tapole	potato (n)	aartappel	terata	wire (n)	draad
tataiso ya thelefone	telephone directory (n)	telefoongids	terata e metsu	barbed wire (n)	doringdraad
tatamolebo	tendril (n)	rankie	terekesutu	tracksuit (n)	sweetpak
-tatelano	chronological (a)	chronologies	terene	train (n)	trein
tatelano	sequence (n)	reeks	terene e lebelo	express (n)	sneltrein
tatso	flavour (n)	geur	terete	tart (n)	tert
tatso	taste (n)	smaak	terompeta	trumpet (n)	trompet
tau	lion (n)	leeu	-teteaneng	dense (a)	dig
tawana	lioness (n)	leeuwyfie	-teteanya	thicken (v)	dik maak
-teana	meet (v)	ontmoet	-tetebela	sink (v)	sink
teano	meeting (n)	ontmoeting	-tetetsa	bruise (v)	kneus
-tebela	sack (v)	afdank	thaabe	hiccough (n)	hik
-tebela	box (v)	boks	thaba	mountain (n)	berg
-tebela	dismiss (v)	ontslaan	-thabile	glad (a)	bly
tebelo	dismissal (n)	ontslag	thabo	pleasure (n)	plesier
tebelo	vigilance (n)	waaksaamheid	thaere	tyre (n)	buiteband
-tebileng	deep (a)	diep	-thahasella	volunteer (v)	vrywillig onderneem
tebiso	reference (n)	verwysing	-thahasellang	keen (a)	toegewyd
teboho	gratitude (n)	dankbaarheid	thaho	kick (n)	skop
tee	tea (n)	tee	thaka ya leihlo	iris (n)	iris
tefello	tariff (n)	tarief	thakgisa	peg (n)	pen
tefello ya leeto	fare (n)	reisgeld	-thakgisa	peg (v)	vaspen
tefiso	fine (n)	boete	-thakgisa sefapanong	crucify (v)	kruisig
tefo	payment (n)	betaling	-thalatsa	glance (v)	vlugtig kyk
-tegeniki	technical (a)	tegnies	thaole	towel (n)	handdoek
-teisela	starch (v)	styf	thapallo	contour (n)	kontoer
-teka	lay (v)	dek	thapallo	parallel (n)	parallel
tekanyi	tape measure (n)	maatband	thapama	afternoon (n)	middag
tekanyo	measure (n)	maat	thapedi	plea (n)	pleidooi
tekanyo ya sehlare	dose (n)	dosis	thapelo	prayer (n)	gebed
tekenikone	technikon (n)	tegnikon	-thapileng	tame (a)	mak
tekenoloji	technology (n)	tegnologie	-thapisa	tame (v)	tem
tekesi	taxi (n)	taxi	thapiso	discipline (n)	dissipline
tekete	ticket (n)	kaartjie	thapo	plait (n)	vlegsel
tekete ya ho paka	parking ticket (n)	parkeerkaartjie	thapollo	exercise (n)	oefening
teko	attempt (n)	poging	tharo	three (n)	drie
teko	test (n)	toets	-thata	hard (a)	hard
teko	trial (n)	verhoor	-thata	difficult (a)	moeilik

T	Sesotho	English	Afrikaans	Sesotho	English	Afrikaans
	-thata	tough (a)	taai	thothokiso	poem (n)	gedig
	-thata	solid (a)	vas	thothomantle	sewerage (n)	riolering
	thato	will (n)	wil	-thothomela	shiver (v)	bewe
	-thea	erect (v)	oprig	-thothomela	tremble (v)	bewe
	thebe	shield (n)	skild	thoto	luggage (n)	bagasie
	-thekesela	stagger (v)	slinger	-thotseng	quiet (a)	stil
	thekiso	sale (n)	uitverkoping	thuana	bedpan (n)	bedpan
	theko	price (n)	prys	-thuha	burgle (v)	inbreek
	thekoise	turquoise (n)	turkoois	thuhlo	giraffe (n)	kameelperd
	thelebeshene	television (n)	televisie	-thulana	collide (v)	bots
	theledi	kneecap (n)	knieskyf	thulano	collision (n)	botsing
	thelefone	telephone (n)	telefoon	thulosi	tool (n)	werktuig
	-thella	slide (v)	gly	-thumisehileng	fine (a)	fyn
	-thellang	slippery (a)	glibberig	-thunya	bloom (v)	blom
	thempone	tampon (n)	tampon	-thunya	fuse (v)	uitbrand
	theo	principle (n)	beginsel	-thunya	shoot (v)	skiet
	-theoha	descend (v)	daal	-thunya	fade (v)	verbleik
	theoho	descent (n)	daling	thunyo	shot (n)	skoot
	-theolela	discount (v)	aftrek	thupelo	instruction (n)	onderrig
	theolelo	discount (n)	afslag	-thusa	assist (v)	bystaan
	thepa	stock (n)	voorraad	-thusa	help (v)	help
	thepa ya ntlo	furniture (n)	meubels	-thusa	aid (v)	help
	thepe	tap (n)	kraan	-thusa	relieve (v)	verlig
	-thesela	bump (v)	stamp	-thusang	helpful (a)	behulpsaam
	-theteha	roll (v)	rol	thuso	assistance (n)	bystand
	thethefatsi	drug (n)	dwelm	thuso	help (n)	hulp
	-thetsa	deceive (v)	bedrieg	thuso	aid (n)	hulp
	-thetsa	flatter (v)	vlei	thuso	relief (n)	verligting
	thetso	fraud (n)	bedrog	thuso ya pele	first aid (n)	noodhulp
	thetso	deceit (n)	bedrog	thuto	lecture (n)	lesing
	thetso	pretext (n)	voorwendsel	thuto	lesson (n)	les
	-thibaneng ditsebe	naughty (a)	stout	thuto	education (n)	opvoeding
	-thibela	block (v)	blokkeer	thuto	sermon (n)	preek
	-thibela	restrain (v)	beperk	thuto ya dinaledi	astronomy (n)	sterrekunde
	-thibela	ban (people) (v)	inperk	thuto ya lefatshe	geography (n)	aardrykskunde
	-thibela	prevent (v)	voorkom	thuto ya puo	grammar (n)	grammatika
	-thibela	ban (things) (v)	verbied	thutswana mollo	match (n)	vuurhoutjie
	-thibela	prohibit (v)	verbied	tieho	delay (n)	vertraging
	-thibela modumo	acoustic (a)	akoesties	-tiileng	firm (a)	ferm
	thibelo	prevention (n)	voorkoming	-tiileng	sure (a)	seker
	thibelo ya pelehi	contraception (n)	voorbehoeding	-tiileng	stable (a)	stabiel
	-thibetse	banned (people) (a)	ingeperk	-tiileng	tight (a)	styf
	-thibetse	banned (things) (a)	verbode	-tiisa	justify (v)	regverdig
	thietha	theatre (n)	teater	-tiisa	tighten (v)	span
	thipa	penknife (n)	knipmes	-tiisa	fasten (v)	vasmaak
	thipa	knife (n)	mes	-tiisetsa	ensure (v)	verseker
	thobeho	fracture (n)	breuk	-tiisetsang	courageous (a)	moedig
	thollo	grain (n)	graan	tiisetso	courage (n)	moed
	tholo	kudu (n)	koedoe	tikoloho	background (n)	agtergrond
	tholwana	nut (n)	neut	tikoloho	environment (n)	omgewing
	tholwana	fruit (n)	vrug	-tima	extinguish (v)	blus
	tholwana	effect (n)	uitwerking	tinare	dinner (n)	hoofmaal
	tholwana ya mohlware	olive (n)	olyf	titjhere	teacher (n)	onderwyser
	thomo	piano (n)	klavier	tjabelo	slap (n)	klap
	thomo	mission (n)	sending	tjale	shawl (n)	tjalie
	thomo	organ (n)	orrel	-tjamela	stare (v)	staar
	-thonya	pick (v)	uitkies	tjamelo	stare (n)	gestaar
	thoriso	praise (n)	lof	-tjeka	dance (v)	dans
	-thotha	cart (v)	karwei	-tjha	new (a)	nuut
	-thothokisa	recite (v)	opsê	-tjha	fresh (a)	vars

Sesotho	English	Afrikaans	Sesotho	English	Afrikaans	T
tjhabo ya letsatsi	sunrise (n)	sonop	-tlatlapa	abuse (v)	misbruik	
tjhadimo	look (n)	blik	-tlatlapa	ill-treat (v)	mishandel	
tjhadimo	view (n)	uitsig	-tlatlapa	antagonise (v)	vyandig maak	
tjhafo	shaft (n)	skag	tlatlapo	affliction (n)	beproewing	
tjhankane	prison (n)	gevangenis	tlatlapo	abuse (n)	misbruik	
tjhankane	jail (n)	tronk	-tlatsa	second (v)	sekondeer	
tjhatene	chutney (n)	blatjang	-tlatsa	fill (v)	vol maak	
tjhefo	poison (n)	gif	-tle	handsome (a)	aantreklik	
tjhefo	venom (n)	venyn	-tle	fair (a)	billik	
-tjheha	set (v)	stel	-tle	pretty (a)	mooi	
-tjheka	dig (v)	spit	-tle	beautiful (a)	pragtig	
tjheke	cheque (n)	tjek	tlelaemete	climate (n)	klimaat	
-tjhekolla	unearth (v)	opgrawe	tlelarinete	clarinet (n)	klarinet	
tjhelete	money (n)	geld	tlelase	class (n)	klas	
tjhelete	cash (n)	kontant	tlelatjhe	clutch (n)	koppelaar	
tjhelete e bolokilweng	savings (n)	spaargeld	tlelenike	clinic (n)	kliniek	
tjhelete ya pampiri	banknote (n)	banknoot	tlelereke	clerk (n)	klerk	
tjhelo	cello (n)	tjello	tleloko	clock (n)	horlosie	
tjhemele	chimney (n)	skoorsteen	-tlepetsa	stone (v)	met klippe gooi	
-tjhentjhana	alternate (v)	afwissel	-tlerola	aloud (adv)	hardop	
-tjhesa	hot (a)	warm	-tletleba	complain (v)	kla	
-tjhesang	warm (a)	warm	tletlebo	grievance (n)	grief	
tjhese	cheese (n)	kaas	tletlebo	complaint (n)	klagte	
-tjhesehelang	enthusiastic (a)	geesdriftig	-tletse	full (a)	vol	
tjheseho	interest (n)	belang	-tletsetletse	plenty (a)	volop	
tjheseho	enthusiasm (n)	geesdrif	tlhabo	injection (n)	inspuiting	
tjhesetso	arson (n)	brandstigting	tlhahala	tumour (n)	gewas	
tjhilise	chilli (n)	brandrissie	tlhahiso	proposal (n)	voorstel	
tjhipise	chip (potato) (n)	skyfie	tlhahlobo	interview (n)	onderhoud	
-tjhitja	round (a)	rond	tlhaho	origin (n)	oorsprong	
tjhoko	chalk (n)	kryt	tlhako	hoof (n)	hoef	
tjhokolete	chocolate (n)	sjokolade	Tlhakubele	March (n)	Maart	
tjhopose	chop (n)	tjop	tlhale	fibre (n)	vesel	
-tjhorisa	adapt (v)	aanpas	tlhalo	divorce (n)	egskeiding	
tjhwehletjhwehle	rattle (n)	ratel	tlhaloso	description (n)	beskrywing	
-tjhwehletsa	jingle (v)	klingel	tlhapa	insult (n)	belediging	
-tjhwehletsa	rattle (v)	ratel	tlhapa	bawdy (a)	onkuis	
tjotjo	bribe (n)	omkoopprys	-tlhapa	vulgar (a)	vulgêr	
-tla	will (v)	sal	tlhapa	curse (n)	vloek	
-tlabola	scorch (v)	skroei	tlhaphohelo	recovery (n)	herstel	
-tlabola	singe (v)	skroei	tlhapi	fish (n)	vis	
tlakasela	shudder (v)	sidder	tlhapinohana	eel (n)	paling	
tlala	famine (n)	hongersnood	tlhase	spark (n)	vonk	
tlala	hunger (n)	honger	tlhaselo	invasion (n)	inval	
-tlaleha	report (v)	berig	tlhatsuong	laundry (n)	wassery	
tlaleho	report (n)	verslag	tlhobaelo	insomnia (n)	slaaploosheid	
-tlama	tie (v)	bind	tlhodisano	competition (n)	wedstryd	
-tlama	chain (v)	vasketting	tlhodiso	pip (n)	pit	
-tlama terata	wire (v)	bedraad	tlhokeho	necessity (n)	noodsaaklikheid	
-tlamehile	must (v)	moet	tlhoko	lack (n)	gebrek	
tlami	hyphen (n)	koppelteken	tlhoko	nipple (n)	tepel	
tlamo	bond (n)	band	tlhoko	teat (n)	tepel	
tlamo	obligation (n)	verpligting	tlhokomelo	maintenance (n)	onderhoud	
-tlanya	type (v)	tik	tlhokomelo	caution (n)	versigtigheid	
tlasa	under (prep)	onder	-tlholeho	failure (n) *	mislukking	
-tlase	down (prep)	af	tlholo	defeat (n)	nederlaag	
-tlase	low (a)	laag	tlholo	triumph (n)	triomf	
-tlase	below (prep)	onder	tlhompho	honour (n)	eer	
-tlase hofeta	lower (a)	laer	tlhompho	respect (n)	respek	
-tlatlapa	rob (v)	beroof	tlhoro	summit (n)	kruin	

T Sesotho	English	Afrikaans	Sesotho	English	Afrikaans
tlhoro	peak (n)	piek	-tsamaisa	control (v)	beheer
-tlhotla	squeeze (v)	druk	-tsamaisa	deliver (v)	aflewer
tlhware	python (n)	luislang	tsamaiso	procedure (n)	prosedure
tlhweko	cleanliness (n)	sindelikheid	-tsamaya	march (v)	marsjeer
-tlisa	bring (v)	bring	-tsamaya	walk (v)	loop
-tlo	come (v)	kom	-tsamaya	move (v)	trek
-tlohela	leave (v)	laat	-tsamaya ka	tiptoe (v)	op die tone loop
-tlohela	omit (v)	weglaat	ditsetsekwame		
tlokotsi	emergency (n)	noodgeval	-tsamayang	moving (a)	bewegend
-tlola	bounce (v)	opspring	-tseba	recognise (v)	herken
-tlola	skip (v)	oorslaan	-tseba	identify (v)	identifiseer
-tlola	trespass (v)	oortree	-tseba	know (v)	weet
-tlola	skip (v)	touspring	-tsebahala	characteristic (a)	kenmerkend
-tlola	jump (v)	spring	-tsebahalang	prominent (a)	prominent
-tlola	spring (v)	spring	-tsebahalang	well-known (a)	welbekend
-tlolatlola	hop (v)	hop	-tsebang	crack (a)	puik
tlolo	jump (n)	sprong	tsebe	ear (n)	oor
-tlosa	subtract (v)	aftrek	-tsebetutu	deaf (a)	doof
-tlotlisa	applaud (v)	toejuig	tsebe-ya-kolobe	arum lily (n)	varkoor
-tlotsa	anoint (v)	salf	-tsebisa	introduce (v)	voorstel
tlotsa ka kerisi	grease (v)	smeer	-tsebisa	announce (v)	aankondig
tlou	elephant (n)	olifant	tsebisa	acquaint (v)	bekend wees
-tlwaela	acquaint (v)	bekend wees	-tsebisa	notify (v)	kennis gee
-tlwaelehileng	plain (a)	gewoon	-tsebisa	inform (v)	meedeel
-tlwaelehileng	common (a)	gewoon	tsebiso	announcement (n)	aankondiging
tlwaelo	habit (n)	gewoonte	tsebiso	information (n)	inligting
-tobileng	direct (a)	direk	tsebiso	notice (n)	kennisgewing
-toboketsa	emphasise (v)	beklemtoon	tsebiso	introduction (n)	voorstelling
toboketso	emphasis (n)	klem	tsebo	knowledge (n)	kennis
toka	justice (n)	geregtigheid	-tse itseng	several (a)	verskeie
-toka	just (a)	regverdig	-tseka	demand (v)	eis
tokisetso	preparation (n)	voorbereiding	tsekahare	index (n)	indeks
tokisetso ya metse e	urbanisation (n)	verstedeliking	-tsekela	wander (v)	dwaal
meholo			-tsekela	giddy (a)	duiselig
tokiso	improvement (n)	verbetering	-tsekela	loiter (v)	rondslenter
tokodiso	accent (n)	aksent	-tsekisana	dispute (v)	betwis
tokodiso	statement (n)	verklaring	tsekisano	dispute (n)	onenigheid
tokollo	release (n)	loslating	tsekiso	controversy (n)	twispunt
tokollo	acquittal (n)	vryspraak	tseko	contest (n)	wedstryd
tokoloho	freedom (n)	vryheid	tsela	road (n)	pad
-tola	bath (v)	bad	tsela	way (n)	pad
-tola	shower (v)	stort	tsela	system (n)	stelsel
-toloka	interpret (v)	vertolk	tsela e potolohang	deviation (n)	ompad
toloko	interpreter (n)	tolk	tsela e potolohang	detour (n)	omweg
tomo	bridle (n)	toom	tselana e kenang	driveway (n)	inrit
tomoso	yeast (n)	gis	tselanyana	path (n)	pad
-tonanahadi	enormous (a)	tamaai	tselathoko	pavement (n)	sypaadjie
tonki	donkey (n)	donkie	-tseparela	clasp (v)	vasklem
-topa	darn (v)	stop	tsetsepelo	stand (n)	stand
toro	dream (n)	droom	-tshaba	afraid (a)	bang
torofeie	cactus (n)	kaktus	-tshaba	apprehensive (a)	bang
torofeie	prickly pear (n)	turksvy	-tshaba	dread (v)	vrees
torong	bunion (n)	knokkeleelt	-tshaba	fear (v)	vrees
toropo	town (n)	dorp	-tshabehang	ghastly (a)	aaklig
tosene	dozen (n)	dosyn	-tshabehang	ominous (a)	onheilspellend
-totobetse	conspicuous (a)	opvallend	-tshabehang	terrible (a)	vreeslik
-totobetse	obvious (a)	vanselfsprekend	tshabo	fear (n)	vrees
-totobetseng	express (a)	uitdruklik	tshaeno	signature (n)	handtekening
totomana	dune (n)	duin	tshebedisano	co-operation (n)	samewerking
tsa ho ngola	stationery (n)	skryfbehoeftes	tshebediso	use (n)	gebruik

Sesotho	English	Afrikaans	Sesotho	English	Afrikaans
tshebediso	consumption (n)	verbruik	tshomo	folklore (n)	volksoorleweringe
tshebetso	activity (n)	bedrywigheid	-tshosa	frighten (v)	skrikmaak
-tshedisa	console (v)	opbeur	-tshosa haholo	terrify (v)	verskrik
-tsheha	laugh (v)	lag	tshosobano	crease (n)	kreukel
-tshehadi	female (a)	vroulik	tshubuhlellano	influx (n)	instroming
-tshehetsa	support (v)	ondersteun	tshukudu	rhinoceros (n)	renoster
-tshehetsa	back (v)	steun	tshupa	weevil (n)	kalander
-tshekalletseng	horizontal (a)	horisontaal	tshupapaka	timetable (n)	rooster
-tshela	cross (v)	kruis	tshuthiso	removal (n)	verwydering
-tshela	pour (v)	skink	tshutshu	steak (n)	biefstuk
-tshela sekontiri	tar (v)	teer	tshutshu	fillet (n)	filet
tshelela	six (n)	ses	-tshwaedisa	immunise (v)	immuniseer
tshenyo	corruption (n)	bedorwenheid	-tshwaedisitswe	immune (a)	onvatbaar
tshenyo	harm (n)	skade	-tshwaetsa	infect (v)	besmet
tshenyo	damage (n)	skade	-tshwaetsang	infectious (a)	besmetlik
tsheola	sleet (n)	ysreën	-tshwaetsang	contagious (a)	aansteeklik
-tshepa	hope (v)	hoop	-tshwana	alike (a)	gelyk
-tshepa	rely (v)	staatmaak	-tshwanang	same (a)	dieselfde
-tshepahalang	trustworthy (a)	betroubaar	-tshwanang	similar (a)	eenders
-tshepahalang	reliable (a)	betroubaar	-tshwanelang	convenient (a)	gerieflik
-tshepahalang	faithful (a)	getrou	tshwanelo	duty (n)	plig
-tshepahalang	honest (a)	eerlik	-tshwanelwa	deserve (v)	verdien
tshepahalo	loyalty (n)	lojaliteit	tshwano	likeness (n)	ooreenkoms
tshepe	bell (n)	klok	-tshwantsha	draw (v)	teken
tshepe	metal (n)	metaal	-tshwantsha	illustrate (v)	illustreer
tshepe	springbok (n)	springbok	-tshwantsha	photograph (v)	fotografeer
tshepe	iron (n)	yster	tshwantshiso	play (n)	toneelstuk
-tshepehang	loyal (a)	lojaal	-tshwara	detain (v)	aanhou
tshepe ya pere	horseshoe (n)	hoefyster	-tshwara	seize (v)	gryp
-tshepisa	promise (v)	belowe	-tshwara	arrest (v)	in hegtenis neem
tshepiso	promise (n)	belofte	-tshwara	handle (v)	hanteer
tshepo	hope (n)	hoop	-tshwara	catch (v)	vang
-tshesane	narrow (a)	smal	-tshwara	grasp (v)	gryp
-tshesane	slender (a)	tingerig	-tshwara	treat (v)	behandel
-tshesane	slim (a)	skraal	-tshwara	contain (v)	bevat
tshila	filth (n)	vuilgoed	-tshwara	hold (v)	hou
tshilafatso	pollution (n)	besoedeling	-tshwarehileng	engaged (a)	beset
tshimo	field (n)	veld	-tshwarela	excuse (v)	verontskuldig
tshireletso	defence (n)	verdediging	-tshwarela	forgive (v)	vergewe
tshisimoso	awe (n)	eerbied	-tshwarela	pardon (v)	vergewe
tshisinyeho	convulsion (n)	rukking	tshwarelo	forgiveness (n)	vergifnis
tshisinyeho ya lefatshe	earthquake (n)	aardbewing	tshwarelo	apology (n)	verskoning
tshitelo	offence (n)	oortreding	tshwarelo	excuse (n)	ekskuus
tshitiso	obstruction (n)	belemmernis	tshwaro	detention (n)	aanhouding
-tshitiso	hindrance (n)	hindernis	tshwaro	hold (n)	vat
tshitiso	interruption (n)	onderbreking	tshwaro	treatment (n)	behandeling
tshito	obstacle (n)	hindernis	-tshwasa	fish (v)	visvang
tshitshidi	bedbug (n)	weeluis	tshwaso ya ditlhapi	fishing (n)	visvang
Tshitwe	December (n)	Desember	-tshwaya	mark (v)	merk
-tsho	black (a)	swart	-tshwaya	tick (v)	tik
-tshoha	panic (v)	paniekerig wees	-tshwaya dintlha	score (v)	punte aanteken
tshoho	terror (n)	terreur	-tshwela	spit (v)	spoeg
tshokelo	threat (n)	dreigement	tshwele	cotton (n)	katoen
tshokoloho	reform (n)	hervorming	tshwele	fishmoth (n)	vismot
tshokoloho	conversion (n)	omsetting	tshwele	thread (n)	draad
-tsholla	spill (v)	mors	tshwele	roughage (n)	vesel
tshomo	fiction (n)	fiksie	tshwelesa	groin (n)	lies
tshomo	fable (n)	fabel	tshwene	baboon (n)	bobbejaan
tshomo	myth (n)	mite	tshwene	monkey (n)	aap
tshomo	ridicule (n)	spottery	tshwetso	disappointment (n)	teleurstelling

Z

Sesotho	English	Afrikaans	Sesotho	English	Afrikaans
-tsietsa	embarrass (v)	verleë maak	tumello	sanction (n)	sanksie
-tsikinya	tickle (v)	kielie	tumello	permit (n)	permit
-tsikitlanya meno	gnash (v)	kners	tumello	approval (n)	goedkeuring
-tsilatsila	hesitate (v)	aarsel	tumelo	faith (n)	geloof
-tsilatsilo	hesitation (n)	aarseling	tumelo	consent (n)	instemming
-tsillama	smirk (v)	grynslag	tumelo	religion (n)	godsdiens
-tsipa	pinch (v)	knyp	-tumileng	famous (a)	beroemd
-tsitlama	grin (v)	gryns	-tumileng	popular (a)	gewild
tsitlamo	grin (n)	grynslag	-turang	costly (a)	kosbaar
-tsitsipaneng	stiff (a)	styf	-turu	expensive (a)	duur
tsitsipano ya mohlahare	tetanus (n)	klem in die kake	-tutla	jerk (v)	ruk
			tweba	mouse (n)	muis
-tsitsitseng	permanent (a)	permanent			
-tsofala	age (v)	verouder	-utlwa	hear (v)	hoor
-tsofetseng	aged (a)	oud	-utlwa bohloko	suffer (v)	ly
-tsohletsohle	miscellaneous (a)	allerlei	-utlwahala	audible (a)	hoorbaar
-tsoka	wag (v)	swaai	-utlwahalang	reasonable (a)	redelik
-tsokotsa	rinse (v)	uitspoel	-utlwahatsa	pronounce (v)	uitspreek
-tsoma	hunt (v)	jag	-utlwang	sensitive (a)	gevoelig
-tsosa	awake (v)	ontwaak	-utlwisisa	understand (v)	verstaan
-tsosa	arouse (v)	opwek	-utswa	loot (v)	plunder
-tsuba	smoke (v)	rook	-utswa	steal (v)	steel
-tsukutla	shake (v)	skud	-utulla	explore (v)	verken
tsuonyana	chicken (n)	hoender			
-tswa	exit (v)	uitgaan	violene	violin (n)	viool
-tswakaneng	synthetic (a)	sinteties	visa	visa (n)	visum
tswalo	birth (n)	geboorte			
-tswa madi	bleed (v)	bloei	-wa	fall (v)	val
tswekere	sugar (n)	suiker	walete	wallet (n)	notetas
tswekeresekgabisi	icing (n)	versiersuiker	watjhe	watch (n)	horlosie
-tswelang pele	progressive (a)	progressief	wena	you (pron)	jy
-tswelang pele	lasting (a)	voortdurend			
-tswela pele	last (v)	voortduur	x-rei	x-ray (n)	x-straal
-tswela pele	continue (v)	vervolg			
-tswela pele	progress (v)	vooruitgaan	-ya	go (v)	gaan
-tswela pele	proceed (v)	voortgaan	-ya	belong (v)	behoort
tswelopele	advancement (n)	vordering	ya-	its (pron)	sy
tswelopele	civilisation (n)	beskawing	ya-	of (prep)	van
tswelopele	advance (n)	vooruitgang	-ya kgweding	menstruate (v)	menstrueer
tswelopele	progress (n)	vooruitgang	Ya matla ohle	Almighty (n)	Almagtige
-tuba	oppress (v)	onderdruk	ya molato	culprit (n)	skuldige
-tuka	alight (a)	aan die brand	ya tsamayang ka maoto	pedestrian (n)	voetganger
-tula	pound (v)	fynstamp			
tulo	place (n)	plek	yena	he (pron)	hy
tulo ya mokgabo	art gallery (n)	kunsgalery	yena	she (pron)	sy
tulo ya tswalo	birthplace (n)	geboorteplek	yena	him (pron)	hom
tumaelo	murmur (n)	gemurmel	yena	her (pron)	haar
tumannotshi	vowel (n)	klinker	yunibesithi	university (n)	universiteit
tumediso	salute (n)	saluut	yunifomo	uniform (n)	uniform
tumellano	agreement (n)	ooreenkoms			
tumellano	pact (n)	verdrag	zaelofone	xylophone (n)	xilofoon
tumello	admission (n)	toelating	zipo	zipper (n)	ritssluiter
tumello	permission (n)	toestemming	zuu	zoo (n)	dieretuin

TSWANA

Geographically, Tswana is the most widely spoken language in southern Africa. It is spoken by the people of Botswana, the northeastern Cape, the central and western Free State and the western Transvaal.

Tswana is a member of the Sotho language group. It consists of different dialect clusters that include different dialects. The southern dialect cluster includes the Rolong, Tlhaping and Tlharo dialects, the eastern cluster the Kwena and Kgatla dialects, the central cluster the Hurutshe dialect, the western cluster the Ngwaketse, Kwena and Kgatla (Botswana) dialects and the northern cluster the Ngwato dialect.

It is important to remember that, in common with other southern African indigenous languages, the structure of Tswana — a tonal language — is very different to Western languages. Tswana is governed by the noun, which is split into various classes. It is what is known as an agglutinating language (a combination of simple word elements to express a specific meaning), with the many suffixes and prefixes used in sentence construction causing sound changes.

PRONUNCIATION

There are four factors that govern the correct pronunciation of Tswana words: speech sounds, syllable structure, tone and length. These combine to form the sound system of the language.

SPEECH SOUNDS

These can be divided into two main categories: vowels and consonants.

Vowels are spoken with the mouth open and without any obstruction by the tongue. The basic vowels − and their approximate sounds − are:

i in **moriri** (*hair*), similar to the English *it*
e in **pele** (*in front*), similar to the English *we*
ê in **selêpe** (*axe*), similar to the Afrikaans *sê*
a in **nama** (*meat*), similar to the English *far*
o in **noko** (*porcupine*), similar to the Afrikaans *lojaal*
ô in **tôrô** (*dream*), similar to the Afrikaans *môre*
u in **kutu** (*stem*) similar to the English *bull*

Vowels pronounced with a higher tongue position may influence how those with a lower tongue position are pronounced.

Consonants are pronounced by using the tongue and lips to block partially or completely the exhalation of air as the sound is made. Different sounds are produced by blocking the air at different points in the mouth. These consonants are classified according to breath control and place of articulation. The consonants, and their approximate sounds, are:

b in **bana** (*children*), similar to the English *able*
d in **madi** (*blood*), similar to the English *doll*
f in **lofofa** (*feather*), similar to the English *after*
g in **segagabi** (*reptile*), similar to the Afrikaans *gaap*
h in **mohumi** (*rich man*), similar to the English *have*
j in **sejo** (*food*), similar to the Cape Flats Afrikaans *jy*
k in **phoka** (*dew*), similar to the English *back*
kg in **dikgomo** (*cattle*), both letters are sounded (no equivalent)
kh in **khiba** (*apron*), aspirated, similar to the English *kindle*
l in **molala** (*neck*), similar to the English *lay*
m in **modi** (*root*), similar to the English *him*
n in **namane** (*calf*), similar to the English *and*
ng in **ngaka** (*doctor*), similar to the English *linger*
ny in **monyadi** (*bridegroom*), similar to the English *Kenya*
p in **pula** (*rain*), similar to the English *lip*
ph in **phala** (*impala*), aspirated, similar to the English *pull*
r in **lerapo** (*bone*), similar to the English *red*
s in **mosese** (*dress*), similar to the English *dress*
š in **mošabele** (*karree tree*), similar to the English *shilling*

t in **tau** (*lion*), similar to the English *at*
th in **thipa** (*knife*), aspirated, similar to the English *till*
tl in **tladi** (*lightning*), similar to the English *little*
tlh in **tlhako** (*hoof*), (no local equivalent, but similar to the Welsh *Llewellyn*)
ts in **letsatsi** (*sun*), similar to the English *sits*
tš in **ntšwa** (*dog*), similar to the English *chirp*
tsh in **tshipi** (*iron*), aspirated, similar to the English *chant*
tšh in **setšhaba** (*a clan of people*), aspirated, similar to the English *church*
w in **nawa** (*bean*), similar to the English *wet*
y in **bolaya** (*kill*), similar to the English *yes*

It is of the utmost importance to distinguish between the aspirated (enunciated with a rush of breath following) and unaspirated consonants in Tswana. They must be regarded as separate speech sounds. Compare the following:
phela! (*live!*)
pela (*rock rabbit*)

Also note that the [w] sound may be used with many of the above sounds. When [w] follows a speech sound, it should be pronounced with rounded lips, and not as a separate sound:
gw in **segwagwa** (*frog*), which approximates the vibration of the Malmesbury [r]
kgw in **kgwale** (*partridge*), similar to the above, but with the [k] sounded quickly too

SYLLABLE STRUCTURE

In most instances the syllable in Tswana ends in a vowel, for example:
se-ru-ru-be-le (*butterfly*)

Where syllabic consonants occur, the unstressed vowel is left out, for example:
molelo: mollo, i.e. **mo-le-lo: mo-l-lo** (*fire*)

The following types of syllables occur in Tswana, where C indicates consonant and V vowel:

-CV- syllables, for example:
pho-lo-go-lo (*wild animal*)
mo-sa-di-mo-go-lo (*old woman*)

-V- syllables, for example:
le-e (*egg*)
le-i-no (*tooth*)

-CCV- syllables, for example:
thwa-ne (*lynx*)
ngwa-na (*child*)

-C- syllables, for example:
m-ma-la (*colour*)
go-l-la (*to cry*)
mo-n-na (*man*)
ba-a-n-nys-tsa (*they despise me*)

TONE

In Tswana each syllable of a word has a specific tone – a specific pitch of voice with which it is pronounced. This is one of the most important factors governing pronunciation, and if not used correctly can cause misunderstanding. The entire meaning of a word can be changed by the mere tone of voice with which it is pronounced, for example:

go rêma (*to chop*) against
go rêma (*to become as thick as milk*),
where the syllable **-rê** of the first word is pronounced with a higher pitch than in the second.

There is no golden rule governing tone in Tswana; you will have to rely on hearing the words being correctly pronounced by the Tswana people themselves.

LENGTH

The length of time taken to pronounce a syllable varies according to the usage. In Tswana, the second last syllable of an individual word or that of the last word in a sentence is longer (indicated phonetically by a colon after the long syllable), for example:

Se:ga (*cut*)
Tsama:ya (*go*)
Sega na:ma (*cut the meat*)
Bana bale ba batla mon:na (*those children are looking for the man*)

TSWANA WORDS

Tswana uses a method known to linguists as 'disjunctive', which means that a word consists of several units. For example, the conjugated verb, **ke a tsamaya** (*I am going*) consists of three different segments.

Language experts call the separate words orthographic (or practical), and the complete words, which consist of at least a root or a root plus other constituent parts (prefix and/or suffix), linguistic. Thus in the example:

Monna o ja bogobe (*the man eats porridge*)
we see four words. But what appears as four separate words are not necessarily separate linguistic words, which in fact are made up of certain groups of syllables that have been separated. In the example there are, in fact, only three linguistic words:

monna, **o ja** and **bogobe**

In Tswana, these linguistic words have a specific independent meaning, consisting of a root, that can be extended by adding a prefix and/or a suffix, and which has a specific function when used in sentences.

The root is the basic part of a word denoting its basic meaning. All of the following words, for example, relate to people (*tho*). As the prefix changes, so does the meaning, all of which, however, are linked to the central meaning of 'people'.

motho (*a person*)
batho (*people*)
setho (*humanely*)
botho (*humanity*)
mothofatsa (*humanise*)
mothonyana (*insignificant person*)

The word that conveys the consistent reference to the concept of 'human' is **tho** – the root in each example. The additional elements are the prefixes and suffixes added to extend the meaning.

In Tswana, the following word classes can be distinguished: noun, pronoun, adjective, relative, quantitative, enumerative, possessive, verb, copulative, adverb, ideophone, conjunctive and interjective.

These in turn may be classified into the following main categories:
Substantives functioning as the subject or object in a sentence (noun, pronoun, possessive, adjective, relative and enumerative);
Predicatives acting as predicates of a sentence (verb, auxiliary, copulative and ideophone);
Qualificatives serving to qualify substantives (adjective, relative, enumerative, possessive, quantitative and demonstrative);
Descriptives modifying predicatives (adverb and ideophone);
Conjunctives (conjunctions); and
Interjectives (interjections).

NOUNS

The main principles on which the structure of Tswana is based are the system of noun classes and agreement.

With certain exceptions, nouns in Tswana are composed of basically two parts: prefix + root:

motho (*people*): **mo-** + **-tho**

The noun can also be composed of a prefix plus a stem — which includes both a root plus one or more suffixes, for example:

morwalo (*load*): **mo-** + **-rwal-** + **o**

morwalelo (*flood*): **mo-** + **-rwal-** + **-el-** + **-o**

The root is more or less a constant element while the prefix might change, for example:

motho batho setho botho

Noun prefixes have three main functions:

To distinguish between different classes of nouns;

To distinguish between singular and plural; and

To determine the form of the corresponding pronouns and grammatical agreement of the sentence in which they are used.

Because of the different noun prefixes, all nouns in Tswana are grouped into 18 noun classes:

Class	Prefix	Tswana	English equivalent
1	**mo-**	**motho**	*person*
2	**ba-**	**batho**	*persons*
1a	**-**	**malome**	*uncle (maternal)*
1b	**bo-**	**bomalome**	*uncle and company/ uncles*
3	**mo-**	**molomo**	*mouth*
4	**me-**	**melomo**	*mouths*
5	**le-**	**legapu**	*watermelon*
6	**ma-**	**magapu**	*watermelons*
7	**se-**	**selêpe**	*axe*
8	**di-**	**dilepe**	*axes*
9	**N-**	**ntwa**	*war*
10	**diN-**	**dintwa**	*wars*
11	**lo-**	**loleme**	*tongue*
14	**bo-**	**bogobe**	*porridge*
15	**go-**	**go bona**	*seeing*
16	**fa-**	**fatshe**	*on the ground*
17	**go-**	**godimo**	*on top of*
18	**mo-**	**morago**	*behind*

In most cases the prefix of one class indicates singular and that of the following class plural (for example, classes 1 and 2). For classes 11 and 14 this is not the case, with class 11 (**lo-**) taking the class prefix of class 10 (**diN-**) in its plural form and class 14 (**bo-**) taking that of class 6 (**ma-**).

The class prefix of class 15 is detached from the stem but this does not mean it is not a prefix like any other, for example:

Go dira ga bana go a itumedisa (*the working of the children makes one happy*)

The class prefix of class 9 (**N-**) precedes only monosyllabic stems beginning with consonants that are formed by using the tip of the tongue to touch the hard ridge behind the upper teeth, for example:

ntsi (*fly*)

With other types of stems it might appear as **n-**, **m-** or not at all, for example:

nku (*sheep*)

mpa (*stomach*)

thipa (*knife*)

The table also indicates how the noun prefixes might determine the agreement between the corresponding qualificative and predicative, as well as the form of the pronouns, for example:

bona: ba- + **-o-** + **-na**

where the **ba-** functions as a prefix in the construction of the absolute pronoun **bona**, referring to a noun from class 2, for example:

Banna ba a ja (*the men are eating*)

Bona ba a ja (*they are eating*)

THE PREDICATIVE

Predicatives are those parts of a sentence or phrase that either describe an action by the subject or object (as in 'the man ran faster') or its state (as in 'the tree is green').

There are two types of predicatives: verbs and copulatives. Verbs are mainly formed from roots that are intrinsically predicative in force; while copulatives are formed from parts of speech that are non-predicative in force (substantives, qualificatives, adverbs and sometimes conjunctives), for example:

Ngwana o nwa metsi (*the child drinks water*), and
Ngwana o tla nna botlhale (*the child will be/become clever*)

Verbs signify the occurrence of an action or the state of a substantive, while copulatives signify only the state of a substantive, for example:

Monna o a thusa (*the man helps*)
Monna o botlhale (*the man is clever*)

The verbal root is the most important part of the verb, the part around which everything has been built. In the example above, the **o-** in **o a thusa**, can be replaced with **ba-** without changing the intrinsic meaning of 'help'. The **-a-** can also be replaced with **-tla-** without changing the intrinsic meaning, to become **ba tla thusa** (*they will help*). The ending of **-thusa** (the **-a**) can also be changed, as in **ga ba thuse** (*they do not help*), again without changing the intrinsic meaning.

However, as soon as the remaining **-thus-** is changed, the verb loses its meaning. So **-thus-** is the verbal root, and in the word list in this book, English verbs have been translated into Tswana with verbal stems, for example:

-tsamaya (*go/walk*)

The user of the word list should thus remember that the verb can be used only with its prefixes or suffixes, except when used as an imperative (an order or direct request):

Batho ba a tsamaya (*the people go/walk*)
Tsamaya! (*go!*)

The subject must be easily identifiable in the verb, for example:

Monna o a ja (*the man is eating*)
O a ja (*he is eating*)

This agreement is in most cases identical to the class of the noun, except when a nasal sound appears in the class prefix and the nasal sound is dropped, for example:

Banna ba a ja (*the men are eating*),
Selêpe se a rema (*the axe is chopping*), but
Motse o a tuka (*the village is burning*)

CONCORDS

The first and second person subject concords (I/we and you/you) are:

1st person singular (I): **-ke-** as in **Nna ke a ja** (*I am eating*)
1st person plural (we): **-re-** as in **Rona re a ja** (*we are eating*)
2nd person singular (you): **-o-** as in **Wena o a ja** (*you are eating*)
2nd person plural (you): **-lo-** as in **Lona lo a ja** (*you are eating*)

The object concord is included in the verb by adding, for example:

Monna o ja nama (*the man is eating/eats meat*) becomes
Monna o a e ja (*the man is eating/eats it*)

The object concord is identical in form to the subject concord except for class 1 nouns where it is **mo**, for example:

Re thusa monna (*we help/are helping the man*) becomes
Re a mo thusa (*we help/are helping him*)

The object pronouns for the first and second person are:

1st person singular (me): **-N-** as in **E a ntoma** (*it is biting me*)
1st person plural (us): **-re-** as in **Ba a re bona** (*they are seeing us*)
2nd person singular (you): **-go-** as in **Ke a go bona** (*I am seeing you*)
2nd person plural (you): **-lo-** as in **Re a lo bona** (*we are seeing you*)

The object concord is usually used when the object is known and is not repeated after the object itself, for example:

Monna o ja nama (*the man eats meat*)
Monna o a e ja (*the man eats it*)

However, when the object is expressed and its object concord is also used in the predicate, the object is emphasised, for example:

Ke bitsa lekau (*I am calling the young man*)
Ke a le bitsa, lekau (*I am calling him, the young man*).

Tswana	English	Afrikaans
-aba	allocate (v)	toewys
-aba	donate (v)	skenk
-abelela	guess (v)	raai
-abula	crawl (v)	kruip
-adima	borrow (v)	leen
-adima	lend (v)	leen
aerisi	iris (n)	iris
-aga	nestle (v)	nestel
-aga	erect (v)	oprig
-aga	build (v)	bou
-akabatsa	embarrass (v)	verleë maak
-akanya	think (v)	dink
-akanya	consider (v)	oorweeg
-akanya	ponder (v)	bepeins
-akanya	reason (v)	redeneer
-akanyang	considerate (a)	bedagsaam
-akaretsa	include (v)	insluit
-akaretsang	inclusive (a)	inklusief
-aketsa	lie (v)	lieg
-akgola	congratulate (v)	gelukwens
-akgola	prize (v)	op prys stel
-akofa	immediate (a)	onmiddellik
akordiono	accordion (n)	trekklavier
alemanaka	calendar (n)	kalender
aletare	altar (n)	altaar
alfabete	alphabet (n)	alfabet
alibi	alibi (n)	alibi
-alosa	wean (v)	speen
-ama	affect (v)	raak
ambilansa	ambulance (n)	ambulans
-amoga	confiscate (v)	beslag lê op
-amogela	adopt (v)	aanneem
-amogela	accept (v)	aanvaar
-amogela	get (v)	kry
-amogela	receive (v)	ontvang
-amogela	earn (v)	verdien
-amogela	welcome (v)	verwelkom
-amogelesegang	acceptable (a)	aanvaarbaar
ampo	or (conj)	of
-anaanela	appreciate (v)	waardeer
-ananya	barter (v)	ruil
-anela	narrate (v)	vertel
-apara	dress (v)	aantrek
-apara	clothe (v)	aantrek
aparata	apparatus (n)	apparaat
-apaya	cook (v)	kook
-apaya	brew (v)	brou
-apola	strip (v)	ontbloot
-apola	undress (v)	uittrek
apole	apple (n)	appel
apolekosi	apricot (n)	appelkoos
-ara	operate (v)	opereer
-araba	reply (v)	antwoord
-araba	echo (v)	weerklink
-araba	answer (v)	antwoord
ase	axle (n)	as
aseine	vinegar (n)	asyn
asorense	assurance (n)	versekering
-ata	multiply (v)	vermenigvuldig
aterese	address (n)	adres

Tswana	English	Afrikaans
atisa	often (adv)	dikwels
-atla	kiss (v)	soen
-atlanega	achieve (v)	presteer
-atlanegisa	recommend (v)	aanbeveel
atlelase	atlas (n)	atlas
atletiki	athletics (n)	atletiek
-atlhola	decide (v)	besluit
-atlhola	judge (v)	oordeel
-atlhola	condemn (v)	veroordeel
-atlhola	assess (v)	skat
baagi	population (n)	bevolking
-baakantsweng	ready (a)	gereed
-baakanya	mend (v)	heelmaak
-baakanya	fix (v)	regmaak
-baakanya	prepare (v)	voorberei
baaki ya tlase	waistcoat (n)	onderbaadjie
-baba	itch (v)	jeuk
-baba	irritate (v)	irriteer
-babalela	protect (v)	beskerm
-babalela	conserve (v)	bewaar
-babalelang	secure (a)	veilig
-babalesega	secure (v)	beveilig
babogedi	bystander (n)	omstander
-babola	singe (v)	skroei
-babola	scorch (v)	skroei
baesekele	bicycle (n)	fiets
baesekopo	cinema (n)	bioskoop
baeyolene	violin (n)	viool
bahumanegi	poor (n)	armes
-baka	cause (v)	veroorsaak
bakene	beacon (n)	baken
baki	jacket (n)	baadjie
-bala	read (v)	lees
-bala	count (v)	tel
balate	ballad (n)	ballade
-balela	calculate (v)	reken
balelapa	family (n)	familie
balono	balloon (n)	ballon
bambusu	bamboo (n)	bamboes
bana	posterity (n)	nageslag
banjo	banjo (n)	banjo
banka	bench (n)	bank
banka	desk (n)	lessenaar
banta	band (n)	groep
-bapala	acquire (v)	aanskaf
-bapang	adjacent (a)	aangrensend
-bapisa	compare (v)	vergelyk
-bapola	crucify (v)	kruisig
bapololano	contest (n)	wedstryd
bara	bar (n)	kroeg
bata	bath (n)	bad
-bata	bath (v)	bad
-bata	slap (v)	klap
batalala	crouch (v)	buk
batho	people (n)	mense
batho	public (n)	publiek
-bathong	public (a)	openbaar
batimamolelo	fire brigade (n)	brandweer
-batla	nearly (adv)	byna

B	Tswana	English	Afrikaans	Tswana	English	Afrikaans
	-batla	track (v)	opspoor	boapeelo	kitchen (n)	kombuis
	-batla	search (v)	soek	-boatla	untidy (a)	slordig
	-batla	want (v)	wil hê	-boatla	careless (a)	nalatig
	-baya	lay (v)	dek	-boatla	clumsy (a)	lomp
	-baya	put (v)	sit	bobe	peril (n)	gevaar
	-baya bubi	flatter (v)	vlei	bobedi	two (n)	twee
	-baya molato	blame (v)	blameer	bobedi	double (n)	dubbel
	-be	ghastly (a)	aaklig	bobedi	pair (n)	paar
	-be	bad (a)	sleg	-bobedi	second (a)	tweede
	bebetsididi	ice cream (n)	roomys	bobesetso	oven (n)	oond
	-beelana	bet (v)	wed	bobetwapelo	temper (n)	humeur
	-bega	inform (v)	meedeel	bobi	cobweb (n)	spinnerak
	Beibele	Bible (n)	Bybel	boboa	wool (n)	wol
	-beilweng	prescribed (a)	voorgeskrewe	boboa jwa podi	mohair (n)	sybokhaar
	beine	wine (n)	wyn	boboi	cowardice (n)	lafhartigheid
	-beisa pelo	postpone (v)	uitstel	boboko	brain (n)	brein
	beke	week (n)	week	-bobolang	ill (a)	siek
	bekepedi	fortnight (n)	twee weke	bobotlana	minimum (n)	minimum
	-bela	fizz (v)	bruis	-bodileng	rotten (a)	verrot
	-bela	ferment (v)	gis	bodilo	floor (n)	vloer
	-bela	boil (v)	kook	bodilo	floor (n)	verdieping
	-belaela	doubt (v)	twyfel	-bodipa	stubborn (a)	koppig
	-belaela	distrust (v)	wantrou	boditse	bristle (n)	steekhaar
	-belaela	suspect (v)	verdink	bodumedi	religion (n)	godsdiens
	-belaelang	uncertain (a)	onseker	bodutu	loneliness (n)	eensaamheid
	-belafalang	boastful (a)	spoggerig	-bodutû	lonely (a)	eensaam
	-beleatanya	squeeze (v)	druk	boe	yolk (n)	eiergeel
	belefo	valve (n)	klep	-boela	return (v)	terugkeer
	belerutwane	guerrilla (n)	guerrilla	boeleele	foolishness (n)	dwaasheid
	-belesetsa	dismiss (v)	ontslaan	-boelela	repeat (v)	herhaal
	bene	panel van (n)	paneelwa	boelela	revise (v)	wysig
	bentlelaka	square (n)	vierkant	boemakepe	harbour (n)	hawe
	-bentlelaka	square (a)	vierkantig	boemeladifofane	airport (n)	lughawe
	-benya	gleam (v)	straal	boepapuso	treason (n)	verraad
	-benyabenya	flicker (v)	flikker	-bofa	fasten (v)	vasmaak
	-beola	shave (v)	skeer	-bofefo	quick (a)	gou
	bera	bear (n)	beer	-bofelela ka keetane	chain (v)	vasketting
	-besa	bake (v)	bak	-bofelo	final (a)	finaal
	-besa	grill (v)	rooster	-bofelo	last (a)	laaste
	bese	bus (n)	bus	-bofelong	ultimate (a)	uiterste
	besete	vest (n)	onderhemp	boferefere	deceit (n)	bedrog
	-beta	strangle (v)	verwurg	-boferefere	cunning (a)	slu
	-beta	drown (v)	verdrink	-bofolola	disconnect (v)	losmaak
	-betagana	overcrowd (v)	oorvol wees	-boga	suffer (v)	ly
	bete	beetroot (n)	beet	bogadikane	polygamy (n)	poligamie
	-betelela	rape (v)	verkrag	bogale	malice (n)	boosaardigheid
	-betla	sculpt (v)	beeldhou	bogale	brave (a)	dapper
	-betolola	pout (v)	pruil	-bogale	sharp (a)	skerp
	-betsa	punch (v)	slaan	-bogale	acute (a)	skerp
	-bidikama	wallow (v)	wentel	-bogale	rage (n)	woede
	-biletsa	dictate (v)	voorskrywe	-bogale	fierce (a)	woes
	-bina	dance (v)	dans	boganana	disobedience (n)	ongehoorsaamheid
	-bipa	cover (v)	dek	boganka	violence (n)	geweld
	bisa	without (adv)	buite	bogare	centre (n)	middel
	bishopo	bishop (n)	biskop	bogobe	paste (n)	pasta
	bisikiti	biscuit (n)	koekie	bogobe	porridge (n)	pap
	-bitala	conceal (v)	verberg	bogodimo	height (n)	hoogte
	-bitsa	summon (v)	ontbied	bogodimo	top (n)	top
	-bitsa	call (v)	roep	bogodimo	level (n)	vlak
	boaka	adultery (n)	owerspel	bogola	bark (v)	blaf

Tswana	English	Afrikaans	Tswana	English	Afrikaans	B
bogolo	adulthood (n)	volwassenheid	boitshwaro	behaviour (n)	gedrag	
-bogolo bogolo	least (a)	minste	boitshwaro	attitude (n)	houding	
-bogologolo	ancient (a)	antiek	boitumelo	delight (n)	blydskap	
-bogologolo	primitive (a)	primitief	boitumelo	happiness (n)	geluk	
bogologolo	age (n)	ouderdom	boitumelo	joy (n)	vreugde	
bogorogoro	delirium (n)	ylhoofdigheid	bojalwa	beer (n)	bier	
bogosi	kingdom (n)	koninkryk	bojalwa	liquor (n)	drank	
bogwata	rash (n)	veluitslag	bojang	lawn (n)	grasperk	
bohibiduhibidu	scarlet (n)	helderrooi	bojarara	anger (n)	kwaadheid	
bohumanegi	poverty (n)	armoede	bojelo	dining room (n)	eetkamer	
-boi	cowardly (a)	lafhartig	-boka	praise (v)	loof	
-boi	timid (a)	skugter	-boka	recite (v)	opsê	
-boi	blunt (a)	stomp	boka	wax (n)	was	
boidiidi	multitude (n)	menigte	bokao	meaning (n)	betekenis	
-boifa	dread (v)	vrees	bokao	disability (n)	gebrek	
-boifa	fear (v)	vrees	bokau/boroba	puberty (n)	puberteit	
-boikanyego	reliable (a)	betroubaar	bokgabisong	art gallery (n)	kunsgalery	
boikanyego	loyalty (n)	lojaliteit	bokgakala	distance (n)	afstand	
-boikanyo	trustworthy (a)	betroubaar	-bokgaolakgang	judicial (a)	regterlik	
boikanyo	fidelity (n)	getrouheid	bokgaolakgang	judiciary (n)	regbank	
boikanyo	honesty (n)	eerlikheid	bokgarebe	virgin (n)	maagd	
-boikanyo	honest (a)	eerlik	bokgoba	slavery (n)	slawerny	
-boikgantsho	conceited (a)	verwaand	bokgogedi	magnetism (n)	magnetisme	
boikgodiso	pride (n)	trots	-bokgola	humid (a)	klam	
boikhutso	rest (n)	rus	bokgola	moisture (n)	vog	
boikhutso	holiday (n)	vakansie	bokgoni	efficiency (n)	doeltreffendheid	
boikokobetso	awe (n)	eerbied	bokgosi	chief (a)	hoof	
boikokobetso	humility (n)	nederigheid	bokgwafo	impertinence (n)	astrantheid	
-boikokobetso	humble (a)	nederig	-bokgwafo	tame (a)	mak	
boikotlhao	regret (n)	spyt	bokhutlo	end (n)	einde	
boikuelo	appeal (n)	beroep	-bokoa	sickly (a)	sieklik	
boima	weight (n)	gewig	bokoa	weakness (n)	swakheid	
-boima	heavy (a)	swaar	-bokoa	weak (a)	swak	
boineelo	surrender (n)	oorgawe	-bokolela	wail (v)	weeklaag	
-boingotlo	modest (a)	beskeie	-bokompa	wholesome (a)	heilsaam	
boipabalelo	caution (n)	versigtigheid	bokone	north (n)	noorde	
boipobolo	confession (n)	belydenis	-bokone	north (a)	noord	
boipolao	suicide (n)	selfmoord	-bokwadi	literary (a)	letterkundig	
-boipuso	independent (a)	onafhanklik	-bokwang	praiseworthy (a)	lofwaardig	
-boitaolo	wilful (a)	moedswillig	-bola	decompose (v)	ontbind	
-boitebalo	unselfish (a)	onselfsugtig	-bola	rot (v)	verrot	
boitekanelo	health (n)	gesondheid	-bola	decay (v)	verrot	
boitekanelo	hygiene (n)	higiëne	boladu	pus (n)	etter	
boiteko	attempt (n)	poging	bolao	bed (n)	bed	
boitemogelo	experience (n)	ervaring	bolao	mattress (n)	matras	
boithomelo	lavatory (n)	toilet	bolaodi	management (n)	bestuur	
boithomelo	toilet (n)	toilet	bolaodi	authority (n)	gesag	
boitimokanyo	pretence (n)	skyn	bolaose	blouse (n)	bloes	
-boitlhaganelo	hasty (a)	haastig	-bolawa ke tlala	starve (v)	honger ly	
boitlhaganelo	haste (n)	haas	-bolaya	kill (v)	doodmaak	
boitlhomo	motive (n)	beweegrede	-bolaya	hurt (v)	seermaak	
boitseanape	science (n)	wetenskap	-bolaya	execute (v)	teregstel	
-boitsemeletso	unwilling (a)	onwillig	-bolaya	murder (v)	vermoor	
boitsheko	purity (n)	suiwerheid	-bolaya	poison (v)	vergiftig	
-boitshepo	holy (a)	heilig	-bolaya ditwatsi	disinfect (v)	ontsmet	
-boitshepo	sacred (a)	heilig	-bolaya mfama	paralyse (v)	verlam	
boitshepo	self-confidence (n)	selfvertroue	-bolaya pelo	frustrate (v)	frustreer	
boitshoko	patience (n)	geduld	-bolea	loose (a)	los	
boitshwarelo	forgiveness (n)	vergifnis	boleele	length (n)	lengte	
boitshwarelo	apology (n)	verskoning	bolekane	companionship (n)	kameraadskap	

329

B

Tswana	English	Afrikaans
-bolela	report (v)	berig
-bolela	tell (v)	vertel
-bolela	state (v)	vermeld
bolele	alga (n)	alg
-bolelo	hot (a)	warm
-bolelo	warm (a)	warm
-bolemi	agricultural (a)	landboukundig
bolemi	agriculture (n)	landbou
boleng	quality (n)	kwaliteit
bolepanaledi	astronomy (n)	sterrekunde
bolepinaledi	astrology (n)	astrologie
-boleta	fine (a)	fyn
-boleta	soft (a)	sag
boletswe	allergy (n)	allergie
boletswe jwa letha la makgwa	pleurisy	borsvliesontsteking
boleyo	existence (n)	bestaan
-boloi	magical (a)	magies
boloi	witchcraft (n)	toorkuns
boloi	magic (n)	towerkuns
-boloka	preserve (v)	bewaar
-boloka	store (v)	bêre
-boloka	keep (v)	hou
-boloka	spare (v)	spaar
-bolokegileng	safe (a)	veilig
-bolokela	deposit (v)	deponeer
bolokololo	analysis (n)	ontleding
-bolotsa	declare (v)	verklaar
bolwetse	sickness (n)	siekte
bolwetse	disease (n)	siekte
bolwetse	illness (n)	siekte
bolwetse jwa sukiri	diabetes (n)	suikersiekte
bomo	bomb (n)	bom
-bomorafe	racist (a)	rassisties
bomo ya mo mmung	landmine (n)	landmyn
-bona	obtain (v)	bekom
-bona	theirs (pron)	hulle s'n
bona	they (pron)	hulle
bona	their (pron)	hulle
bona	them (pron)	hulle
-bona	see (v)	sien
-bona	find (v)	vind
-bona kgwedi	menstruate (v)	menstrueer
-bonako	rapid (a)	vlugtig
-bonala	visible (a)	sigbaar
-bonalang	clear (a)	helder
-bonalatsang	transparent (a)	deurskynend
-bona molato	convict (v)	skuldig bevind
-bonamune	orange (a)	oranje
bonana	tender (n)	tender
bonatla	diligence (n)	fluksheid
-bonegang	concrete (a)	konkreet
bong	gender (n)	geslag
-bongaka	medical (a)	medies
bongola	damp (n)	vogtigheid
bongwana	infancy (n)	kleintyd
-bongwefela	unanimous (a)	eenstemmig
bonna	manhood (n)	manlikheid
bonno	accommodation (n)	huisvesting
bonno	residence (n)	verblyfplek
bonnyane	bit (n)	bietjie
-bonolo	polite (a)	hoflik
-bonolo	easy (a)	maklik
-bonolo	mild (a)	matig
-bonolo	gentle (a)	sagmoedig
bonosi	individual (n)	individu
bontle	beauty (n)	skoonheid
-bontsha	exhibit (v)	uitstal
-bontsha	show (v)	wys
-bontsha	identify (v)	identifiseer
bontsi	plural (n)	meervoud
bonwelo	diving (n)	duikery
-bonya	slow (a)	stadig
bonyana	childhood (n)	kinderjare
bonyelele	rheumatism (n)	rumatiek
-bonyelele	rheumatic (a)	rumaties
bookelo	hospital (n)	hospitaal
-bopa	form (v)	vorm
-bopa	mould (v)	vorm
-bopa	create (v)	skep
bopaki	evidence (n)	getuienis
-bopameng	slim (a)	skraal
-bopameng	lean (a)	maer
bopelokgale	bravery (n)	dapperheid
bopelokgale	courage (n)	moed
bopelompe	cruelty (n)	wreedheid
bopelonomi	charity (n)	liefdadigheid
bopelonomi	kindness (n)	goedheid
bopelotlhomogi	mercy (n)	genade
bophaphathi	breadth (n)	breedte
bophelo	life (n)	lewe
bophelonageng	wildlife (n)	natuurlewe
bophepa	cleanliness (n)	sindelikheid
bophepafatso	refinement (n)	verfyndheid
-bophirima	western (a)	westelik
bophirima	west (n)	weste
bophirima	west (adv)	wes
-bophologolo	brutal (a)	dierlik
bora	bow (n)	boog
borataro	six (n)	ses
borele	spectacles (n)	bril
-borethe	smooth (a)	glad
boroko	sleep (n)	slaap
borongwa	mission (n)	sending
boroso	sausage (n)	wors
borosolo	brush (n)	borsel
borotho	loaf (n)	brood
borotho	bread (n)	brood
borothopate	sandwich (n)	toebroodjie
boroto	plate (n)	bord
boroulo	mourning (n)	rou
borukutlhi	rebellion (n)	opstand
borukutlhi	terror (n)	terreur
borukutlhi	terrorism (n)	terrorisme
borulelo	roof (n)	dak
borutegi	qualification (n)	kwalifikasie
boruti	clergy (n)	geestelikes
-borwa	south (a)	suid
-borwa	southern (a)	suidelik
borwa	south (n)	suide

Tswana	English	Afrikaans
bosa	dawn (n)	dagbreek
bosa	daybreak (n)	dagbreek
bosa	weather (n)	weer
bosaikanyegang	disloyalty (n)	dislojaliteit
bosaitseweng	secrecy (n)	geheimhouding
-bosaitseweng	mysterious (a)	geheimsinnig
bosaitseweng	mystery (n)	misterie
-bosakhuteng	eternal (a)	ewig
bosayenkae	eternity (n)	ewigheid
boseja	side (n)	sy
-bosenabotho	immoral (a)	onsedelik
bosetšhaba	nationalism (n)	nasionalisme
-bosetšhaba	national (a)	nasionaal
-boshushu	deaf (a)	doof
bosigo	night (n)	nag
bosigogare	midnight (n)	middernag
-bosilo	naughty (a)	stout
bosilo	aggressive (a)	aanvallend
bosima	adolescence (n)	adolessensie
bosireletso jwa tlholego	nature reserve	natuurreservaat
-bosisi	numb (a)	dood
-bosula	nasty (a)	gemeen
-bosula	unhappy (a)	ongelukkig
bosula	vice (n)	ondeug
-bosula	tasteless (a)	smaakloos
-bosula	evil (a)	boos
-bosula	unlucky (a)	ongelukkig
bosupaditshwantsho	gallery (n)	galery
bosupi	proof (n)	bewys
bosupi	testimony (n)	getuienis
bosutlha	extravagance (n)	buitensporigheid
bošwa	youth (n)	jeug
boswa	inheritance (n)	erfenis
boswa	heritage (n)	erfenis
boswakgapetla	freezing point (n)	vriespunt
bošweu	white (n)	wit
botala	turquoise (n)	turkoois
-boteng	deep (a)	diep
boteng	depth (n)	diepte
-bothakga	tidy (a)	netjies
bothale	wire (n)	draad
bothata	strength (n)	sterkte
bothata	problem (n)	probleem
bothata	difficulty (n)	moeilikheid
bothibelelo	camping (n)	kampering
-bothitonyana	tepid (a)	lou
bothomo	start (n)	begin
-bothudi	mechanical (a)	meganies
bothumelo	swimming pool (n)	swembad
-botlalo	complete (a)	volledig
botlalogolo	maximum (n)	maksimum
botlamo	bondage (n)	knegskap
-botlana	junior (a)	junior
botlapa	laziness (n)	luiheid
botlase	bottom (n)	bodem
-botlha	sour (a)	suur
botlhabanelo	arena (n)	arena
-botlhabatsatsi	eastern (a)	oostelik
botlhabatsatsi	east (n)	ooste

Tswana	English	Afrikaans
botlhabelo	abattoir (n)	slagplaas
botlhabisa ditlhong	disgrace (n)	skande
botlhaga	vigilance (n)	waaksaamheid
-botlhale	gifted (a)	begaaf
botlhale	intelligence (n)	intelligensie
botlhale	astute (a)	slim
botlhale	wisdom (n)	wysheid
-botlhale	wise (a)	wys
botlhaletlhale	brilliance (n)	helderheid
-botlhaolelong	secluded (a)	afgesonderd
botlhapelo	bathroom (n)	badkamer
botlhatswetso	laundry (n)	wassery
-botlhodi	ominous (a)	onheilspellend
botlhokabotho	obscenity (n)	onbetaamlikheid
-botlhoko	bitter (a)	bitter
-botlhoko	sore (a)	seer
botlhoko	pain (n)	pyn
botlhoko	grief (n)	leed
-botlhokwa	important (a)	belangrik
-botlhokwa	valuable (a)	waardevol
-botlhokwatlhokwa	dear (a)	dierbaar
botlhole	venom (n)	venyn
botlhophi	franchise (n)	kiesreg
botlwaelo	addiction (n)	verslaafdheid
botoka	better (a)	beter
botokololo	membership (n)	lidmaatskap
-botsa	inquire (v)	navraag doen
-botsa	ask (v)	vra
-botsa	question (v)	vra
botsalano	friendship (n)	vriendskap
botsalo	birthday (n)	verjaarsdag
botseno	insanity (n)	kranksinnigheid
botshabelo	refuge (n)	skuiling
botshabelo	asylum (n)	skuilplaas
botshe	nectar (n)	nektar
-botshe	sweet (a)	soet
-botshego	comic (a)	komies
botsho	outcome (n)	uitkoms
botsholo	childbirth (n)	kindergeboorte
botsholong	birthplace (n)	geboorteplek
-botshwakga	indolent (a)	traag
botso	exit (n)	uitgang
-botsolotsa	cross examine (v)	kruisvra
botsuolodi	revolution (n)	revolusie
botswelelopele	advancement (n)	vordering
botswerere	art (n)	kuns
boupe jwa borotho	flour (n)	meel
-boutlwelobotlhoko	sympathetic (a)	simpatiek
boutlwelobotlhoko	sympathy (n)	simpatie
boutu	bolt (n)	bout
bowa	fur (n)	pels
bra	brassiére (n)	bra
-bua	talk (v)	praat
-bua	speak (v)	praat
-buabua	babble (v)	babbel
-buabuang	talkative (a)	spraaksaam
-bua ka pelo	absent-minded (a)	ingedagte
-budule	ripe (a)	ryp
-budulela	inflate (v)	opblaas
-buisa	address (v)	toespreek

B	Tswana	English	Afrikaans	Tswana	English	Afrikaans
	-buisanya	negotiate (v)	onderhandel	-dimokanyang	dazed (a)	bedwelmd
	buka	book (n)	boek	dinata	bunion (n)	knokkeleelt
	bukantswe	dictionary (n)	woordeboek	dingongora	complaint (n)	klagte
	buka ya dijo	menu (n)	spyskaart	dingongora	dissatisfaction (n)	ontevredenheid
	buka ya dinomoro tsa mogala	telephone directory	telefoongids	diogotlelapa	blinkers (n)	oogklappe
				dipalo	arithmetic (n)	rekenkunde
	-bula	open (v)	oopmaak	dipalophatlo	fractions (n)	breuke
	-buledisa	accompany (v)	begelei	Diphalane	October (n)	Oktober
	-buledisa	escort (v)	vergesel	diphatsa	risk (n)	risiko
	-bulegileng	open (a)	oop	dipholo	result (n)	uitslag
	-bulela mafatlha	confide (v)	vertroulik meedeel	diporele tsa letsatsi	sunglasses (n)	sonbril
	-busa	reign (v)	heers	-dira	labour (v)	arbei
	-busa	govern (v)	regeer	-dira	work (v)	werk
	-busa	rule (v)	regeer	-dira	do (v)	doen
	-busetsa	profit (v)	wins maak	-dira	make (v)	maak
	-busetsa	refund (v)	terugbetaal	-dira	perform (v)	uitvoer
	-busetsang	profitable (a)	lonend	-diragatsa	effect (v)	bewerk
	-busolosetsa	avenge (v)	wreek	-direga	happen (v)	gebeur
				-direla	serve (v)	dien
	dekrii	degree (n)	graad	-dirile	done (v)	gedoen
	-dia	detain (v)	aanhou	-dirisa	use (v)	gebruik
	-dia	delay (v)	vertraag	-dirisa e seng ka fa siamong	abuse (v)	misbruik
	diaba	performance (n)	uitvoering			
	diaparo	clothes (n)	klere	-dirisana	co-operate (v)	saamwerk
	dibaga	beadwork (n)	kraalwerk	-dirisiwa	engaged (a)	beset
	dibaketeria	bacteria (n)	bakterie	-disa	guard (v)	bewaak
	dibaole	bowls (n)	rolbal	disiralesedi	blind (n)	blinding
	-dibeletsa	reserve (v)	reserveer	ditaga	drugs (n)	dwelms
	dibetsa	arms (n)	wapens	ditalama	necklace (n)	halssnoer
	didimatsa	silence (v)	stilmaak	diteng	contents (n)	inhoud
	-didimetseng	quiet (a)	stil	ditepese	stairs (n)	trappe
	-didisa	impoverish (v)	verarm	dithoto	luggage (n)	bagasie
	-diga	overthrow (v)	omvergooi	dithoto	goods (n)	goedere
	digaboi	banns (n)	gebooie	dithubegi	crockery (n)	breekware
	-digela ka lemena	mislead (v)	mislei	Dithutlwa	Southern Cross (n)	Suiderkruis
	-digela ka lemena	misleading (a)	misleidend	ditiragalo	proceedings (n)	verrigtinge
	dijego	consumption (n)	verbruik	ditiragalo	history (n)	geskiedenis
	dijo	meal (n)	maal	ditlhomolapelo	tragedy (n)	tragedie
	dijo	nutrition (n)	voeding	ditlhotlhori	roughage (n)	vesel
	dijo	food (n)	kos	-ditsatsa	undesirable (a)	ongewens
	dijotshegare	lunch (n)	middagete	-ditšhaba	international (a)	internasionaal
	dikaelo	index (n)	indeks	-ditšhabatšhaba	multiracial (a)	veelrassig
	-dikanyetsa	surround (v)	omring	ditshebo	gossip (n)	skinderpraatjies
	dikeledi	tears (n)	trane	ditshedi	fauna (n)	fauna
	dikgakologo	spring (n)	lente	ditshego	laughter (n)	gelag
	dikgapo	loot (n)	buit	ditshotlo	sarcasm (n)	sarkasme
	dikgomo	cattle (n)	vee	-duba	knead (v)	knie
	dikhutsafalo	lament (n)	weeklag	-duedisa	fine (v)	beboet
	dikhutsaneng	orphanage (n)	weeshuis	-duela	pay (v)	betaal
	dikiletsokotlhao	sanction (n)	sanksie	-duela	reward (v)	beloon
	dikinane	folklore (n)	volksoorleweringe	-dula setulo	chair (v)	voorsit
	dikobo	bedclothes (n)	beddegoed	-duma	groan (v)	kreun
	dikodu	tonsils (n)	mangels	-duma	moan (v)	kerm
	dikologa	revolve (v)	draai	-dumedisa	greet (v)	groet
	-dikologa	avoid (v)	vermy	-dumela	consent (v)	instem
	-dikologa	circulate (v)	rondgaan	-dumela	believe (v)	glo
	dikwalelo	stationery (n)	skryfbehoeftes	-dumelana	agree (v)	ooreenstem
	dikwalo	literature (n)	letterkunde	-dumelela	admit (v)	toelaat
	-dilola	scowl (v)	suur kyk	-dumelela	authorise (v)	magtig
	dimedi	flora (n)	flora			

Tswana	English	Afrikaans
-ebaeba	loiter (v)	rondslenter
-edimola	yawn (v)	gaap
edimolo	yawn (n)	gaap
eie	onion (n)	ui
-eka	betray (v)	verraai
ekeserei	x-ray (n)	x-straal
ela	along (prep)	langs
-elang tlhoko	observant (a)	oplettend
-elela	flow (v)	vloei
-elelang	liquid (a)	vloeibaar
-elelang	fluid (a)	vloeibaar
-eletsa	wish (v)	wens
-eletsa	aspire (v)	streef
-eletsa	desire (v)	begeer
-eletsa	envy (v)	beny
-eletsa	yearn (v)	hunker
-ema	stop (v)	stop
-ema	stand (v)	staan
-emela	await (v)	wag op
-emela	represent (v)	verteenwoordig
-emela topololo	bail (v)	borg staan
-emeng	stagnant (a)	stagnant
-emeng	stationary (a)	stilstaande
-emisa	park (v)	parkeer
ene	he (pron)	hy
ene	her (pron)	haar
ene	him (pron)	hom
ene	his (pron)	sy
ene	she (pron)	sy
enfelopo	envelope (n)	koevert
eng	what (pron)	wat
enjene	engine (n)	enjin
enke	ink (n)	ink
enta	inoculate (v)	inent
-enta	vaccinate (v)	inent
-epa	convene (v)	byeenroep
-epa	dig (v)	spit
-epolola	unearth (v)	opgrawe
erekisi	pea (n)	ertjie
eriele	aerial (n)	lugdraad
eriele	antenna (n)	lugdraad
esele	ass (n)	donkie
-e seng	never (adv)	nooit
-e seng ka fa molaong	illegal (a)	onwettig
-e seng ka nako	unpunctual (a)	nie stip nie
-e seng sego	unfortunately (adv)	ongelukkig
-esete	acid (a)	suur
esete	acid (n)	suur
-etela	call (v)	besoek
-etela	visit (v)	besoek
-etelela	precede (v)	voorafgaan
-etelela	lead (v)	lei
-ethimola	sneeze (v)	nies
-etsa	ape (v)	na-aap
-etsa	imitate (v)	namaak
fa	if (conj)	as
fa	here (adv)	hier
fa	whether (conj)	of
-fa	present (v)	skenk
-fa	confer (v)	toeken
-fa	supply (v)	verskaf
-fa	give (v)	gee
faboriki	factory (n)	fabriek
faele	file (n)	leêr
fa godimo	over (prep)	oor
-fagola	castrate (v)	kastreer
faki	barrel (n)	vat
-fala	slander (n)	laster
-fala	scrape (v)	skraap
-falala	emigrate (v)	emigreer
-falatsa	scatter (v)	strooi
-falola	escape (v)	ontsnap
fantisi	auction (n)	veiling
-fapaana	cross (v)	kruis
-fapaana	differ (v)	verskil
-fapoga	deviate (v)	afwyk
-farola	slice (v)	skywe sny
-farologanya	distinguish (v)	onderskei
-fatlhosa	enlighten (v)	inlig
-fatshe	low (a)	laag
-fatshefatshe	lower (a)	laer
-fe	which (pron)	watter
-feela	sweep (v)	vee
-fefa	flirt (v)	flirteer
-fegelwa	pant (v)	hyg
feie	figtree (n)	vyeboom
feie	fig (n)	vy
feile	file (n)	vyl
-fekeetsa	overpower (v)	oorweldig
fela	just (adv)	net
fela	only (adv)	slegs
-felang pelo	impatient (a)	ongeduldig
felo	place (n)	plek
felo	scene (n)	toneel
-fema	avert (v)	keer
-femela	defend (v)	verdedig
-femelang	defensive (a)	verdedigend
fenitšhara	furniture (n)	meubels
fensetere	window (n)	venster
-fenya	overcome (v)	te bowe kom
-fenya	defeat (v)	verslaan
-fenya	conquer (v)	verower
-fepa	feed (v)	voer
-fera	hinder (v)	hinder
-ferekana	perturb (v)	verontrus
ferekekere	binoculars (n)	verkyker
-feretlha	riot (v)	oproer maak
-feretlha	disturb (v)	pla
Ferikgong	January (n)	Januarie
-ferosa sebete	disgust (n)	afkeer
-feta	pass (v)	verbygaan
-feta	overtake (v)	verbysteek
-fetelang	contagious (a)	aansteeklik
-fetelelang	infectious (a)	besmetlik
-feteletsa	exaggerate (v)	oordryf
-feteletsa	across (prep)	oor
-fetetsa	infect (v)	besmet
-fetlha	churn (n)	karring
-fetoga	change (v)	verander

F	Tswana	English	Afrikaans	Tswana	English	Afrikaans
	-fetola	vary (v)	varieer	-gagapa	enforce (v)	afdwing
	-fetola	translate (v)	vertaal	-gagapa	dominate (v)	oorheers
	-fetsa	finish (v)	klaarmaak	-gagasetsa	gargle (v)	gorrel
	-fetsa	complete (v)	voltooi	-gago	your (pron)	jou
	fiose	fuse (n)	sekering	-gago	yours (pron)	joune
	-fisa	scald (v)	skroei	-gagola	tear (v)	skeur
	-fitlha	reach (v)	bereik	-gagwe	hers (pron)	hare
	-fitlha	bury (v)	begrawe	-gagwe	his (pron)	syne
	-fitlha	attain (v)	bereik	gagwe	its (pron)	sy
	-fitlha	hide (v)	wegsteek	-gaisa	exceed (v)	oorskry
	-fitlhilweng	hidden (a)	versteek	-gakala	excite (v)	opwind
	-fitshwa	dark (a)	donker	-gakalelang	eager (a)	gretig
	-fodileng tlhogo	sane (a)	verstandig	-gakgamala	wonder (v)	wonder
	-fodisa	heal (v)	genees	-gakgamatsang	radical (a)	radikaal
	-fofa	fly (v)	vlieg	-gakologa	melt (v)	smelt
	-fofora	crumble (v)	verkrummel	-gakologelwa	remember (v)	onthou
	-foka	blow (v)	waai	-gakolola	advise (v)	raad gee
	-fokoletsa	discount (v)	aftrek	-gakololang	advisory (a)	raadgewend
	-fokotsa	lessen (v)	verminder	-galalela	glow (v)	gloei
	-fokotsa	decrease (v)	verminder	galase	glass (n)	glas
	-fola	recover (v)	herstel	galase ya beine	wineglass (n)	wynkelkie
	folaga	flag (n)	vlag	galase ya diporele	contact lens (n)	kontaklens
	foleiki	mouth organ (n)	mondfluitjie	-gale	common (a)	gewoon
	foleiki	harmonica (n)	harmonika	-galetsha	infuriate (v)	woedend maak
	folene	flannel (n)	flanel	-gana	decline (v)	afwys
	-fologa	descend (v)	daal	-gana	object (v)	beswaar maak
	-folosa	unload (v)	aflaai	-gana	disobey (v)	ongehoorsaam wees
	folutu	pennywhistle (n)	kwêlafluitjie	-gana	reject (v)	verwerp
	foo	there (adv)	daar	-gana	refuse (v)	weier
	-fora	deceive (v)	bedrieg	-ganana	protest (v)	protesteer
	foroko	fork (n)	vurk	-gananang	insubordinate (a)	ongehoorsaam
	-forola	cleanse (v)	skoonmaak	-ganela	curb (v)	inhou
	foromo	form (n)	vorm	-ganela	deny (v)	ontken
	-fosa	err (v)	fouteer	-ganetsa	dispute (v)	betwis
	-fosa	miss (v)	mis	-ganetsa	oppose (v)	opponeer
	-foufetseng	blind (a)	blind	-ganetsa	disagree (v)	verskil
	-fudua	stir (v)	roer	-ganetsa	contradict (v)	weerspreek
	-fudugela	immigrate (v)	immigreer	ganetsana	argue (v)	stry
	-fufegang	envious (a)	jaloers	gangwe	once (adv)	een maal
	-fufula	perspire (v)	perspireer	ganse	goose (n)	gans
	-fufula	sweat (v)	sweet	-gapa	loot (v)	plunder
	-fula	pluck (v)	pluk	-gape	extra (a)	ekstra
	-funega	contract (v)	inkrimp	gape	more (a)	meer
	-funela	knot (v)	knoop	gape	also (adv)	ook
	-funyetsa	withdraw (v)	terugtrek	gape	again (adv)	weer
	furu	lining (n)	voering	-gapeletsa	force (v)	forseer
	-futaganeng	double (a)	dubbele	-gapeletsa	compel (v)	dwing
	futshe	hat (n)	hoed	garawe	spade (n)	graaf
				gare	amid (prep)	tussen
	-ga-	own (a)	eie	gare	between (prep)	tussen
	-gaba	scoop (v)	skep	-gasa	broadcast (v)	uitsaai
	ga bedi	twice (n)	twee maal	gase	gas (n)	gas
	-gabela	shred (v)	snipper	-gata	march (v)	marsjeer
	-gadika	fry (v)	bak	-gata	tread (v)	trap
	-gadika	roast (v)	oondbraai	-gata	step (v)	trap
	-gae	civil (a)	burgerlik	-gatelela	emphasise (v)	beklemtoon
	gafole	pitchfork (n)	gaffel	-gatelela	depress (v)	neerdruk
	-gagamatsa	tighten (v)	span	-gatelela	oppress (v)	onderdruk
	-gagametseng	tense (a)	gespanne	-gatelela	subdue (v)	onderwerp
	-gagametseng	tight (a)	styf	-gatelelang pele	progressive (a)	progressief

Tswana	English	Afrikaans	Tswana	English	Afrikaans	G
-gatisa	print (v)	druk	-gologolo	old (a)	oud	
-gatisa	press (v)	pers	-golola	emancipate (v)	vrymaak	
-gatisa	iron (v)	stryk	-golola	extend (v)	uitstrek	
-gatsela	congeal (v)	stol	-golola	release (v)	loslaat	
-gatsela	freeze (v)	vries	-golola	prolong (v)	verleng	
-gaufi	near (adv)	naby	-golola	free (v)	bevry	
gaufi	close (a)	naby	-golola	acquit (v)	vryspreek	
gaumakwe	gall (n)	gal	-gololosegileng	free (a)	vry	
-gebenya	glance (v)	vlugtig kyk	-golwane	senior (a)	senior	
gerama	grammar (n)	grammatika	gomela	about (adv)	rond	
go-	from (prep)	van	gomotsa	console (v)	opbeur	
go	than (conj)	as	-gomotsa	comfort (v)	troos	
go	to (prep)	na	gompieno	today (n)	vandag	
go	for (prep)	vir	-gona	snore (v)	snork	
go-	at (prep)	op	-gonega	shrink (v)	krimp	
go ala diatla	plead (n)	pleit	gone jaana	exact (a)	presies	
go ala diatla	plea (n)	pleidooi	go ngala	strike (n)	staking	
-gobelela	delegate (v)	afvaardig	go ngunanguna	murmur (n)	gemurmel	
-gobola	sip (v)	slurp	-gongwe	distinct (a)	afsonderlik	
-gobua	wade (v)	waad	-gongwe	possible (a)	moontlik	
-godileng	mature (a)	volwasse	gongwe	perhaps (adv)	miskien	
-godileng	adult (a)	volwasse	gongwe	maybe (adv)	miskien	
godimo	high (a)	hoog	gongwe le gongwe	anywhere (adv)	enige plek	
godimo	aloud (adv)	hardop	-go nna seleme	lisp (v)	lispel	
godimodimo	higher (a)	hoër	go opa ga tlhogo	headache (n)	hoofpyn	
-godimodimo	paramount (a)	hoogste	go panya	wink (n)	knipogie	
-godisa	magnify (v)	vergroot	-gopola	recollect (v)	onthou	
go dutla	leak (n)	lek	-gopotsa	remind (v)	herinner	
-goeletsa	announce (v)	aankondig	gore	that (pron)	dat	
go fiswa ke letsatsi	suntan (n)	sonbruin	gore	because (conj)	omdat	
go fitlhelela	until (conj)	tot	go reng	why (adv)	waarom	
-goga	tow (v)	sleep	-goroga	arrive (v)	aankom	
-goga	pull (v)	trek	go rolela hutshe	salute (n)	saluut	
-goga	draw (v)	sleep	-go sa nagangweng	accidental (a)	toevallig	
-goga	smoke (v)	rook	go se ikanyege	dishonesty (n)	oneerlikheid	
-goga	move (v)	skuif	gosele	elsewhere (adv)	elders	
-goga mowa	gasp (v)	snak	go swa bokidi	frostbite (n)	vriesbrand	
-gogoba	drag (v)	sleep	go swa mfama	paralysis (n)	verlamming	
-gogoralang	flatulent (a)	winderig	-gotela	heat (v)	warm maak	
-gogoropa	curl (n)	krul	-gotetseng	inflamed (a)	onsteek	
go ikapaya mokatse	ignorance (n)	onkunde	go thuma	swimming (n)	swem	
go ikutla	retreat (n)	terugtog	go thunya	explosion (n)	ontploffing	
go ikutlwa o le motho	relief (n)	verligting	-gotlha	rub (v)	vryf	
go ja nala	tour (n)	rondreis	-gotlha	grate (v)	rasper	
-gokafala	fornicate (v)	hoereer	-gotlha	chafe (v)	skaaf	
gokelela	attach (v)	aanheg	-gotlha	bare (v)	ontbloot	
go kokota	knock (n)	klop	-gotlha	conflict (v)	bots	
go kwakwaetsa	stammer (v)	gehakkel	-gotlha	scour (v)	skuur	
go kwakwaetsa	stutter (n)	gestotter	go tlhatsa	nausea (n)	naarheid	
-gola	grow (v)	groei	go tlhatswega ngati	contentment (n)	tevredenheid	
-golafatsa	cripple (v)	kreupel maak	-gotlhegileng	bare (a)	kaal	
-golafatsa	maim (v)	vermink	go tlhoka	lack (n)	gebrek	
-golafatsa	deform (v)	vervorm	-gotlhola	cough (v)	hoes	
-gole	remote (a)	afgeleë	go tlhomola pelo	pity (n)	jammerte	
go lebelela	stare (n)	gestaar	go tlhotsa	limp (n)	mankheid	
-golega	handcuff (n)	boei	go tlola	jump (n)	sprong	
-golega	jail (v)	opsluit	go tlwaetsa setoropo	urbanisation (n)	verstedeliking	
-golo	main (a)	vernaamste	-gotsa	ignite (v)	aansteek	
-golo	capital (a)	hoof	go tshwara ditherisano	interview (n)	onderhoud	
go loga	weaving (n)	wewery	go tshwara ditlhapi	fishing (n)	visvang	

335

G	Tswana	English	Afrikaans	Tswana	English	Afrikaans
	gouta	gold (n)	goud	-isa ntle	export (v)	uitvoer
	-go wa ga letlhwa	snow (v)	sneeu	-isegang	agreeable (a)	aangenaam
	granadilla	granadilla (n)	granadilla	-itaya	hit (v)	slaan
	-gwatalalang	adamant (a)	onwrikbaar	-itayang tsebe	shrill (a)	skerp
	-gwela	copulate (v)	kopuleer	-iteka lesego	gamble (v)	dobbel
	-gwetlha	beckon (v)	wink	-itekanela	perfect (a)	volmaak
				-itekanelang	healthy (a)	gesond
	habore	oats (n)	hawer	-ithaopa	volunteer (v)	vrywillig onderneem
	-halofa	halve (v)	halveer	-ithaopang	voluntary (a)	vrywillig
	hambeka	hamburger (n)	hamburger	-ithuta	study (v)	studeer
	hamore	hammer (n)	hamer	-itlamolola	resign (v)	bedank
	hanasekhune	glove (n)	handskoen	-itlhaganela	rush (v)	haas
	haraka	rake (n)	hark	itlhagiso	approach (n)	nadering
	-haraka	rake (v)	hark	-itlhoma	suppose (v)	veronderstel
	harapa	harp (n)	harp	-itlontlolola	misbehave (v)	jou swak gedra
	-hema	breathe (v)	asemhaal	-itoka	excuse (v)	verontskuldig
	-hemela ntle	exhale (v)	uitasem	-itsa	prohibit (v)	verbied
	hempe	shirt (n)	hemp	-itsa	forbid (v)	verbied
	-hibidu	red (a)	rooi	-itsaya	conduct (v)	gedra
	-hira	hire (v)	huur	-itse	know (v)	weet
	-hira	rent (v)	huur	-itsegeng	well-known (a)	welbekend
	hotdog	hot dog (n)	worsbroodjie	-itsegeng	eminent (a)	vooraanstaande
	hotele	hotel (n)	hotel	-itsegeng	ordinary (a)	gewoon
	-huduga	migrate (v)	migreer	-itsegeng	famous (a)	beroemd
	-hudugang	migrant (a)	swerwend	itsegeng le ka la	alias (n)	alias
	huku	fish-hook (n)	vishoek	-itsemeletsang	reluctant (a)	teensinnig
	-humanegileng	poor (a)	arm	-itshoka	persevere (v)	volhard
	-humileng	rich (a)	ryk	-itshola setho	behave (v)	jou gedra
	-hupela	wheeze (v)	hyg	-itshupang	distinguished (a)	vooraanstaande
	-huranya	gnash (v)	kners	-itshupang	conspicuous (a)	opvallend
	-hutsafetseng	sad (a)	treurig	-itshupileng	prominent (a)	prominent
				-itshwarela	pardon (v)	vergewe
	-idibala	faint (v)	flou word	-itshwarela	forgive (v)	vergewe
	-idibetseng	unconscious (a)	bewusteloos	-itsise	notify (v)	kennis gee
	-ikaelela	intend (v)	van plan wees	-itsise	introduce (v)	voorstel
	-ikanya	depend (on) (v)	afhang (van)	-itsisi	disclose (v)	openbaar
	-ikanya	rely (v)	staatmaak	-itumelang	happy (a)	gelukkig
	-ikanyang	dependent (a)	afhanklik	-itumelang	glad (a)	bly
	-ikanyegang	loyal (a)	lojaal			
	-ikanyegang	faithful (a)	getrou	-ja	eat (v)	eet
	-ikgodisang	haughty (a)	hoogmoedig	-ja	dine (v)	hoofmaaltyd eet
	-ikotlhaya	repent (v)	berou hê	-ja	prey (v)	aas
	-ila	abstain (v)	onthou	jaaka	like (prep)	soos
	-ilama	brood (v)	broei	jaale	then (adv)	dan
	-iletsa	ban (things) (v)	verbied	-jaanong	now (adv)	nou
	-iletsa	ban (people) (v)	inperk	-ja boswa	inherit (v)	erf
	-iletsweng	banned (people) (a)	ingeperk	-ja moletlo	feast (v)	feesvier
	-iletsweng	banned (things) (a)	verbode	-ja monate	enjoy (v)	geniet
	-ilwang	hateful (a)	haatlik	-ja monate	savour (v)	geniet
	-ima	conceive (v)	opvat	-ja nala	tour (v)	rondreis
	-ina	immerse (v)	indompel	jang	how (adv)	hoe
	-ina	dip (v)	insteek	-ja pikiniki	picnic (v)	piekniek hou
	-ineela	devote (v)	toewy	jarata	yard (n)	werf
	-ineela	surrender (v)	oorgee	jase	coat (n)	jas
	-inela	soak (v)	week	jase	overcoat (n)	oorjas
	-inoga	emerge (v)	verrys	jase ya pula	raincoat (n)	reënjas
	-ipiletsa	appeal (v)	beroep doen op	ja -siana	race (v)	resies ja
	-ipobola	confess (v)	bely	jeke	jug (n)	beker
	-iposolosetsa	retaliate (v)	vergeld	-jela	credit (v)	krediteer
	isago	future (n)	toekoms	jeme	jam (n)	konfyt

Tswana	English	Afrikaans
jeresi	jersey (n)	trui
-jesa monate	delight (v)	bly maak
Jesu	Jesus (n)	Jesus
-jewa ke tlhong	ashamed (a)	skaam
-jewang	edible (a)	eetbaar
jiminastiki	gymnastics (n)	gimnastiek
joko	yoke (n)	juk
-jwala	sow (v)	saai
-jwala	plant (v)	plant
ka	with (prep)	met
-ka	my (pron)	my
ka	on (prep)	op
ka-	by (prep)	by
kaba	portion (n)	gedeelte
kaba	part (n)	deel
-kaba	plug (v)	toestop
-kabakanya	hesitate (v)	aarsel
kabakanyo	hesitation (n)	aarseling
-kabalanang	breathless (a)	uitasem
ka beke	weekly (a)	weekliks
kabele	cable (n)	kabel
kabelelo	guess (n)	raaiskoot
kabelo	offer (n)	aanbod
kabelo	share (n)	deel
kabelo	ration (n)	rantsoen
kabinete	cabinet (n)	kabinet
ka bomo	deliberate (a)	opsetlik
ka bonako	quickly (adv)	gou
ka bonako	fast (a)	vinnig
ka bonolo	effortless (a)	met gemak
ka bonolo	gently (adv)	saggies
ka bonolo	softly (adv)	saggies
kadimo	loan (n)	lening
kae	where (adv)	waar
-kaela	instruct (v)	onderrig
kaelo	instruction (n)	onderrig
ka ga	about (prep)	oor
kagiso	peace (n)	vrede
kagiso	welfare (n)	welsyn
kago	construction (n)	konstruksie
ka gonne	since (adv)	sedert
ka go sele	otherwise (adv)	anders
kakana	pipe (n)	pyp
kakana	wart (n)	vrat
kakanyo	logic (n)	logika
kakanyo	thought (n)	gedagte
kakanyo	meaning (n)	bedoeling
kakanyo	opinion (n)	mening
-kakara	grasp (v)	gryp
-kakaretso	general (a)	algemeen
kake	cobra (n)	kobra
kaketese	cactus (n)	kaktus
ka kutlo ya tsebe	acoustic (a)	akoesties
kala	branch (n)	tak
kala	twig (n)	takkie
-kala	weigh (v)	weeg
kalafo	cure (n)	genesing
kalaka	lime (n)	kalk
kalaka	whitewash (n)	witkalk
kalakune	turkey (n)	kalkoen
-kalela	hang (v)	hang
-kama	comb (v)	kam
-kamatlela	embrace (v)	omhels
kamatlelo	embrace (n)	omhelsing
kamela	camel (n)	kameel
kamera	camera (n)	kamera
kamo	touch (n)	aanraking
kamo	comb (n)	kam
kamogelo	adoption (n)	aanneming
kamogelo	acceptance (n)	aanvaarding
kamogelo	reception (n)	ontvangs
kamogelo	welcome (n)	welkom
kamore	bedroom (n)	slaapkamer
kamore ya boitapoloso	lounge (n)	sitkamer
ka moso	tomorrow (n)	môre
kampa	camp (n)	kamp
kampa	paddock (n)	veekampie
kana	either (pron)	een van beide
ka nakonyana	instantly (adv)	oombliklik
kanale	canal (n)	kanaal
-ka ne	approximate (a)	geskat
kane	can (v)	kan
-ka nna	may (v)	mag
kano	oath (n)	eed
kanono	cannon (n)	kanon
kanta	lace (n)	kant
kantoro ya dikaraki	box office (n)	kaartjieloket
kantoro ya dithekethe	ticket office (n)	kaartjieskantoor
kapa	rafter (n)	dakbalk
kapetla	fragment (n)	brokstuk
-kapodisa	pronounce (v)	uitspreek
kapodiso	pronunciation (n)	uitspraak
ka puo	verbal (a)	mondeling
karabo	answer (n)	antwoord
karabo	reply (n)	antwoord
karafane	caravan (n)	karavaan
karaje	garage (n)	motorhawe
karaki	cart (n)	kar
karata	card (n)	kaart
karata ya mojela	credit card (n)	kredietkaart
karo	surgery (n)	chirurgie
karo	operation (n)	operasie
karolo	section (n)	afdeling
kase	cheese (n)	kaas
kataloko	catalogue (n)	katalogus
katara	guitar (n)	kitaar
-katisa	coach (v)	afrig
-katisa	train (v)	afrig
-katisa	practise (v)	oefen
-katisa	tame (v)	tem
katlanegiso	recommendation (n)	aanbeveling
katlanego	achievement (n)	prestasie
katlego	success (n)	sukses
katlholelopele	prejudice (n)	vooroordeel
katlholo	judgment (n)	oordeel
katlholo	verdict (n)	uitspraak
katlo	kiss (n)	soen
ka tolamo	just (a)	regverdig

K	Tswana	English	Afrikaans	Tswana	English	Afrikaans
	-katolosa	enlarge (v)	vergroot	-kgama	throttle (v)	wurg
	katsana	kitten (n)	katjie	kgamelo	pail (n)	emmer
	katse	cat (n)	kat	kgamelo	bucket (n)	emmer
	ka tshoganyetso	unexpectedly (adv)	onverwags	kgamorego	daze (n)	bedwelming
	ka tshoganyetso	sudden (a)	skielik	kganelo	prevention (n)	voorkoming
	ka tshoganyo	accidentally (adv)	toevallig	kganetsano	dispute (n)	onenigheid
	kausu	stockings (n)	kouse	kganetsanyo	disagreement (n)	meningsverskil
	kausu	sock (n)	sokkie	kganetso	opposition (n)	opposisie
	-kaya	allege (v)	beweer	kganetso	contradiction (n)	weerspreking
	-kaya	mean (v)	bedoel	kgang	argument (n)	argument
	ke	through (prep)	deur	kgang	discussion (n)	bespreking
	-ke	be (v)	wees	kgang	conversation (n)	gesprek
	ke-	by (prep)	by	kgang	news (n)	nuus
	keetane	chain (n)	ketting	kgang	story (n)	verhaal
	ke fa	then (adv)	toe	kgang e e gotlhang	controversy (n)	twispunt
	keletso	desire (n)	begeerte	-kganna	restrain (v)	beperk
	keletso	envy (n)	naywer	-kganna	restrict (v)	inperk
	keletso	wish (n)	wens	-kganna	prevent (v)	voorkom
	keletso ya dijo	appetite (n)	eetlus	kganno	restriction (n)	inperking
	-kelotlhoko	careful (a)	versigtig	kgano	rejection (n)	verwerping
	kemariso ya	artificial	kunsmatige	kganya	flashlight (n)	flitslig
	maitirelo	insemination (n)	inseminasie	-kganyang	bright (a)	helder
	kemo	standard (n)	standaard	-kgaogana	share (v)	deel
	kepu	crowbar (n)	koevoet	-kgaogana	part (v)	skei
	kere	gear (n)	rat	-kgaoganngweng	separate (a)	afsonderlik
	kereke	church (n)	kerk	kgaogano	parting (n)	paadjie
	kerese	candle (n)	kers	-kgaoganya	segregate (v)	segregeer
	Keresemose	Christmas (n)	Kersfees	-kgaola	amputate (v)	afsit
	Keresete	Christ (n)	Christus	-kgaolela	interrupt (v)	onderbreek
	kerikete	cricket (n)	krieket	kgaolelo	interruption (n)	onderbreking
	kerise	grease (n)	ghries	kgaolo	district (n)	distrik
	kerousara	groceries (n)	kruideniersware	kgaolo	chapter (n)	hoofstuk
	ketapele	preface (n)	voorwoord	kgaolo	area (n)	oppervlakte
	-kete	seem (v)	skyn	kgaolo	region (n)	streek
	-keteka	celebrate (v)	vier	kgaolo	zone (n)	sone
	keteko	celebration (n)	viering	kgaotso	interval (n)	pouse
	ketelelopele	introduction (n)	voorstelling	kgapa	eggshell (n)	eierdop
	-ketla	chip (v)	'n hap kry	kgapeletso	force (n)	krag
	ketlele	kettle (n)	ketel	kgapetla	ice (n)	ys
	ketlele ya tee	teapot (n)	teepot	-kgaphela metsi	row (v)	roei
	kgaba	misfortune (n)	teenspoed	kgara	breastbone (n)	borsbeen
	-kgabaganya	travel (v)	reis	-kgarametsa	push (v)	stoot
	kgabagare	afterwards (adv)	agterna	kgarebe	girlfriend (n)	nooi
	-kgabisa	decorate (v)	versier	kgaro	convulsion (n)	rukking
	kgabiso	ornament (n)	ornament	kgatelelo	pressure (n)	druk
	kgabo	ape (n)	aap	kgatelelo	emphasis (n)	klem
	kgabo	monkey (n)	aap	kgatelelo	oppression (n)	onderdrukking
	kgabo	flame (n)	vlam	kgatelelo ya madi	blood pressure (n)	bloeddruk
	kgaitsadi	sister (n)	suster	kgateletso	accent (n)	aksent
	kgaka	guineafowl (n)	tarentaal	-kgathala	mind (v)	omgee
	kgakala	far (adv)	ver	kgatiso	press (n)	pers
	kgakgamalo	surprise (n)	verrassing	-kgatla	impress (v)	beïndruk
	-kgakologelo	memorial (a)	herdenking	-kgatlha	admire (v)	bewonder
	kgakololo	reminder (n)	herinnering	-kgatlhang	admirable (a)	bewonderenswaardig
	kgakololo	advice (n)	raad	-kgatlhang	interesting (a)	interessant
	-kgala	criticise (v)	kritiseer	kgatlhano	meeting (n)	ontmoeting
	-kgala	admonish (v)	vermaan	kgatlhanong le-	against (prep)	teen
	kgalalelo	glory (n)	glorie	kgatlhanyo	join (n)	lasplek
	kgalemo	warning (n)	waarskuwing	kgatlhatalama	abacus (n)	telraam
	-kgama	choke (v)	verstik	-kgatlhega	interest (v)	interesseer

Tswana	English	Afrikaans	Tswana	English	Afrikaans	K
kgatlhego	admiration (n)	bewondering	kgonotswe	thumb (n)	duim	
kgatlhego	interest (n)	belang	-kgonya	halt (v)	stop	
kgato	beat (n)	ritme	kgoo	scream (n)	gil	
kgato	step (n)	tree	kgoo	cry (n)	kreet	
kgatsha	sprinkle (v)	sprinkel	kgookgoo	whooping cough (n)	kinkhoes	
kgelekiso	rhetoric (n)	retoriek	-kgopa	offend (v)	aanstoot gee	
kgeleswa	gland (n)	klier	kgopa	snail (n)	slak	
-kgetha	tax (v)	belas	-kgopa	trip (v)	struikel	
-kgetha	vote (v)	stem	kgope	bachelor (n)	jongkêrel	
kgetho	vote (n)	stem	-kgope	unmarried (a)	ongetroud	
kgetlane	collarbone (n)	sleutelbeen	-kgopisang	objectionable (a)	aanstootlik	
kgetsi	bag (n)	sak	kgopiso	scandal (n)	skandaal	
kgetsi	sack (n)	sak	-kgopo	obstinate (a)	hardkoppig	
kgetsi ya ga dimo	glovebox (n)	mossienes	-kgopolo	abstract (a)	afgetrokke	
kgobadi	casualty (n)	ongeval	kgopolo	idea (n)	idee	
-kgobela	heap (v)	ophoop	-kgora	satisfy (v)	bevredig	
-kgobokana	gather (v)	byeenkom	-kgoreletsa	obstruct (v)	belemmer	
-kgobola	belch (v)	wind opbreek	kgoreletso	obstruction (n)	belemmernis	
kgobololo	defamation (n)	belastering	kgoreletso	obstacle (n)	hindernis	
kgodisa	hiccough (n)	hik	kgoreletso	hindrance (n)	hindernis	
kgoeletso	announcement (n)	aankondiging	kgoro	gate (n)	hek	
kgofa	tick (n)	luis	kgorogo	arrival (n)	aankoms	
kgogedi	attraction (n)	aantrekking	-kgorotlha	rattle (v)	ratel	
kgogedi	magnet (n)	magneet	kgosana	aristocrat (n)	edelman	
kgogela	whirlpool (n)	maalstroom	kgosana	prince (n)	prins	
-kgogetsa	hook (v)	haak	kgosi	king (n)	koning	
kgogo	fowl (n)	hoender	kgosi	chief (n)	hoofman	
kgogo	hen (n)	hen	kgosigadi	queen (n)	koningin	
kgogolego	erosion (n)	wegvreting	-kgosoba	shuffle (v)	skuifel	
kgogoleloleswe	sewerage (n)	riolering	kgotelo	inflammation (n)	ontsteking	
kgogomelo	bay (n)	baai	-kgotha	jerk (v)	ruk	
-kgokela	pin (v)	vasspeld	kgotla	court (n)	hof	
kgokelelo	attachment (n)	gehegtheid	kgotla	jury (n)	jurie	
kgokelo	safety pin (n)	haakspeld	kgotla ya	supreme court	hooggeregshof	
kgokelo	pin (n)	speld	bokgaolakgang			
-kgokgoetsega	stumble (v)	struikel	kgotlelo	pollution (n)	besoedeling	
-kgokgontsha	ill-treat (v)	mishandel	-kgotlhaganeng	solid (a)	vas	
kgokgotsho	windpipe (n)	gorrelpyp	kgotlhang	conflict (n)	konflik	
kgokgotso	larynx (n)	larinks	kgotlhang	quarrel (n)	twis	
kgolagano	connection (n)	verbinding	kgotlho	brass (n)	geelkoper	
kgole	thong (n)	riem	kgotlho	copper (n)	koper	
kgolegelo	prison (n)	gevangenis	kgotlholo	cough (n)	hoes	
kgolegelo	jail (n)	tronk	kgotsa	either...or (conj)	òf...òf	
kgolego	arrest (n)	inhegtenisneming	kgotso	ignition (n)	ontsteking	
kgololesego	freedom (n)	vryheid	kgotsofalo	satisfaction (n)	bevrediging	
kgololo	release (n)	loslating	-kgotswana	chop (n)	tjop	
kgololo	acquittal (n)	vryspraak	-kgwa	spit (v)	spoeg	
-kgoma	touch (v)	raak	kgwafo	gill (n)	kieu	
-kgomarela	adhere (v)	kleef	kgwanyape	storm (n)	storm	
-kgomarelang	adhesive (a)	klewerig	kgwarapana	gravel (n)	gruis	
-kgomaretsa	paste (v)	plak	kgwatlha	purse (n)	beursie	
kgomo	beast (n)	dier	kgwatlha	sheath (n)	skede	
kgomogadi	cow (n)	koei	kgwebo	trade (n)	handel	
kgomotso	comfort (n)	troos	-kgwebo	commercial (a)	kommersieel	
-kgona	master (v)	bemeester	kgwedi	month (n)	maand	
-kgona	afford (v)	bekostig	kgweditharo	term (n)	termyn	
-kgonang	able (a)	bekwaam	kgwele	ball (n)	bal	
-kgonang	efficient (a)	doeltreffend	kgwethe	lump (n)	klont	
kgono	ability (n)	bekwaamheid	-kgwetlha	challenge (v)	uitdaag	
kgono	persuasion (n)	oorreding	kgwetlho	challenge (n)	uitdaging	

K

Tswana	English	Afrikaans	Tswana	English	Afrikaans
-kgwisa manga	annoying (a)	ergerlik	-kima	thick (a)	dik
khabetshe	cabbage (n)	kool	-kima	stout (a)	geset
khadia	around (adv)	rond	kiriba	wheelbarrow (n)	kruiwa
khai	cloth (n)	doek	kitlano ya meno	tetanus (n)	klem in die kake
khai	material (n)	lap	kitsego	renown (n)	beroemdheid
khaki	khaki (n)	kakie	kitsiso	notice (n)	kennisgewing
khateboto	cardboard (n)	karton	kitsiso	acquaintance (n)	kennismaking
khefi	café (n)	kafee	kitso	knowledge (n)	kennis
khemiso ya	artificial	kunsmatige	kitso	acquaintance (n)	kennis
maitirelo	respiration(n)	asemhaling	-koba	sack (v)	afdank
khemo	respiration (n)	asemhaling	-koba	jilt (v)	afsê
khiba	apron (n)	voorskoot	kobiso	irony (n)	ironie
khiboto	keyboard (n)	klawerbord	kobo	blanket (n)	kombers
kholetshe	college (n)	kollege	kobo ya diphofa	quilt (n)	verekombers
kholifolawa	cauliflower (n)	blomkool	koduntwane	tadpole (n)	paddavissie
kholoro	collar (n)	kraag	kofi	coffee (n)	koffie
khona	bend (n)	buiging	koketso	addition (n)	toevoeging
khona	corner (n)	hoek	koketso	increment (n)	verhoging
khoserete	concert (n)	konsert	koketso	increase (n)	verhoging
khoukhou	cocoa (n)	kakao	koko	chicken (n)	hoender
khuana	wallet (n)	notetas	kokoano	crowd (n)	skare
-khubama	kneel (v)	kniel	-kokobala	float (v)	drywe
khubu	instep (n)	boog	-kokobelang	calm (a)	kalm
khubu	navel (n)	naeltjie	-kokola	skim (v)	afskep
khudu	tortoise (n)	skilpad	kokolohutwe	heron (n)	reier
-khuduego	riotous (a)	wanordelik	-kokona	gnaw (v)	knaag
khudugo	migration (n)	migrasie	-kokonetseng	uneasy (a)	ongerus
khuduthamaga	committee (n)	komitee	-kokorala	bulge (v)	uitbult
khukhwane	bug (n)	gogga	-kokoropana	shrivel (v)	verskrompel
khukhwane	beetle (n)	kewer	-kokota	knock (v)	klop
khunologo	leave (n)	verlof	-kokotela	nail (v)	spyker
khunyelo	contraction (n)	inkrimping	-koloba	convince (v)	oortuig
khupamarama	secret (n)	geheim	kolobe	pig (n)	vark
-khupamarama	confidential (a)	vertroulik	kolobe e namagadi	sow (n)	sog
-khupamarama	confident (a)	vol vertroue	-kolobetsa	baptise (v)	doop
khuparelo	clasp (v)	klem	kolobetso	baptism (n)	doop
khupelo	asthma (n)	asma	kolofo	bat (n)	kolf
khupelo	asphyxia (n)	versmoring	koloi	truck (n)	trok
-khurumetsa	overshadow (v)	oorskadu	koloi	wagon (n)	wa
-khutla	cease (v)	ophou	-kolopa	throw (v)	gooi
-khutla	end (v)	eindig	-kolopa ka matlapa	stone (v)	met klippe gooi
-khutlisa	abolish (v)	afskaf	-kolota	owe (v)	skuld
khutlo	finish (n)	einde	-kolotisa	interrogate (v)	ondervra
khutlo	fullstop (n)	punt	-koma	nod (v)	knik
khutlolo	shrug (n)	skouerophaling	-koma	boast (v)	spog
khutlonne	rectangle (n)	reghoek	komelelo	drought (n)	droogte
khutlopono	horizon (n)	horison	-komota	plain (a)	gewoon
khutlotharo	triangle (n)	driehoek	kompone	compound (n)	kampong
khutlo ya ntwa	ceasefire (n)	skietstilstand	komputara	computer (n)	rekenaar
khutlwana	colon (n)	dubbelpunt	komputara	calculator (n)	rekenaar
khutsafalo	sadness (n)	droefheid	konferense	conference (n)	konferensie
khutsana	orphan (n)	weeskind	kongrese	congress (n)	kongres
khutshwafatsa	shorten (v)	verkort	-konkometsa	pretend (v)	voorgee
khutshwafatso	summary (n)	opsomming	konkreite	concrete (n)	beton
-khutswafaditsweng	brief (a)	beknop	konofole	garlic (n)	knoffel
-khutswafatso	briefly (adv)	kortliks	kontai	conductor (n)	kondukteur
-khutswane	short (a)	kort	konteraka	contract (n)	kontrak
khwaere	choir (n)	koor	kontinente	continent (n)	vasteland
-kiba	stamp (v)	bestempel	konturu	contour (n)	kontoer
kile	ever (adv)	ooit	konyana	lamb (n)	lam

Tswana	English	Afrikaans	Tswana	English	Afrikaans	L
-kopa	beg (v)	bedel	kutlo	reflex (n)	refleks	
-kopa	apply (v)	aansoek doen	kutlobotlhoko	sorrow (n)	smart	
-kopa	peck (v)	pik	kutlwano	agreement (n)	ooreenkoms	
-kopa	charge (price) (v)	vra	kutlwano	relation (n)	verhouding	
-kopa	request (v)	versoek	kutlwano	harmony (n)	harmonie	
-kopa boitshwarelo	apologise (v)	verskoning vra	kutu	stem (n)	stam	
-kopakopa	hop (v)	hop	kwaba	guava (n)	koejawel	
-kopana	meet (v)	ontmoet	kwaba	blot (n)	klad	
-kopana	unite (v)	verenig	kwa botlhabatsatsi	east (adv)	oos	
kopano	meeting (n)	vergadering	-kwadisa	enrol (v)	inskryf	
kopano	union (n)	unie	-kwaisa	aim (v)	mik	
-kopanya	combine (v)	kombineer	-kwakwaetsa	stammer (v)	hakkel	
-kopanya	join (v)	las	-kwakwaetsa	stutter (v)	stotter	
kopanyo	appointment (n)	afspraak	-kwala	record (v)	opteken	
kopela	button (n)	knoop	-kwala	write (v)	skryf	
-kopela	clasp (v)	vasklem	kwa ntle ga	besides (prep)	buiten	
kopelo	song (n)	liedjie	kwatsi	cancer (n)	kanker	
kopelwane	penknife (n)	knipmes	kwena	crocodile (n)	krokodil	
kopere	quince (n)	kweper				
kopi	cup (n)	koppie	Labobedi	Tuesday (n)	Dinsdag	
kopo	request (n)	versoek	Labone	Thursday (n)	Donderdag	
kopo	application (n)	aansoek	Laboraro	Wednesday (n)	Woensdag	
-korobetseng	uncooked (a)	ongaar	Labotlhano	Friday (n)	Vrydag	
korong	wheat (n)	koring	-laela	order (v)	beveel	
-koropa	scrub (v)	skrop	-laetsa	prescribe (v)	voorskryf	
korosetina	concertina (n)	konsertina	-lakasela	sparkle (v)	vonkel	
kota	quarter (n)	kwart	-laletsa	invite (v)	uitnooi	
kota	log (n)	blok	-laola	control (v)	beheer	
-kotama	squat (v)	hurk	-laola	direct (v)	beveel	
kota ya lefeelo	broomstick (n)	besemstok	-laola	manage (v)	bestuur	
kotlhao	penalty (n)	straf	-lapa	tire (v)	moeg word	
kotlhao	punishment (n)	straf	-lapileng	tired (a)	moeg	
kotlhao e e beetsweng thoko	suspended sentence	opgeskorte vonnis	-lapileng	weary (a)	vermoeid	
kotsi	accident (n)	ongeluk	-lapolosa	rest (v)	rus	
-kotsi	dangerous (a)	gevaarlik	-latela	result (v)	volg	
kotsi	danger (n)	gevaar	-latela	follow (v)	volg	
-kotsi	harmful (a)	skadelik	-latelang	next (a)	volgende	
-kotula	reap (v)	oes	-latlha	lose (v)	verloor	
-kua	scream (v)	gil	-latlha	cast (v)	werp	
-kua	howl (v)	tjank	-latofatsa	accuse (v)	beskuldig	
kubakubo	pulse (n)	pols	-latofatsa	charge (law) (v)	aankla	
kubu	hippopotamus (n)	seekoei	Latshipi	Sunday (n)	Sondag	
kudupanyo	spasm (n)	spasma	-latswa	lick (v)	lek	
kudupanyo ya tshika	cramp (n)	kramp	le	and (conj)	en	
-kuelela	applaud (v)	toejuig	le	too (adv)	ook	
-kuka	lift (v)	oplig	Leaforekannere	Afrikaner (n)	Afrikaner	
kuku	tart (n)	tert	leano	plan (n)	plan	
kuku	cake (n)	koek	-leba	gaze (v)	staar	
kumako	reference (n)	verwysing	-leba	look (v)	kyk	
kumo	product (n)	produk	-leba	view (v)	bekyk	
kuranta	newspaper (n)	koerant	lebadi	scar (n)	litteken	
-kuruetsa	whimper (v)	sanik	lebaka	bakery (n)	bakkery	
kuruga	pimple (n)	puisie	lebaka	reason (n)	rede	
-kurukurega	detribalise (v)	ontstam	lebaka	cause (n)	oorsaak	
-kurusa	urge (v)	aanspoor	-lebala	forget (v)	vergeet	
-kurutla	growl (v)	knor	-lebaleba	scout (v)	rondkyk	
kutla	lair (n)	lêplek	-lebaleba	inspect (v)	inspekteer	
kutlo	obedience (n)	gehoorsaamheid	lebanta	belt (n)	gordel	
-kutlo	obedient (a)	gehoorsaam	lebanta la tshireletso	seatbelt (n)	sitplekgordel	
			lebati	door (n)	deur	

341

L	**Tswana**	**English**	**Afrikaans**	**Tswana**	**English**	**Afrikaans**
	lebatsana	plank (n)	plank	lefele	cockroach (n)	kakkerlak
	lebebe	cream (n)	room	lefelo	zero (n)	nul
	lebekere	mug (n)	beker	lefelo la go phaka	parking (n)	parkering
	lebele	breast (n)	bors	lefelo la kampa	camp site (n)	kampeerterrein
	lebele	sorghum (n)	sorghum	lefelo la mapodisa	police station (n)	polisiekantoor
	-lebelela	ascertain (v)	vasstel	lefifi	darkness (n)	donker
	-lebelela	stare (v)	staar	lefika	rock (n)	rots
	lebelo	race (n)	wedren	lefofa	feather (n)	veer
	lebelo	speed (n)	spoed	lefofora	crumb (n)	krummel
	lebelo la dipitse	horserace (n)	perdewedren	lefoko	word (n)	woord
	lebenkele	shop (n)	winkel	lefufa	jealousy (n)	jaloesie
	lebenkele	supermarket (n)	supermark	-lefufa	jealous (a)	jaloers
	lebenya	jewel (n)	juweel	lefuka	wing (n)	vlerk
	lebete	spleen (n)	milt	lefunelo	knot (n)	knoop
	lebitla	tomb (n)	graf	legadima	flash (n)	flits
	leblukomo	bluegum (n)	bloekomboom	legae	home (n)	tuiste
	leboa	mushroom (n)	sampioen	-legae	domestic (a)	huishoudelik
	-leboga	thank (v)	bedank	legae	abode (n)	woonplek
	-lebogang	grateful (a)	dankbaar	legaga	cave (n)	grot
	lebogo	arm (n)	arm	legago	rent (n)	huur
	leboko	poem (n)	gedig	legakabe	crow (n)	kraai
	lebolai	fang (n)	slagtand	legalanyana	cinder (n)	sintel
	lebole	fist (n)	vuis	le gale	however (conj)	maar
	lebolela	sting (n)	steek	le gale	anyhow (adv)	hoe dan ook
	lebone	lamp (n)	lamp	legapa	shell (n)	skulp
	lebone	lantern (n)	lantern	legapu	watermelon (n)	waatlemoen
	lebone	light (n)	lig	legare	razor (n)	skeermes
	lebota	wall (n)	muur	legata	skull (n)	skedel
	lebotlolo	bottle (n)	bottel	legatlapa	coward (n)	lafaard
	lebotsane	paunch (n)	boepmaag	legetla	shoulder (n)	skouer
	ledi	coin (n)	muntstuk	legodimo	heaven (n)	hemel
	ledimo	god (n)	god	legodu	glutton (n)	vraat
	lediri	verb (n)	werkwoord	legodu	thief (n)	dief
	lee	egg (n)	eier	legofi	palm (n)	palm
	leeba	pigeon (n)	duif	legogo	crust (n)	korsie
	leebana	epilepsy (n)	vallende siekte	legong	wood (n)	hout
	leela la mesele	drainpipe (n)	rioolpyp	legong	firewood (n)	brandhout
	-leele	long (a)	lang	legope	shoulderblade (n)	skouerblad
	leele	idiom (n)	idioom	legora	fence (n)	draad
	-leele	tall (a)	lang	legora	hedge (n)	heining
	leemedi	pronoun (n)	voornaamwoord	legora	barrier (n)	versperring
	leepantlo	burglar (n)	inbreker	legotlo	rat (n)	rot
	leeto	visit (n)	besoek	legwafa	armpit (n)	armholte
	leetse	plait (n)	vlegsel	legwaragwara	scoundrel (n)	skobbejak
	le fa	although (conj)	al	legwejana	ankle (n)	enkel
	le fa	even (adv)	selfs	lehihiri	cartilage (n)	kraakbeen
	le fa e le	nor (conj)	nòg	lehuba	tuberculosis (n)	tuberkulose
	lefafa	fin (n)	vin	lehumo	wealth (n)	rykdom
	lefapha	faculty (n)	fakulteit	-lehuti	hollow (a)	hol
	lefapha	department (n)	departement	leina	name (n)	naam
	lefapha la dikepe	navy (n)	vloot	leina	noun (n)	selfstandige naamwoord
	-lefatla	bald (a)	bles			
	lefatlha	twin (n)	tweeling	leinane	fable (n)	fabel
	lefatshe	world (n)	wêreld	leino	molar (n)	kiestand
	lefatshe	land (n)	land	leino	tooth (n)	tand
	lefatshe	earth (n)	aarde	leiso	hearth (n)	haard
	lefaufau	atmosphere (n)	atmosfeer	leiso	fireplace (n)	vuurherd
	lefeelo	broom (n)	besem	leitibolo	firstborn (n)	eersgeborene
	-lefela	vain (a)	ydel	leitlho	eye (n)	oog
	le fela	except (prep)	behalwe	-leka	try (v)	probeer

Tswana	English	Afrikaans	Tswana	English	Afrikaans
-leka	strive (v)	strewe	le mororo	though (conj)	hoewel
-leka	test (v)	toets	lemponempone	dwarf (n)	dwerg
lekakauwe	crab (n)	krap	lenaka	horn (n)	horing
-lekalekanang	even (a)	gelykmatig	lenala	fingernail (n)	vingernael
-lekalekaneng	level (a)	gelyk	lenanatiro	timetable (n)	rooster
-lekana	equal (v)	gelyk wees aan	lenaneo	programme (n)	program
-lekanang	enough (a)	genoeg	lenaneo	program (n)	program
-lekanang	equal (a)	gelyk	lenanetema	agenda (n)	agenda
-lekanang	adequate (a)	voldoende	lenanethuto	syllabus (n)	leerplan
-lekanya	measure (v)	meet	lenao	foot (n)	voet
-lekanya	fit (v)	pas	leng	when (adv)	wanneer
lekau	boyfriend (n)	kêrel	lenga	crack (n)	kraak
lekaulengwe	brother (n)	broer	lengami	groin (n)	lies
lekekema	reef (n)	rif	lengau	cheetah (n)	jagluiperd
lekese	coffin (n)	doodskis	lengena	earring (n)	oorring
lekgaba	hill (n)	heuwel	lengole	knee (n)	knie
lekgabisa	decoration (n)	versiering	lenko	fragrance (n)	geur
-lekgasa	tattered (a)	toiingrig	lenong	vulture (n)	aasvoël
lekgetho	tax (n)	belasting	lente	ribbon (n)	lint
lekgoba	slave (n)	slaaf	lentle	outside (n)	buitekant
lekgolo	century (sport) (n)	honderdtal	lentswe	voice (n)	stem
lekgolo	hundred (n)	honderd	lenyalo	wedding (n)	bruilof
lekgotla	council (n)	raad	lenyalo	marriage (n)	huwelik
lekgotla la boipiletso	appeal court (n)	appélhof	lenyatso	contempt (n)	veragting
lekgwafo	lung (n)	long	lenyenye	maggot (n)	maaier
lekgwamolelo	volcano (n)	vulkaan	lenyora	thirst (n)	dors
lekhubu	wave (n)	brander	leoto	leg (n)	been
lekhubu	ridge (n)	rug	leotwana	wheel (n)	wiel
-lekola	check (v)	nagaan	-lepa	watch (v)	dophou
lekollwane	stork (n)	ooievaar	-lepa	observe (v)	waarneem
lekwalo	letter (n)	brief	lepalo	scab (n)	rofie
lekwalotetla	licence (n)	lisensie	lepele	penis (n)	penis
lekwati	bark (n)	bas	-lepeletsa	suspend (v)	opskort
lekwele	potato (n)	aartappel	lephaka	vacuum (n)	lugleegte
lela	intestine (n)	derm	lephatlo	chip (computer) (n)	vlokkie
-lela	weep (v)	huil	lephothoselo	waterfall (n)	waterval
-lela	ring (v)	lui	lephutshana	butternut (n)	botterskorsie
lela-la-sebi	rectum (n)	rektum	lephutshe	pumpkin (n)	pampoen
lelatlha	battery (n)	battery	lepodisa	policeman (n)	polisieman
lelatlha	coal (n)	steenkool	lepodisi	constable (n)	konstabel
-lelefatsa	elongate (v)	verleng	lepokoso	box (n)	doos
-leleka	pursue (v)	najaag	-lepono	naked (a)	kaal
leleme	tongue (n)	tong	leraga	sediment (n)	sediment
lelengwana	uvula (n)	kleintongetjie	lerago	buttock (n)	boud
leloba	cotton wool (n)	watte	leralalo	disaster (n)	ramp
lelobu	chameleon (n)	verkleurmannetjie	lerang	ray (n)	straal
lelokololo	joint (n)	gewrig	lerang la letsatsi	sunbeam (n)	sonstraal
-lema	cultivate (v)	bewerk	lerapa	rein (n)	leisel
-lema	plough (v)	ploeg	lerapo	bone (n)	been
lemao	knitting needle (n)	breinaald	leratla	noise (n)	geraas
lemao	injection (n)	inspuiting	-leratla	noisy (a)	raserig
lemao	needle (n)	naald	lerato	love (n)	liefde
lemapo	peg (n)	pen	lere	stepladder (n)	trapleer
lemena	pit (n)	gat	lereo	term (n)	term
lemena	ditch (n)	sloot	leriba	ledge (n)	rotslys
lemeno	hem (n)	soom	leribi	dough (n)	deeg
lemeno	fold (n)	vou	leroba	pockmark (n)	pokmerk
-lemoga	recognise (v)	herken	leroba la kopela	buttonhole (n)	knoopsgat
-lemoga	notice (v)	opmerk	lerobananko	nostril (n)	neusgat
lemorago	background (n)	agtergrond	leroborobo	epidemic (n)	epidemie

L

Tswana	English	Afrikaans	Tswana	English	Afrikaans
leroborobo	plague (n)	plaag	letlape	peel (n)	skil
lerole	dust (n)	stof	letlapi	husk (n)	skil
leroo	paw (n)	poot	letlatlana	dusk (n)	skemer
lerophi	blister (n)	blaar	letlha	date (n)	datum
lerothodi	drip (n)	drup	letlhaa	jaw (n)	kaak
lerothodi	raindrop (n)	reëndruppel	letlhafula	autumn (n)	herfs
leru	cloud (n)	wolk	letlhaka	reed (n)	riet
leruarua	whale (n)	walvis	letlhaka	straw (n)	strooi
lerudi	biceps (n)	biseps	letlhalela	wrist (n)	pols
lerumo	bullet (n)	koeël	letlhalosi	adverb (n)	bywoord
lerumo	lead (n)	lood	letlhao	rattle (n)	ratel
lerumo	spear (n)	spies	letlhaodi	adjective (n)	byvoeglike naamwoord
-lesa	omit (v)	weglaat	letlhare	leaf (n)	blaar
lesalela	remainder (n)	oorblyfsel	letlharelegolo	petal (n)	kroonblaar
lesama	cheek (n)	wang	letlhogonolo	fortune (n)	fortuin
lesasupa	fabric (n)	tekstielstof	letlhokwa	match (n)	vuurhoutjie
lesea	baby (n)	baba	letlhole	clot (n)	klont
-lesedi	light (a)	lig	letlhoo	hatred (n)	haat
lesedi la letsatsi	sunlight (n)	sonlig	letlhotlho	discrimination (n)	diskriminasie
lesedi la ngwedi	moonlight (n)	maanlig	letlhotlholo	skeleton (n)	geraamte
lesego	luck (n)	geluk	letlhotlholo	vertebra (n)	werwel
lesego	blessing (n)	seëning	letlhwa	snow (n)	sneeu
leseka	bangle (n)	armband	letlodi	pool (n)	poel
leseka	anklet (n)	enkelring	letlole	organ (n)	orrel
lesekere	famine (n)	hongersnood	letlole	safe (n)	brandkluis
lesela	rag (n)	lap	-letlotla	ramshackle (a)	bouvallig
lesepa	excreta (n)	uitwerpsel	-letobo	dim (a)	dof
lesi	eyelid (n)	ooglid	letonkomane	peanut (n)	grondboontjie
lesika	vein (n)	aar	letsadi	bruise (n)	kneusplek
lesika	nerve (n)	senuwee	-letsa lenaka	hoot (v)	toet
lesika	sinew (n)	sening	letsapa	weariness (n)	moegheid
lesilo	fool (n)	dwaas	letsatsi	sun (n)	son
lesire	veil (n)	sluier	letsatsi	day (n)	dag
leso	death (n)	dood	letseka	detective (n)	speurder
lesokolela	heartburn (n)	sooibrand	letsele	teat (n)	tepel
lesole	soldier (n)	soldaat	letseta	cotton (n)	katoen
lesomo	group (n)	groep	letsetse	flea (n)	vlooi
lesupatsela	scout (n)	verkenner	letsha	lake (n)	meer
-lesuthu	dense (a)	dig	letshanatswai	lagoon (n)	strandmeer
lesutlha	lout (n)	takhaar	letshogo	panic (n)	paniek
leswafe	albino (n)	albino	letsholola	diarrhoea (n)	diarree
-leswe	dirty (a)	vuil	letshololo	dysentery (n)	disenterie
leswe	filth (n)	vuilgoed	letshoroma	influenza (n)	griep
-leta	wait (v)	wag	letshoroma	malaria (n)	malaria
letagwa	alcoholic (n)	alkoholis	letshoroma	fever (n)	koors
letagwa	drunkard (n)	dronklap	letshoroma la mala	typhoid (n)	ingewandskoors
-letela	continue (v)	vervolg	letshotelo	manure (n)	mis
leteng	interior (n)	binneste	letshwao	mark (n)	merk
letheka	waist (n)	middel	letshwaokgwebo	brand (n)	handelsmerk
lethompo	hose (n)	tuinslang	letshwenyo	mischief (n)	kattekwaad
-letla	allow (v)	toestaan	-letshwenyo	mischievous (a)	ondeund
-letla	permit (v)	toelaat	letshwenyo	nuisance (n)	steurnis
letlalo	leather (n)	leer	letsogo	assistant (n)	helper
letlalo	skin (n)	vel	letsogo	sleeve (n)	mou
letlalo la tlhogo	scalp (n)	kopvel	letsoku	ochre (n)	oker
-letlanya	arbitrate (v)	arbitreer	letsuba	wrinkle (n)	plooi
-letlanyang	arbitrary (a)	willekeurig	letsutsuba	crease (n)	kreukel
letlapa	board (n)	bord	letswai	salt (n)	sout
letlapa	stone (n)	klip	letswalo	diaphragm (n)	diafragma
letlapa la phupu	tombstone (n)	grafsteen	letswela	bud (n)	botsel

Tswana	English	Afrikaans		Tswana	English	Afrikaans	**M**
leubelo	fan (n)	waaier		-maatla	vigorous (a)	kragtig	
leungo	fruit (n)	vrug		-maatla	powerful (a)	magtig	
lewatle	ocean (n)	oseaan		maatla	power (n)	mag	
lewatle	sea (n)	see		-maatla	strong (a)	sterk	
-lla	cry (v)	huil		-maatlametlo	excellent (a)	uitmuntend	
llene	linen (n)	linne		-mabela	funny (a)	snaaks	
llere	ladder (n)	leer		-mabela	proud (a)	trots	
lloko	padlock (n)	hangslot		mabitleng	cemetery (n)	begraafplaas	
llori	lorry (n)	vragmotor		mabole	boxing (n)	boks	
-loa	bewitch (v)	toor		mabuka	library (n)	biblioteek	
loa	thicken (v)	dik maak		madi	banknote (n)	banknoot	
loago	society (n)	samelewing		madi	blood (n)	bloed	
loapi	sky (n)	lug		madi	money (n)	geld	
lobaka	chance (n)	kans		madi	cash (n)	kontant	
lobone	torch (n)	flitslig		madilotsana	honeymoon (n)	wittebrood	
loeto	trip (n)	reis		maekorosekopo	microscope (n)	mikroskoop	
-loga	knit (v)	brei		maekorowafe	microwave (n)	mikrogolf	
-loga	weave (v)	weef		maemo	position (n)	posisie	
-loga leano	plan (v)	beplan		maemo	condition (n)	toestand	
logopo	rib (n)	rib		maemo	condition (n)	voorwaarde	
-lokela bothale	wire (v)	bedraad		maemo a bese	bus stop (n)	bushalte	
-lokolola	analyse (v)	ontleed		-mafafa	nervous (a)	senuweeagtig	
lokwalonyana	pamphlet (n)	pamflet		mafafa	nervousness (n)	senuweeagtigheid	
-lolamise	justify (v)	regverdig		-mafega	rude (a)	onbeskof	
-lolea	empty (a)	leeg		mafofonyane	hysterics (n)	histerie	
-loma	sting (v)	steek		mafoko	vocabulary (n)	woordeskat	
-loma	bite (v)	byt		-mafolofolo	enthusiastic (a)	geesdriftig	
-lomagana	connect (v)	verbind		mafolofolo	enthusiasm (n)	geesdrif	
lona	you (pron)	julle		mafulo	pasture (n)	weiveld	
-lona	your (pron)	julle		mafura	fat (n)	vet	
-lona	yours (pron)	julle s'n		mafura	fuel (n)	brandstof	
lonaka	ivory (n)	ivoor		mafura a kolobe	lard (n)	varkvet	
lonala	claw (n)	klou		magagana	battle-axe (n)	strydbyl	
lonala lwa leoto	toenail (n)	toonnael		magalapa	palate (n)	verhemelte	
-lopa	demand (v)	eis		magatwe	hearsay (n)	hoorsê	
-lopa	claim (v)	eis		magawegawe	uproar (n)	lawaai	
-lora	dream (v)	droom		magiseterata	magistrate (n)	landdros	
lorato	affection (n)	toegeneentheid		magogorwane	amateur (n)	amateur	
losi	edge (n)	rand		magogorwane	beginner (n)	beginner	
losi	beach (n)	strand		-magotsane	rough (a)	ru	
losi	eyebrow (n)	winkbrou		-magweregwere	hoarse (a)	hees	
losi	coast (n)	kus		maikaelelo	determination (n)	vasberadenheid	
losotlo	ridicule (n)	spottery		maikaelelo	ambition (n)	ambisie	
losotlo	scorn (n)	veragting		maikaelelo	aim (n)	doel	
loswana	spoon (n)	lepel		-maikaelelo	ideal (a)	ideaal	
-lotlela	lock (v)	sluit		maikaelelo	lust (n)	wellus	
-lotlhanya	antagonise (v)	vyandig maak		maikano	vow (n)	gelofte	
lotseno	income (n)	inkomste		maikemisetso	policy (n)	beleid	
-lwa	battle (v)	veg		-maikgantsho	immodest (a)	onbeskeie	
-lwa	fight (v)	veg		maikutlo	emotion (n)	gevoel	
-lwala	sicken (v)	siek word		maikutlo	mood (n)	bui	
-lwalang	sick (a)	siek		maikutlo	urge (n)	drang	
-lwalang	unhealthy (a)	ongesond		maithuto	academy (n)	akademie	
Lwetse	September (n)	September		maitirelo	artificial (a)	kunsmatig	
				maitlhamelwa	fiction (n)	fiksie	
maabane	yesterday (n)	gister		maitlhomo	goal (n)	doel	
maaka	lie (n)	leuen		maitseboa	evening (n)	aand	
maaka	cliff (n)	krans		maitseo	etiquette (n)	etiket	
maaka	falsehood (n)	onwaarheid		majato	agile (a)	rats	
-maaka	incorrect (a)	onjuis		makakaba	flake (n)	vlokkie	

M	Tswana	English	Afrikaans	Tswana	English	Afrikaans
	-makala	marvel (v)	wonder	-maswe	unclean (a)	onrein
	-makatsa	stun (v)	verstom	-maswe	ugly (a)	lelik
	-makatsa	surprise (v)	verras	-maswe	vulgar (a)	vulgêr
	-makatsa	amaze (v)	verbaas	mašwi	milk (n)	melk
	-makatsang	marvellous (a)	wonderbaarlik	mateng	entrails (n)	ingewande
	-makatsang	amazing (a)	verbasend	mateng	bowels (n)	ingewande
	makatso	amazement (n)	verbasing	matesisi	mathematics (n)	wiskunde
	makgakga	insolence (n)	parmantigheid	-mathaithai	vague (a)	vaag
	-makgakga	impolite (a)	onbeleef	mathata	stress (n)	spanningsdruk
	-makgaphila	messy (a)	morsig	mathe	saliva (n)	speeksel
	makgaphila	mess (n)	gemors	mathikithwane	slum (n)	krotbuurt
	-makgasa	ragged (a)	verflenterd	matlakala	refuse (n)	vullis
	-makgawekgawe	uneven (a)	ongelyk	-matlepetlepe	muddy (a)	modderig
	makidiane	mumps (n)	pampoentjies	-matlhagatlhaga	active (a)	aktief
	makoko	ride (n)	rit	matlhapolosa	nonsense (n)	onsin
	makukunopu	knob (n)	knop	matlhatsa	vomit (n)	vomeersel
	makusa	pantihose (n)	kousbroekie	Matlhatso	Saturday (n)	Saterdag
	malea	puzzle (n)	raaisel	matsale	mother-in-law (n)	skoonmoeder
	-maleba	direct (a)	direk	matsapa	effort (n)	inspanning
	malele	rubbish (n)	vuilgoed	matseno	entry (n)	binnekoms
	malepa	puzzle (n)	legkaart	matshinkilane	nightwatchman (n)	nagwag
	malepa	trick (n)	skelmstreek	matute	juice (n)	sap
	malome	uncle (n)	oom	matute a namune	orange juice (n)	lemoensap
	-mametlelela	glue (v)	gom	-me	mine (pron)	myne
	mametlelelo	appendix (n)	aanhangsel	-megagaru	greedy (a)	gulsig
	mamina	mucus (n)	slym	meiyara	mayor (n)	burgemeester
	mampa-a-kolobe	sundown (n)	sononder	mekhuri	mercury (n)	kwik
	mang	who (pron)	wie	-mena	fold (v)	vou
	mang	whose (pron)	wie se	-mena phatla	grave (a)	gewigtig
	manga	annoyance (n)	ergernis	-menekana	wriggle (v)	wriemel
	mang le mang	anybody (pron)	elkeen	menku	mango (n)	mango
	mankopa	shorts (n)	kortbroek	meno	teeth (n)	tande
	manno	seat (n)	sitplek	meno a maitirelo	dentures (n)	vals tande
	-manobonobo	comfortable (a)	gemaklik	-menoga	capsize (v)	omkantel
	manobonobo	luxury (n)	luukse	mentlele	medal (n)	medalje
	-manontlhotlho	diligent (a)	fluks	-merwalo	pregnant (a)	swanger
	mantle	faeces (n)	uitwerpsel	metara	metre (n)	meter
	manyokenyoke	zigzag (n)	sigsag	metere ya pula	rain gauge (n)	reënmeter
	mapele	genitals (n)	geslagsorgane	metlae	humour (n)	humor
	-maphara	shallow (a)	vlak	metlae	comedy (n)	komedie
	mapodisa	police (n)	polisie	-metsa	swallow (v)	sluk
	maragomagolo	thatch (n)	dekgras	-metsesegae	rural (a)	plattelands
	marakanamantsi	pancreas (n)	pankreas	-metsi	wet (a)	nat
	mareetsane	echo (n)	weerklank	metsi	water (n)	water
	marere	jelly (n)	jellie	mfinyane	shaft (n)	steel
	mariga	winter (n)	winter	mhiri	ring (n)	ring
	marinini	gum (n)	tandvleis	mhure	pod (n)	peul
	-mariri	hairy (a)	harig	mileone	million (n)	miljoen
	-maroka	accurate (a)	noukeurig	mmaba	enemy (n)	vyand
	-maronthotho	spotted (a)	gekol	mmaba	foe (n)	vyand
	marumo	ammunition (n)	ammunisie	mmaditlotlo	accountant (n)	rekenmeester
	-maruru	overcast (a)	bewolk	mmaele	mile (n)	myl
	masakana	brackets (n)	hakies	mmafu	acacia (n)	akasia
	masetete	mustard (n)	mosterd	-mmala	coloured (a)	gekleur
	masole	army (n)	leër	mmala	colour (n)	kleur
	maswabi	disappointment (n)	teleurstelling	-mmalwa	few (a)	min
	maswana	cutlery (n)	eetgerei	-mmalwa	several (a)	verskeie
	-maswe	mean (a)	gemeen	mmamathwane	bat (n)	vlermuis
	-maswe	bawdy (a)	onkuis	-mmamoratwa	favourite (a)	gunsteling
	-maswe	unhygienic (a)	onhigiënies	mmampodi	champion (n)	kampioen

346

Tswana	English	Afrikaans
mmaraka	market (n)	mark
-mmasepala	municipal (a)	munisipaal
mmasepala	municipality (n)	munisipaliteit
mme	lady (n)	dame
mme	anyhow (conj)	in elk geval
mme	but (conj)	maar
mme	mother (n)	moeder
mme	aunt (n)	tante
mmegi	reporter (n)	verslaggewer
mmelaelwa	suspect (n)	verdagte
mmele	body (n)	liggaam
mmelegisi	midwife (n)	vroedvrou
mmemogolo	grandmother (n)	ouma
mmeodi	barber (n)	haarsnyer
mmepe	map (n)	landkaart
mmesi	baker (n)	bakker
mmetli	sculptor (n)	beeldhouer
mmetli	carpenter (n)	timmerman
mmetšhe	mat (n)	mat
mmidi	maize (n)	mielies
mmila	street (n)	straat
mmino	music (n)	musiek
-mmino	musical (a)	musikaal
mmitlwa	thorn (n)	doring
mmitsa	charm (n)	sjarme
mmitsi	caller (n)	roeper
mmobodi	patient (n)	pasiënt
mmogedi	spectator (n)	toeskouer
mmogo	together (adv)	saam
mmoki	poet (n)	digter
mmokwana	measles (n)	masels
mmolai	murderer (n)	moordenaar
mmoni	eyewitness (n)	ooggetuie
mmopa	clay (n)	klei
Mmopi	Creator (n)	Skepper
mmotorokara	motorcar (n)	motor
mmotorokara	car (n)	motor
mmoulo	mule (n)	muil
mmu	soil (n)	grond
mmu	ground (n)	grond
mmudula	pollen (n)	stuifmeel
mmudungwana	stock (n)	voorraad
mmueledi	advocate (n)	advokaat
mmueledi	solicitor (n)	prokureur
mmueledi	attorney (n)	prokureur
mmueledi	lawyer (n)	prokureur
mmueledi	shop steward (n)	segsman
mmuledisi	escort (n)	metgesel
mmusaesi	dictator (n)	diktator
mmusi	ruler (n)	regeerder
mmuso	government (n)	regering
mmutla	rabbit (n)	konyn
mo	up (prep)	op
Moafrika	African (n)	Afrikaan
moagi	architect (n)	argitek
moagi	mason (n)	messelaar
moagi	citizen (n)	burger
moagisani	neighbour (n)	buurman
moago	building (n)	gebou
moaki	liar (n)	leuenaar

Tswana	English	Afrikaans
moanelwa	character (n)	karakter
moaparo	fashion (n)	mode
moapei	cook (n)	kok
moaposetolo	apostle (n)	apostel
moapoteke	pharmacist (n)	apteker
moapoteke	chemist (n)	apteker
moatlhodi	assessor (n)	skatter
moatlhodi	adjudicator (n)	beoordelaar
moatlhodi	judge (n)	regter
mobishopomogolo	archbishop (n)	aartsbiskop
modi	root (n)	wortel
modibonoka	willow (n)	wilgerboom
modidi	pauper (n)	behoeftige
modigedi	waiter (n)	kelner
modiko	circumference (n)	omtrek
modikologo	dizziness (n)	duiseligheid
modilolo	scowl (n)	suur gesig
Modimo	God (n)	God
modingwana	boil (n)	bloedvint
modinyana	radicle (n)	wortel
modiramolato	criminal (n)	misdadiger
modiredi	labourer (n)	arbeider
modirelwa	client (n)	kliënt
modiri	operator (n)	operateur
modiri	employee (n)	werknemer
modiri	worker (n)	werker
modiri	performer (n)	uitvoerder
modiro	ceremony (n)	seremonie
modiro	activity (n)	bedrywigheid
modisa	guard (n)	wag
modisa	shepherd (n)	skaapwagter
moditšhaba	stranger (n)	vreemdeling
moduedi	payer (n)	betaler
modulasetilo wa obedi	vice-chairman	ondervoorsitter
modulasetulo	chairman (n)	voorsitter
modumedi	believer (n)	gelowige
modumo	groan (n)	kreun
modumo	sound (n)	klank
modumo	thunder (n)	donder
modumo	roar (n)	brul
modutela	tributary (n)	takrivier
moduto	calabash (n)	kalbas
moedi	gutter (n)	geut
moedi	stream (n)	stroom
moefanggele	evangelist (n)	evangelis
moela′	current (n)	stroom
moemedi	representative (n)	verteenwoordiger
moemedi	deputy (n)	plaasvervanger
moemedi	agent (n)	agent
moemedi	ambassador (n)	ambassadeur
moengele	angel (n)	engel
moetedi	traveller (n)	reisiger
moeteledipele	leader (n)	leier
moeti	visitor (n)	besoeker
moeti	guest (n)	gas
moeti	caller (n)	besoeker
moetsana	bridesmaid (n)	strooimeisie
moetsi	actor (n)	akteur
moetsigadi	actress (n)	aktrise

M

Tswana	English	Afrikaans	Tswana	English	Afrikaans
mofantisi	auctioneer (n)	afslaer	moikanisi	commissioner of oaths (n)	kommissaris van ede
moferefere	riot (n)	onlus	moikanyi	dependant (n)	afhanklike
mofero	weed (n)	onkruid	moithaopa	volunteer (n)	vrywilliger
mofetoledi	interpreter (n)	tolk	moithuti	student (n)	student
mofetoledi	translator (n)	vertaler	moitimokanyi	hypocrite (n)	skynheilige
mofikela	sneeze (n)	nies	moitlami	nun (n)	non
mofinyana	handle (n)	handvatsel	moitshepi	saint (n)	heilige
mofu	wasp (n)	perdeby	moja	right (n)	regterkant
mofufutso	sweat (n)	sweet	mojabatho	cannibal (n)	mensvreter
mofufutso	perspiration (n)	perspirasie	mojaboswa	heir (n)	erfgenaam
mofuta	make (n)	soort	mojanala	tourist (n)	toeris
mofuta	kind (n)	soort	-mojato	energetic (a)	energiek
mofuta	type (n)	tipe	mojela	credit (n)	krediet
-mofutafuta	varied (a)	gevarieerd	mokabagangwe	seldom (adv)	selde
mofutafuta	variety (n)	verskeidenheid	mokaedi	instructor (n)	instrukteur
mogadibo	sister-in-law (n)	skoonsuster	mokaro	buttermilk (n)	karringmelk
mogaga	lily (n)	lelie	mokasa	block (n)	blok
mogagolwane	shawl (n)	tjalie	mokate	melon (n)	meloen
mogaka	hero (n)	held	mokatisi	coach (n)	afrigter
mogakolodi	adviser (n)	raadgewer	mokento	vaccination (n)	inenting
mogala	cord (n)	koord	mokento	inoculation (n)	inenting
mogala	rope (n)	tou	mokeresete	Christian (n)	Christen
mogala	telegram (n)	telegram	mokgaphe	obligation (n)	verpligting
mogala	telephone (n)	telefoon	mokgatitswane	lizard (n)	akkedis
mogaralefatshe	equator (n)	ewenaar	mokgatlho	co-operation (n)	koöperasie
mogare	germ (n)	kiem	mokgatlho	club (n)	klub
mogateledi	oppressor (n)	onderdrukker	mokgatlho	society (n)	vereniging
mogatla	tail (n)	stert	mokgobe	heap (n)	hoop
mogato	march (n)	mars	mokgono	limb (n)	ledemaat
mogobe	pan (n)	pan	mokgono	forearm (n)	voorarm
mo godimo	above (prep)	bo	mokgopha	aloe (n)	aalwyn
-mogodu	gastric (a)	maag	mokgopha	prickly pear (n)	turksvy
mogogoro	tunnel (n)	tonnel	mokgwa	habit (n)	gewoonte
mogokgo	principal (n)	hoof	mokgwa	method (n)	metode
mogolegwa	prisoner (n)	gevangene	mokgwa	manner (n)	manier
-mogolo	eldest (a)	oudste	mokgwasa	rumour (n)	gerug
mogolo	adult (n)	volwassene	mokgweetsi	driver (n)	bestuurder
mogologolo	ancestor (n)	voorouer	mokgweleo	burden (n)	las
mogoma	plough (n)	ploeg	mokibo wa pelo	heartbeat (n)	hartklop
mo go maswe	badly (adv)	sleg	moko	marrow (n)	murg
mogono	snore (n)	snork	moko	pith (n)	pit
mogope	hut (n)	hut	-mokodue	emaciated (a)	uitgeteer
mogopo	bowl (n)	bak	mokoko	cock (n)	haan
mogorogoro	valley (n)	vallei	mokoko	rooster (n)	hoenderhaan
mogosane	indigestion (n)	slegte spysvertering	mokokotlo	spine (n)	ruggraat
mo go se nang tlhaloganyo	absurd (a)	onsinnig	mokolela	spinal cord (n)	rugmurg
mogote	heat (n)	hitte	mokone	cocoon (n)	kokon
mogwe	son-in-law (n)	skoonseun	-mokong	steep (a)	steil
mogwebisani	partner (n)	vennoot	mokopi	applicant (n)	aansoeker
moheitene	heathen (n)	heiden	mokopi	beggar (n)	bedelaar
moheitene	pagan (n)	heiden	mokoro	boat (n)	boot
-moheitene	pagan (a)	heidens	mokoro	cistern (n)	waterbak
moheitene	unbeliever (n)	ongelowige	mokuane	rump (n)	kruis
mohiri	tenant (n)	bewoner	mokure	castor oil (n)	kasterolie
mohiri	lodger (n)	loseerder	mokutu	coccyx (n)	stuitjiebeen
mohiri	employer (n)	werkgewer	mokwadi	author (n)	skrywer
moidi	antagonist (n)	teenstander	mokwakwa	pavement (n)	sypaadjie
moietsi wa tshelo	cellist (n)	tjellis	mokwaledi	secretary (n)	sekretaris
			mokwalo	handwriting (n)	handskrif

Tswana	English	Afrikaans	Tswana	English	Afrikaans
mokwalo	writing (n)	skrif	molotsana	villain (n)	skurk
mokwatla	back (n)	rug	momela	malt (n)	mout
mola	row (n)	ry	momenagano	roll (n)	rol
mola	queue (n)	tou	mometso	throat (n)	keel
molaetsa	message (n)	boodskap	mometso	gullet (n)	slukderm
molala	neck (n)	nek	mometso	oesophagus (n)	slukderm
molangwa	brother-in-law (n)	swaer	mometso-o-mosweu	diphtheria (n)	witseerkeel
molao	rule (n)	reël	-mona	suck (v)	suig
molao	regulation (n)	regulasie	-monamune	citrus (a)	sitrus
molao	decree (n)	verordening	monang	mosquito (n)	muskiet
molao	law (n)	wet	-monate	nice (a)	aangenaam
-molao	legitimate (a)	wettige	-monate	delicious (a)	heerlik
-molao	lawful (a)	wettig	monate	pleasure (n)	plesier
-molao	legal (a)	wetlik	-monate	savoury (a)	smaaklik
molaodi	manager (n)	bestuurder	mong	owner (n)	eienaar
molaodi	captain (n)	kaptein	mong	landlord (n)	verhuurder
molaotheo	constitution (n)	grondwet	mongato	nappy (n)	babadoek
molapisi	bore (n)	vervelige mens	mongebo	smile (n)	glimlag
molatedi	fan (n)	bewonderaar	mong-gae	host (n)	gasheer
molatedi	disciple (n)	dissipel	mongwegi	deserter (n)	droster
molatedi	follower (n)	volgeling	monkgo	smell (n)	reuk
molato	charge (n)	aanklag	monkgo	stink (n)	stank
molato	crime (n)	misdaad	monko	perfume (n)	parfuum
molato	trouble (n)	moeite	monna	male (n)	man
-molato	guilty (a)	skuldig	monna	man (n)	man
molato	debt (n)	skuld	monnafa	aboriginal (n)	oorspronklike inwoner
molato	guilt (n)	skuld	monokela	gradually (adv)	geleidelik
molatswana	ravine (n)	kloof	monona	husband (n)	man
molebeledi	caretaker (n)	opsigter	monono	abundance (n)	oorvloed
molebo	tendril (n)	rankie	monontsha	fertiliser (n)	kunsmis
molekane	equal (n)	gelyke	monontsha	compost (n)	kompos
molekane	companion (n)	metgesel	monopi	earthworm (n)	erdwurm
molekgotla	councillor (n)	raadslid	monwana	toe (n)	toon
molelo	fire (n)	vuur	monwana	finger (n)	vinger
molelwane	boundary (n)	grenslyn	monyadi	bridegroom (n)	bruidegom
molelwane	border (n)	grens	monyadiwa	bride (n)	bruid
molema	left (n)	linkerkant	-monyela	absorb (v)	absorbeer
-molema	improper (a)	onfatsoenlik	monyo	dew (n)	dou
-molema	left (a)	links	mookana	mimosa (n)	mimosa
molemirui	farmer (n)	boer	mooki	nurse (n)	verpleegster
molemo	favour (n)	guns	mopalami	jockey (n)	jokkie
-molemo	good (a)	goed	mopalami	passenger (n)	passasier
molemo	medicine (n)	medisyne	mopapa	pope (n)	pous
molepera	leper (n)	melaatse	mo pepeneng	obvious (a)	vanselfsprekend
molepi	observer (n)	waarnemer	mo pepeneng	openly (a)	openlik
molete wa molelo	hell (n)	hel	mophato	gang (n)	bende
moletlo	feast (n)	fees	mophato	faction (n)	faksie
moletlo	festival (n)	fees	Mopitlwe	March (n)	Maart
moletsaphala	flautist (n)	fluitspeler	mopomi	hairdresser (n)	haarkapper
moletsiletlole	organist (n)	orrelis	moporofesara	professor (n)	professor
moletsi wa baeyolene	violinist (n)	vioolspeler	moporofiti	prophet (n)	profeet
moletsi wa phala	trumpeter (n)	trompetblaser	morago	after (place) (prep)	agter
moletsi wa piano	pianist (n)	klavierspeler	morago	behind (prep)	agter
molodi	whistle (n)	fluit	-morago	rear (a)	agterste
molomatsebe	informer (n)	verklikker	morago	back (adv)	terug
molomo	bite (n)	hap	Moranang	April (n)	April
molomo	mouth (n)	mond	morara	creeper (n)	klimop
molomo	beak (n)	snawel	moratho	bridge (n)	brug
molora	ash (n)	as	moratho	raft (n)	vlot
molora	soap (n)	seep	morati	lover (n)	minnaar

M	Tswana	English	Afrikaans	Tswana	English	Afrikaans
	morato	margin (n)	kantlyn	mosepele	journey (n)	reis
	more	poison (n)	gif	mosepele	footstep (n)	voetstap
	moreki	buyer (n)	koper	mosese	dress (n)	rok
	Morena	Lord (n)	Here	mosese	skirt (n)	romp
	moreri	preacher (n)	predikant	mosese	petticoat (n)	onderrok
	morero	plot (n)	komplot	mosetlho	groove (n)	groef
	morero	theme (n)	tema	mosetsana	girl (n)	meisie
	moreswedi	martyr (n)	martelaar	mosi	smoke (n)	rook
	moretlwa	raisin (n)	rosyntjie	mosifa	tendon (n)	sening
	moreto	strip (n)	strook	mosifa	muscle (n)	spier
	moriri	hair (n)	hare	mosima	hole (n)	gat
	moriti	shade (n)	skadu	mosima	adolescent (n)	jeugdige
	moriti	shadow (n)	skaduwee	mosimane	lad (n)	knaap
	moritibatsi	drug addict (n)	dwelmslaaf	mosimane	boy (n)	seun
	moro	sauce (n)	sous	mosimegi	official (n)	amptenaar
	moro	gravy (n)	sous	mosito	football (n)	voetbal
	moroba	heifer (n)	vers	mosito	rhythm (n)	ritme
	morodu	rust (n)	roes	-moso	late (a)	oorlede
	morogo	vegetable (n)	groente	mosokologi	convert (n)	bekeerling
	morogo wa seleri	celery (n)	seldery	mosola	use (n)	gebruik
	moroko	seam (n)	naat	-mosola	useful (a)	nuttig
	moroko	bran (n)	semels	mosola	advantage (n)	voordeel
	morokotso	profit (n)	wins	-mosola	beneficial (a)	voordelig
	morongwa	messenger (n)	bode	mosupatsela	guide (n)	gids
	morongwa	missionary (n)	sendeling	mosupi	witness (n)	getuie
	moropa	drum (n)	trom	Mosupologo	Monday (n)	Maandag
	moropana	tambourine (n)	tamboeryn	moswa	newcomer (n)	nuweling
	moroto	urine (n)	urine	moswagadi	widower (n)	wewenaar
	morubisi	owl (n)	uil	mošwe	meerkat (n)	meerkat
	morufa	jar (n)	fles	mosweswe	eczema (n)	ekseem
	morufadišeše	vase (n)	vaas	motala	barbarian (n)	barbaar
	morukutlhi	rebel (n)	rebel	motang	stalk (n)	stingel
	morulaganyi	editor (n)	redakteur	moteketo	assault (n)	aanranding
	morumo	rhyme (n)	rym	motele	motel (n)	motel
	morutabana	teacher (n)	onderwyser	mo teng	in (prep)	in
	moruti	lecturer (n)	dosent	mothalo	line (n)	lyn
	moruti	minister (n)	predikant	mothalo	stripe (n)	streep
	moruti	priest (n)	priester	mothama	mouthful (n)	mondvol
	morutwana	pupil (n)	leerling	mothama	volume (n)	volume
	morwa	son (n)	seun	mothangwana	sip (n)	slukkie
	morwadi	daughter (n)	dogter	Mothatiyotlhe	Almighty (n)	Almagtige
	morwadiaakgosi	princess (n)	prinses	motho	person (n)	persoon
	morwalela	flood (n)	vloed	Mothseganong	May (n)	Mei
	morwalo	load (n)	vrag	mothubiso	purgative (n)	purgeermiddel
	mosadi	wife (n)	vrou	mothudi	mechanic (n)	werktuigkundige
	mosadi	woman (n)	vrou	mothulama	slope (n)	helling
	mosamo	cushion (n)	kussing	mothulego	enema (n)	enema
	mosamo	pillow (n)	kussing	mothumi	swimmer (n)	swemmer
	mosebo	whisper (n)	gefluister	mothuthuntshwane	fungus (n)	swam
	mosegi	tailor (n)	kleremaker	motlae	joke (n)	grap
	moseja	beyond (prep)	oorkant	-motlakase	electric (a)	elektries
	moseja	overseas (n)	oorsee	motlakase	electricity (n)	elektrisiteit
	moseki	accuser (n)	beskuldiger	motlamedi	guardian (n)	voog
	moseki	plaintiff (n)	eiser	motlanyi	typist (n)	tikster
	moseki	complainant (n)	klaer	motlha	occasion (n)	geleentheid
	mosekisi	prosecutor (n)	aanklaer	motlhaba	sand (n)	sand
	mosekisiwa	accused (n)	beskuldigde	motlhagare	toothache (n)	tandpyn
	mosekisiwa	defendant (n)	verweerder	motlhala	afterbirth (n)	nageboorte
	moselammapa	rival (n)	mededinger	motlhala	track (n)	spoor
	mosenyammogo	accomplice (n)	medepligtige	motlhala	footprint (n)	voetspoor

Tswana	English	Afrikaans
motlhala wa monwana	fingerprint (n)	vingerafdruk
-motlha le motlha	daily (a)	daagliks
motlhami	composer (n)	komponis
motlhanka	servant (n)	bediende
motlhape	herd (n)	kudde
motlhape	flock (n)	trop
motlhatlhobatlotlo	auditor (n)	ouditeur
motlhatlhobi	inspector (n)	inspekteur
motlhoboloko	shaft (n)	skag
motlholagadi	widow (n)	weduwee
motlholo	wonder (n)	wonder
motlholo	miracle (n)	wonderwerk
motlhotlheletsi	activist (n)	aktivis
motlhotlheletsi	agitator (n)	opstoker
motlhware	olive (n)	olyf
motlodi	trespasser (n)	oortreder
motlotlo	tale (n)	storie
motlwaetsi	addict (n)	verslaafde
motokwane	cannabis (n)	dagga
motoutwana	weevil (n)	kalander
motoutwane	fishmoth (n)	vismot
motsadi	parent (n)	ouer
motsamao	walk (n)	wandeling
motsamayi	pedestrian (n)	voetganger
-motsana wa dintlha	suburban (a)	voorstedelik
motsana wa dintlha	suburb (n)	voorstad
motse	village (n)	dorpie
motse	town (n)	dorp
motse	household (n)	huishouding
motse	city (n)	stad
motseno	grin (n)	grynslag
motsereganyi	arbiter (n)	arbiter
motsereganyi	mediator (n)	bemiddelaar
motsereganyi	referee (n)	skeidsregter
motshameko	game (n)	spel
motshameko	sport (n)	sport
motshameko	play (n)	toneelstuk
motshamiki wa kerikete	cricketer (n)	krieketspeler
motshamiki wa moropa	drummer (n)	trompeler
motshegare	noon (n)	middag
motšhene wa go roka	sewing machine (n)	naaimasjien
motshewabadimo	rainbow (n)	reënboog
motšhini	machine (n)	masjien
motshwarwa	detainee (n)	aangehoudene
motsietsi	traitor (n)	verraaier
motsitlana	swamp (n)	moeras
motsoko	tobacco (n)	tabak
motsomi	hunter (n)	jagter
-motsopodia	indirect (a)	indirek
motsotso	minute (n)	minuut
-motsotsoropa	slender (a)	tingerig
motsotswana	second (n)	sekonde
motsu	arrow (n)	pyl
motswaiso	flavouring (n)	geursel
motswako	brew (n)	brousel
motswako	mixture (n)	mengsel
motswedi	fountain (n)	fontein
motswedi	source (n)	bron

Tswana	English	Afrikaans
motswere	ironwood (n)	ysterhout
motwane	shin (n)	skeen
-motwenene	straight (a)	reguit
moubo	throb (n)	klopping
mouta	mildew (n)	muf
moutlwalo	taste (n)	smaak
moutlwano	flavour (n)	geur
mouwane	fog (n)	mis
mouwane	mist (n)	mis
mouwane	haze (n)	waas
mowa	breath (n)	asem
mowa	spirit (n)	gees
mowa	soul (n)	siel
mowa	air (n)	lug
-mowafala	evaporate (v)	verdamp
mpa	stomach (n)	maag
mpa	abdomen (n)	buik
mpa	belly (n)	pens
-mpe	terrible (a)	vreeslik
mphe	tapeworm (n)	lintwurm
mpheetšhane	sandal (n)	sandaal
mpho	present (n)	geskenk
-mumu	dumb (a)	stom
-mumura	mutter (v)	mompel
musiamo	museum (n)	museum
-na	rain (v)	reën
naane	myth (n)	mite
naga	veld (n)	veld
naga	state (n)	staat
nagadimo	highveld (n)	hoëveld
naga e e lesuthu	bushveld (n)	bosveld
nagagare	inland (a)	binnelands
nagatlase	lowveld (n)	laeveld
nakedi	polecat (n)	muishond
nakedi	skunk (n)	muishond
nako	tide (n)	gety
nako	time (n)	tyd
nakonyana	moment (n)	oomblik
-na le	own (v)	besit
-na le	consist (v)	bestaan
naledi	star (n)	ster
naledi	planet (n)	planeet
nama	flesh (n)	vleis
nama	meat (n)	vleis
nama e e sitsweng	mince (n)	maalvleis
-namagadi	female (a)	vroulik
namagadi	female (n)	vrou
namane	calf (n)	kalf
namane	foetus (n)	fetus
namaoeme	reserve (n)	reserwe
nama ya diphologolo	venison (n)	wildsvleis
nama ya kgomo	steak (n)	biefstuk
nama ya kgomo	beef (n)	beesvleis
nama ya kolobe	pork (n)	varkvleis
nama ya kolobe	bacon (n)	spek
nama ya kolobe	ham (n)	ham
nama ya namane	veal (n)	kalfsvleis
nama ya nku	mutton (n)	skaapvleis
-na medupe	drizzle (v)	motreën

N

Tswana	English	Afrikaans
-nametsa	encourage (v)	aanmoedig
-namola	rescue (v)	red
namune	orange (n)	lemoen
-nana	young (a)	jong
-nana	tender (a)	teer
-nanganela	penetrate (v)	binnedring
-nangasela	tiptoe (v)	op die tone loop
nariki	naartjie (n)	nartjie
nato	caterpillar (n)	ruspe
nawa	bean (n)	boontjie
-naya	offer (v)	aanbied
-naya motho seditse	acknowledge (v)	erken
-naya pelo	helpless (a)	hulpeloos
-neo	talented (a)	talentvol
neo	talent (n)	talent
-nepagetseng	correct (a)	korrek
nepo	accuracy (n)	noukeurigheid
-nesa pula	acclaim (n)	toejuiging
netefaletso	guarantee (n)	waarborg
-netefatsa	guarantee (v)	waarborg
-ngadileng	angry (a)	kwaad
-ngadisa	anger (v)	kwaad maak
ngaka	doctor (n)	dokter
ngaka	herbalist (n)	kruiekenner
ngaka	witchdoctor (n)	toordokter
ngaka ya karo	surgeon (n)	chirurg
ngaka ya kgaolo	district surgeon (n)	distriksgeneesheer
-ngala	desert (v)	dros
-ngala	strike (v)	staak
ngame	miser (n)	vrek
-ngame	miserly (a)	vrekkerig
ngami	sponge (n)	spons
-ngangabolola	expand (v)	uitbrei
-ngapa	claw (v)	klou
-ngapa	scratch (v)	krap
-ngapa	scrap (v)	skrap
-ngaparela	cling (v)	klou
-ngaparetsa	stick (v)	vasplak
ngata	bundle (n)	bondel
ngata	sheaf (n)	gerf
-ngeba	smile (v)	glimlag
-ngodisa	moisten (v)	natmaak
-ngoka	attract (v)	aantrek
-ngolang	moist (a)	vogtig
-ngomaelang	sullen (a)	nors
-ngongorega	grumble (v)	brom
-ngongorega	complain (v)	kla
-ngongoregang	dissatisfied (a)	ontevrede
ngongorego	grievance (n)	grief
-ngotla	reduce (v)	verminder
ngwaga	year (n)	jaar
-ngwaga	annual (a)	jaarliks
ngwagakgolo	century (n)	eeu
ngwagakgolo wa keteko	centenary (n)	eeufees
ngwagamoleele	leap year (n)	skrikkeljaar
ngwagasome	decade (n)	dekade
ngwana	young (n)	kleintjie
ngwana	child (n)	kind
ngwana	toddler (n)	peuter

Tswana	English	Afrikaans
ngwanaangwanaka	grandchild (n)	kleinkind
Ngwanatseele	November (n)	November
ngwanyana	infant (n)	suigeling
ngwato	spot (n)	kol
-ngwe	another (a)	'n ander
-ngwe	single (a)	enkel
-ngwe	another (a)	nog 'n
-ngwe	some (a)	sommige
ngwedi	moon (n)	maan
ngwe le ngwe	each (pron)	elk(e)
-ngwe le -ngwe	any (a)	enige
ngwetsi	daughter-in-law (n)	skoondogter
-nkga	smell (v)	ruik
-nkga	stink (v)	stink
nkgodi	hawk (n)	valk
nko	nose (n)	neus
nko	muzzle (n)	snoet
-nkong	nasal (a)	nasaal
nku	sheep (n)	skaap
nkwe	leopard (n)	luiperd
nna	I (pron)	ek
nna	me (pron)	my
-nna	sit (v)	sit
nna	self (n)	self
-nna bosutlha	extravagant (a)	buitensporig
-nna le	have (v)	hê
-nna mong-gae	host (v)	gasheer wees
-nna teng	exist (v)	bestaan
-nna teng	occur (v)	voorkom
nne	four (n)	vier
-nnete	valid (a)	geldig
nnete	truth (n)	waarheid
nngwe	one (n)	een
-nngwe-tharong	third (a)	derde
-nnisa	house (v)	huisves
-nnye	small (a)	klein
-nnye	little (a)	klein
-nnye	less (a)	minder
-nnyela	defecate (v)	ontlas
-nnyennye	minute (a)	heel klein
noga	snake (n)	slang
noka	hip (n)	heup
noka	loin (n)	lende
noka	river (n)	rivier
noko	inch (n)	duim
noko	knuckle (n)	kneukel
noko	syllable (n)	lettergreep
noko	porcupine (n)	ystervark
-nolo	simple (a)	eenvoudig
-nonneng	fat (a)	vet
-nonneng	fertile (a)	vrugbaar
-nontsha	fertilise (v)	kunsmis gee
-nontsha	enrich (v)	verryk
nonyane	bird (n)	voël
-nopola	quote (v)	aanhaal
nopolo	quotation (n)	aanhaling
-nosa	irrigate (v)	besproei
-nosa	water (v)	natgooi
-nosa	score (v)	punte aanteken
nosetso	irrigation (n)	besproeiing

Tswana	English	Afrikaans		Tswana	English	Afrikaans	O
-nosi	alone (a)	alleen		ntwa	battlefield (n)	slagveld	
-nosi	only (a)	enigste		-nwa	drink (v)	drink	
-nota	pinch (v)	knyp		-nwela	sink (v)	sink	
notshe	bee (n)	by		-nwela	submerge (v)	onderdompel	
ntatemogolo	grandfather (n)	oupa		-nwela	dive (v)	duik	
-ntha	tough (a)	taai		-nyala	marry (v)	trou	
ntha	ligament (n)	ligament		-nyala	wed (v)	trou	
ntho	injury (n)	besering		-nyatsa	defy (v)	trotseer	
ntho	scratch (n)	krap		-nyatsa	loathe (v)	verafsku	
ntho	wound (n)	wond		-nyatsa	flout (v)	hoon	
-nthsa matlho dinameng	alert (a)	waaksaam		-nyatsa	belittle (v)	verkleineer	
-ntle	handsome (a)	aantreklik		-nyelela	disappear (v)	verdwyn	
-ntle	wonderful (a)	wonderlik		nyelelo	disappearance (n)	verdwyning	
-ntle	attractive (a)	aantreklik		-nyeletsa	exterminate (v)	uitroei	
-ntle	glamorous (a)	bekoorlik		-nyenyane	petty (a)	kleinlik	
-ntle	pretty (a)	mooi		-nyenyefatsa	humiliate (v)	verneder	
-ntle	beautiful (a)	pragtig		-nyorilweng	thirsty (a)	dorstig	
ntle	out (prep)	uit		-nyorolola	quench (v)	les	
ntle ga taolo	fate (n)	lot		nyumonia	pneumonia (n)	longontsteking	
-ntlentle	crack (a)	puik					
ntlha	direction (n)	rigting		oak	oak (n)	eikeboom	
ntlha	phrase (n)	sinsnede		-oba	bend (v)	buig	
ntlha	fact (n)	feit		-obama	bow (v)	buk	
ntlha	point (n)	punt		-obama	stoop (v)	buk	
ntlha	tip (n)	punt		obarolo	overalls (n)	oorpak	
-ntlha	first (a)	eerste		-obola	peel (v)	skil	
ntlhana	item (n)	item		ofisi	office (n)	kantoor	
ntlo	house (n)	huis		-oka	nurse (v)	verpleeg	
ntlo	dwelling (n)	woning		okese	band (n)	orkes	
ntlolehalahala	hall (n)	saal		okesetera	orchestra (n)	orkes	
ntlo ya phemelo	fort (n)	fort		-oketsa	increase (v)	vermeerder	
ntlo ya segosi	palace (n)	paleis		-oketsa	add (v)	byvoeg	
ntlwana	hovel (n)	pondok		-oketsang	additional (a)	bykomend	
ntlwana	cottage (n)	kothuis		-okisa	lure (v)	aanlok	
ntlwana kganya	lighthouse (n)	vuurtoring		-okisa	taunt (v)	uitlok	
ntlwana ya mogala	telephone booth (n)	telefoonhokkie		-okobatsa	quell (v)	demp	
ntsala	nephew (n)	neef		-okofatsa	accelerate (v)	versnel	
ntsala	niece (n)	niggie		-okomela	peep (v)	loer	
-ntse	while (conj)	terwyl		okosijene	oxygen (n)	suurstof	
-ntsenya	involve (v)	betrek		ole	oil (n)	olie	
-ntsha	evict (v)	uitsit		-oma	dry (v)	droogmaak	
-ntsha	subtract (v)	aftrek		-oma	feint (v)	voorgee	
-ntsha	vacate (v)	uittrek		-omana	quarrel (v)	twis	
-ntsha ga tshwene	best (a)	beste		-omanya	scold (v)	uitskel	
ntshane	blade (n)	blad		-omeletseng	arid (a)	dor	
-ntsha ntho	wound (v)	wond		-omileng	dry (a)	droog	
ntshi	eyelash (n)	wimper		-oobedi	both (a)	albei	
-ntsho	black (a)	swart		-opa	ache (v)	pyn	
ntshwe	ostrich (n)	volstruis		-opafatsa	sterilise (v)	steriliseer	
ntsi	fly (n)	vlieg		-opafetseng	sterile (a)	steriel	
-ntsi	much (a)	veel		ope	nobody (pron)	niemand	
-ntsi	many (a)	baie		-opela	sing (v)	sing	
-ntsi	plenty (a)	volop		-ora	bask (v)	koester	
ntsu	eagle (n)	arend		-othuma	nod (n)	knik	
ntswa	dog (n)	hond		-otlhaa	penalise (v)	straf	
ntswagadi	bitch (n)	teef		-otlhaya	regret (v)	spyt hê	
ntswanyana	puppy (n)	klein hondjie		-otlhaya	punish (v)	straf	
ntwa	fight (n)	geveg		-otlhe	every (a)	elke	
ntwa	battle (n)	geveg		-otlhe	entire (a)	hele	
ntwa	war (n)	oorlog		-otobala	wilt (v)	kwyn	

Tswana	English	Afrikaans	Tswana	English	Afrikaans
-otsela	drowse (v)	dommel	-pele	further (a)	verder
-otsela	doze (v)	sluimer	pelegi	birth (n)	geboorte
-otselang	sleepy (a)	vaak	-pelekanya	squint (v)	skeel
			-peleta	spell (v)	spel
paakanyetso	preparation (n)	voorbereiding	pelo	heart (n)	hart
pabalelo	economy (n)	ekonomie	-pelokgale	courageous (a)	moedig
padi	novel (n)	roman	-pelompe	cruel (a)	wreed
-pagama	ride (v)	ry	-pelonolo	meek (a)	gedwee
-pagama	mount (v)	opklim	-pelonomi	kind (a)	goedhartig
-paka	testify (v)	getuig	-pelotelele	patient (a)	geduldig
paka	costume (n)	kostuum	-pelotlhomogi	merciful (a)	genadig
-paka	pack (v)	pak	-pelotshetlha	selfish (a)	selfsugtig
pako	praise (n)	lof	-pelotshweu	generous (a)	vrygewig
palabalo	chatter (n)	gebabbel	pelwana	embryo (n)	embrio
-palama	climb (v)	klim	pene	pen (n)	pen
-palama	scramble (v)	klouter	-penta	paint (v)	verf
-palameng	aboard (adv)	aan boord	pente	paint (n)	verf
palamente	parliament (n)	parlement	peo	coronation (n)	kroning
palo	number (n)	nommer	peo	seed (n)	saad
palogare	average (a)	gemiddeld	pere	pear (n)	peer
palophatlo	fraction (n)	fraksie	perekisi	peach (n)	perske
palo ya batho	census (n)	sensus	perese	purple (a)	pers
pampalamusu	grapefruit (n)	pomelo	pere ya obokado	avocado pear (n)	avokadopeer
pampiri	paper (n)	papier	pesaleme	psalm (n)	psalm
pampiri	writing paper (n)	skryfpapier	petelelo	rape (n)	verkragting
pampiri ya boithomelo	toilet paper (n)	toiletpapier	peterolò	petrol (n)	petrol
panana	banana (n)	piesang	petsana	foal (n)	vulletjie
-panya	blink (v)	knipoog	petso	blow (n)	hou
-panya	wink (v)	knipoog	-phadisana	compete (v)	wedywer
papadi	acquisition (n)	aanskaffing	phadisano	competition (n)	wedstryd
-papana	economise (v)	besuinig	phae	pastry (n)	pastei
papatso	commerce (n)	handel	phaka	park (n)	park
papiso	comparison (n)	vergelyking	phakela	morning (n)	oggend
papo	parallel (n)	parallel	-phakela	early (a)	vroeg
parafene	paraffin (n)	paraffien	phala	flute (n)	fluit
paresele	parsley (n)	pietersielie	phala	trumpet (n)	trompet
paroule	parole (n)	parool	-phala	excel (v)	uitblink
pasa	pass (n)	pas	phalolo	escape (n)	ontsnapping
pateletso	compulsion (n)	dwang	phaloso	rescue (n)	redding
paterone	pattern (n)	patroon	-phamola	snatch (v)	gaps
patlisiso ya loso	inquest (n)	doodsondersoek	phantshara	puncture (n)	lekplek
patlo	search (n)	soektog	-phanya	crack (v)	kraak
-pe	nothing (n)	niks	-phanya	rupture (v)	skeur
peba	mouse (n)	muis	-phanyega	burst (v)	bars
peelano	appointment (n)	aanstelling	-phaphasela	flap (v)	fladder
peelano	bet (n)	weddenskap	-phaphathi	flat (a)	plat
peeletso	deposit (n)	deposito	-phaphathi	wide (a)	wyd
-pega	load (v)	laai	-phaphati	broad (a)	breed
pego e e ikanetsweng	affidavit (n)	beëdigde verklaring	phapogo	deviation (n)	ompad
peinapole	pineapple (n)	pynappel	phapogo	detour (n)	omweg
pejama	pyjamas (n)	pajamas	phaposi	room (n)	kamer
pela	dassie (n)	dassie	pharakano	traffic (n)	verkeer
pelaelo	suspicion (n)	agterdog	phare	cucumber (n)	komkommer
pelaelo	doubt (n)	twyfel	pharo	slice (n)	sny
pelaelo	distrust (n)	wantroue	pharologano	difference (n)	verskil
pele	ahead (adv)	vooruit	-phasalala	publish (v)	uitgee
pele	onward (adv)	voorwaarts	phasalatsa	advertise (v)	adverteer
pele	before (prep)	voor	-phasalatsa	spread (v)	versprei
-pele	front (a)	voor	phasalatso	advertisement (n)	advertensie
pele	forward (adv)	vooruit	phase	trousers (n)	langbroek

Tswana	English	Afrikaans	Tswana	English	Afrikaans
phasele	parcel (n)	pakket	pholetšhe	polish (n)	politoer
phatadikgagane	fern (n)	varing	pholo	ox (n)	os
phatla	forehead (n)	voorhoof	pholo	recovery (n)	herstel
-phatlalala	disperse (v)	verstrooi	phologo	descent (n)	daling
phatlha	gap (n)	opening	phologolo	animal (n)	dier
phatlha	opening (n)	opening	phologolo	antelope (n)	wildsbok
-phatlhalala	adjourn (v)	verdaag	phologolo ya	vertebrate (n)	werweldier
phatlhatiro	vacancy (n)	vakature	mokokotlo		
-phatlhatiro	vacant (a)	vakant	pholosa	save (v)	red
-phatloga	split (v)	splits	-pholosa	deliver (v)	aflewer
-phatsima	glitter (v)	skitter	pholoso	salvation (n)	verlossing
-phatsima	shine (v)	skyn	phone	cheekbone (n)	wangbeen
-phatsimang	shiny (a)	blink	phontshi	bulldog (n)	bulhond
Phatwe	August (n)	Augustus	phoophoo	pawpaw (n)	papaja
phefo	wind (n)	wind	-phophotha legetla	value (v)	waardeer
phefo ya ledimo	gale (n)	stormwind	-phora	fake (a)	vals
phega	bosom (n)	boesem	phoso	mistake (n)	fout
phegelwana	comma (n)	komma	phoso	error (n)	fout
pheke	stallion (n)	hings	-phoso	wrong (a)	verkeerd
-phela	live (v)	leef	phoso	fault (n)	fout
-phelang	lively (a)	lewendig	photi	duiker (n)	duiker
-phelang	alive (a)	lewend	phufudi	vapour (n)	wasem
phelefu	ram (n)	ram	phufudi	steam (n)	stoom
pheletso	consequence (n)	gevolg	phukutsa	purge (v)	skoonmaak
phemelo	defence (n)	verdediging	Phukwi	July (n)	Julie
phensele	pencil (n)	potlood	phupu	grave (n)	graf
phenšene	pension (n)	pensioen	-phutela	wrap (v)	toedraai
phenyo	defeat (n)	nederlaag	-phutha	collect (v)	versamel
phenyo	triumph (n)	triomf	-phuthega	congregate (v)	vergader
-phepa	clean (a)	skoon	phuthego	assembly (n)	vergadering
phepa	pure (a)	suiwer	phuthego	gathering (n)	byeenkoms
-phephafatsa	purify (v)	suiwer	phuthego	congregation (n)	gemeente
-phephafatsa	clean (v)	skoonmaak	-phutholola	interpret (v)	vertolk
phephenene	sheet (n)	laken	phuting	dessert (n)	nagereg
phepheng	scorpion (n)	skerpioen	piano	piano (n)	klavier
pherefere	pepper (n)	peper	pidipidi	duck (n)	eend
pherefere	green pepper (n)	soetrissie	pikiniki	picnic (n)	piekniek
pheretlhego	disturbance (n)	oproer	pila	well (a)	goed
phesente	percent (n)	persent	piletsatshekong	subpoena (n)	dagvaarding
pheswana	breeze (n)	bries	pilisi	pill (n)	pil
phete	sanitary towel (n)	sanitêre doekie	pilisi	tablet (n)	tablet
phetogo	change (n)	verandering	pina	tune (n)	wysie
phetolo	reform (n)	hervorming	pinanyana	lullaby (n)	wiegelied
-phetsega	sprain (v)	verstuit	pina ya bosetshaba	anthem (n)	volkslied
phetsego	sprain (n)	verstuiting	pinki	pink (n)	pienk
phetso	decision (n)	besluit	pino	dance (n)	dans
phetso	conclusion (n)	gevolgtrekking	pipamolomo	bribe (n)	omkoopprys
phifalo	eclipse (n)	verduistering	pipelo	discipline (n)	dissipline
philo	kidney (n)	nier	pipelo	constipation (n)	konstipasie
-phimola	delete (v)	skrap	-pitika	roll (v)	rol
-phimola	erase (v)	uitvee	-pitlaganeng	crowded (a)	propvol
-phimola	wipe (v)	afvee	pitsa	pot (n)	pot
-phimola lerole	dust (n)	afstof	pitsanyana	saucepan (n)	kastrol
phiri-e-thamaga	hyena (n)	hiëna	pitse	horse (n)	perd
phirimo ya letsatsi	sunset (n)	sononder	pitsenamagadi	mare (n)	merrie
phitlho	funeral (n)	begrafnis	pitse ya lebelo	racehorse (n)	renperd
phitlho	burial (n)	begrafnis	pitse-ya-naga	zebra (n)	sebra
phofu	eland (n)	eland	pobe	dimple (n)	kuiltjie
phokojwe	jackal (n)	jakkals	-pobetsa	dent (v)	duik
phokoletso	discount (n)	afslag	podi	buck (n)	bok

Tswana	English	Afrikaans	Tswana	English	Afrikaans
podi	goat (n)	bok	puotlaopo	slang (n)	sleng
podilekgwana	ladybird (n)	lieweheersbesie	pusano	democracy (n)	demokrasie
poelo	gain (n)	wins	puseletso	backwash (n)	terugspoeling
pogisego	affliction (n)	beproewing	puso	reign (n)	bewind
poifo	fear (n)	vrees	pusoloso	vengeance (n)	wraak
polanka ya bonwelo	diving board (n)	duikplank	putlelelo	insurance (n)	versekering
polao	slaughter (n)	slagting			
polao	murder (n)	moord	raborolo	revolver (n)	rewolwer
polase	farm (n)	plaas	radisi	radish (n)	radys
polasetiki	plastic (n)	plastiek	-raga	kick (v)	skop
polelo	statement (n)	verklaring	-raga	boot (v)	skop
polelo	report (n)	verslag	raka	cupboard (n)	kas
polelo	talk (n)	praatjie	raka	shelf (n)	rak
polelo	sentence (n)	sin	rakabi	rugby (n)	rugby
poletiki	politics (n)	politiek	ramakwalo	postman (n)	posbode
-poletšha	polish (v)	poleer	ramatlotlo	treasure (n)	skat
polokelo	bank (n)	bank	rameno	dentist (n)	tandarts
polokelo ya dijo	pantry (n)	spens	rammino	musician (n)	musikant
polokesego	safety (n)	veiligheid	ramolongwana	secretary bird (n)	sekretarisvoël
poloko	savings (n)	spaargeld	-ranola	define (v)	bepaal
-poma	prune (v)	snoei	-raopa	import (v)	invoer
-pompa	pump (v)	pomp	rapalala	across (adv)	dwars
pompo	pump (n)	pomp	-rapameng	horizontal (a)	horisontaal
ponagalo	phenomenon (n)	verskynsel	-rapela	adore (v)	aanbid
ponalo	appearance (n)	verskyning	-rapela	pray (v)	bid
pono	vision (n)	gesigsvermoë	-rarabolola	unravel (v)	ontrafel
pono	view (n)	uitsig	-rarabolola	solve (v)	oplos
pono	sight (n)	sig	-rarolosa	dilute (v)	verdun
pontsho	show (n)	vertoning	raselaga	butcher (n)	slagter
pontsho	show (n)	skou	-rata	favour (v)	begunstig
pontsho	exhibition (n)	uitstalling	-rata	like (v)	hou van
poo	bull (n)	bul	-rata	prefer (v)	verkies
popego	physique (n)	liggaamsbou	-ratega	endear (v)	bemind maak
popelo	womb (n)	baarmoeder	-rategang	popular (a)	gewild
popo	doll (n)	pop	-rategang	affectionate (a)	toegeneë
popoleri	poplar (n)	populier	-rategwang	likeable (a)	beminlik
popoma	dune (n)	duin	-rategwang	lovable (a)	dierbaar
popo ya dinkgo	pottery (n)	pottebakkery	-ratela	stalk (v)	bekruip
poreimi	plum (n)	pruim	-ratha	box (v)	boks
poresidente	president (n)	president	-rathabolola	distribute (v)	versprei
poropo	cork (n)	kurk	-ratile	almost (adv)	amper
poseotore	postal order (n)	posorder	-ratiwa	beloved (a)	bemind
poso	mail (n)	pos	ratsale	father-in-law (n)	skoonvader
poso	post (n)	pos	ratsuru	lemon (n)	suurlemoen
posokarata	postcard (n)	poskaart	-re	say (v)	sê
posong	post office (n)	poskantoor	-rebola	approve (v)	goedkeur
poso ya mowa	airmail (n)	lugpos	-refosana	alternate (v)	afwissel
potata	sweet potato (n)	patat	reisi	rice (n)	rys
potla	pocket (n)	sak	reite	pane (n)	ruit
-potlaka	hurry (v)	jaag	rejisetara	register (n)	register
-potokela	gallop (v)	galop	-reka	buy (v)	koop
-potokwe	round (a)	rond	-reka	shop (v)	inkopies doen
potsane	kid (n)	bokkie	-reka	bribe (v)	omkoop
potso	inquiry (n)	navraag	rekere	rubber (n)	rubber
potso	question (n)	vraag	rekere	elastic (n)	rek
pounama	lip (n)	lip	-reketla	shake (v)	skud
pudula	bubble (n)	borrel	-rekisa	trade (v)	handel dryf
puduloso	inflation (n)	inflasie	-rekisa	sell (v)	verkoop
pula	rain (n)	reën	-rekolola	redeem (v)	goedmaak
puo	language (n)	taal	rekoto	record (n)	rekord

Tswana	English	Afrikaans	Tswana	English	Afrikaans	S
-relela	slide (v)	gly	-ruri	positive (a)	positief	
-relelang	slippery (a)	glibberig	-ruruga	swell (v)	swel	
-rema	chop (v)	kap	-rusa	rust (v)	roes	
-rema	curdle (v)	klonter	-ruta	learn (v)	leer	
-rema	brake (n)	rem	-ruta	educate (v)	opvoed	
-rera	preach (v)	preek	-ruta	lecture (v)	doseer	
-rerisana	consult (v)	raadpleeg	-rutegileng	qualified (a)	gekwalifiseerd	
resetshurente	restaurant (n)	restaurant	-rwala	wear (v)	dra	
-retelelwa	fail (v)	misluk	-rwalela	flood (v)	oorstroom	
-ribama	droop (v)	neerhang				
-ribolola	discover (v)	ontdek	-sa	still (adv)	nog	
-ribolola	invent (v)	uitvind	-sa atlholwang	undecided (a)	onbeslis	
rintlhwe	giant (n)	reus	sabole	sword (n)	swaard	
-roba	harvest (v)	oes	-sa bolokegwang	unsafe (a)	onveilig	
-roba	break (v)	breek	-sa bonweng	invisible (a)	onsigbaar	
-robala	lie (v)	lê	-sa bonweng fela	exotic (a)	eksoties	
-robala	sleep (v)	slaap	-sa diatla	industrial (a)	industrieel	
-robalang	asleep (a)	aan die slaap	-sa duelwang	unrewarded (a)	onbeloond	
robedi	eight (n)	agt	saelefono	xylophone (n)	xilofoon	
robongwe	nine (n)	nege	-saena	sign (v)	teken	
roboto	robot (n)	robot	saese	size (n)	grootte	
-roga	swear (v)	vloek	-sa felang	unfinished (a)	onvoltooid	
-roka	sew (v)	naaldwerk doen	-sa felang	incomplete (a)	onvolledig	
-rokwa	brown (a)	bruin	-sa fetogeng	unalterable (a)	onveranderlik	
-rola tiro	retire (v)	aftree	-šaga	saw (v)	saag	
-rolela hutshe	salute (v)	salueer	-sa ganelwang	undisputed (a)	onbetwis	
-roma	send (v)	stuur	šage	saw (n)	saag	
-romela	post (v)	pos	sa ikanyegang	false (a)	vals	
rona	ourselves (pron)	onsself	-sa ikanyegwang	unfaithful (a)	ontrou	
rona	we (pron)	ons	-sa ipeeng	impersonal (a)	onpersoonlik	
rona	us (pron)	ons	-sa itse	unknowingly (adv)	onwetend	
rona	our (pron)	ons	-sa itsegeng	queer (a)	snaaks	
-rona	ours (pron)	ons s'n	-sa itseng	unaware (a)	onbewus	
-ropologa	erupt (v)	uitbars	-sa itshwarelweng	unforgivable (a)	onvergeeflik	
-rora	roar (v)	brul	šaka	shark (n)	haai	
-roroma	shiver (v)	bewe	sakatuku	handkerchief (n)	sakdoek	
-roroma	tremble (v)	bewe	-sa kgonegwang	unsuccessful (a)	onvoorspoedig	
-rota	urinate (v)	urineer	-sakhutleng	boundless (a)	grensloos	
-rotha	drip (v)	drup	-sala	remain (v)	agterbly	
-roula	mourn (v)	rou	salata	salad (n)	slaai	
rouse	rose (n)	roos	sale	saddle (n)	saal	
rra	father (n)	vader	-sa lebalweng	unforgettable (a)	onvergeetlik	
rramabuka	librarian (n)	bibliotekaris	-sa lekaneng	unequal (a)	ongelyk	
-rua	rear (v)	grootmaak	samente	cement (n)	sement	
-rua	breed (v)	teel	santlhoko	gallbladder (n)	galblaas	
-rua	farm (v)	boer	-šapa	lash (v)	gesel	
rula	ruler (n)	liniaal	-sa pheleng	inanimate (a)	leweloos	
-rulaganya	organise (v)	reël	-sa rutwang	undisciplined (a)	ongedissiplineerd	
-rulaganya	arrange (v)	skik	-sa senolwang	undisclosed (a)	onvermeld	
-rulaganya	tabulate (v)	tabuleer	-sa senyegang	undamaged (a)	onbeskadig	
-rulaganya	edit (v)	redigeer	-sa siameng	unfit (a)	ongeskik	
-rulela	thatch (v)	dek	satane	demon (n)	bose gees	
-ruma	rhyme (v)	rym	satane	devil (n)	duiwel	
-rumola	tease (v)	terg	-sa thibelegeng	inevitable (a)	onvermydelik	
-rupisa	circumcise (v)	besny	-sa tlhabololwang	undeveloped (a)	onontwikkeld	
ruri	actually (adv)	eintlik	-sa tlhalosang	ambiguous (a)	dubbelsinnig	
-ruri	everlasting (a)	ewigdurend	-sa tlhokegwang	unimportant (a)	onbelangrik	
-ruri	permanent (a)	permanent	-sa tlhokomelang	inattentive (a)	onoplettend	
-ruri	sure (a)	seker	-sa tlhomamiswang	unfulfilled (a)	onvervuld	
-ruri	quite (a)	taamlik	-sa tlwaegang	abnormal (a)	abnormaal	

S	Tswana	English	Afrikaans	Tswana	English	Afrikaans
	-sa tlwaelwang	uncommon (a)	ongewoon	Seesemane	English (a)	Engels
	-sa tlwaelwang	unaccustomed (a)	ongewoond	-Seesimane	British (a)	Brits
	-sa tsalweng	unborn (a)	ongebore	Seetebosigo	June (n)	Junie
	-sa tshabeng	unafraid (a)	onbevrees	seetsi	copy (document) (n)	afskrif
	-sa tshepiwang	undependable (a)	onbetroubaar	seetsi	copy (book) (n)	eksemplaar
	-sa tshwanelwang	undeserved (a)	onverdiend	-sefa	sift (v)	sif
	-sa utlwang	inaudible (a)	onhoorbaar	sefako	hail (n)	hael
	šawara	shower (n)	stortbad	sefala	hymn (n)	gesang
	-Seafrika	African (a)	Afrika	sefala	granary (n)	graanskuur
	seako	grain (n)	graan	sefane	surname (n)	van
	seako	bunch (n)	tros	sefapo	bandage (n)	verband
	seamusi	mammal (n)	soogdier	sefatlhego	face (n)	gesig
	seane	proverb (n)	spreekwoord	sefefe	adulterer (n)	owerspeler
	seatla	hand (n)	hand	sefefe	prostitute (n)	prostituut
	-seba	whisper (v)	fluister	sefefe	whore (n)	hoer
	-seba	gossip (v)	skinder	sefikantswe	statue (n)	beeld
	sebabole	sulphur (n)	swawel	sefikantswe	monument (n)	monument
	sebaga	bead (n)	kraal	sefitlholo	breakfast (n)	ontbyt
	sebaka	turn (n)	beurt	sefo	sieve (n)	sif
	sebaka	space (n)	ruimte	sefofane	aeroplane (n)	vliegtuig
	sebala	stain (n)	vlek	sefofane	aircraft (n)	vliegtuig
	sebata	patch (n)	lappie	sefofi	kite (n)	vlieër
	sebata	predator (n)	roofdier	sefokabolea	sleet (n)	ysreën
	sebe	sin (n)	sonde	-sega	cut (v)	sny
	-sebele	personal (a)	persoonlik	segae	assegai (n)	assegaai
	sebete	liver (n)	lewer	segae	vernacular (n)	volkstaal
	sebetsa	weapon (n)	wapen	segakolodi	consciousness (n)	bewussyn
	sebidiso	yeast (n)	gis	segakolodi	conscience (n)	gewete
	sebipo	cover (n)	deksel	segokgo	spider (n)	spinnekop
	seboko	larva (n)	larwe	-segole	disabled (a)	gebreklik
	seboko	worm (n)	wurm	segole	snare (n)	strik
	sebokolodi	millipede (n)	duisendpoot	-segolo	particular (a)	besonder
	sebokolodi	centipede (n)	honderdpoot	segologolo	conservative (a)	konserwatief
	sebolaiwa	victim (n)	slagoffer	segologolo	past (n)	verlede
	sebolawa	prey (n)	prooi	-segompieno	current (a)	huidige
	sebolayaditwatsi	disinfectant (n)	ontsmettingsmiddel	segopa	swarm (n)	swerm
	sebono	anus (n)	anus	segopotsi	souvenir (n)	aandenking
	sebopelo	terrace (n)	terras	segwagwa	toad (n)	brulpadda
	sebopelo	mould (n)	vorm	segwagwa	frog (n)	padda
	sebopiwa	creature (n)	wese	segwai	spirits (n)	spiritus
	seboswa	convict (n)	gevangene	segwapa	biltong (n)	biltong
	sediba	well (n)	put	segwere	bulb (n)	bol
	-sedidi	giddy (a)	duiselig	segwete	carrot (n)	wortel
	-sedifatsa	illuminate (v)	verlig	sehuba	thorax (n)	borskas
	sediko	circle (n)	sirkel	sehuba	chest (n)	borskas
	sedimo	ghost (n)	gees	sehuba	phlegm (n)	fleim
	-sedimo	ancestral (a)	voorvaderlik	sehuba	donation (n)	skenking
	Sedimonthole	December (n)	Desember	sei	silk (n)	sy
	sediri	subject (n)	onderwerp	-se ikanyegeng	dishonest (a)	oneerlik
	sediriswa	tool (n)	werktuig	seile	canvas (n)	seil
	sediriswa	instrument (n)	instrument	seile	sail (n)	seil
	-sedumedi	religious (a)	godsdienstig	seile	tarpaulin (n)	seil
	seduti	hold (n)	vat	seipato	excuse (n)	ekskuus
	seedi	fluid (n)	vloeistof	seipato	pretext (n)	voorwendsel
	seela	liquid (n)	vloeistof	seiphimodi	serviette (n)	servet
	seelamaleka	balance (n)	balans	seipone	mirror (n)	spieël
	-seeleele	stupid (a)	onnosel	sejana	dish (n)	skottel
	seelo	measure (n)	maat	sejaro	aside (adv)	opsy
	seelo	unit (n)	eenheid	-se kae sepe	invalid (a)	ongeldig
	-seemera	incurable (a)	ongeneeslik	sekafo	scarf (n)	serp

Tswana	English	Afrikaans	Tswana	English	Afrikaans	S
sekai	signal (n)	sinjaal	-sele	else (adv)	anders	
sekai	symbol (n)	simbool	-sele	peculiar (a)	eienaardig	
sekai	sign (n)	teken	sele	cell (n)	sel	
sekai	omen (n)	voorteken	-sele	different (a)	verskillend	
sekaka	desert (n)	woestyn	-sele	strange (a)	vreemd	
sekaku	abscess (n)	verswering	seledu	chin (n)	ken	
sekale	scale (n)	skaal	selefera	silver (n)	silwer	
-sekama	lean (v)	leun	-selegae	internal (a)	intern	
-sekama	slant (v)	skuins loop	-selegae	local (a)	plaaslik	
sekaniri	hinge (n)	hingsel	selekano	quantity (n)	hoeveelheid	
sekao	example (n)	voorbeeld	selekanyi	gauge (n)	meter	
-sekaseka	discuss (v)	bespreek	selekanyo	dose (n)	dosis	
sekasetlhake	peninsula (n)	skiereiland	seleme	lisp (n)	gelispel	
sekebekwa	hooligan (n)	skollie	selemo	summer (n)	somer	
sekele	sickle (n)	sekel	selepe	axe (n)	byl	
sekepe	ship (n)	skip	selo	thing (n)	ding	
sekere	scissors (n)	skêr	selo	object (n)	voorwerp	
-sekeresete	Christian (a)	Christelik	selogo	knitting (n)	breiwerk	
sekerete	cigarette (n)	sigaret	seloki	spice (n)	spesery	
sekete	thousand (n)	duisend	selotlele	lock (n)	slot	
-sekete	such (a)	sulke	sematla	idiot (n)	idioot	
seketswana	yacht (n)	seiljag	sematla	birthmark (n)	moedervlek	
sekgamatha	dandruff (n)	skilfers	seme	whip (n)	sweep	
sekgatshi	sprinkler (n)	sprinkelaar	semela	plant (n)	plant	
sekgele	prize (n)	prys	semika	piece (n)	stuk	
sekgomaretsi	glue (n)	gom	semmuso	official (a)	amptelik	
sekgono	elbow (n)	elmboog	semonamone	sweet (n)	lekker	
sekgopi	insult (n)	belediging	-semotseng	urban (a)	stedelik	
sekgopi	offence (n)	oortreding	semphato	uniform (n)	uniform	
sekgwa	forest (n)	bos	sena	after (time) (prep)	na	
sekgwa	bush (n)	bos	senakgodi	pickpocket (n)	sakkeroller	
sekgwa	jungle (n)	oerwoud	-senama	smirk (v)	grynslag	
-sekgwa	overgrown (a)	toegegroei	-se nang boleng	synthetic (a)	sinteties	
sekgwa	wilderness (n)	wildernis	-se nang dibetsa	unarmed (a)	ongewapend	
sekgwage	hook (n)	haak	-se nang fenitšhara	unfurnished (a)	ongemeubileerd	
sekhukhu	umbrella (n)	sambreel	se nang kutlwisiso	misunderstanding (n)	misverstand	
sekhurumelo	lid (n)	deksel	-se nang maitseo	ill-mannered (a)	onmanierlik	
sekhurumelo	cap (n)	deksel	-se nang maitshwarelo	unmerciful (a)	ongenadig	
sekhutlo	angle (n)	hoek	se nang molato	innocent (a)	onskuldig	
-sekisa	prosecute (v)	vervolg	-se nang pelo	uncharitable (a)	onbarmhartig	
sekoka	invalid (n)	invalide	-se nang tebogo	ungrateful (a)	ondankbaar	
sekokonyane	smallpox (n)	waterpokkies	-se nang tiro	unemployed (a)	werkloos	
sekolo	school (n)	skool	-se nang tumelelo	unauthorised (a)	ongemagtig	
sekonopelo sa sipi	zipper (n)	ritssluiter	senate	senate (n)	senaat	
sekontere	tar (n)	teer	-senatla	industrious (a)	vlytig	
sekopo	shovel (n)	skoppie	-se na tlhaga	unwary (a)	onbehoedsaam	
sekoro	score (n)	telling	sengae	vagrant (n)	rondloper	
sekotleleithusetso	bedpan (n)	bedpan	-seng bopelonomi	unkind (a)	onvriendelik	
sekuamokgosi	alarm (n)	alarm	-seng botlalo	imperfect (a)	onvolmaak	
sekuka	lift (n)	hyser	-seng kotsi	harmless (a)	onskadelik	
sekurufu	screw (n)	skroef	-seng loano	unplanned (a)	onbedoeld	
sekuti	depression (n)	bedruktheid	-seng maemo	undignified (a)	onwaardig	
sekwašhe	squash (n)	muurbal	sengwe le sengwe	anything (pron)	enigiets	
-selabe	foreign (a)	vreemd	sengwenyana	gadget (n)	toestelletjie	
selabo	oar (n)	roeispaan	senkgamonate	deodorant (n)	reukweermiddel	
selae	lettuce (n)	blaarslaai	seno	drink (n)	drankie	
selaga	butchery (n)	slagtery	senokwane	robber (n)	rower	
selalelo	supper (n)	aandete	-senola	expose (v)	blootlê	
selatlhelamalele	rubbish bin (n)	vullisblik	-senola	reveal (v)	openbaar	
-sele	other (a)	ander	senotlolo	key (n)	sleutel	

S	Tswana	English	Afrikaans	Tswana	English	Afrikaans
	-sensara	censor (v)	sensor	serwalo	crown (n)	kroon
	sente	cent (n)	sent	sesana	pole (n)	paal
	sentlhaga	nest (n)	nes	sesana	stump (n)	stomp
	sentshamosi	chimney (n)	skoorsteen	-sesane	thin (a)	dun
	senwamaphodi	liqueur (n)	likeur	sesegabojang	lawnmower (n)	grassnyer
	-senya	damage (v)	beskadig	sesenyi	pest (n)	pes
	-senya	corrupt (v)	bederf	sesepa sa go beola	shaving cream (n)	skeerroom
	-senya	demolish (v)	afbreek	sesepa sa meno	toothpaste (n)	tandepasta
	-senya	mess (v)	bemors	seseto	idol (n)	afgod
	-senya	mutilate (v)	skend	seshwiri mo puong	eloquence (n)	welsprekendheid
	-senya	destroy (v)	vernietig	sesiraphefo	windscreen (n)	voorruit
	-senya	devastate (v)	verwoes	sesiro	screen (n)	skerm
	-senya	waste (v)	vermors	sesiro	curtain (n)	gordyn
	-senya maikano	perjure (v)	meineed pleeg	seso	sore (n)	seer
	-senyega	abort (v)	aborteer	seso	acne (n)	aknee
	-senyegang	corrupt (a)	bedorwe	seso	burn (n)	brandplek
	-senyegetsweng	abortive (a)	misluk	-sesole	military (a)	militêre
	-senyegileng	broken (a)	stukkend	sesolo	cheap (a)	goedkoop
	seokofatso	accelerator (n)	brandstofpedaal	sesupanako	watch (n)	horlosie
	-seola	damp (a)	vogtig	sesupanako	clock (n)	horlosie
	seoposengwe	unity (n)	eenheid	sesupo	symptom (n)	simptoom
	seotlwana	pet (n)	troeteldier	sesupo	sample (n)	monster
	sepapetlanyana	wafer (n)	wafel	-sešwa	modern (a)	modern
	-sepe	useless (a)	nutteloos	seswa	newly (adv)	onlangs
	-sepe	trivial (a)	niksbeduidend	-seta	carve (v)	sny
	-sepe	blank (a)	leeg	setabogisa mala	laxative (n)	lakseermiddel
	sepeiti	syringe (n)	spuit	setale	stable (n)	stal
	sepekere	nail (n)	spyker	setampa	samp (n)	stampmielies
	sephatlo	half (n)	helfte	seteisele	starch (n)	stysel
	sephetho	effect (n)	uitwerking	seteišene	station (n)	stasie
	sephimodi	duster (n)	stoflap	setempe	stamp (n)	seël
	sephimodi	eraser (n)	uitveër	setempe	postage stamp (n)	posseël
	sephimola	rubber (n)	wisser	setena	brick (n)	baksteen
	sephinyasapodi	ringworm (n)	ringwurm	seterooberi	strawberry (n)	aarbei
	-sephiri	private (a)	privaat	sethaiso	bow (n)	strik
	-sepoletiki	political (a)	polities	-sethakga	neat (a)	netjies
	seporo	rail (n)	staaf	sethetosekoupo	stethoscope (n)	stetoskoop
	seporo	railway (n)	spoorweg	sethibo	plug (n)	prop
	serai	trap (n)	strik	sethibo	stopper (n)	stopprop
	serala	platform (n)	platform	sethifikheiti	certificate (n)	sertifikaat
	serame	frost (n)	ryp	-setho	humane (a)	mensliewend
	seraopo	import (n)	invoer	-setho	human (a)	menslik
	serašwa	mineral (n)	mineraal	sethoboloko	midday (n)	middag
	sere	substance (n)	stof	sethunya	flower (n)	blom
	seresanta	sergeant (n)	sersant	sethuthuthu	motorcycle (n)	motorfiets
	serethe	butter (n)	botter	setimela	train (n)	trein
	serethe	heel (n)	hak	setimelasegaodi	express (n)	sneltrein
	seretse	mud (n)	modder	-setla	whip (v)	raps
	seripa	segment (n)	segment	-setla	thrash (v)	uitklop
	seriri	mane (n)	maanhare	setlama	herbs (n)	kruie
	seriti	dignity (n)	waardigheid	setlankama	document (n)	dokument
	-seriti	dignified (a)	waardig	setlanyi	typewriter (n)	tikmasjien
	seritibatsi	drug (n)	dwelm	-setlela	establish (v)	vestig
	serolobotlhoko	bushbuck (n)	bosbok	setlha	bladder (n)	blaas
	seromamowa	radio (n)	radio	-setlha	beige (a)	beige
	serope	thigh (n)	dy	-setlha	pale (a)	bleek
	seroto	basket (n)	mandjie	setlha	season (n)	seisoen
	serunya	mole (n)	mol	-setlha	grey (n)	grys
	serurubele	moth (n)	mot	setlhabelo	sacrifice (n)	offerande
	serurubele	butterfly (n)	skoenlapper	setlhabi	ache (n)	pyn

Tswana	English	Afrikaans	Tswana	English	Afrikaans
setlhabi sa tsebe	earache (n)	oorpyn	-sia	flee (v)	vlug
setlhaketlhake	island (n)	eiland	-siame	right (a)	reg
setlhako	shoe (n)	skoen	-siameng	appropriate (a)	geskik
setlhako	boot (n)	stewel	-siameng	eligible (a)	geskik
setlhako	pedal (n)	pedaal	-siametseng	convenient (a)	gerieflik
setlhana	pelvis (n)	bekken	-siamisa	correct (v)	korrigeer
setlhare	tree (n)	boom	-sidilweng	ground (a)	gemaal
setlhatsana	shrub (n)	struik	sikara	cigar (n)	sigaar
setlhatswelo	sink (n)	opwasbak	-sila	grind (v)	maal
setlhoa	apex (n)	spits	siling	ceiling (n)	plafon
setlhodi	spy (n)	spioen	simbala	cymbal (n)	simbaal
setlhogo	title (n)	titel	-sireletsa	shield (v)	beskerm
setlhogo	headline (n)	opskrif	-sisimoga	shun (v)	vermy
setlhokwa	need (n)	behoefte	-sisimogang	sensitive (a)	gevoelig
-setlholo	odd (a)	onewe	-sisimosang	repulsive (a)	walglik
setlhomo	stand (n)	stand	-soka	wring (v)	wring
setlhopa	party (n)	party	-sokameng	crooked (a)	krom
setlhopa	team (n)	span	-sokasoka	persuade (v)	oorreed
setlhopa	class (n)	klas	-sokela motho pelo	plot (v)	saamsweer
setlhora	peak (n)	piek	sokere	soccer (n)	sokker
setlhotsa	cripple (n)	kreupele	-sokolola	convert (v)	omsit
setlo	article (n)	artikel	-sola	gain (v)	wen
setlogolwana	grandson (n)	kleinseun	-solofela	expect (v)	verwag
setlogolwana	granddaughter (n)	kleindogter	-solofela	hope (v)	hoop
setofo	stove (n)	stoof	-solofetsa	promise (v)	belowe
setopo	corpse (n)	lyk	-solofologang	desperate (a)	wanhopig
setoro	store (n)	winkel	somaamabedi	twenty (n)	twintig
setoto	carcass (n)	karkas	somaamane	forty (n)	veertig
setseno	lunatic (n)	waansinnige	somaamarataro	sixty (n)	sestig
setšhaba	nation (n)	nasie	somaarobedi	eighty (n)	tagtig
setshamekiso	toy (n)	speelding	somaarobongwe	ninety (n)	neëntig
setshedi	funnel (n)	tregter	somaasupa	seventy (n)	sewentig
setshego	laugh (n)	lag	somamatlhano	fifty (n)	vyftig
setshego	comic (n)	komiek	some	ten (n)	tien
setshelo	container (n)	houer	some nne	fourteen (n)	veertien
setshoso	threat (n)	dreigement	some nngwe	eleven (n)	elf
setshuu	stew (n)	bredie	some pedi	twelve (n)	twaalf
-setshwakga	lazy (a)	lui	some robedi	eighteen (n)	agtien
setshwano	image (n)	beeld	some robongwe	nineteen (n)	neëntien
setshwano	likeness (n)	ooreenkoms	some supa	seventeen (n)	sewentien
setshwantsho	film (n)	film	some tlhano	fifteen (n)	vyftien
setshwantsho	drawing (n)	tekening	sonobolomo	sunflower (n)	sonneblom
setshwantsho	parable (n)	gelykenis	sopo	soup (n)	sop
setshwantsho	photograph (n)	foto	sorokisi	circus (n)	sirkus
setshwantsho	picture (n)	prent	-sosobana	crease (v)	kreukel
setshwao	label (n)	etiket	-sosobanya	frown (v)	frons
setshwaro sa ditlhapi	fishing rod (n)	visstok	sosobanyo	frown (n)	frons
setshwarwa-sa-ntwa	prisoner-of-war (n)	krygsgevangene	-sotla	ridicule (v)	bespot
setsibosi	stimulus (n)	stimulus	-sotla	scorn (v)	verag
setsidifatsi	freezer (n)	vrieskas	-sotla	mock (v)	bespot
setsidifatsi	radiator (n)	verkoeler	-suga	tan (v)	bruin brand
setsidifatsi	refrigerator (n)	yskas	sukiri	sugar (n)	suiker
setso	culture (n)	kultuur	sukiri	icing (n)	versiersuiker
-setso	ethnic (a)	etnies	-suleng	deceased (a)	oorlede
setswerere	expert (n)	deskundige	-suleng	dead (a)	dood
setulo	chair (n)	stoel	-suma	hiss (v)	sis
seumaka	bile (n)	gal	-sunetsa	sniff (v)	snuif
seyantle	export (n)	uitvoer	-supa	prove (v)	bewys
-se yong	absent (a)	afwesig	-supa	seven (n)	sewe
-sia	win (v)	wen	-supa tlotlo	account (v)	rekenskap gee

S	Tswana	English	Afrikaans
	-supetsa	predict (v)	voorspel
	-supetsa	direct (v)	rig
	-supetsa	demonstrate (v)	betoog
	-sutang	moving (a)	bewegend
	-sutisa	move (v)	trek
	-sutlha	trespass (v)	oortree
	-sutlha	brush (v)	borsel
	-sutlha	cancel (v)	kanselleer
	sutu	suit (n)	pak
	-swa	new (a)	nuut
	-swa	perish (v)	omkom
	-swa	fuse (v)	uitbrand
	-swa	fresh (a)	vars
	-swa	die (v)	doodgaan
	-swa	burn (v)	brand
	-swaba	wither (v)	verlep
	-swabisa	disappoint (v)	teleurstel
	-swedietega	resist (v)	weerstaan
	-swegaswega	inquisitive (a)	nuuskierig
	switshi	switch (n)	skakelaar
	taba	affair (n)	saak
	taba	case (n)	saak
	-taboga	run (v)	hardloop
	taetso	prescription (n)	voorskrif
	tafole	table (n)	tafel
	tafoletuku	tablecloth (n)	tafeldoek
	tagafara	summons (n)	dagvaarding
	tagi	alcohol (n)	alkohol
	-tagisa	intoxicate (v)	bedwelm
	-tagisang	alcoholic (a)	alkoholies
	-tala	blue (a)	blou
	tala	green (n)	groen
	-tala	uneducated (a)	ongeleerd
	-tala	uncivilised (a)	onbeskaaf
	-tala	immature (a)	onvolwasse
	-tala	raw (a)	rou
	-talafeletseng ruri	evergreen (a)	bladhoudend
	talameiti	dynamite (n)	dinamiet
	talelo	ambush (n)	hinderlaag
	taletso	invitation (n)	uitnodiging
	tamati	tomato (n)	tamatie
	tamo	dam (n)	dam
	tampone	tampon (n)	tampon
	tang	pliers (n)	knyptang
	tanka	tank (n)	tenk
	-tantela	screw (v)	skroef
	tao	order (n)	bevel
	taolo	commandment (n)	gebod
	-taologo	elastic (a)	rekbaar
	tapisego	fatigue (n)	vermoeienis
	-tata	impossible (a)	onmoontlik
	tatanyane	fits (n)	stuipe
	tatelano	sequence (n)	reeks
	tatelo	sequel (n)	gevolg
	tatlhegelo	loss (n)	verlies
	tatofatso	accusation (n)	beskuldiging
	tatofatso	blame (n)	blaam
	tau	lion (n)	leeu
	taugadi	lioness (n)	leeuwyfie

Tswana	English	Afrikaans
tawana	cub (n)	welpie
-taya	name (v)	noem
-teatea	wander (v)	dwaal
teatere	theatre (n)	teater
tebo	look (n)	blik
tebo	purpose (n)	oogmerk
tebogo	thanks (n)	dank
tebogo	gratitude (n)	dankbaarheid
tedu	beard (n)	baard
tee	tea (n)	tee
teemane	diamond (n)	diamant
tefiso	fine (n)	boete
-teisela	starch (v)	styf
tekelelo	experiment (n)	proefneming
-teketa	assault (v)	aanrand
teko	test (n)	toets
tekolo	inspection (n)	inspeksie
teleko	dismissal (n)	ontslag
telele	colon (n)	dikderm
telereke ya kamogelo	receptionist (n)	ontvangsklerk
tema	issue (n)	kwessie
tema	paragraph (n)	paragraaf
tema	task (n)	taak
tema	verse (n)	vers
teme	dialect (n)	dialek
temogo	recognition (n)	herkenning
temogo	identity (n)	identiteit
-tena	annoy (v)	vies maak
-tena	bore (v)	verveel
teng	available (a)	beskikbaar
teng	inside (adv)	binne
teng	within (adv)	binne
tente	tent (n)	tent
teradeyuniene	trade union (n)	vakbond
teraetlelini	drycleaner (n)	droogskoonmakery
terata ya mebitlwa	barbed wire (n)	doringdraad
terebe	grape (n)	druiwe
terebe	vine (n)	wingerdstok
terei	tray (n)	skinkbord
terekesutu	tracksuit (n)	sweetpak
terompeta	saxophone (n)	saxofoon
-tetea	bruise (v)	kneus
-teteya	maul (v)	kneus
-tetla	license (v)	lisensieer
tetla	permit (n)	permit
tetla	permission (n)	toestemming
thaba	mountain (n)	berg
-thabang	cheerful (a)	vrolik
-thadisa	express (v)	uitdruk
-thadisang	express (a)	uitdruklik
thae	tie (n)	das
thaelo	temptation (n)	verleiding
-thaepa	type (v)	tik
thaere	tyre (n)	buiteband
thago	kick (n)	skop
-thaisa ditlhapi	fish (v)	visvang
thaiso	set (n)	stel
-thala	sail (v)	seil
thala	testicle (n)	teelbal
thamane	nut (n)	neut

Tswana	English	Afrikaans
thamme	gooseberry (n)	appelliefie
-thamogelwa	convalesce (v)	aansterk
-thanya	awake (v)	ontwaak
-thapa	employ (v)	in diens neem
thapelo	prayer (n)	gebed
thapo	pip (n)	pit
thapo	string (n)	tou
thapo ya go goga	tow rope (n)	sleeptou
thapo ya setlhako	shoelace (n)	skoenveter
tharo	three (n)	drie
thata	energy (n)	energie
-thata	hard (a)	hard
-thata	loud (a)	hard
-thata	very (a)	heel
-thata	hard (a)	moeilik
-thata	difficult (a)	moeilik
thato	will (n)	wil
-thaya	set (v)	stel
thebe	shield (n)	skild
thebolo	approval (n)	goedkeuring
theipi	tape measure (n)	maatband
-thekeletsa	enclose (v)	insluit
thekeniki	technique (n)	tegniek
-thekeniki	technical (a)	tegnies
thekenikono	technikon (n)	tegnikon
thekenoloji	technology (n)	tegnologie
thekesi	taxi (n)	taxi
thekethe	ticket (n)	kaartjie
thekiso	sale (n)	uitverkoping
theko	bribery (n)	omkopery
thele	udder (n)	uier
theledi	kneecap (n)	knieskyf
thelefišene	television (n)	televisie
-thelelelo	fluent (a)	vlot
thelesekopo	telescope (n)	teleskoop
themperetšha	temperature (n)	temperatuur
thenese	tennis (n)	tennis
thenipe	turnip (n)	raap
theo	principle (n)	beginsel
theo	basis (n)	basis
-theo	basic (a)	basies
theo ya kapeo	recipe (n)	resep
thepe	tap (n)	kraan
thero	sermon (n)	preek
thero	conspiracy (n)	sameswering
thetelelo	failure (n)	mislukking
-thetha	brag (v)	grootpraat
-thetha	border (v)	grens
-thetheekela	stagger (v)	slinger
-thiba	block (v)	blokkeer
thibela pelego	contraception (n)	voorbehoeding
-thibelela	camp (v)	kampeer
thipa	knife (n)	mes
-thoba	elope (v)	wegloop
thobane	stick (n)	stok
thobasenotlolo	keyhole (n)	sleutelgat
thobega	chilli (n)	brandrissie
thobego	fracture (n)	breuk
-thobela go	defect (v)	oorloop na
thobo	harvest (n)	oes

Tswana	English	Afrikaans
-thobola	tick (v)	tik
-thobolola	begin (v)	begin
-thobolola	exercise (v)	oefen
thobololo	exercise (n)	oefening
thogo	curse (n)	vloek
thogwa	tissue (n)	weefsel
thoka	ladle (n)	skeplepel
thokgamo	integrity (n)	integriteit
thoko	beside (prep)	langs
thoko	sewing (n)	naaldwerk
-thoko ga	next to (prep)	langs
tholo	kudu (n)	koedoe
thologelo	influx (n)	instroming
-thoma	tackle (v)	aanpak
-thoma	start (v)	begin
-thopa	raid (v)	stroop
-thopa	capture (v)	vang
thopo	raid (n)	strooptog
thoromo ya lefatshe	earthquake (n)	aardbewing
thosola	syphilis (n)	sifilis
thotamadi	bilharzia (n)	bilharzia
thotane	hunchback (n)	boggelrug
thoto	property (n)	eiendom
-thuba	burgle (v)	inbreek
-thuba	spawn (v)	uitbroei
-thuba kobo segole	idle (a)	ledig
thubego	wreck (n)	wrak
-thukhutha	rob (v)	beroof
-thula	bump (v)	stamp
thulaganyo	scheme (n)	skema
thulaganyo	organisation (n)	organisasie
thulaganyo	arrangement (n)	skikking
thulaganyo	system (n)	stelsel
thulaganyo ya beine	winelist (n)	wynkaart
-thulana	collide (v)	bots
thulano	collision (n)	botsing
-thuma	swim (v)	swem
-thunsetsa ntle	eject (v)	uitskiet
-thuntsha	shoot (v)	skiet
-thunya	bloom (v)	blom
-thunya	explode (v)	ontplof
thunyo	shot (n)	skoot
thuo	stud (n)	stoetery
thupa	fillet (n)	filet
thupiso	circumcision (n)	besnydenis
thurugo	swelling (n)	swelsel
-thusa	assist (v)	bystaan
-thusa	aid (v)	help
-thusa	help (v)	help
-thusang	helpful (a)	behulpsaam
thusego	help (n)	hulp
thusego	aid (n)	hulp
thuso	assistance (n)	bystand
thuso ya potlako	first aid (n)	noodhulp
thutafatshe	geography (n)	aardrykskunde
thutatshelo	biology (n)	biologie
thuthubudu	rubbish heap (n)	vullishoop
thutlwa	giraffe (n)	kameelperd
thutlwa	chickenpox (n)	waterpokkies
thuto	lesson (n)	les

T	Tswana	English	Afrikaans	Tswana	English	Afrikaans
	thuto	lecture (n)	lesing	-tlhaba	pierce (v)	deursteek
	thuto	education (n)	opvoeding	-tlhaba	inject (v)	inspuit
	thwadi	figure (n)	figuur	-tlhaba	stab (v)	steek
	thwaiso	commission (n)	kommissie	-tlhaba	slaughter (v)	slag
	tidima	basin (n)	kom	-tlhabela	immunise (v)	immuniseer
	tidimalo	silence (n)	stilte	-tlhabela	sacrifice (v)	opoffer
	tiego	detention (n)	aanhouding	-tlhabetsweng	immune (a)	onvatbaar
	tiego	delay (n)	vertraging	-tlhabiwang ke kgala	shy (a)	skugter
	tikatikwe	centre (n)	middel	tlhabologo	civilisation (n)	beskawing
	tikologo	environment (n)	omgewing	tlhabologo	improvement (n)	verbetering
	tikologo	circulation (n)	omloop	-tlhabolola	civilise (v)	beskaaf
	-tima	extinguish (v)	blus	-tlhabolola	improve (v)	verbeter
	-timela	stray (v)	afdwaal	tlhabololo	amendment (n)	wysiging
	-timelang	lost (a)	verdwaal	tlhabo ya letsatsi	sunrise (n)	sonop
	-timetseng	lost (a)	verlore	tlhadi	lightning (n)	weerlig
	-timpatsa	stain (v)	bevlek	-tlhaeletsa	contact (v)	in aanraking kom
	tinara	dinner (n)	hoofmaal	-tlhafuna	chew (v)	kou
	tiragalo	event (n)	gebeurtenis	tlhaga	grass (n)	gras
	tiragalo	incident (n)	voorval	-tlhaga	natural (a)	natuurlik
	tirisano	co-operation (n)	samewerking	-tlhaga	appear (v)	verskyn
	-tiriso	practical (a)	prakties	-tlhaga	wild (a)	wild
	tiriso	apply (v)	toepas	tlhagafatso	excitement (n)	opwinding
	tiriso e e sa siamang	abuse (n)	misbruik	tlhagala	tumour (n)	gewas
	tiro	employment (n)	werk	tlhagala	ulcer (n)	ulkus
	tiro	duty (n)	plig	-tlhagang	characteristic (a)	kenmerkend
	tiro	job (n)	werk	tlhagelelo	evolution (n)	evolusie
	tiro	work (n)	werk	-tlhagisa	approach (v)	benader
	tiro	labour (n)	arbeid	-tlhagisa	propose (v)	voorstel
	tiro	deed (n)	daad	-tlhagisa	warn (v)	waarsku
	tirolegae	homework (n)	huiswerk	tlhagiso	proposal (n)	voorstel
	tiro ya diatla	handwork (n)	handewerk	tlhago	instinct (n)	instink
	tiro ya maitiso	hobby (n)	stokperdjie	tlhago	tradition (n)	tradisie
	-titina	discourage (v)	ontmoedig	-tlhago	traditional (a)	tradisioneel
	-tla	come (v)	kom	-tlhagola	weed (v)	onkruid uittrek
	-tla	will (v)	sal	-tlhagola	hoe (v)	skoffel
	-tlae	joke (v)	gekskeer	tlhaka	speck (n)	stippel
	-tlaetsa	confuse (v)	verwar	tlhakaina	initial (n)	voorletter
	-tlakisa	appease (v)	bevredig	-tlhakanya tlhogo	puzzle (v)	verwar
	-tlakisa	soothe (v)	kalmeer	tlhako	hoof (n)	hoef
	tlala	hunger (n)	honger	Tlhakole	February (n)	Februarie
	-tlalatlalang	plentiful (a)	talryk	tlhako ya pitse	horseshoe (n)	hoefyster
	-tlalatlalo	abundant (a)	oorvloedig	-tlhala	divorce (v)	skei
	-tlama	tie (v)	bind	tlhale	thread (n)	draad
	tlamanyi	hyphen (n)	koppelteken	tlhale	fibre (n)	vesel
	-tlamela	provide (v)	voorsien	tlhaletsa	amuse (v)	vermaak
	tlamelo	maintenance (n)	onderhoud	-tlhaletsang	amusing (a)	vermaaklik
	tlamo	bond (n)	band	tlhaletso	amusement (n)	vermaaklikheid
	-tlapisa	peg (v)	vaspen	tlhalo	divorce (n)	egskeiding
	tlase	down (prep)	af	-tlhaloganya	understand (v)	verstaan
	tlase	below (prep)	onder	tlhaloganyo	sense (n)	sin
	-tla thari	late (a)	laat	tlhaloganyo	mind (n)	verstand
	-tlatsa	second (v)	sekondeer	-tlhalosa	describe (v)	beskrywe
	-tlatsa	fill (v)	vol maak	-tlhalosa	explain (v)	verduidelik
	tlatso	filling (n)	stopsel	tlhaloso	description (n)	beskrywing
	tleatshe	clutch (n)	koppelaar	tlhaloso	explanation (n)	verduideliking
	tleereke	clerk (n)	klerk	tlhama	compose (v)	komponeer
	tlelapa	slap (n)	klap	tlhamo	composition (n)	komposisie
	tlelarinete	clarinet (n)	klarinet	tlhamo	essay (n)	opstel
	tleniki	clinic (n)	kliniek	tlhamo	invention (n)	uitvinding
	-tletseng	full (a)	vol	tlhano	five (n)	vyf

Tswana	English	Afrikaans	Tswana	English	Afrikaans
-tlhantlha	squash (v)	platdruk	-tlhokegang	precious (a)	kosbaar
-tlhaolegileng	special (a)	spesiaal	-tlhokegang	unavailable (a)	onverkrygbaar
-tlhaologa	dissolve (v)	oplos	-tlhokegang	necessary (a)	noodsaaklik
-tlhapa	shower (v)	stort	-tlhokegang	rare (a)	seldsaam
-tlhapatsa	insult (v)	beledig	tlhokego	essence (n)	essensie
tlhapedi	fun (n)	pret	tlhoko	nipple (n)	tepel
-tlhapedisang	drunk (a)	dronk	-tlhokomela	care (v)	omgee
tlhapi	fish (n)	vis	-tlhokomela	beware (v)	oppas
tlhapisekanoga	eel (n)	paling	-tlhokomologa	neglect (v)	verwaarloos
tlhase	under (prep)	onder	-tlhokomologa	disregard (v)	verontagsaam
tlhase	spark (n)	vonk	-tlhokomologo	negligent (a)	nalatig
-tlhasela	invade (v)	inval	tlhokomologo	negligence (n)	nalatigheid
tlhaselo	attack (v)	aanval	tlhokomologo	omission (n)	weglating
tlhaselo	invasion (n)	inval	-tlhola	spend (v)	bestee
-tlhatlaganya	pile (v)	stapel	tlhola	usually (adv)	gewoonlik
tlhatlaganyo	pile (n)	stapel	tlhola	always (adv)	gedurig
-tlhatlhama	succeed (v)	slaag	-tlhola	spy (v)	spioeneer
-tlhatlhamano	chronological (a)	chronologies	-tlhola	lasting (a)	voortdurend
-tlhatlhamolola	undo (v)	losmaak	-tlholegileng	indigenous (a)	inheems
-tlhatlhoba	examine (v)	ondersoek	tlholego	element (n)	element
tlhatlhobo	examination (n)	eksamen	tlholego	nature (n)	natuur
-tlhatloga	ascend (v)	styg	-tlhoma	appoint (v)	aanstel
-tlhatlosa	raise (v)	ophef	-tlhomagana	queue (v)	toustaan
-tlhatlosa	rise (v)	styg	-tlhomaganya	issue (v)	uitreik
tlhatlosi	stirrup (n)	stiebeuel	-tlhomameng	firm (a)	ferm
tlhatloso	promotion (n)	bevordering	-tlhomameng	stable (a)	stabiel
tlhatloso	rise (n)	styging	-tlhomamisa	ensure (v)	verseker
-tlhatsa	vomit (v)	vomeer	-tlhomamo	standard (a)	standaard
tlhatsisa	nauseate (v)	naar maak	tlhomelela	arm (v)	bewapen
-tlhatswa	dryclean (v)	droogskoonmaak	-tlhomolang pelo	pitiful (a)	jammerlik
-tlhatswa	wash (v)	was	-tlhomolang pelo	tragic (a)	tragies
-tlhatswega ngati	content (a)	tevrede	-tlhonamang	serious (a)	ernstig
tlhatswo	menstruation (n)	menstruasie	tlhong	shame (n)	skaamte
-tlhe	all (beings) (pron)	almal	-tlhopa	classify (v)	klassifiseer
-tlhe	all (things) (pron)	alles	-tlhopa	choose (v)	kies
-tlhe	all (a)	alle	-tlhopa	pick (v)	uitkies
-tlhe	whole (a)	heel	-tlhopha	elect (v)	verkies
tlhetlha	jog (v)	draf	tlhopho	election (n)	verkiesing
-tlhoa	hate (v)	haat	tlhopo	choice (n)	keuse
-tlhoa	detest (v)	verafsku	tlhora	summit (n)	kruin
-tlhoafala	long (v)	verlang	-tlhorang	restless (a)	rusteloos
-tlhoatlhoegang	uncomfortable (a)	ongemaklik	-tlhosetsang	alight (a)	aan die brand
-tlhobaelang	anxious (a)	bekommerd	-tlhotlha	filter (v)	filtreer
-tlhobaelang	sleepless (a)	slapeloos	-tlhotlheletsa	influence (v)	beïnvloed
tlhobaelo	anxiety (n)	kommer	-tlhotlheletsa	dare (v)	uitdaag
tlhobaelo	insomnia (n)	slaaploosheid	tlhotlheletso	influence (n)	invloed
-tlhobega	moult (v)	verhaar	tlhotlheletso	dare (n)	uitdaging
tlhobolo	gun (n)	geweer	-tlhotlholola	discriminate (v)	diskrimineer
tlhobolo	rifle (n)	geweer	-tlhotlhomisa	investigate (v)	ondersoek
-tlhodisa matlho	ignore (v)	ignoreer	tlhotlhomiso	investigation (n)	ondersoek
-tlhoga	sprout (v)	uitloop	tlhotlhwa	price (n)	prys
-tlhogo	intelligent (a)	intelligent	tlhotlhwa	value (n)	waarde
tlhogo	head (n)	kop	-tlhotsa	limp (v)	mank loop
-tlhoka	need (v)	nodig hê	-tlhotsang	lame (a)	mank
tlhokafalo	absence (n)	afwesigheid	tlhware	python (n)	luislang
tlhokafalo	necessity (n)	noodsaaklikheid	-tlhwatlhwa	costly (a)	kosbaar
tlhokamadi	anaemia (n)	bloedarmoede	-tlhwatlhwa	keen (a)	toegewyd
-tlhokang botho	offensive (a)	aanstootlik	tlilemate	climate (n)	klimaat
-tlhokang botho	obscene (a)	onbetaamlik	-tlisa	bring (v)	bring
-tlhokegang	essential (a)	essensieel	tloga	soon (adv)	binnekort

T	Tswana	English	Afrikaans	Tswana	English	Afrikaans
	-tloga	leave (v)	laat	-tsaya	fetch (v)	haal
	-tloga	depart (v)	vertrek	-tsaya	take (v)	neem
	-tlogela	exclude (v)	uitsluit	-tsaya tsia	heed (v)	in ag neem
	-tlogela	abandon (v)	verlaat	tse	this (pron)	dit
	-tlogela kwa ntle	bar (v)	uitsluit	tsebe	page (n)	bladsy
	tlogo	departure (n)	vertrek	tsebe	ear (n)	oor
	-tlola	skip (v)	oorslaan	-tseela	deprive (v)	ontneem
	-tlola	bounce (v)	opspring	-tseela gore	presume (v)	veronderstel
	-tlola	anoint (v)	salf	tsela	path (n)	pad
	-tlola	jump (v)	spring	tsela	road (n)	pad
	-tlola kgati	skip (v)	touspring	tsela	way (n)	pad
	-tlosa	eliminate (v)	verwyder	tsela e e tsenang	driveway (n)	inrit
	-tlosa	remove (v)	verwyder	tsele	those (pron)	daardie
	tloso	removal (n)	verwydering	-tsele le tsele	miscellaneous (a)	allerlei
	-tlotla	chat (v)	gesels	-tsena	enter (v)	binnegaan
	-tlotla	honour (v)	eer	-tsena	grin (v)	gryns
	-tlotla	respect (v)	respekteer	-tsena diphatsa	risk (v)	waag
	-tlotlegang	respectable (a)	fatsoenlik	tseno	attendance (n)	bywoning
	tlotlego	honour (n)	eer	-tsenwang	mad (a)	gek
	tlotlego	respect (n)	respek	-tsenwang	insane (a)	kranksinnig
	tlou	elephant (n)	olifant	-tsenya kakanyo	indoctrinate (v)	indoktrineer
	-tlwaela	adapt (v)	aanpas	-tsenya mo kotsing	endanger (v)	in gevaar stel
	-tlwaela	acquaint (v)	bekend wees	tsenyo	harm (n)	skade
	-tlwaetse	acquaint (v)	bekend wees	tsenyo ya madi	blood transfusion (n)	bloedoortapping
	tokololo	member (n)	lid	-tsepameng	vertical (a)	vertikaal
	-tolamo	fair (a)	billik	-tsereganya	mediate (v)	bemiddel
	tolamo	justice (n)	geregtigheid	tsetse	tsetse fly (n)	tsetsevlieg
	tomo	bridle (n)	toom	-tshabang	afraid (a)	bang
	-tona	big (a)	groot	-tshabegang	apprehensive (a)	bang
	-tona	large (a)	groot	tshabo	flight (n)	vlug
	tona	minister (n)	minister	tshaeno	signature (n)	handtekening
	-tona	huge (a)	reusagtig	-tshameka	play (v)	speel
	-tona	enormous (a)	tamaai	-tshasa	grease (v)	smeer
	-tonanyana	male (a)	manlik	-tshasa sekontere	tar (v)	teer
	-tonanyana	masculine (a)	manlik	tshateni	chutney (n)	blatjang
	-tonatona	giant (a)	reuse	tshedimosetso	information (n)	inligting
	tootso	soapstone (n)	seepsteen	-tshedisa melolwane	exile (v)	verban
	-topa	darn (v)	stop	tshedisomelolwane	exile (n)	verbanning
	topololo	bail (n)	borg	-tshega	laugh (v)	lag
	toro	dream (n)	droom	-tshegatshega	giggle (v)	giggel
	toro e maswe	nightmare (n)	nagmerrie	-tshegetsa	maintain (v)	handhaaf
	tosene	dozen (n)	dosyn	-tshegetsa	uphold (v)	hoog hou
	tota	absolutely (adv)	absoluut	-tshegetsa	support (v)	ondersteun
	tota	absolute (a)	absoluut	-tshegetsa	back (v)	steun
	-tota	undoubted (a)	ongetwyfeld	-tshego	fortunate (a)	gelukkig
	-tota	sincere (a)	opreg	-tshego	lucky (a)	gelukkig
	-tota	true (a)	waar	tshego	cut (n)	sny
	-tota	really (adv)	werklik	-tshegofatsa	bless (v)	seën
	-tota	real (a)	werklik	tsheke	cheque (n)	tjek
	tota	indeed (adv)	werklik	tshekiso	trial (n)	verhoor
	toulo	towel (n)	handdoek	tshekiso	prosecution (n)	vervolging
	-touta	pound (v)	fynstamp	tsheko	cycle (n)	siklus
	-touta	hammer (v)	hamer	-tshela	pour (v)	skink
	tsala	ovary (n)	eierstok	tshele	grudge (n)	wrok
	tsala	friend (n)	vriend	tshelo	cello (n)	tjello
	tsalano	relationship (n)	verhouding	tshenekegi	insect (n)	insek
	tsala ya madi	relation (n)	familielid	tshenyegelo	expenses (n)	onkoste
	-tsamaisa	drive (v)	bestuur	tshenyegelo	damage (n)	skade
	tsamaiso	procedure (n)	prosedure	tshenyegelo ya mpa	abortion (n)	aborsie
	-tsamaya	walk (v)	loop	tshenyego	corruption (n)	bedorwenheid

Tswana	English	Afrikaans
tshenyego	waste (n)	afval
tshenyo	blunder (n)	flater
tshenyo ya maikano	perjury (n)	meineed
tshephe	springbok (n)	springbok
-tshesane	narrow (a)	smal
tshiamelo	opportunity (n)	geleentheid
-tshiamololo	unjust (a)	onregverdig
tshika	blood vessel (n)	bloedvat
tshika	capillary (n)	haarvat
-tshika	turn (v)	draai
tshika	artery (n)	slagaar
-tshikinya	move (v)	beweeg
-tshikinyang	moving (a)	roerend
tshimo	field (n)	veld
tshimologo	beginning (n)	begin
tshimologo	origin (n)	oorsprong
tshimologo	outbreak (n)	uitbreking
tshingwana	garden (n)	tuin
tshipi	bell (n)	klok
tshipi	metal (n)	metaal
tshipi	iron (n)	yster
tshipisi	chip (potato) (n)	skyfie
tshireletso ya dintšwa	kennel (n)	hondehok
tshitabotlhole	antidote (n)	teengif
tshitshiri	bedbug (n)	weeluis
-tshoga	panic (v)	paniekerig wees
-tshoganyetso	unexpected (a)	onverwag
tshoganyetso	emergency (n)	noodgeval
tshoko	chalk (n)	kryt
tshoko	spanner (n)	moersleutel
tshokolete	chocolate (n)	sjokolade
tshokologo	afternoon (n)	middag
tshokologo	conversion (n)	omsetting
-tshola	treat (v)	behandel
-tshola	contain (v)	bevat
-tshola	carry (v)	dra
-tshola	bear (v)	duld
-tshola	accommodate (v)	huisves
-tsholela	cart (v)	karwei
tsholo	treatment (n)	behandeling
tsholofelo	hope (n)	hoop
tsholofetso	promise (n)	belofte
tsholofologo	despair (n)	wanhoop
-tshologa	overflow (v)	oorloop
-tsholola	spill (v)	mors
tshomarelo	thrift (n)	spaarsaamheid
-tshosa	frighten (v)	skrikmaak
-tshosa	terrify (v)	verskrik
tshoswane	ant (n)	mier
tshotlego	misery (n)	ellende
-tshuba	switch (v)	oorskakel
tshubo	arson (n)	brandstigting
tshukudu	rhinoceros (n)	renoster
-tshume	stiff (a)	styf
tshupantla	compass (n)	kompas
tshupatefo	receipt (n)	kwitansie
tshupatiriso	directions (n)	aanwysings
tshupatlotlo	account (n)	rekening
tshupatshwano	reflection (n)	weerkaatsing
tshupetso	demonstration (n)	betoging
tshupetso	reference (n)	getuigskrif
tshupetso	prediction (n)	voorspelling
tshuto	removal (n)	trek
-tshwaka	compress (v)	saampers
-tshwana	resemble (v)	aard na
-tshwana le	same (a)	dieselfde
-tshwanang	similar (a)	eenders
-tshwanang	alike (a)	gelyk
-tshwanelwa	deserve (v)	verdien
-tshwanetse	must (v)	moet
tshwano	analogy (n)	analogie
-tshwantsha	photograph (v)	fotografeer
-tshwantsha	illustrate (v)	illustreer
-tshwantsha	draw (v)	teken
-tshwantsha	imagine (v)	verbeel
tshwantsho	diagram (n)	diagram
tshwantsho	illustration (n)	illustrasie
-tshwara	seize (v)	gryp
-tshwara	arrest (v)	in hegtenis neem
-tshwara	hold (v)	hou
-tshwara	catch (v)	vang
-tshwara ka matsogo	handle (v)	hanteer
-tshwarelela	last (v)	voortduur
-tshwarwa	mount (v)	vassit
-tshwaya	mark (v)	merk
tshwene	baboon (n)	bobbejaan
-tshwenya	pester (v)	pla
-tshwenya	bother (v)	lastig wees
-tshwenya	trouble (v)	kwel
-tshwenya	worry (v)	bekommer
-tshwerweng ke tlala	hungry (a)	honger
-tsibisa	exclaim (v)	uitroep
-tsiboga	respond (v)	respondeer
-tsibosa	arouse (v)	opwek
-tsididi	cold (a)	koud
-tsidifala	cool (v)	afkoel
-tsiditsana	cool (a)	koel
tsie	grasshopper (n)	sprinkaan
tsie	locust (n)	sprinkaan
-tsietsa	cheat (v)	kul
-tsietsa	baffle (v)	verbyster
tsietso	fraud (n)	bedrog
-tsikitla	tickle (v)	kielie
-tsimoga	ooze (v)	sypel
-tsipoga	spring (v)	spring
-tsipoga	shudder (v)	sidder
-tsirimana	jingle (v)	klingel
tsitsibanyo	horror (n)	afsku
-tsofala	age (v)	verouder
-tsofetseng	stale (a)	oud
-tsofetseng	aged (a)	oud
-tsoga	wake (v)	wakker word
-tsoga	arise (v)	opstaan
-tsokotsa	wag (v)	swaai
-tsokotsa	rinse (v)	uitspoel
-tsoma	hunt (v)	jag
tsotlhe	total (n)	totaal
-tsuolola	upset (v)	ontstel
-tsuolola	rebel (v)	rebelleer
-tsuololang	upset (a)	ontsteld

Z

Tswana	English	Afrikaans
tsuololo	sedition (n)	opruiing
tsuololo	revolt (n)	opstand
-tsupa	sulk (v)	dikmond wees
-tsurama	land (v)	land
-tsutsubanya	wrinkle (v)	plooi
-tswa	exit (v)	uitgaan
-tswa	stem (v)	voortspruit
-tswaisa	flavour (v)	geur
-tswaka	mix (v)	meng
-tswala	shut (v)	toemaak
-tswa madi	bleed (v)	bloei
-tswapoga	fade (v)	verbleik
-tswapola	bleach (v)	bleik
-tswelelang pele	prosperous (a)	florerend
-tswelela pele	proceed (v)	voortgaan
-tswelela pele	progress (v)	vooruitgaan
-tswelela pele	prosper (v)	floreer
tswelelopele	advance (n)	vooruitgang
tswelelopele	progress (n)	vooruitgang
-tsweletsa	promote (v)	bevorder
-tswetelela	insist (v)	aandring
tswetelelo	insistence (n)	aandrang
-tswetswe	shut (a)	toe
tswine ya dinotshe	honey (n)	heuning
-tswirinya	whistle (v)	fluit
tuelo	pay (n)	betaling
tuelo	salary (n)	salaris
tuelo	tariff (n)	tarief
tuelo	payment (n)	betaling
tuelo	reward (n)	beloning
tuelo	earnings (n)	loon
tuelo	fare (n)	reisgeld
tuma	moan (n)	gekerm
tumalano	pact (n)	verdrag
tumammogo	consonant (n)	medeklinker
tumanosi	vowel (n)	klinker
tumelelo	visa (n)	visum
tumelelo	admission (n)	toelating
tumelo	consent (n)	instemming
tumelo	faith (n)	geloof
tumo	notoriety (n)	berugtheid
tumo	fame (n)	roem

Tswana	English	Afrikaans
tumuga	donkey (n)	donkie
-turang	expensive (a)	duur
-tutela	fester (v)	sweer
tutlamadi	haemorrhoids (n)	aambeie
tutlamadi	haemorrhage (n)	bloeding
twantshi	antibody (n)	teenliggaam
twantsho	resistance (n)	weerstand
-uma	produce (v)	produseer
-umaka	refer (v)	verwys
-ungwisa	fertilise (v)	bevrug
ura	hour (n)	uur
-usa	drop (v)	laat val
-utlwa	conscious (a)	bewus
-utlwa	obey (v)	gehoorsaam wees
-utlwa	hear (v)	hoor
-utlwa	taste (v)	proe
-utlwa	feel (v)	voel
-utlwagalang	reasonable (a)	redelik
-utlwalang	audible (a)	hoorbaar
-utlwela	misunderstand (v)	misverstaan
-utlwelela	listen (v)	luister
-utswa	abduct (v)	ontvoer
-utswa	hijack (v)	skaak
-utswa	steal (v)	steel
-utulola	explore (v)	verken
-wa	belong (v)	behoort
-wa	fall (v)	val
wa, a, tsa,…	of (prep)	van
-wa dikgora	illegitimate (a)	buite-egtelik
-wela makgwafo	relieve (v)	verlig
wena	you (pron)	jy
-ya	go (v)	gaan
ya semorafe	racial (a)	rasse
yone	it (pron)	dit
yo o molato	culprit (n)	skuldige
yunibeseti	university (n)	universiteit
zuu	zoo (n)	dieretuin

XHOSA

Xhosa, one of the two main Nguni languages, is the home language of approximately 7-million people living in the southern and southwestern Cape, Ciskei and Transkei.

It is important to remember that, in common with other southern African indigenous languages, the structure of Xhosa is very different to Western languages, being governed by the noun, which dominates the sentence. The other words in the sentence must agree with the noun in person, number, gender or case (known as concordial agreement), and this is achieved by adding prefixes to the word stem. Consequently, all the noun forms consist of a prefix plus stem. In addition, the nouns are divided into various classes.

Xhosa is also a tonal language, and the meaning of a particular syllable, word or sentence can change depending on the tone used by the speaker. There are three tone families: namely a high-tone family, a high-falling-tone family and a low-tone family. Every syllable in a word has tone.

PRONUNCIATION

In addition to mastering vowels and consonants, Xhosa speakers also need to master the characteristic clicks, which entered the language through contact with San and Khoi languages centuries ago.

VOWELS

Xhosa has five basic vowels, with the following sounds:
a as in **-thanda** (*love*), similar to the English *father*
e as in **-senga** (*milk*), similar to the English *send*
i as in **imini** (*day*), similar to the English *tea*
o as in **molo** (*hello*), similar to the English *all*
u as in **shushu** (*warm*), similar to the English *to*

CONSONANTS

The following are some Xhosa consonants and their approximate sounds:
b as in **-bala** (*count*), which to the English ear sounds the same as a normal b but softer. To pronounce this sound a little air is drawn into the pharynx and lowered to create a vacuum. Because of the vacuum, there is an implosion.
bh as in **-bhala** (*write*), like the English *buy*
dl as in **-dlala** (*play*), no equivalent, but similar to the Welsh *Llewellyn*.
dy as in **dyobha** (*smear*), almost like the English *duel* but a little further back
g as in **-gula** (*be sick*), like the English *guinea*
gr as in **-grumba** (*dig*), the English sound *r* with voicing
j as in **joja** (*smell*), like the English *Jim*
kh as in **-akha** (*build*), similar to the English *call*, followed by a strong rush of air
kr as in **-krakra** (*bitter*), a compound of k and ch as in the Scottish *loch*, with ejection
ng as in **ingalo** (*arm*), similar to the English *linger*
ntl as in **ntle** (*fine*), (no local equivalent)
ny as in **unyawo** (*frost*), similar to the English *Kenya*
ph as in **iphepha** (*newspaper*), similar to the English *push*, followed by a strong rush of air
rh as in **-rhala** (*greedy*), as in the Scottish *loch*, or Afrikaans *gaan*
sh as in **-shushu** (*hot*), similar to the English *show*
th as in **-thetha** (*speak*), similar to the English *take*, followed by a strong rush of air
ty as in **ilitye** (*stone*), almost like the English *tune* but there is no aspiration
tyh as in **tyhila** (*uncover*), like ty with aspiration
tsh as in **isitshetshe** (*knife*), with a more forceful puff of air than in the English *cheese*
v as in **-vala** (*close*), similar to the English *vain*
w as in **wena** (*you*), similar to the English *woe*
y as in **yena** (*he/she*), similar to the English *you*
z as in **zala** (*give birth*), similar to the English *zoo*

CLICKS

A group of sounds that may pose a challenge for the learner are the clicks, derived from contact with San and Khoi languages. Click sounds are suction sounds made by trapping a body of air between the tongue and the roof of the mouth, i.e. the tongue touches the whole edge of the upper teeth as well as the velum. The middle of the tongue is lowered without this closure being broken. This lessens the pressure of the air in the space between the tongue and the palate. When the closure is broken at any point, the air from outside rushes into this small space, resulting in a click sound.

In order to master the clicks, do not tackle them vertically, but horizontally, that is c, q, x. This will help you to get your tongue in the right position for the respective sets. As you place the tongue in the appropriate position for each of these three, think of the k sound.

For **c**, the dental click as in **-coca** (*cleanse*), press the tip of the tongue against the fror teeth, and then withdraw it sharply, at the same time dropping the back of the tongue from the soft palate. This sound may be compared with the sound you would make when sucking something from your upper teeth, or the sound of sympathy when someone says ts-ts.

For **q**, the palatal click as in **-qala** (*begin*), press the tip of the tongue against the front palate and then follow with the same procedure as for c. This sound may be compared with the sound a person would make when trying to imitate the sound of a cork being pulled from a bottle.

For **x**, the lateral click as in **xukuxa** (*rinse*), place the tip of the tongue against the hard palate as if you were going to produce the n sound. Press one side of the tongue against the side of the jaw. Then, without shifting the tip of the tongue from the hard palate, withdraw the side sharply from the jaw. This sound differs from the other two in that the release takes place at the side(s) of the tongue and not at the front. This sound is sometimes made to express regret or to spur on a horse.

The sharp withdrawal of the tongue has in all cases something of a suck. These three clicks may also be pronounced in different ways. It is advisable that as soon as you have got the three right, to try each one of them with a vowel, taking each of the vowels with each of the clicks one after the other.

Each of the three clicks may
be aspirated (followed by a rush of air),
be nasalised (preceded by a nasal sound),
have delayed voicing (the same as for g above), or be voiced

Dental clicks:
the aspirated **ch** as in **-chaza** (*explain*)
the nasalised **nc** as in **-ncuma** (*smile*)
the delayed **gc** as in **-gcina** (*keep*)

Palatal clicks:
the aspirated **qh** as in **-qhatha** (*cheat*)
the nasalised **nq** as in **inqawa** (*pipe*)
the delayed **gq** as in **gqitha** (*pass*)

Lateral clicks:
the aspirated **xh** as in **-xhoma** (*hang*)
the nasalised **nx** as in **-nxiba** (*dress*)
the breathy voiced **gx** as in **igxalaba** (*shoulder*), which may also be voiced when preceded by a nasal sound

LINGUISTIC STRUCTURE

Xhosa is based on two principles: the system of noun classes and the system of concords.

NOUN CLASSES

Xhosa has 15 noun classes which are arranged according to prefixes. Each person or thing, concrete or abstract, is placed in a specific category or class in Xhosa. Each noun begins with a particular syllable(s) in the singular and each of these syllables is replaced by others in the plural. The rest of the word remains the same.

These syllables that change are called class prefixes of the noun. The part that follows is the noun stem, which remains constant. The different class prefixes give different meaning to the noun:

Class	Prefix	Xhosa	English equivalent
1	um-	umntu	*person*
1a	u-	utata	*my father*
2	aba-	abantu	*people*
2a	oo-	ootata	*fathers*
3	um-	umthi	*tree*
4	imi-	imithi	*trees*
5	ili-	ilitye	*stone*
	i-	isele	*frog*
6	ama-	amasele	*frogs*
7	isi-	isitya	*plate/dish*
	is-	isonka	*bread*
8	izi-	izitya	*plates/dishes*
	iz-	izonka	*breads*
9	in-	intaka	*bird*
	i(n)-	inja	*dog*
	im-	imfene	*baboon*
	i-	ibhokhwe	*goat*
10	iin-	iintaka	*birds*
	izi(n)-	izinja	*dogs*
	iim-	iimfene	*baboons*
	ii-	iibhokhwe	*goats*
10	izim-	izimvo	*opinions*
	iim-	iimfudo	*tortoises*
	iin-	iingcango	*doors*
11	ulu-	uluthi	*stick*
	u-	ufudo	*tortoise*
	u-	ucango	*door*
	ul-	ulonwabo	*happiness*
	ulw-	ulwandle	*sea*
14	ubu-	ububele	*hospitality*
	ub-	ubomi	*life*
15	uku-	ukubhala	*writing*
	ukw-	ukwenza	*doing*
	uk-	ukondla	*feeding*
16	pha-	phandle	*outside*
17	ukw-	ukwindla	*autumn*
	uku	ukunene	*right-hand side*

Xhosa nouns may be divided into weak and strong classes. Classes 1, 3, 4, 6 and 9 are known as the weak classes because their subject concord consists of only a vowel. Classes 2, 5, 7, 8, 10, 11, 14 and 15 are know as the strong classes because their subject concord contains a consonant.

From the outline of classes 1-15, it is noticeable that in most cases:
the plural of Class 1 is Class 2
the plural of Class 3 is Class 4
the plural of Class 5 is Class 6
the plural of Class 7 is Class 8
the plural of Class 9 is Class 10
the plural of Class 11 is Class 10

Thus some classes form the plural of others.

CONCORDS

The importance of the class prefixes does not lie only in that they indicate the noun classes to which the different nouns belong, but also in the fact that they are employed in linking the noun to other words in a sentence. This is done by means of a concord that is derived from the class prefix of the noun and normally bears a close resemblance to the class prefix. This concord is prefixed to the verb in the sentence.

The system of concordial agreement is important because it forms the basis of the whole sentence structure in Xhosa.

In the sentence, *The woman cooks food*, the word for *woman* is **umfazi**, for *cook* is **-pheka** and for *food* is **ukutya**. The subject noun **umfazi** must now be linked with the verb stem **-pheka** by means of a subject concord **-u** which was derived from the class prefix **um-** of the subject noun:
Umfazi upheka ukutya

In most instances, stems cannot be used on their own, which is why they are written with a hyphen in the dictionary.

PRONOUNS

Not only the concords derive from the class prefixes but also the pronouns. In Xhosa several varieties of pronouns are found which show little similarity in their morphological structure. They are grouped together because of their syntactic and semantic similarities, namely:
semantic: a pronoun refers to a noun without actually naming it.
syntactic: a pronoun may be used in place of a noun with the same syntactical functions.
Lo yena ufuna ezi zintle zodwa (*This one only needs these beautiful ones*)

VERBS

The Xhosa verb consists of a root which carries its basic meaning. Unlike European languages, this root cannot be used by itself, but only after certain prefixes and suffixes have been added. When a suffix is added to the root, it becomes a verb stem. The basic verb stem can be used alone only in the imperative:
Thetha! (*Speak!*)

The root **-theth-** has the basic meaning of *speak* and by suffixing different forms, acquires different meanings:
-thetha (*speak*)
-thethela (*speak for*)
-thethile (*have spoken*)
-thethisa (*cause to speak*)
-thethana (*speak to each other*)
-thethisana (*admonish each other*)

When the different prefixes are added to the verb stem, a proper verb is formed. The concords mentioned earlier are also included in the prefixes that can be used with the verb stem:
siyasebenza (*we work*)
basasebenza (*they are still working*)
sasebenza (*we worked*)
usebenzile (*he/she worked*)

Please note that the translations of the words above consist of sentences. This is because Xhosa has an agglutinating morphological structure, which means that it uses morphemes (small segments of language), instead of whole words, to add meaning to the basic form.

The present, future and past tenses appear in various forms in Xhosa. These combine with other formatives to express different aspects of meanings:
Ndiyahamba ngoku (*I am going now*)
Ndiza kuhamba ngoku (*I shall be going now*)
Ndihambe izolo (*I left yesterday*)
Ndiza kuhamba ngomso (*I shall leave tomorrow*)
Basafunda (*They are still learning*)
Sebehambile (*They have already left*)

USING THE DICTIONARY

The Xhosa nouns (n) appear in full, i.e. with a class prefix
and a stem. The verbs (v) are represented by only the stem
and to show that a concord (prefix) is needed before it can be
used as a word, it is preceded by a hyphen. The English
adjectives (a) cannot always be translated by adjectives in
Xhosa. Other parts of speech, especially verb stems, are
often used instead, so they also appear as stems with a
hyphen before them. The adverbs (adv) are mostly complete
words in Xhosa, but again, some make use of other stems in
Xhosa and again are entered with a hyphen. The same
applies to the prepositions and pronouns.

Xhosa	English	Afrikaans	Xhosa	English	Afrikaans	A
-aba	distribute (v)	versprei	amasi	pancreas (n)	pankreas	
abakhaphi	bridesmaid (n)	strooimeisie	amaso	bead (n)	kraal	
abantu	people (n)	mense	amaso	beadwork (n)	kraalwerk	
abashicileli	press (n)	pers	amathambo epiyano	keyboard (n)	klawerbord	
-abela	allocate (v)	toewys	amathe	saliva (n)	speeksel	
Agasti	August (n)	Augustus	amathumbu	bowels (n)	ingewande	
-ahluka	differ (v)	verskil	amava	experience (n)	ervaring	
-ahluka	vary (v)	varieer	amayeza	drugs (n)	dwelms	
-ahluka-hlukene(yo)	varied (a)	gevarieerd	amaza	wave (n)	brander	
-ahlukana	part (v)	skei	amazanana	microwave (n)	mikrogolf	
-ahlukileyo	different (a)	verskillend	amazimba	sorghum (n)	sorghum	
-ahlula	distinguish (v)	onderskei	amazinyo	teeth (n)	tande	
-ahlula	segregate (v)	segregeer	-amkela	accept (v)	aanvaar	
-ahlula	separate (a)	afsonderlik	-amkela	adopt (v)	aanneem	
-ahlulelana	share (v)	deel	-amkela iindwendwe	host (v)	gasheer wees	
akamntu	nobody (pron)	niemand	-amkela	welcome (v)	verwelkom	
-akha	build (v)	bou	-amkelekileyo	acceptable (a)	aanvaarbaar	
-akha	form (v)	vorm	-andisa	enlarge (v)	vergroot	
-akho	personal (a)	persoonlik	-andisa	expand (v)	uitbrei	
-akho	your (pron)	jou	-andisa	extend (v)	uitstrek	
-akho	yours (pron)	joune	-andisa	magnify (v)	vergroot	
-ala	jilt (v)	afsê	-aneleyo	adequate (a)	voldoende	
-ala	object (v)	beswaar maak	-aneleyo	enough (a)	genoeg	
-ala	refuse (v)	weier	-anelisa	satisfy (v)	bevredig	
-alatha	direct (v)	rig	-anelisekile	content (a)	tevrede	
-alatha	identify (v)	identifiseer	-anga	embrace (v)	omhels	
-alatha	prescribe (v)	voorskryf	-angasese	private (a)	privaat	
-alathelwe(yo)	prescribed (a)	voorgeskrewe	anti	aunt (n)	tante	
aleka(yo)	objectionable (a)	aanstootlik	-anya	soak (v)	week	
-alela	ban (things) (v)	verbied	apha	here (adv)	hier	
-alela	deprive (v)	ontneem	-aphukileyo	broken (a)	stukkend	
-alela	forbid (v)	verbied	-aphula	break (v)	breek	
-alela	prohibit (v)	verbied	-aphulela	discount (v)	aftrek	
-alelwayo	banned (things) (a)	verbode	Apreli	April (n)	April	
-ale ndawo	local (a)	plaaslik	-asekhaya	domestic (a)	huishoudelik	
-aluphala	age (v)	verouder	-asemzini	foreign (a)	vreemd	
-alusa	circumcise (v)	besny	-aseNgilane	British (a)	Brits	
amacephe nezitya	cutlery (n)	eetgerei	-asentshona	western (a)	westelik	
amafutha	fat (n)	vet	-asezidolophini	urban (a)	stedelik	
amafutha	polish (n)	politoer	-ayina	iron (v)	stryk	
amafutha ehagu	lard (n)	varkvet	-azi	know (v)	weet	
amahashe	stud (n)	stoetery	-azisa	acquaint (v)	bekend wees	
amalungiselelo	preparation (n)	voorbereiding	-azisa	announce (v)	aankondig	
amampunge	pretext (n)	voorwendsel	-azisa	inform (v)	meedeel	
amandla	biceps (n)	biseps	-azisa	introduce (v)	voorstel	
amandla	energy (n)	energie	-azisa	notify (v)	kennis gee	
amandla	power (n)	mag	-aziswa	acquaint (v)	bekend wees	
amandla	strength (n)	sterkte	-aziwayo	famous (a)	beroemd	
amanqaku	score (n)	telling	-aziwayo	popular (a)	gewild	
amanya	crease (n)	kreukel	-aziwayo	well-known (a)	welbekend	
amanzi	water (n)	water				
amaqhekeza	fractions (n)	breuke	-ba	be (v)	wees	
amashumi alithoba	ninety (n)	neëntig	-ba	belong (v)	behoort	
amashumi amabini	twenty (n)	twintig	-ba	steal (v)	steel	
amashumi amahlanu	fifty (n)	vyftig	ba-	they (pron)	hulle	
amashumi amane	forty (n)	veertig	-bakho	exist (v)	bestaan	
amashumi amathandathu	sixty (n)	sestig	-bala	calculate (v)	reken	
			-bala	count (v)	tel	
amashumi asibhozo	eighty (n)	tagtig	-balaseleyo	eminent (a)	vooraanstaande	
amashumi asixhenxe	seventy (n)	sewentig	-balaseleyo	excellent (a)	uitmuntend	

B

Xhosa	English	Afrikaans	Xhosa	English	Afrikaans
-baleka	run (v)	hardloop	-bhanxa(yo)	stupid (a)	onnosel
-ba ligagu	dare (v)	uitdaag	-bhaqa	discover (v)	ontdek
-balisa	narrate (v)	vertel	-bhaqa	invent (v)	uitvind
-balulekile(yo)	important (a)	belangrik	-bharhileyo	arid (a)	dor
-balulekileyo	distinguished (a)	vooraanstaande	-bheja	gamble (v)	dobbel
-bamba	arrest (v)	in hegtenis neem	-bhekisa	refer (v)	verwys
-bamba	catch (v)	vang	-bhena	appeal (v)	beroep doen op
-bamba	grasp (v)	gryp	-bhengeza	declare (v)	verklaar
-bamba	hold (v)	hou	-bhenguza	flap (v)	fladder
-bamba	seize (v)	gryp	-bhexa	row (v)	roei
-bamba intlanzi	fish (v)	visvang	-bheyila	bail (v)	borg staan
-bamba ipikniki	picnic (v)	piekniek hou	-bhibhidla	babble (v)	babbel
-bamba nkqi	clasp (v)	vasklem	-bhidanisa	confuse (v)	verwar
-bambekayo	concrete (a)	konkreet	-bhijela	wrap (v)	toedraai
-bambelela	cling (v)	klou	-bhityile(yo)	lean (a)	maer
-ba na-	have (v)	hê	-bhityile(yo)	slim (a)	skraal
-banako	afford (v)	bekostig	-bhiyoza	feast (v)	feesvier
-banayo	own (v)	besit	-bhodla	belch (v)	wind opbreek
-bandayo	cold (a)	koud	-bhukuqa	capsize (v)	omkantel
-ba neentloni	ashamed (a)	skaam	-bhukuqa	overthrow (v)	omvergooi
-ba nefuthe	influence (v)	beïnvloed	-bhula	thrash (v)	uitklop
-baneka	light (a)	lig	-bhunga	plot (v)	saamsweer
-ba nembeko	respect (v)	respekteer	-bhunya	strip (v)	ontbloot
-banga	demand (v)	eis	-bi	bad (a)	sleg
-banga	allege (v)	beweer	-bi	nasty (a)	gemeen
-banga	claim (v)	eis	-bi	ugly (a)	lelik
-banga umsindo	infuriate (v)	woedend maak	-bila	boil (v)	kook
-bangela	affect (v)	raak	-bila	perspire (v)	perspireer
-ba ngummi kwelinye ilizwe	immigrate (v)	immigreer	-bila	sweat (v)	sweet
			-bilisa	ferment (v)	gis
-ba ngumphunga	evaporate (v)	verdamp	-bilisa	percolate (v)	perkoleer
-ba nomhlwa	rust (v)	roes	-bini	both (a)	albei
-banzi	wide (a)	wyd	-bini	second (a)	tweede
-bawayo	greedy (a)	gulsig	-biza	call (v)	roep
-baxa	exaggerate (v)	oordryf	-biza	name (v)	noem
-beka	lay (v)	dek	-biza	pronounce (v)	uitspreek
-beka	put (v)	sit	-biza imbizo	convene (v)	byeenroep
-beka ityala	convict (v)	skuldig bevind	-bizela	dictate (v)	voorskrywe
-beka phantsi iintambo	retire (v)	aftree	-bizela enkundleni	summon (v)	ontbied
-bekela	reserve (v)	reserveer	-bo	their (pron)	hulle
-bekelela	pack (v)	pak	-bo	theirs (pron)	hulle s'n
-bengezela	glitter (v)	skitter	-bobosi, -dilikayo	ramshackle (a)	bouvallig
-betha	hit (v)	slaan	-bola	rot (v)	verrot
-betha	lash (v)	gesel	-boleka	borrow (v)	leen
-betha	punch (v)	slaan	-boleka	lend (v)	leen
-betha amanqindi	box (v)	boks	-bolekisana	alternate (v)	afwissel
-betha impempe	whistle (v)	fluit	-bolile (yo)	rotten (a)	verrot
-bethelela	hammer (v)	hamer	-bomvu	red (a)	rooi
-bethelela	nail (v)	spyker	-bona	see (v)	sien
-bethelela	peg (v)	vaspen	bona	them (pron)	hulle
-bhabha	fly (v)	vlieg	-bonakala	seem (v)	skyn
-bhabha	flee (v)	vlug	-bonakalayo	conspicuous (a)	opvallend
-bhadula	wander (v)	dwaal	-bonakalayo	visible (a)	sigbaar
-bhafa	bath (v)	bad	-bonelela	provide (v)	voorsien
-bhaka	bake (v)	bak	-bonelela	supply (v)	verskaf
-bhala	record (v)	opteken	-bonelela nge-	credit (v)	krediteer
-bhala	write (v)	skryf	-bonisa	exhibit (v)	uitstal
-bhalisa	enrol (v)	inskryf	-bonisa	illustrate (v)	illustreer
-bhangisa	abolish (v)	afskaf	-bonisa	show (v)	wys
-bhangisa	quell (v)	demp	-bopha	fasten (v)	vasmaak

Xhosa	English	Afrikaans	Xhosa	English	Afrikaans
-bopha	tie (v)	bind	-cebisayo	advisory (a)	raadgewend
-bopha ngetyathanga	chain (v)	vasketting	-cebula	chip (v)	'n hap kry
-bophelela	attach (v)	aanheg	-cela	request (v)	versoek
-bothoza	dent (v)	duik	-cela umngeni	challenge (v)	uitdaag
brasha	brush (v)	borsel	-cela uxolo	apologise (v)	verskoning vra
-bugcisa	technical (a)	tegnies	-cenga	beg (v)	bedel
-buhlanga	ethnic (a)	etnies	-cenga	persuade (v)	oorreed
-buhlungu	sore (a)	seer	-cengceleza	recite (v)	opsê
-buka	admire (v)	bewonder	-chacha	convalesce (v)	aansterk
-bukhali	acute (a)	skerp	-chaka	tabulate (v)	tabuleer
-bukhali	sharp (a)	skerp	-chama	urinate (v)	urineer
-bukhali	shrill (a)	skerp	-chanekileyo	accurate (a)	noukeurig
-bulala	kill (v)	doodmaak	-chasa	oppose (v)	opponeer
-bulala	murder (v)	vermoor	-chasa	protest (v)	protesteer
-bulala iintsholo-ngwane	disinfect (v)	ontsmet	-chaza	comb (v)	kam
			-chaza	describe (v)	beskrywe
-bulala iintsholo-ngwane	sterilise (v)	steriliseer	-chaza	flout (v)	hoon
			-chaza	define (v)	bepaal
-bulala imithambo	paralyse (v)	verlam	-chitha	spend (v)	bestee
-bulela	thank (v)	bedank	-chitha	spill (v)	mors
-bulisa	greet (v)	groet	-chitha	waste (v)	vermors
-bumba	mould (v)	vorm	-chitha-chitha	disperse (v)	verstrooi
-buna	decay (v)	verrot	-chopha	crouch (v)	buk
-buna	wilt (v)	kwyn	-chopha	squat (v)	hurk
-bunisa	wither (v)	verlep	-chophela	chair (v)	voorsit
-burhalarhume	brutal (a)	dierlik	-chuba	peel (v)	skil
-burhulumente	official (a)	amptelik	-chukumisa	touch (v)	raak
-buthathaka	weak (a)	swak	-chuma	prosper (v)	floreer
-buthuntu	blunt (a)	stomp	-chumileyo	fertile (a)	vrugbaar
-buxoki	fake (a)	vals	-chumisa	fertilise (v)	kunsmis gee
-buxoki	false (a)	vals	-chumisa	fertilise (v)	bevrug
-buya	back (adv)	terug	-chwetheza	type (v)	tik
-buya	return (v)	terugkeer	-cima	delete (v)	skrap
-buza	ask (v)	vra	-cima	extinguish (v)	blus
-buza	cross examine (v)	kruisvra	-cima	erase (v)	uitvee
-buza	interrogate (v)	ondervra	-cinezela	depress (v)	neerdruk
-buza	question (v)	vra	-cinezela	oppress (v)	onderdruk
-buzisa	inquire (v)	navraag doen	-cinga	brood (v)	broei
			-cinga	consider (v)	oorweeg
-cacile(yo)	obvious (a)	vanselfsprekend	-cinga	reason (v)	redeneer
-cacile(yo)	plain (a)	gewoon	-cinga	suppose (v)	veronderstel
-cacileyo	distinct (a)	afsonderlik	-cinga	think (v)	dink
-cacisa	account (v)	rekenskap gee	-cinga ngendlela yakudala	conservative (a)	konserwatief
cacisa	explain (v)	verduidelik			
-cacisa	illuminate (v)	verlig	-cingela(yo)	selfish (a)	selfsugtig
-caleni kwa-	beside (prep)	langs	-coca	clean (v)	skoonmaak
-caleni kwa-	next to (prep)	langs	-coca	purge (v)	skoonmaak
-calula	discriminate (v)	diskrimineer	-cocekile (yo)	neat (a)	netjies
-canda	chop (v)	kap	-cocekile (yo)	tidy (a)	netjies
-canda	split (v)	splits	-cocekileyo	clean (a)	skoon
-canda kubini	halve (v)	halveer	-cola	pound (v)	fynstamp
-candeka	fracture (n)	breuk	-colekileyo	fine (a)	fyn
-caphukela	detest (v)	verafsku	-combulula	unravel (v)	ontrafel
-caphukela	loathe (v)	verafsku	-cothayo	slow (a)	stadig
-caphukisa	annoy (v)	vies maak	-cothela	approach (v)	benader
-caphukisa	irritate (v)	irriteer	-cudisa	press (v)	pers
-caphukisayo	annoying (a)	ergerlik	-cudisa	squeeze (v)	druk
-caphula	quote (v)	aanhaal	-cukuceza	crumble (v)	verkrummel
-ceba	plan (v)	beplan	-cula	sing (v)	sing
-cebisa	advise (v)	raad gee	-cumza	squash (v)	platdruk

C

Xhosa	English	Afrikaans	Xhosa	English	Afrikaans
-cunukisa	taunt (v)	uitlok	ecaleni ku-	along (prep)	langs
-cuthene (yo)	slender (a)	tingerig	-edolophu	municipal (a)	munisipaal
-cwaka	quiet (a)	stil	-ehlomela ledolophu	suburban (a)	voorstedelik
cwangcisa	arrange (v)	skik	emangcwabeni	cemetery (n)	begraafplaas
-cwenga	purify (v)	suiwer	emva	after (place) (prep)	agter
-cwengileyo	pure (a)	suiwer	emva	after (time) (prep)	na
			-emva koko	afterwards (adv)	agterna
-dada	float (v)	drywe	emva kwemini	afternoon (n)	middag
-dada	swim (v)	swem	-endalo	natural (a)	natuurlik
-dala	adult (a)	volwasse	-enu	your (pron)	julle
-dala	aged (a)	oud	-enu	yours (pron)	julle s'n
-dala	create (v)	skep	-enza	cause (v)	veroorsaak
-dala	eldest (a)	oudste	-enza	do (v)	doen
-dala	old (a)	oud	-enza	execute (v)	teregstel
-dala	senior (a)	senior	-enza	perform (v)	uitvoer
-dala	stale (a)	oud	-enza iintloni	embarrass (v)	verleë maak
-dandalaza(yo)	prominent (a)	prominent	-enza ingabi nanto	vacate (v)	uittrek
-danisa	dance (v)	dans	-enza intetho	address (v)	toespreek
-danisa	disappoint (v)	teleurstel	-enza isicelo	apply (v)	aansoek doen
-danisa	frustrate (v)	frustreer	-enza isigqibo	decide (v)	besluit
-de	long (a)	lang	-enza isijwili	wail (v)	weeklaag
-de	tall (a)	lang	-enzakala	hurt (v)	seermaak
-dedela	shun (v)	vermy	-enzakalisa	cripple (v)	kreupel maak
-dela	defy (v)	trotseer	-enzakalisa	wound (v)	wond
-delela	belittle (v)	verkleineer	-enza mdaka	mess (v)	bemors
-denda	eliminate (v)	verwyder	-enza mfutshane	shorten (v)	verkort
-dibana	meet (v)	ontmoet	-enza nkulu	thicken (v)	dik maak
-dibanisa	combine (v)	kombineer	-enza -qingqa	make (v)	maak
-dibanisa	connect (v)	verbind	-enza ubutshaba	antagonise (v)	vyandig maak
-dida	baffle (v)	verbyster	-enza umda	border (v)	grens
-dida	puzzle (v)	verwar	-enza umdla	interest (v)	interesseer
-didekileyo	dazed (a)	bedwelmd	-enza umsindo	anger (v)	kwaad maak
-didiyela	brew (v)	brou	enza uqhushululu	strike (v)	staak
-dika	bore (v)	verveel	-enzeka	happen (v)	gebeur
-dikidiki	tepid (a)	lou	-enzeka	occur (v)	voorkom
-diliza	demolish (v)	afbreek	-enzelela	favour (v)	begunstig
-dinala	dine (v)	hoofmaaltyd eet	-enzelelayo	favourite (a)	gunsteling
-dinayo	tired (a)	moeg	-enzile	done (v)	gedoen
-diniwe(yo)	weary (a)	vermoeid	-enziwe nge-	consist (v)	bestaan
-dinwa	tire (v)	moeg word	-eqhubekayo	current (a)	huidige
-dipozitha	deposit (v)	deponeer	-esisu	gastric (a)	maag
Disemba	December (n)	Desember	-esitrasi	citrus (a)	sitrus
-dityanisiwe(yo)	synthetic (a)	sinteties	-ethu	us (pron)	ons
-diza	disclose (v)	openbaar	eyeKhala	July (n)	Julie
-dla	expensive (a)	duur	eyeSilimela	June (n)	Junie
-dlakadlaka	ragged (a)	verflenterd	eyomQungu	January (n)	Januarie
-dla kancinci	cheap (a)	goedkoop	-eyona	main (a)	vernaamste
-dlala	play (v)	speel	ezinzulwini zobusuku	midnight (n)	middernag
-dlana indlebe	consult (v)	raadpleeg	ezobalo	arithmetic (n)	rekenkunde
-dlula	overtake (v)	verbysteek			
-dlula	pass (v)	verbygaan	-fa	die (v)	doodgaan
-dlwengula	rape (v)	verkrag	-faka	involve (v)	betrek
-drayiklina	dryclean (v)	droogskoonmaak	-faka engozini	endanger (v)	in gevaar stel
-dubula	bloom (v)	blom	-faka engozini	risk (v)	waag
-dubula	shoot (v)	skiet	-faka ucingo	wire (v)	bedraad
-dumba	swell (v)	swel	-famisha	farm (v)	boer
-dwa	alone (a)	alleen	-fana(yo)	similar (a)	eenders
-dwa	lonely (a)	eensaam	-fana na-	resemble (v)	aard na
-dyobha	stain (v)	bevlek	-fanayo	alike (a)	gelyk
			-fanela	deserve (v)	verdien

Xhosa	English	Afrikaans	Xhosa	English	Afrikaans
-fanelekileyo	qualified (a)	gekwalifiseerd	-gcwalisa	fill (v)	vol maak
-feba	fornicate (v)	hoereer	-gezayo	naughty (a)	stout
Febhuwari	February (n)	Februarie	-gibisela	stone (v)	met klippe gooi
-fefa	sprinkle (v)	sprinkel	-gibisela	throw (v)	gooi
-feyinta	faint (v)	flou word	-gigitheka	giggle (v)	giggel
-fifithekisa	squint (v)	skeel	-ginya	swallow (v)	sluk
-fihla	hide (v)	wegsteek	-goba	bend (v)	buig
-fihlakeleyo	hidden (a)	versteek	-goba	bow (v)	buk
-fika	arrive (v)	aankom	-goba	stoop (v)	buk
-fikelela	attain (v)	bereik	-gonya	immunise (v)	immuniseer
-fikelela	reach (v)	bereik	-gonya	vaccinate (v)	inent
-fileyo	dead (a)	dood	-gonyekileyo	immune (a)	onvatbaar
-fileyo	numb (a)	dood	-goso	crooked (a)	krom
-finga iintshiyi	frown (v)	frons	-gqabada	skip (v)	oorslaan
-fota	photograph (v)	fotografeer	-gqabhuka	burst (v)	bars
-fuduka	emigrate (v)	emigreer	-gqabhuka	erupt (v)	uitbars
-fuduka	migrate (v)	migreer	-gqabhuka	explode (v)	ontplof
-fudukayo	migrant (a)	swerwend	-gqabhuka	rupture (v)	skeur
-fulela	thatch (v)	dek	-gqibela (yo)	last (a)	laaste
-fumana	find (v)	vind	-gqibelele(yo)	perfect (a)	volmaak
-fumana	get (v)	kry	-gqibeleyo	complete (a)	volledig
-fumana	receive (v)	ontvang	-gqibezela	complete (v)	voltooi
-fumana	recover (v)	herstel	-gqithisa	exceed (v)	oorskry
-fumana ilifa	inherit (v)	erf	-gquma	cover (v)	dek
-fumana inqaku	score (v)	punte aanteken	-gquma	roar (v)	brul
-fumaneka	available (a)	beskikbaar	-gqwesa	excel (v)	uitblink
-fumba	heap (v)	ophoop	-grenya	gnaw (v)	knaag
-fumba	pile (n)	stapel	-grisa	grease (v)	smeer
-fumile	humid (a)	klam	-gruzula	bruise (v)	kneus
-fumile	damp (a)	vogtig	-gudile (yo)	smooth (a)	glad
-fumile	moist (a)	vogtig	-gudlene	adjacent (a)	aangrensend
-funa	intend (v)	van plan wees	-gula	suffer (v)	ly
-funa	need (v)	nodig hê	-gula(yo)	ill (a)	siek
-funa	search (v)	soek	-gula(yo)	sick (a)	siek
-funa	want (v)	wil hê	-gulayo	sickly (a)	sieklik
-funda	learn (v)	leer	-gulisa	sicken (v)	siek word
-funda	read (v)	lees	-gunyazisa	authorise (v)	magtig
-funda	study (v)	studeer	-gunyazisa	delegate (v)	afvaardig
-fundisa	educate (v)	opvoed	-guqa	kneel (v)	kniel
-fundisa	lecture (v)	doseer	-guqula	convert (v)	omsit
-funekayo	essential (a)	essensieel	-guqulela	translate (v)	vertaal
-funga	fester (v)	sweer	-gusha	conceal (v)	verberg
-funga	vow (n)	gelofte	-gwagwisa	boast (v)	spog
-funga ubuxoki	perjure (v)	meineed pleeg	-gwagwisayo	boastful (a)	spoggerig
-funxa	absorb (v)	absorbeer	-gwayimba	riot (v)	oproer maak
-futha	hiss (v)	sis	-gwayimbile (yo)	riotous (a)	wanordelik
-futshane	brief (a)	beknop	-gweba	condemn (v)	veroordeel
-futshane	short (a)	kort	-gweba	judge (v)	oordeel
			-gwegwa	hook (v)	haak
-gabha	vomit (v)	vomeer	-gxadazela	stagger (v)	slinger
-gada	guard (v)	bewaak	-gxeka	criticise (v)	kritiseer
-galela	pour (v)	skink	-gxeka	scorn (v)	verag
-gantsontso	giant (a)	reuse	-gximfiza	stamp (v)	bestempel
-gcagca	elope (v)	wegloop	-gxininisa	emphasise (v)	beklemtoon
-gcakamela	bask (v)	koester	-gxotha	ban (people) (v)	inperk
-gcina	keep (v)	hou	-gxotha	dismiss (v)	ontslaan
-gcina	spare (v)	spaar	-gxotha	exile (v)	verban
-gcina	store (v)	bêre	-gxotha	reject (v)	verwerp
-gcina eluvalelweni	detain (v)	aanhou	-gxotha	sack (v)	afdank
-gcuma	moan (v)	kerm			

G

Xhosa	English	Afrikaans	Xhosa	English	Afrikaans
-gxothayo	repulsive (a)	walglik	-hlwempuza	impoverish (v)	verarm
-gxothiweyo	banned (people) (a)	ingeperk	hobe	grey (n)	grys
			-hombisa	decorate (v)	versier
-hamba	go (v)	gaan			
-hamba	walk (v)	loop	iadresi	address (n)	adres
-hamba	move (v)	trek	iajenda	agenda (n)	agenda
-hamba ngenqanawa	sail (v)	seil	iakhawunti	account (n)	rekening
-hamba ngoobhontsi	tiptoe (v)	op die tone loop	ialfabhethi	alphabet (n)	alfabet
-hambayo	moving (a)	bewegend	iambulensi	ambulance (n)	ambulans
-hambisa	deliver (v)	aflewer	iapile	apple (n)	appel
-harika	rake (v)	hark	iaprikoso	apricot (n)	appelkoos
-hlaba	inoculate (v)	inent	iarhente	agent (n)	agent
-hlaba	pierce (v)	deursteek	iasi	axle (n)	as
-hlaba	sting (v)	steek	iatlasi	atlas (n)	atlas
-hlaba	stab (v)	steek	iatmosfera	atmosphere (n)	atmosfeer
-hlafuna	chew (v)	kou	iavokhado	avocado (n)	avokado
-hlakula	hoe (v)	skoffel	iayiskrim	ice cream (n)	roomys
-hlala	sit (v)	sit	ibala	field (n)	veld
-hlala	land (v)	land	ibala	spot (n)	kol
-hlala	last (v)	voortduur	ibala	yard (n)	werf
-hlalayo	lasting (a)	voortdurend	ibala lengca	lawn (n)	grasperk
-hlalisa	accommodate (v)	huisves	ibali	story (n)	verhaal
-hlalutya	analyse (v)	ontleed	ibali	tale (n)	storie
-hlamba	menstruate (v)	menstrueer	ibandla	congregation (n)	gemeente
-hlamba	wash (v)	was	ibanjwa	convict (n)	gevangene
-hlambulula	cleanse (v)	skoonmaak	ibele	udder (n)	uier
-hlangana	congregate (v)	vergader	ibhabhathane	butterfly (n)	skoenlapper
-hlangana	gather (v)	byeenkom	ibhadi	springbok (n)	springbok
-hlangana	contact (v)	in aanraking kom	ibhafu	bath (n)	bad
-hlasela	assault (v)	aanrand	ibhaka	bakery (n)	bakkery
-hlasela	tackle (v)	aanpak	ibhakana	beacon (n)	baken
-hlasela	attack (v)	aanval	ibhaladi	ballad (n)	ballade
-hlasela	raid (v)	stroop	ibhalansi	balance (n)	balans
-hlasimla	shudder (v)	sidder	ibhalbhu	bulb (n)	bol
-hlawula	pay (v)	betaal	ibhaloni	balloon (n)	ballon
-hlawula	refund (v)	terugbetaal	ibhanana	banana (n)	piesang
-hle	beautiful (a)	pragtig	ibhandeji	bandage (n)	verband
-hle	glamorous (a)	bekoorlik	ibhanka	bench (n)	bank
-hle	pretty (a)	mooi	ibhanki	bank (n)	bank
-hleba	gossip (v)	skinder	ibhanti	belt (n)	gordel
-hlehlisa	postpone (v)	uitstel	ibhanti	ribbon (n)	lint
-hleka	laugh (v)	lag	ibhanti yesinqe	seatbelt (n)	sitplekgordel
-hlekisa	joke (v)	gekskeer	ibhasi	bus (n)	bus
-hlekisa	ridicule (v)	bespot	ibhaso	prize (n)	prys
-hlekisayo	comic (a)	komies	ibhatata	sweet potato (n)	patat
-hlela	classify (v)	klassifiseer	ibhatyi	jacket (n)	baadjie
-hlela	edit (v)	redigeer	ibhawundri	boundary (n)	grenslyn
-hlikihla	rub (v)	vryf	iBhayibhile	Bible (n)	Bybel
-hloba	curdle (v)	klonter	ibhayisikili	bicycle (n)	fiets
-hlohla	indoctrinate (v)	indoktrineer	ibhayoloji	biology (n)	biologie
-hlokoma	echo (v)	weerklink	ibhere	bear (n)	beer
-hlola	explore (v)	verken	ibhetri	battery (n)	battery
-hlola	inspect (v)	inspekteer	ibheyile	bail (n)	borg
-hloniphekile(yo)	respectable (a)	fatsoenlik	ibhilhazia	bilharzia (n)	bilharzia
-hlubula	bare (v)	ontbloot	ibhishophu	bishop (n)	biskop
-hlukuhla	shake (v)	skud	ibhishophu enkulu	archbishop (n)	aartsbiskop
-hlupha	worry (v)	bekommer	ibhitruthi	beetroot (n)	beet
-hluza	filter (v)	filtreer	ibhodi	board (n)	bord
-hluza	sift (v)	sif	ibhokhwe	goat (n)	bok
-hlwayela	sow (v)	saai	ibhokisi	box (n)	doos

Xhosa	English	Afrikaans	Xhosa	English	Afrikaans	I
ibhola	ball (n)	bal	idlolo	virgin (n)	maagd	
ibhola	football (n)	voetbal	idobo	bushveld (n)	bosveld	
ibhola eqengqwayo	bowls (n)	rolbal	idolo	knee (n)	knie	
ibholiti	bolt (n)	bout	idolo	kneecap (n)	knieskyf	
ibhombu	landmine (n)	landmyn	idolophu	town (n)	dorp	
ibhongo	ambition (n)	ambisie	idonki	ass (n)	donkie	
ibhotile	bottle (n)	bottel	idrayiklina	drycleaner (n)	droogskoonmakery	
ibhotolo	butter (n)	botter	idyasi	overcoat (n)	oorjas	
ibhotwe	palace (n)	paleis	idyasi	coat (n)	jas	
ibhulorho	bridge (n)	brug	idyasi yemvula	raincoat (n)	reënjas	
iBhulu	Afrikaner (n)	Afrikaner	idyokhwe	yoke (n)	juk	
ibhunga	council (n)	raad	idyungudyungu	blister (n)	blaar	
ibhunga ledolophu	municipality (n)	munisipaliteit	iemele	pail (n)	emmer	
ibinzana	phrase (n)	sinsnede	iemere	bucket (n)	emmer	
iblawuzi	blouse (n)	bloes	ierityisi	pea (n)	ertjie	
ibra	brassière	bra	ieriyali	aerial (n)	lugdraad	
ibrashi	brush (n)	borsel	ifama	farm (n)	plaas	
ibrasi	brass (n)	geelkoper	ifanela	funnel (n)	tregter	
ibreki	brake (n)	rem	ifani	surname (n)	van	
ibrukhwe	trousers (n)	langbroek	ifashoni	fashion (n)	mode	
ibubu	swarm (n)	swerm	ifaskoti	apron (n)	voorskoot	
ibunzi	forehead (n)	voorhoof	ifatyi	barrel (n)	vat	
ibuzi	rat (n)	rot	ifayile	file (n)	leêr	
icala	side (n)	sy	ifenitshala	furniture (n)	meubels	
icala	direction (n)	rigting	ifestile	window (n)	venster	
icandelo	section (n)	afdeling	ifestile engaphambili	windscreen (n)	voorruit	
icawa	church (n)	kerk	emotwe			
iCawa	Sunday (n)	Sondag	ifidyoli	violin (n)	viool	
icebo	advice (n)	raad	ifila	file (n)	vyl	
icebo	plan (n)	plan	ifilimu	film (n)	film	
icephe	spoon (n)	lepel	ifiva	fever (n)	koors	
icesina	malaria (n)	malaria	iflegi	flag (n)	vlag	
icesina	typhoid (n)	ingewandskoors	ifleni	flannel (n)	flanel	
ichaphaza	blot (n)	klad	ifleyiti	mouth organ (n)	mondfluitjie	
ichibi	lake (n)	meer	ifleyiti	harmonica (n)	harmonika	
ichibi	pool (n)	poel	ifolokhwe	fork (n)	vurk	
ichibi lokuqubha	swimming pool (n)	swembad	ifolokhwe yokulayisha	pitchfork (n)	gaffel	
icici	earring (n)	oorring	ifoni	telephone (n)	telefoon	
icikilishe	lizard (n)	akkedis	ifoto	photograph (n)	foto	
icuba	tobacco (n)	tabak	ifriji	refrigerator (n)	yskas	
iculo	hymn (n)	gesang	ifuringi	lining (n)	voering	
icwecwe	chip (computer) (n)	vlokkie	ifuthe	influence (n)	invloed	
idada	duck (n)	eend	igadi	guard (n)	wag	
idama	dam (n)	dam	igala	meercat (n)	meerkat	
idamanethi	dynamite (n)	dinamiet	igama	word (n)	woord	
idangatye	flame (n)	vlam	igama	name (n)	naam	
idayafram	diaphragm (n)	diafragma	igama lobuqhetseba	alias (n)	alias	
idayimani	diamond (n)	diamant	igaraji	garage (n)	motorhawe	
idazini	dozen (n)	dosyn	igatha	gutter (n)	geut	
idelo	pasture (n)	weiveld	igatya	lad (n)	knaap	
idemokhrasi	democracy (n)	demokrasie	igazi	blood (n)	bloed	
idemoni	demon (n)	bose gees	igesi	gas (n)	gas	
idesika	desk (n)	lessenaar	igeza	lunatic (n)	waansinnige	
idike	lagoon (n)	strandmeer	igiyeri	gear (n)	rat	
idiliya	grape (n)	druiwe	iglasi	glass (n)	glas	
idinala	dinner (n)	hoofmaal	iglasi yefestile	pane (n)	ruit	
idinga	appointment (n)	afspraak	iglasi yokusela iwayini	wineglass (n)	wynkelkie	
idini	sacrifice (n)	offerande	iglavu	glove (n)	handskoen	
idipozithi	deposit (n)	deposito	igoba	cub (n)	welpie	
idlala	gland (n)	klier	igogotya	miser (n)	vrek	
idlelo	paddock (n)	veekampie				

Xhosa	English	Afrikaans	Xhosa	English	Afrikaans
igolide	gold (n)	goud	ihlonyelwa	suburb (n)	voorstad
igophe	bend (n)	buiging	ihlosi	cheetah (n)	jagluiperd
igophe	angle (n)	hoek	ihlosi	leopard (n)	luiperd
igorila	guerrilla (n)	guerrilla	ihlwempu	poor (n)	armes
igosa	official (n)	amptenaar	ihlwili	clot (n)	klont
igqabi	leaf (n)	blaar	ihobe	pigeon (n)	duif
igqabi	petal (n)	kroonblaar	ihobhil isidlalo	hobby (n)	stokperdjie
igqirha	witchdoctor (n)	toordokter	iholo	hall (n)	saal
igqitha	abscess (n)	verswering	ihotdogi	hot dog (n)	worsbroodjie
igqudu	knob (n)	knop	ihotele	hotel (n)	hotel
igqwetha	advocate (n)	advokaat	ihotele	motel (n)	motel
igqwetha	solicitor (n)	prokureur	ihuku yokuloba	fish-hook (n)	vishoek
igqwetha	lawyer (n)	prokureur	iikawusi	stockings (n)	kouse
igqwetha	attorney (n)	prokureur	iimpahla	goods (n)	goedere
igrabile	gravel (n)	gruis	iimpahla	clothes (n)	klere
igrama	grammar (n)	grammatika	iimpahlana zokuzicoca	toiletries (n)	toiletware
igranadila	granadilla (n)	granadilla			
igrinpepa	green pepper (n)	soetrissie	iimpondo zewayilesi	antenna (n)	lugdraad
igrisi	grease (n)	ghries	iincwadi zokubhalela	stationery (n)	skryfbehoeftes
igubu	drum (n)	trom	iindaba	news (n)	nuus
igumbi	room (n)	kamer	iindleko	expenses (n)	onkoste
igumbi le zobugcisa	art gallery (n)	kunsgalery	iindondo	spectacles (n)	bril
igumbi lokuhlala	lounge (n)	sitkamer	iindondo	sunglasses (n)	sonbril
igumbi lokuhlambela	bathroom (n)	badkamer	iindudumo	thunder (n)	donder
igumbi lokulala	bedroom (n)	slaapkamer	i-infleyishini	inflation (n)	inflasie
igumbi lokutyela	dining room (n)	eetkamer	iingubo	bedclothes (n)	beddegoed
igunya	authority (n)	gesag	i-inki	ink (n)	ink
igusbhere	gooseberry (n)	appelliefie	iinkomo	cattle (n)	vee
igusha	sheep (n)	skaap	iinkuni	firewood (n)	brandhout
igutyana elikhenk-cezayo	tambourine (n)	tamboeryn	iinkuni	wood (n)	hout
			iinqanawa	navy (n)	vloot
igwala	coward (n)	lafaard	i-inshorensi	insurance (n)	versekering
igwava	guava (n)	koejawel	iintlobo ngeentlobo	variety (n)	verskeidenheid
igwegwe	hook (n)	haak	iintlungu	pain (n)	pyn
igwele	yeast (n)	gis	i-intshi	inch (n)	duim
igxalaba	shoulderblade (n)	skouerblad	iintsinga	sinew (n)	sening
ihagu	pig (n)	vark	iinwele	hair (n)	hare
ihambhega	hamburger (n)	hamburger	iinyembezi	tears (n)	trane
ihamile	hammer (n)	hamer	iipolitiki	politics (n)	politiek
ihamte	vacuum (n)	lugleegte	iiveki ezimbini	fortnight (n)	twee weke
iharika	rake (n)	hark	ijaji	judge (n)	regter
ihash'elingevu	syphilis (n)	sifilis	ijaji zelizwe jikelele	judiciary (n)	regbank
ihashe	horse (n)	perd	ijeli	jelly (n)	jellie
ihashe lomdyarho	racehorse (n)	renperd	ijem	jam (n)	konfyt
ihempe	shirt (n)	hemp	ijezi	jersey (n)	trui
ihenjisi	hinge (n)	hingsel	ijografi	geography (n)	aardrykskunde
ihenyukazi	whore (n)	hoer	ijoni	soldier (n)	soldaat
ihenyukazi	prostitute (n)	prostituut	ijoyini	join (n)	lasplek
ihilihili	vagrant (n)	rondloper	ikaki	khaki (n)	kakie
-ihla	descend (v)	daal	ikalika	lime (n)	kalk
ihlakani	accomplice (n)	medepligtige	ikalika	whitewash (n)	witkalk
ihlathi	forest (n)	bos	ikalkuni	turkey (n)	kalkoen
ihlathi	jungle (n)	oerwoud	ikampu	camp (n)	kamp
ihlazo	shame (n)	skaamte	ikamva	background (n)	agtergrond
ihlazo	disgrace (n)	skande	ikamva	future (n)	toekoms
ihlazo	scandal (n)	skandaal	ikastoli	castor oil (n)	kasterolie
ihlebo	secret (n)	geheim	ikatali	guitar (n)	kitaar
ihleza	pelvis (n)	bekken	ikatana	kitten (n)	katjie
ihleza	hip (n)	heup	ikati	cat (n)	kat
ihlobo	summer (n)	somer	ikawusi	sock (n)	sokkie

Xhosa	English	Afrikaans	Xhosa	English	Afrikaans	I
ikayiti	kite (n)	vlieër	iklatshi	clutch (n)	koppelaar	
iketile	kettle (n)	ketel	ikliniki	clinic (n)	kliniek	
ikeyiki ethile	tart (n)	tert	ikofu	coffee (n)	koffie	
ikhabhathi	cupboard (n)	kas	ikoko	cocoa (n)	kakao	
ikhabhinethi	cabinet (n)	kabinet	ikoma	comma (n)	komma	
ikhadi	card (n)	kaart	ikomiti	committee (n)	komitee	
ikhadibhodi	cardboard (n)	karton	ikomkhulu	capital (a)	hoof	
ikhaka	shield (n)	skild	ikomkomire	cucumber (n)	komkommer	
ikhala	aloe (n)	aalwyn	ikompiyuta	computer (n)	rekenaar	
ikhala	cactus (n)	kaktus	ikonofile	garlic (n)	knoffel	
ikhalenda	calendar (n)	kalender	ikonsathi	concert (n)	konsert	
ikhamandela	handcuff (n)	boei	ikopi	copy (document) (n)	afskrif	
ikhamera	camera (n)	kamera	ikopi	copy (book) (n)	eksemplaar	
ikhampasi	compass (n)	kompas	ikopi	cup (n)	koppie	
ikhandlela	candle (n)	kers	ikopolo	copper (n)	koper	
ikhankatha	guardian (n)	voog	ikostina	concertina (n)	konsertina	
ikhaphetshu	cabbage (n)	kool	ikratshi	pride (n)	trots	
ikharavani	caravan (n)	karavaan	iKrismesi	Christmas (n)	Kersfees	
ikhathalogu	catalogue (n)	katalogus	ikumkanikazi	queen (n)	koningin	
ikhaya	home (n)	tuiste	ikwayala	choir (n)	koor	
ikhefi	café (n)	kafee	ikwepile	quince (n)	kweper	
ikhefu	interval (n)	pouse	ikweyita	equator (n)	ewenaar	
ikhefu	holiday (n)	vakansie	ikwiliti	quilt (n)	verekombers	
ikhefu	leave (n)	verlof	ilahle	cinder (n)	sintel	
ikhemesti	chemist (n)	apteker	ilahle	coal (n)	steenkool	
ikhephu	snow (n)	sneeu	ilahleko	loss (n)	verlies	
ikhetini	curtain (n)	gordyn	ilalela	bystander (n)	omstander	
ikhitha	flake (n)	vlokkie	ilamuni	lemon (n)	suurlemoen	
ikhitshi	kitchen (n)	kombuis	ilanga	sun (n)	son	
ikhiwane	fig (n)	vy	ilanga	sunlight (n)	sonlig	
ikhoboka	slave (n)	slaaf	ilanteri	lantern (n)	lantern	
ikhodiyani	accordion (n)	trekklavier	ilaphu	cloth (n)	doek	
ikhohlo	left (n)	linkerkant	ilaphu	fabric (n)	tekstielstof	
ikhola	collar (n)	kraag	ilaphu	material (n)	lap	
ikholeji	college (n)	kollege	ilaphu	nappy (n)	babadoek	
ikholiflawa	cauliflower (n)	blomkool	ilaphu	rag (n)	lap	
ikholoni	colon (n)	dubbelpunt	ilaphu letafile	tablecloth (n)	tafeldoek	
ikholwa	believer (n)	gelowige	ilaphu lokususa uthuli	duster (n)	stoflap	
ikhomedi	comedy (n)	komedie	ilastiki	elastic (n)	rek	
ikhomishini	commission (n)	kommissie	ilatshana lezandla	serviette (n)	servet	
ikhomposi	compost (n)	kompos	ilekese	sweet (n)	lekker	
ikhonkco	bond (n)	band	ileri	ladder (n)	leer	
ikhontakthi lensi	contact lens (n)	kontaklens	ileri	stepladder (n)	trapleer	
ikhonto	contour (n)	kontoer	iletusi	lettuce (n)	blaarslaai	
ikhowa	mushroom (n)	sampioen	ileyibhile	label (n)	etiket	
ikhowa	fungus (n)	swam	ilifa	heritage (n)	erfenis	
ikhredithi khadi	credit card (n)	kredietkaart	ilifa	inheritance (n)	erfenis	
ikhrim yokutsheva	shaving cream (n)	skeerroom	ilifti	lift (n)	hyser	
ikhrowubha	crowbar (n)	koevoet	ilifu	cloud (n)	wolk	
ikhuba	plough (n)	ploeg	iligxa	shoulder (n)	skouer	
ikhulu	century (n)	eeu	ilindle	veld (n)	veld	
ikhulu	hundred (n)	honderd	ilindle	wilderness (n)	wildernis	
ikhulu leminyaka	centenary (n)	eeufees	ilineni	linen (n)	linne	
ikhusi	refuge (n)	skuiling	ilinge	experiment (n)	proefneming	
ikhwapha	armpit (n)	armholte	iliqhwa	sleet (n)	ysreën	
ikhwiniba	bunion (n)	knokkeleelt	ilishwa	misfortune (n)	teenspoed	
ikiriva	wheelbarrow (n)	kruiwa	iliso	eye (n)	oog	
iklabhu	club (n)	klub	ilitha	sunbeam (n)	sonstraal	
iklameti	climate (n)	klimaat	ilitha	ray (n)	straal	
iklasi	class (n)	klas	ilitye	tombstone (n)	grafsteen	

Xhosa	English	Afrikaans	Xhosa	English	Afrikaans
ilitye	stone (n)	klip	imbotyi	bean (n)	boontjie
ilitye lesikhumbuzo	monument (n)	monument	imbovane	ant (n)	mier
ilitye lexabiso	jewel (n)	juweel	imbulambethe	preface (n)	voorwoord
ilitye lexabiso	turquoise (n)	turkoois	imbumbulu	bullet (n)	koeël
iliva	thorn (n)	doring	imeko	mood (n)	bui
iliwa	cliff (n)	krans	imeko	condition (n)	toestand
iliza	antelope (n)	wildsbok	imeko	state (n)	staat
ilizwe	continent (n)	vasteland	imela	knife (n)	mes
ilizwe	world (n)	wêreld	imengo	mango (n)	mango
ilizwi	voice (n)	stem	imephu	map (n)	landkaart
ilokhwe	dress (n)	rok	imetyhuri	mercury (n)	kwik
ilori	lorry (n)	vragmotor	imeyile	mule (n)	muil
ilovane	chameleon (n)	verkleurmannetjie	imfanelo	obligation (n)	verpligting
ilulwane	bat (n)	vlermuis	imfano	analogy (n)	analogie
ilungelo lokuvota	franchise (n)	kiesreg	imfano-ziphelo	rhyme (n)	rym
ilungu	limb (n)	ledemaat	imfazwe	war (n)	oorlog
ilungu	member (n)	lid	imfene	baboon (n)	bobbejaan
ilungu	syllable (n)	lettergreep	imfihlo	secrecy (n)	geheimhouding
ilungu lebhunga	councillor (n)	raadslid	imfuduko	migration (n)	migrasie
-ima	stop (v)	stop	imfuduko	removal (n)	trek
imagi	mug (n)	beker	imfumba	heap (n)	hoop
imakroskopu	microscope (n)	mikroskoop	imfumba	pile (v)	stapel
imali	money (n)	geld	imfundo	education (n)	opvoeding
imali	cash (n)	kontant	imfuneko	need (n)	behoefte
imali egciniweyo	savings (n)	spaargeld	imfuneko	necessity (n)	noodsaaklikheid
imali eliphepha	banknote (n)	banknoot	imfuneko	condition (n)	voorwaarde
imali yokuhamba	fare (n)	reisgeld	imfunxa	sponge (n)	spons
imarike	market (n)	mark	imfuzo	likeness (n)	ooreenkoms
imasisi	measles (n)	masels	imifuno	vegetable (n)	groente
imathematika	mathematics (n)	wiskunde	imimoya	spirits (n)	spiritus
imatshisi	match (n)	vuurhoutjie	iminemaqanda	noon (n)	middag
imayile	mile (n)	myl	iminenkulu	midday (n)	middag
imazi yehagu	sow (n)	sog	imini	day (n)	dag
imazi yehashe	mare (n)	merrie	imitha	metre (n)	meter
imazi yengonyama	lioness (n)	leeuwyfie	imithambo	gymnastics (n)	gimnastiek
imbabala	bushbuck (n)	bosbok	imithombo	malt (n)	mout
imbadada	sandal (n)	sandaal	imivuyo	celebration (n)	viering
imbalela	drought (n)	droogte	imostade	mustard (n)	mosterd
imbali	history (n)	geskiedenis	imoto	motorcar (n)	motor
imbambano	faction (n)	faksie	imoto	car (n)	motor
imbambusi	grapefruit (n)	pomelo	imozulu	weather (n)	weer
imbandezelo	affliction (n)	beproewing	impahla	property (n)	eiendom
imbangi	cause (n)	oorsaak	impahla ethengwe	import (n)	invoer
imbasa	medal (n)	medalje	kwelinye ilizwe		
imbatyisi	oyster (n)	oester	impambano	insanity (n)	kranksinnigheid
imbeko	discipline (n)	dissipline	impambano	delirium (n)	ylhoofdigheid
imbeko	honour (n)	eer	impangele	guineafowl (n)	tarentaal
imbeko	respect (n)	respek	impanza	abortion (n)	aborsie
imbethi-manqindi	boxing (n)	boks	impatho	treatment (n)	behandeling
imbewu	seed (n)	saad	impazamo	error (n)	fout
imbila	dassie (n)	dassie	impazamo	mistake (n)	fout
imbiza	saucepan (n)	kastrol	impefumlelo	artificial	kunsmatige
imbiza	pot (n)	pot		respiration (n)	asemhaling
imbiza yeti	teapot (n)	teepot	impempe	whistle (n)	fluit
imbokotho iliwa	rock (n)	rots	impendulo	reply (n)	antwoord
imbola	ochre (n)	oker	impendulo	answer (n)	antwoord
imboleka	loan (n)	lening	impentshana	pennywhistle (n)	kwêlafluitjie
imbonakalo	appearance (n)	verskyning	impepho	breeze (n)	bries
imbongi	poet (n)	digter	impethu	maggot (n)	maaier
imbongolo	donkey (n)	donkie	impethu	worm (n)	wurm

Xhosa	English	Afrikaans	Xhosa	English	Afrikaans	**I**
impikiswano	dispute (n)	onenigheid	indawo	place (n)	plek	
impikiswano	controversy (n)	twispunt	indawo	position (n)	posisie	
impilo	health (n)	gesondheid	indawo	residence (n)	verblyfplek	
impilo	hygiene (n)	higiëne	indawo	abode (n)	woonplek	
impindezelo	vengeance (n)	wraak	indawo yokubalekela	asylum (n)	skuilplaas	
impofu	eland (n)	eland	indawo yokuhlala	accommodation (n)	huisvesting	
impopo	pump (n)	pomp	indawo yokuhlala	dwelling (n)	woning	
imposiso	fault (n)	fout	indawo yokuhlamba	laundry (n)	wassery	
imposiso	blunder (n)	flater	impahla			
impoxo	sarcasm (n)	sarkasme	indawo yokumisa	parking (n)	parkering	
impucuko	civilisation (n)	beskawing	indawo yokumisa	camp site (n)	kampeerterrein	
impucuko	improvement (n)	verbetering	intente			
impuku	mouse (n)	muis	indawo yokuphefumla	gill (n)	kieu	
impuma	east (n)	ooste	yentlanzi			
impumelelo	achievement (n)	prestasie	indawo yokutyela	restaurant (n)	restaurant	
impumelelo	success (n)	sukses	indelo	contempt (n)	veragting	
impumlo	nose (n)	neus	indibano	meeting (n)	ontmoeting	
impunzi	duiker (n)	duiker	indimla	tonsils (n)	mangels	
imuziyam	museum (n)	museum	indlala	famine (n)	hongersnood	
imvelaphi	source (n)	bron	indlala	hunger (n)	honger	
imveliso	product (n)	produk	indlalifa	heir (n)	erfgenaam	
imvelo	origin (n)	oorsprong	indlanga	tick (n)	luis	
imvisiswano	harmony (n)	harmonie	indlavini	barbarian (n)	barbaar	
imvubu	hippopotamus (n)	seekoei	indlavini	hooligan (n)	skollie	
imvula	rain (n)	reën	indlebe	ear (n)	oor	
imvulophu	envelope (n)	koevert	indledlana	driveway (n)	inrit	
imvume	consent (n)	instemming	indledlana	parting (n)	paadjie	
imvume	licence (n)	lisensie	indledlana	path (n)	pad	
imvume	permit (n)	permit	indledlana yeenyawo	pavement (n)	sypaadjie	
imvume	sanction (n)	sanksie	indlela	way (n)	pad	
imvume	permission (n)	toestemming	indlela	road (n)	pad	
imvumelwano	approval (n)	goedkeuring	indlela yokuvelela	approach (n)	nadering	
-imvumelwano	agreement (n)	ooreenkoms	indlela yokuzikhusela	alibi (n)	alibi	
imvuthuluka	crumb (n)	krummel	indlovu	elephant (n)	olifant	
inaliti	needle (n)	naald	indlu	house (n)	huis	
inaliti	syringe (n)	spuit	indlu	household (n)	huishouding	
inaliti yokunita	knitting needle (n)	breinaald	indlu ekhanyisela	lighthouse (n)	vuurtoring	
inani	number (n)	nommer	inqanawa			
inartyisi	naartjie (n)	nartjie	indlulamthi	giraffe (n)	kameelperd	
incakancaka	uvula (n)	kleintongetjie	indlu yangasese	lavatory (n)	toilet	
incam	tip (n)	punt	indlu yangasese	toilet (n)	toilet	
incam	apex (n)	spits	indlu yenja	kennel (n)	hondehok	
incanda	porcupine (n)	ystervark	indlu yesigcawu	cobweb (n)	spinnerak	
incasa	taste (n)	smaak	indlwana	cottage (n)	kothuis	
inceba	mercy (n)	genade	indlwana yefoni	telephone booth (n)	telefoonhokkie	
incindi	nectar (n)	nektar	indlwane	nest (n)	nes	
incindi	juice (n)	sap	indoda	male (n)	man	
incindi yeorenji	orange juice (n)	lemoensap	indoda	man (n)	man	
inciniba	ostrich (n)	volstruis	indoda- umyeni	husband (n)	man	
incoko	conversation (n)	gesprek	indongomane	peanut (n)	grondboontjie	
incoko	talk (n)	praatjie	indubula	toad (n)	brulpadda	
incopho	summit (n)	kruin	induli	hill (n)	heuwel	
incopho	peak (n)	piek	indulubhatyi	waistcoat (n)	onderbaadjie	
incukuthu	bedbug (n)	weeluis	indumasi	renown (n)	beroemdheid	
incutshe	expert (n)	deskundige	indumiso	psalm (n)	psalm	
incwadana	pamphlet (n)	pamflet	indunduma	dune (n)	duin	
incwadi	book (n)	boek	indutsu	anus (n)	anus	
incwadi	letter (n)	brief	inenekazi	lady (n)	dame	
indadi	swimmer (n)	swemmer	ingalo	arm (n)	arm	
indalo	nature (n)	natuur	ingalo	forearm (n)	voorarm	

Xhosa	English	Afrikaans	Xhosa	English	Afrikaans
ingca	grass (n)	gras	ingxolo	uproar (n)	lawaai
ingcaciso	explanation (n)	verduideliking	ingxolo	rattle (n)	ratel
ingcambu	radicle (n)	wortel	ingxondorha	ravine (n)	kloof
ingcinezelo	oppression (n)	onderdrukking	ingxowa	bag (n)	sak
ingcinga	bud (n)	botsel	ingxowa	sack (n)	sak
ingcinga	thought (n)	gedagte	ingxowa	case (n)	saak
ingcinga	idea (n)	idee	ingxoxo	discussion (n)	bespreking
ingcongconi	mosquito (n)	muskiet	ingxoxo	argument (n)	argument
ingcongconi	tsetse fly (n)	tsetsevlieg	ingxwelerha	casualty (n)	ongeval
ingcongolo	reed (n)	riet	inja	dog (n)	hond
ingcwaba	grave (n)	graf	injakazi	bitch (n)	teef
ingcwaba	tomb (n)	graf	injana	puppy (n)	klein hondjie
ingcwele	saint (n)	heilige	injingalwazi	professor (n)	professor
ingedle	addict (n)	verslaafde	injini	engine (n)	enjin
ingelosi	angel (n)	engel	injongo	meaning (n)	bedoeling
ingeniso	profit (n)	wins	injongo	aim (n)	doel
ingoma	song (n)	liedjie	injongo	purpose (n)	oogmerk
ingoma yosana	lullaby (n)	wiegelied	injongo senzi	object (n)	voorwerp
ingongoma	lump (n)	klont	inkaba	navel (n)	naeltjie
ingono	nipple (n)	tepel	inkabi yenkomo	ox (n)	os
ingono	teat (n)	tepel	inkalakahla	palate (n)	verhemelte
ingonyama	lion (n)	leeu	inkamela	camel (n)	kameel
ingonyana	tune (n)	wysie	inkangeleko	look (n)	blik
ingozi	danger (n)	gevaar	inkanti	bar (n)	kroeg
ingozi	peril (n)	gevaar	inkantsi	cramp (n)	kramp
ingozi	accident (n)	ongeluk	inkantsi	spasm (n)	spasma
ingozi	risk (n)	risiko	inkanuko	lust (n)	wellus
ingozi isehlo	incident (n)	voorval	inkanunu	cannon (n)	kanon
ingqakaqha	smallpox (n)	waterpokkies	inkathazo	annoyance (n)	ergernis
ingqaqambo	ache (n)	pyn	inkathazo	hindrance (n)	hindernis
ingqayi	jar (n)	fles	inkathazo	nuisance (n)	steurnis
ingqesho	rent (n)	huur	inkawu	ape (n)	aap
ingqina	witness (n)	getuie	inkawu	albino (n)	albino
ingqina	eyewitness (n)	ooggetuie	inkawu	monkey (n)	aap
ingqiniba	elbow (n)	elmboog	inkcaso	opposition (n)	opposisie
ingqiniseko	assurance (n)	versekering	inkcaza	comb (n)	kam
ingqiqo	integrity (n)	integriteit	inkcazo	description (n)	beskrywing
ingqiqo	logic (n)	logika	inkcazo	qualification (n)	kwalifikasie
ingqoba	breastbone (n)	borsbeen	inkcitho	waste (n)	afval
ingqokoqwane	weevil (n)	kalander	inkcitho	extravagance (n)	buitensporigheid
ingqolowa	wheat (n)	koring	inkedama	orphan (n)	weeskind
ingqondo	sense (n)	sin	inkohlakalo	cruelty (n)	wreedheid
ingqondo	mind (n)	verstand	inkohliso	deceit (n)	bedrog
ingqosha	collarbone (n)	sleutelbeen	inkokeli	leader (n)	leier
ingqula	larynx (n)	larinks	inkokeli yeqela	captain (n)	kaptein
ingqumbo	rage (n)	woede	inkolo	religion (n)	godsdiens
ingubo	blanket (n)	kombers	inkomfa	conference (n)	konferensie
inguqu	retreat (n)	terugtog	inkomo	cow (n)	koei
ingutyana yokulala	pyjamas (n)	pajamas	inkongolo	congress (n)	kongres
ingwamza	stork (n)	ooievaar	inkonkxa	jug (n)	beker
ingwenya	crocodile (n)	krokodil	inkonkxa	cistern (n)	waterbak
ingxabano	quarrel (n)	twis	inkonkxa yokwenza ibhotolo	churn (n)	karring
ingxaki	trouble (n)	moeite			
ingxaki	problem (n)	probleem	inkonyana yehashe	foal (n)	vulletjie
ingxangxasi	waterfall (n)	waterval	inkonzo ethile	ceremony (n)	seremonie
ingxangxosi	secretary bird (n)	sekretarisvoël	inkophe	eyelid (n)	ooglid
ingxelo	report (n)	verslag	inkosana	prince (n)	prins
ingxelo	result (n)	uitslag	inkosazana	princess (n)	prinses
ingxelo	statement (n)	verklaring	iNkosi	Lord (n)	Here
ingxolo	noise (n)	geraas	inkosi	chief (n)	hoofman

Xhosa	English	Afrikaans	Xhosa	English	Afrikaans
inkqayi	bald (a)	bles	intamo	neck (n)	nek
inkqubela	progress (n)	vooruitgang	intandabuzo	hesitation (n)	aarseling
inkqubela-phambili	advance (n)	vooruitgang	intandabuzo	doubt (n)	twyfel
inkqubo	programme (n)	program	intandane	idol (n)	afgod
inkqubo	program (n)	program	intando	will (n)	wil
inkqubo	procedure (n)	prosedure	intembeko	fidelity (n)	getrouheid
inkqubo	proceedings (n)	verrigtinge	intendelezo	hedge (n)	heining
inkqubo yesizwe	culture (n)	kultuur	intende yesandla	palm (n)	palm
inkuku	fowl (n)	hoender	intenetya	tennis (n)	tennis
inkuku	chicken (n)	hoender	intengiso	advertisement (n)	advertensie
inkulu	firstborn (n)	eersgeborene	intengiso	auction (n)	veiling
inkululeko	freedom (n)	vryheid	intente	tent (n)	tent
inkulungwane	decade (n)	dekade	intesha	paunch (n)	boepmaag
inkulungwane	century (sport) (n)	honderdtal	intethe	locust (n)	sprinkaan
inkundla	court (n)	hof	intethe	grasshopper (n)	sprinkaan
inkundla ephakamileyo	supreme court (n)	hooggeregshof	intetho yesizwana	dialect (n)	dialek
inkundla yezibheno	appeal court (n)	appélhof	intimbo	loot (n)	buit
inkungu	mist (n)	mis	intiyo	hatred (n)	haat
inkungu	fog (n)	mis	intiyo	venom (n)	venyn
inkungu	haze (n)	waas	intlabathi	sand (n)	sand
inkunkuma	rubbish (n)	vuilgoed	intlaba zahlukane	disagreement (n)	meningsverskil
inkunkuma	refuse (n)	vullis	intlala	cartilage (n)	kraakbeen
inkunz'egusha	ram (n)	ram	intlalo-ntle	welfare (n)	welsyn
inkunzana	spanner (n)	moersleutel	intlama	dough (n)	deeg
inkunzi	bull (n)	bul	intlama	paste (n)	pasta
inkunzi yehashe	stallion (n)	hings	intlama yamazinyo	toothpaste (n)	tandepasta
inkuthalo	diligence (n)	fluksheid	intlama yekeyiki	pastry (n)	pastei
inkuthalo	efficiency (n)	doeltreffendheid	intlambo	valley (n)	vallei
inkweli	jockey (n)	jokkie	intlanganiso	assembly (n)	vergadering
inkwenkwe	boy (n)	seun	intlanganiso	meeting (n)	vergadering
inkwenkwezi	star (n)	ster	intlango	desert (n)	woestyn
inkwethu	dandruff (n)	skilfers	intlantsi	spark (n)	vonk
inkxaso	maintenance (n)	onderhoud	intlanzi	fish (n)	vis
inoveli	novel (n)	roman	intlawulo	pay (n)	betaling
inqaba	fort (n)	fort	intlawulo	payment (n)	betaling
inqaku	article (n)	artikel	intlebendwane	gossip (n)	skinderpraatjies
inqaku	fact (n)	feit	intlekele	disaster (n)	ramp
inqaku	goal (n)	doel	intlekele	tragedy (n)	tragedie
inqanawa	ship (n)	skip	intlekisa	ridicule (n)	spottery
inqashela	anklet (n)	enkelring	intlenga	sediment (n)	sediment
inqila	region (n)	streek	intliziyo	heart (n)	hart
inqindi	fist (n)	vuis	intloko	head (n)	kop
inqoba	nut (n)	neut	intloko	subject (n)	onderwerp
inqobo	principle (n)	beginsel	intloko ebuhlungu	headache (n)	hoofpyn
inqugwala	hut (n)	hut	intlokoma	echo (n)	weerklank
inqununu	principal (n)	hoof	intloko yomhlathi	headline (n)	opskrif
inqwelo	cart (n)	kar	intlola	scout (n)	verkenner
inqwelo	wagon (n)	wa	intlondi	mischief (n)	kattekwaad
inqwelomoya	aeroplane (n)	vliegtuig	intlungu	grief (n)	leed
inqwelomoya	aircraft (n)	vliegtuig	intluzo	sieve (n)	sif
intaba	mountain (n)	berg	into	thing (n)	ding
intabamlilo	volcano (n)	vulkaan	into	element (n)	element
intaka	bird (n)	voël	into	item (n)	item
intakumba	flea (n)	vlooi	into	substance (n)	stof
intambo	cable (n)	kabel	into	phenomenon (n)	verskynsel
intambo	cord (n)	koord	intobeko	obedience (n)	gehoorsaamheid
intambo	rein (n)	leisel	into ebambekayo	concrete (n)	beton
intambo	thong (n)	riem	into engekazalwa	foetus (n)	fetus
intambo	rope (n)	tou	into esetyenzisiweyo	consumption (n)	verbruik
intambo yokurhuqa	tow rope (n)	sleeptou	into eyothusayo	alarm (n)	alarm

Xhosa	English	Afrikaans	Xhosa	English	Afrikaans
intombi	daughter (n)	dogter	inyanga	moon (n)	maan
intombi	girl (n)	meisie	inyanga	month (n)	maand
intonga	stick (n)	stok	inyani	truth (n)	waarheid
intonga	rail (n)	staaf	inyathela	step (n)	tree
intonga yokuloba	fishing rod (n)	visstok	inyathelo	footstep (n)	voetstap
intonga yomtshayelo	broomstick (n)	besemstok	inyathelo	advancement (n)	vordering
into yokudlala	toy (n)	speelding	inye	one (n)	een
intsalela	remainder (n)	oorblyfsel	inyewe	affair (n)	saak
intsangu	cannabis (n)	dagga	inyibiba	lily (n)	lelie
intsasa	morning (n)	oggend	inyibiba	arum lily (n)	varkoor
intsebenziso	use (n)	gebruik	inyikima	earthquake (n)	aardbewing
intsebenziswano	co-operation (n)	samewerking	inyoba	canal (n)	kanaal
intshatsheli	champion (n)	kampioen	inyoka	snake (n)	slang
intsholongwane	bacteria (n)	bakterie	inyongo	gall (n)	gal
intsholongwane	germ (n)	kiem	inyongo	bile (n)	gal
intshonalanga	west (n)	weste	inyongo	gallbladder (n)	galblaas
intshulube	tapeworm (n)	lintwurm	inyosi	bee (n)	by
intshumayelo	sermon (n)	preek	inyumoniya	pneumonia (n)	longontsteking
intshwabulo	curse (n)	vloek	inzalelwane	aboriginal (n)	oorspronklike inwoner
intshwaqane	chatter (n)	gebabbel	inzima	difficulty (n)	moeilikheid
intsikelelo	blessing (n)	seëning	inzondo	grudge (n)	wrok
intsimbi	bell (n)	klok	inzululwazi	science (n)	wetenskap
intsimbi	shaft (n)	steel	inzululwazi	astronomy (n)	sterrekunde
intsimbi	iron (n)	yster	ngeenkwenkwezi		
intsimbi yomqala	necklace (n)	halssnoer	inzuzo	acquisition (n)	aanskaffing
intsinekana	grin (n)	grynslag	inzuzo	gain (n)	wins
intsingiselo	meaning (n)	betekenis	iofisi	office (n)	kantoor
intsini	laughter (n)	gelag	iofisi yamatikiti	ticket office (n)	kaartjieskantoor
intsini	gum (n)	tandvleis	iofisi yokuthenga	box office (n)	kaartjieloket
intso	kidney (n)	nier	itiki		
intsomi	fable (n)	fabel	iokhestra	orchestra (n)	orkes
intsomi	fiction (n)	fiksie	ioli	oil (n)	olie
intsomi	myth (n)	mite	ionti	oven (n)	oond
intsongelo	threat (n)	dreigement	iorenji	orange (n)	lemoen
intsula	buttock (n)	boud	iovaroli	overalls (n)	oorpak
intsumpa	wart (n)	vrat	iowutsi	oats (n)	hawer
intswelo	lack (n)	gebrek	ipaka	park (n)	park
intswelo-kwazi	ignorance (n)	onkunde	ipalamente	parliament (n)	parlement
intuku	mole (n)	mol	ipalanga	eel (n)	paling
intungo	ceiling (n)	plafon	ipani	pan (n)	pan
intunja	opening (n)	opening	iparafini	paraffin (n)	paraffien
intuthuzelo	comfort (n)	troos	ipasi	pass (n)	pas
intwana	bit (n)	bietjie	ipasile	parcel (n)	pakket
intwasahlobo	spring (n)	lente	ipayinapile	pineapple (n)	pynappel
intyatyambo	flower (n)	blom	ipensile	pencil (n)	potlood
inxeba	cut (n)	sny	ipentihowusi	pantihose (n)	kousbroekie
inxeba	wound (n)	wond	ipentri	pantry (n)	spens
inxila	alcoholic (n)	alkoholis	ipepile	pepper (n)	peper
inxila	drunkard (n)	dronklap	ipere	pear (n)	peer
inyama	meat (n)	vleis	ipesenti	percent (n)	persent
inyama	flesh (n)	vleis	ipesika	peach (n)	perske
inyama esiliweyo	mince (n)	maalvleis	ipete	pip (n)	pit
inyamakazi	buck (n)	bok	ipetroli	fuel (n)	brandstof
inyamakazi ebuleweyo	carcass (n)	karkas	ipetroli	petrol (n)	petrol
inyama yegusha	mutton (n)	skaapvleis	ipeyinti	paint (n)	verf
inyama yehagu	pork (n)	varkvleis	iphakade	eternity (n)	ewigheid
inyama yenkomo	beef (n)	beesvleis	iphedi	sanitary towel (n)	sanitêre doekie
inyama yenyamakazi	venison (n)	wildsvleis	iphela	cockroach (n)	kakkerlak
inyama yethole	veal (n)	kalfsvleis	iphenyane	boat (n)	boot
inyanga	moonlight (n)	maanlig	iphepha	page (n)	bladsy

Xhosa	English	Afrikaans	Xhosa	English	Afrikaans
iphepha	paper (n)	papier	iqhakuva	pimple (n)	puisie
iphepha lokubhala	writing paper (n)	skryfpapier	iqhalo	proverb (n)	spreekwoord
iphepha lokusula	toilet paper (n)	toiletpapier	iqhawe	hero (n)	held
iphephandaba	newspaper (n)	koerant	iqhekeza	fragment (n)	brokstuk
iphiko	wing (n)	vlerk	iqhekeza	fraction (n)	fraksie
iphiko lentlanzi	fin (n)	vin	iqhina	tie (n)	das
iphini	bat (n)	kolf	iqhina	knot (n)	knoop
iphini	oar (n)	roeispaan	iqhinga	trick (n)	skelmstreek
iphumlo	nostril (n)	neusgat	iqhosha	button (n)	knoop
iphupha	dream (n)	droom	iqhude	kudu (n)	koedoe
iphupha elibi	nightmare (n)	nagmerrie	iqokobhe	eggshell (n)	eierdop
ipikiniki	picnic (n)	piekniek	iqokobhe	shell (n)	skulp
ipilisi	pill (n)	pil	iqombolosha	cocoon (n)	kokon
ipinki	pink (n)	pienk	iqondo	degree (n)	graad
iplamu	plum (n)	pruim	iqondo	point (n)	punt
iplanethi	planet (n)	planeet	iqondo eliphezulu	maximum (n)	maksimum
iplanga	plank (n)	plank	iqondo lomkhenkce	freezing point (n)	vriespunt
iplanga lokuntywila	diving board (n)	duikplank	iqonga	arena (n)	arena
iplanga lophahla	rafter (n)	dakbalk	iqonga	gallery (n)	galery
iplastiki	plastic (n)	plastiek	iqonga	platform (n)	platform
ipleyiti	plate (n)	bord	iqonga	theatre (n)	teater
ipokotho	pocket (n)	sak	iqula	well (n)	put
ipoleni	pollen (n)	stuifmeel	iqula elibizelayo	whirlpool (n)	maalstroom
ipolisa	constable (n)	konstabel	iqumrhu la-	co-operation (n)	koöperasie
ipolisa	policeman (n)	polisieman	iqumrhu labagwebi	jury (n)	jurie
ipolisa	police (n)	polisie	iqunube	strawberry (n)	aarbei
ipopo	pawpaw (n)	papaja	iquphe	knuckle (n)	kneukel
iposi	post (n)	pos	iqwarhashe	zebra (n)	sebra
iposi	mail (n)	pos	iqweqwe	cover (n)	deksel
iposi ehamba ngomoya	airmail (n)	lugpos	irabha	rubber (n)	rubber
			irabha	rubber (n)	wisser
iposi-khadi	postcard (n)	poskaart	iradiyeyitha	radiator (n)	verkoeler
iposofisi	post office (n)	poskantoor	irasentyisi	raisin (n)	rosyntjie
ipostal-oda	postal order (n)	posorder	irayisi	rice (n)	rys
ipowupu	pope (n)	pous	irejista	register (n)	register
iqabaka	frost (n)	ryp	iresiphi	recipe (n)	resep
iqabane	companion (n)	metgesel	ireyi	ride (n)	rit
iqabane	consonant (n)	medeklinker	ireyiza	razor (n)	skeermes
iqabane	partner (n)	vennoot	irhafu	tax (n)	belasting
iqabaza lemvula	raindrop (n)	reëndruppel	irhali	cotton (n)	katoen
iqakamba	cricket (n)	krieket	irhamncwa	predator (n)	roofdier
iqamza	bubble (n)	borrel	irhanisi	goose (n)	gans
iqanda	egg (n)	eier	irhashalala	chickenpox (n)	waterpokkies
iqaqa	polecat (n)	muishond	irhashalala	rash (n)	veluitslag
iqaqa	skunk (n)	muishond	irhawu	amateur (n)	amateur
iqashiso	guess (n)	raaiskoot	irhengqe	sickle (n)	sekel
iqashiso	puzzle (n)	raaisel	irhongo	pockmark (n)	pokmerk
iqashiso	bet (n)	weddenskap	irhorho	bug (n)	gogga
iqatha	ankle (n)	enkel	iringi	ring (n)	ring
iqebengwana	biscuit (n)	koekie	irisiti	receipt (n)	kwitansie
iqebengwana	cake (n)	koek	irobhothi	robot (n)	robot
iqebengwana	sandwich (n)	toebroodjie	irolo	roll (n)	rol
iqela	gang (n)	bende	irostile	grill (v)	rooster
iqela	group (n)	groep	irowuzi	rose (n)	roos
iqela	band (n)	groep	irula	ruler (n)	liniaal
iqela	party (n)	party	isabatha	snare (n)	strik
iqela	team (n)	span	isabelo	portion (n)	gedeelte
iqela lomculo	band (n)	orkes	isabhokhwe	whip (n)	sweep
iqhaga	padlock (n)	hangslot	isabile	sword (n)	swaard
iqhagamshela	hyphen (n)	koppelteken	isabonkolo	tadpole (n)	paddavissie

Xhosa	English	Afrikaans	Xhosa	English	Afrikaans
isacholo	bangle (n)	armband	iseyile	sail (n)	seil
isaci	idiom (n)	idioom	iseyile	reef (n)	rif
isahluko	chapter (n)	hoofstuk	iseyile	tarpaulin (n)	seil
isahlulo	share (n)	deel	iseyile	sale (n)	uitverkoping
isahlulo	part (n)	deel	ishawa	shower (n)	stortbad
isahlulo	quarter (n)	kwart	ishelufu	shelf (n)	rak
isajini	sergeant (n)	sersant	ishiti	sheet (n)	laken
isakhiwo	building (n)	gebou	ishumi	ten (n)	tien
isakhiwo	construction (n)	konstruksie	ishumi elinanye	eleven (n)	elf
isakhiwo	form (n)	vorm	ishumi elinesibhozo	eighteen (n)	agtien
isaladi	salad (n)	slaai	ishumi elinesibini	twelve (n)	twaalf
isalfure	sulphur (n)	swawel	ishumi elinesihlanu	fifteen (n)	vyftien
isali	saddle (n)	saal	ishumi elinesine	fourteen (n)	veertien
isamani	summons (n)	dagvaarding	ishumi	sixteen (n)	sestien
isamani	subpoena (n)	dagvaarding	elinesithandathu		
isambuleni	umbrella (n)	sambreel	ishumi elinesixhenxe	seventeen (n)	sewentien
isamente	cement (n)	sement	ishumi elinethoba	nineteen (n)	neëntien
isampulu	sample (n)	monster	isibali	abacus (n)	telraam
isandi	sound (n)	klank	isibambelelo	tendril (n)	rankie
isandla	hand (n)	hand	isibambi	clasp (n)	klem
isandundu	cheekbone (n)	wangbeen	isibane	lamp (n)	lamp
isango	gate (n)	hek	isibhakabhaka	sky (n)	lug
isango lokungena	entry (n)	binnekoms	isibhanxa	fool (n)	dwaas
isango lokuphuma	exit (n)	uitgang	isibhedlele	hospital (n)	hospitaal
isangqa	circle (n)	sirkel	isibheno	appeal (n)	beroep
isantya	speed (n)	spoed	isibhozo	eight (n)	agt
isaphetha	bow (n)	boog	isibi	speck (n)	stippel
isaphulelo	discount (n)	afslag	isibindi	liver (n)	lewer
isaphuli-mthetho	criminal (n)	misdadiger	isibindi	courage (n)	moed
isarha	saw (n)	saag	isibingelelo	altar (n)	altaar
isayizi	size (n)	grootte	isibini	pair (n)	paar
isazela	conscience (n)	gewete	isibini	two (n)	twee
isaziso	announcement (n)	aankondiging	isibini	twice (n)	twee maal
isaziso	notice (n)	kennisgewing	isibiyeli	brackets (n)	hakies
isaziso somtshato	banns (n)	gebooie	isibizo	noun (n)	selfstandige
isebe	department (n)	departement			naamwoord
isebe	tributary (n)	takrivier	isibonda	pole (n)	paal
isebe	branch (n)	tak	isibonda	mayor (n)	burgemeester
isebe lemfundo	faculty (n)	fakulteit	isibongo	poem (n)	gedig
isefu	safe (n)	brandkluis	isibothwana	toddler (n)	peuter
isekela	deputy (n)	plaasvervanger	isibulala-	disinfectant (n)	ontsmettingsmiddel
isela	thief (n)	dief	ntsholongwane		
isele	frog (n)	padda	isicaka	servant (n)	bediende
iseleri	celery (n)	seldery	isicelo	plea (n)	pleidooi
iseli	cell (n)	sel	isicelo	application (n)	aansoek
iselwa	calabash (n)	kalbas	isicelo	request (n)	versoek
isemilisi	bran (n)	semels	isichazi-magama	dictionary (n)	woordeboek
isende	testicle (n)	teelbal	isichotho	hail (n)	hael
isenethi	senate (n)	senaat	isichumiso	fertiliser (n)	kunsmis
isenta	centre (n)	middel	isiciko	lid (n)	deksel
isenti	cent (n)	sent	isicima-mlilo	fire brigade (n)	brandweer
isenzi	verb (n)	werkwoord	isicimi	eraser (n)	uitveër
isenzo	deed (n)	daad	isicwangciso	arrangement (n)	skikking
isepha	soap (n)	seep	isidalwa	creature (n)	wese
iserityisi	circus (n)	sirkus	isidalwa esanyisayo	mammal (n)	soogdier
iseshini	term (n)	term	isidlele	cheek (n)	wang
iseti	set (n)	stel	isidlo	meal (n)	maal
isetifiketi	certificate (n)	sertifikaat	isidlo sakusasa	breakfast (n)	ontbyt
isetyana	twig (n)	takkie	isidlo sasemini	lunch (n)	middagete
iseyile	canvas (n)	seil	isidubedube	riot (n)	onlus

Xhosa	English	Afrikaans	Xhosa	English	Afrikaans	I
isidudu	porridge (n)	pap	isihlunu	steak (n)	biefstuk	
isifefi	sprinkler (n)	sprinkelaar	isihlunu	fillet (n)	filet	
isifingo	dawn (n)	dagbreek	isihlunu	muscle (n)	spier	
isifo	disease (n)	siekte	isihlunu sehagu	ham (n)	ham	
isifo esosulelayo	epidemic (n)	epidemie	isihlwele	multitude (n)	menigte	
isifombo	hunchback (n)	boggelrug	isihlwele	crowd (n)	skare	
isifo samathambo	rheumatism (n)	rumatiek	isihogo	hell (n)	hel	
isifo sephepha	tuberculosis (n)	tuberkulose	isihombisi-keyiki	icing (n)	versiersuiker	
isifo seswekile	diabetes (n)	suikersiekte	isijungqe	piece (n)	stuk	
isifo sokungalali	insomnia (n)	slaaploosheid	isikali	scale (n)	skaal	
isifo sokuwa	epilepsy (n)	vallende siekte	isikere	scissors (n)	skêr	
isifo sokuxhuzula	fits (n)	stuipe	isikhafu	scarf (n)	serp	
isifo somqala	diphtheria (n)	witseerkeel	isikhalazo	complaint (n)	klagte	
isifuba	chest (n)	borskas	isikhalo	grievance (n)	grief	
isifuba	thorax (n)	borskas	isikhalo	scream (n)	gil	
isifuba	breast (n)	bors	isikhalo	cry (n)	kreet	
isifundo	lesson (n)	les	isikhamiso	vowel (n)	klinker	
isifundo	lecture (n)	lesing	isikhenkcisi	freezer (n)	vrieskas	
isifungo	oath (n)	eed	isikhephe sogqatso	yacht (n)	seiljag	
isiga	cigar (n)	sigaar	isikhohlela	phlegm (n)	fleim	
isigama	vocabulary (n)	woordeskat	isikhokelo	guide (n)	gids	
isiganeko	event (n)	gebeurtenis	isikhongozelo	container (n)	houer	
isigantsontso	giant (n)	reus	isikhonkwane	peg (n)	pen	
isigcawu	spider (n)	spinnekop	isikhonkwane	nail (n)	spyker	
isigcini-sandla	glovebox (n)	mossienes	isikhotsholo	cobra (n)	kobra	
isigebenga	murderer (n)	moordenaar	isikhova	owl (n)	uil	
isigezo	insolence (n)	parmantigheid	isikhukukazi	hen (n)	hen	
isigidi	million (n)	miljoen	isikhukula	flood (n)	vloed	
isigidimi	messenger (n)	bode	isikhululo	station (n)	stasie	
isiginci samagqudwana	xylophone (n)	xilofoon	isikhululo samapolisa	police station (n)	polisiekantoor	
isigodo	log (n)	blok	isikhululo	airport (n)	lughawe	
isigqebelo	irony (n)	ironie	senqwelomoya			
isigqibo	decision (n)	besluit	isikhumbuzo	souvenir (n)	aandenking	
isigqibo	term (n)	termyn	isikhumbuzo	reminder (n)	herinnering	
isigqibo esifungelweyo	affidavit (n)	beëdigde verklaring	isikhundla	lair (n)	lêplek	
isigqubuthelo	veil (n)	sluier	isikhundla	stand (n)	stand	
isigu	trap (n)	strik	isikhuseli	screen (n)	skerm	
isigulana	patient (n)	pasiënt	isikhuseli-buhlungu	antibody (n)	teenliggaam	
isigulo	plague (n)	plaag	isikhusi-mehlo	blinkers (n)	oogklappe	
isigulo	illness (n)	siekte	isikimu	scheme (n)	skema	
isigulo	sickness (n)	siekte	isikolo	school (n)	skool	
isigwebo	judgment (n)	oordeel	isikolo senkcubeko	academy (n)	akademie	
isigwebo	verdict (n)	uitspraak	isikophu	shovel (n)	skoppie	
isigwebo	suspended sentence (n)	opgeskorte vonnis	isikrufu	screw (n)	skroef	
esixhonyiweyo			isilabhasi	syllabus (n)	leerplan	
isihandiba	aristocrat (n)	edelman	isilarha	butchery (n)	slagtery	
isihlahla	wrist (n)	pols	isilarha	abattoir (n)	slagplaas	
isihlahla	bunch (n)	tros	isilayi	slice (n)	sny	
isihlalo	seat (n)	sitplek	isilephere	leper (n)	melaatse	
isihlalo	chair (n)	stoel	isilevu	chin (n)	ken	
-isihlandlo	spell (v)	spel	isilika	silk (n)	sy	
isihlangu	boot (n)	stewel	isilinganisi semvula	rain gauge (n)	reënmeter	
isihlangu	shoe (n)	skoen	isilivere	silver (n)	silwer	
isihlanu	five (n)	vyf	isilo	animal (n)	dier	
isihlekisi	comic (n)	komiek	isilo	beast (n)	dier	
isihlenga	raft (n)	vlot	isilonda	sore (n)	seer	
isihloko	title (n)	titel	isilonda	ulcer (n)	ulkus	
isihlomelo	adverb (n)	bywoord	isilo-qabane	pet (n)	troeteldier	
isihluma	flora (n)	flora	isilumeki	fuse (n)	sekering	
isihluma esizalweni	embryo (n)	embrio	isilumkiso	warning (n)	waarskuwing	

Xhosa	English	Afrikaans	Xhosa	English	Afrikaans
isilungiso	amendment (n)	wysiging	isipho	present (n)	geskenk
isilwanyanya	vertebrate (n)	werweldier	isiphoso	hysterics (n)	histerie
esinomqolo			isiphumo	consequence (n)	gevolg
isimangalo	charge (n)	aanklag	isiphumo	outcome (n)	uitkoms
isimbiwa	mineral (n)	mineraal	isiphumo	effect (n)	uitwerking
isimboli	symbol (n)	simbool	isiphunzi	stump (n)	stomp
isimelabizo	pronoun (n)	voornaamwoord	isipili	mirror (n)	spieël
isimemo	invitation (n)	uitnodiging	isiporho	ghost (n)	gees
isimilo	conduct (v)	gedra	isiporo	horseshoe (n)	hoefyster
isimo sedolophu	urbanisation (n)	verstedeliking	isiporo	railway (n)	spoorweg
isimuncumuncu	dessert (n)	nagereg	isiprofeto	prediction (n)	voorspelling
isinaba	creeper (n)	klimop	isiqabu	relief (n)	verligting
isinambuzane	insect (n)	insek	isiqalo	beginning (n)	begin
isincamathelisi	glue (n)	gom	isiqalo	start (n)	begin
isincoko	essay (n)	opstel	isiqhamo	sequel (n)	gevolg
isindululo	proposal (n)	voorstel	isiqhamo	fruit (n)	vrug
isine	four (n)	vier	isiqhelo	habit (n)	gewoonte
isingci	mane (n)	maanhare	isiqholo	perfume (n)	parfuum
isingcolo	corruption (n)	bedorwenheid	isiqholo	deodorant (n)	reukweermiddel
isi Ngesi	English (a)	Engels	isiqholo	spice (n)	spesery
isingqisho	beat (n)	ritme	isiqhulo	joke (n)	grap
isingqisho	rhythm (n)	ritme	isiqhushumbisi	bomb (n)	bom
isingxi	fullstop (n)	punt	isiqhwala	cripple (n)	kreupele
isingxobo	sheath (n)	skede	isiqingatha	half (n)	helfte
isini	gender (n)	geslag	isiqinisekiso	guarantee (n)	waarborg
isiniki-moya	fan (n)	waaier	isiqithi	island (n)	eiland
isininzi	plural (n)	meervoud	isiqobo	block (n)	blok
isinki	sink (n)	opwasbak	isiqu	stem (n)	stam
isinongo	flavour (n)	geur	isiqwenga	shred (v)	snipper
isinqandamathe	boyfriend (n)	kêrel	isirhovu	glutton (n)	vraat
isinqandi-sifo	antidote (n)	teengif	isisa	charity (n)	liefdadigheid
isinqe	birthplace (n)	geboorteplek	isisa	donation (n)	skenking
isinqe	loin (n)	lende	isiseko	basis (n)	basis
isinqe	waist (n)	middel	isiselo	drink (n)	drankie
isintlakantlakiso	roughage (n)	vesel	isishwankathelo	summary (n)	opsomming
isinxibo	costume (n)	kostuum	isisu	abdomen (n)	buik
isinxilisi	alcohol (n)	alkohol	isisu	stomach (n)	maag
isinxonxo	dimple (n)	kuiltjie	isisu segazi	dysentery (n)	disenterie
isinxusi	parallel (n)	parallel	isitalato	street (n)	straat
isinyanya	ancestor (n)	voorouer	isitali	stable (n)	stal
isinyanzelo	compulsion (n)	dwang	isitatshi	starch (n)	stysel
isinyathelo	pedal (n)	pedaal	isitena	brick (n)	baksteen
isinyi	bladder (n)	blaas	isithabazi	lowveld (n)	laeveld
isinyithi	metal (n)	metaal	isithandathu	six (n)	ses
isinyithi	lead (n)	lood	isithandwa	lover (n)	minnaar
isinyobo	bribe (n)	omkoopprys	isithembiso	promise (n)	belofte
isipaji	purse (n)	beursie	isithembiso sokun-	parole (n)	parool
isipeke	bacon (n)	spek	gabaleki		
isipeliti	safety pin (n)	haakspeld	isithembu	polygamy (n)	poligamie
isipeliti	pin (n)	speld	isithende	heel (n)	hak
isiphango	storm (n)	storm	isithethe	tradition (n)	tradisie
isiphatho	handle (n)	handvatsel	isithetho	slang (n)	sleng
isiphawuli	adjective (n)	byvoeglike naamwoord	isithili	district (n)	distrik
isiphazamiso	interruption (n)	onderbreking	isithintelo	restriction (n)	inperking
isiphazamiso	disturbance (n)	oproer	isithixo	god (n)	god
isipheko	cook (n)	kok	isithiyiseli	fishmoth (n)	vismot
isiphelo	end (n)	einde	isithonga	blow (n)	hou
isiphelo	finish (n)	einde	isithonga	shot (n)	skoot
isiphendu	sedition (n)	opruiing	isithsaba	crown (n)	kroon
isiphilisi	cure (n)	genesing	isithuba	gap (n)	opening

Xhosa	English	Afrikaans	Xhosa	English	Afrikaans	I
isithuba	space (n)	ruimte	isoka	soccer (n)	sokker	
isithuba	vacancy (n)	vakature	isondlo	nutrition (n)	voeding	
isithuko	insult (n)	belediging	isongezelelo	addition (n)	toevoeging	
isithungu	sheaf (n)	gerf	isongezelelo	increase (n)	verhoging	
isithuthuthu	motorcycle (n)	motorfiets	isongololo	millipede (n)	duisendpoot	
isitiya	garden (n)	tuin	isongololo	centipede (n)	honderdpoot	
isitofu	stove (n)	stoof	isonka	bread (n)	brood	
isitsalane	magnet (n)	magneet	isonka	loaf (n)	brood	
isitshanguba	ringworm (n)	ringwurm	isonka somthendeleko	wafer (n)	wafel	
isitshele	stain (n)	vlek	isono	sin (n)	sonde	
isitshisa	heartburn (n)	sooibrand	isophoro	supper (n)	aandete	
isitshixo	key (n)	sleutel	isoseji	sausage (n)	wors	
isitshixo	lock (n)	slot	isothuso	surprise (n)	verrassing	
isitunxa	idiot (n)	idioot	istampu	stamp (n)	seël	
isitya	bowl (n)	bak	istampu sokuposa	postage stamp (n)	posseël	
isitya	basin (n)	kom	istibili	stirrup (n)	stiebeuel	
isitya	dish (n)	skottel	istop sebhasi	bus stop (n)	bushalte	
isityalo	plant (n)	plant	isuntsu	segment (n)	segment	
isitya sokuchamela	bedpan (n)	bedpan	isuti	suit (n)	pak	
isityholo	accusation (n)	beskuldiging	iswekile	sugar (n)	suiker	
isityholo	blame (n)	blaam	iswitshi	switch (n)	skakelaar	
isityholo	slander (n)	laster	itafilana	tablet (n)	tablet	
isityu	stew (n)	bredie	itafile	table (n)	tafel	
isiva	scar (n)	litteken	itakane	kid (n)	bokkie	
isivakalisi	sentence (n)	sin	itakane	lamb (n)	lam	
isivalo	valve (n)	klep	italasi	homosexual (n)	homoseksueel	
isivingco	cork (n)	kurk	italente	talent (n)	talent	
isivingco	plug (n)	prop	itanka	pliers (n)	knyptang	
isivingco	tampon (n)	tampon	-itanki	tank (n)	tenk	
isivingco	stopper (n)	stopprop	itapile	potato (n)	aartappel	
isivuno	harvest (n)	oes	itawuli	towel (n)	handdoek	
isivuseleli	stimulus (n)	stimulus	itayala	tyre (n)	buiteband	
isixeko	village (n)	dorpie	iteksi	taxi (n)	taxi	
isixeko	city (n)	stad	itepu	tap (n)	kraan	
isixhenxe	seven (n)	sewe	itha	tar (n)	teer	
isixhobo	apparatus (n)	apparaat	ithafa	faeces (n)	uitwerpsel	
isixhobo	instrument (n)	instrument	ithafa leduli	battlefield (n)	slagveld	
isixhobo	technique (n)	tegniek	ithala	terrace (n)	terras	
isixhobo	gadget (n)	toestelletjie	ithala leencwadi	library (n)	biblioteek	
isixhobo	weapon (n)	wapen	ithambeka	descent (n)	daling	
isixhobo	tool (n)	werktuig	ithambeka	slope (n)	helling	
isixilongi	stethoscope (n)	stetoskoop	ithambo	bone (n)	been	
isiyilelo -qanda	ovary (n)	eierstok	ithamo	dose (n)	dosis	
isiyolisi	amusement (n)	vermaaklikheid	ithamsanqa	fortune (n)	fortuin	
isiyolo	fun (n)	pret	ithamsanqa	luck (n)	geluk	
isizalo	womb (n)	baarmoeder	ithanga	thigh (n)	dy	
isizalwana	relation (n)	familielid	ithanga	pumpkin (n)	pampoen	
isizathu	motive (n)	beweegrede	ithayimtheyibhili	timetable (n)	rooster	
isizathu	reason (n)	rede	ithebe	rump (n)	kruis	
isizeko	pattern (n)	patroon	itheku	bay (n)	baai	
isiziba	patch (n)	lappie	ithelevizhini	television (n)	televisie	
isizothezothe	nausea (n)	naarheid	ithemba	hope (n)	hoop	
isizukulwana	posterity (n)	nageslag	ithenephu	turnip (n)	raap	
isizunguzane	dizziness (n)	duiseligheid	ithintitha	stammer (n)	gehakkel	
isizwe	nation (n)	nasie	ithoba	nine (n)	nege	
iskwashi	squash (n)	muurbal	ithokazi	heifer (n)	vers	
isohlwayo	fine (n)	boete	ithole	calf (n)	kalf	
isohlwayo	punishment (n)	straf	ithontsi	drip (n)	drup	
isohlwayo	penalty (n)	straf	-ithu	ours (pron)	ons s'n	
isoka	bachelor (n)	jongkêrel	-ithu	our (pron)	ons	

Xhosa	English	Afrikaans	Xhosa	English	Afrikaans
ithuba	turn (n)	beurt	ivisa	visa (n)	visum
ithuba	opportunity (n)	geleentheid	ivolontiya	volunteer (n)	vrywilliger
ithuba	occasion (n)	geleentheid	ivoti	vote (n)	stem
ithuba	chance (n)	kans	ivumba	fragrance (n)	geur
ithuba	moment (n)	oomblik	ivumba	smell (n)	reuk
ithuba lokuxakeka	emergency (n)	noodgeval	ivumba	stink (n)	stank
ithuku	instinct (n)	instink	iwaka	thousand (n)	duisend
ithumba	boil (n)	bloedvint	iwayini	wine (n)	wyn
ithumba	tumour (n)	gewas	iwele	twin (n)	tweeling
ithumbu	intestine (n)	derm	iweyitara	waiter (n)	kelner
ithupha	paw (n)	poot	iwolethi	wallet (n)	notetas
iti	tea (n)	tee	ixabiso	price (n)	prys
itikiti	ticket (n)	kaartjie	ixabiso	value (n)	waarde
ititshala	teacher (n)	onderwyser	ixesha	watch (n)	horlosie
itoliki	interpreter (n)	tolk	ixesha	clock (n)	horlosie
itolofiya	prickly pear (n)	turksvy	ixesha	time (n)	tyd
itolongo itrongo	prison (n)	gevangenis	ixesha ebomini lokufikisa	adolescence (n)	adolessensie
itonela	tunnel (n)	tonnel			
itotshi	torch (n)	flitslig	ixesha eladlulayo	past (n)	verlede
itreksutu	tracksuit (n)	sweetpak	ixesha lobumnandi emvakomtshato	honeymoon (n)	wittebrood
itreyi	tray (n)	skinkbord			
itroko	truck (n)	trok	ixesha lonyaka	season (n)	seisoen
itrongo	jail (n)	tronk	ixhalanga	vulture (n)	aasvoël
itshatini	chutney (n)	blatjang	ixhoba	prey (n)	prooi
itshefu	handkerchief (n)	sakdoek	ixhoba	victim (n)	slagoffer
itsheke	cheque (n)	tjek	ixhobongwana	hovel (n)	pondok
itshilisi	chilli (n)	brandrissie	ixhwele	herbalist (n)	kruiekenner
itshimini	chimney (n)	skoorsteen	ixhwili	hyena (n)	hiëna
itshipsi	chip (potato) (n)	skyfie	ixibhiya	buttermilk (n)	karringmelk
itshivela	villain (n)	skurk	ixilongo	trumpet (n)	trompet
itshizi	cheese (n)	kaas	ixilongo	saxophone (n)	saxofoon
itshokhwe	chalk (n)	kryt	ixilongo	clarinet (n)	klarinet
itshokoleti	chocolate (n)	sjokolade	ixina	cymbal (n)	simbaal
itshopsi	chop (n)	tjop	ixoki	scoundrel (n)	skobbejak
itswele	onion (n)	ui	ixoki	liar (n)	leuenaar
itumata	tomato (n)	tamatie	ixolo	bark (n)	bas
ityala	credit (n)	krediet	ixuxu	lout (n)	takhaar
ityala	offence (n)	oortreding	iyelenqe	conspiracy (n)	sameswering
ityala	guilt (n)	skuld	iyelenqe	plot (n)	komplot
ityala	debt (n)	skuld	iyeza	drug (n)	dwelm
ityala	trial (n)	verhoor	iyeza	herbs (n)	kruie
ityali	shawl (n)	tjalie	iyeza	medicine (n)	medisyne
ityathanga	chain (n)	ketting	iyeza lokuhambisa	laxative (n)	lakseermiddel
ityepusi	cap (n)	deksel	iyeza lokuhambisa	purgative (n)	purgeermiddel
ityhefu	poison (n)	gif	iyonke	total (n)	totaal
ityholo	bush (n)	bos	iyunivesithi	university (n)	universiteit
ityholo	shrub (n)	struik	iyure	hour (n)	uur
ityuwa	salt (n)	sout	-iza	come (v)	kom
ivatala	melon (n)	meloen	izala	rubbish heap (n)	vullishoop
ivatala	watermelon (n)	waatlemoen	izalathisi	directions (n)	aanwysings
ivazi	vase (n)	vaas	izembe	axe (n)	byl
iveki	week (n)	week	izibilini	entrails (n)	ingewande
ivenge	enema (n)	enema	izibi zomzimba	excreta (n)	uitwerpsel
iveni yokusebenza	panel van (n)	paneelwa	izibuko	harbour (n)	hawe
ivenkile	store (n)	winkel	izidubuli	ammunition (n)	ammunisie
ivenkile	shop (n)	winkel	izikhala	haemorrhoids (n)	aambeie
ivesi	verse (n)	vers	iziko	hearth (n)	haard
ivesti	vest (n)	onderhemp	iziko	fireplace (n)	vuurherd
ivili	wheel (n)	wiel	iziko lezilwanyana	zoo (n)	dieretuin
ivinika	vinegar (n)	asyn	iziko lobugcisa	technikon (n)	tegnikon

Xhosa	English	Afrikaans	Xhosa	English	Afrikaans	K
iziko logcino-ndalo	nature reserve (n)	natuurreservaat	-khaliphileyo	brave (a)	dapper	
iziko-mveliso	factory (n)	fabriek	-khalisa	ring (v)	lui	
izila	mourning (n)	rou	-khalisa uphondo	hoot (v)	toet	
izilo	fauna (n)	fauna	-khangela	check (v)	nagaan	
izim	cannibal (n)	mensvreter	-khanya	shine (v)	skyn	
izinxonxo	dentures (n)	vals tande	-khanyayo	shiny (a)	blink	
izinyo	fang (n)	slagtand	-khanyela	deny (v)	ontken	
izinyo	tooth (n)	tand	-khanyisela	enlighten (v)	inlig	
izinyo	toothache (n)	tandpyn	-khapa	kick (v)	skop	
izipheko imenyu	menu (n)	spyskaart	-khapha	accompany (v)	begelei	
iziphu	zipper (n)	ritssluiter	-khapha	escort (v)	vergesel	
izitepu	stairs (n)	trappe	-khathalela	care (v)	omgee	
izithuthi	traffic (n)	verkeer	-khathalela	mind (v)	omgee	
izitya	crockery (n)	breekware	-khathali(yo)	negligent (a)	nalatig	
izixhobo	arms (n)	wapens	-khathaza	bother (v)	lastig wees	
izolo	yesterday (n)	gister	-khathaza	hinder (v)	hinder	
izulu	heaven (n)	hemel	-khathaza	perturb (v)	verontrus	
			-khathaza	pester (v)	pla	
-jacekileyo	tattered (a)	toiingrig	-khathaza	trouble (v)	kwel	
-jala	pout (v)	pruil	-khawuleza(yo)	quick (a)	gou	
-jamela	scowl (v)	suur kyk	-khawulezayo	express (a)	uitdruklik	
-javujavu	tasteless (a)	smaakloos	-khawulezayo	fast (a)	vinnig	
-jija	wring (v)	wring	-khawulezayo	rapid (a)	vlugtig	
-jika	turn (v)	draai	-khawulezile(yo)	sudden (a)	skielik	
-jikelele	general (a)	algemeen	-khawulezisa	accelerate (v)	versnel	
-jikeleza	revolve (v)	draai	-khazimla	gleam (v)	straal	
-jikelezisa	circulate (v)	rondgaan	-khazimla	sparkle (v)	vonkel	
-jinga	droop (v)	neerhang	-khe	hers (pron)	hare	
-jiwula	wag (v)	swaai	-khe	his (pron)	sy	
-jiyisa	congeal (v)	stol	-khe	his (pron)	syne	
-jolisa	aim (v)	mik	-khe	its (pron)	sy	
-jonga	gaze (v)	staar	-khefuza	gasp (v)	snak	
-jonga	look (v)	kyk	-khefuzela	pant (v)	hyg	
-jonga	view (v)	bekyk	-khenkca	freeze (v)	vries	
-joyina	join (v)	las	-khenkceza	jingle (v)	klingel	
-jubalaza	wriggle (v)	wriemel	-khenketha	tour (v)	rondreis	
			-khephuza	snow (v)	sneeu	
kabani	whose (pron)	wie se	-khetha	choose (v)	kies	
-kade	late (a)	laat	-khetha	pick (v)	uitkies	
-kakubi	badly (adv)	sleg	-khetha	prefer (v)	verkies	
kakuhle	well (a)	goed	-khohlakeleyo	cruel (a)	wreed	
kambe	anyhow (conj)	in elk geval	-khohlela	cough (v)	hoes	
-kancinci	gradually (adv)	geleidelik	-khohlisa	deceive (v)	bedrieg	
-kanga	much (a)	veel	-khohlisa	flatter (v)	vlei	
-kangaka	approximate (a)	geskat	-khohlo	left (a)	links	
kanje	just (adv)	net	-khokela	lead (v)	lei	
kanye	absolute (a)	absoluut	-khokela	precede (v)	voorafgaan	
-kanye	exact (a)	presies	-kholelwa	believe (v)	glo	
kanye	indeed (adv)	werklik	-kholiwe(yo)	religious (a)	godsdienstig	
kanye	once (adv)	een maal	-kholwa	like (v)	hou van	
-kawonke-wonke	public (a)	openbaar	-khomokazi	female (a)	vroulik	
-kazwelonke	international (a)	internasionaal	-khonkotha	bark (v)	blaf	
-kekela	slant (v)	skuins loop	-khonkotha	howl (v)	tjank	
-kha	scoop (v)	skep	-khonza	serve (v)	dien	
-khaba	boot (v)	skop	-khotha	lick (v)	lek	
-khahlela	salute (v)	salueer	-khubeka	stumble (v)	struikel	
-khala	cry (v)	huil	-khubeka	trip (v)	struikel	
-khala	lament (n)	weeklag	-khubekisa	offend (v)	aanstoot gee	
-khala	scream (v)	gil	-khubekisayo	offensive (a)	aanstootlik	
-khalaza	complain (v)	kla	-khucula	bleach (v)	bleik	

395

K

Xhosa	English	Afrikaans
-khuhla	grate (v)	rasper
-khuhla	scour (v)	skuur
-khuhla	scrub (v)	skrop
-khukhumala	bulge (v)	uitbult
-khula	grow (v)	groei
-khule gqitha	overgrown (a)	toegegroei
-khulile(yo)	mature (a)	volwasse
-khulisa	rear (v)	grootmaak
-khulu	big (a)	groot
-khulu	enormous (a)	tamaai
-khulu	huge (a)	reusagtig
-khulu	large (a)	groot
-khulu	thick (a)	dik
-khulu	very (a)	heel
-khulula	acquit (v)	vryspreek
-khulula	disconnect (v)	losmaak
-khulula	emancipate (v)	vrymaak
-khulula	free (v)	bevry
-khulula	release (v)	loslaat
-khulula	undo (v)	losmaak
-khulula	undress (v)	uittrek
-khululekileyo	free (a)	vry
-khululekile(yo)	loose (a)	los
-khumbula	long (v)	verlang
-khumbula	recollect (v)	onthou
-khumbula	remember (v)	onthou
-khumbuza	remind (v)	herinner
-khupha	eject (v)	uitskiet
-khupha	issue (v)	uitreik
-khuphe endlwini	evict (v)	uitsit
-khuphisana	compete (v)	wedywer
-khusela	defend (v)	verdedig
-khusela	protect (v)	beskerm
-khusela	secure (v)	beveilig
-khusela	shield (v)	beskerm
-khuselayo	defensive (a)	verdedigend
-khuselekileyo	secure (a)	veilig
-khuthaza	encourage (v)	aanmoedig
-khutheleyo	diligent (a)	fluks
-khutheleyo	efficient (a)	doeltreffend
-khutheleyo	industrious (a)	vlytig
-khuthula	chafe (v)	skaaf
-khuthuza	rob (v)	beroof
-khwankqisa	stun (v)	verstom
-khwaza	exclaim (v)	uitroep
-khweba	beckon (v)	wink
-khwebula	avoid (v)	vermy
-khwela	climb (v)	klim
-khwina	whimper (v)	sanik
kodwa	but (conj)	maar
kodwa	however (conj)	maar
-krakra	bitter (a)	bitter
-krazula	tear (v)	skeur
-krele-krele	intelligent (a)	intelligent
-krelekrele	transparent (a)	deurskynend
-kreqa	defect (v)	oorloop na
-kroba	peep (v)	loer
-kroxoma	rattle (v)	ratel
-kruneka	sprain (v)	verstuit
-krwada	raw (a)	rou
-krwada	rude (a)	onbeskof
-krwaqula	glance (v)	vlugtig kyk
-krwela	tick (v)	tik
-krwela	scrape (v)	skraap
-krwela	scratch (v)	krap
-krwempa	claw (v)	klou
-krwitsha	throttle (v)	wurg
-krwitsha	strangle (v)	verwurg
ku-	from (prep)	van
ku-	to (prep)	na
-kude	far (adv)	ver
-kude	remote (a)	afgeleë
kude	until (conj)	tot
-kufutshane	close (a)	naby
kufutshane	near (adv)	naby
kuna-	than (conj)	as
kungekudala	soon (adv)	binnekort
kungenjalo	otherwise (adv)	anders
kunye, na-	and (conj)	en
-kuphela	only (a)	enigste
kuphela	only (adv)	slegs
-kuqala	first (a)	eerste
-kusasa	early (a)	vroeg
kwakhona	again (adv)	weer
kwakhona	still (adv)	nog
-kwamsinya	immediate (a)	onmiddellik
kwaza	then (adv)	dan
kwaza	then (adv)	toe
-kwazi	able (a)	bekwaam
-kwazi	can (n)	kan
kwenye indawo	elsewhere (adv)	elders
-lahleka (yo)	lost (a)	verdwaal
-lahlekayo	stray (v)	afdwaal
-lahlekelwa	lose (v)	verloor
-lahlekelwe ziingqondo	unconscious (a)	bewusteloos
lahlekile (yo)	lost (a)	verlore
-lala	lie (v)	lê
-lala	doze (v)	sluimer
-lala	sleep (v)	slaap
-lamba	starve (v)	honger ly
-lambathayo	vain (a)	ydel
-lambile(yo)	hungry (a)	honger
-lamla	mediate (v)	bemiddel
-landela	follow (v)	volg
-landela	pursue (v)	najaag
-landela	stalk (v)	bekruip
-landela	track (v)	opspoor
-landelayo	next (a)	volgende
-landelelana ngamaxesha	chronological (a)	chronologies
-langazelela	aspire (v)	streef
-langazelela	yearn (v)	hunker
-lawula	control (v)	beheer
-lawula	govern (v)	regeer
-lawula	manage (v)	bestuur
-lawula	master (v)	bemeester
-lawula	reign (v)	heers
-lawula	rule (v)	regeer

Xhosa	English	Afrikaans	Xhosa	English	Afrikaans
le	this (pron)	dit	-lungileyo	fit (v)	pas
-leleyo	asleep (a)	aan die slaap	-lungisa	correct (v)	korrigeer
leya	those (pron)	daardie	-lungisa	fix (v)	regmaak
-libala	forget (v)	vergeet	-lungisa	justify (v)	regverdig
-libazisa	delay (v)	vertraag	-lungiselela	adapt (v)	aanpas
-lihlebo	confidential (a)	vertroulik	-lungiselela	prepare (v)	voorberei
-lihlwempu	poor (a)	arm	-luphawu	characteristic (a)	kenmerkend
-lila	weep (v)	huil	-lushwaca	sullen (a)	nors
-lima	plough (v)	ploeg	-lusizi	sad (a)	treurig
-lima	cultivate (v)	bewerk	-luzizi	dim (a)	dof
-limaza	deform (v)	vervorm	-lwa	battle (v)	veg
-limaza	maim (v)	vermink			
-limaza	mutilate (v)	skend	-ma	halt (v)	stop
-limeleyo	disabled (a)	gebreklik	-ma	stand (v)	staan
-linda	wait (v)	wag	-mamela	listen (v)	luister
-lindela	await (v)	wag op	-mandulo	ancient (a)	antiek
-lindela	expect (v)	verwag	-mangalelwa	charge (law) (v)	aankla
-lingana(yo)	level (a)	gelyk	-mangalisa	amaze (v)	verbaas
-linganayo	even (a)	gelykmatig	-mangalisa	marvel (v)	wonder
-linganayo	equal (a)	gelyk	-mangalisa	wonder (v)	wonder
-linganisa	ape (v)	na-aap	-mangalisayo	amazing (a)	verbasend
-linganisa	equal (v)	gelyk wees aan	-mangalisa(yo)	marvellous (a)	wonderbaarlik
-linganisa	imitate (v)	namaak	-mangalisayo	mysterious (a)	geheimsinnig
-linganisa	measure (v)	meet	-mangalisa (yo)	wonderful (a)	wonderlik
-linganisela	weigh (v)	weeg	-manya	unit (n)	eenheid
-lingisa	feint (v)	voorgee	-manzi	wet (a)	nat
-londoloza	conserve (v)	bewaar	-manzisa	moisten (v)	natmaak
-londoloza	preserve (v)	bewaar	-manzisa	water (v)	natgooi
-lubhelu-mdaka	beige (a)	beige	-maphandleni	rural (a)	plattelands
-luhlaza	blue (a)	blou	-matsha	march (v)	marsjeer
-luhlaza njalo	evergreen (a)	bladhoudend	-ma umtya	queue (v)	toustaan
-lukhuni	hard (a)	hard	-mbalwa	few (a)	min
-lukuhla	mislead (v)	mislei	-mbeko	polite (a)	hoflik
-lukuhla(yo)	misleading (a)	misleidend	-mbolombini	ambiguous (a)	dubbelsinnig
-lula	effortless (a)	met gemak	-mbombozela	grumble (v)	brom
-lula	easy (a)	maklik	-mbombozela	mutter (v)	mompel
-lula	simple (a)	eenvoudig	-mbuna	tame (a)	mak
-lulamile(yo)	humble (a)	nederig	-mcaba	flat (a)	plat
-lulamile(yo)	meek (a)	gedwee	-mdaka	brown (a)	bruin
-lulamile(yo)	modest (a)	beskeie	-mdaka	dirty (a)	vuil
-lulamisa	tame (v)	tem	-mdaka	unclean (a)	onrein
-lulwelo	liquid (a)	vloeibaar	-mdaka	untidy (a)	slordig
-luma	bite (v)	byt	-mela	represent (v)	verteenwoordig
-lumeka	ignite (v)	aansteek	-mele	must (v)	moet
-lumka	heed (v)	in ag neem	-mema	invite (v)	uitnooi
-lumka	beware (v)	oppas	-mfuneko	necessary (a)	noodsaaklik
-lumkile (yo)	wise (a)	wys	-mfusa	purple (a)	pers
-lumkileyo	astute (a)	slim	-mgangatho	standard (a)	standaard
-lumkileyo	careful (a)	versigtig	-mgqakhwe	illegitimate (a)	buite-egtelik
-lumkisa	admonish (v)	vermaan	mhlawumbi	maybe (adv)	miskien
-lumkisa	warn (v)	waarsku	mhlawumbi	perhaps (adv)	miskien
-lumla	wean (v)	speen	-mhlophe	clear (a)	helder
-lunga	ready (a)	gereed	-mihla yonke	daily (a)	daagliks
-lungeleyo	convenient (a)	gerieflik	-mileyo	stationary (a)	stilstaande
-lungile	good (a)	goed	-mileyo	stagnant (a)	stagnant
-lungile (yo)	fair (a)	billik	-misa	assess (v)	skat
-lungile (yo)	mild (a)	matig	-misa	erect (v)	oprig
-lungile(yo)	right (a)	reg	-misa	park (v)	parkeer
-lungileyo	appropriate (a)	geskik	-misa intente	camp (v)	kampeer
-lungileyo	correct (a)	korrek	-misela ixesha elizayo	adjourn (v)	verdaag

M

Xhosa	English	Afrikaans	Xhosa	English	Afrikaans
-miwa	choke (v)	verstik	-ncinci	less (a)	minder
mna	me (pron)	my	-ncinci	least (a)	minste
mna	self (n)	self	-nciphile(yo)	thin (a)	dun
-mnandi	delicious (a)	heerlik	-nciphisa	lessen (v)	verminder
-mnandi	nice (a)	aangenaam	-nciphisa	reduce (v)	verminder
-mnyama	black (a)	swart	-nciphisa	decrease (v)	verminder
-mnyama	dark (a)	donker	-ncokola	chat (v)	gesels
-monela	envy (v)	beny	-ncokolisa	flirt (v)	flirteer
-mpompa	pump (v)	pomp	-ncoma	recommend (v)	aanbeveel
-mpuma	east (adv)	oos	-ncoma	praise (v)	loof
-mpuma	eastern (a)	oostelik	-ncoma	appreciate (v)	waardeer
-mpumlo	nasal (a)	nasaal	-ncomeka(yo)	praiseworthy (a)	lofwaardig
-mqengqelezi	steep (a)	steil	-ncomekayo	admirable (a)	bewonderendswaardig
-msulwa	honest (a)	eerlik	-ncomekayo	best (a)	beste
-msulwa	innocent (a)	onskuldig	-ncuma	smile (v)	glimlag
mthubi bomvu	tan (v)	bruin brand	-ncwina	groan (v)	kreun
-mthuzubala	pale (a)	bleek	-ndala	primitive (a)	primitief
-mtyaba	horizontal (a)	horisontaal	ndi-	I (pron)	ek
-mtyibilizi	slippery (a)	glibberig	-ndilekileyo	dignified (a)	waardig
-muncu	acid (a)	suur	-nduluka	leave (v)	laat
-muncu	sour (a)	suur	-nduluka	depart (v)	vertrek
-mxinwa	narrow (a)	smal	-ndulula	propose (v)	voorstel
-myinga	average (a)	gemiddeld	-ndwebile (yo)	wild (a)	wild
			-neentloni	shy (a)	skugter
-na	rain (v)	reën	-nekratshi	conceited (a)	verwaand
na-	too (adv)	ook	-nempumelelo	prosperous (a)	florerend
na-	also (adv)	ook	-nencasa	savoury (a)	smaaklik
-nabani	anybody (pron)	elkeen	-nenceba	merciful (a)	genadig
-nabungozi	harmless (a)	onskadelik	-nencilikithi	giddy (a)	duiselig
-nakana	recognise (v)	herken	-nengeniso	profitable (a)	lonend
-namandla	energetic (a)	energiek	-nengozi	dangerous (a)	gevaarlik
-namandla	powerful (a)	magtig	-nengqondo	reasonable (a)	redelik
-namandla	strong (a)	sterk	-nengqondo	sane (a)	verstandig
-nambitha	savour (v)	geniet	-nenkani	stubborn (a)	koppig
namhlanje	today (n)	vandag	-nenkani	wilful (a)	moedswillig
nangona	although (conj)	al	-nenkcitho	extravagant (a)	buitensporig
-nanisa	barter (v)	ruil	-nenkqubela	progressive (a)	progressief
-nanjani	anyhow (adv)	hoe dan ook	-nentlondi	mischievous (a)	ondeund
nantoni	anything (pron)	enigiets	-nentsingiselo	mean (a)	gemeen
naphi	anywhere (adv)	enige plek	-nesibindi	courageous (a)	moedig
naxa	though (conj)	hoewel	-nesikhumbuzo	memorial (a)	herdenking
-nayiphi	any (a)	enige	-nesiphiwo	gifted (a)	begaaf
-ncama	abandon (v)	verlaat	-netalente	talented (a)	talentvol
-ncamathela	adhere (v)	kleef	-nethamsanqa	lucky (a)	gelukkig
-ncamathela	stick (v)	vasplak	-nethamsanqa	fortunate (a)	gelukkig
-ncamathelayo	adhesive (a)	klewerig	-netyala	guilty (a)	skuldig
-ncamathelisa	glue (v)	gom	-nexabiso	valuable (a)	waardevol
-ncamathisela	paste (v)	plak	-nga	through (prep)	deur
-ncanca	suck (v)	suig	-nga	by (prep)	by
-nceda	assist (v)	bystaan	-nga	may (v)	mag
-nceda	aid (v)	help	nga-	about (prep)	oor
-nceda	help (v)	help	nga-	with (prep)	met
-nceda	rescue (v)	red	nga(m)nye	each (pron)	elk(e)
-ncedayo	helpful (a)	behulpsaam	-ngabhekisi mntwini	impersonal (a)	onpersoonlik
-ncedayo	beneficial (a)	voordelig	-ngabom	deliberate (a)	opsetlik
-ncinane	petty (a)	kleinlik	-ngabonakali(yo)	invisible (a)	onsigbaar
-ncinane	minute (a)	heel klein	-ngaboniyo	blind (a)	blind
-ncinci	little (a)	klein	-ngacacanga	vague (a)	vaag
-ncinci	small (a)	klein	-ngacetywanga	unplanned (a)	onbedoeld
-ncinci	junior (a)	junior	-ngadalwanga	artificial (a)	kunsmatig

Xhosa	English	Afrikaans	Xhosa	English	Afrikaans	N
ngafane	seldom (adv)	selde	-ngaqhelekanga	queer (a)	snaaks	
-ngafanelanga	undeserved (a)	onverdiend	-ngaqhelekanga	funny (a)	snaaks	
-ngafanelekanga	unfit (a)	ongeskik	-ngaqhelekanga	strange (a)	vreemd	
-ngafanelekanga	improper (a)	onfatsoenlik	-ngaqinisekanga	uncertain (a)	onseker	
-ngafumanekiyo	unavailable (a)	onverkrygbaar	-ngaqondanga	unaware (a)	onbewus	
-ngafundanga	uneducated (a)	ongeleerd	-ngaqondi kakuhle	misunderstand (v)	misverstaan	
-ngafuniyo	unwilling (a)	onwillig	-ngase	by (prep)	by	
-ngagcini xesha	unpunctual (a)	nie stip nie	-ngasecaleni	aside (adv)	opsy	
-ngagqibekanga	incomplete (a)	onvolledig	-ngathembakalanga	undependable (a)	onbetroubaar	
-ngagqibelelanga	imperfect (a)	onvolmaak	-ngathembekanga	dishonest (a)	oneerlik	
-ngagqitywanga	unfinished (a)	onvoltooid	-ngathembekanga	unfaithful (a)	ontrou	
-ngagunyaziswanga	unauthorised (a)	ongemagtig	-ngathembi	distrust (v)	wantrou	
-ngajikiyo	unalterable (a)	onveranderlik	-ngatshatanga	unmarried (a)	ongetroud	
-ngakhathaleli	neglect (v)	verwaarloos	-ngatyhilwanga	undisclosed (a)	onvermeld	
-ngakhathaliyo	careless (a)	nalatig	-ngavakali(yo)	inaudible (a)	onhoorbaar	
-ngalibalekiyo	unforgettable (a)	onvergeetlik	-ngavumelani	disagree (v)	verskil	
-ngalindelekanga	unexpected (a)	onverwag	-ngavuzwanga	unrewarded (a)	onbeloond	
-ngalinganiyo	unequal (a)	ongelyk	-ngaxhobanga	unarmed (a)	ongewapend	
-ngalinganiyo	uneven (a)	ongelyk	-ngaxhomekekanga	independent (a)	onafhanklik	
-ngalunganga	incorrect (a)	onjuis	-ngaxolelekiyo	unforgivable (a)	onvergeeflik	
-ngalunganga	wrong (a)	verkeerd	-ngazalisekanga	unfulfilled (a)	onvervuld	
-ngamameli(yo)	inattentive (a)	onoplettend	-ngazelwanga	unborn (a)	ongebore	
-ngamandla	vigorous (a)	kragtig	-ngazicingeliyo	unselfish (a)	onselfsugtig	
-ngamanzi	fluid (a)	vloeibaar	-ngcamla	taste (v)	proe	
-nganelisekanga	dissatisfied (a)	ontevrede	-ngcangcazela	tremble (v)	bewe	
-nganqwenelekiyo	undesirable (a)	ongewens	-ngcangcazela	shiver (v)	bewe	
-nganyangekiyo	incurable (a)	ongeneeslik	-ngcatsha	betray (v)	verraai	
ngaphakathi	within (adv)	binne	-ngciba	mend (v)	heelmaak	
ngaphakathi	inside (adv)	binne	-ngcolile (yo)	evil (a)	boos	
-ngaphakathi	inland (a)	binnelands	-ngcolileyo	corrupt (a)	bedorwe	
-ngaphakathi	eternal (a)	ewig	-ngcolileyo	obscene (a)	onbetaamlik	
-ngaphakathi	internal (a)	intern	-ngcolisa	corrupt (v)	bederf	
-ngaphambili	ahead (adv)	vooruit	-ngcothoza	spy (v)	spioeneer	
ngaphandle	except (prep)	behalwe	-ngcwaba	bury (v)	begrawe	
ngaphandle	without (adv)	buite	-ngcwele	holy (a)	heilig	
-ngaphantsi	below (prep)	onder	-ngcwele	sacred (a)	heilig	
ngaphantsi	under (prep)	onder	-ngekakhuli	immature (a)	onvolwasse	
-ngaphaphamanga	unwary (a)	onbehoedsaam	-ngekasetyenziswa	undeveloped (a)	onontwikkeld	
-ngaphathekiyo	abstract (a)	afgetrokke	-ngekho mfumamfuma	uncomfortable (a)	ongemaklik	
ngaphaya	across (prep)	oor	-ngekho mthethweni	illegal (a)	onwettig	
-ngaphaya	beyond (prep)	oorkant	-ngekhoyo	absent (a)	afwesig	
-ngaphefumliyo	breathless (a)	uitasem	-ngele kwa-	besides (prep)	buiten	
-ngaphekwanga	uncooked (a)	ongaar	ngelishwa	unfortunately (adv)	ongelukkig	
-ngapheliyo	everlasting (a)	ewigdurend	ngelixa	while (conj)	terwyl	
-ngaphezulu	more (a)	meer	-ngemva	behind (prep)	agter	
ngaphezulu	over (prep)	oor	-ngena	enter (v)	binnegaan	
-ngaphezulu	aboard (adv)	aan boord	-ngenabhawundri	boundless (a)	grensloos	
-ngaphikiswa(yo)	undisputed (a)	onbetwis	-ngenabubele	unkind (a)	onvriendelik	
-ngaphilanga	unhealthy (a)	ongesond	-ngenabulungisa	unjust (a)	onregverdig	
-ngaphiliyo	inanimate (a)	leweloos	-ngenafenitshala	unfurnished (a)	ongemeubileerd	
-ngaphucukanga	uncivilised (a)	onbeskaaf	-ngenakuthandatyuzwa	undoubted (a)	ongetwyfeld	
-ngaphumelelanga	unsuccessful (a)	onvoorspoedig	-ngenakwenzeka	impossible (a)	onmoontlik	
-ngaphumeleli	fail (v)	misluk	-ngenaluncedo	helpless (a)	hulpeloos	
-ngaqeqeshekanga	undisciplined (a)	ongedissiplineerd	-ngenambeko	impolite (a)	onbeleef	
-ngaqeshwanga	unemployed (a)	werkloos	-ngenambeko	ill-mannered (a)	onmanierlik	
-ngaqhelanga	unaccustomed (a)	ongewoond	-ngenambulelo	ungrateful (a)	ondankbaar	
-ngaqhelekanga	abnormal (a)	abnormaal	-ngenamfesane	uncharitable (a)	onbarmhartig	
-ngaqhelekanga	peculiar (a)	eienaardig	-ngenampilo	unhygienic (a)	onhigiënies	
-ngaqhelekanga	exotic (a)	eksoties	-ngenamsebenzi	trivial (a)	niksbeduidend	
-ngaqhelekanga	uncommon (a)	ongewoon	-ngenamsebenzi	useless (a)	nutteloos	

N	Xhosa	English	Afrikaans		Xhosa	English	Afrikaans
	-ngenanceba	unmerciful (a)	ongenadig		-ngquba	bump (v)	stamp
	-ngenangozi	safe (a)	veilig		-ngqubana	collide (v)	bots
	-ngenanto	vacant (a)	vakant		-ngqukuva	round (a)	rond
	-ngenasigqibo	undecided (a)	onbeslis		-ngquzulana	conflict (v)	bots
	-ngenasithozela	undignified (a)	onwaardig		-ngumlwelwe	invalid (a)	ongeldig
	-ngenathamsanqa	unlucky (a)	ongelukkig		-ngumnqakathi	odd (a)	onewe
	-ngenazintsholongwane	sterile (a)	steriel		-ngxama	rush (v)	haas
	-ngenela	invade (v)	inval		-ngxama	hurry (v)	jaag
	-ngenela umdyarho	race (v)	resies ja		-ngxamileyo	hasty (a)	haastig
	-ngenelela	arbitrate (v)	arbitreer		-ngxola (yo)	loud (a)	hard
	-ngenene	absolutely (adv)	absoluut		-ngxolayo	noisy (a)	raserig
	-ngengozi	accidentally (adv)	toevallig		-ngxolisa	scold (v)	uitskel
	-ngenkani	adamant (a)	onwrikbaar		-ngxubevange	miscellaneous (a)	allerlei
	-ngenzeka	possible (a)	moontlik		-nika	give (v)	gee
	-ngenzeka	practical (a)	prakties		-nika	confer (v)	toeken
	-ngevayo	deaf (a)	doof		-nika imbeko	honour (v)	eer
	-ngevayo	obstinate (a)	hardkoppig		-nika ingxelo	report (v)	berig
	-ngevayo	insubordinate (a)	ongehoorsaam		-nika iphepha-mvume	license (v)	lisensieer
	-ngeveki	weekly (a)	weekliks		-nikela	offer (v)	aanbied
	-ngobugogotya	miserly (a)	vrekkerig		-nikela	devote (v)	toewy
	-ngobugwala	cowardly (a)	lafhartig		-nikela ngesisa	donate (v)	skenk
	-ngobuncutshe	crack (a)	puik		-nikezela	surrender (v)	oorgee
	-ngobungozi	accidental (a)	toevallig		-nikezela	sacrifice (v)	opoffer
	-ngokomatshini	mechanical (a)	meganies		nina	you (pron)	julle
	ngoku	now (adv)	nou		nini	when (adv)	wanneer
	ngokuba	because (conj)	omdat		-ninzi	many (a)	baie
	ngokuba	why (adv)	waarom		-ninzi	abundant (a)	oorvloedig
	-ngokufutshane	briefly (adv)	kortliks		-ninzi	plentiful (a)	talryk
	ngokuhlwa	evening (n)	aand		-nita	knit (v)	brei
	-ngokujikeleyo	about (adv)	rond		njalo	often (adv)	dikwels
	-ngokujikelezayo	around (adv)	rond		njani	how (adv)	hoe
	ngokukhawuleza	quickly (adv)	gou		nje	just (a)	regverdig
	ngokukhawuleza	instantly (adv)	oombliklik		njenga	such (a)	sulke
	-ngokukhwaza	aloud (adv)	hardop		njenga	like (prep)	soos
	-ngokulingana	even (adv)	selfs		-nkcenkceshela	irrigate (v)	besproei
	ngokungalindelekanga	unexpectedly (adv)	onverwags		-nke	every (a)	elke
	-ngokungathanga ngqo	indirect (a)	indirek		-nke	entire (a)	hele
	ngokungazi	unknowingly (adv)	onwetend		-nkqo	vertical (a)	vertikaal
	-ngokungxamela	eager (a)	gretig		-nkqonkqoza	knock (v)	klop
	ngokuqhelekileyo	usually (adv)	gewoonlik		-nkulelane	indigenous (a)	inheems
	ngokuthamba	softly (adv)	saggies		-nkwantya (yo)	timid (a)	skugter
	-ngokuxwesa	across (adv)	dwars		-noboya	hairy (a)	harig
	ngokuzolile yo	gently (adv)	saggies		-nobubele	kind (a)	goedhartig
	-ngokwenene	actually (adv)	eintlik		-nobuciko	fluent (a)	vlot
	ngokwenyani	really (adv)	werklik		-nobudibi	shallow (a)	vlak
	ngokwesithethe	traditional (a)	tradisioneel		-nobudoda	masculine (a)	manlik
	ngomso	tomorrow (n)	môre		-nobudoda	male (a)	manlik
	-ngonakelanga	undamaged (a)	onbeskadig		-nobugqi	magical (a)	magies
	-ngoncwadi	literary (a)	letterkundig		-nobuhenyu	bawdy (a)	onkuis
	-ngonwabanga	uneasy (a)	ongerus		-nobuhiba	absurd (a)	onsinnig
	-ngonwabanga	unhappy (a)	ongelukkig		-nobuhlanga	racist (a)	rassisties
	-ngonwabanga	restless (a)	rusteloos		-nobuhlanga	racial (a)	rasse
	-ngonyaka	annual (a)	jaarliks		-nobungozi	unsafe (a)	onveilig
	-ngoqoqosho	commercial (a)	kommersieel		-nobuntlekele	tragic (a)	tragies
	-ngoyikiyo	unafraid (a)	onbevrees		-nobuntu	humane (a)	mensliewend
	-ngqina	prove (v)	bewys		-nobupolitika	political (a)	polities
	-ngqina	testify (v)	getuig		-nobuqhokolo	cunning (a)	slu
	-ngqiyama	lean (v)	leun		-nobuxelegu	clumsy (a)	lomp
	-ngqiyama	against (prep)	teen		-nobuzwe	national (a)	nasionaal
	-ngqoqo	spotted (a)	gekol		-nodaka	muddy (a)	modderig

Xhosa	English	Afrikaans	Xhosa	English	Afrikaans	O
noko	quite (a)	taamlik	-nxwema	exclude (v)	uitsluit	
-nokuba nguwuphi	either (pron)	een van beide	-nxwema	secluded (a)	afgesonderd	
nokuba okanye	either...or (conj)	òf...òf	-nyala	immoral (a)	onsedelik	
-nokunyulwa	eligible (a)	geskik	-nyamalala	perish (v)	omkom	
-nokusetyenziswa	useful (a)	nuttig	-nyanisekile(yo)	loyal (a)	lojaal	
-noluvo lotshintsho olugqibeleleyo	radical (a)	radikaal	-nyanisile(yo)	true (a)	waar	
			-nyanzela	compel (v)	dwing	
-nombala	coloured (a)	gekleur	-nyanzela	force (v)	forseer	
-nombulelo	grateful (a)	dankbaar	-nyanzelisa	enforce (v)	afdwing	
-nomculo	musical (a)	musikaal	-nyanzelisa	insist (v)	aandring	
-nomdla	enthusiastic (a)	geesdriftig	-nyathela	step (v)	trap	
-nomdla	interesting (a)	interessant	-nyathela	tread (v)	trap	
-nomdla	keen (a)	toegewyd	-nye	another (a)	'n ander	
-nomkhitha	handsome (a)	aantreklik	-nye	another (a)	nog 'n	
-nomona	envious (a)	jaloers	-nye	else (adv)	anders	
-nomona	jealous (a)	jaloers	-nye	other (a)	ander	
-nomonde	patient (a)	geduldig	-nye	same (a)	dieselfde	
-nomsa	affectionate (a)	toegeneë	-nye	single (a)	enkel	
-nomsindo	angry (a)	kwaad	-nye	some (a)	sommige	
-nomtsalane	attractive (a)	aantreklik	-nyibilika	dissolve (v)	oplos	
-nonga	flavour (v)	geur	-nyibilika	melt (v)	smelt	
-novelwano	considerate (a)	bedagsaam	-nyoba	bribe (v)	omkoop	
-novelwano	pitiful (a)	jammerlik	-nyovula	wade (v)	waad	
-novelwano	sympathetic (a)	simpatiek	-nyuka	ascend (v)	styg	
nozakuzaku	ambassador (n)	ambassadeur	-nyula	elect (v)	verkies	
-nqaba	prevent (v)	voorkom	-nyumbaza	tickle (v)	kielie	
-nqabile(yo)	rare (a)	seldsaam	-nyusa	raise (v)	ophef	
-nqanda	avert (v)	keer	-nyusa	rise (v)	styg	
-nqanda	bar (v)	uitsluit	-nyusela	promote (v)	bevorder	
-nqanda	curb (v)	inhou	-nzima	difficult (a)	moeilik	
-nqasha	whip (v)	raps	-nzima	hard (a)	moeilik	
-nqenayo	idle (a)	ledig	-nzima	heavy (a)	swaar	
-nqenayo	indolent (a)	traag	-nzima	pregnant (a)	swanger	
-nqenayo	reluctant (a)	teensinnig	-nzulu	deep (a)	diep	
-nqinileyo	emaciated (a)	uitgeteer				
-nqola	peck (v)	pik	-obugqirha	medical (a)	medies	
-nqwala	nod (v)	knik	-obuhedeni	pagan (a)	heidens	
-nqwena	desire (v)	begeer	-obuKrestu	Christian (a)	Christelik	
-nqwena	wish (v)	wens	-obuza	moult (v)	verhaar	
ntathu	three (n)	drie	-odwa	special (a)	spesiaal	
-ntla	north (a)	noord	-ohlwaya	fine (v)	beboet	
ntoni	what (pron)	wat	-ohlwaya	penalise (v)	straf	
-ntsha	modern (a)	modern	-ohlwaya	punish (v)	straf	
ntshona	west (adv)	wes	-oja	roast (v)	oondbraai	
-ntshula	sprout (v)	uitloop	okanye	nor (conj)	nòg	
-ntwebekayo	elastic (a)	rekbaar	okanye	or (conj)	of	
-ntyuntya	jog (v)	draf	Oktobha	October (n)	Oktober	
-ntywila	dive (v)	duik	-okugqibela	final (a)	finaal	
-ntywilisa	immerse (v)	indompel	-okugqibela	ultimate (a)	uiterste	
-ntywilisa	submerge (v)	onderdompel	-olimo	agricultural (a)	landboukundig	
-nuka	stink (v)	stink	-olula	elongate (v)	verleng	
-nukisa	smell (v)	ruik	-olula	prolong (v)	verleng	
-nxaniwe (yo)	thirsty (a)	dorstig	-oluntu	civil (a)	burgerlik	
-nxiba	dress (v)	aantrek	-olwayo	aggressive (a)	aanvallend	
-nxiba	clothe (v)	aantrek	-omba	dig (v)	spit	
-nxiba	wear (v)	dra	-ombane	electric (a)	elektries	
-nxilile	drunk (a)	dronk	-omeleleyo	stout (a)	geset	
-nxilisa	intoxicate (v)	bedwelm	-omelele(yo)	tough (a)	taai	
-nxilisayo	alcoholic (a)	alkoholies	-omhlola	ominous (a)	onheilspellend	
-nxungupheleyo	anxious (a)	bekommerd	-omileyo	dry (a)	droog	

O

Xhosa	English	Afrikaans
-omisa	dry (v)	droogmaak
-omkhosi	military (a)	militêre
-omlomo	verbal (a)	mondeling
-omntu	human (a)	menslik
-omxhelomnye	unanimous (a)	eenstemmig
-onakalisa	damage (v)	beskadig
-onakalisayo	harmful (a)	skadelik
-onakeleyo	messy (a)	morsig
-onga	nurse (v)	verpleeg
-ongamele(yo)	paramount (a)	hoogste
-ongeza	add (v)	byvoeg
-ongeza	increase (v)	vermeerder
-ongezelelweyo	additional (a)	bykomend
-ongezelelweyo	extra (a)	ekstra
-ongula	skim (v)	afskep
-ongumAfrika	African (a)	Afrika
-onke	all (a)	alle
-onke	all (beings) (pron)	almal
-onke	all (things) (pron)	alles
-onwabela	enjoy (v)	geniet
-onwabileyo	cheerful (a)	vrolik
-onwabisayo	delight (v)	bly maak
-opha	bleed (v)	bloei
-ophayo	generous (a)	vrygewig
-ophula umthetho	trespass (v)	oortree
-orenji	orange (a)	oranje
-othusa	surprise (v)	verras
-oyika	dread (v)	vrees
-oyika	fear (v)	vrees
-oyikayo	afraid (a)	bang
-oyikeka(yo)	fierce (a)	woes
-oyikeka (yo)	ghastly (a)	aaklig
-oyikekayo	terrible (a)	vreeslik
-oyikisa	frighten (v)	skrikmaak
-oyikisa	terrify (v)	verskrik
-oyikisayo	apprehensive (a)	bang
-oyisa	conquer (v)	verower
-oyisa	defeat (v)	verslaan
-oyisa	overcome (v)	te bowe kom
-oyisa	overpower (v)	oorweldig
-oyisa	subdue (v)	onderwerp
-ozela	drowse (v)	dommel
-ozelayo	sleepy (a)	vaak
-papasha	publish (v)	uitgee
-pha	present (v)	skenk
-phakamile(yo)	high (a)	hoog
-phakamile(yo)	higher (a)	hoër
-phakamisa	lift (v)	oplig
phakathi	in (prep)	in
-phakathi	between (prep)	tussen
phakathi kwa-	amid (prep)	tussen
-phakuzela(yo)	nervous (a)	senuweeagtig
-phala	gallop (v)	galop
-phambeneyo	insane (a)	kranksinnig
-phambene (yo)	mad (a)	gek
-phambi	before (prep)	voor
phambi	front (a)	voor
-phambili	further (a)	verder
phambili	forward (adv)	vooruit
phambili	onward (adv)	voorwaarts
-phambuka	deviate (v)	afwyk
-phanda	investigate (v)	ondersoek
-phandle	openly (a)	openlik
phandle	out (prep)	uit
-phanga	loot (v)	plunder
-phangaleleyo	broad (a)	breed
phantse	nearly (adv)	byna
-phantse	almost (adv)	amper
-phantsi	down (prep)	af
-phanza	abort (v)	aborteer
-phanzileyo	abortive (a)	misluk
-phaphamileyo	alert (a)	waaksaam
-phaphamisa	awake (v)	ontwaak
-phaphazela	panic (v)	paniekerig wees
-phatha	handle (v)	hanteer
-phatha	treat (v)	behandel
-phatha kakubi	ill-treat (v)	mishandel
-phawula	mark (v)	merk
phaya	there (adv)	daar
-phazama	err (v)	fouteer
-phazamisa	disturb (v)	pla
-phazamisa	interrupt (v)	onderbreek
-phazamisa	upset (v)	ontstel
-phazamisekile(yo)	upset (a)	ontsteld
-phefumla	exhale (v)	uitasem
-phefumla	breathe (v)	asemhaal
-phehlelela	baptise (v)	doop
-pheka	cook (v)	kook
-phela	finish (v)	klaarmaak
-phela	end (v)	eindig
-phelelwe lithemba	desperate (a)	wanhopig
-phelisa unxano	quench (v)	les
-phendula	answer (v)	antwoord
-phendula	reply (v)	antwoord gee
-phendula	respond (v)	respondeer
-phengulula	revise (v)	wysig
phesheya	overseas (n)	oorsee
-phethula	roll (v)	rol
-pheza	cease (v)	ophou
phezu	on (prep)	op
phezu; kwa- e-	at (prep)	op
-phezulu	above (prep)	bo
phezulu	up (prep)	op
phi	where (adv)	waar
-phikisana	dispute (v)	betwis
-phila	heal (v)	genees
-phila	live (v)	leef
-phila(yo)	lively (a)	lewendig
-philile	healthy (a)	gesond
-philile(yo)	wholesome (a)	heilsaam
-philileyo	alive (a)	lewend
-phinda	repeat (v)	herhaal
-phinda-phinda	multiply (v)	vermenigvuldig
-phindeneyo	double (a)	dubbele
-phindezela	avenge (v)	wreek
-phindisa	retaliate (v)	vergeld
-phola	cool (v)	afkoel
-pholileyo	cool (a)	koel
-phosa	cast (v)	werp
-phosa	miss (v)	mis

Xhosa	English	Afrikaans	Xhosa	English	Afrikaans	**R**
-photha	weave (v)	weef	-qhubeka	continue (v)	vervolg	
-phoxa	mock (v)	bespot	-qhubela phambili	progress (v)	vooruitgaan	
phoxa	humiliate (v)	verneder	-qhula	tease (v)	terg	
-phucukileyo	better (a)	beter	-qhuma	smoke (v)	rook	
-phucula	civilise (v)	beskaaf	-qhwaba	slap (v)	klap	
-phucula	improve (v)	verbeter	-qhwabela	applaud (v)	toejuig	
-phuma	exit (v)	uitgaan	-qhwalela	limp (v)	mank loop	
-phuma ku-	result (v)	volg	-qhwalela (yo)	lame (a)	mank	
-phumelela	succeed (v)	slaag	-qhwanyaza	flicker (v)	flikker	
-phumezo	effect (v)	bewerk	-qhwanyaza	blink (v)	knipoog	
-phumla	rest (v)	rus	-qhwesha	desert (v)	dros	
-phupha	dream (v)	droom	-qhwesha	escape (v)	ontsnap	
-phuphuma	overflow (v)	oorloop	-qina	starch (v)	styf	
-phuthuma	fetch (v)	haal	-qingqa	sculpt (v)	beeldhou	
-phuza	kiss (v)	soen	-qingqiweyo	grave (a)	gewigtig	
-posa	post (v)	pos	-qinile(yo)	solid (a)	vas	
-pula	rinse (v)	uitspoel	-qinile(yo)	tight (a)	styf	
			-qinileyo	stiff (a)	styf	
-qaba	paint (v)	verf	-qinisa	mount (v)	vassit	
-qaba	polish (v)	poleer	-qinisa	tighten (v)	span	
-qaba itha	tar (v)	teer	-qinisekile(yo)	positive (a)	positief	
-qabela	mount (v)	opklim	-qinisekile(yo)	sure (a)	seker	
-qabula	relieve (v)	verlig	-qinisekisa	convince (v)	oortuig	
-qakathisa	bounce (v)	opspring	-qinisekisa	guarantee (v)	waarborg	
-qala	begin (v)	begin	qinisekisa	ascertain (v)	vasstel	
-qala	start (v)	begin	-qinisekisa	ensure (v)	verseker	
-qamba	compose (v)	komponeer	-qoba iliso	wink (v)	knipoog	
-qaphela	notice (v)	opmerk	-qokelela	collect (v)	versamel	
-qaphela	observe (v)	waarneem	-qonda	conceive (v)	opvat	
-qaphelayo	observant (a)	oplettend	-qonda	understand (v)	verstaan	
-qaqamba	ache (v)	pyn	-qoqosha	economise (v)	besuinig	
-qaqamba	glow (v)	gloei	-qukanisa	include (v)	insluit	
-qaqambileyo	bright (a)	helder	-qukile(yo)	inclusive (a)	inklusief	
-qashela	guess (v)	raai	-qukuqela	flow (v)	vloei	
-qashisa	bet (v)	wed	-qulatha	contain (v)	bevat	
-qavileyo	inquisitive (a)	nuuskierig	-qulatha	house (v)	huisves	
-qela	several (a)	verskeie	-qumba	sulk (v)	dikmond wees	
-qeqesha	coach (v)	afrig	-qumbelayo	flatulent (a)	winderig	
-qeqesha	train (v)	afrig	-ququzelela	organise (v)	reël	
-qesha	rent (v)	huur	-quthuma	nestle (v)	nestel	
-qesha	employ (v)	in diens neem	-qwalasela	watch (v)	dophou	
-qesha	hire (v)	huur	-qwayitekile	sleepless (a)	slapeloos	
-qhankqalaza	demonstrate (v)	betoog	-qwenga	maul (v)	kneus	
-qhankqalaza	rebel (v)	rebelleer	-qweqwedisa	hijack (v)	skaak	
-qhaqha	operate (v)	opereer				
-qhatha	cheat (v)	kul	-rayima	rhyme (v)	rym	
-qhawula umtshato	divorce (v)	skei	-reya	ride (v)	ry	
-qhayisa	brag (v)	grootpraat	-rhabaxa	rough (a)	ru	
-qhekeza	burgle (v)	inbreek	-rhabaxa	hoarse (a)	hees	
-qhekeza	crack (v)	kraak	-rhabula	sip (v)	slurp	
-qhelekile(yo)	ordinary (a)	gewoon	-rhafisa	tax (v)	belas	
-qhelekileyo	common (a)	gewoon	-rhanela	suspect (v)	verdink	
-qhelisa	practise (v)	oefen	-rhangqa	surround (v)	omring	
-qhelisa	exercise (v)	oefen	-rharhaza	gargle (v)	gorrel	
-qhina	knot (v)	knoop	-rhawula	singe (v)	skroei	
-qhobosha	pin (v)	vasspeld	-rhawuzela	itch (v)	jeuk	
-qhola	anoint (v)	salf	-rhaxwa	drown (v)	verdrink	
-qhotsa	fry (v)	bak	-rhogola	sniff (v)	snuif	
-qhuba	drive (v)	bestuur	-rhona	snore (v)	snork	
-qhuba	proceed (v)	voortgaan	-rhoxa	resign (v)	bedank	

R

Xhosa	English	Afrikaans	Xhosa	English	Afrikaans
-rhoxa	withdraw (v)	terugtrek	-sindisa	redeem (v)	goedmaak
-rhoxisa	cancel (v)	kanselleer	-sindisa	save (v)	red
-rhubuluza	crawl (v)	kruip	-sineka	grin (v)	gryns
-rhuqa	drag (v)	sleep	-sineka	smirk (v)	grynslag
-rhuqa	draw (v)	sleep	-singisela	mean (v)	bedoel
-rhuqa	tow (v)	sleep	-sisimumu	dumb (a)	stom
-rhwaqela	contract (v)	inkrimp	-sisiseko	basic (a)	basies
-rhweba	trade (v)	handel dryf	-sitha	overshadow (v)	oorskadu
			-sithela	disappear (v)	verdwyn
-sala	remain (v)	agterbly	-sithela	fade (v)	verbleik
-sandula	newly (adv)	onlangs	-skrufela	screw (v)	skroef
-sarha	saw (v)	saag	-soloko	always (adv)	gedurig
-sasaza	broadcast (v)	uitsaai	Somandla	Almighty (n)	Almagtige
-sasaza	scatter (v)	strooi	-songa	fold (v)	vou
-sasaza	spread (v)	versprei	sonke	together (adv)	saam
-sebenza	labour (v)	arbei	soze	never (adv)	nooit
-sebenza	work (v)	werk	-sukuhoya	disregard (v)	verontagsaam
-sebenzayo	active (a)	aktief	-sukunaka	ignore (v)	ignoreer
-sebenzisa	apply (v)	toepas	-sukuthobela	disobey (v)	ongehoorsaam wees
-sebenzisa	use (v)	gebruik	-sula	wipe (v)	afvee
-sebenzisana	co-operate (v)	saamwerk	-sulela	infect (v)	besmet
-sebeza	whisper (v)	fluister	-sulelayo	contagious (a)	aansteeklik
-secaleni	impertinence (n)	astrantheid	-sulelayo	infectious (a)	besmetlik
-sela	drink (v)	drink	-susa	scrap (v)	skrap
-semthethweni	judicial (a)	regterlik	-susa ukhula	weed (v)	onkruid uittrek
-se mthethweni	lawful (a)	wettig	-sutu	sweet (a)	soet
-semthethweni	legal (a)	wetlik	-swelekile (yo)	late (a)	oorlede
-semthethweni	legitimate (a)	wettige	-swelekileyo	deceased (a)	oorlede
-semva	rear (a)	agterste	-switsha	switch (v)	oorskakel
-sengqondweni	ideal (a)	ideaal			
-seta	set (v)	stel	-teketa	lisp (v)	lispel
-sezingqondweni	conscious (a)	bewus	-thabatha	subtract (v)	aftrek
-shawarisha	shower (v)	stort	-thabatha uhambo	travel (v)	reis
-shenxa	move (v)	skuif	-thabathekisa	impress (v)	beïndruk
-shenxisa	remove (v)	verwyder	-thakatha	bewitch (v)	toor
-shicilela	print (v)	druk	-thambile (yo)	tender (a)	teer
-shixiza	shuffle (v)	skuifel	-thambileyo	agile (a)	rats
-shiya	omit (v)	weglaat	-thambile(yo)	soft (a)	sag
-shukuma	move (v)	beweeg	-thanda	adore (v)	aanbid
shukumayo	moving (a)	roerend	-thandabuza	doubt (v)	twyfel
-shumayela	preach (v)	preek	-thandabuza	hesitate (v)	aarsel
-shunqula	amputate (v)	afsit	-thandaza	pray (v)	bid
-shushu	hot (a)	warm	-thandekayo	beloved (a)	bemind
-shushu	warm (a)	warm	-thandekayo	likeable (a)	beminlik
-shushubeza	heat (v)	warm maak	-thandekayo	lovable (a)	dierbaar
-shwabana	shrink (v)	krimp	-thandekayo	dear (a)	dierbaar
-shwabanisa	crease (v)	kreukel	-thandisa	endear (v)	bemind maak
-shwabanisa	shrivel (v)	verskrompel	-thatha	take (v)	neem
-shwabanisa	wrinkle (v)	plooi	-thathu	third (a)	derde
sibali	brother-in-law (n)	swaer	-thelekelela	imagine (v)	verbeel
-sibekele	overcast (a)	bewolk	-thelekisa	compare (v)	vergelyk
-sigxina	permanent (a)	permanent	-themba	hope (v)	hoop
-sika	cut (v)	sny	-thembekile(yo)	reliable (a)	betroubaar
-sika	carve (v)	sny	-thembekile(yo)	sincere (a)	opreg
-sika	slice (v)	skywe sny	-thembekile(yo)	trustworthy (a)	betroubaar
sikelela	bless (v)	seën	-thembela	confide (v)	vertroulik meedeel
-sikremblisha	scramble (v)	klouter	-thembela	rely (v)	staatmaak
-sila	grind (v)	maal	-thembisa	promise (v)	belowe
-sileyo	immodest (a)	onbeskeie	-thena	prune (v)	snoei
-siliweyo	ground (a)	gemaal	-thena	castrate (v)	kastreer

Xhosa	English	Afrikaans	Xhosa	English	Afrikaans
-thenga	buy (v)	koop	-tsha	young (a)	jong
-thenga	shop (v)	inkopies doen	-tshabalalisa	exterminate (v)	uitroei
-thenga kwelinye ilizwe	import (v)	invoer	-tshabalalisa	destroy (v)	vernietig
-thengisa	advertise (v)	adverteer	-tshabalalisa	devastate (v)	verwoes
-thengisa	sell (v)	verkoop	-tshata	marry (v)	trou
-the nqo	direct (a)	direk	-tshata	wed (v)	trou
-thetha	speak (v)	praat	-tshayela	sweep (v)	vee
-thetha	talk (v)	praat	-tshayo	alight (a)	aan die brand
-thethathethana	negotiate (v)	onderhandel	-tsheva	shave (v)	skeer
-thethayo	talkative (a)	spraaksaam	-tshica	spit (v)	spoeg
-the tse	straight (a)	reguit	-tshileyo	inflamed (a)	onsteek
-thi	say (v)	sê	-tshintsha	change (v)	verander
-thile	particular (a)	besonder	-tshisa	burn (v)	brand
-thimba	capture (v)	vang	-tshisa	fuse (v)	uitbrand
-thimba	confiscate (v)	beslag lê op	-tshisa	scorch (v)	skroei
-thimla	sneeze (v)	nies	-tshiseka(yo)	impatient (a)	ongeduldig
thina	ourselves (pron)	onsself	-tshixa	lock (v)	sluit
thina	we (pron)	ons	-tshixizisa	gnash (v)	kners
-thi ndwanya	stare (v)	staar	-tshona	sink (v)	sink
-thi nkxu	dip (v)	insteek	-tshutshisa	prosecute (v)	vervolg
-thintela	obstruct (v)	belemmer	-tsiba	hop (v)	hop
-thintela	restrain (v)	beperk	-tsiba	jump (v)	spring
-thintela	restrict (v)	inperk	-tsiba	skip (v)	touspring
-thintitha	stutter (v)	stotter	-tsiba	spring (v)	spring
-thintitha	stammer (v)	hakkel	-tswikila	pinch (v)	knyp
-thitshisa ubuhlanga	detribalise (v)	ontstam	-tswina	wheeze (v)	hyg
-thi tshu	fizz (v)	bruis	-tya	eat (v)	eet
-thiya	hate (v)	haat	-tyabula	scald (v)	skroei
-thiyileyo	hateful (a)	haatlik	-tyala	plant (v)	plant
-thobekile(yo)	obedient (a)	gehoorsaam	-tyala	owe (v)	skuld
-thobela	obey (v)	gehoorsaam wees	-tyatyamba(yo)	rheumatic (a)	rumaties
-thobileyo	faithful (a)	getrou	-tyebile (yo)	rich (a)	ryk
-thomalalisa	soothe (v)	kalmeer	-tyebileyo	fat (a)	vet
-thontsiza	drip (v)	drup	-tyebisa	enrich (v)	verryk
-thuka	insult (v)	beledig	-tyekayo	edible (a)	eetbaar
-thuka	swear (v)	vloek	-tyelela	call (v)	besoek
-thukayo	vulgar (a)	vulgêr	-tyelela	visit (v)	besoek
-thula	unload (v)	aflaai	-tyhafisa	discourage (v)	ontmoedig
-thulisa	silence (v)	stilmaak	-tyhala	push (v)	stoot
-thululeka	ooze (v)	sypel	-tyhefa	poison (v)	vergiftig
-thuma	send (v)	stuur	-tyhila	expose (v)	blootlê
-thumela ngendlela	express (v)	uitdruk	-tyhila	reveal (v)	openbaar
ekhawulezayo			-tyhola	accuse (v)	beskuldig
-thundeza	urge (v)	aanspoor	-tyhola	blame (v)	blameer
-thunga	darn (v)	stop	-tyhutyha	penetrate (v)	binnedring
-thunga	sew (v)	naaldwerk doen	-tyibilika	slide (v)	gly
-thutha	cart (v)	karwei	-tyikitya	sign (v)	teken
-thuthuzela	comfort (v)	troos	-tyisa	feed (v)	voer
-thuthuzela	console (v)	opbeur	-tyumba	appoint (v)	aanstel
-thwala	abduct (v)	ontvoer			
-thwala	bear (v)	duld	ubalo lwabantu	census (n)	sensus
-thwala	carry (v)	dra	ubambo	rib (n)	rib
-thwalisa	load (v)	laai	ubani	who (pron)	wie
-tofa	inject (v)	inspuit	ubawomkhulu	grandfather (n)	oupa
-tofotofo	comfortable (a)	gemaklik	ubawozala	father-in-law (n)	skoonvader
-tolika	interpret (v)	vertolk	ubhantom	ladybird (n)	lieweheersbesie
-tsala	attract (v)	aantrek	ubhontsi	thumb (n)	duim
-tsala	pull (v)	trek	ubhubhane	pest (n)	pes
-tsha	fresh (a)	vars	ubilo	rest (n)	rus
-tsha	new (a)	nuut	ubisi	milk (n)	melk

Xhosa	English	Afrikaans	Xhosa	English	Afrikaans
ubizo	mission (n)	sending	ubungabikho	nothing (n)	niks
ubizo	pronunciation (n)	uitspraak	ubungakanani	quantity (n)	hoeveelheid
ubomi	life (n)	lewe	ubungedle	addiction (n)	verslaafdheid
ubomi basendle	wildlife (n)	natuurlewe	ubungqina	evidence (n)	getuienis
ubovu	pus (n)	etter	ubungqina	proof (n)	bewys
uboya	wool (n)	wol	ubungqina	record (n)	rekord
uboya beseyibhokhwe	mohair (n)	sybokhaar	ubungqina	testimony (n)	getuienis
ububanzi	breadth (n)	breedte	ubuninzi	abundance (n)	oorvloed
ububele	kindness (n)	goedheid	ubunqolobi	terrorism (n)	terrorisme
ububhanxa	foolishness (n)	dwaasheid	ubunto	essence (n)	essensie
ububhovubhovu	violence (n)	geweld	ubuntsundu	suntan (n)	sonbruin
ububomvu	scarlet (n)	helderrooi	ubuntu	humility (n)	nederigheid
ubuchopho	brain (n)	brein	ubuntwana	childhood (n)	kinderjare
ubuchule	ability (n)	bekwaamheid	ubuntwana	infancy (n)	kleintyd
ubuciko	eloquence (n)	welsprekendheid	ubunye	union (n)	unie
ubuciko	rhetoric (n)	retoriek	ubunzima	weight (n)	gewig
ubudala	age (n)	ouderdom	ubunzulu	depth (n)	diepte
ubudala	adulthood (n)	volwassenheid	ubuphaku-phaku	nervousness (n)	senuweeagtigheid
ubude	length (n)	lengte	ubuqabane	companionship (n)	kameraadskap
ubudoda	manhood (n)	manlikheid	ubuqhetseba	fraud (n)	bedrog
ubugagu	dare (n)	uitdaging	ubuqhwala	limp (n)	mankheid
ubugcisa	art (n)	kuns	uburharha	humour (n)	humor
ubugebenga	murder (n)	moord	ubusa	daybreak (n)	dagbreek
ubugogotya	misery (n)	ellende	ubushushu	heat (n)	hitte
ubugqi	magic (n)	towerkuns	ubushushu	temperature (n)	temperatuur
ubugqirha	surgery (n)	chirurgie	ubusi	honey (n)	heuning
ubugqwirha	witchcraft (n)	toorkuns	ubusika	winter (n)	winter
ubugwala	cowardice (n)	lafhartigheid	ubuso	face (n)	gesig
ubuhedeni	heathen (n)	heiden	ubusuku	night (n)	nag
ubuhle	beauty (n)	skoonheid	ubuthathaka	weakness (n)	swakheid
ubuhlobo	friendship (n)	vriendskap	ubuthintitha	stutter (n)	gestotter
ubuhlwempu	poverty (n)	armoede	ubutsalane	magnetism (n)	magnetisme
ubukhalipha	bravery (n)	dapperheid	ubutyebi	treasure (n)	skat
ubukho	attendance (n)	bywoning	ubutyebi	wealth (n)	rykdom
ubukho	existence (n)	bestaan	ubutyobo	wreck (n)	wrak
ubukhoboka	bondage (n)	knegskap	ubuvila	laziness (n)	luiheid
ubukhoboka	slavery (n)	slawerny	ubuvuvu	nonsense (n)	onsin
ubukrele-krele	intelligence (n)	intelligensie	ubuxhifilili	slum (n)	krotbuurt
ubukumkani	kingdom (n)	koninkryk	ubuxoki	lie (n)	leuen
ubulelwe	disability (n)	gebrek	ubuxoki	falsehood (n)	onwaarheid
ubulembu	alga (n)	alg	ubuyengeyenge	fluid (n)	vloeistof
ubulolo	loneliness (n)	eensaamheid	ubuzwe	nationalism (n)	nasionalisme
ubulumko	wisdom (n)	wysheid	ucalulo	discrimination (n)	diskriminasie
ubulungisa	justice (n)	geregtigheid	ucango	door (n)	deur
ubulungu	membership (n)	lidmaatskap	ucekiseko	disgust (n)	afkeer
ubumbaxa	compound (n)	kampong	ucelemba	battle-axe (n)	strydbyl
ubumbeko	mould (n)	vorm	uchatha	increment (n)	verhoging
ubumdaka	filth (n)	vuilgoed	uchukumiso	touch (n)	aanraking
ubumdaka	mess (n)	gemors	ucinezelo	depression (n)	bedruktheid
ubume bendawo	environment (n)	omgewing	ucingo	fence (n)	draad
ubumenemene	dishonesty (n)	oneerlikheid	ucingo	telegram (n)	telegram
ubumfama	blind (n)	blinding	ucingo	wire (n)	draad
ubumhlophe	white (n)	wit	ucingo olunameva	barbed wire (n)	doringdraad
ubumnandi	pleasure (n)	plesier	ucoceko	cleanliness (n)	sindelikheid
ubumnandi	luxury (n)	luukse	ucwaka	silence (n)	stilte
ubumnyama	darkness (n)	donker	ucwambu	cream (n)	room
ubumsulwa	honesty (n)	eerlikheid	udade	sister (n)	suster
ubumuncu	acid (n)	suur	udaka	mud (n)	modder
ubuncinane	minimum (n)	minimum	udakada	spleen (n)	milt
ubungabikho	absence (n)	afwesigheid	udevu	beard (n)	baard

Xhosa	English	Afrikaans	Xhosa	English	Afrikaans	U
udini	margin (n)	kantlyn	ukhenketho	tour (n)	rondreis	
udino	fatigue (n)	vermoeienis	ukhetho	choice (n)	keuse	
udiza	straw (n)	strooi	ukhetshe	hawk (n)	valk	
udladla	granary (n)	graanskuur	ukhohlokhohlo	cough (n)	hoes	
udliwano-ndlebe	interview (n)	onderhoud	ukhoko	crust (n)	korsie	
udlwengulo	rape (n)	verkragting	ukhoko	scab (n)	rofie	
udonga	wall (n)	muur	ukholo	faith (n)	geloof	
udongwe	clay (n)	klei	ukhozi	eagle (n)	arend	
udwayi	pauper (n)	behoeftige	ukhozo	grain (n)	graan	
udyakalashe	jackal (n)	jakkals	ukhozo lwemali	coin (n)	muntstuk	
ufele	fur (n)	pels	ukhuko	mat (n)	mat	
ufele	leather (n)	leer	ukhukuliseko	erosion (n)	wegvreting	
ufele	skin (n)	vel	ukhula	weed (n)	onkruid	
ufele lwentloko	scalp (n)	kopvel	ukhululo	release (n)	loslating	
ufudo	tortoise (n)	skilpad	ukhuphiswano	contest (n)	wedstryd	
ufulelo	thatch (n)	dekgras	ukhuphiswano	competition (n)	wedstryd	
ufundo	astrology (n)	astrologie	ukhuphu	acne (n)	aknee	
ngeenkwenkwezi			ukhuseleko	safety (n)	veiligheid	
ufunxo-gazi	blood transfusion (n)	bloedoortapping	ukhuselo	defence (n)	verdediging	
ufunzeweni	activist (n)	aktivis	ukhwalimanzi	heron (n)	reier	
ufuthaniselo	asphyxia (n)	versmoring	ukopha	haemorrhage (n)	bloeding	
ugesi	x-ray (n)	x-straal	ukralo lwenwebu-	pleurisy (n)	borsvliesontsteking	
ugonyo	vaccination (n)	inenting	miphunga			
ugqabhuko-dubulo	explosion (n)	ontploffing	ukrebe	shark (n)	haai	
ugqirha	doctor (n)	dokter	uKrestu	Christ (n)	Christus	
ugqirha	surgeon (n)	chirurg	ukrexezo	adultery (n)	owerspel	
ugqirha wamazinyo	dentist (n)	tandarts	ukuba	if (conj)	as	
ugqirha wesithili	district surgeon (n)	distriksgeneesheer	ukuba	that (pron)	dat	
ugqoloma	python (n)	luislang	ukuba	whether (conj)	of	
uguqulo	conversion (n)	omsetting	ukubaluleka	fame (n)	roem	
ugwali	harp (n)	harp	ukubamba	hold (n)	vat	
ugwetyelo	acquittal (n)	vryspraak	ukuba	consciousness (n)	bewussyn	
ugxeko	scorn (n)	veragting	sezingqondweni			
ugxininiso	emphasis (n)	klem	ukubeleka	childbirth (n)	kindergeboorte	
ugxininiso	stress (n)	spanningsdruk	ukubhala	handwriting (n)	handskrif	
ugxotho	exile (n)	verbanning	ukubhekisa	reference (n)	verwysing	
ugxotho	dismissal (n)	ontslag	ukubona	sight (n)	sig	
uhadi	piano (n)	klavier	ukubonga	acclaim (n)	toejuiging	
uhadi	organ (n)	orrel	ukubophelela	attachment (n)	gehegtheid	
uhambo	trip (n)	reis	ukubuza	inquiry (n)	navraag	
uhambo	journey (n)	reis	ukucaphula	quotation (n)	aanhaling	
uhambo ngomoya	flight (n)	vlug	ukucenga	persuasion (n)	oorreding	
uhili	dwarf (n)	dwerg	ukuchaneka	accuracy (n)	noukeurigheid	
uhlalutyo	analysis (n)	ontleding	ukucokisa	refinement (n)	verfyndheid	
uhlangothi	edge (n)	rand	ukucwenga	purity (n)	suiwerheid	
uhlaselo	assault (n)	aanranding	ukudada	swimming (n)	swem	
uhlaselo	invasion (n)	inval	ukudaleka	evolution (n)	evolusie	
uhlaselo	raid (n)	strooptog	ukudanisa	disappointment (n)	teleurstelling	
uhlaza	green (n)	groen	ukudideka	daze (n)	bedwelming	
uhlaziyo	reform (n)	hervorming	ukudideka	puzzle (n)	legkaart	
uhlobo	kind (n)	soort	ukudinwa	weariness (n)	moegheid	
uhlobo	make (n)	soort	ukuduma	notoriety (n)	berugtheid	
uhlobo	type (n)	tipe	ukudumba	swelling (n)	swelsel	
uhlobo lokuthetha	accent (n)	aksent	ukudumzela	murmur (n)	gemurmel	
uhlobo lomvundla	rabbit (n)	konyn	ukufa	death (n)	dood	
uhlolo	inspection (n)	inspeksie	ukufaka etrongweni	arrest (n)	inhegtenisneming	
ujikojiko	zigzag (n)	sigsag	ukufana	identity (n)	identiteit	
ujongilanga	sunflower (n)	sonneblom	ukufana	uniform (n)	uniform	
ukhahlelo	salute (n)	saluut	ukufika	arrival (n)	aankoms	
ukhakayi	skull (n)	skedel	ukufikisa	puberty (n)	puberteit	

U

Xhosa	English	Afrikaans	Xhosa	English	Afrikaans
ukufuma	damp (n)	vogtigheid	ukuqale ugwebe	prejudice (n)	vooroordeel
ukufuma	moisture (n)	vog	ukuqamba	composition (n)	komposisie
ukufumana	recovery (n)	herstel	ukuqaqamba	brilliance (n)	helderheid
ukufuna	search (n)	soektog	ukuqaqamba	earache (n)	oorpyn
ukufunga ubuxoki	perjury (n)	meineed	kwendlebe		
ukufunyanwa	invention (n)	uitvinding	ukuqhina	constipation (n)	konstipasie
ukugabha	vomit (n)	vomeersel	ukuqhwaba	slap (n)	klap
ukugcisa	thrift (n)	spaarsaamheid	ukurhabula	sip (n)	slukkie
ukugcuma	moan (n)	gekerm	ukurhona	snore (n)	snork
ukuhlamba	menstruation (n)	menstruasie	ukurhwaqela	contract (n)	kontrak
ukuhleka	laugh (n)	lag	ukusebenzisa kakubi	abuse (n)	misbruik
ukuhlwa	sundown (n)	sononder	ukusithela	disappearance (n)	verdwyning
ukujala	frown (n)	frons	ukusukela	since (adv)	sedert
ukujama	scowl (n)	suur gesig	ukuteketa	lisp (n)	gelispel
ukukhaba	kick (n)	skop	ukuthimla	sneeze (n)	nies
ukukhangela	reference (n)	getuigskrif	ukutshona kwelanga	sunset (n)	sononder
ukukhanya	light (n)	lig	ukutya	blade (n)	blad
ukukhapha	escort (n)	metgesel	ukutya	groceries (n)	kruideniersware
ukukhusela	contraception (n)	voorbehoeding	ukutya	food (n)	kos
ukukhutywa	hiccough (n)	hik	ukutyumba	appointment (n)	aanstelling
ukukrala	inflammation (n)	ontsteking	ukuvuma	confession (n)	belydenis
ukukruneka	sprain (n)	verstuiting	ukuwa	failure (n)	mislukking
ukulahla	rejection (n)	verwerping	ukuxhathisa	resistance (n)	weerstand
ukulahla ithemba	despair (n)	wanhoop	ukuxhela	slaughter (n)	slagting
ukulala	sleep (n)	slaap	ukuzala	birth (n)	geboorte
ukulalela	ambush (n)	hinderlaag	ukuzamla	yawn (n)	gaap
ukuloba	fishing (n)	visvang	ukuzenzekela	reflex (n)	refleks
ukulumeka	ignition (n)	ontsteking	ukuzenzisa	pretence (n)	skyn
ukumatsha	march (n)	mars	ukuzibhijabhija	wallow (v)	wentel
ukumisa intente	camping (n)	kampering	ukuzibulala	suicide (n)	selfmoord
ukumkani	king (n)	koning	ukuzigwebela	excuse (n)	ekskuus
ukunene	right (n)	regterkant	ukuzimisela	determination (n)	vasberadenheid
ukungakhathali	negligence (n)	nalatigheid	ukuziphatha	behaviour (n)	gedrag
ukungalungelani	allergy (n)	allergie	ukuziphatha	etiquette (n)	etiket
nempilo			ukuziphatha	manner (n)	manier
ukunganeliseki	dissatisfaction (n)	ontevredenheid	ukuziphikisa	contradiction (n)	weerspreking
ukunganyaniseki	disloyalty (n)	dislojaliteit	ukuziqhelisa	exercise (n)	oefening
ukungaqondani	misunderstanding (n)	misverstand	ukuzisola	regret (n)	spyt
ukungasebenzi kwe-	paralysis (n)	verlamming	ukuzithemba	self-confidence (n)	selfvertroue
lungu lomzimba			ukuzithethela	plead (n)	pleit
ukungathembi	distrust (n)	wantroue	ukwakhiwa komzimba	physique (n)	liggaamsbou
ukungathobeli	disobedience (n)	ongehoorsaamheid	ukwamkela	adoption (n)	aanneming
ukungcola	obscenity (n)	onbetaamlikheid	ukwaneliseka	contentment (n)	tevredenheid
ukungcoliseka	pollution (n)	besoedeling	ukwanga	embrace (n)	omhelsing
ukungena	influx (n)	instroming	ukwazisa	introduction (n)	voorstelling
ukungetyisi	indigestion (n)	slegte spysvertering	ukwenza	performance (n)	uitvoering
ukungongoza	heartbeat (n)	hartklop	ukwenzakala	injury (n)	besering
ukungunda	mildew (n)	muf	ukwindla	autumn (n)	herfs
ukungxama	haste (n)	haas	ulandelelwano	sequence (n)	reeks
ukunikezela	surrender (n)	oorgawe	ulawulo	reign (n)	bewind
ukunkqonkqoza	knock (n)	klop	ulawulo	management (n)	bestuur
ukunqwala	nod (n)	knik	ulibaziso	delay (n)	vertraging
ukunyaniseka	loyalty (n)	lojaliteit	ulimo	agriculture (n)	landbou
ukuphakama	height (n)	hoogte	ulingano	equal (n)	gelyke
ukuphaphama	vigilance (n)	waaksaamheid	ulingo	temptation (n)	verleiding
ukuphaphazela	panic (n)	paniek	uloliwe	train (n)	trein
ukuphefumla	respiration (n)	asemhaling	uloliwe okhawulezayo	express (n)	sneltrein
ukuphotha	weaving (n)	wewery	ulonwabo	delight (n)	blydskap
ukuphuma kwelanga	sunrise (n)	sonop	uloyiko	horror (n)	afsku
ukuphuza	kiss (n)	soen	uloyiko	awe (n)	eerbied

Xhosa	English	Afrikaans
uloyiko	terror (n)	terreur
uloyiko	fear (n)	vrees
uloyiso	defeat (n)	nederlaag
uloyiso	triumph (n)	triomf
ulucu	tissue (n)	weefsel
uluhlu lwamagama	index (n)	indeks
uluhlu lwamaxabiso	tariff (n)	tarief
uluhlu lweentlobo zewayini	winelist (n)	wynkaart
ulundi	horizon (n)	horison
uluntu	population (n)	bevolking
uluntu	society (n)	samelewing
ulunya	malice (n)	boosaardigheid
ulutsha	youth (n)	jeug
ulutya	tape measure (n)	maatband
uluvo	emotion (n)	gevoel
uluvo	attitude (n)	houding
uluvo	opinion (n)	mening
ulwaluko	circumcision (n)	besnydenis
ulwamkelo	acceptance (n)	aanvaarding
ulwamkelo	reception (n)	ontvangs
ulwamkelo	admission (n)	toelating
ulwamkelo	welcome (n)	welkom
ulwamvila	sting (n)	steek
ulwandle	ocean (n)	oseaan
ulwandle	sea (n)	see
ulwaneliseko	satisfaction (n)	bevrediging
ulwaphulo-mthetho	crime (n)	misdaad
ulwazano	acquaintance (n)	kennismaking
ulwazano	acquaintance (n)	kennis
ulwazi	information (n)	inligting
ulwazi	knowledge (n)	kennis
ulwazi ngobugcisa	technology (n)	tegnologie
ulwelo	liquid (n)	vloeistof
ulwesiBini	Tuesday (n)	Dinsdag
ulwesi Hlanu	Friday (n)	Vrydag
uLwesine	Thursday (n)	Donderdag
uLwesithathu	Wednesday (n)	Woensdag
ulwimi	tongue (n)	tong
ulwimi	language (n)	taal
ulwimi lwemveli	vernacular (n)	volkstaal
umabonakude	telescope (n)	teleskoop
umabonakude	binoculars (n)	verkyker
umAfrika	African (n)	Afrikaan
umahluko	difference (n)	verskil
umakhi	mason (n)	messelaar
umakhulu	grandmother (n)	ouma
umalume	uncle (n)	oom
umalusi	shepherd (n)	skaapwagter
umama	mother (n)	moeder
umamkeli	receptionist (n)	ontvangsklerk
umamkelo	income (n)	inkomste
umandlalo	bed (n)	bed
umandlalo	mattress (n)	matras
umantshingilane	nightwatchman (n)	nagwag
umantyi	magistrate (n)	landdros
umanyano	unity (n)	eenheid
umanyano	unite (v)	verenig
umanyano lwabase-benzi	trade union (n)	vakbond

Xhosa	English	Afrikaans
umaphuli-mthetho	trespasser (n)	oortreder
umashini	machine (n)	masjien
umashini wokubala	calculator (n)	rekenaar
umashini wokuchwetheza	typewriter (n)	tikmasjien
uMatshi	March (n)	Maart
umatshini wokucheba ingca	lawnmower (n)	grassnyer
umatshini wokuthunga	sewing machine (n)	naaimasjien
umayime	ceasefire (n)	skietstilstand
umazisi	informer (n)	verklikker
umba	issue (n)	kwessie
umbala	colour (n)	kleur
umbane	flashlight (n)	flitslig
umbane	electricity (n)	elektrisiteit
umbane	lightning (n)	weerlig
umbanjwa	detainee (n)	aangehoudene
umbanjwa	prisoner (n)	gevangene
umbanjwa wemfazwe	prisoner-of-war (n)	krygsgevangene
umbaxa	rifle (n)	geweer
umbefu	asthma (n)	asma
umbeko	reserve (n)	reserwe
umbelekisikazi	midwife (n)	vroedvrou
umbethe	dew (n)	dou
umbethi-gubu	drummer (n)	tromspeler
umbhali	author (n)	skrywer
umbhali-mali	accountant (n)	rekenmeester
umbhalo	writing (n)	skrif
umbhexeshi	conductor (n)	kondukteur
umbhinqo	skirt (n)	romp
umbhobho	pipe (n)	pyp
umbhobho	drainpipe (n)	rioolpyp
umbhobho	hose (n)	tuinslang
umbhumbutho	bundle (n)	bondel
umbilini	pulse (n)	pols
umbilo	perspiration (n)	perspirasie
umbilo	sweat (n)	sweet
umbimbi	wrinkle (n)	plooi
umbindi	centre (n)	middel
umbingeleli	priest (n)	priester
umbizane	lure (v)	aanlok
umbizi	caller (n)	roeper
umbona	maize (n)	mielies
umboniso	illustration (n)	illustrasie
umboniso	show (n)	skou
umboniso	exhibition (n)	uitstalling
umboniso	show (n)	vertoning
umboniso bhanya-bhanya	cinema (n)	bioskoop
umbono	vision (n)	gesigsvermoë
umbono	scene (n)	toneel
umbono	view (n)	uitsig
umboxo	rugby (n)	rugby
umbukeli	spectator (n)	toeskouer
umbulelo	gratitude (n)	dankbaarheid
umbulelo	thanks (n)	dank
umbungu	caterpillar (n)	ruspe
umbungu	larva (n)	larwe
umbutho	organisation (n)	organisasie
umbutho	society (n)	vereniging

U

Xhosa	English	Afrikaans	Xhosa	English	Afrikaans
umbuzo	question (n)	vraag	umfelakholo	martyr (n)	martelaar
umcebisi	adviser (n)	raadgewer	umfiki	newcomer (n)	nuweling
umcebi wezakhiwo	architect (n)	argitek	umfisi	fern (n)	varing
umceli	applicant (n)	aansoeker	umfundi	student (n)	student
umcephe	accelerator (n)	brandstofpedaal	umfundisi	clergy (n)	geestelikes
umcephe	ladle (n)	skeplepel	umfundisi	minister (n)	predikant
umchachazo	spine (n)	ruggraat	umfungi	commissioner of oaths (n)	kommissaris van ede
umchamo	urine (n)	urine			
umchasi	rival (n)	mededinger	umfuno	parsley (n)	pietersielie
umchasi	antagonist (n)	teenstander	umfuno onegaqa	radish (n)	radys
umchebi	barber (n)	haarsnyer	umgama	distance (n)	afstand
umchebi	hairdresser (n)	haarkapper	umgamtriya	bluegum (n)	bloekomboom
umchongi	adjudicator (n)	beoordelaar	umgangatho	quality (n)	kwaliteit
umchweli	carpenter (n)	timmerman	umgangatho	standard (n)	standaard
umchwethezi	typist (n)	tikster	umgangatho	floor (n)	vloer
umcinezeli	oppressor (n)	onderdrukker	umgangatho	floor (n)	verdieping
umcu	strip (n)	strook	umgangatho	level (n)	vlak
umculi	musician (n)	musikant	umgaqo	policy (n)	beleid
umculo	music (n)	musiek	umgaqo	method (n)	metode
umcuphi	detective (n)	speurder	umgaqo-siseko	constitution (n)	grondwet
umda	border (n)	grens	umgca	row (n)	ry
umDali	Creator (n)	Skepper	umgca	stripe (n)	streep
umdaniso	dance (n)	dans	umgca okroliweyo	groove (n)	groef
umdibaniso	unimportant (a)	onbelangrik	umgcinindawo	caretaker (n)	opsigter
umdibano	joint (n)	gewrig	umgobo	hem (n)	soom
umdiliya	vine (n)	wingerdstok	umgotywana	penknife (n)	knipmes
umdisipile	disciple (n)	dissipel	umgqalisela	caution (n)	versigtigheid
umdiza	cigarette (n)	sigaret	uMgqibelo	Saturday (n)	Saterdag
umdla	interest (n)	belang	umgqomo	rubbish bin (n)	vullisblik
umdla	enthusiasm (n)	geesdrif	umgquba	manure (n)	mis
umdlali	actress (n)	aktrise	umgqumo	roar (n)	brul
umdlali	actor (n)	akteur	umgqwetho	fold (n)	vou
umdlali-fidyoli	violinist (n)	vioolspeler	umgruzulo	bruise (n)	kneusplek
umdlali-fluti	flautist (n)	fluitspeler	umgubo	flour (n)	meel
umdlali -hadi	organist (n)	orrelis	umgudlo	soapstone (n)	seepsteen
umdlalihadi	pianist (n)	klavierspeler	umguquki	convert (n)	bekeerling
umdlalimrhubhe	cellist (n)	tjellis	umguquli	translator (n)	vertaler
umdlali weqakamba	cricketer (n)	krieketspeler	umgwegwelezo	detour (n)	omweg
umdlali-xilongo	trumpeter (n)	trompetblaser	umgwejelo	corner (n)	hoek
umdlalo	game (n)	spel	umgxobhozo	swamp (n)	moeras
umdlalo	sport (n)	sport	umhambi	passenger (n)	passasier
umdlalo	play (n)	toneelstuk	umhambi	traveller (n)	reisiger
umdlalo wobaleko	athletics (n)	atletiek	umhambi ngeenyawo	pedestrian (n)	voetganger
umdumba	pod (n)	peul	umhambo	walk (n)	wandeling
umdyarho	horserace (n)	perdewedren	umhanahanisi	hypocrite (n)	skynheilige
umdyarho	race (n)	wedren	umhedeni	pagan (n)	heiden
umenye	flash (n)	flits	umhla	date (n)	datum
umenyezelo	reflection (n)	weerkaatsing	umhlaba	land (n)	land
umenzi	performer (n)	uitvoerder	umhlaba	earth (n)	aarde
uMeyi	May (n)	Mei	umhlaba	soil (n)	grond
umfama	farmer (n)	boer	umhlaba	ground (n)	grond
umfanekiso	figure (n)	figuur	umhlakulo	spade (n)	graaf
umfanekiso	picture (n)	prent	umhlalaphantsi	pension (n)	pensioen
umfanekiso -ntelekelelo	image (n)	beeld	umhlali-ngaphambili	chairman (n)	voorsitter
			umhlaliswa	lodger (n)	loseerder
umfanekiso oqingqiweyo	statue (n)	beeld	umhlambi	flock (n)	trop
			umhlambi	herd (n)	kudde
umfazi	woman (n)	vrou	umhlangano	gathering (n)	byeenkoms
umfazi	wife (n)	vrou	umhlathi	jaw (n)	kaak
umfazi	female (n)	vrou	umhlathi	molar (n)	kiestand

Xhosa	English	Afrikaans	Xhosa	English	Afrikaans
umhlathi	paragraph (n)	paragraaf	umlawuli	manager (n)	bestuurder
umhla wokuzalwa	birthday (n)	verjaarsdag	umlawuli	ruler (n)	regeerder
umhlawuli	payer (n)	betaler	umlebe	lip (n)	lip
umhlaza	cancer (n)	kanker	umlenze	leg (n)	been
umhleli	editor (n)	redakteur	umlibo	stock (n)	voorraad
umhlobo	friend (n)	vriend	umlilo	fire (n)	vuur
umhlobokazi	girlfriend (n)	nooi	umlinganiselo	measure (n)	maat
umhlohli	lecturer (n)	dosent	umlinganiso	gauge (n)	meter
umhlohlo	filling (n)	stopsel	umlinganiswa	character (n)	karakter
umhlola	omen (n)	voorteken	umlo	fight (n)	geveg
umhloli	inspector (n)	inspekteur	umlo	battle (n)	geveg
umhloli-ncwadi	auditor (n)	ouditeur	umlomo	mouth (n)	mond
umhlolo	widower (n)	wewenaar	umlomo wentaka	beak (n)	snawel
umhlolokazi	widow (n)	weduwee	umlomo wesilwanyana	muzzle (n)	snoet
umhluzi	soup (n)	sop	umlwelwe	invalid (n)	invalide
umhluzi	sauce (n)	sous	ummandla	area (n)	oppervlakte
umhluzi	gravy (n)	sous	ummandla	zone (n)	sone
umhluzi weendaba	censor (v)	sensor	ummandla omathafa	highveld (n)	hoëveld
umhlwa	rust (n)	roes	ummangalelwa	accused (n)	beskuldigde
umhobe	anthem (n)	volkslied	ummangalelwa	defendant (n)	verweerder
umhombiso	ornament (n)	ornament	ummangali	accuser (n)	beskuldiger
umhombiso	decoration (n)	versiering	ummangali	plaintiff (n)	eiser
umingimingi	rumour (n)	gerug	ummangali	complainant (n)	klaer
umiso	system (n)	stelsel	ummangaliso	mystery (n)	misterie
umjelo wezibi	sewerage (n)	riolering	ummangaliso	amazement (n)	verbasing
umjikelezo	circulation (n)	omloop	ummangaliso	wonder (n)	wonder
umjikelo	circumference (n)	omtrek	ummangaliso	miracle (n)	wonderwerk
umjikelo	cycle (n)	siklus	ummeli	shop steward (n)	segsman
umjiko	curl (n)	krul	ummeli	representative (n)	verteenwoordiger
umkhaba	belly (n)	pens	ummelwane	neighbour (n)	buurman
umkhala	bridle (n)	toom	ummi	citizen (n)	burger
umkhandi	mechanic (n)	werktuigkundige	ummiselo	fate (n)	lot
umkhango	birthmark (n)	moedervlek	ummiselo	decree (n)	verordening
umkhaya	afterbirth (n)	nageboorte	ummisi	assessor (n)	skatter
umkhenkce	ice (n)	ys	ummizo	gullet (n)	slukderm
umkhenkethi	tourist (n)	toeris	ummizo	oesophagus (n)	slukderm
umkhombe	rhinoceros (n)	renoster	umnakwethu	brother (n)	broer
umkhombe	ironwood (n)	ysterhout	umncedi	assistant (n)	helper
umkhono	sleeve (n)	mou	umncwino	groan (n)	kreun
umkhonto	assegai (n)	assegaai	umndwendwelwa	host (n)	gasheer
umkhonto	spear (n)	spies	umnenga	whale (n)	walvis
umkhosi	army (n)	leër	umnga	acacia (n)	akasia
umkhuba	vice (n)	ondeug	umnga	mimosa (n)	mimosa
umkhuhlane	influenza (n)	griep	umngcatshi	traitor (n)	verraaier
umkhumbi	coffin (n)	doodskis	umngcunube	willow (n)	wilgerboom
umkhumezelo	drizzle (v)	motreën	umngcwabo	funeral (n)	begrafnis
umkhuthuzi	pickpocket (n)	sakkeroller	umngcwabo	burial (n)	begrafnis
umkhuthuzi	robber (n)	rower	umngeni	challenge (n)	uitdaging
umkhwenyana	son-in-law (n)	skoonseun	umngqibi	beggar (n)	bedelaar
umkra	appetite (n)	eetlus	umngqusho	samp (n)	stampmielies
umKrestu	Christian (n)	Christen	umngxuma	pit (n)	gat
umkrexezi	adulterer (n)	owerspeler	umngxuma	hole (n)	gat
umkrwelo	scratch (n)	krap	umngxuma weqhosha	buttonhole (n)	knoopsgat
umlambo	anaemia (n)	bloedarmoede	umngxuma wesitshixo	keyhole (n)	sleutelgat
umlambo	river (n)	rivier	umngxunyana	puncture (n)	lekplek
umlambo	stream (n)	stroom	umnikelo	offer (n)	aanbod
umlamli	mediator (n)	bemiddelaar	umniki-ngxelo	reporter (n)	verslaggewer
umlamli	arbiter (n)	arbiter	umnini	owner (n)	eienaar
umlandeli	follower (n)	volgeling	umnini-ndlu	landlord (n)	verhuurder
umlanyakazi	sister-in-law (n)	skoonsuster	umnqamlezo	cross (v)	kruis

U	Xhosa	English	Afrikaans	Xhosa	English	Afrikaans
	uMnqamlezo wase-mZantsi	Southern Cross (n)	Suiderkruis	umphindwa	double (n)	dubbel
				umphini	shaft (n)	skag
	umnqathe	root (n)	wortel	umphotho	plait (n)	vlegsel
	umnqathe	carrot (n)	wortel	umphula	wax (n)	was
	umnqonqo	spinal cord (n)	rugmurg	umphunga	lung (n)	long
	umnqophiso	pact (n)	verdrag	umphunga	steam (n)	stoom
	umnquma	olive (n)	olyf	umphunga	vapour (n)	wasem
	umnqwazi	hat (n)	hoed	umpostile	apostle (n)	apostel
	umnqweno	desire (n)	begeerte	umprofeti	prophet (n)	profeet
	umnqweno	wish (n)	wens	umpu	gun (n)	geweer
	umntla	north (n)	noorde	umpu	revolver (n)	rewolwer
	umntu	individual (n)	individu	umqala	windpipe (n)	gorrelpyp
	umntu	person (n)	persoon	umqala	throat (n)	keel
	umntu ofikisayo	adolescent (n)	jeugdige	umqali	beginner (n)	beginner
	umntu omdala	adult (n)	volwassene	umqambi	composer (n)	komponis
	umntu ongakholwayo	unbeliever (n)	ongelowige	umqamelo	cushion (n)	kussing
	-umntu oxhomeke-kileyo	dependant (n)	afhanklike	umqamelo	pillow (n)	kussing
				umqapheli	observer (n)	waarnemer
	umntu wasemzini	stranger (n)	vreemdeling	umqeqeshi	coach (n)	afrigter
	umntwana	baby (n)	baba	umqeshi	tenant (n)	bewoner
	umntwana	young (n)	kleintjie	umqeshi	employer (n)	werkgewer
	umntwana	child (n)	kind	umqeshwa	employee (n)	werknemer
	umntwana	pupil (n)	leerling	umqhagi	cock (n)	haan
	umntwana	infant (n)	suigeling	umqhagi	rooster (n)	hoenderhaan
	umnwe	fingerprint (n)	vingerafdruk	umqhaphu	cotton wool (n)	watte
	umnwe	finger (n)	vinger	umqhaqhi	operator (n)	operateur
	umnxaxhi	rebel (n)	rebel	umqhekezi	burglar (n)	inbreker
	umnyadala	festival (n)	fees	umqhubi	driver (n)	bestuurder
	umnyama	iris (n)	iris	umqhwayi	agitator (n)	opstoker
	umnyama	rainbow (n)	reënboog	umqhweshi	deserter (n)	droster
	umnyama	eclipse (n)	verduistering	umqingqi	sculptor (n)	beeldhouer
	umnyazi	basket (n)	mandjie	umqobo	obstacle (n)	hindernis
	umnyiki	stalk (n)	stingel	umqobo	barrier (n)	versperring
	umoki	oak (n)	eikeboom	umqolo	ridge (n)	rug
	umolokazana	daughter-in-law (n)	skoondogter	umqolo	back (n)	rug
	umona	jealousy (n)	jaloesie	umqolo	vertebra (n)	werwel
	umona	envy (n)	naywer	umqolomba	cave (n)	grot
	umonakalo	damage (n)	skade	umqondiso	signal (n)	sinjaal
	umonakalo	harm (n)	skade	umqukumbelo	appendix (n)	aanhangsel
	umonde	patience (n)	geduld	umqukumbelo	conclusion (n)	gevolgtrekking
	umongameli	president (n)	president	umqukumbelo	lace (n)	kant
	umongameli	tender (n)	tender	umququ	husk (n)	skil
	umongikazi	nurse (n)	verpleegster	umqwayito	biltong (n)	biltong
	umongo	marrow (n)	murg	umrhanelwa	suspect (n)	verdagte
	umongo, ipete	pith (n)	pit	umrhawuzelelane	eczema (n)	ekseem
	umongomoya	oxygen (n)	suurstof	umrhubhe	banjo (n)	banjo
	umoni	culprit (n)	skuldige	umrhubhe	cello (n)	tjello
	umoya	air (n)	lug	umsa	affection (n)	toegeneentheid
	umoya	wind (n)	wind	umsebe	eyelash (n)	wimper
	umphakathi	interior (n)	binneste	umsebenzi	labour (n)	arbeid
	umphakatho	groin (n)	lies	umsebenzi	labourer (n)	arbeider
	umphambili-nqanawa	bow (n)	strik	umsebenzi	duty (n)	plig
	umphandle	outside (n)	buitekant	umsebenzi	task (n)	taak
	umphantsi	genitals (n)	geslagsorgane	umsebenzi	employment (n)	werk
	umphathiswa	minister (n)	minister	umsebenzi	job (n)	werk
	umphefumlo	breath (n)	asem	umsebenzi	worker (n)	werker
	umphefumlo	spirit (n)	gees	umsebenzi	work (n)	werk
	umphefumlo	soul (n)	siel	umsebenzi wasekhaya	homework (n)	huiswerk
	umphezulu	top (n)	top	umsebenzi wezandla	handwork (n)	handewerk
	umphezulu wonyawo	instep (n)	boog	umsebenzi wodongwe	pottery (n)	pottebakkery

Xhosa	English	Afrikaans	Xhosa	English	Afrikaans	U
umsele	ditch (n)	sloot	umtshutshisi	prosecutor (n)	aanklaer	
umshumayeli	preacher (n)	predikant	umtsi	jump (n)	sprong	
umsi	smoke (n)	rook	umtya	thread (n)	draad	
umsiki wempahla	tailor (n)	kleremaker	umtya	line (n)	lyn	
umsila	tail (n)	stert	umtya	queue (n)	tou	
umsinandozele	bore (n)	vervelige mens	umtya	string (n)	tou	
umsindo	anger (n)	kwaadheid	umtya wesihlangu	shoelace (n)	skoenveter	
umsindo	temper (n)	humeur	umtyholi	devil (n)	duiwel	
umsinga	tide (n)	gety	umtyikityo	signature (n)	handtekening	
umsinga	backwash (n)	terugspoeling	umvangeli	evangelist (n)	evangelis	
umsinga	current (n)	stroom	uMvulo	Monday (n)	Maandag	
umsintsila	coccyx (n)	stuitjiebeen	umvuzo	reward (n)	beloning	
umsipha	ligament (n)	ligament	umvuzo	earnings (n)	loon	
umsipha	tendon (n)	sening	umvuzo	salary (n)	salaris	
umsitho	feast (n)	fees	umxhasi	fan (n)	bewonderaar	
umsundululu	earthworm (n)	erdwurm	umxhasi	client (n)	kliënt	
umthambo	vein (n)	aar	umxhelo	bosom (n)	boesem	
umthambo	artery (n)	slagaar	umxhesho	ration (n)	rantsoen	
umthambo-luvo	nerve (n)	senuwee	umxholo	theme (n)	tema	
umthambo wegazi	blood vessel (n)	bloedvat	umxhuzulo	convulsion (n)	rukking	
umthamo	bite (n)	hap	umxube	mixture (n)	mengsel	
umthamo	contents (n)	inhoud	umxube weentlanga	multiracial (a)	veelrassig	
umthamo	mouthful (n)	mondvol	umyaleli	instructor (n)	instrukteur	
umthamo	volume (n)	volume	umyalelo	order (n)	bevel	
umthandazo	prayer (n)	gebed	umyalelo	commandment (n)	gebod	
umthanjana	capillary (n)	haarvat	umyalelo	instruction (n)	onderrig	
umthengi	buyer (n)	koper	umyalelo	prescription (n)	voorskrif	
umthengisi	auctioneer (n)	afslaer	umyalezo	message (n)	boodskap	
umthetho	rule (n)	reël	umyeni	bridegroom (n)	bruidegom	
umthetho	regulation (n)	regulasie	umyotywa	drug addict (n)	dwelmslaaf	
umthetho	law (n)	wet	umzali	parent (n)	ouer	
umthi	tree (n)	boom	umzamo	effort (n)	inspanning	
umthika	fly (n)	vlieg	umzamo	attempt (n)	poging	
umthi webhambu	bamboo (n)	bamboes	umzantsi	bottom (n)	bodem	
umthi wekhiwane	figtree (n)	vyeboom	umzantsi	south (n)	suide	
umthi wepampiri	poplar (n)	populier	umzekeliso	parable (n)	gelykenis	
umthombo	fountain (n)	fontein	umzekelo	example (n)	voorbeeld	
umthondo	penis (n)	penis	umzila	track (n)	spoor	
umthubi	yolk (n)	eiergeel	umzima	body (n)	liggaam	
umthumeli	export (n)	uitvoer	umzimba	corpse (n)	lyk	
umthungo	knitting (n)	breiwerk	umzingeli	hunter (n)	jagter	
umthungo	seam (n)	naat	umzi weenkedama	orphanage (n)	weeshuis	
umthungo	sewing (n)	naaldwerk	umzobo	diagram (n)	diagram	
umthunywa umfundisi	missionary (n)	sendeling	umzobo	drawing (n)	tekening	
umthunzi	shadow (n)	skaduwee	umzukulwana	granddaughter (n)	kleindogter	
umthunzi	shade (n)	skadu	umzukulwana	grandson (n)	kleinseun	
umthwalo	luggage (n)	bagasie	umzukulwana	grandchild (n)	kleinkind	
umthwalo	burden (n)	las	umzuzu	minute (n)	minuut	
umthwalo	load (n)	vrag	umzuzwana	second (n)	sekonde	
umtsalane	attraction (n)	aantrekking	unakano	recognition (n)	herkenning	
umtsalane	charm (n)	sjarme	unceda	help (n)	hulp	
umtshakazi	bride (n)	bruid	uncedo	assistance (n)	bystand	
umtshana	nephew (n)	neef	uncedo	favour (n)	guns	
umtshana	niece (n)	niggie	uncedo	aid (n)	hulp	
umtshato	wedding (n)	bruilof	uncedo	rescue (n)	redding	
umtshato	marriage (n)	huwelik	uncedo	advantage (n)	voordeel	
umtshayelo	broom (n)	besem	uncedo lokuqala	first aid (n)	noodhulp	
umtshaza	frostbite (n)	vriesbrand	uncomo	recommendation (n)	aanbeveling	
umtshingo	flute (n)	fluit	uncomo	admiration (n)	bewondering	
umtshiso	burn (n)	brandplek	uncomo	praise (n)	lof	

Xhosa	English	Afrikaans	Xhosa	English	Afrikaans
uncumo	smile (n)	glimlag	unyawo	footprint (n)	voetspoor
uncwadi	literature (n)	letterkunde	unyeliso	defamation (n)	belastering
uncwadi lomlomo	folklore (n)	volksoorleweringe	unyobo	bribery (n)	omkopery
undiliseko	dignity (n)	waardigheid	unyulo	election (n)	verkiesing
undiva	hearsay (n)	hoorsê	unyuselo	promotion (n)	bevordering
undloku	colon (n)	dikderm	unyuso	rise (n)	styging
undloku, undonci	rectum (n)	rektum	unyuso-magxa	shrug (n)	skouerophaling
undondozelo	throb (n)	klopping	uphahla	roof (n)	dak
unduluko	departure (n)	vertrek	uphahla	skeleton (n)	geraamte
undwanya	stare (n)	gestaar	uphambuko	deviation (n)	ompad
undwendwe	visitor (n)	besoeker	uphando	inquest (n)	doodsondersoek
undwendwe	caller (n)	besoeker	uphando	investigation (n)	ondersoek
undwendwe	guest (n)	gas	uphawu	brand (n)	handelsmerk
ungcatsho	treason (n)	verraad	uphawu	mark (n)	merk
ungcothoza	spy (n)	spioen	uphawu	symptom (n)	simptoom
ungqameko	ledge (n)	rotslys	uphawu	sign (n)	teken
ungqubano	collision (n)	botsing	uphehlelelo	baptism (n)	doop
ungquzulwano	conflict (n)	konflik	uphondo	horn (n)	horing
ungxengxezo	apology (n)	verskoning	uphondo lwendlovu	ivory (n)	ivoor
uninazala	mother-in-law (n)	skoonmoeder	uphuphu	hoof (n)	hoef
unkcenkcesho	irrigation (n)	besproeiing	uqhagamshelo	connection (n)	verbinding
unkonkonko	whooping cough (n)	kinkhoes	uqhambuko	outbreak (n)	uitbreking
unobhaka	baker (n)	bakker	uqhankqalazo	demonstration (n)	betoging
unobhala	clerk (n)	klerk	uqhaqho	operation (n)	operasie
unobhala	secretary (n)	sekretaris	uqhawulo-mtshato	divorce (n)	egskeiding
unobumba	initial (n)	voorletter	uqhushululu	strike (n)	staking
unokhemesti	pharmacist (n)	apteker	uqhwanyazo	wink (n)	knipogie
unomadudwane	scorpion (n)	skerpioen	uqhwesho	escape (n)	ontsnapping
unomasinana	bulldog (n)	bulhond	uqhwithela	gale (n)	stormwind
unomathotholo	radio (n)	radio	uqino-mihlathi	tetanus (n)	klem in die kake
unomeva	wasp (n)	perdeby	uqongqothwane	beetle (n)	kewer
unomtidili	petticoat (n)	onderrok	uqoqosho	economy (n)	ekonomie
unomyayi	crow (n)	kraai	uqoqosho	commerce (n)	handel
unoncwadi	librarian (n)	bibliotekaris	uqweqwe	peel (n)	skil
unongendi	nun (n)	non	uqwilikane	mumps (n)	pampoentjies
unongo	flavouring (n)	geursel	urhano	suspicion (n)	agterdog
unonkala	crab (n)	krap	urhatya	dusk (n)	skemer
unopopi	doll (n)	pop	urhudo	diarrhoea (n)	diarree
unoposi	postman (n)	posbode	urhulumente	government (n)	regering
unosilarha	butcher (n)	slagter	urhwaqelo	contraction (n)	inkrimping
unothi	zero (n)	nul	urhwebo	trade (n)	handel
uNovemba	November (n)	November	usapho	family (n)	familie
unqando	prevention (n)	voorkoming	usebezo	whisper (n)	gefluister
unsebenzi	activity (n)	bedrywigheid	usekela-sihlalo	vice-chairman (n)	ondervoorsitter
untozonke	supermarket (n)	supermark	usenza	butternut (n)	botterskorsie
untywilo	diving (n)	duikery	uSeptemba	September (n)	September
unwele	bristle (n)	steekhaar	ushenxiso	removal (n)	verwydering
unxano	thirst (n)	dors	ushiyi	eyebrow (n)	winkbrou
unxantathu	triangle (n)	driehoek	ushiyo	omission (n)	weglating
unxulumano	relation (n)	verhouding	ushoti	shorts (n)	kortbroek
unxulumano	relationship (n)	verhouding	usiba	feather (n)	veer
unxunguphalo	anxiety (n)	kommer	usiba	pen (n)	pen
unxweme	coast (n)	kus	usindiso	salvation (n)	verlossing
unxweme	beach (n)	strand	usinga	fibre (n)	vesel
unyaka	year (n)	jaar	usingasiqithi	peninsula (n)	skiereiland
unyakande	leap year (n)	skrikkeljaar	usinyeke	snail (n)	slak
unyana	son (n)	seun	usizi	sorrow (n)	smart
unyanzelo	insistence (n)	aandrang	usizi	pity (n)	jammerte
unyanzelo	force (n)	krag	usizi	sadness (n)	droefheid
unyawo	foot (n)	voet	usompempe	referee (n)	skeidsregter

Xhosa	English	Afrikaans	Xhosa	English	Afrikaans	X
utata	father (n)	vader	-vakalela(yo)	sensitive (a)	gevoelig	
uthanda	leak (n)	lek	-vakalelwa	feel (v)	voel	
uthanda	crack (n)	kraak	-vala	shut (v)	toemaak	
uthando	love (n)	liefde	-valela	jail (v)	opsluit	
uthelekiso	comparison (n)	vergelyking	-valela	enclose (v)	insluit	
uthintelo	obstruction (n)	belemmernis	-valile(yo)	shut (a)	toe	
uThixo	God (n)	God	-vavanya	examine (v)	ondersoek	
uthuli	dust (n)	stof	-vavanya	test (v)	toets	
uthumelo kwelinye ilizwe	export (v)	uitvoer	-vela	appear (v)	verskyn	
			-vela	emerge (v)	verrys	
uthundezo	urge (n)	drang	-velela	dominate (v)	oorheers	
uthuthu	ash (n)	as	-velisa	produce (v)	produseer	
uthweso	coronation (n)	kroning	-vilaphayo	lazy (a)	lui	
utofo	inoculation (n)	inenting	-vingca	block (v)	blokkeer	
utofo	injection (n)	inspuiting	-vingca	plug (v)	toestop	
utolo	arrow (n)	pyl	-vota	vote (v)	stem	
utshaba	foe (n)	vyand	-vuka	arise (v)	opstaan	
utshaba	enemy (n)	vyand	-vuka	wake (v)	wakker word	
utshintsho	change (n)	verandering	-vula	open (v)	oopmaak	
utshiso	arson (n)	brandstigting	-vulekile(yo)	open (a)	oop	
utshutshiso	prosecution (n)	vervolging	-vuma	acknowledge (v)	erken	
utyelelo	visit (n)	besoek	-vuma	agree (v)	ooreenstem	
utywala	beer (n)	bier	-vuma	confess (v)	bely	
utywala	brew (n)	brousel	-vuma	consent (v)	instem	
utywala	liquor (n)	drank	-vuma	stem (v)	voortspruit	
utywala	liqueur (n)	likeur	-vumbulula	unearth (v)	opgrawe	
uvalelo	detention (n)	aanhouding	-vumela	allow (v)	toestaan	
uvavanyo	test (n)	toets	-vumela	permit (v)	toelaat	
uvavanyo	examination (n)	eksamen	-vumelana	approve (v)	goedkeur	
uvelwano	sympathy (n)	simpatie	-vumelanayo	agreeable (a)	aangenaam	
uvivingane	moth (n)	mot	-vuna	reap (v)	oes	
uvukelo	revolt (n)	opstand	-vuna	harvest (v)	oes	
uvukelo	revolution (n)	revolusie	-vunda	decompose (v)	ontbind	
uvukelo	rebellion (n)	opstand	-vungama	growl (v)	knor	
uvuyo	joy (n)	vreugde	-vusa	arouse (v)	opwek	
uvuyo	excitement (n)	opwinding	-vusa	leak (v)	lek	
uvuyo	happiness (n)	geluk	-vuthela	inflate (v)	opblaas	
uwonke-wonke	public (n)	publiek	-vuthela	blow (v)	waai	
uxakaxa	mucus (n)	slym	-vuthiwe (yo)	ripe (a)	ryp	
uxande	rectangle (n)	reghoek	-vuthulula	dust (v)	afstof	
uxande	square (n)	vierkant	-vuya	glad (a)	bly	
uxhongo	shin (n)	skeen	-vuyayo	happy (a)	gelukkig	
uxinzelelo	pressure (n)	druk	-vuyela	celebrate (v)	vier	
uxinzelelo lwegazi	blood pressure (n)	bloeddruk	-vuyisa	excite (v)	opwind	
uxolo	peace (n)	vrede	-vuyisana	congratulate (v)	gelukwens	
uxolo	forgiveness (n)	vergifnis	-vuza	reward (v)	beloon	
uxwebhu	document (n)	dokument				
uYesu	Jesus (n)	Jesus	-wa	fall (v)	val	
uzaliso	artificial insemination (n)	kunsmatige inseminasie	wakha	ever (adv)	ooit	
			wena	you (pron)	jy	
uzipho	toenail (n)	toonnael	-wisa	drop (v)	laat val	
uzipho	fingernail (n)	vingernael				
uzipho lwentaka	claw (n)	klou	-xabana	quarrel (v)	twis	
uzuko	glory (n)	glorie	-xabisa	charge (price) (v)	vra	
uzwane	toe (n)	toon	-xabisa	prize (v)	op prys stel	
uzwilakhe	dictator (n)	diktator	-xabisa	value (v)	waardeer	
			-xabisayo	costly (a)	kosbaar	
-va	hear (v)	hoor	-xabisekile (yo)	precious (a)	kosbaar	
-vakalayo	acoustic (a)	akoesties	-xabisekile(yo)	valid (a)	geldig	
-vakalayo	audible (a)	hoorbaar	-xakekile	engaged (a)	beset	

Z	Xhosa	English	Afrikaans		Xhosa	English	Afrikaans
	-xande	square (a)	vierkantig		-yolisayo	amusing (a)	vermaaklik
	-xazulula	solve (v)	oplos		yona	it (pron)	dit
	-xela	predict (v)	voorspel		yonke	whole (a)	heel
	-xela	tell (v)	vertel		-yoshishino	industrial (a)	industrieel
	-xela	state (v)	vermeld				
	-xhalile (yo)	tense (a)	gespanne		-za	will (v)	sal
	-xhalisekile(yo)	serious (a)	ernstig		-zabalaza	strive (v)	strewe
	xhasa	back (v)	steun		-za kwenzeka	inevitable (a)	onvermydelik
	-xhasa	maintain (v)	handhaaf		-zala	spawn (v)	uitbroei
	-xhasa	second (v)	sekondeer		-zalisa	breed (v)	teel
	-xhasa	support (v)	ondersteun		-zalisa ngamanzi	flood (v)	oorstroom
	-xhasa	uphold (v)	hoog hou		-zama	try (v)	probeer
	-xhathisa	resist (v)	weerstaan		-zamisa	stir (v)	roer
	-xhela	slaughter (v)	slag		-zamla	yawn (v)	gaap
	-xhoba	arm (v)	bewapen		-zantsana	lower (a)	laer
	-xhoma	crucify (v)	kruisig		-zantsi	low (a)	laag
	-xhoma	hang (v)	hang		-zantsi	southern (a)	suidelik
	-xhoma	suspend (v)	opskort		-zantsi	south (a)	suid
	-xhomekeka	depend (on) (v)	afhang (van)		-ze	bare (a)	kaal
	-xhomekekileyo	dependent (a)	afhanklik		-ze	blank (a)	leeg
	-xhuzula	jerk (v)	ruk		-ze	empty (a)	leeg
	-xhwila	snatch (v)	gaps		-ze	hollow (a)	hol
	-xhwitha	pluck (v)	pluk		-ze	naked (a)	kaal
	-xinanisa	overcrowd (v)	oorvol wees		-zeka	copulate (v)	kopuleer
	-xineneyo	dense (a)	dig		-zele	plenty (a)	volop
	-xineneyo	crowded (a)	propvol		-zeleyo	full (a)	vol
	-xinzelela	compress (v)	saampers		-zenzisa	pretend (v)	voorgee
	-xoka	lie (v)	lieg		-zidla(yo)	proud (a)	trots
	-xolela	excuse (v)	verontskuldig		-zifunelayo	arbitrary (a)	willekeurig
	-xolela	forgive (v)	vergewe		-zikisa	ponder (v)	bepeins
	-xolela	pardon (v)	vergewe		-zila	mourn (v)	rou
	-xolisa	appease (v)	bevredig		-zindla	presume (v)	veronderstel
	-xovula	knead (v)	knie		-zingela	hunt (v)	jag
	-xoxa	argue (v)	stry		-zingela	prey (v)	aas
	-xoxa	discuss (v)	bespreek		-zingela	scout (v)	rondkyk
	-xuba	dilute (v)	verdun		-zingisa	persevere (v)	volhard
	-xuba	mix (v)	meng		-zinzile(yo)	firm (a)	ferm
					-zinzile(yo)	stable (a)	stabiel
	-ya	for (prep)	vir		-zinzisa	establish (v)	vestig
	ya-	of (prep)	van		-ziphakamisileyo	haughty (a)	hoogmoedig
	-yabula	loiter (v)	rondslenter		-ziphatha kakubi	misbehave (v)	jou swak gedra
	-ya endle	defecate (v)	ontlas		-ziphathe	behave (v)	jou gedra
	-yala	decline (v)	afwys		-ziphikise	contradict (v)	weerspreek
	-yalela	direct (v)	beveel		-zisa	bring (v)	bring
	-yalela	instruct (v)	onderrig		-zisole	regret (v)	spyt hê
	-yalela	order (v)	beveel		-zithandelayo	voluntary (a)	vrywillig
	yam	mine (pron)	myne		-zithandele	volunteer (v)	vrywillig onderneem
	yam	my (pron)	my		-zithembileyo	confident (a)	vol vertroue
	yam	own (a)	eie		-zoba	draw (v)	teken
	-yamkela	admit (v)	toelaat		zohlwaya	repent (v)	berou hê
	-yeka	abstain (v)	onthou		-zolileyo	calm (a)	kalm
	yena	he (pron)	hy		-zolile (yo)	gentle (a)	sagmoedig
	yena	her (pron)	haar		-zotha	nauseate (v)	naar maak
	yena	him (pron)	hom		-zungubala	absent-minded (a)	ingedagte
	yena	she (pron)	sy		-zuza	achieve (v)	presteer
	-yezinyanya	ancestral (a)	voorvaderlik		-zuza	acquire (v)	aanskaf
	-yilwa	fight (v)	veg		-zuza	earn (v)	verdien
	-yintloko	chief (a)	hoof		-zuza	gain (v)	wen
	-yinyani, -nene	real (a)	werklik		-zuza	obtain (v)	bekom
	yiphi	which (pron)	watter		-zuza	profit (v)	wins maak
	-yolisa	amuse (v)	vermaak		-zuza	win (v)	wen

ZULU

Zulu, or isiZulu as it is known among its speakers, is understood by approximately 10- to 12-million people in southern Africa, from the Cape to Zimbabwe. Only in the western parts of southern Africa and in the far northern Transvaal is Zulu not generally understood.

There are four major Bantu language groups in southern Africa: Nguni, Sotho, Tsonga and Venda. Zulu is the written language of the Northern Nguni, i.e. the people of Natal, KwaZulu, the eastern Free State and the south and southeastern Transvaal.

It is important to remember that, in common with other southern African indigenous languages, the structure of Zulu – a tonal language – is very different to Western languages. Zulu is governed by the noun, which is split into various classes. It is what is known as an agglutinating language (a combination of suffixes and prefixes to express a compound meaning).

PRONUNCIATION

In addition to mastering vowels and consonants, Zulu speakers also need to master the characteristic clicks, which entered the language through contact with San and Khoi languages.

VOWELS
The Zulu vowels, and their approximate sounds, are:

a as in **abafazi** (*women*), similar to the English *father*
e as in **-sebenza** (*work*), similar to the English *end*
i as in **insimbi** (*an iron*), similar to the English *tea*
o as in **inkomo** (*head of cattle*), similar to the English *all*
u as in **umuntu** (*a person*), similar to the English *to*

CONSONANTS
The Zulu consonants, and their approximate sounds, are:

b as in **ubaba** (*father*), which to the English ear sounds the same as a normal **b** but softer, and pronounced with less force, and easily confused with **bh**
dl as in **-dlala** (*play*), no local equivalent, but somewhat similar to the Welsh *Llewellyn*
f as in **-funa** (*want/seek*), similar to the English *fat*
h as in **-hahama** (*growl*), similar to the first sound in the Afrikaans *gaan*; a softer **h**, similar to the English *how*, may be substituted
hh as in **ihhashi** (*a horse*), similar to the English *hotel*
hl in **-hlala** (*sit*), no local equivalent, but similar to the Welsh *Llewellyn*
k as in **ukulwa** (*to fight*), similar to the **g** in the English *good*
kh as in **-khokha** (*take out*), similar to the first consonant in the English *call*, followed by a strong rush of air
l as in **-lala** (*sleep*), similar to the English *lull*
m as in **umama** (*mother*), similar to the English *mum*
n as in **nina** (*you (pl.)*), similar to the English *nun*
ng as in **ngena** (*enter*), similar to the English *linger*
ny as in **unyawo** (*foot*), similar to the English *Kenya*
ph as in **-phapha** (*fly*), similar to the first consonant in the English *push*, followed by a strong rush of air occurs only in borrowed words
s as in **-susa** (*take away*), similar to the English *say*
sh as in **-shaya** (*hit*), similar to the English *show*
th as in **-thatha** (*take*), similar to the first consonant in the English *take*, followed by a strong rush of air
v as in **-vala** (*close*), similar to the English *vain*
w as in **wawa** (*he/she fell*), similar to the English *well*
y as in **yebo** (*yes*), similar to the English *yes*
z as in **-zala** (*give birth*), similar to the English *zoo*

The following group of sounds, called ejectives, appear to be sharper and shorter than similar sounds in English. They may also be pronounced with a lot of tension in the speech organs.

k as in **ikati** (*a cat*), similar to the final sound in *tick*, but sharper
kl as in **-klwebha** (*scratch*), it would be similar to a combination of a **k** and the first sound in the Welsh *Llewellyn*, but sharper
p as in **ipipi** (*a smoking pipe*), similar to the final **p** in *tip*, but sharper
t as in **into** (*a thing*), similar to the final sound in *pot*, but sharper
ts as in **-tsatsaza** (*spurt*), no English equivalent, sharper than the final sound in *pots*
tsh as in **itshe** (*a stone*), similar to the first sound in *church*

Some voiced consonants in Zulu have a peculiar type of voicing which is often difficult to reproduce. The best way to learn to pronounce these sounds is to make a break in the voicing before saying the sound, i.e. pronounce it as if it is the first sound of a word, even when it occurs in the middle of a word. Thus, try to pronounce the **g** in **ugogo** (*a grandmother*) as if it is the first sound of the word — make a break in the voicing before you pronounce it and let it be followed by a voiced **h**: **u-go-go**. Examples are:

bh as in **isibhamu** (*a rifle*); **ibhayisikobhu** (*a bioscope*)
d as in **idada** (*a duck*); **-deda** (*get out of the way*)
g as in **ugogo** (*a grandmother*); **-gada** (*guard*)
j as in **ijuba** (*a dove*); **uju** (honey), similar to the English *join*

CLICKS

Another group of sounds will also pose problems for the learner of the language. These are the click sounds introduced to Zulu by the San and Khoi languages. Click sounds are suction sounds made by trapping a body of air between the tongue and the roof of the mouth, i.e. the tongue touches the whole of the upper teeth ridge as well as the velum. The middle of the tongue is then lowered without this closure being broken. This lessens the pressure of the air in the space between the tongue and the palate. When the closure is broken at any point, the air from outside rushes into this small space, resulting in a click sound.

c the dental click as in **-caca** (*open*), may be compared with the sound you would make when sucking something from your upper front teeth, or the sound of sympathy when someone says *ts-ts*. The tip of the tongue releases the air when it is pulled away from the upper front teeth.

q the palatal click as in **-qala** (*begin*), may be compared with the sound a person would make when trying to imitate the sound of a cork being pulled from a bottle. The front part of the tongue moves away from the area behind the upper gums to cause the release.

x the lateral click as in **-xoxa** (*talk*) differs from the other two in that the release takes place at the side(s) of the tongue and not at the front. This sound is sometimes used to express regret or to spur on a horse.

These three clicks may also be pronounced in different ways and each may be:
aspirated (followed by a rush of air);
nasalised (preceded by a nasal sound);
have delayed voicing (the same as for **d** and **g** above); or
voiced.

The three ways are:

Dental clicks:
the aspirated **ch** as in **-chitha** (*pour*)
the nasalised **nc** as in **-ncela** (*suck*)
the delayed **gc** as in **-gcina** (*end*). When preceded by a nasal sound as in **ingcosana** (*a few/little*), it is voiced.

Palatal clicks:
the aspirated **qh** as in **iqhawe** (*warrior*)
the nasalised **nq** as in **-nquma** (*cut throat*)
the delayed **gq** as in **-gqiba** (*bury*), which may also be voiced when preceded by a nasal sound as in **-ngqangqa** (*tremble with anger*)

Lateral clicks:
the aspirated **xh** as in **isixhafuxhafu** (*a mannerless person*)
the nasalised **nx** as in **inxakanxaka** (*a confusion*)
the breathy-voiced **gx** as in **-gxagxaza** (*leaking a lot*), which may also be voiced when preceded by a nasal sound as in **-ngxangxasha** (*hop about*)

LINGUISTIC STRUCTURE

Zulu is based on two principles: the system of noun classes and the system of concords.

NOUN CLASSES

Each person or thing, concrete or abstract, is placed in a specific category or class in Zulu. Each word begins with a particular syllable(s) in the singular and each of these syllables is replaced by others in the plural. The rest of the word remains the same.

The syllables that change are called class prefixes of the noun. The part that follows is the noun stem, which remains constant. The different class prefixes give different meaning to the word.

Class	Prefix	Zulu	English equivalent
1	umu-	umuntu	*person*
1a	u-	ubaba	*my father*
2	aba-	abantu	*people*
2a	o-	obaba	*fathers*
3	umu-	umuthi	*tree*
4	imi-	imithi	*trees*
5	ili-/i-	ilitshe	*stone*
6	ama-	amatshe	*stones*
7	isi-	isitsha	*plate*
8	izi-	izitsha	*plates*
9	in-	inja	*dog*
10	izin-	izinja	*dogs*
11	ulu-/u-	uthi	*stick*
14	ubu-	ubukhulu	*size*
15	uku-	ukubona	*to see*
15a	uku-	ukunene	*the right-hand side*
16	pha-	phandle	*outside*
17	ku-	kumama	*to/at/by mother*

Thus it is clear that some classes form the plural of others (e.g. class 2 contains the plurals for class 1).

CONCORDS

The class prefixes indicate the classes to which the different nouns belong. From these prefixes a formative is derived which is used to link the noun to other words in the sentence. This formative is called the concord. This concord is prefixed to the verb or to other words in the sentence. Without the concord, any sentence in Zulu would be grammatically incorrect.

In the sentence, *The woman cooks food*, the word for *the woman* in Zulu is **inkosikazi**, for *cook* it is **-pheka** and for *food* it is **ukudla**. The subject noun **inkosikazi** must now be linked with the verb stem **-pheka** by means of a subject concord **i-**, which was derived from the class prefix **in-** of the subject noun:

Inkosikazi ipheka ukudla

In many cases, stems cannot be used on their own, which is why they are written with a hyphen in the dictionary.

PRONOUNS

Not only the concords derive from the class prefixes of the nouns, but also the pronouns:

Izicathulo zona lezi umbala wazo muhle (*These shoes, their colour is beautiful*)

VERBS

The Zulu verb consists of a root which carries its basic meaning. Unlike European languages, this root cannot be used by itself, but only after certain prefixes and suffixes have been added. When a suffix is added to the root, it becomes a verb stem. The basic verb stem can be used alone only in the imperative:

Hamba! (*Go!*)

The root **-fund-** has the basic meaning of *learn* and by suffixing different forms, it acquires different meanings:

-funda (*learn*)
-fundela (*learn for*)
-fundile (*have learnt*)
-fundisa (*cause to learn/teach*)
-fundana (*learn together*)
-fundisana (*teach one another*)

When the different prefixes are added to the verb stem, a proper verb is formed. The concords mentioned earlier are also included in the prefixes that can be used with the verb stem:

siyasebenza (*we work*)
basasebenza (*they are still working*)
nizosebenza (*you are going to work*)
sasebenza (*we worked*)
usebenzile (*he/she has worked*)

Note that the translations of the 'words' above consist of sentences. This is because Zulu uses morphemes, i.e. small segments of language instead of whole words, to add meaning to the basic form.

The present, future and past tenses appear in various forms in Zulu. These combine with other forms and formatives to express different aspects of meanings.

Ngiyadla manje (*I eat now*)
Ngizokudla manje (*I shall eat now*)
Ngidle izolo (*I ate yesterday*)
Ngizohamba kusasa (*I shall leave tomorrow*)
Ngisazohamba kusasa (*I am still leaving tomorrow*)
Basafunda (*They are still learning*)
Sengiyahamba (*I am going now*)

USING THE DICTIONARY

The Zulu nouns (n) appear in full, i.e. with a class prefix and a stem. The verbs (v) are represented by only the stem and to show that a concord (prefix) is needed before it can be used as a word, it is preceded by a hyphen. The English adjectives (a) cannot always be translated by adjectives in Zulu. Other parts of speech, especially verb stems, are often used instead so they also appear as stems with a hyphen before them. The adverbs (adv) are mostly complete words in Zulu, but again, some make use of other stems in Zulu and again are entered with a hyphen. The same applies to the prepositions and pronouns.

Zulu	English	Afrikaans	Zulu	English	Afrikaans
-a-	own (a)	eie	amandla	force (n)	krag
-a-	of (prep)	van	amandla	power (n)	mag
abacimimlilo	fire brigade (n)	brandweer	amandla	strength (n)	sterkte
abampofu	poor (n)	armes	amandla kazibuthe	magnetism (n)	magnetisme
abantu	people (n)	mense	amanga	lie (n)	leuen
abavalelwe umlomo	banned (people) (a)	ingeperk	amanga	falsehood (n)	onwaarheid
abefundisi	clergy (n)	geestelikes	-amanje	current (a)	huidige
-abela	allocate (v)	toewys	amanyikwe	pancreas (n)	pankreas
abethu	ours (pron)	ons s'n	amanzi	water (n)	water
abomuzi bonke	household (n)	huishouding	amaphahla	pair (n)	paar
-ahluka	deviate (v)	afwyk	amaphijama	pyjamas (n)	pajamas
-ahlukana	differ (v)	verskil	amaphoyisa	police (n)	polisie
-ahlukananisa	part (v)	skei	amaqhezu	fractions (n)	breuke
-ahlukanisa	classify (v)	klassifiseer	amashumi ayisishiyagalombili	eighty (n)	tagtig
-ahlukanisa	disconnect (v)	losmaak	amashumi amabili	twenty (n)	twintig
-ahlukanisa	segregate (v)	segregeer	amashumi amahlanu	fifty (n)	vyftig
-ahlukanisa	distinguish (v)	onderskei	amashumi amane	forty (n)	veertig
-ahlukene	distinct (a)	afsonderlik	amashumi ayishiyagalolunye	ninety (n)	neëntig
-ahlukene	separate (a)	afsonderlik	amashumi ayisikhombisa	seventy (n)	sewentig
-ahlukile	different (a)	verskillend	amashumi ayisithupha	sixty (n)	sestig
-ahlula	subdue (v)	onderwerp	amasiko nezinganekwane	folklore (n)	volksoorleweringe
-ahlula	overpower (v)	oorweldig	amasimba	faeces (n)	uitwerpsel
-ahlula	overcome (v)	te bowe kom	amasimba	excreta (n)	uitwerpsel
-ahlula	excel (v)	uitblink	amasokisi abesifazane	pantihose (n)	kousbroekie
-ahlula	master (v)	bemeester	amasokisi amade	stockings (n)	kouse
-ahlula	conquer (v)	verower	amasonto amabili	fortnight (n)	twee weke
-ahlula	baffle (v)	verbyster	amasotsha asemkhunjini	navy (n)	vloot
-akha	erect (v)	oprig	amatata	nervousness (n)	senuweeagtigheid
-akha	build (v)	bou	amathe	saliva (n)	speeksel
-akha kwelinye izwe	migrate (v)	migreer	amathe onyawo	instep (n)	boog
-akhe yedwa	private (a)	privaat	amathezane	delirium (n)	ylhoofdigheid
-akhona	local (a)	plaaslik	amathumbu	entrails (n)	ingewande
-akubantu	popular (a)	gewild	amathumbu	bowels (n)	ingewande
akukho-muntu	nobody (pron)	niemand	amazinyo	teeth (n)	tande
-ala	jilt (v)	afsê	amazolo	dew (n)	dou
-ala	refuse (v)	weier	-ami	mine (pron)	myne
-ala	forbid (v)	verbied	-amukela	receive (v)	ontvang
-alo	its (pron)	sy	-amukela	accept (v)	aanvaar
-aluka	weave (v)	weef	-amukelekayo	acceptable (a)	aanvaarbaar
-alukile	absent-minded (a)	ingedagte	-amukezela	distribute (v)	versprei
amabele	sorghum (n)	sorghum	-andisa	enlarge (v)	vergroot
amabholi	bowls (n)	rolbal	-andisa	exaggerate (v)	oordryf
amadela	abattoir (n)	slagplaas	-andulela	precede (v)	voorafgaan
amadlala asemphinjweni	tonsils (n)	mangels	-anele	enough (a)	genoeg
amafutha	fat (n)	vet	-anele	adequate (a)	voldoende
amafutha engulube	lard (n)	varkvet	-anelisa	satisfy (v)	bevredig
amagama	vocabulary (n)	woordeskat	-aphuca	deprive (v)	ontneem
amagogolosi	sunglasses (n)	sonbril	-asendle	wild (a)	wild
amagrebhisi	grape (n)	druiwe	-asendlini	domestic (a)	huishoudelik
amahemuhemu	rumour (n)	gerug	-asendulo	primitive (a)	primitief
amahemuhemu	gossip (n)	skinderpraatjies	-aseningizimu	south (a)	suid
amahloni	shame (n)	skaamte	-asenyakatho	north (a)	noord
amahluba	husk (n)	skil	ayina	iron (v)	stryk
amajaji	judiciary (n)	regbank	-azi	know (v)	weet
amajaji okugcina	appeal court (n)	appélhof	-azisa	acquaint (v)	bekend wees
amakha	fragrance (n)	geur			
amakhoba	bran (n)	semels			
amalahle	coal (n)	steenkool			
amalungiselelo	apparatus (n)	apparaat			

A	Zulu	English	Afrikaans	Zulu	English	Afrikaans
	-azisa	notify (v)	kennis gee	-bheka	look (v)	kyk
	-azisa	inform (v)	meedeel	-bhema	smoke (v)	rook
	-azisa	advertise (v)	adverteer	-bheyila	bail (v)	borg staan
	-azisa	acquaint (v)	bekend wees	-bhicika	ooze (v)	sypel
	-azisisa	ascertain (v)	vasstel	-bhikisha	demonstrate (v)	betoog
				-bhixiza	mess (v)	bemors
	-ba	be (v)	wees	-bhoboza	pierce (v)	deursteek
	-babaza	admire (v)	bewonder	-bhodla	belch (v)	wind opbreek
	-babaza	flatter (v)	vlei	-bhohoza	wheeze (v)	hyg
	-babazekile	admirable (a)	bewonderendswaardig	-bhosha	defecate (v)	ontlas
	-bala	count (v)	tel	-bhovumula	growl (v)	knor
	-baleka	escape (v)	ontsnap	-bhoxoza	wade (v)	waad
	-baleka	elope (v)	wegloop	-bhubha	perish (v)	omkom
	-baleka	flee (v)	vlug	-bhuduza	crumble (v)	verkrummel
	-balekela	shun (v)	vermy	-bhukuda	swim (v)	swem
	-balisisa	calculate (v)	reken	-bhulasha	brush (v)	borsel
	-balisisa	account (v)	rekenskap gee	-bhungula	detribalise (v)	ontstam
	-bamba	grasp (v)	gryp	-bhuqa	devastate (v)	verwoes
	-bamba	seize (v)	gryp	-bhuqa	destroy (v)	vernietig
	-bamba	hold (v)	hou	-bi	evil (a)	boos
	-bamba	catch (v)	vang	-bi	nasty (a)	gemeen
	-bamba	capture (v)	vang	-bi	ugly (a)	lelik
	-bambekile	engaged (a)	beset	-bi	bad (a)	sleg
	-bambela	reserve (v)	reserveer	-bibitheka	whimper (v)	sanik
	-ba- na-	own (v)	besit	-bika	report (v)	berig
	(-ba-) na-	have (v)	hê	-bika	declare (v)	verklaar
	-bandlululayo ngokwezinhlanga	racist (a)	rassisties	-bikezela	predict (v)	voorspel
				-bila	ferment (v)	gis
	-banga	dispute (v)	betwis	-bilisa	boil (v)	kook
	-banga isidumo	riot (v)	oproer maak	-binda	choke (v)	verstik
	-banzi	broad (a)	breed	-bingelela	greet (v)	groet
	-banzi	wide (a)	wyd	-biza	claim (v)	eis
	-befuzela	gasp (v)	snak	-biza	demand (v)	eis
	-beka	deposit (v)	deponeer	-biza	name (v)	noem
	-beka	store (v)	bêre	-biza	summon (v)	ontbied
	-beka	put (v)	sit	-biza	call (v)	roep
	-beka	set (v)	stel	-biza	charge (price) (v)	vra
	-beka icala	charge (law) (v)	aankla	-bizela	dictate (v)	voorskrywe
	-beka icala	accuse (v)	beskuldig	-bo-	must (v)	moet
	-beka inani	value (v)	waardeer	bobabili	both (a)	albei
	-bekezela	bear (v)	duld	-bocoza	dent (v)	duik
	-bekile	meek (a)	gedwee	-bola	decompose (v)	ontbind
	-bekile	patient (a)	geduldig	-bola	rot (v)	verrot
	-bekile	mild (a)	matig	-bola	decay (v)	verrot
	-benyezela	glitter (v)	skitter	-boleka	borrow (v)	leen
	-bethela	hammer (v)	hamer	-bolekisa	lend (v)	leen
	-bethela	nail (v)	spyker	-bolile	rotten (a)	verrot
	-bethela	peg (v)	vaspen	-bolile	corrupt (v)	bederf
	-bhabhadisa	baptise (v)	doop	-bomvu	red (a)	rooi
	-bhabhazisa	flap (v)	fladder	-bomvu klebhu	scarlet (n)	helderrooi
	-bhadazela	stagger (v)	slinger	-bona	see (v)	sien
	-bhadla	bubble (n)	borrel	bona	they (pron)	hulle
	-bhadla	roar (v)	brul	-bona	recognise (v)	herken
	-bhaka	bake (v)	bak	bona	their (pron)	hulle
	-bhakela	box (v)	boks	bona	them (pron)	hulle
	-bhakela	punch (v)	slaan	-bonakala	appear (v)	verskyn
	-bhala	write (v)	skryf	-bonakala	visible (a)	sigbaar
	-bhamuza	boast (v)	spog	-bonakele	obvious (a)	vanselfsprekend
	-bheja	bet (v)	wed	-bonda	stir (v)	roer
	-bheka	watch (v)	dophou	-bonga	thank (v)	bedank

Zulu	English	Afrikaans
-bonga	praise (v)	loof
-bongayo	grateful (a)	dankbaar
-bongekayo	praiseworthy (a)	lofwaardig
-bonisa	persuade (v)	oorreed
-bonisa	prove (v)	bewys
-bopha	chain (v)	vasketting
-bopha	jail (v)	opsluit
-bopha	arrest (v)	in hegtenis neem
-bopha	detain (v)	aanhou
-bopha	tie (v)	bind
-bopha	fasten (v)	vasmaak
-bopha ifindo	knot (v)	knoop
-bopha ngesipeleti	pin (v)	vasspeld
-bubula	groan (v)	kreun
-bubuza	moan (v)	kerm
-buhlungu	sore (a)	seer
-buka	view (v)	bekyk
-bukekayo	handsome (a)	aantreklik
-bukekayo	beautiful (a)	pragtig
-bukeza	revise (v)	wysig
-bukhali	sharp (a)	skerp
-bukisa	exhibit (v)	uitstal
-bulala	kill (v)	doodmaak
-bulala	murder (v)	vermoor
-bulala imbewu yokufa	disinfect (v)	ontsmet
-bulala ngomthetho	execute (v)	teregstel
-bumba	form (v)	vorm
-bunjwa	consist (v)	bestaan
-bunxele	left (a)	links
-busa	rule (v)	regeer
-busa	govern (v)	regeer
-busa	dominate (v)	oorheers
-busa	reign (v)	heers
-bushelelezi	slippery (a)	glibberig
-bushelezi	smooth (a)	glad
-busisa	bless (v)	seën
-buthana	congregate (v)	vergader
-butheleka	overcrowd (v)	oorvol wees
-buthuntu	blunt (a)	stomp
-buyisela	refund (v)	terugbetaal
-buyisile	overcast (a)	bewolk
-buza	ask (v)	vra
-buza	question (v)	vra
-buza	inquire (v)	navraag doen
-buzisisa	interrogate (v)	ondervra
-buzisisa	cross examine (v)	kruisvra
-cabanga	consider (v)	oorweeg
-cabanga	reason (v)	redeneer
-cabanga	imagine (v)	verbeel
-cabanga	suppose (v)	veronderstel
-cabanga	ponder (v)	bepeins
-cabanga	think (v)	dink
-cabangelayo	considerate (a)	bedagsaam
-cacisa umbalo omhlophe	bleach (v)	bleik
-canula	nauseate (v)	naar maak
-canulayo	annoying (a)	ergerlik
-caphuna	quote (v)	aanhaal
-casula	annoy (v)	vies maak
-casula	irritate (v)	irriteer
-caza kabili	halve (v)	halveer
-cazelana	share (v)	deel
-ceba	plot (v)	saamsweer
-cebisa	enrich (v)	verryk
-cela	request (v)	versoek
-cela	apply (v)	aansoek doen
-cela inselele	challenge (v)	uitdaag
-chachile	clear (a)	helder
-chama	urinate (v)	urineer
-chaza	explain (v)	verduidelik
-chela ngenkhasa	irrigate (v)	besproei
-chelela	water (v)	natgooi
-chichima	overflow (v)	oorloop
-chinineka	percolate (v)	perkoleer
-chitha	spill (v)	mors
-chukuluza	taunt (v)	uitlok
-chuma	prosper (v)	floreer
-chumile	prosperous (a)	florerend
-cijile	acute (a)	skerp
-cijile	keen (a)	toegewyd
-cima	extinguish (v)	blus
-cindezela	oppress (v)	onderdruk
-cindezela	compress (v)	saampers
-cindezela	squeeze (v)	druk
-cindezela	force (v)	forseer
-cindezela	depress (v)	neerdruk
-cindizela	press (v)	pers
-cindizela	print (v)	druk
-cinga	search (v)	soek
-cishe	almost (adv)	amper
-cishe	nearly (adv)	byna
-coliweyo	fine (a)	fyn
-consa	drip (v)	drup
-cula	sing (v)	sing
-cunula	offend (v)	aanstoot gee
-cunulayo	offensive (a)	aanstootlik
-cuthene	slender (a)	tingerig
-cwayiza	wink (v)	knipoog
-cwenga	skim (v)	afskep
-cwila	dive (v)	duik
-cwilisa	submerge (v)	onderdompel
-cwilisa	immerse (v)	indompel
-cwilisa	dip (v)	insteek
-cwilisa	soak (v)	week
-dabukela	regret (v)	spyt hê
-dabukile	sad (a)	treurig
-dabula	cross (v)	kruis
-dabula	tear (v)	skeur
-daka	intoxicate (v)	bedwelm
-dakisayo	alcoholic (a)	alkoholies
-dakiwe	drunk (a)	dronk
-dala	old (a)	oud
-dala	senior (a)	senior
-dala	create (v)	skep
-dala kakhulu	eldest (a)	oudste
-dana	darn (v)	stop
-de	tall (a)	lang
-de	long (a)	lang

425

D	Zulu	English	Afrikaans		Zulu	English	Afrikaans
	-debeselwe	neglect (v)	verwaarloos		-eba	steal (v)	steel
	-deka	lay (v)	dek		-edlula	overtake (v)	verbysteek
	-dela	sacrifice (v)	opoffer		-eduka	stray (a)	afdwaal
	-delela	insubordinate (a)	ongehoorsaam		-eduze	near (adv)	naby
	-delela	disregard (v)	verontagsaam		eduze	close (a)	naby
	-delela	naughty (a)	stout		-ehla	descend (v)	daal
	-dephisa	extend (v)	uitstrek		-ehlelo lezikhathi	chronological (a)	chronologies
	-dephisa	prolong (v)	verleng		zemilando		
	-dida	confuse (v)	verwar		-ehlile	low (a)	laag
	-dida	puzzle (v)	verwar		-ehlulela	judge (v)	oordeel
	-dika	belittle (v)	verkleineer		-ekhala	nasal (a)	nasaal
	-dikibalisa	frustrate (v)	frustreer		ekuqaleni	start (n)	begin
	-dikiza	feast (v)	feesvier		ekuseni	morning (n)	oggend
	-diliza	demolish (v)	afbreek		e-, kwa-	at (prep)	op
	-dinda	thrash (v)	uitklop		-elapha	heal (v)	genees
	-dingekile	necessary (a)	noodsaaklik		-elapha	treat (v)	behandel
	-dingisa	exile (v)	verban		-elaphayo	medical (a)	medies
	-dinisayo	bore (v)	verveel		-elula	elongate (v)	verleng
	-divosa	divorce (v)	skei		-emaNgisi	British (a)	Brits
	-dla	eat (v)	eet		-embesa	clothe (v)	aantrek
	-dla	confiscate (v)	beslag lê op		-embuka	rebel (v)	rebelleer
	-dla idina	dine (v)	hoofmaaltyd eet		emkhunjini	aboard (adv)	aan boord
	-dlala	play (v)	speel		-empi	military (a)	militêre
	-dledlezela	jog (v)	draf		-emuka	depart (v)	vertrek
	-dlekayo	edible (a)	eetbaar		-emuka	move (v)	trek
	-dlelezela	defy (v)	trotseer		-emukela	welcome (v)	verwelkom
	-dlukuza	jerk (v)	ruk		emuva	back (adv)	terug
	-dlula	exceed (v)	oorskry		emuva	behind (prep)	agter
	-dlula	pass (v)	verbygaan		emuva kwa-	after (time) (prep)	na
	-dlulayo konke	best (a)	beste		emuva kwa-	after (place) (prep)	agter
	-dlulisela	refer (v)	verwys		-enamile	content (a)	tevrede
	-dlwengula	rape (v)	verkrag		-enanela	echo (v)	weerklink
	-doba	fish (v)	visvang		-endoda	masculine (a)	manlik
	-donsa	draw (v)	sleep		-enezela	add (v)	byvoeg
	-donsa	tow (v)	sleep		-engama	overshadow (v)	oorskadu
	-donsa	pull (v)	trek		enhla kwa-	above (prep)	bo
	-drayiklina	dryclean (v)	droogskoonmaak		-enhlamba	bawdy (a)	onkuis
	-dubhuza	bump (v)	stamp		-enile	overgrown (a)	toegegroei
	-dubula	shoot (v)	skiet		-enqaba	reject (v)	verwerp
	-duduza	appease (v)	bevredig		entshonalanga	west (adv)	wes
	-duduza	soothe (v)	kalmeer		-enyanya	loathe (v)	verafsku
	-duduza	comfort (v)	troos		-enyanya	detest (v)	verafsku
	-dukisa	mislead (v)	mislei		-enyanyekayo	repulsive (a)	walglik
	-dukisayo	misleading (a)	misleidend		-enyelisa	sprain (v)	verstuit
	-dulile	costly (a)	kosbaar		-enyuka	ascend (v)	styg
	-dulile	expensive (a)	duur		-enyula	prefer (v)	verkies
	-duma	tasteless (a)	smaakloos		-enyusa	promote (v)	bevorder
	-dumaza	disappoint (v)	teleurstel		-enza	make (v)	maak
	-dumaza	humiliate (v)	verneder		-enza	do (v)	doen
	-dumba	bulge (v)	uitbult		-enza	perform (v)	uitvoer
	-dumile	famous (a)	beroemd		-enza	cause (v)	veroorsaak
	-dumileyo	well-known (a)	welbekend		-enza kubeluhlonzi	thicken (v)	dik maak
	-dumileyo	prominent (a)	prominent		-enza kubengcono	improve (v)	verbeter
	-duvile	stale (a)	oud		-enzekayo	possible (a)	moontlik
	-dwa	alone (a)	alleen		-enziwe	done (v)	gedoen
	-dwa	only (a)	enigste		-enziweyo nje	artificial (a)	kunsmatig
	-dwa-nje	odd (a)	onewe		-ephabhuliki	public (a)	openbaar
	-dweba	draw (v)	teken		-ephuka	break (v)	breek
					-eqa	skip (v)	oorslaan
					-eqa	spring (v)	spring

Zulu	English	Afrikaans	Zulu	English	Afrikaans	G
-eqa umthetho	trespass (v)	oortree	-finyanisa	embarrass (v)	verleë maak	
-esaba	fear (v)	vrees	-fiphala	fade (v)	verbleik	
-esabekayo	terrible (a)	vreeslik	-fiphele	dark (a)	donker	
-esabekayo	ghastly (a)	aaklig	-fiphele	dim (a)	dof	
-esibili	second (a)	tweede	-fisa	wish (v)	wens	
-esikhundla	official (a)	amptelik	-fithizile	ambiguous (a)	dubbelsinnig	
-esilisa	male (a)	manlik	-fiyuza	fuse (v)	uitbrand	
-esithathu	third (a)	derde	-fudumele	warm (a)	warm	
-esizwe	national (a)	nasionaal	-fudumele	tepid (a)	lou	
-ethasiselayo	additional (a)	bykomend	-fudumele	hot (a)	warm	
-ethemba	expect (v)	verwag	-fudumeza	heat (v)	warm maak	
-ethemba	hope (v)	hoop	-fukama	brood (v)	broei	
-ethukayo	timid (a)	skugter	-fulela	thatch (v)	dek	
-ethula	introduce (v)	voorstel	-fumanisa	discover (v)	ontdek	
-ethula	unload (v)	aflaai	-fumbathisa	bribe (v)	omkoop	
-ethula emkhunjini	land (v)	land	-funa	want (v)	wil hê	
-ethusa	frighten (v)	skrikmaak	-funda	learn (v)	leer	
-ethusa	terrify (v)	verskrik	-funda	study (v)	studeer	
-ethusa	perturb (v)	verontrus	-funda	read (v)	lees	
-etshisa	deliberate (a)	opsetlik	-fundisa	train (v)	afrig	
-eyama	depend (on) (v)	afhang (van)	-fundisa	lecture (v)	doseer	
-eyisa	scorn (v)	verag	-fundisa	instruct (v)	onderrig	
ezingavunyelwa	banned (things) (a)	verbode	-fundisa	educate (v)	opvoed	
-ezizwe ngezizwe	international (a)	internasionaal	-fundisa	coach (v)	afrig	
-ezohwebo	commercial (a)	kommersieel	-funekayo	essential (a)	essensieel	
			-fungela amanga	perjure (v)	meineed pleeg	
-fa	die (v)	doodgaan	-funza ngemfundiso ethile	indoctrinate (v)	indoktrineer	
-fafaza	sprinkle (v)	sprinkel				
-faka	include (v)	insluit	-fushane	short (a)	kort	
-faka engozini	endanger (v)	in gevaar stel	-fushane	brief (a)	beknop	
-faka isihlungu	poison (v)	vergiftig	-fushanisa	shorten (v)	verkort	
-faka itiyela	tar (v)	teer	-futha	pump (v)	pomp	
-faka ucingo	wire (v)	bedraad	-futha	inflate (v)	opblaas	
-faka uzankosi	handcuff (n)	boei	futhi	again (adv)	weer	
-fakaza	testify (v)	getuig	futhi	too (adv)	ook	
-fana	resemble (v)	aard na	futhi	also (adv)	ook	
-fanayo	same (a)	dieselfde	-fuya	breed (v)	teel	
-fanayo	alike (a)	gelyk				
-fanayo	similar (a)	eenders	-gabaza	brag (v)	grootpraat	
-fanela	deserve (v)	verdien	-gada	guard (v)	bewaak	
-fanele	just (a)	regverdig	-gamele	positive (a)	positief	
-fanelekile	eligible (a)	geskik	-gawula	chop (v)	kap	
-faneleyo	reasonable (a)	redelik	-gaya	grind (v)	maal	
-fanisa	imitate (v)	namaak	-gayiweyo	ground (a)	gemaal	
-feba	fornicate (v)	hoereer	-gcaba	vaccinate (v)	inent	
-fefeza	lisp (v)	lispel	-gcina	end (v)	eindig	
-fehleka	wilt (v)	kwyn	-gcina	keep (v)	hou	
-feza	effect (v)	bewerk	-gcinayo	last (a)	laaste	
-feza	achieve (v)	presteer	-gcizelela	insist (v)	aandring	
-fica	reach (v)	bereik	-gcizelela	emphasise (v)	beklemtoon	
-fihla	hide (v)	wegsteek	-gcoba	grease (v)	smeer	
-fihla	conceal (v)	verberg	-gcoba	anoint (v)	salf	
-fihlakele	mysterious (a)	geheimsinnig	-gcona	tease (v)	terg	
-fihliwe	hidden (a)	versteek	-gculisa	convince (v)	oortuig	
-fika	arrive (v)	aankom	-gcwalisa	fill (v)	vol maak	
-fika ezweni	immigrate (v)	immigreer	-gcwele	full (a)	vol	
-file	broken (a)	stukkend	-gedla	gnash (v)	kners	
-file	dead (a)	dood	-gegedla	gnaw (v)	knaag	
-fingciza	wrinkle (v)	plooi	-geja	miss (v)	mis	
-fingqana	contract (v)	inkrimp	-gejile	abortive (a)	misluk	

G	Zulu	English	Afrikaans		Zulu	English	Afrikaans
	-gembula	gamble (v)	dobbel		-hhuka	hook (v)	haak
	-gemenca	flirt (v)	flirteer		-hlaba	criticise (v)	kritiseer
	-geza	wash (v)	was		-hlaba	inject (v)	inspuit
	-gibela	ride (v)	ry		-hlaba	sting (v)	steek
	-gigitheka	giggle (v)	giggel		-hlaba	slaughter (v)	slag
	-gijima	run (v)	hardloop		-hlaba	stab (v)	steek
	-gingqika	roll (v)	rol		-hlaba ihele	queue (v)	toustaan
	-goba	bend (v)	buig		-hlafuna	chew (v)	kou
	-goba	bow (v)	buk		-hlahlela	analyse (v)	ontleed
	-gobhoza	flow (v)	vloei		-hlakaniphile	astute (a)	slim
	-goduka	return (v)	terugkeer		-hlakaniphile	sane (a)	verstandig
	-goga	cripple (v)	kreupel maak		-hlakaniphile	wise (a)	wys
	-gogobala	crouch (v)	buk		-hlakaniphile	talented (a)	talentvol
	-goma	immunise (v)	immuniseer		-hlakanyeka	shudder (v)	sidder
	-gona	embrace (v)	omhels		-hlakaza	disperse (v)	verstrooi
	-gonyiwe	immune (a)	onvatbaar		-hlakula	hoe (v)	skoffel
	-gqabuka	rupture (v)	skeur		-hlakula	weed (v)	onkruid uittrek
	-gqekeza	burgle (v)	inbreek		-hlala	sit (v)	sit
	-gqoka	wear (v)	dra		-hlala isikhathi	last (v)	voortduur
	-gqokisa	dress (v)	aantrek		-hlala phansi	retire (v)	aftree
	-gqoloza	stare (v)	staar		-hlalayo	permanent (a)	permanent
	-gqugquzela	urge (v)	aanspoor		-hlalayo	lasting (a)	voortdurend
	-gubha umkhosi	celebrate (v)	vier		-hlalisa	house (v)	huisves
	-gudleka	chafe (v)	skaaf		-hlambulula	dilute (v)	verdun
	-guga	age (v)	verouder		-hlangana	convene (v)	byeenroep
	-gugile	aged (a)	oud		-hlangana	copulate (v)	kopuleer
	-gula	ill (a)	siek		-hlangana	gather (v)	byeenkom
	-gulayo	sick (a)	siek		-hlangana na-	meet (v)	ontmoet
	-gulisa	sicken (v)	siek word		-hlanganisa	combine (v)	kombineer
	-gumbeqeka	capsize (v)	omkantel		-hlanganisa	join (v)	las
	-gunquza	rattle (v)	ratel		-hlanganisa	pack (v)	pak
	-guqa	kneel (v)	kniel		-hlanganisa	connect (v)	verbind
	-guquka	repent (v)	berou hê		-hlanganisa	unite (v)	verenig
	-gweda	perfect (a)	volmaak		-hlanganisa	attach (v)	aanheg
	-gwedla	row (v)	roei		-hlangene	together (adv)	saam
	-gwema	avoid (v)	vermy		-hlanyayo	insane (a)	kranksinnig
	-gwinya	swallow (v)	sluk		-hlanza	cleanse (v)	skoonmaak
	-gxoba	pound (v)	fynstamp		-hlanza	clean (v)	skoonmaak
	-gxoba ngamatshe	stone (v)	met klippe gooi		-hlanza	vomit (v)	vomeer
					-hlanza	purge (v)	skoonmaak
	-habula	sip (v)	slurp		-hlanza	purify (v)	suiwer
	-hahaza	gargle (v)	gorrel		-hlanzekile	clean (a)	skoon
	-halalisa	applaud (v)	toejuig		-hlaphazayo	extravagant (a)	buitensporig
	-halalisela	congratulate (v)	gelukwens		-hlasela	invade (v)	inval
	-hamba	walk (v)	loop		-hlasela	assault (v)	aanrand
	-hamba	travel (v)	reis		-hlasela	attack (v)	aanval
	-hamba	step (v)	trap		-hlasela	raid (v)	stroop
	-hamba	tour (v)	rondreis		-hlaselayo	aggressive (a)	aanvallend
	-hamba ngamazwani	tiptoe (v)	op die tone loop		-hlawula	fine (v)	beboet
	-hamba phambili	lead (v)	lei		-hlawulisa	penalise (v)	straf
	-hambisanayo	parallel (n)	parallel		-hle	fair (a)	billik
	-hanguza	singe (v)	skroei		-hle	ideal (a)	ideaal
	-hawukela	envy (v)	beny		-hle	pretty (a)	mooi
	-hawukelayo	envious (a)	jaloers		-hle	good (a)	goed
	-heha	attract (v)	aantrek		-hleba	slander (n)	laster
	-hela	sniff (v)	snuif		-hleba	whisper (v)	fluister
	-hemuza	gossip (v)	skinder		-hlebela	confide (v)	vertroulik meedeel
	-hhala	rake (v)	hark		-hlehlisa	suspend (v)	opskort
	-hhewula	howl (v)	tjank		-hlehlisa	postpone (v)	uitstel
					-hlehlisa	adjourn (v)	verdaag

428

Zulu	English	Afrikaans	Zulu	English	Afrikaans
-hleka	ridicule (v)	bespot	i-asidi	acid (n)	suur
-hleka	laugh (v)	lag	i-athletiki	athletics (n)	atletiek
-hle kakhulu	excellent (a)	uitmuntend	i-atmosfiye	atmosphere (n)	atmosfeer
-hleka uzulu	flout (v)	hoon	i-awa	hour (n)	uur
-hlekisayo	funny (a)	snaaks	i-ayisingi	icing (n)	versiersuiker
-hlekisayo	comic (a)	komies	ibala	spot (n)	kol
-hlela	edit (v)	redigeer	ibala	stain (n)	vlek
-hlela	arrange (v)	skik	ibalana	speck (n)	stippel
-hlela	organise (v)	reël	ibandla	council (n)	raad
-hlenga	redeem (v)	goedmaak	ibandla	congregation (n)	gemeente
-hlihla	fizz (v)	bruis	ibandla	assembly (n)	vergadering
-hlikihla	rub (v)	vryf	ibandla labasizi bejaji	jury (n)	jurie
-hlinza	operate (v)	opereer	ibanga	distance (n)	afstand
-hlobisa	decorate (v)	versier	ibanga lokukhula	adolescence (n)	adolessensie
-hlokoma	murmur (n)	gemurmel	ibele	teat (n)	tepel
-hlola	investigate (v)	ondersoek	ibhakede	bucket (n)	emmer
-hlola	inspect (v)	inspekteer	ibhakthiriya	bacteria (n)	bakterie
-hlola	test (v)	toets	ibhala	wheelbarrow (n)	kruiwa
-hlola	spy (v)	spioeneer	ibhalbhu	bulb (n)	bol
-hlola	explore (v)	verken	ibhamuza	balloon (n)	ballon
-hlola	scout (v)	rondkyk	ibhamuza	blister (n)	blaar
-hlolisisa	check (v)	nagaan	ibhande	belt (n)	gordel
-hloma	arm (v)	bewapen	ibhande lemoto	seatbelt (n)	sitplekgordel
-hlonipha	honour (v)	eer	ibhange	bank (n)	bank
-hlonipha	respect (v)	respekteer	ibhantshi	jacket (n)	baadjie
-hlosa	intend (v)	van plan wees	ibhantshi	coat (n)	jas
-hluba	strip (v)	ontbloot	ibhasi	bus (n)	bus
-hluba	moult (v)	verhaar	ibhathanathi	butternut (n)	botterskorsie
-hluba	peel (v)	skil	ibhavulumu	bathroom (n)	badkamer
-hlukana	vary (v)	varieer	ibhawodi	bolt (n)	bout
-hlula	defeat (v)	verslaan	iBhayibheli	Bible (n)	Bybel
-hluleka	fail (v)	misluk	ibhayisikili	bicycle (n)	fiets
-hluma	sprout (v)	uitloop	ibhayisikobho	cinema (n)	bioskoop
-hlupheka	suffer (v)	ly	ibhayoloji	biology (n)	biologie
-hluphekile	unhappy (a)	ongelukkig	ibheja	bear (n)	beer
-hluthulela	lock (v)	sluit	ibhendi	band (n)	orkes
-hlwitha	snatch (v)	gaps	ibhenjo	banjo (n)	banjo
-holobha	gallop (v)	galop	ibhentshi	bench (n)	bank
-hona	snore (v)	snork	ibhethili	battery (n)	battery
-hoshozile	hoarse (a)	hees	ibheyili	bail (n)	borg
-hudula	drag (v)	sleep	ibhikawozi	bakery (n)	bakkery
-humusha	interpret (v)	vertolk	ibhilihaziya	bilharzia (n)	bilharzia
-humusha	translate (v)	vertaal	ibhilikosi	apricot (n)	appelkoos
-huquza	wallow (v)	wentel	ibhiskidi	biscuit (n)	koekie
-hwamuka	evaporate (v)	verdamp	ibhithi	beat (n)	ritme
-hwaqabala	frown (v)	frons	ibhithrudi	beetroot (n)	beet
-hwaqabala	scowl (v)	suur kyk	ibhodi	board (n)	bord
-hweba	trade (v)	handel dryf	ibhodlela	bottle (n)	bottel
-hweba	barter (v)	ruil	ibhodwe	pot (n)	pot
			ibhokisi	box (n)	doos
i-abakhusi	abacus (n)	telraam	ibhola	ball (n)	bal
i-ajenda	agenda (n)	agenda	ibhomu	bomb (n)	bom
i-akhawunti	account (n)	rekening	ibhomu eligqitshwayo	landmine (n)	landmyn
i-aleji	allergy (n)	allergie	ibhotela	butter (n)	botter
i-alfabhethi	alphabet (n)	alfabet	ibhu	moth (n)	mot
i-algi	alga (n)	alg	ibhubesi	lion (n)	leeu
i-alibi	alibi (n)	alibi	ibhubesi lensikazi	lioness (n)	leeuwyfie
i-ambulense	ambulance (n)	ambulans	ibhulakufesi	breakfast (n)	ontbyt
i-antena	antenna (n)	lugdraad	ibhulashi	brush (n)	borsel
i-apula	apple (n)	appel	ibhulawozi	blouse (n)	bloes

Zulu	English	Afrikaans	Zulu	English	Afrikaans
ibhulayindi	blind (n)	blinding	idwala	rock (n)	rots
ibhuliki	brake (n)	rem	i-ekseli	axle (n)	as
ibhuloho	bridge (n)	brug	i-engele	angle (n)	hoek
ibhulukwe	trousers (n)	langbroek	i-eriya	area (n)	oppervlakte
ibhungane	beetle (n)	kewer	ifa	inheritance (n)	erfenis
iBhunu	Afrikaner (n)	Afrikaner	ifa	heritage (n)	erfenis
ibika	omen (n)	voorteken	ifasitela	window (n)	venster
ibizo	noun (n)	selfstandige naamwoord	ifasitela lemoto langaphambili	windscreen (n)	voorruit
ibizo	term (n)	term	ifayili	file (n)	vyl
ibizo	title (n)	titel	ifektri	factory (n)	fabriek
ibololwane	swarm (n)	swerm	ifenisha	furniture (n)	meubels
ibunzi	forehead (n)	voorhoof	ifilimu	film (n)	film
ibutho	band (n)	groep	ifindo	knot (n)	knoop
ibuya	tide (n)	gety	ifiyuzi	fuse (n)	sekering
ibuya	backwash (n)	terugspoeling	ifoliji	oats (n)	hawer
icala	charge (n)	aanklag	ifosholo	shovel (n)	skoppie
icala	edge (n)	rand	ifriji	refrigerator (n)	yskas
icala	side (n)	sy	ifu	cloud (n)	wolk
icala	guilt (n)	skuld	ifuku	hovel (n)	pondok
icala elibekwayo	accusation (n)	beskuldiging	ifulagi	flag (n)	vlag
icala lokushisa	arson (n)	brandstigting	ifulanela	flannel (n)	flanel
icansi	mat (n)	mat	igagasi	wave (n)	brander
icasha	birthmark (n)	moedervlek	igalaji	garage (n)	motorhawe
icebo	plot (n)	komplot	igalari	gallery (n)	galery
icebo	pretext (n)	voorwendsel	igalari yokobuciko	art gallery (n)	kunsgalery
ichaphazela	blot (n)	klad	igama	name (n)	naam
ichibi	lake (n)	meer	igama	word (n)	woord
ichibi	pool (n)	poel	igama mbumbulu	alias (n)	alias
ichibi lokuhlamba	swimming pool (n)	swembad	igatha	gutter (n)	geut
ichilo	scandal (n)	skandaal	igatsha	branch (n)	tak
ichweba	lagoon (n)	strandmeer	igatshana	twig (n)	takkie
icici	earring (n)	oorring	igayidi	guide (n)	gids
icilongo	trumpet (n)	trompet	igazi	blood (n)	bloed
icimbi	caterpillar (n)	ruspe	igedlela	kettle (n)	ketel
iconsi	drip (n)	drup	igeja	plough (n)	ploeg
iconsi	raindrop (n)	reëndruppel	igeji	gauge (n)	meter
iculo	song (n)	liedjie	igeli	gear (n)	rat
icwecwe lepulangwe lokucwila	diving board (n)	duikplank	igengi	gang (n)	bende
idada	duck (n)	eend	igenqeza	rattle (n)	ratel
idamu	dam (n)	dam	igesi	gas (n)	gas
idayabhithizi	diabetes (n)	suikersiekte	igilavu	glove (n)	handskoen
idayimani	diamond (n)	diamant	igilibhufuluthi	grapefruit (n)	pomelo
idazini	dozen (n)	dosyn	igilosa	groceries (n)	kruideniersware
idesiki	desk (n)	lessenaar	igobolondo	shell (n)	skulp
idethi	date (n)	datum	igobolondo leqanda	eggshell (n)	eierdop
idili	feast (n)	fees	igolide	gold (n)	goud
idimoni	demon (n)	bose gees	igorila	guerrilla (n)	guerrilla
idina	dinner (n)	hoofmaal	igotshwa	penknife (n)	knipmes
idina	lunch (n)	middagete	igqubu	grudge (n)	wrok
idivosi	divorce (n)	egskeiding	igquma	dune (n)	duin
idlala	gland (n)	klier	igquma	hill (n)	heuwel
idlelo	container (n)	houer	igrama	grammar (n)	grammatika
idlelo	pasture (n)	weiveld	igrisi	grease (n)	ghries
idolo	knee (n)	knie	igugu	treasure (n)	skat
idolobha	town (n)	dorp	iguma	waist (n)	middel
idolobha	city (n)	stad	igundane	mouse (n)	muis
idolobhana	village (n)	dorpie	igundane	rat (n)	rot
idube	zebra (n)	sebra	igunya	authority (n)	gesag
iduku	handkerchief (n)	sakdoek	igwababa	crow (n)	kraai

Zulu	English	Afrikaans	Zulu	English	Afrikaans	**I**
igwala	coward (n)	lafaard	ikhabe	watermelon (n)	waatlemoen	
igwinci	zigzag (n)	sigsag	ikhabethe	cupboard (n)	kas	
ihalavu	spade (n)	graaf	ikhabishi	cabbage (n)	kool	
ihansi	goose (n)	gans	ikhadi	card (n)	kaart	
ihawa	shield (n)	skild	ikhadibhodi	cardboard (n)	karton	
ihayifini	hyphen (n)	koppelteken	ikhadi lokukweleta	credit card (n)	kredietkaart	
ihele	queue (n)	tou	ikhala	nostril (n)	neusgat	
ihembe	shirt (n)	hemp	ikhala	nose (n)	neus	
ihemubhega	hamburger (n)	hamburger	ikhalenda	calendar (n)	kalender	
ihhala	rake (n)	hark	ikhalothi	carrot (n)	wortel	
ihhashi	horse (n)	perd	ikhambi	herbs (n)	kruie	
ihhashi lomjaho	racehorse (n)	renperd	ikhamela	camel (n)	kameel	
ihholo	hall (n)	saal	ikhamera	camera (n)	kamera	
ihhotela	hotel (n)	hotel	ikhanda	head (n)	kop	
ihhovisi	office (n)	kantoor	ikhandlela	candle (n)	kers	
ihhovisilamathikithi	ticket office (n)	kaartjieskantoor	ikharavani	caravan (n)	karavaan	
ihhuku	hook (n)	haak	ikhasi	page (n)	bladsy	
ihilikiqi	scoundrel (n)	skobbejak	ikhasi	leaf (n)	blaar	
ihinji	hinge (n)	hingsel	ikhasi	peel (n)	skil	
ihlanze	bushveld (n)	bosveld	ikhasimende	client (n)	kliënt	
ihlanze	lowveld (n)	laeveld	ikhathalogi	catalogue (n)	katalogus	
ihlathi	bush (n)	bos	ikhaya	home (n)	tuiste	
ihlathi	forest (n)	bos	ikhaya	dwelling (n)	woning	
ihlathi	jungle (n)	oerwoud	ikhaya lezintandane	orphanage (n)	weeshuis	
ihlawulo	penalty (n)	straf	ikhayithi	kite (n)	vlieër	
ihlaya	joke (n)	grap	ikhefana	comma (n)	komma	
ihlazo	disgrace (n)	skande	ikhefi	café (n)	kafee	
ihlelo	district (n)	distrik	ikhefu	interval (n)	pouse	
ihlelo	system (n)	stelsel	ikhekhe	cake (n)	koek	
ihlelo lemali	tariff (n)	tarief	ikhekhe	tart (n)	tert	
ihlobo	summer (n)	somer	ikheli	address (n)	adres	
ihlombe	shoulder (n)	skouer	ikhethini	curtain (n)	gordyn	
ihodogi	hot dog (n)	worsbroodjie	ikhilikithi	cricket (n)	krieket	
iholide	holiday (n)	vakansie	ikhilisi	crease (n)	kreukel	
iholo	income (n)	inkomste	ikhishi	kitchen (n)	kombuis	
iholo	salary (n)	salaris	ikhiwane	fig (n)	vy	
ihubo	hymn (n)	gesang	ikhofi	coffee (n)	koffie	
ihubo	psalm (n)	psalm	ikhofini	coffin (n)	doodskis	
ihubo lesizwe	anthem (n)	volkslied	ikholiji	college (n)	kollege	
ijaji	judge (n)	regter	ikholoni	colon (n)	dubbelpunt	
ijazi	overcoat (n)	oorjas	ikholwa	believer (n)	gelowige	
ijazi lemvula	raincoat (n)	reënjas	ikhomedi	comedy (n)	komedie	
ijele	prison (n)	gevangenis	ikhomishani	commission (n)	kommissie	
ijele	jail (n)	tronk	ikhompasi	compass (n)	kompas	
ijemu	germ (n)	kiem	ikhomputha	computer (n)	rekenaar	
ijezi	jersey (n)	trui	ikhona	corner (n)	hoek	
ijoka	yoke (n)	juk	ikhonsathi	concert (n)	konsert	
ijuba	pigeon (n)	duif	ikhophi	copy (document) (n)	afskrif	
ijubane	speed (n)	spoed	ikhophi	copy (book) (n)	eksemplaar	
ijusi	juice (n)	sap	ikhositshumu	costume (n)	kostuum	
ijwabu lehlo	eyelid (n)	ooglid	ikhowe	mushroom (n)	sampioen	
ikalikuni	turkey (n)	kalkoen	ikhukhamba	cucumber (n)	komkommer	
ikalishi	cart (n)	kar	ikhulu	century (sport) (n)	honderdtal	
ikamelo	room (n)	kamer	ikhulu	hundred (n)	honderd	
ikamelo lokudlela	dining room (n)	eetkamer	ikhulu leminyaka	century (n)	eeu	
ikamelo lokulala	bedroom (n)	slaapkamer	ikhunkulo	rheumatism (n)	rumatiek	
ikamu	comb (n)	kam	ikhwapha	armpit (n)	armholte	
ikati	cat (n)	kat	ikhwelo	whistle (n)	fluit	
iketanga	chain (n)	ketting	ikhwilithi	quilt (n)	verekombers	
ikhabe	melon (n)	meloen	ikilobhu	club (n)	klub	

I	Zulu	English	Afrikaans	Zulu	English	Afrikaans
	iklarinethi	clarinet (n)	klarinet	imbobo kakhiye	keyhole (n)	sleutelgat
	iklashi	clutch (n)	koppelaar	imbobo yenkinobho	buttonhole (n)	knoopsgat
	iklasi	class (n)	klas	imbongi	poet (n)	digter
	iklayimethi	climate (n)	klimaat	imbongolo	donkey (n)	donkie
	ikliniki	clinic (n)	kliniek	imbongolo	ass (n)	donkie
	iklogo	clock (n)	horlosie	imbubuzi	moan (n)	gekerm
	ikomiti	committee (n)	komitee	imbuka	rebel (n)	rebel
	iKrestu	Christian (n)	Christen	imbuka	traitor (n)	verraaier
	ikusasa	future (n)	toekoms	imbuki	deserter (n)	droster
	ikwata	quarter (n)	kwart	imbungulu	bedbug (n)	weeluis
	ikwaya	choir (n)	koor	imbuzi	goat (n)	bok
	ilabhulali	library (n)	biblioteek	imeli	mare (n)	merrie
	ilahle	cinder (n)	sintel	imendlela	medal (n)	medalje
	ilanga	sun (n)	son	imenyu	menu (n)	spyskaart
	ilangabi	flame (n)	vlam	imephu	map (n)	landkaart
	ilathi	altar (n)	altaar	imeya	mayor (n)	burgemeester
	ilawunji	lounge (n)	sitkamer	imfanelo	duty (n)	plig
	ilayisense	licence (n)	lisensie	imfene	baboon (n)	bobbejaan
	ilebula	label (n)	etiket	imfengwane	pennywhistle (n)	kwêlafluitjie
	ilesheni	ration (n)	rantsoen	imfeshini	fashion (n)	mode
	iletha lokuqala	initial (n)	voorletter	imfihlakalo	mystery (n)	misterie
	ileveli	level (n)	vlak	imfihlo	secret (n)	geheim
	ilifi	lift (n)	hyser	imfiliji	mouth organ (n)	mondfluitjie
	ilitshe	stone (n)	klip	imfingo	shark (n)	haai
	ilivi	leave (n)	verlof	imfiva	fever (n)	koors
	ilojiki	logic (n)	logika	imfologo	fork (n)	vurk
	ilokwe	dress (n)	rok	imfologo yotshani	pitchfork (n)	gaffel
	iloli	lorry (n)	vragmotor	imfoloko	pockmark (n)	pokmerk
	ilondolo	laundry (n)	wassery	imfulomu	lining (n)	voering
	ilulwane	bat (n)	vlermuis	imfuluyenza	influenza (n)	griep
	ilunga	syllable (n)	lettergreep	imfunda-makhwele	amateur (n)	amateur
	ilunga	member (n)	lid	imfundo	education (n)	opvoeding
	ilungelo	qualification (n)	kwalifikasie	imfundo ephakeme	academy (n)	akademie
	ilungelo lokuvota	franchise (n)	kiesreg	imibhalo	literature (n)	letterkunde
	ilungu	element (n)	element	imigilingwane	gymnastics (n)	gimnastiek
	ilungu lasebandla	councillor (n)	raadslid	yokuzivivinya		
	imagi	mug (n)	beker	imini	midday (n)	middag
	imakethe	market (n)	mark	imini	noon (n)	middag
	imakhroweyivi	microwave (n)	mikrogolf	iminithi	minute (n)	minuut
	imali	money (n)	geld	iminyaka eyishumi	decade (n)	dekade
	imali eholwayo	earnings (n)	loon	imitha	metre (n)	meter
	imali elondoloziwe	savings (n)	spaargeld	imithombo	malt (n)	mout
	imali yephepha	banknote (n)	banknoot	imizoko	haemorrhoids (n)	aambeie
	imali yokukhwela	fare (n)	reisgeld	imnyuziyamu	museum (n)	museum
	imashi	march (n)	mars	imothela	motel (n)	motel
	imathimathiki	mathematics (n)	wiskunde	imoto	motorcar (n)	motor
	imayela	mile (n)	myl	imoto	car (n)	motor
	imbali	flower (n)	blom	impahla	property (n)	eiendom
	imbandezeka	anxiety (n)	kommer	impahla	stock (n)	voorraad
	imbangela	stimulus (n)	stimulus	impahla yendlela	luggage (n)	bagasie
	imbangi	rival (n)	mededinger	impakatha	deputy (n)	plaasvervanger
	imbangi	antagonist (n)	teenstander	impama	slap (n)	klap
	imbazo	axe (n)	byl	impambano	disagreement (n)	meningsverskil
	imbemba	battle-axe (n)	strydbyl	impande	root (n)	wortel
	imbewu	seed (n)	saad	impande	radicle (n)	wortel
	imbila	dassie (n)	dassie	impangele	guineafowl (n)	tarentaal
	imbilapho	groin (n)	lies	impatho eqinileyo	discipline (n)	dissipline
	imbizana	jar (n)	fles	impela	quite (a)	taamlik
	imbobo	leak (n)	lek	impela	indeed (adv)	werklik
	imbobo	puncture (n)	lekplek	impelamehlo	horizon (n)	horison

Zulu	English	Afrikaans	Zulu	English	Afrikaans	I
impelesi	bridesmaid (n)	strooimeisie	indawo	scene (n)	toneel	
impenduko	conversion (n)	omsetting	indawo ehlanganisiweyo	join (n)	lasplek	
impendulo	answer (n)	antwoord	indawo engenampilo	slum (n)	krotbuurt	
impendulo	reply (n)	antwoord	indawo yamathuna	cemetery (n)	begraafplaas	
impesheni	pension (n)	pensioen	indawo yasendle	field (n)	veld	
impethu	worm (n)	wurm	indawo yokuhlala	accommodation (n)	huisvesting	
impi	battle (n)	geveg	nokulala			
impi	war (n)	oorlog	indawo yokuthenga	box office (n)	kaartjieloket	
impi	army (n)	leër	amathikithi			
impilo	health (n)	gesondheid	indawo yokuzalwa	birthplace (n)	geboorteplek	
impilo	life (n)	lewe	indebe	ladle (n)	skeplepel	
impilo yasendle	wildlife (n)	natuurlewe	indelelo	contempt (n)	veragting	
impindiselo	vengeance (n)	wraak	indesheni	salute (n)	saluut	
impisi	hyena (n)	hiëna	indida	puzzle (n)	legkaart	
impofu	eland (n)	eland	indikimba	theme (n)	tema	
impohlo	bachelor (n)	jongkêrel	indima	verse (n)	vers	
impophoma	waterfall (n)	waterval	indishi	dish (n)	skottel	
impoqa	terrorism (n)	terrorisme	indiza	aircraft (n)	vliegtuig	
impova	pollen (n)	stuifmeel	indizamshini	aeroplane (n)	vliegtuig	
impubumpubu	lout (n)	takhaar	indlala	famine (n)	hongersnood	
impucuko	civilisation (n)	beskawing	indlalifa	heir (n)	erfgenaam	
impukane	fly (n)	vlieg	indle	veld (n)	veld	
impumalanga	east (n)	ooste	indle	wilderness (n)	wildernis	
impumelelo	sequel (n)	gevolg	indlebe	ear (n)	oor	
impumelelo	achievement (n)	prestasie	indlela	path (n)	pad	
impumelelo	success (n)	sukses	indlela	way (n)	pad	
impumulo	muzzle (n)	snoet	indlela yenqubo	procedure (n)	prosedure	
impungushe	jackal (n)	jakkals	indlovu	elephant (n)	olifant	
impunzi	duiker (n)	duiker	indlovukazi	queen (n)	koningin	
imvalamlomo	bribery (n)	omkopery	indlu	house (n)	huis	
imvelo	nature (n)	natuur	indlulamithi	giraffe (n)	kameelperd	
imvilophu	envelope (n)	koevert	indlu yenja	kennel (n)	hondehok	
imvu	sheep (n)	skaap	indlu yokudlela	restaurant (n)	restaurant	
imvubelo	yeast (n)	gis	indlwana	cottage (n)	kothuis	
imvubu	hippopotamus (n)	seekoei	indoda	man (n)	man	
imvula	rain (n)	reën	indodana	son (n)	seun	
imvume	approval (n)	goedkeuring	indololwane	elbow (n)	elmboog	
imvume	permission (n)	toestemming	indophi	rope (n)	tou	
imvumelano	contract (n)	kontrak	indophi enohlonze	cable (n)	kabel	
imvumelwano	rhyme (n)	rym	indudumela yomhlaba	earthquake (n)	aardbewing	
imvuso	alarm (n)	alarm	induduzo	comfort (n)	troos	
imvuthu	crumb (n)	krummel	indudwane	weevil (n)	kalander	
inalidi yokunitha	knitting needle (n)	breinaald	induku	stick (n)	stok	
inaliti	needle (n)	naald	indumalo	disappointment (n)	teleurstelling	
inani	value (n)	waarde	induna	chief (n)	hoofman	
inani labantu	population (n)	bevolking	indwandwe	heron (n)	reier	
inantshi	naartjie (n)	nartjie	indwangu	cloth (n)	doek	
incasiselo	explanation (n)	verduideliking	indwangu	material (n)	lap	
incazelo	meaning (n)	betekenis	indwangu yetafula	tablecloth (n)	tafeldoek	
incwadi	book (n)	boek	inephi	nappy (n)	babadoek	
incwadi	letter (n)	brief	ingadi	garden (n)	tuin	
incwadi efungelwe	affidavit (n)	beëdigde verklaring	ingalo	arm (n)	arm	
incwadi yamabalazwe	atlas (n)	atlas	ingalo	forearm (n)	voorarm	
indaba	case (n)	saak	ingane	toddler (n)	peuter	
indaba	story (n)	verhaal	ingane esancelayo	infant (n)	suigeling	
indaba elotshiweyo	essay (n)	opstel	inganekwane	tale (n)	storie	
indali	auction (n)	veiling	ingaphakathi	interior (n)	binneste	
indali	sale (n)	uitverkoping	ingaphansi	bottom (n)	bodem	
indandatho	ring (n)	ring	ingcili	tapeworm (n)	lintwurm	
indawo	place (n)	plek	ingcino	wax (n)	was	

Zulu	English	Afrikaans
ingele	sleet (n)	ysreën
ingelosi	angel (n)	engel
ingide	padlock (n)	hangslot
ingilazi	glass (n)	glas
ingilazi yewayini	wineglass (n)	wynkelkie
ingilazi yezibuko	contact lens (n)	kontaklens
ingoma	ballad (n)	ballade
ingono	nipple (n)	tepel
ingosi yethelefoni	telephone booth (n)	telefoonhokkie
ingozi	injury (n)	besering
ingozi	peril (n)	gevaar
ingozi	danger (n)	gevaar
ingozi	accident (n)	ongeluk
ingozi	casualty (n)	ongeval
ingozi	emergency (n)	noodgeval
ingozi	risk (n)	risiko
ingqangasi	bristle (n)	steekhaar
ingqapheli	observer (n)	waarnemer
ingqikithi	essence (n)	essensie
ingqondo	meaning (n)	bedoeling
ingqondo	purpose (n)	oogmerk
ingqondo	sense (n)	sin
ingquza	anus (n)	anus
ingqwababa	collarbone (n)	sleutelbeen
ingqwele	champion (n)	kampioen
ingubo	blanket (n)	kombers
ingulube	pig (n)	vark
ingulube yensikazi	sow (n)	sog
ingulule	cheetah (n)	jagluiperd
ingungumbane	porcupine (n)	ystervark
inguquko	change (n)	verandering
ingutshana yokubopha amabele	brassière (n)	bra
ingwe	leopard (n)	luiperd
ingwenya	crocodile (n)	krokodil
ingxabulela	sandal (n)	sandaal
ingxibongo	smallpox (n)	waterpokkies
ingxoxo	discussion (n)	bespreking
ingxoxo	interview (n)	onderhoud
ingxoxo	talk (n)	praatjie
inhlakanipho	intelligence (n)	intelligensie
inhlakanipho	wisdom (n)	wysheid
inhlalakahle	welfare (n)	welsyn
inhlama	dough (n)	deeg
inhlamba	insult (n)	belediging
inhlamba	obscenity (n)	onbetaamlikheid
inhlambi	swimmer (n)	swemmer
inhlamvu	bullet (n)	koeël
inhlamvu kaphizi	pea (n)	ertjie
inhlamvu yomuthi eqathwayo	nut (n)	neut
inhlangano	congress (n)	kongres
inhlangano	organisation (n)	organisasie
inhlangano	society (n)	vereniging
inhlangano yamathambo	joint (n)	gewrig
inhlangano yobambiswano	co-operation (n)	koöperasie
inhlanhla	luck (n)	geluk
inhlansi	spark (n)	vonk
inhlanzeko	hygiene (n)	higiëne
inhlanzi	fish (n)	vis
inhlaselo	invasion (n)	inval
inhlawulo	fine (n)	boete
inhliziyo	heart (n)	hart
inhliziyo	humour (n)	humor
inhloli	spy (n)	spioen
inhloli	scout (n)	verkenner
inhlolo	test (n)	toets
inhlonhla	diaphragm (n)	diafragma
inhlonhlo	peninsula (n)	skiereiland
inhlonipho	honour (n)	eer
inhloso	aim (n)	doel
inhlumba	bunion (n)	knokkeleelt
inhlupheko	affliction (n)	beproewing
inhlwathi	python (n)	luislang
iningizimu	south (n)	suide
inja	dog (n)	hond
injabulo	delight (n)	blydskap
injabulo	happiness (n)	geluk
injabulo	pleasure (n)	plesier
injabulo	joy (n)	vreugde
injakazi	bitch (n)	teef
injini	engine (n)	enjin
injoloba	elastic (n)	rek
injoloba	rubber (n)	wisser
injongo	goal (n)	doel
injwayelo	habit (n)	gewoonte
inkaba	navel (n)	naeltjie
inkabazwe	equator (n)	ewenaar
inkabi	ox (n)	os
inkalankala	crab (n)	krap
inkambu	camp (n)	kamp
inkambu	paddock (n)	veekampie
inkangala	highveld (n)	hoëveld
inkantini	bar (n)	kroeg
inkantolo	court (n)	hof
inkantolo yamaJaji	supreme court (n)	hooggeregshof
inkanuko	desire (n)	begeerte
inkanuko	appetite (n)	eetlus
inkanuko	lust (n)	wellus
inkanyezi	star (n)	ster
inkasa	irrigation (n)	besproeiing
inkathazo	trouble (n)	moeite
inkathazo	plague (n)	plaag
inkathazo	pest (n)	pes
inkathazo	nuisance (n)	steurnis
inkawu	monkey (n)	aap
inkazimulo	glory (n)	glorie
inkemba	sword (n)	swaard
inkhohliso	deceit (n)	bedrog
inkinga	problem (n)	probleem
inkinobho	button (n)	knoop
inkintshela yokuhlobisa	bow (n)	strik
inkohliso	fraud (n)	bedrog
inkohliso	dishonesty (n)	oneerlikheid
inkohliso	trick (n)	skelmstreek
inkokhelo	payment (n)	betaling
inkokhelo	pay (n)	betaling
inkolo	religion (n)	godsdiens

434

Zulu	English	Afrikaans	Zulu	English	Afrikaans
inkomazi	cow (n)	koei	insonge	curl (n)	krul
inkomba	index (n)	indeks	insumo	fable (n)	fabel
inkomishi	cup (n)	koppie	insumo	myth (n)	mite
inkomponi	compound (n)	kampong	insumpa	wart (n)	vrat
inkondlo	poem (n)	gedig	insunsumba	pimple (n)	puisie
inkonsitini esalupiyani	accordion (n)	trekklavier	inswelo	need (n)	behoefte
inkonyane	calf (n)	kalf	intaba	mountain (n)	berg
inkonyane	dimple (n)	kuiltjie	intabamlilo	volcano (n)	vulkaan
inkonyane yehhashi	foal (n)	vulletjie	intambama	afternoon (n)	middag
iNkosi	Lord (n)	Here	intambo	line (n)	lyn
inkosi	king (n)	koning	intambo	thong (n)	riem
inkosikazi	lady (n)	dame	intambo	string (n)	tou
inkositini	concertina (n)	konsertina	intambo yesicathulo	shoelace (n)	skoenveter
inkukhu	chicken (n)	hoender	intambo yokudonsa	tow rope (n)	sleeptou
inkukhu	fowl (n)	hoender	intamo	neck (n)	nek
inkululeko	release (n)	loslating	intandane	orphan (n)	weeskind
inkululeko	freedom (n)	vryheid	intandela	creeper (n)	klimop
inkulumo	conversation (n)	gesprek	intando	will (n)	wil
inkulungwane	thousand (n)	duisend	intebe	arum lily (n)	varkoor
inkumbela	bow (n)	boog	intela	tax (n)	belasting
inkume	centipede (n)	honderdpoot	intela	rent (n)	huur
inkundla	arena (n)	arena	intende yesandla	palm (n)	palm
inkundla yempi	battlefield (n)	slagveld	intengo	price (n)	prys
inkundla yezindiza	airport (n)	lughawe	interika	typhoid (n)	ingewandskoors
inkunga	fog (n)	mis	intethe	locust (n)	sprinkaan
inkungu	mist (n)	mis	intethe	grasshopper (n)	sprinkaan
inkunzi	bull (n)	bul	intinginono	secretary bird (n)	sekretarisvoël
inkunzi yehhashi	stallion (n)	hings	into	article (n)	artikel
inkuthalo	diligence (n)	fluksheid	into	thing (n)	ding
inkwantshu	cramp (n)	kramp	into	object (n)	voorwerp
inombolo	number (n)	nommer	intobeko	humility (n)	nederigheid
inoveli	novel (n)	roman	into engamanzi	fluid (n)	vloeistof
inqaba	asylum (n)	skuilplaas	into ephothwe yabayingubo	fabric (n)	tekstielstof
inqama	ram (n)	ram	intolibhantshi	waistcoat (n)	onderbaadjie
inqe	vulture (n)	aasvoël	intombazane	girl (n)	meisie
inqindi	fist (n)	vuis	intombi	daughter (n)	dogter
inqola	wagon (n)	wa	intombi	girlfriend (n)	nooi
inqolobane	granary (n)	graanskuur	intombi emsulwa	virgin (n)	maagd
inqubekela-phambili	advancement (n)	vordering	intongomane	peanut (n)	grondboontjie
inqubeko	progress (n)	vooruitgang	into yokucindizela	press (n)	pers
inqubulunjwana	chickenpox (n)	waterpokkies	into yokudlala	toy (n)	speelding
inqulu	hip (n)	heup	intsha	adolescent (n)	jeugdige
inqumbi yezibi	rubbish heap (n)	vullishoop	intshe	ostrich (n)	volstruis
inqwaba	heap (n)	hoop	intshonalanga	west (n)	weste
insalela	remainder (n)	oorblyfsel	intshumayelo	sermon (n)	preek
insangu	cannabis (n)	dagga	intuthu	smoke (n)	rook
inselele	challenge (n)	uitdaging	intuthwane	ant (n)	mier
insephe	springbok (n)	springbok	intuva	dandruff (n)	skilfers
inshuwarensi	insurance (n)	versekering	intwabi	hiccough (n)	hik
insimbi	bell (n)	klok	intwasahlobo	spring (n)	lente
insimbi	metal (n)	metaal	-inu	your (pron)	julle
insimbi	iron (n)	yster	inxeba	wound (n)	wond
insimbi yokosa	grill (v)	rooster	inxenye	portion (n)	gedeelte
insini	laughter (n)	gelag	inxusa	ambassador (n)	ambassadeur
insini	gum (n)	tandvleis	inyakatho	north (n)	noorde
insipho	soap (n)	seep	inyama	meat (n)	vleis
insithamehlo	blinkers (n)	oogklappe	inyama	flesh (n)	vleis
inso	kidney (n)	nier	inyama egayiweyo	mince (n)	maalvleis
insolo	suspicion (n)	agterdog	inyama ethambileyo	fillet (n)	filet
insolo	complaint (n)	klagte			

Zulu	English	Afrikaans	Zulu	English	Afrikaans
inyama yemvu	mutton (n)	skaapvleis	iphepha	paper (n)	papier
inyama yengulube	pork (n)	varkvleis	iphepha lasetholethe	toilet paper (n)	toiletpapier
inyama yenkomo	beef (n)	beesvleis	iphepha lokubhala	writing paper (n)	skryfpapier
inyama yenkonyane	veal (n)	kalfsvleis	iphephandaba	newspaper (n)	koerant
inyama yenyamazane	venison (n)	wildsvleis	iphesenti	percent (n)	persent
inyamazane	buck (n)	bok	iphethini	pattern (n)	patroon
inyamazane	antelope (n)	wildsbok	iphevumente	pavement (n)	sypaadjie
inyamazane edliwayo	prey (n)	prooi	ipheya	pear (n)	peer
inyanga	month (n)	maand	iphiko	wing (n)	vlerk
inyanga	moon (n)	maan	iphiko lenhlanzi	fin (n)	vin
inyanga yamakhambi	herbalist (n)	kruiekenner	iphilisi	pill (n)	pil
inyanga yamazinyo	dentist (n)	tandarts	iphilisi	tablet (n)	tablet
inyoka	snake (n)	slang	iphini	bat (n)	kolf
inyongo	gallbladder (n)	galblaas	ipholisiteshi	police station (n)	polisiekantoor
inyongo	bile (n)	gal	iphomende	permit (n)	permit
inyongo	gall (n)	gal	iphosiso	fault (n)	fout
inyoni	bird (n)	voël	iphoyisa	constable (n)	konstabel
inyonyana yezisebenzi	trade union (n)	vakbond	iphoyisa	policeman (n)	polisieman
inyosi	bee (n)	by	iphunga	smell (n)	reuk
inyufomu	uniform (n)	uniform	iphunga elibi	stink (n)	stank
inyunyana	union (n)	unie	iphupho	dream (n)	droom
inyuwane	beginner (n)	beginner	iphupho elesabisayo	nightmare (n)	nagmerrie
inyuwane	newcomer (n)	nuweling	ipikiniki	picnic (n)	piekniek
inzalo	family (n)	familie	ipipi	pipe (n)	pyp
inzawu	fang (n)	slagtand	ipitikoti	petticoat (n)	onderrok
inzika	sediment (n)	sediment	iplanethi	planet (n)	planeet
inzondo	hatred (n)	haat	ipolitiki	politics (n)	politiek
inzululwane	dizziness (n)	duiseligheid	iposi	post office (n)	poskantoor
inzuzo	advantage (n)	voordeel	iposi	post (n)	pos
inzuzo	profit (n)	wins	iposi	mail (n)	pos
inzuzo	gain (n)	wins	iposi elihamba ngezindiza	airmail (n)	lugpos
inzwabethi	hearsay (n)	hoorsê			
i-ogani	organ (n)	orrel	iposikhadi	postcard (n)	poskaart
i-okhestra	orchestra (n)	orkes	iposoda	postal order (n)	posorder
i-oki	oak (n)	eikeboom	iprogramu	programme (n)	program
i-oksijini	oxygen (n)	suurstof	iprogramu	program (n)	program
i-olivi	olive (n)	olyf	ipulamu	plum (n)	pruim
i-ovaloli	overalls (n)	oorpak	ipulangwe	plank (n)	plank
i-oyili	oil (n)	olie	ipulastiki	plastic (n)	plastiek
ipaki	park (n)	park	ipulatifomu	platform (n)	platform
ipani	saucepan (n)	kastrol	ipulazi	farm (n)	plaas
ipani	pan (n)	pan	iqakala	ankle (n)	enkel
ipasi	pass (n)	pas	iqakathi	plait (n)	vlegsel
ipasili	parsley (n)	pietersielie	iqako	menstruation (n)	menstruasie
ipayipi	drainpipe (n)	rioolpyp	iqanda	egg (n)	eier
ipayipi lendle	sewerage (n)	riolering	iqanda	zero (n)	nul
ipeni	pen (n)	pen	iqaqa	skunk (n)	muishond
ipensele	pencil (n)	potlood	iqaqa	polecat (n)	muishond
ipetshisi	peach (n)	perske	iqele	slope (n)	helling
iphabhuliki	public (n)	publiek	iqhawe	hero (n)	held
iphakethe	parcel (n)	pakket	iqhezu	fraction (n)	fraksie
iphalamende	parliament (n)	parlement	iqhude	cock (n)	haan
iphalasi	palace (n)	paleis	iqhude	rooster (n)	hoenderhaan
iphalishi	porridge (n)	pap	iqhugwane	hut (n)	hut
iphamfulethe	pamphlet (n)	pamflet	iqhwa	snow (n)	sneeu
iphampu	pump (n)	pomp	iqhwa	ice (n)	ys
iphandolo	pantry (n)	spens	iqiniso	fact (n)	feit
iphansi	floor (n)	vloer	iqiniso	truth (n)	waarheid
iphaphu	lung (n)	long	iqonqela	miser (n)	vrek
iphela	cockroach (n)	kakkerlak	iqoqo	summary (n)	opsomming

Zulu	English	Afrikaans	Zulu	English	Afrikaans
iqupha	knuckle (n)	kneukel	isenethe	senate (n)	senaat
irabha	rubber (n)	rubber	isenta	centre (n)	middel
iradiyetha	radiator (n)	verkoeler	isenta	centre (n)	middel
iragbhi	rugby (n)	rugby	isenti	cent (n)	sent
irayisi	rice (n)	rys	isenwishi	sandwich (n)	toebroodjie
ireferense	reference (n)	getuigskrif	isenyelo	sprain (n)	verstuiting
irejista	register (n)	register	isenzeko	phenomenon (n)	verskynsel
irekhodi	record (n)	rekord	isenzo	deed (n)	daad
ireza	razor (n)	skeermes	isenzo	verb (n)	werkwoord
iribhini	ribbon (n)	lint	isephephezelo	fan (n)	waaier
irisidi	receipt (n)	kwitansie	isephulelo emalini	discount (n)	afslag
irobhothi	robot (n)	robot	isesulo	duster (n)	stoflap
iroza	rose (n)	roos	isesulo	eraser (n)	uitveër
irula	ruler (n)	liniaal	isethi	set (n)	stel
isabelo	share (n)	deel	isethi lamazinyo	dentures (n)	vals tande
isabelo	reserve (n)	reserwe	afakwayo		
isabhebhe	suburb (n)	voorstad	isetho	funnel (n)	tregter
isabizwana	pronoun (n)	voornaamwoord	isetifikethi	certificate (n)	sertifikaat
isaga	proverb (n)	spreekwoord	iseviyethe	serviette (n)	servet
isaha	saw (n)	saag	ishalofu	shelf (n)	rak
isahluko	chapter (n)	hoofstuk	ishatini	chutney (n)	blatjang
isaka	sack (n)	sak	ishawa	shower (n)	stortbad
isaka	bag (n)	sak	isheki	cheque (n)	tjek
isakhamuzi	citizen (n)	burger	ishelo	cello (n)	tjello
isakhiwo	building (n)	gebou	ishidi	sheet (n)	laken
isaladi	salad (n)	slaai	ishiphu	chip (computer) (n)	vlokkie
isalufa	sulphur (n)	swawel	ishiya	eyebrow (n)	winkbrou
isamaniso	summons (n)	dagvaarding	ishobhisi	chop (n)	tjop
isamaniso	subpoena (n)	dagvaarding	ishongololo	millipede (n)	duisendpoot
isamba	total (n)	totaal	ishumi	ten (n)	tien
isambulela	umbrella (n)	sambreel	ishumi nambili	twelve (n)	twaalf
isampula	sample (n)	monster	ishumi nane	fourteen (n)	veertien
isandiso	adverb (n)	bywoord	ishumi nanye	eleven (n)	elf
isandla	hand (n)	hand	ishumi nesihlanu	fifteen (n)	vyftien
isandla	handwriting (n)	handskrif	ishumi nesikhombisa	seventeen (n)	sewentien
isando	hammer (n)	hamer	ishumi	nineteen (n)	neëntien
isanduleliso	preface (n)	voorwoord	nesishiyagalolunye		
isaneliso	satisfaction (n)	bevrediging	ishumi	eighteen (n)	agtien
isango	gate (n)	hek	nesishiyagalombili		
isansimbi	mineral (n)	mineraal	ishwa	misfortune (n)	teenspoed
isapha	supper (n)	aandete	isibambo	handle (n)	handvatsel
isayensi	science (n)	wetenskap	isibanda	scar (n)	litteken
isazani	acquaintance (n)	kennis	isibani	lamp (n)	lamp
isazela	instinct (n)	instink	isibashu	burn (n)	brandplek
isazi	expert (n)	deskundige	isibasi	fuel (n)	brandstof
isaziso	advertisement (n)	advertensie	isibeko	deposit (n)	deposito
isazi somculo	musician (n)	musikant	isibeletho	womb (n)	baarmoeder
isehlakalo	event (n)	gebeurtenis	isibhadalala	epidemic (n)	epidemie
isekeni	second (n)	sekonde	isibhakabhaka	sky (n)	lug
isekisi	circus (n)	sirkus	isibhakela	boxing (n)	boks
iseksafoni	saxophone (n)	saxofoon	isibhamu	gun (n)	geweer
isela	thief (n)	dief	isibhamu	rifle (n)	geweer
isele	toad (n)	brulpadda	isibhaxelo	apron (n)	voorskoot
isele	frog (n)	padda	isibhedlela	hospital (n)	hospitaal
iselekelelo	assistance (n)	bystand	isibheqe	patch (n)	lappie
iseli	cell (n)	sel	isibhidli	abundance (n)	oorvloed
iseluleko	directions (n)	aanwysings	isibhinqo	irony (n)	ironie
iseluleko	advice (n)	raad	isibhixi	mess (n)	gemors
iselwa	calabash (n)	kalbas	isibiba	antidote (n)	teengif
isende	testicle (n)	teelbal	isibili	two (n)	twee

Zulu	English	Afrikaans	Zulu	English	Afrikaans
isibindi	liver (n)	lewer	isifuba	chest (n)	borskas
isibindi	courage (n)	moed	isifuba	thorax (n)	borskas
isibonakaliso	symptom (n)	simptoom	isifuba	bosom (n)	boesem
isibonakaliso	sign (n)	teken	isifuba	breast (n)	bors
isibonelo	example (n)	voorbeeld	isifumbu	hunchback (n)	boggelrug
isibongo	surname (n)	van	isifunda	region (n)	streek
isiboniso	illustration (n)	illustrasie	isifunda	zone (n)	sone
isibopho	obligation (n)	verpligting	isifundo	lesson (n)	les
isiboshwa	detainee (n)	aangehoudene	isifundo	lecture (n)	lesing
isiboshwa	convict (n)	gevangene	isifungo	vow (n)	gelofte
isiboshwa	prisoner (n)	gevangene	isifungo	oath (n)	eed
isibubulungu	lighthouse (n)	vuurtoring	isigaba	section (n)	afdeling
isibukeli	bystander (n)	omstander	isigaba	department (n)	departement
isibukeli	eyewitness (n)	ooggetuie	isigaba	faculty (n)	fakulteit
isibukeli	spectator (n)	toeskouer	isigaba	paragraph (n)	paragraaf
isibuko	mirror (n)	spieël	isigalelo	blow (n)	hou
isibungu	larva (n)	larwe	isigameko	incident (n)	voorval
isibungu	maggot (n)	maaier	isigaxa	block (n)	blok
isibusiso	blessing (n)	seëning	isigaxa	lump (n)	klont
isicanucanu	nausea (n)	naarheid	isigaxa	clot (n)	klont
isicasulo	disgust (n)	afkeer	isigcebe sembali	petal (n)	kroonblaar
isicathulo	shoe (n)	skoen	isigcini-magilavu	glovebox (n)	mossienes
isicelo	application (n)	aansoek	isigcino	final (a)	finaal
isicelo	request (n)	versoek	isigcizelelo	insistence (n)	aandrang
isichazimazwi	dictionary (n)	woordeboek	isigcizelelo	accent (n)	aksent
isichwe	dwarf (n)	dwerg	isigebengu	criminal (n)	misdadiger
isichwensi	hooligan (n)	skollie	isigebengu	villain (n)	skurk
isici	mark (n)	merk	isigejane samazwi	phrase (n)	sinsnede
isicubu	tissue (n)	weefsel	isigidi	million (n)	miljoen
isicunulo	offence (n)	oortreding	isiginali	signal (n)	sinjaal
isicupho	trap (n)	strik	isiginxi	guitar (n)	kitaar
isidakamizwa	drug (n)	dwelm	isigodi	valley (n)	vallei
isidakwa	alcoholic (n)	alkoholis	isigqi	rhythm (n)	ritme
isidakwa	drunkard (n)	dronklap	isigqila	slave (n)	slaaf
isidalwa	creature (n)	wese	isigqili sesidakamizwa	drug addict (n)	dwelmslaaf
isidingo	necessity (n)	noodsaaklikheid	isigqizo	bangle (n)	armband
isidladla	paw (n)	poot	isigqizo	anklet (n)	enkelring
isidlakadlaka	violence (n)	geweld	isigqoko	hat (n)	hoed
isidleke	nest (n)	nes	isigubhu	drum (n)	trom
isidlo	meal (n)	maal	isiguli	patient (n)	pasiënt
isidlwabidlwabi	barbarian (n)	barbaar	isigungu sikahulumeni	cabinet (n)	kabinet
isidolobha	slang (n)	sleng	isigwegwe	bend (n)	buiging
isidumbu	corpse (n)	lyk	isigxobo	pole (n)	paal
isidumbu sesilwane	carcass (n)	karkas	isihambi	traveller (n)	reisiger
isidumo	riot (n)	onlus	isihambi	tourist (n)	toeris
isidumo	disaster (n)	ramp	isihawu	mercy (n)	genade
isidwedwe	rag (n)	lap	isihlabathi	sand (n)	sand
isifafazo	sprinkler (n)	sprinkelaar	isihlabo	file (n)	leêr
isifanekiso	statue (n)	beeld	isihlahlana	shrub (n)	struik
isifanekiso esidwe-tshiweyo	diagram (n)	diagram	isihlakala	wrist (n)	pols
isifanelisano	analogy (n)	analogie	isihlalo	seat (n)	sitplek
isifazane	female (n)	vrou	isihlalo	saddle (n)	saal
isifebe	whore (n)	hoer	isihlalo	chair (n)	stoel
isifebe	prostitute (n)	prostituut	isihlangu	boot (n)	stewel
isificezelo	compulsion (n)	dwang	isihlanu	five (n)	vyf
isifiso	wish (n)	wens	isihlathi	cheek (n)	wang
isifo	disease (n)	siekte	isihlebo	defamation (n)	belastering
isifo esivimbanisa umphimbo	diphtheria (n)	witseerkeel	isihlehle	cactus (n)	kaktus
			isihlehle	prickly pear (n)	turksvy
			isihleke	bunch (n)	tros

Zulu	English	Afrikaans
isihlenga	raft (n)	vlot
isihlephu	bit (n)	bietjie
isihlobo	relation (n)	familielid
isihloko	point (n)	punt
isihloko	headline (n)	opskrif
isihloko	tip (n)	punt
isihloko	peak (n)	piek
isihloko	top (n)	top
isihlungu	poison (n)	gif
isihlungu	venom (n)	venyn
isihluthulelo	lock (n)	slot
isihosha	ravine (n)	kloof
isihudo	dysentery (n)	disenterie
isijeziso	punishment (n)	straf
isijeziso esilengisiwe	suspended sentence (n)	opgeskorte vonnis
isikali	scale (n)	skaal
isikaniso	fort (n)	fort
isikela	sickle (n)	sekel
isikelo	scissors (n)	skêr
isiketekete	lantern (n)	lantern
isiketi	skirt (n)	romp
isikhafu	scarf (n)	serp
isikhala	gap (n)	opening
isikhala	space (n)	ruimte
isikhala	vacancy (n)	vakature
isikhala esingenamoya	vacuum (n)	lugleegte
isikhali	weapon (n)	wapen
isikhali somsebenzi	instrument (n)	instrument
isikhalo	appeal (n)	beroep
isikhalo	grievance (n)	grief
isikhalo	cry (n)	kreet
isikhanda	knob (n)	knop
isikhathi	time (n)	tyd
isikhathi esidlulileyo	past (n)	verlede
isikhathi sokuthomba	puberty (n)	puberteit
isikhathi sonyaka	season (n)	seisoen
isikhaxelisi	gadget (n)	toestelletjie
isikhindi	shorts (n)	kortbroek
isikhomane	fern (n)	varing
isikhombisa	seven (n)	sewe
isikhonkwane	peg (n)	pen
isikhonkwane somdabuli	beacon (n)	baken
isikhonzi	dependant (n)	afhanklike
isikhonzi	minister (n)	minister
isikhova	owl (n)	uil
isikhukhukazi	hen (n)	hen
isikhukhula	flood (n)	vloed
isikhumba	leather (n)	leer
isikhumba	skin (n)	vel
isikhumba sekhanda	scalp (n)	kopvel
isikhumbuziso	souvenir (n)	aandenking
isikhumbuzo	memorial (a)	herdenking
isikhumbuzo	reminder (n)	herinnering
isikhundla	lair (n)	lêplek
isikhundla	abode (n)	woonplek
isikhunta	mildew (n)	muf
isikhunta	fungus (n)	swam
isikhupha	pulse (n)	pols
isikhupha seqanda	yolk (n)	eiergeel

Zulu	English	Afrikaans
isikhutha	mould (n)	vorm
isikhwama	pocket (n)	sak
isikhwama semali	purse (n)	beursie
isikhwehlela	phlegm (n)	fleim
isikhwehlela	mucus (n)	slym
isikhwele	jealousy (n)	jaloesie
isikhwelo	ladder (n)	leer
isikigi	bedpan (n)	bedpan
isikole	school (n)	skool
isiko lezizukulwane	tradition (n)	tradisie
isikolo	score (n)	telling
isikulufo	screw (n)	skroef
isikwashi	squash (n)	muurbal
isikwele	square (n)	vierkant
isikwenethu	loan (n)	lening
isikwenetu	debt (n)	skuld
isilaha	butchery (n)	slagtery
isilevu	beard (n)	baard
isilevu	chin (n)	ken
isilibazisi	interruption (n)	onderbreking
isilibaziso	delay (n)	vertraging
isililo	mourning (n)	rou
isililo	lament (n)	weeklag
isilima	fool (n)	dwaas
isilima	idiot (n)	idioot
isilinda	invalid (n)	invalide
isilinganiso	measure (n)	maat
isilinganiso semvula	rain gauge (n)	reënmeter
isilingi	ceiling (n)	plafon
isilisa	male (n)	man
isiliva	silver (n)	silwer
isilomo	aristocrat (n)	edelman
isilonda	sore (n)	seer
isilonda	ulcer (n)	ulkus
isilungulela	heartburn (n)	sooibrand
isilwane	beast (n)	dier
isilwane	animal (n)	dier
isilwane esincelisayo	mammal (n)	soogdier
isilwane esiphangayo	predator (n)	roofdier
isilwanyakazane	bug (n)	gogga
isimangaliso	surprise (n)	verrassing
isimangaliso	wonder (n)	wonder
isimangaliso	miracle (n)	wonderwerk
isimbali	cymbal (n)	simbaal
isimemela	subject (n)	onderwerp
isimemezelo	announcement (n)	aankondiging
isimemezelo	decree (n)	verordening
isimemo	invitation (n)	uitnodiging
isimenywa	guest (n)	gas
isiminzi	glutton (n)	vraat
isimiselo	fate (n)	lot
isimiselo	condition (n)	voorwaarde
isimo	attitude (n)	houding
isimo	position (n)	posisie
isimo	form (n)	vorm
isimo sempucuko	culture (n)	kultuur
isimungumungwane	measles (n)	masels
isinamathelisi	glue (v)	gom
isinambuzane	insect (n)	insek
isinandisi	flavour (n)	geur

Zulu	English	Afrikaans	Zulu	English	Afrikaans
isineke sokonga	thrift (n)	spaarsaamheid	isiqumbi	group (n)	groep
isinengiso	annoyance (n)	ergernis	isiqumbi	crowd (n)	skare
isingeniso	introduction (n)	voorstelling	isirinji	syringe (n)	spuit
isiNgisi	English (a)	Engels	isisebenzi	servant (n)	bediende
isinkwa	bread (n)	brood	isisebenzi	labourer (n)	arbeider
isinkwa	loaf (n)	brood	isisebenzi	worker (n)	werker
isinqandakufa egazini	antibody (n)	teenliggaam	isisebenzi	employee (n)	werknemer
isinqe	buttock (n)	boud	isisefo	safe (n)	brandkluis
isinqe	rump (n)	kruis	isisefo	sieve (n)	sif
isinqumo	decision (n)	besluit	isisekelo	basis (n)	basis
isinqumo	judgment (n)	oordeel	isisele	groove (n)	groef
isinqumo	verdict (n)	uitspraak	isishiyagalolunye	nine (n)	nege
isinxibi	beggar (n)	bedelaar	isishiyagalombili	eight (n)	agt
isinyathelo	pedal (n)	pedaal	isisho	idiom (n)	idioom
isinyathelo	step (n)	tree	isisihla	bruise (n)	kneusplek
isinyathelo	footstep (n)	voetstap	isisindo	weight (n)	gewig
isinye	bladder (n)	blaas	isisitela	nun (n)	non
isipanela	spanner (n)	moersleutel	isisitho	screen (n)	skerm
isipanji	sponge (n)	spons	isisu	abdomen (n)	buik
isipayisi	spice (n)	spesery	isisu	stomach (n)	maag
isipelete	safety pin (n)	haakspeld	isisu	belly (n)	pens
isipeleti	pin (n)	speld	isisusa	motive (n)	beweegrede
isiphambeko	blunder (n)	flater	isisusa	cause (n)	oorsaak
isiphanga	shoulderblade (n)	skouerblad	isiswebhu	whip (n)	sweep
isiphathimandla	official (n)	amptenaar	isitabane	homosexual (n)	homoseksueel
isiphawulo	adjective (n)	byvoeglike naamwoord	isitadi	stud (n)	stoetery
isiphephelo	refuge (n)	skuiling	isitaki	pile (n)	stapel
isiphepho	gale (n)	stormwind	isitaladi	street (n)	straat
isiphetho	conclusion (n)	gevolgtrekking	isitambu	samp (n)	stampmielies
isiphethu	whirlpool (n)	maalstroom	isitashi	starch (n)	stysel
isiphicaphicwano	puzzle (n)	raaisel	isitebele	stable (n)	stal
isiphingi	adulterer (n)	owerspeler	isitebhisi	stepladder (n)	trapleer
isipho	present (n)	geskenk	isiteki	steak (n)	biefstuk
isiphosiso	error (n)	fout	isiteleka	strike (n)	staking
isiphosiso	mistake (n)	fout	isitembu	stamp (n)	seël
isiphunzi	stump (n)	stomp	isitembu	postage stamp (n)	posseël
isiphuzo	drink (n)	drankie	isiteshi	station (n)	stasie
isipikili	nail (n)	spyker	isitetimente	statement (n)	verklaring
isipirithi	spirits (n)	spiritus	isitezi	stairs (n)	trappe
isipoki	ghost (n)	gees	isitezi	floor (n)	verdieping
isipolo	track (n)	spoor	isitha	enemy (n)	vyand
isipolo sehhashi	horseshoe (n)	hoefyster	isitha	foe (n)	vyand
isipuni	accelerator (n)	brandstofpedaal	isithako	prescription (n)	voorskrif
isiqa	substance (n)	stof	isithandwa	lover (n)	minnaar
isiqalekiso	curse (n)	vloek	isithasiselo	appendix (n)	aanhangsel
isiqandisi	freezer (n)	vrieskas	isithelo	product (n)	produk
isiqapheliso	warning (n)	waarskuwing	isithelo	fruit (n)	vrug
isiqapheliso	caution (n)	versigtigheid	isithembiso	promise (n)	belofte
isiqhephu	piece (n)	stuk	isithembiso	offer (n)	aanbod
isiqhingi	island (n)	eiland	isithembiso	parole (n)	parool
isiqhoma	cheekbone (n)	wangbeen	sokungabaleki		
isiqhotho	hail (n)	hael	isithembu	polygamy (n)	poligamie
isiqinisekiso	guarantee (n)	waarborg	isithende	heel (n)	hak
isiqiwu	nature reserve (n)	natuurreservaat	isithimuka	sneeze (n)	nies
isiqongo	summit (n)	kruin	isithixo	idol (n)	afgod
isiqongo	apex (n)	spits	isithixo	god (n)	god
isiqophi sezwi	video recorder (n)	videokassetopnemer	isithiyo	hindrance (n)	hindernis
nezithombe			isithiyo	barrier (n)	versperring
isiqu	degree (n)	graad	isitho	limb (n)	ledemaat
isiqu	stem (n)	stam	isithole	heifer (n)	vers

Zulu	English	Afrikaans	Zulu	English	Afrikaans	I
isithombe	image (n)	beeld	isolo	blame (n)	blaam	
isithombe	photograph (n)	foto	isondlo	maintenance (n)	onderhoud	
isithombo	plant (n)	plant	isondo	hoof (n)	hoef	
isithrasi	citrus (a)	sitrus	isondo	wheel (n)	wiel	
isithungu	sheaf (n)	gerf	isongozo	proposal (n)	voorstel	
isithunywa	messenger (n)	bode	isono	sin (n)	sonde	
isithunzi	shadow (n)	skaduwee	iSonto	Sunday (n)	Sondag	
isithupha	thumb (n)	duim	isonto	church (n)	kerk	
isithupha	six (n)	ses	isositshi	sausage (n)	wors	
isithupha	fingerprint (n)	vingerafdruk	isotsha	soldier (n)	soldaat	
isithuthuthu	motorcycle (n)	motorfiets	iSouthern Cross	Southern Cross (n)	Suiderkruis	
isithuthwane	fits (n)	stuipe	isu	plan (n)	plan	
isithuthwane	epilepsy (n)	vallende siekte	isudi	suit (n)	pak	
isithwathwa	frost (n)	ryp	isu lokupheka	recipe (n)	resep	
isitibili	stirrup (n)	stiebeuel	isuphamakethe	supermarket (n)	supermark	
isitimela	train (n)	trein	iswidi	sweet (n)	lekker	
isitimu	steam (n)	stoom	iswitshi	switch (n)	skakelaar	
isitini	brick (n)	baksteen	itafula	table (n)	tafel	
isitobhi	bus stop (n)	bushalte	itangi	cistern (n)	waterbak	
isitofu	stove (n)	stoof	ithambo	bone (n)	been	
isitolo	shop (n)	winkel	ithambo lekhanda	skull (n)	skedel	
isitolo	store (n)	winkel	ithambo lesifuba	breastbone (n)	borsbeen	
isitrobheli	strawberry (n)	aarbei	ithamborini	tambourine (n)	tamboeryn	
isitsha	plate (n)	bord	ithamo elilinganisiweyo	dose (n)	dosis	
isitsha	bowl (n)	bak	ithanga	thigh (n)	dy	
isitsha	basin (n)	kom	ithanga	pumpkin (n)	pampoen	
isitshudeni	student (n)	student	ithangi	tank (n)	tenk	
isitshulu	stew (n)	bredie	ithawula	towel (n)	handdoek	
isivakashi	caller (n)	besoeker	ithawula lokusubela	sanitary towel (n)	sanitêre doekie	
isivakashi	visitor (n)	besoeker	ithaya	tyre (n)	buiteband	
isivalo	cover (n)	deksel	ithayiphisi	typist (n)	tikster	
isivalo	lid (n)	deksel	ithebe	pelvis (n)	bekken	
isivalo	cap (n)	deksel	ithekinikhoni	technikon (n)	tegnikon	
isivimbelo	obstacle (n)	hindernis	ithekiniki	technique (n)	tegniek	
isivimbo	plug (n)	prop	ithekisi	taxi (n)	taxi	
isivimbo	stopper (n)	stopprop	itheknoloji	technology (n)	tegnologie	
isivini	vine (n)	wingerdstok	itheku	bay (n)	baai	
isivumelwano	agreement (n)	ooreenkoms	itheku	harbour (n)	hawe	
isivumelwano	pact (n)	verdrag	ithelefoni	telephone (n)	telefoon	
isivunguvungu	storm (n)	storm	ithelegrama	telegram (n)	telegram	
isivuno	harvest (n)	oes	ithelevishini	television (n)	televisie	
isivuthela	inflation (n)	inflasie	ithelisikobho	telescope (n)	teleskoop	
isixexelegu	faction (n)	faksie	ithemba	faith (n)	geloof	
isixhakathisi	clasp (n)	klem	ithemba	hope (n)	hoop	
isixoliso	apology (n)	verskoning	ithemponi	tampon (n)	tampon	
isiyayo	young (n)	kleintjie	ithemu	term (n)	termyn	
isiyengo	temptation (n)	verleiding	ithenda	tender (n)	tender	
isiyingi	circle (n)	sirkel	ithende	tent (n)	tent	
isiyingi seso	iris (n)	iris	ithenisi	tennis (n)	tennis	
isiza sekambu	camp site (n)	kampeerterrein	ithephu	tape measure (n)	maatband	
isizathu	reason (n)	rede	itheresi	terrace (n)	terras	
isizinda	background (n)	agtergrond	ithethanusi	tetanus (n)	klem in die kake	
isizotha	dignity (n)	waardigheid	ithikithi	ticket (n)	kaartjie	
isizuku	multitude (n)	menigte	ithimu	team (n)	span	
isizungu	loneliness (n)	eensaamheid	ithiphothi	teapot (n)	teepot	
isizwe	nation (n)	nasie	ithiyetha	theatre (n)	teater	
iso	eye (n)	oog	itholethe	toilet (n)	toilet	
isobho	soup (n)	sop	itholethe	lavatory (n)	toilet	
isoka	boyfriend (n)	kêrel	ithonela	tunnel (n)	tonnel	
isokisi	sock (n)	sokkie	ithonya	influence (n)	invloed	

I	**Zulu**	**English**	**Afrikaans**	**Zulu**	**English**	**Afrikaans**
	ithoshi	flashlight (n)	flitslig	iyadi	yard (n)	werf
	ithoshi	torch (n)	flitslig	iyintshi	inch (n)	duim
	ithreyi	tray (n)	skinkbord	iyunivesiti	university (n)	universiteit
	-ithu	our (pron)	ons	izaba	excuse (n)	ekskuus
	ithuba	turn (n)	beurt	izambane	potato (n)	aartappel
	ithuba	opportunity (n)	geleentheid	izayilofoni	xylophone (n)	xilofoon
	ithuba	chance (n)	kans	ize	nothing (n)	niks
	ithubulela	swelling (n)	swelsel	izenge	segment (n)	segment
	ithulusi	tool (n)	werktuig	izeze	flea (n)	vlooi
	ithumba	boil (n)	bloedvint	izibalo	arithmetic (n)	rekenkunde
	ithumba	tumour (n)	gewas	izibhobo	pneumonia (n)	longontsteking
	ithumba	abscess (n)	verswering	izibi	waste (n)	afval
	ithumbu	intestine (n)	derm	izibi	rubbish (n)	vuilgoed
	ithumbu	hose (n)	tuinslang	izibi	refuse (n)	vullis
	ithuna	tomb (n)	graf	izibiyelo	brackets (n)	hakies
	ithuna	grave (n)	graf	izibuko	spectacles (n)	bril
	ithunga	pail (n)	emmer	izibulo	firstborn (n)	eersgeborene
	ithunga	can (n)	kan	izidakamizwa	drugs (n)	dwelms
	ithusi	brass (n)	geelkoper	izikhali	arms (n)	wapens
	ithusi	copper (n)	koper	iziko	hearth (n)	haard
	itiye	tea (n)	tee	iziko	fireplace (n)	vuurherd
	itiyela	tar (n)	teer	izilwane	fauna (n)	fauna
	itologo	truck (n)	trok	izimemezelo zomshadu	banns (n)	gebooie
	itomu	rein (n)	leisel	izimpahla	goods (n)	goedere
	itomu	bridle (n)	toom	izimpahla zokubhala	stationery (n)	skryfbehoeftes
	itrefiki	traffic (n)	verkeer	izimu	cannibal (n)	mensvreter
	itrekisudi	tracksuit (n)	sweetpak	izindaba	news (n)	nuus
	itsetse	tsetse fly (n)	tsetsevlieg	izindleko	expenses (n)	onkoste
	itshali	shawl (n)	tjalie	izindubulo	ammunition (n)	ammunisie
	itshana eliyigugu	jewel (n)	juweel	izinga-qhwa	freezing point (n)	vriespunt
	itshe eliluhlaza	turquoise (n)	turkoois	izingilazi zokubuka kude	binoculars (n)	verkyker
	itshe lesikhumbuzo	monument (n)	monument	izingubo	clothes (n)	klere
	itshe lethuna	tombstone (n)	grafsteen	izingubo zokulala	bedclothes (n)	beddegoed
	itswayi	salt (n)	sout	izinhlobonhlobo	variety (n)	verskeidenheid
	iva	thorn (n)	doring	izinhlobo zemithi	flora (n)	flora
	ivalfu	valve (n)	klep	izinkomo	cattle (n)	vee
	ivayolini	violin (n)	viool	izinkonyane	biceps (n)	biseps
	ivazi	vase (n)	vaas	izinkuni	firewood (n)	brandhout
	iveli	veil (n)	sluier	izinsuko zonke	daily (a)	daagliks
	iveni	panel van (n)	paneelwa	izinsunsu	acne (n)	aknee
	ivesti	vest (n)	onderhemp	izinto ezenziwe ngezandla	handwork (n)	handewerk
	ivi	kneecap (n)	knieskyf	izinto okudliwa ngazo	cutlery (n)	eetgerei
	iviki	week (n)	week	izinwele	hair (n)	hare
	ivisa	visa (n)	visum	izinyane	kid (n)	bokkie
	ivolovolo	revolver (n)	rewolwer	izinyane	lamb (n)	lam
	ivukusi	mole (n)	mol	izinyane lekati	kitten (n)	katjie
	ivumo	tune (n)	wysie	izinyembezi	tears (n)	trane
	iwa	cliff (n)	krans	izinyo	tooth (n)	tand
	iwalethi	wallet (n)	notetas	izinyo lendlovu	ivory (n)	ivoor
	iwashi	watch (n)	horlosie	izinyo lomhlathi	molar (n)	kiestand
	iwayalense	radio (n)	radio	izipho lozwani	toenail (n)	toonnael
	iwayini	wine (n)	wyn	iziphu	zipper (n)	ritssluiter
	iwele	twin (n)	tweeling	izipopolo	stethoscope (n)	stetoskoop
	iwindi	pane (n)	ruit	izithako zikagologo	liqueur (n)	likeur
	iwolintshi	orange (n)	lemoen	izitho zobulili	genitals (n)	geslagsorgane
	iwundlu	cub (n)	welpie	izitsha	crockery (n)	breekware
	ixhaphozi	swamp (n)	moeras	izizalo	ovary (n)	eierstok
	ixolo	bark (n)	bas	izizukulwane ezizayo	posterity (n)	nageslag
	iX-reyi	x-ray (n)	x-straal			
	ixube	mixture (n)	mengsel			

Zulu	English	Afrikaans
izolo	yesterday (n)	gister
izondo	malice (n)	boosaardigheid
izongwe lomhlandla	vertebra (n)	werwel
izu	zoo (n)	dieretuin
izulu	weather (n)	weer
izulu	heaven (n)	hemel
izwekazi	continent (n)	vasteland
izwi	voice (n)	stem
-jabulela	enjoy (v)	geniet
-jabulile	glad (a)	bly
-jabulisa	delight (v)	bly maak
-jaha	race (v)	resies ja
-jantiza	glance (v)	vlugtig kyk
-jezisa	punish (v)	straf
-jika	turn (v)	draai
-jiya	curdle (v)	klonter
-jiyelwe	disabled (a)	gebreklik
-jobulukayo	elastic (a)	rekbaar
-jolozela	gaze (v)	staar
-jova	inoculate (v)	inent
-joyina	enrol (v)	inskryf
-juluka	perspire (v)	perspireer
-juluka	sweat (v)	sweet
-kabani	whose (pron)	wie se
kabi	badly (adv)	sleg
kabili	twice (n)	twee maal
kabusha	newly (adv)	onlangs
kafushane	briefly (adv)	kortliks
-kagesi	electric (a)	elektries
kahle	well (a)	goed
kakhulu	very (a)	heel
-kala	weigh (v)	weeg
kalula	effortless (a)	met gemak
-kama	comb (v)	kam
-kamasipalati	municipal (a)	munisipaal
kamuva	afterwards (adv)	agterna
kancane	seldom (adv)	selde
kancane	softly (adv)	saggies
kancane	slow (a)	stadig
kaningi	often (adv)	dikwels
kanjani	how (adv)	hoe
-kansela	cancel (v)	kanselleer
kanye	once (adv)	een maal
-kha	pluck (v)	pluk
-kha	scoop (v)	skep
-khafula	spit (v)	spoeg
-khahlela	kick (v)	skop
-khahlela	boot (v)	skop
-khala	appeal (v)	beroep doen op
-khala	complain (v)	kla
-khala	weep (v)	huil
-khala	cry (v)	huil
-khala	ring (v)	lui
-khala	wail (v)	weeklaag
-khalima	stem (v)	voortspruit
-khaliphile	intelligent (a)	intelligent
-khama	strangle (v)	verwurg
-khama	throttle (v)	wurg

Zulu	English	Afrikaans
-khangayo	glamorous (a)	bekoorlik
-khangayo	express (a)	uitdruklik
-khanuka	desire (v)	begeer
-khanya	shine (v)	skyn
-khanyayo	shiny (a)	blink
-khanyayo	transparent (a)	deurskynend
-khanyayo	light (a)	lig
-khanyisa	illuminate (v)	verlig
-khanyisela	enlighten (v)	inlig
-khaphela	betray (v)	verraai
-khasa	crawl (v)	kruip
-khathala	tire (v)	moeg word
-khathala nga-	mind (v)	omgee
-khathaza	trouble (v)	kwel
-khathaza	bother (v)	lastig wees
-khathaza	pester (v)	pla
-khathazeka	worry (v)	bekommer
-khathazekile	anxious (a)	bekommerd
-khathele	tired (a)	moeg
-khathele	weary (a)	vermoeid
-khawula	cease (v)	ophou
-khazimula	gleam (v)	straal
-khazimula	sparkle (v)	vonkel
-khazimulayo	bright (a)	helder
-khefuzelayo	breathless (a)	uitasem
-khehlezelayo	ramshackle (a)	bouvallig
-kheleza	hop (v)	hop
-khetha	favour (v)	begunstig
-khetha	discriminate (v)	diskrimineer
-khetha	choose (v)	kies
-khetha	pick (v)	uitkies
-khethekayo	favourite (a)	gunsteling
-khethiwe	elect (v)	verkies
-khipha	withdraw (v)	terugtrek
-khipha isisu	abort (v)	aborteer
-khipha umoya	exhale (v)	uitasem
-khisila	hiss (v)	sis
-khithika	snow (v)	sneeu
-khiza	drizzle (v)	motreën
-kho	your (pron)	jou
-khohlisa	deceive (v)	bedrieg
-khohlisa	cheat (v)	kul
-khohlisayo	dishonest (a)	oneerlik
-khohlisayo	false (a)	vals
-khohlwa	forget (v)	vergeet
-khokha	pay (v)	betaal
-khokha	spend (v)	bestee
-kholiwe	religious (a)	godsdienstig
-kholwa	believe (v)	glo
-khomba	identify (v)	identifiseer
-khomba	aim (v)	mik
-khombisa	show (v)	wys
-khona	exist (v)	bestaan
khona-manje	instantly (adv)	oombliklik
-khonkotha	bark (v)	blaf
-khononda	grumble (v)	brom
-khonondayo	dissatisfied (a)	ontevrede
-khosela	nestle (v)	nestel
-khotha	lick (v)	lek
-khothama	stoop (v)	buk

K

443

K	Zulu	English	Afrikaans
	-khubeka	trip (v)	struikel
	-khubeka	stumble (v)	struikel
	-khubeza	discourage (v)	ontmoedig
	-khuhla	grate (v)	rasper
	-khuhla	scour (v)	skuur
	-khuhla	scrub (v)	skrop
	-khuhlumezayo	brutal (a)	dierlik
	-khukhula	flood (v)	oorstroom
	-khula	increase (v)	vermeerder
	-khulekela	adore (v)	aanbid
	-khulelwe	pregnant (a)	swanger
	-khulile	mature (a)	volwasse
	-khulisa	rear (v)	grootmaak
	-khulisa	expand (v)	uitbrei
	-khulisa	magnify (v)	vergroot
	-khulu	big (a)	groot
	-khulu	large (a)	groot
	-khulu	chief (a)	hoof
	-khulu	capital (a)	hoof
	-khulu	main (a)	vernaamste
	-khulu kakhulu	maximum (n)	maksimum
	-khulukazi	enormous (a)	tamaai
	-khulu kunakho konke	paramount (a)	hoogste
	-khulula	free (v)	bevry
	-khulula	release (v)	loslaat
	-khulula	emancipate (v)	vrymaak
	-khulula	acquit (v)	vryspreek
	-khululekile	free (a)	vry
	-khuluma	speak (v)	praat
	-khuluma	talk (v)	praat
	-khuluma	address (v)	toespreek
	-khuluphele	stout (a)	geset
	-khuluphele	fat (a)	vet
	-khumbula	remember (v)	onthou
	-khumbula	recollect (v)	onthou
	-khumbuza	remind (v)	herinner
	-khumula	undress (v)	uittrek
	-khunsa	sulk (v)	dikmond wees
	-khuphuka	rise (v)	styg
	-khutha	mould (v)	vorm
	-khuthaza	encourage (v)	aanmoedig
	-khuthazela	persevere (v)	volhard
	-khuthele	active (a)	aktief
	-khuthele	energetic (a)	energiek
	-khuthele	diligent (a)	fluks
	-khuthele	industrious (a)	vlytig
	-khuza	restrain (v)	beperk
	-khuza	curb (v)	inhou
	-khuza	console (v)	opbeur
	-khuza	admonish (v)	vermaan
	-khweba	beckon (v)	wink
	-khwehlela	cough (v)	hoes
	-khwela	climb (v)	klim
	-khwela	mount (v)	opklim
	-khwelezayo	jealous (a)	jaloers
	-kitaza	tickle (v)	kielie
	-klabalasa	scream (v)	gil
	-klama	plan (v)	beplan
	-klewuka	crack (v)	kraak
	-klinile	mischievous (a)	ondeund

Zulu	English	Afrikaans
-kloloda	mock (v)	bespot
-klomela	prize (v)	op prys stel
-klomela	reward (v)	beloon
-klwebha	scratch (v)	krap
kodwa	but (conj)	maar
-kohlobo lobuzwe	ethnic (a)	etnies
-kokubili	either (pron)	een van beide
-kokugcina	ultimate (a)	uiterste
-komuntu uqobo lwakhe	personal (a)	persoonlik
konke	all (things) (pron)	alles
konyaka	annual (a)	jaarliks
ku-	to (prep)	na
-kude	remote (a)	afgeleë
kude	far (adv)	ver
-kulufa	screw (v)	skroef
kungathi	seem (v)	skyn
-kungenjalo	else (adv)	anders
kuphela	only (adv)	slegs
kusasa	tomorrow (n)	môre
kusuka ku-	from (prep)	van
kuthathu	three (n)	drie
kuze	until (conj)	tot
-kwa-	belong (v)	behoort
kwalasha	hell (n)	hel
-kwase-Afrika	African (a)	Afrika
-kwasempumalanga	eastern (a)	oostelik
-kwaseningizimu	southern (a)	suidelik
-kweleta	owe (v)	skuld
-kwemibhalo	literary (a)	letterkundig
-kwemisindo	acoustic (a)	akoesties
-kwemvelo	indigenous (a)	inheems
-kwenye indawo	elsewhere (adv)	elders
-kwezakhamizi	civil (a)	burgerlik
-kwezizwe ezinye	foreign (a)	vreemd
-lahla	waste (v)	vermors
-lahla ngecala	convict (v)	skuldig bevind
-lahlekelwa	lose (v)	verloor
-lahlekelwe	lost (a)	verlore
-lahlekelwe	lost (a)	verdwaal
-lala	lie (v)	lê
-lala	sleep (v)	slaap
-lalela	listen (v)	luister
-lalela	obey (v)	gehoorsaam wees
-lalelayo	obedient (a)	gehoorsaam
-lamba	starve (v)	honger ly
-lambile	hungry (a)	honger
-lamula	arbitrate (v)	arbitreer
-lamula	mediate (v)	bemiddel
-landa	describe (v)	beskrywe
-landa	fetch (v)	haal
-landa	recite (v)	opsê
-landa	tell (v)	vertel
-landa	narrate (v)	vertel
-landela	result (v)	volg
-landela	follow (v)	volg
-landela isipolo	track (v)	opspoor
-landelayo	next (a)	volgende
-landelisa	pursue (v)	najaag

Zulu	English	Afrikaans	Zulu	English	Afrikaans
-langazela	yearn (v)	hunker	-lulekayo	advise (v)	raad gee
-langazela	long (v)	verlang	-luma	bite (v)	byt
-langazela	aspire (v)	streef	-lumula	wean (v)	speen
lapha	here (adv)	hier	-lunge nomthetho	standard (a)	standaard
lapho	there (adv)	daar	-lungile	ready (a)	gereed
lapho	then (adv)	dan	-lungile	correct (a)	korrek
-layeza	direct (v)	beveel	-lungile	valid (a)	geldig
-layeza	prescribe (v)	voorskryf	-lungisa	correct (v)	korrigeer
-layeza	order (v)	beveel	-lungisa	fix (v)	regmaak
-lele	asleep (a)	aan die slaap	-lungisa	prepare (v)	voorberei
-lengisa	hang (v)	hang	-lungisa	mend (v)	heelmaak
-letha	bring (v)	bring	-lungisiwe	tidy (a)	netjies
-libala	loiter (v)	rondslenter	-lunguza	peep (v)	loer
-libazisa	delay (v)	vertraag	-lunywa	itch (v)	jeuk
-ligobongo	hollow (a)	hol	-lwa	fight (v)	veg
-liKrestu	Christian (a)	Christelik	-lwa	battle (v)	veg
-lilela	mourn (v)	rou			
-lima	farm (v)	boer	-ma	stand (v)	staan
-lima	cultivate (v)	bewerk	-ma	halt (v)	stop
-lima	plough (v)	ploeg	-mabalabala	spotted (a)	gekol
-limaza	maim (v)	vermink	-magwegwe	crooked (a)	krom
-limaza	wound (v)	wond	-mahhadla	rough (a)	ru
-limaza	hurt (v)	seermaak	-mahlikihliki	untidy (a)	slordig
-limaza	damage (v)	beskadig	-maka	mark (v)	merk
-linda	wait (v)	wag	-makhaza	cold (a)	koud
-lindela	await (v)	wag op	-mamatheka	smile (v)	glimlag
-lingana	fit (v)	pas	-mangala	wonder (v)	wonder
-lingana na-	equal (v)	gelyk wees aan	-mangalela	prosecute (v)	vervolg
-linganisa	measure (v)	meet	-mangalisa	surprise (v)	verras
-linganiselwe	approximate (a)	geskat	-mangalisa	amaze (v)	verbaas
-lingene	level (a)	gelyk	-mangalisa	marvel (v)	wonder
-lingene	equal (a)	gelyk	-mangalisayo	peculiar (a)	eienaardig
-lingene	even (a)	gelykmatig	-mangalisayo	queer (a)	snaaks
-lingisa	ape (v)	na-aap	-mangalisayo	amazing (a)	verbasend
-liphuzana	beige (a)	beige	-mangalisayo	wonderful (a)	wonderlik
-liqiniso	real (a)	werklik	-mangalisayo	marvellous (a)	wonderbaarlik
-livila	lazy (a)	lui	-manikiniki	tattered (a)	toiingrig
-loba ngezinhla	tabulate (v)	tabuleer	-manikiniki	ragged (a)	verflenterd
lokho	those (pron)	daardie	manje	now (adv)	nou
lokhu	this (pron)	dit	manje	immediate (a)	onmiddellik
lokhu	it (pron)	dit	-manzana	humid (a)	klam
-lokotha	dare (v)	uitdaag	-manzana	damp (a)	vogtig
-londekile	safe (a)	veilig	-manzana	moist (a)	vogtig
-londekile	secure (a)	veilig	-manzi	wet (a)	nat
-londoloza	preserve (v)	bewaar	-manzi	liquid (a)	vloeibaar
-londoloza	secure (v)	beveilig	-manzisa	moisten (v)	natmaak
-lontoza	flicker (v)	flikker	-maphandleni	rural (a)	plattelands
-luhlanya	mad (a)	gek	-masha	march (v)	marsjeer
-luhlaza	green (n)	groen	masinya	sudden (a)	skielik
-luhlaza	immature (a)	onvolwasse	masinyane	soon (adv)	binnekort
-luhlaza	uncooked (a)	ongaar	-masinyane	fast (a)	vinnig
-luhlaza	raw (a)	rou	-masisha	early (a)	vroeg
-luhlwibi	sullen (a)	nors	-mba	dig (v)	spit
-lukhuni	stiff (a)	styf	-mbanyile	miserly (a)	vrekkerig
-lukhuni	tough (a)	taai	-mbuka	desert (v)	dros
-lukhuni	hard (a)	hard	-mcingo	narrow (a)	smal
-lula	easy (a)	maklik	-mculo	musical (a)	musikaal
-lula	agile (a)	rats	-mela	represent (v)	verteenwoordig
-lulama	convalesce (v)	aansterk	-melana na-	oppose (v)	opponeer
-lulekayo	advisory (a)	raadgewend	-mema	invite (v)	uitnooi

445

M	Zulu	English	Afrikaans		Zulu	English	Afrikaans
	-memethekayo	contagious (a)	aansteeklik		-namathelisa	paste (v)	plak
	-memeza	exclaim (v)	uitroep		namuhla	today (n)	vandag
	-memezela	announce (v)	aankondig		-nandisa	flavour (v)	geur
	mhlawumbe	perhaps (adv)	miskien		nanini	ever (adv)	ooit
	mhlawumbe	maybe (adv)	miskien		-naphakade	eternal (a)	ewig
	-mhlophe	white (n)	wit		-ncamasha	lean (v)	leun
	-mhloshana	pale (a)	bleek		-ncane	minute (a)	heel klein
	-mi	my (pron)	my		-ncane	junior (a)	junior
	-mila	grow (v)	groei		-ncane	little (a)	klein
	mina	me (pron)	my		-ncane	young (a)	jong
	-mi ndawonye	stagnant (a)	stagnant		-ncane	small (a)	klein
	-mi ndawonye	stationary (a)	stilstaande		-ncane	unimportant (a)	onbelangrik
	-minyene	dense (a)	dig		-ncane	few (a)	min
	-minyene	crowded (a)	propvol		-ncane kakhulu	minimum (n)	minimum
	-minza	drown (v)	verdrink		-ncane kakhulu	least (a)	minste
	-misa	establish (v)	vestig		-ncane kuna-	less (a)	minder
	-misa	mount (v)	vassit		-ncenceza	jingle (v)	klingel
	-misa inkambu	camp (v)	kampeer		-ncenceza	tick (v)	tik
	-mitha	conceive (v)	opvat		-ncibilika	melt (v)	smelt
	-mnandi	agreeable (a)	aangenaam		-ncibilikisa	dissolve (v)	oplos
	-mnandi	nice (a)	aangenaam		-ncinyane	petty (a)	kleinlik
	-mnandi	savoury (a)	smaaklik		-ncipha	decline (v)	afwys
	-mnandi	delicious (a)	heerlik		-ncipha	decrease (v)	verminder
	-mnene	gentle (a)	sagmoedig		-nciphile	emaciated (a)	uitgeteer
	-mnyama	black (a)	swart		-nciphisa	discount (v)	aftrek
	-mpofu	poor (a)	arm		-nciphisa	reduce (v)	verminder
	-mpompa	babble (v)	babbel		-nciphisa	lessen (v)	verminder
	-mpunga	grey (n)	grys		-ncishanayo	mean (a)	gemeen
	-msulwa	pure (a)	suiwer		-ncoma	recommend (v)	aanbeveel
	-msulwa	innocent (a)	onskuldig		-ncoma	appreciate (v)	waardeer
	-mtoti	sweet (a)	soet		-ncweba	pinch (v)	knyp
	-mukela	admit (v)	toelaat		-ndaxandaxa	clumsy (a)	lomp
	-mukisa	dismiss (v)	ontslaan		-ndiyazisa	stun (v)	verstom
	-mukula	slap (v)	klap		-ndiza	fly (v)	vlieg
	-munca	absorb (v)	absorbeer		nebhadi	unlucky (a)	ongelukkig
	-muncu	bitter (a)	bitter		-necala	guilty (a)	skuldig
	-muncu	acid (a)	suur		-nelungelo	qualified (a)	gekwalifiseerd
	-munqazela	mutter (v)	mompel		-nemba	direct (v)	rig
	-munya	sour (a)	suur		-nemihlola	ominous (a)	onheilspellend
	-munya	suck (v)	suig		nenani eliphakeme	valuable (a)	waardevol
					-nengozi	dangerous (a)	gevaarlik
	-na	rain (v)	reën		-nengozi	unsafe (a)	onveilig
	na-	than (conj)	as		-nengozi	harmful (a)	skadelik
	na-	and (conj)	en		-nenhlamba	obscene (a)	onbetaamlik
	na-	even (adv)	selfs		-nenhlanhla	lucky (a)	gelukkig
	-naka	heed (v)	in ag neem		-nenhlanhla	fortunate (a)	gelukkig
	-naka	notice (v)	opmerk		-nenhlazane	inquisitive (a)	nuuskierig
	-nakekele	careful (a)	versigtig		-nenkani	stubborn (a)	koppig
	nakuphi	anywhere (adv)	enige plek		-nenkani	obstinate (a)	hardkoppig
	-namaduma	uneven (a)	ongelyk		-nesa	nurse (v)	verpleeg
	-namahloni	modest (a)	beskeie		-nesibhixi	messy (a)	morsig
	-namahloni	ashamed (a)	skaam		-nesibindi	courageous (a)	moedig
	-namahloni	shy (a)	skugter		-nesihawu	merciful (a)	genadig
	-namandla	powerful (a)	magtig		-nesimo esincane	slim (a)	skraal
	-namandla	strong (a)	sterk		-nesithunzi	respectable (a)	fatsoenlik
	-namatata	nervous (a)	senuweeagtig		-nesithunzi	dignified (a)	waardig
	-namathela	adhere (v)	kleef		-nesizungu	lonely (a)	eensaam
	-namathela	stick (v)	vasplak		-nesizunguzane	giddy (a)	duiselig
	-namathelayo	adhesive (a)	klewerig		-nethezekile	comfortable (a)	gemaklik
	-namathelisa	glue (n)	gom		nga-	by (prep)	by

Zulu	English	Afrikaans	Zulu	English	Afrikaans	N
nga-	through (prep)	deur	-ngaphucuzekile	uncivilised (a)	onbeskaaf	
nga-	by (prep)	by	-ngaphumelelanga	unsuccessful (a)	onvoorspoedig	
-nga-	may (v)	mag	-ngaqediwe	unfinished (a)	onvoltooid	
nga-	with (prep)	met	ngasese	aside (adv)	opsy	
nga-	about (adv)	rond	-ngasezwa	numb (a)	dood	
nga-	for (prep)	vir	-ngashonile	shallow (a)	vlak	
-ngabaza	uncertain (a)	onseker	-ngasile	absurd (a)	onsinnig	
-ngabongi	ungrateful (a)	ondankbaar	-ngasizi	useless (a)	nutteloos	
-ngabongwanga	unrewarded (a)	onbeloond	-ngathandeki	objectionable (a)	aanstootlik	
-ngadlulisiyo	conservative (a)	konserwatief	-ngathandi	unwilling (a)	onwillig	
-ngafanele	improper (a)	onfatsoenlik	-ngathandi	reluctant (a)	teensinnig	
-ngafanele	undeserved (a)	onverdiend	-ngathembeki	undependable (a)	onbetroubaar	
-ngafekethisiwe	plain (a)	gewoon	-ngathembekile	unfaithful (a)	ontrou	
-ngafeziwe	unfulfilled (a)	onvervuld	-ngathembi	distrust (v)	wantrou	
-ngafundile	uneducated (a)	ongeleerd	-ngathethelelwa	unforgivable (a)	onvergeeflik	
-ngafuneki	undesirable (a)	ongewens	-ngatholakali	unavailable (a)	onverkrygbaar	
-ngaganile	unmarried (a)	ongetroud	-ngathuthukile	undeveloped (a)	onontwikkeld	
-ngagcinisikhathi	unpunctual (a)	nie stip nie	-ngavamile	abnormal (a)	abnormaal	
-ngagunyaziwe	unauthorised (a)	ongemagtig	-ngavamile	uncommon (a)	ongewoon	
-ngaguquki	unalterable (a)	onveranderlik	-ngavamile	rare (a)	seldsaam	
-ngahleliwe	unplanned (a)	onbedoeld	-ngavamile	special (a)	spesiaal	
-ngahlomile	unarmed (a)	ongewapend	-ngavezwanga	undisclosed (a)	onvermeld	
-ngahloniphi	ill-mannered (a)	onmanierlik	-ngavunyelwa	ban (things) (v)	verbied	
-ngahloniphi	rude (a)	onbeskof	-ngawohlokisi amakhasi	evergreen (a)	bladhoudend	
-ngahloniphi	impolite (a)	onbeleef	-ngawuza	peck (v)	pik	
-ngajwayele	unaccustomed (a)	ongewoond	-ngaxwayile	unwary (a)	onbehoedsaam	
-ngakazalwa	unborn (a)	ongebore	-ngaziwa	strange (a)	vreemd	
-ngakhohlwa	unforgettable (a)	onvergeetlik	-ngcolile	immoral (a)	onsedelik	
-ngalaleli	inattentive (a)	onoplettend	-ngcolile	unclean (a)	onrein	
-ngalaleli	disobey (v)	ongehoorsaam wees	-ngcolile	dirty (a)	vuil	
-ngalimalanga	undamaged (a)	onbeskadig	-ngcono	better (a)	beter	
-ngalingene	unequal (a)	ongelyk	-ngcwaba	bury (v)	begrawe	
-ngalungele	unfit (a)	ongeskik	-ngcwele	sacred (a)	heilig	
-ngalungile	unjust (a)	onregverdig	-ngcwele	holy (a)	heilig	
-ngalungile	incorrect (a)	onjuis	-ngejubane	rapid (a)	vlugtig	
-ngalungile	wrong (a)	verkeerd	-ngeke	never (adv)	nooit	
ngamabomu	wilful (a)	moedswillig	-ngekho	absent (a)	afwesig	
-ngamandla	vigorous (a)	kragtig	-ngelishwa	unfortunately (adv)	ongelukkig	
-ngamanzi	fluid (a)	vloeibaar	ngempela	absolute (a)	absoluut	
-nganaki	ignore (v)	ignoreer	ngempela	absolutely (adv)	absoluut	
-nganaki	unaware (a)	onbewus	ngempela	actually (adv)	eintlik	
-nganaki	careless (a)	nalatig	-ngempela	really (adv)	werklik	
-nganaki	negligent (a)	nalatig	-ngemuva	rear (a)	agterste	
-nganaki umthetho	arbitrary (a)	willekeurig	-ngena	penetrate (v)	binnedring	
-nganethezekile	uncomfortable (a)	ongemaklik	-ngena	enter (v)	binnegaan	
ngani	why (adv)	waarom	-ngenabuthongo	sleepless (a)	slapeloos	
ngaphakathi	within (adv)	binne	-ngenakuphikiswa	undisputed (a)	onbetwis	
ngaphakathi	internal (a)	intern	-ngenakuvinjelwa	inevitable (a)	onvermydelik	
ngaphakathi	between (prep)	tussen	-ngenakuzwa	deaf (a)	doof	
ngaphambili	ahead (adv)	vooruit	-ngenakwelashwa	incurable (a)	ongeneeslik	
ngaphambili	forward (adv)	vooruit	-ngenakwenzeka	impossible (a)	onmoontlik	
ngaphandle	without (adv)	buite	-ngenalutho	empty (a)	leeg	
ngaphandle komthetho	illegitimate (a)	buite-egtelik	-ngenalutho	vacant (a)	vakant	
ngaphandle kwa-	except (prep)	behalwe	-ngenamagciwane	sterile (a)	steriel	
-ngaphansana	lower (a)	laer	-ngenamahloni	vulgar (a)	vulgêr	
-ngaphathelene nabantu	impersonal (a)	onpersoonlik	-ngenamandla	invalid (a)	ongeldig	
-ngaphelele	imperfect (a)	onvolmaak	-ngenamandla	weak (a)	swak	
-ngaphelele	incomplete (a)	onvolledig	-ngenamhawu	uncharitable (a)	onbarmhartig	
-ngaphezulu	extra (a)	ekstra	-ngenamhawu	unmerciful (a)	ongenadig	
-ngaphilile	unhealthy (a)	ongesond	-ngenamkhawulo	boundless (a)	grensloos	

Zulu	English	Afrikaans	Zulu	English	Afrikaans
-ngenamsebenzi	unemployed (a)	werkloos	-nitha	knit (v)	brei
-ngenamthetho	undisciplined (a)	ongedissiplineerd	njalo	always (adv)	gedurig
-ngenamusa	unkind (a)	onvriendelik	-nje	such (a)	sulke
-ngenangozi	harmless (a)	onskadelik	-njenga-	like (prep)	soos
-ngenanhlanzeko	unhygienic (a)	onhigiënies	-njengomthetho	lawful (a)	wettig
-ngenasithunzi	undignified (a)	onwaardig	-njunjuza	ache (v)	pyn
-ngenayo ifenisha	unfurnished (a)	ongemeubileerd	-nkamunkamu	enthusiastic (a)	geesdriftig
-ngenazinhloni	immodest (a)	onbeskeie	-nkamunkamu	eager (a)	gretig
ngengozi	accidentally (adv)	toevallig	-nke	all (a)	alle
-ngenisa	import (v)	invoer	-nke	every (a)	elke
ngenkathi	while (conj)	terwyl	-nkemuzela	glow (v)	gloei
-ngenomkhuba	accidental (a)	toevallig	-noboya	hairy (a)	harig
-ngentando	voluntary (a)	vrywillig	-nobugwala	cowardly (a)	lafhartig
-ngenzi lutho	idle (a)	ledig	-nobungcweti	gifted (a)	begaaf
-ngesabi	unafraid (a)	onbevrees	-nobunono	neat (a)	netjies
ngesikhathi	then (adv)	toe	-nobupolitiki	political (a)	polities
ngeviki	weekly (a)	weekliks	-nobuqhawe	brave (a)	dapper
-ngezwa	misunderstand (v)	misverstaan	-nobuqili	cunning (a)	slu
-ngezwakali	inaudible (a)	onhoorbaar	-nobuthekiniki	technical (a)	tegnies
-ngezwakali kahle	vague (a)	vaag	-nobuthongo	sleepy (a)	vaak
-ngezwayo	inanimate (a)	leweloos	-nodaka	muddy (a)	modderig
ngi-	I (pron)	ek	-nodweshu	riotous (a)	wanordelik
-ngingiza	stammer (v)	hakkel	-nohlonze	thick (a)	dik
-ngingiza	stutter (v)	stotter	nokho	however (conj)	maar
ngoba	because (conj)	omdat	nokho	anyhow (conj)	in elk geval
ngobunono	gently (adv)	saggies	nokho	though (conj)	hoewel
ngokulinganisene	along (prep)	langs	nokuba	although (conj)	al
ngokungazi	unknowingly (adv)	onwetend	nokunye	another (a)	nog 'n
ngokunye	otherwise (adv)	anders	-nokuphana	generous (a)	vrygewig
ngokushesha	quickly (adv)	gou	-nokwazi	able (a)	bekwaam
ngokuvamileyo	usually (adv)	gewoonlik	-nokwenzeka	practical (a)	prakties
ngokuya-ngokuya	gradually (adv)	geleidelik	-nolaka	fierce (a)	woes
ngokuzuma	unexpectedly (adv)	onverwags	noma	any (a)	enige
ngokuzungezile	around (adv)	rond	noma	whether (conj)	of
ngokwesiko	traditional (a)	tradisioneel	noma	nor (conj)	nòg
-ngokwezinhlanga	racial (a)	rasse	noma	or (conj)	of
-ngomlomo	verbal (a)	mondeling	noma kunjani	anyhow (adv)	hoe dan ook
-ngqatha	skip (v)	touspring	noma muphi	either...or (conj)	òf...òf
-ngqazukayo	crack (a)	puik	noma ubani	anybody (pron)	elkeen
-ngqongqoza	knock (n)	klop	noma yini	anything (pron)	enigiets
-ngunaphakade	everlasting (a)	ewigdurend	-nombela	cling (v)	klou
-ngundabeni	talkative (a)	spraaksaam	-nomhawu	moving (a)	bewegend
-nhliziyombili	undecided (a)	onbeslis	-nomhawu	pitiful (a)	jammerlik
-nhlobonhlobo	varied (a)	gevarieerd	-nomhawu	unselfish (a)	onselfsugtig
-nika	provide (v)	voorsien	-nomhawu	selfish (a)	selfsugtig
-nika	supply (v)	verskaf	-nomlingo	magical (a)	magies
-nika	donate (v)	skenk	-nommango	steep (a)	steil
-nika	confer (v)	toeken	-nomsebenzi	useful (a)	nuttig
-nika ilayisense	license (v)	lisensieer	-nomsindo	noisy (a)	raserig
-nika indawo	accommodate (v)	huisves	nomsindo	aloud (adv)	hardop
-nikeza	deliver (v)	aflewer	-nomsindo	loud (a)	hard
nina	you (pron)	julle	-nomusa	kind (a)	goedhartig
-ninda	stain (v)	bevlek	-nomusa	humane (a)	mensliewend
-ningana	several (a)	verskeie	-nonya	cruel (a)	wreed
-ningi	many (a)	baie	-nosizi	tragic (a)	tragies
-ningi	plentiful (a)	talryk	-nothile	rich (a)	ryk
-ningi	plenty (a)	volop	-novalo	apprehensive (a)	bang
-ningi	much (a)	veel	-novalo	uneasy (a)	ongerus
-ningi ngokudlula	more (a)	meer	-novalo	afraid (a)	bang
nini	when (adv)	wanneer	-nozwela	sensitive (a)	gevoelig

Zulu	English	Afrikaans	Zulu	English	Afrikaans	**P**
-nqaba	protest (v)	protesteer	okunakisayo	interesting (a)	interessant	
-nqabela	prohibit (v)	verbied	okune	four (n)	vier	
-nqabile	precious (a)	kosbaar	okungabonakali	invisible (a)	onsigbaar	
-nqamuleza	crucify (v)	kruisig	-okungaphatheka	concrete (a)	konkreet	
-nqanda	restrict (v)	inperk	-okungenalutho	blank (a)	leeg	
-nqekuza	nod (v)	knik	okuphindiweyo	double (n)	dubbel	
-nqoba	score (v)	punte aanteken	-okuqala	first (a)	eerste	
-nquma	amputate (v)	afsit	okuqanjiwe	fiction (n)	fiksie	
-nquma	assess (v)	skat	okuqukethwe	contents (n)	inhoud	
-nquma	prune (v)	snoei	okuqungiwe	brew (n)	brousel	
-nquma	define (v)	bepaal	-okusengqondweni kuphela	abstract (a)	afgetrokke	
-nquma	decide (v)	besluit				
-nqumanquma	mutilate (v)	skend	okusesiswini	gastric (a)	maag	
-nqunu	naked (a)	kaal	okuthathelwanayo	infectious (a)	besmetlik	
-nqunu	bare (a)	kaal	okwabo	theirs (pron)	hulle s'n	
-nqwabela	heap (v)	ophoop	okwakhe	hers (pron)	hare	
-nsundu	tan (v)	bruin brand	okwakhe	his (pron)	syne	
-nsundu	brown (a)	bruin	okwakhe	his (pron)	sy	
-ntanta	float (v)	drywe	okwakho	yours (pron)	joune	
-ntontolozayo	shrill (a)	skerp	-okwasendulo	ancient (a)	antiek	
-ntshonalanga	western (a)	westelik	okwenu	yours (pron)	julle s'n	
-ntweza	sail (v)	seil	okwesabekayo	horror (n)	afsku	
-nuka	smell (v)	ruik	olingene na-	equal (n)	gelyke	
-nuka kabi	stink (v)	stink	-oma	wither (v)	verlep	
-nwepha	claw (v)	klou	-omile	dry (a)	droog	
-nxiba	beg (v)	bedel	-omile	arid (a)	dor	
-nxwema	squint (v)	skeel	-omile	thirsty (a)	dorstig	
-nyakazayo	moving (a)	roerend	-omisa	dry (v)	droogmaak	
-nyakazisa	shake (v)	skud	-omsebenzi wamajaji	judicial (a)	regterlik	
-nyakazisa	disturb (v)	pla	-omshini	mechanical (a)	meganies	
-nyakazisa	move (v)	beweeg	-omthetho	legal (a)	wetlik	
-nyamalala	disappear (v)	verdwyn	-ona isimo	deform (v)	vervorm	
-nyathela	tread (v)	trap	-onakele	corrupt (a)	bedorwe	
-nye	single (a)	enkel	-ondla	maintain (v)	handhaaf	
-nye	other (a)	ander	-onga	spare (v)	spaar	
-nye	another (a)	'n ander	-onga	conserve (v)	bewaar	
-nyonyobela	stalk (v)	bekruip	-onga	economise (v)	besuinig	
-nyukuza	move (v)	skuif	ongakholiwe	unbeliever (n)	ongelowige	
-nzima	grave (a)	gewigtig	-ongamela	chair (v)	voorsit	
-nzima	difficult (a)	moeilik	ongcwele	saint (n)	heilige	
-nzima	hard (a)	moeilik	-opha	bleed (v)	bloei	
			-osa	roast (v)	oondbraai	
-obala	openly (a)	openlik	-osekhulile	adult (a)	volwasse	
-obuhedeni	pagan (a)	heidens	osolwayo	suspect (n)	verdagte	
-obuntu	human (a)	menslik	-otha	bask (v)	koester	
-ofehlane	rheumatic (a)	rumaties	-owesifazane	female (a)	vroulik	
ohlangothini lwa-	beside (prep)	langs	-ozela	drowse (v)	dommel	
-okhangayo	attractive (a)	aantreklik	-ozela	doze (v)	sluimer	
-okhela	ignite (v)	aansteek				
-okhele	alight (v)	aan die brand	-paka	park (v)	parkeer	
-okhokho	ancestral (a)	voorvaderlik	-pathelene nesabhebhe	suburban (a)	voorstedelik	
-okomkhuba	characteristic (a)	kenmerkend	-pela	spell (v)	spel	
okomsebenzi wohwebo	industrial (a)	industrieel	-penda	paint (v)	verf	
-okudumbile	inflamed (a)	onsteek	-pha	present (v)	skenk	
-okufanele	appropriate (a)	geskik	-pha	give (v)	gee	
okugcwalisayo	filling (n)	stopsel	-pha amandla	authorise (v)	magtig	
okuhlekisayo	comic (n)	komiek	-phakamisa	uphold (v)	hoog hou	
okukweletwayo	credit (n)	krediet	-phakamisa	raise (v)	ophef	
-okulingene	average (a)	gemiddeld	-phakamisa	lift (v)	oplig	
-okumbala	coloured (a)	gekleur	-phakathi	inclusive (a)	inklusief	

P	**Zulu**	**English**	**Afrikaans**	**Zulu**	**English**	**Afrikaans**
	phakathi	inside (adv)	binne	-phephetha	blow (v)	waai
	phakathi kwa-	amid (prep)	tussen	phesheya	over (prep)	oor
	phakathi kwa-	in (prep)	in	phesheya	across (prep)	oor
	phakathi kwamabili	midnight (n)	middernag	-phesheya	beyond (prep)	oorkant
	-phakathi nezwe	inland (a)	binnelands	phesheya	overseas (n)	oorsee
	-phakela	feed (v)	voer	-phethela	border (v)	grens
	-phakeme	high (a)	hoog	-phethwe	dependent (a)	afhanklik
	-phakeme	distinguished (a)	vooraanstaande	phezu kwa-	about (prep)	oor
	-phakeme	eminent (a)	vooraanstaande	phezu kwa-	on (prep)	op
	-phakeme kakhudlwana	higher (a)	hoër	phezulu	up (prep)	op
	-phakula	castrate (v)	kastreer	-phi	which (pron)	watter
	-phala	scrape (v)	skraap	-phi	where (adv)	waar
	-phambana	disagree (v)	verskil	-phika	deny (v)	ontken
	-phambana	conflict (v)	bots	-phikisa	object (v)	beswaar maak
	phambana na-	antagonise (v)	vyandig maak	-phikisa	contradict (v)	weerspreek
	phambana na-	across (adv)	dwars	-phikisana	argue (v)	stry
	-phambanisiweyo	alternate (v)	afwissel	-phila	live (v)	leef
	-phambene na-	against (prep)	teen	-philile	healthy (a)	gesond
	-phambene nomthetho	illegal (a)	onwettig	-philile	alive (a)	lewend
	phambi kwa-	before (prep)	voor	-philile	whole (a)	heel
	phambili	front (a)	voor	-philisayo	wholesome (a)	heilsaam
	phambili	onward (adv)	voorwaarts	-phinda	multiply (v)	vermenigvuldig
	phambili	further (a)	verder	-phinda	repeat (v)	herhaal
	phandle	out (prep)	uit	-phindisa	retaliate (v)	vergeld
	phandle kwa-	besides (prep)	buiten	-phindisela	avenge (v)	wreek
	-phanga	prey (v)	aas	-phindiwe	double (v)	dubbele
	-phanga	loot (v)	plunder	-phofisa	impoverish (v)	verarm
	-phanga	rob (v)	beroof	-phola	cool (v)	afkoel
	-phangayo	greedy (a)	gulsig	-pholile	cool (a)	koel
	-phangelana	scramble (v)	klouter	-pholisha	polish (v)	poleer
	-phangisa	hurry (v)	jaag	-phonsa	throw (v)	gooi
	phansi	down (prep)	af	-phonsa	cast (v)	werp
	phansi	under (prep)	onder	-phoqa	compel (v)	dwing
	phansi kwa-	below (prep)	onder	-phoqa	enforce (v)	afdwing
	-phaphama	wake (v)	wakker word	-phosisa	err (v)	fouteer
	-phaphazela	panic (v)	paniekerig wees	-phucuza	civilise (v)	beskaaf
	-phatha	control (v)	beheer	-phukula umlomo	pout (v)	pruil
	-phatha	manage (v)	bestuur	-phukuzekile	stupid (a)	onnosel
	-phatha	contain (v)	bevat	-phuma	exit (v)	uitgaan
	-phatha	handle (v)	hanteer	-phuma	emerge (v)	verrys
	-phatha kabi	ill-treat (v)	mishandel	-phuma ipikiniki	picnic (v)	piekniek hou
	-phazima	blink (v)	knipoog	-phumelela	succeed (v)	slaag
	-pheca	fold (v)	vou	-phumisa	issue (v)	uitreik
	-phefumula	breathe (v)	asemhaal	-phumisela	pronounce (v)	uitspreek
	-phefuzela	pant (v)	hyg	-phumula	rest (v)	rus
	-phehla	churn (n)	karring	-phupha	dream (v)	droom
	-pheka	cook (v)	kook	-phuphuthekisa	dazed (a)	bedwelmd
	-phekuzayo	lively (a)	lewendig	-phuza	drink (v)	drink
	-phelayo	entire (a)	hele	-phuzile	late (a)	laat
	-pheleleyo	complete (a)	volledig	-pitshiza	squash (v)	platdruk
	-phelelwe yithemba	desperate (a)	wanhopig	-popoza	hoot (v)	toet
	-phelezela	accompany (v)	begelei	-posa	post (v)	pos
	-phelezela	escort (v)	vergesel	-potshoza	eject (v)	uitskiet
	-phelisa	finish (v)	klaarmaak			
	-phendukisa	convert (v)	omsit	-qabula	kiss (v)	soen
	-phendula	reply (v)	antwoord gee	-qaka	menstruate (v)	menstrueer
	-phendula	respond (v)	respondeer	-qala	tackle (v)	aanpak
	-phendula	answer (v)	antwoord	-qala	begin (v)	begin
	-phendula ecaleni	plead (n)	pleit	-qala	start (v)	begin
	-phenya	examine (v)	ondersoek	-qalekile	unconscious (a)	bewusteloos

Zulu	English	Afrikaans	Zulu	English	Afrikaans	S
-qamba	compose (v)	komponeer	-qoshama	squat (v)	hurk	
-qamba	invent (v)	uitvind	-qotho	sincere (a)	opreg	
-qamba amanga	lie (v)	lieg	-qotho	honest (a)	eerlik	
-qanda	split (v)	splits	-qukethe	serious (a)	ernstig	
-qandela	guess (v)	raai	-quleka	faint (v)	flou word	
-qandisa	freeze (v)	vries	-qumbile	flatulent (a)	winderig	
-qanjiwe	synthetic (a)	sinteties	-qunga	brew (v)	brou	
-qaphela	observe (v)	waarneem				
-qaphela	beware (v)	oppas	-sa-	still (adv)	nog	
-qaphelayo	observant (a)	oplettend	-saha	saw (v)	saag	
-qaphisa	warn (v)	waarsku	-sakaza	scatter (v)	strooi	
-qaqa	solve (v)	oplos	-sakaza	spread (v)	versprei	
-qaqa	undo (v)	losmaak	-sakaza	broadcast (v)	uitsaai	
-qaqa	unravel (v)	ontrafel	-sala	remain (v)	agterbly	
-qasha	rent (v)	huur	-sanda	just (adv)	net	
-qasha	hire (v)	huur	-sayina	sign (v)	teken	
-qasha	employ (v)	in diens neem	-sebenza	labour (v)	arbei	
-qasha	appoint (v)	aanstel	-sebenza	exercise (v)	oefen	
-qavile	important (a)	belangrik	-sebenza	work (v)	werk	
-qeda ukoma	quench (v)	les	-sebenzela	serve (v)	dien	
-qedela	complete (v)	voltooi	-sebenzisa	use (v)	gebruik	
-qembuka	defect (v)	oorloop na	-sebenzisa	apply (v)	toepas	
-qeqeshekile	efficient (a)	doeltreffend	-seceleni kwa-	next to (prep)	langs	
-qhakaza	bloom (v)	blom	-sefa	sift (v)	sif	
-qhamile	conspicuous (a)	opvallend	-sekela	assist (v)	bystaan	
-qhaqhazela	shiver (v)	bewe	-sekela	support (v)	ondersteun	
-qhaqhazela	tremble (v)	bewe	-sekela	second (v)	sekondeer	
-qhathanisa	compare (v)	vergelyk	-sekela	back (v)	steun	
-qhephula	chip (v)	'n hap kry	-semadolobheni	urban (a)	stedelik	
-qholoshile	boastful (a)	spoggerig	-sempumalanga	east (adv)	oos	
-qhubeka	progress (v)	vooruitgaan	-seza	reveal (v)	openbaar	
-qhubeka	proceed (v)	voortgaan	-sha	new (a)	nuut	
-qhubekelayo	progressive (a)	progressief	-sha	fresh (a)	vars	
-qhubisa	continue (v)	vervolg	-shabalalisa	exterminate (v)	uitroei	
-qhudelana	compete (v)	wedywer	-shada	wed (v)	trou	
-qhugayo	lame (a)	mank	-shadisa	marry (v)	trou	
-qhuma	explode (v)	ontplof	-shanela	sweep (v)	vee	
-qhuma	burst (v)	bars	-shaqekile	tense (a)	gespanne	
-qhuma	erupt (v)	uitbars	-shawa	shower (v)	stort	
-qinile	firm (a)	ferm	-shaya	hit (v)	slaan	
-qinile	tight (a)	styf	-shaya ikhwelo	whistle (v)	fluit	
-qinile	solid (a)	vas	-shaya indesheni	salute (v)	salueer	
-qinile mbe	stable (a)	stabiel	-shayana	collide (v)	bots	
-qinisa	tighten (v)	span	-shayela	drive (v)	bestuur	
-qiniseka	ensure (v)	verseker	-shefa	shave (v)	skeer	
-qinisekile	sure (a)	seker	-shelela	slide (v)	gly	
-qinisekisa	guarantee (v)	waarborg	-sheshayo	quick (a)	gou	
-qinisile	true (a)	waar	-sheshisa	hasty (a)	haastig	
-qinisile	exact (a)	presies	-sheshisa	rush (v)	haas	
-qokiwe	prescribed (a)	voorgeskrewe	-sheshisa	accelerate (v)	versnel	
-qonda	mean (v)	bedoel	-shibhile	cheap (a)	goedkoop	
-qonda	understand (v)	verstaan	-shicilela	publish (v)	uitgee	
-qonde ngqo	accurate (a)	noukeurig	-shikashika	maul (v)	kneus	
-qonde phezulu	vertical (a)	vertikaal	-shintsha	switch (v)	oorskakel	
-qondile	direct (a)	direk	-shintsha	change (v)	verander	
-qondile	right (a)	reg	-shisa	burn (v)	brand	
-qondile	straight (a)	reguit	-shisa	scorch (v)	skroei	
-qopha	record (v)	opteken	-shisa	scald (v)	skroei	
-qopha amatshe	sculpt (v)	beeldhou	-shiya	resign (v)	bedank	
-qoqa	collect (v)	versamel	-shiya	leave (v)	laat	

Zulu	English	Afrikaans	Zulu	English	Afrikaans
-shiya	omit (v)	weglaat	-taka	pile (v)	stapel
-sho	allege (v)	beweer	-tasha	starch (v)	styf
-sho	say (v)	sê	-tekula	joke (v)	gekskeer
-sho	state (v)	vermeld	-teleka	strike (v)	staak
-shobashoba	wriggle (v)	wriemel	-thakathela	bewitch (v)	toor
-shona	sink (v)	sink	-thambile	tame (a)	mak
-shonile	deep (a)	diep	-thambile	soft (a)	sag
-shonile	late (a)	oorlede	-thambile	tender (a)	teer
-shonileyo	deceased (a)	oorlede	-thambisa	tame (v)	tem
-shuba	congeal (v)	stol	-thanda	like (v)	hou van
-shudula	shuffle (v)	skuifel	-thandaza	pray (v)	bid
-shumayela	preach (v)	preek	-thandekayo	lovable (a)	dierbaar
-shwabana	crease (v)	kreukel	-thandekayo	affectionate (a)	toegeneë
-shwabana	shrink (v)	krimp	-thandekayo	likeable (a)	beminlik
-shwabana	shrivel (v)	verskrompel	-thandekisa	endear (v)	bemind maak
-sicila	bruise (v)	kneus	-thandiwe	dear (a)	dierbaar
-sicilela	stamp (v)	bestempel	-thandiwe	beloved (a)	bemind
-sidlakela	giant (a)	reuse	-thatha	take (v)	neem
-sika	slice (v)	skywe sny	-thatha isithombe	photograph (v)	fotografeer
-sika	cut (v)	sny	-thatheka	interest (v)	interesseer
-sika	shred (v)	snipper	-thayipha ngomshini	type (v)	tik
-sika	carve (v)	sny	-thekelisa	export (n)	uitvoer
-sina	dance (v)	dans	-thela	surrender (v)	oorgee
-sinda	heavy (a)	swaar	-thela	produce (v)	produseer
-sinda	recover (v)	herstel	-thela	pour (v)	skink
-sindisa	rescue (v)	red	-thela umanyolo	fertilise (v)	kunsmis gee
-sindisa	save (v)	red	-thelela	infect (v)	besmet
-sineka	grin (v)	gryns	-thelisa	tax (v)	belas
-sineka	smirk (v)	grynslag	-themba	rely (v)	staatmaak
-sithekile	secluded (a)	afgesonderd	-thembayo	confident (a)	vol vertroue
-siza	help (v)	help	-thembekile	trustworthy (a)	betroubaar
-siza	aid (v)	help	-thembekile	loyal (a)	lojaal
-siza	relieve (v)	verlig	-thembekile	reliable (a)	betroubaar
-sizana	co-operate (v)	saamwerk	-thembekile	faithful (a)	getrou
-sizayo	helpful (a)	behulpsaam	-thembisa	promise (v)	belowe
-sizayo	beneficial (a)	voordelig	-thembisa	offer (v)	aanbied
-sobala	undoubted (a)	ongetwyfeld	-thena	sterilise (v)	steriliseer
-sobala	simple (a)	eenvoudig	-thenga	buy (v)	koop
-soka	circumcise (v)	besny	-thenga	shop (v)	inkopies doen
-sola	doubt (v)	twyfel	-thengisa	sell (v)	verkoop
-sola	condemn (v)	veroordeel	-thethisa	scold (v)	uitskel
-sola	suspect (v)	verdink	-thikameza	interrupt (v)	onderbreek
-sola	blame (v)	blameer	-thile	particular (a)	besonder
-sondelene	adjacent (a)	aangrensend	-thimula	sneeze (v)	nies
-songa	wrap (v)	toedraai	thina	we (pron)	ons
-songoza	propose (v)	voorstel	thina	us (pron)	ons
sonke	all (beings) (pron)	almal	thina	ourselves (pron)	onsself
-sontiza	wring (v)	wring	-thinta	touch (v)	raak
-sula	erase (v)	uitvee	-thinta	affect (v)	raak
-sula	dust (v)	afstof	-thinthana	contact (v)	in aanraking kom
-sula	wipe (v)	afvee	-thithibele	helpless (a)	hulpeloos
-sunduza	push (v)	stoot	-thiya	hinder (v)	hinder
-susa	eliminate (v)	verwyder	-thize	some (a)	sommige
-susa	remove (v)	verwyder	-thobekile	polite (a)	hoflik
-susa	delete (v)	skrap	-thobile	humble (a)	nederig
-susa	abolish (v)	afskaf	-thokozile	cheerful (a)	vrolik
-susa	subtract (v)	aftrek	-thokozile	happy (a)	gelukkig
-swela	need (v)	nodig hê	-thokozisa	amuse (v)	vermaak
			-thokozisayo	amusing (a)	vermaaklik
			-thola	adopt (v)	aanneem

Zulu	English	Afrikaans	Zulu	English	Afrikaans
-thola	get (v)	kry	uboya	fur (n)	pels
-thola	find (v)	vind	uboya bembuzi yaseAngora	mohair (n)	sybokhaar
-tholakalayo	available (a)	beskikbaar	ububanzi	breadth (n)	breedte
-thola njengefa	inherit (v)	erf	ububhibhi	meercat (n)	meerkat
-thomba	rust (v)	roes	ubuchopho	brain (n)	brein
-thonya	influence (v)	beïnvloed	ubuciko	art (n)	kuns
-thosa	fry (v)	bak	ubuciko	rhetoric (n)	retoriek
-thuka	insult (v)	beledig	ubucwazicwazi	brilliance (n)	helderheid
-thuka	swear (v)	vloek	ubudala	age (n)	ouderdom
-thukuthele	angry (a)	kwaad	ubude	length (n)	lengte
-thukuthelisa	infuriate (v)	woedend maak	ubudlewane	bond (n)	band
-thukuthelisa	anger (v)	kwaad maak	ubudoda	manhood (n)	manlikheid
-thulile	calm (a)	kalm	ubufakazi	proof (n)	bewys
-thulile	quiet (a)	stil	ubufakazi	evidence (n)	getuienis
-thulisa	quell (v)	demp	ubufakazi	testimony (n)	getuienis
-thulisa	silence (v)	stilmaak	ubugebengu	crime (n)	misdaad
-thuma	send (v)	stuur	ubugevugevu	chatter (n)	gebabbel
-thuma	delegate (v)	afvaardig	ubugqila	slavery (n)	slawerny
-thunga	sew (v)	naaldwerk doen	ubugwala	cowardice (n)	lafhartigheid
-thunukalisa	upset (v)	ontstel	ubuhlalu	bead (n)	kraal
-thunukele	upset (a)	ontsteld	ubuhlanzo	vomit (n)	vomeersel
-thutha	vacate (v)	uittrek	ubuhle	beauty (n)	skoonheid
-thutha	cart (v)	karwei	ubuhle	charm (n)	sjarme
-thuthela kwelinye izwe	migrant (a)	swerwend	ubuhlungu	ache (n)	pyn
-thuthela kwelinye izwe	emigrate (v)	emigreer	ubuhlungu	pain (n)	pyn
-thwala	carry (v)	dra	ubuhlungu bendlebe	earache (n)	oorpyn
-thwala	load (v)	laai	ubuhlungu bezinyo	toothache (n)	tandpyn
-thwala	abduct (v)	ontvoer	ubukhizikhizi	luxury (n)	luukse
-thwebula	paralyse (v)	verlam	ubukhona	existence (n)	bestaan
-thwele ikhanda	haughty (a)	hoogmoedig	ubukhosi	kingdom (n)	koninkryk
-thwibila	lash (v)	gesel	ubukhulu	size (n)	grootte
-thwisha	whip (v)	raps	ubukhulu ba-	volume (n)	volume
-thwishikile	horizontal (a)	horisontaal	ubukhuphekhuphe	activity (n)	bedrywigheid
-tshala	sow (v)	saai	ubulembu	cobweb (n)	spinnerak
-tshala	plant (v)	plant	ubulili	gender (n)	geslag
-tsheka	slant (v)	skuins loop	ubulima	foolishness (n)	dwaasheid
-tshikizisa	wag (v)	swaai	ubulunga	membership (n)	lidmaatskap
			ubulungisa	justice (n)	geregtigheid
u-anyanisi	onion (n)	ui	ubumanzi	moisture (n)	vog
u-Aprili	April (n)	April	ubumanzi	damp (n)	vogtigheid
u-ayisikhilimu	ice cream (n)	roomys	ubumba	clay (n)	klei
ubaba	father (n)	vader	ubumina	self (n)	self
ubabamkhulu	grandfather (n)	oupa	ubumnyama	darkness (n)	donker
ubabezala	father-in-law (n)	skoonvader	ubumpofu	poverty (n)	armoede
ubambo	rib (n)	rib	ubundubundu	paste (n)	pasta
ubani	who (pron)	wie	ubunene	right (n)	regterkant
ubende	spleen (n)	milt	ubungako	quantity (n)	hoeveelheid
ubhabhulini	poplar (n)	populier	ubungane	companionship (n)	kameraadskap
ubhanana	banana (n)	piesang	ubungane	infancy (n)	kleintyd
ubhasikidi	basket (n)	mandjie	ubungane	friendship (n)	vriendskap
ubhatata	sweet potato (n)	patat	ubungcono	improvement (n)	verbetering
ubhavu	bath (n)	bad	ubuningi	plural (n)	meervoud
ubhejane	rhinoceros (n)	renoster	ubunjalo bendawo	environment (n)	omgewing
ubhekeni	bacon (n)	spek	ubunjani	quality (n)	kwaliteit
ubhontshisi	bean (n)	boontjie	ubunjani	condition (n)	toestand
ubhova	bulldog (n)	bulhond	ubunkamunkamu	enthusiasm (n)	geesdrif
ubhusha	butcher (n)	slagter	ubunsomi	purple (a)	pers
ubisi	milk (n)	melk	ubuntwana	childhood (n)	kinderjare
ubonono	cleanliness (n)	sindelikheid	ubunxele	left (n)	linkerkant
ubovu	pus (n)	etter			

U	Zulu	English	Afrikaans	Zulu	English	Afrikaans
	ubunye	unity (n)	eenheid	ugibe	snare (n)	strik
	ubunzima	difficulty (n)	moeilikheid	uginindela	granadilla (n)	granadilla
	ubuphakade	eternity (n)	ewigheid	ugobhozi	skeleton (n)	geraamte
	ubuqaphuqaphu	eloquence (n)	welsprekendheid	ugodo	log (n)	blok
	ubuqhawe	bravery (n)	dapperheid	ugogo	grandmother (n)	ouma
	ubuqotho	honesty (n)	eerlikheid	ugologo	alcohol (n)	alkohol
	ubuqotho	integrity (n)	integriteit	ugologo	liquor (n)	drank
	ubusha	youth (n)	jeug	ugovane	uvula (n)	kleintongetjie
	ubusika	winter (n)	winter	ugqoko	keyboard (n)	klawerbord
	ubuso	face (n)	gesig	ugqumgqumu	gooseberry (n)	appelliefie
	ubusuku	night (n)	nag	ugu	coast (n)	kus
	ubuthakathi	witchcraft (n)	toorkuns	ugwavu	guava (n)	koejawel
	ubuthongo	sleep (n)	slaap	ugwayi	tobacco (n)	tabak
	ubuvila	laziness (n)	luiheid	uhabhu	harp (n)	harp
	ubuzwe	nationalism (n)	nasionalisme	uhambo	trip (n)	reis
	ucezu	blade (n)	blad	uhambo	journey (n)	reis
	ucezu	slice (n)	sny	uhambo	tour (n)	rondreis
	ucezu	chip (potato) (n)	skyfie	uhele	hawk (n)	valk
	ucezwana	fragment (n)	brokstuk	uhemu	ham (n)	ham
	uchatho	enema (n)	enema	uhhafu	half (n)	helfte
	ucingo	fence (n)	draad	uhhavini	oven (n)	oond
	ucingo	thread (n)	draad	uhlabo	injection (n)	inspuiting
	ucingo	wire (n)	draad	uhla lwamawayini	winelist (n)	wynkaart
	ucingo lwewayilense	aerial (n)	lugdraad	uhlamvu	grain (n)	graan
	ucingo olunameva	barbed wire (n)	doringdraad	uhlamvu	unit (n)	eenheid
	ucwecwana	flake (n)	vlokkie	uhlamvu	pip (n)	pit
	ucwecwane	wafer (n)	wafel	uhlamvu lwemali	coin (n)	muntstuk
	udaba	issue (n)	kwessie	uhlanya	lunatic (n)	waansinnige
	udaba	affair (n)	saak	uhlaselo	assault (n)	aanranding
	udade	sister (n)	suster	uhlaza	vegetable (n)	groente
	udaka	mud (n)	modder	uhlelo	scheme (n)	skema
	udalimede	dynamite (n)	dinamiet	uhlelo	arrangement (n)	skikking
	udebe	lip (n)	lip	uhlelo lwesikhathi	timetable (n)	rooster
	uDisemba	December (n)	Desember	uhlelo lwezifundo	syllabus (n)	leerplan
	udlawu	pliers (n)	knyptang	uhlobo	manner (n)	manier
	udobo	fish-hook (n)	vishoek	uhlobo	kind (n)	soort
	udokotela	doctor (n)	dokter	uhlobo	make (n)	soort
	udokotela kahulumeni	district surgeon (n)	distriksgeneesheer	uhlobo	type (n)	tipe
	udokotela ohlinzayo	surgeon (n)	chirurg	uhlobo logubhu	harmonica (n)	harmonika
	udoli	doll (n)	pop	uhlobo lwebumba	ochre (n)	oker
	udonga	wall (n)	muur	uhlobo lwenkawu engenamsila	ape (n)	aap
	udoti	filth (n)	vuilgoed			
	udumo	renown (n)	beroemdheid	uhlu	row (n)	ry
	udumo	fame (n)	roem	uhudu	diarrhoea (n)	diarree
	udumo olubi	notoriety (n)	berugtheid	uhulumeni	government (n)	regering
	udweshu	conflict (n)	konflik	uhulumeni	state (n)	staat
	ufakazi	witness (n)	getuie	uhwebo	commerce (n)	handel
	ufasimbe	haze (n)	waas	ujamu	jam (n)	konfyt
	uFebhuwali	February (n)	Februarie	uJanuwari	January (n)	Januarie
	ufezela	scorpion (n)	skerpioen	ujeke	jug (n)	beker
	ufuba	tuberculosis (n)	tuberkulose	ujeli	jelly (n)	jellie
	ufudu	tortoise (n)	skilpad	uJesu	Jesus (n)	Jesus
	ufulawa	flour (n)	meel	ujikanelanga	sunflower (n)	sonneblom
	ugaba	stalk (n)	stingel	ujoki	jockey (n)	jokkie
	ugadi	nightwatchman (n)	nagwag	uju	honey (n)	heuning
	ugadi	guard (n)	wag	uju	nectar (n)	nektar
	ugaliki	garlic (n)	knoffel	uJulayi	July (n)	Julie
	ugcunsula	syphilis (n)	sifilis	uJuni	June (n)	Junie
	ugedla	gravel (n)	gruis	ujusi kawolintshi	orange juice (n)	lemoensap
	ugesi	electricity (n)	elektrisiteit	ukaputeni	captain (n)	kaptein

Zulu	English	Afrikaans
uketshezi	liquid (n)	vloeistof
ukhakhi	khaki (n)	kakie
ukhalifulawa	cauliflower (n)	blomkool
ukhalo	loin (n)	lende
ukhasitowela	castor oil (n)	kasterolie
ukheshe	cash (n)	kontant
ukhetho	election (n)	verkiesing
ukhezo	spoon (n)	lepel
ukhilimu wokushefa	shaving cream (n)	skeerroom
uKhisimusi	Christmas (n)	Kersfees
ukhiye	key (n)	sleutel
ukhohlokhohlo	whooping cough (n)	kinkhoes
ukhokho	cocoa (n)	kakao
ukhokho	cork (n)	kurk
ukhokho	crust (n)	korsie
ukhokho	ancestor (n)	voorouer
ukhola	collar (n)	kraag
ukhondakta	conductor (n)	kondukteur
ukhonkolo	concrete (n)	beton
ukhonondo	dissatisfaction (n)	ontevredenheid
ukhophe	eyelash (n)	wimper
ukhozi	eagle (n)	arend
ukhula	weed (n)	onkruid
ukhuni	wood (n)	hout
ukhwathu	oyster (n)	oester
ukokheleka	ignition (n)	ontsteking
ukolo	wheat (n)	koring
ukoma	thirst (n)	dors
ukomisa kwezulu	drought (n)	droogte
ukonakala	corruption (n)	bedorwenheid
ukondliwa komzimba	nutrition (n)	voeding
ukoniwa	abuse (n)	misbruik
ukotini	cotton (n)	katoen
uKrestu	Christ (n)	Christus
ukubabaza	admiration (n)	bewondering
ukubakhona	attendance (n)	bywoning
ukubaleka	flight (n)	vlug
ukubalwa kwabantu	census (n)	sensus
ukubamba	hold (n)	vat
ukubamba inkunzi	hijack (v)	skaak
ukubekezela	patience (n)	geduld
ukubeletha	childbirth (n)	kindergeboorte
ukubhadla	roar (n)	brul
ukubhava	bath (v)	bad
ukubheja	bet (n)	weddenskap
ukubheka	look (n)	blik
ukubhikisha	demonstration (n)	betoging
ukubhukuda	swimming (n)	swem
ukubona	vision (n)	gesigsvermoë
ukubona	recognition (n)	herkenning
ukubonakala	appearance (n)	verskyning
ukubonga	thanks (n)	dank
ukubonga	gratitude (n)	dankbaarheid
ukubonga	praise (n)	lof
ukubonisa	persuasion (n)	oorreding
ukuboshwa	detention (n)	aanhouding
ukuboshwa	arrest (n)	inhegtenisneming
ukubuka	sight (n)	sig
ukubukisa	show (n)	vertoning
ukubulala umuntu	murder (n)	moord

Zulu	English	Afrikaans
ukubungaza izivakashi	host (v)	gasheer wees
ukubusa	reign (n)	bewind
ukubusa ngentando yabantu	democracy (n)	demokrasie
ukubuyiswa	reflection (n)	weerkaatsing
ukubuza	inquiry (n)	navraag
ukucaphuna	quotation (n)	aanhaling
ukucindezela	oppression (n)	onderdrukking
ukucindizela	pressure (n)	druk
ukucindizelwa	stress (n)	spanningsdruk
ukucinga	search (n)	soektog
ukucophelela	accuracy (n)	noukeurigheid
ukucwayiza	wink (n)	knipogie
ukucwila	diving (n)	duikery
ukudabuka	sadness (n)	droefheid
ukudabukela	regret (n)	spyt
ukudikiza	convulsion (n)	rukking
ukudingiswa	exile (n)	verbanning
ukudla	food (n)	kos
ukudlala	fun (n)	pret
ukudla okugcinwa ngakho	dessert (n)	nagereg
ukudliwa	consumption (n)	verbruik
ukudlulisela	reference (n)	verwysing
ukudlwengula	rape (n)	verkragting
ukudoba	fishing (n)	visvang
ukudubula	shot (n)	skoot
ukuduma	thunder (n)	donder
ukudumba	inflammation (n)	ontsteking
ukufa	death (n)	dood
ukufana	likeness (n)	ooreenkoms
ukufefeza	lisp (n)	gelispel
ukufihleka	secrecy (n)	geheimhouding
ukufika	arrival (n)	aankoms
ukufinyeza	contraction (n)	inkrimping
ukufumbathiswa	bribe (n)	omkoopprys
ukufundwa kwezinkanyezi	astrology (n)	astrologie
ukufungela amanga	perjury (n)	meineed
ukufutha	throb (n)	klopping
ukugcina	end (n)	einde
ukugcizelela	emphasis (n)	klem
ukugcotshwa	coronation (n)	kroning
ukugibela	ride (n)	rit
ukugingqika	roll (n)	rol
ukugona	embrace (n)	omhelsing
ukugongobala	spasm (n)	spasma
ukugqoloza	stare (n)	gestaar
ukugqunqa	suntan (n)	sonbruin
ukugula	sickness (n)	siekte
ukugula	illness (n)	siekte
ukuguquka	reform (n)	hervorming
ukugwaliza	asphyxia (n)	versmoring
ukugwenguka	reflex (n)	refleks
ukuhamba	walk (n)	wandeling
ukuhambelana	relationship (n)	verhouding
ukuhebhuka	erosion (n)	wegvreting
ukuheha	attraction (n)	aantrekking
ukuhlaba	sting (n)	steek
ukuhlaba	slaughter (n)	slagting

455

U

Zulu	English	Afrikaans	Zulu	English	Afrikaans
ukuhlakanipha	talent (n)	talent	ukulimaza	damage (n)	skade
ukuhlangana	meeting (n)	ontmoeting	ukulimaza	prejudice (n)	vooroordeel
ukuhlangana	society (n)	samelewing	ukulinga	experiment (n)	proefneming
ukuhlangana	connection (n)	verbinding	ukulinganisa	figure (n)	figuur
ukuhlanganiswa	addition (n)	toevoeging	ukulondeka	safety (n)	veiligheid
ukuhlanya	insanity (n)	kranksinnigheid	ukuluma	bite (n)	hap
ukuhlanzeka	purity (n)	suiwerheid	ukulungisela	preparation (n)	voorbereiding
ukuhlaphaza	extravagance (n)	buitensporigheid	ukulutha	addiction (n)	verslaafdheid
ukuhlasela	raid (n)	strooptog	ukulwa	fight (n)	geveg
ukuhleba	whisper (n)	gefluister	ukuma	stand (n)	stand
ukuhlehlela	retreat (n)	terugtog	ukuma kwenhliziyo	mood (n)	bui
ukuhleka	laugh (n)	lag	ukumamatheka	smile (n)	glimlag
ukuhleka	ridicule (n)	spottery	ukumangala	amazement (n)	verbasing
ukuhlinza	operation (n)	operasie	ukumangalelwa	prosecution (n)	vervolging
ukuhlinzwa	surgery (n)	chirurgie	ukumelana	opposition (n)	opposisie
ukuhlokoma	acclaim (n)	toejuiging	ukumisa	constitution (n)	grondwet
ukuhlola	inspection (n)	inspeksie	ukumukiswa	dismissal (n)	ontslag
ukuhlola	investigation (n)	ondersoek	ukunakelela	care (v)	omgee
ukuhlolwa	examination (n)	eksamen	ukunamathelana	attachment (n)	gehegtheid
ukuhlolwa kwem- bangela yokufa	inquest (n)	doodsondersoek	ukunandisa	flavouring (n)	geursel
ukuhlonga	lack (n)	gebrek	ukuncoma	recommendation (n)	aanbeveling
ukuhlonipha	respect (n)	respek	ukungabikho	absence (n)	afwesigheid
ukuhlubuka	disloyalty (n)	dislojaliteit	ukungahloniphi	insolence (n)	parmantigheid
ukuhlupheka	misery (n)	ellende	ukungalaleli	disobedience (n)	ongehoorsaamheid
ukuhlwa	evening (n)	aand	ukunganaki	negligence (n)	nalatigheid
ukuhona	snore (n)	snork	ukungaqini	weakness (n)	swakheid
ukuhwalala	dusk (n)	skemer	ukungathembi	distrust (n)	wantroue
ukuhwaqabala	frown (n)	frons	ukungazi	ignorance (n)	onkunde
ukuhwaqabala	scowl (n)	suur gesig	ukungcolisa	pollution (n)	besoedeling
ukuhweba	trade (n)	handel	ukungena	entry (n)	binnekoms
ukujiyelwa	disability (n)	gebrek	ukungezwani	misunderstanding (n)	misverstand
ukujula	depth (n)	diepte	ukungingiza	stutter (n)	gestotter
ukukampa	camping (n)	kampering	ukungingiza	stammer (n)	gehakkel
ukukhahlela	kick (n)	skop	ukungqongqoza	knock (v)	klop
ukukhanya	light (n)	lig	ukunitha	knitting (n)	breiwerk
ukukhanya kwelanga	sunlight (n)	sonlig	ukunqamuka kokudubula	ceasefire (n)	skietstilstand
ukukhathala	weariness (n)	moegheid	ukunqanda	restriction (n)	inperking
ukukhathala	fatigue (n)	vermoeienis	ukunqekuza	nod (n)	knik
ukukhetha	discrimination (n)	diskriminasie	ukunqoba	triumph (n)	triomf
ukukhetha	choice (n)	keuse	ukunquma nentaba	contour (n)	kontoer
ukukhinyabeza	sanction (n)	sanksie	ukunqumelana isikhathi	appointment (n)	afspraak
ukukhombisa	direction (n)	rigting	ukuntoko	pet (n)	troeteldier
ukukhula	increase (n)	verhoging	ukunyakaza	disturbance (n)	oproer
ukukhula	adulthood (n)	volwassenheid	ukunyamalala	disappearance (n)	verdwyning
ukukhulelisa ngokujova	artificial insemination (n)	kunsmatige inseminasie	ukunye	one (n)	een
ukukhululwa	acquittal (n)	vryspraak	ukupaka	parking (n)	parkering
ukukhuphuka	rise (n)	styging	ukuphakama	height (n)	hoogte
ukukhwehlela	cough (n)	hoes	ukuphambuka	deviation (n)	ompad
ukuklabalasa	scream (n)	gil	ukuphaphatheka kwegazi	anaemia (n)	bloedarmoede
ukuklina	mischief (n)	kattekwaad	ukuphaphazela	panic (n)	paniek
ukukweletisa	credit (v)	krediteer	ukuphathana	relation (n)	verhouding
ukulahlekelwa	loss (n)	verlies	ukuphathwa	management (n)	bestuur
ukulalela	obedience (n)	gehoorsaamheid	ukuphathwa ikhanda	headache (n)	hoofpyn
ukulamba	hunger (n)	honger	ukuphefumula	respiration (n)	asemhaling
ukulanda	description (n)	beskrywing	ukuphefumulisa	artificial respiration (n)	kunsmatige asemhaling
ukulandelana	sequence (n)	reeks			
ukulangazela	ambition (n)	ambisie			
ukulimala	harm (n)	skade	ukuphela	finish (n)	einde

Zulu	English	Afrikaans	Zulu	English	Afrikaans
ukuphela ithemba	despair (n)	wanhoop	ukuthola	adoption (n)	aanneming
ukuphendula ecaleni	plea (n)	pleidooi	ukuthomba	rust (n)	roes
ukuphikisa	contradiction (n)	weerspreking	ukuthula	silence (n)	stilte
ukuphikisana	argument (n)	argument	ukuthula	peace (n)	vrede
ukuphikisana	controversy (n)	twispunt	ukuthumbeka	bondage (n)	knegskap
ukuphila isidolobha	urbanisation (n)	verstedeliking	ukuthungwa kobuhlalu	beadwork (n)	kraalwerk
ukuphilisa	cure (n)	genesing	ukuthunywa	mission (n)	sending
ukuphokophela	urge (n)	drang	ukuthutha	removal (n)	trek
ukuphucuka	refinement (n)	verfyndheid	ukuthutheleka	influx (n)	instroming
ukuphuma	exit (n)	uitgang	ukuvakashela	visit (n)	besoek
ukuphuma kwelanga	sunrise (n)	sonop	ukuvelela	approach (n)	nadering
ukuphumisela	pronunciation (n)	uitspraak	ukuvikelwa	defence (n)	verdediging
ukuphumula	rest (n)	rus	ukuvimbela	obstruction (n)	belemmernis
ukuphuphuma isisu	abortion (n)	aborsie	ukuvimbela	prevention (n)	voorkoming
ukuphuphutheka	daze (n)	bedwelming	ukuvota	vote (n)	stem
ukuqabula	kiss (n)	soen	ukuvukela	revolt (n)	opstand
ukuqala	beginning (n)	begin	ukuvukela umbuso	revolution (n)	revolusie
ukuqanjwa	invention (n)	uitvinding	ukuvukela umbuso	sedition (n)	opruiing
ukuqaphela	vigilance (n)	waaksaamheid	ukuvula	opening (n)	opening
ukuqashwa	appointment (n)	aanstelling	ukuvuma	confession (n)	belydenis
ukuqeqesheka	efficiency (n)	doeltreffendheid	ukuvuma	consent (n)	instemming
ukuqhamuka	outbreak (n)	uitbreking	ukuxabana	quarrel (n)	twis
ukuqhathanisa	comparison (n)	vergelyking	ukuxhuga	limp (n)	mankheid
ukuqhikiza	shrug (n)	skouerophaling	ukuxhuma	jump (n)	sprong
ukuqhubeka	advance (n)	vooruitgang	ukuya kwelinye izwe	migration (n)	migrasie
ukuqhuma	explosion (n)	ontploffing	ukuyingiliza	cycle (n)	siklus
ukuqhutshwa kweholo	increment (n)	verhoging	ukuzabalaza	resistance (n)	weerstand
ukuqumba	constipation (n)	konstipasie	ukuzalwa	birth (n)	geboorte
ukuqwasha	insomnia (n)	slaaploosheid	ukuzamula	yawn (n)	gaap
ukusa	daybreak (n)	dagbreek	ukuze	that (pron)	dat
ukusa	dawn (n)	dagbreek	ukuzenzisa	pretence (n)	skyn
ukusayina	signature (n)	handtekening	ukuzibulala	suicide (n)	selfmoord
ukushaya kwenhliziyo	heartbeat (n)	hartklop	ukuzidla	pride (n)	trots
ukushayisana	collision (n)	botsing	ukuzimelela	balance (n)	balans
ukusheshisa	haste (n)	haas	ukuzimisela	determination (n)	vasberadenheid
ukushisa	heat (n)	hitte	ukuzindela	hesitation (n)	aarseling
ukushisa	temperature (n)	temperatuur	ukuziphatha	behaviour (n)	gedrag
ukushiya	omission (n)	weglating	ukuzithemba	self-confidence (n)	selfvertroue
ukushona kwelanga	sundown (n)	sononder	ukuzivala	contraception (n)	voorbehoeding
ukushona kwelanga	sunset (n)	sononder	ukuzungeleza	circulation (n)	omloop
ukusina	dance (n)	dans	ukuzuza	acquisition (n)	aanskaffing
ukusinda	recovery (n)	herstel	ukuzwana	harmony (n)	harmonie
ukusindisa	rescue (n)	redding	ukuzwangomlomo	taste (n)	smaak
ukusineka	grin (n)	grynslag	ukwahlukana	parting (n)	paadjie
ukusithibala	eclipse (n)	verduistering	ukwahluleka	defeat (n)	nederlaag
ukusizana	co-operation (n)	samewerking	ukwahluleka	failure (n)	mislukking
ukusoka	circumcision (n)	besnydenis	ukwakha	composition (n)	komposisie
ukusola	doubt (n)	twyfel	ukwakha	construction (n)	konstruksie
ukusombuluka kwendalo	evolution (n)	evolusie	ukwaluka	weaving (n)	wewery
ukusukela kwa-	since (adv)	sedert	ukwambuka	rebellion (n)	opstand
ukususa	removal (n)	verwydering	ukwambuka	treason (n)	verraad
ukuthasiselwa igazi	blood transfusion (n)	bloedoortapping	ukwamukela	acceptance (n)	aanvaarding
ukuthekelisa	export (v)	uitvoer	ukwamukelwa	reception (n)	ontvangs
ukuthela	surrender (n)	oorgawe	ukwamukelwa	admission (n)	toelating
ukuthembeka	loyalty (n)	lojaliteit	ukwaphuka	fracture (n)	breuk
ukuthethwa kwecala	trial (n)	verhoor	ukwatapeya	avocado (n)	avokado
ukuthethwa kwecala	proceedings (n)	verrigtinge	ukwazana	acquaintance (n)	kennismaking
ukuthinta	touch (n)	aanraking	ukwazi	ability (n)	bekwaamheid
ukuthokozisa	amusement (n)	vermaaklikheid	ukwazi	consciousness (n)	bewussyn
			ukwazi ngezinkanyezi	astronomy (n)	sterrekunde

457

U

Zulu	English	Afrikaans
ukwehla	descent (n)	daling
ukwelapha	treatment (n)	behandeling
ukwemuka	departure (n)	vertrek
ukwemukela	welcome (n)	welkom
ukwenama	contentment (n)	tevredenheid
ukwenqaba	rejection (n)	verwerping
ukwenyuswa	promotion (n)	bevordering
ukwenza	performance (n)	uitvoering
ukweqa	escape (n)	ontsnapping
ukwesaba	fear (n)	vrees
ukwesabisa	terror (n)	terreur
ukwethembeka	fidelity (n)	getrouheid
ukweyisa	impertinence (n)	astrantheid
ukweyisa	scorn (n)	veragting
ukwindla	autumn (n)	herfs
ukwipili	quince (n)	kweper
ulaka	temper (n)	humeur
ulaka	anger (n)	kwaadheid
ulaka	rage (n)	woede
ulamula	lemon (n)	suurlemoen
ulaza	cream (n)	room
uletisi	lettuce (n)	blaarslaai
uleyisi	lace (n)	kant
ulimi	tongue (n)	tong
ulimi	language (n)	taal
ulimi	vernacular (n)	volkstaal
ulimi lwesigodi	dialect (n)	dialek
ulimo	agriculture (n)	landbou
ulineni	linen (n)	linne
uloliwe	railway (n)	spoorweg
ulwandle	ocean (n)	oseaan
ulwandle	sea (n)	see
ulwanga	palate (n)	verhemelte
ulwazi	experience (n)	ervaring
ulwazi	knowledge (n)	kennis
ulwembu	spider (n)	spinnekop
uLwesibili	Tuesday (n)	Dinsdag
uLwesihlanu	Friday (n)	Vrydag
uLwesine	Thursday (n)	Donderdag
ulwesithathu	Wednesday (n)	Woensdag
uma	if (conj)	as
umabhalana	clerk (n)	klerk
umAfrika	African (n)	Afrikaan
umahluka	difference (n)	verskil
umahluli	adjudicator (n)	beoordelaar
umakhelwane	neighbour (n)	buurman
umakheniki	mechanic (n)	werktuigkundige
umakoti	bride (n)	bruid
umakoti	daughter-in-law (n)	skoondogter
umalume	uncle (n)	oom
umalusi wezimvu	shepherd (n)	skaapwagter
umama	mother (n)	moeder
umamezala	mother-in-law (n)	skoonmoeder
umamncane	aunt (n)	tante
uMandulo	August (n)	Augustus
umango	mango (n)	mango
umanqulwane	ladybird (n)	lieweheersbesie
umantshi	magistrate (n)	landdros
umanyolo	fertiliser (n)	kunsmis
uMashi	March (n)	Maart

Zulu	English	Afrikaans
umashiqela	dictator (n)	diktator
umasikilopu	microscope (n)	mikroskoop
umasipalati	municipality (n)	munisipaliteit
umasitadi	mustard (n)	mosterd
umata	partner (n)	vennoot
umatilasi	mattress (n)	matras
umbala	colour (n)	kleur
umbala	shin (n)	skeen
umbala wesiphofu	pink (n)	pienk
umbala wewolintshi	orange (a)	oranje
umbandamu	ringworm (n)	ringwurm
umbandela	amendment (n)	wysiging
umbangalusizi	tragedy (n)	tragedie
umbango	dispute (n)	onenigheid
umbango	contest (n)	wedstryd
umbani	flash (n)	flits
umbani	lightning (n)	weerlig
umbankwa	lizard (n)	akkedis
umbayimbayi	cannon (n)	kanon
umbazi	carpenter (n)	timmerman
umbefu	asthma (n)	asma
umbele	udder (n)	uier
umbelethisi	midwife (n)	vroedvrou
umbhabhadiso	baptism (n)	doop
umbhabhalala	wreck (n)	wrak
umbhaki	baker (n)	bakker
umbhali	author (n)	skrywer
umbhali wamakhawunti	accountant (n)	rekenmeester
umbhalo	document (n)	dokument
umbhalo	writing (n)	skrif
umbhede	bed (n)	bed
umbhedo	nonsense (n)	onsin
umbheki	caretaker (n)	opsigter
umbhishobhi	bishop (n)	biskop
umbhishobhi omkhulu	archbishop (n)	aartsbiskop
umbhobe	buttermilk (n)	karringmelk
umbhongo	groan (n)	kreun
umbhuqo	sarcasm (n)	sarkasme
umbiki	reporter (n)	verslaggewer
umbiko	message (n)	boodskap
umbiko	information (n)	inligting
umbiko	prediction (n)	voorspelling
umbiko	report (n)	verslag
umbokwane	eel (n)	paling
umbonisici	censor (v)	sensor
umbono	opinion (n)	mening
umbukiso	show (n)	skou
umbukiso	view (n)	uitsig
umbukiso	exhibition (n)	uitstalling
umbulali	murderer (n)	moordenaar
umbungu	foetus (n)	fetus
umbungu	embryo (n)	embrio
umbusi	ruler (n)	regeerder
umbuzo	question (n)	vraag
umcabanago	thought (n)	gedagte
umcabango	idea (n)	idee
umcako	lime (n)	kalk
umcako	whitewash (n)	witkalk
umcamelo	pillow (n)	kussing
umcebi	informer (n)	verklikker

Zulu	English	Afrikaans	Zulu	English	Afrikaans
umceli	applicant (n)	aansoeker	umfuthi wecilongo	trumpeter (n)	trompetblaser
umchamo	urine (n)	urine	umfutho	energy (n)	energie
umchilo	cord (n)	koord	umfutho wegazi	blood pressure (n)	bloeddruk
umcibisholo	arrow (n)	pyl	umgankla	kudu (n)	koedoe
umcimbi	item (n)	item	umgathini	bluegum (n)	bloekomboom
umcimbi	party (n)	party	umgaxo	necklace (n)	halssnoer
umcindezeli	oppressor (n)	onderdrukker	umgcabo	vaccination (n)	inenting
umculo	music (n)	musiek	umgede	cave (n)	grot
umcwali	hairdresser (n)	haarkapper	umgibeli	passenger (n)	passasier
umcwaningi wezimali	auditor (n)	ouditeur	umgidi	ceremony (n)	seremonie
umdabu	origin (n)	oorsprong	umgodi	hole (n)	gat
umdaka	bushbuck (n)	bosbok	umgodi	pit (n)	gat
uMdali	Creator (n)	Skepper	umgodi	shaft (n)	skag
umdayisi endalini	auctioneer (n)	afslaer	umgodi onomthombo	well (n)	put
umdidi	rectum (n)	rektum	umgodlo	sheath (n)	skede
umdlali	actor (n)	akteur	umgogodla	spine (n)	ruggraat
umdlalikazi	actress (n)	aktrise	umgomo	policy (n)	beleid
umdlali wekhilikithi	cricketer (n)	krieketspeler	umgomo	standard (n)	standaard
umdlali we-ogani	organist (n)	orrelis	umgqekezi	burglar (n)	inbreker
umdlalo	sport (n)	sport	uMgqibelo	Saturday (n)	Saterdag
umdlalo	play (n)	toneelstuk	umgqomo wezibi	rubbish bin (n)	vullisblik
umdlalo	game (n)	spel	umgudlo	soapstone (n)	seepsteen
umdlavuza	cancer (n)	kanker	umgwaqo	road (n)	pad
umdlwane	puppy (n)	klein hondjie	umgwaqo oya endlini	driveway (n)	inrit
umdondoshiya	giant (n)	reus	umgwedli	oar (n)	roeispaan
umdrayiklini	drycleaner (n)	droogskoonmakery	umgxala	crowbar (n)	koevoet
umdumba	pod (n)	peul	umhabulo	sip (n)	slukkie
umdweshu	strip (n)	strook	umhambiphansi	pedestrian (n)	voetganger
umdweshu	bandage (n)	verband	umhawu	pity (n)	jammerte
umemukeli-bahambeli	receptionist (n)	ontvangsklerk	umhawu	envy (n)	naywer
umentshisi	match (n)	vuurhoutjie	umhawu	charity (n)	liefdadigheid
umenzeli	agent (n)	agent	umhayizo	hysterics (n)	histerie
umenzi	performer (n)	uitvoerder	umhedeni	heathen (n)	heiden
umeqi	trespasser (n)	oortreder	umhedeni	pagan (n)	heiden
umesaso	excitement (n)	opwinding	umhhadlazo	roughage (n)	vesel
umese	knife (n)	mes	umhlaba	aloe (n)	aalwyn
umeselane	mason (n)	messelaar	umhlaba	earth (n)	aarde
uMeyi	May (n)	Mei	umhlaba	land (n)	land
umfana	lad (n)	knaap	umhlaba	world (n)	wêreld
umfana	boy (n)	seun	umhlabathi	soil (n)	grond
umfanekiso	picture (n)	prent	umhlabathi	ground (n)	grond
umfanekiso	drawing (n)	tekening	umhlahlelo	analysis (n)	ontleding
umfazi	woman (n)	vrou	umhlambi	herd (n)	kudde
umfece	cocoon (n)	kokon	umhlambi	flock (n)	trop
umfelokazi	widow (n)	weduwee	umhlane	back (n)	rug
umfelukholo	martyr (n)	martelaar	umhlanga	reed (n)	riet
umfelwa	widower (n)	wewenaar	umhlangano	gathering (n)	byeenkoms
umfingcizo	wrinkle (n)	plooi	umhlangano	conference (n)	konferensie
umfokazi	stranger (n)	vreemdeling	umhlangano	meeting (n)	vergadering
umfowethu	brother (n)	broer	umhlanganyeli	companion (n)	metgesel
umfudlana	stream (n)	stroom	umhlapho	afterbirth (n)	nageboorte
umfula	river (n)	rivier	umhlathi	jaw (n)	kaak
umfundi	pupil (n)	leerling	umhlatshelo	victim (n)	slagoffer
umfundisi	lecturer (n)	dosent	umhleli	editor (n)	redakteur
umfundisi	instructor (n)	instrukteur	umhlobiso	ornament (n)	ornament
umfundisi	minister (n)	predikant	umhlobiso	decoration (n)	versiering
umfundisi	missionary (n)	sendeling	umhloli	inspector (n)	inspekteur
umfungisi	commissioner of oaths (n)	kommissaris van ede	umhlubukisi	agitator (n)	opstoker
			umhluzi	sauce (n)	sous
umfunkulu	spinal cord (n)	rugmurg	umhluzi	gravy (n)	sous

U

Zulu	English	Afrikaans	Zulu	English	Afrikaans
umhlwenga	mane (n)	maanhare	umlotha	ash (n)	as
umholi	leader (n)	leier	umluleki	adviser (n)	raadgewer
umhumushi	interpreter (n)	tolk	umlutha	addict (n)	verslaafde
umhumushi	translator (n)	vertaler	ummangaleli	prosecutor (n)	aanklaer
umhwamuko	vapour (n)	wasem	ummangaleli	complainant (n)	klaer
umiyane	mosquito (n)	muskiet	ummangalelwa	accused (n)	beskuldigde
umjaho	race (n)	wedren	ummangali	accuser (n)	beskuldiger
umjaho wamahhashi	horserace (n)	perdewedren	ummangali	plaintiff (n)	eiser
umjibe	rafter (n)	dakbalk	ummbila	maize (n)	mielies
umjikelezo wesiyingi	circumference (n)	omtrek	ummeli	advocate (n)	advokaat
umjovo	inoculation (n)	inenting	ummeli	lawyer (n)	prokureur
umjuluko	perspiration (n)	perspirasie	ummeli	attorney (n)	prokureur
umjuluko	sweat (n)	sweet	ummeli	solicitor (n)	prokureur
umkhaba	paunch (n)	boepmaag	ummeli	representative (n)	verteenwoordiger
umkhamba	acacia (n)	akasia	ummeli-zisebenzi	shop steward (n)	segsman
umkhasi	festival (n)	fees	ummemo	echo (n)	weerklank
umkhaza	tick (n)	luis	umminzo	oesophagus (n)	slukderm
umkhemisi	pharmacist (n)	apteker	ummpunyumpunyu	mercury (n)	kwik
umkhemisi	chemist (n)	apteker	umnako	interest (n)	belang
umkhiwane	figtree (n)	vyeboom	umnako	notice (n)	kennisgewing
umkhokhi	payer (n)	betaler	umncele	border (n)	grens
umkhoma	whale (n)	walvis	umncele	boundary (n)	grenslyn
umkhono	sleeve (n)	mou	umncomeli	fan (n)	bewonderaar
umkhonto	assegai (n)	assegaai	umnduze	lily (n)	lelie
umkhonto	spear (n)	spies	umnenke	snail (n)	slak
umkhosi	occasion (n)	geleentheid	umngane	friend (n)	vriend
umkhosi	celebration (n)	viering	umngcwabo	burial (n)	begrafnis
umkhosi wekhulu leminyaka	centenary (n)	eeufees	umngcwabo	funeral (n)	begrafnis
umkhuba	method (n)	metode	umngenela	tributary (n)	takrivier
umkhuba omubi	vice (n)	ondeug	umnikazi	owner (n)	eienaar
umkhumbi	boat (n)	boot	umnikelo	sacrifice (n)	offerande
umkhumbi	yacht (n)	seiljag	umnikelo	donation (n)	skenking
umkhumbi	ship (n)	skip	umninindlu	host (n)	gasheer
umkhuthazi	activist (n)	aktivis	umnkantsha	marrow (n)	murg
umkhuthuzi	pickpocket (n)	sakkeroller	umnkenke	crack (n)	kraak
umkhwenyana	son-in-law (n)	skoonseun	umnotho	economy (n)	ekonomie
umklami wezindlu	architect (n)	argitek	umnotho	fortune (n)	fortuin
umklomelo	reward (n)	beloning	umnotho	wealth (n)	rykdom
umklomelo	prize (n)	prys	umnqumi wenani	assessor (n)	skatter
umlalelo	ambush (n)	hinderlaag	umntwana	baby (n)	baba
umlamu	sister-in-law (n)	skoonsuster	umntwana	child (n)	kind
umlamu	brother-in-law (n)	swaer	umnyango	door (n)	deur
umlamuli	arbiter (n)	arbiter	umnyezane	willow (n)	wilgerboom
umlamuli	mediator (n)	bemiddelaar	umnyinyitheko	depression (n)	bedruktheid
umlandeli	disciple (n)	dissipel	umnyuzi	mule (n)	muil
umlandeli	follower (n)	volgeling	umondli	guardian (n)	voog
umlando	history (n)	geskiedenis	umongameli	president (n)	president
umlekeleli	accomplice (n)	medepligtige	umongo	pith (n)	pit
umlenze	leg (n)	been	umoni	culprit (n)	skuldige
umlephero	leper (n)	melaatse	umopho	haemorrhage (n)	bloeding
umliba	tendril (n)	rankie	umoya	air (n)	lug
umlilo	fire (n)	vuur	umoya	wind (n)	wind
umlimi	farmer (n)	boer	umphandle	outside (n)	buitekant
umlingiswa	character (n)	karakter	umphangi	robber (n)	rower
umlingo	magic (n)	towerkuns	umphango	loot (n)	buit
umlokothi	dare (n)	uitdaging	umphathi	manager (n)	bestuurder
umlolozelo	lullaby (n)	wiegelied	umphathi welabhulali	librarian (n)	bibliotekaris
umlomo	mouth (n)	mond	umpheco	fold (n)	vou
umlomo wenyoni	beak (n)	snawel	umphefumulo	breath (n)	asem
			umphefumulo	spirit (n)	gees

Zulu	English	Afrikaans
umphefumulo	soul (n)	siel
umpheki	cook (n)	kok
umphelezeli	escort (n)	metgesel
umphenduki	convert (n)	bekeerling
umphimbo	throat (n)	keel
umphimbo	larynx (n)	larinks
umphimbo	gullet (n)	slukderm
umphini	shaft (n)	steel
umphongolo	barrel (n)	vat
umphostoli	apostle (n)	apostel
umphuci	barber (n)	haarsnyer
umphumela	consequence (n)	gevolg
umphumela	outcome (n)	uitkoms
umphumela	effect (n)	uitwerking
umphumela	result (n)	uitslag
umphungo	disinfectant (n)	ontsmettingsmiddel
umpompi	tap (n)	kraan
umpristi	priest (n)	priester
umprofethi	prophet (n)	profeet
umqambi	composer (n)	komponis
umqambi-manga	liar (n)	leuenaar
umqamelo	cushion (n)	kussing
umqandelo	guess (n)	raaiskoot
umqashi	tenant (n)	bewoner
umqashi	lodger (n)	loseerder
umqashi	employer (n)	werkgewer
umqashisi	landlord (n)	verhuurder
umqeqeshi	coach (n)	afrigter
umqhele	crown (n)	kroon
umqhubi-msebenzi	operator (n)	operateur
umqhudelwano	competition (n)	wedstryd
umqondo	mind (n)	verstand
umqophi	sculptor (n)	beeldhouer
umqothu	desert (n)	woestyn
umquba	compost (n)	kompos
umqubo	manure (n)	mis
umqubuko	rash (n)	veluitslag
umqulu	bundle (n)	bondel
umqumbe	bud (n)	botsel
umqwayiba	biltong (n)	biltong
umsebe	ray (n)	straal
umsebenzana wokuzilibazisa	hobby (n)	stokperdjie
umsebenzi	employment (n)	werk
umsebenzi	work (n)	werk
umsebenzi	labour (n)	arbeid
umsebenzi	exercise (n)	oefening
umsebenzi	task (n)	taak
umsebenzi	use (n)	gebruik
umsebenzi	job (n)	werk
umsebenzi wasekhaya	homework (n)	huiswerk
umsebenzi wokubumba	pottery (n)	pottebakkery
umsebe welanga	sunbeam (n)	sonstraal
umsele	ditch (n)	sloot
umselekazi wamanzi	canal (n)	kanaal
umseshi	detective (n)	speurder
umshado	wedding (n)	bruilof
umshado	marriage (n)	huwelik
umshana	nephew (n)	neef
umshanakazi	niece (n)	niggie
umshanelo	broom (n)	besem
umshayeli	driver (n)	bestuurder
umshayi-mitshingo	flautist (n)	fluitspeler
umshayi-vayolina	cellist (n)	tjellis
umshayivayolini	violinist (n)	vioolspeler
umshayi wesigubhu	drummer (n)	tromspeler
umshayi wopiyane	pianist (n)	klavierspeler
umshayo	rail (n)	staaf
umshazo	frostbite (n)	vriesbrand
umshekelelo	detour (n)	omweg
umshini	machine (n)	masjien
umshini wokubala	calculator (n)	rekenaar
umshini wokusika utshani	lawnmower (n)	grassnyer
umshini wokuthayipha	typewriter (n)	tikmasjien
umshini wokuthunga	sewing machine (n)	naaimasjien
umshumayeli	preacher (n)	predikant
umshuwalense	assurance (n)	versekering
umsiko	cut (n)	sny
umsila	tail (n)	stert
umsimbithi	ironwood (n)	ysterhout
umsindo	noise (n)	geraas
umsindo	sound (n)	klank
umsindo	uproar (n)	lawaai
umsinga	current (n)	stroom
umsinsila	coccyx (n)	stuitjiebeen
umsipha	ligament (n)	ligament
umsipha	sinew (n)	sening
umsipha	tendon (n)	sening
umsipha	muscle (n)	spier
umsizi	assistant (n)	helper
uMsombuluko	Monday (n)	Maandag
umsundu	earthworm (n)	erdwurm
umthakathi	witchdoctor (n)	toordokter
umthambo	vein (n)	aar
umthambo	artery (n)	slagaar
umthambo wegazi	blood vessel (n)	bloedvat
umthamo	mouthful (n)	mondvol
umthandazo	prayer (n)	gebed
umthanjana	capillary (n)	haarvat
umthengi	buyer (n)	koper
umthetho	principle (n)	beginsel
umthetho	regulation (n)	regulasie
umthetho	rule (n)	reël
umthetho	law (n)	wet
umthofu	lead (n)	lood
umthombo	source (n)	bron
umthombo	fountain (n)	fontein
umthondo	penis (n)	penis
umthungi	tailor (n)	kleremaker
umthungo	seam (n)	naat
umthungo	sewing (n)	naaldwerk
umthungo	hem (n)	soom
umthunjwa	prisoner-of-war (n)	krygsgevangene
umthunzi	shade (n)	skadu
umthwalo	burden (n)	las
umthwalo	load (n)	vrag
umtshingo	flute (n)	fluit
umudwa	scratch (n)	krap
umumo womhlaba	geography (n)	aardrykskunde

461

	Zulu	English	Afrikaans
U	umunga	mimosa (n)	mimosa
	umuntu	person (n)	persoon
	umuntu munye	individual (n)	individu
	umuntu obizayo	caller (n)	roeper
	umuntu odinisayo	bore (n)	vervelige mens
	umuntu osekhulile	adult (n)	volwassene
	umuntu oyinkawu	albino (n)	albino
	umuntu weposi	postman (n)	posbode
	umuntu womdabu	aboriginal (n)	oorspronklike inwoner
	umunwe	finger (n)	vinger
	umunxa	part (n)	deel
	umusa	kindness (n)	goedheid
	umusa	favour (n)	guns
	umusho	sentence (n)	sin
	umushu	stripe (n)	streep
	umuthi	tree (n)	boom
	umuthi	medicine (n)	medisyne
	umuthi wamazinyo	toothpaste (n)	tandepasta
	umuthi wokuhlam-bulula isisu	laxative (n)	lakseermiddel
	umuthi wokuhudisa	purgative (n)	purgeermiddel
	umuthi wokuqeda iphunga elibi	deodorant (n)	reukweermiddel
	umuvi	wasp (n)	perdeby
	umuzi	residence (n)	verblyfplek
	umuzwa	nerve (n)	senuwee
	umvangeli	evangelist (n)	evangelis
	umvikeli	defendant (n)	verweerder
	umvunya	fishmoth (n)	vismot
	umyalezo	order (n)	bevel
	umyalo	commandment (n)	gebod
	umyalo	instruction (n)	onderrig
	umyeni	bridegroom (n)	bruidegom
	umyeni	husband (n)	man
	umzali	parent (n)	ouer
	umzamo	effort (n)	inspanning
	umzamo	attempt (n)	poging
	umzekeliso	parable (n)	gelykenis
	umzenzisi	hypocrite (n)	skynheilige
	umzimba	physique (n)	liggaamsbou
	umzimba	body (n)	liggaam
	umzingeli	hunter (n)	jagter
	umzukulu	grandchild (n)	kleinkind
	umzukulu wesifazane	granddaughter (n)	kleindogter
	umzukulu wesilisa	grandson (n)	kleinseun
	umzuzu	moment (n)	oomblik
	umzwelo	emotion (n)	gevoel
	unembeza	conscience (n)	gewete
	unesi	nurse (n)	verpleegster
	ungqi	fullstop (n)	punt
	ungwaqa	consonant (n)	medeklinker
	ungwengwe	lawn (n)	grasperk
	unhloko	principal (n)	hoof
	unjongwe	indigestion (n)	slegte spysvertering
	unkamisa	vowel (n)	klinker
	unkosikazi	wife (n)	vrou
	uNkulunkulu	God (n)	God
	unobhala	secretary (n)	sekretaris
	unobhutshuzwayo	soccer (n)	sokker
	unobhutshuzwayo	football (n)	voetbal

Zulu	English	Afrikaans
unogolantethe	stork (n)	ooievaar
unogwaja	rabbit (n)	konyn
unompempe	referee (n)	skeidsregter
uNovemba	November (n)	November
unqenqema	ledge (n)	rotslys
unqenqema	ridge (n)	rug
unwabu	chameleon (n)	verkleurmannetjie
unxande	rectangle (n)	reghoek
unxantathu	triangle (n)	driehoek
unya	cruelty (n)	wreedheid
unyaka	year (n)	jaar
unyaka onezinsuku ezingu-	leap year (n)	skrikkeljaar
unyawo	footprint (n)	voetspoor
unyawo	foot (n)	voet
unyele	breeze (n)	bries
unyezi	moonlight (n)	maanlig
unyonga	cripple (n)	kreupele
u-Okthoba	October (n)	Oktober
upelepele	chilli (n)	brandrissie
upelepele	pepper (n)	peper
upelepele oluhlaza	green pepper (n)	soetrissie
upende	paint (n)	verf
upetroli	petrol (n)	petrol
uphahla	roof (n)	dak
uphalafini	paraffin (n)	paraffien
uphanqu	pauper (n)	behoeftige
uPhapha	pope (n)	pous
uphaphe	feather (n)	veer
uphawu	brand (n)	handelsmerk
uphawu	symbol (n)	simbool
uphayinaphu	pineapple (n)	pynappel
uphempethwane	cobra (n)	kobra
uphingo	adultery (n)	owerspel
upholishi	polish (n)	politoer
uphondo	horn (n)	horing
upiyane	piano (n)	klavier
upopo	pawpaw (n)	papaja
upopopo	colon (n)	dikderm
uprinsesi	princess (n)	prinses
uprinsi	prince (n)	prins
uprofesa	professor (n)	professor
uqalo	bamboo (n)	bamboes
uqhoqhoqho	windpipe (n)	gorrelpyp
uqhuqho	malaria (n)	malaria
uqobo lwa-	identity (n)	identiteit
uqwanga	cartilage (n)	kraakbeen
uqweqwe	scab (n)	rofie
uqweqwe lukaphayi	pastry (n)	pastei
uradishi	radish (n)	radys
urezini	raisin (n)	rosyntjie
uSathane	devil (n)	duiwel
usayitsheni	sergeant (n)	sersant
usebe	margin (n)	kantlyn
usebe lolwandle	beach (n)	strand
usekelasihlalo	vice-chairman (n)	ondervoorsitter
useleri	celery (n)	seldery
usemende	cement (n)	sement
usende	perfume (n)	parfuum
uSepthemba	September (n)	September

Zulu	English	Afrikaans	Zulu	English	Afrikaans
useyili	sail (n)	seil	uzungu	conspiracy (n)	sameswering
useyili	canvas (n)	seil	uzwani	toe (n)	toon
useyili	tarpaulin (n)	seil	uzwelo	sympathy (n)	simpatie
ushikishi	express (n)	sneltrein	-vakasha	call (v)	besoek
ushimula	chimney (n)	skoorsteen	-vakashela	visit (v)	besoek
ushisi	cheese (n)	kaas	-vala	cover (v)	dek
ushobishobi	tadpole (n)	paddavissie	-vala	shut (v)	toemaak
ushoki	chalk (n)	kryt	-valela ngaphandle	exclude (v)	uitsluit
ushokolethe	chocolate (n)	sjokolade	-valiweyo	shut (a)	toe
ushukela	sugar (n)	suiker	-valwa umlomo	ban (people) (v)	inperk
usigazi	cigar (n)	sigaar	-vamile	general (a)	algemeen
usihlalo	chairman (n)	voorsitter	-vamile	ordinary (a)	gewoon
usikilidi	cigarette (n)	sigaret	-vamile	common (a)	gewoon
usikothi	etiquette (n)	etiket	-vela	occur (v)	voorkom
usilika	silk (n)	sy	-vela	happen (v)	gebeur
usindiso	salvation (n)	verlossing	-vele kwelinye izwe	exotic (a)	eksoties
usinki	sink (n)	opwasbak	-velela	approach (v)	benader
usizi	grief (n)	leed	-veza	bare (v)	ontbloot
usizi	sorrow (n)	smart	-veza	disclose (v)	openbaar
usizo	relief (n)	verligting	-veza	afford (v)	bekostig
usizo	help (n)	hulp	-veza	expose (v)	blootlê
usizo	aid (n)	hulp	-veza iziboniso	illustrate (v)	illustreer
usizo lokuqala	first aid (n)	noodhulp	-vika	avert (v)	keer
uSomandla	Almighty (n)	Almagtige	-vikela	shield (v)	beskerm
usongo	threat (n)	dreigement	-vikela	defend (v)	verdedig
usuku	day (n)	dag	-vikela	protect (v)	beskerm
usuku lokuzalwa	birthday (n)	verjaarsdag	-vikelayo	defensive (a)	verdedigend
utamatisi	tomato (n)	tamatie	-vimba	plug (v)	toestop
uthando	affection (n)	toegeneentheid	-vimba	stop (v)	stop
uthando	love (n)	liefde	-vimbela	obstruct (v)	belemmer
uthango	hedge (n)	heining	-vimbela	block (v)	blokkeer
uthayi	tie (n)	das	-vimbela	bar (v)	uitsluit
utheniphu	turnip (n)	raap	-vimbela	prevent (v)	voorkom
uthi lokudoba	fishing rod (n)	visstok	-volontiya	volunteer (v)	vrywillig onderneem
uthi lomshanelo	broomstick (n)	besemstok	-vota	vote (v)	stem
uthingo lwenkosazane	rainbow (n)	reënboog	-vova	filter (v)	filtreer
uthisha	teacher (n)	onderwyser	-vuka	arise (v)	opstaan
uthuli	dust (n)	stof	-vuka	awake (v)	ontwaak
uthunge lwamatshe	reef (n)	rif	-vula	open (v)	oopmaak
utshani	grass (n)	gras	-vuliwe	open (a)	oop
utshani bokufulela	thatch (n)	dekgras	-vuma	acknowledge (v)	erken
utshani obomileyo	straw (n)	strooi	-vuma	consent (v)	instem
utshwala	beer (n)	bier	-vuma	confess (v)	bely
utwayi	eczema (n)	ekseem	-vumbulula	unearth (v)	opgrawe
uvalo	awe (n)	eerbied	-vumekayo	convenient (a)	gerieflik
uvalo	dread (v)	vrees	-vumela	approve (v)	goedkeur
uvemvane	butterfly (n)	skoenlapper	-vumela	justify (v)	regverdig
uvinika	vinegar (n)	asyn	-vumela	permit (v)	toelaat
uvolo	wool (n)	wol	-vumela	allow (v)	toestaan
uvolo	cotton wool (n)	watte	-vumelana	agree (v)	ooreenstem
uvolontiya	volunteer (n)	vrywilliger	-vumelana	rhyme (v)	rym
uweta	waiter (n)	kelner	-vumelanisa	adapt (v)	aanpas
uxolo	forgiveness (n)	vergifnis	-vumelene	unanimous (a)	eenstemmig
uyinki	ink (n)	ink	-vuna	harvest (v)	oes
uzagiga	mumps (n)	pampoentjies	-vuna	reap (v)	oes
uzi	fibre (n)	vesel	-vunda	fester (v)	sweer
uzibuthe	magnet (n)	magneet	-vundile	fertile (a)	vrugbaar
uzipho	claw (n)	klou	-vunyelwe ngumthetho	legitimate (a)	wettige
uzipho lomunwe	fingernail (n)	vingernael	-vusa	arouse (v)	opwek
uzulane	vagrant (n)	rondloper			

463

Zulu	English	Afrikaans
-vusa	excite (v)	opwind
-vuthiwe	ripe (a)	ryp
-vuvuka	swell (v)	swel
-vuza	leak (v)	lek
-wa	fall (v)	val
wena	you (pron)	jy
-wina	win (v)	wen
-wisa	overthrow (v)	omvergooi
-wisa	drop (v)	laat val
-xabana	quarrel (v)	twis
-xegezela	loose (a)	los
-xhakathisa	clasp (v)	vasklem
-xhamazele	impatient (a)	ongeduldig
-xhaphakile	abundant (a)	oorvloedig
-xhomondela	presume (v)	veronderstel
-xhuga	limp (v)	mank loop
-xhuma	bounce (v)	opspring
-xhuma	jump (v)	spring
-xhwalile	sickly (a)	sieklik
-xolela	excuse (v)	verontskuldig
-xolela	forgive (v)	vergewe
-xolela	pardon (v)	vergewe
-xolisa	apologise (v)	verskoning vra
-xosha	sack (v)	afdank
-xosha	evict (v)	uitsit
-xova	knead (v)	knie
-xoxa	chat (v)	gesels
-xoxisana	negotiate (v)	onderhandel
-xoxisana	consult (v)	raadpleeg
-xoxisana nga-	discuss (v)	bespreek
-xubana	mix (v)	meng
-xwayile	alert (a)	waaksaam
-ya	go (v)	gaan
-yakaza	rinse (v)	uitspoel
-yaluzayo	restless (a)	rusteloos
-yeka	abstain (v)	onthou
-yeka	scrap (v)	skrap
-yeka	abandon (v)	verlaat
yena	her (pron)	haar
yena	he (pron)	hy
yena	him (pron)	hom
yena	she (pron)	sy
-yenda	droop (v)	neerhang
-yenga	lure (v)	aanlok
-yesimanje	modern (a)	modern
yilowo	each (pron)	elk(e)
-yimfeketho	trivial (a)	niksbeduidend
-yimpandla	bald (a)	bles
-yimpumputhe	blind (a)	blind
-yimvelo	natural (a)	natuurlik
-yindilinga	round (a)	rond
-yingqamundi	fluent (a)	vlot
-yinhlanganisela	miscellaneous (a)	allerlei
yini	what (pron)	wat
-yinkohliso	fake (a)	vals
-yisibhidli	huge (a)	reusagtig
-yisicaba	flat (a)	plat
-yisifuba	confidential (a)	vertroulik
-yisikwele	square (a)	vierkantig
-yisimungulu	dumb (a)	stom
-yisisekelo	basic (a)	basies
-yitshe	adamant (a)	onwrikbaar
-yivila	indolent (a)	traag
-za	come (v)	kom
-zabalaza	resist (v)	weerstaan
-zacile	thin (a)	dun
-zacile	lean (a)	maer
-zalela	spawn (v)	uitbroei
-zalisa	fertilise (v)	bevrug
-zama	strive (v)	strewe
-zama	try (v)	probeer
-zamula	yawn (v)	gaap
-zenzisa	feint (v)	voorgee
-zenzisa	pretend (v)	voorgee
-zidlayo	proud (a)	trots
-zifaka engozini	risk (v)	waag
-zijwayeza	practise (v)	oefen
-zimele	independent (a)	onafhanklik
-zimisa	behave (v)	jou gedra
-zindela	hesitate (v)	aarsel
-zingela	hunt (v)	jag
-zinhlangangezinhlanga	multiracial (a)	veelrassig
-zinikela ku-	devote (v)	toewy
-ziphatha kabi	misbehave (v)	jou swak gedra
-ziphatha kahle	conduct (v)	gedra
-ziqhayisa	conceited (a)	verwaand
-ziqhenya	vain (a)	ydel
-zo-	will (v)	sal
-zokulima	agricultural (a)	landboukundig
-zombelezayo	indirect (a)	indirek
-zonda	hate (v)	haat
-zondekayo	hateful (a)	haatlik
-zongolozela	involve (v)	betrek
-zula	wander (v)	dwaal
-zulucwathile	blue (a)	blou
-zumayo	unexpected (a)	onverwag
-zungeleza	circulate (v)	rondgaan
-zungeza	revolve (v)	draai
-zungeza	surround (v)	omring
-zungezeleka	enclose (v)	insluit
-zuza	gain (v)	wen
-zuza	earn (v)	verdien
-zuza	acquire (v)	aanskaf
-zuza	attain (v)	bereik
-zuza	obtain (v)	bekom
-zuza	profit (v)	wins maak
-zuzisayo	profitable (a)	lonend
-zwa	feel (v)	voel
-zwa	taste (v)	proe
-zwa	hear (v)	hoor
-zwa	savour (v)	geniet
-zwakalayo	audible (a)	hoorbaar
-zwelayo	sympathetic (a)	simpatiek
-zwile	conscious (a)	bewus
-zwisisa	impress (v)	beïndruk

PHRASES

English	Afrikaans	N Sotho	Sesotho
General	Algemeen	Kakaretšo	Tse akaretsang
I am/have/want	Ek is/het/wil hê	Nna ke/ke na le/ke nyaka	Nna ke/ke na le/ke batla
You are/have/want	Jy is/het/wil hê	Wena o/o na le/o nyaka	Wena o/o na le/o batla
We are/have/want	Ons is/het/wil hê	Rena re/re na le/re nyaka	Rona re/re na le/re batla
You are/have/want	Julle is/het/wil hê	Lena le/le na la/le nyaka	Lona le/le na le/le batla
They are/have/want	Hulle is/het/wil hê	Bona ba/ba na le/ba nyaka	Bona ba/ba na le/ba batla
Here is …	Hier is …	… šo	Ke -na …
Where is …?	Waar is …?	… o kae?	-kae …?
What is this/that?	Wat is dit/daardie?	Ke eng se/seo?	Ke eng hona/hono?
Why?	Hoekom?	Ka baka lang?	Hobaneng?
Do/don't do that	Doen dit/moenie dit doen nie	Dira bjalo/se dire bjalo	Etsa/Se etse hoo
I know/don't know	Ek weet/weet nie	Ke a tseba/ga ke tsebe	Ke a tseba/ha ke tsebe
I think/don't think so	Ek dink so/dink nie so nie	Ke gopola bjalo/ga ke gopole bjalo	Ke nahana jwalo/ha ke nahane jwalo
I am tired	Ek is moeg	Ke lapile	Ke kgathetse
I am glad/annoyed	Ek is bly/kwaad	Ke thabile/ke befetšwe	Ke thabile/halefile
I am sorry	Ek is jammer	Ke kgopela tshwarelo	Ke mohau
I am grateful	Ek is dankbaar	Ke lebogile	Ke a leboha
Listen	Luister	Theetša	Mamela
Look out	Pasop	Hlokomela	Hlokomela
Not so fast	Nie so vinnig nie	E sego ka lebelo bjalo	Butle
Do you speak …?	Praat jy …?	Na o bolela …?	Na o a bua …?
I speak …	Ek praat …	Ke bolela …	Ke a bua …
I don't understand	Ek verstaan nie	Ga ke kwišiše/ga ke hlaloganye	Ha ke utlwisise
What do you mean?	Wat bedoel jy?	O ra bjang?	O bolelang?
Can you explain?	Kan jy verduidelik?	A o ka hlaloša?	Na o ka hlalosa?
Will you write it down, please?	Sal jy dit asseblief neerskryf?	Ako e ngwale hle	Ako e ngole fatshe hle
Please speak slowly	Praat asseblief stadig	Anke o bolele ka go iketla	Ako bue butle (hle)
Please repeat that	Herhaal dit, asseblief	Anke o boeletše	Ako phete hoo (hle)
Yes	Ja	Ee	E!
Please	Asseblief	Hle …/… hle	(Ka kopo) hle
No	Nee	Aowa	Tjhe
Thank you	Dankie	Ke a leboga	Ke a leboha
Excuse me	Verskoon my	Tshwarelo	Ntshwarele
Pardon me, what did you say?	Ekskuus, wat het jy gesê?	Tshwarelo, o ile wa reng?	Ntshwarele hle, o itseng?
Good morning	Goeiemôre	Thobela/dumela	Dumela(ng)
Good afternoon	Goeiemiddag	Thobela/dumela	Dumela(ng)
Good evening	Goeienaand	Thobela/dumela	Fonaneng
Goodbye	Totsiens	Šala gabotse/sepela gabotse	Sala(ng) hantle
See you later	Sien jou later	Re tla bonana	Re tla bonana
Until we meet again	Tot siens	Go fihla re kopana gape	Ho fihlela re bonana
He sends his regards	Hy stuur groete	A re le dumeleng	O a dumedisa
May I introduce you to …?	Kan ek jou aan … voorstel?	A nka go tsebiša …?	Ke rata ho o/le tsebisa …
How do you do	Aangename kennis	Ke leboga go le tseba	Ke thabela ho o tseba
How are you?	Hoe gaan dit?	Le kae?	O/le sa phela?
I am fine, thank you	Dit gaan goed, dankie	Re gona	Ke phela hantle
Does … live here?	Woon … hier?	Na … o dula mo?	Na … o dula mona?
Is he at home?	Is hy tuis?	Na o gona mo gae?	Ebe o lapeng?
May I see him?	Kan ek hom sien?	Na nka mmona?	Na nka mmona?
He won't be long	Hy sal nie lank neem nie	A ka se diege	Ha a tlo dieha
Please tell him I called	Sê vir hom ek het hom gesoek	Ako mmotše gore ke be ke mo etetše	Ako mo jwetse hore ke ne ke tlile
I shall be glad to help you	Ek sal jou met graagte help	Nka thabela go go thuša	Ke tla thabela ho o thusa
Who is there?	Wie is daar?	Ke mang moo?	Ke mang moo?
Come in	Kom binne	Tsena	Kena
Please open the door	Maak asseblief die deur oop	Anke o bule lemati	Ako bule monyako hle
Please shut the door	Maak asseblief die deur toe	Anke o tswalele lemati	Ako kwale monyako hle

Tswana	Xhosa	Zulu	English
Kakaretso	**Jikelele**	**Vamile**	**General**
Nna ke/ke na le/ke batla	Ndi-/-na/-funa	Ngingu-(Ngiyi-)/ngina-/ngifuna	I am/have/want
Wena o/o na le/o batla	U-/-na/-funa	Ungu-(Uyi-)/una-/-ufuna	You are/have/want
Rona re/re na le/re batla	Si-/-na/-funa	Singa-(Siyi-)/sina-/sifuna	We are/have/want
Lona le/le na le/le batla	U-/-na/-funa	Niba-(Niyi-)/nina-/nifuna	You are/have/want
Bona ba/ba na le/ba batla	Ba-/-na/-funa	Banga-(Bayi-)/bana-/bafuna	They are/have/want
...ke...	Apha	Nakhu ...	Here is ...
...kae?	Iphi ...?	-kuphi?	Where is ...?
Ke eng?	Yintoni le/leyo?	Kuyini lokhu/lokho?	What is this/that?
Go reng?	Ngokuba?	Kungani?	Why ...?
Dira jalo/se dire jalo	Enza/sukwenza	Yenza/Musa ukwenza lokho	Do/don't do that
Ke a itse/Ga ke itse	Ndiyazi/andazi	Ngiyazi/Angazi	I know/don't know
Ke nagana jalo/ga ke nagane jalo	Ndiyacinga/andicingi	Ngicabanga/Angisho	I think/don't think so
Ke lapile	Ndidiniwe	Ngikhathele	I am tired
Ke e itumetse/Ke galefile	Ndiyavuya/ndicaphukile	Ngiyajabula/ngithukuthele	I am glad/annoyed
Intshwarele	Ndiva into embi	Uxolo	I am sorry
Ke a leboga	Ndinombulelo	Ngiyathokoza	I am grateful
Utlwelela	Phulaphula	Lalela	Listen
Tlhokomela	Lumka	Qaphela	Look out
E seng ka bonako jalo	Ngokungakhawulezi kangaka	Kancane	Not so fast
A o a bua ...?	Uyathetha ...?	Ukhuluma isi-...?	Do you speak ...?
Ke a bua ...	Ndithetha ...	Ngikhuluma isi-...	I speak ...
Ga ke tlhaloganye	Andiqondi	Angizwa	I don't understand
O kaya eng?	Uthetha ukuthini?	Usho ukuthini?	What do you mean?
A o ka tlhalosa?	Ungakhe ucacise?	Ungachaza na?	Can you explain?
A o ka se kwala?	Unganceda uyibhale phantsi?	Uxolo, ngicela ukubhale phansi	Will you write it down, please?
Bua ka iketlo, tsweetswee	Nceda uthethe ngokucothayo	Mawukhulume kancane	Please speak slowly
Boeletsa, tsweetswee	Nceda khawuyiphinde	Mawuphinde usho lokho	Please repeat that
Ee	Ewe	Yebo	Yes
Tsweetswee	Nceda	Uxolo	Please
Nnyaa	Hayi	Cha	No
Ke a leboga	Enkosi	Ngiyabonga	Thank you
Intshwarele	Uxolo	Uxolo	Excuse me
Intshwarele, o ne o reng?	Uxolo, ubusithini?	Uxolo, utheni?	Pardon me, what did you say?
Dumela	Molo/bhota	Sawubona	Good morning
Dumela	Molo/bhoto	Sawubona	Good afternoon
Dumela	Molo/bhota	Sawubona	Good evening
Sala sentle	Nisale kakuhle	Sala kahle	Goodbye
Ke tla go bona	Sobe sibonane	Sizobanana	See you later
Go fitlhelela re bonana gape	De sibonane kwakhona	Size sibonane futhi	Until we meet again
O a dumedisa	Uyabulisa	Ukhonzile	He sends his regards
A nka go itsise ...	Ndingakwazisa ku ...	Mangikwethule ku ...	May I introduce you to ...?
O tsogile jang?	Kunjani	Ninjani?	How do you do
O tsogile jang?	Kunjani ?	Ninjani?	How are you?
Ke tsogile sentle	Ndiphilile, enkosi	Ngisaphila	I am fine, thank you
... o nna fa?	Ingaba ... uhlala apha?	U... uhlala lapha?	Does ... live here?
A o teng?	Ingaba ukhona?	Ukhona ekhaya?	Is he at home?
A nka mmona?	Ndingambona?	Ngingambona na?	May I see him?
Ga a kake a tsaya nako	Akazi kuba mde	Uzoba yisikhashana	He won't be long
Mmolele gore ke ne ke mmatla	Maze umxelele ukuba bendikhe ndaza kuvela	Mtshele ukuthi bengimfuna	Please tell him I called
Ke tla itumelela go go thusa	Ndingavuya ukukunceda	Ngingajabula ukukusiza	I shall be glad to help you
Ke mang?	Ngubani olapho?	Kukhona ubani?	Who is there?
Tsena	Ngena	Ngena	Come in
Bula lebati tlhe	Nceda vula ucango	Ngicela uvule umnyango	Please open the door
Tswala lebati tlhe	Nceda vala ucango	Ngicela uvale umnyango	Please shut the door

English	Afrikaans	N Sotho	Sesotho
General	**Algemeen**	**Kakaretšo**	**Tse akaretsang**
I am busy	Ek is besig	Ke swaregile	Ke sa tshwarehile
Am I interrupting you?	Onderbreek ek jou?	A ke a go tshwenya?	Na ke o kena hanong?
How long must I wait?	Hoe lank moet ek wag?	Ke swanetše go ema lebaka le lekakang?	Na ke eme nako e kae?
Tell him to wait	Sê hy moet wag	Mmotše gore a eme	Ere a eme
Wait a minute, please	Wag asseblief 'n bietjie	Anke o eme gannyane	Ema hanyenyane hle
Would you like something to drink/eat?	Wil jy iets hê om te drink/eet?	Na o nyaka sa go nwa/ja?	Na o tla thabela se nowang/jewang?
Would you like some tea/coffee?	Wil jy tee/koffie hê?	Na o nyaka teye/kofi?	Na o tla thabela tee/kofi
Do you take milk?	Drink jy melk?	Na o nwa maswi?	Na o nwa lebese?
How much sugar?	Hoeveel suiker?	Na o nyaka swikiri e kakang?	Ke tshele tswekere e kae?
Two spoons of sugar, please	Twee lepels suiker, asseblief	Anke o ntšhelele malepola a mabedi a swikiri	Kgaba tse pedi tsa tswekere, hle
Please don't go to any trouble	Moet asseblief nie moeite doen nie	Se itshwenye hle	Se ikgathatse hle
I hope it is not inconvenient	Ek hoop nie dit is ongerieflik nie	Ke holofela gore le ka se tshwenyege	Ke a tshepa ha ke o sitise
What is the matter?	Wat is verkeerd?	Molato keng?	Molato ke eng?
What is that for?	Waarvoor is dit?	Ke sa go dira eng?	Ke hwa eng hoo?
What is your name?	Wat is jou naam?	Leina la gago ke mang?	O mang na?
My name is …	My naam is …	Leina la ka ke …	Lebitso la ka ke …
How old are you?	Hoe oud is jy?	O na le mengwaga ye mekae?	Dilemo tsa hao di kae?
I am … years old	Ek is … jaar oud	Ke na le mengwaga ye …	Dilemo tsa ka di …
Are you married?	Is jy getroud?	A o nyetše? (m)/nyetšwe? (f)	Na o nyetse? (m)/nyetswe? (f)
I am single/divorced	Ek is ongetroud/geskei	Ga ke a nyala (m)/nyalwa (f)/ke hladile	Ha ke eso nyale (m)/nyalwe (f)/ke hladile
Do you have any children?	Het jy kinders?	Na o na le bana?	Na o na le bana?
Where do you live?	Waar woon jy?	O dula kae?	O dula kae?
I live …	Ek woon …	Ke dula …	Ke dula …
Where do you work?	Waar werk jy?	O šoma kae?	O sebetsa kae?
I work …	Ek werk …	Ke šoma …	Ke sebetsa …
What is your postal address?	Wat is jou posadres?	Aterese ya gago ya poso ke efe?	Aterese ya poso ya hao ke efe?
My postal address is …	My posadres is …	Aterese ya ka ya poso ke …	Aterese ya poso ya ka ke …
What is your telephone number?	Wat is jou telefoonnommer?	Nomoro ya gago ya mogala ke efe?	Nomoro ya hao ya fonofono ke eng na?
My telephone number is …	My telefoonnommer is …	Nomoro ya ka ya mogala ke …	Nomoro ya ka ya fonofono ke …
What number did you want?	Watter nommer wou jy gehad het?	O be o nyaka nomoro efe?	O ne o batla nomoro efeng?
What number did you dial?	Watter nommer het jy geskakel?	O leleditše nomoro efe?	O letseditse nomorong efeng?
You have the wrong number	Jy het die verkeerde nommer	Nomoro ye ga se ye o e nyakago	O letseditse nomorong esele
Whom do you want to speak to?	Met wie wil jy praat?	O nyaka go bolela le mang?	Na o rata ho bua le mang?
Where are you going?	Waarheen gaan jy?	O ya kae?	Na o ya kae?
I am going to …	Ek gaan na …	Ke ya …	Ke ya …
Where have you come from?	Waarvandaan het jy gekom?	O tšwa kae?	O tswa kae na?
I have come from …	Ek het van … af gekom	Ke tšwa …	Ke tswa …

Tswana	Xhosa	Zulu	English
Kakaretso	**Jikelele**	**Vamile**	**General**
Ke sa dira	Ndixakekile	Ngiyasebenza	I am busy
A ke a go kgaosetsa?	Ndiyakuphazamisa?	Ngiyakuphazamisa na?	Am I interrupting you?
Ke eme nako e kana kang?	Ndilinde ixesha elingakanani?	Ngizolinda isikhathi esingakanani?	How long must I wait?
Mmolele gore a lete	Mxelele alinde	Mtshele alinde	Tell him to wait
Leta go le gonnye, tsweetswee	Khawulinde kancinci	Mawulindalinde kancane	Wait a minute, please
A o batla sengwe sa go nwa/ja?	Kukho nto onqwenela ukuyisela?	Ufuna okokuphuza na?	Would you like something to drink/eat?
A o batla tee/kofi?	Kunjani ngeti/ngekofu?	Ufuna itiye/ikhofi?	Would you like some tea/coffee?
A o nwa mašwi?	Uyalusela ubisi?	Uphuza ubisi?	Do you take milk?
Sukiri e kana kang?	Iswekile engakanani?	Ushukela ongakanani?	How much sugar?
Maswana a mabedi a sukiri, tsweetswee	Amacephe nje amabini	Izinkezo ezimbili	Two spoons of sugar, please
Se itsenye mo mathateng	Nceda ungazihluphi	Ungakhathazeki	Please don't go to any trouble
Ke solofela gore ga se mathata	Ndiyathemba akuhlupheki	Ngikholwa ukuthi angikuphazamisi	I hope it is not inconvenient
Molato ke eng?	Kutheke ni?	Yini ndaba?	What is the matter?
Ke sa go dira eng?	Yeyantoni loo nto?	Ngokwani lokho?	What is that for?
Leina la gago ke mang?	Ngubani igama lakho?	Ungubani igama lakho?	What is your name?
Leina la me ke …	Igama lam ngu …	Igama lami ngingu …	My name is …
O na le dingwaga tse kae?	Umdala kangakanani?	Uneminyaka emingaki?	How old are you?
Ke na le dingwaga tse …	Ndine … (le) minyaka ubudala	Ngineminyaka eyi-	I am … years old
A o nyetse? (m)/A o nyetswe? (f)	Ingaba utshatile?	Uganile?	Are you married?
Ga ke a nyala/ke tlhadile	Ndilisoka/ndiqhawule	Angishadile/Ngehlukanisile	I am single/divorced
A o na le bana?	Unabo abantwana?	Unabo abantwana?	Do you have any children?
O nna kae?	Uhlala phi?	Uhlalaphi?	Where do you live?
Ke nna …	Ndihlala e …	Ngihlala …	I live …
O bereka kae?	Usebenza phi?	Usebenzaphi?	Where do you work?
Ke bereka …	Ndesebenza …	Ngisebenza …	I work …
Aterese ya gago ke efe?	Idilesi yakho ithini?	Lithini ikheli lakho leposi?	What is your postal address?
Aterese ya me ke …	Idilesi yam yeposi i…	Ikheli lami lithi …	My postal address is …
Nomoro ya gago ya mogala ke efe?	Inambari yakho yefoni ithini?	Iyini inamba yocingo lwakho?	What is your telephone number?
Nomoro ya me ya mogala ke …	Inambari yam yefoni i…	Inamba yami ingu …	My telephone number is …
O ne o batla nomoro efe?	Ufuna eyiphi inambari?	Ufuna yiphi inamba?	What number did you want?
O leditse nomoro efe?	Ubutsale eyiphi inambari?	Ushaye yiphi inamba?	What number did you dial?
O tshotse nomoro e e phoso	Uphume kwinambari engeyiyo	Ushaye inamba okungeyona	You have the wrong number
O batla go bua le mang?	Ufuna ukuthetha nabani?	Ufuna ukukhuluma nobani?	Whom do you want to speak to?
O ya kae?	Uyaphi?	Uyaphi?	Where are you going?
Ke ya …	Ndiya e …	Ngiya …	I am going to …
O ne o tswa kae?	Uvela phi?	Uphumaphi?	Where have you come from?
Ke ne ke tswa …	Bendivela e…	Ngibuya …	I have come from …

English	Afrikaans	N Sotho	Sesotho
Time	**Tyd**	**Nako**	**Nako**
What is the date today/tomorrow?	Wat is vandag/môre se datum?	Ke dikae lehono/gosasa?	Kgwedi e matsatsi a makae kajeno/hosane?
What was the date yesterday?	Wat was gister se datum?	Maabane e be e le dikae?	Kgwedi e ne e le matsatsi a makae maobane?
What day is it? It is Monday/Tuesday/Wednesday/ Thursday/Friday/Saturday/Sunday	Watter dag is dit? Dit is Maandag/Dinsdag/Woensdag/ Donderdag/Vrydag/Saterdag/Sondag	Ke la bokae? Ke Mošupologo/Labobedi/Laboraro/ Labone/Labohlano/Mokibelo/ Lamorena	Ke la bokae kajeno? Ke Mantaha/Labobedi/Laboraro/ Labone/Labohlano/Moqebelo/Sontaha
What month is it? It is January/February/March/April/ May/June/July/August/September/ October/November/December	Watter maand is dit? Dit is Januarie/Februarie/Maart/April/ Mei/Junie/Julie/Augustus/September/ Oktober/November/Desember	Ke kgwedi efe? Ke Janaware/Fepereware/Matšhe/ Aprele/Mei/June/Julae/Agostose/ Setemere/Oktobore/Nofemere/ Desemerε	Kgwedi ena ke mang? Ke Pherekgong/Hlakubele/Hlakola/ Mesa/Motsheanong/Phupu/Phupjane/ Phatwe/Lwetse/Mphalane/ Pudungwane/Tshitwe
What time is it? The time is one/two/three/four/five/ six/seven/eight/nine/ten/eleven/twelve o'clock	Hoe laat is dit? Dit is een-/twee-/drie-/vier-/vyf-/ ses-/sewe-/agt-/nege-/tien-/elf-/ twaalfuur	Ke nako mang? Ke iri ya pele/bobedi/boraro/bone/ bohlano/boselela/bošupa/seswai/ senyane/lesome/lesometee/lesomepedi	Ke nako mang? Ke hora ya pele/bobedi/boraro/bone/ bohlano/botshelela/bosupa/borobedi/ borobong/leshome/leshome le motso/ leshome le metso e mmedi
The time is half past one	Dit is halftwee	Nako ke metsotso ye masometharo go tšwa go iri ya pele	Ke metsotso e mashome a maroro ka mora hora ya pele
The time is quarter past one	Dit is kwart oor een	Nako ke metsotso ye lesomehlano morago ga iri ya pele	Ke metsotso e leshome le metso e mehlano ka mora hora ya pele
The time is quarter to one	Dit is kwart voor een	Nako ke metsotso ye lesomehlano pele ga iri ya pele	Ke kotara pele ho hora ya pele
My watch is fast/slow	My horlosie is voor/agter	Sešupanako sa ka se pele/morago ga nako	Orolosi ya ka e pele/morao
It is late/early	Dit is laat/vroeg	Nako e ile/nako e sa le gona	Nako e ile/e sa le teng
Is it time to go?	Is dit tyd om te gaan?	Ke nako ya go sepela?	Na ke nako ya ho tsamaya?
I am in a hurry	Ek is haastig	Ke itlhaganetše	Ke tatile
What time are you leaving?	Hoe laat vertrek jy?	O sepela ka nako mang?	O tsamaya ka nako mang?
What time will you be back?	Hoe laat sal jy terug wees?	O tla be ɔ boile ka nako mang?	O tla kgutla ka nako mang?

Tswana	Xhosa	Zulu	English
Nako	**Ixesha**	**Isikhathi**	**Time**
Ke dikae gompieno/ka moso?	Umhla uthini namhlanje/ngomso?	Yizingaki namuhla/kusasa?	What is the date today/tomorrow?
Go ne go le dikae maabane?	Ibiyintoni umhla izolo?	Izolo kwakuyizingaki?	What was the date yesterday?
Ke la bokae?	Kungolwesingaphi?	Olwesingaki namuhla?	What day is it?
Ke Masupologo/Labobedi/Laboraro/ Labone/Labotlhano/Lamatlhatso/ Latshipi	Kungo Mvulo/Lwesibini/Lwesithathu/ Lwesine/Lwesihlanu/Mgqibelo/Cawa	NguMsombuluko/Ngolwesibili/ Ngolwesithathu/Ngolwesine/ Ngolwesihlanu/NguMgqibelo/YiSonto	It is Monday/Tuesday/Wednesday/ Thursday/Friday/Saturday/Sunday
Ke kgwedi efe?	Yeyiphi inyanga?	Iyiphi le nyanga?	What month is it?
Ke kgwedi ya Ferikong/Tlhakole/ Mopitlwe/Moranang/Motsheganong/ Seetebosigo/Phukwi/Phatwe/Lwetse/ Diphalane/Ngwanatsele/Sedimonthole	Janyuwari/Febhuwari/Matshi/Epreli/ Meyi/Juni/Julayi/Agasti/Septemba/ Oktobha/Novemba/Disemba	NguJanuwari/NguFebruwari/ NguMashi/NguAprele/NguMeyi/ NguJuni/NguJulayi/Ngu-Agoste/ NguSeptemba/Ngu-Oktoba/ NguNovemba/NguDisemba	It is January/February/March/April/ May/June/July/August/September/ October/November/December
Ke nako mang?	Ngubani ixesha?	Yisikhathi sini?	What time is it?
Ke ura ya ntlha/bobedi/boraro/bone/ botlhano/borataro/bosupa/borobedi/ borobongwe/lesome/somenngwe/ somepedi	Ixesha yintsimbi/yokuqala/yesibini/ yesithathu/yesine/yesihlanu/ yesithandathu/yesixhenxe/yesibhozo/ yethoba/yeshumi	Yihora lokuqala/lesibili/lesithathu/ lesine/lesihlanu/lesithupha/ lesikhombisa/lesishiyagalombili/ lesishiyagalolunye/leshumi/leshumi nanye/leshumi nambili	The time is one/two/three/four/five/six/ seven/eight/nine/ten/eleven/twelve o'clock
Nako ke metsoso e le someamararo go tswa ureng ya bongwe	Ixesha licala emva kweyokuqala	Isikhathu yisigamu emva kwehóra lokuqala	The time is half past one
Nako ke metsotso e le sometlhano morago ga ura ya ntlha	Ixesha ngumkhono emva kweyokuqala	Imizuzu iyishumi nanhlanu emva kwehora lokuqala	The time is quarter past one
Nako ke metsotso e le sometlhano pele ga ura ya ntlha	Ixesha ngumkhono phambi kweyokuqala	Imizuzu iyishumi nanhlanu ngaphambi kwehora lokuqala	The time is quarter to one
Tshupanako ya me e bonako/bonya	Iwotshi yam iyabaleka/iyacotha	Iwashi lami liphambili/lisemuva	My watch is fast/slow
Nako e ile/sa le teng	Kusemva kwexesha/kuphambi	Isikhathi sesishayilo/sisekahle	It is late/early
Ke nako ya go tsamaya?	Lixesha lokuba kuhanjwe ?	Yisikhathi sokuhamba na?	Is it time to go?
Ke itlhaganetse	Ndingxamile	Ngijahile	I am in a hurry
O tsamaya nako mang?	Uhamba ngabani ixesha?	Uhamba ngasikhathi sini?	What time are you leaving?
O tla boa ka nako mang?	Uya kubuya ngabani ixesha?	Uzobuya ngasikhathi sini?	What time will you be back?

English	Afrikaans	N Sotho	Sesotho
Household	**Die Huis**	**Tša lapa**	**Lapeng**
I will make lunch/supper	Ek sal middag-/aandete voorberei	Ke tla apea dijo tša matena/tša go lalela	Ke tla pheha dijo tsa motsheare/mantsiboya
I will bake a cake	Ek sal 'n koek bak	Ke tla paka kuku	Ke tla baka kuku
I will make tea/coffee	Ek sal tee/koffie maak	Ke tla dira teye/kofi	Ke tla etsa tee/kofi
Please put on the kettle	Skakel asseblief die ketel aan	Anke o tšhume ketlele	Beha ketlele ifo hle
The washing up must be done	Die skottelgoed moet gewas word	Dibjana di swanetše go hlatswiwa	Dijana di tshwanetse ho hlatsuwa
I will dry up	Ek sal afdroog	Nna ke tla phumola	Ke tla di phumola
Please put the dishes away	Bêre asseblief die borde	Anke o boloke dibjana	Hleka dijana hle
The table must be set for lunch/supper	Die tafel moet vir middag-/aandete gedek word	Tafola e swanetše go tekelwa dijo tša matena/tša go lalela	Tafole e tlamehile ho lokisetswa dijo tsa motsheare/mantsiboya
The silverware must be cleaned	Die messegoed moet skoongemaak word	Malepola, dithipa le diforoko di swanetše go hlwekišwa	Dithipa di tlamehile ho hlwekiswa
The refrigerator needs defrosting	Die yskas moet ontvries word	Setšidifatši se swanetše go tingwa gore lehlwa le tologe se be se hlwekišwe	Foriji e hloka ho ntshwa leqhwa
The oven must be cleaned	Die oond moet skoongemaak word	Onto e swanetše go hlwekišwa	Onto e tlamehile ho hlwekiswa
The house needs cleaning	Die huis moet skoongemaak word	Ntlo e swanetše go hlwekišwa	Ntlo e tlamehile ho hlwekiswa
The windows need washing	Die vensters moet gewas word	Mafesetere a swanetše go hlatswiwa	Difensetere di tlamehile ho hlatsuwa
The floor needs sweeping/cleaning/polishing	Die vloer moet gevee/skoongemaak/gepoleer word	Lebato le swanetše go swielwa/hlwekišwa/pholišwa	Foluru e tlamehile ho fielwa/hlwekiswa/poleshwa
The carpets need vacuuming	Die matte moet skoongemaak word	Mebetso e swanetše go hlwekišwa	Khapete e hloka ho hlwekiswa
The beds must be made	Die beddens moet opgemaak word	Malao a swanetše go alwa	Dibethe di tlamehile ho alolwa
The washing must be hung out to dry	Die wasgoed moed opgehang word om droog te word	Mašela a swanetše go anegwa gore a ome	Washing e tlamehille ho fanyehwa hore e ome
The ironing must be done	Die strykwerk moet gedoen word	Go swanetše go šidilwe	Ho tereka ho tlamehile ho etsuwa
Hang up your clothes	Hang jou klere op	Fega diaparo tša gago	Fanyeha diaparo tsa hao
Put your clothes away	Bêre jou klere	Boloka diaparo tša gago	Beha diaparo tsa hao
The light bulb has blown	Die gloeilamp het geblaas	Lebone le timile	Tleloupo ya lebone e thuntse
The light bulb must be replaced	Die gloeilamp moet vervang word	Go nyakega tleloupo ye mpsha	Re tlamehile ho kenya tleloupo e nngwe
The yard needs sweeping	Die werf moet gevee word	Jarata e swanetše go swielwa	Jarete e tlamehile ho fielwa
The garden needs watering	Die tuin moet natgelei word	Serapana se swanetše go nošetšwa	Serapa se hloka ho nwesetswa
The flowerbeds need weeding	Die onkruid moet uit die blombeddings uitgetrek word	Diloto tša matšoba di swanetše go hlagolwa	Dipalesa di tlamehile ho hlaolelwa
I will pick some flowers	Ek sal blomme pluk	Ke tla kga matšoba	Ke tla kga dipalesa
Arrange the flowers in a vase	Rangskik die blomme in die blompot	Beakanya matšoba ka sebjaneng sa ona	Hlophisa dipalesa ka pitsaneng
The lawn must be mowed	Die gras moet gesny word	Sehlwa se/lone e swanetše go segwa	Jwang bo tlamehile ho helwa
The hedge needs trimming	Die heining moet gesnoei word	Legora le swanetše go kgothwa	Seotlwana se tlamehile ho kutwa
The wall needs painting	Die muur moet geverf word	Leboto le nyaka go pentwa	Lebota le hloka ferefe

Tswana	Xhosa	Zulu	English
Ntlong	**Ezendlu**	**Okwasekhaya**	**Household**
Ke tla apaya dijo tsa motshegare/ dilalelo	Ndiza kwenza ilantshi/isopholo	Ngizopheka ilantshi/isapha	I will make lunch/supper
Ke tla baka kuku	Ndiza kubhaka ikeyiki	Ngizobhaka ikhekhe	I will bake a cake
Ke tla apaya tee/kofi	Ndiza kwenza iti/ikofu	Ngizokwenza itiye/ikhofi	I will make tea/coffee
Tshuba ketlele	Nceda layita iketile	Ngicela wokhele ugesi wegedlela	Please put on the kettle
O tlhatswe dijana	Kufuneka zihlanjwe izitya	Kumele kugezwe izitsha	The washing up must be done
Ke tla phimola dijana	Ndiza kusula	Ngizozesula	I will dry up
O beye dilwana tsa go jela	Nceda qoqosha izitya	Ngicela ungibekele izitsha	Please put the dishes away
O bakanye tafole mo dijong tsa motshegare/dilalelo	Makulungiselelwe ilantshi/isopholo	Itafula lifanele lilungiselwe ilantshi/isapha	The table must be set for lunch/supper
Dithipa di tshwanetse go tlhatswiwa	Izitya zesilivere mazicocwe	Kumele khuhlanzwe izinto zesiliva	The silverware must be cleaned
Setsidifatse se tshwanetse go nyerololwa	Ifriji ifuna ukunyityilikiswa	Kumele kuncibilikiswe iqhwa efrijini	The refrigerator needs defrosting
O tlhatswe onto	Ioveni kufuneka icocwe	Uhhavini udinga ukuhlanzwa	The oven must be cleaned
Ntlo e tlhoka go phephafatswa	Indlu ifuna ukucocwa	Indlu idinga ukuhlanzwa	The house needs cleaning
Mafensetere a tshwanetswe go tlhatswa	Iifestile zifuna ukuhlanjwa	Amafasitele amelwe ukugezwa	The windows need washing
Bodilo bo feelwe/phephafatswe/tshaswe pholetšhe	Umgangatho ufuna ukutshayelwa/ ukucocwa/ukupolishwa	Iphansi lidinga ukushanelwa/ ukuhlanzwa/ukupholishwa	The floor needs sweeping/cleaning/ polishing
Dimata di tlhotlhorwe	Iikhapeti zifuna ukucocwa	Amakhaphethe adinga ukuhlanzwa	The carpets need vacuuming
Malao a alwe	Iibhedi mazandlulwe	Imibhede idinga ukwendlulwa	The beds must be made
Dikhai/diaparo di anegwe go oma	Impahla ehlanjiweyo mayixhonywe phandle izokoma	Iwšhingi idinga ukwenekwa izokoma	The washing must be hung out to dry
Go tereikiwe	Impahla mayolulwe	Kudingeka ku-ayinwe	The ironing must be done
Phutha diaparo tsa gago	Xhoma iimpahla zakho	Phanyeka izingubo zakho	Hang up your clothes
Baya diaparo tsa gago	Qoqosha iimpahla zakho	Beka izingubo zakho	Put your clothes away
Lobone le senyegile	Ibhalbhu yesibane iqhushumbile	Igilobhi lifile	The light bulb has blown
Lobone lo fetolwe	Makufakelwe enye ibhalbhu yesibane	Kumele kufakwe elinye igilobhi	The light bulb must be replaced
Lelapa le feelwe	Iyadi ifuna ukucocwa	Iyadi lifanele lishanelwe	The yard needs sweeping
Tshingwana e nosetswe	Igadi ifuna ukunkcenkceshelwa	Ingadi idinga ukuniselwa	The garden needs watering
Mo dišhešeng go tlhagolwe	Iziqendwana zeentyatyambo zifuna ukususwa ukhula	Izimbali zidinga ukuhlakulelwa	The flowerbeds need weeding
Ke tla kgetla dišheše	Ndiza kukha iintyatyambo	Ngizokha izimbali	I will pick some flowers
Rulaganya dišheše	Cwangcisa iintyatyambo evazini	Faka lezi zimbali evasini	Arrange the flowers in a vase
Bojang bo segiwe	Ingca kufuneka ichetywe	Utshani bufanele ukusikwa	The lawn must be mowed
Legora le kgaolwe	Uthango lwemithi lufuna ukulungelelaniswa	Uthango kumele luncwelwe	The hedge needs trimming
Mabotana a pentiwe	Udonga lufuna ukuqatywa/ ukupeyintwa	Udonga lumele lupendwe	The wall needs painting

473

English	Afrikaans	N Sotho	Sesotho
Recreation	**Ontspanning**	**Maitišo**	**Boikgathollo**
What games/sport do you play?	Wat se speletjies speel jy?/sport beoefen jy?	Na o raloka dipapadi dife?	Dipapadi/papadi eo o e bapalang ke efe?
I don't play any games/sport	Ek speel geen speletjies nie/doen geen sport nie	Ga go papadi ye ke e ralokago	Ha ho na papadi eo ke e bapalang
Where is the nearest tennis court/golf course/squash court/swimming pool?	Waar is die naaste tennisbaan/gholfbaan/muurbalbaan/swembad?	Lebala la kgauswi la thenese/kolofo/sekwaše le kae?/bothinthelo bja kgauswi bo kae?	Lebala le haufiufi la tenese/kolofo/sekwashe/ho sesa le kae?
I want to go to rugby/soccer/cricket	Ek wil rugby/sokker/krieket toe gaan	Ke nyaka go ya go bogela rakbi/kgwele ya maoto/krikhete	Ke batla ho ya rakebing/bolong/keriketeng
How do you reach the ground?	Hoe kom 'n mens by die veld?	Motho o sepela bjang go fihla lebaleng?	O ya lebaleng leo jwang?
Two tickets for the stands, please	Twee pawiljoenkaartjies, asseblief	A nka hwetša dithekethe tše pedi go dula madulong a a šireleditšwego hle	Ditekete tse pedi ka pabilejone hle
I want to go fishing	Ek wil gaan visvang	Ke nyaka go yo rea dihlapi	Ke batla ho ya tshwasa ditlhapi
Where can I buy bait?	Waar kan ek aas koop?	Nka reka kae sa go bea kobing?	Moo nka rekang sa ho tshwasa ke kae?
I need a new tennis racket	Ek het 'n nuwe tennisrakket nodig	Ke nyaka rakete ye mpsha ya thenese	Ke hloka rekete e ntjha
I have brought my golf clubs	Ek het my gholfstokke gebring	Ke tlile le ditshipi tša ka tša kolofo	Ke tlile le melangwana ya kolofo
Which way is the beach?	Hoe kom 'n mens by die strand?	A nka fihla bjang lebopong?	Tsela e yang bitjheng ke efe?
Can you swim?	Kan jy swem?	A o tseba go rutha?	Na o tseba ho sesa?
Is this beach dangerous?	Is die strand gevaarlik?	A lebopo le le kotsi?	Na bitjhe e kotsi?
Are there lifesavers?	Is daar lewensredders?	A go na le baphološabaruthi?	Bapholosi ba teng?
Where is the change-room?	Waar is die kleedkamer?	Boaparelo bo kae?	Phaposi ya ho tjhentjha diaparo e kae?
I want to go to the theatre/cinema	Ek wil teater/bioskoop toe gaan	Ke nyaka go ya teatereng/paesekopong	Ke batla ho ya baesekopong
What do you want to see?	Wat wil jy gaan kyk?	A o nyaka go yo bona eng?	O batla ho bona eng?
Two tickets for the late show, please	Twee kaartjies vir die laat vertoning, asseblief	Ke kgopela dithekete tše pedi tša pontšho ya morago hle	Ditekete tse pedi tsa shou ya bosiu hle
I want tickets on the aisle/near the back	Ek wil plek teen die paadjie/agterlangs hê	Ke nyaka madulo hleng ga tsejana/go ya morago	Ke batla ditekete tsa pela tselana/ka morao
The show is fully booked	Die vertoning is volbespreek	Dithekethe tša pontšho ye di fedile	Shou e beheleditswe ka botlalo
Where is the nearest library/museum/art gallery?	Waar is die naaste biblioteek/museum/kunsgalery?	Bokgobapuku bja kgauswi bo kae?/musiamo wa kgauswi o kae?/lefelo la pontšho ya bokgabo la kgauswi le kae?	Laeborari/musiamo/pontsho ya mekgabo e kae?
Can I join the library?	Kan ek by die biblioteek aansluit?	A nka ba leloko la bokgobapuku?	Na nka ba setho sa laeborari?
I want to borrow a book	Ek wil 'n boek uitneem	Ke nyaka go adima puku	Ke batla ho adima buka

Tswana	Xhosa	Zulu	English
Boitiso	**Ezolonwabo**	**Ukudlala**	**Recreation**
O tshameka motshameko ofe?	Yeyiphi imidlalo/umdlalo owudlalayo?	Udlala mdlalo muni?	What games/sport do you play?
Ga ke tshameke ope	Andidlali midlalo/mdlalo	Angidlali lutho mina	I don't play any games/sport
Lefelo la thenese/golofo/sekwase/go thuma le le gaufi le kae?	Liphi ibala letenesi/ibala legolufa/ibala lesikwashi/iqula lokuqubha elikufutshane?	Ikuphu inkundla eseduze yethenisi/yegalofu/yesikwashi/Sikuphi isiziba sokubhukuda?	Where is the nearest tennis court/golf course/squash court/swimming pool?
Ke batla go ya rakabing/kgwele ya maoto/keriketeng	Ndifuna ukuya embhoxweni/kwisoka/kwiqakamba	Ngifuna ukuya emdlalweni weragbhi/kanobhutshuzwayo/wekhilikithi	I want to go to rugby/soccer/cricket
O fitlha jang kwa botshamekelong?	Uya njani ebaleni?	Uhamba ngani ukuya enkundleni?	How do you reach the ground?
Dithekete tse pedi tsa bodulo jo bo sireleditsweng, tsweetswee	Ndincede ngama tikiti amabini asemaqongeni	Ngicela amathikithi amabili	Two tickets for the stands, please
Ke batla go ya go thaisa ditlhapi	Ndifuna ukuya kubambisela intlanzi	Ngifuna ukuyodoba izinhlanzi	I want to go fishing
Ke kgona go reka kae dithaisi tsa ditlhapi?	Ndingayithenga phi into yokuthiyisela?	Ngingakuthengaphi ukudla kokudoba?	Where can I buy bait?
Ke thoka rakete ya thenese e ntshwa	Ndifuna ibhadi elitsha letenesi	Ngidinga ilakhethe lethenisi elisha	I need a new tennis racket
Ke tlile le dikotana tsa golofo tsa me	Ndiwaphethe amagqudu am egolufa	Ngize nezagila zami zegalofu	I have brought my golf clubs
Motho o fitlha jang kwa lebopong?	Lungaphi unxweme?	Ibhishi lingakuphi?	Which way is the beach?
O kgona go thuma?	Uyakwazi ukuqubha?	Uyakwazi ukubhukuda?	Can you swim?
A bothumelo bo bo kotsi?	Lunengozi na olu nxweme?	Lelibhishi linengozi na?	Is this beach dangerous?
A go na le bathusibathumi?	Bakhona na abahlanguli?	Bakhona ababhekimpilo?	Are there lifesavers?
Boaparelo bo kae?	Liphi igumbi lokunxibela?	Ikuphi indlu yokushintsha?	Where is the change-room?
Ke batla go ya dibaesekopong/teatereng	Ndifuna ukuya ethiyetha/kumboniso bhanya-bhanya	Ngifuna ukuya ethiyetha/ebhayiskobho	I want to go to the theatre/cinema
O batla go ya go bona eng?	Ufuna ukubona ntoni?	Ufuna ukuyobonani?	What do you want to see?
Dithekete tse pedi mo setshwantshong sa bosigo	Nceda ngamatikiti amabini eshowu yasebusuku	Ngicela amathikithi amabili omboniso wakamuva	Two tickets for the late show, please
Ke batla manno gaufi le tselana/kwa morago	Ndifuna amatikiti asepasejini/angasemva	Ngifuna amathikithi angasemhubheni/angasemuva	I want tickets on the aisle/near the back
Ga go na manno mo setshwantshong se	Indawo iphelile	Embukisweni kugcwele nswi	The show is fully booked
Laeborari/Mmisiami/Artgalari e e gaufi e kae?	Ilayibhri ekufutshane indawoni imuziyem/iart gallery?	Ikuphi ilabhulali/imnyuziyamu/i-athigalari eseduze?	Where is the nearest library/museum/art gallery?
A ke kgona go nna tokololo/leloko la laeborari?	Ndingangena elayibhri?	Ngingajoyina ilabhulali?	Can I join the library?
Ke batla go adima buka	Ndifuna ukuboleka incwadi	Ngifuna ukuboleka incwadi	I want to borrow a book

English	Afrikaans	N Sotho	Sesotho
Shopping	**Inkopies**	**Go reka**	**Ho reka**
Where is the nearest shop/shopping centre/supermarket?	Waar is die naaste winkel/winkelsentrum/supermark?	Lebenkele la kgauswi le kae?/marekelo a kgauswi a kae?/supamakethe ya kgauswi e kae?	Lebenkele le/setsi sa mabenkele se/suphamakete e haufiufi e kae?
I want to buy …	Ek wil … koop	Ke nyaka go reka …	Ke batla ho reka …
What colours do you have?	Watter kleure het u?	A o swere mebala efe?	O na le mebala efe?
I want size …	Ek wil nommer … hê	Ke nyaka saese …	Ke batla nomoro ya …
May I try this on?	Kan ek dit aanpas?	Nka e lekanya?	Na nka itekanya?
This does not fit me	Dit pas nie vir my nie	Ga e ntekanye	Ha se ntekane
This does not suit me	Dit pas my nie	Ga e ntshwanele	Hona ha ho ntshwanele
This is not my size	Dit is nie my grootte nie	Ga se saese ya ka	Hona ha se nomoro ya ka
I want something smaller/larger	Ek wil iets kleiner/groter hê	Ke nyaka ye nnyane/kgolo go ye	Ke batla ho honyenyane/holwanyane
This is too small/big	Dit is te klein/groot	Ke ye nnyane/kgolo	Hona ho honyenyane/hoholo haholo
This is too short/long	Dit is te kort/lank	Ke ye kopana/telele	Hona ho hokgutshwanyane/holelele
This is too narrow/wide	Dit is te nou/wyd	E a pitlagana/mpheta	Hona ho hosesane/batsi haholo
The collar is too tight/loose	Die kraag is te styf/los	Kholoro e a nkgama/ke ye kgolo	Kholloro e tiile/kgwehlile haholo
I want something cheaper	Ek wil iets goedkoper hê	Ke nyaka ya theko ya fase	Ke batla ho kang ho theko e tlase
Will this shrink/stretch?	Sal dit krimp/rek?	A e tla hunyela/ngangega?	Na hona ho a honyela/saroloha?
What are the washing instructions?	Wat is die wasaanwysings?	Ditaelo tša go hlatswa ke dife?	Ditaelo tsa ho hlatswa ke dife?
Will the colour run?	Sal die kleur afgee?	A mmala o tla tšwa?	Na mmala o tla thunya?
Must this be drycleaned?	Moet 'n mens dit droogskoonmaak?	A e swanetše go hlatswiwa ke mohlwekišaoma?	Na hoo ho tlameha ho iswa teraetleleneng?
How much does it cost?	Hoeveel kos dit?	Ke bokae?	Ke bokae?
It costs …	Dit kos …	E bitša …	Ho ja …
How much money do you have on you?	Hoeveel geld het jy by jou?	O swere bokae?	O tshwere tjhelete e kae?
Do you have any money on you?	Het jy geld by jou?	A o swere tšhelete?	A o tshwere tjhelete?
Do you have any change?	Het jy kleingeld?	A o swere tšhentši?	A o na le tjhentjhe?
May I pay by cheque/credit card?	Kan ek met 'n tjek/kredietkaart betaal?	A nka lefa ka tšheke/karatakhodi?	Na nka lefa ka tjheke/karete ya melato?
Put it on my account	Sit dit op my rekening	E tsenye molatong wa ka	E ngole akhaonteng ya ka
What are the instalments?	Hoeveel is die paaiemente?	Se lefelwa bokae ka kgwedi?	Mekgahlelo ke bokae?
I want to lay-by this item	Ek wil hierdie artikel bêrekoop	Ke nyaka go beeletša selo se	Ke batla ho beheletsa ntho ena
I want to take this item on appro	Ek wil hierdie artikel op sig neem	Ke nyaka go tšea selo se ke tle ke se lefele ka morago	Ke batla ho hlahloba ntho ena
Do you give student/pensioner's discount?	Gee u afslag aan studente/pensioenarisse?	A o fokoletša baithuti/baamogelaphenšene?	Na le theolela baithuti/maqheku?
Pay at the till	Betaal by die kassier	Lefa go moamogelatšhelete	Lefa ho kheshiare
Where can I get this repaired?	Waar kan ek hierdie artikel laat herstel?	A selo se se ka lokišwa kae?	Ntho ena e ka lokiswa kae?
This needs mending	Dit moet heelgemaak word	Se swanetše go lokišwa	Hona ho hloka ho rokwa
Can you mend this?	Kan u dit heelmaak?	A o ka se lokiša?	Na o ka roka moo?
My watch has stopped	My horlosie het gaan staan	Sešupanako sa ka se eme	Watjhe ya ka e eme
The glass is broken	Die glas is gebreek	Galase e pšhatlegile	Kgalase ena e pshatlehile
The watch needs cleaning	Die horlosie moet skoongemaak word	Sešupanako se se swanetše go hlwekišwa	Watjhe ena e hloka ho hlwekiswa
My radio does not work	My radio werk nie	Seyalemoya sa ka ga se lle	Radio ya ka ha e bapale
How much do you charge?	Hoeveel vra u?	O bitša bokae?	O lefisa bokae?
When will it be ready?	Wanneer sal dit gereed wees?	Se tla be se lokile neng?	E tla loka neng?
Do you deliver?	Lewer u af?	A o išetša bareki dilo gae?	Na le tla e tlisa?
I shall come back for it	Ek sal dit kom haal	Ke tla tla ke se tšea	Ke tla tla e lata
I shall wait for it	Ek sal daarvoor wag	Ke tla se letela	Ke tla e emela
I want my hair cut	Ek wil my hare laat sny	Ke nyaka go kota moriri wa ka	Ke batla ho kutwa moriri
I want my hair done	Ek wil my hare laat doen	Ke nyaka gore o beakanye moriri wa ka	Ke batla ho hlophiswa moriri
I want my hair permed/straightened	Ek wil my hare laat kartel/reguit maak	Ke nyaka go phema/kgopamolla moriri wa ka	Ke batla ho phema/otlollwa moriri

Tswana	Xhosa	Zulu	English
Ditheko	**Intengo**	**Ukuthenga**	**Shopping**
Lebenkele/Mabenkele/Lebenkelekgolo le le gaufi le kae?	Iphi na ivenkile ekufutshane/indawo eneevenkile/isuphamakethi?	Sikuphi isitolo/inxanxathela yezitolo/ isuphamakethe eseduze?	Where is the nearest shop/shopping centre/supermarket?
Ke batla go reka …	Ndifuna ukuthenga …	Ngifuna ukuthenga …	I want to buy …
O na le mebala efe?	Yeyiphi imibala onayo?	Unezingubo ezinemibala enjani?	What colours do you have?
Ke batla ya saese …	Ndifuna usayizi …	Ngifuna usayizi …	I want size …
A ke ka e lekeletsa?	Ndingasilinganisa esi?	Ngingakulinganisa lokhu?	May I try this on?
Ga e ntekane	Le ayindilingani	Lokhu akungilingani	This does not fit me
Ga e ntshwanne	Le ayindifaneli	Lokhu akungifaneli	This does not suit me
Ga se saese ya me	Asiyosayizi yam le	Akusiwo usayizi wami lokhu	This is not my size
Ke batla sengwe se se nnye/tona	Ndifuna ebuncinane/enkulwana	Ngifuna okuncanyana/okukhudlwana	I want something smaller/larger
E nnye/kgolo thata	Le incinci kakhulu/inkulu kakhulu	Lokhu kuncane/kukhulu kakhulu	This is too small/big
E khutswane/telele thata	Le imfutshane kakhulu/inde kakhulu	Lokhu kufisha/kude kakhulu	This is too short/long
E a ntshwara/E tona	Le imxinwa kakhulu/ivuleke kakhulu	Lokhu kuncane/kubanzi kakhulu	This is too narrow/wide
Kholoro e a nkgama/e tona	Umqala (wehempe) uqinile/ukhululekile	Ikhola iqina/ixega kakhulu	The collar is too tight/loose
Ke batla sengwe se se tlhotlhwatlase	Ndifuna into exabisa kancinci	Ngifuna okushibhashibhile	I want something cheaper
A se tla gonyela/repa?	Ingaba le nto iza kushwabana/kuntwebeka ?	Kuyofinyela/Kuyonwebeka yini lokhu?	Will this shrink/stretch?
Se tlhatswiwa jang?	Ithini imigaqo yokuhlamba?	Kugezwa kanjani lokhu?	What are the washing instructions?
A mmala o tla tswa?	Ingaba umbala uza kuphuma?	Umbala uzophuma yini?	Will the colour run?
A se tlhatsiwe ka teraetlhilini?	Kufuneka le ihlanjwe ngaphandle kwamanzi na?	Kumele kudrayikilinwe?	Must this be drycleaned?
Se ja bokae?	Ixabisa malini?	Kubiza malini?	How much does it cost?
Se ja …	Ixabisa …	Kubiza …	It costs …
O na le madi a le kae mo go wena?	Unamalini apha kuwe?	Uphethe malini?	How much money do you have on you?
A o na le madi mo go wena?	Unayo imali apha kuwe?	Unayo imali?	Do you have any money on you?
A o na le madimannye?	Unayo na itshintshi?	Unawo ushintshi?	Do you have any change?
A nka duela ka tšheke/karata ya melato?	Ndingahlawula ngetsheki/ngekhredit khadi?	Ngingakhokha ngesheki/ngekhadi lokuthatha ngesikweletu?	May I pay by cheque/credit card?
Se beye mo tshupamolatong ya me?	Yifake kwiakhawunti yam	Faka ku-akhawunti yami	Put it on my account
Dikarolotuelo ke bokae?	Zithini/Yintoni izavenge?	Malini ekhokhwa ngamanconzunconzu?	What are the instalments?
Ke batla go beeletsa selwana se	Ndifuna ukuleyibhaya le nto	Ngifuna ukukhokha isibambiso kulempahla	I want to lay-by this item
Ke batla go isa selo se gae ke ye go se lekeletsa	Ndifuna ukuthatha le nto okwexesha ndiyokuyilinganisa	Le mpahla ngifuna ukuyithatha kengiyoyihlolo kuqala	I want to take this item on appro
A o fa baithuti/bagolo phokoletso?	Uyabanika na abafundi/abadla umhlalaphantsi isaphulelo?	Sikhona yini isephulelo sezitshudeni/ salabo abahola impesheni?	Do you give student/pensioner's discount?
Duela kwa boduelong	Hlawula ethilini	Khokha emshinini	Pay at the till
Nka tlhamaganyetsa selwana se kae?	Ndingayilungisisa phi le nto?	Kungalungiswa kuphi lokhu?	Where can I get this repaired?
Se se baakanngwe	Le nto ifuna ukungcitywa	Lokhu kudinga ukuchitshelwa	This needs mending
A o kgona go baakanya se?	Ungayingciba na le nto?	Ungakuchibela lokhu?	Can you mend this?
Tshupanako ya me e eme	Iwotshi yam imile	Iwashi lami limile	My watch has stopped
Galase e thubegile	Iglasi yaphukile	Kuphuke ingilazi	The glass is broken
Tshupanako e tshwanetse go tlhatswiwa	Iwotshi ifuna ukucocwa	Iwashi lidinga ukuhlanzwa	The watch needs cleaning
Seromamoa sa me se senyegile	Iradio yam ayisebenzi	Iwayilense yami ayidlali	My radio does not work
O duedisa bokae?	Ubiza malini na?	Ubiza malini?	How much do you charge?
E tla siama leng?	Iya kulunga nini?	Izolunga nini?	When will it be ready?
A o a romela?	Uyazizisa na?	Uyadiliva?	Do you deliver?
Ke tla se boela	Ndiza kube ndiyibuyele	Ngizobuya ngikulande	I shall come back for it
Ke tla se emela	Ndiza kuyilinda	Ngizokulindela	I shall wait for it
Ke batla go beola moriri	Ndifuna ukucheba iinwele	Ngifuna ukugunda	I want my hair cut
Ke batla go baakanya moriri	Ndifuna ukulungiswa iinwele	Ngifuna ukucwalwa izinwele	I want my hair done
Ke batla go phema/tlhamalatswa moriri	Ndifuna ukuphema/ukolula iinwele	Ngifuna ukuphema/ukwelula izinwele	I want my hair permed/straightened

English	Afrikaans	N Sotho	Sesotho
Bank	**Bank**	**Panka**	**Banka**
Where is the nearest bank/building society?	Waar is die naaste bank/bouvereniging?	Panka ya kgauswi e kae/mokgatlokago wa kgauswi o kae?	Banka/mokgatlo wa meaho e/o haufiufi e/o hokae?
When do the banks open/close?	Wanneer maak die banke oop/toe?	Dipanka di bulwa/tswalelwa neng?	Dibanka di bulwa/kwalwa neng?
What is the exchange rate?	Wat is die wisselkoers?	Na tšhelete ya naga ye e lekana le tšhelete e kakang ya dinaga tše dingwe?	Ditefello tsa dijeho tsa banka ke bokae?
I want to open an account	Ek wil 'n rekening oopmaak	Ke nyaka go bula tšhupaletlotlo	Ke batla ho bula akhaonte
I want to close my account	Ek wil my rekening sluit	Ke nyaka go tswalela tšhupaletlotlo	Ke batla ho kwala akhaonte ya ka
I want to apply for a cheque book	Ek wil om 'n tjekboek aansoek doen	Ke nyaka go kgopela tšhekepuku	Ke batla ho etsa kopo ya buka ya ditjheke
I want to apply for a credit card	Ek wil om 'n kredietkaart aansoek doen	Ke nyaka go kgopela karatakhodi	Ke batla ho etsa kopo ya karete ya melato
I want to apply for an overdraft	Ek wil om 'n oortrekking aansoek doen	Ke nyaka go kgopela tšhelete mo pankeng	Ke batla ho etsa kopo ya ho fetisa tjhelete e teng
I want to apply for a loan	Ek wil om 'n lening aansoek doen	Ke nyaka go kgopela tšheletekadimo	Ke batla ho etsa kopo ya kadimo
I want change	Ek wil kleingeld hê	Ke nyaka tšhentšhi	Ke batla tjhentjhe
I want to draw money	Ek wil geld trek	Ke nyaka go goga tšhelete	Ke batla ho ntsha tjhelete
How much would you like to draw?	Hoeveel wil u trek?	O nyaka go goga bokae?	O batla ho ntsha bokae?
I want to deposit money	Ek wil geld deponeer	Ke nyaka go boloka	Ke batla ho boloka tjhelete
How much would you like to deposit?	Hoeveel wil u deponeer?	O nyaka go boloka?	O batla ho boloka bokae?
What is the balance in my account?	Wat is die balans op my rekening?	Go na le bokae tšhupaletlotlong ya ka?	Tjhelete e setseng akhaonteng ya ka ke bokae?
I want to cash a cheque	Ek wil 'n tjek wissel	Ke nyaka go tšhentšha tšheke	Ke batla ho tjhentjha tjheke
I want to draw a cheque	Ek wil 'n tjek trek	Ke nyaka go goga tšheke	Ke batla ho ngola tjheke
Where do I sign?	Waar moet ek teken?	Ke swanetše go saena kae?	Ke saena kae?

Tswana	Xhosa	Zulu	English
Banka	**Ibhanki**	**Ebhange**	**Bank**
Banka e e gaufi e kae?	Iphi ibhanki ekufutshane/ibuilding sosayiti?	Yiliphi ibhange/ibhildingi sosayathi eseduze?	Where is the nearest bank/building society?
Dibanka di bulwa/tswalwa ka nako mang?	Iibhanki zivulwa/zivalwa nini?	Amabhange avula/avala nini?	When do the banks open/close?
Tuelo ya kananyomadi ke bokae?	Ithini na ireyiti yotshintshiselwano?	Yini inani lokushintshisana ngemali?	What is the exchange rate?
Ke batla go bula tshupamolato	Ndifuna ukuvula iakhawunti	Ngifuna ukuvula i-akhawunti	I want to open an account
Ke batla go tswala tshupamolato ya me	Ndifuna ukuyivala iakhawunti yam	Ngifuna ukuvala i-akhawunti yami	I want to close my account
Ke batla go kopa buka ya ditšheke	Ndifuna ukwenza isicelo sencwadi yeetsheke	Ngifuna ukucela ibhuku lamasheke	I want to apply for a cheque book
Ke batla go kopa karata ya molato	Ndifuna ukwenza isicelo sekhredithi khadi	Ngifuna ukucela ikhadi lokuthenga ngesikweletu	I want to apply for a credit card
Ke batla go kopa pheteletso ya madi mo bankeng	Ndifuna ukwenza isicelo seowuva drafti	Ngifuna ukucela i-ovadrafu	I want to apply for an overdraft
Ke batla go dira kadimo	Ndifuna ukuboleka imali	Ngifuna ukweboleka imali	I want to apply for a loan
Ke batla madipotlana	Ndifuna itshintshi	Ngifuna ushintshi	I want change
Ke batla go goga madi	Ndifuna ukukhupha imali	Ngifuna ukukhipha imali	I want to draw money
O batla go goga bokae?	Ufuna ukukhupha malini?	Ufuna ukukhipha malini?	How much would you like to draw?
Ke batla go boloka madi	Ndifuna ukufaka imali	Ngifuna ukulondoloza imali	I want to deposit money
O batla go boloka bokae?	Ufuna ukufaka malini?	Ufuna ukulondoloza malini?	How much would you like to deposit?
Go na le madi a makae mo tshupatlotlong ya me?	Kusele malini kwiakhawunti yam?	Malini eyibhalansi ku-akhawunti yami?	What is the balance in my account?
Ke batla go fetolola tšheke go madi	Ndifuna ukutshintsha itsheke	Ngifuna ukukhesha isheki	I want to cash a cheque
Ke batla go goga tšheke	Ndifuna ukwenzelwa itsheke	Ngifuna ukukhipha isheki	I want to draw a cheque
Ke kwala fa kae?	Ndisayine phi?	Ngimele ngisayine kuphi?	Where do I sign?

English	Afrikaans	N Sotho	Sesotho
Post Office	**Poskantoor**	**Poso**	**Posong**
Where is the nearest post office?	Waar is die naaste poskantoor?	Poso ya kgauswi e kae?	Poso e haufiufi le mona e kae?
Which counter must I go to?	Na watter toonbank toe moet ek gaan?	Ke swanetše go ya khaontereng efe?	Ke lokela ho ya khaontareng efe?
Join the queue	Staan in die ry	Ema mothalading	Kena moleng
Where can I telephone?	Waar kan ek bel?	Nka letša mogala kae?	Nka letsa kae?
Do you have a telephone directory?	Het u 'n telefoongids?	A o na le puku ya dinomoro tša mogala?	Na o na le bukana ya ditelefone?
I want to post a letter	Ek wil 'n brief pos	Ke nyaka go posa lengwalo	Ke batla ho posa lengolo
When does the last post go?	Wanneer gaan die laaste pos uit?	Poso ya mafelelo e sepela neng?	Poso ya ho qetela e tswa neng?
Can you please post this letter for me?	Sal u asseblief die brief vir my pos?	A o ka mposetša lengwalo le hle?	A o ka mposetsa lengolo lee?
I want to buy postage stamps	Ek wil posseëls koop	Ke nyaka go reka ditempe	Ke batla ho reka setempe
How much is the postage to …?	Hoeveel is die posgeld na … toe?	Tšhelete ya poso ke bokae go ya …?	Setempe se yang … ke bokae?
I want to send this letter/parcel surface mail/airmail/express mail/registered mail	Ek wil hierdie brief/pakket gewone pos/lugpos/spoedpos/per aangetekende pos stuur	Ke nyaka go romela lengwalo le/phasela ye ka poso ya ka mehla/posomoya/posotlhaganelo/posongwadišwa	Ke batla ho romela lengolo lena/phasele ena ka poso/sefofane/poso e potlakang/poso e rejisitaruweng
I want to insure this letter/parcel	Ek wil die brief/pakket verseker	Ke nyaka go inšora lengwalo le/phasela ye	Ke batla ho inshora lengolo lena/phasele ena
This parcel is fragile	Hierdie pakket is breekbaar	Diteng tša phasela ye di ka pšhatlega	Phasele ena e a thueha/pshatleha
I want to collect a parcel	Ek wil 'n pakket afhaal	Ke tlile go tšea phasela	Ke tlilo lata phasele
I want to send a telegram	Ek wil 'n telegram stuur	Ke nyaka go romela thelekramo	Ke batla ho romela thelekeramo/mohala
I want to apply for a telephone	Ek wil aansoek doen om 'n telefoon	Ke nyaka go kgopela go fiwa mogala	Ke batla ho etsa kopo ya telefone
I want to apply to transfer a telephone	Ek wil aansoek doen om 'n telefoon oor te dra	Ke nyaka go kgopela go šuthišetšwa mogala	Ke batla ho etsa kopo ya ho suthisa telefone
I want to apply for a post office box	Ek wil aansoek doen om 'n posbus	Ke nyaka go kgopela go fiwa lepokisi la poso	Ke batla ho etsa kopo ya lebokose la poso
I want to pay my telephone account/television licence	Ek wil my telefoonrekening/televisielisensie betaal	Ke nyaka go lefa tšhupamolato ya mogala/laesense ya thelebišene	Ke batla ho lefella akhaonte ya telefone/laesense ya telebishine
I want to change my address	Ek wil my adres verander	Ke nyaka go fetola aterese ya ka	Ke batla ho fetola aterese ya ka

Tswana	Xhosa	Zulu	English
Posong	**Iposofisi**	**Eposini**	**Post Office**
Poso e e gaufi e kae?	Iphi iposi ekufutshane?	Likuphi iposi eliseduze?	Where is the nearest post office?
Ke ye go khauntareng efe?	Ndiye kweyiphi ikhawuntari?	Ngimele ngiye kuliphi ikhawunta?	Which counter must I go to?
Ema mo mokolokong	Ngena emgceni	Ngena edilesini	Join the queue
Ke kgona go letsa mogala kae?	Ndingafona phi?	Ngingalushaya kuphi ucingo?	Where can I telephone?
O na le buka ya dinomoro tsa mogala?	Unayo incwadi yefoni ?	Unayo inkomba yethelefoni?	Do you have a telephone directory?
Ke batla go romela lokwala	Ndifuna ukuposa ileta	Ngifuna ukuposa incwadi	I want to post a letter
Poso ya bofelo e tswa leng?	Iposi yamva ihamba nini?	Iposi lokugcina liphuma nini?	When does the last post go?
A o ka nthomelela lekwalo le?	Ungandinceda undiposele le leta?	Ngicela ungiposele le ncwadi ?	Can you please post this letter for me?
Ke batla go reka ditempe	Ndifuna ukuthenga izitampu zokuposa	Ngifuna ukuthenga izitembu	I want to buy postage stamps
Madi a poso go ya … ke bokae?	Kuposwa ngamalini ukuya e …?	Libiza malini iposi ukuya e …?	How much is the postage to …?
Ke batla go romela lekwalo/phasele le/e ka poso/pososefofane/posobonako/ posotshireletso	Ndifuna ukuthumela le leta/ipasile/ iposi yomoya/iposi engxamisekileyo/ iposi ngerejista	Ngifuna ukuthumela le ncwadi/leli phasela ngeposi/leli posi ngendiza/leli posi nge-ekspresi	I want to send this letter/parcel surface mail/airmail/express mail/registered mail
Ke batla go putlelela lekwalo/phasele le/e	Ndifuna ukuqinisekisa ileta/ipasile	Ngifuna ukuposa le ncwadi/leli phasela ngesiqinisekiso	I want to insure this letter/parcel
Phasele e ke ya dilo tse di ka thubegang	Le pasile iyaphuka	Leli phasela lingaphuka	This parcel is fragile
Ke batla go tsaya phasele	Ndifuna ukuthatha ipasile	Ngilande iphasela	I want to collect a parcel
Ke batla go romela thelekerama	Ndifuna ukuthumela ucingo	Ngifuna ukuthumela ithelegrama	I want to send a telegram
Ke batla go kopa mogala	Ndifuna ukwenza isicelo sefoni	Ngifuna ukucela ithelefoni	I want to apply for a telephone
Ke batla go kopa pheteletso ya mogala	Ndifuna ukutshintshela kwenye indawo ifoni	Ngifuna ukucela ukwedlulisela ithelefoni	I want to apply to transfer a telephone
Ke batla go kopa bokoso ya poso	Ndifuna ukwenza isicelo sebhokisi yeposi	Ngifuna ukucela ibhokisi leposi	I want to apply for a post office box
Ke batla go duela mogala/laesense ya thelebišene	Ndifuna ukuhlawula iakhawunti yefoni/ilayisenisi yethelevizhini	Ngifuna ukukhokha i-akhawunti yethelefoni/nelayisense yethelevishini	I want to pay my telephone account/ television licence
Ke batla go fetola aterese ya me	Ndifuna ukutshintsha iadresi yam	Ngifuna ukushintsha ikheli lami	I want to change my address

English	Afrikaans	N Sotho	Sesotho
Restaurant	**Restourant**	**Bojelo**	**Resetjhurente**
I am hungry/thirsty	Ek is honger/dors	Ke swerwe ke tlala/lenyora	Ke lapile/nyorilwe
Where is the nearest restaurant?	Waar is die naaste restourant?	Bojelo bja kgauswi bo kae?	Resetjhurente e haufiufi e hokae?
Is this restaurant licensed?	Is hierdie restourant gelisensieerd?	A bojelo bjo bo rekiša bjala?	Na resetjhurente ena e na le laesense?
Is this restaurant self-service?	Is dit 'n selfdiensrestourant?	A bojelong bjo motho o a ithuša?	Na motho o a iphepa resetjhurenteng ena?
Do you serve takeaways?	Bedien u wegneemetes?	A le rekiša dijo tše motho a ka sepelago le tšona?	Na le na le dijo tseo nka tsamayang le tsona?
Do you have a table for …?	Het u 'n tafel vir …?	A o na le tafola ye e lekanago batho ba …?	O na le tafole ya …?
I have booked a table	Ek het 'n tafel bespreek	Ke beeleditše tafola	Ke beheleditse tafole
Is this table taken?	Is hierdie tafel geneem?	Tafola ye e tšerwe?	Na tafole ena e nkilwe?
May I share this table?	Kan ek hierdie tafel deel?	A nka kopanela tafola ye le ba bangwe?	Na nka dula le lona tafoleng ena?
May I have a table at the window?	Kan ek 'n tafel by die venster kry?	A nka hwetša tafola lefesetereng?	A nka fumana tafole e fensetereng?
There is a draught here	Daar is 'n trek hier	Go foka phefo mo	Ho na le moya o matla mona
May I see a menu/winelist?	Kan ek die spyskaart/wynlys sien?	A nka bona menyu/lenaneowaene?	A nka bona lenane la dijo/beine?
May I see the waiter/wine steward/manager?	Kan ek die kelner/wynkelner/bestuurder spreek?	A nka bona weitara/weitara ya dino/molaodi?	Na nka bua le mofepi/moqhatsetsi wa beine/motsamaisi?
Where is the ladies'/men's toilet?	Waar is die dames-/manstoilet?	Boithomelo bja banna/basadi bo kae?	Ntlwana ya bomme/bontate e kae?
Are you ready to order?	Is u gereed om te bestel?	A o nyaka go orotela?	A o se o loketse ho bitsa?
What is your speciality?	Wat is u spesialiteit?	Sejo sa lena še se kgethegilego ke sefe?	O rata eng haholo?
What do you recommend?	Wat beveel u aan?	Wena o ka re ke kgethe eng?	Wena o reng?
Do you serve children's portions?	Bedien u kinderporsies?	A le sola dikabelo tša bana?	Na le na le dijo tsa bana?
Do you serve vegetarian meals?	Bedien u vegetariese etes?	A le solela dijamorogo?	A le fana ka dijo tsa meroho feela?
I would like …	Ek wil graag … hê	Ke nyaka …	Ke tla thabela …
I would like my steak rare/medium/well done	Ek wil graag my biefstuk halfgaar/medium/goedgaar hê	Ke nyaka nama ya ka e butšwe gannyane/e butšwe/e butšwe gabotse	Tshutshu ya ka e tlabolwe/e be mahareng/e butswe hantle
I would like a baked potato/chips	Ek wil graag gebakte aartappel/skyfies hê	Ke nyaka letapola le le gadikilwego/ditapola	Ke tla thabela ditapole tse phehilweng/hadikilweng
I would like boiled/fried/scrambled/poached eggs/an omelette	Ek wil graag gekookte/gebakte/roer-/geposjeerde eiers/'n omelet hê	Ke nyaka mae a a apeilwego/gadikilwego/huduilwego/a a apeilwego a pšhatlilwe/omelete	Ke tla thabela mahe a bedisitsweng/hadikilweng/fuduuweng/bedisi tsweng ntle ho dikgaketlana/omolete
I would like grilled/fried fish	Ek wil graag geroosterde/gebakte vis hê	Ke nyaka hlapi ye e bešitšwego/gadikilwego	Ke tla thabela tlhapi e besitsweng/hadikilweng
May I have some bread and butter?	Kan ek brood en botter kry?	A o ka mpha borotho le potoro?	A nka fumana borotho le botoro?
May I have some water?	Kan ek water kry?	A o ka mpha meetse a go nwa?	A nka fumana metsi?
May I have some salt and pepper?	Kan ek sout en peper kry?	A o ka mpha letswai le pepere?	A nka fumana letswai le pepere?
May I have some dressing?	Kan ek slaaisous kry?	A o ka mpha dikhanakhana tša selae?	A nka fumana moro wa selae?
May I have a serviette?	Kan ek 'n servet kry?	A o ka mpha sebiete?	A nka fumana sakatuku?
The food is cold/overdone/not properly cooked	Die kos is koud/doodgekook/halfrou	Dijo di a tonya/di budule kudu/ga di a butšwa	Dijo di a bata/butswitse haholo/ha di a butswa
Take this away	Neem dit weg	Di tloše	Di tlose
This isn't clean	Dit is nie skoon nie	Ye ga e a hlweka	Ntho ena ha e a hlweka
Would you like something else?	Wil u graag iets anders hê?	A o ka rata se sengwe?	A o tla thabela ho hong hape?
I would like to see the dessert menu	Wys my asseblief die nagereg-spyskaart	Ke nyaka go bona lenaneo la phuting	Ke tla thabela ho bona lenane la phuting
No thank you, I have had sufficient	Nee dankie, ek het genoeg gehad	Aowa, ke a leboga, ke khoše	Tjhe, ke a leboha, ke kgotshe
May I have the bill?	Kan ek die rekening kry?	Nka hwetša tšhupamolato?	Ditshenyehelo di reng?
I think there is a mistake here	Ek dink daar is 'n fout hier	Ke bona nke go na le phošo mo	Ke hopola hore ho na le phoso mona
We shall pay separately	Ons sal afsonderlik betaal	Yo mongwe le yo mongwe o tla itefela	Ke tla lefa ka thoko
Is service included?	Is die diensgeld ingesluit?	Tefelotirelo e akareditšwe?	Na le matsoho a balelletswe?
The tip is for the waiter	Die fooi is vir die kelner	Tšhelete ye ke ya weitara	Thipe ke ya mofepi
Did you enjoy the meal?	Het u die ete geniet?	A o ipshinne ka dijo?	A o natefetswe ke dijo tsee?

482

Tswana	Xhosa	Zulu	English
Bojelo	**Irestyu**	**Irestoranti**	**Restaurant**
Ke bolailwe ke tlala/Ke nyorilwe	Ndilambile/ndinxaniwe	Ngilambile/Ngomile	I am hungry/thirsty
Bojelo jo bo gaufi bo kae?	Iphi na irestyu ekufutshane?	Ikuphi irestoranti eseduze?	Where is the nearest restaurant?
A bojelo bo bo rekisa dino?	Isemthethweni na le restyu?	Le restoranti inalo ilayisense lotshwala?	Is this restaurant licensed?
A ke bojelo jo motho a ithusang?	Uyazinceda umntu kule restyu?	Le restoranti ingumazithathele yini?	Is this restaurant self-service?
A le tsholela dijo tse o ka tsamayang ka tsona ?	Niyamnceda umntu othenga ahambe?	Niyakuthengisa ukudla okuhanjwa nakho?	Do you serve takeaways?
A o na le tafole mo go ka nnang batho ba le ...?	Ninayo itafile ya ...?	Unalo itafula elingahlala ...?	Do you have a table for ...?
Ke beeleditse tafole	Ndigcinelwe itafile	Ngilibhukile itafula	I have booked a table
A tafole e e tserwe?	Seyinomntu na le tafile?	Lithathiwe leli tafula?	Is this table taken?
A nka kgaoganya tafole e?	Ndingahlalisana kule tafile?	Singahlalisana kuleli tafula na?	May I share this table?
A nka fiwa tafole fa lefensetereng?	Ndingafumana itafile esefestileni?	Ngicela itafula elingasefasiteleni ?	May I have a table at the window?
Go foka phefo fa	Kukho umoya apha	Kunomoya lapha	There is a draught here
A nka bona bukana ya dijo/ya dino?	Ndingayibona imenyu?	Ngicela ukubona imenyu/uhla wewayini?	May I see a menu/winelist?
A nka bona modiredi/radino/ motsamaisi?	Ndingabona neweyitara/umfo nezisedo/umanejara?	Ngicela ukukhuluma noweta/noweta wewayini/nomeneja?	May I see the waiter/wine steward/ manager?
Boithusetso jwa basadi/banna bo kae?	Iphi indawo yangasese yamanenekazi/ yamanene?	Likuphi itholethe labesifazane/ labesilisa?	Where is the ladies'/men's toilet?
A o setse o batla go bitsa?	Sowukulungele ukuodola?	Usufuna uku-oda na?	Are you ready to order?
O rata eng thata?	Yeyiphi into eyodwa ekukholisayo?	Yikuphi ukudla okuyisipesheli sosuku?	What is your speciality?
Wena o atlanegisa eng?	Ucebisa ntoni na?	Uncomani wena?	What do you recommend?
A o tshola dikarolwana tsa bana?	Niyabaphakela abantwana?	Niyakuphaka yini okulingene abantwana?	Do you serve children's portions?
O tshola dijo tsa bajamerogo?	Niyakuphaka ukutya kodlamfuno?	Ninakho ukudla kwalabo abangayidli inyama?	Do you serve vegetarian meals?
Ke batla ...	Ndingathanda ...	Ngizocela ...	I would like ...
Ke batla nama ya me e besitswe go le gonnye/fa gare/thata	Ndisifuna isiqam sam senyama singavuthwanga/siphakathi/sivuthiwe	Ngithanda inyama yami ivuze igazi/ ivuthwe kahle/ivuthwe lushu	I would like my steak rare/medium/ well done
Ke batla tapole e e apeilweng/ditshipisi	Ndingathanda itapile elibhakiweyo/ itshipsi	Ngifuna izambane elibhakiwe/ amashiphusi	I would like a baked potato/chips
Ke batla mae a a apeilweng/besitsweng/ gadikilweng/bedesitsweng/omolete	Ndifuna iqanda elibilisiweyo/ eliqhotsiweyo/eliqhuqhiweyo/ elibhadlisiweyo/iomlethi	Ngithanda iqanda elibilisiwe/ elithosiwe/eliphehliwe/eliyiphoshi/ i-omilethe	I would like boiled/fried/scrambled/ poached eggs/an omelette
Ke batla tlhapi e e besitsweng/ gadikilweng	Ndingathanda intlanzi eyosiweyo/ eqhotsiweyo	Ngithanda inhlanzi egriliwe/ethosiwe	I would like grilled/fried fish
A nka fiwa borotho le botoro?	Ndingafumana isonka kunye nebhotolo?	Ngicela isinkwa nebhotela?	May I have some bread and butter?
A nka fiwa metsi?	Ndingafumana amanzi?	Ngicela amanzi?	May I have some water?
A nka bona letswai le pepere?	Ndingafumana ityuwa nepepile?	Ngicela itswayi nopelepele?	May I have some salt and pepper?
A nka bona moro wa selae?	Ndingafumana iisaladi?	Ngicela umhluzi wesaladi?	May I have some dressing?
A nka fiwa seiphomodi?	Ndingafumana ilatshana lezandla?	Ngicela iseviyethe?	May I have a serviette?
Dijo di tsididi/apeilwe thata/ga di a butsa	Ukutya kuyabanda/kuvuthwe kakhulu/ akuphekekanga	Ukudla kuyabanda/kuvuthwe lushu/ kuseluhlaza	The food is cold/overdone/not properly cooked
Di tlose	Yithathe uhambe	Kususe lokhu	Take this away
Se ga se a phephafatswa	Le ayicocekanga	Akumsulwa lokhu	This isn't clean
A o batla selo sengwe?	Kukho enye into oyifunayo?	Usafuna okunye na?	Would you like something else?
Ke batla go bona menu ya disubitsi	Ndicela ukubona imenyu yezimuncu- muncu	Ngicela ukubona imenyu yephudingi	I would like to see the dessert menu
Ke a leboga, ke siame	Hayi enkosi, sendanele	Ngiyabonga, sengesuthi	No thank you, I have had sufficient
A nka bona molato ?	Ndingafumana iakhawunti?	Ngicela i-akhawunti?	May I have the bill?
O ka re go na le phoso fa	Ndicinga ukuba kukho impazamo apha	Ngicabanga ukuthi kukhona iphutha lapha	I think there is a mistake here
Re tla duela mongwe le mongwe	Siza kuhlawula ngokwahlukeneyo	Sizokhokha ngokwehlukana	We shall pay separately
A madi a go direlwa a akareditswe?	Ingaba imali yenkonzo iqukanisiwe?	Ukuseva nakho kubaliwe yini?	Is service included?
Tebogo ke ya modiredi	Ibhaswana leleweyitara	Ithiphu ikaweta	The tip is for the waiter
A lo itumeletse dijo?	Ingaba utye kamnandi?	Udle kamnandi na?	Did you enjoy the meal?

English	Afrikaans	N Sotho	Sesotho
Medical	**Medies**	**Tša kalafo**	**Kalafo**
I want to see the doctor	Ek wil die dokter spreek	Ke nyaka go bona ngaka	Ke batla ho bona ngaka
I want to see the dentist	Ek wil die tandarts spreek	Ke nyaka go bona rameno	Ke batla ho bona ngaka ya meno
I want to have my eyes tested	Ek wil my oë laat toets	Ke nyaka gore mahlo a ka a hlahlobje	Ke batla mahlo a ka a hlahlojwe
Make an appointment to see the doctor	Maak 'n afspraak om die dokter te spreek	Bea nako ya go bona ngaka	Beheletsa ho bonana le ngaka
Go to the casualty department	Gaan na die ongevalleafdeling toe	Eya karolong ya bagobadidikotsing	Eya ho ba okelwang ntle
Go to the out-patients	Gaan na buitepasiënte toe	Eya karolong ya balwetši ba ka ntle	Eya ho ba okelwang ntle
Do you have medical aid?	Het u 'n mediese hulpskema?	A o leloko la mokgatlothušo wa kalafo?	Na o na le thuso ya kalafo?
I need new glasses	Ek het 'n nuwe bril nodig	Ke nyaka digalase tšê mpsha	Ke hloka diborele tse ntjha
I have lost my contact lenses	Ek het my kontaklense verloor	Ke timeditše digalasanakaleihlong tša ka	Ke lahlehetswe ke dikgalase tsa ka
I have lost my dentures	Ek het my valstande verloor	Ke timeditše meno a ka a maitirelo	Ke lahlehetswe ke meno a ka
I have toothache	Ek het tandpyn	Ke thunywa ke leino	Leino la ka le bohloko
I have broken a tooth	Ek het 'n gebreekte tand	Leino la ka le kgetlogile	Leino la ka le robehile
I have eyestrain	My oë is moeg	Mahlo a ka a lapile	Mahlo a ka a kgathetse
I am sick	Ek is siek	Ke a lwala	Ke a kula
This person is sick	Hierdie mens is siek	Motho yo o a lwala	Motho enwa o a kula
I am injured	Ek is beseer	Ke gobetše	Ke tswile kotsi
This person is injured	Hierdie mens is beseer	Motho yo o gobetše	Motho enwa o tswile kotsi
Where does it hurt?	Waar is dit seer?	O kwa bohloko kae?	Ho bohloko kae?
It hurts me to move	Dit is seer as ek beweeg	Go bohloko ge ke itšhikinya	Ho bohloko ha ke sisinyeha
How long have you been ill?	Hoe lank is jy al siek?	E šetše e le lebaka le lekakang o lwala?	Ke nako e kae o kula?
It hurts when I cough/breathe/swallow	Dit is seer as ek hoes/asemhaal/sluk	Go bohloko ge ke gohlola/buša moya/metša	Ho bohloko ha ke kgohlola/phefumoloha/kwenya
I have a pain here	Dit is hier seer	Go bohloko mo	Ke na le sehlabi mona
I have heart trouble	Ek het hartprobleme	Ke na le bolwetši bja pelo	Ke na le lefu la pelo
I have a headache/sore throat/temperature	Ek het hoofpyn/'n seer keel/koors	Ke opiwa ke hlogo/mogolo wa ka o bohloko/mmele wa ka o a fiša	Hlooho/mmetso e/o bohloko, ke a tjhesa
I have something in my eye	Ek het iets in my oog	Ke fahlilwe	Ke na le ntho ka leihlong
I have been stung by an insect/a bee/a bluebottle	Ek is deur 'n insek/by gesteek/Ek is deur 'n bloublasie gebrand	Ke lomilwe ke khunkhwane/nose/khunkhwane ya lewatle	Ke lomilwe ke kokonyana/notshi/ke tlabotswe ke lelakabe
I have been bitten by a dog/scratched by a cat	'n Hond het my gebyt/'n Kat het my gekrap	Ke lomilwe ke mpša/ke ngapilwe ke katse	Ke lomilwe ke ntja/ke ngwapilwe ke katse
I have been bitten by a snake	'n Slang het my gepik	Ke lomilwe ke noga	Ke lomilwe ke noha
I have sprained my wrist/ankle	Ek het my gewrig/enkel verstuit	Ke thinyegile lenakaila/kokoilane	Ke nonyetsehile letsoho/leqaqailana
I have broken my arm/leg	Ek het my arm/been gebreek	Ke robegile letsogo/leoto	Ke robehile sephaka/leoto
I have lost blood	Ek het bloed verloor	Ke tšwele madi a mantši	Ke lahlehetswe ke madi
I have brought up blood/bile	Ek het bloed/gal opgebring	Ke hlatšitše madi/nyoko	Ke hlatsitse madi/nyooko
I have diarrhoea	Ek het diarree	Ke swerwe ke letšhollo	Ke a tsholla
I am constipated	Ek is hardlywig	Ke bipetšwe	Ke sibilwe
I feel nauseous	Ek voel naar	Ke feroga dibete	Pelo ya ka e a nyeka
I feel feverish	Ek voel koorsig	Mmele wa ka o a fiša	Ke a tjhesa
I feel very weak	Ek voel baie swak	Ke a fokola/Ke ikwa ke le bohwefo	Ke ikutlwa ke fokola haholo
I feel dizzy	Ek voel duiselig	Ke a dikologa	Ke a tsekela
I fainted	Ek het flou geword	Ke ile ka idibala	Ke akgehile
I can't breathe	Ek kan nie asemhaal nie	Ke palelwa ke go buša moya	Ke sitwa ho hema
I can't sleep	Ek kan nie slaap nie	Ga ke kgone go robala	Ha ke na boroko
I have an infection	Ek het 'n infeksie	Ke swerwe ke phetetšo	Ke tshwaeditswe
I have a rash	Ek het 'n uitslag	Ke tshwenywa ke mogorogo	Ke na le lekgopho
I am deaf	Ek is doof	Ke sefoa	Ha ke utlwe
I have a splinter	Ek het 'n splinter	Ke hlabilwe ke phatša	Ke na le sepolintere

Tswana	Xhosa	Zulu	English
Tsa bongaka	**Ezobugqirha**	**Mayelana nemithi**	**Medical**
Ke batla go bona ngaka	Ndifuna ukubonana noqgirha	Ngifuna ukubona udokotela	I want to see the doctor
Ke batla go bona rameno	Ndifuna ukubonana noqgirha wamazinyo	Ngifuna ukubona inyanga yamanzinyo	I want to see the dentist
Ke batla gore matlho a me a lekeletswe	Ndifuna ukuhlolisa amehlo	Ngifuna ukuhlolwa amehlo ami	I want to have my eyes tested
Dira peelano go bona ngaka	Yenza idinga lokubonana noqgirha	Nquma usuku nesikhathi sokubonana nodokotela	Make an appointment to see the doctor
Eya kwa lefapeng la dikotsi	Yiya kwicandelo labalimeleyo	Yiya kumnyango wabalimele	Go to the casualty department
Eya kwa balwetsing ba kwa ntle	Yiya kwicandelo labagula behamba	Yiya egumbini labagulela ngaphandle	Go to the out-patients
A o na le sekema sa thuso sa bolwetsi?	Ulilungu lombutho onceda ngonyango na?	Unawo yaini unshuwalense wabagulayo?	Do you have medical aid?
Ke tlhoka diborele tse dintšhwa	Ndifuna iindondo/iiglasi zamehlo ezintsha	Ngidinga izibuko ezintsha	I need new glasses
Ke latlhegetswe ke dilense tsa matlho	Ndilahlekelwe ziindondo zam ezinxitywa elisweni	Izingilazi zami zezibuko zilahlekile	I have lost my contact lenses
Ke latlhegetswe ke menotekanyo	Ndilahlekelwe ngamazinyo am enziweyo	Amazinyo ami afakwayo alahlekile	I have lost my dentures
Ke opiwa ke meno	Ndiqaqanjelwa lizinyo	Ngiphethwe yizinyo	I have toothache
Ke robegile leino	Ndinezinyo elaphukileyo	Izinyo lami liphukile	I have broken a tooth
Matlho a me a lapile	Amehlo am adiniwe	Amehlo ami adonsekile	I have eyestrain
Ke a lwala	Ndiyagula	Ngiyagula	I am sick
Motho yo o a lwala	Lo mntu uyagula	Lo muntu uyagula	This person is sick
Ke ronkgetswe	Ndenzakele	Ngilimele	I am injured
Motho yo o ronkgetswe	Lo mntu wenzakele	Lo muntu ulimele	This person is injured
Go botlhoko kae?	Kubuhlungu ndawoni?	Kubuhlungu kuphi?	Where does it hurt?
Go botlhoko fa ke itshikinya	Kubuhlungu ndakushukuma	Kubuhlungu uma nginyakaza	It hurts me to move
Ke lebaka le le kae o lwala?	Lithuba elingakanani ugula?	Unesikhathi esingakanani ugula?	How long have you been ill?
Go botlhoko fa ke gotlhola/hema/metsa	Kubuhlungu ndakukhohlela/ndakuphefumla/ndakuginya	Kubuhlungu nxa ngikhwehlela/ngiphefumula/ngigwinya	It hurts when I cough/breathe/swallow
Ke na le setlhabi fa	Kubuhlungu apha	Kubuhlungu lapha	I have a pain here
Ke na le botlhoko jwa pelo	Ndikhathazwa yintliziyo	Ngikhathazwa yinhliziyo	I have heart trouble
Ke opiwa ke tlhogo/Ke na le mometso o o botlhoko/Ke na le letshoroma	Ndinentloko ebuhlungu/umqala/ubushushu	Ngiphethwe yikhanda/umphimbo/ukushisa	I have a headache/sore throat/temperature
Ke na le sengwe mo leitlhong	Ndinento eselisweni	Ngixhoshiwe	I have something in my eye
Ke lomilwe ke tshenekegi/notshe/khukwane	Ndilunywe sisinambuzane/yinyosi/nguhodoshe	Ngitinyelwe yisinambuzane/yinyosi/yimvimvi	I have been stung by an insect/a bee/a bluebottle
Ke lomilwe/ngapilwe ke ntšwa/katse	Ndilunywe yinja/ndikrwentshwe yikati	Ngilunywe yinja/Ngiklwetshwe yikati	I have been bitten by a dog/scratched by a cat
Ke lomilwe ke noga	Ndityiwe yinyoka	Ngilunywe yinyoka	I have been bitten by a snake
Ke tsipotse letlhalela/lenginana la me	Ndikruneke isihlahla/iqatha	Ngenyele isihlakala/iqakala	I have sprained my wrist/ankle
Ke robegile letsogo/leoto	Ndaphuke ingalo/umlenze	Ngephuke umkhono/umlenze	I have broken my arm/leg
Ke dule madi	Ndophe kakhulu	Ngiyopha	I have lost blood
Ke ne ke tlhatsa madi/gala	Ndikhupha igazi/inyongo	Ngihlanze igazi/inyongo	I have brought up blood/bile
Ke tshwerwe ke letshololo	Ndinesisu esihambisayo/ndiyarhuda	Ngiphethwe yisihudo	I have diarrhoea
Ke a bipelwa	Ndiqhinile	Ngiqumbile	I am constipated
Ke batla go tlhatsa	Ndinesicefecefe/isizothezothe	Nginesicanucanu	I feel nauseous
Ke na le letshoroma	Ndinemfuxane	Ngiyashisa	I feel feverish
Ke utlwa bokoa	Ndiwe amandla	Anginamandla	I feel very weak
Ke a tsibikela	Ndinesiyezi	Ngiphethwe yinzululwane	I feel dizzy
Ke ne ke idibetse	Ndiwe isiqaqa	Ngiqulekile	I fainted
Ga ke kgone go hema	Andikwazi ukuphefumla	Angikwazi ukuphefumula	I can't breathe
Ga ke kgone go robala	Andikwazi ukulala	Angikwazi ukulala	I can't sleep
Ke tsenwe ke dithwatsi	Ndosulelwe sisifo	Ngingenwe wukufa	I have an infection
Ke na le bogwata	Ndinerhashalala	Nginomqubuko	I have a rash
Ga ke utlwe	Ndisisithulu	Angizwa	I am deaf
Ke na le sesana	Ndichachambe ithambo	Ngivaveke ithambo	I have a splinter

English	Afrikaans	N Sotho	Sesotho
Medical	**Medies**	**Tša kalafo**	**Kalafo**
Do you have any allergies?	Het jy enige allergieë?	A o lwatšwa ke dilo tše di itšego?	Na ho na le ho hananang le wena?
I am allergic to penicillin	Ek is allergies vir penisilline	Peneseline e a ntwatša	Ke hanana le penicillin
I take this medicine	Ek neem hierdie medisyne	Ke nwa sehlare se	Ke nwa moriana ona
Take this prescription to the chemist	Neem hierdie voorskrif apteek toe	Iša taetšo ye/lengwalotaetšo le khemeseng	Isa ditaelo tsena khemiseng
Please make up this prescription	Maak asseblief die voorskrif op	Anke o phethe tša taetšo ye	Mphethele ditaelo tsena hle
Take this medicine once/twice/three times a day	Neem hierdie medisyne een-/twee-/drie keer per dag	Nwaa sehlare se gatee/gabedi/gararo ka letšatši	Nwa moriana ona hang/habedi/hararo ka letsatsi
Take this medicine after/before meals	Neem hierdie medisyne na/voor ete	Nwaa sehlare se pele/morago ga dijo	Nwa moriana ona ka mora/pele ho dijo
What can I eat/drink?	Wat kan ek eet/drink?	A nka ja/nwa eng?	Nka jang/nwang?
I am going to give you an injection	Ek gaan jou inspuit	Ke ile go hlabela kurumane	Ke tla o hlaba
Must I stay in bed?	Moet ek in die bed bly?	Ke hlwe malaong?	Ke robale?
Stay in bed for one day/two/three/four/five/six/seven days	Bly in die bed vir een/twee/drie/vier/vyf/ses/sewe dae	Hlwaa malaong lebaka la letšatši/matšatši a mabedi/a mararo/a mane/a mahlano/a a selelago/a a šupago	Robala letsatsi/a mabedi/a mararo/a mane/a mahlano/a tsheletseng/a supileng
Come back in … days	Kom oor … dae terug	Boa morago ga matšatši a …	O tlo kgutle ka mora matsatsi a …

Tswana	Xhosa	Zulu	English
Tsa bongaka	**Ezobugqirha**	**Mayelana Nemithi**	**Medical**
A c lwatswa ke dilo dingwe?	Unezinto ezalanayo nempilo yakho na?	Unayo i-aleji?	Do you have any allergies?
Ke lwatswa ke peneselene	Ndiyalana nephenisilini	Ngine-aleji kuphenisilini	I am allergic to penicillin
Ke nwa molemo o	Ndiyalisela eli yeza	Ngiphuza lo muthi	I take this medicine
Isa sesupetso se kwa khemiseng	Yisa lo myalelo ekhemisti	Thatha lesi sithako uye ekhemisi	Take this prescription to the chemist
Mphe molemo o o kailweng	Nceda ulungise lo myalelo	Ngicela ungixubele lesisithako	Please make up this prescription
Nwa molemo o gangwe/gabedi/gararo ka lelatsi	Sela iyeza kube kanye/kabini/kathathu ngemini	Phuza lo muthi kanye/kabili/kathathu ngelanga	Take this medicine once/twice/three times a day
Nwa molemo o pele o ja/fa o sena go ja	Sela iyeza emva/phambi kokutya	Phuza lo muthi ngaphambili kokudla/ngemuva kokudla	Take this medicine after/before meals
Nka ja/nwa eng?	Ndingatya/sela ntoni?	Ngimele ngidleni/ngiphuzeni?	What can I eat/drink?
Ke tlile go go tlhaba lemao	Ndiza kukuhlaba	Ngizokujova	I am going to give you an injection
A ke nne mo dikobong?	Kufuneka ndizigcine ezingubeni na?	Ngimele ngihlale embhedeni na?	Must I stay in bed?
Nna mo dikobong lelatsi le le lengwe/malatsi a le mabedi/mararo/mane/matlhano/marataro/supa	Zigcine ezingubeni usuku/iintsuku ezimbini/ezintathu/ezine/ezintlanu/ezisixhenxe	Hlala embhedeni usuku lunye/izinsuku ezimbili/ezintathu/ezine/ezinhlanu/eziyisithupha/eziyisikhombisa	Stay in bed for one day/two/three/four/five/six/seven days
Boa morago ga malatsi a le …	Buya emva kweentsuku ezi …	Ubuye ezinsukwini ezingu …	Come back in … days

English	Afrikaans	N Sotho	Sesotho
Travel	Reis	Leeto	Leeto
Where is the airport?	Waar is die lughawe?	Boemafofane bo kae?	Difofaneng ke kae?
Where is the departures/arrivals hall?	Waar is die vertrek-/aankomssaal?	Holo ya go tloga/ya bogorogelo e kae?	Holo eo ba tsamayang/fihlang ba yang ho yona e kae?
Where must I check in?	Waar moet ek inweeg?	Ke swanetše go ipega kae?	Sekaleng ke kae?
What luggage may I take on board?	Wat se bagasie kan ek aan boord neem?	Ke merwalo ya mohuta mang yeo nka namelago sefofane le yona?	Thoto eo nka palamang le yona ke efe?
Can I fly direct?	Kan ek direk vlieg?	Na nka fofela gona thwii?	Na nka fofa ka ho otloloha?
Is there transport to the city?	Is daar vervoer stad toe?	Na go na le dinamelwa tše di yago toropong?	Na ho na le dipalangwang ho ya motseng?
I want to cancel my reservation	Ek wil my bespreking kanselleer	Ke nyaka go khantshela peeletšo ya ka	Ke batla ho hula peheletso ya ka
May I change my seat?	Kan ek my sitplek verander?	Na nka fetoša madulo a ka?	Na nka fuwa setulo se seng sesele?
I want a window seat	Ek wil 'n venstersitplek hê	Ke nyaka go dula lefesetereng	Ke batla ho dula fensetereng
I suffer from travel sickness	Ek kry reissiekte	Ke tshwenywa ke go ferogwa dibete ge ke fofa	Ke na le lefu la leeto
Please fasten your seatbelts	Maak asseblief u sitplekgordels vas	Anke le ipofeng ka mapanta madulong a lena	Tlamang mabanta a lona hle
Where is the emergency exit?	Waar is die nooduitgang?	Lematitšhoganyetšo le kae?	Monyako wa kotsing o kae?
Where is the station?	Waar is die stasie?	Seteišene se kae?	Seteishene se hokae?
Where is the bus stop?	Waar is die bushalte?	Boemapese bo kae?	Setopo sa bese se hokae?
What time does the train/bus/aeroplane leave?	Hoe laat vertrek die trein/bus/vliegtuig?	Setimela se/pese e/sefofane se tloga ka nako mang?	Terene e/bese e/sefofane se tloha ka nako mang?
What time does the train/bus/aeroplane arrive?	Hoe laat kom die trein/bus/vliegtuig aan?	Setimela se/pese e/sefofane se goroga ka nako mang?	Terene e/bese e/sefofane se fihla ka nako mang?
The train is about to leave	Die trein is op die punt om te vertrek	Setimela se kgauswi le go tloga	Terene e haufi le ho tsamaya
What time is the next bus?	Hoe laat is die volgende bus?	Pese ye e latelago ke ya nako mang?	Bese e latelang e fihla ka nako mang?
What platform does the train leave from?	Van watter platform af vertrek die trein?	Setimela se tloga polatefomong efe?	Terene e tla ema polateforomong efe?
Which way is platform …?	Watter kant toe is platform …?	Polatefomo ya … e thokong efe?	Polateforomo e ka hokae?
Where is the timetable?	Waar is die tydrooster?	Tšhupadinako ya ditimela e kae?	Manane a dinako a kae?
I want to buy a single/return ticket to …	Ek wil 'n enkel-/retoerkaartjie … toe koop	Ke nyaka go reka thekethe ya go ya/ya go ya le go boa …	Ke batla ho reka tekete ya ho ya/ya ho ya le ho kgutla …
How much is a ticket to …?	Hoeveel kos 'n kaartjie … toe?	Thekethe ya go ya … ke bokae?	Tekete ya ho ya … ke bokae?
Is there a dining car/sleeper?	Is daar 'n eet-/slaapwa?	Setimela se na le letorokisi la go jela/robalela?	Na ho na le koloi ya dijo/boroko?
Where does the train stop?	Waar stop die trein?	Setimela se ema kae?	Terene e ema kae?
Is it an express train?	Is dit 'n sneltrein?	Ke setimela sa mafofonyane?	Na ke terene ya lebelo?
Where is the station master?	Waar is die stasiemeester?	Raseteišene o kae?	Raseteishene o kae?
Where is the conductor?	Waar is die kondukteur?	Kontai o kae?	Khate e kae?
Is there a porter?	Is daar 'n kruier?	Morwalamerwalo o gona?	Na ho na le mothothadithoto?
Where can I leave my luggage?	Waar kan ek my bagasie laat?	Merwalo ya ka nka e tlogela kae?	Nka beha thoto ya ka kae?
Please keep an eye on my things	Hou asseblief 'n ogie oor my goed	Anke o hlokomele dilo tša ka	Beha leihlo dinthong tsa ka hle
Where is the left luggage office?	Waar is die kantoor vir verlore goedere?	Ofisi ya merwalo ye e lahlegilwego e kae?	Ofisi ya thoto tse lahlehileng e kae?
May I have an upper/lower berth?	Kan ek 'n boonste/onderste slaapbank kry?	Nka robala mpeteng wa ka godimo/tlase?	Na nka fumana banka e ka tlase/hodimo?
Put my luggage under the seat/on the rack	Sit my bagasie onder die sitplek/op die rak	Beka merwalo ya ka fase ga madulo/godimo ga raka	Beha thoto ya ka ka tlasa setulo/mohaolwaneng
May I open the window?	Kan ek die venster oopmaak?	Na nka bula lefesetere?	Na nka bula fensetere?
Please shut the window	Maak asseblief die venster toe	Anke o tswalele lefesetere	Kwala fensetere hle
Here is my ticket	Hier is my kaartjie	Thekethe ya ka še	Tekete ya ka ke ena
Where can I hire a car?	Waar kan ek 'n motor huur?	Na nka hira/lefela koloi kae?	Moo nka hirang koloi teng ke kae?
Here is my driver's licence	Hier is my rybewys	Laesense ya ka ya go otlela koloi še	Lengolo la ka la ho kganna ke lena
Where can I get a taxi?	Waar kan ek 'n taxi kry?	Kolointefe nka e hwetša kae?	Nka fumana tekise kae?
What is the fare to …?	Hoeveel kos dit … toe?	Ke bokae go ya …?	Ditefello ho ya … ke bokae?
How far is it?	Hoe ver is dit?	Ke bokgole bjo bokakang?	Ho bo hole bo bokae?
How long will it take?	Hoe lank sal dit neem?	Go tla tšea sebaka se sekakang?	E tla ba nako e kae?

Tswana	Xhosa	Zulu	English
Loeto	**Uhambo**	**Uhambo**	**Travel**
Boemadifofane bo kae?	Siphi isikhululo senqwelo moya?	Ikuphi inkundla yezindiza?	Where is the airport?
Holo ya go tloga-/goroga e kae?	Iphi indawo yokunduluka/fikela?	Likuphi ihholo lokwemuka/likufika?	Where is the departures/arrivals hall?
Ke ye go netefatsa kae?	Iphi indawo yokutsheka?	Kumele ngingene kuphi?	Where must I check in?
Ke kgona go tsaya dithoto dife le nna?	Ndikhwele nawuphi umthwalo?	Ngingagibela naziphi izimpahla?	What luggage may I take on board?
A nka kgona go tsaya loeto le le tlhamaletseng ka sefofane?	Ndingabhabha ngqo ngenqwelo-moya?	Ikhona indiza eqonda lapho ngiya knona?	Can I fly direct?
A go na le dipalangwa go ya motseng?	Zikhona izithuthi eziya edolophini?	Ikhona intilasiposi yokuya edolobheni?	Is there transport to the city?
Ke batla go phimola peelelo ya me	Ndifuna ukurhoxisa indawo ebigciniwe	Ngifuna ukukhansela ithikithi lami	I want to cancel my reservation
A ke ka kgona go fetola bonno jwa me?	Ndingasitshintsha isihlalo sam?	Ngingashintsha isihlalo sami?	May I change my seat?
Ke batla manno fa lefesetereng	Ndifuna isihlalo esingasefestileni	Ngifuna isihlalo esingasefasiteleni	I want a window seat
Ke na le bokao jwa go tsamaya mesepele	Ndinesigulo sohambo	Ukuhamba kuyangigulisa	I suffer from travel sickness
Bofang mabanta a itshireletso a lona, tsweetswee	Ncedani nibophe iibhanti	Bophani amabhande ezihlalo zenu	Please fasten your seatbelts
Lebatitshoganyetso le kae?	Iphi indawo yokuphuma ngethuba lokuxakeka?	Uphi umnyango wokuphuma ngokuphuthuma?	Where is the emergency exit?
Seteišene se kae?	Siphi isikhululo?	Sikuphi isiteshi?	Where is the station?
Boemelo ba dibese bo kae?	Siphi istopu sebhasi?	Sikuphi isitophu sebhasi?	Where is the bus stop?
Setimela/Bese/Sefofane se/e/se tloga ka nako mang?	Induluka ngabani ixesha itreyini/ibhasi/inqwelo-moya?	Isitimela sihamba/Ibhasi lihamba/Indiza ihamba ngasikhathi sini?	What time does the train/bus/aeroplane leave?
Setimela/Bese/Sefofane se/e/se goroga leng?	Ifika ngabani ixesha itreyini/ibhasi/inqwelo-moya?	Isitimela sifika/Ibhasi lifika/Indiza ifika ngasikhathi sini?	What time does the train/bus/aeroplane arrive?
Setimela se tloga se tsamaya	Itreyini seyiza kuhamba	Isitimela sesizohamba manje	The train is about to leave
Bese e e latelang e tla ka nako mang?	Linini ixesha lebhasi elandelayo?	Ibhasi elinye lizofika ngasikhathi sini?	What time is the next bus?
Setimela se tloga mo seraleng sefe?	Indulukela kweyiphi iplatfomu itreyini?	Isitimela sisuka kuyiphi ipulatfomu?	What platform does the train leave from?
Serala sa … se thokong efe?	Ikweliphi icala iplatfomu …?	Ipulatfomu … ingakuphi?	Which way is platform …?
Lenanetiro le kae?	Abhalwe phi amaxesha?	Ithebula lezikhathilikuphi?	Where is the timetable?
Ke batla go reka thekethe ya go ya/le go boa go …	Ndifuna ukuthenga itikiti eliyisingili/eliya libuye e…	Ngifuna ukthenga ithikithi eliyisingili/eliyiritheni …	I want to buy a single/return ticket to …
Thekethe ya go ya … ke bokae?	Yimalini itikiti eliya …?	Limalini ithikithi eliya e …?	How much is a ticket to …?
Go na le koloi ya go ja/robala?	Ikhona indawo yokutyela/yokulala?	Ikhona inqola yokudla/yokulala?	Is there a dining car/sleeper?
Setimela se ema kae?	Imisa phi itreyini?	Sima kuphi isitimela?	Where does the train stop?
A ke setimelasegaodi?	Ingaba yitreyini ekhawulezayo?	Yisitimela esingumasheshisa na?	Is it an express train?
Moeteledipele wa seteišene o kae?	Uphi usositishi?	Uphi umphathisiteshi?	Where is the station master?
Kontai o kae?	Uphi umhloli-matikiti?	Uphi ukhondaktha?	Where is the conductor?
A morwaladithoto o teng?	Ukhona umthuthi mpahla?	Kukhona othutha izimpahla?	Is there a porter?
Nka tlogela dithoto tsa me kae?	Ndingayishiya phi impahla yam?	Ngingazishiyaphi izimpahla zami?	Where can I leave my luggage?
A o ke o ntlhokomele dilwana tsa me	Nceda undigcinele izinto zam	Ngicela ungibhekela izinto zami	Please keep an eye on my things
Kantoro ya dilo tse di latlhegileng e kae?	Iphi iofisi yokushiya imithwalo?	Liphi ihhouvisi lezimpahla ezilahlekileyo?	Where is the left luggage office?
A o ka mpha marobalo kwa godimo/tlase?	Ndingafumana iqonga elingentla?	Ngicela ukulala embhedini ophezulu/ophansi?	May I have an upper/lower berth?
Baya dithoto tsa me ka fa tlase ga manno/mo rakeng	Beka umthwalo wam phantsi kwesihlalo/erakini	Beka izimpahla zami ngaphansi kwesihlalo/phezulu eshalofini	Put my luggage under the seat/on the rack
A nka bula lefensetere?	Ndingayivula ifestile?	Ngingalivula ifasitela na?	May I open the window?
A o ke o tswale lefensetere, tsweetswee	Khawuvale ifestile	Ngicela uvale ifasitela	Please shut the window
Thekethe ya me ke e	Nali itikiti lam	Nanti ithikithi lami	Here is my ticket
Nka hira mmotorokara kae?	Ndingayiqesha phi imoto?	Ngingayiqashaphi imoto?	Where can I hire a car?
Lekwalotetla la go kgweetsa la me ke le	Nazi iincwadi zam zokuqhuba	Nansi ilayisense yami	Here is my driver's licence
Theksi nka e bona kae?	Ndingayifumana phi iteksi?	Ngingayitholaphi itekisi?	Where can I get a taxi?
Ke bokae go ya …?	Yimalini ukuya e …?	Kumalini ukuya e …?	What is the fare to …?
Go bokgakala jo bo kana kang?	Kukude kangakanani?	Kukude kangakanani?	How far is it?
Go tla tsaya nako e kana kang?	Kuza kuthatha ixesha elingakanani?	Kuyothatha isikhathi eside kangakanani?	How long will it take?

Travel woes

English	Afrikaans	N Sotho	Sesotho
Travel woes	Reisprobleme	Mathata a leeto	Mathata a maeto
I have lost my way	Ek het verdwaal	Ke timetše	Ke lahlehile
Can you show me the way to …?	Hoe kom ek by …?	A o ka mpontsha tsela ye e yago …?	Na o ka mpontsha tsela e yang …?
Is this the right road to …?	Is dit die regte pad … toe?	A ke yona tsela ye e yago …?	Na ke yona tsela e yang …?
Which is the right road to …?	Watter pad is die regte een … toe ?	Tsela ye e yago … ke efe?	Tsela e yang … ke efe?
Where does this road lead to?	Waarheen gaan hierdie pad?	Tsela ye e ya kae?	Tsela ena e ya kae?
How far is it to …?	Hoe ver is dit tot by …?	Ke bokgole bjo bokakang go ya …?	Ho ya … ho bo hole bo bokae?
Do you have a map?	Het jy 'n kaart?	A o na le mmapa?	Na o na le mmapa?
What is the condition of the road?	In wat se toestand is die pad?	Maemo a tsela a bjang?	Boemo ba tsela bo jwang?
Is the road passable?	Is die pad begaanbaar?	A tsela e a sepelega?	Na tsela e a tsamaeha?
Is the road suitable for a caravan?	Is hierdie pad geskik vir 'n karavaan?	A tsela ye e loketše karabane?	Na tsela eo e loketse karavane?
Is the road steep/bumpy?	Is die pad steil/stamperig?	A tsela ye ke morotoga/ga e a lekanela?	Na tsela e moepa/kgehlepa?
The bridge is under water	Die brug is onder water	Leporogo le nweletše	Borokgo bo kwahetswe ke metsi
Take a detour	Neem 'n ompad	Tšea tsela ye e fapogago	Nka tsela e kgelohang
Carry straight on	Gaan reguit aan	Tšwela pele thwii	Tsamaya jwalo
First left/right	Eerste links/regs	Pele go la nngele/go la go ja	O thinyetse ka leqeleng/ho le letona pele
I have lost my car keys	Ek het my motorsleutels verloor	Ke timeditše dinotlelo tša koloi ya ka	Ke lahlile dinotlolo tsa koloi
I have locked my keys in the car	Ek het my sleutels in die motor toegesluit	Ke notleletše dinotlelo tša koloi ka gare ga yona	Ke notlelletse dinotlolo tsa ka ka koloing
My car has been stolen	My motor is gesteel	Koloi ya ka e utswitšwe	Koloi ya ka e utswitswe
My car has been broken into	Daar is by my motor ingebreek	Koloi ya ka e thubilwe	Koloi ya ka e thuhilwe
My car has broken down	My motor is stukkend	Koloi ya ka e senyegile	Koloi ya ka e robehile
My car will not start	My motor wil nie vat nie	Koloi ya ka e gana go duma	Koloi ya ka e hana ho duma
The lights won't work	Die ligte wil nie werk nie	Mabone a gana go tuka	Mabone ha a bonese
My car has a flat battery	My motor se battery is pap	Peteri ya koloi ya ka e fedile maatla	Beteri ya koloi ya ka e kgathetse
The fuses have blown	Die smeltdrade is uitgebrand	Difiuse di swele	Difiosi di tjhele
The windscreen is shattered	Die vooruit is fyngebreek	Seširaphefo se pšhatlegile	Kgalase ya ka pele e thuehile
My car has run out of petrol	My motor is sonder petrol	Koloi ya ka e feletšwe ke peterolo	Koloi ya ka e felletswe ke peterole
My car needs water in its radiator	My motor het verkoelerwater nodig	Koloi ya ka e hloka meetse ka radietareng	Koloi ya ka e hloka metsi
My car has a broken fanbelt	My motor se waaierband is stukkend	Lepanta la sefokišamoya sa koloi ya ka le kgaogile	Fenebelete ya koloi ya ka e kgaohile
My car has a puncture	My motor het 'n pap wiel	Leotwana la koloi ya ka le phontšhitše	Lebidi la koloi ya ka le tswile moya
My car is stuck	My motor sit vas	Koloi ya ka e tantšwe lerageng	Koloi ya ka e eme
Can you tow my car to the nearest town?	Kan jy my motor na die naaste dorp insleep?	A o ka gogela koloi ya ka toropong ya kgauswi?	Na o ka hulela koloi ya ka toropong e haufiufi?
Can you give me a lift to the nearest town?	Kan ek met jou saamry na die naaste dorp toe?	A o ka nnametša go fihla toropong ya kgauswi?	Na o ka mpalamisa ho ya toropong e haufiufi?
Where is the nearest garage?	Waar is die naaste motorhawe?	Karatšhe ya kgauswi e kae?	Karatjhe e haufiufi e kae?
Please call a breakdown service to come here as soon as possible	Vra asseblief 'n insleepdiens om so gou moontlik hiernatoe te kom	Anke o kgopele bagogadikoloi gore ba tle mono ka pelapela	Mpitsetse koloi e ka nkgulang ka potlako
Please fill the car	Maak asseblief die motor vol	Anke o tlatše koloi ka makhura	Tlatsa koloi ya ka hle
Please check the oil/water/tyres	Gaan asseblief die olie/water/bande na	Anke o lekole oli/meetse/dithaere	Hlahloba oli/metsi/dithaere hle
Please wash the car	Was asseblief die motor	Anke o hlatswe koloi	O ka hlatswa koloi hle
How much will it cost to repair the car?	Hoeveel sal dit kos om die motor te herstel?	Na e ka ba bokae go lokiša koloi ye?	Ho lokisa koloi e tla ba bokae?
How long will it take?	Hoe lank sal dit neem?	Go ka tšea sebaka se sekakang?	Ho tla nka nako e kae?
My bicycle has a puncture	My fiets het 'n pap wiel	Leotwana la paesekela ya ka le phontšhitše	Baesekele ya ka e pantjhitse

Tswana	Xhosa	Zulu	English
Mathata a loeto	**Iinkathazo zohambo**	**Okokuhamba**	**Travel woes**
Ke timetse	Ndilahlekene nendlela yam	Ngedukile	I have lost my way
A o kgona go ntshupetsa go ya …?	Ungandibonisa indlela eya …?	Ngicela indlela eya …?	Can you show me the way to …?
A ke tsela e e yang …?	Yindlela eya e … le?	Yiyo yini indlela eya …?	Is this the right road to …?
Ke tsela efe e e yang …?	Yeyiphi eyona ndlela iya e … ?	Iyiphi indlela eya …?	Which is the right road to …?
Tsela e e ya kae?	Iyaphi le ndlela?	Iyaphi le ndlela?	Where does this road lead to?
Go bokgakala jo bo kana kang go ya …?	Kukude kangakanani ukuya e …?	Kukude kangakanani e …?	How far is it to …?
A o na le mmepe?	Unayo imephu?	Unayo imephu?	Do you have a map?
Boemo jwa tsela bo ntse jang?	Imeko yendlela injani?	Unjani umgwaqo?	What is the condition of the road?
Go ka fetwa ka tsela e?	Iyahambeka indlela?	Kungahanjwa kulomgwaqo?	Is the road passable?
A karabene e ka feta ka tsela e?	Ingaba indlela izilungele ikharavani?	Ingahamba ikhereveni kulomgwaqo?	Is the road suitable for a caravan?
A tsela e mokong/mesima ?	Ingaba indlela imqengqelezi/inezigingqi?	Umgwaqo uyakhuphukela unezigingqi na?	Is the road steep/bumpy?
Ke borogo e khupeditswe ke metsi	Ibhulorho igqunywe ngamanzi	Ibhuloho limbozwe ngamanzi	The bridge is under water
Tsaya tsela e e dikologang	Hamba ngokugwegweleza	Hamba ngendlela ephambukayo	Take a detour
Tlhamalala fela	Hamba ngqo ungajiki	Qhubeka uqonde phambili	Carry straight on
Pele molema/moja	Qala ngekhohlo/ngokunene	Emgwaqeni wokuqala ujikele ngakwesokudla/ngakwesokunxele	First left/right
Ke latlhegetswe ke dinotlolo tsa mmotorokara	Ndilahle izitshixo zemoto	Ngilahlekelwe isikhiye zemoto yami	I have lost my car keys
Ke notleletse dinotlolo mo mmotorokareng	Nditshixele izitshixo zam emotweni	Ngikhiyele izikhiye zami emotweni	I have locked my keys in the car
Mmotorokara wa me o utswitswe	Imoto yam ibiwe	Imoto yami yebiwe	My car has been stolen
Mmotorokara wa me o thubilwe	Imoto yam iqhekeziwe	Imoto yami igqekeziwe	My car has been broken into
Mmotorokara wa me o robegile	Imoto yam yaphukile	Imoto yami ifile	My car has broken down
Mmotorokara wa me o gana go duma	Imoto yam ayiqhwithi	Imoto yami ayifuna ukustada	My car will not start
Mabone ga a batle go tshuba	Izibane azisebenzi	Izibane azikhanyisi	The lights won't work
Mmotorokara wa me o feleletswe ke lelatlha	Ibhetri yemoto yam ifleti	Ibhetri yemoto yami iphelile	My car has a flat battery
Difiuse di swele	Iifiyuzi ziqhushumbile	Amafiyuzi ashile	The fuses have blown
Letlhabaphefo le thubegile	Ifestile yangaphambili yaphukile	Ifasitela langa phamabili lephukile	The windscreen is shattered
Mmotorokara wa me o feleletswe ka mafura	Imoto yam iphelelwe ngamafutha	Imoto yami iphelelwe upetroli	My car has run out of petrol
Mmotorokara wa me o tlhoka metsi mo setsidifatsing	Imoto yam ifuna amanzi kwiradiyeyitha	Imoto yami idinga amanzi kurediyetha	My car needs water in its radiator
Lebanta la sefoki sa mmotorokara wa me le kgaogile	Imoto yam iqhawukelwe yefeni bhelti	Ifenbelti yemoto yami idabukile	My car has a broken fanbelt
Leotwana la mmotorokara wa me le dule mowa	Imoto yam igqajukelwe livili	Isondo lemoto yami liphantshile	My car has a puncture
Mmotorokara wa me o tshwerwe	Imoto yam ixingile	Imoto yami ibhajiwe	My car is stuck
A o ka kgona go nkgogela mmotorokara wa me mo motseng o o gaufi?	Ungayisala imoto yam ukuya kwidolophu ekufutshane?	Ngicela ungidonsele imoto yami edolobheni eliseduze?	Can you tow my car to the nearest town?
A o ka kgona go mpalamisa go fitlha mo motseng o o gaufi?	Ungandikhwelisa ukuya kwidolophu ekufutshane?	Ngicela ungigibelise uyongibeka edolobheni eliseduze?	Can you give me a lift to the nearest town?
Karaje e e gaufi e kae?	Iphi igaraji ekufutshane?	Likuphi igalaji eliseduze?	Where is the nearest garage?
A ke o bitse segogadikoloi go tla kwano ka bonako	Nceda ubize isilenga size apha ngokukhawuleza	Ngicela ungibizele imoto ezongidonsa ngokushesha okukhulu	Please call a breakdown service to come here as soon as possible
A o ke o tlatse mmotorokara	Nceda yizalise imoto ngepetroli	Ngicela uyigcwalise imoto	Please fill the car
Tlhola oli/metsi/dithaere, tsweetswee	Khawukhangele ioyile/amanzi/amavili	Ngicela ubheke uwoyela/amanzi/amasondo	Please check the oil/water/tyres
Tlhatswa mmotorokara, tsweetswee	Khawuhlambe imoto	Ngicela ugeze imoto	Please wash the car
Go tla ja bokae go baakanya mmotorokara?	Kuya kubiza malini ukulungisa imoto?	Kuzobiza malini ukulungisa imoto?	How much will it cost to repair the car?
Go tla tsaya nako e kana kang?	Kuya kuthatha ixesha elingakanani?	Kuzoba isikhathi esingakanani?	How long will it take?
Baesekele ya me e na le leotwana le le duleng mowa	Ibhayisikili yam igqajukelwe livili	Ibhayisikili lami liphantshile	My bicycle has a puncture

English	Afrikaans	N Sotho	Sesotho
Travel woes	**Reisprobleme**	**Mathata a leeto**	**Mathata a maeto**
There has been an accident	Daar was 'n ongeluk	Go diregile kotsi	Ho hlahile kotsi
Are you hurt?	Het jy seergekry?	A o gobetše?	Na o tswile kotsi?
No one is seriously injured	Niemand het ernstig seergekry nie	Ga go motho yo a gobetšego kudu	Ha ho motho ya tswileng kotsi e mpe
This person is injured	Hierdie persoon is beseer	Motho yo o gobetše	Motho enwa o tswile kotsi
Don't move this person	Moenie hierdie persoon beweeg nie	Se šuthiše motho yo	Se ka sisinya motho enwa
Can I help?	Kan ek help?	Nka thuša?	Na nka thusa?
Do you have a first aid kit?	Het jy noodhulptoerusting?	Na o na le didirišwa tša thušo ya tlhaganelo?	Na o na le lebokose la thuso ya kotsing?
Please call a doctor/an ambulance/the police to come here as soon as possible	Ontbied asseblief 'n dokter/'n ambulans/die polisie om so gou moontlik te kom	Anke o bitše ngaka/amalanse/maphodisa gore e/e/a tle mono ka pelapela hle	Bitsa ngaka/ambulense/mapolesa ho tla kwano ka potlako hle
Where is the nearest doctor/hospital/police station/telephone?	Waar is die naaste dokter/hospitaal/polisiestasie/telefoon?	Ngaka ya kgauswi e kae?/Sepetlele sa kgauswi se kae?/Seteišene sa maphodisa sa kgauswi se kae?/Mogala wa kgauswi o kae?	Ngaka/sepetlele/mapoleseng/telefone e haufiufi e kae?
Please write down your name and address	Skryf asseblief jou naam en adres neer	Anke o ngwale leina la gago le aterese ya gago	Ngola lebitso le aterese ya hao hle
Please write down details of your insurance company	Skryf asseblief besonderhede van jou versekeringsmaatskappy neer	Anke o ngwale dintlha tše bohlokwa ka ga khamphani ya inšorentshe ya gago	Ngola tsohle tsa inshorense ya hao hle
Will you take a breathalyser test?	Sal jy 'n asemtoets ondergaan?	Na o ka re dumelela go hlahloba moya wa gago?	A ko etse teko ya moya hle?
I want to report an accident	Ek wil 'n ongeluk aanmeld	Ke nyaka go bega kotsi	Ke batla ho tlaleha tsa kotsi
I want to make a statement	Ek wil 'n verklaring aflê	Ke nyaka go bea mantšu a pego	Ke batla ho etsa tlhaloso
I want an interpreter	Ek wil 'n tolk hê	Ke nyaka mofetoledi	Ke batla toloko
You are under arrest	Jy is onder arres	O swerwe	O tshwerwe
You may call a lawyer	Jy kan 'n prokureur inroep	O ka kgopela thušo ya agente	O ka mema mmuelli
You must appear in court	Jy moet in die hof verskyn	O swanetše go hlaga kgorong ya tsheko	O lokela ho ya kgotla

Tswana	Xhosa	Zulu	English
Mathata a loeto	**Iinkathazo zohambo**	**Okokuhamba**	**Travel woes**
Go ne go na le kotsi	Bekukho ingozi	Kuvele ingozi	There has been an accident
A o utlwile botlhoko?	Ingaba wenzakele?	Ulimele na?	Are you hurt?
Ga go na ope yo o utlwileng botlhoko thata	Akukho bani wenzakele kakhulu	Abekho abalimele kakhulu	No one is seriously injured
Motho yo o utlwile botlhoko	Lo mntu wenzakele	Umuntu lo ulimele	This person is injured
Se sutise motho yo	Musa ukumshenxisa lo mntu	Ningamnyakazisi lo muntu	Don't move this person
A nka thusa?	Ndinganceda?	Ngingasiza na?	Can I help?
O na le dilwana tsa thuso ya ntlha?	Unazo izixhobo zoncedo lokuqala?	Unawo yini umgodla wezinto zosizo lokuqala?	Do you have a first aid kit?
A o ke o bitse ngaka/ambilansa/mapodisa go tla kwano ka bonako	Nceda ubize ugqirha/iambhulensi/amapolisa eze apha ngokukhawuleza	Ngicela ubize udokotela/i-ambulense/amaphoyisa eze lapha ngokushesha	Please call a doctor/an ambulance/the police to come here as soon as possible
Ngaka/sepetlele/mapodisa/mogala e e/se se/a a/o o gaufi e/se/a/o kae?	Undawoni ugqirha/isibhedlele/isikhululo samapolisa/ifoni ekufutshane?	Ukuphi udokotela/uthelefoni oseduzane?/Sikuphi isibhedlela/isiteshi samaphoyisa esiseduzane?	Where is the nearest doctor/hospital/police station/telephone?
Nkwalele leina le aterese ya gago, tsweetswee	Nceda ubhale igama lakho kunye neadresi	Bhala phansi igama nekheli lakho	Please write down your name and address
Nkwalele ditshedimosetso tsa kompani ya insorense ya gago	Nceda ubhale iinkcukacha zeinshorensi yakho	Bhala phansi imininingwane yomshuwalense wakho	Please write down details of your insurance company
A o tla tsaya teko ya mowa?	Ungenza uvavanyo lomphefumlo?	Singakuhlola umoya na?	Will you take a breathalyser test?
Ke batla go le bega ka ga kotsi	Ndifuna ukwenza ingxelo ngengozi	Ngizobika ingozi	I want to report an accident
Ke batla go dira bosupi	Ndifuna ukwenza ingxelo	Ngizokwethula isitatimende	I want to make a statement
Ke batla mofetoledi	Ndifuna itoliki	Ngifuna umhumushi	I want an interpreter
O tshwerwe	Ubanjiwe	Uboshiwe	You are under arrest
O ka bitsa mmueledi	Ungafuna igqwetha	Ungabiza ummeli	You may call a lawyer
O tshwanetse go ya kgotlatshekelo	Kufuneka uvele enkundleni yamatyala	Kumele uze enkantolo	You must appear in court

English	Afrikaans	N Sotho	Sesotho
Accommodation	**Huisvesting**	**Marobalo**	**Bodulo**
Where is the nearest hotel/motel?	Waar is die naaste hotel/motel?	Hotele/motele ya kgauswi e kae?	Hotele e/motele o haufiufi e/ho kae?
I have a booking	Ek het 'n bespreking	Ke beeleditše marobalo	Ke beheleditse
Do you have any vacancies?	Het jy nog plek?	A go sa na le marobalo?	Na sebaka se teng?
I want a single/double room	Ek wil 'n enkel-/dubbelkamer hê	Ke nyaka phapoši ya motho o tee/batho ba babedi	Ke hloka kamore/kamore ya ba babedi
I want a room with a bathroom	Ek wil 'n kamer met 'n badkamer hê	Ke nyaka phapoši ye e nago le bohlapelo	Ke hloka kamore e nang le batekamore
Does the room have television?	Het die kamer televisie?	Na phapoši ye e na le thelebišene?	Na kamore eo e na le telebishine?
Does the room have air conditioning?	Het die kamer lugversorging?	Na phapoši ye e na le setontšhamoya?	Na kamore eo e na le moya o phodileng/futhumetseng?
May I see the room?	Kan ek die kamer sien?	A nka bona phapoši ya gona?	Na nka bona kamore eo?
Do you have a quieter room?	Het jy 'n stiller kamer?	A go na le phapoši yeo e sa tsenyego lešata kudu?	Na kamore e kgutsitseng ho feta ena e teng?
Do you have anything cheaper?	Het jy iets goedkoper?	A o na le (phapoši) ya tefo ya tlase?	Na ho na le e tefello e tlasenyana?
Are animals allowed?	Word diere toegelaat?	Na diruiwa di a dumelelwa?	Na diphoofolo di dumelletswe?
What is the hotel tariff?	Wat is die hoteltarief?	Hotele e lefelwa bokae ka letšatši?	Ditefello tsa hotele ke bokae?
Does the tariff include breakfast/lunch/dinner?	Sluit die tarief ontbyt/middagete/aandete in?	Na tefo ya hotele e akaretša le dijo tša go fihlola/tša mosegare/tša go lalela?	Na ditefello di balella borakafese/dijo tsa motshehare/dijo tsa mantsiboya?
Is there a special rate for children?	Is daar 'n spesiale tarief vir kinders?	Na go na le tefo ye e kgethilwego ya bana?	Na ho na le ditefello tse ikgethang baneng?
May I have my room key?	Kan ek my kamersleutel kry?	A nka hwetša senotlelo sa phapoši ya ka?	Na nka fumana senotlolo sa kamore ya ka?
Please sign the register	Teken asseblief die register	Anke o saene retšistara	Saena rejisetara hle
Where can I park my car?	Waar kan ek parkeer?	Nka emiša koloi ya ka kae?	Koloi ya ka nka e emisa kae?
Where is the dining room?	Waar is die eetkamer?	Na phapoši ya bojelo e kae?	Phaposi ya dijo e kae?
Where is the bar?	Waar is die kroeg?	Na phapoši ya bonwelo/para e kae?	Bareng ke kae?
May I have room service?	Kan ek kamerdiens kry?	A nka fiwa tirelophapošing?	Na nka tlisetswa dijo kamoreng?
May I have valet service?	Kan ek 'n kamerbediende kry?	A nka fiwa modiredi wa ka phapošing?	Na nka fumantshwa mothusi kamoreng?
Is there a message for me?	Is daar 'n boodskap vir my?	A le ntshwaretše molaetša?	Na ke na le molaetsa?
I shall be leaving at …	Ek sal … vertrek	Ke tla tloga ka …	Ke tla tsamaya ka …
May I have my bill?	Kan ek my rekening kry?	O ka mpha tšhupamolato ya ka?	Molato wa ka ke bokae?
May I have a receipt?	Kan ek 'n kwitansie kry?	O ka mpha rasiti?	Na nka fumana rasite?
Please collect my luggage	Bring asseblief my bagasie	Anke o ntlišetše merwalo ya ka	Tlo le morwalo wa ka hle
Please call a taxi	Ontbied asseblief 'n taxi	Anke o mpiletše kolointefe	Mpitsetse tekisi hle
Where is the nearest caravan/camp site?	Waar is die naaste woonwapark/kampeerterrein?	Boemakarabane/bokampelo bja kgauswi bo kae?	Sebaka se haufiufi sa dikaravane/khemping se kae?
What is the charge per site?	Wat is die tarief vir 'n staanplek?	Tefo ya boemo ke bokae?	Ditefello tsa ho ba moo ke bokae?
Where is the ablution block?	Waar is die toilet- en wasgeriewe?	Moago wa boithomelo le bohlapelo o kae?	Sebaka sa matlwana le moo ho hlatswetswang teng ke kae?
Is there electricity?	Is daar elektrisiteit?	A go na le mohlagase?	Na motlakase o teng?
Where must I dispose of rubbish?	Waar moet ek vullis weggooi?	Ditšhila ke di lahle kae?	Ditshila di lahlelwa kae?
May I light a fire?	Kan ek vuurmaak?	Ke dumeletšwe go gotša mollo?	Na nka besa mollo?
Is the water drinkable?	Is die water drinkbaar?	A meetse a a a nwega?	Na metsi a a nweha?
Where can I empty my chemical toilet?	Waar kan ek my chemiese toilet leegmaak?	Nka tšholla kae diteng tša boithomelo bja ka bja dikhemikale?	Moo nka tshollelang mantle a ntlwana ya ka ke kae?
Where can I refill my gas cylinder?	Waar kan ek my gassilinder volmaak?	Nka tlaleletša silintara sa ka sa gase kae?	Na moo nka tlatsang pitsana ya kgase ke kae?
Is there a shop?	Is daar 'n winkel?	A go na le lebenkele?	Na lebenkele le teng?

Tswana	Xhosa	Zulu	English
Manno	**Indawo**	**Indawo yokuhlala nokulala**	**Accommodation**
Hotele/Motele e e gaufi e kae?	Iphi ihotele/indawo yabahambi ekufutshane?	Likuphi ihhotela eliseduze?	Where is the nearest hotel/motel?
Ke dirile peelelo	Ndigcinelwe indawo	Ngibhukile	I have a booking
A o sa na le manno?	Ingaba unazo izithuba?	Unayo indawo?	Do you have any vacancies?
Ke batla kamore ya motho a le mongwe/ba babedi	Ndifuna igumbi lomntu omnye/lababini	Ngifuna ikamelo eliyisingili/eliyidabuli	I want a single/double room
Ke batla kamore e e nang botlhapelo	Ndifuna igumbi elinegunjana lokuhlambela	Ngifuna ikamelo elinebhavulumu	I want a room with a bathroom
A kamore e na le thelebišene?	Ingaba igumbi linayo itelevizhini?	Ikamelo linayo ithelevishini?	Does the room have television?
A kamore e na le sefokisamowa?	Ingaba igumbi linaso isiphephelisi?	Ikhono i-ekhondishini ekamelweni?	Does the room have air conditioning?
A nka bona kamore?	Ndingalibona igumbi?	Ngingalibona ikamelo na?	May I see the room?
A o na le kamore e e setu?	Unalo igumbi elisendaweni ethe cwaka?	Unalo ikamelo elingenamsindo kangako?	Do you have a quieter room?
O na le sengwe sa madi a a kwa tlase?	Unayo into exabisa kancinci?	Awunakho okushibhashibhile?	Do you have anything cheaper?
A diruiwa di a dumelwa?	Ingaba zivunyelwe na izilwanyana?	Izilwane ziyavunyelwa?	Are animals allowed?
Madi a hotele ke bokae?	Athini na amaxabiso ehotele?	Libiza malini ihhotela?	What is the hotel tariff?
A tuelo e akaretsa difitlholo/dijo tsa motshegare/dilalelo?	Ingaba ixabiso liqukanisa ibrakfesi/ilantshi/idinara?	Ngabe imali ebizwayo nebhulakufesi/nelantshi/nedina?	Does the tariff include breakfast/lunch/dinner?
A go na le tuelo e e rileng ya bana?	Kukho isibonelelo sexabiso sabantwana na?	Abantwana banalo inani lezibiza eliyisipesheli?	Is there a special rate for children?
A o ka mpha senotlolo sa kamore ya me?	Ndingasifumana isitshixo segumbi lam?	Ngicela isikhiye sekamelo lami?	May I have my room key?
Kwala leina mo bukaineng, tsweetswee	Nceda usayine irejista	Ngicela usayine irejesta	Please sign the register
Ke ka emisa koloi kae?	Ndingayimisa phi na imoto yam?	Ngingayibeka kuphi imoto yami?	Where can I park my car?
Bojelo bo kae?	Liphi na igumbi lokutyela?	Likuphi ikamelo lokudlela?	Where is the dining room?
Bonwelo bo kae?	Liphi na igumbi lokusela?	Ikuphi inkantini?	Where is the bar?
A o ka mpha phepelo kwa dikamoreng?	Ndingaziselwa izinto egumbini lam na?	Ngicela ukulethelwa ukudla ekamelweni?	May I have room service?
A o ka mpha modiredi wa dikamore?	Ndingancedwa ngomntu wokundiququzelela?	Ngicela isisebenzi sokungisiza ekamelweni?	May I have valet service?
A ke amogetse molaetsa?	Kukho umyalezo wam na?	Ukhona yini umlayezo wami?	Is there a message for me?
Ke tla tloga ka …	Ndiza kuhamba ng …	Ngizohamba ng …	I shall be leaving at …
A nka amogela molato wa me?	Khawundiphe iakhawunti yam?	Ngicela i-akhwunti yami?	May I have my bill?
A nka amogela rasiti?	Khawundiphe isiphetshana?	Ngicela iriside?	May I have a receipt?
Tlisa dithoto tsa me, tsweetswee	Khawundiphathise umthwalo wam	Ngicela ungilethele izimpahla zami	Please collect my luggage
Leletsa thekesi mogala gore e tle	Nceda ubize iteksi	Ngicela ungibizele ithekisi	Please call a taxi
Kampa ya dikarabene/maitiso e e gaufi e kae?	Iphi ikharavani/indawo yeekharavani ekufutshane?	Ikuphi indawo eseduze yekharavani/yokukampa?	Where is the nearest caravan/camp site?
Maemo a ja bokae?	Isiza sibiza malini?	Ibiza malini indawo yokukampa?	What is the charge per site?
Botlhapelo/Boithusetso bo kae?	Iphi indawo yangasese nokuhlambela?	Akuphi amatholethe nendawo yokugeza?	Where is the ablution block?
A motlakase o teng?	Ukhona na umbane?	Ukhona ugesi?	Is there electricity?
Ke latlhele matlakala kae?	Ndiyilahle phi na inkunkuma?	Ngizilahlaphi izibi?	Where must I dispose of rubbish?
Nka gotsa molelo?	Ndingabasa na?	Kuyavunyelwa ukubasa umlilo?	May I light a fire?
A metsi a ka nowa?	Ayaselwa na amanzi?	Singawaphuza amanzi na?	Is the water drinkable?
Nka tshololela boithusetso jwa dikhemikale kae?	Ndingawalahla phi na amachiza?	Ngingalithululela kuphi itholethe lami elinamakhemikhali?	Where can I empty my chemical toilet?
Nka tlatsa gase kae?	Ndingayizalisa phi na igesi?	Ngingaligcwalisa kuphi ibhodlela legesi?	Where can I refill my gas cylinder?
A go na le lebenkele?	Ikhona na ivenkile?	Sikhona isitolo?	Is there a shop?

Colour separations by Hirt & Carter, Cape Town
Printed and bound by Colorgraphic, Durban